CANADIAN FOOTBALL LEAGUE ®

FACTS FIGURES AND RECORDS ®

1994 Edition

A Canadian Football League Publication © 1994

Triumph Books
CHICAGO

CANADIAN FOOTBALL LEAGUE

1994 FACTS FIGURES AND RECORDS

All material contained herein has been compiled by the CFL Communications Department.

CFL Vice President Communications: Michael J. Murray
Managing Directors & Creative Co-ordinators: Diane Mihalek, Jim Neish
Editorial Assistant: Marcel Desjardins

Special thanks to the Club Media/Public Relations Directors for their input and where required, pictorial assistance.

Typesetting/Layout/Creative Assistance by Spalding/Ilesic Advertising Dimensions, 321 Evans Avenue, Toronto, ON M8Z 1K2 416/255-9433; FAX 416/252-6547
Printed by Spalding/Ilesic Advertising Dimensions, 321 Evans Avenue, Toronto, ON M8Z 1K2 416/255-9433; FAX 416/252-6547

Distribution in Canada by Canadian Football League Properties/Publications,
110 Eglinton Avenue West, Fifth Floor, Toronto, ON M4R 1A3 416/322-9650; FAX 416/322-9651

and General Publishing, 30 Lesmill Road, Toronto, ON M3B 2T6 416/445-3333 FAX 416/445-5991

Distribution in U.S.A. by Triumph Books, 644 South Clark Street, Chicago, Illinois 60605
312/939-3330; FAX 312/663-3557

Photo Credits: cover photos, CFL personnel photos, player head shots, some regular season and Grey Cup game action photos taken by John Sokolowski; player head shots, Most Outstanding Player Award photos and some Grey Cup game action photos taken by Brad Watson; Officials' signals, some regular season and playoff game action photos taken by CFL photographer Art Martin; All-time Canadian Football Hall of Fame Inductee photos and Trophy photos supplied by the Canadian Football Hall of Fame and Museum; Caravan photos courtesy of CFL photo library; Montreal Caravan/Expos photo taken by Cormier photos; John Candy photo taken by Steve Schapiro; Las Vegas Posse photos taken by Randy Becker, Elite Photography, Inc.; Baltimore CFL Colts photo taken by Rick Preski; television crews' photos courtesy of the CBC, TSN and RDS.

Front Cover: 1993 CFL Most Outstanding Player Doug Flutie, Calgary Stampeders; 1993 Runner-up CFL Most Outstanding Player Matt Dunigan, Winnipeg Blue Bombers; Quarterback David Archer, expansion Sacramento Gold Miners.

ISBN 1-880141-72-8

The Canadian Football League
Fifth Floor
110 Eglinton Avenue West
Toronto, Ontario Canada
M4R 1A3
416/322-9650 FAX 416/322-9651

TABLE OF CONTENTS

LARRY W. SMITH

COMMISSIONER

Larry W. Smith was appointed the ninth Commissioner of the Canadian Football League on Thursday, February 27, 1992, taking office on April 1, 1992.

The forty-three-year-old played nine seasons at running back and slotback with the Montreal Alouettes between 1972 and 1980. After being selected first overall in the 1972 Draft, Smith went on to play in 140 consecutive regular season, 13 playoff and five Grey Cup games.

Smith began his business career with positions in sales, marketing and human resources. In 1983, he joined Industrial Life Technical Services as General Manager - Montreal Branch. The following year, he assumed responsibility for the Multi-Products Division and in 1985, he became Senior Vice-President - Central Region. Between 1985 and 1991, Smith held several executive positions with various divisions of John Labatt Ltd., the most recent being President of the Frozen Bakery Division of Ogilvie Mills Ltd.

Larry Smith's solid background as a businessman, as a player and as a fan, as well as his in-depth knowledge of the Canadian Football League, will enable him to guide the CFL in the years ahead. He feels that the CFL is a valuable part of the Canadian sporting tradition and that the best is yet to come.

Since his arrival, Smith has led the League into a new era. He was instrumental in the establishment of new ownerships in Hamilton and Vancouver in 1991 as well as in Ottawa and Toronto earlier this year. Smith also pioneered the first expansion of the CFL since the B.C. Lions joined the League in 1954. On January 12, 1993 the Sacramento Gold Miners were introduced as the first-ever United States-based team to play in the Canadian Football League. Since then, three additional teams have joined the League. In July 1993, the Las Vegas Posse became the second franchise from outside of Canada to join the CFL. And in February 1994, the Baltimore CFL Colts and the Shreveport Pirates became the third and fourth expansion teams of the decade.

Smith, who is bilingual, was born on April 28, 1951 in Montreal, Quebec and attended Bishop's University, graduating with a Bachelor of Arts in Economics and Business in 1972. In 1976, he received a Bachelor of Civil Law degree from McGill University. He served as Past President, Bishop's Alumni Association and is a member of the Corporation of Bishop's University's Board of Governors. Smith and his wife Leesa have three children, Wesley - 16, Ashley - 14 and Bradley - 10.

JOHN H. TORY

CHAIRMAN

John H. Tory was appointed as Chairman of the Canadian Football League Board of Governors on February 28, 1992.

Tory is a partner and member of the Executive Committee in the law firm of Tory Tory DesLauriers and Binnington in Toronto, with a particular interest in legislative, regulatory and government related matters.

He also maintains an active interest in the business community and serves as a member of the Boards of Directors of John Labatt Limited (majority owners of the Toronto Blue Jays), Rogers Broadcasting Limited and Multilingual Television (Toronto) Limited, Cam Vec Limited and the Ontario Chamber of Commerce.

Tory has also maintained an active interest in politics over a period of 25 years, serving as a campaign manager 8 times for candidates at all three levels of government.

In 1982, he was appointed Principal Secretary to the Premier of Ontario, and he served in that role, and as Associate Secretary of the Ontario Cabinet for almost four years.

Tory has remained involved in the community through membership on the Boards of Directors of a large number of community and charitable organizations. He is a Past President of the Osgoode Hall Law School Alumni Association and he is also a member of the Advisory Board of the Salvation Army.

He is host of Reaction, a weekly cable TV program shown across Southern Ontario. He is also a regular television and radio commentator on national and provincial affairs.

Tory is married and has four children.

CANADIAN FOOTBALL LEAGUE

Canadian Football League Building,
Fifth Floor, 110 Eglinton Avenue West
Toronto, Ontario Canada M4R 1A3
Telephone: (416) 322-9650 Fax: (416) 322-9651

COMMISSIONER - LARRY W. SMITH

GREGORY B. FULTON
Secretary-Treasurer
Born December 8, 1919 in Winnipeg, Manitoba. He served overseas with the Armed Forces from 1940-45 and then attended the University of Alberta in 1946-48, where he was deeply involved in sport. While working for the Taxation Department in Calgary, he became the original statistician for the Stampeders in 1950. In 1963, he was appointed to the CFL Rules Committee and has been secretary since 1967. In 1966, he compiled the first record manual.

DONALD H. BARKER
Director of Officiating
Born November 28, 1929 in Edmonton, Alberta. Barker joined the Canadian Football League Office as Director of Officiating in April, 1985 following a 21-year career as a game official. He officiated in 390 Regular Season and Playoff games, including 10 Grey Cup Games between 1960 and 1981. Barker became Director of Operations/Officiating in June, 1988.

PAUL MIHALEK
Controller
Born September 28, 1958 in Toronto, Ontario. A Bachelor of Commerce Graduate from the University of Toronto, Mihalek has been involved with the CFL since 1982, when he worked with the League's Auditors. He is in his ninth season with the CFL after assuming his current duties in Finance and Administration in October, 1985.

PAUL F. BRULÉ
Vice President Business Development
Born February 1, 1945. Brulé joined the CFL on March 1, 1994 after several years as Vice-President of Sales for the Recognition Division of Jostens Canada Ltd. Prior to Jostens, he was National Sales Manager at Bauer as well as Corporate Marketing Manager for the Montreal Olympics Organizing Committee. Following an outstanding college career with the St. Francis Xavier football team, he was a 1st round Draft Choice by Ottawa in 1968 and was then traded to Winnipeg, where he played defensive back until 1972. He ended his career with Montreal in '73.

MICHAEL J. MURRAY
Vice President Communications
Joined the CFL on June 1, 1992 after having spent nine years with the Canadian Amateur Hockey Association. He was involved with Canada's National Jr. Team from 1984-92 including being the General Manager in 1989-'90 when Canada won the Gold medal in Helsinki, Finland. Prior to joining the C.A.H.A., Murray spent time coaching at Concordia University and at the University of Ottawa before joining the Coaching Association of Canada.

EDWARD S. CHALUPKA
Vice President Football Operations
Began with the CFL on February 1, 1993 in a newly-created position. Ed has a solid business background in real estate sales and management. He has held several positions with the CFL Players' Association, including five years as President and was Managing Director of the Canadian Football Hall of Fame & Museum prior to the CFL. Chalupka was an all-star guard with the Hamilton Tiger-Cats and was the Most Outstanding Offensive Lineman in '74 and '75.

DIANE MIHALEK
Communications Coordinator

JIM NEISH
Communications Coordinator

MAGGIE HERMANT
Events Manager

RICHARD STAMPER
Retail Licensing Manager

LINDA PISCIONE
Executive Assistant

MARCEL DESJARDINS
Communications Assistant

SANDRA TAYLOR
Marketing Coordinator

DAVE BOWEN
Corporate Sales

ROSHAN PEIRIS
Accountant

NATALIE WAY
Sales and Marketing Administrator

SUE HUTCHINSON
Receptionist

1994 CFL COMMITTEES

ADVISORY BOARD

The Hon. William G. Davis, Toronto, Ontario
Leo W. Gerard, Toronto, Ontario
H. Earl Joudrie, Toronto, Ontario
John H. Tory, Toronto, Ontario
The Hon. Mr. Justice Warren Winkler, Toronto, Ontario

BOARD OF GOVERNORS

Chairman - John H. Tory
Commissioner - Larry W. Smith
Vice-Chairman - John Lipp, Saskatchewan Roughriders

Governors - Bruce Firestone, Ottawa Rough Riders
Paul Beeston, Toronto Argonauts
Roger Yachetti, Hamilton Tiger-Cats
Reginald Low, Winnipeg Blue Bombers
James L. Speros, Baltimore CFL Colts
Bernard Glieberman, Shreveport Pirates
Larry Ryckman, Calgary Stampeders
John C. Ramsey, Edmonton Eskimos
Bill Comrie, B.C. Lions
Fred Anderson, Sacramento Gold Miners
Nick Mileti, Las Vegas Posse

Secretary-Treasurer - Gregory B. Fulton

Alternates - Phil Kershaw, Ottawa Rough Riders
Gordon Craig, Toronto Argonauts
John Michaluk, David MacDonald, Hamilton Tiger-Cats
Cal Murphy, Bruce Robinson, Winnipeg Blue Bombers
Lonie Glieberman, John Ritchie, Shreveport Pirates
Alan Ford, Saskatchewan Roughriders
Wally Buono, Calgary Stampeders
Hugh Campbell, Edmonton Eskimos
Al Swyrypa, Peter Classon, B.C. Lions
Tom Bass, Sacramento Gold Miners

MANAGEMENT COUNCIL

Chairman - Larry W. Smith

Secretary - Gregory B. Fulton

Members - Phil Kershaw, Ottawa Rough Riders
Bob O'Billovich, Toronto Argonauts
John Gregory, Hamilton Tiger-Cats
Cal Murphy, Winnipeg Blue Bombers
James L. Speros, Baltimore CFL Colts
J.I. Albrecht, Shreveport Pirates
Alan Ford, Saskatchewan Roughriders
Wally Buono, Calgary Stampeders
Hugh Campbell, Edmonton Eskimos
Eric Tillman, B.C. Lions
Tom Bass, Sacramento Gold Miners
Nick Mileti, Las Vegas Posse

EXECUTIVE COMMITTEE

Commissioner - Larry W. Smith
Chairman - Bill Comrie, B.C. Lions
Members - Bernard Glieberman, Shreveport Pirates
John C. Ramsey, Edmonton Eskimos

PLAYER RELATIONS COMMITTEE

Chairman - Hugh Campbell, Edmonton Eskimos
Members - Alan Ford, Saskatchewan Roughriders
Tom Bass, Sacramento Gold Miners
Edward Chalupka, CFL
David Wakely, CFL Advisor

PENSION PLAN COMMITTEE

Chairman - Fred James
Members - Reginald Low, Winnipeg Blue Bombers
Alan Ford, Saskatchewan Roughriders

SAVINGS COMMITTEE

Chairman - Larry W. Smith
Members - Hugh Campbell, Edmonton Eskimos
Alan Ford, Saskatchewan Roughriders
Bob O'Billovich, Toronto Argonauts

1996 GREY CUP COMMITTEE

Chairman - Reginald Low, Winnipeg Blue Bombers
Members - John Lipp, Saskatchewan Roughriders
Fred Anderson, Sacramento Gold Miners

RULES COMMITTEE

Chairman - Larry W. Smith
Secretary - Gregory B. Fulton
Members - Donald H. Barker, CFL Officials
Bob O'Billovich, Toronto Argonauts
John Gregory, Hamilton Tiger-Cats
Cal Murphy, Winnipeg Blue Bombers
Alan Ford, Saskatchewan Roughriders
Wally Buono, Calgary Stampeders
Hugh Campbell, Edmonton Eskimos
Tom Huiskens, Sacramento Gold Miners
Neil Payne, CFL Officials
Ian Sinclair, CFL Players' Association

EXPANSION COMMITTEE

Chairman - Larry Ryckman, Calgary Stampeders
Members - Roger Yachetti, Hamilton Tiger-Cats
John Lipp, Saskatchewan Roughriders
Bruce Firestone, Ottawa Rough Riders
James L. Speros, Baltimore CFL Colts
David MacDonald, CFL Consultant

MARKETING COMMITTEE

Chairman - Nick Mileti, Las Vegas Posse
Members - Reginald Low, Winnipeg Blue Bombers
Bruce Firestone, Ottawa Rough Riders
James L. Speros, Baltimore CFL Colts
John Ritchie, Consultant

CFL PLAYERS' ASSOCIATION

EXECUTIVE COMMITTEE

PRESIDENT
Dan Ferrone
Toronto, ON

1ST VICE-PRESIDENT
Ian Sinclair
Vancouver, B.C.

2ND VICE-PRESIDENT
Stu Laird
Calgary, AB

SECRETARY
Randy Ambrosie
Edmonton, AB

MEMBER AT LARGE
Don Moen
Toronto, ON

LEGAL COUNSEL
Ed Molstad
Edmonton, AB

BENEFITS CHAIRMAN
Fred James
Calgary, AB

TREASURER
Oskar Kruger
Edmonton, AB

TOM PATE MEMORIAL AWARD

Presented annually by the Canadian Football League Players' Association since 1976 to the Player who demonstrates outstanding sportsmanship and dedication to the League and the community, as selected by members of the Canadian Football League Players' Association.

1993	Michael Clemons	Toronto Argonauts
1992	Danny Barrett	B.C. Lions
1991	Stu Laird	Calgary Stampeders
1990	Ritchie Hall	Saskatchewan Roughriders
1989	Matt Dunigan	B.C. Lions
1988	Hector Pothier	Edmonton Eskimos
1987	Nick Arakgi	Montreal Alouettes
1986	Tyrone Crews	B.C. Lions
1985	Jerry Friesen	Saskatchewan Roughriders
1984	Bruce Walker	Ottawa Rough Riders
1983	Henry Wazczuk	Hamilton Tiger-Cats
1982	David Boone	Edmonton Eskimos
1981	Ken McEachern	Saskatchewan Roughriders
1980	Jim Coode	Ottawa Rough Riders
1979	Peter Muller	Toronto Argonauts
1978	John Helton	Calgary Stampeders
1977	Ron Lancaster	Saskatchewan Roughriders
1976	George Reed	Saskatchewan Roughriders

1993 COMMISSIONER'S AWARD

Every year, the top players and coaches in sport are recognized by awards and All-Star nominations. In 1990, a new award was presented by then-Commissioner Donald Crump, to honour the top performers behind the scenes for their achievements. The Commissioner's Award is presented annually to the person, or persons, who have made an outstanding contribution to Canadian Football.

The 1993 recipient of the award is Mr. Reg Wheeler, a man who is certainly no stranger to those who have been involved in Canadian Football. The native of Hamilton, Ontario has contributed significantly to the development of football in Canada. His love of football started back in the 1930s and 1940s when he played with the Hamilton Tigers and Wildcats. This gentleman served his community for many years by being active with numerous charities; he is currently Chairman of the Kiwanis Music Festival and sells programs at Hamilton Tiger-Cat home games. From 1960 to 1985, he was an Alderman with the City of Hamilton. This year's Commissioner's Award winner was Chairman of the Canadian Hall of Fame Induction Committee for 21 consecutive years (1972-1993) and has been a member of the Hall of Fame Management Committee since the 1960s. He is currently vice-chairman and an honourary life member of the Management Committee.

Reg Wheeler receiving Commissioner's Award from Larry Smith

IN MEMORY OF...

John Candy

1950-94

1994 CFL TELEVISION BROADCAST CREWS

CBC SPORTS

SCOTT OAKE
HOST
9TH SEASON

DON WITTMAN
PLAY-BY-PLAY
33RD SEASON

DAN KEPLEY
COLOUR
4TH SEASON

MARK LEE
HOST
3RD SEASON

CHRIS CUTHBERT
PLAY-BY-PLAY
4TH SEASON

JAMES CURRY
COLOUR
2ND SEASON

THE SPORTS NETWORK

GORD MILLER
HOST
4TH SEASON

JOHN WELLS
PLAY-BY-PLAY
8TH SEASON

LEIF PETTERSEN
COLOUR
8TH SEASON

RÉSEAU DES SPORTS

PIERRE DURIVAGE
HOST/PLAY-BY-PLAY
5TH SEASON

JACQUES DUSSAULT
COLOUR
3RD SEASON

ESPN/ESPN2

MO DAVENPORT
COORDINATING PRODUCER

OTTAWA ROUGH RIDERS FOOTBALL CLUB

301 Moodie Drive, Suite 102
Nepean, Ontario
K2H 9C4
Telephone Numbers: Administration (613) 721-2255
Ticket Office (613) 721-2200/1-800-985-2225
Fax: Administration (613) 721-2250 Coaches (613) 563-4658

EXECUTIVE

Chairman/Governor: Bruce M. Firestone
President and Alternate Governor: Phil Kershaw
Vice-Chairman: Barry G. Lett
Vice-Chairman: Dennis Ruffo
Vice-President of Communications: Dawn Firestone
Assistant to the Chairman: Connie Cochran
Assistant to the President: Anne Cox

FOOTBALL OPERATIONS

Director of Football Operations/Head Coach: Adam Rita
Assistant Coaches:
Urban Bowman, Assistant Head Coach and Defensive Coordinator
Jim Hilles, Defensive Front Seven Coach
Don Blackwelder, Running Backs and Receivers Coach
Charlie Carpenter, Offensive Line Coach
Paul Chryst, Special Teams Coach
Player Personnel Consultant: Mike McCarthy
Player Personnel Coordinator: Crista Bazos
Equipment Manager: Steve McCoy
Athletic Therapist: Gerry "Kurly" Kurylowich
Doctors: Dr. Mark Aubry, Club Physician, Dr. Gary Greenberg, Club Physician, Dr. Don Johnson, Orthopedic Surgeon, Dr. Rob Beattie, Orthopedic Surgeon
Football Operations Secretary: Martha Wurtele

ADMINISTRATION

Director of Operations: Paul Blinn
Director of Communications: Robert W. Gialloreto
Director of Corporate Properties: Hughes Gibeault
Director of Corporate Sales: Mark Worobey
Director of Ticket Sales: Luigi Porcari
Receptionist: Lisa Estensen
Director of Marketing/Merchandise: Marc Seaman
Fan Relations Co-ordinator: Mark Russett
Fan Relations Co-ordinator: Chris Stewart
Financial Controller: Elaine Harrison

FAST FACTS

Home Stadium: Frank Clair Stadium
Stadium Address: Frank Clair Stadium, Ottawa, Ontario K1S 3W7
Club Colours: Red, Gold & Blue
Club Name: Ottawa Rough Riders
Training Camp Site: Collège Militaire Royal de Saint-Jean, Montreal, PQ
Press Box Location: North Side; Enter via Arena Gate 1
Dressing Room Locations: Home Team - Southwest Corner, enter via stadium gate 11
Visiting Team - Under South stands, enter stadium gate 11
Radio Broadcasts: TBA
P.A. Announcer: TBA
Statistician: Richard Dupuis (Assistants - Alain Labelle/Pierre Tremblay)
Offensive Spotter: Ed Saikeley
Defensive Spotter: Dan Mooney
Typists: Michel Lefebvre/Christian Dorion
Timekeeper: Drew Shouldice
Scorekeeper: Bill Hart
Assistant Timekeeper/Scorekeeper: Ray Kealey
Communications Co-Ordinator: Doug Shouldice

NINE GREY CUP VICTORIES FOR OTTAWA-BASED TEAMS

Senators (2) - 1925, 1926
Rough Riders (7) - 1940, 1951, 1960, 1968, 1969, 1973, 1976

Frank Clair Stadium Facts 'n Figures

Capacity: 30,927
Largest Regular Season One Game Attendance: 35,289 - Ottawa 46, Montreal 6 (November 2, 1975)
Largest Playoff One Game Attendance: 33,003 - Montreal 20, Ottawa 10 (November 15, 1975)
Largest Grey Cup Attendance: 50,604 - Winnipeg 22, B.C. 21 (November 27, 1988)

Club History: 1876 Ottawa Football Club is formed...1898 formal organization of the Rough Riders as a football club...1883 the Rough Riders enter the newly formed Ontario Rugby Football Union...1924 club name changed from the Rough Riders to the Senators following a merger with the St. Brigit's Club...returned to the name Rough Riders in 1926...renamed stadium to Frank Clair Stadium in March, 1993.

OTTAWA CLUB RECORDS SINCE 1946
Regular Season

- CFL Record
- Ties CFL Record
() - Figures in Brackets represent Year(s) Club mark set

Most Points Scored One Season (minimum 14 games) - 540 ('90)
Most Points Scored Against One Season (minimum 14 games) - 630 ('89)
Fewest Points Against One Season (minimum 14 games) - 177 ('66)
Most Points Scored One Game - 56 -
- Hamilton at Ottawa 07/09/75 Final: 56-31
Most Points Scored Against One Game - 65 -
- at Winnipeg 07/09/84 Final: 65-25
Most Wins One Season (minimum 14 games) - 11 ('66, '69, '72, '78)
Most Losses One Season (minimum 14 games) - #16 ('88)
Highest Shutout - 36-0 - Ottawa at Toronto 31/10/64
Highest Shutout Against - 45-0 - at Hamilton 02/10/54
Most Touchdowns One Season (minimum 14 games) - 59 ('90)
Most Touchdowns One Game - 8 - Hamilton at Ottawa 07/09/75
Most Converts One Season (minimum 14 games) - 55 ('90)
Most Converts One Game - 8 - Hamilton at Ottawa 07/09/75
Most Field Goals One Season (minimum 14 games) - 46 ('91)
Most Field Goals One Game - 7 - Saskatchewan at Ottawa 24/09/89
Most First Downs One Season - 411 ('90)
Most First Downs One Game - 42 - Toronto at Ottawa 19/08/58
Most Yards Total Offence One Season - 7,331 ('91)
Most Yards Total Offence One Game - 655 - Toronto at Ottawa 19/08/58
Most Yards Rushing One Game - #468 - at Montreal 10/10/60
Most Times Carried One Game - 64 - Toronto at Ottawa 14/09/60

Most Touchdowns Rushing One Game - #7 - at Montreal 10/10/60
Most Yards Passing One Game - 471 - at Montreal 29/07/82
Most Passes Thrown One Game - 51 - at Edmonton 12/10/81
Most Completions One Game - 30 - at Toronto 20/07/88
Most Touchdown Passes One Game - 5 - Montreal at Ottawa 29/07/82
- at Hamilton 17/09/89

OTTAWA INDIVIDUAL RECORDS SINCE 1946
Regular Season

Points (Career) - 1,462 - Gerry Organ
Points (Season) - 202 - Terry Baker ('91)
Points (Game) - 24 -
- Ken Charlton, Hamilton at Ottawa 09/11/46
- Dave Thelen, Toronto at Ottawa 16/09/59
- Ron Stewart, at Montreal 10/10/60
- Art Green, Hamilton at Ottawa 07/09/75
- Dean Dorsey, Saskatchewan at Ottawa 24/09/89

Touchdowns (Career) - 70 - Bob Simpson
Touchdowns (Season) - 18 - Alvin (Skip) Walker ('82)
Touchdowns (Game) - 5 - Tom Burgess, Toronto at Ottawa 09/07/92
Field Goals (Career) - 318 - Gerry Organ
Field Goals (Season) - 46 - Terry Baker ('91)
Field Goals (Game) - 7 -
- Dean Dorsey - Saskatchewan at Ottawa 24/09/89

Longest Field Goal - 55 - Dean Dorsey - at Saskatchewan 07/07/85
Passes Thrown (Career) - 2,530 - Russ Jackson
Passes Thrown (Season) - 546 - Damon Allen ('91)
Passes Thrown (Game) - 51 - J.C. Watts - at Edmonton 12/10/81
Passes Completed (Career) - 1,356 - Russ Jackson
Passes Completed (Season) - 329 - Tom Burgess ('93)
Passes Completed (Game) - 30 - Tom Burgess - vs. Hamilton 16/08/93
Passes Intercepted (Game) - 6 - Tom Burgess - at Saskatchewan 11/09/93
Passing Yards (Career) - 25,264 - Tom Burgess
Passing Yards (Season) - 5,063 - Tom Burgess ('93)
Passing Yards (Game) - 471 - Chris Isaac - Montreal at Ottawa 29/07/82
Touchdown Passes Thrown (Career) - 185 - Russ Jackson
Touchdown Passes Thrown (Season) - 34 - Damon Allen ('90)
Touchdown Passes Thrown (Game) - 5 -
- Chris Isaac - Montreal at Ottawa 29/07/82
- Damon Allen - Edmonton at Ottawa 26/07/90

No. of Carries (Career) - 1,211 - Dave Thelen
No. of Carries (Season) - 291 - Reggie Barnes ('91)
No. of Carries (Game) - 33 - Dave Thelen - Toronto at Ottawa 14/09/60
Yards Rushing (Career) - 6,917 - Dave Thelen
Yards Rushing (Season) - 1,486 - Reggie Barnes ('91)
Yards Rushing (Game) - #287 - Ron Stewart - at Montreal 10/10/60
Touchdowns by Rushing (Career) - 54 - Russ Jackson
Touchdowns by Rushing (Season) - 15 - Ron Stewart ('60)
Touchdowns by Rushing (Game) - 4 -
- Ken Charlton - Hamilton at Ottawa 09/11/46
- Dave Thelen - Toronto at Ottawa 16/09/59
- Ron Stewart - at Montreal 10/10/60
- Art Green - Hamilton at Ottawa 07/09/75

Passes Caught (Career) - 444 - Tony Gabriel
Passes Caught (Season) - 94 - Marc Lewis ('87)
Passes Caught (Game) - 13 - Mark Barousse - at Hamilton 03/07/86
Pass Reception Yards (Career) - 7,484 - Tony Gabriel
Pass Reception Yards (Season) - 1,471 - Gerald Alphin ('89)
Pass Reception Yards (Game) - 258 -
- Bob Simpson - Toronto at Ottawa 29/09/56

Touchdown Passes Caught (Career) - 65 - Bob Simpson
Touchdown Passes Caught (Season) - 14 - Tony Gabriel ('76)
Touchdown Passes Caught (Game) - 3 -
- Ted Watkins - Montreal at Ottawa 12/08/63
- Whit Tucker - Hamilton at Ottawa 01/08/68
- Whit Tucker - Saskatchewan at Ottawa 14/08/68
- Tony Gabriel - Saskatchewan at Ottawa 24/09/78
- Martin Cox - Montreal at Ottawa 29/08/79
- Kelvin Kirk - Montreal at Ottawa 29/07/82
- Tyron Gray - Ottawa at Montreal 21/07/84
- Mark Barousse - Ottawa at Edmonton 17/07/86
- Stephen Jones - Toronto at Ottawa 09/07/92

First Quarterback in Club History and second in the CFL to rush for over 1000 yards - Damon Allen (1,036 yards)

OTTAWA'S RECORD AGAINST OTHER CLUBS

(REGULAR SEASON)

		GP	W	L	T	F	A	PTS
Versus Toronto	(Since 1946)	160	81	76	3	3331	3105	165
Versus Hamilton	(Since 1946)	165	78	86	1	3343	3376	157
Versus Winnipeg	(Since 1961)	54	24	29	1	1337	1513	49
Versus Saskatchewan	(Since 1961)	47	19	28	0	1078	1239	38
Versus Calgary	(Since 1961)	46	18	28	0	1010	1166	36
Versus Edmonton	(Since 1961)	47	19	26	2	1150	1361	40
Versus B.C.	(Since 1961)	46	17	27	2	1033	1187	36
Versus Sacramento	(Since 1993)	2	1	1	0	47	70	2
OTTAWA VS OPPOSITION		567	257	301	9	12329	13017	523

Chairman and Governor: Bruce M. Firestone

Bruce Firestone has continually shown his commitment to the sporting community of Ottawa. From 1990 to 1993 Bruce was the Chairman and Governor for the Ottawa Senators, and was the key player in bringing the Senators back to the capital. Bruce served on the National Hockey League Board of Governors, NHL Executive Advisory Committee and as a member of the NHL Marketing and Public Relations Committee and the NHL Expansion Committee. He currently owns and is Chairman of Bretton Woods Entertainment Incorporated in Ottawa. Bruce Studied at McGill University, receiving his B. Eng (Civil), University of New South Wales, Sydney (M. Eng), and Australian National University, Canberra (Phd.). Bruce also studied at the University of Laval, University of Western Ontario, and Harvard, and in 1982 joined Terrace Investments Limited, which his father founded in 1956. Bruce and his wife Dawn have five children and this year Mr. Firestone will be a Sessional Lecturer and Research Associate teaching "The Management of Real Estate Development", at the Schools of Architecture and Business, Carleton University. Bruce is an avid art collector and is Director, Gallery of Arts Court and the Firestone Group of Seven Art Collection. Bruce is also an active supporter of many valuable organizations in the National Capital Region and serves as Chairman of the Bruce M. Firestone Atom Invitational Tournament, Scouts Canada, Salvation Army, Terry Fox Foundation, CHEO Foundation and St. John's Anglican Church of March. Bruce will serve on the CFL's Expansion and Television/Marketing Committees. Bruce M. Firestone is not only committed to building a competitive Rough Riders team, but also to building a strong, growing, and vibrant North American-wide football league.

Vice Chairman: Barry G. Lett

Barry was born in December of 1943 in Ottawa, Ontario. He graduated from Ryerson Polytechnical Institute, 1966, in Civil Engineering Technology. Barry has been Director of Land Development in both Ottawa and Calgary and served three years as executive management of an independent housing and land development company branch office. In the Ottawa area, he has been involved in numerous prestige residential developments and while in Calgary, directed the early development of the Millrise community and strategically significant parts of the Strathcona Heights areas. Barry is currently President and C.E.O. of Bretton Woods Entertainment Inc., with responsibilities for real estate management and sales, venue site developments, and feasibility investigations.

Vice Chairman: Dennis A. Ruffo

Dennis is one of the premier entertainment people in Canada. From 1978 to 1981, he worked in the Ottawa area as a partner in Rodas Productions, promoting various entertainment events including the premier Ottawa performances by "The Nylons", a series of Blues concerts with the likes of Muddy Waters, James Cotton and John Lee Hooker. All this led to his 13-year tenure at Bass Clef Entertainments. Along with his responsibilities in marketing, advertising and promotion of various entertainment events, he has established himself in this market as a senior concert promoter. Some of the events he has been involved with over the years have included the Central Canada Exhibition Grandstand series, the largest rock concerts in the City of Ottawa with David Bowie and Pink Floyd, and promoting many touring Broadway productions such as Cats, Evita, Camelot and Jesus Christ Superstar. He is currently Vice President of Bretton Woods Entertainment Inc. where his responsibilities include the development of venues for presentation of unique entertainment events.

President and Alternate Governor: Phil Kershaw

Born November 25, 1948 in London, England. Comes to Ottawa as the new President of the Rough Riders. He served three consecutive terms as President of the Saskatchewan Roughriders from 1990 to 1992. Phil was appointed CFL Chairman in 1991 and served briefly as Interim Commissioner prior to the appointment of Larry Smith. Phil is yet another member of the new Riders' management team who wears a Grey Cup ring, bringing a wealth of experience and enthusiasm to the Nation's Capital. His leadership will ensure a first class operation, resulting in quality entertainment for all fans.

Director of Football Operations and Head Coach: Adam Rita

Born on September 21, 1947 in Honolulu, Hawaii. Comes to the Riders from the Edmonton Eskimos, where he was the Offensive Coordinator last season for the 1993 Grey Cup Champions. Prior to that, he spent three years in Toronto. He joined the Argonauts in 1990 as offensive coordinator and was named head coach in 1991. The Argos had a 13-5 record and won the Grey Cup game in Winnipeg that season. Adam was then named CFL Coach of the Year. Prior to 1990 he was with the B.C. Lions as an assistant coach and ran their offense from 1983 through 1988 and helped the Lions to three Grey Cup appearances and a championship in 1985. He was the defensive co-ordinator at UBC for the 1989 season. Came to the CFL after holding assistant coaching positions in college football at the University of Hawaii (1979-82), Nevada-Las Vegas (1976-78) and Boise State (1969-75). He was born September 21, 1947 in Honolulu and grew up on the Hawaiian Island of Kauai. He is a graduate of Boise State University.

Player Personnel Consultant: Michael McCarthy

Born March 21, 1953 in Oneida, N.Y. Joined the Argonauts on November 30, 1989 after spending the previous five seasons as the Director of Player Personnel for the Hamilton Tiger-Cats and Assistant to the General Manager, Joe Zuger. Was instrumental in building the Ti-Cats, who appeared in the Grey Cup Championship 3 times under his tenure. He has signed numerous stars to the CFL, including Tony Champion, Earl Winfield, Mike Kerrigan and Raghib "Rocket" Ismail. He began coaching with the University of Oklahoma Sooners in 1976 until 1979, was a scout with the NFL New England Patriots from 1980-82; Director of Player Personnel for the USFL Chicago Blitz from 1982-84. In 1984, he joined the Oakland Invaders before coming to the CFL in 1985. In 1991 he earned the distinction of becoming the youngest General Manager in CFL history to win a Grey Cup.

Assistant Coaches

Urban Bowman, Assistant Head Coach and Defensive Coordinator. Born November 16, 1937 in Westminster, Maryland. Comes to the Riders from the Winnipeg Blue Bombers. Graduate of the University of Delaware and has a Masters degree in Education from Colorado State University. Previous coaching experience includes University of Delaware (1961), University of Dayton (1962), one season at Lebanon Valley College and six years at Colorado State. Began his coaching career in the CFL with the Hamilton Tiger-Cats (1971) and the Edmonton Eskimos (1972-73). Took an eight-year coaching hiatus (1974 to 1981). Assistant coach at Bemidgi State University 1981 to 1983. Linebacker coach at Purdue University 1984. Defensive line and special teams coach with the Blue Bombers 1985 to 1988. Offensive line coach with the Ottawa Rough Riders in 1989. Defensive line coach with the Edmonton Eskimos in 1990. Joined the Blue Bombers in March 1991 as defensive line and special teams coach and spent most of the '92 season as interim head coach.

Charlie Carpenter, Offensive Line Coach. Born October 3, 1948 in Cincinnati, Ohio. Joins the Riders after spending two seasons in the same capacity with the Blue Bombers. Spent five seasons (1987-91) at Murray State University, where he was the offensive line coach. Prior to his Murray State position, Carpenter served at Cumberland College in Williamsburg, Ky., where he helped establish the school's football program. His coaching career began as an assistant coach at Mayfield High (Ky) and Reading High (Oh). He also spent eight years as head coach at Amelia High (Oh), prior to joining the college ranks. As a player, Charlie was a three-time All-Ohio Valley Conference selection as an offensive lineman at Murray State University and had pro tryouts with the Philadelphia Eagles and Memphis of the WFL. A four-year letterman for the Racers, he served as team captain in his junior and senior years.

Paul Chryst, Special Teams Coach. Born November 17, 1965 in Madison Wisconsin. Joins the staff as special teams coach working along with Urban Bowman. Paul worked with receivers under Adam Rita as a guest coach with the Edmonton Eskimos last season. In 1991 and 1992, Paul coached under Mike Riley with the San Antonio Riders of the World League of American Football.

Jim Hilles, Defensive Line Coach. Born September 24, 1936 in Warren, Ohio. Joined the Argonauts in 1991 after coaching for the University of Kansas from 1988-1990 as the Defensive Coordinator/Linebacker Coach. Previous coaching experience includes Kent State University, Defensive Coordinator/Linebacker Coach (1987), Head Football Coach, University of Wisconsin-Madison (1986) and Assistant Coach (1978-85), Ball State University, Defensive Coordinator (1971-78). Holds a Bachelor of Science Degree in Physical Education from Ohio University, as well as a Master of Arts in Secondary Administration from Westminster College. Has coached numerous players that have gone on to play in the NFL.

Don Blackwelder, Running Backs and Receivers Coach. Born December 9, 1946. Joins the staff as an assistant after spending the last two years as the head coach of the Bergamo Lions, who won the 1993 National Championship of the Professional Football League in Italy. Served as an assistant for Adam Rita in Toronto in 1991, working with the quarterbacks the year the Argos last won the Grey Cup.

OTTAWA ROUGH RIDERS
1994 CURRENT ROSTER AS OF APRIL 30, 1994
RETURNING PLAYERS

* Denotes Import

	Player	Pos.	Ht.	Wt.	Born	University/ Junior Affiliate	Yrs CFL	Yrs OTT
	BAKER, Terry	QB	6.01	210	08 MAY 62	Mt. Allison	8	5
*	BARNES, Reggie	RB	5.09	210	10 OCT 67	Delaware State	5	5
	BEATON, Bruce	OT	6.06	300	13 JUN 68	Acadia	2	2
*	BENEFIELD, Daved	LB	6.03	225	16 FEB 67	Northridge State	3	3
*	BONNER, Brian	LB	6.01	235	09 OCT 65	Minnesota	4	4
	BURKE, Patrick	CB	5.11	180	06 NOV 68	Fresno College	2	2
	CHAYTORS, Dave	DT	6.02	235	12 OCT 69	Utah	2	2
	CHRONOPOLOUS, D.	OG	6.04	290	12 JUN 68	Purdue	3	3
	CLIMIE, Jock	SB	6.01	185	28 SEP 68	Queen's	5	4
	CRIFO, Rob	WR	6.06	230	10 NOV 65	Toronto	6	2
	CUMMINGS, Burtland	DB	5.08	165	10 NOV 65	North Dakota	5	2
	DAYMOND, Irv	C	6.04	265	09 OCT 62	Western Ontario	9	9
*	DOWDEN, Cory	DB	5.10	190	18 OCT 68	Tulane	1	1
	ELLINGSON, James	SB	6.01	205	18 MAY 63	UBC	9	5
*	FLEETWOOD, Marquel	QB	6.01	195	23 JAN 70	Minnesota	2	2
	GIOSKOS, Chris	G	6.02	275	15 DEC 67	Ottawa	5	2
*	GORDON, Charles	DB	6.00	185	30 JUL 68	Eastern Michigan	4	4
*	GRAYBILL, Michael	T	6.07	280	14 OCT 66	Boston	2	2
*	HINTON, Patrick	LB	6.01	230	11 FEB 68	South Carolina	2	2
*	JONES, Stephen	WR	6.00	190	08 JUN 60	Central Michigan	10	5
	JOSEPH, Darren	RB	6.00	200	29 AUG 68	Ottawa Jrs.	3	3
*	KROPKE, John	DT	6.05	280	03 JAN 66	Illinios State	6	6
	KULKA, Glenn	DE	6.03	265	03 MAR 64	Bakersfield	9	5
	LAMY, Michel	G	6.02	265	25 JUN 67	Sequoias	6	6
	LEVY, Nigel	WR	6.03	195	18 FEB 69	Western Ontario	2	2
	MOREAU, Jacques	G	6.03	265	19 JUN 67	Concordia	2	2
	NOEL, Dean	RB	5.11	200	21 FEB 67	Delaware State	2	2
	RABY, Michel	DT	6.05	265	17 DEC 68	Ottawa	4	4
*	ROBINSON, Lybrant	DE	6.04	250	31 AUG 64	Delaware State	4	4
*	SARDO, Joe	DB	6.01	210	07 NOV 69	Hawaii	3	3
	SCHRAMAYR, Ernie	FB	5.10	215	07 JUL 66	Purdue	6	2
*	SHAVERS, Tyrone	SB	6.03	210	09 FEB 68	Lamar	2	2
*	SNIPES, Angelo	LB	6.01	235	01 NOV 63	West Georgia	4	4
*	STANLEY, Walter	WR	5.10	180	05 NOV 62	Mesa College	2	2
	STEWART, Andrew	DE	6.05	265	20 NOV 65	Cincinnati	2	2
	STEWART, Dean	RB	5.07	180	07 JAN 69	Mansfield	2	2
*	THORNTON, Reggie	WR	5.11	180	26 SEP 67	Bowling Green	2	2
	TIERNEY, Brad	G	6.04	265	06 MAY 65	Acadia	6	5
	WALCOTT, Ken	DB	6.00	205	01 MAY 9	Saint Mary's	2	2
	WEBER, Gordon	LB	6.03	210	12 FEB 65	Ottawa	5	5
	WETMORE, Paul	LB	6.03	225	10 OCT 66	Acadia	6	2
*	YOUNG, Brett	DB	5.10	185	03 APR 67	Oregon	5	5

NEW PLAYERS

	Player	Pos.	Ht.	Wt.	Born	University/ Junior Affiliate	Yrs CFL
*	BARRETT, Danny	QB	5.11	195	18 DEC 61	Cincinnati	11
*	BRASWELL, Jeff	LB	6.02	230	23 NOV 64	Iowa State	6
*	BROOKS, Horace	WR	5.09	170	12 DEC 70	Alabama State	1
*	BULLOCK, Randy	LB	6.02	245	23 NOV 69	NW Louisiana	1
*	CALLOWAY, Ernest	WR	5.08	155	19 JAN 70	Purdue	1
*	COLLINS, Gerry	RB	5.07	190	04 JUN 69	Penn State	1
*	ELLIS, Donnie	DB	5.11	170	14 NOV 69	Texas Southern	1
	FERRY, Robert	FB	6.01	230	17 JUN 71	McMaster	1
	FREDERICK, Albert	CB	6.01	210	18 JUL 69	Livingston	1
*	GARDNER, Donnie	DE	6.04	265	17 FEB 68	Kentucky	1
*	GILBERT, Freddie	SB	5.09	175	03 SEP 69	Houston	1
	GRANT, Warren	WR	5.09	185	22 OCT 70	Ottawa	1
*	HABERSHAM, Shoun	WR	5.11	185	04 APR 68	Tenn-Chattanooga	1
*	HARDY, Darryl	LB	6.03	215	22 NOV 68	Tennessee	1
*	HENRY, Maurice	LB	6.00	225	12 MAR 67	Kansas State	1
*	LATSON, Lawann	WR	5.07	180	11 MAR 71	NW Louisiana	1
	MAZZOLI, Nick	WR	5.11	185	08 AUG 68	Simon Fraser	4
*	McPHERSON, Don	QB	6.01	190	02 APR 65	Syracuse	4
*	PARKS, Vincent	WR	5.09	165	30 JAN 70	Middle Tennessee	1
*	RICHARDSON, Mike	RB	5.11	200	13 OCT 69	Louisiana Tech	4
*	SMALL, Jessie	LB	6.04	245	30 NOV 66	Eastern Kentucky	1
*	STEWART, Andrew	DE	6.05	265	20 NOV 65	Cincinnati	1

TORONTO ARGONAUTS FOOTBALL CLUB

Executive Offices: SkyDome Gate 7
P.O. Box 188, Station C
Toronto, Ontario M6J 3M9
Telephone Number: (416) 595-9600
Fax: (416) 595-8232
Ticket Office: (416) 595-1131 Fax: (416) 595-0797

EXECUTIVE

Owners: TSN Enterprises
President: Paul Beeston
Executive Vice President: Bob Nicholson

FOOTBALL OPERATIONS

General Manager and Head Coach: Bob O'Billovich
Assistant Coaches:
Dennis Meyer, Defensive Coordinator
Joe Moss, Defensive Line Coach
Tommy Lee, Offensive Backs and Receivers Coach
Tony Marciano, Offensive Line Coach
Director of Player Personnel: John Peterson
Executive Assistant, Football Operations: Cathie Burns
Administrative Assistant: Lorraine Tuck
Athletic Therapist: Gerry Townend
Assistant Athletic Therapist: Don Alexander
Equipment Manager: Danny Webb
Assistant Equipment Manager: Jason Colero
Senior Medical Advisor: Dr. Jerry Shklar
Team Orthopedic Surgeon: Dr. Wayne Marshall
Dentist: Dr. Paul Piccinnini
Scouts: Nick Volpe, Bernie Custis, Gerry Sazio, Dominik Machek, Jack O'Billovich

ADMINISTRATION

Vice President, Finance: Stephen Prest
Vice President, Communications: David P. Watkins
Director of Communications: Michael Cosentino
Director of Promotions: Sarah Higgins
Accounting Assistant: Jeannette Abela

TICKET SALES - SKYDOME

Director of Ticket Sales: Steve Shiffman
Box Office Manager: Janet Fletcher

MARKETING & COMMUNITY SERVICE CENTRE

95 Wellington Street West
Ground Floor, P.O. Box 55
Toronto, Ontario M5J 2N7
Telephone: (416) 862-7722 Fax: (416) 862-7725
Corporate Sales Executives: Don Moen, Patricia Pilot
Corporate Sales Coordinator: Tosha Rehak

***"END ZONE"* MERCHANDISE STORE**

151 Front Street West
Toronto, Ontario M5J 2N1
Telephone: (416) 601-4820 Fax: (416) 601-1760
Store Manager: Adam Zeleski

FAST FACTS

Home Stadium: SkyDome
300 Bremner Blvd.
Toronto, Ontario M5V 3B2
Ticket Office: SkyDome, Gate 7,
P.O. Box 188, Station C
Toronto, ON M6J 3M9
Club Colours: Oxford Blue, Cambridge Blue
Training Camp Site: University of Guelph
Press Box Location: West Side of Dome
Dressing Room Locations: Home Team - Southeast Corner
Visiting Team - Southwest Corner
Radio Broadcasts: CFRB 1010
P.A. Announcer: Bill Sturrup
Statistician: Victor Gosselin

SkyDome Facts 'n Figures

Capacity: 50,377
Largest Regular Season One Game Attendance: 44,209 Hamilton 36, Toronto 25 (November 4, 1989)
Largest Playoff One Game Attendance: 50,386 Toronto 42, Winnipeg 3 (November 17, 1991)
Largest Grey Cup Attendance: 54,088 Saskatchewan 43, Hamilton 40 (November 26, 1989)

FAST FACTS (Cont'd)

Offensive Spotters: Larry Aicken/Mark Warden
Defensive Spotter: Corey Gibson
Typist: Doug Aicken

Club History: 1873 formation of the Toronto Argonaut football team by the Toronto Argonaut Rowing Club. Argonauts play University of Toronto on October 11. Argonauts move to SkyDome in 1989. Last Grey Cup win was on November 24, 1991 in Winnipeg.

NINETEEN GREY CUP VICTORIES FOR TORONTO-BASED TEAMS

University of Toronto (4) - 1909, 1910, 1911, 1920
Argonauts (12) - 1914, 1921, 1933, 1937, 1938, 1945, 1946, 1947, 1950,1952, 1983, 1991
Balmy Beach (2) - 1927, 1930
RCAF Hurricanes (1) - 1942

TORONTO CLUB RECORDS SINCE 1946
Regular Season

- CFL Record
- Ties CFL Record
( ) - Figures in Brackets represent Year(s) Club mark set

Most Points Scored One Season (minimum 14 games) - #689 ('90)
Most Points Scored Against One Season (minimum 14 games) - 526 ('91)
Fewest Points Against One Season (minimum 14 games) - 231 ('73)
Most Points Scored One Game - 70 - Calgary at Toronto 09/20/90 Final: 70-18
Most Points Scored Against One Game - 61 - at Edmonton 24/10/81 Final: 61-7
Most Wins One Season (minimum 14 games) - 14 ('88)
Most Consecutive Wins at Home - 12 - (10/20/90 - 07/16/92)
Most Losses One Season (minimum 14 games) - 14 ('81)
Highest Shutout - 53-0 - Winnipeg at Toronto 08/10/67
Highest Shutout Against - 50-0 - Calgary at Toronto 22/09/63
Most Touchdowns One Season (minimum 14 games) - #81 ('90)

Most Touchdowns One Game - 10 - Calgary at Toronto 09/20/90
Most Converts One Season (minimum 14 games) - #77 ('90)
Most Converts One Game - 10 - Calgary at Toronto 09/20/90
Most Field Goals One Season (minimum 14 games) - 55 ('91)
Most Field Goals One Game - 6 - vs. Edmonton 23/08/86
Most Field Goals One Game - 6 - vs. Winnipeg 08/11/87
Most First Downs One Game - 38 - Ottawa at Toronto 29/10/55
Most Yards Total Offense One Game - 677 - Montreal at Toronto 30/10/60
Most Yards Rushing One Game - 433 - Montreal at Toronto 02/11/57
Most Touchdowns Rushing One Season - 21 ('91, '90)
Most Times Carried One Game - 60 - Ottawa at Toronto 19/10/57
Most Touchdowns Rushing One Game - 4 - B.C. at Toronto 16/07/81
Most Yards Passing One Game - 524 - Montreal at Toronto 19/08/60
Most Passes Thrown One Game - 56 - at Calgary 07/07/83;
Most Passes Thrown One Game - 56 - at Winnipeg 08/07/84
Most Completions One Game - 38 - Montreal at Toronto 19/08/60
Most Touchdown Passes One Game - 7 - Montreal at Toronto 01/10/60
Most Touchdown Passes One Game - 7 - Montreal at Toronto 30/10/60
Most Touchdown Passes One Game - 7 - Hamilton at Toronto 29/09/90

TORONTO INDIVIDUAL RECORDS SINCE 1946
Regular Season

Points (Career) - 1,498 - Lance Chomyc
Points (Season) - #236 - Lance Chomyc ('91)
Points (Game) - 27 -
- Chester (Cookie) Gilchrist - Montreal at Toronto 30/10/60
Touchdowns (Career) - 91 - Dick Shatto
Touchdowns (Season) - ##20 - Darrell K. Smith ('90)
Touchdowns (Game) - 4 -
- Dick Shatto - Hamilton at Toronto 13/10/58
- Bill Symons - Toronto at Ottawa 07/09/70
Converts (Career) - 412 - Lance Chomyc
Converts (Season) - ##76 - Lance Chomyc ('90)
Converts (Game) - ##9 - Lance Chomyc - Calgary at Toronto 20/09/90
Field Goals (Career) - 337 - Lance Chomyc
Field Goals (Season) - 55 - Lance Chomyc ('91)
Field Goals (Game) - 7 -
- Lance Chomyc - Toronto at Calgary 30/09/88
- Lance Chomyc - Ottawa at Toronto 14/10/88
Longest Field Goal - 57 - Zenon Andrusyshyn - at Saskatchewan 14/09/80
Kickoff Yards (Career) - 30,385 - Hank Ilesic
Kickoff Yards (Season) - 5,688 - Lance Chomyc ('90)
Kickoff Yards (Game) - 749 - Hank Ilesic - B.C. at Toronto 16/07/92
Kickoffs (Game) - 12 - Hank Ilesic - B.C. at Toronto 16/07/92
Passes Thrown (Career) - 1,988 - Condredge Holloway
Passes Thrown (Season) - 527 - Gilbert Renfroe ('88)
Passes Thrown (Game) - 54 - Tobin Rote - Montreal at Toronto 19/08/60
Passes Completed (Career) - 1,149 - Condredge Holloway
Passes Completed (Season) - 299 - Condredge Holloway ('82)
Passes Completed (Game) - 38 - Tobin Rote - Montreal at Toronto 19/08/60
Passing Yards (Career) - 16,619 - Condredge Holloway
Passing Yards (Season) - 4,661 - Condredge Holloway ('82)
Passing Yards (Game) - 524 - Tobin Rote - Montreal at Toronto 19/08/60
Touchdown Passes Thrown (Career) - 98 - Condredge Holloway
Touchdown Passes Thrown (Season) - 38 - Tobin Rote ('60)
Touchdown Passes Thrown (Game) - 7 -
- Tobin Rote - Montreal at Toronto 01/10/60
- Tobin Rote - Montreal at Toronto 30/10/60
- Rickey Foggie - Hamilton at Toronto 29/09/90
No. of Carries (Career) - 1,322 - Dick Shatto
No. of Carries (Season) - 245 - Gill Fenerty ('89)
No. of Carries (Game) - #37 - Doyle Orange - Hamilton at Toronto 13/08/75
Yards Rushing (Career) - 6,958 - Dick Shatto
Yards Rushing (Season) - 1,247 - Gill Fenerty ('89)
Yards Rushing (Game) - 215 - Gill Fenerty - Calgary at Toronto 31/08/88
Yards Rushing Quarterback (Season) - 644 - Rickey Foggie ('91)
Yards Rushing Quarterback (Game) - 135 -
- Rickey Foggie - Toronto at Calgary 9/15/91
Touchdowns by Rushing (Career) - 39 - Dick Shatto
Touchdowns by Rushing (Season) - 12 - Gill Fenerty ('87)
Touchdowns by Rushing (Game) - 3 -
- Bill Symons - Toronto at Ottawa 07/09/70
- Gill Fenerty - Hamilton at Toronto 20/09/87

Passes Caught (Career) - 466 - Dick Shatto
Passes Caught (Season) - 113 - Terry Greer ('83)
Passes Caught First Year Player - 64 - Raghib Ismail ('91)
Passes Caught (Game) - #16 - Terry Greer - Toronto at Ottawa 19/08/83
Pass Reception Yards (Career) - 8,144 - Darrell K. Smith
Pass Reception Yards (Season) - #2,003 - Terry Greer ('83)
Pass Reception Yards First Year Player - 1,300 - Raghib Ismail ('91)
Pass Reception Yards (Game) - 246 -
- Terry Greer - Hamilton at Toronto 10/09/82
Touchdown Passes Caught (Career) - 52 - Dick Shatto
Touchdown Passes Caught (Season) - 15 - Al Pfeifer ('55)
Touchdown Passes Caught (Game) - 4 -
- Darrell K. Smith - Hamilton at Toronto 29/09/90

TORONTO'S RECORD AGAINST OTHER CLUBS (REGULAR SEASON)

		GP	W	L	T	F	A	PTS
Versus Ottawa	(Since 1946)	160	76	81	3	3105	3331	155
Versus Hamilton	(Since 1946)	170	67	99	4	3210	3508	45
Versus Winnipeg	(Since 1961)	52	22	29	1	1130	1170	45
Versus Saskatchewan	(Since 1961)	46	21	24	1	1116	1068	43
Versus Calgary	(Since 1961)	46	21	24	1	1092	1152	43
Versus Edmonton	(Since 1961)	46	20	25	1	1037	1217	41
Versus B.C.	(Since 1961)	46	19	25	2	1191	1251	40
Versus Sacramento	(Since 1993)	2	1	1	0	61	73	2
TORONTO VS OPPOSITION		568	247	308	13	11942	12770	412

President and CEO, JLL Broadcast Group: Gordon Craig

Born in Winnipeg, Manitoba, in 1936, Gordon Craig began his broadcast career with the Canadian Broadcasting Corporation in 1955 where he held progressively senior positions with the company including Executive Producer, TV Sports (1966-68), Deputy Head, and then Head of TV Sports (1968-76), Director of Television for the province of British Columbia (1976-81) and Director of Operations, English Services Division (1981-83). Craig was responsible for the extensive coverage of the 1976 Olympic Games in Montreal when he earned accolades for the most comprehensive coverage of an international sporting event ever offered to Canadians. He was also the Executive Producer of the Winter Olympics in Grenoble, France (1968), and in Saporo, Japan (1972). In 1983, Craig joined the Houston Group Communications Ltd. as Vice-President and General Manager. Craig became President and General Manager of The Sports Network, Canada's only 24-hour all-sports TV network. He led the TSN team through the television process, and launched the network on September 1, 1984. In 1988, Craig became the President and CEO of the JLL Broadcast Group, consisting of The Sports Network (TSN), Dome Productions, Le Réseau des sports (RDS), TSN Enterprises and The Rep Shoppe.

President, Toronto Argonauts Football Club: Paul Beeston

Born June 20, 1945 in Welland, Ontario. He graduated from the University of Western Ontario in 1968 with a Bachelor of Arts degree, majoring in economics and political science. He began working with Coopers and Lybrand in London, Ont. in 1968 and received his chartered accountant designation three years later. Beeston became a manager with Coopers and Lybrand in 1973 and was named the first employee of the Toronto Blue Jays Baseball Club on May 10, 1976, only 11/2 months after the granting of the franchise. He became the Blue Jays' VP, Administration, went on to be named VP, Business Operations Nov. 24, 1977 and assumed the title of Chief Operating Officer on Jan. 10, 1989. He received the designation of Fellow of the Institute of Chartered Accountants of Ontario, March 23, 1988. He was appointed to the Board of Directors for the Stratford Festival. In 1994, he was selected the 20th most powerful person in sports, chosen by The Sporting News. He was named President of the Toronto Argonauts Football Club Thurs., May 5, 1994 by JLL Broadcast Group President Gordon Craig. Paul and wife Kaye have two children, Aimee (19) and David (16), and reside in Toronto.

General Manager and Head Coach: Bob O'Billovich

Born on June 30, 1940 in Butte, Montana. Attended the University of Montana. Selected by the NFL's St. Louis Cardinals in the 1962 Draft. With the NFL Denver Broncos before joining the Ottawa Rough Riders from 1963 to 1967 as a defensive back and quarterback. Retired in 1968 and went on to coach football and basketball at Algonquin College, Carleton University and the University of Ottawa. Assistant coach with the Rough Riders from 1976 to 1981. In 1981 he became head coach of the Argonauts. O'Billovich then joined the B.C. Lions in September, 1990, where he stayed until

1992. Rejoined the Argonauts in September of last year. In his first stint with the Argonauts, the team appeared in three Grey Cups, winning one, and made it to the playoffs six times. O'Billovich was the inaugural inductee into the Butte (Montana) Sports Hall of Fame in 1982.

Assistant Coaches

Dennis Meyer, Defensive Coordinator. Born April 8, 1950 in Jefferson City, Missouri. Returns to his position as defensive coordinator after a stint as head coach, when he replaced Adam Rita on September 21, 1992. He is the only member of the Argonauts' football operation to have shared in both the 1983 and 1991 Grey Cup victories. Joined the Argonauts on February 8, 1982 as Defensive Backs Coach and worked for eight seasons as the Defensive Secondary Coach. Under head coach Don Matthews (1990), he specialized as Linebacker Coach and was then appointed Defensive coordinator when Adam Rita became Head Coach in 1991. He is a graduate of Arkansas State University, where he earned a BSE Degree in Physical Education and Sociology. His academic standing earned him Academic All-American accolades and a scholarship where he later earned a Masters Degree in Secondary School Administration from Georgia State. He was a sixth-round Draft selection of the NFL Pittsburgh Steelers in 1972 and played Defensive Back for the Calgary Stampeders for three seasons beginning in 1975. Meyer began his coaching career with Calgary in 1978 before returning to the U.S. to coach at the High School level until 1980. He rejoined Calgary as Coach of Defensive Backs and Specialty Teams in 1980-81.

Joe Moss, Defensive Line Coach. Born April 9, 1930 in Elkins, West Virginia. Returns for his fourth stint with the Toronto Argonauts, having previously spent some time there from 1973-76, 1983-84 and lastly from 1987-89. Comes from the Hamilton Tiger-Cats where he coordinated the defensive unit and the defensive backs from 1990-93. Moss is a graduate of the University of Maryland where he played offensive line (1949-52) and was a member of the 1952 Washington Redskins. His coaching career began in the college ranks with the University of Maryland in 1956, then on to Texas Tech in 1957-59, West Texas State (1960) and United States Air Force Academy (1961-68). Began his professional coaching career with the Philadelphia Eagles of the NFL in 1969. After entering the CFL with the Argonauts, he moved to Saskatchewan for the 1977 season, then went on to Ottawa from 1978-81. He returned to Toronto in '83 then served as head coach of the Ottawa club from 1985 to 1987. Following three years back with the Argonauts, he joined Hamilton where he remained until last season.

Tommy Lee, Offensive Backs and Receivers Coach. Born September 11, 1942 in Honolulu, Hawaii. Lee last served as a pro coach in 1992, his second season as receivers coach for the San Antonio Riders of the WLAF. He spent five years (1986-90) as offensive coordinator at the University of Montana. Before that, Lee worked as offensive coordinator and recruiting coordinator at Portland State University from 1983-85. He served as Head Coach and Athletic Director at Willamette University (Salem, Oregon) from 1974-82. Prior to that, he worked as a coaching assistant at Willamette in '72-'73 and was head coach at Central Catholic High School in Portland from 1969-71. Played quarterback for the Ottawa Rough Riders in 1962 after earning his Bachelor's and Master's Degrees in Physical Education at Willamette.

Tony Marciano, Offensive Line Coach. Born June 14, 1956 in Scranton, Pennsylvania. Graduated from Indiana University of Pennsylvania (IUP) in 1978 with a Bachelor of Science Degree in Elementary Education. Began his coaching career as an assistant at Dunmore (PA.) High School and at IUP before accepting a position as Assistant Offensive Line Coach at Texas Christian University, where he also spent two years as the Director of Strength and Conditioning Programs. Following that, he moved on to Southern Methodist University, where he spent from 1981 to 1987 working with the tackles, tight ends and kickers. Served as a guest coach at the Ottawa Rough Rider training camp in '87 and then was named Offensive Coordinator at Brown University for two seasons. Spent 1988 to 1990 as the Offensive Coordinator at the University of Richmond and then served as the Assistant Head Coach at Kent State University (1991-92) before joining the Argonauts this season.

TORONTO ARGONAUTS
1994 CURRENT ROSTER AS OF APRIL 30, 1994
RETURNING PLAYERS

* Denotes Import

Player	Pos.	Ht.	Wt.	Born	University/ Junior Affiliate	Yrs CFL	Yrs TOR
BELANGER, Francois	T	6.06	290	21 FEB 68	McGill	4	2
* BRANCH, Darrick	WR	6.00	200	10 FEB 70	Hawaii	2	2
CAMPBELL, Michael	DT	6.01	260	19 SEP 65	Slippery Rock	6	6
CASTELLO, Keith	LB	6.02	215	31 MAY 64	Oshawa Jrs.	7	5
CHOMYC, Lance	K	6.00	195	2 MAR 63	Toronto	10	10
* CLARK, Reggie	LB	6.02	225	17 OCT 67	North Carolina	2	2
* CLARK, Robert	WR	5.10	180	6 AUG 65	N Carolina Central	2	2
* CLEMONS, Michael	RB	5.06	170	15 JAN 65	William & Mary	6	6
COULTER, Carl	G	6.01	275	14 NOV 66	Carleton	5	1
CRANMER, Paul	SB	6.01	195	27 NOV 69	Grand Valley State	2	1
* GORDON, Robert	WR	5.10	185	9 JUL 68	Nebraska-Omaha	4	2
* HALLMAN, Harold	DT	6.00	255	10 DEC 62	Auburn	9	7
* HARDING, Rodney	DT	6.02	250	1 AUG 62	Oklanoma State	10	10
* HARDY, John	DB	5.11	175	11 JUN 68	California	2	2
* HAZARD, Manny	SB	5.08	175	22 JUL 69	Houston	2	2
* HENRY, Tommy	DB	6.02	175	4 NOV 69	Florida State	2	1
HOULDER, Mark	LB	6.01	230	22 AUG 67	York	2	2
HUDSON, Warren	FN	6.02	215	25 MAY 62	Guelph	10	7
* HUGHES, Darren	DB	6.01	180	3 JUN 67	Carson Newman	2	2
* JACKSON, Enis	DB	5.09	175	16 MAY 63	Memphis State	5	2
* JACKSON, Pat	RB	5.09	180	8 JUL 69	Kansas State	2	2
* KERRIGAN, Mike	QB	6.04	215	27 APR 60	Northwestern	9	3
KING, Lorne	RB	6.00	210	12 APR 67	Toronto	3	2
LAMMLE, Wayne	PK	6.04	220	10 APR 69	Utah	3	2
* LEWIS, Tahaun	CB	5.11	180	29 SEP 68	Nebraska	2	2
MASOTTI, Paul	WR	6.00	185	10 MAR 65	Acadia	7	7
MCCURDY, Brian	DB	6.01	180	11 JUN 67	Northern Arizona	2	2
MOEN, Don	LB	6.02	235	29 APR 60	UBC	13	13
MURRAY, Andrew	SB	6.03	200	15 JUL 64	Carleton	7	5
NIMAKO, George	DB	5.10	195	9 MAR 69	Liberty	2	2
* OLIVER, Travis	CB	6.00	180	10 MAR 68	California	3	2
PARTCHENKO, Peter	T	6.04	285	30 JAN 70	Michigan State	2	2
* PLEASANT, Reggie	CB	5.09	175	1 MAY 62	Clemson	8	8
RICHARDS, Dwight	RB	5.10	200	7 SEP 69	Weber State	2	2
RODEHUTSKORS, Steven	T	6.06	265	27 NOV 63	Calgary	8	2
SCHMIDT, Blaine	DE	6.04	285	23 AUG 63	Guelph	8	8
SCHULTZ, Chris	T	6.08	290	16 FEB 60	Arizona	9	9
* SLACK, Reggie	QB	6.02	220	2 MAY 68	Auburn	3	2
SMELLIE, Kevin	RB	5.10	190	27 JUL 66	Massacusetts	4	4
THOMAS, Andrew	DB	5.11	185	5 OCT 66	Massachusetts	5	2
VERCHEVAL, Pierre	G	6.01	275	22 NOV 64	Western Ontario	7	2
* WHITLEY, Kevin	DB	5.10	190	26 FEB 70	Georgia Southern	2	2
YLI-RENKO, Kari	T	6.05	270	17 NOV 59	Cincinnati	10	2

NEW PLAYERS

* Denotes Import

Player	Pos.	Ht.	Wt.	Born	University/ Jr. Affiliate	Yrs. CFL
AZCONA, Eddie	K	5.10	180	11 NOV 67	Michigan	1
* BELL, Billy	DB	5.10	175	16 JAN 61	Lamar	2
BENNETT, Jamie	DT	6.03	265	25 MAR 70	Fresno State	1
* BENSON, Maurice	DB	6.00	200	27 NOV 70	Missouri	1
BOLES, Todd	LB	6.03	215	18 MAR 69	N/A	1
* BRUHIN, John	OG	6.03	285	9 DEC 64	Tennessee	1
* BURGOS, Joe	OL	6.03	290	12 MAR 71	Temple	1
* CARROLL, Kevin	DE	6.03	265	17 JUN 69	Knoxville College	1
CASOLA, Norm	WR	6.03	225	4 AUG 69	Windsor	1
* CECCHINI, David	DB	5.10	175	9 MAR 72	Lehigh	1
CHARLES, Hency	DB	5.10	200	4 OCT 70	Ottawa	1
* CRESPINA, Keita	CB	5.08	185	25 FEB 71	Temple	1
CRIFO, Dan	OL	6.04	290	17 FEB 72	McGill	1
* DAVIS, Bo	DT	6.03	290	17 MAY 70	Louisiana State	1
* DEAN, Orlando	DE	6.00	260	16 AUG 71	Savannah State	1
* EDMOND, Corey	LB	6.01	240	15 FEB 69	North Carolina State	1
FAIRHOLM, Jeff	SB	5.11	190	7 NOV 65	Arizona	7
* FRANKS, Carl	DB	5.10	180	30 APR 70	Montana	1
* GRAHAM, Boris	LB	6.03	240	21 JAN 69	West Virginia	1
* HAYS, Todd	LB	6.02	225	21 MAY 6	Tulsa	1
* HILL, Tim	CB	5.08	175	16 SEP 69	Kansas	1
* JACOBS, Joe	DE	6.04	265	21 SEP 70	Utah	1
JAGAS, Frank	K	5.10	210	8 JAN 71	Western Ontario	1
JOVANOVICH, Mike	T	6.06	290	11 MAY 67	Boston College	3
* KENT, Phillip	LB	6.00	240	6 MAY 7	Mississippi	1
LAING, Trac	DL	6.04	275	3 SEP 71	Cisco JC	1
* SHAMBURGER, Anthony	LB	6.03	230	19 JAN 69	Alabama State	1
* SHIPLEY, Stephen	WR	6.05	225		Texas Christian	1
* WALKER, David	RB	5.09	215	4 DEC 69	Syracuse	1
* WAUFORD, Jon	DE	6.03	265	11 FEB 70	Miami of Ohio	1
* WILLIAMS, Keith	RB	5.08	185	20 SEP 71	Utah	1
* WRIGHT, Eric	WR				Stephen F. Austin	1

HAMILTON TIGER-CAT FOOTBALL CLUB

Administrative Office:
Lloyd D. Jackson Square
2 King St. West
Hamilton, Ontario L8P 1A1
Tel.: (905) 521-5666
Fax: (905) 527-5332

Football Operations:
Ivor Wynne Stadium
75 Balsam Ave. N.
Hamilton, Ontario L8L 8C1
Tel.: (905) 547-2418
Fax: (905) 549-6610

Ticket Office Phone: (905) 527-1508

EXECUTIVE

Chairman: Roger Yachetti, Q.C.
President and Chief Executive Officer: John Michaluk
Directors: Roger Yachetti, John Michaluk, Mayor Bob Morrow, Regional Chairman Reg Whynott, Gordon Bullock, Sam Mercanti.

FOOTBALL OPERATIONS

Director of Football Operations and Head Coach: John Gregory
Assistant Coaches:
Jim Clark, Linebacker/Special Teams Coach
Gary Durchik,Offensive Coordinator/Quarterbacks and Receivers Coach
John Salavantis,Offensive Line Coach
Don Sutherin, Defensive Coordinator/Defensive Back Coach
Don Wnek, Defensive Line Coach
Asst. Director of Football Operations: Greg Mohns
Trainer: Al Scott
Equipment Manager/Strength and Conditioning Coach: Issac Wright
Assistant Equipment Manager: Rob Whitehouse
Canadian Scout: Bob Krouse
Receptionist/Secretary: Laurie Wade
Medical Staff: Dr. J.W. Charters, Dr. D. Levy, Dr. N. Siksay
Dental Staff: Dr. J.E. Durran, Dr. W.R. Barlow

BUSINESS OPERATIONS

Controller: Robert Agopian
Vice President, Marketing and Sales: Neil Lumsden
Corporate Marketing and Sales: Don Edwards
Communications Director: Norm Miller
Operations Director: Todd Crocker
Accounting: Josephine Barlow
Ticket Manager: Matthew Moreland
Ticket Sales: Denise Carron
Merchandising Manager: Michelle Plant

FAST FACTS

Club Colours: Black, Gold and White. Black jerseys for home games, white jerseys for away games.
Stadium: Ivor Wynne Stadium
P.A. Announcer: Bill Sturrup, Bill Kelly, Ann Riches
City Stadium Manager: Dave Cowan
Training Camp Site: Ivor Wynne Stadium, Hamilton, Ontario
Press Box Location: South Side of Stadium, via Gate 10, Section 26
Dressing Room Locations: Home Team - Under South side of stands
Visiting Team - Under South-East side of stands
Radio Broadcasts: CHML-AM 900 Play-By-Play - Bob Bratina
Colour Commentary - John Bonk
Statistician/Producer - Bob Hooper
Reporters - Al Craig, Ted Michaels
Statistician: Ron Novakovich
Spotters: Ric Wood, Dennis Cooke
Typist: Mary Tinson
Timekeeper: Leo Dunn
Scorekeeper: Don Roberts

Club History: 1869 Hamilton Tigers were formed. In 1907, they joined the Interprovincial Rugby Football Union . . . 1914 amalgamation of the Hamilton Alerts and the Hamilton Tigers to continue playing under the name Tigers . . . Tigers suspended play for WW II . . . 1948 Hamilton Wildcats joined the IRFU to replace the Tigers who joined the Ontario Rugby Football Union . . . 1950 Tigers and Wildcats amalgamate to form the Hamilton Tiger-Cats in the IRFU.

Ivor Wynne Stadium Facts 'n Figures

Capacity: 29,123
Largest Regular Season One Game Attendance: 35,394
Hamilton 18, Toronto 0 (November 7, 1976)
Largest Playoff One Game Attendance: 29,656
Hamilton 24, Montreal 13 (November 16, 1980)
Largest Grey Cup Attendance: 33,993
Hamilton 13, Saskatchewan 10 (December 3, 1972)

FOURTEEN GREY CUP VICTORIES FOR HAMILTON-BASED TEAMS

Alerts (1) - 1912
Tigers (5) - 1913, 1915, 1928, 1929, 1932
Flying Wildcats (1) - 1943
Tiger Cats (7) - 1953, 1957, 1963, 1965, 1967, 1972, 1986

HAMILTON CLUB RECORDS SINCE 1946

Regular Season

- CFL Record
( ) - Figures in Brackets represent Year(s) Club mark set

Most Points Scored One Season (minimum 14 games) - 536 ('92)
Most Points Scored Against (minimum 14 games) - 628 ('90)
Fewest Points Against One Season (minimum 14 games) - 153 ('65)
Most Points Scored One Game - 67 -
- Saskatchewan at Hamilton - 15/10/62. Final: 67-21
Most Points Scored Against One Game -#82 -
- at Montreal 20/10/56. Final: 82-14.
Most Wins One Season (minimum 14 games) - 12 ('89)
Most Losses One Season (minimum 14 games) - 15 ('91)
Highest Shutout - 45-0 - Ottawa at Hamilton 02/10/54
Highest Shutout Against - 37-0 - at Toronto 13/10/58
Most Touchdowns One Season (minimum 14 games) - 55 - ('92)
Most Touchdowns One Game - 10 - Saskatchewan at Hamilton 15/10/62
Most Converts One Season (minimum 14 games) - 52 ('92)
Most Converts One Game - 8 - Toronto at Hamilton 25/07/81
Most Field Goals One Season (minimum 14 games) - 54 ('89)
Most Field Goals One Game - 6 - Toronto at Hamilton 07/09/87
- Winnipeg at Hamilton 07/20/89
- Edmonton at Hamilton 10/08/90
Most First Downs One Game - 42 - Hamilton at Toronto 21/08/87
Most Yards Total Offence One Game - 680 -
- Saskatchewan at Hamilton 15/10/62
Most Yards Rushing One Game - 397 - at Montreal 04/11/63

Most Times Carried One Game - 65 - Ottawa at Hamilton 15/10/55
Most Touchdowns Rushing One Game - 6 - Toronto at Hamilton 05/09/55
Most Yards Passing One Game - 572 -
- Saskatchewan at Hamilton 15/10/62
Most Passes Thrown One Game - 58 - Saskatchewan at Hamilton 08/07/84
Most Completions One Game - 37 - Saskatchewan at Hamilton 08/07/84
Most Touchdown Passes One Game -#10 -
- Saskatchewan at Hamilton 15/10/62

HAMILTON INDIVIDUAL RECORDS SINCE 1946

Regular Season

Points (Career) - 1,237 - Paul Osbaldiston
Points (Season) - 233 - Paul Osbaldiston ('89)
Points (Game) - 26 - Terry Evanshen - at Ottawa 07/09/75
Touchdowns (Career) - 56 - Garney Henley, Earl Winfield
Touchdowns (Season) - 15 - Tony Champion ('89)
Touchdowns (Game) - 4 - Garney Henley - at Winnipeg 02/09/70
- Terry Evanshen - at Ottawa 07/09/75
Field Goals (Career) - 281 - Paul Osbaldiston
Field Goals (Season) - 54 - Paul Osbaldiston ('89)
Field Goals (Game) - 6 - Bernie Ruoff - Toronto at Hamilton 07/09/87
- Paul Osbaldiston - Winnipeg at Hamilton 07/20/89
- Paul Osbaldiston - Edmonton at Hamilton 10/08/90
Longest Field Goal - 57 - Bernie Ruoff - at Calgary 20/07/84
Passes Thrown (Career) - 2,238 - Mike Kerrigan
Passes Thrown (Season) - 561 - Dieter Brock ('84)
Passes Thrown (Game) - 58 -
- Dieter Brock - Saskatchewan at Hamilton 08/07/84
Passes Completed (Career) - 1,185 - Mike Kerrigan
Passes Completed (Season) - 356 - Tom Clements ('82)
Passes Completed (Game) - 37 -
- Dieter Brock - Saskatchewan at Hamilton 08/07/84
Passing Yards (Career) - 17,425 - Bernie Faloney
Passing Yards (Season) - 4,706 - Tom Clements ('82)
Passing Yards (Game) - 475 -
- Joe Zuger - Saskatchewan at Hamilton 15/10/62
Touchdown Passes Thrown (Career) - 121 - Bernie Faloney
Touchdown Passes Thrown (Season) - 27 - Tom Clements ('81)
Touchdown Passes Thrown (Game) -#8 -
- Joe Zuger - Saskatchewan at Hamilton 15/10/62
No. of Carries (Career) - 845 - Gerry McDougall
No. of Carries (Season) - 263 - Dave Buchanan ('72)
No. of Carries (Game) - 33 - Obie Graves - Toronto at Hamilton 01/09/80
Yards Rushing (Career) - 4,270 - Gerry McDougall
Yards Rushing (Season) - 1,581 - Jimmy Edwards ('77)
Yards Rushing (Game) - 213 -
- Gerry McDougall - Montreal at Hamilton - 28/09/57
Touchdowns by Rushing (Career) - 29 - Gerry McDougall
Touchdowns by Rushing (Season) - 11 - Derrick McAdoo ('89)
Touchdowns by Rushing (Game) - 3
- Bucky McElroy - Toronto at Hamilton 05/09/55
- Walter Bender - Montreal at Hamilton 01/09/86
Passes Caught (Career) - #706 - Rocky DiPietro
Passes Caught (Season) - 95 - Tony Champion ('89)
Passes Caught (Game) - 13 - Jimmy Edwards - at B.C. 29/07/76
Pass Reception Yards (Career) - 9,762 - Rocky DiPietro
Pass Reception Yards (Season) - 1,656 - Tony Champion ('89)
Pass Reception Yards (Game) - 228 -
- Hal Patterson - Saskatchewan at Hamilton 15/10/62
Touchdown Passes Caught (Career) - 51 - Tommy Grant
Touchdown Passes Caught (Season) - 15 - Tony Champion ('89)
Touchdown Passes Caught (Game) - 4
- Garney Henley - Saskatchewan at Hamilton 15/10/62
- Terry Evanshen - at Ottawa 07/09/75
Quarterback Sacks (Career) - #157 - Grover Covington
Quarterback Sacks (Season) - 25 - Grover Covington ('88)

HAMILTON'S RECORD AGAINST OTHER CLUBS (REGULAR SEASON)

		GP	W	L	T	F	A	PTS
Versus Ottawa	(Since 1946)	165	86	78	1	3376	3343	173
Versus Toronto	(Since 1946)	170	99	67	4	3508	3210	202
Versus Winnipeg	(Since 1961)	51	23	28	0	1072	1291	46
Versus Saskatchewan	(Since 1961)	46	24	18	4	1212	1057	52
Versus Calgary	(Since 1961)	47	18	29	0	1058	1250	36
Versus Edmonton	(Since 1961)	46	14	31	1	914	1190	29
Versus B.C.	(Since 1961)	46	21	22	3	1039	1161	45
Versus Sacramento	(Since 1993)	2	1	1	0	40	60	2
HAMILTON VS OPPOSITION		573	286	274	13	12219	12562	585

Chairman: Roger Yachetti, Q.C.

Born April 14, 1940, in Hamilton, Ontario, the son of Anna and Americo Yachetti. Senior partner in the law firm of Yachetti, Lanza & Restivo. Bencher of the Law Society of Upper Canada for the past 14 years. Very active in many legal associations including The Canadian Bar Association, The Advocates' Society, The Criminal Lawyers' Association, The Hamilton Lawyers' Club, The Hamilton Criminal Lawyers' Association, and others. Attended Hamilton's Cathedral High School. Graduated from the University of Western Ontario with a Bachelor of Arts in 1961 and a Bachelor of Laws in 1964 (Gold Medalist) and was called to the Bar at Osgoode Hall in 1966 (Treasurer's Medalist). Actively involved in many community organizations including the St. Joseph's Community Health Centre Fund Drive and the Villa Italia project of the Sons of Italy. Named Chairman of the Board of Directors for the Hamilton Tiger-Cats in August, 1992.

President and Chief Executive Officer: John Michaluk

Born to Ukranian parents in Hamilton, Ontario on September 14th, 1942. Graduated from Hamilton public and high schools before attending Kent State University, Kent, Ohio where he obtained his Bachelor of Business Administration degree while playing collegiate football. Began his business career with the Royal Bank of Canada in 1966. In over twenty years with Canada's leading bank, held a variety of positions in the lending, administrative, and marketing areas. For four seasons, between 1966 and 1969, while employed at the Royal, he was also a linebacker and centre with the Tiger-Cats and played on the Grey Cup Championship team of 1967, Canada's Centennial year. Very active in the community, he is Past President of the Hamilton Chamber of Commerce, a director of the Royal Botanical Gardens, and a member of Rotary. Was a free-lance broadcaster with radio station 900 CHML for 21 years and was their long-time colour analyst for Tiger-Cat games and host of the popular Fifth-Quarter post game phone-in show. Tiger-Cat President and Chief Executive Officer since August 27th, 1992.

Director of Football Operations and Head Coach: John Gregory

Born November 22, 1938 in Webster City, Iowa. Entering his fourth season in Hamilton. Appointed Director of Football Operations and Head Coach in January, 1993. Joined the Tiger-Cats in mid-season in 1991 after having been Head Coach with the Saskatchewan Roughriders from 1987 to 1991. Head coaching record currently reads 56 wins, 70 losses and 1 tie. Winner of the Annis Stukus Trophy as the CFL Coach of the Year for 1989 after leading the Roughriders to their first Grey Cup win since 1966. Began his CFL coaching career as an assistant with Winnipeg Blue Bombers in 1983. Graduated with a B.A. from Univ. of Northern Iowa where he was a three-year letterman in football. Also holds a Master Degree from Mankota State Univ. Also coached at the collegiate level with South Dakota State Univ. and Univ. of Northern Iowa. Officially became Tiger-Cat Head Coach on August 31, 1991.

Assistant Coaches

Jim Clark, Linebacker/Special Teams Coach. Born March 22, 1942 in St. Thomas, Ontario. Entering his first season in Hamilton and is responsible for the coaching of the Tiger-Cat linebackers and special teams. In 1992 and '93, Clark coached the running backs for the

Ottawa Rough Riders. Prior to going to Ottawa, he was personnel assistant and college scout for the Calgary Stampeders from 1986 to 1988. From 1985 to '86, he performed the same duties with the B.C. Lions. Prior to 1985, he was Head Coach of the University of Ottawa for 2 seasons. From 1979 to '82, he was an assistant coach with U. of O. From 1976 to '79, Clark was head football coach at St. Mary's University in Halifax, Nova Scotia. Before 1976, he coached 4 years at Clearwater High School in Clearwater, Florida. From 1970 to '72, he was a graduate assistant at the University of Tennessee. Began his coaching career as a graduate assistant coach at Acadia University in 1968. Graduated from Acadia with a Bachelor of Business Administration in 1970.

Gary Durchik, Offensive Coordinator/Quarterback and Receivers Coach. Born May 30, 1944 in Martinsburg, West Virginia. Entering his fourth season in Hamilton. Coordinates the Tiger-Cat offensive unit and coaches the quarterbacks and receivers. Played defensive end at the University of Miami (Ohio) 1962-1966. Began coaching as an assistant at Chillicothe High in Ohio in 1966 and named Head Coach in 1969. Moved to the collegiate level at Miami (Ohio) in 1973. Also coached at Colorado (1975-77), University of Illinois (1978-79), and Northern Illinois (1980-83). Coached 4 Bowl games (California, Blue Bonnet, Orange and Tangerine). Joined the CFL with Montreal in 1984 and promoted to Head Coach during the 1985 season. Spent four seasons with the Edmonton Eskimos as Offensive Line Coach (1987-90). Joined Tiger-Cat staff on February 1, 1991.

John Salavantis, Offensive Line Coach. Returns to the Tiger-Cats for his seventh season as an assistant coach after a previous stop that lasted from 1985 to 1990. During that time, the 'Cats won the Grey Cup in 1986, the Eastern Championship in '85 and '89, and qualified for postseason play five of the six sesaons. Previously with Hamilton, he served as Co-offensive Coordinator. Last season, Salavantis joined the Ottawa Rough Riders on September 1, 1993 and for the remainder of the season, was the Offensive Backfield Coach. He joined the CHML Broadcast crew midway through the 1992 season and until his departure to accept the Ottawa job, served as colour commentator and co-hosted the Fifth Quarter. In 1991, he coached with the Montreal Machine of the WLAF. His first exposure to the CFL came in 1983 when he was a guest coach with the Saskatchewan Roughriders under Joe Faragalli. Has over 24 years of coaching experience. In 1983 and '84, he coached at Garden City Community College and was at Missouri Southern University from 1980 to '82. Salavantis has also held head coaching positions with Independence Junior College, Pratt Junior College, and Ottawa (Kansas) University. He won two junior college league titles in Kansas and led teams to the Junior college Mid-American Bowl in 1971 and the Junior College Wool Bowl in 1977.

Don Sutherin, Defensive Coordinator/Defensive Back Coach. Born February 29, 1936 in Toronto, Ohio. Entering his first season as an assistant coach with the Tiger-Cats after serving with the Calgary Stampeders for the last three seasons. A former Tiger-Cat great, Sutherin was inducted to the Canadian Football Hall of Fame as a Player in 1992. Joined the Stampeders in 1991, after spending a number of months coaching with the Montreal Machine of the WLAF. Prior to that, he served as an Assistant Coach with the Edmonton Eskimos from 1985 to 1990. Sutherin's coaching career began at the high school level in Uniontown, Ohio. Following that stint, he was guest coach of the defensive secondary at Kent State University and scouted for the NFL Pittsburgh Steelers for five years. His CFL coaching career began with the Ottawa Rough Riders, where he was an assistant from 1981 to '84. As a coach, Sutherin has been in six Grey Cup Championships, winning twice. Played under collegiate coaching legend Woody Hayes at Ohio State University and kicked the winning field goal in the 1958 Rose Bowl versus the University of Oregon. Was selected to the All Big Ten All-Star Team on two occasions. Played one season with the Tiger-Cats in 1958, before moving on to the NFL where he spent single seasons with the New York Giants and Pittsburgh. Returned to the 'Cats from 1961-66, played in Ottawa from 1967-69 and was with the Toronto Argonauts for part of '70. He played in 8 Grey Cups and won five.

Don Wnek, Defensive Line Coach. Born May 4, 1951 in Chicago, Illinois. Entering his fourth season as defensive line coach with the Tiger-Cats. Defensive line coach with the San Antonio Riders of the WLAF in 1991 and 1992. Began his coaching career at Winnebago High School (Illinois) in 1974. Moved to the collegiate level in 1977 with Northern Illinois University and transferred to the University of Nevada at Reno in 1982 where he remained for eight seasons (1982-1990). Played collegiate football at Northern Illinois University where he was a three-year letterman at the outside linebacker position. Joined the Tiger-Cat staff on June 11, 1991.

HAMILTON TIGER-CATS
1994 CURRENT ROSTER AS OF APRIL 30, 1994
RETURNING PLAYERS

* Denotes Import

	Player	Pos.	Ht.	Wt.	Born	University/ Jr. Affiliate	Yrs. CFL	Yrs. HAM
*	ANDREWS, Romel	DT	6.05	255	4 JUL 63	Tennessee Martin	8	6
*	BATES, Stephen	DE	6.04	245	28 JUN 66	James Madison	3	3
*	BURBAGE, Cornell	WR	5.10	185	20 FEB 65	Kentucky	2	2
	BUSHEY, Paul	FB	6.02	235	8 APR 66	Colgate	5	4
*	COFIELD, Tim	DE	6.02	257	8 MAY 63	Elizabeth City State	4	2
*	DAWSON, Bobby	DB	5.11	210	18 FEB 66	Illinois	5	5
*	DILLON, Todd	QB	6.00	195	6 JAN 62	Long Beach State	9	6
	DINNALL, Dave	RB	5.11	190	4 SEP 69	Burlington Juniors	3	3
	DOUGLAS, Scott	T	6.03	265	22 NOV 67	Western Ontario	4	4
*	ERVIN, Corris	CB	5.11	185	30 AUG 66	Central Florida	4	4
	EVRAIRE, Ken	SB	6.01	205	17 JUL 65	Wilfrid Laurier	7	5
*	FIELDS, Jeff	DT	6.03	300	3 JUL 67	Arkansas State	4	4
	GIFTOPOULOS, Peter	OL	6.03	240	14 JUNE 65	Penn State	7	7
	HARLE, Darrell	T	6.02	270	4 MAR 66	Eastern Michigan	6	6
	HENNIG, Roger	DB	6.00	190	3 OCT 66	UBC	3	3
*	HILL, Lonzell	WR	5.11	190	25 SEP 65	Washington	3	3
*	JACKSON, Tim	DB	6.00	190	7 NOV 65	Nebraska	4	4
	JAUCH, James	DB	6.01	180	25 JUN 65	North Carolina	5	3
	KNIGHT, Lee	SB	6.03	230	8 FEB 65	Burlington Juniors	8	8
	MARTIN, Peter J.	FB	6.00	230	1 MAY	Wilfrid Laurier	2	2
*	MOTTON, John	LB	6.01	235	20 JUN 67	Akron	4	4
	NURSE, Richard	WR	5.11	185	16 MAR 67	Canisius	5	5
	O'SHEA, Michael	LB	6.03	225	21 SEP 70	Guelph	2	2
	OSBALDISTON, Paul	K	6.03	210	27 APR 64	Western Montana	9	9
*	PERKINS, Bruce	RB	6.03	225	14 AUG 67	Arizona State	2	2
	RICHARDSON, Dave	T	6.04	275	1 JUL 67	Edmonton Jrs.	7	5
*	ROGERS, Reggie	DE	6.06	280	21 JAN 64	Washington	2	2
*	ROYAL, Rickey	CB	5.10	185	26 JUL 66	Sam Houston State	4	4
	SANDERSON, Dale	C	6.04	285	12 DEC 61	Tennessee	10	10
	SCOTT, Mark	LB	6.01	215	19 DEC 68	Virginia Tech	3	2
	TORRANCE, Bob	QB	6.01	209	4 JUN 68	Calgary	4	2
*	WALLOW, Rob	T	6.04	285	16 OCT 62	NE Louisiana	2	2
*	WILKERSON, Gary	CB	6.00	180	11 OCT 65	Penn State	5	5
*	WILLIAMS, Brett	DE	6.03	260	23 MAY 59	Austin Peay	10	3
*	WINFIELD, Earl	WR	5.11	185	6 AUG 61	North Carolina	8	8
*	WRIGHT, Terry	CB	6.00	195	17 JUL 65	Temple	4	4

NEW PLAYERS

* Denotes Import

	Player	Pos.	Ht.	Wt.	Born	University/ Jr. Affiliate	Yrs. CFL
*	BAILEY, Hassan	LB	6.00	205	28 JAN 71	Kansas	1
	BRAITENBACK, Jeremy	SB	6.01	195	1 MAR 71	Saskatchewan	1
*	CAMPBELL, Joe	RB	5.09	180	14 JAN 70	Middle Tennessee	1
	CHEVERS, Michael	LB	6.02	230	17 JUL 71	Wilfrid Laurier	1
	COULDERY, Robert	OG	6.03	275	13 AUG 70	Snow College	1
*	CRUDUP, Derrick	DB	6.02	215	15 FEB 69	Oklahoma	1
	D'AGOSTINO, Anthony	WR	5.05	175	9 OCT 67	McMaster	1
*	DUFFEY, Gerald	WR	5.11	210	23 AUG 70	Florida A & M	1
*	EVANS, Fernando	WR	6.02	185	12 OCT 69	Alcorn State	1
	FISCHER, Richard	DE	6.02	260	30 DEC 69	Toronto	1
	GISBORN, Peter	T	6.02	275	12 NOV 69	Wilfrid Laurier	1
	GRIGG, Andrew	WR	6.00	175	25 APR 71	Ottawa	1
	HARRIS, Chris	DB	5.10	170	27 APR 72	Simon Fraser	1
*	HUNTER, Arthur	DB	5.11	200	24 JAN 67	Ohio Central	1
*	KIMBROUGH, Anthony	QB	6.00	190	20 JAN 64	Western Michigan	5
*	MAULDIN, Joe	QB	6.02	235	26 NOV 70	Los Angeles Valley	1
	MCKEE, Steve	LB	6.02	220	13 NOV 69	Guelph	1
*	MCMILLAN, Curtis	LB	6.01	220	28 NOV 70	Miami of Ohio	1
*	MEANS, Kelvin	WR	5.211	185	27 OCT 69	Fresno State	1
*	MORGAN, Mark	WR	6.00	190	18 MAR 70	Ricks College	1
*	MOSSBURG, Darrell	LB	6.03	225	28 DEC 69	Toledo	1
	NICHOL, Geoff	LB	6.02	226	19 DEC 72	Colgate	1
*	O'NEAL, Andreas	DE	6.04	260	29 DEC 69	North Carolina State	1
*	ODEGARD, Don	CB	5.11	185	22 NOV 66	Nevada Las Vegas	1
*	ROSENBACH, Timm	QB	6.02	215	27 OCT 66	Washington State	1
	RYSAVY, Dallas	DB	5.10	1285	30 JUN 71	North Dakota	1
*	SNOW, Carlos	RB	5.08	200	24 OCT 68	Ohio State	1
*	STURDIVANT, Michael	WR	6.02	195	17 APR 69	Virginia Tech	1
	TAYLOR, Simon	OL	6.06	270	27 JUN 69	Toronto	1
*	TENNER, Mylai	DE	6.02	250	21 MAR 71	SW Minnesota	1
*	WALCZAK, Mark	SB	6.06	245	26 APR 62	Arizona	1
*	WALKER, Kenny	DE	6.03	260	6 APR 67	Nebraska	1
	WILLIAMS, Nigel	WR	6.03	200	16 AUG 71	Burlington Jrs.	1
	ZATYLNY, Walter	SB	5.09	180	25 MAR 63	Bishop's	7

WINNIPEG BLUE BOMBER FOOTBALL CLUB

1465 Maroons Road
Winnipeg, Manitoba R3G 0L6
Telephone Number: (204) 784-2583
Fax (204) 783-5222 Tickets (204) 780-7328
The Bomber Shop (204) 784-2589

EXECUTIVE

Owner: Community Owned
President: Reg Low
Executive Committee: Ken Houssin, Don Cozine, Lynn Bishop, Bob Filuk, Brian Cook, Don Taylor, Mark Fenny, Barry Loudon, Ken Bishop, Bruce Robinson
Governor: Reg Low **Alternate:** Cal Murphy, Bruce Robinson

FOOTBALL OPERATIONS

General Manager & Head Coach: Cal Murphy
Assistant General Manager: Lyle Bauer
Assistant Coaches:
Mike Kelly, Receivers and Offensive Backfield Coach
Mike Roach, Defensive Secondary Coach
Jim Gilstrap, Offensive Line Coach
John Jenkins, Linebackers Coach
Trainer: Ross Hodgkinson
Doctors: Dr. Garth Carrick, Dr. Bert Longstaffe, Dr. John Peterson, Dr. Jan S. Brown (Dentist), Dr. Neville Winograd (Dentist)
Director of Player Personnel: Paul Jones
Director of Canadian Personnel: Mike Kelly
American Scouts: Pat Martin, Brian Husted

ADMINISTRATION

Director of Marketing: Rick Titarniuk
Director of Media and Public Relations: Kevin O'Donovan
Marketing/Merchandising : Dave Read
Marketing and Sales : Wayne Antonishin
Marketing Assistant : J.D. Boyd
Business Manager: Bill Christie
Controller : Darryle Lidtke
Administrative Secretary: Joyce Murphy
Secretary to the Coaches: Barbara Ledyard
Business Manager's Secretary: Olive Kostyshyn
Ticket Supervisor: Jean Love
Receptionist: Jane Garvie
Tickets & Game Day Assistant: Bev Hobson
Game Day Assistant: Gerald Hobson

FAST FACTS

Home Stadium: Winnipeg Stadium
Stadium Address: 1465 Maroons Road, Winnipeg, Manitoba R3G 0L6
Club Colours: Royal Blue & Old Gold
Club Name: Winnipeg Blue Bombers
Training Camp Sites: Brandon, Man. & Winnipeg Stadium
Press Box Location: West Side, between Upper & Lower decks, Media Pass Gate is located on West side of Stadium
Dressing Room Locations: Home Team - On West side of Stadium
Visiting Team - On West side of Stadium
Radio Broadcasts: CJOB Radio - Bob Irving, Play-by-Play
Joe Poplawski, Colour
Press Box Host: Stew MacPherson
P.A. Announcer: Mo Renaud
Statistician: Paul Friesen
Offensive Spotter: Delbert Pedrick
Defensive Spotter: Derek Kolowca
Typist: Melanie Verhaeghe

Club History: 1880 formation of the Winnipeg Rugby Football Club...1892 formation of the Manitoba Rugby Football Union including such teams as the Victorias, The Winnipeg Rowing Club and the St. John's...1930 the Winnipeg Football Club becomes known as the Winnipegs...1933 the Winnipegs and the St. John's amalgamate to form the 'Pegs...1936 formation of the Western Interprovincial Football Union which the 'Pegs joined under the new team name the Blue Bombers.

Winnipeg Stadium Facts 'n Figures

Capacity: 32,648
Largest Regular Season One Game Attendance: 35,959
Winnipeg 41, Saskatchewan 23 (September 12, 1993)
Largest Playoff One Game Attendance: 32,946
Toronto 19, Winnipeg 3 (November 22, 1987)
Largest Grey Cup Game Attendance: 51,985
Toronto 36, Calgary 21 (November 24, 1987)

TEN GREY CUP VICTORIES FOR WINNIPEG-BASED TEAMS

Winnipegs (1) - 1935
Blue Bombers (9) - 1939, 1941, 1958, 1959, 1961, 1962, 1984, 1988, 1990

WINNIPEG CLUB RECORDS SINCE 1946
Regular Season

- CFL Record
- Tie for CFL Record
() - Figures in Brackets represent Year(s) mark set

Most Points Scored One Season (minimum 14 games) - 646 ('93)
Most Points Scored Against One Season (minimum 14 games) - 499 ('91)
Fewest Points Against One Season (minimum 14 games) - 156 ('50)
Most Points Scored One Game - 68 -
- Hamilton at Winnipeg 19/10/91 Final: 68-14
Most Points Scored Against One Game - 55 -
- at Saskatchewan 02/09/90 Final: 55-11
Most Wins One Season (minimum 14 games) - 14 ('60, '93)
Most Losses One Season (minimum 14 games) - 14 ('64)
Highest Shutout - #56-0 - vs. Saskatchewan 05/07/86
Highest Shutout Against - 53-0 - at Toronto 08/10/67
Most Touchdowns One Season (minimum 14 games) - 71 ('93)
Most Touchdowns One Game - 9 - at Saskatchewan 29/08/59
- Ottawa at Winnipeg 07/09/84
Most Converts One Season (minimum 14 games) - 68 ('93)
Most Converts One Game - ##9 - Ottawa at Winnipeg 07/09/84
Most Field Goals One Season (minimum 14 games) - 47 ('92)
Most Field Goals One Game - 7 - Toronto at Winnipeg 11/10/81
Most First Downs One Game - 41 - at Ottawa 03/10/81
Most Yards Total Offence One Game - 681 -
- Ottawa at Winnipeg 07/09/84
Most Yards Rushing One Game - 349 - Hamilton at Winnipeg 24/09/75
Most Times Carried One Game - 65 - Edmonton at Winnipeg 06/10/56
Most Touchdowns Rushing One Game - 5 - B.C. at Winnipeg 07/09/72
Most Yards Passing One Game - 510 - Calgary at Winnipeg 08/10/84

Most Passes Thrown One Game - 55 - Calgary at Winnipeg 28/08/90
Most Completions One Game -#41 - at Ottawa 03/10/81
Most Touchdown Passes One Game - 8 - at Saskatchewan 29/08/59
Most Yards Interception Returns One Season - 692 ('91)
Most Penalties One Season - #216 ('91)
Most Yards Penalized One Season - #1,822 ('91)
Fewest Sacks Against One Season - 20 ('93)

WINNIPEG INDIVIDUAL RECORDS SINCE 1946
Regular Season

Points (Career) - 1,840 - Trevor Kennerd
Points (Season) - 209 - Troy Westwood ('93)
Points (Game) -#36 - Bob McNamara - at B.C. 13/10/56
Touchdowns (Career) - 75 - Leo Lewis
Touchdowns (Season) - 19 - Gerry James ('57)
Touchdowns (Game) -#6 - Bob McNamara - at B.C. 13/10/56
Field Goals (Career) - 394 - Trevor Kennerd
Field Goals (Season) - 47 - Troy Westwood ('92)
Field Goals (Game) - 7 - Trevor Kennerd - Toronto at Winnipeg 11/10/81
Longest Field Goal - 58 - Bernie Ruoff - at Calgary 12/08/75
Passes Thrown (Career) - 3,777 - Dieter Brock
Passes Thrown (Season) - 600 - Matt Dunigan ('93)
Passes Thrown (Game) - 53 -
- Tom Clements - Edmonton at Winnipeg 24/07/87
Passes Completed (Career) - 2,168 - Dieter Brock
Passes Completed (Season) - 354 - Dieter Brock ('81)
Passes Completed (Game) - #41 - Dieter Brock - at Ottawa 03/10/81
Passing Yards (Career) - 29,623 - Dieter Brock
Passing Yards (Season) - 4,796 - Dieter Brock ('81)
Passing Yards (Game) - 464 -
- Tom Burgess - Saskatchewan at Winnipeg 09/08/91
Touchdown Passes Thrown (Career) - 177 - Dieter Brock
Touchdown Passes Thrown (Season) - 36 - Matt Dunigan ('93)
Touchdown Passes Thrown (Game) - 7 -
- Jim Van Pelt - at Saskatchewan 29/08/59
No. of Carries (Career) - 1,351 - Leo Lewis
No. of Carries (Season) - 326 - Robert Mimbs ('91)
No. of Carries (Game) - 31 - Michael Richardson
- Toronto at Winnipeg 25/10/92
Yards Rushing (Career) - 8,861 - Leo Lewis
Yards Rushing (Season) - 1,769 - Robert Mimbs ('91)
Yards Rushing (Game) - 221 -
- Willard Reaves - Ottawa at Winnipeg 07/09/84
Most 100-Yard Rushing Games - #10 - Willard Reaves ('84)
- Robert Mimbs ('91)
Touchdowns by Rushing (Career) - 57 - Gerry James
Touchdowns by Rushing (Season) - ##18 - Gerry James ('57)
Touchdowns by Rushing (Game) - 4 -
- Bob McNamara - at B.C. 13/10/56
- Willard Reaves - Hamilton at Winnipeg 15/09/84
Passes Caught (Career) - 573 - James Murphy
Passes Caught (Season) - 116 - James Murphy ('86)
Passes Caught (Game) - 15 -
- Eugene Goodlow - Calgary at Winnipeg 01/11/81
Pass Reception Yards (Career) - 9,036 - James Murphy
Pass Reception Yards (Season) - 1,746 - James Murphy ('86)
Pass Reception Yards (Game) - 229 -
- James Murphy - Winnipeg at Hamilton 16/10/88
Touchdown Passes Caught (Career) - 54 - Ernie Pitts
Touchdown Passes Caught (Season) - 16 - Ernie Pitts ('59)
Touchdown Passes Caught (Game) -#5 -
- Ernie Pitts - at Saskatchewan 29/08/59
Kicks Blocked (Career) - ##7 - Rod Hill
Touchdowns on Fumble Returns (Career) - #5 - Michael Allen

WINNIPEG'S RECORD AGAINST OTHER CLUBS (REGULAR SEASON)

		GP	W	L	T	F	A	PTS
Versus Toronto	(Since 1946)	160	81	76	3	3331	3105	165
Versus Ottawa	(Since 1961)	54	29	24	1	1513	1337	59
Versus Toronto	(Since 1961)	52	29	22	1	1170	1130	59
Versus Hamilton	(Since 1961)	51	28	23	0	1291	1072	56
Versus Saskatchewan	(Since 1961)	161	93	65	3	3352	2919	189
Versus Calgary	(Since 1946)	151	78	73	0	3036	2794	156
Versus Edmonton	(Since 1949)	137	62	73	2	2714	2845	126
Versus B.C.	(Since 1954)	118	65	51	2	2575	2286	132
Versus Sacramento	(Since 1993)	2	2	0	0	63	44	4
WINNIPEG VS OPPOSITION		726	386	331	9	15714	14427	781

President: Reginald Low

Born May 14, 1939 in Regina, Saskatchewan. Reg will serve as the Blue Bomber Governor to the CFL Board of Directors on behalf of the Winnipeg Football Club. He will also act as Chairman of the Planning and Policy Committees in addition to working with the Club's management as a liaison with the major corporate sponsors. Reg will also liaise with the General Manager on a Public Relations Committee on behalf of the Board of Directors. He joined the Directorship in 1983 and is the President of Sound Concepts Canada Inc. Reg and his wife Judy have two children, Janet and David.

General Manager & Head Coach: Cal Murphy

Born March 12, 1932 in Winnipeg, Manitoba. Begins his sixth season as General Manager and seventh as Head Coach of the Winnipeg Blue Bombers. He previously had been a CFL Head Coach for 5 1/2 years with Winnipeg and the B.C. Lions. His career regular season Head Coaching record is 67-40-3. Played as a Quarterback with the University of British Columbia Thunderbirds and tried out as a Defensive Back in 1956 with the Lions. Head Coach at Notre Dame High School, Vancouver from 1956 to 1959 and Vancouver College from 1960 to 1964. Assistant Coach, Eastern Washington University from 1965 to 1967, then the University of Hawaii from 1968 to 1972 and San Jose State University in 1973. His Pro Coaching career began in 1974 as an Offensive Line Coach with the B.C. Lions. Named Head Coach of the Lions in August, 1975. Joined Montreal Alouettes as Offensive Line Coach in 1977 and held the same position with the Edmonton Eskimos from 1978 to 1982. 1990's Grey Cup win provided Murphy with his 9th Grey Cup ring; 1 with Montreal, 5 with Edmonton and 3 with the Bombers. Named winner of Annis Stukus Trophy as CFL Coach of the Year for second consecutive year in 1984. One of five head coaches to win the honour more than once. Murphy is the first Canadian Head Coach to win the Grey Cup since Teddy Morris in 1947. Named Head Coach of Winnipeg, January 25, 1983. Named General Manager January 2, 1987 and added coaching duties on March 31, 1992.

Assistant General Manager: Lyle Bauer

Born August 22, 1958 in Saskatoon, Saskatchewan. Was named assistant general manager in February, 1992 upon his retirement as a player. A ten-year veteran of the Blue Bombers, he was the offensive team captain from 1987 to 1991 and was selected to the Eastern All-Star Team in 1990. In 1988, he was nominated as the team's Most Outstanding Offensive Lineman. Played in 161 regular season games and won three Grey Cups (1984, 1988 and 1990). Holds his B.A. in Business Administration from Weber State College, and has been in the real estate industry since 1982. Most recently, he was a Broker/Manager with NRS Block Bros. Realty since 1990. Also served as the CFLPA's representative with the Bombers. Is involved with numerous charitable organizations throughout Manitoba.

Assistant Coaches

Jim Gilstrap, Offensive Line Coach. Born May 11, 1942 in South Bend, Indiana. Returns to Winnipeg from the Toronto Argonauts where he served in the same capacity in 1993. Prior to that, he spent 1991-'92 with the San Antonio Riders of the WLAF. As offensive line coach under Mike Riley, the Riders compiled an 11-9 record over those 2 years. Served as the Argonauts' Offensive Backs and Receivers coach from 1987-1989. Gilstrap left the Argonauts to join Winnipeg in 1990. After two decades of college coaching experience, he got his first taste of CFL action in 1986 when he joined the Saskatchewan Roughriders in 1984 as defensive coordinator/linebacker coach. He spent the next two seasons as the offensive line coach. His football coaching career began at Southern Illinois University, and was followed by stops at Fort Hayes State, Western Michigan, Kansas State, Edinboro State College, Illinois State and Case Western Reserve Universities. He was a graduate of Western Michigan University, where he played centre and linebacker for the Broncos.

Mike Kelly, Receivers and Offensive Backfield Coach. Born February 11, 1958. Joins the Bomber staff after spending the past two seasons at San Francisco State University, where he was their Associate Head Coach in 1991, responsible for the receivers and special teams, as well as recruiting and academics. Prior to that he spent three years at Capital University in Columbus, Ohio as their offensive coordinator and head baseball coach. Also served as offensive coordinator and recruiting coordinator at Ohio Wesleyan in 1986, running back coach at Marietta College from 1983-1985 and assistant football coach at Ridgedale High School in Marion, Ohio. Played college football at Bluffton College in Ohio, and is still ranked in the school's top ten listings for QBs. Holds a B.A. in Health/Phys. Ed/Recreation from Bluffton and a Master's Degree in Secondary School Education from Edinboro University, where he worked as a graduate assistant football coach. Joined the Bombers in April, 1992.

Mike Roach, Defensive Secondary Coach. Born October 4, 1943 in Rapid City, South Dakota. Entering his first season with the Blue Bombers, coming from Ottawa where he was defensive coordinator and secondary coach. Rejoined the Riders in 1993 after having spent the year before as Defensive Coordinator and Linebackers Coach with the B.C. Lions. First coached with the Rough Riders in January, 1989, following three seasons as the linebackers coach with the Edmonton Eskimos from 1986-'88, earning a Grey Cup ring in 1987. A former defensive lineman at South Dakota State University, he began his coaching career at Rapid City High School in 1963 and moved to coaching university ball at South Dakota from 1975 to 1981. Joined the CFL with the Calgary Stampeders in 1982 as an assistant coach on defence.

WINNIPEG BLUE BOMBERS
1994 CURRENT ROSTER AS OF APRIL 30, 1994
RETURNING PLAYERS

* Denotes Import

	Player	Pos.	Ht.	Wt.	Born	University/ Jr. Affiliate	Yrs. CFL	Yrs. WPG
*	ALPHIN, Gerald	SB	6.03	215	21 MAY 64	Kansas State	7	3
	BENJAMIN, Nick	G	6.03	280	29 MAY 61	Concordia	10	6
*	BETHUNE, George	LB	6.04	240	30 MAR 67	Alabama	2	2
	BLACK, David	T	6.03	280	13 APR 62	Laurier	10	10
*	BOLTON, Nathaniel	WR	5.11	200	1 JUL 68	Mississippi College	2	2
*	BOOKER, Vaughn	DE	6.05	260	24 FEB 68	Cincinnati	3	3
	BOYKO, Allan	FB	5.11	175	02 MAR 67	Western Michigan	3	2
*	BRYANT, Blaise	RB	6.01	205	23 NOV 69	Iowa State	2	2
	CAMERON, Bob	K	6.00	185	18 JUL 55	Acadia	15	15
*	CLARK, Greg	LB	6.00	225	05 MAR 65	Arizona	2	2
	DAVIDSON, Rob	DT	6.04	275	10 MAY 67	Toronto	5	2
*	DUNIGAN, Matt	QB	5.11	190	6 DEC 60	Louisiana Tech	12	3
	DZIKOWICZ, Jayson	DB	5.11	185	11 APR 68	Manitoba	3	3
*	EVANS, Bobby	DB	6.02	195	1 DEC 67	Southern Arkansas	5	5
*	GARZA, Sammy	QB	6.01	185	10 JUL 65	Texas El Paso	6	6
	GORRELL, Miles	T	6.08	305	16 OCT 55	Ottawa	17	3
	GRANT, Steve	DT	6.03	245	3 OCT 69	Simon Fraser	4	4
	HATZIIOANNOU, Leon	DT	6.01	250	28 MAR 65	Simon Fraser	7	7
*	JACKSON, Alfred	DB	6.00	185	10 JUL 67	San Diego State	2	2
	JOHNSTONE, Chris	RB	6.03	215	12 DEC 63	Bakersfield	9	2
*	LEWIS, Loyd	DE	6.03	265	23 FEB 62	Texas A & I	10	2
*	LYLES, Del	LB	6.01	220	7 SEP 70	Utah State	2	2
	MACNEIL, Brett	G	6.05	290	27 NOV 67	Boston	3	3
	MAGNUSON, Quinn	G	6.05	275	08 MAR 71	Washington State	2	2
	MARTIN, Andrew	WR	6.01	200	31 MAR 70	Cornell	3	3
*	MCCANT, Keithen	QB	6.02	205	8 MAR 69	Nebraska	2	2
	MIKAWOS, Stan	DT	6.04	265	11 MAY 58	North Dakota	13	13
	PEARCE, Matt	FB	6.02	205	22 APR 67	UBC	6	6
*	PHILLIPS, Kim	DB	5.10	190	28 OCT 66	North Texas	3	3
*	PORRAS, Tom	QB	6.03	210	28 MAR 58	Washington	9	2
*	RANDOLPH, Paul	LB	6.00	235	22 JUN 66	Tennessee Martin	6	6
*	ROGERS, Brendan	LB	6.01	235	25 FEB 68	Eastern Washington	4	4
*	SAMPSON, Darryl	DB	6.02	175	21 SEP 63	York	9	9
*	SMITH, Donald	DB	6.00	185	21 FEB 68	Liberty	3	3
	TSANGARIS, Chris	LB	6.02	240	20 JUL 68	Long Beach State	3	3
	VANKOUGHNETT, Dave	G	6.03	260	1 APR 66	Boise State	5	5
	WALBY, Chris	T	6.07	305	23 OCT 56	Dickinson State	14	14
	WETMORE, Alan	LB	6.03	225	17 MAY 70	Acadia	2	2
	WILCOX, Gerald	SB	6.02	215	08 JUL 66	Weber State	6	3
*	WILLIAMS, David	WR	6.04	195	10 JUN 64	Illinois	7	2

NEW PLAYERS

* Denotes Import

	Player	Pos.	Ht.	Wt.	Born	University/ Jr. Affiliate	Yrs. CFL
*	ANDERSON, Herbie	DB	5.10	195	19 NOV 68	Texas A & I	1
*	BOLDEN, Tunji	DE	6.02	245	31 OCT 70	Texas Christian	1
*	BRADLEY, James	WR	6.01	200	24 NOV 68	Michigan State	1
*	BROWN, John	WR	6.03	200	07 JUL 68	Houston	1
*	BURRESS, Ken	CB	5.11	180	16 FEB 70	Bowling Green	1
*	CHILDRESS, Fred	OL	6.05	310	17 SEP 66	Arkansas	1
	CUTLER, John	K	5.11	180	06 JAN 71	Alberta	1
*	FAISON, Derrick	WR	6.04	210	24 AUG 67	Howard	1
*	FRALEY, Charles	LB	6.01	210	21 APR 69	Washington	1
*	GRAYS, Jeffery	LB	6.02	225	21 JAN 71	Angelo State	1
*	HADLEY, Darius	DB	6.01	190	09 SEP 71	South Carolina St.	1
*	HAMLET, Anthony	DE	6.03	230	31 JUL 69	Miami	1
*	HOLLAND, Jamie	WR	6.01	195	01 FEB 64	Ohio State	1
*	JOHNSON, Antonio	WR	5.08	180	18 APR 69	Syracuse	1
	KAURIC, Jerry	K	6.01	215	28 JUN 63	Windsor Jrs.	5
*	MAYES, Michael	CB	5.11	180	17 AUG 66	Louisiana State	1
*	McCOLLINS, Bill	DE	6.05	265	11 APR 70	Livingston	1
*	McMAHON, Cotie	WR	5.09	175	20 APR 70	Utah State	1
*	MILLER, Eddie	WR	5.11	190	20 JUN 69	South Carolina	1
*	PERRY, Ronald	LB	6.03	235	28 DEC 70	Grambling	1
*	RICHARDS, James	WR	6.01	195	03 MAY 70	Greenville College	1
*	SMITH, Kelvin	LB	6.01	235	23 MAR 69	Florida State	1
	SMYRL, Jim	G	6.03	290	13 DEC 69	Manitoba	1
*	SPENCER, James	DE	6.06	285	09 JAN 70	Syracuse	1
*	TEMPLE, Tawan	LB	6.01	235	16 JAN 69	East Mississippi	1
*	THOMAS, Norris	DB	5.11	195	16 JAN 69	Wiscon. La Crosse	1
*	WARD, Fred	WR	5.11	180	26 AUG 71	Mississippi State	1
*	WILLIAMS, Sean	WR	5.11	170	10 JAN 71	Utah	1
*	WILSON, Walter	WR	6.00	185	06 OCT 66	East Carolina	1
*	WOODSIDE, Keith	RB	5.11	205	29 JUL 64	Texas A & M	1

#63 T Chris Walby

BALTIMORE CFL COLTS FOOTBALL CLUB

Memorial Stadium
1000 East 33rd Street
Baltimore, Maryland 21218
Telephone: (410) 554-1010
Fax: (410) 554-1015
Ticket Office: (410) 554-1040

EXECUTIVE

Owner/President: James L. Speros
Vice-President, Operations: Joe Namath
Vice-President, Marketing: Tom Matte
Special Advisor: Irv Cross
Governor: James Speros **Alternate:** TBA

FOOTBALL OPERATIONS

Director of Football Operations/Head Coach: Don Matthews
Assistant Coaches:
Joe Barnes, Quarterbacks Coach
Steve Buratto, Offensive Coordinator/Offensive Line Coach
Daryl Edralin, Linebackers and Special Teams Coach
Don Hill, Receivers Coach
Marty Long, Defensive Line Coach
Bob Price, Defensive Coordinator and Defensive Backs Coach
Director of Player Personnel: Jim Popp
Equipment Manager: Tracy Solem
Assistant Equipment Manager: Brad Melland
Athletic Trainer: John Lopez
Doctor: Dr. Kenneth Gertsen
Football Operations Secretary: Dava Ansell

ADMINISTRATION

Director of Marketing/Sales: David Julian
Director of Public Relations: Mike Gathagan
Director of Special Projects: E.J. Narcise
Director of Community Relations: Bonnie Downing
Advertising Consultant: Bob Leffler
Director of Facilities: Jobie Waldt
Marketing Representatives: Dave Stack, Dave Miller, Jim Wise
Administrative Assistant - Marketing: Laura Jennings
Administrative Assistant - Business: Tim Dunnigan
Ticket Consultant: Paul Blaber
Receptionist/Secretary: Twana Miller

FAST FACTS

Home Stadium: Memorial Stadium
Stadium Address: 1000 East 33rd Street, Baltimore, MD 21218
Club Colors: Royal Blue, Silver, Black, White
Club Name: Baltimore CFL Colts
Training Camp Location: Townson State University
Press Box Location: West Side, Sections 10-11
Dressing Room Location: Home - West side, Section 5, Visitor - East Side, Section 38
Radio Broadcasts: TBA
P.A. Announcer: TBA
Statistician: Dan O'Connell
Offensive Spotter: Chuck Acquisto
Defensive Spotter: Bob Hough
Typist: TBA
Timekeeper: TBA
Scorekeeper: TBA

Memorial Stadium Facts'n Figures

Capacity: 54,600
Largest Regular Season One Game Attendance:
60,763 vs Oakland 12/24/77 (NFL Baltimore Colts vs. Oakland Raiders)

Club History: On February 17, 1994, the City of Baltimore was granted the third American franchise in CFL history. The CFL Colts begin their inaugural season on July 7, 1994 in Toronto against the Argonauts. Their first home game will be played on July 16 against the Calgary Stampeders at Memorial Stadium.

President and Owner: James L. Speros

Born February 17, 1959 in Potomac, Maryland. On his 35th birthday, Jim Speros became the owner of the Baltimore CFL Colts. A graduate of Clemson University, Speros started at Linebacker for the Tigers' 1981 National Championship team. After a brief stay with the Montreal Alouettes in 1982, Speros coached with the Washington Redskins (1982-83) and the Buffalo Bills (1984-85) of the NFL. Jim left football and by 1988, he was one of the top real estate brokers in the Washington, D.C. area. In 1989, Jim co-founded Champions Sports, Inc., which owns, licences, and franchises 23 "Champions" Sports bars across the United States. An additional 12 Champions bars are located in Marriott Hotels. Speros never did leave football. In 1990, he began pursuing a football team for the district in the World League of American Football. After securing the franchise in 1991, the League folded before Speros' team played a down.

Director of Football Operations and Head Coach: Don Matthews

Born June 22, 1939 in Amesbury, Massachusetts. The sixth winningest coach in CFL history, Don Matthews brings his "Living on the edge" philosophy to Baltimore. A winner wherever he goes, he is entering his 17th season coaching in the CFL. From 1977 to 1982, Matthews was the defensive coordinator for the Edmonton Eskimos. In Don's 6 seasons in Edmonton, the Eskimos won 5 Grey Cups. In 1983, Matthews took over as the head coach of the B.C. Lions. In his five seasons in Vancouver, Don's record was 56-23-1 and included the 1985 Grey Cup title and the 1985 Coach of the Year award. He also made it to the 1983 Grey Cup. In 1990, he took over the Toronto Argonauts and in his only season with the Argos, Toronto went 10-8 and made it to the Eastern Final. Following one season with the Orlando Thunder of the World League, Don took over the Saskatchewan Roughriders in August 1991 and in 2 1/2 seasons in Regina, his team went 25-22. A former marine, Matthews played football at the University of Idaho and made All-West Coast his senior year.

Assistant Coaches

Joe Barnes, Quarterbacks Coach. Born December 18, 1951 in Fort Worth, Texas. One of the greatest quarterbacks in CFL history, Joe returns to the League for the first time since retiring after the 1986 season. In 11 seasons with four teams, Barnes passed for 18,491 yards and 94 touchdowns. Joe played in five Grey Cups, winning two. He was named MVP of the 1983 Grey Cup when his last minute TD pass beat Don Matthews and the B.C. Lions 18-17. A CFL All-Star in 1984, Barnes played at Texas Tech and spent 2 years with the NFL Chicago Bears before coming to the CFL. Joe spent the last year working at North Texas State University in the Athletic Administration Office.

Steve Buratto, Offensive Coordinator and Offensive Line Coach. Born September 22, 1943 in Seattle, Washington. A former teammate of Don Matthews at Idaho, Buratto is working with the head coach for the fourth time; first in 1983 as the defensive line coach with the B.C.Lions, in 1986-87 as the Lions' offensive coordinator, and in 1993 as the Saskatchewan's offensive line coach. Buratto was the head coach of the Calgary Stampeders in 1984 and part of 1985. An All-Big Sky performer at Idaho, Buratto spent 2 training camps with the NFL Green Bay Packers. He also had a pair of coaching tenures at Boise State University.

Daryl Edralin, Linebackers and Special Teams Coach. Born January 28, 1955 in Oahu, Hawaii. For the fifth straight season, Edralin will work with Head Coach Matthews. Daryl spent the last 2 seasons with Saskatchewan after spending the 1991 campaign in Orlando of the WLAF. During the 1990 season, he worked with the Toronto Argonauts during training camp. Edralin began his coaching career at his alma mater, the University of Hawaii. He spent 11 years as the Rainbows' linebacker, running backs and special teams coach. Edralin played fullback and captained the special teams at Hawaii.

Don Hill, Receivers' Coach. Born July 29, 1969. He has been the Receivers' Coach at Hampton University in Virginia for the last two years. Prior to coaching at Hampton, Hill spent six seasons at Virginia Union, three as the quarterback and three as an assistant coach. He is finishing up a Masters' degree in counselling at Hampton.

Marty Long, Defensive Line Coach. Born January 8, 1964. Spent eight years at The Citadel in Charleston, South Carolina as the defensive ends coach and recruiting coordinator. A 1986 graduate of The Citadel and a former Bulldog player, Long started coaching at his alma mater in 1987 as a graduate assistant with the outside linebackers. He became a full-time coach in 1988 and has coached the defensive ends and been the program's recruiter for the last five years. Hark working and enthusiastic, Long was a favourite with the Bulldog players. He also coached a season at Western Kentucky.

Bob Price, Defensive Coordinator and Defensive Backs Coach. Born July 24, 1955 in New York City, New York. Price enters his third season working with Coach Matthews. He spent the past two seasons as Saskatchewan's defensive coordinator and secondary coach. In 1991, Price coached Ottawa's defensive backs. Prior to that, Price coached at Cal-Berkeley, University of Nevada-Reno, College of Eastern Utah, University of Las Vegas and Idaho State. Bob played linebacker in college - first at Idaho State then at Cal Poly-Pomona.

#8 QB Tracy Ham

BALTIMORE COLTS
1994 CURRENT ROSTER AS OF APRIL 30, 1994
NEW PLAYERS

* Denotes Import

	Player	Pos.	Ht.	Wt.	Born	University/ Junior Affiliate	Yrs CFL
*	BADGETT, Marcus	WR	6.00	185	09 FEB 70	Maryland	1
*	BALLARD, Keith	T	6.04	300	16 DEC 70	Minnesota	1
*	BARBOUR, Anthony	RB	5.08	180	03 DEC 69	North Carolina State	1
*	BAYLIS, Jearld	DT	6.00	280	12 AUG 62	Southern Mississippi	8
*	BEALS, Shawn	WR	5.10	180	16 AUG 66	Idaho State	4
*	BECTON, Jesse	LB	6.00	200	03 JUN 69	New Mexico	1
*	BENSON, Kenneth	LB	6.02	220	04 MAR 69	Arkansas	3
*	BRIGANCE, O.J.	LB	6.00	220	29 SEP 69	Rice	4
*	BROWN, Norris	CB	5.11	195	14 DEC 69	Clemson	1
*	BUCKLES, Carlton	CB	5.09	175	13 SEP 69	Louisiana State	1
*	BURCH, Swift	DT	6.04	265	08 MAY 69	Temple	1
*	BYRD, Melendez	LB	6.01	225	11 MAR 71	Virginia Tech	1
*	CAESAR, Ivan	LB	6.02	240	07 JAN 67	Boston College	1
*	CAMPBELL, Donte	OL	6.03	295	03 DEC 69	Morehouse College	1
*	CAMPBELL, Mark	CB	5.10	180	19 OCT 68	East New Mexico	1
*	CANLEY, Sheldon	RB	5.09	200	19 APR 68	San Jose State	1
*	CLARK, Brad	DB	5.11	200	05 NOV 67	Brigham Young	1
*	COLLIER, Cornell	LB	6.02	230	17 AUG 69	California	1
*	CONGEMI, John	QB	5.11	190	19 JUN 64	Pittsburgh	7
*	DAVIS, Paul	CB	5.10	180	17 AUG 69	Western Michigan	1
*	DOCTOR, Sean	FB	6.01	235	10 JUL 66	Marshall	1
*	DOLLY, Richard	DT	6.03	280	21 NOV 69	West Virginia	1
*	DRIVER, Clayton	SB	6.00	200	02 MAY 71	East Carolina	1
*	DYKES, Scott	WR	6.01	175	22 AUG 71	East Tennessee State	1
*	FARMER, Jamal	RB	5.11	225	13 MAY 70	Hawaii	1
*	FIELDS, Earnest	LB	5.11	240	15 OCT 68	Tennessee	1
*	FLESCH, Jeb	G	6.03	280	21 FEB 69	Clemson	1
*	FORT, Neal	T	6.07	310	12 APR 68	Brigham Young	1
*	GOODMAN, Bobby	QB	5.11	210	12 MAY 70	Virginia	1
*	GOODWIN, Malcolm	LB	6.02	235	15 JUL 70	Iowa State	1
*	GOODWIN, Marcus	WR	5.08	160	20 MAR 70	Toledo	1
*	GOODWIN, Matt	DB	6.02	205	15 JUL 70	Iowa State	1
*	GREER, Casey	HB	6.01	200	28 NOV 69	Miami	1
*	GUARANTANO, James	WR	5.10	175	30 JUL 69	Rutgers	1
*	HAM, Tracy	QB	5.11	195	05 JAN 64	Georgia Southern	8
*	HARBISON, James	DB	6.00	180	12 MAY 70	Gardner Webb	1
*	HARMON, Eric	T	6.03	290	03 MAR 67	Clemson	1
*	HARRIS, Anthony	WR	6.03	190	02 NOV 67	North Carolina Central	1
*	HART, Randy	DT	6.05	290	26 NOV 70	Auburn	1
*	HENRY, Robert	WR	6.03	195	18 NOV 69	Florida State	1
*	HICKERSON, Eric	LB	6.03	220	04 OCT 65	Indiana	1
*	HILL, Andrew	WR	6.05	210	01 JUN 69	Indiana-Penn	1
*	HOWFIELD, Ian	K	6.02	215	04 JUN 66	Tennessee	1
*	IGWEBUIKE, Donald	K	5.09	185	27 DEC 60	Clemson	1
*	JOHNSON, Jarrod	C	6.01	280	29 MAR 69	Lehigh	1
*	KEATON, David	WR	5.11	180	06 MAY 70	Glenville State	1
*	KING, William	LB	5.09	210	30 OCT 71	Marshall	1
*	LOCKRIDGE, Dietrich	G	6.03	290	09 MAY 68	Jackson State	1
*	LONG, Terry	G	6.00	280	21 JUL 59	East Carolina	1
*	MAGGIO, Kirk	K	6.00	170	18 SEP 67	UCLA	1
*	MASTERS, C. J.	DB	6.00	210	26 FEB 70	Kansas State	1
*	MILLER, Scott	DE	6.04	285	22 APR 68	Rutgers	1
*	NARCISSE, Shawn	WR	5.09	175	06 DEC 70	Praire View	1
*	NEALY, Otis	LB	6.00	225	18 SEP 69	Texas A&M	1
*	OBERG, Andrew	T	6.07	295	02 FEB 69	North Carolina	1
*	PADDOCK, Jim	DB	6.00	210	12 DEC 70	Lindenwood College	1
*	PALOMINO, Michal	TE	6.03	230	16 NOV 69	Portland State	1
*	PARHAM, Felix	LB	6.02	220	27 DEC 70	Tennessee Tech	1
*	PATRICK, Greg	LB	6.01	220	12 JUN 69	Brown	1
*	PAWLAWSKI, Mike	QB	6.02	204	18 JUL 69	California	1
*	PEGRAM, Victor	RB	5.07	190	15 OCT 68	Prairie View	1
*	PINKERTON, Steve	K	6.02	205	10 MAR 70	Lindenwood College	1
*	PORTER, Rapier	T	6.04	285	14 AUG 66	Ark - Pine Bluff	1
*	POURDANESH, Shahriar	T	6.06	290	19 JUL 70	Nevada	1
*	PRESBURY, Robert	DE	6.03	285	18 JUL 65	Delaware State	1
*	RINGOEN, Leif Erik	LB	6.03	235	01 JUL 68	Hofstra	2
*	ROBINSON, Reggie	DB	5.11	175	04 DEC 69	Taft	1
*	SANDS, Everett	FB	5.10	215	28 JUL 71	The Citadel	1
*	SHARP, Jerry	G	6.03	290	08 OCT 69	Syracuse	1
*	SIMS, Robert	K	6.01	210	29 MAR 71	Pennsylvania	1
*	SMITH, Jackie	QB	6.02	210	16 APR 71	Clark Atlanta	1
*	SMITH, James	DB	6.02	210	18 NOV 69	Richmond	1
*	SMITH, Kwame	CB	5.09	180	01 JAN 71	West Virginia	1
*	SMITH, Tim	RB	5.11	210	21 JAN 64	Texas Tech	1
*	STEELE, Derek	DL	6.04	265	27 DEC 65	Maryland	2
*	TALLMAN, Aaron	DE	6.03	260	04 FEB 70	Tulsa	1
*	TELLINGTON, Tony	DB	5.09	175	09 OCT 68	Youngstown State	1
*	TUIPULOTU, Peter	FB	5.11	215	20 FEB 69	Brigham Young	1
*	URSIN, Jerry	WR	6.02	210	29 JUL 70	Tulane	1
*	VAUGHN, Andre	S	6.02	200	01 MAR 70	Maryland	1
*	WASHINGTON, Joe	WR	6.03	200	16 JAN 70	Tuskegee	1
*	WATSON, Ken	DB	6.02	200	10 NOV 66	Livingston	6
*	WEATHERSPOON, John	RB	5.08	220	03 JUL 68	Houston	1
*	WEBB, David	DE	6.04	240	14 NOV 69	Southern California	1
*	WILLIAMS, Wayne	DB	5.09	180	14 OCT 69	Louisiana State	1
*	WOODS, Jerry	DB	5.10	195	13 FEB 66	Northern Michigan	1
*	YANCY, Kelly	RB	6.00	210	08 MAY 71	Morningside	1
*	YOUNGBLOOD, Jason	G	6.03	275	18 DEC 70	Houston	1

CFL Caravan '94

Mayor Kurt L. Schmoke with Owner Jim Speros February/94

SHREVEPORT PIRATES FOOTBALL CLUB

Administration
505 Travis Street, Suite 602
Shreveport, Louisiana 71101
Administration Office Tel.: (318) 222-3000
Fax: (318) 222-4271
Tickets: (800) 575-4235

Football Office
3701 Hudson Street
Shreveport, Louisiana 71109
Tel: (318) 635-8466
Fax: (318) 635-4080

EXECUTIVE

Owner: Bernie Glieberman
President: Lonie Glieberman

FOOTBALL OPERATIONS

Executive Vice-President/Football Operations: J.I. Albrecht
General Manager/Director of Player Development: Dean Albrecht
Head Coach: John Huard
Assistant Coaches:
George Brancato, Offensive Backfield & Quarterbacks
Steve Dennis, Defensive Backs
Bob Surace, Offensive Line
Mark Hedgecock, Quality Control
Equipment Manager: Jim Rempel
Athletic Trainer: TBA
Doctors: Dr. Craig Springmeyer, Dr. William Webb, Dr. Edward Anglin, Dr. Carl Goodman
Assistant, Football Operations: Luther Wilson
Football Operations Secretary: Paula Herwick

ADMINISTRATION

Executive VP/Marketing and Sales: Rudi Schiffer
Director of Entertainment and Events: Robert Jackson
Director of Public/Media Relations and Publications: Missy Setters
Corporate and Retail Sales: Kay Brown
Group Sales: Ann Pringle
Corporate Sales: Pat Booras, Steve Effler, Edd Wilbanks
Director of Corporate & Legal Affairs/Community Relations: Cheryl Gray
Ticket Manager: Shelly Ragle
Assistant Ticket Manager: Marshall McInnis
Office Manager: Karen Sepulvado
Retail Sales Manager: Jim Kittler
Director/Choreographer KTUX 99 Shreveport Pirates Cheerleaders: Jamie DeRamus
Telemarketing Manager: Trina Anderson
Receptionist: Nina Robinson

FAST FACTS

Home Stadium: Independence Stadium
Stadium Address: I-20 at Hearne or Jewella Exits
Club Colors: Purple, Orange, Silver and Black
Club Name: Shreveport Pirates
Training Camp Location: State Fair Grounds
Press Box Location: West Side
Dressing Room Location: Home team and visiting team in North end zone
Radio Broadcasts: KLKL FM 92.1 - John James Marshall - play-by-play; Ben Marshall - color; Joe Ferguson - analyst.
P.A. Announcer: Dennis Brodie
Statistician: Kevin Schweers
Offensive Spotter: Jeff Conrad
Defensive Spotter: Lewis Calligas
Typist: Laura Sullivan
Timekeeper: TBA
Scorekeeper: TBA

Independence Stadium Facts 'n Figures

Capacity: 40,000

Club History: On February 18, 1994, the city of Shreveport joined the CFL as the fourth American-based team. The name "Pirates" was chosen in mid-January because "we're a Pirate team in a Pirate League," said Lonie Glieberman, President of the Club. The Pirates begin their inaugural season on July 6, 1994 at Frank Clair Stadium in Ottawa. The first regular season Canadian Football League game to be played in Shreveport is slated for July 16 against the Toronto Argonauts.

Owner/Chairman: Bernard Glieberman

Born September 23, 1939 in Detroit, Michigan. Is sole owner and president of several companies engaged in real estate development: Crosswinds Communities, Inc.; Crosswinds Realty; Greenpointe Condominiums, Inc.; and Tralon Corporation. He has become one of Michigan's best-known and respected builders and developers, building more than 5,000 homes, plus some 2,000 condominiums. He was recently named Builder of the Year South East Michigan, by the National Home Builders Association Local Chapter. Is also known as one of the foremost national authorities in classic and antique Mercedes Benz Automobiles. He has assembled one of the world's most significant collections of Mercedes Benz automobiles, including a one-of-a-kind 1939 Short Chassis, Special Roadster. Joined the League in October 1991 when he purchased the Ottawa Rough Riders. Bernie sold the Club in February 1994 and made a bid for an expansion franchise in the U.S. He was finally successful and on February 18th, the Shreveport Pirates were introduced as the fourth U.S.-based team to play in the CFL, beginning this July.

President: Lonie Glieberman

Born February 1, 1968 in Detroit, Michigan. Lonie is a graduate of Michigan State University where he received a degree in tele-communications. Prior to becoming president of the Ottawa Rough Riders in 1991, Lonie was the Director of Marketing for Crosswinds Communities where he was involved in several major development projects. During the fall months, Lonie did extensive research and found Shreveport to be a strong market for CFL football. He is an ardent believer in CFL-style football and a proponent of U.S. expansion for the game he loves.

Executive Vice-President of Football Operations: J.I. Albrecht

Born February 15, 1930. He brings 44 years of football experience to the table at the highest level of competition - Canadian and U.S. College, CFL, the old AFL and NFL. J.I. was the first-ever Director of Player Personnel in the CFL (Montreal Alouettes, 1960) and earned a reputation for his recruiting coups. Two of his very first signees wound up in the Hall of Fame - Marv Luster - and the youngest inductee - Terry Evanshen. Included among his proteges are CFL Commissioner Larry Smith and CFL "Coach of the Year" Wally Buono of the Calgary Stampeders. The Pirates have 3 of his former recruits on staff - Head Coach John Huard and Assistants George Brancato and Steve Dennis. Between service with the Montreal organization (1960-62, 1970-73), J.I. was with the Oakland Raiders, Dallas Cowboys, San Francisco 49ers and Denver Broncos of the NFL. He was Manager of Football Operations with the Toronto Argonauts from 1975-77 following a tour of duty with the New England Patriots as their Executive Assistant/Player Personnel. He was named the "All-Time GM of the Alouettes" in the CFL-sponsored national poll last year.

General Manager and Director of Player Development: Dean Albrecht

The youngest son of J.I. Albrecht was hand-picked for his present post by Pirates' owner Bernie Glieberman and his son, Lonie, the President of the Club, in concert with the senior Albrecht and Coach Huard, ironically one of Dean's own clients. At age 29, he is the youngest GM in pro football, thus following in his father's footsteps. Dean graduated from Acadia, where he played for Coach Huard and represented most of his teammates in their pro contract negotiations with CFL and NFL clubs, with a degree in Political Science. He also represented new Ottawa Head Coach Adam Rita. Along with Steve Arnold of the Las Vegas Posse, he is one of the few day-to-day operators who have seen service on both sides of the desk.

Head Coach: John Huard

Born March 9, 1944. Comes to the Pirates from Maine Maritime Academy in Castine, Maine, where he coached his team to a 9-1 record and the Eastern Collegiate Athletic Conference Northeast and New England Football Conference Championships during the 1993 season. In his first head coaching job at Acadia University in Nova Scotia, his teams won two national championships in 1979 and 1981. Huard was drafted in 1967 in the fifth round by the NFL Denver Broncos as a linebacker. He was later traded to the New Orleans Saints, where he played one season. From there, he went to the Montreal Alouettes as a player/coach. He also served as special teams coach with the Chicago Blitz of the USFL.

Assistant Coaches

George Brancato, Offensive Backfield/Quarterbacks Coach. Born May 27, 1931. Broke into professional football with the old Chicago Cardinals of the NFL. Following a leg injury in his rookie season, he jumped to the CFL with the Montreal Alouettes. After one year, he was traded to the Ottawa Rough Riders, where he played both ways. He began his coaching career in 1964 with the Quebec Rifles. He developed into one of the foremost coaches in the CFL as head coach of the Ottawa Rough Riders as well as the Saskatchewan Roughriders. He led his teams to two Grey Cups, winning one and losing one. In eleven years as head coach, his teams missed the playoffs only once. For the past several years, he coached various teams in the Arena Football League, including two years with the Providence Steamrollers and one each with the Chicago Bruisers, Dallas Texans and the Charlotte Rage.

Steve Dennis, Defensive Backs Coach. Born July 25, 1951. Comes to the Pirates from Grambling University. Dennis, known as "Stick", played with the Toronto Argonauts, under coach Bob Ward. He finished his football playing career with the Saskatchewan Roughriders and then entered the college coaching ranks at Grambling, where he served as defensive backfield coach for the past eight years.

Bob Surace, Offensive Line Coach. Born April 25, 1968. Surace will coach the Pirates' offensive line. A Princeton University graduate, he was an All-Ivy League selection as a center, is considered to be one of the truly bright young forces in football today. A history major, he holds a minor degree in Sports Management from Springfield College in Massachusetts. He is a computer expert and served with Coach Huard's Division III National Championship team at Maine Maritime Academy.

Mark Hedgecock, Quality Control Coach. Born September 20, 1956. Mark will be in charge of quality control, a post created by the NFL Dallas Cowboys a few decades ago. Considered one of the most important factors in professional football today. The University of San Diego History major also holds a master's degree in Education and coached at the high school and junior college level in both California and Oklahoma before joining Huard at Maine Maritime.

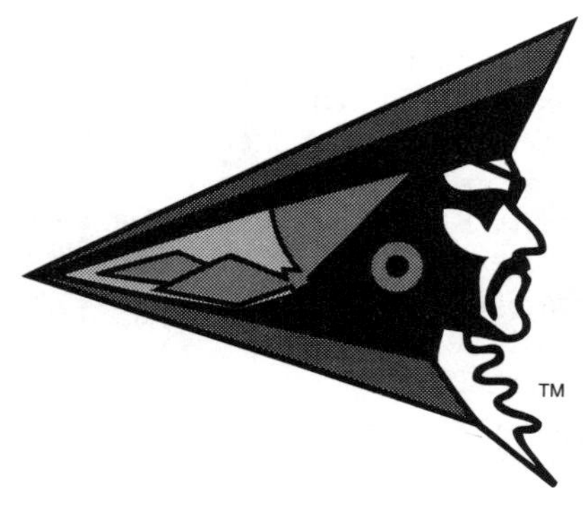

SHREVEPORT PIRATES
1994 CURRENT ROSTER AS OF APRIL 30, 1994
NEW PLAYERS

* Denotes Import

Player	Pos.	Ht.	Wt.	Born	University/ Junior Affiliate	Yrs CFL
* AUSTIN, Schredrick	—	na				1
* BAMBURG, Dennis	WR	5.11	175		NE Louisiana	1
* BARRETT, Kelly	DL				Carson Newman	1
* BRIGGS, Tom	DE	6.05	250	12 MAY 70	West Virginia	1
* BROUDY, Carey	CB	6.02	200		Louisiana Tech	1
* CAMERA, Christian	T	6.05	255	12 APR 69	Hofstra	1
* CATO, Eric	—	na				1
* COOLEY, Anthony	WR	5.09	175	19 AUG 65	North Carolina Central	1
* DEAN, Walter	RB	6.00	185		Grambling	1
* DOUGLAS, Steven	DB				Northern Arizona	1
* DUPER, Mark	WR	5.09	190	25 JAN59	NW Louisiana	1
* DYSON, Ron	WR	5.10	180		Grambling	1
* FENERTY, Gill	RB	6.00	195	24 AUG 63	Holy Cross	4
* FISHER, Luke	TE	6.02	235	21 NOV 68	East Carolina	1
* FOURCADE, John	QB	6.01	220	11 OCT 60	Mississippi	3
* FRAGER, Tim	RB	5.09	185		Boston College	1
* FREEMAN, Jamie	—	na				1
* FULLER, Joe	CB	5.11	180	25 SEP 64	Northern Iowa	4
* GAINES, Brad	FB	6.00	225		Vanderbilt	1
* GOVI, Mark	G	6.04	290	11 AUG 70	Tulsa	1
* GREER, Brett	DE	6.03	235	01 JAN 68	Youngstown State	1
* GRIFFIN, Thomas	LB	6.00	245	11 MAR 68	Grambling	1
* HAISLEY, Glen	—	na				1
* HARRISON, Nathaniel	—	na				1
* HASTON, Henry	TE	6.02	220		Florida	1
* HAYES, Jason	QB	6.04	225		Cape Breton	1
* HILK, Brian	LB	6.00	225	23 APR 69	Akron	3
* HILL, Derek	WR	6.02	200	04 NOV 67	Arizona	1
* JONES, Terrence	QB	6.01	210	18 JUN 66	Tulane	6
* KANNER, Aaron	K	6.02	215		Catawba	1
* KOLODZIEY, Chris	K				No College	1
* LATTIMORE, Brian	RB				SE Missouri	1
* LOYD, Demise	DB	6.01	200		Louisiana Tech	1
* MANLEY, Dexter	DE	6.03	270	02 FEB 59	Oklahoma State	3
* MCADOO, Steven	T	6.02	295		Middle Tennessee	1
* McCONNELL, Wesley	—	na				1
* McGILL, Reggie	RB				Arizona	1
* McGRATH, Ryan	—	na				1
* McGUIRK, Pat	DB	5.11	180	22 JUL 67	Cal Poly Obispo	1
* McKINNON, David	DL	6.05	280		Long Beach State	1
* MERO, Joe	DB	5.11	185	08 FEB 68	Louisiana State	3
* MITCHELL, Brian	—	na				1
* MOKWUAH, Gabe	LB	6.02	255	28 NOV 70	American International	1
* MOSS, Tony	WR	5.08	175		Louisiana State	1
* NAIL, Michael	DB	6.00	175	29 JUL 69	Grambling	1
* NASH, Harold	CB	5.09	180	05 MAY 70	SW Louisiana	1
* NITTMO, Bjorn	K	5.11	185	26 JUL 66	Appalachian State	1
* PALAZZI, David	QB				Massachusetts	1
* PAYTON, Elfrid	LB	6.01	230	22 SEP 67	Grambling	4
* PEARCE, Mark	DE	6.06	265	25 MAY 67	Cape Breton	2
* PEARCE, Marlon	WR	5.08	165		NE Louisiana	1
* RALEY, Tyson	—	na				1
* RENFROE, Gilbert	QB	6.01	195	18 FEB 63	Tennessee State	1
* RICHARD, Henry	RB	5.10	205	03 OCT 68	NE Louisiana	1
* RODGERS, Kacy	DE	6.03	255	27 JUN 69	Tennessee	1
* RUSSO, Anthony	RB				St John's NY	1
* SANCHEZ, Eros	QB	5.11	195	11 AUG 67	Virginia	2
* SAVAGE, Raymond	LB	6.01	240	01 MAR 68	Virginia	1
* SCOTT, Johnny	—	na				1
* SETTERS, Ross	OL				Louisiana State	1
* SHANNON, John	DT	6.03	265		Kentucky	1
* SIGN, Matt	—	na				1
* SIGN, Robert	—	na				1
* SKAGGS, Luther	—	na				1
* SMITH, Brian	DB	5.09	180	10 SEP 66	Idaho	2
* SMITH, Darrell K.	SB	6.02	190	05 NOV 61	Ohio Central	9
* SMITH, Jeff	SB	6.04	180	28 MAY 63	Cal Poly Obispo	6
* SMITH, Terry	WR	5.08	170	29 JUL 69	Penn State	1
* STAUROVSKY, Jason	K	5.09	170	23 MAR 63	Tulsa	1
* STOWELL, Mike	T	6.02	280		Tennessee	1
* STUMON, Greg	LB	6.00	235	26 MAY 63	Southern Arkansas	9
* THOMPSON, Charles	RB	5.09	185	28 MAY 68	Ohio Central	2
* THORNTON, Randy	DE	6.04	250	23 DEC 64	Houston	2
* WALKER, Wayne	WR	5.08	165	27 DEC 66	Texas Tech	3
* WASHINGTON, Eric	—	na				1
* WILEY, John	DB	6.00	195	08 AUG 69	Auburn	2
* WORTHMAN, Antoine	CB	5.10	190	20 JUN 70	Illinois State	3
* ZENO, Marc	WR	6.03	205	21 JUN 65	Tulane	3

LB Elfrid Payton - '93 Eastern Division Most Outstanding Defensive Player

QB Terrence Jones

SASKATCHEWAN ROUGHRIDER FOOTBALL CLUB

2940 - 10th Avenue,
P.O. Box 1277
Regina, Saskatchewan S4P 3B8
Telephone Numbers: Main Office (306) 569-2323
Ticket Office (306) 525-2181 "The Store" (306) 522-8989
Fax (306) 522-7075

EXECUTIVE

Owner: Community Owned
Executive Committee:
President - John Lipp
Vice-President - Fred Wagman
Treasurer - Tom Shepherd
Executive Members - Gunnar Pedersen, Don McDougall, Frank Buck, Wendy Kelly, Dan Marce
Special Advisor - Paul Hill
Governor: John Lipp **Alternate:** Alan Ford
General Manager and Chief Operating Officer: Alan Ford

FOOTBALL OPERATIONS

Head Coach and Offensive Coordinator: Ray Jauch
Assistant Coaches:
Jim Daley - Defensive Coordinator and Linebackers
Richie Hall - Defensive Backs
Greg Marshall - Defensive Line
Pat Perles - Offensive Line
Bob Vespaziani - Offensive Backs and Receivers
Director of Football Operations: Dan Rambo
Player Personnel Assistant: Brendan Taman
Head Trainer: Ivan Gutfriend
Equipment Manager: Norm Fong
Team Doctors:
Dr. Jack Alexander, Dr. Ron Ailsby, Dr. Donovan Brown
Dr. James Fraser
Team Dentist: Dr. H. Baumann, Dr. B. Mang
US Scout: Mike MacCagnan

MARKETING/BUSINESS OPERATIONS

Director of Marketing: Barry Taman
Director of Business Operations: Jill McDougall
Controller: Blair Watson
Media/Public Relations Coordinator: Tony Playter
Marketing/Special Events Coordinator: Stacey Cattell
Ticket Office Manager: Vickie Poitras
Ticket Office Staff: Carol Hoeving
Player Personnel/Admin. Assistant: Patti Jackson
Receptionist/Marketing Assistant: Cheryl McLean
Manager of Computer Systems: Dave Dunster
Store Manager: Liz Measner

FAST FACTS

Home Stadium: Taylor Field
Stadium Address: 2940 - 10th Avenue, P.O. Box 1277, Regina, Saskatchewan S4P 3B8
Club Colours: Green & White
Club Name: Saskatchewan Roughriders
Training Camp Site: Taylor Field, Regina
Press Box Location: West Side of Taylor Field
Dressing Room Locations: Home Team - Under West side stands, South end
Visiting Team - Under West side stands, use main entrance
Radio Broadcasts: 980 CKRM-AM - Geoff Currier, Play-by-Play
P.A. Announcer: Roy Brown
Statistician: Jim Stirr
Offensive Spotter: Steve Stirr
Defensive Spotter: Jim Hutchinson
Typist: Dave Taylor
Timekeeper: Del Jones
Scorekeeper: John Grundy

TWO GREY CUP VICTORIES FOR REGINA-BASED TEAMS

Saskatchewan Roughriders (2) - 1966, 1989

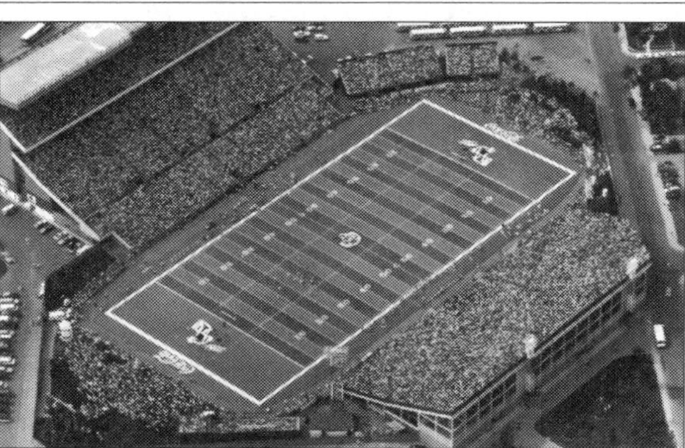

Taylor Field Facts 'n Figures

Capacity: 27,637
Largest Regular Season One Game Attendance: 33,032
Saskatchewan 26, Sacramento 23 (August 27, 1993)
Largest Playoff One Game Attendance: 26,229
B.C. 42, Saskatchewan 18 (November 13, 1988)

Club History:

1890 the first recorded game of football in Saskatchewan played by the North West Mounted Police . . . 1895 Fort Saskatchewan plays its first series of organized games . . . 1910 the Regina Rugby Club forms in the new Saskatchewan Rugby Football Union . . . 1924 Regina Rugby Club changes name to Regina Roughriders . . . 1946 name again changed to the Saskatchewan Roughriders popularly although this was not legally changed until 1950

SASKATCHEWAN CLUB RECORDS SINCE 1946
Regular Season

- CFL Record
- Ties CFL Record
( ) - Figures in Brackets represent Year(s) Club mark set

Most Points Scored One Season (minimum 14 games) - 606 ('91)
Most Points Scored Against One Season (minimum 14 games) - 710 ('91)
Fewest Points Against One Season (minimum 14 games) - 102 ('49)
Most Points Scored One Game - 58 -
- Ottawa at Saskatchewan 07/08/89 Final: 58-22
Most Points Scored Against One Game - 67 -
- at Hamilton 15/10/62 Final: 67-21
Most Wins One Season (minimum 14 games) - 14 ('70)
Most Losses One Season (minimum 14 games) - 15 ('59)
Highest Shutout - 47-0 - at Winnipeg 15/10/49
Highest Shutout Against -#56-0 - at Winnipeg 05/07/86
Most Touchdowns One Season (minimum 14 games) - 62 ('91)
Most Touchdowns One Game - 8 -
- at Winnipeg 15/10/49
- at Edmonton 28/08/64
Most Converts One Season (minimum 14 games) - 54 ('91)
Most Converts One Game - 7 -
- at B.C. 16/08/58
- at Edmonton 28/08/64
- B.C. at Saskatchewan 24/10/71
- Ottawa at Saskatchewan 07/08/89
- Winnipeg at Saskatchewan 02/09/90
- Hamilton at Saskatchewan 26/07/91
- Winnipeg at Saskatchewan 01/09/91

Most Field Goals One Season (minimum 14 games) - #59 ('90)
Most Field Goals One Game - #8 - at Ottawa - 29/07/84
- vs. Edmonton 23/07/88
Most First Downs One Game - #46 - at B.C. 13/08/92
Most Yards Total Offence One Game -721 at B.C. - 13/08/92
Most Yards Rushing One Game - 374 -
- Edmonton at Saskatchewan 20/08/62
Most Times Carried One Game - 58 -
- Edmonton at Saskatchewan 01/11/58
Most Touchdowns Rushing One Game - 4 -
- at Winnipeg 26/10/59
- Edmonton at Saskatchewan 30/10/68
- at Winnipeg 31/08/88
Most Yards Passing One Game - 558 - at B.C. - 13/08/92
Most Passes Thrown One Game - #65 -
- Edmonton at Saskatchewan 15/09/91
Most Completions One Game - 41 at Toronto - 31/10/93
Most Touchdown Passes One Game - 6 - at B.C. - 21/09/91

SASKATCHEWAN INDIVIDUAL RECORDS SINCE 1946
Regular Season

Points (Career) - 2,018 - Dave Ridgway
Points (Season) - 233 - Dave Ridgway ('90)
Points (Game) - 30 - Ferd Burket - at Winnipeg 26/10/59
Touchdowns (Career) - #137 - George Reed
Touchdowns (Season) - 18 - Ken Carpenter ('55)
Touchdowns (Game) - 5 - Ferd Burket - at Winnipeg 26/10/59
Field Goals (Career) - 501 - Dave Ridgway
Field Goals (Season) - #59 - Dave Ridgway ('90)
Field Goals (Game) - #8 - Dave Ridgway - at Ottawa 29/07/84
- vs. Edmonton 23/07/88
Longest Field Goal - #60 -
- Dave Ridgway - Winnipeg at Saskatchewan 06/09/87
Passes Thrown (Career) - 5,834 - Ron Lancaster (Note: Lancaster's Career Total with Saskatchewan and Ottawa is #6,233)
Passes Thrown (Season) - #770 - Kent Austin ('92)
Passes Thrown (Game) - #65 -
- Kent Austin - Edmonton at Saskatchewan 15/09/91
Passes Completed (Career) - 3,186 - Ron Lancaster (Note: Lancaster's Career Total with Saskatchewan and Ottawa is #3,384)
Passes Completed (Season) - 459 - Kent Austin ('92)
Passes Completed (Game) - 41 -
- Kent Austin - at Toronto - 31/10/93
Passing Yards (Career) - 46,710 - Ron Lancaster (Note: Lancaster's Career Total with Saskatchewan and Ottawa is #50,535)
Passing Yards (Season) - 6,225 - Kent Austin ('92)
Passing Yards (Game) - 558 - Kent Austin - at B.C. 13/08/92
Touchdown Passes Thrown (Career) - 299 - Ron Lancaster (Note: Lancaster's Career Total with Saskatchewan and Ottawa is #333)
Touchdown Passes Thrown (Season) - 35 - Kent Austin ('92)
Touchdown Passes Thrown (Game) - 6 -
- Kent Austin - at B.C. 21/09/91
No. of Carries (Career) - #3,243 - George Reed
No. of Carries (Season) - 323 - George Reed ('75)
No. of Carries (Game) - 34 -
- George Reed - at Hamilton 08/08/70
- George Reed - at Winnipeg 12/10/75
Yards Rushing (Career) - #16,116 - George Reed
Yards Rushing (Season) - 1,768 - George Reed ('65)
Yards Rushing (Game) - 268 - George Reed - at B.C. 24/10/65
Touchdowns by Rushing (Career) - #134 - George Reed
Touchdowns by Rushing (Season) - 16 - George Reed ('68)
Touchdowns by Rushing (Game) - 4 -
- Ferd Burket - at Winnipeg 26/10/59
- George Reed - Edmonton at Saskatchewan 30/10/68
- Milson Jones - at Winnipeg 31/08/88
Passes Caught (Career) - 694 - Ray Elgaard
Passes Caught (Season) - 102 - Joey Walters ('82)
- Craig Ellis ('85)
Passes Caught (Game) - 15 - Don Narcisse - at Toronto 31/10/93
- Craig Ellis - Mtl. at Sask. 19/07/85
Pass Reception Yards (Career) - 9,860 - Ray Elgaard
Pass Reception Yards (Season) - 1,715 - Joey Walters ('81)
Pass Reception Yards (Game) - 260 -
- Chris DeFrance at Edmonton 05/08/83
Touchdown Passes Caught (Career) - 69 - Ray Elgaard
Touchdown Passes Caught (Season) - 17 - Hugh Campbell ('66)
Touchdown Passes Caught (Game) - 3 -
- Jack Hill - at B.C. 29/09/58
- Bob Renn - Calgary at Saskatchewan 26/09/60
- Hugh Campbell - at Edmonton 28/08/64
- Hugh Campbell - Winnipeg at Saskatchewan 07/08/65
- Hugh Campbell - at Edmonton 29/07/66
- Hugh Campbell - Winnipeg at Saskatchewan 07/08/66
- Joey Walters - at Edmonton 30/08/81
- Joey Walters - Edmonton at Saskatchewan 18/10/81
- Ray Elgaard - at B.C. 16/09/88
- Jeff Fairholm - at B.C. 21/09/91

SASKATCHEWAN'S RECORD AGAINST OTHER CLUBS (REGULAR SEASON)

		GP	W	L	T	F	A	PTS
Versus Ottawa	(Since 1961)	47	28	19	0	1239	1078	56
Versus Toronto	(Since 1961)	46	24	21	1	1068	1116	49
Versus Hamilton	(Since 1961)	46	18	24	4	1057	1212	40
Versus Winnipeg	(Since 1961)	161	65	93	3	2919	3352	133
Versus Calgary	(Since 1946)	126	66	53	7	2978	3307	139
Versus Edmonton	(Since 1949)	143	61	80	2	2763	3340	124
Versus B.C.	(Since 1954)	124	67	53	4	2767	2842	138
Versus Sacramento	(Since 1993)	3	2	1	0	79	80	4
SASKATCHEWAN VS OPPOSITION		696	331	344	21	14870	16327	683

President: John Lipp

Born January 27, 1939 in Germany. John Lipp was elected President of the Club on January 21, 1993. John has been a member of the Executive since 1987 and served as the Club's Vice-President for three seasons before becoming Club President. John is the 20th modern era President of the Riders. John represents the Roughriders on the CFL's Board of Governors. John is currently serving his second term as a member of the Regina City Council. He has a long history of commitment to the community as a businessman, a volunteer and as a member and Chairperson of the Regina Separate School Board.

General Manager and Chief Operating Officer: Alan Ford

Born July 2, 1943 in Regina, Saskatchewan. Became the twelfth General Manager of the Roughriders when he was promoted from Assistant General Manager on January 5, 1989. After playing high school football in Regina, he headed to the University of the Pacific in California. His CFL playing career started in 1965 and he retired in 1976. After retiring, he became a teacher in Regina. In 1979 he joined the 'Rider coaching staff as an assistant responsible for the Secondary and Special Teams. After one season he returned to teaching until August of 1981. He then became a project officer with Canada Pioneer Realty. In 1985 he rejoined the 'Riders as the Director of Administration and Canadian Player Development.

Head Coach: Ray Jauch

Born February 11, 1938 in Mendota, Illinois. Was named Head Coach of the 'Riders on January 18, 1994. Received a B.Sc. degree in Physical Education from Iowa in 1960, and played two seasons with the Winnipeg Blue Bombers before suffering a career-ending injury in the 1961 Grey Cup Game. Became an assistant coach with the Edmonton Eskimos from 1966 to 1969. Was named Head Coach of the Eskimos in 1970. In 12 years as a Head Coach in the CFL, he had 111 wins, 78 losses and 4 ties. Was the Annis Stukus Trophy winner as CFL Coach of the Year after his rookie season as Head Coach of Edmonton and ten years later in 1980 with Winnipeg. Three times he coached his team to the Grey Cup, winning it in 1975 while with the Eskimos. Became Director of Football Operations in 1977 but returned to coaching a year later in Winnipeg. After the 1982 season, he left the Blue Bombers to become Head Coach and General Manager of the USFL Washington Federals in 1983 and 1984. Spent the 1987 season as the

Head Coach of the Chicago Bruisers in the Arena Football League. Was the Director of Football Operations of the Arena Football League in 1988 and '89. Spent the 1990 season as Head Coach at St. Ambrose University in Davenport, Iowa. Joined Saskatchewan on April 11, 1991.

Assistant Coaches

Jim Daley, Defensive Line Coach and Special Teams Coordinator. Born July 15, 1954 in Ottawa, Ontario. Comes to the Western Riders after a three-year stint with the Eastern Riders. During his tenure in Ottawa, Daley spent time with the Running Backs, Defensive Line and Special Teams. Prior to joining the Rough Riders in April 1991, was the Head Coach at the University of Ottawa from 1985-1990. During that time, he was OQIFC Coach of the Year in 1986 and 1988. From 1982 to 1984, was Head Coach of the Ottawa Sooners and was selected OFC Coach of the Year in both 1982 and 1984. In his final year as the Sooners' Head Coach, Jim directed the Club to the 1984 National Title and was selected North East Regional Association Coach of the Year. Prior to 1982, was an assistant coach at Carleton University and St. Pius X High School. Began his coaching career as a Head Coach at St. Patrick's High School in 1976.

Richie Hall, Defensive Backs Coach. Born October 4, 1960 in San Antonio, Texas. Begins his first stint as an assistant coach in the professional ranks. Was a member of the O'Neill Titans coaching staff under head coach Darrell Puscus in 1993. Has been a guest coach at training camps at Colorado State University, his alma mater, over the last few years. Signed with the Calgary Stampeders in 1983 before being dealt to the Roughriders in May 1988. He was a member of the 1989 Grey Cup Champions, was named to the Western All-Star team 4 times (1983, '86, '88 and '90) and to the CFL All-Star team in 1983. Richie was voted the Roughriders' Most Popular Player in 1988 by Saskatchewan fans and was also named the Club's nominee as Outstanding Defensive Player. In 1991, he was the recipient of the Tom Pate Award, given by the CFL Players' Association, for his outstanding dedication to the CFL, the community as well as his performance on the field.

Greg Marshall, Defensive Line. Born September 9, 1956 in Beverly, Massachussetts. Spent the past three seasons handling the Head Coaching duties with the Ottawa Sooners, guiding them to a CJFL National Championship in 1992. Has been a guest coach at the Ottawa Rough Rider training camp for the past two seasons, looking after the defensive line. In 1991, Greg spent training camp coaching and evaluating defensive line talent for the Toronto Argonauts. Also spent two seasons coaching the Ottawa Bootleggers in the American Football Alliance. His coaching career began in 1978 as a graduate assistant with his Alma Mater, Oregon State University. Greg was originally drafted by the NFL Philadelphia Eagles in the seventh round of the 1978 Draft. Spent time with the Eagles and the Baltimore Colts before heading to the CFL, where he was named to the Eastern All-Star team four times ('81-'84) as well as the CFL All-Star team ('81, '83) and was voted the Most Outstanding Defensive Player in 1983 while a member of the Eastern Riders from 1980 to 1988.

Pat Perles, Offensive Line Coach. Born October 2, 1963 in Pittsburgh, Pennsylvania. Joins Saskatchewan from Michigan State University where he assisted with the Spartans' defensive secondary. Son of legendary Michigan State Football coach George Perles. Has coaching experience in the NCAA, where he also implemented a defensive strategy for the Stunt 4-3 defense at the University of Toledo, and the NFL, spending some time assisting the defensive and offensive lines, and special teams with the Los Angeles Rams from 1992 to 1993.

Bob Vespaziani, Receivers and Running Backs. Born June 15, 1935 in Mount Vernon, New York. This is his second stint with the Green and White, after being a guest coach during the 1990 training camp. Spent the 1993 training camp as a guest coach of the Winnipeg Blue Bombers, prior to which he coached the defensive front-seven. Prior to that, Bob was with the B.C. Lions in 1985 and again from 1988 to 1991. Was the Calgary Stampeders' head coach from 1986 to 1987. Began coaching in the CFL in 1979 with Winnipeg, where he remained until 1984, winning the Grey Cup that same year. Began coaching at the collegiate level in 1969 at Acadia University as an assistant, before he was promoted to head coach in 1971, staying there until 1978. During his stay at Acadia, he was named the AUAA Coach of the Year three times ('72, '75 and '76).

SASKATCHEWAN ROUGHRIDERS
1994 CURRENT ROSTER AS OF APRIL 30, 1994
RETURNING PLAYERS

* Denotes Import

	Player	Pos.	Ht.	Wt.	Born	University/ Jr. Affiliate	Yrs. CFL	Yrs. SASK
	ANDERSON, Michael	C	6.03	260	15 AUG 61	San Diego State	11	11
	BERNARD, Ray	LB	6.01	220	29 MAY 67	Bishop's	3	3
	BOYKO, Bruce	SB	6.01	210	2 MAR 67	Western Michigan	5	5
*	BRANTLEY, Sean	DT	6.00	245	30 JUL 69	Florida A & M	2	2
*	BROWN, Albert	CB	6.00	180	19 DEC 63	Western Illinois	8	8
	BROWN, Errol	CB	5.08	170	4 JAN 71	Saskatchewan	2	2
*	CRUM, Maurice	LB	6.00	220	19 APR 69	Miami	2	2
*	DONELSON, Ventson	DB	5.11	180	2 FEB 68	Michigan State	4	4
	ELGAARD, Ray	SB	6.03	225	29 AUG 59	Utah	12	12
	FARTHING, Dan	SB	5.10	180	11 OCT 69	Saskatchewan	4	4
	HENDRICKSON, Scott	C	6.03	275	25 JAN 70	Minnesota	3	3
*	JONES, Warren	QB	6.02	200	23 SEP 66	Hawaii	5	3
*	JURASIN, Bobby	DE	6.01	235	26 AUG 64	Northern Michigan	9	9
*	LANCE, Carlton	CB	6.00	195	3 OCT 70	SW Minnesota	2	2
*	LEWIS, Gary	DT	6.03	270	14 JAN 61	Oklahoma State	10	10
	MACCALLUM, Tom	T	6.03	270	22 DEC 70	Minot State	2	2
	MATICH, Brent	K	6.01	190	5 DEC 66	Calgary	6	3
*	NARCISSE, Donald	WR	5.09	170	26 FEB 65	Texas Southern	8	8
	PITCHER, David	SB	6.02	220	29 JAN 67	Okanagan Juniors	5	5
	RASHOVICH, Dan	LB	6.01	220	30 NOV 60	Simon Fraser	11	8
	RIDGWAY, David	K	6.01	190	24 APR 59	Toledo	13	13
*	SAUNDERS, Mike	RB	5.10	200	3 OCT 69	Iowa	3	3
	SUITOR, Glen	DB	6.00	190	24 NOV 62	Simon Fraser	11	11
	VAJDA, Paul	G	6.02	265	27 JUL 66	Concordia	4	4

NEW PLAYERS

* Denotes Import

	Player	Pos.	Ht.	Wt.	Born	University/ Jr. Affiliate	Yrs. CFL
*	BARBER, Wolf	CB	6.00	185	20 APR 70	California	1
*	BATTLE, Kevin	DT	6.05	305	11 JUN 70	Georgia Tech.	1
*	BECKHAM, Terry	WR	5.07	160	07 AUG 72	Clark Atlanta	1
*	BURGESS, Tom	QB	6.00	200	06 MAR 64	Colgate	9
*	CAMPBELL, Christopher	WR	6.00	190	17 APR 70	Virginia Tech	1
*	CLARK, Steve	DE	6.05	265	15 MAY 70	Houston	1
*	DAVIS, John	DB	6.02	220	12 FEB 71	Florida State	1
*	DRAWHORN, Anthony	DB	5.09	175	27 JUL 65	Nevada Las Vegas	7
*	FREENEY, William	DB	5.10	200	23 FEB 70	Northern Iowa	1
*	GETHERS, Ivory	LB	6.02	225	11 MAR 70	Penn State	1
*	GOETZ, Ron	LB	6.03	230	08 FEB 68	Minnesota	2
*	GRANT, Marcus	WR	5.09	165	12 SEP 70	Houston	1
*	GRIFFITH, Robert	DB	6.00	195	30 NOV 70	San Diego State	1
*	HALIBURTON, Sheldon	T	6.06	305	31 JAN 68	Texas A & I	1
	HARMER, Robert	DT	6.01	235	26 FEB 69	Edinboro	1
*	HARRIS, Stephen	CB	6.00	185	30 DEC 68	Houston	1
	HULL, Bart	RB	5.11	210	13 FEB 69	Boise State	2
*	JOHNSON, Michael	QB	6.02	185	02 MAY 67	Akron	2
*	JOSEPH, Dale	CB	5.11	180	03 AUG 67	Howard Payne	1
*	KEMP, Dane	DT	6.07	310	03 MAY 69	Indiana	1
*	KING, Ulric	WR	5.11	205	31 DEC 70	Western Michigan	1
	KOZAN, Paul	RB	6.00	205	01 MAY 71	Queen's	1
*	LESTER, Greg	WR	5.10	180	16 DEC 70	Georgia Tech	1
*	PAYTON, Michael	QB	6.01	220	05 MAR 70	Marshall	1
*	PETRY, Stan	CB	6.00	170	14 AUG 66	Texas Christian	1
*	PIERCE, Bennie	DE	6.02	245	25 SEP 69	Auburn	1
*	POLLARD, William	WR	6.05	225	19 FEB 71	Notre Dame	1
*	RANDOLPH, Joe	WR	5.07	160	30 APR 71	Elon College	1
*	REESE, Julius	WR	6.03	195	05 JUN 71	North Carolina	1
*	ROGERS, Gary	LB	6.03	225	18 SEP 70	Vanderbilt	1
*	RUFFIN, Aaron	CB	5.10	171	17 MAY 69	Nicholls State	2
	SERKE, Travis	T	6.03	290	12 JUN 68	Saskatchewan	1
*	SMITH, Lester	DB	5.10	180	04 AUG 70	The Citadel	1
*	THOMAS, Alex	DB	6.01	220	20 MAY 68	Auburn	1

CALGARY STAMPEDER FOOTBALL CLUB

McMahon Stadium
1817 Crowchild Trail N.W.
Calgary, Alberta T2M 4R6
Administration: (403) 289-0205 Fax (403) 289-7850
Ticket Office (403) 289-0258 Fax (403) 289-6828
Stamp Store: (403) 289-4441

OWNERSHIP

Owner/President: Larry Ryckman
Personal Assistant to Owner: Linda Gagnon
Governor: Larry Ryckman **Alternate:** Wally Buono

FOOTBALL OPERATIONS

General Manager and Head Coach: Wally Buono
Assistant General Manager/Player Personnel: Roy Shivers
Assistant Coaches:
Tom Higgins, Defensive Line
George Cortez, Offensive Line
John Hufnagel, Offensive Co-ordinator & Quarterbacks Coach
Frank Spaziani, Defensive Secondary Coach
Chuck McMann, Wide Receivers and Running Backs Coach
Football Administration: Chuck McMann
Executive Assistant Football: Jane Mawby
Head Therapist, Travel and Training Camp Coordinator: Pat Clayton
Assistant Therapist: Chris Fleming
Equipment Manager: George Hopkins
Video Coordinator/Equipment Assistant: Ross Folan
Team Doctors: Dr. Vince Murphy, Dr. L. Van Zuiden, Dr. P. McMurtry, Dr. J. Mackenzie
Team Dentist: Dr. B. Tomimoto, Dr. L. Brooks

MARKETING/BUSINESS OPERATIONS

Vice President of Marketing and Communications: Ron Rooke
Vice President of Business Operations: Maurice Strul
Executive Director of Sales: Brian Wilson
Special Events and Promotions Coordinator: Karen Wilkinson
Media Relations/Community Events Coordinator: Tania Van Brunt
Marketing Representatives: Linda Orr, Sugarfoot Anderson, Doug Armstrong, Scott Harvey
Ticket Office Manager: Annette Vogelsang
Ticketing Assistant: Brenda Fentiman
Red and White Club: Vickie Chase
Stamp Store and Merchandising Manager: Alan Harvie
Stamp Store: Mike Hardiman
Controller: Peter Glass
Accountant: Kerry Martinuk
Receptionist: Joanne Gauthier
Office Assistant: Kelly Turner
Alumni President: Herm Harrison
McMahon Stadium General Manager: John Haverstock

FAST FACTS

Home Stadium: McMahon Stadium
Stadium Address: 1817 Crowchild Trail N.W., Calgary, Alberta T2M 4R6
Club Colours: Red, White & Black
Club Name: Calgary Stampeders
Training Camp Location: McMahon Stadium
Press Box Location: West Side of Stadium via South-West Pass Gate to Press Box (Elevator on West Side)
Dressing Room Location: Home Team at South Side, Visiting team under stands on West side
Radio Broadcasts: QR77 AM Radio - Mike Lownsbrough, Don Siler, Marshall Toner
Public Announcer: Dan Carson
Statistician: Paulette Slade
Volunteer Statistician: Daryl Slade
Offensive Spotters: Darren Haynes
Defensive Spotter: Nate DiLeandro
Typist: Susan Mills
Timekeeper: John Semkuley
Scorekeeper: Merv Piling

McMahon Stadium Facts 'n Figures

Capacity: 37,317
Largest Regular Season One Game Attendance: 38,205
Edmonton 34, Calgary 21 (September 7, 1992)
Calgary 33, Edmonton 13 (September 6, 1993)
Largest Playoff One Game Attendance: 31,923
Edmonton 43, Calgary 23 (November 18, 1990)
Largest Grey Cup Attendance: 50,035
Edmonton 33, Winnipeg 23 (November 28, 1993)

Club History: 1891 first Edmonton and Calgary home and home series . . . 1908 formation of the Calgary Tigers . . . 1924 disbanding of the Calgary Tigers for war, replaced by the 50th Battalion and later the Calgary Altomas . . . Calgary Bronks formed in 1935 . . . 1945 team name changed to the Stampeders . . . 1948 the Stampeders won the Grey Cup and turned the annual fall classic into a national festival . . . Stampeders won their 3rd Grey Cup in 1992 in Toronto, a 24-10 win over Winnipeg.

THREE GREY CUP VICTORIES FOR CALGARY-BASED TEAMS

Stampeders (3) - 1948, 1971, 1992

CALGARY CLUB RECORDS SINCE 1946
Regular Season

- CFL Record
() - Figures in Brackets represent Year(s) Club mark set

Most Points Scored One Season (minimum 14 games) - 646 ('93)
Most Points Scored Against One Season (minimum 14 games) - 566 ('90)
Fewest Points Against One Season (minimum 14 games) - #77 ('49)
Most Points Scored One Game - 57 -
- Winnipeg at Calgary 20/9/92
Most Points Scored Against One Game - 70 -
- Calgary at Toronto 20/09/90 Final: 18-70
Most Wins One Season (minimum 14 games) - 15 ('93)
Most Losses One Season (minimum 14 games) - 13 ('85)
Highest Shutout - 50-0 - at Toronto 22/09/63
Highest Shutout Against - 52-0 - at Edmonton 22/09/56
Most Touchdowns One Season (minimum 14 games) - 70 ('93)
Most Touchdowns One Game - 8 - Saskatchewan at Calgary 10/10/59
Most Converts One Season (minimum 14 games) - 63 ('92, '93)
Most Converts One Game - 7 - Hamilton at Calgary 17/10/82
Most Field Goals One Season (minimum 14 games) - 48 ('89)
Most Field Goals One Game - 6 - B.C. at Calgary 31/10/82
- Calgary at B.C. 11/07/91

Most First Downs One Game - 42 - Saskatchewan at Calgary 10/10/59
Most Yards Total Offence One Game - 661 -
- Saskatchewan at Calgary 10/10/59
Most Yards Rushing One Game - 387 - at B.C. 16/08/62
Most Times Carried One Game - 48 - at Saskatchewan 16/09/79
Most Touchdowns Rushing One Game - 5 - Calgary at Hamilton 21/10/90
- Edmonton at Calgary 03/09/62
- Saskatchewan at Calgary 23/07/80
Most Yards Passing One Game - 556 - Calgary at Ottawa 06/08/93
Most Passes Thrown One Game - 63 - Calgary at Saskatchewan 07/08/92
Most Completions One Game - 37 - Calgary at B.C. 23/10/93
Most Touchdown Passes One Game - 6 - Winnipeg at Calgary 15/10/67

CALGARY INDIVIDUAL RECORDS SINCE 1946
Regular Season

Points (Career) - 1,275 - J.T. Hay
Points (Season) - 215- Mark McLoughlin ('93)
Points (Game) - 30 - Earl Lunsford - Edmonton at Calgary 03/09/62
Touchdowns (Career) - 62 - Tom Forzani
Touchdowns (Season) - 17 - Terry Evanshen ('67)
Touchdowns (Game) - 5 - Earl Lunsford - Edmonton at Calgary 03/09/62
Field Goals (Career) - 274 - J.T. Hay
Field Goals (Season) - 48 - Mark McLoughlin ('89)
Field Goals (Game) - 6 - J.T. Hay - B.C. at Calgary 31/10/82
- Mark McLoughlin - Calgary at B.C. 11/07/91
Longest Field Goal - 58 -
- Mark McLoughlin - Calgary at Saskatchewan 09/10/88
Passes Thrown (Career) - 1,971 - Peter Liske
Passes Thrown (Season) - 703- Doug Flutie ('93)
Passes Thrown (Game) - 63 -
- Doug Flutie - Calgary at Saskatchewan 07/08/92
Passes Completed (Career) - 1,145 - Peter Liske
Passes Completed (Season) - 416 - Doug Flutie ('93)
Passes Completed (Game) - 37 - Doug Flutie - Calgary at Saskatchewan 23/11/93
Passing Yards (Career) - 16,741 - Peter Liske
Passing Yards (Season) - 6,092 - Doug Flutie ('93)
Passing Yards (Game) - 556 -
- Doug Flutie - Calgary at Ottawa 08/06/93
Touchdown Passes Thrown (Career) - 106 - Peter Liske
Touchdown Passes Thrown (Season) - #44 - Doug Flutie ('93)
Touchdown Passes Thrown (Game) - 6 - Peter Liske
- Winnipeg at Calgary 15/10/67
No. of Carries (Career) - 1,242 - Willie Burden
No. of Carries (Season) - #332 - Willie Burden ('75)
No. of Carries (Game) - 36 - Lovell Coleman - at Winnipeg 12/08/63
Yards Rushing (Career) - 6,994 - Earl Lunsford
Yards Rushing (Season) -#1,896 - Willie Burden ('75)
Yards Rushing (Game) - 238 -
- Lovell Coleman - Calgary at Hamilton 15/09/64
- Willie Burden - Winnipeg at Calgary 02/11/75
Touchdowns by Rushing (Career) - 56 - Earl Lunsford
Touchdowns by Rushing (Season) - 13 -
- Earl Lunsford ('60)
- Lovell Coleman ('63)
- James Sykes ('78)
Touchdowns by Rushing (Game) - #5 -
- Earl Lunsford - Edmonton at Calgary 03/09/62
Passes Caught (Career) - 553 - Tom Forzani
Passes Caught (Season) - #118 - Allen Pitts ('91)
Passes Caught (Game) - 16 - Brian Wiggins - Calgary at Saskatchewan 23/11/93
Pass Reception Yards (Career) - 8,285 - Tom Forzani
Pass Reception Yards (Season) - 1,764 - Allen Pitts ('91)
Pass Reception Yards (Game) - 237 - Herman Harrison
- Saskatchewan at Calgary 29/09/68
Touchdown Passes Caught (Career) - 62 - Tom Forzani
Touchdown Passes Caught (Season) - 17 - Terry Evanshen ('67)
Touchdown Passes Caught (Game) - 4 - Herman Harrison
- at Winnipeg 02/09/70

CALGARY'S RECORD AGAINST OTHER CLUBS
(REGULAR SEASON)

		GP	W	L	T	F	A	PTS
Versus Ottawa	(Since 1961)	46	28	18	0	1166	1010	56
Versus Toronto	(Since 1961)	46	24	21	1	1152	1092	49
Versus Hamilton	(Since 1961)	47	29	18	0	1250	1058	58
Versus Winnipeg	(Since 1946)	151	73	78	0	2794	3036	146
Versus Saskatchewan	(Since 1946)	126	53	66	7	3307	2978	113
Versus Edmonton	(Since 1949)	153	54	95	4	2853	3470	112
Versus B.C.	(Since 1954)	122	69	49	4	2809	2422	142
Versus Sacramento	(Since 1993)	2	2	0	0	79	44	4
CALGARY VS OPPOSITION		693	332	345	16	15410	15110	680

President and Owner: Larry Ryckman

Born in Toronto in 1955, but having resided in Calgary for the last 22 years, Larry Ryckman is listed in the Who's Who of Canada. Mr. Ryckman is one of Western Canada's most prominent businessmen, whose companies employ over 750 people in the province of Alberta. He currently holds positions as President and Owner of the Calgary Stampeders, President and CEO of Consolidated Cambridge Mines Ltd., President and CEO of AABBAX Financial Corporation and is the President and Director of Ryckman Financial Corporation. Larry also owns the Calgary franchise of professional Roller Hockey and recently purchased the Max Bell Centre in Calgary. In addition, he has financial interests in Fox Hollow Golf Course and Golf Dome, thoroughbred race horses, and real estate. On October 23, 1991, he purchased the financially troubled Stampeders and became the first private owner of the team. His efforts to rejuvenate the Stampeders have been successful as the team has participated in two Grey Cups, winning in 1992 in Toronto 24-10 over Winnipeg. Mr. Ryckman is very active in the community and with charitable organizations in Calgary. He was the honorary chairman for the 1992 Easter Seals Calgary campaign & the "Ride for Sight" campaign in 1993. Hobbies include tennis, golf, skiing and riding his motorcycle. Larry and his wife Elaine have three chidren ranging in age from three to eight years. Larry was recently named a 1993 Vanier Award winner that honours young Canadians for their tremendous business and community achievements.

General Manager and Head Coach: Wally Buono

Born February 7, 1950 in Potenza, Italy. On March 19th, 1992, Buono was elevated to the position of General Manager and Head Coach. He became the 20th Head Coach in Stampeder history on January 4th, 1990. Prior to his appointment, was an assistant coach for 3 years (1987-1989). Wally has been involved in the CFL for the past 21 years: 10 as a player, 7 as an assistant coach and 4 as a head coach. In 1992, he guided the Stampeders to a Grey Cup championship, the club's first since 1971. Was named the CFL Coach of the Year for 1992 and 1993. Began coaching career in 1982 with the Montreal Jr. Concordes. Following year joined the Alouettes and was with the Montreal franchise as an assistant coach until 1986. Came to the Stampeders as an Assistant Coach in 1987 and was elevated to Defensive Co-ordinator in 1989. As a player, he played in Montreal from 1972 to 1981, playing outside and inside linebacker. Also participated in 152 consecutive games. Played in 5 Grey Cup games, earning rings on two occasions, in 1974 and 1977. Played college ball at Idaho State University from 1968 to 1971.

Assistant General Manager and Director of Player Personnel: Roy Shivers

Born in Las Vegas. This season will be Roy's 5th season with the Stampeders. Prior to joining the Stampeders in December of 1989, Roy spent 7 years (1983-1989) with the B.C. Lions before joining the Stampeders. In 1983 and '84 was an assistant coach in charge of running backs. In 1985 he became the Director of Player Personnel. While in B.C. the Lions competed in two Grey Cups and participated in 6 Western Finals. In 11 years of CFL involvement the team Roy played in the Western Final on 10 occasions. Handles the recruiting and signing of import talent for the Stampeders. In 1966, following a successful career at Utah State, he became a first round supplemental draft pick of the NFL St. Louis Cardinals. Played with St. Louis from 1966 to 1973. Following his playing career he spent the 1974 season as Head Coach of Merritt Junior College in Oakland, California. In 1975 became the running back coach at the University of Hawaii. In 1976 he held the same capacity for the University of Nevada at Las Vegas until 1983.

Assistant Coaches

George Cortez, Offensive Line Coach. Born February 11, 1951 in Port Arthur, Texas. Joined the Stampeders on January 12, 1992 as Offensive Line Coach. The 1994 season will be George's 17th year of coaching at the professional or college level. Spent 1990 and 1991 as the Defensive Line and Special Team coach with the Ottawa Rough Riders. Spent four seasons with the Montreal Alouettes/Concordes (1983 to 1986). Enjoyed coaching stints at Lamar University (1987 to 1989) and at Rice University from (1978 to 1982). At both US based college programs was responsible for coaching the offensive line. Began coaching career at C.E. King High School in 1973 and coached until 1978. George graduated from Texas A&M with a Bachelor of Science in Physical Education in 1973. For the next two years he pursued post graduate studies at Lamar University, the University of Houston and Sam Houston State University.

Tom Higgins, Defensive Line Coach. Born July 13, 1954 in Newark, New Jersey. This season will be Tom's 10th year as a member of the Stampeder coaching staff. Has coached linebackers, defensive line, offensive line, and special teams. This year, he will continue to instruct the defensive line and overlook special teams. Played professionally with the Stampeders in 1976 and 1977. He then headed south to play with the NFL New York Giants and also with the Buffalo Bills. Tom returned to the CFL in 1980 joining the Saskatchewan Roughriders and retired at the end of the season. In 1981 Tom coached football at Crescent Heights High School in Calgary. From 1982 to 1984, he joined the coaching staff of the University of Calgary Dinosaurs and helped the Dinos capture two conference titles and in 1983 won the Vanier Cup. At North Carolina State, Tom won the All-ACC (Atlantic Coast Conference) honour during his junior and senior years. Was voted Third Team All-American in 1975, was honoured with the Academic All-ACC that same year and then repeated the next season. Tom played in Peach Bowl games in '72 and '75, the Liberty Bowl in '73 and the Blue Bonnet Bowl in '74. He also lettered four years in wrestling, winning the 1976 ACC Heavyweight Championship along with the All-American NCAA top heavyweight honours.

John Hufnagel, Offensive Co-ordinator & Quarterbacks Coach. Born September 13, 1951 in Corapolis, Pennsylvania. This is John's fifth year as Offensive Co-ordinator in charge of Quarterbacks and the Offensive Game Plan. Began his coaching career as a player/coach for Saskatchewan in 1987. In 1988, he returned to Calgary and began working in real estate. John served as a guest coach for Saskatchewan in 1988 and 1989. During this time, he volunteered his coaching services to the University of Calgary for the two seasons. Joined the Stampeders early in 1990 and under his guidance the club has established several team records in various offensive categories. During his 12-year playing career, he spent his first four years in Calgary ('76-'79), five years in Saskatchewan ('80-'83, plus '87) and three years in Winnipeg ('84-'86). Huffer also spent 3 years with the Denver Broncos of the NFL before coming to Calgary. Was an All-American at Penn State and led them to a Cotton Bowl his Junior year and Sugar Bowl in his senior year. Also in his final year, John participated in the Hula Bowl.

Chuck McMann, Football Administrator/Receivers and Running Backs Coach. Born May 11, 1951 in Toronto, Ontario. Chuck joined the Stampeders on February 24th, 1992. Has three seasons of pro coaching experience under his belt, that in 1985, when he was a playing coach with the Montreal Alouettes, and the past two years with the Stampeders. In 1990 and 1991 was a guest coach at the Stampeder training camp. Most recently Chuck was the Defensive Coordinator at the University of Waterloo from 1988 to 1991. Played 10 years in the Canadian Football League with the Montreal Alouettes and Concordes. Chuck played in 130 career CFL games and made 80 catches for 1150 yards and 4 touchdowns as a slotback. A graduate of Wilfrid Laurier, he coached High School football in Montreal with Vanier CEGEP and Vieux Montreal.

Frank Spaziani, Defensive Secondary Coach. Born April 1, 1947 in Clark, New Jersey. In his first season with the Stampeders, he provides extensive coaching and playing experience for the secondary. He joined the Stampeders in February 1994 after spending two years coaching the defensive backs with the Winnipeg Blue Bombers. His coaching career began in 1969 where he was an assistant coach at Penn State. He was an assistant coach with Carteret High School for three years following and then took on the Head Coaching duties at Hempstead High in 1973, and at Raritan High in '74. Frank spent the next seven years at the U.S. Naval Academy coaching the offensive line for 2 years and then the defensive secondary for 5 years. The next stop in his coaching career was at the University of Virginia where he spent nine years as defensive backs coach and then the defensive coordinator before joining the Blue Bombers in 1992. He was a member of the 1967 team that tied Florida State in the Gator Bowl and defeated Kansas in the 1969 Orange Bowl. Besides playing football, he was a pitcher for the Nittany Lions baseball team for two seasons and has his Masters Degree in Education from Seton Hall University.

CALGARY STAMPEDERS
1994 CURRENT ROSTER AS OF APRIL 30, 1994
RETURNING PLAYERS

* Denotes Import

	Player	Pos.	Ht.	Wt.	Born	University/ Jr. Affiliate	Yrs. CFL	Yrs. CAL
	BIGGS, Raymond	LB	6.01	220	20 OCT 68	New Mexico State	2	2
*	BRITTON, Eddie	WR	5.09	165	01 DEC 68	Ohio Central	2	2
	COVERNTON, Bruce	T	6.05	295	12 AUG 66	Weber State	3	3
*	CRAFT, Douglass	DB	6.00	193	23 JUL 68	Southern	2	2
*	CRAWFORD, Derrick	WR	5.11	180	3 SEP 61	Memphis State	5	5
	CRYSDALE, Jamie	C	6.04	280	14 DEC 68	Cincinnati	2	2
	DAVIES, Doug	C	6.04	270	22 DEC 64	Simon Fraser	7	6
	DMYTRYSHYN, Duane	SB	6.01	215	11 JUN 71	Saskatchewan	2	2
	DUBE, Marc	LB	6.02	230	23 FEB 68	Maine	3	3
*	EAGLIN, Greg	DB	6.02	200	14 NOV 67	Ark. Pine Buff	2	2
	FINLAY, Matt	LB	6.02	225	28 SEP 62	Eastern Michigan	9	8
*	FLUTIE, Doug	QB	5.10	175	23 OCT 62	Boston College	5	3
	FRERS, Greg	DB	5.11	188	04 AUG 71	Simon Fraser	2	2
*	JOHNSON, Alondra	LB	5.11	225	22 JUL 65	West Texas State	6	4
*	JOHNSON, Eric	DE	6.03	245	11 MAR 70	Stephen F. Austin	2	2
*	JOHNSON, Will	DE	6.05	245	4 DEC 64	NE Louisiana	6	6
	KNOX, Greg	DB	6.00	180	6 DEC 69	Wilfrid Laurier	3	3
	LAIRD, Stuart	DT	6.02	255	8 JUL 60	Calgary	10	10
*	LEONARD, Kenton	CB	5.09	170	2 MAY 68	Nicholls State	4	4
	MAHON, Patrick	C	6.03	250	24 AUG 68	Western Ontario	2	2
	MAROF, Frank	SB	6.00	190	30 SEP 68	Guelph	3	3
	MARTINO, Tony	K	6.00	190	9 JUN 66	Kent State	6	3
	MCLOUGHLIN, Mark	K	6.01	193	26 OCT 65	South Dakota	7	7
	MCVEY, Andy	FB	6.01	215	6 JUN 63	Toronto	8	8
	MOORE, Ken	T	6.05	250	27 JAN 61	Hawaii	12	6
*	MOORE, Will	WR	6.02	180	21 FEB 70	Texas Southern	3	3
*	PITTS, Allen	SB	6.04	200	28 JUN 63	Fullerton State	5	5
*	POPE, Marvin	LB	6.01	240	18 JAN 69	Ohio Central	3	3
	ROMANO, Rocco	G	6.04	270	23 JAN 63	Concordia	8	4
	SAPUNJIS, David	SB	6.01	185	7 SEP 67	Western Ontario	5	5
*	SMITH, Peewee	WR	6.01	180	3 JAN 68	Miami	5	5
*	STEWART, Tony	RB	6.01	206	30 JAN 68	Iowa	2	2
	STORME, Todd	T	6.05	275	16 OCT 64	Utah State	5	3
*	TAYLOR, Steve	QB	6.00	205	7 JAN 67	Nebraska	6	4
*	THURMAN, Junior	CB	6.00	185	8 SEP 64	Southern California	6	6
*	VAUGHN, Gerald	DB	6.03	195	08 APR 70	Mississippi	2	2
*	WIGGINS, Brian	WR	5.11	182	14 JUN 68	Texas Southern	2	2
	ZERR, Blair	RB	6.00	200	22 NOV 65	San Jose State	3	3
	ZIZAKOVIC, Srecko	DT	6.05	260	13 AUG 66	Ohio State	5	5

NEW PLAYERS

* Denotes Import

	Player	Pos.	Ht.	Wt.	Born	University/ Jr. Affiliate	Yrs. CFL
*	BLOUNT, Eric	LB	6.00	240	20 APR 70	Houston	1
*	BRINKLEY, Lester	DE	6.06	255	13 MAY 65	Mississippi	2
*	GREEN, Michael	WR	6.00	185	11 OCT 71	Southern	1
*	HARRIS, Darrin	RB	5.11	205	16 MAY 69	Morehead State	1
*	HOOKS, Greg	WR	6.02	200	06 SEP 72	Utah	1
	KALIN, John	DB	6.00	190	18 JUL 70	Calgary	1
	McNEIL, Jay	G	6.04	285	20 AUG 70	Kent State	1
	MEYER, Tohn	OL	6.03	265	17 JAN 72	Calgary	1
	PANDELIDIS, Bobby	G	6.02	290	04 MAY 68	Eastern Michigan	1
*	RAGIN, Harold	DB	6.02	190	14 JAN 71	Utah	1
	REID, Bruce	FB	5.10	220	05 JUL 71	Simon Fraser	1
	REINSON, Roger	LB	6.00	215	19 APR 68	Calgary	1
*	SCOTT, Lindsey	RB	5.09	190	19 MAR 71	Southern	1
*	SMITH, Michael	WR	5.09	160	21 NOV 70	Kansas State	1
	VENIERIS, William	C	6.01	260	06 JUN 68	Concordia	1
*	WIGGINS, Shawn	WR	5.11	165	08 AUG 68	Wyoming	1
	ZIZAKOVIC, Lubo	DT	6.08	270	28 FEB 68	Maryland	3

#25 SB David Sapunjis

EDMONTON ESKIMO FOOTBALL CLUB

9023 - 111 Avenue
Edmonton, Alberta
T5B 0C3
Administration Office (403) 448-1525, Fax (403) 429-3452
Ticket Office (403) 448-ESKS Fax (403) 448-2531

EXECUTIVE

Owner: Community Owned
Board of Directors:
President - John C. Ramsey
Directors - K.F. Bailey, D.M. Erker, G.C. Gent, S.E. LeLacheur, D.H. Sprague, E.F. Stevens, R.J. Turner Q.C., R.B. Young
Governor: John C. Ramsey **Alternate:** Hugh Campbell
General Manager: Hugh Campbell

FOOTBALL OPERATIONS

Head Coach: Ron Lancaster
Assistant Coaches:
Bill MacDermott, Offensive Line Coach
Mark Nelson, Special Teams/Running Back Coach
Greg Newhouse, Defensive Line
Joe Paopao, Offensive Coordinator
Rich Stubler, Defensive Coordinator
Trainer/Therapist: Ian Hallworth
Equipment Manager: Dwayne Mandrusiak
Doctors:
Dr. Peter Boucher
Dr. Boris Boyko
Dr. Dick Cherry
Dr. Rob Ross
Dr. David Reid
Physical Therapist Consultant: Dr. David Magee
Dentist: Dr. Terry Horne
Director of Operations: TBA

BUSINESS OPERATIONS

Marketing and Communications: Allan Watt
Accountant: Cathy Presniak
Administrative Assistant: Pam Monastyrskyj
Ticket Office Supervisor: Shona Wards
Coaches' Secretary: Karen Livingstone
Merchandise Manager: Jason Hatch

FAST FACTS

Home Stadium: Commonwealth Stadium
Stadium Address: 11000 Stadium Road, Edmonton, Alberta T5J 2R7
Club Colours: Green & Gold
Club Name: Edmonton Eskimos
Training Camp Site: Concordia College, Edmonton
Press Box Location: West Side, Concourse Level, Commonwealth Stadium; Access through Gate 2, South-West side of Stadium
Dressing Room Locations: Lower Level, Recreation Centre; Access down Marathon Ramp off Stadium Road
Radio Broadcasters: 630 CHED - Play-by-Play, Bryan Hall
Statistician/Typist: Lorne Lindenberg/Gerry Hunt/Greg Robinson
Permanent Crew: Herb McLachlin, Albert Munro, Dave Holmberg, Dale Cocks
Timekeeper: Ernie Wynychuk
Scorekeeper: Lee Fairbanks

Club History: 1891 first Calgary and Edmonton home and home series . . . 1895 Edmonton plays first series of organized games with the formation of the Alberta Rugby Football Union . . . 1907 the name Eskimaux coined . . . 1910 club officially named the Edmonton Eskimos

ELEVEN GREY CUP VICTORIES FOR EDMONTON-BASED TEAMS

Eskimos (11) - 1954, 1955, 1956, 1975, 1978, 1979, 1980, 1981, 1982, 1987, 1993

Commonwealth Stadium Facts 'n Figures

Capacity: 60,081
Largest Regular Season One Game Attendance: 59,921
Edmonton 30, B.C. 1 (October 10, 1982 when Stadium capacity was 59,921)
Largest Playoff One Game Attendance: 52,709
Edmonton 22, B.C. 16 (November 15, 1981 when Stadium capacity was 52,709)
Largest Grey Cup Attendance: 60,081
Winnipeg 47, Hamilton 17 (November 18, 1984)

EDMONTON CLUB RECORDS SINCE 1949
Regular Season

- CFL Record
- Ties CFL Record
( ) - Figures in Brackets represent Year(s) Club mark set

Most Points Scored One Season (minimum 14 games) - 671 ('91)
Most Points Scored Against One Season (minimum 14 games) - 569 ('91)
Fewest Points Against One Season (minimum 14 games) - 117 ('55)
Most Points Scored One Game - 62 - Montreal at Edmonton 26/09/80
Most Points Scored Against One Game - 56 - at Saskatchewan 28/08/64
Most Wins One Season (minimum 14 games) -#16 ('89)
Most Losses One Season (minimum 14 games) - 14 ('63)
Highest Shutout -55-0 - Saskatchewan at Edmonton 24/08/59
Highest Shutout Against - 40-0 - at Saskatchewan 15/08/76
Most Touchdowns One Season (minimum 14 games) -77 ('91)
Most Touchdowns One Game - 8 -
- B.C. at Edmonton 22/10/56
- Saskatchewan at Edmonton 24/08/59
- Montreal at Edmonton 26/09/81
- Toronto at Edmonton 24/10/81
Most Converts One Season (minimum 14 games) - 75 ('91)
Most Converts One Game - 8 -
- Montreal at Edmonton 26/09/81
- Toronto at Edmonton 24/10/81
Most Field Goals One Season (minimum 14 games) - 50 ('77)
Most Field Goals One Game - 6 - Saskatchewan at Edmonton 22/10/72
- B.C. at Edmonton 13/07/89
Most First Downs One Game -#44 - Hamilton at Edmonton 11/09/83
Most Yards Total Offence One Game - 698 -
- Hamilton at Edmonton 11/09/83
Most Yards Rushing One Game - 441 - at Calgary 15/09/51
Most Times Carried One Game -#67 - at Winnipeg 25/08/51

Most Touchdowns Rushing One Game - 6 - B.C. at Edmonton 22/10/56
Most Yards Passing One Game - 555 - Montreal at Edmonton 15/10/83
Most Passes Thrown One Game - 52 - Montreal at Edmonton 15/10/83
Most Completions One Game - 37 - Hamilton at Edmonton 11/09/83
Most Touchdown Passes One Game - 6 -
- Saskatchewan at Edmonton 05/11/89
Most Quarterback Sacks One Game - #13 -
- Toronto at Edmonton 18/08/93

EDMONTON INDIVIDUAL RECORDS SINCE 1949
Regular Season

Points (Career) - 2,237 - Dave Cutler
Points (Season) - 224 - Jerry Kauric ('89)
Points (Game) - 24 -
- Jim Germany - Hamilton at Edmonton 01/08/81
- Brian Kelly - Ottawa at Edmonton 30/06/84
Touchdowns (Career) - 97 - Brian Kelly
Touchdowns (Season) - 20 - Blake Marshall ('91)
Touchdowns (Game) - 4 -
- Jim Germany - Hamilton at Edmonton 01/08/81
- Brian Kelly - Ottawa at Edmonton 30/06/84
Field Goals (Career) -#464 - Dave Cutler
Field Goals (Season) - 50 - Dave Cutler ('77)
Field Goals (Game) - 6 - Dave Cutler
- Saskatchewan at Edmonton 22/10/72
- Saskatchewan at Edmonton 18/11/73
Longest Field Goal - 59 - Dave Cutler - at Saskatchewan 28/10/70
Passes Thrown (Career) - 2,433 - Tracy Ham
Passes Thrown (Season) -#664 - Warren Moon ('83)
Passes Thrown (Game) - 51 -
- Tom Wilkinson - Winnipeg at Edmonton 18/07/77
- Warren Moon - Montreal at Edmonton 15/10/83
Passes Completed (Career) - 1,613 - Tom Wilkinson
Passes Completed (Season) -#380 - Warren Moon ('83)
Passes Completed (Game) - 36 - Warren Moon
- Hamilton at Edmonton 11/09/83
Longest Pass Completion - 102 - Henry Williams
- Ottawa at Edmonton 16/10/93
Passing Yards (Career) - 21,228 - Warren Moon
Passing Yards (Season) -#5,648 - Warren Moon ('83)
Passing Yards (Game) - 555 - Warren Moon
- Montreal at Edmonton 15/10/83
Touchdown Passes Thrown (Career) - 144 - Warren Moon
Touchdown Passes Thrown (Season) - 36 - Warren Moon ('82)
- Tracy Ham ('90)
Touchdown Passes Thrown (Game) - 5 -
- Warren Moon - Montreal at Edmonton 15/10/83
- Tracy Ham - Toronto at Edmonton 21/08/91
No. of Carries (Career) - 1,770 - Johnny Bright
No. of Carries (Season) - 296 - Johnny Bright ('58)
No. of Carries (Game) - 30 -
- Normie Kwong - Calgary at Edmonton 29/10/55
Yards Rushing (Career) - 9,966 - Johnny Bright
Yards Rushing (Season) - 1,722 - Johnny Bright ('58)
Yards Rushing (Season) by a Quarterback - #1,096 - Tracy Ham ('90)
Yards Rushing (Game) - 192 -
- Normie Kwong - Calgary at Edmonton 29/10/55
Touchdowns by Rushing (Career) - 73 - Normie Kwong
Touchdowns by Rushing (Season) -##18 - Jim Germany ('81)
Touchdowns by Rushing (Game) - 4 -
- Jim Germany - Hamilton at Edmonton 01/08/81
Passes Caught (Career) - 575 - Brian Kelly
Passes Caught (Season) - 106 - Craig Ellis ('90)
Passes Caught (Game) - 15 -
- George McGowan - at Saskatchewan 03/09/73
Pass Reception Yards (Career) -#11,169 - Brian Kelly
Pass Reception Yards (Season) - 1,812 - Brian Kelly ('83)
Pass Reception Yards (Game) - 266 -
- Brian Kelly - Montreal at Edmonton 15/10/83
Touchdown Passes Caught (Career) -#97 - Brian Kelly
Touchdown Passes Caught (Season) - 18 -Brian Kelly ('84)
Touchdown Passes Caught (Game) - 4 -
- Brian Kelly - Ottawa at Edmonton 30/06/84

EDMONTON'S RECORD AGAINST OTHER CLUBS (REGULAR SEASON)

		GP	W	L	T	F	A	PTS
Versus Ottawa	(Since 1961)	47	26	19	2	1361	1150	54
Versus Toronto	(Since 1961)	46	25	20	1	1217	1037	51
Versus Hamilton	(Since 1961)	46	31	14	1	1190	914	63
Versus Winnipeg	(Since 1949)	137	73	62	2	2845	2714	148
Versus Saskatchewan	(Since 1949)	143	80	61	2	3340	2763	162
Versus Calgary	(Since 1949)	153	95	54	4	3470	2853	194
Versus B.C.	(Since 1954)	123	75	44	4	2700	2240	154
Versus Sacramento	(Since 1993)	3	3	0	0	90	36	6
EDMONTON VS OPPOSITION		698	408	274	16	16213	13707	832

President: John C. Ramsey

Named President of the Edmonton Eskimo Board of Directors on February 17, 1993. Mr. Ramsey was born in Edmonton and received a degree in Engineering from the University of Alberta, followed by an MBA from McMaster University. He worked in the engineering field in Eastern Canada and in the United States until 1972 when he became President, Chairman and C.E.O. of Ramsey Brokerage Co. Ltd. He is also a partner in two auto dealer groups in the Edmonton area. John has served as president of the Alberta Food Brokers Association, Chairman of the Grant MacEwan Community College, on the Board of Directors of Edmonton Northlands, as Board Chairman of Economic Development Edmonton, and President of the Kinsmen Club of Edmonton. John was also a member of the 1984 Edmonton Grey Cup Committee and the 1978 Commonwealth Games Committee. John is married with three daughters.

General Manager: Hugh Campbell

Born May 21, 1941 in San Jose, California, Hugh played his collegiate football at Washington State University from 1959-1962. He was an outstanding wide receiver at Washington State and following his senior year he played in the East-West Shrine game, Hula Bowl, College All-Star game and Coaches All America game. He was named Most Valuable Player in both the Coaches All America and East-West Shrine games. Hugh holds a Bachelor of Science Degree in Education and Physical Education (1963) and a Masters Degree (1966), both from Washington State. Drafted by the San Francisco 49ers in 1963 in the 4th round, he began his pro career with the Saskatchewan Roughriders and became a brilliant receiver in the CFL. During his 6 years as a Roughrider (1963-67, 1969), he established Roughrider records for Most Career Touchdown Receptions (60), Most Touchdowns in the Season (17) and Most Yards Receiving in a career, 5,425. Hugh played in the 1966, '67 and '69 Grey Cup Games and was All-Western All-Star in 1964 and 1969 and All-Canadian in 1965 and 1966. Three seasons, (1964, 1965 and 1966) he was over 1,000 yards in receiving. Interrupted his playing career in 1968 to become an assistant coach at Washington State. His first head coaching job was at Whitworth College in Spokane, Washington in 1970. Became the Head Coach of the Los Angeles Express of the United States Football League in 1983 and after 1 season in Los Angeles, he was named Head Coach of the NFL Houston Oilers and spent '84 and '85 as head coach in Houston. Hugh was named General Manager of the Eskimos on March 18, 1986. He returned to the Eskimo organization after a three-year absence. From 1977 to 1982 he was Head Coach of the Eskimo Football Club and that 6-year period was the most successful any coach has enjoyed in CFL history. The Eskimos went to the Grey Cup all 6 seasons and won the championship 5 consecutive years (1978-1982).

Head Coach: Ron Lancaster

Born October 14, 1938 in Fairchance, Pennsylvania. Was named head coach of the Eskimos on Monday, February 4, 1991, and that season guided the Eskimos to a 12-6 record and first place in the West. Ron's second year, the Eskimos finished 10-8, second in the West. 1993 proved to be a winner with the Eskimos finishing the season second in their division with a 12-6 record, capturing the championship title for the 11th time in club history. Ron's overall Eskimo record is now 34-20. He became the 12th head coach in Eskimo history (1948). This is Ron's 2nd position as head coach, having guided the Saskatchewan Roughriders from October of 1976 to the end of the 1980 season. Ron maintained a complete knowledge of the CFL for the next ten years as a football colour commentator on CBC Television's CFL coverage. In fact, he not only excelled as a football broadcaster, but travelled to the 1988 Olympic Games in Seoul, Korea as the CBC's basketball play-by-play broadcaster at the Olympic games. Became a head coach the day he retired as a player after 16 glorious years with the Saskatchewan Roughriders, for a total of 19 seasons as a CFL quarterback. He began his career in 1960 with the Ottawa Rough Riders and they won the Grey Cup that year. Following 2 more seasons in Ottawa, sharing the quarterback duties with Russ Jackson, he was traded to Saskatchewan and guided the Roughriders to the playoffs 14 of the next 16 years. The Riders won 170 games in that span, an average of 10 a season. He was the All-Canadian quarterback in 1970, '73, '75 and '76 and was named a Western All-Star seven times. Ron was selected winner of the Schenley Award as Most Outstanding Player in 1970 and 1976. The final award came in May of 1982, when he was named to the Canadian Football Hall of Fame. In 1985 Ron was also named to Canada's Sports Hall of Fame. Taught high school in Regina for 7-1/2 years while playing for the Riders, then became a player-coach from 1972 through 1978. For the '77 and '78 seasons, he was offensive coordinator, in addition to his duties as starting Saskatchewan quarterback. Played his college football at Wittenberg University in Springfield, Ohio and established school passing records and total offense marks over three and one-half years.

Assistant Coaches

Bill MacDermott, Offensive Line Coach. Born May 14, 1936 in Providence, Rhode Island. Bill joined the Eskimos directly from Montreal where he had been coaching in the World League Championship game with the Orlando Thunder. Bill had been in Orlando for the previous two seasons ('91 and '92) as offensive line coach. He went to the World League from Toronto in the spring of 1991 when Don Matthews left the Argos to become head coach in Orlando. Bill had been on the Argo Staff for the 1990 season. He was a guest coach in Edmonton in 1989 and the Montreal Alouette training camp in 1987. He was the assistant head coach and offensive line coach at California Poly State University at San Luis Obispo for the 1987, '88 and '89 seasons and was formerly the head coach at Wesleyan University in Middletown University in Middletown, Connecticut for 16 years.

Mark Nelson, Special Teams/Running Back Coach. Born July 25, 1957 in Edmonton, Alberta. Mark played with the Calgary Stampeders from 1980 to 1986 as a linebacker and fullback, then finished his playing career with one year (1986) in Saskatchewan. He then began a coaching career in the high school system in Choctaw, Oklahoma. He moved to Independence Community College in 1987 as the defensive line coach and became the defensive coordinator in 1988 and the head coach in 1990. Along the way he stayed in touch with the CFL by attending the 1989 Rough Rider camp as a guest coach and the 1990 and '91 Stampeder training camps. Mark is the son of Roger Nelson who enjoyed a brilliant 13 year career with the Eskimos and was inducted in the Canadian Football Hall of Fame in 1986.

Greg Newhouse, Defensive Line Coach. Born February 9, 1952 in Long Beach, California. The World League was home to Greg for the 1991 and '92 seasons where he was the defensive coordinator of the San Antonio Riders. He spent 1991 in Vancouver with the Lions as a defensive assistant and was also in B.C. from 1984 through 1987 as defensive coordinator, and 1983 as an assistant. During that period, the Lions finished first three times and won the 1985 Grey Cup. He left the Lions in 1988 and joined the staff at the University of Hawaii for two seasons then to the University of New Mexico for 1990. He began his coaching career at the University of Nevada-Reno in 1975 as a graduate assistant, then moved to Chaffey (California) Junior College for 1976. In '77 he returned to Nevada-Reno then to UNLV for two years, and to Cal State Fullerton for 1980-82. Greg has a Bachelor's degree in education from the University of Nevada-Reno.

Joe Paopao, Offensive Coordinator. Born June 6, 1955 in Honolulu, Hawaii. Joe began his football career at Long Beach State in California as a quarterback. He joined the B.C. Lions in 1978 and played for six years in Vancouver before signing in Saskatchewan as a free agent in 1983, and on to the Ottawa Rough Riders in 1987. He retired as a player and joined the Lions' coaching staff as offensive backfield coach in 1989. In 1990, he returned to quarterback the Lions and completed the '90 season as their starting quarterback. For the past two seasons, Joe has been the offensive coordinator with B.C.

Rich Stubler, Defensive Coordinator. Born August 4, 1949. Spent seven years in Hamilton as a defensive coordinator, from 1983 to 1989. He moved to Toronto for the 1990 season with the Argos. Prior to joining the CFL, Stubler was at the University of Colorado, where his college coaching career originally began in 1974. Rich began coaching at the high school level at Roaring Fork High School in Carbondale, Colorado from 1971 through 1973. In 1975, he moved to New Mexico State University and spent three years there. In 1978, he joined the Southern Methodist University Mustangs as a defensive backfield coach and spent one season there before moving to Colorado State for three seasons.

EDMONTON ESKIMOS
1994 CURRENT ROSTER AS OF APRIL 30, 1994
RETURNING PLAYERS

* Denotes Import

	Player	Pos.	Ht.	Wt.	Born	University/ Jr. Affiliate	Yrs. CFL	Yrs. EDM
*	ALLEN, Damon	QB	6.01	170	29 JUL 63	Fullerton State	10	5
	AMBROSIE, Randy	G	6.04	260	16 MAR 63	Manitoba	10	6
*	BERRY, Ed	CB	5.10	185	28 SEP 63	Utah State	7	2
	BLUGH, Leroy	LB	6.02	230	14 MAY 66	Bishop's	6	6
	BOURGEAU, Michel	DT	6.05	275	28 JUN 61	Boise State	11	6
*	BROWN, Eddie	WR	5.11	175	8 MAY 66	Iowa State	5	2
	BROWN, Trent	DB	5.11	190	7 OCT 66	Alberta	4	4
	CHORNEY, Terris	OL	6.01	240	11 NOV 69	Nebraska	2	2
	CHRISTENSEN, Jay	SB	6.04	205	19 NOV 63	Okanagan Juniors	9	3
	CONNOP, Rod	C	6.06	265	4 JUN 59	Wilfrid Laurier	13	13
	CROONEN, Jeff	G	6.03	240	02 SEP 66	Western Ontario	6	1
	DERMOTT, Blake	T	6.03	270	10 SEP 61	Alberta	12	12
	DICKSON, Bruce	LB	6.02	225	11 OCT 67	Simon Fraser	4	2
	DUMARESQ, Mike	G	6.05	265	4 SEP 65	Western Ontario	5	5
	FLEMING, Sean	K	6.03	190	19 MAR 70	Wyoming	3	3
*	FLOYD, Lucius	RB	6.00	195	07 APR 66	Nevada	5	2
*	FOGGIE, Rickey	QB	6.02	190	15 JUL 66	Minnesota	7	2
*	GOODS, Bennie	DT	6.03	255	20 FEB 68	Alcorn State	5	5
	HARPER, Glenn	K	6.00	175	12 SEP 62	Washington State	9	4
*	HOLLAND, John	CB	5.10	185	18 JUL 65	Sacramento State	3	2
*	HUNTER, Malvin	LB	6.03	230	20 NOV 69	Wisconsin	2	2
	IZQUIERDO, J.P.	RB	5.11	195	12 MAR 69	Calgary	4	2
*	JOHNSON, Leonard	DT	6.06	255	17 MAY 63	Georgia Military	4	2
*	JONES, Ricky	QB	6.00	185	12 FEB 70	Alabama State	2	2
	KRUPEY, Steve	G	6.03	265	16 MAR 65	Western Ontario	4	4
*	LOLAR, Morris	DB	5.11	185	18 DEC 70	Friends College	2	2
	MARTIN, Errol	LB	6.02	210	25 MAR 68	Utah	2	2
	MORRIS, Chris	T	6.05	285	13 SEP 68	Toronto	3	3
	MORRIS, Gary	WR	6.02	185	26 JUN 68	Norfolk State	2	2
*	MUECKE, Tom	QB	6.01	205	20 AUG 63	Baylor	7	4
	MURPHY, Dan	DB	6.03	205	28 AUG 68	Acadia	4	4
*	PLESS, Willie	LB	5.11	210	21 FEB 64	Kansas	9	4
	ROBERTS, Jed	DE	6.02	230	10 NOV 67	Northern Colorado	5	5
*	ROGERS, Glenn	CB	6.00	180	08 JUN 69	Memphis State	2	2
*	SANDUSKY, Jim	WR	5.09	180	9 SEP 61	San Diego State	9	5
	SOLES, Michael	FB	6.01	215	8 NOV 66	McGill	6	6
	THOMAS, Jeff	OT	6.08	305	31 JAN 66	Cal Poly Pomona	2	2
	WALLING, Brian	FB	5.08	185	16 SEP 63	Acadia	8	6
*	WILLIAMS, Henry	WR	5.06	185	31 MAY 62	East Carolina	8	8
*	WILSON, Don	DB	6.02	195	28 JUL 61	North Carolina St.	8	5
*	WOODS, Clinton	DT	6.04	275	19 MAR 66	Oklahoma	2	2
	WRUCK, Larry	LB	6.00	220	29 OCT 62	Saskatoon Juniors	10	10

NEW PLAYERS

* Denotes Import

	Player	Pos.	Ht.	Wt.	Born	University/ Jr. Affiliate	Yrs. CFL
	BAILEY, Walter	DB	5.11	195	16 MAR 70	Washington	1
	BENOIT, Jeff	RB	5.10	205	10 DEC 70	Mansfield	1
	CARLSON, Chad	WR	6.00	185	14 AUG 71	Lewis & Clark	1
*	CRAYTON, Estrus	RB	6.02	195	09 SEP 71	Southern California	1
*	DAVIS, Charles J.	WR	6.00	185	04 SEP 69	Washington State	1
	DAY, Stephen	DB	6.01	195	26 DEC 70	Alberta	1
	FRIDD, Darryl	OL	6.04	270	26 MAY 71	Alberta	1
*	NAPOSKI, Eric	LB	6.02	250	20 DEC 66	Connecticut	1
*	SAMUELS, Robert	DB	6.01	190	03 JAN 70	Penn State	2
*	SEUMALO, Joe	DE	6.04	250	23 AUG 66	Hawaii	2
	TOBERT, Marc	WR	5.11	190	08 MAR 71	Alberta	1
*	VARGAS, Chris	QB	5.11	170	29 JAN 71	Nevada	1
	WESSELING, Rob	T	6.03	290	21 JAN 71	Guelph	1
	WIENS, Raymond	C	6.03	285	07 JUL 68	Saskatchewan	2
	ZACHARIAS, Brad	RB	5.09	205	24 DEC 70	Acadia	1

#24 DB Dan Murphy

BRITISH COLUMBIA LIONS FOOTBALL TEAM

10605 135th St.
Surrey, B.C. V3T 4C8
Telephone: (604) 583-7747
Fax: (604) 583-7882
Ticket Office: (604) 589-7627

EXECUTIVE

Owner: Bill Comrie
President: Peter Classon
General Manager: Eric Tillman

FOOTBALL OPERATIONS

Head Coach: Dave Ritchie
Director of Player Personnel: Bill Quinter
Assistant Coaches:
John Payne, Offensive Coordinator
Jody Allen, Receivers
Gary Hoffman, Offensive Line
Gene Gaines, Defensive Secondary
Dave Easley, Linebackers
Michael Gray, Defensive Line
Head Trainer: Bill Reichelt
Equipment Manager: Creighton O'Malley
Assistant Equipment Manager: Ken "Kato" Kasuya
Doctors: Dr. Ken Appleby (Chief Medical Officer), Dr. B. McCormack, Dr. Graham Pate, Dr. Bill Ragen, Dr. Phil Lee, Dr. Nis Schmidt, Dr. John Wilson, Dr. Orville Wright
Director of Media/Public Relations: Roger Kelly
Executive Assistant: Lillian Hum
Football Administrative Assistant: Louise Anderson

BUSINESS OPERATIONS

Director of Business Operations: Gord Robertson
Director of Marketing: George Chayka
Director of Ticket Sales: Duncan Caulfield
Director of Advertising/Promotions: Marianne O'Reilly
Director of Finance: Julia Gowe

FAST FACTS

Home Stadium: B.C. Place Stadium
Stadium Address: 777 Pacific Blvd. S., Vancouver, B.C. V6B 2Y9
Club Colours: Burnt Orange, Black & Silver
Club Name: B.C. Lions
Training Facility: 10605 - 135th Street
Surrey, B.C. V3T 4C8
Telephone Number: (604) 583-7747
Fax Number: (604) 583-7882
Training Camp Site: Kamloops, B.C.
Press Box Location: Level 3 Concourse on the North Side of B.C. Place Stadium; Enter via Media Entrance only, located at Ground level (level 1) at the North-West corner of the Stadium off Pacific Blvd. North.
Dressing Room Location: Home Team - Level 1 (Field Level) at the West End of the Stadium on the North side of tunnel.
Visiting Team - Level 1 (Field Level) at the West End of the Stadium on the South side of tunnel.
P.A. Announcer: TBA
Radio Broadcasts: CKNW - J. Paul McConnell, Play-by-Play
Tom Larscheid, Neil Macrae, Lee Powell, Ron Barnett
Statistician: Joe Frizzell
Spotters: Denis DeBray, Leagh Farrell, Mario Voci, Irving Buckwold
Typist: Don Weimer
Timekeeper: Bill Reid
Scorekeeper: Jack Cuthbert

Club History: 1941 the Vancouver Grizzlies play a single season in the Western Interprovincial Football Union . . . 1952 application made to the WIFU for a football team in Vancouver . . . 1953 first annual meeting of the B.C. Lions . . . 1954 B.C. Lions play their first game.

B.C. Place Facts 'n Figures

Capacity: 59,478 (Regular Season - 40,800)
Largest Regular Season One Game Attendance: 59,478
B.C. 10, Winnipeg 31 (October 11, 1985)
Largest Playoff One Game Attendance: 59,478
Winnipeg 22, B.C. 42 (November 17, 1985)
Largest Grey Cup Attendance: 59,621
Hamilton 39, Edmonton 15 (November 30, 1986)

TWO GREY CUP VICTORIES FOR VANCOUVER-BASED TEAMS

B .C. Lions (2) - 1964, 1985

B.C. LIONS CLUB RECORDS SINCE 1954
Regular Season

\# - CFL Record
\## - Ties CFL Record
( ) - Figures in Brackets represent Year(s) Club mark set

Most Points Scored One Season (minimum 14 games) - 661 ('91)
Most Points Scored Against One Season (minimum 14 games) - 667 ('92)
Fewest Points Against One Season (minimum 14 games) - 168 ('64)
Most Points Scored One Game - 55 - vs. Toronto 12/08/93
Most Points Scored Against One Game - 68 - at Toronto 01/09/90
Most Wins One Season (minimum 14 games) - 13 ('85)
Most Losses One Season (minimum 14 games) - 15 ('54, '92)
Highest Shutout - 38-0 - Saskatchewan at B.C. 29/10/60
Highest Shutout Against - 42-0 - at Calgary 18/08/58
Most Touchdowns One Season (minimum 14 games) - 74 ('91)
Most Touchdowns One Game - 7 - at Edmonton 29/09/62
- at Edmonton 19/09/64
- vs. Edmonton 29/10/88
Most Converts One Season (minimum 14 games) - 67 ('91)
Most Converts One Game - 7 - at Edmonton 19/09/64
- vs. Edmonton 29/10/88
Most Field Goals One Season (minimum 14 games) - 52 ('87)
Most Field Goals One Game - 7 - Toronto at B.C. 06/09/85
Most First Downs One Game - 32 - at Ottawa 28/08/90
Most First Downs One Season - #508 ('91)
Most Yards Total Offence One Season - #9117 ('91)
Most Yards Total Offence One Game - 620 - vs Toronto 12/08/93
Most Yards Rushing One Game - 377 - at Calgary 22/08/60
Most Times Carried One Game - 52 - at Edmonton 17/08/59

Most Touchdowns Rushing One Game - 4 -
- Saskatchewan at B.C. 16/08/58
- at Calgary 22/08/60 at Calgary 31/07/81
Most Yards Passing One Season - #6714 ('91)
Most Kickoff Returns One Season - #126 ('91)
Most Yards Passing One Game - #601 - vs Toronto 12/08/93
Most Passes Thrown One Game - 59 - at Ottawa 28/08/90
Most Passes Completed One Season - #470 ('91)
Most Completions One Game - 37 - at Saskatchewan 21/08/91
Most Touchdown Passes One Game - 6 - at Edmonton 29/09/62

B.C. INDIVIDUAL RECORDS SINCE 1954
Regular Season

Points (Career) - #2,829 - Lui Passaglia
Points (Season) - 214 - Lui Passaglia ('87)
Points (Game) - 25 - Willie Fleming - Saskatchewan at B.C. 29/10/60
Touchdowns (Career) - 86 - Willie Fleming
Touchdowns (Season) - ##20 - Jon Volpe ('91)
Touchdowns (Game) - 4 -
- Willie Fleming - Saskatchewan at B.C. 29/10/60
- Larry Key - at Calgary 31/07/81
- Mervyn Fernandez - Edmonton at B.C. 06/07/84
- Mervyn Fernandez - at Ottawa 13/10/84
- Mervyn Fernandez - Calgary at B.C. 17/08/85
- David Williams - Edmonton at B.C. 29/10/88
Touchdowns First Year Player - #20 - Jon Volpe ('91)
Converts (Career) - #744 - Lui Passaglia
Consecutive Converts - #436 - Lui Passaglia
Field Goals (Career) - #609 - Lui Passaglia
Field Goals (Season) - 52 - Lui Passaglia ('87)
Field Goals (Game) - 7 - Lui Passaglia - Toronto at B.C. 06/09/85
Longest Field Goal - 54 - Lui Passaglia
- Saskatchewan at B.C. 08/07/80
- at Saskatchewan 05/08/84
Singles (Career) - #252 - Lui Passaglia
Times Punted (Career) - #2,301 - Lui Passaglia
Yards Punted (Career) - #99,329 - Lui Passaglia
Passes Thrown (Career) - 2,898 - Roy Dewalt
Passes Thrown (Season) - #730 - Doug Flutie ('91)
Passes Thrown (Game) - 56 - Tony Kimbrough - vs. Hamilton 08/06/92
Passes Completed (Career) - 1,705 - Roy Dewalt
Passes Completed (Season) - #466 - Doug Flutie ('91)
Passes Completed (Game) - 37 - Doug Flutie - at Saskatchewan 21/08/91
Passing Yards (Career) - 26,718 - Roy Dewalt
Passing Yards (Season) - #6,619 - Doug Flutie ('91)
Passing Yards (Game) - #601 - Danny Barrett - vs. B.C. 12/08/93
Touchdown Passes Thrown (Career) - 129 - Roy Dewalt
Touchdown Passes Thrown (Season) - 38 - Doug Flutie ('91)
Touchdown Passes Thrown (Game) - 6 -
- Joe Kapp - at Edmonton 29/09/62
No. of Carries (Career) - 1,151 - Jim Evenson
No. of Carries (Season) - 260 - Jim Evenson ('71)
No. of Carries (Game) - 32 - Jim Evenson - Winnipeg at B.C. 19/10/68
Yards Rushing (Career) - 6,125 - Willie Fleming
Yards Rushing (Season) - 1,395 - Jon Volpe ('91)
Yards Rushing (Game) - 206 - Keyvan Jenkins - at Toronto 01/08/85
Touchdowns by Rushing (Career) - 47 - Larry Key
Touchdowns by Rushing (Season) - 17 - Larry Key ('81)
Touchdowns by Rushing (Game) - 4 - Larry Key - at Calgary 31/07/81
Passes Caught (Career) - 552 - Jim Young
Passes Caught (Season) - 104 - Ray Alexander ('91)
Passes Caught (Game) - 14 - Eric Streater - vs. Hamilton 06/10/89
Passes Caught First Year Player - #79 - Matt Clark ('91)
Pass Reception Yards (Career) - 9,248 - Jim Young
Pass Reception Yards (Season) - 1,727 - Mervyn Fernandez ('85)
Pass Reception Yards (Game) - 270 - Tyron Gray - at Edmonton 12/09/81
Pass Reception Yards First Year Player - #1,530 - Matt Clark ('91)
Touchdown Passes Caught (Career) - 65 - Jim Young
Touchdown Passes Caught (Season) - 18 - David Williams ('88)
Touchdown Passes Caught (Game) - 4 -
- Mervyn Fernandez - Edmonton at B.C. 06/07/84
- Mervyn Fernandez - at Ottawa 13/10/84
- Mervyn Fernandez - Calgary at B.C. 17/08/85
- David Williams - Edmonton at B.C. 29/10/88

B.C.'S RECORD AGAINST OTHER CLUBS (REGULAR SEASON)

		GP	W	L	T	F	A	PTS
Versus Ottawa	(Since 1961)	46	27	17	2	1187	1033	56
Versus Toronto	(Since 1961)	46	25	19	2	1251	1191	52
Versus Hamilton	(Since 1961)	46	22	21	3	1161	1039	47
Versus Winnipeg	(Since 1954)	118	51	65	2	2286	2575	104
Versus Saskatchewan	(Since 1954)	124	53	67	4	2842	2767	110
Versus Calgary	(Since 1954)	122	49	69	4	2422	2809	102
Versus Edmonton	(Since 1954)	123	44	75	4	2240	2700	92
Versus Sacramento	(Since 1993)	2	0	2	0	50	91	0
B.C. VS OPPOSITION		627	271	335	21	13439	14205	563

Owner: Bill Comrie

Born June 29, 1950 in Edmonton Alberta. Purchased the B.C. Lions in September, 1992. He abruptly ended his promising hockey career at the age of 19 and with no business background, took over the family business (a small furniture store) in 1969. He opened Bill Comrie's Furniture Warehouse in 1971 and a year later he launched the "Midnight Madness" concept. In 1976, he moved the business to a well-known brick warehouse in Edmonton which had come to be known as the "brick", from which he kept the name and thus, "The Brick Furniture Warehouse" was born. By 1982, he expanded to three stores and two years later, three more outlets were opened in Toronto. Today, there are 42 "The Brick" stores across Canada. Bill is also involved in sports. He owns, with his two brothers, the San Diego Gulls of the International Hockey League and served on the board of the Edmonton Eskimos for six years. He is also deeply involved in charities and serves as host of the annual International Super Novice Hockey Tournament in Edmonton.

President: Peter R. Classon

Born September 29, 1944 in Cardiff, Wales. Emigrated to Canada as the son of a war bride in 1946. After graduating from high school in Summerside, PEI, he spent 4 years with the Bank of Nova Scotia before entering Mount Allison University where he completed a Bachelor of Commerce degree in 1970 with first class honours. After graduating from Mt. A, Peter joined H.R. Doane and Company and received his CA designation in 1972. In 1977 he became President and minority shareholder of MacCulloch & Co. Ltd., a Nova Scotia based corporation involved in cable television, retail building materials, and commercial and residential real estate development. He joined Shaw Communications Inc. (the third largest Canadian cable television company) in 1982 as Executive VP and a director of the public company. In addition to his management consulting company, Corporate Consulting, Peter owns and continues to be involved in a successful manufacturing facility located in Penticton, B.C. Peter assumed the role of President of the B.C. Lions in July, 1993.

General Manager: Eric Tillman

Born July 24, 1957 in Gulfport, Mississippi. Graduated from the University of Mississippi with a degree in journalism. He worked in the Ole Miss athletic department before leaving for the Houston Oilers of the NFL where he worked in public relations and administration for two years. In 1983, he headed to the Montreal Concordes under Joe Galat, who was the head coach at the time, where he served as the Director of Player Personnel. For the next two seasons, he was the Director of U.S. Scouting. In May 1985, he was named the Executive Director of the Senior Bowl (the only college all-star game associated with the NFL) in Mobile, Alabama, where he worked until joining the Lions on December 10, 1992. He was very successful in his position, with his responsibilities being extensive and ranging from marketing and promoting the event to recruiting the best college seniors in the country to play in the game. When he entered the picture, the Senior Bowl was in financial difficulty with flagging interest and poor attendance. Before long, things had turned around. In 1986, the game sold out for the first time in six years and has remained a sellout ever since.

Head Coach: Dave Ritchie

Born September 3, 1938 in New Bedford, Massachusetts. Was named to his first pro head coaching position in January, 1993 with the Lions. Graduate of the University of Cincinnati where he played linebacker and fullback. Was the Linebackers' Coach with the Winnipeg Blue Bombers in 1990 and 1991. Prior to that, he spent the 1989 season at Marshall University in Huntington,

West Virginia as Defensive Coordinator and Outside Linebacker Coach. The previous two years, he was at the University of Cincinnati as the Defensive Coordinator. Spent four seasons with the Montreal Alouettes from 1983-1986, responsible for the defensive backs and was Head Coach at Fairmont State College from 1978-1982. Worked with the Ottawa Rough Riders for the 1992 season as Defensive Coordinator and Defensive Secondary Coach.

ASSISTANT COACHES

Jody Allen, Receivers Coach. Born in Atlanta, Georgia. Entering his first season with the Lions. Played defensive end at Marion Military Institute in 1979-80, moving to Catawba College in 1981 and Valdosta State College in 1982. Began his coaching career as the offensive line coach at Marion (Ala.) Military Institute Junior College in 1983. Following that, he spent two years (1986-87) as receivers coach at the University of Alabama under Ray Perkins before Perkins departed for the NFL Tampa Bay Buccaneers. He then moved on to the University of Mississippi where he coached running backs and receivers, and he stayed for five years. Allen was a guest coach at the Lions' training camp in Kelowna in 1993 while he served as the offensive coordinator and quarterbacks coach at Arkansas State University.

Dave Easley, Linebackers Coach. Moves from the defensive line where he spent the 1993 season with the Lions. Joined B.C. from the Toronto Argonauts where he earned a Grey Cup ring as a defensive assistant in 1991. Before joining Toronto, Easley was a defensive coach at the University of British Columbia in 1989-90 and defensive back/linebackers coach from 1983 to '87. He gained pro experience as a guest coach with the Saskatchewan Roughriders in 1984 and with B.C. in 1985 and '86. He also spent some time coaching the Adelaide Eagles in Australia from 1987 to '88. Was one of the top players in the CFL, being named Rookie of the Year in 1969 while with the Lions. He then moved to Hamilton in 1973 and finished his playing career with Edmonton in 1976.

Gene Gaines, Defensive Secondary. Born June 26, 1938 in Los Angeles, California. Entering his fourth season with Lions. Began his career as Defensive Back and Halfback at UCLA, where he graduated with a Bachelor of Science degree. Played for the Montreal Alouettes in 1961, the Ottawa Rough Riders from 1962-69, and returned to Montreal from 1970-76. Retired in 1976 and coached in Montreal until joining the Edmonton Eskimos for the 1982 season. Was Linebacker Coach for the Los Angeles Express of the USFL in 1983. Joined the NFL Houston Oilers as Special Teams and Linebackers Coach in 1984. Returned to the CFL in 1986 with the Winnipeg Blue Bombers. Signed with B.C. in January, 1991. Gaines is being inducted into the Canadian Football Hall of Fame in 1994.

Michael Gray, Defensive Line Coach. Born February 11, 1960 in Baltimore, Maryland. Begins his coaching career following an outstanding career as a defensive tackle with the B.C. Lions (1985-86) and the Winnipeg Blue Bombers (1987-92). Was selected as the CFL Most Outstanding Rookie in 1985, recording 13 sacks. He was selected by Ottawa in the Equalization Draft in 1987, and then signed with Winnipeg later that year, where he remained until 1992. Gray earned a total of three Grey Cup rings in eight seasons.

Gary Hoffman, Offensive Line Coach. Born February 22, 1944 in Olivia, Minnesota. Graduate Westman College (B.A.) 1966 and University of South Dakota (Masters) 1971. Entering his second season with the Lions after spending six seasons with Saskatchewan Roughriders as the Offensive Line Coach. Began coaching with ten seasons in the Iowa, Minnesota and South Dakota high school systems. Defensive Line Coach 1980, Offensive Line Coach 1981-82. Offensive Co-ordinator and Backfield Coach 1983-86 all with the South Dakota State University. Offensive Line guest coach Winnipeg Blue Bombers 1983-86. Joined Saskatchewan for his first coaching position in the professional ranks on January 19, 1987.

John Payne, Offensive Coordinator. Born May 15, 1933 in Schoolton, Oklahoma. Payne is a sixteen-year veteran of the CFL. He most recently was the offensive line coach with the Sacramento Gold Miners in 1993 after spending the 1992 season in the same capacity with the Toronto Argonauts and the '91 season with Winnipeg Blue Bombers. Served as the Head Coach at Abilene Christian University in Abilene, Texas from 1985-1990. Spent the 1983 season with the Chicago Blitz and 1984 with the Arizona Wranglers, both of the USFL. Prior to that, he was on staff with the Detroit Lions of the NFL. His CFL coaching career included stops in Winnipeg, Edmonton, Saskatchewan and Hamilton. As head coach, he appeared in Grey Cup games in 1976 with Saskatchewan and 1980 with Hamilton. He also served as offensive coordinator at Texas Christian University and at Brigham Young University. Was honoured as the Oklahoma High School Coach of the Year in 1962. Received his bachelor's degree from Oklahoma State University and his master's degree from Central State University in Oklahoma.

B.C. LIONS
1994 CURRENT ROSTER AS OF APRIL 30, 1994
RETURNING PLAYERS

* Denotes Import

	Player	Pos.	Ht.	Wt.	Born	University/ Jr. Affiliate	Yrs. CFL	Yrs. B.C.
*	ALEXANDER, Ray	WR	6.04	205	8 JAN 62	Florida A & M	7	5
*	ALLEN, Zock	LB	6.01	220	12 JUN 68	Texas A & I	4	4
*	BAYSINGER, Freeman	WR	5.09	170	22 DEC 69	Humboldt State	2	2
*	BROWNE, Less	CB	5.11	170	12 JUL 59	Colorado State	11	2
	CARAVATTA, Giulio	QB	6.00	220	20 MAR 66	Simon Fraser	4	4
	CLARK, Matt	WR	6.00	180	14 MAY 68	Montana	4	4
	CLARKE, Matt	LB	6.00	225	6 APR 68	UBC	4	4
	EUROPE, Tom	DB	5.11	195	27 JUL 70	Bishop's	2	2
*	FLUTIE, Darren	WR	5.10	180	18 NOV 66	Boston College	4	4
	FOUDY, Sean	DB	6.03	195	25 OCT 65	York	6	2
*	FRANCIS, Andre	CB	5.08	170	5 OCT 60	New Mexico State	12	6
	FURDYK, Todd	T	6.07	305	10 DEC 69	Rocky Mountain	2	2
*	GRIER, Derek	CB	6.00	175	4 MAR 70	Marshall	2	2
	GROENEWEGEN, Leo	G	6.05	270	13 AUG 65	UBC	8	6
	HANSON, Ryan	RB	6.01	215	17 JAN 64	Slippery Rock	7	5
	HOCKING, Doug	LB	6.00	230	16 OCT 69	Surrey Juniors	4	4
*	JACKSON, Jeff	LB	6.01	235	10 SEP 61	Auburn	4	2
	LORENZ, Tim	DE	6.02	240	12 FEB 65	Santa Barbara	7	3
	MACCREADY, Derek	DT	6.05	265	4 MAY 67	Ohio State	6	6
*	MACNEILL, John	DT	6.04	260	15 NOV 68	Michigan State	3	3
	McCALLUM, Paul	K	5.11	185	07 JAN 70	Surrey Jrs.	2	2
	MCLENNAN, Spencer	WR	5.10	190	16 OCT 69	Imperial Valley	4	4
*	McMANUS, DANNY	QB	6.00	200	17 JUN 65	Florida State	5	2
	MILLINGTON, Sean	RB	6.02	225	1 FEB 68	Simon Fraser	4	4
*	MURPHY, Yo	WR	5.10	170	11 MAY 71	Idaho	2	2
	PASSAGLIA, Lui	K	5.11	190	7 JUN 54	Simon Fraser	19	19
*	PHILPOT, Cory	RB	5.09	185	15 MAY 70	Mississippi	2	2
	SCRIVENER, Glen	DT	6.04	275	14 JUL 67	William Jewell	4	3
*	SIMS, Kelly	DB	5.10	190	10 NOV 70	Cinncinatti	2	2
	SINCLAIR, Ian	C	6.04	260	22 JUL 60	Miami	10	10
	SKINNER, Chris	RB	6.00	220	18 DEC 61	Bishop's	10	4
	SMITH, Robert J.	G	6.04	270	3 OCT 58	Utah State	14	5
	STEVENSON, Victor	T	6.04	255	22 SEP 60	Calgary	12	2
	TARAS, Jamie	G	6.02	260	31 JAN 66	Western Ontario	8	8
*	TREVATHAN, Mike	WR	6.01	205	26 MAR 68	Montana	4	4
*	TURNER, Lonnie	WR	5.07	170	31 AUG 60	Cal Poly Pomona	2	2
	WARNOCK, Kent	DT	6.07	260	03 JUN 64	Calgary	8	2
*	WILLIAMS, Arnie	LB	6.01	235	04 AUG 70	Southern Miss.	2	2
	WRIGHT, Donovan	LB	6.03	200	16 OCT 66	Slippery Rock	6	3

NEW PLAYERS

* Denotes Import

	Player	Pos.	Ht.	Wt.	Born	University/ Jr. Affiliate	Yrs. CFL
*	AMOS, Dwayne	DB	5.11	180	07 APR 70	Mississippi	1
*	AUSTIN, Kent	QB	6.01	195	25 JUN 63	Mississippi	8
*	BENTON, Gerald	WR	5.05	165	24 AUG 70	Kansas State	1
*	BROOKS, Earl	LB	6.00	215	17 DEC 71	Missouri	1
*	CHATHAM, Kefa	DE	6.04	265	30 MAR 72	Texas A & M	1
*	CHATMAN, Tyrone	LB	5.08	220	12 APR 71	Arkansas	1
*	CRYER, Lionel	LB	6.00	220	22 APR 71	Grambling	1
*	FERNANDEZ, Mervyn	WR	6.03	215	29 DEC 59	San Jose State	6
*	HARRIS, Tony	DB	6.00	205		Mississippi State	1
*	JACKSON, Tony	RB	5.08	170	04 AUG 71	Vanderbilt	1
*	JADLOT, Mike	WR	6.04	200	26 JAN 71	Missouri	1
*	JONES, Shawn	DB	5.10	185	19 JUL 70	Kutztown	2
*	JORDAN, Sean	WR	5.09	180	14 JUN 68	US Military Acadamy	1
*	KING, Shannon	LB	5.09	240	25 FEB 72	Marshall	1
*	LOWERY, David	QB	6.00	200	30 MAY 71	San Diego State	1
	MANTYKA, Cory	T	6.05	275	31 MAY 70	Jamestown	2
*	MATSUZAKI, Micah	WR	5.11	185	23 JUN 71	Bringham Young	1
*	McCLUNG, Marcus	LB	6.02	225	26 NOV 71	Virginia Tech	1
*	NEWBY, Henry	LB	6.02	230	21 JUN 68	Fairmont State	1
	PALMER, Kensley	FB	5.11	230	16 FEB 67	Manitoba	4
*	PEARSON, Matthew	DE	6.04	260	11 SEP 68	Baylor	1
*	PLATE, Scott	DB	5.11	195	01 JUL 70	Iowa	1
*	POOL, Charles	LB	5.10	210	24 JUN 71	SW Louisiana	1
*	ROBERTS, Craig	CB	5.08	185	07 FEB 71	SW Louisiana	1
*	ROBERTSON, Virgil	LB	6.02	225	09 NOV 66	Nicholls State	3
*	SHAMBURGER, Anthony	LB	6.03	230	19 JAN 69	Alabama State	1
*	SHIPLEY, Stephen	WR	6.05	225	17 MAY 71	Texas Christian	1
*	WALKER, David	RB	5.09	215	04 DEC 69	Syracuse	1
*	WAUFORD, Jon	DE	6.03	265	11 FEB 70	Miami of Ohio	1
*	WILLIAMS, Keith	RB	5.08	185	20 SEP 71	Utah	1
*	WRIGHT, Eric	WR	6.00	195	04 AUG 69	Stephen F. Austin	1

SACRAMENTO GOLD MINERS FOOTBALL CLUB

Business Office
14670 Cantova Way, Suite 200
Rancho Murieta, CA 95683
Tel.: (916) 354-1000
Fax: (916) 354-3244

Sales/Ticket Office
Hornet Field
6020 Hornet Drive
Sacramento, CA 95819
Tel.: (916) 456-5925
Fax: (916) 456-1306

MANAGEMENT

Chairman-CEO: Fred Anderson
President/Chief Operating Officer: Tom Bass
Executive Vice-President & Director: Dave Lucchetti
Vice President & Director: Jim Anderson

FOOTBALL OPERATIONS

Head Coach/Director of Football Operations: Kay Stephenson
Assistant Coaches:
Bill Bradley, Defensive Backs
Bob Mattos, Special Teams/Running Backs
Jim Niblack, Defensive Line
Bill Urbanik, Defensive Coordinator
Mike Bender, Offensive Line
Director of Player Personnel: Rick Mueller
Trainer: Tony Griffith
Assistant Trainer: Joe Hubbard
Equipment Manager: Marc Miller
Assistant Equipment Manager: Jason Pierce
Video Director: Mark Hobbs
Team Physicians: Dr. Timothy Mar, Dr. Harold Strauch, Dr. Ron Sockolov
Coaching/Administrative Assistant: Megan Lucchetti

ADMINISTRATION

General Manager: Tom Huiskens
Assistant General Manager: Bob Herrfeldt
Controller: Cathy Castaneda
Director of Media Relations: Tim McDowd
Director of Promotions: Randy Greenfield
Director of Sponsorships and Corporate Sales: Mike Preacher
Director of Ticket Sales: Bob Welton
Ticket Manager: Jason Best
Promotions Assistant/Community Relations: Kelly Silveira
Box Office Manager: Lynne Thompson
Administrative Assistant: Carol Howle
Administrative Assistant/Receptionist: Penny Steuben

FAST FACTS

Home Stadium: Hornet Field
Stadium Address: Hornet Field, 6020 Hornet Drive, Sacramento, CA 95819
Club Colors: Aqua and Old Gold
Club Name: Sacramento Gold Miners
Training Camp Location: Yuba College
Press Box Location: West Grandstands (Elevator on West Side of Grandstands)
Dressing Room Location: Home team /visiting team in North end zone
Radio Broadcasts: KFBK 1530-AM (Play-by-play - Tim Roye; Color Commentator - Lee Grosscup)
P.A. Announcer: Fred Anderson
Statistician: Dave Kranz
Offensive Spotter: Dick Kranz, Matt Matushefski
Defensive Spotter: Jeff Kranz
Typist: Vicky Boyd
Timekeeper: Jim Mancini
Scorekeeper: Dave Kranz

Club History: On February 26, 1993, the city of Sacramento became the first United States-based CFL franchise. The name "Gold Miners" was chosen on January 15, 1993 to describe the hard-working and prosperity-minded people involved during the euphoric days of the California Gold Rush. The team logo depicts the power of a Gold Miner's pick axe striking the earth and the energy that has been created by the skill and hard work of these historic Californians. In keeping with the beauty of California and its people, the team colors of aqua and gold represent two valuable and historic commodities to Sacramento and California: water and gold. The Gold Miners

Hornet Field Facts 'n Figures

Capacity: 24,000
Largest CFL Regular Season One Game Attendance: 20,082
Sacramento Gold Miners 36, Calgary Stampeders 38 (July 17, 1993)

Club history (cont'd)
improved steadily throughout the first season of CFL play finishing the year with a 6-12 record. The Gold Miners' six wins broke a CFL record for the most wins by a first-year team. Gold Miner home games are played at Hornet Field on the campus of California State University, Sacramento.

SACRAMENTO CLUB RECORDS SINCE 1993
Regular Season

- CFL Record
- Ties CFL Record
( ) - Figures in Brackets represent Year(s) Club mark set

Most Points Scored One Season (minimum 14 games) - 498 ('93)
Most Points Scored Against One Season (minimum 14 games) - 511 ('93)
Fewest Points Scored Against One Season (minimum 14 games) - 498 ('93)
Most Points Scored One Game - 64- vs. B.C. 06/11/93 Final: 64-27
Most Points Scored Against One Game - 43- Edmonton at Sacramento 31/7/93 Final: 43-11
Most Wins One Season (minimum 14 games) - 6 ('93)
Most Losses One Season (minimum 14 games) - 12 ('93)
Highest Shutout - none to date of publication
Highest Shutout Against - none to date of publication
Most Touchdowns One Season (minimum 14 games) - 56 ('93)
Most Touchdowns One Game - 9 - vs. B.C. 6/11/93
Most Converts One Season (minimum 14 games) - 56 ('93)
Most Converts One Game - 9 - vs. B.C. 6/11/93
Most Field Goals One Season (minimum 14 games) - 28 ('93)
Most Field Goals One Game - 4 - vs. Ottawa 11/9/93 vs. Hamilton 14/8/93
Most First Downs One Game - 31 - vs. Calgary 17/7/93
Most First Downs One Season (minimum 14 games) - 407 - 1993
Most Yards Total Offence One Season- 7,798 ('93)
Most Yards Total Offence One Game - 614 - vs. B.C. 6/11/93
Most Yards Rushing One Game - 588 - vs. B.C., 11/6/93
Most Times Carried One Game - 21 - vs. Saskatchewan, 7/24/93 and vs. Ottawa, 9/11/93
Most Touchdowns Rushing One Game - 2 - three times - at Toronto, 5/8/93, vs. Ottawa, 11/9/93, and vs. B.C., 6/11/93

Most Yards Passing One Season - 737 - 1993
Most Kickoff Returns One Season - 89 - 1993
Most Yards Passing One Game - 496 - at Winnipeg, 21/8/93
Most Passes Thrown One Game - 53 - at Hamilton, 10/7/93
Most Passes Completed One Season- 425 - 1993
Most Completions One Game - 33 - vs. Calgary, 17/7/93
Most Touchdown Passes One Game - 4 - vs. Toronto, 23/10/93 & vs. B.C., 6/11/93

SACRAMENTO INDIVIDUAL RECORDS SINCE 1993
Regular Season (CFL Statistics Only)

Points (Career) - 156 - Jim Crouch
Points (Season) - 156 - Jim Crouch - 1993
Points (Game) - 18 - Carl Parker - (3TDs) vs. B.C., 6/11/93
Touchdowns (Career) - 13 - Mike Oliphant
Touchdowns (Season) - 13 - Mike Oliphant - 1993
Touchdowns (Game) - 3 - Carl Parker - vs. B.C.,6/11/93
Converts (Career) - 56 - Jim Crouch
Converts (Game) - ##9 - Jim Crouch
Consecutive Converts - 56 - Jim Crouch - vs. B.C., 6/11/93
Field Goals (Career) - 28 - Jim Crouch
Field Goals (Season) - 28 - Jim Crouch - 1993
Field Goals (Game) - 4 - Jim Crouch - vs. Ottawa, 11/9/93
Longest Field Goal - 42 - Jim Crouch
Singles (Career) - 18 - Jim Crouch- (15 missed on Field Goals, and 3 on Kickoffs)
Times Punted (Career) - 77 - Pete Gardere
Passes Thrown (Career) - 701 - Dave Archer
Passes Thrown (Season) - 701 - Dave Archer - 1993
Passes Thrown (Game) - 53 - Dave Archer - at Hamilton, 10/7/93
Passes Completed (Career) - 403 - Dave Archer
Passes Completed (Season) - 403 - Dave Archer - 1993
Passes Completed (Game) - 33 - Dave Archer - vs. Calgary, 17/7/93
Passing Yards (Career) - 6,023 - Dave Archer
Passing Yards (Season) - 6,023 - Dave Archer - 1993
Passing Yards (Game) - 496 - Dave Archer - vs. Winnipeg, 21/8/93
Touchdown Passes Thrown (Career) - 35 - Dave Archer
Touchdown Passes Thrown (Season) - 35 - Dave Archer - 1993
Touchdown Passes Thrown (Game) - 4 - Dave Archer - vs. Toronto, 23/10/93 and vs. B.C., 6/11/93
No. of Carries (Career) - 116 - Mike Oliphant
No. of Carries (Season) -116 - Mike Oliphant - 1993
No. of Carries (Game) - 12 - Mike Oliphant - vs. Ottawa, 11/9/93
Yards Rushing (Career) - 760 - Mike Oliphant
Yards Rushing (Season)- 760 - Mike Oliphant - 1993
Yards Rushing (Game) - 173 - Mike Oliphant - vs. Ottawa, 11/9/93
Touchdowns by Rushing (Career) - 8 - Mike Oliphant
Touchdowns by Rushing (Season) - 8 - Mike Oliphant - 1993
Touchdowns by Rushing (Game) - 2 - Mike Oliphant - at Toronto, 8/5/93 and vs. Ottawa, 11/9/93; Mike Pringle - vs. B.C., 11/6/93
Passes Caught (Career) - 90 - Rod Harris
Passes Caught (Season) - 90 - Rod Harris - 1993
Passes Caught (Game) - 10 - Mike Oliphant - at Saskatchewan, 27/8/93
Passes Caught Rookie Player - 12 - Charles Thompson
Pass Reception Yards (Career) - 1,379 - Rod Harris
Pass Reception Yards (Season) - 1,379 - Rod Harris - 1993
Pass Reception Yards (Game) - 200 - Mike Oliphant - vs. Winnipeg, 21/8/93
Pass Reception Yards Rookie Player - 143 - Charles Thompson
Touchdown Passes Caught (Career) - 7 - Rod Harris
Touchdown Passes Caught (Season) - 7 - Rod Harris
Touchdown Passes Caught (Game) - 3 - Carl Parker - vs. B.C., 6/11/93

SACRAMENTO'S RECORD AGAINST OTHER CLUBS (REGULAR SEASON)

		GP	W	L	T	F	A	PTS
Versus Ottawa	(Since 1993)	2	1	1	0	70	47	2
Versus Toronto	(Since 1993)	2	1	1	0	73	61	2
Versus Hamilton	(Since 1993)	2	1	1	0	60	40	2
Versus Winnipeg	(Since 1993)	2	0	2	0	44	63	0
Versus Saskatchewan	(Since 1993)	3	1	2	0	80	79	2
Versus Calgary	(Since 1993)	2	0	2	0	44	79	0
Versus Edmonton	(Since 1993)	3	0	3	0	36	90	0
Versus B.C.	(Since 1993)	2	2	0	0	91	50	4
SACRAMENTO VS OPPOSITION		18	6	12	0	498	509	12

Chaiman-CEO: Fred Anderson

Born on May 11, 1924, in Sacramento, California. Fred Anderson's efforts to bring professional sports to Sacramento reached a new level in 1993 when the Sacramento Gold Miners became the first and only American team in the CFL. As Chairman-CEO of the Gold Miners, he is a well-respected businessman and leader in the Sacramento community. As former owner of the World League champion Surge and minority owner of the NBA Kings, Anderson has the experience and persistence necessary to participate as an active force in today's volatile professional sports market. In his latest sports venture, Anderson has stepped up Sacramento's efforts to complete the existing stadium near Arco Arena and has vowed to place a Single A baseball team and his Gold Miners in the venue by the year 1996. Over the past 40 years, Anderson has built one of America's largest privately-owned companies, Pacific Coast Building Products, Inc. A fourth generation Sacramentan, and the original founder of the company, he now serves as the chairman of the Board. Anderson served in the United States Air Force during World War II as a meterologist and returned after the war to complete his degree in engineering from Stanford University.

President/Chief Operating Officer: Tom Bass

Born on August 2, 1943, at March Air Force Base in California. Bass was named the Gold Miners President and Chief Operating Officer on February 28, 1994 after serving as a personal advisor to Head Coach Stephenson in Gold Miners' first season. Bass will coordinate each aspect of the organization and will be involved in all Club business and football matters. In '92, Bass was the Vice President of Player Assistance/Pro Personnel for the New England Patriots. He originally joined the Patriots as the Vice President of Public Relations/Pro Player Assistance. Bass has been involved with many start-up franchises including the Cincinnati Bengals and the Tampa Bay Buccaneers. He was the first coach hired by NFL owner, Paul Brown, to help operate the expansion Bengals. From 1976-81, Bass was responsible for the signing and drafting of college players and pro personnel. He served as the San Diego Chargers' defensive coordinator on 2 different occasions, 1964-'68 and then from 1982-85. He also wrote Play Football the NFL Way, the first ever 'how to' book authorized by the NFL. Bass has published 2 books of poetry, Pro Football from the Inside, and Fly Free My Love.

General Manager: Tom Huiskens

Born July 14, 1950 in Bay City, Michigan. Huiskens was named General Manager of the Gold Miners prior to Sacramento's inaugural season. As General Manager, Huiskens is responsible for the Gold Miners business management efforts. Huiskens is working his 4th consecutive season with Chairman-CEO Fred Anderson. Huiskens joined the WL Sacramento Surge in 1991 as Gameday and Facilities Coordinator. Prior to the 1992 Surge season, Huiskens was responsible for the enormous task of renovating Hornet Field, with an original capacity of 6,500 to the current capacity of 25,000 seats. He has been a licensed contractor since '77 in the Sea Ranch area of California. Huiskens attended the University of Michigan on a football scholarship. He played in the 1969 Rose Bowl as a sophomore at the quick end position.

Head Coach: Kay Stephenson

Born December 17, 1944, in DeFuniak Springs, Florida. Kay Stephenson enters his 2nd season with the Gold Miners and his 4th season as a head coach for a Sacramento-based professional football team. In 1993, Stephenson was named Head Coach of the first U.S.expansion team in the CFL. Prior to that, Stephenson helped orchestrate one of the finest turnarounds of any professional football squad. He directed a 3-2 WL Sacramento Surge team to seven consecutive victories, five in regular season, two in post-season play, as the Surge captured the World Bowl '92 championship with a 21-17 victory over the Orlando Thunder in Montreal's Olympic Stadium. Stephenson was the quarterbacks coach with both the NFL Los Angeles Rams and NFL Buffalo Bills. In 1983, Stephenson's offensive ingenuity helped elevate him to the Bills' head coaching position. In two plus years with a team in complete transition, Stephenson's overall record was 10-26. He played QB at the University of Florida before making the jump to the pros. Stephenson's pro career lasted three years while playing for both the San Diego Chargers and the Buffalo Bills, 1967-70.

Assistant Coaches

Bill Urbanik, Defensive Coordinator. Born on December 27, 1947, in Donora, Pennsylvania. Urbanik was named defensive coordinator in the Gold Miners' inaugural season. He joined Sacramento and the CFL via the Los Angeles Raiders where he spent 2 years in the player personnel department. He joined the Raiders in 1989 serving as their defensive line coach after five seasons in the same capacity with the Cincinnati Bengals. 1991 marked Urbanik's first season in the player personnel department. Urbanik coached the defensive line and special teams at Wake Forest from 1979-83. From 1975-77, he was the defensive coordinator at Northern Illinois. He began coaching in 1970 as a student assistant at Ohio State University where he was a three-year letterman under Woody Hayes. Urbanik was the offensive line coach at Marshall University from 1971-73, where he earned his master's degree.

Jim Niblack, Defensive Line Coach. Born in Americus, Georgia. Niblack returns to Sacramento for his third season. He was the only returning assistant coach last season from Kay Stephenson's '92 WL championship season. He has over 35 years of coaching experience which has ranged through many leagues. He coached Kay Stephenson in 1973-74 when Stephenson was the QB with the WFL Jacksonville Sharks. Niblack and Stephenson were reunited in Buffalo in 1983-84 when Niblack coached the offensive line for Stephenson. He served at offensive coordinator of the USFL Orlando Renegades in 1985 and has been involved with the Arena League Chicago Bruisers, 1987-88, Detroit Drive, 1990, and the Orlando Predators, 1991. He has coached at the Universities of Florida and Kentucky.

Bill Bradley, Defensive Backs Coach. Born on January 24, 1947 in Palestine, Texas. Bradley has the most CFL experience of all Gold Miner coaches. In 1991-'92, he coached the defensive backs with the WL San Antonio Riders. He served as the Calgary Stampeders' defensive coordinator in 1990 and was their defensive backs and special teams coach in 1988-'89. Bradley became a personnel assistant with the USFL San Antonio Gunslingers in 1983. The next year, he began his 1st coaching job as the Gunslingers' secondary coach and was later promoted to assistant head coach. Bradley went on to coach the defensive backs with the USFL Memphis Showboats before moving to the University of Texas as a volunteer assistant coach in 1987. He was an NFL All-Pro safety three times, 1971-73, with the NFL Philadelphia Eagles during his ten-year playing career.

Bob Mattos, Special Teams Coordinator/Running Backs Coach. Born on September 28, 1941 in Modesto, California. Mattos begins his 2nd year of coaching in the pros as he returns to the Gold Miners to coach the special teams and serve as an offensive assistant to coach Stephenson. Mattos was head coach at California State University, Sacramento for 15 seasons before joing the Gold Miners. He is Sacramento State's all-time winningest coach with an overall record of 84-73-2. From 1978-'92, his coached teams consistently were ranked among the nation's top 20 in several offensive categories. Within his 15 years he saw 95 individual and team records broken. Mattos was quarterback and linebacker for the 1962 and '63 Sacramento State teams. He began coaching at his prep alma mater Orestimba High School in Newman, California where after just one season as the assistant coach was promoted to his first head coaching position.

Mike Bender, Offensive Line Coach. Born on April 21, 1943 in Strong, Arkansas. Bender joins the Gold Miners from the University of Nevada, Las Vegas (UNLV) where he was the Assistant Head Coach and Offensive Line Coach in 1992-93. Makes the jump to the professional ranks after spending 24 seasons coaching college football. Bender spent 3 seasons (1989-91) as the offensive line coach at Rice University and 6 seasons at the University of South Carolina. After playing 2 seasons in the NFL, both on the offensive line and as a defensive end with the Atlanta Falcons, Bender returned to Arkansas to complete his undergraduate studies. He began his collegiate coaching career in 1979 at his alma mater Arkansas, serving as an assistant under Lou Holtz. He moved on to New Mexico, working as an assistant from 1980-82, before becoming offensive line coach at South Carolina.

Rick Mueller, Director of Player Personnel. Born on December 4, 1967, in Spokane, Washington. In his 3rd year with Kay Stephenson, Mueller takes on added duties as director of player personnel. With the Gold Miners in '93, Mueller coached the wide receivers and was an assistant in the player personnel department. Mueller joined Coach Stephenson in 1992 with the WL Sacramento Surge. After the '92 World Bowl in Montreal, Mueller became a scout for the WL. In 1990, Mueller joined the Washington State University coaching staff as a graduate assistant/quarterback coach. Mueller played collegiate football at the University of Puget Sound.

SACRAMENTO GOLD MINERS
1994 CURRENT ROSTER AS OF APRIL 30, 1994
RETURNING PLAYERS

* Denotes Import

Player	Pos.	Ht.	Wt.	Born	University/ Jr. Affiliate	Yrs. CFL	Yrs. SAC
* ARCHER, David	QB	6.02	208	15 FEB 62	Iowa State	2	
* BELL, Kerwin	QB	6.03	211	15 JUN 65	Florida	2	
* BOUYER, Willie	WR	6.03	196	24 SEP 66	Michigan State	2	
* BROWN, Hurlie	DB	6.01	200	21 JUN 69	Miami	2	
* CROUCH, Jim	K	6.03	180	13 SEP 68	Sacramento State	2	
* DAVIS, Darrick	DB	5.08	165	29 SEP 69	Idaho	2	
* DAVIS, Paschall	LB	6.03	230	5 JUN 69	Texas A & M	2	
* DIAZ-INFANTE, David	OG	6.02	295	31 MAR 64	San Jose State	2	
* DRESSEL, Robert	C	6.04	270	19-AUG 69	Purdue	2	
* DYKO, Chris	T	6.06	280	16 MAR 66	Washington	2	
* EVERETT, Tre	WR	5.10	172	12 OCT 69	Florida State	2	
* FRANK, Garry	G	6.02	310	20 DEC 64	Mississippi State	2	
* FREEMAN, Corian	LB	6.03	225`	16 AUG 68	Florida State	2	
* GABBARD, Steve	OL	6.04	295	19 JUL 68	Florida State	2	
* GARDERE, Peter	QB	6.00	190	28 SEP 69	Texas	2	
* HAMMOND, Vance	DL	6.06	290	4 DEC 67	Clemson	2	
* HARPER, James	G	6.03	285	6 SEP 66	Alcorn State	2	
* HARRIS, Rod	WR	5.10	185	14 NOV 66	Texas A & M	2	
* HENKE, Brad	OL	6.04	295	10 APR 67	Arizona	2	
* HUMPHERY, Bobby	DB	5.10	180	23 AUG 61	New Mexico State	2	
* JACKSON, Byron	WR	5.07	160	16 FEB 68	San Jose State	2	
* JENNINGS, Jim	OT	6.04	294	04 APR 69	San Diego State	2	
* JOELSON, Greg	DE	6.03	270	22 AUG 66	Arizona State	3	
* JOHNSON, Joe Howard	WR	5.08	170	21 DEC 62	Notre Dame	2	
* KING, Emanuel	DT	6.04	270	15 AUG 63	Alabama	2	
* KISELAK, Michael	C	6.03	290	9 MAR 67	Maryland	2	
* LEDBETTER, Mark	DE	6.03	235	14 DEC 66	Washington State	2	
* MILLER, Muarice	LB	6.03	220	06 SEP 69	Wake Forest	2	
* MILLS, Troy	RB	6.02	215	7 JAN 66	Sacramento State	2	
* MOORE, Curtis	LB	6.02	235	11 FEB 67	Kansas	2	
* NELSON, Leonard	LB	6.01	220	21 NOV 69	Wake Forest	2	
* OLIPHANT, Mike	RB	5.09	171	19 MAY 63	Puget Sound	2	
* PARRISH, Doug	CB	6.00	190	25 FEB 68	San Fransisco State	4	
* PRINGLE, Mike	RB	5.10	190	1 SEP 67	Fullerton State	3	
* PRUITT, James	WR	6.03	205	29 JAN 64	Fullerton State	3	
* PULERI, Charles	QB	6.02	208	01 MAR 69	New Mexico State	2	
* ROGERS, Ernie	G	6.05	305	03 JAN 68	California	2	
* SHIPLEY, Ron	C	6.04	285	17 AUG 68	New Mexico	2	
* TEXADA, Kip	CB	5.09	180	15 JAN 68	McNeese State	2	
* THIENEMAN, Chris	DT	6.04	270	06 JUN 66	Louisville	2	
* WALLACE, Jason	CB	5.10	170	28 AUG 69	Virginia	2	
* WESTBROOKS, David	DE	6.04	265	23 MAR 68	Howard	2	
* WHITE, Brent	DL	6.05	275	28 FEB 67	Michigan	2	
* WHITE, Robb	DL	6.05	270	26 MAY 65	South Dakota	2	
* WISE, Myron	WR	6.01	170	26 JUN 72	Palomar JC	2	

NEW PLAYERS

* Denotes Import

Player	Pos.	Ht.	Wt.	Born	University/ Jr. Affiliate	Yrs. CFL
* ANDERSON, Roman	K	5.10	190	19 APR 69	Houston	1
* BUDDENBERG, John	OL	6.05	280	9 Oct 65	Akron	1
* DICKERSON, Rodney	RB	6.02	240	18 Jul 71	Humboldt State	1
* DILLON, Jerry	LB	6.04	235	17 Sep 69	East Carolina	1
* DIXON, Titus	WR	5.08	160	15 Jun 66	Troy State	1
* DOUGLAS, John	DE	6.00	210	17 Aug 71	Abilene Christian	1
* ESTY, Charles	OL	6.05	300	30 Dec 68	St Lawrence	1
* FEARS, Willie	DE	6.05	285	4 Jun 64	NW Louisiana	3
* FRANK, Malcolm	DB	5.08	180	5 Nov 68	Baylor	1
* GERHART, Tommy	DB	6.01	190	24 Feb 65	Ohio	1
* GREENE, Brian	DB	5.11	185	15 Feb 72	Western Oregon	1
* HARPER, David	LB	6.02	225	5 May 66	Humboldt State	1
* HAWKINS, Wayne	WR	5.11	185	13 Aug 69	Southwest Minnesota	1
* KENNEDY, Tony	RB	5.10	215	3 Mar 70	Virginia Tech	1
* KING, James	DE	6.00	230	9 Feb 68	Texas A&I	3
* LeSURE, Mike	WR	6.02	190	23 Oct 69	Ball State	1
* McCURTY, Gary	RB	5.06	210	29 May 71	Puget Sound	2
* McWRIGHT, Robert	CB	5.08	170	10 Nov 66	Texas Christian	1
* MILES, Charles	RB	5.10	185	12 Oct 70	East Carolina	1
* O'BRIEN, Kevin	LB	6.04	235	1 Jul 70	Bowling Green	1
* PRICE, Aaron	K	5.10	190	17 Jun 70	Washington State	1
* ROBINSON, David	CB	5.09	185	3 Feb 68	East Carolina	1
* SHORTS, Peter	OL	6.07	280	12 Jul 66	Illinois State	1
* SMITH, Tommy	LB	6.02	225	7 Aug 71	Washington	1
* STEVENSON, Robert	OL	6.02	290	20 Dec 69	Florida State	1
* THOMAS, Dee	DB	5.10	180	7 Nov 67	Nicholls State	1
* THOMAS, Harvey	DE	6.04	230	22 Mar 69	Florida	1
* TURNER, Robert	DB	6.03	200	5 Sep 70	Washington State	1
* TURRAL, Eric	WR	5.10	180	8 Oct 70	Florida State	1
* WALKER, Johnny R.	WR	6.01	190	18 Nov 68	Texas	1
* WILHITE, Kenny	CB	5.08	180	26 Jul 70	Nebraska	1

LAS VEGAS MAJOR LEAGUE SPORTS, INC.
(dba) LAS VEGAS POSSE

Administration
1204 East Desert Inn Rd.
Las Vegas, Nevada 89109
(702) 242-4200
Fax: (702) 893-0105

Football Operations
3750 E. Flamingo Rd.
Las Vegas, Nevada 89121
(702) 898-8200
Fax: (702) 898-7312

EXECUTIVE

Owner/Chairman and C.E.O.: Nick J. Mileti

FOOTBALL OPERATIONS

Head Coach: Ron Meyer
Assistant Coaches:
Ron Smeltzer, Offensive Coordinator
Al Tanara, Offensive Line Coach
John Chura, Linebackers Coach
Jeff Reinebold, Secondary Coach
Director of Player Personnel: Steve Arnold
Director of Football Operations & Scouting: Lannie Julias
Team Physician: Dr. Tim Sutherland
Equipment Manager: Marty Daly
Assistant Equipment Manager: Ray Sterling
Trainer: Joe Bradshaw
Assistant Trainer: Joe Rainone
Physical Therapists: Keith Klevin, Jack Close
Video Coordinator: Kent Anderson
Coaches' Secretary: Cuinn Maxham

ADMINISTRATION

Chief Financial Officer: Ronald F. Ryan
Director of Marketing: David Humm
Sales Manager: Lee Meade
Program Sales: Mark Borgognoni
Posse Roundup Sales: John Buonaugurio
Group Sales: Dave Porter
Director of Communications: George McCabe
Media Coordinator: Amy Joy Slade
Merchandise Manager: Jim Coyle
Ticket Manager: Denise Moran Korach
Assistant Ticket Manager: Laura Horde

FAST FACTS

Home Stadium: Sam Boyd Stadium
Stadium Address: 7000 E. Russell Rd., Henderson, NV 89122
Club Colors: Desert Sand, Black and White
Club Name: Las Vegas Posse
Training Camp Location: Riviera Hotel & Casino, Las Vegas
Press Box Location: West Grandstands (Enter through Portal 17-21)
Dressing Room Location: Home and visiting team in the North end zone
Radio Broadcasts: KVEG (840 AM)
TV Broadcasts: KLAS-TV (CBS) Channel 8
P.A. Announcer: TBA
Statistician: TBA
Offensive Spotter: TBA
Defensive Spotter: TBA
Typist: TBA
Timekeeper: TBA
Scorekeeper: TBA

Sam Boyd Stadium Facts 'n Figures

Capacity: 31,000
Largest One Game Attendance: 32,206 on September 20, 1986 (UNLV 17, Wisconsin 7)

Club History: The fastest growing city in the United States became the home of the Las Vegas Posse on July 26, 1993. The Posse was the second American team to join the League and is now one of four cities South of the border. The name Posse was chosen by Janet Negrete of Las Vegas. More than 1,200 people sent in over 2,000 name suggestions, including six for Posse. Negrete was declared the winner because besides choosing the name, she also picked the Posse's official colors - desert sand, black and white - the same colors you would see looking at the terrain around the city. Negrete said she chose the name Posse because when she moved to Las Vegas from Toronto 32 years ago, "it was just a cowboy town". The logo was originally designed by Brad Burch of Merica, Burch and Dickerson, and later finalized by Chris Sharp, the art director at Caliendo-Savio Enterprises. Las Vegas is slated to begin its first season on Friday, July 8, 1994 at Sacramento against the Gold Miners in the first-ever all-American CFL game.

Owner/Chairman/Chief Executive Officer: Nick J. Mileti

Born April 22, 1931 in Cleveland, Ohio. Graduated from Bowling Green State University with a B.A. degree in 1953 and The Ohio State College of Law with a JD in 1956. In private law practice from 1958 to 1962, serving as prosecutor for the City of Lakewood, Ohio from 1960-62. From 1963-67 he was a consultant to non-profit groups focusing on construction of housing and activity centers for older persons. Entered the field of sports in 1968 when he purchased the Cleveland Barons of the American Hockey League and the Cleveland

Arena, serving as President and Chief Operating Officer of both entities. In 1970, he was awarded an expansion franchise for the Cleveland Cavaliers in the National Basketball Association and was President and COO of the Cavaliers for 10 years. In 1973, he founded and served as Managing General Partner of the Cleveland Crusaders of the World Hockey Association. In the early '70s, he put together a group to buy the Cleveland Indians baseball club of the American League, and kept the team from moving out of Cleveland. In 1979, he moved to Beverly Hills, California, where he was an inverstor-partner with three other NBA team owners in SLM, a company which financed feature motion pictures with MGM and Twentieth Century Fox. In 1987, he purchased and operated radio stations WVEC and KPGA in San Luis Obispo, California. He sold the stations and retired in Rome in 1989, but returned to the U.S. in 1992 and began his quest for a CFL franchise. The Las Vegas expansion franchise was awarded to him on July 26, 1993.

Head Coach: Ron Meyer

Born February 17, 1941 in Westerville, Ohio. His first coaching position was as Head Coach of Penn High School in Mishawaka, Indiana in 1964. In 1965, he returned to Purdue University, where he was a defensive back for four years, as an offensive assistant in charge of the backfield, receivers and overall passing game. He was the recipient of Purdue's Nobel Kizer Award for athletic and academic achievements, was selected on the All-Big Ten Academic team and won the Big Ten Medal of honor in 1963. Received both his Bachelor of Science and Master of Science from Purdue. He stayed at Purdue through the 1970 season. Meyer accepted his first professional coaching job with the Dallas Cowboys in 1971. During his first two years with the Cowboys, they were 21-7 and won Super Bowl VI with a 24-3 victory over the Miami Dolphins. After his stint with Dallas, Meyer coached the University of Nevada at Las Vegas to a 27-8 record in three years. He returned to Dallas in 1976, taking over a struggling Southern Methodist University football program. After four building seasons at SMU, Meyer's Mustangs compiled an 8-4 record in 1980 and went 10-1 in '81, winning the Southwest Conference. Meyer moved to the NFL in 1982, joining the New England Patriots until 1984. He then coached the Indianapolis Colts in 1986, where he stayed for more than three seasons. Twice he was named American Football Conference "Coach of the Year", once with New England, and the other time with Indianapolis. He was an analyst on CNN's "NFL Preview" before he joined the Posse as their first head coach on January 12, 1994.

Assistant Coaches

Ron Smeltzer, Offensive Coordinator. Born October 29, 1941 in York, Pennsylvania. Ron enters his first season with the Posse after two seasons at the helm of the Ottawa Rough Riders. During his rookie season, the team put together their best season in more than a decade with a .500 mark. Smeltzer was the offensive line coach under Ron Meyer at UNLV from 1973-75 when the Rebels won 27 of 35 games and made post-season trips to the Grantland Rice Bowl in 1974 and the Rubber Bowl in 1976. He played center and linebacker at West Chester State (Pennsylvania) and was a graduate assistant coach with West Chester's 1967 Tangerine Bowl team. Coached two years while completing his Masters Degree in Physical Education at the University of Colorado in 1968. Coached the offensive line at University of California Santa Barbara ('70-'71) and then coached the offensive line at UNLV. He coached at Servite High in Anaheim, California from 1979-83, winning two state titles and earning a No. 4 national ranking in 1982. He moved to the professional ranks in 1984, serving as offensive line coach with the B.C. Lions for two seasons, with the Lions winning the Grey Cup in 1985. He then joined the Calgary Stampeders for two seasons (1986-87) as offensive coordinator and returned to B.C. in 1988 as the offensive line coach and coordinated the entire offense in 1989. Following a year as the Athletic Director and Head Coach of Holy Cross High School in Surrey, B.C., he joined the Edmonton Eskimos as offensive line coach in 1991.

John Chura, Defensive Coordinator. Born July 13, 1943 in Chicago, Illinois. Was a two-year letterman at Purdue University, where he graduated in 1965. Was a graduate assistant coach at Purdue the following season, before becoming a high school coach at Daytona Beach, Fla. from 1967 to 1973. Became an assistant coach under Ron Meyer at UNLV in 1973 and 1974 and then moved to Chaparral High School in Las Vegas, where he was an assistant coach for five years and head coach for 10 years. While at Chaparral, he compiled a 68-40 record, was named Coach of the Year five times, and won a state championship. Was an assistant coach at Cimarron-Memorial High School in Las Vegas in 1991 before moving to the professional ranks. Was a guest coach for two months with the Calgary Stampeders in 1984. Was Linebackers' Coach with the Ottawa Rough Riders in 1992. Joined the B.C. Lions in 1993 as linebackers coach, where they had the second-leading quarterback sacks in the CFL. Chura received his Bachelor of Science in 1965, and his Master of Science in 1966 from Purdue.

Jeff Reinebold, Secondary Coach. Born November 19, 1957 in South Bend, Indiana. Joins the Posse after spending three seasons with the B.C. Lions as their special teams coordinator. Was a guest coach of the Lions in 1988 and 1989. Before moving to the professional ranks, Reinebold was an assistant at the University of New Mexico, University of Pennsylvania (during which time the team won the Ivy League title twice - '86 and '88), University of Montana, Dartmouth College and Western Montana College and head coach at Rocky Mountain College. While at Rocky Mountain College, his team was conference runner-up after finishing last the previous three seasons. Rocky Mountain led the NAIA District XII and Frontier Conference in passing offense and set records for total offense and passing offense. At Montana, his team played in the Mirage Bowl. Western Montana led the Frontier Conference in passing offense and claimed school records in passing offense and efficiency while Reinebold was on staff. He played defensive back at the University of Maine from 1977 to 1980. Graduated cum laude from Indiana University with a Bachelor of Arts in 1981.

Al Tanara, Offensive Line Coach. Born March 7, 1942 in Pottstown, Pennsylvania. Tanara broke into the coaching ranks in 1965 as freshman coach at the University of Tennessee, where he was a three-year leterman. In 1966-67, he coached football and basketball at Merritt Island High School in Florida. After one year at the University of Hawaii in Honolulu and Pasadena City College, he became the offensive line coach at Arizona State University. He spent six years at Texas Tech University and one year at the University of Utah as offensive line coach, and then three years as assistant coach at UNLV. Tanara was the offensive line coach at San Diego State University before coming back to Las Vegas to be head coach of the Gamblers, a semi-pro football team, compiling a 10-0 record. Other coaching highlights while Tanara was on staff include a 11-2 record and a California Bowl win at UNLV in '84, an 8-2-1 record at the University of Utah in '81, the team's best record since 1964, a 10-1 record and co-champs of the Southwest Conference at Texas Tech in '76, four Western Athletic Conference Championships and four bowl victories while at ASU. The Sun Devils also had three NCAA National Titles in total offense and led the nation in scoring in 1972-73. While on staff at Pasadena City College, the team was 8-0-1, ranked No. 1 in California and third in the nation. Tanara graduated from the University of Tennessee with a Bachelor of Science degree in physical education and zoology.

LAS VEGAS POSSE
1994 CURRENT ROSTER AS OF APRIL 30, 1994
NEW PLAYERS

* Denotes Import

	Player	Pos.	Ht.	Wt.	Born	University/ Junior Affiliate	Yrs CFL
*	ADAMS, Stefan	DB	5.10	190	11 AUG 63	East Carolina	1
*	ARMSTRONG, Chris	SB	6.02	200	28 AUG 67	Fayetteville State	3
*	ASHLEY, Tyrone	RB	6.01	210	03 MAY 70	Mississippi	1
*	BATTLE, Greg	LB	6.01	225	14 APR 64	Arizona State	8
*	BELL, Richard	WR	5.11	180	03 MAY 67	Nebraska	1
*	BENSON, Mitchell	DT	6.04	290	30 MAY 67	Texas Christian	1
*	BLUE, Anthony	DB	5.09	190	19 SEP 64	Nevada Las Vegas	1
*	BRICE, Romero	LB	6.03	210		Illinois	1
*	BROADY, Timothy	LB	6.00	215	20 FEB 66	Murray State	1
*	BULLOCK, James	WR	5.10	190		Arizona	1
*	BURCHETTE, Nathan	WR	6.02	190	20 AUG 70	Weber State	1
*	BURSE, Tony	RB	6.00	220	04 APR 65	Middle Tennessee	1
*	CALVILLO, Anthony	QB	6.02	185	23 AUG 72	Utah State	1
*	CAREY, Richard	CB	5.09	185	06 MAY 68	Idaho	1
*	CARRON, Andre	LB	6.00	220	11 SEP 68	Northwestern Louisiana	1
*	CARRUTHERS, Kirk	LB	6.01	225	15 JUL 70	Florida State	1
*	CHEEVERS, Shawn	K	5.10	200	30 SEP 70	Long Beach State	1
*	CLARK, Michael	DB	5.11	188	07 MAR 70	Oklahoma	1
*	CLARK, Waldy Jay	WR	5.11	180	21 APR 69	Boston College	1
*	COBB, Glenn	LB	6.00	200	14 OCT 66	Illinois	2
*	COOK, Lance	DE	6.02	225	02 OCT 60	The Citadel	1
*	CRAWFORD, Cedric	DB	5.09	185		Utah	1
*	DALE, Ron	K	6.03	195		Southern California	1
*	DAVIS, Darrell	LB	6.02	230	10 MAR 66	Texas Christian	1
*	DAVIS, Michael	DE	6.03	250	05 FEB 68	North Texas	1
*	DICKEY, Terry	SB	5.07	170	06 SEP 70	DePauw	2
*	DINZEO, Marcol	DL	6.04	280		St Cloud State	1
*	DUCKENS, Mark	DE	6.04	270	04 MAR 65	Arizona State	1
*	EDMONDS, Bobby Joe	WR	5.11	190	26 SEP 64	Arkansas	1
*	EKONOMOU, Nick	T	6.03	290	03 NOV 67	Florida State	1
*	EZOR, Blake	RB	5.10	185	11 OCT 66	Michigan State	2
*	GARBER, Jon	T	6.03	305	06 SEP 67	Western Washington	2
*	GATLIN, Fred	QB	6.01	176	23 JUN 71	Nevada	1
*	GIBSON, Craig	C	6.03	245	28 MAY 71	Southern California	1
*	GILLETTE, Mike	K	6.00	180	17 MAR 67	Michigan	1
*	GOMES, Len	DL	6.02	260	20 MAY 71	Brigham Young	1
*	GOODE, James	LB	6.04	250	21 JAN 68	Oklahoma	1
*	GOSAR, Peter	LB	6.01	225	29 DEC 69	Wyoming	1
*	GREEDY, Garrett	LB	6.04	245	28 JAN 71	UCLA	1
*	GRISBY, Kevin	DB	6.03	210	24 MAY 68	Bethune-Cookman	1
*	HAGAN, Darian	QB	5.09	190	01 FEB 70	Colorado	2
*	HALL, Danny	DB	6.00	180		McPherson College	1
*	HARDWICK, Jesse	DL	6.05	310	21 JUN 70	Fresno State	1
*	HARRIS, Ike	T	6.04	260	14 DEC 67	South Carolina	1
*	HARRY, Carl	WR	5.09	170	26 OCT 67	Utah	1
*	HART, Roy	DT	6.00	285	10 JUL 65	South Carolina	2
*	HAYNES, Haywood	G	6.03	280	29 JUN 67	Florida State	1
*	HILL, Gavin	LB	6.04	225	09 JUL 70	Arizona State	1
*	HOUSTON, Brandon	T	6.04	290	02 APR 69	Oklahoma	1
*	HUERTA, Carlos	K	5.07	160	29 JUN 69	Miami	1
*	HUFF, Brent	DB	6.01	190		Oregon State	1
*	HUNTER, Bradley	DT	6.06	280	16 AUG 66	Brigham Young	1
*	JEFFERSON, Ben	OL	6.10	315		Maryland	1
*	JOINER, Jim	LB	6.04	215	14 NOV 70	California	1
*	JONES, Claude	G	6.02	290	12 SEP 69	Miami	2
*	JONES, Larry	DL	6.03	295	03 MAR 67	Hawaii	1
*	JORDAN, Al	DB	6.01	185	25 FEB 70	UCLA	1
*	KEEN, Robbie	K	6.05	215	28 AUG 68	California	1
*	KELLY, Maurice	DB	6.00	190		East Tennessee	1
*	KELSON, Derrick	CB	6.00	190	15 MAY 68	Purdue	3
*	LACOMBE, Brad	DL	5.11	240		St Cloud State	1
*	LEGGETT, Brad	C	6.05	270	16 JAN 66	Southern California	1
*	LEWIS, Ernie	LB	6.03	210		East Carolina	1
*	LOOTS, Jeff	QB	6.02	200	19 MAY 70	SW Minnesota	1
*	MARXSON, Herkey	K	5.08	185	04 MAR 68	Southern Utah	1
*	MATTHEWS, Keilan	LB	6.01	220	30 DEC 67	Sacramento State	2
*	MAYFIELD, Curtis	WR	6.00	175	23 MAR 68	Oklahoma State	1
*	McDONALD, Quintus	LB	6.03	240	14 DEC 66	Penn State	1
*	MICKLES, Joe	RB	5.09	225	25 DEC 65	Mississippi	1
*	MIMBS, Robert	RB	6.00	195	06 AUG 64	Kansas	5
*	MITCHEL, Eric	RB	5.11	212	13 FEB 67	Oklahoma	3
*	MODKINS, Curtis	RB	5.08	185	15 NOV 70	Texas Christian	1
*	MONROE, Stacy	LB	6.01	215	23 OCT 68	Nevada Las Vegas	1
*	NAPOLEON, Eugene	RB	5.10	176	17 FEB 66	West Virginia	1
*	NEE, John	OL	6.06	300	21 NOV 67	Elon College	1
*	NICHOLSON, Calvin	DB	5.11	187	09 JUL 67	Oregon State	1
*	OBERDORF, Todd	OL	6.05	305	21 JAN 67	Indiana	1
*	PARVIN, Brian	K	5.10	170	18 SEP 71	Nevada Las Vegas	1
*	PESEK, Jim	T	6.04	295	28 OCT 69	Illinois	1
*	PLUMMER, Bruce	DB	6.01	195	01 SEP 64	Mississippi State	3
*	PORTER, Charles	DB	6.02	200		Texas A&I	1
*	PROCTOR, Basil	LB	6.04	245	06 OCT 67	West Virginia	3
*	RAY, Corey	WR	5.09	180		Northern Illinois	1
*	RAY, Darryl	DB				Georgia Tech	1
*	REED, Clifford	WR	6.04	215		New Mexico State	1
*	REED, Roderick	LB	6.02	230	27 APR 68	Southern Mississippi	1
*	RENTIE, Caesar	T	6.03	290	10 NOV 64	Oklahoma	1
*	REX, Byron	TE	6.02	230		Brigham Young	1
*	RICHARDS, James	T	6.04	290	07 NOV 69	California	1
*	RIX, Zachary	DT	6.02	250	10 DEC 70	Fresno State	1
*	ROBERTS, Kenny	WR	5.08	170	27 NOV 63	Mississippi State	1
*	ROBERTSON, Derrell	DE	6.06	270	22 SEP 67	Mississippi State	1
*	ROBINSON, Stacey	DB	6.00	190		Northern Illinois	1
*	ROBINSON, William	QB	6.01	185	31 MAR 70	Mississippi State	1
*	ROBINSON, Zedrick	RB	5.09	180	19 FEB 71	Southern Utah	1
*	ROSS, Scott	LB	6.03	225	07 DEC 68	Southern California	1
*	SALTZ, Lee	QB	6.01	210	25 SEP 63	Temple	4
*	SARGENT, Tony	DB	5.10	185	01 DEC 66	Miami	1
*	SAWYER, Jeff	LB	6.03	235	13 APR 70	Memphis State	1
*	SERFAS, Nick	DE	6.04	245	27 OCT 69	Fresno State	1
*	SHEPARD, Derrick	WR	5.10	190	22 JAN 64	Oklahoma	1
*	SILEO, Dan	DT	6.01	280	03 MAR 66	Miami	1
*	SIMS, Travis	RB	5.10	225	28 JAN 70	Hawaii	1
*	SITALA, Time	OL	6.02	290	27 JUN 71	Long Beach City	1
*	SLACK, Ron	RB	5.11	205	07 DEC 67	San Diego State	1
*	STEELE, Norman	DL	6.06	245	18 JUN 70	New Mexico State	1
*	TAGOIA, Junior	LB	6.01	215		Hawaii	1
*	TAYLOR, Preston	LB	6.02	225		Cameron	1
*	TAYLOR, Treamelle	WR	5.10	180	08 NOV 69	Nevada	2
*	TEZENO, Quinton	DB	5.11	205		New Mexico State	1
*	THOMPSON, Larry	WR	5.11	170	25 MAY 71	Solano College	2
*	TUCKER, Greg	LB	6.01	220	23 DEC 68	Northern Colorado	1
*	VANOVER, Tamarick	WR	6.01	215	25 FEB 74	Florida State	1
*	VERDUZCO, Jason	QB	5.09	190	03 APR 70	Illinois	2
*	VINES, Ken	C	6.05	290	03 MAY 67	Ohio Central	1
*	WAGNER, Steve	T	6.07	310	02 MAY 70	Delaware Valley	1
*	WALKER, Adrian	RB	5.11	200		Texas	1
*	WIMBLEY, Prince	WR	5.09	175	22 SEP 70	Alabama	1
*	WINTERS, Scott	DB	6.00	180	29 MAR 71	SW Baptist	1
*	WOODS, Thomas	WR	5.10	185	21 FEB 65	Tennessee	1
*	WRIGHT, T C	RB	5.10	170		San Jose State	1

Commissioner Smith with Owner Nick Mileti
CFL CARAVAN '94

1994 CFL DRAFT - MARCH 5, VANCOUVER, B.C.

BAILEY

BURNS

CAREY

DANIELSEN

PHILION

ST. GERMAIN

BONUS ROUND*

NO.	CLUB	PLAYER	POS.	SCHOOL
1.	HAMILTON	Val St. Germain	OL	McGill University
2.	SASKATCHEWAN	Chris Burns	OT	Portland State University
3.	CALGARY	Vince Danielsen	WR	U of British Columbia
4.	WINNIPEG	Ryan Carey	DB	Acadia University

FIRST ROUND

NO.	CLUB	PLAYER	POS.	SCHOOL
5.	OTTAWA	Tony Bailey	DE	Saint Mary's University
6.	B.C.	Trevor Shaw	WR	Weber State University
	(acquired from Toronto)			
7.	OTTAWA	Rod Murphy	LB	Idaho State University
8.	CALGARY	John Kalin	DB/QB	University of Calgary
	(acquired from Hamilton)			
9.	B.C.	Stefan Ptasek	WR	Wilfrid Laurier University
10.	SASKATCHEWAN	Matthiew Quiviger	OT	McGill University
11.	CALGARY	Ed Philion	DL	Ferris State University
12.	WINNIPEG	Mitch Berger	P/K	University of Colorado
13.	EDMONTON	Rob Wessling	OT	University of Guelph

SECOND ROUND

NO.	CLUB	PLAYER	POS.	SCHOOL
14.	TORONTO	Claudio Berton	FB	Lehigh University
15.	OTTAWA	Mike Malott	RB	University of Waterloo
16.	HAMILTON	Jeremy Braitenback	WR	U. of Saskatchewan
17.	B.C.	Mike Morreale	WR	McMaster University
18.	SASKATCHEWAN	Andrew Greene	OL	University of Indiana
19.	CALGARY	Phil Yeboah-Kodie	LB	Penn State University
20.	WINNIPEG	Ken Browne	OL	University of Colorado
21.	EDMONTON	Pat McNerney	TE/OL	Weber State University

THIRD ROUND

NO.	CLUB	PLAYER	POS.	SCHOOL
22.	TORONTO	Mike Campbell	OT	Idaho State University
23.	OTTAWA	Glenn McCausland	WR	University of Toronto
24.	HAMILTON	Ainsworth Morgan	WR	University of Toledo
25.	B.C.	Mike Bromilow	DT	Simon Fraser University
26.	CALGARY	Ken Rayner	OL	Weber State University
	(acquired from Saskatchewan)			
27.	CALGARY	Craig Brenner	SB/FB	Wilfrid Laurier University
28.	HAMILTON	Tim Tindale	FB	U. of Western Ontario
	(acquired from Winnipeg)			
29.	EDMONTON	Darryl Fridd	DL	University of Alberta

FOURTH ROUND

NO.	CLUB	PLAYER	POS.	SCHOOL
30.	TORONTO	Dave Irwin	WR	University of Guelph
31.	OTTAWA	Obie Spanic	DT	Weber State University
32.	HAMILTON	Chris Harris	CB	Simon Fraser University
	B.C.	(choice forfeited in 1993 supplemental draft)		
33.	SASKATCHEWAN	Andrew Walters	DB	U. of British Columbia
34.	CALGARY	Jay McNeil	OL	Kent State University
35.	WINNIPEG	Ed Kucy	OG	University of Arizona
36.	EDMONTON	Brad Zacharias	RB	Acadia University

FIFTH ROUND

NO.	CLUB	PLAYER	POS.	SCHOOL
37.	TORONTO	Jamie Bennett	DT	Fresno State University
	OTTAWA	(choice forfeited in 1993 supplemental draft)		
38.	HAMILTON	Michael Cheevers	LB	Wilfrid Laurier University
39.	B.C.	Paul Blackwood	FB	University of Cincinnati
40.	SASKATCHEWAN	Tony Tighe	OL	Edinboro U. -Penn
41.	CALGARY	Roger Reinson	LB	University of Calgary
42.	WINNIPEG	Kevin Robson	OL	University of N. Dakota
43.	EDMONTON	Stephen Day	LB	University of Alberta

SIXTH ROUND

NO.	CLUB	PLAYER	POS.	SCHOOL
44.	TORONTO	Norm Casola	WR	University of Windsor
	OTTAWA	(choice forfeited in 1993 supplemental draft)		
45.	HAMILTON	Geoff Nichol	LB	Colgate University
46.	B.C.	Paul Zuccato	LB	Simon Fraser University
47.	SASKATCHEWAN	Paul Kozan	RB	Queen's University
48.	CALGARY	Cooper Harris	LB	Pitt State University
49.	WINNIPEG	Scott Mitchell	QB	University of Toronto
	EDMONTON	(choice forfeited in 1993 supplemental draft)		

SCHOOL-BY-SCHOOL BREAKDOWN

School	No.	School	No.
Acadia	2	McMaster	1
Alberta	2	North Dakota	1
Arizona	1	Penn State	1
British Columbia	2	Pitt	1
Calgary	2	Portland State	1
Cincinnati	1	Queen's	1
Colgate	1	Saint Mary's	1
Colorado	2	Saskatchewan	1
Edinboro - Pennsylvania	1	Simon Fraser	3
Ferris State	1	Toledo	1
Fresno State	1	Toronto	2
Guelph	2	Waterloo	1
Idaho State	2	Weber State	4
Indiana	1	Western Ontario	1
Kent State	1	Wilfrid Laurier	3
Lehigh	1	Windsor	1
McGill	2		49

PLAYER POSITION BREAKDOWN

Position	No.	Position	No.
Offensive Linemen	13	Linebackers	8
Defensive Linemen	6	Slotbacks	1
Wide Receivers	9	Quarterbacks	1
Defensive Backs	4	Full Backs	3
Punters/Kickers	1		49
Running Backs	3		

VANIER CUP CHAMPIONS
(CANADIAN INTERCOLLEGIATE ATHLETIC UNION CHAMPIONS)

1993 - Toronto
1992 - Queen's
1991 - Wilfrid Laurier
1990 - Saskatchewan
1989 - Western
1988 - Calgary
1987 - McGill
1986 - UBC
1985 - Calgary
1984 - Guelph
1983 - Calgary
1982 - UBC
1981 - Acadia
1980 - Alberta
1979 - Acadia
1978 - Queen's
1977 - Western
1976 - Western
1975 - Ottawa
1974 - Western
1973 - St. Mary's
1972 - Alberta
1971 - Western
1970 - Manitoba
1969 - Manitoba
1968 - Queen's
1967 - Alberta
1966 - St. Francis Xavier
1965 - Toronto

*** Bonus round is awarded by the Commissioner to those clubs who have complied with the competitive Expenditure Cap.**

EAST VS. WEST INTERLOCKING SCHEDULE RESULTS

YEAR-BY-YEAR

	EAST				WEST			
	GP	W	L	T	GP	W	L	T
1961	20	11	7	2	20	7	11	2
1962	20	7	12	1	20	12	7	1
1963	20	10	10	0	20	10	10	0
1964	20	10	8	2	20	8	10	2
1965	20	7	13	0	20	13	7	0
1966	20	13	7	0	20	7	13	0
1967	20	9	11	0	20	11	9	0
1968	20	11	8	1	20	8	11	1
1969	20	14	5	1	20	5	14	1
1970	20	12	8	0	20	8	12	0
1971	20	11	9	0	20	9	11	0
1972	20	11	9	0	20	9	11	0
1973	20	13	6	1	20	6	13	1
1974	20	8	11	1	20	11	8	1
1975	20	7	10	3	20	10	7	3
1976	20	10	9	1	20	9	10	1
1977	20	8	12	0	20	12	8	0
1978	20	6	12	2	20	12	6	2
1979	20	9	10	1	20	10	9	1
1980	20	7	12	1	20	12	7	1
1981	40	9	30	1	40	30	9	1
1982	40	12	26	2	40	26	12	2
1983	40	18	22	0	40	22	18	0
1984	40	13	24	3	40	24	13	3
1985	40	17	23	0	40	23	17	0
1986	40	10	28	2	40	28	10	2
1987	38	16	21	1	38	21	16	1
1988	36	16	20	0	36	20	16	0
1989	32	10	22	0	32	22	10	0
1990	32	15	17	0	32	17	15	0
1991	32	12	20	0	32	20	12	0
1992	32	17	15	0	32	15	17	0
1993	40	11	29	0	40	29	11	0

TOTALS AS OF 1993:

Games Played - 882
East wins/West losses - 370
West wins/East losses - 486
Ties - 26
Points for East/Against West - 19,853
Points for West/Against East - 22,293

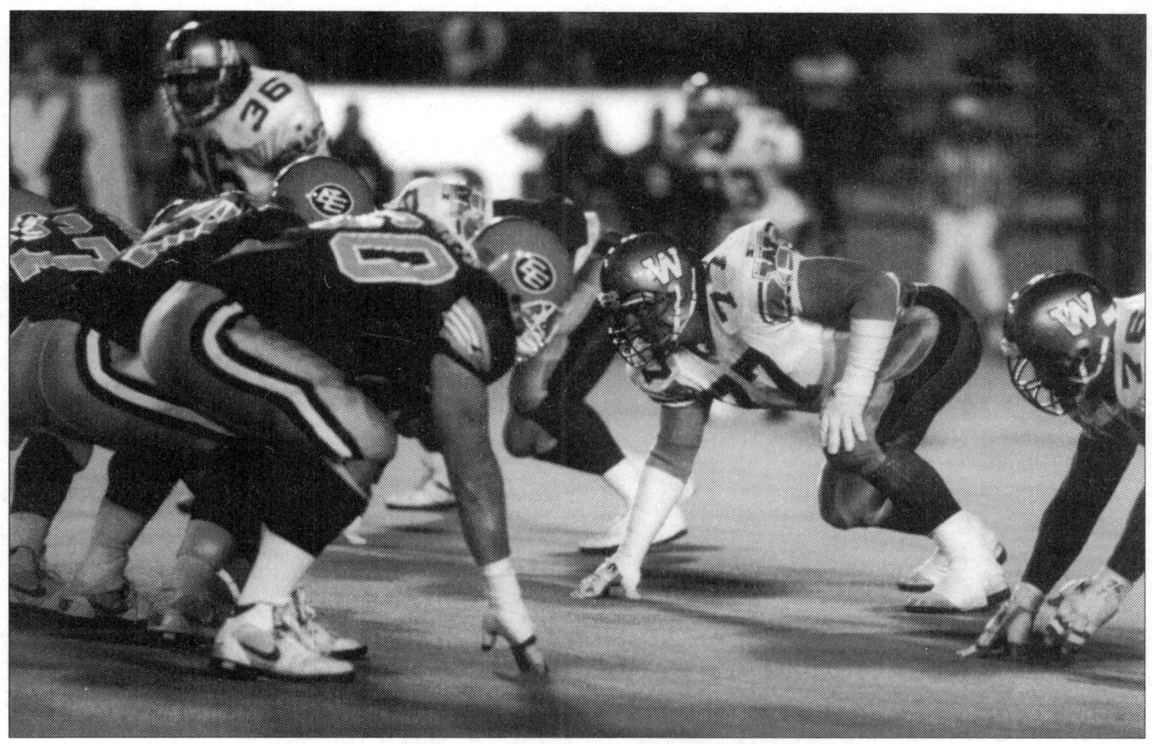

Grey Cup '93 Winnipeg vs. Edmonton
November 28, 1993 - McMahon Stadium

CFL CARAVAN '94

CFL CARAVAN '94 AND THE MONTREAL EXPOS

CFL CARAVAN '94 IN BALTIMORE, MARYLAND

CFL CARAVAN '94 IN SACRAMENTO, CALIFORNIA

1994 PLAYER PROFILES

NOTE: The 1994 Player Register lists all players that are on a Club's active roster, or were on a 1993 Final CFL Roster. Trades and roster changes are current as of April 15, 1994.

Abbreviations: ATT - Attempts; **AVE** - Average; **C** - Convert; **COMP** - Completions; **FG**-Field Goal; **G** -Good; **GP**-Games Played; **INT**-Interceptions; **L**-Lost; **LG** -Longest; **LK**- Longest Kick; **LR** - Longest Return; **NO** - Number; **OFR**-Own Fumbles Recovered; **P**- Punt; **PCT**-Percentage; **QB Sacks**-Quarterback Sacks; **S**-Single; **T**- Tried; **TB**-Total Blocked; **TC**-Total Carries; **TD**-Touchdown; **TP**-Total Points; **X**-2-point convert; **YDS**-Yards.

ALEXANDER, RAY

Born: January 8, 1962
Birthplace: Miami, Florida
Wide Receiver. 6'4", 205 lbs. Import
Last Amateur Club: Florida A & M University
Acquired: Selected by Tampa Bay in the 1984 USFL Territorial Draft. Signed as a free agent by the NFL Denver Broncos in May, 1984. Released in September, 1984. Signed as a free agent by the Calgary Stampeders in September, 1985. Signed as a free agent by the NFL Dallas Cowboys in March, 1987 and was released in 1989. Signed as a free agent by the B.C. Lions in March, 1990. Released in June, 1992. Re-signed by B.C. in August, 1992.

	Scoring						Pass Receiving					Fumbles	
	Team	**GP**	**TD**	**C**	**FG**	**S**	**TP**	**NO**	**YDS**	**AVE**	**LG**	**TD**	**NO**	**LOST**
1985	Cal.	8	1	0	0	0	6	22	361	16.4	44	1	1	1
1986a	Cal.	18	10	x1	0	0	62	88	1590	18.1	59	10	3	1
1987			NFL							NFL				NFL
1988			NFL							NFL				NFL
1989			NFL							NFL				NFL
1990a	B.C.	15	9	0	0	0	54	65	1120	17.2	44	9	1	1
1991ab	B.C.	16	3	0	0	0	18	104	1650	15.4	31	3	1	1
1992	B.C.	10	2	0	0	0	12	56	786	14.0	44	2	3	3
1993	B.C.	15	4	0	0	0	24	77	1300	16.9	43	4	0	0
CFL TOTALS		**82**	**29**	**x1**	**0**	**0**	**176**	**412**	**6762**	**16.4**	**59**	**29**	**9**	**7**

Rushing - 1 for 5 yards with B.C. in 1992.
CFL Total Rushing - 1 for - 5 yards.

Blocked Kicks - 1 Field Goal with B.C. in 1993.
CFL Total Blocked Kicks - 1 (1 Field Goal).

Passing - 1 attempt, 1 made for 26 yards with B.C. in 1991.
CFL Total Passing - 1 attempt, 1 made for 26 yards.

Own Fumbles Recovered - 1 with B.C. in 1993.
CFL Total OFR - 1.

Defensive Tackles - 2 with B.C. in 1990; 1 in 1991 and 1 in 1992.
CFL Total Defensive Tackles - 4.

a - All-Western All-Star.
b - CFL All-Star

Playoffs

Games Played - 1 with Calgary in 1986; 1 with B.C. in 1991 and 1 with B.C. in 1993
CFL Total Playoff GP - 3

Pass Receiving - 4 for 63 yards, 15.8 average, longest 18 yards with Calgary in 1986; 7 for 132 yards, 18.9 average, longest 42 yards with B.C. in 1991 and 5 for 61 yards, 12.2 average, longest 18 yards with B.C. in 1993.
CFL Total Playoff Pass Receiving - 16 for 256 yards, 16.0 average, longest 42 yards.

ALLEN, DAMON

Born: July 29, 1963
Birthplace: San Diego, California
Quarterback. 6'0". 170 lbs. Import
Last Amateur Club: Cal State University at Fullerton
Acquired: Signed as a free agent by the Edmonton Eskimos in May, 1985. Signed as a free agent by the Ottawa Rough Riders in March, 1989. Granted free agency status, February 15, 1992. Signed as a free agent by the Hamilton Tiger-Cats in May, 1992. Traded to Edmonton in February, 1993 in exchange for quarterback De Chane Cameron, linebacker DeWayne Odom, linebacker Michael O'Shea and the negotiation list rights to linebacker William Freeney.

	Scoring						Rushing				
	Team	**GP**	**TD**	**C**	**FG**	**S**	**TP**	**NO**	**YDS**	**AVE**	**LG**	**TD**
1985	Edm.	16	5	0	0	0	30	36	190	5.3	18	5
1986	Edm.	18	6	0	0	0	36	31	245	7.9	39	6
1987	Edm.	18	6	0	0	0	36	66	562	8.5	40	6
1988	Edm.	10	1	0	0	0	6	33	130	3.9	13	1
1989	Ott.	13	1	x1	0	0	8	75	532	7.1	51	1
1990	Ott.	17	7	0	0	0	42	124	776	6.3	41	7
1991a	Ott.	18	8	x1	0	0	50	129	1036	8.0	42	8
1992	Ham.	18	7	0	0	0	42	111	850	7.7	37	7
1993	Edm.	18	6	0	0	0	36	120	920	7.7	43	6
CFL TOTALS		**146**	**47**	**x2**	**0**	**0**	**286**	**725**	**5241**	**7.2**	**51**	**47**

	Passing								Fumbles		
	Team	**ATT**	**COMP**	**YDS**	**PCT**	**INT**	**LG**	**TD**	**NO**	**LOST**	**OFR**
1985	Edm.	98	48	661	49.0	3	54	3	3	0	3
1986	Edm.	87	49	878	56.3	3	75	8	2	1	0
1987	Edm.	287	150	2670	52.3	13	97	17	8	6	3
1988	Edm.	218	94	1309	43.1	12	44	4	5	4	0
1989	Ott.	434	209	3093	48.2	16	78	17	7	5	1
1990	Ott.	528	276	3883	52.3	23	74	34	9	3	3
1991a	Ott.	546	282	4275	51.6	31	70	24	6	2	1
1992	Ham.	523	266	3858	50.9	14	82	19	18	8	6
1993	Edm.	400	214	3394	53.5	10	102	25	8	4	1
CFL TOTALS		**3121**	**1588**	**24021**	**50.9**	**125**	**102**	**151**	**66**	**33**	**18**

2-Pt Converts - 1 attempt, 0 complete with Edmonton in 1986; 1 attempt, 0 complete in 1987; 1 attempt, 1 complete in 1988; 6 attempts, 2 complete, 1 made good with Ottawa in 1989; 4 attempts, 0 complete in 1990 and 4 attempts, 2 complete, 1 made good in 1991. **CFL Total 2-Pt. Converts - 17 attempts, 5 complete, 2 made good.**

Fumble Returns - 1 for 0 yards with Hamilton in 1992.
CFL Total Fumble Returns - 1 for 0 yards.

Tackles - 1 defensive with Edmonton in 1987; 4 defensive with Ottawa in 1989; 2 defensive in 1990; 2 defensive in 1991; 1 special teams with Hamilton in 1992 and 1 defensive with Edmonton in 1993.
CFL Total Tackles - 11 (10 defensive and 1 special teams)

a - All-Eastern All-Star

Playoffs

	Scoring						Rushing				
	Team	**GP**	**TD**	**C**	**FG**	**S**	**TP**	**NO**	**YDS**	**AVE**	**LG**	**TD**
1985	Edm.	1	1	0	0	0	6	9	44	4.9	13	1
1986	Edm.	2	0	0	0	0	0	4	33	8.3	15	0
1987	Edm.	2	0	0	0	0	0	0	0	0.0	0	0
1988	Edm.	1	0	0	0	0	0	0	0	0.0	0	0
1990	Ott.	1	1	0	0	0	6	10	84	8.4	32	1
1991	Ott.	1	0	0	0	0	0	7	34	4.9	17	0
1992	Ham.	2	0	0	0	0	0	9	35	3.9	17	0
1993	Edm.	2	0	0	0	0	0	12	116	9.7	23	0
CFL TOTALS		**12**	**2**	**0**	**0**	**0**	**12**	**51**	**346**	**6.8**	**32**	**2**

	Fumbles			Passing						
	Team	**NO**	**LOST**	**OFR**	**ATT**	**COMP**	**YDS**	**PCT**	**INT**	**LG**	**TD**
1985	Edm.	1	1	0	29	11	156	37.9	2	32	0
1986	Edm.	0	0	0	7	2	42	28.6	0	29	0
1987	Edm.	0	0	0	0	0	0	0.0	0	0	0
1988	Edm.	0	0	0	0	0	0	0.0	0	0	0
1990	Ott.	0	0	0	35	20	326	57.1	1	62	1
1991	Ott.	3	2	1	31	15	150	48.4	2	21	1
1992	Ham.	3	2	1	47	22	312	46.0	6	40	2
1993	Edm.	1	0	1	43	23	444	53.5	1	73	7
CFL TOTALS		**8**	**5**	**3**	**192**	**93**	**1430**	**48.4**	**12**	**73**	**11**

Grey Cup

	Scoring						Rushing					Fumbles		
	Team	**GP**	**TD**	**C**	**FG**	**S**	**TP**	**NO**	**YDS**	**AVE**	**LG**	**TD**	**NO**	**LOST**	**OFR**
1986	Edm.	1	1	x1	0	0	8	4	20	5.0	6	1	1	1	0
1987	Edm.	1	1	0	0	0	6	6	46	7.7	17	1	2	1	1
1993	Edm.	1	0	0	0	0	0	14	90	6.4	17	0	1	0	1
CFL TOTALS		**3**	**2**	**x1**	**0**	**0**	**14**	**24**	**156**	**6.5**	**17**	**2**	**4**	**2**	**2**

	Passing								2-Pt. Converts		
	Team	**ATT**	**COMP**	**YDS**	**PCT**	**INT**	**LG**	**TD**	**TRIED**	**GOOD**	**PCT**
1986	Edm.	12	7	128	58.3	1	39	1	1	1	100.0
1987	Edm.	20	15	225	75.0	0	39	2	0	0	0.0
1993	Edm.	29	17	226	58.6	1	52	1	0	0	0.0
CFL TOTALS		**61**	**39**	**609**	**63.9**	**2**	**52**	**4**	**1**	**1**	**100.0**

Tackles - 1 defensive with Edmonton in 1993.
Grey Cup Tackles - 1 (1 defensive)

Grey Cup Game Offensive Star in 1987.
Grey Cup MVP in 1993.

ALLEN, MICHAEL

Born: August 1, 1964
Birthplace: Clarendon, Jamaica
Defensive Back. 5'11", 165 lbs. Non-import
Last Amateur Club: Carleton University (OQIFC)
Acquired: Selected in the fourth round (29th overall) by the Winnipeg Blue Bombers in the 1988 CFL College Draft. Traded to the Ottawa Rough Riders in June, 1992 in exchange for offensive lineman Brett MacNeil. Traded to the B.C. Lions in August, 1993 in exchange for defensive back Burtland Cummings. Granted free agency status on February 15, 1994.

ALLEN, MICHAEL

		Scoring						Punt Returns				
	Team	GP	TD	C	FG	S	TP	NO	YDS	AVE	LG	TD
1988	Wpg.	17	3	0	0	0	18	1	3	3.0	3	0
1989	Wpg.	16	1	0	0	0	6	0	0	0.0	0	0
1990	Wpg.	18	0	0	0	0	0	1	20	20.0	20	0
1991a	Wpg.	12	1	0	0	0	6	0	0	0.0	0	0
1992	Ott.	18	0	0	0	0	0	0	0	0.0	0	0
1993	Ott.	5	0	0	0	0	0	0	0	0.0	0	0
	B.C.	9	0	0	0	0	0	0	0	0.0	0	0
CFL TOTALS		**95**	**5**	**0**	**0**	**0**	**30**	**2**	**23**	**11.5**	**20**	**0**

		Kickoff Returns					Fumble Returns				
	Team	NO	YDS	AVE	LG	TD	NO	YDS	AVE	LG	TD
1988	Wpg.	13	241	18.5	37	0	4	66	16.5	35	3
1989	Wpg.	0	0	0.0	0	0	2	7	3.5	7	1
1990	Wpg.	0	0	0.0	0	0	0	0	0.0	0	0
1991	Wpg.	2	44	22.0	24	0	1	43	43.0	43	1
1992	Ott.	1	5	5.0	5	0	0	0	0.0	0	0
1993	Ott.	0	0	0.0	0	0	0	0	0.0	0	0
	B.C.	0	0	0.0	0	0	0	0	0.0	0	0
CFL TOTALS		**16**	**290**	**18.1**	**37**	**0**	**7**	**116**	**16.6**	**43**	**5**

Own Fumbles Recovered - 1 with Winnipeg in 1991. **CFL Total OFR - 1**

Interception Returns - 2 for 25 yards, 12.5 average, longest 16 yards with Winnipeg in 1989 and 1 for 37 yards in 1991. **CFL Total Interception Returns - 3 for 62 yards, 20.7 average, longest 37 yards.**

Quarterback Sacks - 1 with Winnipeg in 1991. **CFL Total QB Sacks - 1.**

Tackles - 27 defensive with Winnipeg in 1989; 4 defensive in 1990; 22 defensive and 16 special teams in 1991; 1 defensive and 18 special teams with Ottawa in 1992; 9 defensive and 2 special teams with Ottawa and 4 defensive and 4 special teams with B.C. in 1993. **CFL Total Tackles - 107 (67 defensive and 40 special teams).**

a - Set CFL Record for Most Career Fumble Return TDs.

Playoffs

Games Played - 1 with Winnipeg 1988; 2 in 1989; 1 in 1990; 2 in 1991; 1 with Ottawa in 1992 and 1 with B.C. in 1993. **CFL Total Playoff GP - 8**

Blocked Kicks - 1 punt with Winnipeg in 1989
CFL Total Playoff Blocked Kicks - 1 punt.

Tackles - 4 defensive and 2 special teams with Winnipeg in 1991; 1 defensive and 1 special teams with Ottawa in 1992 and 1 defensive and 1 special teams with B.C. in 1993. **CFL Total Playoff Tackles - 10 (6 defensive and 4 special teams).**

Grey Cup

Games Played - 1 with Winnipeg in 1988 and 1 in 1990. **Total Grey Cup GP - 2.**

Defensive Tackles - 1 with Winnipeg in 1990
Total Grey Cup Defensive Tackles - 1.

ALLEN, ZOCK

Born: June 12, 1968
Birthplace: Madisonville, Texas
Linebacker. 6'1", 220 lbs. Import
Last Amateur Club: Texas A & I University
Acquired: Signed by the B.C. Lions as a free agent in May, 1991. Released by B.C. in August, 1991. Re-signed by B.C. in March, 1992

Games Played - 6 with B.C. in 1991; 3 in 1992 and 15 in 1993. **CFL Total GP - 24.**

Fumble Returns - 1 for 0 yards with B.C. in 1991 and 1 for 1 yard in 1993.
CFL Total Fumble Returns - 2 for 1 yard.

Quarterback Sacks - 2 with B.C. in 1991 and 2 for 11 yards lost in 1993.
CFL Total QB Sacks - 4 for 11 yards lost.

Tackles - 24 defensive and 7 special teams with B.C. in 1991; 11 defensive and 2 special teams in 1992 and 59 defensive and 8 special teams in 1993.
CFL Total Tackles - 111 (94 defensive and 17 special teams).

Tackles for Losses - 2 for 3 yards with B.C. in 1991 and 5 for 11 yards in 1993.
CFL Total Tackles for Losses - 7 for 14 yards.

Playoffs

Games Played - 1 with B.C. in 1993. **CFL Total Playoff GP - 1.**

Fumble Returns - 1 for 0 yards with B.C. in 1993.
CFL Total Playoff Fumble Returns - 1 for 0 yards.

Tackles - 4 defensive with B.C. in 1993.
CFL Total Playoff Tackles - 4 (4 defensive).

ALPHIN, GERALD

Born: May 21, 1964
Birthplace: Portland, Oregon
Wide Receiver. 6'3", 211 lbs, Import
Last Amateur Club: Kansas State University
Acquired: Signed as a free agent by the NFL Los Angles Raiders in May, 1986. Released by Los Angeles in August, 1986. Signed as a free agent by the Montreal Alouettes in September 1986. Signed as a free agent by Ottawa Rough Riders in June, 1987. Granted free agency status in March, 1990. Signed as a free agent by the NFL New Orleans Saints in March, 1990. Released by New Orleans in October, 1991. Signed as a free agent by the NFL Dallas Cowboys in March, 1992. Released by Dallas following training camp in 1992 and signed as a free agent by the Winnipeg Blue Bombers in September 1992.

		Scoring						Pass Receiving					Fumbles	
	Team	GP	TD	C	FG	S	TP	NO	YDS	AVE	LG	TD	NO	LOST
1986	Mtl.	6	2	0	0	0	12	20	409	20.5	55	2	1	1
1987	Ott.	14	8	0	0	0	48	67	1029	15.4	57	8	4	4
1988a	Ott.	15	5	x1	0	0	32	64	1307	20.4	61	5	2	2
1989	Ott.	17	10	0	0	0	60	68	1471	21.6	78	10	0	0
1990			NFL						NFL					
1991			NFL						NFL					
1992	Wpg.	9	2	0	0	0	12	26	507	19.5	73	2	0	0
1993	Wpg.	16	4	0	0	0	24	55	1052	19.1	54	4	2	2
CFL TOTALS		**77**	**31**	**x1**	**0**	**0**	**188**	**300**	**5775**	**19.3**	**132**	**31**	**9**	**9**

		Rushing					Passing						
	Team	NO	YDS	AVE	LG	TD	ATT	COMP	YDS	PCT	INT	LG	TD
1987	Ott.	4	12	3.0	9	0	1	1	14	100.0	0	14	0
1988a	Ott.	1	-2	-2.0	-2	0	0	0	0	0.0	0	0	0
1989	Ott.	3	9	3.0	14	0	1	1	14	100.0	0	14	1
1990				NFL					NFL				
1991				NFL					NFL				
1992	Wpg.	0	0	0.0	0	0	0	0	0	0.0	0	0	0
1993	Wpg.	0	0	0.0	0	0	1	1	28	100.0	0	28	0
CFL TOTALS		**8**	**19**	**2.4**	**14**	**0**	**3**	**3**	**56**	**100.0**	**0**	**28**	**1**

Kickoff Returns - 10 for 189 yards, 18.9 average, longest 32 yards with Ottawa in 1987 and 1 for 0 yards with Winnipeg in 1993.
CFL Total Kickoff Returns - 11 for 189 yards, 17.2 average, longest 32 yards.

Defensive Tackles- 2 with Ottawa in 1987; 4 in 1989; 3 with Winnipeg in 1992 and 2 with Winnipeg in 1993.
CFL Total Defensive Tackles - 11

a - All-Eastern All-Star

Playoffs

		Scoring						Pass Receiving					Fumbles	
	Team	GP	TD	C	FG	S	TP	NO	YDS	AVE	LG	TD	NO	LOST
1992	Wpg.	1	1	0	0	0	6	2	49	24.5	30	1	0	0
1993	Wpg.	1	0	0	0	0	0	2	24	12.0	13	0	1	1
CFL TOTALS		**2**	**1**	**0**	**0**	**0**	**6**	**4**	**73**	**18.3**	**30**	**1**	**1**	**1**

Grey Cup

		Scoring						Pass Receiving				
	Team	GP	TD	C	FG	S	TP	NO	YDS	AVE	LG	TD
1992	Wpg.	1	1	0	0	0	6	5	103	20.6	36	1
1993	Wpg.	1	0	0	0	0	0	3	55	18.3	24	0
CFL TOTALS		**2**	**1**	**0**	**0**	**0**	**6**	**8**	**158**	**19.8**	**36**	**1**

AMBROSIE, RANDY

Born: March 16, 1963
Birthplace: Winnipeg, Manitoba
Guard. 6'4", 260 lbs. Non-import
Last Amateur Club: University of Manitoba (WIFL)
Acquired: Selected in the first round (second overall) by the Calgary Stampeders in the 1985 CFL College Draft. Traded to Toronto Argonauts for the club's second round selection in the 1988 CFL College Draft (wide receiver Wayne Yearwood; 13th overall) in July, 1987. Draft choice was originally traded to Toronto by Winnipeg Blue Bombers for defensive lineman Mark Seale. Traded to Edmonton Eskimos in June, 1989 for defensive tackle Branko Vincic.

Games Played - 13 in 1985 with Calgary; 17 in 1986; 4 in 1987; 13 with Toronto in 1987; 15 in 1988; 18 with Edmonton in 1989; 13 in 1990; 18 in 1991; 18 in 1992 and 13 in 1993. **CFL Total GP - 142.**

Pass Receiving - 1 for 0 yards in 1985 with Calgary.
CFL Total Pass Receiving - 1 for 0 yards.

Kickoff Returns - 1 for 0 yards in 1985 with Calgary and 1 for 0 yards in 1990.
CFL Total Kickoff Returns - 2 for 0 yards.

Own Fumbles Recovered - 1 with Edmonton in 1989 and 1 in 1993.
CFL Total OFR - 2

AMBROSIE, RANDY

Defensive Tackles - 2 with Toronto in 1988; 1 with Edmonton in 1989; 3 in 1990; 1 in 1991 and 1 in 1992. **CFL Total Defensive Tackles - 8.**

Playoffs

Games Played- 1 with Calgary in 1986; 1 with Toronto in 1987; 1 in 1988; 1 with Edmonton in 1989; 1 in 1991; 2 in 1992 and 2 in 1993.
CFL Total Playoff GP - 9

Grey Cup

Games Played - 1 with Toronto in 1987 and 1 with Edmonton in 1993.
Total Grey Cup GP - 2.

ANDERSON, MIKE
Born: August 15, 1961
Birthplace: Regina, Saskatchewan
Offensive Lineman. 6'3", 260 lbs. Non-import
Last Amateur Club: San Diego State University
Acquired: Territorial Exemption by the Saskatchewan Roughriders in 1984. Released by Saskatchewan in February, 1993. Re-signed by Saskatchewan in June, 1993.

Games Played - 9 with Saskatchewan in 1984; 16 in 1985; 18 in 1986; 18 in 1987; 18 in 1988; 18 in 1989; 18 in 1990; 18 in 1991; 18 in 1992 and 18 in 1993.
CFL Total GP - 169.

Fumble Returns - 1 for 0 yards with Saskatchewan in 1985.
CFL Total Fumble Returns - 1 for 0 yards.

Own Fumbles Recovered - 1 with Saskatchewan in 1988 and 1 in 1993.
CFL Total OFR - 2.

Defensive Tackles - 1 with Saskatchewan in 1987; 1 in 1990 and 1 in 1993.
CFL Total Defensive Tackles - 3.

Playoffs

Games Played - 1 with Saskatchewan in 1988; 2 in 1989; 1 in 1990; 1 in 1992 and 1 in 1993. **CFL Total Playoff GP - 6**

Grey Cup

Games Played - 1 with Saskatchewan in 1989.
Total Grey Cup GP - 1.

All-Western All-Star in 1988.

ANDREWS, ROMEL
Born: July 4, 1963
Birthplace: Ripley, Tennessee
Defensive Tackle. 6'5", 255 lbs. Import
Last Amateur Club: University of Tennessee at Martin
Acquired: Signed by the Hamilton Tiger-Cats in 1986. Released by Hamilton in August 1988. Signed as a free agent by Winnipeg Blue Bombers in August, 1988. Granted free agency status in March, 1990. Subsequently signed with the NFL Washington Redskins but was released after Training Camp. Signed with Hamilton as a free agent in September, 1990. Was released by Hamilton in July, 1993 and was re-signed by Hamilton later that month.

Games Played - 4 with Hamilton in 1986; 8 with Winnipeg in 1988; 18 in 1989; 10 with Hamilton in 1990; 12 in 1991; 4 in 1992 and 11 in 1993.
CFL Total GP - 67.

Interception Returns - 0 for 6 yards with Hamilton in 1986.
CFL Total Interception Returns - 0 for 6 yards.

Fumble Returns - 1 for 12 yards with Winnipeg in 1989 and 1 for 0 yards with Hamilton in 1992. **CFL Total Fumble Returns - 2 for 12 yards, 6.0 average, longest 12 yards.**

Quarterback Sacks - 2 with Hamilton in 1986; 2 with Winnipeg in 1988; 9 in 1989; 7 with Hamilton in 1990; 5 in 1991; 1 for 2 yards lost in 1992 and 4 for 30 yards lost in 1993. **CFL Total QB Sacks - 30.**

Tackles - 9 defensive with Hamilton in 1986; 7 defensive with Winnipeg in 1988; 31 defensive in 1989; 18 defensive with Hamilton in 1990; 22 defensive and 2 special teams in 1991; 4 defensive in 1992 and 11 defensive in 1993.
CFL Total Tackles - 104 (102 defensive and 2 special teams).

Tackles for Losses - 4 for 13 yards with Hamilton in 1991; 1 for 3 yards in 1992 and 1 for 3 yards in 1993. **CFL Total Tackles for Losses - 6 for 19 yards.**

Playoffs

Games Played - 2 with Winnipeg in 1988; 2 in 1989 and 2 with Hamilton in 1993.
CFL Total Playoff GP - 6

Quarterback Sacks - 1 with Winnipeg in 1988 and 1 in 1989.
CFL Total Playoff QB Sacks - 2.

Tackles - 4 defensive with Winnipeg in 1988; 3 defensive in 1989 and 5 defensive and 1 special teams with Hamilton in 1993.
CFL Total Playoff Tackles - 13 (12 defensive and 1 special teams).

Tackles for Losses - 1 for 5 yards with Hamilton in 1993.
CFL Total Playoff Tackles for Losses - 1 for 5 yards.

Fumble Returns - 1 for 0 yards with Hamilton in 1993.
CFL Total Playoff Fumble Returns - 1 for 0 yards.

Grey Cup

Games Played - 1 with Winnipeg in 1988. **Total Grey Cup GP - 1.**

Defensive Tackles - 4 with Winnipeg in 1988.
Total Grey Cup Defensive Tackles - 4.

ANTHONY, CHARLES
Born: October 12, 1968
Birthplace: Las Vegas, Nevada
Defensive Back. 6'2", 195 lbs. Import
Last Amateur Club: University of Nevada Las Vegas
Acquired: Signed as a free agent by the Calgary Stampeders in June 1991. Awarded on waivers to the Saskatchewan Roughriders in July, 1992. Was granted free agency status on February 15, 1994.

			Interception Returns					Fumbles		
	Team	GP	NO	YDS	AVE	LG	TD	NO	LOST	OFR
1991	Cal.	2	0	0	0.0	0	0	0	0	0
1992	Sask.	16	3	17	5.7	17	0	1	0	0
1993ab	Sask.	18	5	10	2.0	6	0	0	0	0
CFL TOTALS		**34**	**8**	**27**	**3.4**	**17**	**0**	**1**	**0**	**0**

Scoring - 1 TD for 6 points with Saskatchewan in 1993.
CFL Total Scoring - 1 TD for 6 points.

Fumble Returns - 1 for 0 yards with Saskatchewan in 1992 and 6 for 137 yards, 22.8 average, longest 92 yards and 1 TD**. CFL Total Fumble Returns - 7 for 137 yards, 19.6 average, longest 92 yards and 1 TD.**

Blocked Kicks - 2 with Saskatchewan in 1993.
CFL Total Blocked Kicks - 2.

Tackles - 5 defensive and 3 special teams with Calgary in 1991; 43 defensive and 4 special teams with Saskatchewan in 1992 and 48 defensive and 8 special teams in 1993. **CFL Total Tackles - 111 (96 defensive and 15 special teams).**

Tackles for Losses - 1 for 4 yards with Saskatchewan in 1992 and 1 for 1 yard in 1993. **CFL Total Tackles for Losses - 2 for 5 yards.**

a - Tied for CFL lead in Fumble Returns with 6.
b - Led CFL in Fumble Return Yardage with 137.

Playoffs

Games Played - 1 with Saskatchewan in 1992 and 1 in 1993.
CFL Total Playoff GP - 2.

Tackles - 2 defensive with Saskatchewan in 1992 and 1 defensive and 3 special teams in 1993.
CFL Total Playoff Tackles - 6 (3 defensive and 3 special teams).

ANTHONY, KARL
Born: March 14, 1967
Birthplace: Lafayette, Louisiana
Defensive Back. 5'9", 175 lbs. Import
Last Amateur Club: Southwest Missouri State University
Acquired: Signed as a free agent by the Calgary Stampeders in October, 1990. Granted free agency status in February, 1994.

Games Played - 1 with Calgary in 1990; 15 in 1991; 18 in 1992 and 18 in 1993.
CFL Total GP - 52.

Scoring - 1 TD for 6 points with Calgary in 1992 and 1 TD for 6 points in 1993.
CFL Total Scoring - 2 TDs for 12 points.

Interception Returns - 3 for 83 yards, 27.7 average, longest 51 yards with Calgary in 1991; 5 for 110 yards, 22.0 average, longest 47 yards and 1 TD in 1992 and 6 for 145 yards, 24.2 average, longest 115 yards and 1 TD in 1993.
CFL Total Interception Returns - 14 for 338 yards, 24.1 average, longest 115 yards and 1 TD.

Blocked Kicks - 1 punt with Calgary in 1993.
CFL Total Blocked Kicks - 1 (1 punt).

Fumble Returns - 1 for 0 yards with Calgary in 1991; 1 for 0 yards in 1992 and 1 for 0 yards in 1993. **CFL Total Fumble Returns - 3 for 0 yards.**

Own Fumbles Recovered - 1 with Calgary in 1993.
CFL Total OFR - 1.

Tackles for Losses - 1 for 1 yard with Calgary in 1991 and 1 for 3 yards in 1992.
CFL Total Tackles for Losses - 2 for 4 yards.

ANTHONY, KARL

Tackles - 3 defensive with Calgary in 1990; 37 defensive and 6 special teams in 1991; 48 defensive and 6 special teams in 1992 and 64 defensive and 5 special teams in 1993.
CFL Total Tackles - 169 (152 defensive and 17 special teams).

All-Western All-Star in 1993.
CFL All-Star in 1993.

Playoffs

Games played - 2 with Calgary in 1991; 1 in 1992 and 2 in 1993.
CFL Total Playoff GP - 5.

Tackles - 4 defensive with Calgary in 1991; 1 defensive and 1 special teams in 1992 and 5 defensive in 1993.
CFL Total Playoff Tackles - 11 (10 defensive and 1 special teams).

Grey Cup

Games Played - 1 with Calgary in 1991 and 1 in 1992. **Total Grey Cup GP - 2**

Tackles - 1 defensive with Calgary in 1991.
Total Grey Cup Tackles - 1 (1 defensive).

ARCHER, DAVID
Born: February 15, 1962
Birthplace: Fayetteville, NC
Quarterback. 6'2", 208 lbs., Import
Last Amateur Club: Iowa State
Acquired: Signed as a free agent by the NFL Atlanta Falcons in 1984. Waived by the Falcons in February 1988. Attended Miami Dolphins 1988 training camp and was released during pre-season. Signed as a free agent by the Washington Redskins on September 22, 1988. Was waived by Washington in October. Signed as a free agent by the San Diego Chargers in March, 1989. Was waived by the Chargers in August, 1990. Signed as a free agent by the NFL Philadelphia Eagles on December 12, 1991. Was selected by the Sacramento Surge of the WLAF in the 1992 Supplemental Draft. Returned to the Eagles following the 1992 WLAF Season. Signed as a free agent by the Sacramento Gold Miners in March, 1993.

	Team	GP	Scoring TD	C	FG	S	TP	ATT	Rushing NO	YDS	AVE	LG	TD
1993	Sac.	18	2	0	0	0	12	701	60	287	4.8	18	2
CFL TOTALS		**18**	**2**	**0**	**0**	**0**	**12**	**701**	**60**	**287**	**4.8**	**18**	**2**

	Team	Passing ATT	COMP	YDS	AVE	INT	LG	TD	Fumbles NO	LOST	OFR
1993	Sac.	701	403	6023	57.5	23	90	35	8	3	2
CFL TOTALS		**701**	**403**	**6032**	**57.5**	**23**	**90**	**35**	**8**	**3**	**2**

Own Fumble Recovered - 2 with Sacramento in 1993. **CFL Total OFR - 2.**

AUSTIN, KENT
Born: June 25 1963
Birthplace: Natick, Mississippi
Quarterback. 6'1", 195 lbs. Import
Last Amateur Club: University of Mississippi
Acquired: Signed as a free agent by the Saskatchewan Roughriders in October, 1987. Traded to the Ottawa Rough Riders in exchange for defensive back Anthony Drawhorn, linebacker Ron Goetz and defensive end Paul Yatkowski and was in turn then traded to the B.C. Lions in exchange for quarterback Danny Barrett and defensive back Cory Dowden in March, 1994.

	Team	GP	Scoring TD	C	FG	S	TP	Rushing NO	YDS	AVE	LG	TD
1987	Sask.	5	0	0	0	0	0	24	138	5.8	31	0
1988	Sask.	14	2	0	0	0	12	51	258	5.1	34	2
1989	Sask.	18	3	0	0	0	18	42	168	4.0	18	3
1990abcde	Sask.	16	5	0	0	0	30	50	158	3.2	17	5
1991	Sask.	13	6	0	0	0	36	21	10	0.5	-9	6
1992cdefg	Sask.	18	11	0	0	0	66	71	200	2.8	17	11
1993dh	Sask.	17	7	0	0	0	42	32	88	2.8	21	7
CFL TOTALS		**101**	**34**	**0**	**0**	**0**	**204**	**291**	**1020**	**3.5**	**34**	**34**

	Team	Passing ATT	COMP	YDS	PCT	INT	LG	TD	Fumbles NO	LOST	OFR
1987	Sask.	156	93	1172	59.6	10	51	3	6	3	1
1988	Sask.	277	162	2084	58.5	12	66	8	7	5	2
1989	Sask.	323	183	2650	56.7	12	74	16	4	3	1
1990	Sask.	618	360	4604	58.3	27	107	27	4	2	1
1991	Sask.	554	302	4137	54.5	18	99	32	2	1	1
1992	Sask.	770	459	6225	59.6	30	91	35	4	3	1
1993	Sask.	715	405	5754	56.6	25	78	31	3	2	0
CFL TOTALS		**3413**	**1964**	**26626**	**57.5**	**134**	**107**	**152**	**30**	**19**	**7**

2-Pt. Converts - 1 attempt, 1 complete with Saskatchewan in 1989; 3 attempts, 2 complete in 1990; 3 attempts, 0 complete in 1991 and 5 attempts, 3 complete in 1992. **CFL Total 2-Pt. Converts - 12 attempts, 6 complete.**

Punting - 1 for 39 yards with Saskatchewan in 1990.
CFL Total Punting - 1 for 39 yards.

Defensive Tackles - 1 with Saskatchewan in 1990 and 1 in 1993.
CFL Total Defensive Tackles - 2.

a - All-Western All-Star.
b - CFL All-Star.
c - Led CFL in Passing Yards.
d - Led CFL in Passing Attempts.
e - Led CFL in Passing Completions.
f - Set CFL Record for Most Passes Thrown One Season.
g - Led CFL in Passing TDs.
h - Tied CFL Record for Most Completions in One Game (41).

Playoffs

	Team	GP	Rushing NO	YDS	AVE	LG	TD	Passing ATT	COMP	YDS	PCT	INT	LG	TD
1988	Sask.	1	0	0	0.0	0	0	0	0	0	0.0	0	0	0
1989	Sask.	2	4	25	6.3	12	0	52	29	263	55.8	4	19	1
1990	Sask.	1	0	0	0.0	0	0	35	22	208	62.9	2	48	1
1992	Sask.	1	1	1	1.0	1	0	46	32	468	69.6	1	55	2
1993	Sask.	1	0	0	0.0	0	0	37	26	303	70.3	0	34	1
CFL TOTALS		**6**	**5**	**26**	**5.2**	**12**	**0**	**170**	**109**	**1242**	**64.1**	**7**	**55**	**5**

Fumbles - 1 and 0 lost with Saskatchewan in 1990.
CFL Total Playoff Fumbles - 1 and 0 lost.

Grey Cup

	Team	GP	Rushing NO	YDS	AVE	LG	TD	Passing ATT	COMP	YDS	PCT	INT	LG	TD
1989	Sask.	1	2	8	4.0	6	0	41	26	474	63.4	1	75	3
CFL TOTALS		**1**	**2**	**8**	**4.0**	**6**	**0**	**41**	**26**	**474**	**63.4**	**1**	**75**	**3**

Grey Cup Game Offensive Star in 1989.

BAILEY, DAVID
Born: September 3, 1965
Birthplace: Coatesville, Pennsylvania
Defensive End. 6'4", 265 lbs. Import
Last Amateur Club: Oklahoma State University
Acquired: Signed as a free agent by the NFL Philadelphia Eagles in April, 1989. Released by Philadelphia in December, 1990. Selected in the second round (20th defensive lineman overall) by the San Antonio Riders in the 1991 WLAF Positional Draft. Signed as a free agent by the NFL Kansas City Chiefs in June, 1991. Released by Kansas City during training camp and signed as a free agent by the Hamilton Tiger-Cats in September, 1991. Granted free agency status in February, 1993. Re-signed by the Tiger-Cats in June 1993. Released by Hamilton in October 1993.

Games Played - 9 with Hamilton in 1991; 18 in 1992 and 13 in 1993.
CFL Total GP - 40

Interception Returns - 1 for 3 yards with Hamilton in 1992.
CFL Total Interception Returns - 1 for 3 yards.

Fumble Returns - 2 for 26 yards, 13.0 average, longest 26 yards with Hamilton in 1991; 1 for 11 yards, 11.0 average, longest 6 yards in 1992 and 2 for 1 yard, 0.5 average, longest 1 yard in 1993. **CFL Total Fumble Returns - 5 for 38 yards, 7.6 average, longest 26 yards.**

Quarterback Sacks - 6 with Hamilton in 1991; 6 for 44 yards lost in 1992 and 8 for 53 yards lost in 1993. **CFL Total QB Sacks - 20.**

Tackles - 21 defensive with Hamilton in 1991; 32 defensive and 1 special teams in 1992 and 16 defensive in 1993.
CFL Total Tackles - 70 (69 defensive and 1 special teams).

Tackles for Losses - 4 for 15 yards with Hamilton in 1992 and 2 for 5 yards in 1993.
CFL Total Tackles for Losses - 6 for 20 yards.

Playoffs

Games Played - 2 with Hamilton in 1992.
CFL Total Playoff GP - 2.

Fumble Returns - 1 for 0 yards with Hamilton in 1992.
CFL Total Playoff Fumble Returns - 1 for 0 yards.

Tackles - 9 defensive with Hamilton in 1992.
CFL Total Playoff Tackles - 9 (9 defensive).

BAILEY, WALTER
Born: March 16, 1970
Birthplace: Portland, Oregon
Defensive Back. 5'11", 195 lbs. Import
Last Amateur Club: University of Washington
Acquired: Signed as a free agent by the Sacramento Gold Miners in July, 1993. Traded to the Edmonton Eskimos in exchange for defensive back Doug Parrish in March, 1994.

	Team	GP	Interception Returns NO	YDS	AVE	LG	TD	Fumbles NO	LOST	OFR
1993	Sac.	15	2	29	14.5	29	0	1	0	1
CFL TOTALS		**15**	**2**	**29**	**14.5**	**29**	**0**	**1**	**0**	**1**

BAILEY, WALTER

		Kickoff Returns					Fumble Returns				
	Team	NO	YDS	AVE	LG	TD	NO	YDS	AVE	LG	TD
1993	Sac.	1	37	37.0	37	0	1	0	0.0	0	0
CFL TOTALS		**1**	**37**	**37.0**	**37**	**0**	**1**	**0**	**0.0**	**0**	**0**

Quarterback Sacks - 2 for 25 yards lost with Sacramento in 1993.
CFL Total QB Sacks - 2 for 25 yards lost.

Tackles - 17 defensive and 12 special teams with Sacramento in 1993.
CFL Total Tackles - 29 (17 defensive and 12 special teams).

BAKER, TERRY

Born: May 8, 1962
Birthplace: Bridgewater, Nova Scotia
Kicker. 6'1", 210 lbs. Non-import
Last Amateur Club: Mount Allison University (AUAA)
Acquired: Selected in the eighth round (65th overall) by the Montreal Concordes in the 1984 Canadian College Draft. Transferred to the Retired List in May, 1984. Released by Montreal in February, 1985 and signed as a free agent by the Edmonton Eskimos in the same month. Released by Edmonton in June, 1985 and signed as a free agent by the Toronto Argonauts in April, 1986. Released in June, 1986 and signed by the Montreal Alouettes as a free agent in January, 1987. Signed as a free agent by the Saskatchewan Roughriders in July, 1987. Traded to Ottawa Rough Riders in March, 1990 for defensive lineman Scott Camper, punter Mike Lazecki and cornerback Charles McCree. Released by Ottawa in November, 1993. Re-signed by Ottawa in March, 1994.

		Scoring						Kickoffs				
	Team	GP	TD	C	FG	S	TP	NO	YDS	AVE	LK	S
1987	Sask.	15	0	0	0	6	6	0	0	0.0	0	0
1988	Sask.	18	0	0	0	4	4	4	173	43.3	61	0
1989	Sask.	18	0	0	0	7	7	0	0	0.0	0	0
1990	Ott.	18	0	0	0	4	4	3	139	46.3	53	0
1991	Ott.	18	0	45	46	19	202	94	5339	56.8	82	1
1992	Ott.	18	0	48	40	16	184	82	4517	55.1	90	1
1993a	Ott.	11	0	24	18	11	89	44	2491	56.6	86	1
CFL TOTALS		**116**	**0**	**117**	**104**	**67**	**496**	**227**	**12659**	**55.8**	**90**	**3**

		Field Goals						Converts		
	Team	T	G	YDS	AVE	LK	PCT	T	G	PCT
1991	Ott.	60	46	1427	31.0	53	76.7	46	45	97.8
1992	Ott.	57	40	1246	31.2	50	70.2	48	48	100.0
1993	Ott.	30	18	556	30.9	50	60.0	24	24	100.0
CFL TOTALS		**147**	**104**	**3229**	**31.1**	**53**	**70.8**	**118**	**117**	**99.2**

		Punting					Fumbles		
	Team	NO	YDS	AVE	LK	S	NO	LOST	OFR
1987	Sask.	137	5603	40.9	94	6	2	1	0
1988	Sask.	154	6118	39.7	75	4	4	4	0
1989	Sask.	142	5699	40.1	88	7	5	4	1
1990	Ott.	149	5935	39.8	81	4	2	2	1
1991	Ott.	126	5476	43.5	78	5	4	4	1
1992	Ott.	153	6526	42.7	75	5	2	1	1
1993	Ott.	91	4142	45.5	68	2	1	1	0
CFL TOTALS		**952**	**39499**	**41.5**	**94**	**33**	**20**	**17**	**4**

		Rushing					Field Goal Attempts				
	Team	NO	YDS	AVE	LG	TD	NO	YDS	AVE	LK	S
1987	Sask.	1	-2	-2.0	-2	0	0	0	0.0	0	0
1988	Sask.	2	1	0.5	1	0	0	0	0.0	0	0
1989	Sask.	3	-9	-3.0	-13	0	0	0	0.0	0	0
1990	Ott.	0	0	0.0	0	0	0	0	0.0	0	0
1991	Ott.	2	35	17.5	34	0	14	641	45.8	52	13
1992	Ott.	0	0	0.0	0	0	17	736	43.3	60	10
1993	Ott.	1	7	7.0	7	0	12	559	46.6	54	8
CFL TOTALS		**9**	**32**	**3.5**	**34**	**0**	**48**	**1936**	**45.0**	**60**	**31**

Net Punting - 129 for 4233 yards, 32.8 average with Ottawa in 1991, 155 for 5403 yards, 34.9 average in 1992 and 92 for 3340 yards, 36.3 average in 1993.
CFL Total Net Punting - 376 for 12976 yards, 34.5 average.

Passing - 1 attempt, 0 complete with Ottawa in 1990; 3 attempts, 2 complete for 36 yards, 66.7 percent complete, longest 28 yards in 1991 and 2 attempts, 1 complete for 18 yards, 50.0 percent complete, longest 18 yards in 1992.
CFL Total Passing - 6 attempts, 3 complete for 54 yards, 50 percent complete, longest 28 yards.

Pass Receiving - 1 for -1 yard with Ottawa in 1991.
CFL Total Pass Receiving - 1 for -1 yard.

Own Punts Recovered - 1 for 17 yards with Saskatchewan in 1988; 1 for 15 yards in 1989; 1 for 0 yards with Ottawa in 1990; 1 for 0 yards in 1991 and 1 for 0 yards in 1992. **CFL Total Own Punts Recovered - 5 for 32 yards, 6.4 average, longest 17 yards.**

Punt Returns - 1 for 0 yards with Ottawa in 1991.
CFL Total Punt Returns - 1 for 0 yards.

Tackles - 7 special teams with Ottawa in 1991; 5 special teams in 1992 and 1 defensive and 6 special teams in 1993.
CFL Total Tackles - 19 (1 defensive and 18 special teams).

a - Led CFL in Punting Average

Playoffs

		Scoring						Fumbles			Kickoffs				
	Team	GP	TD	C	FG	S	TP	NO	LOST	OFR	NO	YDS	AVE	LK	S
1988	Sask.	1	0	0	0	0	0	0	0	0	0	0	0.0	0	0
1989	Sask.	2	0	0	0	1	1	0	0	0	0	0	0.0	0	0
1990	Ott.	1	0	0	0	0	0	0	0	0	0	0	0.0	0	0
1991	Ott.	1	0	0	0	2	2	1	0	1	1	12	12.0	12	0
1992	Ott.	1	0	3	1	2	8	0	0	0	5	249	49.8	60	0
CFL TOTALS		**6**	**0**	**3**	**1**	**5**	**11**	**1**	**0**	**1**	**6**	**261**	**43.5**	**60**	**0**

		Punting					Field Goals					
	Team	NO	YDS	AVE	LK	S	T	G	YDS	AVE	LK	PCT
1988	Sask.	8	250	31.3	37	0	0	0	0	0.0	0	0.0
1989	Sask.	17	629	37.0	48	1	0	0	0	0.0	0	0.0
1990	Ott.	9	416	46.2	58	0	0	0	0	0.0	0	0.0
1991	Ott.	10	412	41.2	70	1	1	0	0	0.0	0	0.0
1992	Ott.	9	371	41.2	52	1	4	1	37	37.0	37	25.0
CFL TOTALS		**53**	**2078**	**39.2**	**70**	**3**	**5**	**1**	**37**	**37.0**	**37**	**20.0**

Net Punting - 11 for 306 yards, 27.8 average with Ottawa in 1991 and 9 for 302 yards, 33.6 average in 1992.
CFL Total Net Punting - 20 for 608 yards, 30.4 average.

Field Goal Attempts - 1 for 48 yards and 1 single with Ottawa in 1991 and 3 for 126 yards, 42.0 average, longest 46 yards and 1 single in 1992.
CFL Total Field Goal Attempts - 4 for 174 yards, 43.5 average and 2 singles.

Grey Cup

			Punting				
	Team	GP	NO	YDS	AVE	LK	S
1989	Sask.	1	6	279	46.5	62	1
CFL TOTALS		**1**	**6**	**269**	**46.5**	**62**	**1**

BARNES, REGGIE

Born: October 19, 1967
Birthplace: Philadelphia, Pennsylvania
Running Back. 5'9", 210 lbs. Import
Last Amateur Club: Delaware State University
Acquired: Attended the New York Jets (NFL) 1989 training camp and was released prior to the season. Signed as a free agent by the Ottawa Rough Riders in May, 1990. Granted free agency status in February, 1993. Re-signed by Ottawa in May, 1993, then released in July, 1993. Re-signed by Ottawa in October, 1993.

		Scoring							Pass Receiving				
	Team	GP	TD	C	FG	S	TP		NO	YDS	AVE	LG	TD
1990ab	Ott.	14	6	0	0	0	36		29	360	12.4	74	1
1991	Ott.	18	13	x1	0	0	80		33	246	7.5	26	3
1992	Ott.	17	3	0	0	0	18		22	168	7.6	22	1
1993	Ott.	4	0	0	0	0	0		11	128	11.6	40	0
CFL TOTALS		**53**	**22**	**x1**	**0**	**0**	**134**		**95**	**902**	**9.5**	**74**	**5**

		Rushing					Kickoff Returns				
	Team	NO	YDS	AVE	LG	TD	NO	YDS	AVE	LG	TD
1990	Ott.	211	1260	6.0	58	5	16	359	22.4	42	0
1991	Ott.	291	1486	5.1	57	10	7	135	19.3	38	0
1992	Ott.	204	926	4.5	38	2	0	0	0.0	0	0
1993	Ott.	45	233	5.2	28	0	0	0	0.0	0	0
CFL TOTALS		**751**	**3905**	**5.2**	**58**	**17**	**23**	**494**	**21.5**	**42**	**0**

Punt Returns - 1 for 6 yards with Ottawa in 1992.
CFL Total Punt Returns - 1 for 6 yards.

Fumbles - 12 and 6 lost with Ottawa in 1990; 7 and 2 lost in 1991 and 5 and 4 lost in 1992.
CFL Total Fumbles - 24 and 12 lost.

Own Fumbles Recovered - 4 with Ottawa in 1990; 2 in 1991 and 1 in 1992.
CFL Total OFR - 7.

Fumble Returns - 1 for 0 yards with Ottawa in 1990.
CFL Total Fumble Returns - 1 for 0 yards.

2-Pt. Converts - 1 made with Ottawa in 1991.
CFL Total 2-Pt. Converts - 1 made.

Tackles - 2 defensive with Ottawa in 1990; 2 defensive and 1 special teams in 1991 and 1 defensive in 1992. **CFL Total Tackles - 6 (5 defensive and 1 special teams).**

a - CFL Most Outstanding Rookie.
b - Winner of the Frank M. Gibson Trophy, Outstanding Rookie, Eastern Division.

Playoffs

			Pass Receiving					Rushing				
	Team	GP	NO	YDS	AVE	LG	TD	NO	YDS	AVE	LG	TD
1990	Ott.	1	5	45	9.0	12	0	15	47	3.1	12	0
1991	Ott.	1	0	0	0.0	0	0	13	18	1.4	14	0
1992	Ott.	1	1	7	7.0	7	0	31	151	4.9	35	1
1993	Ott.	1	10	73	7.3	15	0	12	39	3.3	13	0
CFL TOTALS		**4**	**16**	**125**	**7.8**	**15**	**0**	**71**	**255**	**3.6**	**35**	**1**

BARNES, REGGIE

Fumbles - 1 and 0 lost with Ottawa in 1991, 1 and 1 lost in 1992 and 2 and 1 lost in 1993. **CFL Total Playoff Fumbles - 4 and 2 lost.**

Tackles - 1 defensive with Ottawa in 1991.
CFL Total Playoff Tackles - 1 (1 defensive).

BARRETT, DANNY
Born: December 18, 1961
Birthplace: Boynton Beach, Florida
Quarterback. 5'11", 195 lbs. Import
Last Amateur Club: University of Cincinnati
Acquired: Signed as a free agent by the Calgary Stampeders in May, 1983. Traded to the Toronto Argonauts in September, 1985 for Toronto's third round selection in the 1986 CFL College Draft, linebacker Dave Pappin. Signed with USFL New Jersey Generals in 1986. Released and signed as a free agent with Toronto in March, 1987. Traded to Calgary Stampeders in July, 1989 in exchange for future considerations. Traded to B.C. Lions in April, 1992 in exchange for offensive lineman Rocco Romano and the rights to offensive lineman Jamie Crysdale. Traded to the Ottawa Rough Riders along with defensive back Cory Dowden in exchange for quarterback Kent Austin in March, 1994.

		Scoring						Rushing					Fumbles		
	Team	GP	TD	C	FG	S	TP	NO	YDS	AVE	LG	TD	NO	LOST	OFR
1983	Cal.	2	0	0	0	0	0	6	26	4.3	10	0	0	0	0
1984	Cal.	10	0	0	0	0	0	14	90	6.4	22	0	1	1	0
1985	Cal.	8	2	0	0	0	12	1	2	2.0	2	0	2	2	1
	Tor.	4	1	0	0	0	6	9	29	3.2	8	1	2	2	0
1986		USFL						USFL					USFL		
1987	Tor.	13	1	0	0	0	6	65	345	5.3	24	1	4	3	0
1988	Tor.	4	0	0	0	0	0	3	22	7.3	13	0	0	0	0
1989	Cal.	13	5	0	0	0	30	64	421	6.6	29	5	7	5	2
1990	Cal.	13	7	0	0	0	42	57	295	5.2	46	7	5	2	1
1991	Cal.	13	6	0	0	0	36	50	263	5.3	18	6	7	2	2
1992	B.C.	10	3	0	0	0	18	37	125	3.4	12	3	3	0	1
1993a	B.C.	18	4	0	0	0	24	42	162	3.9	15	4	5	2	2
CFL TOTALS		**108**	**29**	**0**	**0**	**0**	**174**	**348**	**1780**	**5.1**	**46**	**27**	**36**	**19**	**9**

		Passing							Pass Receiving				
	Team	ATT	COMP	YDS	PCT	INT	LG	TD	NO	YDS	AVE	LG	TD
1983	Cal.	23	8	213	34.8	1	56	1	0	0	0.0	0	0
1984	Cal.	79	34	319	43.0	8	31	2	0	0	0.0	0	0
1985	Cal.	1	1	15	100.0	0	15	0	32	455	14.2	35	2
	Tor.	30	18	193	60.0	0	20	0	2	46	23.0	59	0
1986			USFL				USFL				USFL		
1987	Tor.	226	120	1453	53.1	3	49	7	0	0	0.0	0	0
1988	Tor.	23	10	154	43.5	2	34	1	0	0	0.0	0	0
1989	Cal.	333	160	2608	48.0	13	80	16	0	0	0.0	0	0
1990	Cal.	295	155	2677	52.5	13	67	19	0	0	0.0	0	0
1991	Cal.	438	249	3453	56.8	5	83	19	0	0	0.0	0	0
1992	B.C.	306	172	2206	56.2	10	57	7	0	0	0.0	0	0
1993	B.C.	513	293	4097	57.1	12	70	24	0	0	0.0	0	0
CFL TOTALS		**2267**	**1220**	**17388**	**53.8**	**67**	**83**	**96**	**34**	**501**	**14.7**	**59**	**2**

2-Pt. Converts - 2 attempts, 0 complete with Calgary in 1991; 2 attempts, 1 complete with B.C. in 1992 and 1 attempt, 0 complete in 1993.
CFL Total 2-Pt. Converts - 5 attempts, 1 complete.

Net Punting - 1 for 29 yards with B.C. in 1993.
CFL Total Net Punting - 1 for 29 yards.

Defensive Tackles - 1 with Calgary in 1990; 2 with B.C. in 1992 and 1 in 1993.
CFL Total Defensive Tackles - 4.

a - Set CFL Record for Most Passing Yards in One Game (601).

Playoffs

			Rushing					Passing						
	Team	GP	NO	YDS	AVE	LG	TD	ATT	COMP	YDS	PCT	INT	LG	TD
1987	Tor.	2	2	10	5.0	9	0	4	1	-1	25.0	0	-1	0
1988	Tor.	1	0	0	0.0	0	0	0	0	0	0.0	0	0	0
1989	Cal.	1	6	31	5.2	10	0	18	6	175	33.3	3	58	0
1990	Cal.	1	4	43	10.8	18	0	38	15	188	39.5	2	31	1
1991	Cal.	2	13	83	6.4	18	1	67	43	793	64.2	1	67	7
1993	B.C.	1	6	23	3.8	6	0	42	24	339	57.1	2	45	0
CFL TOTALS		**8**	**31**	**190**	**6.1**	**18**	**1**	**169**	**89**	**1494**	**52.7**	**8**	**67**	**8**

Fumbles - 1 and 0 lost with B.C. in 1993.
CFL Total Playoff Fumbles - 1 and 0 lost.

Grey Cup

			Scoring					Rushing				
	Team	GP	TD	C	FG	S	TP	NO	YDS	AVE	LG	TD
1987	Tor.	1	1	0	0	0	6	1	25	25.0	25	1
1991	Cal.	1	1	0	0	0	6	9	14	1.6	77	1
CFL TOTALS		**2**	**2**	**0**	**0**	**0**	**12**	**10**	**39**	**3.9**	**77**	**2**

		Passing							Fumbles		
	Team	ATT	COMP	YDS	PCT	INT	LG	TD	NO	LOST	OFR
1987	Tor.	12	4	60	33.3	0	25	0	0	0	0
1991	Cal.	56	34	377	60.7	3	31	1	1	0	1
CFL TOTALS		**68**	**38**	**437**	**55.9**	**3**	**31**	**1**	**1**	**0**	**1**

2-Pt. Converts - 1 attempt, 0 complete with Toronto in 1987.
CFL Total Playoff Fumbles - 1 and 0 lost.

BARY, OUSMANE
Born: January 22, 1968
Birthplace: Bordeaux, France
Defensive Back. 6'0", 200 lbs. Non-import
Last Amateur Club: Syracuse University
Acquired: Selected by the Winnipeg Blue Bombers in the fifth round, (36th overall) in the 1992 CFL College Draft. Released by Winnipeg in September, 1993.

Games Played - 12 with Winnipeg in 1993. **CFL Total GP - 12.**

Interception Returns -1 for -7 yards with Winnipeg in 1993.
CFL Total Interception Returns - 1 for -7 yards.

Tackles - 11 defensive and 2 special teams with Winnipeg in 1993.
CFL Total Tackles - 13 (11 defensive and 2 special teams).

BATES, STEVE
Born: June 28, 1966
Birthplace: Pittsburgh, Pennsylvania
Defensive End. 6'4", 245 lbs. Import
Last Amateur Club: James Madison University
Acquired: Selected in the 10th round (272nd overall) by the Los Angeles Rams in the 1990 NFL Draft. Released by Los Angeles after training camp in 1990. Signed as a free agent by the NFL Indianapolis Colts in 1990 and released after the 1991 season. Played for the Orlando Thunder of the World League of American Football in the 1992 season. Signed as a free agent by the Hamilton Tiger-Cats in September, 1992.

Games Played - 3 with Hamilton in 1992 and 2 in 1993. **CFL Total GP - 5.**

Quarterback Sacks - 3 for 30 yards lost with Hamilton in 1992 and 1 for 4 yards lost in 1993. **CFL Total QB Sacks - 4 for 34 yards lost.**

Tackles - 8 defensive and 2 special teams with Hamilton in 1992 and 7 defensive in 1993. **CFL Total Tackles - 17 (15 defensive and 2 special teams).**

Playoffs

Games Played - 2 with Hamilton in 1992 and 2 in 1993.
CFL Total Playoff GP - 4.

Quarterback Sacks - 2 for 5 yards lost with Hamilton in 1993.
CFL Total Playoff QB Sacks - 2 for 5 yards lost.

Fumble Returns - 1 for 0 yards with Hamilton in 1993.
CFL Total Playoff Fumble Returns - 1 for 0 yards.

Tackles - 5 defensive with Hamilton in 1992 and 5 defensive in 1993.
CFL Total Playoff Tackles - 10 (10 defensive).

Tackles for Losses - 1 for 1 yard with Hamilton in 1993.
CFL Total Playoff Tackles for Losses - 1 for 1 yard.

BATTLE, GREG
Born: April 14, 1964
Birthplace: Long Beach, California
Linebacker. 6'1", 225 lbs. Import
Last Amateur Club: Arizona State University
Acquired: Signed as a free agent by the NFL Denver Broncos in 1986. Signed as a free agent by the Winnipeg Blue Bombers in May, 1987. Granted free agency status in February, 1994. Signed as a free agent by the Las Vegas Posse in March, 1994.

			Interception Returns					QB Sacks	Fumbles		
	Team	GP	NO	YDS	AVE	LG	TD	NO	NO	LOST	OFR
1987	Wpg.	6	1	25	25.0	25	0	3	0	0	1
1988	Wpg.	18	1	12	12.0	12	0	5	1	0	0
1989abc	Wpg.	18	3	15	5.0	9	0	2	1	1	0
1990abde	Wpg.	18	3	14	4.7	14	0	4	0	0	1
1991abde	Wpg.	17	3	31	10.3	24	0	0	0	0	0
1992	Wpg.	17	4	59	14.8	33	0	3	2	1	1
1993	Wpg.	16	4	53	13.3	34	1	2	1	1	0
CFL TOTALS		**110**	**19**	**209**	**11.0**	**34**	**1**	**19**	**5**	**3**	**3**

Scoring - 1 TD for 6 points with Winnipeg in 1988; 1 TD for 6 points in 1992 and 2 TDs for 12 points in 1993.
CFL Total Scoring - 4 TDs for 24 points.

Pass Receiving - 2 for 52 yards, 26.0 average, longest 30 yards with Winnipeg in 1989. **CFL Total Pass Receiving - 2 for 52 yards, 26.0 average, longest 30 yards.**

Blocked Kicks - 1 convert with Winnipeg in 1990.
CFL Total Blocked Kicks - 1 convert.

BATTLE, GREG

Kickoff Returns - 1 for 25 yards with Winnipeg in 1989; 0 for 5 yards in 1990, 1 for 13 yards in 1991 and 3 for 36 yards, 12.0 average, longest 19 yards in 1993. **CFL Total Kickoff Returns - 5 for 79 yards, 15.8 average, longest 25 yards.**

Punt Returns - 1 for 18 yards with Winnipeg in 1992. **CFL Total Punt Returns - 1 for 18 yards.**

Fumble Returns - 4 for 66 yards, 16.5 average, longest 66 yards and 1 TD with Winnipeg in 1988; 2 for 19 yards, 9.5 average, longest 19 yards in 1989; 5 for 30 yards, 6.0 average, longest 30 yards in 1990; 4 for 24 yards, 6.0 average, longest 20 yards in 1991; 3 for 61 yards, 20.3 average, longest 55 yards and 1 TD in 1992 and 2 for 41 yards, 20.5 average, longest 41 yards and 1 TD in 1993. **CFL Total Fumble Returns - 20 for 241 yards, 12.1 average, longest 66 yards and 3 TDs.**

Tackles - 20 defensive with Winnipeg in 1987; 54 defensive in 1988; 108 defensive in 1989; 100 defensive in 1990; 97 defensive and 3 special teams in 1991; 81 defensive in 1992 and 45 defensive and 2 special teams in 1993. **CFL Total Tackles - 510 (505 defensive and 5 special teams).**

Tackles for Losses - 6 for 15 yards with Winnipeg in 1991, 2 for 3 yards in 1992, and 2 for 3 yards in 1993. **CFL Total Tackles for Losses - 10 for 21 yards.**

a - All-Eastern All-Star
b - Winner James P. McCaffrey Trophy as Outstanding Defensive Player, Eastern Division
c - Runner-up CFL Most Outstanding Defensive Player
d - CFL All-Star
e - CFL Most Outstanding Defensive Player

Playoffs

Games Played - 1 with Winnipeg in 1987; 1 in 1988; 2 in 1989; 1 in 1990; 2 in 1991; 1 in 1992 and 1 in 1993. **CFL Total Playoff GP - 9.**

Pass Receiving - 1 for 6 yards with Winnipeg in 1989. **CFL Total Playoff Pass Receiving - 1 for 6 yards.**

Interception Returns - 1 for 30 yards with Winnipeg in 1990 and 1 for 31 yards in 1992. **CFL Total Playoff Interception Returns - 2 for 61 yards, 30.5 average, longest 31 yards.**

Quarterback Sacks - 1 with Winnipeg in 1988 and 1 in 1991. **CFL Total Playoff QB Sacks - 2.**

Kickoff Returns - 1 for 14 yards with Winnipeg in 1989. **CFL Total Playoff Kickoff Returns - 1 for 14 yards.**

Tackles - 5 defensive with Winnipeg in 1987; 1 defensive in 1988; 10 defensive in 1989; 4 defensive in 1990; 11 defensive in 1991; 6 defensive in 1992 and 2 defensive in 1993. **CFL Total Playoff Tackles - 39 (39 defensive).**

Tackles for Losses - 1 for 1 yard with Winnipeg in 1991. **CFL Total Playoff Tackles for Losses - 1 for 1 yard.**

Grey Cup

Games Played - 1 with Winnipeg in 1990, 1 in 1992 and 1 in 1993. **Total Grey Cup GP - 3.**

Interception Returns - 2 for 88 yards, 44.0 average, longest 56 yards, 1 TD with Winnipeg in 1990. **Total Grey Cup Interception Returns - 2 for 88 yards, 44.0 average, longest 56 yards and 1 TD.**

Quarterback Sacks - 2 for 6 yards lost with Winnipeg in 1993. **Total Grey Cup QB Sacks - 2 for 6 yards lost.**

Own Fumbles Recovered - 1 with Winnipeg in 1990. **Total Grey Cup OFR - 1.**

Fumbles - 1 and 0 lost with Winnipeg in 1990. **Total Grey Cup Fumbles - 1 and 0 lost.**

Defensive Tackles - 4 with Winnipeg in 1990; 7 in 1992 and 3 in 1993. **Total Grey Cup Defensive Tackles - 14.**

Grey Cup Game Defensive Star in 1990.
Set CFL Record for All-Time Most Defensive Tackles in Grey Cup with 14 in 1993.

BAYLIS, JEARLD

Born: August 12, 1962
Birthplace: Jackson, Mississippi
Defensive Tackle. 6'0", 245 lbs. Import
Last Amateur Club: University of Southern Mississippi
Acquired: Selected by New Orleans in the 1984 USFL Territorial Draft. Moved to Portland with the franchise transfer. Released and signed as a free agent by the Toronto Argonauts in August, 1986. Traded to the B.C. Lions with quarterback Rick Johnson, linebackers Willie Pless and Tony Visco, slotback Emanuel Tolbert and defensive back Todd Wiseman in March, 1990 in exchange for quarterback Matt Dunigan. Retired during the 1990 season due to injury. Came out of retirement for the 1991 season. Released by B.C. in October, 1991. Signed as a free agent by the Saskatchewan Roughriders in June, 1992. Granted free agency status in February 1994. Signed as a free agent by the Baltimore CFL Colts in April, 1994.

Games Played - 9 with Toronto in 1986; 16 in 1987; 10 in 1988; 16 in 1989; 7 with B.C. in 1991; 18 with Saskatchewan in 1992 and 18 in 1993. **CFL Total GP - 94.**

Fumble Returns - 2 for 0 yards with Toronto in 1987; 1 for 4 yards in 1989; 1 for 0 yards with B.C. in 1991; 1 for 0 yards with Saskatchewan in 1992 and 4 for 1 yard in 1993. **CFL Total Fumble Returns - 9 for 5 yards, 0.6 average, longest 4 yards.**

Own Fumbles Recovered - 1 with Toronto in 1987. **CFL Total OFR - 1.**

Blocked Kicks - 1 punt with Toronto in 1989. **CFL Total Blocked Kicks - 1 punt.**

Quarterback Sacks - 5 with Toronto in 1986; 7 in 1987; 4 in 1988; 1 with B.C. in 1991; 8 for 58 yards lost with Saskatchewan in 1992 and 11 for 79 yards lost in 1993. **CFL Total QB Sacks - 36.**

Tackles - 47 defensive with Toronto in 1987; 22 defensive in 1988; 65 defensive in 1989; 14 defensive and 2 special teams with B.C. in 1991; 53 defensive with Saskatchewan in 1992 and 56 defensive and 1 special teams in 1993. **CFL Total Tackles - 260 (257 defensive and 3 special teams).**

Tackles for Losses - 3 for 3 yards with B.C. in 1991; 10 for 38 yards with Saskatchewan in 1992 and 18 for 36 yards in 1993. **CFL Total Tackles for Losses - 31 for 77 yards.**

All-Eastern All-Star in 1987.
All-Western All-Star in 1992 and 1993.
CFL All-Star in 1987, 1992 and 1993.
Norm Fieldgate Trophy, Most Outstanding Defensive Player in Western Division in 1993.
CFL Outstanding Defensive Player in 1993.

Playoffs

Games Played - 2 with Toronto in 1986; 2 with Toronto in 1987; 1 in 1988; 1 in 1989; 1 with Saskatchewan in 1992 and 1 with Saskatchewan in 1993. **CFL Total Playoff GP - 8.**

Quarterback Sacks - 1 with Toronto in 1988; 1 in 1989 and 1 for 5 yards lost with Saskatchewan in 1992. **CFL Total Playoff QB Sacks - 3.**

Tackles - 6 defensive with Toronto in 1987; 3 defensive in 1988; 3 defensive in 1989; 6 defensive with Saskatchewan in 1992 and 7 defensive in 1993. **CFL Total Playoff Tackles - 25 (25 defensive).**

Grey Cup

Games Played - 1 with Toronto in 1987. **Total Grey Cup GP - 1.**

Quarterback Sacks - 1 with Toronto in 1987. **Total Grey Cup QB Sacks - 1.**

Tackles - 2 defensive with Toronto in 1987. **Total Grey Cup Tackles - 2 (2 defensive).**

BAYSINGER, FREEMAN

Born: December 22, 1969
Birthplace: Oakland, California
Slotback. 5'9", 170 lbs. Import
Last Amateur Club: Humbolt State University
Acquired: Selected in the 12th Round (333rd overall) by the New England Patriots in the 1992 NFL Draft. Was released by the Patriots in August, 1992. Signed as a free agent by the Sacramento Gold Miners in April, 1993. Traded to the B.C. Lions in exchange for the rights to two of B.C.'s Negotiation List players in October, 1993.

		Scoring						Pass Receiving				
	Team	GP	TD	C	FG	S	TP	NO	YDS	AVE	LG	TD
1993	Sac.	13	4	0	0	0	24	48	736	15.3	83	3
	B.C.	3	0	0	0	0	0	5	97	19.4	42	0
CFL TOTALS		**16**	**4**	**0**	**0**	**0**	**24**	**53**	**833**	**15.7**	**83**	**3**

		Punt Returns					Kickoff Returns				
	Team	NO	YDS	AVE	LG	TD	NO	YDS	AVE	LG	TD
1993	Sac.	52	402	7.8	59	1	0	0	0.0	0	0
	B.C.	12	99	8.3	20	0	18	385	21.4	47	0
CFL TOTALS		**64**	**504**	**7.9**	**59**	**1**	**18**	**385**	**21.4**	**47**	**0**

		Unsuccessful Field Goal Returns					Fumbles		
	Team	NO	YDS	AVE	LG	TD	NO	LOST	OFR
1993	Sac.	4	114	28.5	63	0	1	1	0
	B.C.	0	0	0.0	0	0	2	2	0
CFL TOTALS		**4**	**114**	**28.5**	**63**	**0**	**3**	**3**	**0**

Tackles - 1 defensive with Sacramento and 1 defensive with B.C. in 1993. **CFL Total Tackles - 2 (2 defensive).**

Playoffs

Games Played - 1 with B.C. in 1993. **CFL Total Playoff GP - 1.**

Punt Returns - 4 for 14 yards, 3.5 average, longest 6 yards with B.C. in 1993. **CFL Total Playoff Punt Returns - 4 for 14 yards, 3.5 average, longest 6 yards.**

Kickoff Returns - 3 for 54 yards with B.C. in 1993. **CFL Total Playoff Kickoff Returns - 3 for 54 yards.**

BEATON, BRUCE
Born: June 13, 1968
Birthplace: Port Hood, Nova Scotia
Defensive End. 6'5", 285 lbs. Non-import
Last Amateur Club: Acadia University (AUAA)
Acquired: Was selected in the first round (8th overall) by the B.C. Lions in the 1991 CFL College Draft. Traded to the Otawa Rough Riders in exchange for defensive back Brett Young in September, 1992.

Games Played - 16 with Ottawa in 1993. **CFL Total GP - 16.**

BEAVERS, DARRELL
Born: November 24, 1967
Birthplace: Joliet, Illinois
Linebacker. 6'3", 230 lbs. Import
Last Amateur Club: Morehead State University
Acquired: Selected in the 12th round (329th overall) by the Philadelphia Eagles in the 1991 NFL Draft. Was signed as a free agent by the Hamilton Tiger-Cats in April, 1993. Released by Hamilton in November, 1993.

Games Played - 7 with Hamilton in 1993. **CFL Total GP - 7.**

Own Fumbles Recovered - 1 with Hamilton in 1993. **CFL Total OFR - 1.**

Tackles - 5 defensive and 5 special teams with Hamilton in 1993. **CFL Total Tackles - 10 (5 defensive and 5 special teams).**

BELANGER, FRANCOIS
Born: February 21, 1968
Birthplace: Ste. Foy, Quebec
Offensive Tackle. 6'6", 290 lbs. Non-import
Last Amateur Club: McGill University (OQIFC)
Acquired: Selected in the eighth round (57th overall) by the Hamilton Tiger-Cats in the 1991 CFL College Draft. Released by Hamilton in October, 1992. Signed as a free agent by the Winnipeg Blue Bombers in November, 1992. Released by Winnipeg in July, 1993. Signed as a free agent by the Toronto Argonauts in July, 1993.

Games Played - 1 with Hamilton in 1991; 12 in 1992 and 12 with Toronto in 1993. **CFL Total GP - 25.**

Own Fumbles Recovered - 1 with Hamilton in 1992. **CFL Total OFR - 1.**

BELL, KERWIN
Born: June 15, 1965
Birthplace: Live Oak, Florida
Quarterback. 6'3", 211 lbs. Import
Last Amateur Club: University of Florida
Acquired: Selected in the 7th round (180th overall) by the Miami Dolphins in the 1988 NFL Draft. Released in August, 1988 and then signed as a free agent by the Atlanta Falcons. Was released by the Falcons during the pre-season and was subsequently re-signed by Atlanta in October, 1988. Was again released by the Falcons and signed as a free agent by the Tampa Bay Buccaneers where he was released prior to the start of the 1989 season. Was then re-signed by the Buccaneers in October, 1989 and released again in November. Re-signed by Tampa Bay in December and was subsequently waived by the Buccaneers in April, 1990. Was selected in the first round (6th overall) by the Orlando Thunder in the 1991 WLAF Positional Draft. Signed as a free agent by the Sacramento Gold Miners in May 1993.

			Passing							Rushing				
	Team	GP	ATT	COMP	YDS	AVE	INT	LG	TD	NO	YDS	AVE	LG	TD
1993	Sac.	18	34	22	296	64.7	1	58	2	4	13	3.3	8	0
CFL TOTALS		**18**	**34**	**22**	**296**	**64.7**	**1**	**58**	**2**	**4**	**13**	**3.3**	**8**	**0**

BELLAMY, MIKE
Born: June 28, 1966
Birthplace: New York City, New York
Wide Receiver. 6'1", 190 lbs. Import
Last Amateur Club: University of Illinois
Acquired: Selected in the second round (50th overall), by the Philadelphia Eagles in the 1990 NFL Draft. Released by Philadelphia and signed as a free agent by the Indianapolis Colts in February, 1992. Released by Indianapolis in August, 1992. Signed as a free agent by the Winnipeg Blue Bombers in January, 1993. Released by Winnipeg in November, 1993.

			Pass Receiving					Rushing				
	Team	GP	NO	YDS	AVE	LG	TD	NO	YDS	AVE	LG	TD
1993	Wpg.	7	12	104	8.7	17	0	3	13	4.3	8	0
CFL TOTALS		**7**	**12**	**104**	**8.7**	**17**	**0**	**3**	**13**	**4.3**	**8**	**0**

Kickoff Returns - 1 for 32 yards with Winnipeg in 1993. **CFL Total Kickoff Returns - 1 for 32 yards.**

BENEFIELD, DAVED
Born: August 28, 1967
Birthplace: Los Angeles, California
Linebacker. 6'3", 222 lbs. Import
Last Amateur Club: California State University at Northridge
Acquired: Signed as a free agent by the Edmonton Eskimos in November, 1990. Released by Edmonton in July, 1991. Signed as a free agent by the Ottawa Rough Riders in June, 1992.

Games Played - 2 with Ottawa in 1992 and 11 in 1993. **CFL Total GP - 13.**

Blocked Kicks - 1 punt with Ottawa in 1993. **CFL Total Blocked Kicks - 1 punt.**

Quarterback Sacks - 2 for 13 yards lost with Ottawa in 1992 and 6 for 63 yards lost in 1993. **CFL Total QB Sacks - 8 for 76 yards lost.**

Tackles - 7 defensive and 2 special teams with Ottawa in 1992 and 8 defensive and 6 special teams in 1993. **CFL Total Tackles - 23 (15 defensive and 8 special teams).**

Tackles for Losses - 2 for 6 yards with Ottawa in 1992. **CFL Total Tackles for Losses - 2 for 6 yards.**

BENJAMIN, NICK
Born: May 29, 1961
Birthplace: Trinidad
Offensive Guard. 6'2", 270 lbs. Non-import
Last Amateur Club: Concordia University (OQIFC)
Acquired: Selected in the first round (first overall) by the Ottawa Rough Riders in the 1985 CFL College Draft. Traded to the Winnipeg Blue Bombers for Defensive Lineman Willie Fears and Offensive Lineman Brad Tierney in August, 1989. Granted free agency status February, 1991. Re-signed by Winnipeg in March, 1991.

Games Played - 16 with Ottawa in 1985; 10 in 1986; 17 in 1987; 18 in 1988, 2 in 1989; 6 with Winnipeg in 1989; 17 in 1990; 18 in 1991; 11 in 1992 and 12 in 1993. **CFL Total GP - 127.**

Scoring - 1 TD for 6 points with Winnipeg in 1991. **CFL Total Scoring - 1 TD for 6 points.**

Fumbles - 1 and 0 lost with Winnipeg in 1991; 2 and 0 lost in 1992 and 2 and 0 lost in 1993. **CFL Total Fumbles - 5 and 0 lost.**

Own Fumbles Recovered - 3 with Ottawa in 1988 and 1 in 1989. **CFL Total OFR - 4.**

Fumble Returns - 2 for 2 yards, 1.0 average, longest 2 yards and 1 TD with Winnipeg in 1991. **CFL Total Fumble Returns - 2 for 2 yards, 1.0 average, longest 2 yards and 1 TD.**

Tackles - 1 defensive with Ottawa in 1987; 4 defensive in 1988; 4 defensive with Winnipeg in 1990; 2 defensive and 8 special teams in 1991; 1 defensive and 5 special teams in 1992 and 2 defensive and 8 special teams in 1993. **CFL Total Tackles - 35 (14 defensive and 21 special teams).**

Winner of the Frank M. Gibson Trophy, Outstanding Rookie Eastern Division in 1985.
Runner-up Schenley Most Outstanding Rookie in 1985.

Playoffs

Games Played - 1 with Ottawa in 1985; 1 with Winnipeg in 1990; 2 in 1991; 1 in 1992 and 1 in 1993. **CFL Total Playoff GP - 6.**

Tackles - 2 special teams with Winnipeg in 1991 and 1 special teams in 1993. **CFL Total Playoff Tackles - 3 (3 special teams).**

Grey Cup

Games Played - 1 with Winnipeg in 1990; 1 in 1992 and 1 in 1993. **Total Grey Cup GP - 3.**

Fumbles - 1 and 0 lost with Winnipeg in 1990. **Total Grey Cup Fumbles - 1 and 0 lost.**

BENSON, KEN
Born: March 4, 1969
Birthplace: Kansas City, Kansas
Linebacker. 6'2", 220 lbs. Import
Last Amateur Club: University of Arkansas
Acquired: Signed as a free agent by the NFL Philadelphia Eagles in 1991. Was later released and signed as a free agent by the Toronto Argonauts in April, 1992. Granted free agency status in February, 1994. Signed as a free agent by the Baltimore CFL Colts in March, 1994.

Games Played - 18 with Toronto in 1992 and 18 in 1993. **CFL Total GP - 36.**

Kickoff Returns - 1 for 0 yards with Toronto in 1992. **CFL Total Kickoff Returns - 1 for 0 yards.**

Fumble Returns - 2 for 0 yards with Toronto in 1993. **CFL Total Fumble Returns - 2.**

Own Fumbles Recovered - 1 with Toronto in 1992. **CFL Total OFR - 1.**

BENSON, KEN

Interception Returns - 1 for 2 yards with Toronto in 1993.
CFL Total Interception Returns - 1 for 2 yards.

Quarterback Sacks - 2 for 10 yards lost with Toronto in 1992 and 5 for 30 yards lost in 1993. **CFL Total QB Sacks - 7 for 40 yards lost.**

Tackles - 68 defensive and 24 special teams with Toronto in 1992 and 80 defensive and 8 special teams with Toronto in 1993.
CFL Total Tackles - 190 (148 defensive and 42 special teams).

Tackles for Losses - 3 for 11 yards with Toronto in 1992 and 4 for 11 yards in 1993. **CFL Total Tackles for Losses - 7 for 22 yards.**

Led CFL in Combined Tackles in 1993.

BERNARD, RAY
Born: May 29, 1967
Birthplace: Laval, Quebec
Linebacker. 6'1", 220 lbs. Non-import
Last Amateur Club: Bishop's University (OQIFC)
Acquired: Selected in the second round (10th overall) of the 1992 CFL College Draft by the Saskatchewan Roughriders.

Games Played - 16 with Saskatchewan in 1992 and 18 in 1993.
CFL Total GP - 34.

Quarterback Sacks - 1 for 10 yards lost with Saskatchewan in 1993.
CFL Total QB Sacks - 1 for 10 yards lost.

Fumble Returns - 3 for 0 yards with Saskatchewan in 1993.
CFL Total Fumble Returns - 3 for 0 yards.

Tackles - 16 defensive and 32 special teams with Saskatchewan in 1992; 92 defensive and 6 special teams in 1993.
CFL Total Tackles - 146 (108 defensive and 38 special teams).

Tackles for Losses - 2 for 3 yards with Saskatchewan in 1993.
CFL Total Tackles for Losses - 2 for 3 yards.

Led CFL in defensive tackles in 1993.

Playoffs

Games Played - 1 with Saskatchewan in 1992 and 1 in 1993.
CFL Total Playoff GP - 2.

Tackles - 6 defensive and 1 special teams with Saskatchewan in 1992 and 10 defensive in 1993. **CFL Total Playoff Tackles - 17 (16 defensive and 1 special teams).**

BERRY, ED
Born: September 28, 1963
Birthplace: San Francisco, California
Cornerback. 5'10", 185 lbs. Import
Last Amateur Club: Utah State University
Acquired: Selected by the Green Bay Packers in the seventh round (183rd overall) of the 1987 NFL Draft. Released by Green Bay prior to the start of the 1987 season. Signed with the NFL San Diego Chargers as a replacement player during the NFL strike in 1987. Signed as a free agent with the Toronto Argonauts in September, 1988. Traded to the Edmonton Eskimos in January, 1993 along with wide receiver Eddie Brown, linebacker Bruce Dickson, quarterback Rickey Foggie, slotback J.P. Izquierdo, defensive lineman Leonard Johnson, slotback Darrell K. Smith and defensive back Don Wilson in exchange for defensive lineman Cameron Brosseau, linebacker John Davis, slotback Craig Ellis, quarterback Tracy Ham, defensive back Enis Jackson, running back Chris Johnstone, defensive back Travis Oliver and wide receiver Ken Winey.

		Scoring						Interception Returns				
	Team	GP	TD	C	FG	S	TP	NO	YDS	AVE	LG	TD
1988	Tor.	6	1	0	0	0	6	2	115	57.5	77	1
1989a	Tor.	14	1	0	0	0	6	5	147	29.4	75	0
1990	Tor.	18	1	0	0	0	6	7	153	21.9	62	1
1991	Tor.	16	1	0	0	0	6	4	78	19.5	59	1
1992	Tor.	17	1	0	0	0	6	9	97	10.8	62	1
1993	Edm.	14	0	0	0	0	0	2	26	13.0	16	0
CFL TOTALS		**85**	**5**	**0**	**0**	**0**	**30**	**29**	**616**	**21.2**	**77**	**4**

Blocked Kicks - 1 punt with Toronto in 1989.
CFL Total Blocked Kicks - 1 punt.

Punt Returns - 1 for 1 yard with Toronto in 1992.
CFL Total Punt Returns - 1 for 1 yard.

Kickoff Returns - 6 for 64 yards, 10.7 average, longest 21 yards with Toronto in 1992.
CFL Total Kickoff Returns - 6 for 64 yards, 10.7 average, longest 21 yards.

Fumble Returns - 1 for 0 yards with Toronto in 1988; 3 for 13 yards, 4.3 average, longest 13 yards and 1 TD in 1989; 1 for 0 yards in 1991 and 1 for 2 yards with Edmonton in 1993. **CFL Total Fumble Returns - 6 for 15 yards, 2.5 average, longest 13 yards and 1 TD.**

Tackles - 16 defensive with Toronto in 1988; 66 defensive in 1989; 72 defensive in 1990; 66 defensive and 3 special teams in 1991; 46 defensive and 4 special teams in 1992 and 44 defensive and 3 special teams with Edmonton in 1993.
CFL Total Tackles - 320 (310 defensive and 10 special teams).

a - All-Eastern All-Star

Playoffs

Games Played - 1 with Toronto in 1988; 2 in 1990; 1 in 1991 and 1 with Edmonton in 1993. **CFL Total Playoff GP - 5.**

Interception Returns - 2 for 27 yards, 13.5 average, longest 27 yards with Toronto in 1991. **CFL Total Playoff Interception Returns - 2 for 27 yards, 13.5 average, longest 27 yards.**

Fumble Returns - 1 for 37 yards with Edmonton in 1993.
CFL Total Playoff Fumble Returns - 1 for 37 yards.

Tackles - 3 defensive with Toronto in 1988; 6 defensive in 1990 and 1 defensive and 1 special teams in 1991.
CFL Total Playoff Tackles - 11 (10 defensive and 1 special teams).

Grey Cup

Games Played - 1 with Toronto in 1991. **Total Grey Cup GP - 1.**

Scoring - 1 TD for 6 points with Toronto in 1991.
Total Grey Cup Scoring - 1 TD for 6 points.

Interception Returns - 1 for 50 yards and 1 TD with Toronto in 1991.
Total Grey Cup Interception Returns - 1 for 50 yards and 1 TD.

BETHUNE, GEORGE
Born: March 30, 1967
Birthplace: Fort Watton Beach, Florida
Defensive End. 6'4", 265 lbs. Import
Last Amateur Club: University of Alabama
Acquired: Selected in the seventh round (88th overall) by the Los Angeles Rams in the 1989 NFL Draft. Released by the Rams in August, 1991. Selected in the first round (1st overall) by the Sacramento Surge in the 1992 WLAF Draft. Signed as a free agent by the Houston Oilers in July, 1992 and was released later that month. Signed as a free agent by the Green Bay Packers in February, 1993. Was released by Green Bay and signed as a free agent by the Winnipeg Blue Bombers in September, 1993.

Games Played - 1 with Winnipeg in 1993. **CFL Total GP - 1.**

BIGGS, RAYMOND
Born: October 20, 1968
Birthplace: Toronto, Ontario
Linebacker. 6'1", 218 lbs. Non-import
Last Amateur Club: New Mexico State University
Acquired: Signed as free agent by the Calgary Stampeders in March, 1993.

			Interception Returns					Fumble Returns				
	Team	GP	NO	YDS	AVE	LG	TD	NO	YDS	AVE	LG	TD
1993	Cal.	18	1	26	26.0	26	0	3	21	7.0	15	0
CFL TOTALS		**18**	**1**	**26**	**26.0**	**26**	**0**	**3**	**21**	**7.0**	**15**	**0**

Tackles - 11 defensive and 17 special teams with Calgary in 1993.
CFL Total Tackles - 28 (11 defensive and 17 special teams).

Tackles For Losses - 1 for 3 yards with Calgary in 1993.
CFL Total Tackles for Losses - 1 for 3 yards.

Playoffs

Games Played - 2 with Calgary in 1993.
CFL Total Playoff GP - 2.

Tackles - 1 special teams with Calgary in 1993.
CFL Total Playoff Tackles - 1 (1 special teams).

BLACK, DAVID
Born: April 13, 1962
Birthplace: Oshawa, Ontario
Offensive Tackle. 6'3", 245 lbs. Non-import
Last Amateur Club: Wilfrid Laurier University (OUAA)
Acquired: Selected in the third round, (34th overall), by the Winnipeg Blue Bombers in the 1984 CFL College Draft.

Games Played - 10 with Winnipeg in 1985; 11 in 1986; 18 in 1987; 18 in 1988; 17 in 1989; 18 in 1990; 17 in 1991; 18 in 1992 and 18 in 1993. **CFL Total GP - 145.**

Own Fumbles Recovered - 1 with Winnipeg in 1992. **CFL Total OFR - 1.**

BLACK, DAVID

Defensive Tackles - 1 with Winnipeg in 1987; 2 in 1990; 2 in 1991; 1 in 1992 and 2 in 1993. **CFL Total Defensive Tackles - 8.**

All-Eastern All-Star in 1989 and 1993.
CFL All-Star in 1993.

Playoffs

Games Played - 2 with Winnipeg in 1985; 1 in 1986; 1 in 1987; 2 in 1988; 2 in 1989; 1 in 1990; 2 in 1991; 1 in 1992 and 1 in 1993. **CFL Total Playoff GP - 13.**

Grey Cup

Games Played - 1 with Winnipeg in 1988; 1 in 1990; 1 in 1992 and 1 in 1993. **Total Grey Cup GP - 4.**

BLUGH, LEROY
Born: May 14, 1966
Birthplace: St. Vincent (Caribbean)
Linebacker. 6'2", 230 lbs. Non-import
Last Amateur Club: Bishop's University (OQIFC)
Acquired: Selected in the first round (seventh overall) in the 1989 CFL College Draft by the Edmonton Eskimos. Edmonton acquired the pick from the B.C. Lions along with wide receiver Jim Sandusky in June, 1988 in exchange for quarterback Matt Dunigan. Edmonton completed the deal in January, 1989 by acquiring linebackers Gregg Stumon and Jeff Braswell, running back Reggie Taylor and defensive back Andre Francis.

Games Played - 18 with Edmonton in 1989; 14 in 1990; 18 in 1991; 18 in 1992 and 18 in 1993. **CFL Total GP - 86.**

Scoring - 1 TD for 6 points with Edmonton in 1992. **CFL Total Scoring - 1 TD for 6 points.**

Pass Receiving - 2 for 30 yards, 15.0 average, longest 16 yards with Edmonton in 1991. **CFL Total Pass Receiving - 2 for 30 yards, 15.0 average, longest 16 yards.**

Fumble Returns - 1 for 0 yards with Edmonton in 1989; 2 for 2 yards and 1 TD in 1992 and 2 for 30 yards in 1993. **CFL Total Fumble Returns - 4 for 32 yards, 8 average, longest 30 yards and 1 TD.**

Own Fumbles Recovered - 1 with Edmonton in 1989. **CFL Total OFR - 1.**

Interception Returns - 1 for 3 yards with Edmonton in 1990. **CFL Total Interception Returns - 1 for 3 yards.**

Kickoff Returns - 1 for 9 yards with Edmonton in 1990 and 1 for 12 yards in 1992. **CFL Total Kickoff Returns - 2 for 21 yards, 10.5 average, longest 12 yards.**

Quarterback Sacks - 3 with Edmonton in 1990; 7 in 1991; 7 for 41 yards lost in 1992 and 7 for 41 yards lost in 1993. **CFL Total QB Sacks - 24.**

Tackles - 8 defensive with Edmonton in 1989; 28 defensive in 1990; 31 defensive and 3 special teams in 1991; 44 defensive in 1992 and 46 defensive and 1 special teams in 1993. **CFL Total Tackles - 161 (157 defensive and 4 special teams).**

Tackles for Losses - 4 for 13 yards with Edmonton in 1991; 5 for 17 yards in 1992 and 3 for 6 yards in 1993. **CFL Total Tackles for Losses - 12 for 36 yards.**

Playoffs

Games Played - 1 with Edmonton in 1989; 2 in 1990; 1 in 1991; 2 in 1992 and 2 in 1993. **CFL Total Playoff GP - 8.**

Fumble Returns - 1 for 0 yards with Edmonton in 1993. **CFL Total Playoff Fumble Returns - 1 for 0 yards.**

Quarterback Sacks - 1 with Edmonton in 1990; 1 in 1991 and 1 for 8 yards lost in 1993. **CFL Total Playoff QB Sacks - 3.**

Tackles - 1 defensive with Edmonton in 1989; 1 defensive in 1990; 2 defensive in 1991; 7 defensive in 1992 and 7 defensive in 1993. **CFL Total Playoff Tackles - 18 (18 defensive).**

Grey Cup

Games Played - 1 with Edmonton in 1990 and 1 in 1993. **Total Grey Cup GP - 2.**

Quarterback Sacks - 1 with Edmonton in 1990. **Total Grey Cup QB Sacks - 1.**

Defensive Tackles - 3 with Edmonton in 1990 and 3 in 1993. **Total Grey Cup Defensive Tackles - 6.**

Tackles for Losses - 1 for 1 yard with Edmonton in 1993. **Total Grey Cup Tackles for Losses - 1 for 1 yard.**

BOLTON, NATHANIEL
Born: July 1, 1968
Birthplace: Mobile, Alabama
Wide Receiver. 5'11", 195 lbs. Import
Last Amateur Club: Mississippi College
Acquired: Signed as free agent by the NFL Cleveland Browns in 1991. Released by the Browns and signed as a free agent by the NFL New Orleans Saints in July, 1991. Released in August, 1991 and was subsequently re-signed by New Orleans in the off-season. Released by New Orleans and signed as a free agent by the Winnipeg Blue Bombers in January, 1993.

	Team	Scoring GP	TD	C	FG	S	TP
1993	Wpg.	12	6	0	0	0	36
CFL TOTALS		**12**	**6**	**0**	**0**	**0**	**36**

	Pass Receiving NO	YDS	AVE	LG	TD
1993	42	713	17.0	57	5
CFL TOTALS	**42**	**713**	**17.0**	**57**	**5**

	Team	Rushing NO	YDS	AVE	LG	TD
1993	Wpg.	2	6	3.0	17	0
CFL TOTALS		**2**	**6**	**3.0**	**17**	**0**

	Punt Returns NO	YDS	AVE	LG	TD
1993	49	325	6.6	71	1
CFL TOTALS	**49**	**325**	**6.6**	**71**	**1**

	Team	Kickoff Returns NO	YDS	AVE	LG	TD
1993	Wpg.	20	494	24.7	55	0
CFL TOTALS		**20**	**494**	**24.7**	**55**	**0**

	Fumbles NO	LOST	OFR
1993	1	0	0
CFL TOTALS	**1**	**0**	**0**

Tackles - 2 defensive and 1 special teams with Winnipeg in 1993. **CFL Total Tackles - 3 (2 defensive and 1 special teams).**

BONNER, BRIAN
Born: October 9, 1965
Birthplace: Minneapolis, Minnesota
Linebacker. 6'2", 228 lbs. Import
Last Amateur Club: University of Minnesota
Acquired: Selected in the ninth round (247th overall) by the San Francisco 49ers in the 1988 NFL Draft. Released and signed by the NFL Washington Redskins in June, 1988. On injured reserved through October 1989. Released during training camp in 1990. Signed as a free agent by the Ottawa Rough Riders in May, 1991. Granted free agency status in February, 1993. Signed as a free agent by the Saskatchewan Roughriders in July, 1993. Transferred to the Ottawa Rough Riders in September, 1993. Was released by Ottawa in December, 1993. Re-signed by Ottawa in April, 1994.

Games Played - 15 with Ottawa in 1991; 15 in 1992 and 7 with Ottawa and 10 with Saskatchewan in 1993. **CFL Total GP - 47.**

Fumble Returns - 3 for 0 yards with Ottawa in 1991; 1 for 0 yards in 1992 and 1 for 0 yards in 1993. **CFL Total Fumble Returns - 5 for 0 yards.**

Quarterback Sacks - 9 with Ottawa in 1991; 4 for 24 yards lost in 1992; 3 for 12 yards lost with Ottawa and 1 for 8 yards lost with Saskatchewan in 1993. **CFL Total QB Sacks - 17.**

Tackles - 68 defensive and 16 special teams with Ottawa in 1991; 44 defensive and 5 special teams in 1992; 20 defensive and 7 special teams with Ottawa and 39 defensive and 1 special teams with Saskatchewan in 1993. **CFL Total Tackles - 200 (171 defensive and 29 special teams).**

Tackles for Losses - 2 for 5 yards with Ottawa in 1991; 6 for 9 yards in 1992 and 2 for 2 yards with Saskatchewan in 1993. **CFL Total Tackles for Losses - 10 for 16 yards.**

All-Eastern All-Star in 1991.

Playoffs

Games Played - 1 with Ottawa in 1992 and 1 in 1993. **CFL Total Playoff GP - 2.**

Quarterback Sacks - 1 for 4 yards lost with Ottawa in 1993. **CFL Total Playoff QB Sacks - 1 for 4 yards lost.**

Tackles - 3 defensive with Ottawa in 1992 and 4 defensive in 1993. **CFL Total Playoff Tackles - 7 (7 defensive).**

BOOKER, VAUGHN
Born: February 24, 1968
Birthplace: Cincinnati, Ohio
Defensive End. 6'5", 260 lbs. Import
Last Amateur Club: University of Cincinnati
Acquired: Signed as a free agent by the Winnipeg Blue Bombers in June, 1992.

	Team	GP	Kickoff Returns NO	YDS	AVE	LG	TD
1992	Wpg.	15	1	3	3.0	3	0
1993	Wpg.	9	0	0	0	0	0
CFL TOTALS		**24**	**1**	**3**	**3.0**	**3**	**0**

	Fumble Returns NO	YDS	AVE	LG	TD
1992	4	1	0.3	1	0
1993	0	0	0.0	0	0
CFL TOTALS	**4**	**1**	**0.3**	**1**	**0**

Quarterback Sacks - 2 for 7 yards lost with Winnipeg in 1992 and 4 for 16 yards lost in 1993. **CFL Total QB Sacks - 6 for 23 yards lost.**

Tackles - 29 defensive and 7 special teams with Winnipeg in 1992 and 18 defensive in 1993. **CFL Total Tackles - 54 (47 defensive and 7 special teams).**

Tackles for Losses - 4 for 13 yards with Winnipeg in 1992 and 2 for 15 yards in 1993. **CFL Total Tackles for Losses - 6 for 28 yards.**

Playoffs

Games Played - 1 with Winnipeg in 1992 and 1 in 1993. **CFL Total Playoff GP - 2.**

Quarterback Sacks - 2 for 13 yards lost with Winnipeg in 1992. **CFL Total Playoff QB Sacks - 2 for 13 yards lost.**

BOOKER, VAUGHN

Tackles - 1 defensive with Winnipeg in 1992 and 6 defensive in 1993.
CFL Total Playoff Tackles - 7 (7 defensive).

Tackles for Losses - 2 for 3 yards with Winnipeg in 1993.
CFL Total Playoff Tackles for Losses - 2 for 3 yards.

Grey Cup

Games Played - 1 with Winnipeg in 1992 and 1 in 1993.
Total Grey Cup GP - 2.

Tackles - 5 defensive with Winnipeg in 1992 and 6 defensive in 1993.
Total Grey Cup Tackles - 11 (11 defensive).

BOURGEAU, MICHEL
Born: June 28, 1961
Birthplace: Montreal, Quebec
Tackle. 6'5", 275 lbs. Non-import
Last Amateur Club: Boise State University
Acquired: First 1984 Territorial Exemption by the Ottawa Rough Riders and 11th round selection of the New Orleans Saints in the 1984 NFL Draft. The exemption was acquired from the Montreal Concordes for fullback Mike Murphy. Released by Ottawa and signed as a free agent by the Edmonton Eskimos in August, 1989.

Games Played - 6 with Ottawa in 1984; 16 in 1985; 17 in 1986; 14 in 1987; 13 in 1988; 16 with Edmonton in 1989; 12 in 1990; 13 in 1991; 18 in 1992 and 17 in 1993.
CFL Total GP - 142.

Fumble Returns - 1 with Ottawa in 1984; 1 in 1985; 2 in 1987; 1 in 1988; 3 in 1990 and 1 in 1993. **CFL Total Fumble Returns - 9.**

Interception Returns - 1 with Ottawa in 1985.
CFL Total Interception Returns - 1.

Quarterback Sacks - 4 with Ottawa in 1985; 4 in 1986; 4 in 1987; 3 in 1988; 2 with Edmonton in 1990; 4 in 1991 and 1 for 8 yards lost in 1992.
CFL Total QB Sacks - 22.

Tackles - 40 defensive with Ottawa in 1987; 24 defensive in 1988; 8 defensive with Edmonton in 1989; 13 defensive in 1990; 19 defensive in 1991; 9 defensive and 6 special teams in 1992 and 4 defensive and 10 special teams in 1993.
CFL Total Tackles - 133 (117 defensive and 16 special teams).

Tackles for Losses - 3 for 11 yards with Edmonton in 1991 and 1 for 6 yards in 1992.
CFL Total Tackles for Losses - 4 for 17 yards.

Playoffs

Games Played - 1 with Ottawa in 1985; 1 with Edmonton in 1989; 2 in 1990; 1 in 1991; 2 in 1992 and 2 in 1993. **CFL Total Playoff GP - 9.**

Quarterback Sacks - 1 with Edmonton in 1989.
CFL Total Playoff QB Sacks - 1.

Tackles - 7 defensive with Edmonton in 1990; 1 defensive in 1991; 1 special teams in 1992 and 2 special teams in 1993.
CFL Total Playoff Tackles - 11 (8 defensive and 3 special teams).

Grey Cup

Games Played - 1 with Edmonton in 1990 and 1 in 1993.
Total Grey Cup GP - 2.

Defensive Tackles - 2 with Edmonton in 1990.
Total Grey Cup Defensive Tackles - 2.

BOUYER, WILLIE
Born: September 24,. 1966
Birthplace: Detroit, Michigan
Wide Receiver. 6'3", 196 lbs. Import
Last Amateur Club: Michigan State University
Acquired: Signed as a free agent by the NFL Seattle Seahawks in 1989. Released by Seattle in October, 1990. Selected in the first round (eighth overall) by the Birmingham Fire in the 1991 WLAF Positional Draft. Signed as a free agent by the Sacramento Gold Miners in April, 1993.

		Scoring						Pass Receiving				
	Team	GP	TD	C	FG	S	TP	NO	YDS	AVE	LG	TD
1993	Sac.	6	2	0	0	0	12	15	175	11.7	31	2
CFL TOTALS		**6**	**2**	**0**	**0**	**0**	**12**	**15**	**175**	**11.7**	**31**	**2**

Fumbles - 1 and 1 lost with Sacramento in 1993.
CFL Total Fumbles - 1 and 1 lost.

Tackles - 2 defensive with Sacramento in 1993.
CFL Total Tackles - 2 (2 defensive).

BOYKO, ALLAN
Born: March 2, 1967
Birthplace: Hamilton, Ontario
Slotback. 6'2", 175 lbs. Non-import
Last Amateur Club: Western Michigan University
Acquired: Selected by the Winnipeg Blue Bombers in the third round (19th overall) in the 1990 CFL College Draft. Rights were traded to the Saskatchewan Roughriders in July, 1990 along with quarterback Lee Saltz and Winnipeg's first round draft choices in the 1991 and 1992 CFL College Draft in December 1991 in exchange for quarterback Tom Burgess and future considerations. Traded back to Winnipeg along with a first round draft pick (acquired previously from Winnipeg) in exchange for linebacker Tyrone Jones and future considerations.

		Scoring						Pass Receiving				
	Team	GP	TD	C	FG	S	TP	NO	YDS	AVE	LG	TD
1993	Wpg.	17	3	0	0	0	18	7	108	15.4	27	3
CFL TOTALS		**17**	**3**	**0**	**0**	**0**	**18**	**7**	**108**	**15.4**	**27**	**3**

		Punt Returns					Kickoff Returns				
	Team	NO	YDS	AVE	LG	TD	NO	YDS	AVE	LG	TD
1993	Wpg.	63	299	4.7	20	0	27	446	16.5	43	0
CFL TOTALS		**63**	**299**	**4.7**	**20**	**0**	**27**	**446**	**16.5**	**43**	**0**

Interception Returns - 1 for 30 yards with Winnipeg in 1993.
CFL Total Interception Returns - 1 for 30 yards.

Tackles - 3 defensive and 7 special teams with Winnipeg in 1993.
CFL Total Tackles - 10 (3 defensive and 7 special teams).

Playoffs

Games Played - 1 with Winnipeg in 1993.
CFL Total Playoff GP - 1.

Punt Returns - 2 for 33 yards, 16.5 average, longest 17 yards with Winnipeg in 1993.
CFL Total Playoff Punt Returns - 2 for 33 yards, 16.5 average, longest 17 yards.

Unsuccessful Field Goal Returns - 1 for 21 yards with Winnpeg in 1993.
CFL Total Playoff Unsuccessful Field Goal Returns - 1 for 21 yards.

Kickoff Returns - 1 for 14 yards with Winnipeg in 1993.
CFL Total Playoff Kickoff Returns - 1 for 14 yards.

Grey Cup

Games Played - 1 with Winnipeg in 1993.
Total Grey Cup GP - 1.

Punt Returns - 5 for 16 yards, 3.2 average, longest 9 yards with Winnipeg in 1993.
Total Grey Cup Punt Returns - 5 for 16 yards, 3.2 average, longest 9 yards.

Kickoff Returns - 1 for 9 yards with Winnipeg in 1993.
Total Grey Cup Kickoff Returns - 1 for 9 yards.

BOYKO, BRUCE
Born: March 2, 1967
Birthplace: Hamilton, Ontario
Slotback. 6'3", 210 lbs. Non-import
Last Amateur Club: Western Michigan University
Acquired: Selected in the second round (9th overall) in the 1990 CFL College Draft by the Saskatchewan Roughriders.

		Rushing						Pass Receiving				
	Team	GP	NO	YDS	AVE	LG	TD	NO	YDS	AVE	LG	TD
1990	Sask.	18	1	2	2.0	2	0	18	259	14.4	24	0
1991	Sask.	18	0	0	0.0	0	0	5	44	8.8	12	0
1992	Sask.	17	0	0	0.0	0	0	1	19	19.0	19	0
1993	Sask.	18	20	72	3.6	10	0	30	299	10.0	28	2
CFL TOTALS		**71**	**21**	**74**	**3.5**	**10**	**0**	**54**	**621**	**11.5**	**28**	**2**

Scoring - 2 TDs for 12 points with Saskatchewan in 1993.
CFL Total Scoring - 2 TDs for 12 points.

Blocked Kicks - 1 punt with Saskatchewan in 1990. **CFL Total Blocked Kicks - 1 punt.**

Kickoff Returns - 2 for -7 yards, -3.5 average, longest -13 yards with Saskatchewan in 1991; 2 for 0 yards in 1992 and 2 for 1 yard, 0.5 average, longest 1 yard in 1993. **CFL Total Kickoff Returns - 6 for -6 yards, -1.0 average, longest 1 yard.**

Fumbles - 2 and 2 lost with Saskatchewan in 1993. **CFL Total Fumbles - 2 and 2 lost.**

Own Fumbles Recovered - 2 with Saskatchewan in 1993. **CFL Total OFR - 2.**

Fumble Returns - 1 for 0 yards with Saskatchewan in 1990; 1 for 0 yards in 1991; 1 for 0 yards in 1992 and 1 for 54 yards in 1993.
CFL Total Fumble Returns - 4 for 54 yards.

Tackles - 1 defensive and 27 special teams with Saskatchewan in 1991; 1 defensive and 25 special teams in 1992 and 13 special teams in 1993.
CFL Total Tackles - 67 (2 defensive and 65 special teams).

BOYKO, BRUCE

Playoffs

Games Played - 1 with Saskatchewan in 1990; 1 in 1992 and 1 in 1993.
CFL Total Playoff GP - 3.

Scoring - 1 TD for 6 points with Saskatchewan in 1993.
CFL Total Playoff Scoring - 1 TD for 6 points.

Pass Receiving - 5 for 77 yards, 15.4 average, longest 24 yards and 1 TD with Saskatchewan in 1993.
CFL Total Playoff Pass Receiving - 5 for 77 yards, 15.4 average, longest 24 yards and 1 TD.

Tackles - 4 special teams with Saskatchewan in 1992.
CFL Total Playoff Tackles - 4 (4 special teams).

BRANCH, DARRICK
Born: February 10, 1970
Birthplace: Dallas, Texas
Wide Receiver. 5'11", 195 lbs. Import
Last Amateur Club: University of Hawaii
Acquired: Selected in the eighth round (220th overall) by the Tampa Bay Buccaneers in the 1993 NFL Draft. Released during training camp. Signed as a free agent by the Toronto Argonauts in October, 1993.

			Kickoff Returns				
	Team	GP	NO	YDS	AVE	LG	TD
1993	Tor.	2	2	41	20.5	31	0
CFL TOTALS		**2**	**2**	**41**	**20.5**	**31**	**0**

BRANTLEY, SEAN
Born: June 30, 1969
Birthplace: Washington, D.C.
Defensive Tackle. 6'1", 285 lbs. Import
Last Amateur Club: Florida A & M University
Acquired: Signed as a free agent by the Saskatchewan Roughriders in May, 1993.

Games Played - 3 with Saskatchewan in 1993. **CFL Total GP - 3.**

Quarterback Sacks - 1 for 7 yards lost with Saskatchewan in 1993.
CFL Total QB Sacks - 1 for 7 yards lost.

Tackles - 7 defensive with Saskatchewan in 1993.
CFL Total Tackles - 7 (7 defensive).

Tackles for Losses - 3 for 8 yards with Saskatchewan in 1993.
CFL Total Tackles for Losses - 3 for 8 yards.

BRIGANCE, O.J.
Born: September 29, 1969
Birthplace: Houston, Texas
Linebacker. 6'0", 220 lbs. Import
Last Amateur Club: Rice University
Acquired: Signed as a free agent by the B.C. Lions in May, 1991. Granted free agency status in February, 1994. Signed as a free agent by the Baltimore CFL Colts in April, 1994.

Games Played - 18 with B.C. in 1991; 18 in 1992 and 18 in 1993.
CFL Total GP - 54.

Kickoff Returns - 5 for 40 yards, 8.0 average, longest 13 yards with B.C. in 1992.
CFL Total Kickoff Returns - 5 for 40 yards, 8.0 average, longest 13 yards.

Interception Returns - 1 for 7 yards with B.C. in 1991.
CFL Total Interception Returns - 1 for 7 yards.

Fumble Returns - 3 for 0 yards with B.C. in 1992 and 1 for 27 yards in 1993.
CFL Total Fumble Returns - 4 for 27 yards.

Quarterback Sacks - 2 with B.C. in 1991 and 20 for 131 yards lost in 1993.
CFL Total QB Sacks - 22.

Tackles - 92 defensive and 20 special teams with B.C. in 1991; 87 defensive and 7 special teams in 1992 and 46 defensive and 13 special teams in 1993.
CFL Total Tackles - 265 (225 defensive and 40 special teams).

Tackles for Losses - 3 for 4 yards with B.C. in 1991; 8 for 16 yards in 1992 and 10 for 32 yards in 1993.
CFL Total Tackles for Losses - 21 for 73 yards.

All-Western All-Star in 1991 and 1993.

Playoffs

Games Played - 1 with B.C. in 1991 and 1 in 1993. **CFL Total Playoff GP - 2.**

Quarterback Sacks - 2 for 22 yards lost with B.C. in 1993.
CFL Total Playoff QB Sacks - 2 for 22 yards lost.

Tackles - 8 defensive with B.C. in 1991 and 4 defensive and 1 special teams in 1993. **CFL Total Playoff Tackles - 13 (12 defensive and 1 special teams).**

BRITTON, EDDIE
Born: January 12, 1968
Birthplace: Chicago, Illinois
Wide Receiver. 5'9", 160 lbs. Import
Last Amateur Club: Central State of Ohio University
Acquired: Signed as a free agent by the NFL Indianapolis Colts in 1991 and was subsequently released during training camp. Spent the 1992 season with the WLAF Birmingham Fire. Signed as a free agent by the Calgary Stampeders in December, 1992.

Games Played - 2 with Calgary in 1993. **CFL Total GP - 2.**

Pass Receiving - 1 for 27 yards with Calgary in 1993.
CFL Total Pass Receiving - 1 for 27 yards.

BROWN, ALBERT
Born: December 19, 1963
Birthplace: Omaha, Nebraska
Wide Receiver. 6'0", 180 lbs. Import
Last Amateur Club: Western Illinois University
Acquired: Signed as a free agent by the Saskatchewan Roughriders in April, 1987.

			Scoring					Fumbles		
	Team	GP	TD	C	FG	S	TP	NO	LOST	OFR
1987	Sask.	2	0	0	0	0	0	0	0	0
1988	Sask.	11	0	0	0	0	0	0	0	0
1989a	Sask.	17	3	0	0	0	18	0	0	0
1990	Sask.	17	0	0	0	0	0	1	0	1
1991	Sask.	15	1	0	0	0	6	2	0	0
1992	Sask.	16	1	0	0	0	6	0	0	1
1993	Sask.	18	1	0	0	0	6	0	0	0
CFL TOTALS		**96**	**6**	**0**	**0**	**0**	**36**	**3**	**0**	**2**

		Kickoff Returns					Unsuccessful Field Goal Returns				
	Team	NO	YDS	AVE	LG	TD	NO	YDS	AVE	LG	TD
1987	Sask.	3	69	23.0	23	0	0	0	0.0	0	0
1988	Sask.	18	395	21.9	51	0	0	0	0.0	0	0
1989	Sask.	21	600	28.6	65	0	9	164	18.2	50	0
1990	Sask.	33	589	17.8	43	0	9	251	27.9	72	0
1991	Sask.	30	675	22.5	97	1	3	44	14.7	22	0
1992	Sask.	17	290	17.1	44	0	1	21	21.0	21	0
1993	Sask.	0	0	0.0	0	0	3	169	56.3	108	1
CFL TOTALS		**122**	**2618**	**21.5**	**97**	**1**	**25**	**649**	**26.0**	**108**	**1**

		Interception Returns					Punt Returns				
	Team	NO	YDS	AVE	LG	TD	NO	YDS	AVE	LG	TD
1987	Sask.	0	0	0.0	0	0	0	0	0.0	0	0
1988	Sask.	1	58	58.0	58	0	14	208	14.9	54	0
1989	Sask.	8	176	22.0	96	1	73	849	11.6	87	2
1990	Sask.	5	42	8.4	20	0	45	416	9.2	33	0
1991	Sask.	4	30	7.5	18	0	3	15	5.0	9	0
1992	Sask.	6	150	25.0	68	1	19	68	3.6	21	0
1993	Sask.	3	20	6.7	20	0	5	23	4.6	8	0
CFL TOTALS		**27**	**476**	**17.6**	**96**	**2**	**159**	**1579**	**9.9**	**87**	**2**

Rushing - 1 for 1 yard with Saskatchewan in 1987.
CFL Total Rushing - 1 for 1 yard.

Pass Receiving - 1 for 4 yards with Saskatchewan in 1987.
CFL Total Pass Receiving - 1 for 4 yards.

Fumble Returns - 1 for 0 yards with Saskatchewan in 1991 and 1 for 0 yards in 1992. **CFL Total Fumble Returns - 2 for 0 yards.**

2-Pt. Converts - 1 tried, 0 made with Saskatchewan in 1989.
CFL Total 2-Pt. Converts - 1 tried, 0 made.

Own Kickoffs Recovered - 1 for 5 yards with Saskatchewan in 1989 and 1 for 0 yards in 1990. **CFL Total Own Kickoffs Recovered - 2 for 5 yards.**

Tackles - 50 defensive with Saskatchewan in 1989; 59 defensive in 1990; 25 defensive and 4 special teams in 1991; 29 defensive and 3 special teams in 1992 and 39 defensive and 2 special teams in 1993.
CFL Total Tackles - 211 (202 defensive and 9 special teams).

a - Led the League in unsuccessful field goal returns

Playoffs

Games Played - 1 with Saskatchewan in 1990; 1 in 1992 and 1 in 1993.
CFL Total Playoff GP - 3.

Punt Returns - 1 for 2 yards with Saskatchewan in 1990.
CFL Total Playoff Punt Returns - 1 for 2 yards.

Kickoff Returns - 1 for 11 yards with Saskatchewan in 1990.
CFL Total Playoff Kickoff Returns - 1 for 11 yards.

Tackles - 6 defensive with Saskatchewan in 1990; 2 defensive in 1992 and 3 defensive in 1993. **CFL Total Playoff Tackles - 11 (11 defensive).**

BROWN, ANDRE
Born: August 21, 1966
Birthplace: Chicago, Illinois
Slotback. 6'3", 210 lbs. Import
Last Amateur Club: University of Miami
Acquired: Signed as a free agent by the NFL Miami Dolphins in April, 1989. Released by the Dolphins following the 1990 season. Signed as a free agent by the Ottawa Rough Riders in June, 1993. Released by Ottawa in September, 1993 and signed as a free agent by the Toronto Argonauts in October, 1993. Released by Toronto in November, 1993.

	Team	Scoring GP	TD	C	FG	S	TP	Pass Receiving NO	YDS	AVE	LG	TD
1993	Ott.	8	0	0	0	0	0	19	287	15.1	31	0
	Tor.	2	1	0	0	0	6	5	84	16.8	35	1
CFL TOTALS		**10**	**1**	**0**	**0**	**0**	**6**	**24**	**371**	**15.5**	**35**	**1**

Own Fumbles Recovered - 1 with Ottawa in 1993. **CFL Total OFR - 1.**

Tackles - 1 defensive and 1 special teams with Ottawa in 1993. **CFL Total Tackles - 2 (1 defensive and 1 special teams).**

BROWN, EDDIE
Born: August 6, 1966
Birthplace: Topeka, Kansas
Wide Receiver. 5'11", 175 lbs. Import
Last Amateur Club: Iowa State University
Acquired: Signed as a free agent by the Calgary Stampeders in April, 1990. Released in September, 1990 and signed as a free agent by the Ottawa Rough Riders in December, 1990. Released by Ottawa in January, 1992. Spent the 1992 season with the Sacramento Surge of the World League of American Football. Signed as a free agent by the Toronto Argonauts in August, 1992. Traded to the Edmonton Eskimos in January, 1993, along with defensive back Ed Berry, linebacker Bruce Dickson, quarterback Rickey Foggie, slotback J.P. Izquierdo, defensive lineman Leonard Johnson, slotback Darrell K. Smith and defensive back Don Wilson in exchange for defensive lineman Cameron Brosseau, linebacker John Davis, slotback Craig Ellis, quarterback Tracy Ham, defensive back Enis Jackson, running back Chris Johnstone, defensive back Travis Oliver and wide receiver Ken Winey.

	Team	Scoring GP	TD	C	FG	S	TP	Rushing NO	YDS	AVE	LG	TD
1990	Cal.	10	1	0	0	0	6	1	-12	-12.0	-12	0
1991	Ott.	11	4	0	0	0	24	2	9	4.5	7	0
1992	Tor.	10	5	0	0	0	30	1	12	12.0	12	0
1993ab	Edm.	18	15	0	0	0	90	3	19	6.3	21	0
CFL TOTALS		**49**	**25**	**0**	**0**	**0**	**150**	**7**	**28**	**4.0**	**21**	**0**

	Team	Pass Receiving NO	YDS	AVE	LG	TD	Punt Returns NO	YDS	AVE	LG	TD
1990	Cal.	23	357	15.5	56	1	19	166	8.7	29	0
1991	Ott.	21	458	21.8	70	4	22	171	7.8	51	0
1992	Tor.	31	571	18.4	72	5	7	-11	-1.6	29	0
1993	Edm.	67	1378	20.6	75	15	15	119	7.9	49	0
CFL TOTALS		**142**	**2764**	**19.5**	**75**	**25**	**63**	**445**	**7.1**	**51**	**0**

	Team	Kickoff Returns NO	YDS	AVE	LG	TD	Fumbles NO	LOST	OFR
1990	Cal.	7	104	14.9	27	0	2	1	0
1991	Ott.	1	14	14.0	14	0	3	3	0
1992	Tor.	8	149	18.6	25	0	1	0	1
1993	Edm.	0	0	0.0	0	0	3	3	0
CFL TOTALS		**16**	**267**	**16.7**	**27**	**0**	**9**	**7**	**1**

Tackles - 1 defensive with Toronto in 1992 and 3 defensive with Edmonton in 1993. **CFL Total Tackles - 4 (4 defensive).**

a - Tied for CFL Points - Touchdowns
b - Tied for CFL Lead - Receiving Touchdowns

Playoffs

	Team	Scoring GP	TD	C	FG	S	TP	Pass Receiving NO	YDS	AVE	LG	TD
1991	Ott.	1	0	0	0	0	0	1	21	21.0	21	0
1993	Edm.	2	3	0	0	0	18	6	110	18.3	32	3
CFL TOTALS		**3**	**3**	**0**	**0**	**0**	**18**	**7**	**131**	**19.3**	**32**	**3**

Tackles - 1 defensive with Ottawa in 1991. **CFL Total Playoff Tackles - 1 (1 defensive).**

Grey Cup

	Team	GP	Pass Receiving NO	YDS	AVE	LG	TD	Fumbles NO	LOST	OFR
1993	Edm.	1	4	114	28.5	52	0	1	1	0
CFL TOTALS		**1**	**4**	**114**	**28.5**	**52**	**0**	**1**	**1**	**0**

BROWN, ERROL
Born: January 4, 1971
Birthplace: Wolverhampton, England
Defensive Back, 5'8", 170 lbs, Non-import
Last Amateur Club: University of Saskatchewan
Acquired: Selected in the third round (17th overall) by the Saskatchewan Roughriders in the 1993 CFL College Draft. Released by Saskatchewan in October, 1993 and signed as a free agent by the Winnipeg Blue Bombers in November, 1993. Traded to the Saskatchewan Roughriders in exchange for future considerations in April, 1994.

	Team	GP	Punt Returns NO	YDS	AVE	LG	TD	Kickoff Returns NO	YDS	AVE	LG	TD
1993	Wpg.	2	5	23	4.6	16	0	1	12	12.0	12	0
	Sask.	14	22	158	7.2	26	0	8	144	18.0	26	0
CFL TOTALS		**16**	**27**	**181**	**6.7**	**26**	**0**	**9**	**156**	**17.3**	**26**	**0**

Own Kickoffs Recovered - 1 with Saskatchewan in 1993. **CFL Total OKR - 1.**

Tackles - 4 defensive and 4 special teams with Saskatchewan and 2 defensive with Winnipeg in 1993. **CFL Total Tackles - 10 (6 defensive and 4 special teams).**

Playoffs

Games Played - 1 with Winnipeg in 1993. **CFL Total Playoff GP - 1**

Punt Returns - 5 for 15 yards, 3.0 average, longest 13 yards with Winnipeg in 1993. **CFL Total Playoff Punt Returns - 5 for 15 yards, 3.0 average, longest 13 yards.**

Interception Returns - 1 for 31 yards with Winnipeg in 1993. **CFL Total Playoff Interception Returns - 1 for 31 yards.**

Fumbles - 1 and 1 lost with Winnipeg in 1993. **CFL Total Playoff Fumbles - 1 and 1 lost.**

Tackles - 2 defensive with Winnipeg in 1993. **CFL Total Playoff Tackles - 2 (2 defensive).**

Grey Cup

Games Played - 1 with Winnipeg in 1993. **Total Grey Cup GP - 1**

Tackles - 3 defensive with Winnipeg in 1993. **Total Grey Cup Tackles - 3 (3 defensive).**

BROWN, HURLIE
Born: June 21, 1969
Birthplace: Rockledge, Florida
Linebacker. 6'1", 200 lbs. Import
Last Amateur Club: University of Miami
Acquired: Signed as a free agent by the NFL Washington Redskins in 1992. Released by Washington and signed as a free agent by the NFL San Francisco 49ers. Released by San Francisco and signed as a free agent by the Sacramento Gold Miners in September, 1993.

Games Played - 1 with Sacramento in 1993. **CFL Total GP - 1.**

Quarterback Sacks - 1 for 6 yards lost with Sacramento in 1993. **CFL Total QB Sacks - 1 for 6 yards lost.**

Tackles - 4 defensive with Sacramento in 1993. **CFL Total Tackles - 4 (4 defensive).**

BROWN, TRENT
Born: October 7, 1966
Birthplace: Edmonton, Alberta
Defensive Back. 5'11", 190 lbs. Non-import
Last Amateur Club: University of Alberta (CWAA)
Acquired: Signed as a free agent by the Edmonton Eskimos in January, 1991.

Games Played - 12 with Edmonton in 1991; 18 in 1992 and 16 in 1993. **CFL Total GP - 46.**

Kickoff Returns - 0 for -6 yards with Edmonton in 1991. **CFL Total Kickoff Returns - 0 for -6 yards.**

Fumble Returns - 2 for 29 yards, 14.5 average, longest 17 yards with Edmonton in 1991 and 1 for 4 yards in 1992. **CFL Total Fumble Returns - 3 for 33 yards, 11.0 average, longest 17 yards.**

Interception Returns - 2 for 38 yards, 19.0 average, longest 20 yards with Edmonton in 1992. **CFL Total Interception Returns - 2 for 38 yards, 19.0 average, longest 20 yards.**

Quarterback Sacks - 1 for 7 yards lost with Edmonton in 1993. **CFL Total QB Sacks - 1 for 7 yards lost.**

Tackles - 13 defensive and 6 special teams with Edmonton in 1991; 36 defensive and 16 special teams in 1992 and 8 defensive and 20 special teams in 1993.**CFL Total Tackles - 99 (57 defensive and 42 special teams).**

BROWN, TRENT

Playoffs

Games Played - 2 with Edmonton in 1992 and 2 in 1993.
CFL Total Playoff GP - 4.

Tackles - 4 defensive with Edmonton in 1992 and 2 defensive and 2 special teams in 1993.
CFL Total Playoff Tackles - 8 (6 defensive and 2 special teams).

Grey Cup

Games Played - 1 with Edmonton in 1993.
Total Grey Cup GP - 1.

Fumble Returns - 1 for 0 yards with Edmonton in 1993.
Total Grey Cup Fumble Returns - 1 for 0 yards.

Tackles - 2 special teams with Edmonton in 1993.
Total Grey Cup Tackles - 2 (2 special teams).

BROWNE, LESS

Born: December 7, 1959
Birthplace: East Liverpool, Ohio
Defensive Back. 5'10", 165 lbs. Import
Last Amateur Club: Colorado State University
Acquired: Selected in the 13th round by the Pittsburgh Maulers of the USFL in 1984 American College Draft. Signed as a free agent with the Hamilton Tiger-Cats in April, 1984. Released by Hamilton in October, 1988. Signed as a free agent by the Edmonton Eskimos in March, 1989. Released by Edmonton and signed as a free agent by Winnipeg Blue Bombers in June, 1989. Traded to the Ottawa Rough Riders in May, 1992 in exchange for slotback Gerald Wilcox. Traded to the B.C. Lions in April, 1993 along with offensive tackle tackle Rob Smith and linebacker Patrick Wayne in exchange for offensive linesman Carl Coulter and Chris Gioskos, kicker Wayne Lammle, cornerback Joe Mero and linebacker Mark Scott.

		Scoring						Fumbles		
	Team	GP	TD	C	FG	S	TP	NO	LOST	OFR
1984	Ham.	8	0	0	0	0	0	2	1	0
1985abc	Ham.	15	0	0	0	0	0	0	0	0
1986ab	Ham.	17	1	0	0	0	6	1	0	1
1987	Ham.	16	1	0	0	0	6	0	0	0
1988	Ham.	15	0	x1	0	0	2	0	0	0
1989	Wpg.	17	0	0	0	0	0	0	0	0
1990abdef	Wpg.	18	1	0	0	0	6	0	0	1
1991abde	Wpg.	16	0	0	0	0	0	1	0	0
1992abdeg	Ott.	17	0	0	0	0	0	0	0	1
1993	B.C.	18	2	0	0	0	12	0	0	0
CFL TOTALS		**157**	**5**	**x1**	**0**	**0**	**32**	**4**	**1**	**3**

		Kickoff Returns					Fumble Returns				
	Team	NO	YDS	AVE	LG	TD	NO	YDS	AVE	LG	TD
1984	Ham.	2	72	36.0	31	0	0	0	0.0	0	0
1985	Ham.	2	13	6.5	10	0	1	0	0.0	0	0
1986	Ham.	20	520	26.0	61	0	0	0	0.0	0	0
1987	Ham.	1	26	26.0	26	0	0	0	0.0	0	0
1988	Ham.	1	62	62.0	62	0	2	16	8.0	16	0
1989	Wpg.	1	5	5.0	5	0	0	0	0.0	0	0
1990	Wpg.	0	0	0.0	0	0	2	1	0.5	1	0
1991	Wpg.	3	57	19.0	25	0	2	0	0.0	0	0
1992	Ott.	1	15	15.0	15	0	1	0	0.0	0	0
1993	B.C.	0	0	0.0	0	0	1	85	85.0	85	1
CFL TOTALS		**31**	**770**	**24.8**	**62**	**0**	**9**	**102**	**11.3**	**85**	**1**

		Punt Returns					Interception Returns				
	Team	NO	YDS	AVE	LG	TD	NO	YDS	AVE	LG	TD
1984	Ham.	0	0	0.0	0	0	0	0	0.0	0	0
1985	Ham.	5	42	8.4	25	0	12	165	13.8	34	0
1986	Ham.	1	111	111.1	47	0	8	128	16.0	42	1
1987	Ham.	1	82	82.0	75	1	5	32	6.4	19	0
1988	Ham.	0	0	0.0	0	0	8	90	11.3	27	0
1989	Wpg.	5	-8	-1.6	6	0	3	31	10.3	19	0
1990	Wpg.	1	2	2.0	2	0	14	273	19.5	45	1
1991	Wpg.	2	15	7.5	9	0	10	267	26.7	55	0
1992	Ott.	0	0	0.0	0	0	11	259	23.5	76	0
1993	B.C.	1	0	0.0	0	0	5	140	28.0	52	1
CFL TOTALS		**16**	**244**	**16.3**	**75**	**1**	**76**	**1385**	**18.2**	**76**	**3**

		QB Sacks	Blocked Punts	Unsuccessful Field Goal Returns				
	Team	NO	NO	NO	YDS	AVE	LG	TD
1984	Ham.	0	0	0	0	0.0	0	0
1985	Ham.	1	1	0	0	0.0	0	0
1986	Ham.	1	2	2	70	35.0	50	0
1987	Ham.	0	0	4	41	10.3	20	0
1988	Ham.	0	0	8	111	13.9	54	0
1989	Wpg.	0	0	5	100	20.0	41	0
1990	Wpg.	0	0	0	0	0.0	0	0
1991	Wpg.	0	0	0	0	0.0	0	0
1992	Ott.	0	3	0	0	0.0	0	0
1993	B.C.	0	0	0	0	0.0	0	0
CFL TOTALS		**2**	**6**	**19**	**322**	**16.9**	**54**	**0**

Own Kickoffs Recovered - 1 for 0 yards with Ottawa in 1992.
CFL Total Own Kickoffs Recovered - 1 for 0 yards.

Pass Receiving - 1 for 19 yards with Winnipeg in 1991.
CFL Total Pass Receiving - 1 for 19 yards.

Tackles - 45 defensive with Hamilton in 1987; 42 defensive in 1988; 32 defensive with Winnipeg in 1989; 42 defensive in 1990; 33 defensive and 5 special teams in 1991; 40 defensive and 8 special teams with Ottawa in 1992 and 49 defensive with B.C. in 1993.
CFL Total Tackles - 296 (283 defensive and 13 special teams).

Tackles for Losses - 1 for 1 yard with Ottawa in 1992 and 2 for 15 yards with B.C. in 1993. **CFL Total Tackles for Losses - 3 for 16 yards.**

a - All-Eastern All-Star
b - CFL All-Star
c - Shared the lead for the most interceptions in the season with Paul Bennett of the Hamilton Tiger-Cats.
d - Led CFL in Interceptions
e - Led CFL in Interception Return Yards.
f - Set CFL Record for Most Interception Return Yards in One Season.
g - Set CFL Record for Most Career Interceptions and Interception Return Yards.

Playoffs

Games Played - 1 with Hamilton in 1985; 1 in 1986; 1 in 1987; 2 with Winnipeg in 1989; 1 in 1990; 2 in 1991; 1 with Ottawa in 1992 and 1 with B.C. in 1993.
CFL Total Playoff GP - 10.

Fumble Returns - 1 for 0 yards with Winnipeg in 1991.
CFL Total Playoff Fumble Returns - 1 for 0 yards.

Punt Returns - 11 for 104 yards, 9.5 average, longest 46 yards with Winnipeg in 1991. **CFL Total Playoff Punt Returns - 11 for 104 yards, 9.5 average, longest 46 yards.**

Kickoff Returns - 1 for 31 yards with Hamilton in 1986; 1 for 17 yards with Hamilton in 1987; 1 for 89 yards with Winnipeg in 1991 and 1 for 9 yards with B.C. in 1993. **CFL Total Playoff Kickoff Returns - 4 for 146 yards, 36.5 average, longest 89 yards.**

Interception Returns - 1 for 10 yards with Winnipeg in 1989; 3 for 14 yards, 4.7 average, longest 9 yards in 1991 and 1 for 0 yards with Ottawa in 1992.
CFL Total Playoff Interception Returns - 4 for 24 yards, 6.0 average, longest 9 yards.

Tackles - 1 defensive with Hamilton in 1987; 3 defensive with Winnipeg in 1989; 4 defensive in 1991 and 1 defensive with Ottawa in 1992.
CFL Total Playoff Tackles - 9 (9 defensive).

Grey Cup

Games Played - 1 with Hamilton in 1985 and 1 with Winnipeg in 1990.
Total Grey Cup GP - 2.

Defensive Tackles - 2 with Winnipeg in 1990.
Total Grey Cup Defensive Tackles - 2.

BROWNLEE, VINCENT

Born: December 20, 1969
Birthplace: Armory, Mississippi
Wide Receiver. 6'0", 188 lbs. Import
Last Amateur Club: University of Mississippi
Acquired: Selected in the eighth round (29th overall) by the New York Jets in the 1992 NFL Draft. Signed as a free agent by the B.C. Lions in July, 1993. Released by B.C. in August, 1993.

			Pass Receiving					Punt Returns				
	Team	GP	NO	YDS	AVE	LG	TD	NO	YDS	AVE	LG	TD
1993	B.C.	2	2	41	20.5	36	0	5	29	5.8	21	0
CFL TOTALS		**2**	**2**	**41**	**20.5**	**36**	**0**	**5**	**29**	**5.8**	**21**	**0**

		Kickoff Returns					Fumbles		
	Team	NO	YDS	AVE	LG	TD	NO	LOST	OFR
1993	B.C.	9	160	17.8	36	0	1	1	0
CFL TOTALS		**9**	**160**	**17.8**	**36**	**0**	**1**	**1**	**0**

Unsuccessful Field Goal Returns - 1 for 0 yards with B.C. in 1993.
CFL Total Unsuccessful Field Goal Returns - 1 for 0 yards.

BRYANT, BLAISE

Born: November 23, 1969
Birthplace: Huntington Beach, California
Running Back. 6'0", 205 lbs. Import
Last Amateur Club: Iowa State University
Acquired: Selected in the sixth round (148th overall) by the New York Jets in the 1991 NFL Draft. Released by New York in August, 1992. Signed as a free agent by the Winnipeg Blue Bombers in April, 1993. Released by Winnipeg in August, 1993 and was subsequently signed as a free agent by the Saskatchewan Roughriders in September, 1993. Transfered back to Winnipeg in October, 1993.

			Scoring					Pass Receiving				
	Team	GP	TD	C	FG	S	TP	NO	YDS	AVE	LG	TD
1993	Wpg.	8	1	0	0	0	6	31	252	8.1	31	0
	Sask.	2	0	0	0	0	0	16	132	8.3	35	0
CFL TOTALS		**10**	**1**	**0**	**0**	**0**	**6**	**47**	**384**	**8.2**	**35**	**0**

BRYANT, BLAISE

	Team	Rushing NO	YDS	AVE	LG	TD	Kickoff Returns NO	YDS	AVE	LG	TD
1993	Wpg.	62	313	5.0	68	1	1	31	31.0	31	0
	Sask.	16	132	8.3	35	0	4	88	22.0	28	0
CFL TOTALS		**47**	**384**	**8.2**	**35**	**0**	**5**	**119**	**23.8**	**31**	**0**

Fumbles - 3 and 3 lost with Winnipeg and 2 and 2 lost with Saskatchewan in 1993. **CFL Total Fumbles - 5 and 5 lost.**

Tackles - 1 defensive with Winnipeg in 1993. **CFL Total Tackles - 1 (1 defensive).**

Playoffs

Games Played - 1 with Winnipeg in 1993. **CFL Total Playoff GP - 1**

Tackles - 1 special teams with Winnipeg in 1993. **CFL Total Playoff Tackles - 1 (1 special teams).**

Grey Cup

Games Played - 1 with Winnipeg in 1993. **Total Grey Cup GP - 1.**

Kickoff Returns - 2 for 22 yards with Winnipeg in 1993. **Total Grey Cup Kickoff Returns - 2 for 22 yards.**

Fumbles - 1 and 1 lost with Winnipeg in 1993. **Total Grey Cup Fumbles - 1 and 1 lost.**

Tackles - 1 special teams with Winnipeg in 1993. **Total Grey Cup Tackles - 1 (1 special teams).**

BURBAGE, CORNELL

Born: February 22, 1965
Birthplace: Lexington, Kentucky
Wide Receiver. 5'10", 185 lbs. Import
Last Amateur Club: University of Kentucky
Acquired: Signed as a free agent by the Dallas Cowboys in April, 1987. Was subsequently released and re-signed as a replacement player by Dallas in September, 1987. Granted unconditional free agency in February 1990 and was subsequently signed as a free agent by the NFL Minnesota Vikings. Was released by Minnesota and was selected in the first round (seventh overall) by the New York/New Jersey Knights in the 1991 WLAF Positional Draft. Signed as a free agent by the Hamilton Tiger-Cats in April, 1993.

	Team	Scoring GP	TD	C	FG	S	TP	Pass Receiving NO	YDS	AVE	LG	TD
1993	Ham.	12	3	0	0	0	18	31	367	11.8	31	3
CFL TOTALS		**12**	**3**	**0**	**0**	**0**	**18**	**31**	**367**	**11.8**	**31**	**3**

	Team	Punt Returns NO	YDS	AVE	LG	TD	Kickoff Returns NO	YDS	AVE	LG	TD
1993	Ham.	16	126	7.9	45	0	35	597	17.1	43	0
CFL TOTALS		**16**	**126**	**7.9**	**45**	**0**	**35**	**397**	**17.1**	**43**	**0**

	Team	Unsuccessful Field Goal Returns NO	YDS	AVE	LG	TD	Fumbles NO	LOST	OFR
1993	Ham.	1	4	4.0	4	0	1	0	1
CFL TOTALS		**1**	**4**	**4.0**	**4**	**0**	**1**	**0**	**1**

Tackles - 5 defensive and 1 special teams with Hamilton in 1993. **CFL Total Tackles - 6 (5 defensive and 1 special teams).**

Playoffs

Games Played - 2 with Hamilton in 1993. **CFL Total Playoff GP - 2.**

Pass Receiving - 6 for 65 yards, 10.8 average, longest 27 yards with Hamilton in 1993. **CFL Total Playoff Pass Receiving - 6 for 65 yards, 10.8 average, longest 27 yards.**

Punt Returns - 6 for 28 yards, 4.7 average, longest 17 yards with Hamilton in 1993. **CFL Total Playoff Punt Returns - 6 for 28 yards, 4.7 average, longest 17 yards.**

Kickoff Returns - 2 for 66 yards, 33.0 average, longest 39 yards with Hamilton in 1993. **CFL Total Playoff Kickoff Returns - 2 for 66 yards, 33.0 average, longest 39 yards.**

Fumbles - 1 and 0 lost with Hamilton in 1993.**CFL Total Playoff Fumbles - 1 and 0 lost.**

BURGESS, TOM

Born: March 6, 1964
Birthplace: Newark, New Jersey
Quarterback. 6'0", 195 lbs. Import
Last Amateur Club: Colgate University
Acquired: Signed as a free agent by the Ottawa Rough Riders in March, 1986. Traded to Saskatchewan for quarterback Joe Paopao in April, 1987. Traded to Winnipeg Blue Bombers in July, 1990 in exchange for quarterback Lee Saltz and the rights to wide receiver Allan Boyko, as well as Winnipeg's first round draft choices in the 1991 and 1992 CFL College Draft. Granted free agency status in February, 1992. Signed as a free agent by Ottawa in May, 1992. Traded to the Saskatchewan Roughriders along with defensive back Anthony Drawhorn, linebacker Ron Goetz and defensive end Paul Yatkowski in exchange for quarterback Kent Austin and offensive lineman Andrew Greene in March, 1994.

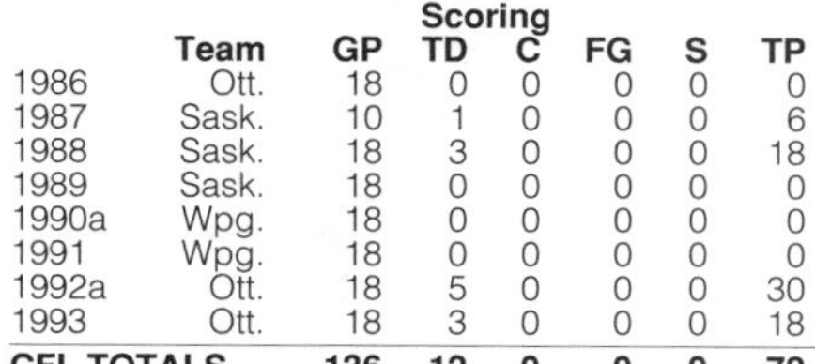

	Team	Scoring GP	TD	C	FG	S	TP
1986	Ott.	18	0	0	0	0	0
1987	Sask.	10	1	0	0	0	6
1988	Sask.	18	3	0	0	0	18
1989	Sask.	18	0	0	0	0	0
1990a	Wpg.	18	0	0	0	0	0
1991	Wpg.	18	0	0	0	0	0
1992a	Ott.	18	5	0	0	0	30
1993	Ott.	18	3	0	0	0	18
CFL TOTALS		**136**	**12**	**0**	**0**	**0**	**72**

	Team	Rushing NO	YDS	AVE	LG	TD	Passing ATT	COMP	YDS	PCT	INT	LG	TD
1986	Ott.	26	113	4.4	14	0	199	95	1199	47.7	12	68	5
1987	Sask.	26	114	4.4	14	1	243	127	1691	52.3	14	62	7
1988	Sask.	61	249	4.1	25	3	331	159	2575	48.0	14	79	19
1989	Sask.	48	209	4.4	28	0	342	162	2540	47.4	18	58	22
1990	Wpg.	70	260	3.7	26	0	574	330	3958	57.5	27	75	25
1991	Wpg.	73	326	4.5	19	0	525	261	4212	49.7	29	104	27
1992	Ott.	68	348	5.1	19	5	511	276	4026	54.0	24	71	29
1993	Ott.	75	347	4.6	18	3	591	329	5063	55.7	25	98	30
CFL TOTALS		**447**	**1966**	**4.4**	**28**	**12**	**3316**	**1739**	**25264**	**52.4**	**163**	**104**	**164**

	Team	Fumbles NO	LOST	OFR	2-Pt. Converts TRIED	GOOD	PCT
1986	Ott.	1	1	0	2	0	0.0
1987	Sask.	4	4	1	1	0	0.0
1988	Sask.	2	1	1	1	1	100.0
1989	Sask.	2	2	0	1	0	0.0
1990	Wpg.	6	5	2	1	1	100.0
1991	Wpg.	8	6	2	2	1	50.0
1992	Ott.	10	8	2	1	1	100.0
1993	Ott.	11	2	6	1	0	0.0
CFL TOTALS		**44**	**29**	**14**	**10**	**4**	**40.0**

Defensive Tackles - 1 with Saskatchewan in 1988; 1 in 1989; 2 with Winnipeg in 1990; 3 with Ottawa in 1992 and 2 in 1993. **CFL Total Defensive Tackles - 9.**

a - All-Eastern All-Star.

Playoffs

	Team	GP	Passing ATT	COMP	YDS	PCT	INT	LG	TD	Rushing NO	YDS	AVE	LG	TD
1988	Sask.	1	42	20	276	47.6	1	33	1	8	30	3.8	11	0
1989	Sask.	2	12	9	120	75.0	0	47	2	7	8	1.1	8	0
1990	Wpg.	1	40	24	230	60.0	1	19	1	7	49	7.0	31	0
1991	Wpg.	2	40	15	171	37.5	3	24	1	8	38	4.8	14	0
1992	Ott.	1	22	12	161	54.5	0	43	1	6	21	3.5	11	0
1993	Ott.	1	42	25	338	13.5	0	75	1	4	11	2.8	9	0
CFL TOTALS		**8**	**198**	**105**	**1296**	**53.0**	**5**	**75**	**7**	**40**	**157**	**3.9**	**31**	**0**

Fumbles - 1 and 0 lost with Winnipeg in 1990. **CFL Total Playoff Fumbles - 1 and 0 lost.**

Own Fumbles Recovered - 1 with Winnipeg in 1990. **CFL Total Playoff OFR - 1.**

Grey Cup

Games Played - 1 with Saskatchewan in 1989 and 1 with Winnipeg in 1990. **Total Grey Cup GP - 2.**

	Team	Passing ATT	COMP	YDS	PCT	INT	LG	TD	Rushing NO	YDS	AVE	LG	TD
1990	Wpg.	31	18	286	58.1	0	55	3	7	26	3.7	11	0
CFL TOTALS		**31**	**18**	**286**	**58.1**	**0**	**55**	**3**	**7**	**26**	**3.7**	**11**	**0**

Grey Cup Game Offensive Star in 1990.

BURKE, PATRICK

Born: November 6, 1968
Birthplace: Willowdale, Ontario
Safety. 5'11", 180 lbs. Non-import
Last Amateur Club: Fresno College
Acquired: Selected in the first round (first overall) by the B.C. Lions in the 1993 CFL College Draft. Traded to the Ottawa Rough Riders in June, 1993 in exchange for defensive back Ken Hailey.

	Team	GP	Interception Returns NO	YDS	AVE	LG	TD	Kickoff Returns NO	YDS	AVE	LG	TD
1993	Ott.	18	1	0	0.0	0	0	27	415	15.4	30	0
CFL TOTALS		**18**	**1**	**0**	**0.0**	**0**	**0**	**27**	**415**	**15.4**	**30**	**0**

Tackles - 36 defensive and 8 special teams with Ottawa in 1993. **CFL Total Tackles - 44 (36 defensive and 8 special teams).**

Tackles for Losses - 1 for 6 yards with Ottawa in 1993. **CFL Total Tackles for Losses - 1 for 6 yards.**

Playoffs

Games Played - 1 with Ottawa in 1993. **CFL Total Playoff GP - 1.**

BURKE, PATRICK

Kickoff Returns - 1 for 14 yards with Ottawa in 1993.
CFL Total Playoff Kickoff Returns - 1 for 14 yards.

Tackles - 3 defensive with Ottawa in 1993.
CFL Total Playoff Tackles - 3 (3 defensive).

BUSHEY, PAUL
Born: April 9, 1966
Birthplace: Hamilton, Ontario
Fullback. 6'1", 219 lbs. Non-import
Last Amateur Club: Colgate University
Acquired: Selected in the fourth round (32nd overall) by the Saskatchewan Roughriders in the 1990 CFL College Draft. Released and signed as a free agent by the Hamilton Tiger-Cats in September, 1991. Granted free agency status in February, 1993. Re-signed by Hamilton in June, 1993.

	Team	GP	Scoring TD	C	FG	S	TP
1990	Sask.	14	0	0	0	0	0
1991	Sask.	9	1	0	0	0	6
	Ham.	6	0	x1	0	0	2
1992	Ham.	8	0	0	0	0	0
1993	Ham.	15	1	0	0	0	6
CFL TOTALS		**52**	**2**	**x1**	**0**	**0**	**14**

	Team	Rushing NO	YDS	AVE	LG	TD	Fumbles NO	LOST	OFR
1990	Sask.	5	28	5.6	18	0	0	0	0
1991	Sask.	13	81	6.2	25	1	1	1	0
	Ham.	2	8	4.0	6	0	0	0	0
1992	Ham.	5	48	9.6	23	0	0	0	1
1993	Ham.	15	60	4.0	12	1	1	1	0
CFL TOTALS		**40**	**225**	**5.6**	**25**	**2**	**2**	**2**	**1**

	Team	Kickoff Returns NO	YDS	AVE	LG	TD	Pass Receiving NO	YDS	AVE	LG	TD
1990	Sask.	7	95	13.6	23	0	0	0	0.0	0	0
1991	Sask.	1	11	11.0	11	0	3	21	7.0	9	0
	Ham.	3	45	15.0	20	0	1	5	5.0	5	0
1992	Ham.	2	22	11.0	15	0	12	163	13.6	22	0
1993	Ham.	2	23	11.5	13	0	18	135	7.5	30	0
CFL TOTALS		**15**	**196**	**13.1**	**23**	**0**	**34**	**324**	**9.5**	**30**	**0**

Punting - 1 for 40 yards with Hamilton in 1992.
CFL Total Punting - 1 for 40 yards.

Net Punting - 1 for 34 yards, 34.0 average with Hamilton in 1993.
CFL Total Net Punting - 1 for 34 yards, 34.0 average.

Tackles - 1 defensive with Saskatchewan in 1990; 10 special teams in 1991; 1 defensive and 20 special teams with Hamilton in 1991; 2 defensive and 15 special teams in 1992 and 1 defensive and 19 special teams in 1993.
CFL Total Tackles - 69 (5 defensive and 64 special teams).

Playoffs

	Team	GP	Rushing NO	YDS	AVE	LG	TD	Kickoff Returns NO	YDS	AVE	LG	TD
1990	Sask.	1	-1	-1	-1.0	-1	0	4	60	15.0	27	0
1993	Ham.	2	2	9	4.5	6	0	0	0	0.0	0	0
CFL TOTALS		**3**	**1**	**8**	**8.0**	**6**	**0**	**4**	**60**	**15.0**	**27**	**0**

	Team	Punt Returns NO	YDS	AVE	LG	TD	Pass Receiving NO	YDS	AVE	LG	TD
1990	Sask.	1	5	5.0	5	0	0	0	0.0	0	0
1993	Ham.	0	0	0.0	0	0	2	14	7.0	9	0
CFL TOTALS		**1**	**5**	**5.0**	**5**	**0**	**2**	**14**	**7.0**	**9**	**0**

Tackles - 8 special teams with Hamilton in 1993.
CFL Total Playoff Tackles - 8 (8 special teams).

BUTLER, WAYDE
Born: December 25, 1969
Birthplace: Beaumont, Texas
Wide Receiver. 5'11", 180 lbs. Non-import
Last Amateur Club: SW Louisiana University
Acquired: Signed as a free agent by the Edmonton Eskimos in October, 1993.

Games Played - 3 with Edmonton in 1993. **CFL Total GP - 3.**

Pass Receiving -1 for 7 yards with Edmonton in 1993.
CFL Total Pass Receiving - 1 for 7 yards.

Tackles - 1 defensive with Edmonton in 1993.
CFL Total Tackles - 1 (1 defensive).

CAFAZZO, LOU
Born: June 14, 1966
Birthplace: Hamilton, Ontario
Offensive Lineman. 6'3", 250 lbs. Non-import
Last Amateur Club: Eastern Michigan University
Acquired: Selected in the third round (18th overall) by the Calgary Stampeders in the 1989 CFL College Draft. Traded to the Hamilton Tiger-Cats in exchange for defensive lineman Lubo Zizakovic in April, 1994.

Games Played - 6 with Calgary in 1989; 1 in 1990; 5 in 1991; 18 in 1992 and 12 in 1993. **CFL Total GP - 42.**

Blocked Kicks - 1 punt with Calgary in 1993.
CFL Total Blocked Kicks - 1 punt.

Fumble Returns - 1 for 0 yards with Calgary in 1993.
CFL Total Fumble Returns - 1 for 0 yards.

Tackles - 1 defensive with Calgary in 1989; 5 special teams in 1991; 1 defensive in 1992 and 1 defensive in 1993.
CFL Total Tackles - 8 (3 defensive and 5 special teams).

Playoffs

Games Played - 2 with Calgary in 1991; 1 in 1992 and 2 in 1993.
CFL Total Playoff GP - 5.

Tackles - 1 special teams with Calgary in 1991.
CFL Total Playoff Tackles - 1 (1 special teams).

Grey Cup

Games Played - 1 with Calgary in 1991 and 1 in 1992.
Total Grey Cup GP - 2.

Tackles - 1 special teams with Calgary in 1991 and 1 defensive in 1992.
Total Grey Cup Tackles - 2 (1 defensive and 1 special teams).

CAMERON, BOB
Born: July 18, 1955
Birthplace: Hamilton, Ontario
Kicker. 6'0", 185 lbs. Non-import
Last Amateur Club: Acadia University (AUAA)
Acquired: Selected in the first round (sixth overall) by the Edmonton Eskimos in the 1977 CFL College Draft. Signed as a free agent by the Winnipeg Blue Bombers in December, 1979.

	Team	GP	Scoring TD	C	FG	S	TP	Punting NO	YDS	AVE	LK	S
1980	Wpg.	15	0	0	0	2	2	104	4432	42.6	78	2
1981	Wpg.	16	0	0	0	2	2	96	4249	44.3	69	2
1982	Wpg.	16	0	0	0	5	5	130	5635	43.3	83	5
1983	Wpg.	16	0	0	0	8	8	135	6337	46.9	75	8
1984a	Wpg.	16	0	0	0	5	5	113	5176	45.8	65	5
1985	Wpg.	16	0	0	0	8	8	117	5256	44.9	95	8
1986	Wpg.	18	0	0	0	11	11	133	5617	42.2	72	11
1987	Wpg.	18	0	0	0	7	7	165	6904	41.8	77	7
1988abcde	Wpg.	18	0	0	0	6	6	188	8214	43.7	82	6
1989bc	Wpg.	18	0	0	0	12	12	175	7425	42.4	77	12
1990bc	Wpg.	18	0	0	0	10	10	160	6724	42.0	65	10
1991	Wpg.	18	0	4	0	8	12	147	5902	40.1	65	8
1992	Wpg.	18	0	0	0	6	6	161	6780	42.1	84	6
1993bc	Wpg.	18	0	0	0	5	5	141	5916	42.0	70	5
CFL TOTALS		**239**	**0**	**4**	**0**	**95**	**99**	**1965**	**84567**	**43.2**	**95**	**95**

	Team	Passing ATT	COMP	YDS	PCT	INT	LG	TD	Fumbles NO	LOST	OFR
1980	Wpg.	0	0	0	0.0	0	0	0	2	1	1
1981	Wpg.	0	0	0	0.0	0	0	0	1	1	0
1982	Wpg.	0	0	0	0.0	0	0	0	1	1	0
1983	Wpg.	2	2	29	100.0	0	25	0	1	1	0
1984	Wpg.	3	1	24	33.3	1	24	0	0	0	0
1985	Wpg.	0	0	0	0.0	0	0	0	2	2	0
1986	Wpg.	0	0	0	0.0	0	0	0	2	2	0
1987	Wpg.	1	1	18	100.0	0	18	0	1	1	1
1988	Wpg.	2	0	0	0.0	0	0	0	1	0	1
1989	Wpg.	3	1	18	33.3	0	18	0	2	1	0
1990	Wpg.	2	1	32	50.0	0	32	0	3	1	2
1991	Wpg.	1	0	0	0.0	0	0	0	1	1	1
1992	Wpg.	0	0	0	0.0	0	0	0	4	4	2
1993	Wpg.	0	0	0	0.0	0	0	0	3	1	4
CFL TOTALS		**14**	**6**	**121**	**42.9**	**1**	**32**	**0**	**24**	**17**	**12**

Net Punting - 148 for 5150 yards, 34.8 average with Winnipeg in 1991; 165 for 5658 yards, 34.3 average in 1992 and 142 for 5026 yards, 35.4 average in 1993. **CFL Total Net Punting - 455 for 15834 yards, 34.8 average.**

CAMERON, BOB

Kickoffs - 6 for 291 yards, 48.5 average, longest 52 yards with Winnipeg in 1991. **CFL Total Kickoffs - 6 for 291 yards, 48.5 average, longest 52 yards.**

Rushing - 1 for 8 yards with Winnipeg in 1992. **CFL Total Rushing - 1 for 8 yards.**

Punt Returns - 1 for -3 yards with Winnipeg in 1984. **CFL Total Punt Returns - 1 for -3 yards.**

Unsuccessful Field Goal Returns - 1 for 1 yard with Winnipeg in 1991. **CFL Total Unsuccessful Field Goal Returns - 1 for 1 yard.**

Own Punts Recovered - 1 with Winnipeg in 1982 and 1 in 1990. **CFL Total Own Punts Recovered - 2.**

1-Pt. Converts - 4 tried, 4 good with Winnipeg in 1991. **CFL Total 1-Pt. Converts - 4 tried, 4 good.**

2-Pt. Converts - 1 tried, 0 made with Winnipeg in 1988 and 1 tried, 0 made in 1990. **CFL Total 2-Pt. Converts - 2 tried, 0 made.**

Tackles - 1 defensive with Winnipeg in 1988; 1 defensive in 1989; 1 special teams in 1991 and 2 special teams in 1993. **CFL Total Tackles - 5 (2 defensive and 3 special teams).**

a - All-Western All-Star
b - All-Eastern All-Star
c - CFL All-Star
d - Set CFL Record Most Punting Yardage One Season
e - Set CFL Record Most Punts One Season

Playoffs

			Scoring					Punting					Fumbles	
	Team	GP	TD	C	FG	S	TP	NO	YDS	AVE	LK	S	NO	LOST
1980	Wpg.	2	0	0	0	1	1	15	635	42.3	58	1	0	0
1981	Wpg.	1	0	0	0	1	1	14	551	39.4	51	1	0	0
1982	Wpg.	2	0	0	0	1	1	18	727	40.4	61	1	0	0
1983	Wpg.	2	0	0	0	1	1	12	550	45.8	56	1	1	1
1984	Wpg.	2	0	0	0	1	1	11	448	40.7	57	1	0	0
1985	Wpg.	2	0	0	0	1	1	19	808	42.5	59	1	0	0
1986	Wpg.	1	0	0	0	0	0	10	452	45.2	52	0	0	0
1987	Wpg.	1	0	0	0	0	0	9	383	42.6	64	0	0	0
1988	Wpg.	2	0	0	0	1	1	15	587	39.1	58	1	0	0
1989	Wpg.	2	0	0	0	4	4	28	1149	41.0	57	4	0	0
1990	Wpg.	1	0	0	0	0	0	6	210	35.0	45	0	0	0
1991	Wpg.	2	0	0	0	0	0	20	792	39.6	55	0	0	0
1992	Wpg.	1	0	0	0	0	0	6	214	35.7	42	0	0	0
1993	Wpg.	1	0	0	0	1	1	10	346	34.6	68	1	0	0
CFL TOTALS		**22**	**0**	**0**	**0**	**12**	**12**	**193**	**7852**	**40.7**	**68**	**12**	**1**	**1**

Net Punting - 20 for 574 yards, 28.7 average with Winnipeg in 1991; 6 for 192 yards, 32.0 average in 1992 and 10 for 295, 29.5 average in 1993. **CFL Total Playoff Net Punting - 36 for 1061 yards, 29.5 average.**

Own Punts Recovered - 1 with Winnipeg in 1981. **CFL Total Playoff Own Punts Recovered - 1.**

Tackles - 1 special teams with Winnipeg in 1992. **CFL Total Playoff Tackles - 1 (1 special teams).**

Grey Cup

			Punting					Fumbles	
	Team	GP	NO	YDS	AVE	LK	S	NO	LOST
1984	Wpg.	1	4	172	43.0	49	0	0	0
1988	Wpg.	1	12	567	47.3	61	2	0	0
1990	Wpg.	1	7	296	42.3	52	0	0	0
1992	Wpg.	1	10	437	43.7	55	0	0	0
1993	Wpg.	1	7	317	45.3	57	0	1	1
CFL TOTALS		**5**	**40**	**1789**	**44.7**	**61**	**2**	**1**	**1**

CAMPBELL, MICHAEL

Born: September 19, 1965
Birthplace: North York, Ontario
Defensive Tackle. 6'1", 260 lbs. Non-import
Last Amateur Club: Slippery Rock University
Acquired: Selected in the second round (10th overall) by the Toronto Argonauts in the 1989 CFL College Draft. The choice was acquired from Calgary Stampeders along with defensive tackle Harald Hallman in exchange for linebacker Doug Landry. Granted free agency status in February, 1993. Re-signed by the Argonauts in June, 1993.

Games Played - 13 with Toronto in 1989; 12 in 1990; 18 in 1991; 17 in 1992 and 17 in 1993. **CFL Total GP - 77.**

Scoring - 1 TD for 6 points with Toronto in 1990 and 1 TD for 6 points in 1991. **CFL Total Scoring - 2 TDs for 12 points.**

Pass Receiving - 1 for 41 yards and 1 TD with Toronto in 1990. **CFL Total Pass Receiving - 1 for 41 yards and 1 TD.**

Fumble Returns - 2 for 38 yards, 19.0 average, longest 38 yards and 1 TD with Toronto in 1991 and 1 for 0 yards in 1992. **CFL Total Fumble Returns - 3 for 38 yards, 12.7 average, longest 38 yards and 1 TD.**

Quarterback Sacks - 1 with Toronto in 1989; 1 in 1990; 13 in 1991; 6 for 44 yards lost in 1992 and 5 for 21 yards in 1993. **CFL Total QB Sacks - 21.**

Blocked Kicks - 1 punt with Toronto in 1989. **CFL Total Blocked Kicks - 1 punt.**

Tackles - 2 defensive with Toronto in 1989; 11 defensive in 1990; 27 defensive and 1 special teams in 1991; 40 defensive in 1992 and 21 defensive in 1993. **CFL Total Tackles - 102 (101 defensive and 1 special teams).**

Tackles for Losses - 3 for 20 yards with Toronto in 1991; 5 for 12 yards in 1992 and 2 for 7 yards in 1993. **CFL Total Tackles for Losses - 10 for 39 yards.**

All-Eastern All-Star in 1991 and 1992.
CFL All-Star in 1991.

Playoffs

Games Played - 2 with Toronto in 1990 and 1 in 1991. **CFL Total Playoff GP - 3.**

Quarterback Sacks - 1 with Toronto in 1991. **CFL Total Playoff QB Sacks - 1.**

Defensive Tackles - 2 with Toronto in 1990 and 2 in 1991. **CFL Total Playoff Defensive Tackles - 4.**

Grey Cup

Games Played - 1 with Toronto in 1991. **Total Grey Cup GP - 1.**

Quarterback Sacks - 1 with Toronto in 1991. **Total Grey Cup QB Sacks - 1.**

Defensive Tackles - 2 with Toronto in 1991. **Total Grey Cup Defensive Tackles - 2.**

CARAVATTA, GIULIO

Born: March 20, 1966
Birthplace: Toronto, Ontario
Quarterback/Kicker. 6'0", 220 lbs. Non-import
Last Amateur Club: Simon Fraser University (EVCO)
Acquired: Signed as a free agent by the Winnipeg Blue Bombers in April, 1990. Released by Winnipeg in June, 1990. Signed as a free agent by the B.C. Lions in February, 1991.

			Kickoffs					Punting				
	Team	GP	NO	YDS	AVE	LK	S	NO	YDS	AVE	LK	S
1991	B.C.	18	91	4841	53.2	90	1	0	0	0.0	0	0
1992	B.C.	15	10	518	51.8	62	0	22	767	34.9	52	0
1993	B.C.	6	0	0	0.0	0	0	8	331	41.4	49	0
CFL TOTALS		**39**	**101**	**5359**	**53.1**	**90**	**1**	**30**	**1098**	**36.6**	**52**	**0**

Scoring - 1 single with B.C. in 1991. **CFL Total Scoring - 1 single.**

Rushing - 2 for 5 yards, 2.5 average, longest 5 yards with B.C. in 1992. **CFL Total Rushing - 2 for 5 yards, 2.5 average, longest 5 yards.**

Passing - 8 attempts, 3 complete for 27 yards, 37.5 percent complete, longest 13 yards with B.C. in 1992. **CFL Total Passing - 8 attempts, 3 complete for 27 yards, 37.5 percent complete, longest 13 yards.**

Net Punting - 22 for 627 yards, 28.5 average with B.C. in 1992 and 8 for 302 yards, 37.8 average in 1993. **CFL Total Net Punting - 30 for 929 yards, 31.0 average.**

Fumbles - 1 and 0 lost with B.C. in 1992. **CFL Total Fumbles - 1 and 0 lost.**

Tackles - 3 special teams with B.C. in 1991 and 2 special teams in 1992. **CFL Total Tackles - 5 (5 special teams).**

Playoffs

Games Played - 1 with B.C. in 1991 and 1 in 1993. **CFL Total Playoff GP - 2.**

CASTELLO, KEITH

Born: May 31, 1964
Birthplace: Toronto, Ontario
Linebacker. 6'2", 215 lbs. Non-import
Last Amateur Club - Oshawa Jrs. (OJFC)
Acquired: Signed as a free agent by the Hamilton Tiger-Cats in May, 1988. Released in July, 1990 and signed as a free agent by Toronto Argonauts that same month.

Games Played - 1 with Hamilton in 1988; 13 in 1989; 16 with Toronto in 1990; 15 in 1991; 17 in 1992 and 18 in 1993. **CFL Total GP - 80.**

Scoring - 1 TD for 6 points with Toronto in 1990 and 1 TD for 6 points in 1992. **CFL Total Scoring - 2 TDs for 12 points.**

Pass Receiving - 1 for 5 yards with Toronto in 1993. **CFL Total Pass Receiving - 1 for 5 yards.**

Fumble Returns - 2 for 34 yards, 17.0 average, longest 34 yards and 1 TD in 1990 with Toronto and 1 for 84 yards and 1 TD in 1992. **CFL Total Fumble Returns - 3 for 118 yards, 39.3 average, longest 84 yards and 2 TDs.**

CASTELLO, KEITH

Own Fumbles Recovered - 1 with Toronto in 1992. **CFL Total OFR - 1.**

Own Kickoffs Recovered - 1 for 0 yards with Toronto in 1992.
CFL Total Own Kickoffs Recovered - 1 for 0 yards.

Quarterback Sacks - 1 with Toronto in 1990 and 1 for 5 yards lost in 1992.
CFL Total QB Sacks - 2.

Tackles - 1 defensive with Hamilton in 1989; 12 defensive with Toronto in 1990; 5 defensive and 23 special teams in 1991; 15 defensive and 15 special teams in 1992 and 30 defensive and 9 special teams in 1993.
CFL Total Tackles - 110 (63 defensive and 47 special teams).

Tackles for Losses - 1 for 8 yards with Toronto in 1991 and 5 for 9 yards in 1993. **CFL Total Tackles for Losses - 6 for 17 yards.**

Playoffs

Games Played - 2 with Toronto in 1990 and 1 in 1991.
CFL Total Playoff GP - 3.

Fumble Returns - 1 for 0 yards with Toronto in 1990.
CFL Total Playoff Fumble Returns - 1 for 0 yards.

Tackles - 1 defensive with Toronto in 1990 and 2 special teams in 1991.
CFL Total Playoff Tackles - 3 (1 defensive and 2 special teams).

Grey Cup

Games Played - 1 with Hamilton in 1989 and 1 with Toronto in 1991.
Total Grey Cup GP - 2.

Fumble Returns - 2 for 4 yards, 2.0 average, longest 4 yards with Toronto in 1991.
Total Grey Cup Fumble Returns - 2 for 4 yards, 2.0 average, longest 4 yards.

Tackles - 1 defensive and 1 special teams with Toronto in 1991.
Total Grey Cup Tackles - 2 (1 defensive and 1 special teams).

CHAYTORS, DAVE

Born: October 12, 1969
Birthplace: Calgary, Alberta
Defensive Tackle. 6'2:", 258 lbs. Non-import
Last Amateur Club: Utah University
Acquired: Selected in the third round (19th overall) by the Ottawa Rough Riders in the 1992 CFL College Draft.

Games Played - 13 with Ottawa in 1993. **CFL Total GP - 13.**

Fumble Returns - 1 for 0 yards with Ottawa in 1993.
CFL Total Fumble Returns - 1 for 0 yards.

Tackles - 8 defensive and 1 special teams with Ottawa in 1993.
CFL Total Tackles - 9 (8 defensive and 1 special teams).

CHOMYC, LANCE

Born: March 2, 1963
Birthplace: Edmonton, Alberta
Kicker. 6'0", 195 lbs. Non-import
Last Amateur Club: University of Toronto (OUAA)
Acquired: Ottawa's sixth round selection, (46th overall), in the 1985 CFL College Draft. Released by Ottawa and signed as a free agent by Saskatchewan in July, 1985. Released by Saskatchewan and signed as a free agent by Toronto in July, 1985.

		Scoring						Field Goals					
	Team	GP	TD	C	FG	S	TP	T	G	YDS	AVE	LK	PCT
1985	Tor.	12	0	21	14	9	72	26	14	423	30.2	47	53.8
1986ab	Tor.	18	0	38	37	8	157	48	37	1194	32.3	49	77.1
1987c	Tor.	18	0	44	47	8	193	64	47	1700	36.2	55	73.4
1988	Tor.	18	0	58	48	5	207	59	48	1467	30.6	51	81.4
1989	Tor.	18	0	35	33	10	144	50	33	1031	31.2	50	66.0
1990de	Tor.	18	0	76	38	10	100	52	38	1093	28.8	52	73.1
1991abfghij	Tor.	18	0	64	55	7	236	65	55	1634	29.7	53	84.6
1992	Tor.	18	0	41	35	8	154	49	35	1259	36.0	53	71.4
1993	Tor.	18	0	35	30	10	135	44	30	984	32.8	52	68.3
CFL TOTALS		**156**	**0**	**412**	**337**	**75**	**1498**	**457**	**337**	**10785**	**32.0**	**55**	**73.7**

		Field Goal Attempts					Punting					Converts		
	Team	NO	YDS	AVE	LK	S	NO	YDS	AVE	LK	S	T	G	PCT
1985	Tor.	12	557	46.4	60	9	1	37	37.0	37	0	21	21	100.0
1986	Tor.	11	500	45.5	65	6	0	0	0.0	0	0	38	38	100.0
1987	Tor.	17	718	42.2	54	8	1	45	45.0	45	0	44	44	100.0
1988	Tor.	11	502	45.6	56	5	0	0	0.0	0	0	58	58	100.0
1989	Tor.	17	727	42.8	53	9	17	691	40.6	54	0	35	35	100.0
1990	Tor.	14	648	46.3	52	10	0	0	0.0	0	0	77	76	98.7
1991	Tor.	10	443	44.3	60	7	13	434	33.4	48	0	64	64	100.0
1992	Tor.	14	616	44.0	55	8	17	618	36.4	43	0	42	41	97.6
1993	Tor.	14	595	42.5	55	10	3	77	25.7	34	0	35	35	100.0
CFL TOTALS		**120**	**5306**	**44.2**	**65**	**72**	**52**	**1902**	**36.6**	**54**	**0**	**414**	**412**	**99.5**

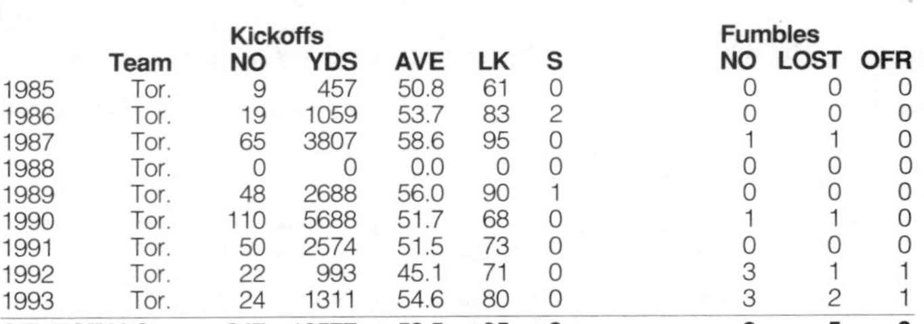

		Kickoffs					Fumbles		
	Team	NO	YDS	AVE	LK	S	NO	LOST	OFR
1985	Tor.	9	457	50.8	61	0	0	0	0
1986	Tor.	19	1059	53.7	83	2	0	0	0
1987	Tor.	65	3807	58.6	95	0	1	1	0
1988	Tor.	0	0	0.0	0	0	0	0	0
1989	Tor.	48	2688	56.0	90	1	0	0	0
1990	Tor.	110	5688	51.7	68	0	1	1	0
1991	Tor.	50	2574	51.5	73	0	0	0	0
1992	Tor.	22	993	45.1	71	0	3	1	1
1993	Tor.	24	1311	54.6	80	0	3	2	1
CFL TOTALS		**347**	**18577**	**53.5**	**95**	**3**	**8**	**5**	**3**

Passing - 1 attempt and 0 complete with Toronto in 1990.
CFL Total Passing - 1 attempt and 0 complete.

Own Kickoffs Recovered - 1 with Toronto in 1990.
CFL Total Own Kickoffs Recovered - 1.

Pass Receiving - 1 for 22 yards with Toronto in 1990.
CFL Total Pass Receiving - 1 for 22 yards.

Net Punting - 13 for 373 yards, 28.7 average with Toronto in 1991; 18 for 531 yards, 29.5 average in 1992 and 3 for 68 yards, 22.7 average in 1993.
CFL Total Net Punting - 34 for 972 yards, 28.5 average.

Tackles - 2 special teams with Toronto in 1991 and 1 special teams in 1992.
CFL Total Tackles - 3 (3 special teams).

a - All-Eastern All-Star
b - CFL All-Star
c - Tied Dave Cutler's record of 6 Field Goals in 1 Playoff Game.
d - Set CFL Record for Most Converts in one season.
e - Tied CFL Record for Most Converts in one game.
f - Winner of Lew Hayman Trophy as Outstanding Canadian, Eastern Division.
g - Led the League in Scoring
h - Set League record for most points in one season.
i - Led the League in Field Goals
j - Runner-up GMC Most Outstanding Canadian.

Playoffs

		Scoring						Field Goals					Converts		
	Team	GP	TD	C	FG	S	TP	T	G	YDS	AVE	LK	T	G	PCT
1986	Tor.	2	0	6	4	0	18	5	4	126	31.5	43	6	6	100.0
1987	Tor.	2	0	3	7	1	25	8	7	170	24.3	34	3	3	100.0
1988	Tor.	1	0	1	1	0	4	1	1	39	39.0	39	1	1	100.0
1989	Tor.	1	0	1	0	0	1	0	0	0	0.0	0	1	1	100.0
1990	Tor.	2	0	5	5	1	21	6	5	155	31.0	38	5	5	100.0
1991	Tor.	1	0	5	1	0	8	1	1	24	24.0	24	5	5	100.0
CFL TOTALS		**9**	**0**	**21**	**18**	**2**	**77**	**21**	**18**	**514**	**28.6**	**43**	**21**	**21**	**100.0**

		Field Goal Attempts					Kickoffs				
	Team	NO	YDS	AVE	LK	S	NO	YDS	AVE	LK	S
1986	Tor.	1	44	44.0	44	0	4	198	49.5	53	0
1987	Tor.	1	32	32.0	32	1	0	0	0.0	0	0
1988	Tor.	0	0	0.0	0	0	0	0	0.0	0	0
1989	Tor.	0	0	0.0	0	0	2	109	54.5	70	0
1990	Tor.	1	45	45.0	45	1	0	0	0.0	0	0
1991	Tor.	0	0	0.0	0	0	0	0	0.0	0	0
CFL TOTALS		**3**	**121**	**40.3**	**45**	**2**	**6**	**307**	**51.2**	**70**	**0**

Punting - 1 for 42 yards with Toronto in 1991.
CFL Total Playoff Punting - 1 for 42 yards.

Grey Cup

		Scoring						Field Goals				
	Team	GP	TD	C	FG	S	TP	T	G	YDS	AVE	LK
1987	Tor.	1	0	3	3	0	12	5	3	116	38.7	50
1991	Tor.	1	0	4	2	2	12	4	2	46	23.0	27
CFL TOTALS		**2**	**0**	**7**	**5**	**2**	**24**	**9**	**5**	**162**	**32.4**	**50**

		Converts			Field Goal Attempts				
	Team	T	G	PCT	NO	YDS	AVE	LK	S
1987	Tor.	3	3	100.0	2	88	44.0	44	0
1991	Tor.	4	4	100.0	2	77	38.5	39	2
CFL TOTALS		**7**	**7**	**100.0**	**4**	**165**	**41.3**	**44**	**2**

CHORNEY, TERRIS

Born: November 11, 1969
Birthplace: Ituna, Saskatchewan
Offensive Lineman. 6'1", 240 lbs. Non-import
Last Amateur Club: University of Nebraska
Acquired: Selected in the 4th round (26th overall) by the Edmonton Eskimos in the 1992 CFL College Draft. The choice was acquired from Saskatchewan.

Games Played - 9 with Edmonton in 1993. **CFL Total GP - 9.**

CHRISTENSEN, JAY

Born: November 19, 1963
Birthplace: Vancouver, B.C.
Slotback. 6'4", 215 lbs. Non-import
Last Amateur Club: Okanagan Sun Juniors (BCJFL)
Acquired: Signed as a free agent by the Calgary Stampeders in September, 1986. Released by Calgary and signed as a free agent by the B.C. Lions in February, 1990. Released by B.C. in July, 1992. Signed as a free agent by the Edmonton Eskimos in August, 1992

	Team	GP	Scoring TD	C	FG	S	TP	Pass Receiving NO	YDS	AVE	LG	TD
1986	Cal.	4	0	0	0	0	0	3	29	9.7	21	0
1987	Cal.	13	1	0	0	0	6	13	178	13.7	37	1
1988	Cal.	18	2	0	0	0	12	14	179	12.8	27	2
1989	Cal.	16	0	0	0	0	0	5	59	11.8	19	0
1990a	B.C.	18	8	x2	0	0	52	62	1036	16.7	48	8
1991	B.C.	16	9	x1	0	0	56	45	630	14.0	53	8
1992	Edm.	8	1	0	0	0	6	14	238	17.0	50	1
1993	Edm.	9	0	0	0	0	0	16	273	17.1	38	0
CFL TOTALS		**102**	**21**	**x3**	**0**	**0**	**132**	**172**	**2622**	**15.2**	**53**	**20**

Rushing - 1 for 10 yards and 1 TD with B.C. in 1991.
CFL Total Rushing - 1 for 10 yards and 1 TD.

Passing - 1 attempt, 0 complete with B.C. in 1991.
CFL Total Passing - 1 attempt, 0 complete.

Punting - 1 for 23 yards with B.C. in 1991. **CFL Total Punting - 1 for 23 yards.**

Kickoff Returns - 1 for 0 yards with Calgary in 1988; 2 for 1 yard, 0.5 yards average, longest 1 yard with B.C. in 1990 and 1 for 0 yards in 1991.
CFL Total Kickoff Returns - 4 for 1 yard, 0.3 average, longest 1 yard.

Fumble Returns - 1 for 0 yards with Calgary in 1988.
CFL Total Fumble Returns - 1 for 0 yards.

Own Fumbles Recovered - 1 with Calgary in 1987; 1 in 1988; 1 with B.C. in 1990 and 1 in 1991. **CFL Total OFR - 4.**

Fumbles - 2 and 2 lost with B.C. in 1990 and 1 and 1 lost in 1991.
CFL Total Fumbles - 3 and 3 lost.

Tackles - 1 defensive with Calgary in 1987; 1 defensive in 1988; 2 defensive with B.C. in 1990; 1 defensive in 1991; 1 special teams with Edmonton in 1992 and 1 defensive and 3 special teams in 1993.
CFL Total Tackles - 10 (6 defensive and 4 special teams).

a - Tied CFL Record for Most 2-Pt. Converts One Game (2).

Playoffs

	Team	GP	Scoring TD	C	FG	S	TP	Pass Receiving NO	YDS	AVE	LG	TD
1987	Cal.	1	0	0	0	0	0	1	6	6.0	6	0
1992	Edm.	2	0	0	0	0	0	1	17	17.0	17	0
1993	Edm.	2	1	0	0	0	6	2	27	13.5	16	1
CFL TOTALS		**5**	**1**	**0**	**0**	**0**	**6**	**4**	**50**	**12.5**	**17**	**1**

Grey Cup

	Team	GP	Pass Receiving NO	YDS	AVE	LG	TD
1993	Edm.	1	2	25	12.5	19	0
CFL TOTALS		**1**	**2**	**25**	**12.5**	**19**	**0**

CHRONOPOULOS, DENNY

Born: June 12, 1968
Birthplace: Montreal, Quebec
Offensive Guard. 6'4", 289 lbs. Non-import
Last Amateur Club: Purdue University
Acquired: Selected in the first round (third overall) of the 1992 CFL College Draft by the Ottawa Rough Riders.

Games Played - 18 with Ottawa in 1992 and 18 in 1993. **CFL Total GP - 36**

Own Fumbles Recovered - 2 with Ottawa in 1993. **CFL Total OFR - 2.**

Defensive Tackles - 1 with Ottawa in 1993.
CFL Total Defensive Tackles - 1.

All-Eastern All-Star in 1993.

Playoffs

Games Played - 1 with Ottawa in 1992 and 1 in 1993. **CFL Total Playoff GP - 2.**

Tackles - 1 defensive with Ottawa in 1992 and 1 special teams in 1993.
CFL Total Playoff Tackles - 2 (1 defensive and 1 special teams).

CLARK, GREG

Born: March 5, 1965
Birthplace: Los Angeles, California
Linebacker, 6'0", 220 lbs. Import
Last Amateur Club: Arizona State University
Acquired: Selected in the 12th round (329th overall) by the Chicago Bears in the 1988 NFL Draft. Signed as a free agent by the NFL Miami Dolphins in March, 1989. Released by Miami prior to the start of the 1989 season. Signed as a free agent by the NFL Green Bay Packers in March, 1990. Released by Green Bay in September 1990. Signed as a free agent by the NFL Los Angeles Rams in September, 1990. Released and signed as a free agent by the Green Bay Packers in April, 1991. Claimed on waivers by the San Diego Chargers in September, 1991. Released by San Diego in August, 1992. Signed as a free agent by the NFL Seattle Seahawks in September, 1992. Released by Seattle and signed as a free agent by the NFL Pittsburgh Steelers in March, 1993. Released by Pittsburgh and signed as a free agent by the Winnipeg Blue Bombers in September, 1993.

Games Played - 4 with Winnipeg in 1993. **CFL Total GP - 4.**

Quarterback Sacks - 1 for 2 yards lost with Winnipeg in 1993.
CFL Total QB sacks - 1 for 2 yards lost.

Tackles - 12 defensive and 6 special teams with Winnipeg in 1993.
CFL Total Tackles - 18 (12 defensive and 6 special teams).

Playoffs

Games Played - 1 with Winnipeg in 1993.
CFL Total Playoff GP - 1.

Tackles - 4 defensive and 1 special teams with Winnipeg in 1993.
CFL Total Playoff Tackles - 5 (4 defensive and 1 special teams).

Grey Cup

Games Played - 1 with Winnipeg in 1993.
Total Grey Cup GP - 1.

Fumble Returns - 1 for 3 yards with Winnipeg in 1993.
Total Grey Cup Fumble Returns - 1 for 3 yards.

Tackles - 8 defensive and 1 special teams with Winnipeg in 1993.
Total Grey Cup Tackles - 9 (8 defensive and 1 special teams).

Tackles for Losses - 1 for 2 yards with Winnipeg in 1993.
Total Grey Cup Tackles for Losses - 1 for 2 yards.

CLARK, MATT

Born: May 14, 1968
Birthplace: Calgary, Alberta
Wide Receiver. 6'0", 180 lbs. Non-import
Last Amateur Club: University of Montana
Acquired: Selected in the first round (second overall) by the B.C. Lions in the 1991 CFL Supplementary Draft. Signed with B.C. in May, 1991.

	Team	GP	Scoring TD	C	FG	S	TP	Pass Receiving NO	YDS	AVE	LG	TD
1991abcd	B.C.	18	10	x1	0	0	62	80	1530	19.4	89	10
1992	B.C.	18	5	0	0	0	30	49	718	14.7	37	5
1993	B.C.	16	4	0	0	0	24	74	970	13.1	55	4
CFL TOTALS		**52**	**19**	**x1**	**0**	**0**	**116**	**202**	**3218**	**15.9**	**89**	**19**

Rushing - 4 for 28 yards, 7.0 average, longest 12 yards with B.C. in 1991.
CFL Total Rushing - 4 for 28 yards, 7.0 average, longest 12 yards.

Kickoff Returns - 1 for 13 yards with B.C. in 1991.
CFL Total Kickoff Returns - 1 for 13 yards.

Fumbles - 3 and 2 lost with B.C. in 1991; 2 and 1 lost in 1992 and 2 and 2 lost in 1993. **CFL Total Fumbles - 7 and 5 lost.**

Own Fumbles Recovered - 1 with B.C. in 1991. **CFL Total OFR - 1.**

Tackles - 1 defensive with B.C. in 1991; 3 defensive in 1992 and 1 defensive in 1993. **CFL Total Tackles - 5 (5 defensive).**

a - All-Western All-Star Team
b - All-CFL All-Star Team
c - Set CFL record for Most Pass Receptions One Season by a First-Year Player.
d - Set CFL record for Most Yards Receiving One Season by a First-Year Player.

CLARK, REGGIE

Born: October 17, 1967
Birthplace: Charlotte, North Carolina
Linebacker. 6'2", 225 lbs. Import
Last Amateur Club: University of North Carolina
Acquired: Signed as a free agent by the NFL New England Patriots in April, 1991. Released during training camp. Spent the 1991 season on New England's practice squad. Re-signed as a free agent by the New England Patriots in February, 1992. Was allocated to the Montreal Machine of the WLAF during the off-season. Signed as a free agent by the Toronto Argonauts in September, 1993.

Games Played - 2 with Toronto in 1993. **CFL Total GP - 2.**

Tackles - 3 defensive and 1 special teams with Toronto in 1993.
CFL Total Tackles - 4 (3 defensive and 1 special teams).

CLARK, ROBERT
Born: August 6, 1965
Birthplace: Pittsboro, North Carolina
Wide Receiver. 5'10" 180 lbs. Import
Last Amateur Club: N.C. Central University
Acquired: Selected in the 10th round (263rd overall) by the New Orleans Saints in the 1987 NFL Draft. Signed as a free agent by the NFL Detroit Lions in February, 1989. Signed as a plan B free agent by the NFL Miami Dolphins in March, 1992. Signed as a free agent by the Toronto Argonauts in May, 1993.

		Scoring						Pass Receiving				
	Team	GP	TD	C	FG	S	TP	NO	YDS	AVE	LG	TD
1993	Tor.	13	3	0	0	0	18	50	900	18.0	64	3
CFL TOTALS		**13**	**3**	**0**	**0**	**0**	**18**	**50**	**900**	**18.0**	**64**	**3**

Tackles - 3 defensive with Toronto in 1993. **CFL Total Tackles - 3 (3 defensive).**

CLARKE, MATT
Born: April 6, 1968
Birthplace: Vancouver, B.C.
Linebacker. 6'0", 225 lbs. Non-import
Last Amateur Club: University of British Columbia (CWAA)
Acquired: Signed as a free agent by the B.C. Lions in June, 1991.

Games Played - 18 with B.C. in 1991; 18 in 1992 and 18 in 1993.
CFL Total GP - 54.

Tackles - 1 defensive and 6 special teams with B.C. in 1991; 9 special teams in 1992 and 1 defensive and 2 special teams in 1993.
CFL Total Tackles - 19 (2 defensive and 17 special teams).

Playoffs

Games Played - 1 with B.C. in 1991 and 1 in 1993.
CFL Total Playoff GP - 2.

CLEMONS, MICHAEL
Born: January 15, 1965
Birthplace: Tampa Bay, Florida
Running Back. 5'6", 170 lbs. Import
Last Amateur Club: College of William and Mary.
Acquired: Selected in the eighth round (218th overall) by the Kansas City Chiefs in the 1987 NFL Draft. Had a tryout with NFL Tampa Bay Buccaneers in 1988. Signed as a free agent by the Toronto Argonauts in June, 1989.

		Scoring						Rushing					Fumbles		
	Team	GP	TD	C	FG	S	TP	NO	YDS	AVE	LG	TD	NO	LOST	OFR
1989	Tor.	10	2	0	0	0	12	28	134	4.8	23	1	5	2	2
1990abcdef	Tor.	16	14	0	0	0	84	105	519	4.9	62	4	8	5	2
1991	Tor.	11	6	0	0	0	36	64	443	6.9	64	3	4	3	0
1992	Tor.	18	5	x1	0	0	32	148	572	3.9	20	0	5	5	1
1993a	Tor.	18	6	x1	0	0	38	89	481	5.4	32	1	6	5	3
CFL TOTALS		**73**	**33**	**x2**	**0**	**0**	**202**	**434**	**2149**	**5.0**	**64**	**9**	**28**	**20**	**8**

		Pass Receiving					Punt Returns				
	Team	NO	YDS	AVE	LG	TD	NO	YDS	AVE	LG	TD
1989	Tor.	1	2	2.0	2	0	50	507	10.1	48	1
1990	Tor.	72	905	12.6	65	8	74	1045	14.1	92	2
1991	Tor.	38	417	11.0	28	2	32	440	13.8	94	1
1992	Tor.	46	559	12.2	52	5	34	279	8.2	32	0
1993	Tor.	32	313	9.8	31	3	77	716	9.3	79	2
CFL TOTALS		**189**	**2196**	**11.6**	**65**	**18**	**267**	**2987**	**11.2**	**94**	**6**

		Kickoff Returns					Unsuccessful Field Goal Returns				
	Team	NO	YDS	AVE	LG	TD	NO	YDS	AVE	LG	TD
1989	Tor.	13	356	27.4	45	0	6	158	26.3	44	0
1990	Tor.	39	831	21.3	51	0	0	0	0.0	0	0
1991	Tor.	19	216	11.4	23	0	1	-10	-10.0	-10	0
1992	Tor.	15	295	19.7	38	0	0	0	0.0	0	0
1993	Tor.	30	604	20.1	41	0	3	31	10.3	14	0
CFL TOTALS		**116**	**2302**	**19.9**	**51**	**0**	**10**	**179**	**17.9**	**44**	**0**

Passing - 1 attempt, 1 complete for 18 yards and 1 TD with Toronto in 1989 and 1 attempt, 0 complete in 1993.
CFL Total Passing - 2 attempts, 1 complete for 18 yards and 1 TD.

Fumble Returns - 1 for 0 yards with Toronto in 1993. **CFL Total Fumble Returns - 1 for 0 yards.**

2-Pt. Converts - 1 made for 2 points with Toronto in 1992 and 1 made for 2 points in 1993. **CFL Total 2-Pt. Converts - 2 for 4 points.**

Defensive Tackles - 1 with Toronto in 1989; 4 in 1990; 5 in 1992 and 3 in 1993.
CFL Total Defensive Tackles - 13.

Punting - 1 for 28 yards with Toronto in 1993.
CFL Total Punting - 1 for 28 yards.

a - All-Eastern All-Star, Specialty Teams
b - CFL All-Star, Specialty Teams
c - Jeff Russel Memorial East Division Outstanding Player Trophy
d - CFL Most Outstanding Player Award Winner
e - Set CFL Record for Most Combined Yards in a Season with 3300, (519 rushing, 905 receiving, 1045 punt returns, 831 kickoff returns)
f - Led CFL in Punt Return Yards.

Playoffs

			Scoring					Rushing				
	Team	GP	TD	C	FG	S	TP	NO	YDS	AVE	LG	TD
1989	Tor.	1	0	0	0	0	0	0	0	0.0	0	0
1990	Tor.	2	1	0	0	0	6	21	177	8.4	41	1
1991	Tor.	1	1	0	0	0	6	1	-2	-2.0	-2	0
CFL TOTALS		**4**	**2**	**0**	**0**	**0**	**12**	**22**	**175**	**8.0**	**41**	**1**

		Pass Receiving					Punt Returns				
	Team	NO	YDS	AVE	LG	TD	NO	YDS	AVE	LG	TD
1989	Tor.	0	0	0.0	0	0	5	26	5.2	11	0
1990	Tor.	6	62	10.3	20	0	12	129	10.8	54	0
1991	Tor.	4	104	26.0	70	1	3	40	13.3	34	0
CFL TOTALS		**10**	**166**	**16.6**	**70**	**1**	**20**	**195**	**9.8**	**54**	**0**

		Kickoff Returns					Fumbles	
	Team	NO	YDS	AVE	LG	TD	NO	LOST
1989	Tor.	3	37	12.3	16	0	0	0
1990	Tor.	6	130	21.7	36	0	2	1
1991	Tor.	1	39	39.0	39	0	0	0
CFL TOTALS		**10**	**206**	**20.6**	**39**	**0**	**2**	**1**

Grey Cup

		Rushing					Pass Receiving				
	Team	NO	YDS	AVE	LG	TD	NO	YDS	AVE	LG	TD
1991	Tor.	3	-2	-0.7	-1	0	1	7	7.0	7	0
CFL TOTALS		**3**	**-2**	**-0.7**	**-1**	**0**	**1**	**7**	**7.0**	**7**	**0**

Kickoff Returns - 1 for 43 yards with Toronto in 1991.
Total Grey Cup Kickoff Returns - 1 for 43 yards

Punt Returns - 2 for 12 yards, 6.0 average, longest 7 yards with Toronto in 1991.
Total Grey Cup Punt Returns - 2 for 12 yards, 6.0 average, longest 7 yards.

Tackles - 1 special teams with Toronto in 1991.
Total Grey Cup Tackles- 1 (1 special teams).

CLIMIE, JOCK
Born: September 28, 1968
Birthplace: Toronto, Ontario
Slotback. 6'1", 185 lbs. Non-import
Last Amateur Club: Queen's University (OQIFC)
Acquired: Selected in the first round (fourth overall) by the Toronto Argonauts in the 1990 CFL College Draft. Released in July, 1990 and signed as a free agent by the Ottawa Rough Riders in August, 1990.

			Scoring					Pass Receiving				
	Team	GP	TD	C	FG	S	TP	NO	YDS	AVE	LG	TD
1990	Tor.	2	0	0	0	0	0	2	20	10.0	16	0
1991	Ott.	16	1	0	0	0	6	32	599	18.7	62	1
1992	Ott.	18	6	x1	0	0	38	57	901	15.8	50	6
1993a	Ott.	18	11	0	0	1	67	67	1281	19.1	89	11
CFL TOTALS		**54**	**18**	**x1**	**0**	**1**	**111**	**158**	**2801**	**17.7**	**89**	**18**

Rushing - 2 for 2 yards, 1.0 average, longest 4 yards with Ottawa in 1991 and 0 for 21 yards, longest 16 yards in 1992.
CFL Total Rushing - 2 for 23 yards, 11.5 average, longest 16 yards.

Punt Returns - 8 for 42 yards, 5.3 average, longest 18 yards with Ottawa in 1991.
CFL Total Punt Returns - 8 for 42 yards, 5.3 average, longest 18 yards.

Kickoff Returns - 1 for 0 yards with Ottawa in 1991.
CFL Total Kickoff Returns - 1 for 0 yards.

2-Pt. Converts - 1 made for 2 points with Ottawa in 1992.
CFL Total 2-Pt. Converts - 1 for 2 points.

Punting - 1 for 16 yards with Ottawa in 1992 and 15 for 506 yards; 33.7 average, longest 55 yards and 1 single in 1993.
CFL Total Punting - 16 for 522 yards, 32.6 average, longest 55 yards and 1 single.

Net Punting - 1 for 16 yards with Ottawa in 1992 and 15 for 424 yards, 28.3 average in 1993. **CFL Total Net Punting - 16 for 440 yards, 27.5 average.**

CLIMIE, JOCK

Unsuccessful Field Goal Returns - 1 for 17 yards with Ottawa in 1992.
CFL Total Unsuccessful Field Goal Returns - 1 for 17 yards.

Fumbles - 1 and 1 lost with Ottawa in 1991; 1 and 0 lost in 1992 and 2 and 2 lost in 1993. **CFL Total Fumbles - 4 and 3 lost.**

Own Fumbles Recovered - 1 with Ottawa in 1991 and 1 in 1993.
CFL Total OFR - 2.

Tackles - 1 defensive with Toronto in 1990; 3 defensive and 11 special teams with Ottawa in 1991; 2 defensive and 2 special teams in 1992 and 1 defensive and 6 special teams in 1993.
CFL Total Defensive Tackles - 26 (7 defensive and 19 special teams).

a - All-Eastern All-Star

Playoffs

	Team	Scoring GP	TD	C	FG	S	TP	Pass Receiving NO	YDS	AVE	LG	TD
1992	Ott.	1	1	0	0	0	6	4	47	11.8	27	1
1993	Ott.	1	0	0	0	0	0	2	30	15.0	19	0
CFL TOTALS		**2**	**1**	**0**	**0**	**0**	**6**	**6**	**77**	**12.8**	**27**	**1**

Tackles - 1 defensive with Ottawa in 1993.
CFL Total Playoff Tackles - 1 (1 defensive).

COFIELD, TIM
Born: May 8, 1963
Birthplace: Murfreesboro, North Carolina
Defensive End. 6'2", 245 lbs. Import
Last Amateur Club: Elizabeth City State University
Acquired: Selected in the sixth round (45th overall) by the Baltimore Stars in the 1986 USFL Draft. Signed as a free agent by the NFL Kansas City Chiefs in May, 1986. Granted unconditional free agency status by Kansas City in February, 1989. Signed as a free agent by the NFL New York Jets in March, 1989. Released by New York in October, 1989 and awarded on waivers to the NFL Buffalo Bills. Released by Buffalo in September, 1990. Signed as a free agent by the NFL Los Angeles Raiders in February, 1991 and was released after training camp. Signed as a free agent by the Calgary Stampeders in October, 1991. Traded to the Hamilton Tiger-Cats in July 1993 in exchange for a 2nd round Draft Choice.

Games Played - 4 with Calgary in 1991; 14 in 1992 and 18 with Hamilton in 1993. **CFL Total GP - 36.**

Fumble Returns - 2 for 0 yards with Calgary in 1991 and 2 for 0 yards with Hamilton in 1993. **CFL Total Fumble Returns - 4 for 0 yards.**

Quarterback Sacks - 2 with Calgary in 1991; 6 for 30 yards lost in 1992 and 19 for 150 yards lost with Hamilton in 1993. **CFL Total QB Sacks - 27.**

Defensive Tackles - 17 with Calgary in 1991; 24 in 1992 and 30 with Hamilton in 1993. **CFL Total Defensive Tackles - 71.**

Tackles for Losses - 2 for 24 yards with Hamilton in 1993.
CFL Total Tackles for Losses - 2 for 24 yards.

All-Eastern All-Star in 1993
CFL All-Star in 1993
Tied CFL Record for Most Quarterback Sacks in One Game (5) in 1993.

Playoffs

Games Played - 2 with Calgary in 1991; 1 in 1992 and 2 with Hamilton in 1993.
CFL Total Playoff GP - 5.

Quarterback Sacks - 2 for 10 yards lost with Calgary in 1992.
CFL Total Playoff QB Sacks - 2.

Defensive Tackles - 13 with Calgary in 1991; 1 in 1992 and 7 with Hamilton in 1993. **CFL Total Playoff Defensive Tackles - 21.**

Grey Cup

Games Played - 1 with Calgary in 1991. **Total Grey Cup GP - 1.**

Fumble Returns - 1 for 3 yards with Calgary in 1991.
Total Grey Cup Fumble Returns - 1 for 3 yards.

Defensive Tackles - 2 with Calgary in 1991.
Total Grey Cup Defensive Tackles - 2.

COLAR, HESHIMU
Born: October 15, 1970
Birthplace: Shreveport, Louisiana
Defensive Back. 5'10", 195 lbs. Import
Last Amateur Club: San Jose State University
Acquired: Signed as a free agent by the NFL Denver Broncos in 1992. Released by Denver prior to the start of the 1992 season. Signed as a free agent by the Sacramento Gold Miners in July, 1993. Released by Sacramento in November, 1993.

Games Played - 6 with Sacramento in 1993. **CFL Total GP - 6.**

Tackles - 11 defensive and 3 special teams with Sacramento in 1993.
CFL Total Tackles - 14 (11 defensive and 3 special teams).

CONNOP, ROD
Born: June 4, 1959
Birthplace: Burnaby, B.C.
Centre. 6'6", 245 lbs. Non-import
Last Amateur Club: Wilfrid Laurier University (OUAA)
Acquired: Selected in the first round (ninth overall) by the Edmonton Eskimos in the 1982 CFL College Draft.

Games Played - 16 with Edmonton in 1982; 14 in 1983; 16 in 1984; 16 in 1985; 18 in 1986; 18 in 1987; 18 in 1988; 18 in 1989; 18 in 1990; 18 in 1991; 18 in 1992 and 18 in 1993. **CFL Total GP - 206.**

Own Fumbles Recovered - 1 with Edmonton in 1982; 1 in 1983; 1 in 1987 and 1 in 1991. **CFL Total OFR - 4.**

Rushing - 1 for - 4 yards with Edmonton in 1984.
CFL Total Rushing - 1 for -4 yards.

Kickoff Returns - 1 for 7 yards with Edmonton in 1984 and 1 for 20 yards in 1987. **CFL Total Kickoff Returns - 2 for 27 yards, 13.5 average, longest 20 yards.**

Fumbles - 1 and 0 lost with Edmonton in 1987 and 1 and 0 lost in 1989.
CFL Total Fumbles - 2 and 0 lost.

Tackles - 3 defensive with Edmonton in 1990; 4 defensive and 2 special teams in 1991; 3 defensive in 1992 and 2 defensive in 1993.
CFL Total Tackles - 14 (12 defensive and 2 special teams).

All-Western All-Star in 1987; 1989; 1990; 1991; 1992 and 1993.
CFL All-Star in 1987; 1989; 1990; 1991; 1992 and 1993.
Winner of the DeMarco-Becket Memorial Trophy in 1989.
Winner of the CFL Most Oustanding Offensive Lineman in 1989.

Playoffs

Games Played 1 with Edmonton in 1982; 1 in 1983; 1 in 1984; 1 in 1985; 2 in 1986; 2 in 1987; 1 in 1988; 1 in 1989; 2 in 1990; 1 in 1991; 2 in 1992 and 2 in 1993. **CFL Total Playoff GP - 17.**

Fumble Returns - 1 with Edmonton in 1985. **CFL Total Playoff Fumble Returns -1.**

Defensive Tackles - 1 with Edmonton in 1988.
CFL Total Playoff Defensive Tackles - 1.

Grey Cup

Games Played - 1 with Edmonton in 1986; 1 in 1987; 1 in 1990 and 1 in 1993.
Total Grey Cup GP - 4.

COOK, LANCE
Born: October 2, 1970
Birthplace: Atlanta, Georgia
Defensive End. 6'2", 225 lbs. Import
Last Amateur Club: The Citadel
Acquired: Signed as a free agent by the Saskatchewan Roughriders in June, 1992. Released by Saskatchewan in July, 1993. Signed as a free agent by the Las Vegas Posse in February, 1994.

Games Played - 8 with Saskatchewan in 1992 and 1 in 1993. **CFL Total GP - 9.**

Interception Returns - 1 for 10 yards with Saskatchewan in 1992. **CFL Total Interception Returns - 1 for 10 yards.**

Fumble Returns - 1 for 0 yards with Saskatchewan in 1992.
CFL Total Fumble Returns - 1 for 0 yards.

Quarterback Sacks - 5 for 41 yards lost with Saskatchewan in 1992.
CFL Total QB Sacks - 5.

Blocked Kicks - 1 punt with Saskatchewan in 1992.
CFL Total Blocked Kicks - 1 punt.

Tackles - 17 defensive with Saskatchewan in 1992.
CFL Total Tackles - 17 (17 defensive).

Tackles for Losses - 1 for 2 yards with Saskatchewan in 1992.
CFL Total Tackles for Losses - 1 for 2 yards.

COULTER, CARL
Born: November 14, 1966
Birthplace: Lindsay, Ontario
Centre. 6'1", 275 lbs. Non-import
Last Amateur Club: Carleton University (OQIFC)
Acquired: Selected in the fourth round (26th overall) by the B.C. Lions in the 1990 CFL College Draft. Traded to the Ottawa Rough Riders in April, 1993 along with Offensive Lineman Chris Gioskos, Kicker Wayne Lammle, Cornerback Joe Mero and Linebacker Mark Scott in exchange for Cornerback Less Browne, Offensive Tackle Rob Smith and linebacker Patrick Wayne. Granted free agency status in February, 1994. Signed as a free agent by the Toronto Argonauts in March, 1994.

COULTER, CARL

Games Played - 18 with B.C. in 1990; 18 in 1991; 18 in 1992 and 1 with Ottawa in 1993. **CFL Total GP - 55.**

Scoring - 1 TD for 6 points with B.C. in 1992. **CFL Total Scoring - 1 TD for 6 points.**

Pass Receiving - 1 for 3 yards and 1 TD with B.C. in 1992. **CFL Total Pass Receiving - 1 for 3 yards and 1 TD.**

Fumbles - 1 and 0 lost with B.C. in 1990. **CFL Total Fumbles - 1 and 0 lost in 1990.**

Own Fumbles Recovered - 1 with B.C. in 1992. **CFL Total OFR - 1.**

Kickoff Returns - 1 for 18 yards with B.C. in 1990; 2 for 13 yards, 6.5 average, longest 8 yards in 1991 and 3 for 30 yards, 10.0 average, longest 13 yards in 1992. **CFL Total Kickoff Returns - 6 for 61 yards, 10.2 average, longest 18 yards.**

Tackles - 1 defensive with B.C. in 1990; 1 special teams with Ottawa in 1991; 3 defensive and 20 special teams in 1992 and 1 special teams with Ottawa in 1993. **CFL Total Tackles - 25 (4 defensive and 21 special teams).**

Playoffs

Games Played - 1 with B.C. in 1991. **CFL Total Playoff GP - 1.**

COVERNTON, BRUCE

Born: August 12, 1966
Birthplace: Morris, Manitoba
Offensive Tackle. 6'5", 292 lbs. Non-import
Last Amateur Club: Weber State University
Acquired: Selected in the first round (first overall) of the 1992 CFL College Draft by the Calgary Stampeders.

Games Played - 18 with Calgary in 1992 and 18 in 1993. **CFL Total GP - 36.**

Pass Receiving - 0 for 5 yards with Calgary in 1993. **CFL Total Pass Receiving - 0 for 5 yards.**

Own Fumbles Recovered - 1 with Calgary in 1993. **CFL Total OFR - 1.**

Tackles - 1 defensive with Calgary in 1992. **CFL Total Tackles - 1 (1 defensive).**

Winner Jackie Parker Trophy for Most Outstanding Rookie, Western Division in 1992.
Runner-up CFL Most Outstanding Rookie in 1992.
All-Western All-Star in 1993.
CFL All-Star in 1993.
Winner DeMarco-Becket Memorial Trophy for Most Outstanding Offensive Lineman in the Western Division in 1993.
Runner-up CFL Most Outstanding Offensive Lineman in 1993.

Playoffs

Games Played - 1 with Calgary in 1992 and 2 in 1993. **CFL Total Playoff GP - 3.**

Rushing - 0 for 3 yards with Calgary in 1993. **CFL Total Playoff Rushing - 0 for 3 yards.**

Own Fumbles Recovered - 1 with Calgary in 1993. **CFL Total Playoff OFR - 1.**

Grey Cup

Games Played - 1 with Calgary in 1992. **Total Grey Cup GP - 1.**

CRAFT, DOUG

Born: July 23, 1968
Birthplace: Houghton, Louisiana
Defensive Back. 6'0", 195 lbs. Import
Last Amateur Club: Southern University
Acquired: Signed as a free agent by the NFL Seattle Seahawks in 1991. Released prior to the start of the regular season. Signed as a free agent by the Dallas Texans of the Arena Football League. Signed as a free agent by the Calgary Stampeders in June, 1993.

		Scoring						Interception Returns				
	Team	GP	TD	C	FG	S	TP	NO	YDS	AVE	LG	TD
1993	Cal.	8	1	0	0	0	6	2	104	52.0	64	1
CFL TOTALS		**8**	**1**	**0**	**0**	**0**	**6**	**2**	**104**	**52.0**	**64**	**1**

Fumble Returns - 1 for 0 yards with Calgary in 1993. **CFL Total Fumble Returns - 1 for 0 yards.**

Tackles - 28 defensive and 8 special teams with Calgary in 1993. **CFL Total Tackles - 36 (28 defensive and 8 special teams).**

CRANMER, PAUL

Born: November 27, 1969
Birthplace: Calgary, Alberta
Slotback. 6'1", 193 lbs. Non-import
Last Amateur Club: Grand Valley State University
Acquired: Selected in the fourth round (25th overall) by the Saskatchewan Roughriders in the 1993 CFL College Draft. Released by Saskatchewan in December, 1993. Signed as a free agent by the Toronto Argonauts in March, 1994.

Games Played - 1 with Saskatchewan in 1993. **CFL Total GP - 1.**

Tackles - 1 special teams with Saskatchewan in 1993. **CFL Total Tackles - 1 (1 special teams).**

CRAWFORD, DERRICK

Born: September 3, 1961
Birthplace: Memphis, Tennessee
Wide Receiver. 5'11", 180 lbs. Import
Last Amateur Club: Memphis State University
Acquired: Selected by USFL Memphis Showboats in 1984 USFL Territorial Draft. Selected by San Francisco 49ers in 1st round (24th overall) of 1984 NFL Supplemental Draft. Granted free agency when USFL suspended operations August, 1986. Signed by San Francisco 49ers in August, 1986. Was on injured reserve list most of 1986 and 1987. Released in August, 1988 and signed as a free agent by NFL Cleveland Browns in March, 1989. Released in August, 1988 and signed as a free agent by NFL Cleveland Browns in March, 1989. Signed as a free agent by the Calgary Stampeders in May, 1990.

		Scoring						Pass Receiving				
	Team	GP	TD	C	FG	S	TP	NO	YDS	AVE	LG	TD
1990a	Cal.	18	15	0	0	0	90	57	1096	19.2	58	11
1991	Cal.	5	1	0	0	0	6	13	209	16.1	50	1
1992	Cal.	17	5	0	0	0	30	47	714	15.2	68	5
1993	Cal.	18	11	x2	0	0	70	57	1007	17.7	75	10
CFL TOTALS		**58**	**32**	**x2**	**0**	**0**	**196**	**174**	**3026**	**17.4**	**75**	**27**

		Punt Returns					Kickoff Returns				
	Team	NO	YDS	AVE	LG	TD	NO	YDS	AVE	LG	TD
1990	Cal.	56	796	14.2	82	3	23	734	31.9	88	1
1991	Cal.	8	52	6.5	21	0	6	81	13.5	19	0
1992	Cal.	7	24	3.4	8	0	18	392	21.8	52	0
1993	Cal.	65	589	9.1	70	1	24	462	19.3	40	0
CFL TOTALS		**136**	**1461**	**10.7**	**82**	**4**	**71**	**1669**	**23.5**	**88**	**1**

		Unsuccessful Field Goal Returns					Fumbles		
	Team	NO	YDS	AVE	LG	TD	NO	LOST	OFR
1990	Cal.	1	7	7.0	7	0	4	3	1
1991	Cal.	0	0	0.0	0	0	1	1	0
1992	Cal.	0	0	0.0	0	0	1	0	1
1993	Cal.	4	136	34.0	51	0	3	1	1
CFL TOTALS		**5**	**143**	**28.6**	**51**	**0**	**9**	**5**	**3**

Rushing - 4 for 19 yards, 4.8 average, longest 7 yards with Calgary in 1993. **CFL Total Rushing - 4 for 19 yards, 4.8 average, longest 7 yards.**

2-Pt. Converts - 1 complete, 2 made with Calgary in 1993. **CFL Total 2-Pt. Converts - 1 complete, 2 made.**

Tackles - 3 defensive with Calgary in 1992 and 1 defensive in 1993. **CFL Total Tackles - 4 (4 defensive).**

a - All-Western All-Star.

Playoffs

Games Played - 1 with Calgary in 1990; 1 in 1992 and 2 in 1993. **CFL Total Playoff GP - 4.**

Pass Receiving - 1 for 14 yards with Calgary in 1990 and 3 for 62 yards, 20.7 average, longest 41 yards in 1993. **CFL Total Playoff Pass Receiving - 4 for 76 yards, 19.0 average, longest 41 yards.**

Rushing - 0 for 30 yards with Calgary in 1992. **CFL Total Playoff Rushing - 0 for 30 yards.**

Punt Returns - 4 for 50 yards, 12.5 average, longest 21 yards with Calgary in 1990; 2 for 54 yards, 27.0 average, longest 54 yards in 1992 and 4 for 52 yards, 13.0 average, longest 29 yards in 1993. **CFL Total Playoff Punt Returns - 10 for 156 yards, 15.6 average, longest 54 yards.**

Kickoff Returns - 3 for 25 yards, 8.3 average, longest 12 yards with Calgary in 1992 and 4 for 52 yards, 8.0 average, longest 19 yards in 1993. **CFL Total Playoff Kickoff Returns - 7 for 77 yards, 11.0 average, longest 19 yards.**

Grey Cup

Games Played - 1 with Calgary in 1992. **Total Grey Cup GP - 1.**

Pass Receiving - 6 for 162 yards, 27.0 average, longest 41 yards with Calgary in 1992. **Total Grey Cup Pass Receiving - 6 for 162 yards, 27.0 average, longest 41 yards.**

Punt Returns - 7 for 70 yards, 10.0 average, longest 23 yards with Calgary in 1992. **Total Grey Cup Punt Returns - 7 for 70 yards, 10.0 average, longest 23 yards.**

CRIFO, ROBERT
Born: November 10, 1965
Birthplace: Toronto, Ontario
Wide Receiver. 6'6", 215 lbs. Non-import
Last Amateur Club: University of Toronto (OUAA)
Acquired: Selected by Winnipeg Blue Bombers in the third round (21st overall) of the 1988 CFL College Draft. Released by Winnipeg in September, 1993 and was signed as a free agent by the Ottawa Rough Riders later that month.

		Scoring						Pass Receiving				
	Team	GP	TD	C	FG	S	TP	NO	YDS	AVE	LG	TD
1989	Wpg.	3	0	0	0	0	0	2	17	8.5	14	0
1990	Wpg.	11	0	0	0	0	0	5	147	29.4	51	0
1991a	Wpg.	18	4	0	0	0	24	39	775	19.9	47	4
1992a	Wpg.	18	5	0	0	0	30	53	798	15.1	55	5
1993	Wpg.	4	0	x1	0	0	2	2	21	10.5	11	0
	Ott.	7	2	0	0	0	12	15	252	16.8	39	2
CFL TOTALS		**61**	**11**	**x1**	**0**	**0**	**68**	**116**	**2010**	**17.3**	**55**	**11**

Kickoff Returns - 1 for 0 yards with Winnipeg in 1992.
CFL Total Kickoff Returns - 1 for 0 yards.

2-Pt. Converts - 1 made for 2 points with Winnipeg in 1993.
CFL Total 2-Pt. Converts - 1 made for 2 points.

Fumbles - 1 and 0 lost with Winnipeg in 1991 and 2 and 1 lost in 1992.
CFL Total Fumbles - 3 and 1 lost.

Own Fumbles Recovered - 1 with Winnipeg in 1991. **CFL Total OFR - 1.**

Defensive Tackles - 1 with Winnipeg in 1991; 5 in 1992 and 2 with Ottawa in 1993.
CFL Total Defensive Tackles - 8.

a - All-Eastern All-Star

Playoffs

Games Played - 1 with Winnipeg in 1990; 2 in 1991; 1 in 1992 and 1 with Ottawa in 1993. **CFL Total Playoff GP - 5.**

Pass Receiving - 2 for 31 yards, 15.5 average, longest 24 yards with Winnipeg in 1992 and 4 for 97 yards, 24.4 average, longest 29 yards with Ottawa in 1993.
CFL Total Playoff Pass Receiving - 6 for 128 yards, 21.3 average, longest 29 yards.

Grey Cup

Games Played - 1 with Winnipeg in 1990 and 1 in 1992. **Total Grey Cup GP - 2.**

Pass Receiving - 2 for 14 yards, 7.0 average, longest 10 yards with Winnipeg in 1992.
Total Grey Cup Pass Receiving - 2 for 14 yards, 7.0 average, longest 10 yards.

CROONEN, JEFF
Born: September 2, 1966
Birthplace: Hamilton, Ontario
Linebacker. 6'3", 240 lbs. Non-import
Last Amateur Club: University of Western Ontario (OUAA)
Acquired: Selected by Winnipeg Blue Bombers in the fifth round (40th overall) of the 1989 CFL College Draft. Released by Winnipeg in July, 1991. Signed as a free agent by the Hamilton Tiger-Cats in July, 1991. Released by Hamilton in August, 1991. Signed as a free agent by the Toronto Argonauts in January, 1992. Released by Toronto in August, 1993. Signed as a free agent by the Edmonton Eskimos in December, 1993.

Games Played - 8 with Winnipeg in 1989; 16 in 1990; 4 with Hamilton in 1991; 4 with Toronto in 1992 and 3 in 1993. **CFL Total GP - 35.**

Interception Returns - 0 for 39 yards with Winnipeg in 1990.
CFL Total Interception Returns - 0 for 39 yards.

Rushing - 1 for 2 yards with Toronto in 1993. **CFL Total Rushing - 1 for 2 yards.**

Tackles - 6 defensive with Winnipeg in 1990; 3 defensive and 1 special teams with Hamilton in 1991; 5 special teams with Toronto in 1992 and 3 special teams in 1993. **CFL Total Tackles - 18 (9 defensive and 9 special teams).**

Playoffs

Games Played - 1 with Winnipeg in 1990. **CFL Total Playoff GP - 1**

Grey Cup

Games Played - 1 with Winnipeg in 1990. **Total Grey Cup GP - 1.**

CROUCH, JIM
Born: January 6, 1968
Birthplace: Sacramento, California
Kicker/Punter. 6'4", 175 lbs. Import
Last Amateur Club: California State University at Sacramento
Acquired: Signed as a free agent by the Buffalo Bills in 1992. Released during training camp. Signed as a free agent by the Sacramento Gold Miners in May, 1993.

		Scoring						Kickoffs				
	Team	GP	TD	C	FG	S	TP	NO	YDS	AVE	LK	S
1993a	Sac.	18	0	56	28	16	156	78	4441	56.9	95	3
CFL TOTALS		**18**	**0**	**56**	**28**	**16**	**156**	**78**	**4441**	**56.9**	**95**	**3**

		Punting					Field Goals					
	Team	NO	YDS	AVE	LK	S	T	M	YDS	AVE	LK	PCT
1993	Sac.	34	1220	35.9	58	0	45	28	711	25.4	42	62.2
CFL TOTALS		**34**	**1220**	**35.9**	**58**	**0**	**45**	**28**	**711**	**25.4**	**42**	**62.2**

		Field Goal Attempts					Converts			Fumbles		
	Team	NO	YDS	AVE	LK	S	T	G	PCT	NO	LOST	OFR
1993	Sac.	17	775	45.6	59	13	56	56	100.0	3	2	1
CFL TOTALS		**17**	**775**	**45.6**	**59**	**13**	**56**	**56**	**100.0**	**3**	**2**	**1**

Net Punting - 34 for 1025 yards with Sacramento in 1993.
CFL Total Net Punting - 34 for 1025 yards.

Fumble Returns - 1 for 0 yards with Sacramento in 1993.
CFL Total Fumble Returns - 1 for 0 yards.

Tackles - 1 special teams with Sacramento in 1993.
CFL Total Tackles - 1 (1 special teams).

a - Tied CFL record for Most Converts in One Game (9).

CRUM, MAURICE
Born: April 19, 1969
Birthplace: Tampa, Florida
Linebacker. 5'11", 230 lbs. Import
Last Amateur Club: University of Miami
Acquired: Signed as a free agent by the NFL Tampa Bay Buccaneers in 1991. Released by Tampa Bay and signed as a free agent by the Orlando Thunder of the WLAF in 1992. Signed as a free agent by the NFL Dallas Cowboys during 1992 training camp. Signed as a free agent by the Saskatchewan Roughriders in March, 1993.

Games Played - 18 with Saskatchewan in 1993. **CFL Total GP - 18.**

Interception Returns - 1 for 0 yards with Saskatchewan in 1993.
CFL Total Interception Returns - 1 for 0 yards.

Kickoff Returns - 1 for 1 yard with Saskatchewan in 1993.
CFL Total Kickoff Returns - 1 for 1 yard.

Fumble Returns - 1 for 65 yards with Saskatchewan in 1993.
CFL Total Fumble Returns - 1 for 65 yards.

Blocked Kicks - 2 converts with Saskatchewan in 1993.
CFL Total Blocked Kicks - 2 (2 converts).

Quarterback Sacks - 1 for 9 yards lost with Saskatchewan in 1993.
CFL Total QB Sacks - 1 for 9 yards lost.

Tackles - 80 defensive and 7 special teams with Saskatchewan in 1993.
CFL Total Tackles - 87 (80 defensive and 7 special teams).

Tackles for Losses - 7 for 16 yards lost with Saskatchewan in 1993.
CFL Total Tackles for Losses - 7 for 16 yards lost.

Playoffs

Games Played - 1 with Saskatchewan in 1993.
CFL Total Playoff GP - 1

Tackles - 1 defensive and 2 special teams with Saskatchewan in 1993.
CFL Total Playoff Tackles - 3 (1 defensive and 2 special teams).

CRYSDALE, JAMIE
Born: December 14, 1968
Birthplace:Toronto, Ontario
Centre. 6'4", 289 lbs. Non-import
Last Amateur Club: University of Cincinnati
Acquired: Signed as a free agent by the Calgary Stampeders in September, 1993.

Games Played - 7 with Calgary in 1993. **CFL Total GP - 7.**

Playoffs

Games Played - 2 with Calgary in 1993. **CFL Total Playoff GP - 2.**

CULPEPPER, WILLIE
Born: March 27, 1967
Birthplace: Jacksonville, Florida
Wide Receiver. 5'10", 150 lbs. Import
Last Amateur Club: University of Southwestern Louisiana
Acquired: Signed with the New Orleans Night of the Arena Football League in 1991. Signed as a free agent by the NFL Tampa Bay Buccaneers prior to training camp in 1992. Was placed on Tampa Bay's Developmental Squad halfway through the season. Signed as a free agent by the Cleveland Thunderbolts of the Arena Football League prior to the 1993 season. Signed as a free agent by the Saskatchewan Roughriders in May, 1993. Placed on Suspension List in October, 1993. Released by Saskatchewan in November, 1993.

		Scoring						Pass Receiving				
	Team	GP	TD	C	FG	S	TP	NO	YDS	AVE	LG	TD
1993	Sask.	3	1	0	0	0	6	6	95	15.8	34	1
CFL TOTALS		**3**	**1**	**0**	**0**	**0**	**6**	**6**	**95**	**15.8**	**34**	**1**

CULPEPPER, WILLIE

	Team	Punt Returns NO	YDS	AVE	LG	TD	Kickoff Returns NO	YDS	AVE	LG	TD
1993	Sask.	2	16	8.0	14	0	2	42	21.0	24	0
CFL TOTALS		**2**	**16**	**8.0**	**14**	**0**	**2**	**42**	**21.0**	**24**	**0**

Unsuccessful Field Goal Returns - 1 for 21 yards with Saskatchewan in 1993. **CFL Total Unsuccessful Field Goal Returns - 1 for 21 yards.**

Fumbles - 1 and 1 lost with Saskatchewan in 1993. **CFL Total Fumbles - 1 and 1 lost.**

CUMMINGS, BURT
Born: November 19, 1965
Birthplace: London, England
Defensive Back. 5'8", 175 lbs. Non-import
Last Amateur Club: University of North Dakota
Acquired: Selected by Hamilton Tiger-Cats in the fourth round (27th overall) of the 1988 CFL College Draft. Released in July, 1989. Signed as a free agent by Winnipeg Blue Bombers in October, 1989. Spent the 1992 season on the injured list. Claimed on waivers by the B.C. Lions in July, 1993. Traded to the Ottawa Rough Riders in August, 1993 in exchange for defensive back Michael Allen.

Games Played - 4 with Winnipeg in 1989; 3 in 1990; 12 in 1991; 3 with B.C. and 6 with Ottawa in 1993. **CFL Total GP - 28.**

Punt Returns - 6 for 16 yards, 2.7 average, longest 11 yards with Winnipeg in 1991. **CFL Total Punt Returns - 6 for 16 yards, 2.7 average, longest 11 yards.**

Interception Returns - 1 for 6 yards with Ottawa in 1993. **CFL Total Interception Returns - 1 for 6 yards.**

Kickoff Returns - 5 for 71 yards, 14.2 average, longest 24 yards with Winnipeg in 1991. **CFL Total Kickoff Returns - 5 for 71 yards, 14.2 average, longest 24 yards.**

Fumble Returns - 1 for 0 yards with Winnipeg in 1989 and 1 for 4 yards with Ottawa in 1993. **CFL Total Fumble Returns - 2 for 4 yards.**

Tackles - 12 defensive with Winnipeg in 1989; 2 defensive in 1990; 1 defensive and 9 special teams in 1991 and 5 defensive and 3 special teams with Ottawa in 1993. **CFL Total Tackles - 32 (20 defensive and 12 special teams).**

Playoffs

Games Played - 2 with Winnipeg in 1989 and 1 with Ottawa in 1993. **CFL Total Playoff GP - 3.**

Tackles - 1 defensive with Winnipeg in 1989 and 2 defensive and 1 special teams with Ottawa in 1993. **CFL Total Playoff Tackles - 4 (3 defensive and 1 special teams).**

DANIELS, SHAWN
Born: September 3, 1966
Birthplace: Montreal, Quebec
Fullback. 5'11", 240 lbs. Non-import
Last Amateur Club: Bowling Green University
Acquired: Selected in the third round (19th overall) by the Hamilton Tiger-Cats in the 1988 CFL College Draft. Attended the NFL Dallas Cowboy's training camp in August, 1989. Released and signed by the Saskatchewan Roughriders in September, 1989 after his rights were traded from Hamilton along with a first round draft pick in the 1989 CFL College Draft (cornerback Andrew Thomas) for linebacker Pete Giftopoulos. Traded with slotback James Ellingson to the Ottawa Rough Riders for running back Orville Lee in August, 1990. Granted free agency status in February, 1994.

	Team	Scoring GP	TD	C	FG	S	TP	Rushing NO	YDS	AVE	LG	TD
1989	Sask.	10	0	0	0	0	0	20	48	2.4	7	0
1990	Ott.	2	0	0	0	0	0	4	23	5.8	8	0
1991	Ott.	16	6	0	0	0	36	52	229	4.4	26	5
1992	Ott.	14	0	0	0	0	0	9	79	5.4	31	0
1993	Ott.	18	3	0	0	0	18	52	238	4.6	20	2
CFL TOTALS		**60**	**9**	**0**	**0**	**0**	**54**	**137**	**587**	**4.3**	**31**	**7**

	Team	Pass Receiving NO	YDS	AVE	LG	TD	Kickoff Returns NO	YDS	AVE	LG	TD
1989	Sask.	10	100	10.0	19	0	2	41	20.5	33	0
1990	Ott.	1	8	8.8	8	0	0	0	0.0	0	0
1991	Ott.	4	38	9.5	25	1	1	0	0.0	0	0
1992	Ott.	10	41	4.1	12	0	0	0	0.0	0	0
1993	Ott.	43	326	7.6	28	1	0	0	0.0	0	0
CFL TOTALS		**68**	**513**	**7.5**	**28**	**2**	**3**	**41**	**13.7**	**33**	**0**

Fumbles - 3 and 2 lost with Saskatchewan in 1989; 1 and 1 lost with Ottawa in 1991 and 2 and 2 lost in 1993. **CFL Total Fumbles - 6 and 5 lost.**

Own Fumbles Recovered - 1 with Ottawa in 1993. **CFL Total OFR - 1.**

Tackles - 8 special teams with Ottawa in 1991; 1 defensive and 5 special teams in 1992 and 2 defensive and 3 special teams in 1993. **CFL Total Tackles- 19 (3 defensive and 16 special teams).**

Playoffs

Games Played - 2 with Saskatchewan in 1989; 1 with Ottawa in 1991; 1 in 1992 and 1 in 1993. **CFL Total Playoff GP - 5**

Rushing - 4 for 39 yards, 9.8 average, longest 24 yards with Ottawa in 1991 and 1 for 4 yards in 1993. **CFL Total Playoff Rushing - 5 for 43 yards, 8.6 average, longest 24 yards.**

Kickoff Returns - 1 for 13 yards with Ottawa in 1993. **CFL Total Playoff Kickoff Returns - 1 for 13 yards.**

Fumbles - 1 and 1 lost with Ottawa in 1991 and 1 and 1 lost in 1993. **CFL Total Playoff Fumbles - 2 and 2 lost.**

Own Fumbles Recovered - 1 with Ottawa in 1991. **CFL Total Playoff OFR - 1.**

Tackles - 1 special teams with Ottawa in 1992 and 1 defensive in 1993. **CFL Total Playoff Tackles - 2 (1 defensive and 1 special teams).**

Grey Cup

Games Played - 1 with Saskatchewan in 1989. **Total Grey Cup GP 1.**

DAVIDSON, ROB
Born: May 10, 1967
Birthplace: Montreal, Quebec
Defensive Tackle. 6'4", 275 lbs. Non-import
Last Amateur Club: University of Toronto (OUAA)
Acquired: Selected in the sixth round, (45th overall), by the Edmonton Eskimos in the 1989 CFL College Draft. Returned to school in 1989 and signed by Edmonton in April, 1990. Released by Edmonton in July, 1993. Signed as a free agent by the Winnipeg Blue Bombers in August,1993.

Games Played - 15 with Edmonton in 1990; 11 in 1991; 18 in 1992 and 6 with Winnipeg in 1993. **CFL Total GP - 50**

Kickoff Returns - 1 for 0 yards with Winnipeg in 1993. **CFL Total Kickoff Returns - 1 for 0 yards.**

Fumble Returns - 1 for 0 yards with Edmonton in 1991. **CFL Total Fumble Returns - 1 for 0 yards.**

Fumbles - 1 and 0 lost with Winnipeg in 1993. **CFL Total Fumbles - 1 and 0 lost**

Quarterback Sacks - 3 with Edmonton in 1991 and 5 for 21 yards lost in 1992. **CFL Total QB Sacks - 8.**

Tackles - 6 defensive with Edmonton in 1990; 7 defensive and 8 special teams in 1991; 31 defensive and 2 special teams in 1992 and 1 defensive and 2 special teams with Winnipeg in 1993. **CFL Total Tackles - 57 (45 defensive and 12 special teams).**

Tackles for Losses - 6 for 10 yards with Edmonton in 1992. **CFL Total Tackles for Losses - 6 for 10 yards.**

Playoffs

Games Played - 2 with Edmonton in 1990; 1 in 1991 and 2 in 1992. **CFL Total Playoff GP - 5**

Defensive Tackles - 1 with Edmonton in 1990 and 2 in 1992. **CFL Total Defensive Tackles - 3.**

Grey Cup

Games Played - 1 with Edmonton in 1990. **Total Grey Cup GP -1.**

DAVIES, DOUG
Born: December 2, 1964
Birthplace: Toronto, Ontario
Offensive Lineman. 6'4", 270 lbs. Non-import
Last Amateur Club: Simon Fraser University (EVCO)
Acquired: Selected in the second round (11th overall) by the Montreal Alouettes in the 1987 CFL College Draft. Signed as a free agent in May, 1988 by the Hamilton Tiger-Cats. Selected by Calgary Stampeders in the 1989 Equalization Draft. Was injured for the 1989 season.

Games Played - 17 with Hamilton in 1988; 18 with Calgary in 1990; 18 in 1991; 18 in 1992 and 18 in 1993. **CFL Total GP - 89**

Pass Receiving - 0 for 5 yards with Calgary in 1993. **CFL Total Pass Receiving - 0 for 5 yards.**

Fumbles - 1 and 0 lost with Calgary in 1990 and 1 and 1 lost in 1991. **CFL Total Fumbles - 2 and 1 lost.**

Fumble Returns - 1 for 0 yards with Hamilton in 1988 and 2 for 0 yards with Calgary in 1992. **CFL Total Fumble Returns - 3 for 0 yards.**

DAVIES, DOUG

Tackles - 1 defensive with Calgary in 1990; 4 special teams in 1991; 3 special teams in 1992 and 2 special teams in 1993. **CFL Total Tackles - 10 (1 defensive and 9 special teams).**

Playoffs

Games Played - 1 with Hamilton in 1988; 1 with Calgary in 1990; 2 in 1991; 1 in 1992 and 2 in 1993. **CFL Total Playoff GP - 7.**

Fumble Returns - 1 for 0 yards with Calgary in 1992. **CFL Total Playoff Fumble Returns - 1 for 0 yards.**

Grey Cup

Games Played - 1 with Calgary in 1991 and 1 in 1992. **Total Grey Cup GP - 2**

DAVIS, DARRICK
Born: September 29, 1969
Birthplace: Chicago, Illinois
Cornerback. 5'8", 165 lbs. Import
Last Amateur Club: University of Idaho
Acquired: Signed as a free agent by the Sacramento Gold Miners in August, 1993.

Games Played - 9 with Sacramento in 1993. **CFL Total GP - 9.**

Tackles - 27 defensive and 1 special teams with Sacramento in 1993. **CFL Total Tackles - 28 (27 defensive and 1 special teams).**

DAVIS, PASCHALL
Born: May 7, 1969
Birthplace: Bryan, Texas
Linebacker. 6'2", 220 lbs. Import
Last Amateur Club: Texas A & M University
Acquired: Signed as a free agent by the Sacramento Gold Miners in March, 1993.

	Team	Scoring GP	TD	C	FG	S	TP	Interception Returns NO	YDS	AVE	LG	TD
1993	Sac.	18	1	0	0	0	6	2	46	23.0	39	1
CFL TOTALS		**18**	**1**	**0**	**0**	**0**	**6**	**2**	**46**	**23.0**	**39**	**1**

	Team	Kickoff Returns NO	YDS	AVE	LG	TD	Fumble Returns NO	YDS	AVE	LG	TD
1993	Sac.	1	13	13.0	13	0	1	0	0.0	0	0
CFL TOTALS		**1**	**13**	**13.0**	**13**	**0**	**1**	**0**	**0.0**	**0**	**0**

Tackles - 13 defensive and 15 special teams with Sacramento in 1993. **CFL Total Tackles - 28 (13 defensive and 15 special teams).**

Tackles For Losses - 1 for 2 yards with Sacramento in 1993. **CFL Total Tackles For Losses - 1 for 2 yards.**

DAWSON, BOBBY
Born: February 18, 1966
Birthplace: Sacramento, California
Defensive Back. 5'11", 210 lbs. Import
Last Amateur Club: University of Illinois
Acquired: Selected in the 11th round of the 1988 NFL College Draft by the Pittsburgh Steelers and attended their training camp in 1988. Signed as a free agent by the Hamilton Tiger-Cats in March, 1990.

	Team	GP	Interception Returns NO	YDS	AVE	LG	TD	Fumble Returns NO	YDS	AVE	LG	TD
1990	Ham.	15	3	8	2.7	8	0	0	0	0.0	0	0
1991	Ham.	15	5	34	6.5	22	0	2	22	11.0	12	0
1992	Ham.	18	4	52	13.0	25	0	1	25	25.0	25	1
1993	Ham.	11	2	35	17.5	29	1	0	0	0.0	0	0
CFL TOTALS		**59**	**14**	**129**	**9.2**	**29**	**1**	**3**	**47**	**15.7**	**25**	**1**

Scoring - 1 TD for 6 points with Hamilton in 1992 and 1 TD for 6 points in 1993. **CFL Total Scoring - 2 TDs for 12 points.**

Kickoff Returns - 1 for 18 yards with Hamilton in 1992. **CFL Total Kickoff Returns - 1 for 18 yards.**

Blocked Kicks - 1 punt with Hamilton in 1991. **CFL Total Blocked Kicks - 1 punt.**

Quarterback Sacks - 1 for 17 yards lost with Hamilton in 1992. **CFL Total QB Sacks - 1.**

Tackles - 51 defensive with Hamilton in 1990; 72 defensive and 2 special teams in 1991; 76 defensive and 1 special teams in 1992 and 33 defensive and 1 special teams in 1993. **CFL Total Tackles - 236 (232 defensive and 4 special teams).**

Tackles for Losses - 4 for 18 yards with Hamilton in 1991 and 1 for 1 yard in 1992. **CFL Total Tackles for Losses - 5 for 19 yards.**

Playoffs

Games Played - 2 with Hamilton in 1992 and 2 in 1993. **CFL Total Playoff GP - 4.**

Tackles - 6 defensive with Hamilton in 1992 and 7 defensive in 1993. **CFL Total Playoff Tackles - 13 (13 defensive).**

Quarterback Sacks - 1 for 8 yards lost with Hamilton in 1993. **CFL Total Playoff QB Sacks - 1 for 8 yards lost.**

DAYMOND, IRV
Born: October 9, 1962
Birthplace: St. Thomas, Ontario
Offensive Centre. 6'5", 265 lbs. Non-import
Last Amateur Club: University of Western Ontario,(OUAA)
Acquired: Selected in the sixth round, (53th overall), in the 1984 CFL College Draft by the B.C. Lions. Released in May, 1984. Signed as a free agent with the Calgary Stampeders in March, 1986. Released in June, 1986 and signed as a free agent by the Ottawa Rough Riders in October, 1986. Released by Ottawa in April, 1993. Re-signed by Ottawa in June, 1993.

Games Played - 3 with Ottawa in 1986; 16 in 1987; 12 in 1988; 18 in 1989; 18 in 1990; 17 in 1991; 17 in 1992 and 12 in 1993. **CFL Total GP - 113.**

Own Fumbles Recovered - 1 with Ottawa in 1987. **CFL Total OFR - 1.**

Fumbles - 1 and 1 lost with Ottawa in 1989 and 1 and 0 lost in 1992. **CFL Total Fumbles - 2 and 1 lost.**

Defensive Tackles - 1 with Ottawa in 1987; 1 in 1988; 4 in 1989; 8 in 1990; 4 in 1991; 3 in 1992 and 4 in 1993. **CFL Total Defensive Tackles - 25.**

All-Eastern All-Star in 1991 and 1992.

Playoffs

Games Played - 1 with Ottawa in 1990; 1 in 1991 and 1 in 1992. **CFL Total Playoff GP - 3.**

DENNIS, MARK
Born: October 25, 1967
Birthplace: Windsor, Ontario
Linebacker. 6'2", 235 lbs. Non-import
Last Amateur Club: Central Michigan University
Acquired: Selected in the first round (seventh overall) by the Hamilton Tiger-Cats in the 1990 CFL College Draft. Signed as a free agent by the NFL New York Giants and was released after training camp. Signed by Hamilton in September, 1990. Granted free agency status in February, 1993. Re-signed by Hamilton in May, 1993 and was subsequently released in October, 1993.

Games Played - 5 with Hamilton in 1990; 17 in 1991; 14 in 1992 and 1 in 1993. **CFL Total GP - 37**

Fumble Returns - 1 for 0 yards with Hamilton in 1991 and 2 for 0 yards in 1992. **CFL Total Fumble Returns - 3 for 0 yards.**

Quarterback Sacks - 1 with Hamilton in 1991 and 1 for 12 yards lost in 1992. **CFL Total QB Sacks - 2.**

Tackles - 18 defensive with Hamilton in 1990; 22 defensive and 4 special teams in 1991; 4 defensive and 18 special teams in 1992 and 2 defensive with Hamilton in 1993. **CFL Total Tackles - 68 (46 defensive and 22 special teams).**

DERMOTT, BLAKE
Born: September 10, 1961
Birthplace: Edmonton, Alberta
Centre. 6'3", 255 lbs. Non-import
Last Amateur Club: University of Alberta (WIFL)
Acquired: Territorial Exemption by the Edmonton Eskimos in 1983.

Games Played - 15 with Edmonton in 1983; 16 in 1984; 16 in 1985; 18 in 1986; 18 in 1887; 18 in 1988; 18 in 1989; 18 in 1990; 18 in 1991; 17 in 1992 and 18 in 1993. **CFL Total GP - 190.**

Fumble Returns - 1 with Edmonton in 1983. **CFL Total Fumble Returns - 1.**

Own Fumbles Recovered - 1 with Edmonton in 1984; 2 in 1985; 1 in 1986; 1 in 1989; 1 in 1990 and 1 in 1991. **CFL Total OFR - 7.**

Tackles - 2 defensive with Edmonton in 1988; 1 defensive in 1990; 1 defensive and 1 special teams in 1991 and 2 special teams in 1992. **CFL Total Tackles - 7 (4 defensive and 3 special teams).**

All-Western All-Star in 1989

DERMOTT, BLAKE

Playoffs

Games Played - 1 with Edmonton in 1983; 1 in 1984; 1 in 1985; 2 in 1986; 2 in 1987; 1 in 1989; 2 in 1990; 1 in 1991; 2 in 1992 and 2 in 1993.
CFL Total Playoff GP - 15.

Tackles - 1 defensive with Edmonton in 1992.
CFL Total Playoff Tackles - 1 (1 defensive).

Grey Cup

Games Played - 1 with Edmonton in 1986; 1 in 1987; 1 in 1990 and 1 in 1993.
Total Grey Cup GP - 4

DIAZ-INFANTE, DAVID
Born: March 31, 1964
Birthplace: San Jose, California
Offensive Guard, 6'2", 278 lbs. Import
Last Amateur Club: San Jose State University
Acquired: Signed as a free agent by the NFL San Diego Chargers prior to the 1987 NFL season. Released by San Diego and later re-signed as a replacement player. Released by San Diego in October, 1987. Signed as a free agent by the NFL Los Angeles Rams in 1989. Released by Los Angeles during pre-season. Selected by the Frankfurt Galaxy in the 3rd round (24th overall) in the 1991 WLAF Positional Draft. Signed as a free agent by the Sacramento Gold Miners in September, 1993.

Games Played - 8 with Sacramento in 1993. **CFL Total GP - 8.**

DICKEY, TERRY
Born: September 6, 1970
Birthplace: Columbus, Ohio
Slotback/Running Back, 5'7", 170 lbs., Import
Last Amateur Club: Depauw University
Acquired: Signed as a free agent by the Toronto Argonauts in September, 1993. Was released by Toronto in September, 1993. Signed as a free agent by the Las Vegas Posse in March, 1994.

			Rushing					Kickoff Returns				
	Team	GP	NO	YDS	AVE	LG	TD	NO	YDS	AVE	LG	TD
1993	Tor.	6	3	10	3.3	4	0	9	98	10.9	20	0
CFL TOTALS		**6**	**3**	**10**	**3.3**	**4**	**0**	**9**	**98**	**10.9**	**20**	**0**

		Pass Receiving				Punt Returns				
	Team	NO	YDS	AVE	LG	TD	NO	YDS	AVE	LG	TD
1993	Tor.	16	136	8.5	24	0	2	11	5.5	9	0
CFL TOTALS		**16**	**136**	**8.5**	**24**	**0**	**2**	**11**	**5.5**	**9**	**0**

Fumbles - 1 and 0 lost with Toronto in 1993. **CFL Total Fumbles - 1 and 0 lost.**

Tackles - 1 defensive with Toronto in 1993. **CFL Total Tackles - 1 (1 defensive).**

DICKSON, BRUCE
Born: October 11, 1967
Birthplace: Hamilton, Ontario
Linebacker. 6'2", 225 lbs. Non-import
Last Amateur Club: Simon Fraser University (CFA)
Acquired: Selected in the third round (18th overall) by the Toronto Argonauts in the 1991 CFL College Draft. The selection was acquired from the B.C. Lions to complete a deal for the rights to defensive back Andrew Thomas. Traded to the Edmonton Eskimos in January, 1993 along with cornerback Ed Berry, wide receiver Eddie Brown, quarterback Rickey Foggie, slotback J.P. Izquierdo, defensive lineman Leonard Johnson, slotback Darrel K. Smith and defensive back Don Wilson in exchange for defensive lineman Cameron Brosseau, linebacker John Davis slotback Craig Ellis, quarterback Tracy Ham, defensive back Enis Jackson, running back Chris Johnstone, defensive back Travis Oliver, and wide receiver Ken Winey.

Games Played - 3 with Toronto in 1991; 12 in 1992 and 15 with Edmonton in 1993.
CFL Total GP - 30

Interception Returns - 1 for 22 yards with Edmonton in 1993.
CFL Total Interception Returns - 1 for 22 yards.

Kickoff Returns - 1 for 0 yards with Edmonton in 1993.
CFL Total Kickoff Returns - 1 for 0 yards.

Fumble Returns - 1 for 0 yards with Toronto in 1992 and 1 for 0 yards with Edmonton in 1993. **CFL Total Fumble Returns - 2 for 0 yards.**

Fumbles - 1 and 0 lost with Edmonton in 1993. **CFL Total Fumbles - 1 and 0 lost.**

Own Fumbles Recovered - 1 with Edmonton in 1993. **CFL Total OFR - 1.**

Blocked Kicks - 1 punt with Edmonton in 1993.
CFL Total Blocked Kicks - 1 (1 punt)

Quarterback Sacks - 1 for 6 yards lost with Edmonton in 1993.
CFL Total QB Sacks - 1 for 6 yards lost.

Tackles - 2 special teams with Toronto in 1991; 1 defensive and 14 special teams in 1992 and 6 defensive and 20 special teams with Edmonton in 1993.
CFL Total Tackles - 43 (7 defensive and 36 special teams).

Tackles for Losses - 1 for 2 yards with Toronto in 1992.
CFL Total Tackles for Losses - 1 for 2 yards.

Playoffs

Games Played - 2 with Edmonton in 1993. **CFL Total Playoff GP - 2.**

Tackles - 1 defensive and 6 special teams with Edmonton in 1993.
CFL Total Playoff Tackles - 7 (1 defensive and 6 special teams).

Grey Cup

Games Played - 1 with Edmonton in 1993. **Total Grey Cup GP - 1.**

Fumble Returns - 1 for 0 yards with Edmonton in 1993.
Total Grey Cup Fumble Returns - 1 for 0 yards.

Blocked Kicks - 1 punt with Edmonton in 1993.
Total Grey Cup Blocked Kicks - 1 (1 punt).

DILLON, TODD
Born: January 6, 1962
Birthplace: Modesto, California
Linebacker. 6'0", 195 lbs. Import
Last Amateur Club: Long Beach State University
Acquired: Selected by Los Angeles in the 1984 USFL Territorial Draft. Traded to the Houston Gamblers in February, 1984 for past considerations. Released by the Gamblers and signed as a free agent by the New Jersey Generals. Released and signed as a free agent by the Ottawa Rough Riders in August, 1986. Released in August, 1988 and signed as a free agent by the Hamilton Tiger-Cats in October, 1988. Placed on the suspension list in June, 1993. Granted free agency status in February, 1994. Re-signed by Hamilton in March, 1994.

			Scoring					Rushing				
	Team	GP	TD	C	FG	S	TP	NO	YDS	AVE	LG	TD
1986	Ott.	12	0	0	0	0	0	4	6	1.5	3	0
1987	Ott.	14	0	0	0	0	0	29	228	7.9	19	0
1988	Ott.	7	3	0	0	0	18	16	109	6.8	37	3
1989	Ham.	18	0	0	0	0	0	22	106	4.8	32	0
1990	Ham.	18	0	0	0	0	0	14	59	4.2	18	0
1991	Ham.	17	2	0	0	0	12	39	243	6.2	25	0
1992	Ham.	18	0	0	0	0	0	7	47	6.7	23	0
1993	Ham.	1	0	0	0	0	0	5	23	4.6	11	0
CFL TOTALS		**105**	**5**	**0**	**0**	**0**	**30**	**136**	**821**	**6.0**	**37**	**5**

		Passing							Fumbles		
	Team	ATT	COMP	YDS	PCT	INT	LGT	TD	NO	LOST	OFR
1986	Ott.	186	102	1279	54.8	12	47	3	1	0	0
1987	Ott.	402	222	2901	55.2	18	57	14	4	2	3
1988	Ott.	185	97	1211	52.4	8	72	4	3	1	0
1989	Ham.	191	105	1368	55.0	3	53	5	4	2	1
1990	Ham.	193	113	135	58.5	10	48	7	0	0	0
1991	Ham.	246	125	1551	50.8	10	75	8	1	0	0
1992	Ham.	46	20	371	43.5	2	53	2	2	0	2
1993	Ham.	22	14	192	63.6	1	46	1	1	1	0
CFL TOTALS		**147**	**798**	**10,224**	**54.2**	**64**	**421**	**44**	**16**	**6**	**6**

2-Pt. Converts - 3 attempts, 0 made with Ottawa in 1987 and 1 attempt, 0 made with Hamilton in 1990; 2 attempts, 1 made in 1991 and 1 attempt, 0 made in 1992. **CFL Total 2-Pt. Converts - 7 attempts, 1 made.**

Tackles - 2 defensive with Ottawa in 1988; 1 defensive and 1 special teams with Hamilton in 1991 and 1 defensive and 2 special teams in 1992.
CFL Tackles - 6 (3 defensive and 3 special teams).

Playoffs

			Rushing					Passing						
	Team	GP	NO	YDS	AVE	LG	TD	ATT	COMP	YDS	PCT	INT	LG	TD
1988	Ham.	1	2	11	5.5	9	1	11	7	75.	63.6	0	14	0
1989	Ham.	1	0	0	0.0	0	0	20	11	151	55.0	0	23	0
1992	Ham.	2	0	0	0.0	0	0	0	0	0	0.0	0	0	0
1993	Ham.	2	9	13	1.4	6	0	73	45	479	61.6	2	42	2
CFL TOTALS		**6**	**11**	**24**	**2.2**	**15**	**1**	**104**	**63**	**705**	**60.6**	**2**	**42**	**2**

Own Fumbles Recovered - 1 with Hamilton in 1993.
CFL Total Playoff OFR - 1.

Fumbles - 1 and 0 lost with Hamilton in 1993.
CFL Total Playoff Fumbles - 1 and 0 lost

Grey Cup

Games Played - 1 with Hamilton in 1989. **Total Grey Cup GP - 1.**

DINNALL, DAVE
Born: September 4, 1969
Birthplace: London, England
Running Back. 5'11", 190 lbs. Non-import
Last Amateur Club: Burlington Braves (OJFC)
Acquired: Attended the 1991 Toronto Argonaut training camp. Was released and returned to juniors for 1991. Signed as a free agent by the Hamilton Tiger-Cats in May, 1992

	Team	Scoring GP	TD	C	FG	S	TP	Kickoff Returns NO	YDS	AVE	LG	TD
1992	Ham.	3	2	0	0	0	12	4	71	14.8	30	0
1993	Ham.	15	0	0	0	0	0	1	16	16.0	16	0
CFL TOTALS		**18**	**2**	**0**	**0**	**0**	**12**	**5**	**87**	**17.4**	**30**	**0**

	Team	Rushing NO	YDS	AVE	LG	TD	Passing NO	YDS	AVE	LG	TD
1992	Ham.	0	0	0.0	0	0	0	0	0.0	0	0
1993	Ham.	12	117	9.8	63	1	2	23	11.5	14	0
CFL TOTALS		**12**	**117**	**9.8**	**63**	**1**	**2**	**23**	**11.8**	**14**	**0**

	Team	Fumble Returns NO	YDS	AVE	LG	TD	Fumbles NO	YDS	OFR
1992	Ham.	0	0	0.0	0	0	0	0	0
1993	Ham.	1	20	20.0	20	0	1	1	0
CFL TOTALS		**1**	**20**	**20.0**	**20**	**0**	**1**	**1**	**0**

Tackles - 4 special teams with Hamilton in 1992 and 2 defensive and 13 special teams in 1993. **CFL Total Tackles - 19 (2 defensive and 17 special teams).**

Playoffs

	Team	Scoring GP	TD	C	FG	S	TP	Rushing NO	YDS	AVE	LG	TD
1993	Ham.	2	2	0	0	0	12	31	130	4.2	34	2
CFL TOTALS		**2**	**2**	**0**	**0**	**0**	**12**	**31**	**130**	**4.2**	**34**	**2**

	Team	Pass Receiving NO	YDS	AVE	LG	TD	Fumbles NO	LOST	OFR
1993	Ham.	5	39	738	14	0	4	4	0
CFL TOTALS		**5**	**39**	**738**	**14**	**0**	**4**	**4**	**0**

DIXON, TITUS
Born: June 15, 1966
Birthplace: Clewiston, Florida
Wide Receiver, 5'7", 160 lbs. Import
Last Amateur Club: Troy State University
Acquired: Selected by the New York Jets in the sixth round (153rd overall) in the 1989 NFL Draft. Released by New York in September, 1989. Signed as a free agent by the NFL Indianapolis Colts in October, 1989 and was subsequently released by Indianapolis later that month. Signed as a free agent by the NFL Atlanta Falcons in April, 1990 and was released by Atlanta in August, 1990. Signed as a free agent by the NFL Kansas City Chiefs in April, 1991 and was released by Kansas City in August, 1991. Selected by the San Antonio Riders in the fourth round (36th overall) in the 1992 WLAF Draft. Signed as a free agent by the Sacramento Gold Miners in July, 1993.

	Team	Scoring GP	TD	C	FG	S	TP	Pass Receiving NO	YDS	AVE	LG	TD
1993	Sac.	15	5	0	0	0	30	61	1074	17.6	90	5
CFL TOTALS		**15**	**5**	**0**	**0**	**0**	**30**	**61**	**1074**	**17.6**	**90**	**5**

	Team	Punt Returns NO	YDS	AVE	LG	TD	Kickoff Returns NO	YDS	AVE	LG	TD
1993	Sac.	3	6	2.0	6	0	31	602	19.4	42	0
CFL TOTALS		**3**	**6**	**2.0**	**6**	**0**	**31**	**602**	**19.4**	**42**	**0**

Own Fumbles Recovered - 1 with Sacramento in 1993. **CFL Total OFR - 1.**

Fumbles - 3 and 1 lost with Sacremento in 1993. **CFL Total Fumbles - 3 and 1 lost.**

Tackles - 2 defensive with Sacramento in 1993. **CFL Total Tackles - 2 (2 defensive).**

DMYTRYSHYN, DUANE
Born: June 11, 1971
Birthplace: Saskatoon, Saskatchewan
Slotback, 6'1", 210 lbs. Non-import
Last Amateur Club: University of Calgary (CWAA)
Acquired: Selected in the 3rd round (21st overall) by the Calgary Stampeders in the 1993 CFL College Draft. The choice was acquired from the Winnipeg Blue Bombers in exchange for full-back Duane Forde.

Games Played - 1 with Calgary in 1993. **CFL Total GP - 1.**

DONELSON, VENTSON
Born: February 2, 1968
Birthplace: Rock Island, Illinois
Cornerback. 5'11", 180 lbs. Import
Last Amateur Club: Michigan State University
Acquired: Selected in the 12th round (309th overall) by the NFL New England Patriots in the 1990 NFL Draft. Spent the 1990 season on the injured list. Signed as a free agent by the NFL Green Bay Packers in March, 1991 and was released after training camp. Signed as a free agent by the Saskatchewan Roughriders in September, 1991. Released by Saskatchewan in February, 1994. Re-signed by Saskatchewan in April, 1994.

Games Played - 3 with Saskatchewan in 1991; 18 in 1992 and 14 in 1993. **CFL Total GP - 35.**

Kickoff Returns - 2 for 46 yards, 23.0 average, longest 25 yards with Saskatchewan in 1991 and 1 for 0 yards in 1992. **CFL Total Kickoff Returns - 3 for 46 yards, 15.3 average, longest 25 yards.**

Interception Returns - 3 for 7 yards, 2.3 average, longest 3 yards with Saskatchewan in 1992. **CFL Total Interception Returns - 3 for 7 yards, 2.3 average, longest 3 yards.**

Fumbles - 1 and 1 lost with Saskatchewan in 1991. **CFL Total Fumbles - 1 and 1 lost.**

Fumble Returns - 1 for 9 yards with Saskatchewan in 1992. **CFL Total Fumble Returns - 1 for 9 yards.**

Blocked Kicks - 1 punt with Saskatchewan in 1992. **CFL Total Blocked Kicks - 1 (1 punt).**

Quarterback Sacks - 1 for 4 yards lost with Saskatchewan in 1993. **CFL Total QB Sacks - 1 for 4 yards lost.**

Tackles - 8 defensive and 2 special teams with Saskatchewan in 1991; 64 defensive and 8 special teams in 1992 and 35 defensive and 8 special teams in 1993. **CFL Total Tackles - 125 (107 defensive and 18 special teams).**

Tackles for Losses - 1 for 3 yards with Saskatchewan in 1992 and 1 for 2 yards in 1993. **CFL Total Tackles for Losses - 2 for 5 yards.**

Playoffs

Games Played - 1 with Saskatchewan in 1992 and 1 in 1993. **CFL Total Playoff GP - 2.**

Tackles - 5 defensive with Saskatchewan in 1992 and 1 defensive in 1993. **CFL Total Playoff Tackles - 6 (6 defensive).**

DOUGLAS, SCOTT
Born: November 22, 1967
Birthplace: Windsor, Ontario
Offensive Lineman. 6'3", 265 lbs. Non-import
Last Amateur Club: University of Western Ontario (OUAA)
Acquired: Selected in the fifth round (39th overall) by the Hamilton Tiger-Cats in the 1990 CFL College Draft. Signed by Hamilton in December, 1990. Granted free agency status in February, 1994. Re-signed by Hamilton in March, 1994.

Games Played - 18 with Hamilton in 1991; 16 in 1992 and 18 in 1993. **CFL Total GP - 52.**

Tackles - 1 defensive and 1 special teams with Hamilton in 1991. **CFL Total Tackles - 2 (1 defensive and 1 special teams).**

Playoffs

Games Played - 2 with Hamilton in 1992 and 2 in 1993. **CFL Total Playoff GP - 4.**

Own Fumbles Recovered - 1 with Hamilton in 1992. **CFL Total Playoff OFR - 1.**

Tackles - 1 defensive with Hamilton in 1993. **CFL Total Playoff Tackles - 1 (1 defensive).**

DRAWHORN, ANTHONY
Born: July 27, 1965
Birthplace: Los Angeles, California
Defensive Back. 5'9", 175 lbs. Import
Last Amateur Club: University of Nevada at Las Vegas
Acquired: Signed as a free agent by B.C. Lions in June, 1988. Released in July, 1991 and signed as a free agent by the Ottawa Rough Riders. Traded to the Saskatchewan Roughriders along with quarterback Tom Burgess and defensive end Paul Yatkowski in exchange for quarterback Kent Austin and offensive lineman Andrew Greene in March 1994.

	Team	Scoring GP	TD	C	FG	S	TP	Interception Returns NO	YDS	AVE	LG	TD
1988	B.C.	18	1	0	0	0	6	5	93	18.6	31	0
1989	B.C.	5	0	0	0	0	0	1	10	10.0	10	0
1990	B.C.	9	0	0	0	0	0	1	70	70.0	70	0
1991a	Ott.	17	2	0	0	0	12	5	128	25.6	63	2
1992ab	Ott.	18	1	0	0	0	6	8	77	9.6	40	1
1993	Ott.	18	0	0	0	0	0	3	28	9.3	28	0
CFL TOTALS		**85**	**4**	**0**	**0**	**0**	**24**	**23**	**406**	**17.7**	**70**	**3**

DRAWHORN, ANTHONY

	Team	Punt Returns NO	YDS	AVE	LG	TD	Kickoff Returns NO	YDS	AVE	LG	TD
1988	B.C.	8	60	7.5	23	0	31	691	22.3	57	0
1989	B.C.	0	0	0.0	0	0	9	221	24.6	53	0
1990	B.C.	1	13	13.0	13	0	4	38	9.5	19	0
1991	Ott.	75	677	9.0	50	0	54	1095	20.3	70	0
1992	Ott.	38	166	4.4	16	0	13	233	17.9	25	0
1993	Ott.	52	334	6.4	28	0	6	100	16.7	26	0
CFL TOTALS		**174**	**1250**	**7.2**	**78**	**0**	**117**	**2378**	**20**	**96**	**0**

	Team	Fumble Returns NO	YDS	AVE	LG	TD	Fumbles NO	LOST	OFR
1988	B.C.	3	46	15.3	24	1	0	0	0
1989	B.C.	0	0	0.0	0	0	0	0	0
1990	B.C.	3	3	1.0	3	0	2	1	1
1991	Ott.	1	0	0.0	0	0	3	0	2
1992	Ott.	0	0	0.0	0	0	1	0	1
1993	Ott.	0	0	0.0	0	0	4	3	1
CFL TOTALS		**7**	**49**	**7.0**	**24**	**1**	**10**	**4**	**5**

Unsuccessful Field Goal Returns - 2 for 8 yards, 4.0 average, longest 20 yards with Ottawa in 1991; 2 for 19 yards, 9.5 average, longest 14 yards in 1992 and 8 for 70 yards, 8.8 average, longest 29 yards in 1993. **CFL Total Unsuccessful Field Goal Returns - 12 for 97 yards, 8.1 average, longest 29 yards.**

Own Kickoffs Recovered - 1 for 0 yards in 1992. **CFL Total Own Kickoffs Recovered - 1.**

Tackles - 61 defensive with B.C. in 1988; 10 defensive in 1989; 37 defensive in 1990; 36 defensive and 10 special teams with Ottawa in 1991; 53 defensive and 3 special teams in 1992 and 52 defensive and 1 special teams in 1993. **CFL Total Tackles - 263 (249 defensive and 14 special teams).**

Quarterback Sacks - 1 with B.C. in 1989; 1 with Ottawa in 1991 and 1 for 9 yards lost in 1992. **CFL Total QB Sacks - 4.**

Tackles for Losses - 1 for 1 yard with Ottawa in 1993. **CFL Total Tackles for Losses - 1 for 1 yard.**

a - All-Eastern All-Star.
b - CFL All-Star.

Playoffs

	Team	GP	Punt Returns NO	YDS	AVE	LG	TD	Kickoff Returns NO	YDS	AVE	LG	TD
1988	B.C.	2	8	102	12.8	29	0	4	137	34.2	56	0
1991	Ott.	1	4	42	10.5	41	0	2	13	6.5	10	0
1992	Ott.	1	0	0	0.0	0	0	0	0	0.0	0	0
1993	Ott.	1	1	7	7.0	7	0	0	15	0.0	15	0
CFL TOTALS		**5**	**13**	**151**	**11.6**	**41**	**0**	**6**	**165**	**25.0**	**56**	**0**

Fumbles - 1 and 0 lost with B.C. in 1988. **CFL Total Playoff Fumbles - 1 and 0 lost.**

Fumble Returns - 1 for 0 yards with Ottawa in 1991. **CFL Total Playoff Fumble Returns - 1 for 0 yards.**

Tackles - 13 defensive with B.C. in 1988; 5 defensive with Ottawa in 1991; 8 defensive in 1992 and 3 defensive and 1 special teams in 1993. **CFL Total Playoff Tackles - 30 (29 defensive and 1 special teams).**

Grey Cup

	Team	GP	Punt Returns NO	YDS	AVE	LG	TD	Kickoff Returns NO	YDS	AVE	LG	TD
1988	B.C.	1	8	21	2.6	10	0	5	134	26.8	38	0
CFL TOTALS		**1**	**8**	**21**	**2.6**	**10**	**0**	**5**	**134**	**26.8**	**38**	**0**

Fumbles - 1 and 1 lost with B.C. in 1988. **Total Grey Cup Fumbles - 1 and 1 lost.**

Defensive Tackles - 3 with B.C. in 1988. **Total Grey Cup Defensive Tackles - 3**

DRESSEL, BOB

Born: August 19, 1969
Birthplace: Glendale, Arizona
Offensive Guard/Tackle. 6'4", 295 lbs. Import
Last Amateur Club: Purdue University
Acquired: Signed as a free agent by the Sacramento Gold Miners in September 1993.

Games Played - 5 with Sacramento in 1993. **CFL Total GP - 5.**

DRINKWALTER, WAYNE

Born: April 23, 1966
Birthplace: Thunder Bay, Ontario
Defensive Lineman. 6'3", 265 lbs. Non-import
Last Amateur Club: Thunder Bay Giants (MJFC)
Acquired: Selected in the third round (19th overall) by the Hamilton Tiger-Cats in the 1989 CFL College Draft. Traded to the Saskatchewan Roughriders in exchange for offensive lineman Darrel Harle in July, 1989. Granted free agency status in February, 1993. Re-signed by Saskatchewan in June, 1993.

Games Played - 18 with Saskatchewan in 1989; 18 in 1990; 18 in 1991; 18 in 1992 and 18 in 1993. **CFL Total GP - 90.**

Own Fumbles Recovered - 1 with Saskatchewan in 1989. **CFL Total OFR - 1.**

Fumble Returns - 1 for 0 yards with Saskatchewan in 1990 and 1 for 10 yards in 1991. **CFL Total Fumble Returns - 2 for 10 yards, 5.0 average, longest 10 yards.**

Blocked Kicks - 1 field goal with Saskatchewan in 1993. **CFL Total Blocked Kicks - 1 field goal.**

Interception Returns - 1 for 9 yards with Saskatchewan in 1990. **CFL Total Interception Returns - 1 for 9 yards.**

Quarterback Sacks - 2 with Saskatchewan in 1990; 5 in 1991 and 1 for 7 yards lost in 1993. **CFL Total QB Sacks - 8.**

Tackles - 8 defensive with Saskatchewan in 1989; 4 defensive in 1990; 12 defensive and 1 special teams in 1991; 2 defensive and 7 special teams in 1992 and 1 defensive and 9 special teams in 1993. **CFL Total Tackles - 44 (27 defensive and 17 special teams).**

Playoffs

Games Played - 2 with Saskatchewan in 1989; 1 in 1990; 1 in 1992 and 1 in 1993. **CFL Total Playoff GP - 5.**

Tackles - 2 defensive with Saskatchewan in 1992. **CFL Total Playoff Tackles - 2 (2 defensive).**

Grey Cup

Games Played - 1 with Saskatchewan in 1989. **Total Grey Cup GP - 1.**

DUBE, MARC

Born: February 23, 1968
Birthplace: Gloucester, Ontario
Linebacker. 6'2", 230 lbs. Non-import
Last Amateur Club: University of Maine
Acquired: Selected in the third round (24th overall) by the Toronto Argonauts in the 1992 CFL College Draft. Signed by Toronto in May, 1992 and released in June, 1992. Signed as a free agent by the Calgary Stampeders in September, 1992.

Games Played - 1 with Calgary in 1992 and 10 in 1993. **CFL Total GP - 11.**

Tackles - 1 special teams with Calgary in 1992 and 1 defensive and 13 special teams in 1993. **CFL Total Tackles - 15 (1 defensive and 14 special teams).**

DuMARESQ, MIKE

Born: September 4, 1965
Birthplace: Toronto, Ontario
Defensive Tackle. 6'5", 265 lbs. Non-import
Last Amateur Club: University of Western Ontario (OUAA)
Acquired: Signed as a free agent by the Edmonton Eskimos in March, 1990

Games Played - 6 with Edmonton in 1990; 10 in 1991; 18 in 1992 and 18 in 1993. **CFL Total GP - 52.**

Tackles - 2 defensive with Edmonton in 1992 and 1 defensive in 1993. **CFL Total Tackles - 3 (3 defensive).**

Playoffs

Games Played - 2 with Edmonton in 1990: 2 in 1992 and 2 in 1993. **CFL Total Playoff GP - 6**

Grey Cup

Games Played - 1 with Edmonton in 1990 and 1 in 1993. **Total Grey Cup GP - 2.**

DUNIGAN, MATT

Born: December 6, 1960
Birthplace: Lakewood, Ohio
Quarterback. 5'11", 180 lbs. Import
Last Amateur Club: Louisiana Tech University
Acquired: Signed as a free agent with the Edmonton Eskimos in January, 1983. Traded to B.C. Lions for wide receiver Jim Sandusky and future considerations in June, 1988. Linebackers Jeff Braswell and Gregg Stumon, running back Reggie Taylor, defensive back Andre Francis and B.C.'s 1st round draft choice in the 1989 CFL College Draft, Leroy Blugh, completed the deal in January, 1989. Traded to Toronto Argonauts for quarterback Rick Johnson, linebackers Willie Pless and Tony Visco, slotback Emanuel Tolbert, defensive back Todd Wiseman and defensive tackle Jearld Baylis in March, 1990. Granted free agency status in February, 1992. Signed as a free agent by the Winnipeg Blue Bombers in June, 1992.

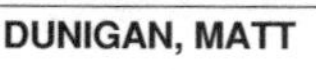

DUNIGAN, MATT

Year	Team	GP	TD	C	FG	S	TP	Rushing NO	YDS	AVE	LG	TD
1983	Edm.	16	0	0	0	0	0	4	23	5.8	20	0
1984a	Edm.	13	9	x1	0	0	56	89	732	8.2	69	9
1985	Edm.	14	9	0	0	0	54	113	737	8.2	69	9
1986	Edm.	18	4	0	0	0	24	118	594	5.0	24	4
1987	Edm.	13	4	0	0	0	24	51	287	5.6	33	4
1988bc	B.C.	17	6	0	0	0	36	97	501	5.2	31	6
1989def	B.C.	18	10	0	0	0	60	70	397	5.7	21	10
1990	Tor.	8	7	0	0	0	42	48	218	4.5	24	7
1991	Tor.	8	2	0	0	0	12	34	190	5.6	14	2
1992	Wpg	18	3	0	0	0	18	42	238	5.7	24	3
1993hijk	Wpg.	16	11	0	0	0	66	84	517	6.2	37	11
CFL TOTALS		**159**	**65**	**x1**	**0**	**0**	**392**	**750**	**4434**	**5.9**	**106**	**65**

(Scoring: GP–TP; Rushing: NO–TD)

Year	Team	Passing ATT	COMP	YDS	PCT	INT	LGT	TD	Fumbles NO	LOST	OFR	2-Pt. Converts T	G	PCT
1983	Edm.	26	14	239	53.9	2	54	4	4	0	0	1	0	0.0
1984	Edm.	412	220	3273	53.4	19	81	21	7	5	4	3	1	33.3
1985	Edm.	405	242	3410	59.7	22	89	19	9	2	2	1	0	0.0
1986	Edm.	485	275	3648	56.7	14	68	25	11	4	1	1	0	0.0
1987	Edm.	326	175	2823	53.7	19	89	21	4	2	0	0	0	0.0
1988	B.C.	471	268	3776	56.9	22	76	26	11	8	3	3	2	66.7
1989	B.C.	597	331	4509	55.4	20	83	27	9	6	2	4	0	0.0
1990	Tor.	262	144	2028	55.0	14	53	17	3	0	0	1	0	0.0
1991	Tor.	196	121	2011	61.7	10	89	16	4	3	1	1	1	100.0
1992	Wpg.	411	205	2857	49.9	15	60	17	5	3	0	0	0	0.0
1993	Wpg.	600	334	4682	55.7	18	75	36	7	4	1	2	1	50.0
CFL TOTALS		**4191**	**2329**	**33256**	**55.6**	**175**	**164**	**226**	**71**	**37**	**14**	**17**	**5**	**29.4**

Pass Receiving - 1 for 0 yards with Edmonton in 1986 and 1 for 28 yards with Winnipeg in 1993. **CFL Total Pass Receiving - 2 for 28 yards, 14.0 average, longest 28 yards.**

Fumble Returns - 1 for 0 yards with Edmonton in 1983. **CFL Total Fumble Returns - 1.**

Defensive Tackles - 1 with B.C. in 1988; 3 in 1989; 1 with Toronto in 1990; 2 in 1991; 2 with Winnipeg in 1992 and 5 in 1993. **CFL Total Defensive Tackles - 14.**

a - Set CFL record for rushing yardage by a quarterback in a season (since eclipsed by Ken Hobart, Tracy Ham and Damon Allen)
b - All-Western All-Star
c - CFL All-Star
d - Led CFL in Completions
e - Led CFL in Attempts
f - Led CFL in Passing Yards
g - Tied CFL Record for Most Passes Intercepted in One Game with 7.
h - All-Eastern All-Star
i - Tied for CFL Lead in Rushing TD's
j - Jeff Russell Memorial Trophy - Most Outstanding Player of Eastern Division
k - Runner up - CFL Most Outstanding Player

Playoffs

Year	Team	GP	TD	C	FG	S	TP	Rushing NO	YDS	AVE	LG	TD
1983	Edm.	1	0	0	0	0	0	0	0	0.0	0	0
1984	Edm.	1	1	0	0	0	6	3	5	1.7	2	1
1985	Edm.	1	0	0	0	0	0	0	0	0.0	0	0
1986	Edm.	2	2	0	0	0	12	25	186	7.4	43	2
1987	Edm.	2	0	0	0	0	0	8	47	5.9	17	0
1988	B.C.	2	0	0	0	0	0	3	15	5.0	8	1
1991	Tor.	1	0	0	0	0	0	2	24	12.0	12	0
1992	Wpg	1	0	0	0	0	0	3	22	7.3	9	0
CFL TOTALS		**11**	**3**	**0**	**0**	**0**	**18**	**44**	**299**	**6.8**	**43**	**4**

(Scoring: GP–TP; Rushing: NO–TD)

Year	Team	Passing ATT	COMP	YDS	PCT	INT	LG	TD	Fumbles NO	LOST
1983	Edm.	5	2	52	40.0	0	31	0	0	0
1984	Edm.	30	19	264	63.3	3	45	1	1	1
1985	Edm.	0	0	0	0.0	0	0	0	0	0
1986	Edm.	46	31	504	67.4	1	98	3	1	1
1987	Edm.	57	28	567	49.1	4	80	3	0	0
1988	B.C.	61	37	435	60.7	3	73	4	1	0
1991	Tor.	22	11	188	50.0	1	7	3	0	0
1992	Wpg.	24	11	197	45.8	0	57	1	0	0
CFL TOTALS		**248**	**139**	**2207**	**56.7**	**12**	**98**	**15**	**3**	**2**

Grey Cup

Year	Team	GP	Rushing NO	YDS	AVE	LG	TD
1986	Edm.	1	7	27	3.9	14	0
1987	Edm.	1	3	18	6.0	14	0
1988	Edm.	1	7	49	7.0	19	0
1991	Tor.	1	7	44	6.3	11	0
1992	Wpg.	1	2	9	4.5	7	0
CFL TOTALS		**5**	**26**	**147**	**5.7**	**19**	**0**

Year	Team	Passing ATT	COMP	YDS	PCT	INT	LGT	TD	Fumbles NO	LOST
1986	Edm.	26	11	158	42.3	1	46	0	3	3
1987	Edm.	12	8	104	66.7	1	19	0	1	1
1988	B.C.	32	14	196	43.8	2	41	1	0	0
1991	Tor.	29	12	142	41.4	0	48	2	3	2
1992	Wpg.	19	6	47	31.6	0	15	0	0	0
CFL TOTALS		**118**	**51**	**647**	**43.2**	**4**	**48**	**3**	**7**	**6**

DUNN, KASEY

Born: July 22, 1969
Birthplace: San Diego, California
Wide Receiver. 6'2", 200 lbs. Import
Last Amateur Club: University of Idaho
Acquired: Signed as a free agent by the B.C. Lions in July, 1992. Released by B.C. in August, 1992. Signed as a free agent by the Edmonton Eskimos in October, 1992. Released by Edmonton in September, 1993.

Year	Team	GP	TD	C	FG	S	TP	Pass Receiving NO	YDS	AVE	LG	TD
1992	B.C.	4	2	0	0	0	12	15	222	14.8	31	2
	Edm.	2	1	0	0	0	6	5	91	18.2	31	1
1993	Edm.	7	1	0	0	0	6	7	90	12.9	28	1
CFL TOTALS		**13**	**4**	**0**	**0**	**0**	**24**	**27**	**403**	**14.9**	**31**	**4**

(Scoring: GP–TP)

Punt Returns - 1 for 2 yards with B.C. in 1992. **CFL Total Punt Returns - 1 for 2 yards.**

Tackles - 1 defensive with B.C. in 1992 and 1 special teams with Edmonton in 1993. **CFL Total Tackles - 2 (1 defensive and 1 special teams).**

Playoffs

Year	Team	GP	Pass Receiving NO	YDS	AVE	LG	TD
1993	Edm.	1	4	55	13.8	20	0
CFL TOTALS		**1**	**4**	**55**	**13.8**	**20**	**0**

DYKO, CHRIS

Born: March 16, 1966
Birthplace: Champaign, Illinois
Offensive Tackle. 6'6", 280 lbs. Import
Last Amateur Club: Washington State University
Acquired: Selected by the NFL Chicago Bears in the eighth round (221st overall) in the 1989 NFL Draft. Released by Chicago in September, 1990. Signed as a free agent by the NFL Seattle Seahawks in September, 1990. Spent the 1990 season on the Injured Reserve List. Granted free agency status in January, 1991. Released by Seattle in August, 1991. Selected by the New York/New Jersey Knights in the second round (16th overall) of the 1992 WLAF Draft. Signed as a free agent by the NFL New York Giants in June, 1992. Signed as a free agent by the Sacramento Gold Miners in March, 1993.

Games Played - 16 with Sacramento in 1993. **CFL Total GP - 16.**

DZIKOWICZ, JAYSON

Born: April 11, 1968
Birthplace: Winnipeg, Manitoba
Defensive Back. 5'11", 190 lbs. Non-import
Last Amateur Club: University of Manitoba (CWAA)
Acquired: Selected by Winnipeg in the seventh round (56th overall) of the 1991 CFL College Draft.

Year	Team	GP	Interception Returns NO	YDS	AVE	LG	TD	Kickoff Returns NO	YDS	AVE	LG	TD
1992	Wpg.	14	3	40	13.3	32	0	3	32	10.7	14	0
1993	Wpg.	16	2	20	10.0	19	0	0	0	0.0	14	0
CFL TOTALS		**30**	**5**	**60**	**12.0**	**51**	**0**	**3**	**32**	**10.7**	**14**	**0**

Year	Team	Punt Returns NO	YDS	AVE	LG	TD	Fumbles NO	LOST
1992	Wpg.	1	0	0.0	0	0	2	2
1993	Wpg.	1	1	1.0	1	0	0	0
CFL TOTALS		**2**	**1**	**0.5**	**1**	**0**	**2**	**2**

Quarterback Sacks - 1 for 9 yards lost with Winnipeg in 1992. **CFL Total QB Sacks - 1.**

Tackles - 10 defensive and 7 special teams with Winnipeg in 1992 and 24 defensive and 12 special teams in 1993. **CFL Total Tackles - 53 (34 defensive and 19 special teams).**

DZIKOWICZ, JAYSON

Playoffs

Games Played - 1 with Winnipeg in 1992. **CFL Total Playoff GP - 1.**

Grey Cup

Games Played - 1 with Winnipeg in 1992 and 1 in 1993. **Total Grey GP - 2.**

Tackles - 3 special teams with Winnipeg in 1992.
Total Grey Cup Tackles - 3 (3 special teams).

EAGLIN, GREG

Born: November 14, 1967
Birthplace: Cleveland, Texas
Cornerback. 6'2", 190 lbs. Import
Last Amateur Club: University of Arkansas (Pine-Buff)
Acquired: Attended the NFL Philadelphia Eagles' 1991 Training Camp. Selected by the San Antonio Riders in the 28th round (273rd overall) in the 1992 WLAF Draft. Signed as a free agent by the Hamilton Tiger-Cats in June 1992. Released by Hamilton in October, 1993 and was signed as a free agent by the Calgary Stampeders later that month.

		Scoring						Fumble Returns				
	Team	GP	TD	C	FG	S	TP	NO	YDS	AVE	LG	TD
1993	Ham.	9	1	0	0	0	6	2	75	37.5	75	1
	Cal.	6	0	0	0	0	0	0	0	0.0	0	0
CFL TOTALS		**15**	**1**	**0**	**0**	**0**	**6**	**2**	**75**	**37.5**	**75**	**1**

Interception Returns - 1 for 14 yards with Calgary in 1993.
CFL Total Interception Returns - 1 for 14 yards.

Tackles - 33 defensive and 2 special teams with Hamilton and 8 defensive and 8 special teams with Calgary in 1993.
CFL Total Tackles - 51 (41 defensive and 10 special teams).

Tackles For Losses - 1 for 36 yards with Hamilton in 1993.
CFL Total Tackles For Losses - 1 for 36 yards.

Playoffs

Games Played - 2 with Calgary in 1993. **CFL Total Playoff GP - 2.**

Quarterback Sacks - 1 with Calgary in 1993. **CFL Total Playoff QB Sacks - 1.**

Tackles - 5 defensive with Calgary in 1993.
CFL Total Playoff Tackles - 5 (5 defensive).

ELGAARD, RAY

Born: August 29, 1959
Birthplace: Edmonton, Alberta
Slotback. 6'3", 220 lbs. Non-import
Last Amateur Club: University of Utah
Acquired: Selected in the second round (12th overall), by the Saskatchewan Roughriders in the 1983 CFL College Draft

		Scoring						Pass Receiving				
	Team	GP	TD	C	FG	S	TP	NO	YDS	AVE	LG	TD
1983	Sask.	15	1	x1	0	0	8	7	41	5.9	17	1
1984	Sask.	16	3	0	0	0	18	45	744	16.5	48	3
1985ab	Sask.	15	4	0	0	0	24	79	1193	15.1	44	4
1986	Sask.	16	4	0	0	0	24	55	1003	18.2	59	4
1987a	Sask.	18	4	0	0	0	24	63	865	13.7	51	4
1988abcd	Sask.	18	6	0	0	0	36	69	1290	18.7	75	6
1989	Sask.	13	6	0	0	0	36	40	717	17.9	44	6
1990ace	Sask.	16	11	x1	0	0	68	94	1494	15.9	81	11
1991	Sask.	13	11	0	0	0	66	62	1069	17.2	59	11
1992abcef	Sask.	18	11	0	0	0	66	91	1444	15.9	51	11
1993abg	Sask.	18	8	0	0	0	48	89	1393	15.7	64	8
CFL TOTALS		**176**	**69**	**x2**	**0**	**0**	**418**	**694**	**11253**	**16.2**	**64**	**69**

		Kickoff Returns					Rushing					Fumbles		
	Team	NO	YDS	AVE	LG	TD	NO	YDS	AVE	LG	TD	NO	LOST	OFR
1983	Sask.	3	50	16.7	25	0	2	7	3.5	6	0	0	0	0
1984	Sask.	3	0	0.0	4	0	0	0	0.0	0	0	0	0	1
1985	Sask.	0	0	0.0	0	0	1	5	5.0	5	0	2	1	0
1986	Sask.	0	1	0.0	1	0	1	-1	-1.0	-1	0	0	0	0
1987	Sask.	0	0	0.0	0	0	0	0	0.0	0	0	2	2	1
1988	Sask.	0	0	0.0	0	0	0	0	0.0	0	0	0	0	0
1989	Sask.	0	0	0.0	0	0	0	0	0.0	0	0	0	0	0
1990	Sask.	1	6	6.0	6	0	3	23	7.7	16	0	3	3	0
1991	Sask.	0	0	0.0	0	0	0	0	0.0	0	0	0	0	1
1992	Sask.	0	0	0.0	0	0	2	6	3.0	5	0	2	2	0
1993	Sask.	0	0	0.0	0	0	0	19	0.0	19	0	1	1	0
CFL TOTALS		**7**	**57**	**8.1**	**25**	**0**	**11**	**91**	**8.3**	**34**	**0**	**11**	**10**	**3**

Passing - 1 attempt, 0 complete for 0 yards with Saskatchewan in 1988 and 1 attempt, 0 complete for 0 yards in 1989.
CFL Total Passing - 2 attempts, 0 complete.

Fumble Returns - 2 for 0 yards with Saskatchewan in 1986; 1 for 0 yards in 1991 and 1 for 0 yards in 1993.
CFL Total Fumble Returns - 4 for 0 yards.

Tackles - 1 defensive with Saskatchewan in 1986; 4 defensive and 3 special teams in 1991; 5 defensive and 1 special teams in 1992 and 1 defensive and 7 special teams in 1993.
CFL Total Tackles - 22 (11 defensive and 11 special teams).

a - All-Western All-Star
b - CFL All-Star
c - Dr. Beattie Martin West Division Canadian Player Trophy
d - Schenley Most Outstanding Canadian Player
e - Most Outstanding Canadian Winner
f - Tied CFL Record for Most Career 1000-yard Pass Receiving Seasons(6)
g - Set CFL Record for Most Career 1000-yard Pass Receiving Seasons

Playoffs

		Pass Receiving					
	Team	GP	NO	YDS	AVE	LG	TD
1988	Sask.	1	4	76	19.0	33	0
1989	Sask.	1	4	44	11.0	20	2
1990	Sask.	1	2	26	13.0	13	0
1992	Sask.	1	3	34	11.3	13	0
1993	Sask.	1	6	104	17.3	31	0
CFL TOTALS		**5**	**19**	**184**	**14.9**	**33**	**2**

Grey Cup

Games Played - 1 with Saskatchewan in 1989.
Total Grey Cup GP - 1.

Pass Receiving - 6 for 73 yards, 12.2 average, longest 20 yards and 1 TD with Saskatchewan in 1989.
Total Grey Cup Pass Receiving - 6 for 73 yards, 12.2 average, longest 20 yards and 1 TD.

ELLINGSON, JAMES

Born: May 18, 1963
Birthplace: Calgary, Alberta
Slotback. 6'1", 205 lbs. Non-import
Last Amateur Club: Richmond Raiders Jrs. (BCJFL)
Acquired: Selected in the second round, (11th overall), in the 1986 CFL College Draft by the Saskatchewan Roughriders. Traded to the Ottawa Rough Riders with fullback Shawn Daniels in August, 1990 in exchange for running back Orville Lee.

		Scoring						Pass Receiving				
	Team	GP	TD	C	FG	S	TP	NO	YDS	AVE	LG	TD
1986	Sask.	4	0	0	0	0	0	1	10	10.0	10	0
1987	Sask.	10	0	0	0	0	0	3	24	8.0	10	0
1988	Sask.	18	0	x1	0	0	2	17	223	13.1	27	0
1989	Sask.	18	2	0	0	0	12	22	288	13.1	41	2
1990	Sask.	6	0	0	0	0	0	18	244	13.6	34	0
	Ott.	12	1	0	0	0	6	31	391	12.6	25	1
1991	Ott.	14	0	0	0	0	0	15	222	14.8	28	0
1992	Ott.	18	9	0	0	0	54	54	797	14.8	71	9
1993	Ott.	18	2	0	0	0	12	25	281	11.2	23	2
CFL TOTALS		**118**	**14**	**x1**	**0**	**0**	**86**	**186**	**2480**	**13.3**	**71**	**14**

Fumble Returns - 1 for 0 yards with Saskatchewan in 1987 and 1 for 0 yards in 1989. **CFL Total Fumble Returns - 2 for 0 yards.**

Fumbles - 1 and 0 lost with Ottawa in 1991 and 1 and 0 lost in 1992.
CFL Total Fumbles - 2 and 0 lost.

Rushing - 1 for 10 yards with Saskatchewan in 1990.
CFL Total Rushing - 1 for 10 yards.

Kickoff Returns - 1 for 9 yards with Saskatchewan in 1989 and 1 for 0 yards with Ottawa in 1990.
CFL Total Kickoff Returns - 2 for 9 yards, 4.5 average, longest 9 yards.

Punting - 1 for 5 yards with Ottawa in 1992. **CFL Total Punting - 1 for 5 yards.**

Net Punting - 1 for -13 yards with Ottawa in 1992.
CFL Total Net Punting - 1 for -13 yards.

Defensive Tackles - 1 with Saskatchewan in 1989; 1 with Ottawa in 1992 and 1 in 1993. **CFL Total Defensive Tackles - 3.**

Playoffs

Games Played - 1 with Saskatchewan in 1988; 2 in 1989; 1 with Ottawa in 1990; 1 in 1991; 1 in 1992 and 1 in 1993. **CFL Total Playoff GP - 7.**

Pass Receiving - 1 for 21 yards, 21.0 average, longest 21 yards and 1 TD with Saskatchewan in 1988; 3 for 25 yards, 8.3 average, longest 11 yards in 1989; 4 for 91 yards, 22.8 average, longest 27 yards with Ottawa in 1990; 4 for 45 yards, 11.3 average, longest 13 yards in 1991 and 2 for 19 yards, 9.5 average, longest 11 yards in 1993.
CFL Total Playoff Pass Receiving - 14 for 201 yards, 14.4 average, longest 27 yards and 1 TD.

ELLINGSON, JAMES

Grey Cup

Games Played - 1 with Saskatchewan in 1989. **Total Grey Cup GP - 1.**

Pass Receiving - 5 for 64 yards, 12.8 average, longest 18 yards with Saskatchewan in 1989. **Total Grey Cup Pass Receiving - 5 for 64 yards, 12.8 average, longest 18 yards.**

ELLIOTT, BRUCE
Born: November 27, 1964
Birthplace: Willowdale, Ontario
Linebacker. 6'3", 240 lbs. Non-import
Last Amateur Club: University of Western Ontario (OUAA)
Acquired: Selected in the sixth round, (48th overall), in the 1986 CFL College Draft by the Toronto Argonauts. Released by Toronto in November, 1993.

			Fumble Returns					Fumbles		
	Team	GP	NO	YDS	AVE	LG	TD	NO	LOST	OFR
1987	Tor.	15	0	0	0.0	0	0	1	0	0
1988	Tor.	18	1	0	0.0	0	0	0	0	0
1989	Tor.	14	1	0	0.0	0	0	0	0	0
1990	Tor.	18	2	2	1.0	2	0	0	0	1
1991	Tor.	13	1	5	5.0	5	0	0	0	0
1992	Tor.	8	0	0	0.0	0	0	0	0	0
1993	Tor.	17	1	5	5.0	5	0	0	0	0
CFL TOTALS		**103**	**6**	**12**	**2.0**	**5**	**0**	**1**	**0**	**1**

Punt Returns - 1 for 6 yards with Toronto in 1990.
CFL Total Punt Returns - 1 for 6 yards.

Blocked Kicks - 1 punt with Toronto in 1993. **CFL Total Blocked Kicks - 1 (1 punt).**

Own Kickoffs Recovered - 1 for 0 yards with Toronto in 1987.
CFL Total Own Kickoffs Recovered - 1 for 0 yards.

Quarterback Sacks - 1 with Toronto in 1988; 1 in 1989; 2 in 1990 and 2 for 13 yards lost in 1992. **CFL Total QB Sacks - 6.**

Tackles - 2 defensive with Toronto in 1987; 6 defensive in 1988; 8 defensive in 1989; 26 defensive in 1990; 6 defensive and 19 special teams in 1991 and 4 defensive and 9 special teams in 1992.
CFL Total Tackles - 80 (52 defensive and 28 special teams).

Playoffs

Games Played - 2 with Toronto in 1987; 1 in 1988; 1 in 1989; 2 in 1990 and 1 in 1991. **CFL Total Playoff GP - 7.**

Grey Cup

Games Played - 1 with Toronto in 1987 and 1 in 1991. **Total Grey Cup GP - 2.**

Tackles - 2 defensive with Toronto in 1987 and 3 special teams in 1991.
Total Grey Cup Tackles - 5 (2 defensive and 3 special teams).

ELLIS, CRAIG
Born: January 26, 1961
Birthplace: Los Angeles, California
Running Back/Slotback. 5'11", 195 lbs. Import
Last Amateur Club: San Diego State University
Acquired: Signed by the NFL San Francisco 49ers in 1982. Signed as a free agent by the Winnipeg Blue Bombers in September, 1982. Signed as a free agent by Edmonton Eskimos in January, 1983. Released by Edmonton and signed by Calgary Stampeders in August, 1983. Claimed on waivers by Saskatchewan Roughriders in October, 1983. Signed as a free agent by Toronto Argonauts in 1986. Released by Toronto and played for NFL Miami Dolphins in 1986. In 1987 played for NFL L.A. Raiders during the strike. Attended the NFL Dallas Cowboys Camp in 1988. Signed as a free agent by Edmonton in February, 1989. Traded to the Toronto Argonauts in January, 1993 along with defensive lineman Cameron Brosseau, linebacker John Davis, quarterback Tracy Ham, defensive back Enis Jackson, running back Chris Johnstone, defensive back Travis Oliver and wide receiver Ken Winey in exchange for cornerback Ed Berry, wide receiver Eddie Brown, linebacker Bruce Dickson, quarterback Rickey Foggie, slotback J.P. Izquierdo, defensive lineman Leonard Johnson, slotback Darrell K. Smith and defensive back Don Wilson. Released by Toronto in August, 1993.

			Scoring					Rushing				
	Team	GP	TD	C	FG	S	TP	NO	YDS	AVE	LG	TD
1982	Wpg.	1	0	0	0	0	0	0	0	0.0	0	0
1983	Cal.	9	3	X1	0	0	20	82	413	5.0	29	1
1984abcd	Sask.	16	12	0	0	0	72	141	690	4.9	65	8
1985aef	Sask.	16	17	0	0	0	102	149	569	3.8	45	14
1986	Tor.	10	10	0	0	0	60	113	381	3.4	18	7
1987			NFL						NFL			
1988			NFL						NFL			
1989bg	Edm.	15	9	0	0	0	54	5	22	4.4	12	0
1990abghi	Edm.	18	17	0	0	0	102	3	20	6.7	14	0
1991j	Edm.	18	10	0	0	0	60	0	0	0.0	0	0
1992k	Edm.	17	10	0	0	0	60	0	0	0.0	0	0
1993	Tor.	1	0	0	0	0	0	0	0	0.0	0	0
CFL TOTALS		**121**	**88**	**x1**	**0**	**0**	**530**	**493**	**2095**	**4.2**	**65**	**30**

		Pass Receiving					Kickoff Returns				
	Team	NO	YDS	AVE	LG	TD	NO	YDS	AVE	LG	TD
1982	Wpg.	0	0	0.0	0	0	0	0	0.0	0	0
1983	Cal.	30	451	15.0	86	2	4	102	25.5	39	0
1984	Sask.	91	871	9.6	37	4	42	1040	24.8	92	0
1985	Sask.	102	977	9.6	36	3	12	223	18.6	25	0
1986	Tor.	41	338	8.2	28	3	26	548	21.1	45	0
1987			NFL						NFL		
1988			NFL						NFL		
1989	Edm.	80	1264	15.8	59	9	0	0	0.0	0	0
1990	Edm.	106	1654	15.6	63	17	0	0	0.0	0	0
1991	Edm.	66	1133	17.2	52	10	31	644	20.8	34	0
1992	Edm.	62	1018	16.4	41	10	16	250	15.6	40	0
1993	Tor.	2	51	25.5	38	0	0	0	0.0	0	0
CFL TOTALS		**580**	**7757**	**13.4**	**86**	**58**	**131**	**2807**	**21.4**	**92**	**0**

		Punt Returns					Fumbles		
	Team	NO	YDS	AVE	LG	TD	NO	LOST	OFR
1982	Wpg.	0	0	0.0	0	0	0	0	0
1983	Cal.	10	119	11.9	40	0	7	6	1
1984	Sask.	1	14	14.0	14	0	11	9	1
1985	Sask.	4	29	7.3	11	0	6	4	2
1986	Tor.	0	0	0.0	0	0	6	5	2
1987			NFL					NFL	
1988			NFL					NFL	
1989	Edm.	1	7	7.0	7	0	0	0	0
1990	Edm.	0	0	0.0	0	0	1	1	0
1991	Edm.	0	0	0.0	0	0	1	1	0
1992	Edm.	0	0	0.0	0	0	0	0	0
1993	Tor.	0	0	0.0	0	0	0	0	0
CFL TOTALS		**16**	**169**	**10.6**	**40**	**0**	**32**	**26**	**6**

Tackles - 1 defensive with Edmonton in 1989; 2 defensive in 1990; 2 defensive in 1991 and 3 defensive and 1 special teams in 1992.
CFL Total Tackles - 9 (8 defensive and 1 special teams).

a - Led CFL in number of Pass Receptions.
b - All-Western All-Star.
c - Led CFL in number of Kickoff Returns.
d - Led CFL in Kickoff Return Yardage.
e - Led CFL in Touchdown Scoring.
f - Led CFL in Rushing Touchdowns.
g - CFL All-Star.
h - Most Outstanding Player Runner Up.
i - Winner of the Jeff Nicklin Trophy, Most Outstanding Player, Western Division.
j - Tied CFL Record for Most Seasons Catching Passes All Games (7).
k - Set CFL Record for Most Seasons Catching Passes All Games (8).

Playoffs

Games Played - 1 with Edmonton in 1989; 2 in 1990; 1 in 1991 and 2 in 1992.
CFL Total Playoff GP - 6.

Scoring - 2 TDs for 12 points with Edmonton in 1990; 1 TD for 6 points in 1991 and 1 TD for 6 points in 1992. **CFL Total Playoff Scoring - 4 TDs for 24 points.**

Pass Receiving - 3 for 48 yards, 16.0 average, longest 26 yards with Edmonton in 1989; 5 for 91 yards, 18.2 average, longest 34 yards and 2 TDs in 1990; 3 for 61 yards, 20.3 average, longest 39 yards and 1 TD in 1991 and 5 for 48 yards, 9.6 average, longest 20 yards and 1 TD in 1992.
CFL Total Playoff Pass Receiving - 16 for 248 yards, 15.5 average, longest 39 yards and 4 TDs.

Punt Returns - 1 for 8 yards with Edmonton in 1991.
CFL Total Playoff Punt Returns - 1 for 8 yards.

Kickoff Returns - 3 for 61 yards, 20.3 average, longest 30 yards with Edmonton in 1991. **CFL Total Playoff Kickoff Returns - 3 for 61 yards, 20.3 average, longest 30 yards.**

Grey Cup

Games Played - 1 with Edmonton in 1990. **Total Grey Cup GP - 1.**

Pass Receiving - 8 for 131 yards, 16.4 average, longest 29 yards with Edmonton in 1990.
Total Grey Cup Pass Receiving - 8 for 131 yards, 16.4 average, longest 29 yards.

Fumbles - 2 and 2 lost with Edmonton in 1990.
Total Grey Cup Fumbles - 2 and 2 lost.

ERVIN, CORRIS
Born: August 30, 1966
Birthplace: Pompano Beach, Florida
Cornerback. 5'11", 185 lbs. Import
Last Amateur Club: University of Central Florida
Acquired: Selected in the fifth round by the Denver Broncos in the 1988 NFL Draft. Released in pre-season. Re-signed as a free agent by Denver in 1989. Released during training camp and signed as a free agent by the NFL San Francisco 49ers. Released by San Francisco in September, 1989. Signed by the NFL Dallas Cowboys in November, 1989 for the developmental squad. Released by Dallas in January, 1990. Selected in the first round (first defensive back) by the London Monarchs in the 1991 WLAF positional draft. Signed as a free agent by the Hamilton Tiger-Cats in June, 1991. Granted free agency status in February, 1993. Signed as a free agent by the Toronto Argonauts in July, 1993. Released by Toronto in September, 1993. Signed as a free agent by the Hamilton Tiger-Cats in September, 1993.

ERVIN, CORRIS

	Team	GP	Interception Returns NO	YDS	AVE	LG	TD	Fumble Returns NO	YDS	AVE	LG	TD
1991	Ham.	18	3	34	11.3	23	0	3	12	4.0	12	0
1992	Ham.	18	3	63	21.0	28	0	2	22	11.0	22	0
1993	Tor.	6	0	0	0.0	0	0	0	0	0.0	0	0
	Ham.	7	3	31	10.3	16	0	0	0	0.0	0	0
CFL TOTALS		**49**	**9**	**128**	**14.2**	**28**	**0**	**5**	**34**	**6.8**	**22**	**0**

Blocked Kicks - 1 punt and 1 field goal with Hamilton in 1992.
CFL Total Blocked Kicks - 2 (1 punt and 1 field goal).

Tackles - 62 defensive and 4 special teams with Hamilton in 1991; 51 defensive in 1992 and 25 defensive with Toronto and 24 defensive with Hamilton in 1993. **CFL Total Tackles - 166 (162 defensive and 4 special teams).**

Tackles for Losses - 2 for 3 yards with Hamilton in 1992.
CFL Total Tackles for Losses - 2 for 3 yards.

Playoffs

Games Played - 2 with Hamilton in 1992 and 2 in 1993.
CFL Total Playoff GP - 4.

Tackles - 8 defensive with Hamilton in 1992 and 8 defensive in 1993.
CFL Total Playoff Tackles - 16 (16 defensive).

Fumbles Returned - 1 for 0 yards with Hamilton in 1993.
CFL Total Playoff Fumble Returns - 1 for 0 yards.

EUROPE, TOM

Born: July 27, 1970
Birthplace: Toronto, Ontario
Defensive Back. 5'11", 195 lbs. Non-import
Last Amateur Club: Bishop's University (OQIFC)
Acquired: Selected in the second round (9th overall) by the B.C. Lions in the 1993 CFL College Draft.

	Team	GP	Interception Returns NO	YDS	AVE	LG	TD	Unsuccessful Field Goal Returns NO	YDS	AVE	LG	TD
1993	B.C.	18	2	35	17.5	23	0	3	35	11.7	35	0
CFL TOTALS		**18**	**2**	**35**	**17.5**	**23**	**0**	**3**	**35**	**11.7**	**35**	**0**

Fumble Returns - 1 for 0 yards with B.C. in 1993.
CFL Total Fumble Returns - 1 for 0 yards.

Tackles - 44 defensive and 10 special teams with B.C. in 1993.
CFL Total Tackles - 54 (44 defensive and 10 special teams).

Playoffs

Games Played - 1 with B.C. in 1993. **CFL Total Playoff GP - 1.**

Tackles - 7 defensive with B.C. in 1993.
CFL Total Playoff Tackles - 7 (7 defensive).

EVANS, BOBBY

Born: December 2, 1967
Birthplace: Haynesville, Louisiana
Defensive Back. 6'2", 195 lbs. Import
Last Amateur Club: Southern Arkansas University
Acquired: Signed as a free agent by the Winnipeg Blue Bombers in April, 1990.

	Team	GP	Scoring TD	C	FG	S	TP	Interception Returns NO	YDS	AVE	LG	TD
1990	Wpg.	3	0	0	0	0	0	0	0	0.0	0	0
1991	Wpg.	18	0	0	0	0	0	2	10	5.0	10	0
1992	Wpg.	16	1	0	0	0	6	4	66	16.5	34	1
1993a	Wpg.	18	0	0	0	0	0	5	43	8.6	32	0
CFL TOTALS		**55**	**1**	**0**	**0**	**0**	**6**	**11**	**43**	**10.8**	**34**	**1**

Kickoff Returns - 1 for 11 yards with Winnipeg in 1991.
CFL Total Kickoff Returns - 1 for 11 yards.

Fumbles - 1 and 1 lost with Winnipeg in 1993.
CFL Total Fumbles - 1 and 1 lost.

Fumble Returns - 2 for 0 yards with Winnipeg in 1991 and 1 for 0 yards in 1992.
CFL Total Fumble Returns - 3 for 0 yards.

Unsuccessful Field Goal Returns - 1 for 0 yards with Winnipeg in 1993.
CFL Total Unsuccessful Field Goal Returns - 1 for 0 yards.

Quarterback Sacks - 1 with Winnipeg in 1991 and 2 for 10 yards lost in 1992 and 1 for 9 yards lost in 1993. **CFL Total QB Sacks - 4.**

Tackles - 7 defensive with Winnipeg in 1990; 60 defensive and 17 special teams in 1991; 39 defensive and 13 special teams in 1992 and 60 defensive and 13 special teams in 1993. **CFL Total Tackles - 209 (166 defensive and 43 special teams).**

Tackles for Losses - 2 for 5 yards with Winnipeg in 1991; 2 for 6 yards in 1992 and 3 for 5 yards in 1993.
CFL Total Tackles for Losses - 7 for 16 yards.

Playoffs

Games Played - 2 with Winnipeg in 1991; 1 in 1992 and 1 in 1993.
CFL Total Playoff GP - 4.

Fumble Returns - 1 for 0 yards with Winnipeg in 1991.
CFL Total Playoff Fumble Returns - 1 for 0 yards.

Interception Returns - 1 for 9 yards with Winnipeg in 1992.
CFL Total Playoff Interception Returns - 1 for 9 yards.

Tackles - 4 defensive with Winnipeg in 1991; 1 defensive in 1992 and 1 defensive and 1 special teams in 1993.
CFL Total Playoff Tackles - 7 (6 defensive and 1 special teams).

Grey Cup

Games Played - 1 with Winnipeg in 1992 and 1 in 1993. **Total Grey Cup GP - 2.**

Tackles - 5 defensive with Winnipeg in 1992 and 3 defensive and 1 special teams in 1993.
Total Grey Cup Tackles - 9 (8 defensive and 1 special teams).

a - All-Eastern All-Star.

EVERETT, TRE

Born: December 10, 1969
Birthplace: Washington, D.C.
Wide Receiver, 5'9", 170 lbs, Import
Last Amateur Club: University of Florida
Acquired: Signed as a free agent by the Saskatchewan Roughriders in August, 1993 and was later released and signed as a free agent by the Sacramento Gold Miners in October, 1993.

	Team	GP	Scoring TD	C	FG	S	TP	Pass Receiving NO	YDS	AVE	LG	TD
1993	Sask.	4	1	0	0	0	6	11	127	11.5	44	1
	Sac.	4	1	0	0	0	6	2	10	5.0	13	1
CFL TOTALS		**8**	**2**	**0**	**0**	**0**	**12**	**13**	**137**	**10.5**	**44**	**2**

	Team	Punt Returns NO	YDS	AVE	LG	TD	Kickoff Returns NO	YDS	AVE	LG	TD
1993	Sask.	6	44	7.3	13	0	2	29	14.5	17	0
	Sac.	0	0	0.0	0	0	0	0	0.0	0	0
CFL TOTALS		**6**	**44**	**7.3**	**13**	**0**	**2**	**29**	**14.5**	**17**	**0**

Fumbles - 1 and 1 lost with Saskatchewan and 1 and 1 lost with Sacramento in 1993. **CFL Total Fumbles - 2 and 2 lost.**

Tackles - 2 defensive with Saskatchewan and 1 special teams with Sacramento in 1993. **CFL Total Tackles - 3 (2 defensive and 1 special teams).**

EVRAIRE, KEN

Born: July 17, 1965
Birthplace: Toronto, Ontario
Slotback. 6'1", 205 lbs. Non-import
Last Amateur Club: Wilfrid Laurier University (OUAA)
Acquired: Selected in the second round (ninth overall) by the Saskatchewan Roughriders in the 1988 CFL College Draft. Traded to the Ottawa Rough Riders in August, 1988 for a second round draft choice in the 1989 CFL College Draft, defensive tackle Dan Payne and future considerations. Released and signed as a free agent by the Hamilton Tiger-Cats in September, 1990.

	Team	GP	Scoring TD	C	FG	S	TP	Pass Receiving NO	YDS	AVE	LG	TD
1988	Ott.	11	1	0	0	0	6	8	74	9.3	16	1
1989	Ott.	15	4	x1	0	0	26	26	427	16.4	44	4
1990	Ott.	7	2	0	0	0	12	22	315	14.3	30	2
	Ham.	4	0	0	0	0	0	0	0	0.0	0	0
1991	Ham.	15	4	0	0	0	24	31	491	15.8	65	4
1992abc	Ham.	18	3	0	0	0	18	61	1081	17.7	53	3
1993	Ham.	15	0	0	0	0	0	41	679	16.6	64	0
CFL TOTALS		**85**	**14**	**x1**	**0**	**0**	**86**	**189**	**3067**	**16.2**	**65**	**14**

Rushing - 1 for 9 yards with Ottawa in 1989; 1 for 5 yards in 1990 and 1 for -1 yards with Hamilton in 1991.
CFL Total Rushing - 3 for 13 yards, 4.3 average, longest 9 yards.

Punt Returns - 1 for 12 yards with Ottawa in 1989.
CFL Total Punt Returns - 1 for 12 yards.

Kickoff Returns - 1 for 2 yards with Hamilton in 1993.
CFL Total Kickoff Returns - 1 for 2 yards.

EVRAIRE, KEN

Fumbles - 1 and 1 lost with Hamilton in 1991 and 1 and 0 lost in 1993.
CFL Total Fumbles - 2 and 1 lost.

Fumble Returns - 1 for 6 yards with Ottawa in 1989 and 1 for 0 yards in 1990.
CFL Total Fumble Returns - 2 for 6 yards, 3.0 average, longest 6 yards.

Tackles - 1 defensive with Ottawa in 1988; 5 defensive in 1989; 1 defensive and 10 special teams with Hamilton in 1991; 4 defensive in 1992 and 4 defensive in 1993.
CFL Total Defensive Tackles - 25 (15 defensive and 10 special teams).

a - All-Eastern All-Star
b - Winner Lew Hayman Trophy, Most Outstanding Canadian Player, Eastern Division
c - Runner-up Most Outstanding Canadian Player

Playoffs

		Scoring						Pass Receiving				
	Team	GP	TD	C	FG	S	TP	NO	YDS	AVE	LG	TD
1992	Ham.	2	2	0	0	0	12	4	58	14.5	28	2
1993	Ham.	2	0	0	0	0	0	6	7	12.7	19	0
CFL TOTALS		**4**	**2**	**0**	**0**	**0**	**12**	**10**	**65**	**13.4**	**47**	**2**

Fumbles - 1 and 1 lost with Hamilton in 1993. **CFL Total Playoff Fumbles - 1 and 1 lost.**

FAIRHOLM, JEFF

Born: November 7, 1965
Birthplace: Montreal, Quebec
Slotback. 5'11", 190 lbs. Non-import
Last Amateur Club: University of Arizona
Acquired: Selected in the first round (second overall) by the Saskatchewan Roughriders in the 1988 CFL College Draft. Granted free agency status in February, 1994. Signed as a free agent by the Toronto Argonauts in March, 1994.

		Scoring						Rushing					Fumbles		
	Team	GP	TD	C	FG	S	TP	NO	YDS	AVE	LG	TD	NO	LOST	OFR
1988ab	Sask.	18	10	0	0	0	60	4	32	8.0	15	0	1	0	1
1989cde	Sask.	15	11	0	0	0	66	5	43	8.6	14	0	0	0	0
1990	Sask.	10	4	0	0	0	24	0	0	0.0	0	0	0	0	1
1991	Sask.	18	13	0	0	0	78	11	102	9.3	26	0	1	1	1
1992	Sask.	17	6	0	0	0	36	3	10	3.3	8	0	0	0	3
1993	Sask.	18	9	0	0	0	54	3	7	2.3	7	0	1	1	0
CFL TOTALS		**96**	**53**	**0**	**0**	**0**	**318**	**26**	**194**	**7.5**	**26**	**0**	**3**	**2**	**6**

		Pass Receiving					Kickoff Returns				
	Team	NO	YDS	AVE	LG	TD	NO	YDS	AVE	LG	TD
1988	Sask.	45	833	18.5	79	10	0	6	0.0	6	0
1989	Sask.	45	893	19.8	73	11	0	0	0.0	0	0
1990	Sask.	34	471	13.9	107	4	0	0	0.0	0	0
1991	Sask.	70	1239	17.7	99	13	2	24	12.0	24	0
1992	Sask.	74	1344	18.2	76	6	0	0	0.0	0	0
1993	Sask.	72	1391	19.3	78	9	0	0	0.0	0	0
CFL TOTALS		**340**	**6171**	**18.2**	**107**	**53**	**2**	**30**	**15.0**	**24**	**0**

Punting - 1 for 28 yards with Saskatchewan in 1991.
CFL Total Punting - 1 for 28 yards.

Fumble Returns - 1 for 0 yards with Saskatchewan in 1989.
CFL Total Fumble Returns - 1 for 0 yards.

Tackles - 3 defensive with Saskatchewan in 1988; 6 defensive in 1989; 1 defensive in 1990; 1 defensive in 1991; 3 defensive in 1992 and 4 defensive in 1993. **CFL Total Tackles - 18 (18 defensive).**

a - Jackie Parker West Division Rookie Trophy
b - Runner-up Schenley Most Outstanding Rookie
c - All-Western All-Star
d - Winner Dr. Beattie Martin Trophy, Most Outstanding Canadian, Western Division
e - Runner-up CFL Most Outstanding Canadian Player

Playoffs

		Scoring						Pass Receiving				
	Team	GP	TD	C	FG	S	TP	NO	YDS	AVE	LG	TD
1988	Sask.	1	0	0	0	0	0	5	66	13.0	26	0
1989	Sask.	2	1	0	0	0	6	6	94	15.7	47	1
1990	Sask.	1	1	0	0	0	6	3	84	28.0	48	1
1992	Sask.	1	0	0	0	0	0	6	103	17.2	49	0
1993	Sask.	1	0	0	0	0	0	6	58	9.7	34	0
CFL TOTALS		**6**	**2**	**0**	**0**	**0**	**12**	**26**	**405**	**15.6**	**49**	**2**

Grey Cup

Games Played - 1 with Saskatchewan in 1989. **Total Grey Cup GP - 1.**

Scoring - 1 TD for 6 points with Saskatchewan in 1989.
Total Grey Cup Scoring - 1 TD for 6 points.

Pass Receiving - 2 for 97 yards, 48.5 average, longest 75 yards and 1 TD with Saskatchewan in 1989.
Total Grey Cup Pass Receiving - 2 for 97 yards, 48.5 average, longest 75 yards and 1 TD.

FARTHING, DAN

Born: October 11, 1969
Birthplace: Saskatoon, Saskatchewan
Slotback. 5'11", 190 lbs. Non-import
Last Amateur Club: University of Saskatchewan (CWAA)
Acquired: Selected in the first round (second overall) by the Saskatchewan Roughriders in the 1991 CFL College Draft.

		Scoring						Pass Receiving				
	Team	GP	TD	C	FG	S	TP	NO	YDS	AVE	LG	TD
1991	Sask.	5	1	0	0	0	6	11	142	12.9	21	1
1992	Sask.	16	1	0	0	0	6	17	182	10.7	31	1
1992	Sask.	18	0	0	0	0	0	22	192	8.7	25	0
CFL TOTALS		**39**	**2**	**0**	**0**	**0**	**12**	**50**	**516**	**10.3**	**31**	**2**

		Kickoff Returns					Punt Returns				
	Team	NO	YDS	AVE	LG	TD	NO	YDS	AVE	LG	TD
1991	Sask.	1	12	12.0	12	0	0	0	0.0	0	0
1992	Sask.	4	35	8.8	19	0	5	28	5.6	10	0
1993	Sask.	5	54	10.8	21	0	5	43	8.6	12	0
CFL TOTALS		**10**	**101**	**10.1**	**21**	**0**	**10**	**71**	**7.1**	**12**	**0**

Own Fumbles Recovered - 1 with Saskatchewan in 1993. **CFL Total OFR - 1**

Tackles - 1 defensive with Saskatchewan in 1991; 2 defensive and 1 special teams in 1992 and 1 defensive and 7 special teams in 1993.
CFL Total Tackles - 12 (4 defensive and 8 special teams).

Playoffs

			Pass Receiving				
	Team	GP	NO	YDS	AVE	LG	TD
1992	Sask.	1	3	50	16.7	20	0
1993	Sask.	1	2	22	11.0	13	0
CFL TOTALS		**2**	**5**	**72**	**14.4**	**20**	**0**

Tackles - 1 defensive and 1 special teams with Saskatchewan in 1993.
Total CFL Playoff Tackles - 2 (1 defensive and 1 special teams).

FIELDS, JEFF

Born: July 3, 1967
Birthplace: Jackson, Mississippi
Defensive Tackle. 6'3", 300 lbs. Import
Last Amateur Club: Arkansas State University
Acquired: Selected in the ninth round (228th overall) by the Los Angeles Rams in the 1991 NFL Draft. Released by Los Angeles after training camp. Signed as a free agent by the Hamilton Tiger-Cats in October, 1991. Granted free agency status in February, 1993. Re-signed as a free agent by Hamilton in October, 1993.

Games Played - 5 with Hamilton in 1991; 18 in 1992 and 5 in 1993.
CFL Total GP - 28.

Scoring - 1 TD for 6 points with Hamilton in 1992.
CFL Total Scoring - 1 TD for 6 points.

Interception Returns - 1 for 10 yards and 1 TD with Hamilton in 1992.
CFL Total Interception Returns - 1 for 10 yards and 1 TD.

Fumble Returns - 1 for 10 yards with Hamilton in 1992 and 1 for 8 yards in 1993.
CFL Total Fumble Returns - 2 for 18 yards, 9.0 average, longest 10 yards.

Quarterback Sacks - 2 with Hamilton in 1991; 7 for 44 yards lost in 1992 and 2 for 13 yards lost in 1993. **CFL Total QB Sacks - 11.**

Tackles - 14 defensive and 1 special teams with Hamilton in 1991; 52 defensive in 1992 and 16 defensive in 1993.
CFL Total Tackles - 83 (82 defensive and 1 special teams).

Tackles for Losses - 2 for 11 yards with Hamilton in 1991; 6 for 16 yards in 1992 and 3 for 7 yards in 1993.
CFL Total Tackles for Losses - 11 for 34 yards.

All-Eastern All-Star in 1992.

Playoffs

Games Played - 2 with Hamilton in 1992 and 2 in 1993. **CFL Total Playoff GP - 4.**

Tackles - 16 defensive with Hamilton in 1992 and 11 defensive in 1993.
CFL Total Playoff Tackles - 27 (27 defensive).

Tackles for Losses - 2 for 4 yards with Hamilton in 1992 and 2 for 4 yards in 1993.
CFL Total Playoff Tackles for Losses - 4 for 8 yards.

FINCH, LONNIE
Born: November 27, 1967
Birthplace: Longview, Texas
Defensive Back. 6'0", 180 lbs. Import
Last Amateur Club: University of Oklahoma
Acquired: Signed as a free agent by the NFL San Francisco 49ers in 1989. Placed on the 49ers Developmental roster prior to being waived by the club. Signed by the NFL Cleveland Browns in 1989 and was later released. Signed as a free agent by the NFL Buffalo Bills in 1990 and was released by the Bills prior to the start of training camp. Signed as a free agent by the NFL Houston Oilers prior to their 1990 training camp and was subsequently released during the pre-season. Signed as a free agent by the B.C. Lions in 1990. Released by B.C. in October, 1990. Selected by the Frankfurt Galaxy in the 4th round (37th overall) in the 1991 WLAF Positional Draft. Re-signed by the B.C. Lions in September, 1991. Released following the 1991 season. Spent the 1992 season with the Frankfurt Galaxy of the WLAF. Signed as a free agent by the Hamilton Tiger-Cats in May, 1993. Released by Hamilton in November, 1993.

Games Played - 2 with B.C. in 1990; 5 in 1991 and 8 with Hamilton in 1993.
CFL Total GP - 15.

Interception Returns - 1 for 0 yards with B.C. in 1990; 1 for 0 yards in 1991 and 2 for 0 yards with Hamilton in 1993.
CFL Total Interception Returns - 4 for 0 yards.

Tackles - 6 defensive with B.C. in 1990; 22 defensive and 4 special teams in 1991 and 18 defensive with Hamilton in 1993.
CFL Total Tackles - 50 (46 defensive and 4 special teams).

Fumble Returns - 1 for 0 yards with B.C. in 1990.
CFL Total Fumble Returns - 1 for 0 yards.

Playoffs

Games Played - 1 with B.C. in 1991.
CFL Total Playoff GP - 1.

Tackles - 3 defensive with B.C. in 1991.
CFL Total Playoff Tackles - 3 (3 defensive).

FINDLAY, BROOKS
Born: December 22, 1970
Birthplace: Vancouver, B.C.
Linebacker. 6'4", 235 lbs. Non-import
Last Amateur Club: Portland State University
Acquired: Selected by the Saskatchewan Roughriders in the second round (ninth overall) in the 1993 CFL College Draft.

Games Played - 18 with Saskatchewan in 1993. **CFL Total GP - 18.**

Tackles - 17 special teams with Saskatchewan in 1993.
CFL Total Tackles - 17 (17 special teams).

Playoffs

Games Played - 1 with Saskatchewan in 1993. **CFL Total Playoff GP - 1.**

FINLAY, MATT
Born: September 28, 1962
Birthplace: Toronto, Ontario
Linebacker. 6'2", 225 lbs. Non-import
Last Amateur Club: University of Eastern Michigan
Acquired: Selected in the first round (fifth overall) of the 1986 CFL College Draft by the Montreal Alouettes. Selected by the Toronto Argonauts in the first round (third overall) of the Alouettes dispersal draft in June, 1987. Traded to Calgary Stampeders in July, 1987 for defensive back Rick Ryan.

Games Played - 18 with Montreal in 1986; 1 with Toronto in 1987; 15 with Calgary in 1987; 17 in 1988; 18 in 1989; 18 in 1990; 14 in 1991; 18 in 1992 and 16 in 1993. **CFL Total GP - 135.**

Scoring - 1 TD for 6 points with Calgary in 1990. **CFL Total Scoring - 1 TD for 6 points.**

Interception Returns - 2 for 65 yards, 32.5 average, longest 58 yards and 1 TD with Calgary in 1990; 1 for 8 yards in 1991 and 1 for 29 yards in 1993.
CFL Total Interception Returns - 4 for 102 yards, 25.5 average, longest 58 yards and 1 TD.

Kickoff Returns - 1 for 12 yards with Montreal in 1986; 1 for 18 yards with Calgary in 1989; 1 for 32 yards in 1990 and 1 for 0 yards in 1991.
CFL Total Kickoff Returns - 4 for 62 yards, 15.5 average, longest 32 yards.

Blocked Kicks - 1 punt with Calgary in 1993. **CFL Total Blocked Kicks - 1 (1 punt).**

Fumble Returns - 1 for 0 yards with Montreal in 1986; 1 for 0 yards with Calgary in 1987; 2 for 0 yards in 1988; 1 for 0 yards in 1989; 1 for 0 yards in 1990; 2 for 11 yards, 5.5 average, longest 11 yards in 1991; 2 for 69 yards, 34.5 average, longest 69 yards in 1992 and 1 for 21 yards in 1993.
CFL Total Fumble Returns - 11 for 101 yards, 9.2 average, longest 69 yards.

Quarterback Sacks - 1 with Montreal in 1986; 1 with Calgary in 1987; 1 in 1988; 1 in 1989; 3 in 1990; 5 in 1991 and 2 for 22 yards lost in 1992.
CFL Total QB Sacks - 14.

Tackles - 6 defensive with Toronto in 1987; 31 defensive with Calgary in 1987; 56 defensive in 1988; 57 defensive in 1989; 80 defensive in 1990; 56 defensive and 7 special teams in 1991; 88 defensive and 12 special teams in 1992 and 61 defensive in 1993.
CFL Total Tackles - 454 (435 defensive and 19 special teams).

Tackles for Losses - 5 for 6 yards with Calgary in 1991; 8 for 18 yards in 1992 and 2 in 1993.
CFL Total Tackles for Losses - 15 for 26 yards.

All-Western All-Star in 1992.

Playoffs

Games Played - 1 with Calgary in 1987; 1 in 1989; 1 in 1990; 2 in 1991; 1 in 1992 and 2 in 1993.
CFL Total Playoff GP - 8.

Interception Returns - 1 for 1 yard with Calgary in 1989.
CFL Total Playoff Interception Returns - 1 for 1 yard.

Quarterback Sacks - 2 with Calgary in 1991 and 1 for 3 yards lost in 1993.
CFL Total Playoff QB Sacks - 3.

Tackles - 1 defensive with Calgary in 1987; 8 defensive in 1989; 6 defensive in 1990; 8 defensive in 1991; 4 defensive and 1 special teams in 1992 and 8 defensive in 1993.
CFL Total Playoff Tackles - 36 (35 defensive and 1 special teams).

Grey Cup

Games Played - 1 with Calgary in 1991 and 1 in 1992. **Total Grey Cup GP - 2.**

Fumble Returns - 1 for 5 yards with Calgary in 1991.
Total Grey Cup Fumble Returns - 1 for 5 yards.

Tackles - 4 defensive with Calgary in 1991 and 3 defensive and 1 special teams in 1992. **Total Grey Cup Tackles - 8 (7 defensive and 1 special teams).**

FLEETWOOD, MARQUEL
Born: January 23, 1970
Birthplace: Atlanta, Georgia
Quarterback. 6'0", 192 lbs. Import
Last Amateur Club: University of Minnesota
Acquired: Signed as a free agent by the Ottawa Rough Riders in April, 1993.

Games Played - 14 with Ottawa in 1993. **CFL Total GP - 14.**

Rushing - 1 for 5 yards with Ottawa in 1993.
CFL Total Rushing - 1 for 5 yards.

Passing - 5 attempts, 2 complete for 7 yards, 40.0 percent complete, 1 interception, longest 5 yards with Ottawa in 1993.
CFL Total Passing - 5 attempts, 2 complete for 7 yards, 40.0 percent complete, 1 interception, longest 5 yards.

Playoffs

Games Played - 1 with Ottawa in 1993. **CFL Total Playoff GP - 1.**

FLEMING, SEAN
Born: March 19, 1970
Birthplace: Burnaby, British Columbia
Kicker/Punter. 6'3", 190 lbs. Non-import
Last Amateur Club: University of Wyoming
Acquired: Selected in the first round (sixth overall) of the 1992 CFL College Draft by the Edmonton Eskimos.

		Scoring						Field Goals					
	Team	GP	TD	C	FG	S	TP	T	G	YDS	AVE	LK	PCT
1992	Edm.	18	0	60	30	14	164	49	30	803	26.8	53	61.2
1993	Edm.	18	0	54	34	10	166	48	34	1132	33.3	58	70.8
CFL TOTALS		**36**	**0**	**114**	**64**	**24**	**330**	**97**	**64**	**1935**	**30.2**	**58**	**66.0**

		Kickoffs					Fumbles		
	Team	NO	YDS	AVE	LK	S	NO	LOST	OFR
1992	Edm.	102	5732	56.2	70	1	1	0	0
1993	Edm.	82	4908	59.9	74	0	0	0	0
CFL TOTALS		**184**	**10640**	**57.8**	**74**	**0**	**1**	**0**	**0**

FLEMING, SEAN

	Team	Field Goal Attempts NO	YDS	AVE	LK	S	Converts T	G	PCT
1992	Edm.	19	856	45.1	53	13	61	60	98.4
1993	Edm.	14	690	49.3	63	10	54	54	100.0
CFL TOTALS		**33**	**1546**	**46.9**	**63**	**23**	**115**	**114**	**99.1**

Rushing - 1 for 0 yards with Edmonton in 1992.
CFL Total Rushing - 1 for 0 yards.

Fumble Returns - 1 for 0 yards with Edmonton in 1992.
CFL Total Fumble Returns - 1 for 0 yards.

Tackles - 6 special teams with Edmonton in 1992 and 8 special teams in 1993.
CFL Total Tackles - 14 (14 special teams).

Playoffs

	Team	Scoring GP	TD	C	FG	S	TP	Field Goals T	G	YDS	AVE	LK	PCT
1992	Edm.	2	0	5	2	2	13	4	2	82	41.0	44	50.0
1993	Edm.	2	0	10	3	0	19	3	3	101	33.7	37	100.0
CFL TOTALS		**4**	**0**	**15**	**5**	**2**	**32**	**7**	**5**	**183**	**36.6**	**44**	**71.4**

	Team	Kickoffs NO	YDS	AVE	LK	S	Field Goal Attempts NO	YDS	AVE	LK	S	Converts T	G	PCT
1992	Edm.	6	286	47.7	64	0	2	89	44.5	46	2	5	5	100.0
1993	Edm.	12	624	52.0	65	0	0	0	0	0	0	10	10	100.0
CFL TOTALS		**18**	**910**	**50.6**	**65**	**0**	**2**	**89**	**44.5**	**46**	**2**	**15**	**15**	**100.0**

Grey Cup

	Team	Scoring GP	TD	C	FG	S	TP	Field Goals T	G	YDS	AVE	LK	PCT
1993	Edm.	1	0	2	6	1	21	7	6	182	30.3	45	85.7
CFL TOTALS		**1**	**0**	**2**	**6**	**1**	**21**	**7**	**6**	**182**	**30.3**	**45**	**85.7**

	Team	Kickoffs NO	YDS	AVE	LK	S	Field Goal Attempts NO	YDS	AVE	LK	S	Converts T	G	PCT
1993	Edm.	3	167	55.7	62	0	1	59	59.0	59	1	2	2	100.0
CFL TOTALS		**3**	**167**	**55.7**	**62**	**0**	**1**	**59**	**59.0**	**59**	**1**	**2**	**2**	**100.0**

Grey Cup Canadian Player of the Game in 1993 (Dick Suderman Trophy).
Tied Grey Cup Record for Most FGs in One Game (6).

FLORENCE, ANTHONY
Born: December 11, 1966
Birthplace: Del Ray Beach, Florida
Defensive Back. 5'11", 185 lbs. Import
Last Amateur Club: Bethune-Cookman College
Acquired: Selected by the NFL Tampa Bay Buccaneers in the fourth round (90th overall) in the 1989 NFL Draft. Released by Tampa Bay in September, 1990 and assigned to their Developmental Squad. Released by Tampa Bay in January, 1990. Signed as a free agent by the NFL Cleveland Browns in 1990. Released by Cleveland in August, 1990. Re-signed by the Browns in 1991 and was again subsequently released in October, 1991. Re-signed by Cleveland in November, 1991 and assigned to their practice roster. Released by the Browns in November, 1991. Signed as a free agent by the NFL New Orleans Saints and assigned to their practice squad. Signed as a free agent by the Winnipeg Blue Bombers in August, 1993.

Games Played - 3 with Winnipeg in 1993. **CFL Total GP - 3.**

Tackles - 3 defensive with Winnipeg in 1993. **CFL Total Tackles - 3 (3 defensive).**

FLOYD, LUCIUS
Born: April 7, 1966
Birthplace: Inglewood, California
Running Back. 6'0", 195 lbs. Import
Last Amateur Club: University of Nevada-Reno
Acquired: Attended the 1988 and 1989 training camps of the NFL Seattle Seahawks. Released and signed as a free agent by the Saskatchewan Roughriders in March ,1990. Released by Saskatchewan in July, 1993. Signed as a free agent by the Edmonton Eskimos in September, 1993.

	Team	Scoring GP	TD	C	FG	S	TP	Pass Receiving NO	YDS	AVE	LG	TD
1990	Sask.	13	5	0	0	0	30	73	811	11.1	78	5
1991	Sask.	17	6	0	0	0	36	84	720	8.6	47	3
1992	Sask.	14	6	0	0	0	36	74	645	8.7	33	2
1992	Edm.	8	4	0	0	0	24	29	262	9.0	25	2
CFL TOTALS		**52**	**21**	**0**	**0**	**0**	**126**	**260**	**2438**	**9.4**	**78**	**12**

	Team	Rushing NO	YDS	AVE	LG	TD	Kickoff Returns NO	YDS	AVE	LG	TD
1990	Sask.	91	421	4.6	37	0	1	19	19.0	19	0
1991	Sask.	117	677	5.8	59	3	3	33	11.0	21	0
1992	Sask.	92	373	4.1	38	4	3	61	20.3	22	0
1993	Edm.	81	423	5.2	35	2	17	360	21.2	44	0
CFL TOTALS		**381**	**1894**	**5.0**	**59**	**9**	**24**	**493**	**19.7**	**44**	**0**

Fumbles - 4 and 4 lost with Saskatchewan in 1990; 4 and 3 lost in 1991 and 4 and 4 lost with Edmonton in 1993. **CFL Total Fumbles - 12 and 11 lost.**

Passing - 1 attempt, 1 complete for 20 yards and 1 TD with Saskatchewan in 1990 and 1 attempt, 0 complete in 1992. **CFL Total Passing - 2 attempts, 1 complete for 20 yards, 50.0 percent complete and 1 TD.**

Tackles - 2 defensive with Saskatchewan in 1990; 2 defensive and 6 special teams in 1991; 3 defensive and 4 special teams in 1992 and 2 defensive with Edmonton in 1993. **CFL Total Tackles - 19 (9 defensive and 10 special teams).**

Winner of the Jackie Parker Trophy for Outstanding Rookie, Western Division in 1990.
Runner-up CFL Most Outstanding Rookie in 1990

Playoffs

	Team	Scoring GP	TD	C	FG	S	TP	Rushing NO	YDS	AVE	LG	TD
1990	Sask.	1	0	0	0	0	0	6	4	0.7	3	0
1993	Edm.	2	2	0	0	0	12	46	251	5.5	20	2
CFL TOTALS		**3**	**2**	**0**	**0**	**0**	**12**	**52**	**254**	**4.9**	**20**	**2**

	Team	Pass Receiving NO	YDS	AVE	LG	TD	Punt Returns NO	YDS	AVE	LG	TD
1990	Sask.	8	28	3.5	7	0	0	0	0.0	0	0
1993	Edm.	5	70	14.0	32	0	5	103	20.6	33	0
CFL TOTALS		**13**	**98**	**7.5**	**32**	**0**	**5**	**103**	**20.6**	**33**	**0**

Fumbles - 1 and 0 lost with Edmonton in 1993.
CFL Total Playoff Fumbles - 1 and 0 lost.

Own Fumbles Recovered - 1 with Edmonton in 1993.
CFL Total Playoff OFR - 1.

Grey Cup

	Team	GP	Pass Receiving NO	YDS	AVE	LG	TD	Rushing NO	YDS	AVE	LG	TD
1993	Edm.	1	3	17	5.4	14	0	15	41	2.7	10	1
CFL TOTALS		**1**	**3**	**17**	**5.4**	**14**	**0**	**15**	**41**	**2.7**	**10**	**1**

	Team	Kickoff Returns NO	YDS	AVE	LG	TD	Fumbles NO	LOST	OFR
1993	Edm.	4	94	23.4	28	0	1	1	0
CFL TOTALS		**4**	**94**	**23.4**	**28**	**0**	**1**	**1**	**0**

FLUTIE, DARREN
Born: November 18, 1966
Birthplace: Manchester, Maryland
Wide Receiver. 5'10", 180 lbs. Import
Last Amateur Club: Boston College
Acquired: Signed as a free agent by the NFL San Diego Chargers in May, 1988. Released in September 1989. Signed as a free agent by the NFL Phoenix Cardinals in May, 1990. Was injured through the 1990 season. Released following the 1991 training camp. Signed as a free agent by the B.C. Lions in September, 1991.

	Team	Scoring GP	TD	C	FG	S	TP	Pass Receiving NO	YDS	AVE	LG	TD
1991	B.C.	8	6	0	0	0	36	52	860	16.5	51	6
1992a	B.C.	18	4	0	0	0	24	90	1336	14.8	76	4
1993	B.C.	17	5	0	0	0	30	79	1068	13.5	45	5
CFL TOTALS		**43**	**15**	**0**	**0**	**0**	**90**	**221**	**3264**	**14.8**	**76**	**15**

	Team	Kickoff Returns NO	YDS	AVE	LG	TD	Fumbles NO	LOST	OFR
1991	B.C.	14	292	20.9	30	0	3	2	1
1992	B.C.	4	65	16.3	24	0	1	1	3
1993	B.C.	11	122	11.1	26	0	0	0	1
CFL TOTALS		**29**	**479**	**16.5**	**30**	**0**	**4**	**3**	**5**

Passing - 1 attempt, 0 complete with B.C. in 1991; 1 attempt, 0 complete and 1 interception in 1992 and 3 attempts, 1 complete for 42 yards, 33.3 percent complete in 1993.
CFL Total Passing - 5 attempts, 1 complete for 42 yards, 20.0 percent complete and 1 interception.

Punt Returns - 1 for 5 yards with B.C. in 1991; 15 for 104 yards, 6.9 average, longest 24 yards in 1992 and 11 for 84 yards, 7.6 average, longest 25 yards in 1993. **CFL Total Punt Returns - 27 for 193 yards, 7.2 average, longest 25 yards.**

Unsuccessful Field Goal Returns - 2 for -18 yards, longest 0 yards with B.C. in 1992 and 1 for 0 yards in 1993. **CFL Total Unsuccessful Field Goal Returns - 3 for -18 yards, -9.0 average, longest 0 yards.**

Tackles - 1 defensive with B.C. in 1991; 5 defensive in 1992 and 2 defensive in 1993. **CFL Total Tackles - 8 (8 defensive).**

a - All-Western All-Star

FLUTIE, DARREN

Playoffs

		Pass Receiving						Fumbles		
	Team	GP	NO	YDS	AVE	LG	TD	NO	LOST	OFR
1991	B.C.	1	3	30	10.0	13	0	1	1	0
1993	B.C.	1	7	125	17.9	45	0	0	0	0
CFL TOTALS		**2**	**10**	**155**	**15.5**	**45**	**0**	**1**	**1**	**0**

		Kickoff Returns				
	Team	NO	YDS	AVE	LG	TD
1991	B.C.	1	32	32.0	32	0
1993	B.C.	0	0	0.0	0	0
CFL TOTALS		**1**	**32**	**32.0**	**32**	**0**

FLUTIE, DOUG
Born: October 23, 1962
Birthplace: Manchester, Maryland
Quarterback. 5'10", 175 lbs. Import
Last Amateur Club: Boston College
Acquired: Selected by USFL New Jersey Generals in 1985 USFL Territorial Draft. Signed by New Jersey in February, 1985. Selected in the 11th round (285th overall) by the NFL Los Angeles Rams in the 1985 NFL Draft. Added to the Los Angeles developmental squad in June, 1985 and spent the entire season on it. Traded in October, 1986 to the NFL Chicago Bears along with a 4th round draft choice in the 1987 draft in exchange for 3rd and 6th round draft choices in the 1987 Draft. Signed by Chicago in October, 1986. Traded in October, 1987 to the NFL New England Patriots in exchange for an 8th round draft choice in the 1988 Draft. Released by New England after the 1989 season. Signed as a free agent by the B.C. Lions in June, 1990. Granted free agency status in February, 1992. Signed as a free agent by the Calgary Stampeders in March, 1992.

			Scoring					Rushing				
	Team	GP	TD	C	FG	S	TP	NO	YDS	AVE	LG	TD
1990	B.C.	16	3	0	0	0	18	79	662	8.4	32	3
1991abcdefghi	B.C.	18	14	x1	0	0	86	120	610	5.1	32	14
1992aghij	Cal.	18	11	0	0	0	66	96	669	7.0	44	11
1993abcdeghikl	Cal.	18	11	0	0	0	66	74	373	5.0	50	11
CFL TOTALS		**70**	**39**	**x1**	**0**	**0**	**236**	**369**	**2314**	**6.3**	**50**	**34**

		Passing							Fumbles		
	Team	ATT	COMP	YDS	PCT	INT	LG	TD	NO	LOST	OFR
1990	B.C.	392	207	2960	52.8	19	55	16	6	3	1
1991	B.C.	730	466	6619	63.8	24	89	38	7	4	3
1992	Cal.	688	396	5945	57.6	30	81	32	5	4	3
1993	Cal.	703	416	6092	59.2	17	75	44	5	5	1
CFL TOTALS		**2513**	**1485**	**21616**	**59.1**	**90**	**89**	**130**	**23**	**16**	**8**

2-Pt. Converts - 4 attempts, 2 complete, 0 made with B.C. in 1990; 7 attempts, 2 complete, 1 made in 1991 and 5 attempts, 1 complete and 0 made with Calgary in 1993.
CFL Total 2-Pt. Converts - 18 attempts, 5 complete, 1 made.

Pass Receiving - 1 for -11 yards with Calgary in 1993.
CFL Total Pass Receiving - 1 for -11 yards.

Tackles - 4 defensive with Calgary in 1992 and 1 defensive in 1993.
CFL Total Tackles - 5 (5 defensive).

a - Winner of Jeff Nicklin Memorial Trophy for Outstanding Player, Western Division.
b - Led the League in passing attempts.
c - Led the League in passing completions.
d - Led the League in passing yards.
e - Led the League in touchdown passes.
f - Set League record for passing attempts, completions and yards in one season.
g - CFL Most Outstanding Player Award Winner.
h - All-Western All-Star.
i - CFL All-Star.
j - Grey Cup Most Valuable Player.
k - Led the League in Passing Efficiency Rating.
l - Tied for CFL Lead in Rushing TDs.

Playoffs

			Scoring					Rushing				
	Team	GP	TD	C	FG	S	TP	NO	YDS	AVE	LG	TD
1991	B.C.	1	1	0	0	0	6	9	45	5.0	13	1
1992	Cal.	1	2	0	0	0	12	13	94	7.2	19	2
1993	Cal.	2	0	0	0	0	0	18	127	7.1	16	0
CFL TOTALS		**4**	**3**	**0**	**0**	**0**	**18**	**40**	**266**	**6.7**	**19**	**3**

		Passing							Fumbles		
	Team	ATT	COMP	YDS	PCT	INT	LG	TD	NO	LOST	OFR
1991	B.C.	32	17	257	53.1	1	42	0	0	0	0
1992	Cal.	27	13	185	48.1	1	39	0	3	1	2
1993	Cal.	73	36	421	49.3	1	41	1	1	0	0
CFL TOTALS		**132**	**66**	**863**	**50.0**	**3**	**42**	**1**	**4**	**1**	**2**

Grey Cup

			Passing							Rushing				
	Team	GP	ATT	COMP	YDS	PCT	INT	LG	TD	NO	YDS	AVE	LG	TD
1992	Cal.	1	49	33	480	67.3	0	41	2	4	20	5.0	12	0
CFL TOTALS		**1**	**49**	**33**	**480**	**67.3**	**0**	**41**	**2**	**4**	**20**	**5.0**	**12**	**0**

Fumbles - 1 and 0 lost with Calgary in 1992. **Total Grey Cup Fumbles - 1 and 0 lost.**

Own Fumbles Recovered - 1 with Calgary in 1992. **Total Grey Cup OFR - 1.**

FOGGIE, RICKEY
Born: July 15, 1966
Birthplace: Laurens, South Carolina
Quarterback. 6'1", 185 lbs. Import
Last Amateur Club: University of Minnesota
Acquired: Signed as a free agent by the B.C. Lions in April, 1988. Released by B.C. in August, 1990. Signed by the Toronto Argonauts as a free agent in August, 1990. Traded to the Edmonton Eskimos in January, 1993 along with cornerback Ed Berry, wide receiver Eddie Brown, linebacker Bruce Dickson, slotback J.P. Izquierdo, defensive lineman Leonard Johnson, slotback Darrell K. Smith and defensive back Don Wilson in exchange for defensive lineman Cameron Brosseau, linebacker John Davis, slotback Craig Ellis, quarterback Tracy Ham, defensive back Enis Jackson, running back Chris Johnstone, defensive back Travis Oliver and wide receiver Ken Winey.

			Scoring					Rushing				
	Team	GP	TD	C	FG	S	TP	NO	YDS	AVE	LG	TD
1988	B.C.	18	3	0	0	0	18	34	177	5.2	20	3
1989	B.C.	18	0	x1	0	0	2	10	89	8.9	16	0
1990a	B.C.	5	0	0	0	0	0	9	69	7.7	18	0
	Tor.	10	5	0	0	0	30	59	674	11.4	65	5
1991	Tor.	18	8	0	0	0	48	95	644	6.8	61	8
1992	Tor.	18	8	0	0	0	48	67	444	6.6	25	8
1993	Edm.	18	2	0	0	0	12	12	32	2.7	14	2
CFL TOTALS		**105**	**26**	**x1**	**0**	**0**	**158**	**286**	**2129**	**7.4**	**65**	**26**

		Passing							Converts (2 pts.)		
	Team	ATT	COMP	YDS	PCT	INT	LG	TD	Tried	Comp	Made
1988	B.C.	78	29	438	37.2	5	77	4	2	0	0
1989	B.C.	53	26	419	49.1	3	62	5	1	0	1
1990	B.C.	41	20	252	48.8	3	35	2	0	0	0
	Tor.	169	89	1676	52.7	5	76	21	1	1	0
1991	Tor.	352	171	3108	48.6	19	89	21	0	0	0
1992	Tor.	482	215	3507	44.6	25	89	18	3	2	0
1993	Edm.	96	42	738	43.8	4	64	4	1	0	0
CFL TOTALS		**1271**	**592**	**10138**	**46.6**	**64**	**89**	**75**	**8**	**3**	**1**

Fumbles - 3 and 1 lost with B.C. in 1988; 1 and 1 lost in 1989; 2 and 1 lost with B.C.; 5 and 2 lost with Toronto in 1990; 8 and 4 lost in 1991; 8 and 4 lost in 1992 and 1 and 1 lost with Edmonton in 1993.
CFL Total Fumbles - 28 and 14 lost.

Own Fumbles Recovered - 1 with B.C. in 1988; 1 with B.C. in 1990; 1 with Toronto in 1991 and 2 in 1992. **CFL Total OFR - 5.**
Tackles - 2 defensive with Toronto in 1992. **CFL Total Tackles - 2 (2 defensive).**

a - Set CFL Record for Most 100-Yard Rushing Games by a Quarterback One Season with 4.

Playoffs

			Passing							Rushing				
	Team	GP	ATT	COMP	YDS	PCT	INT	LG	TD	NO	YDS	AVE	LG	TD
1988	B.C.	2	0	0	0	0.0	0	0	0	0	0	0.0	0	0
1990	Tor.	1	5	3	60	60.0	0	45	0	0	0	0.0	0	0
1991	Tor.	1	18	10	143	55.6	1	24	0	2	19	9.5	13	0
1993	Edm.	2	0	0	0	0.0	0	0	0	0	0	0.0	0	0
CFL TOTALS		**6**	**23**	**13**	**203**	**56.5**	**1**	**45**	**0**	**2**	**19**	**9.5**	**13**	**0**

Fumbles - 1 and 1 lost with Toronto in 1990.
CFL Total Playoff Fumbles - 1 and 1 lost.

Grey Cup

Games Played - 1 with B.C. in 1988; 1 with Toronto in 1991 and 1 with Edmonton in 1993. **Total Grey Cup GP - 3.**

FORDE, DUANE
Born: May 8, 1969
Birthplace: Mississauga, Ontario
Fullback. 6'0", 230 lbs. Non-import
Last Amateur Club: University of Western Ontario (OUAA)
Acquired: Selected in the first round (fifth overall) by the Calgary Stampeders in the 1991 CFL College Draft. Traded to the Winnipeg Blue Bombers in March, 1993 in exchange for Winnipeg's third round selection (21st overall) in the 1993 CFL College Draft, slotback Dwayne Dmytryshyn. Granted free agency status in February, 1994.

			Rushing					Pass Receiving				
	Team	GP	NO	YDS	AVE	LG	TD	NO	YDS	AVE	LG	TD
1991	Cal.	3	0	0	0.0	0	0	0	0	0.0	0	0
1992	Cal.	18	9	26	2.9	10	0	9	86	9.6	18	0
1993	Wpg.	13	2	6	3.0	5	0	0	0	0.0	0	0
CFL TOTALS		**34**	**11**	**32**	**2.9**	**10**	**0**	**9**	**86**	**9.6**	**18**	**0**

FORDE, DUANE

Kickoff Returns - 1 for 4 yards with Calgary in 1992.
CFL Total Kickoff Returns - 1 for 4 yards.

Tackles - 4 special teams with Calgary in 1991; 2 special teams in 1992 and 6 special teams in 1993.
CFL Total Tackles - 12 (12 special teams).

Playoffs

Games Played - 1 with Calgary in 1992 and 1 with Winnipeg in 1993.
CFL Total Playoff GP - 2.

Grey Cup

Games Played - 1 with Calgary in 1992 and 1 with Winnipeg in 1993.
Total Grey Cup GP - 2.

Tackles - 1 defensive with Winnipeg in 1993. **CFL Grey Cup Total Tackles - 1.**

FOUDY, SEAN
Born: October 25, 1966
Birthplace: Toronto, Ontario
Defensive Back. 6'3", 193 lbs. Non-import
Last Amateur Club: York University (OUAA)
Acquired: Selected in the third round (17th overall) by the Ottawa Rough Riders in the 1989 CFL College Draft. Granted free agency status in February, 1993. Signed as a free agent by the B.C. Lions in March, 1993.

Games Played - 6 with Ottawa in 1989; 9 in 1990; 18 in 1991; 18 in 1992 and 9 with B.C. in 1993. **CFL Total GP - 60.**

Interception Returns - 1 for 19 yards with Ottawa in 1992.
CFL Total Interception Returns - 1 for 19 yards.

Own Kickoffs Recovered - 1 for 2 yards with Ottawa in 1989.
CFL Total Own Kickoffs Recovered - 1 for 2 yards.

Own Fumbles Recovered - 1 with Ottawa in 1992. **CFL Total OFR - 1.**

Unsuccessful Field Goal Returns - 1 for 9 yards with Ottawa in 1989.
CFL Total Unsuccessful Field Goal Returns - 1 for 9 yards.

Blocked Kicks - 1 punt with Ottawa in 1989; 2 punts in 1992 and 1 punt with B.C. in 1993. **CFL Total Blocked Kicks - 4 punts.**

Fumble Returns - 1 for 0 yards with Ottawa in 1989; 1 for 68 yards in 1991; 2 for 0 yards in 1992 and 2 for 0 yards with B.C. in 1993.
CFL Total Fumble Returns - 6 for 68 yards, 11.3 average, longest 68 yards.

Quarterback Sacks - 1 for 3 yards lost with Ottawa in 1992.
CFL Total QB Sacks - 1 for 3 yards lost.

Tackles - 10 defensive with Ottawa in 1989; 7 defensive in 1990; 2 defensive and 22 special teams in 1991; 38 defensive and 14 special teams in 1992 and 26 defensive and 3 special teams with B.C. in 1993.
CFL Total Tackles - 122 (83 defensive and 39 special teams).

Tackles for Losses - 1 for 1 yard with Ottawa in 1992 and 1 for 2 yards with B.C. in 1993. **CFL Total Tackles for Losses - 2 for 3 yards.**

Playoffs

Games Played - 1 with Ottawa in 1990; 1 in 1991 and 1 in 1992.
CFL Total Playoff GP - 3.

Interception Returns - 1 for 40 yards with Ottawa in 1992.
CFL Total Playoff Interception Returns - 1 for 40 yards.

Tackles - 1 defensive and 2 special teams with Ottawa in 1991 and 2 defensive and 1 special teams in 1992.
CFL Total Playoff Tackles - 6 (3 defensive and 3 special teams).

FRANCIS, ANDRE
Born: October 5, 1961
Birthplace: Kingston, Jamaica
Cornerback. 5'8", 170 lbs. Import
Last Amateur Club: New Mexico State University
Acquired: Signed as a free agent by Montreal Alouettes in February, 1983. Traded to the Saskatchewan Roughriders in September, 1985 for Saskatchewan's third round selection in the 1986 CFL College Draft. Saskatchewan traded defensive back Terry Irvin to Montreal in February, 1986 to reacquire this pick and selected defensive back Dave McEachern. Released by Saskatchewan in September, 1985 and signed as a free agent by the B.C. Lions in August, 1986. Traded with linebackers Jeff Braswell and Greg Stumon, wide receiver Jim Sandusky, running back Reggie Taylor and 1st round draft choice (Leroy Blugh) to Edmonton for quarterback Matt Dunigan. Deal completed in February, 1989. Granted free agency status in February, 1991. Signed as a free agent by Ottawa Rough Riders in March, 1991. Released by Ottawa in June, 1992. Signed as a free agent by B.C. in August, 1992.

		Scoring						Blocked Kicks	Interception Returns				
	Team	GP	TD	C	FG	S	TP	NO	NO	YDS	AVE	LG	TD
1983	Mtl.	16	0	0	0	0	0	1	5	108	21.6	79	0
1984	Mtl.	16	0	0	0	0	0	1	3	84	28.0	28	0
1985	Mtl.	9	0	0	0	0	0	0	0	0	0.0	0	0
	Sask.	1	0	0	0	0	0	0	0	0	0.0	0	0
1986	B.C.	10	0	0	0	0	0	0	2	23	11.5	23	0
1987	B.C.	18	1	0	0	0	6	0	5	117	23.4	49	1
1988	B.C.	18	1	0	0	0	6	0	7	101	14.4	77	1
1989a	Edm.	18	0	0	0	0	0	1	5	101	20.2	35	0
1990a	Edm.	18	0	0	0	0	0	1	7	137	19.6	42	0
1991	Ott.	18	0	0	0	0	0	0	1	0	0.0	0	0
1992	B.C.	14	1	0	0	0	6	0	5	106	21.2	69	1
1993bc	B.C.	16	1	0	0	0	6	0	8	153	19.1	71	1
CFL TOTALS		**172**	**4**	**0**	**0**	**0**	**24**	**4**	**48**	**930**	**19.4**	**79**	**4**

Kickoff Returns - 7 for 143 yards, 20.4 average, longest 30 yards with Montreal in 1984 and 1 for 13 yards with B.C. in 1986.
CFL Total Kickoff Returns - 8 for 156 yards, 19.5 average, longest 30 yards.

Punt Returns - 0 for 34 yards, longest 20 yards with Montreal in 1984 and 1 for 1 yard with B.C. in 1987.
CFL Total Punt Returns - 1 for 35 yards, 35.0 average, longest 20 yards.

Fumble Returns - 3 for 15 yards, 5.0 average, longest 12 yards with B.C. in 1987; 1 for 0 yards with Ottawa in 1991 and 1 for 0 yards in 1992.
CFL Total Fumble Returns - 5 for 15 yards, 3.0 average, longest 12 yards.

Fumbles - 1 and 0 lost with B.C. in 1988; 1 and 0 lost in 1992 and 1 and 1 lost in 1993. **CFL Total Fumbles - 3 and 1 lost.**

Own Fumbles Recovered - 1 with B.C. in 1988 and 1 with Edmonton in 1990.
CFL Total OFR - 2.

Defensive Tackles - 60 with B.C. in 1987; 39 in 1988; 42 with Edmonton in 1989; 45 in 1990; 34 with Ottawa in 1991; 19 with B.C. in 1992 and 37 in 1993.
CFL Total Defensive Tackles - 276.

Tackles for Losses - 1 for 1 yard with B.C. in 1993.
CFL Total Tackles for Losses - 1 for 1 yard.

a - All-Western All-Star
b - Led CFL in Interception Return Yards.
c - Led CFL in Interception Returns.

Playoffs

Games Played - 1 with Montreal in 1984; 1 with B.C. in 1986; 1 in 1987; 2 in 1988; 1 with Edmonton in 1989; 2 in 1990; 1 with Ottawa in 1991 and 1 with B.C. in 1993.
CFL Total Playoff GP - 10.

Interception Returns - 1 for 38 yards with B.C. in 1988.
CFL Total Playoff Interception Returns - 1 for 38 yards.

Defensive Tackles - 3 with B.C. in 1988; 2 with Edmonton in 1989; 3 in 1990; 1 with Ottawa in 1991 and 3 with B.C. in 1993.
CFL Total Playoff Defensive Tackles - 12.

Grey Cup

Games Played - 1 with B.C. in 1988 and 1 with Edmonton in 1990.
Total Grey Cup GP - 2.

Defensive Tackles - 3 with B.C. in 1988 and 2 with Edmonton in 1990.
Total Grey Cup Defensive Tackles - 5.

FRANCIS, RON
Born: April 7, 1964
Birthplace: Galveston, Texas
Defensive Back. 5'9", 188 lbs. Import
Last Amateur Club: Baylor University
Acquired: Selected in the second round (39th overall) of the 1987 NFL Draft by the NFL Dallas Cowboys. Signed by Dallas in July, 1987. Traded to the NFL New England Patriots in April, 1991 along with linebackers Eugene Lockhart and David Howard to complete a deal in which Dallas traded first and second 1991 draft picks to New England for first-round pick in 1991 draft. Released by New England after training camp in 1991. Signed as a free agent by the Calgary Stampeders in May, 1992 and was released in July, 1992. Signed as a free agent by the B.C. Lions in August, 1992. Released by B.C. in July, 1993.

Games Played - 9 with B.C. in 1992 and 2 in 1993. **CFL Total GP - 11.**

Scoring - 1 TD for 6 points with B.C. in 1992. **CFL Total Scoring - 1 TD for 6 points.**

Kickoff Returns - 6 for 95 yards, 15.8 average, longest 31 yards with B.C. in 1992. **CFL Total Kickoff Returns - 6 for 95 yards, 15.8 average, longest 31 yards.**

Fumble Returns - 2 for 85 yards, 42.5 average, longest 85 yards and 1 TD with B.C. in 1992. **CFL Total Fumble Returns - 2 for 85 yards, 42.5 average, longest 85 yards and 1 TD.**

Quarterback Sacks - 1 for 9 yards lost with B.C. in 1992.
CFL Total QB Sacks - 1 for 9 yards lost.

FRANCIS, RON

Tackles - 20 defensive with B.C. in 1992 and 8 defensive in 1993.
CFL Total Tackles - 28 (28 defensive).

FRANK, GARY
Born: December 20, 1964
Birthplace: Berlin, Wisconsin
Offensive Guard. 6'2", 310 lbs. Import
Last Amateur Club: Mississippi State University
Acquired: Signed as a free agent by the Sacramento Gold Miners in March, 1993.

Games Played - 4 with Sacramento in 1993. **CFL Total GP - 4.**

FRANKS, CHARLES
Born: January 11, 1970
Birthplace: Oklahoma City, Oklahoma
Cornerback. 5'10", 185 lbs. Import
Last Amateur Club: University of Oklahoma
Acquired: Attended the NFL Los Angeles Rams' 1992 training camp as a free agent and was subsequently released during the camp. Signed as a free agent by the Sacramento Gold Miners in March, 1993. Released by Sacramento in November, 1993.

Games Played - 10 with Sacramento in 1993. **CFL Total GP - 10.**

Interception Returns - 3 for 93 yards, 31.0 average,longest 53 yards with Sacramento in 1993.
CFL Total Interception Returns - 3 for 93 yards, 31.0 average, longest 53 yards.

Fumbles - 1 and 1 lost with Sacramento in 1993. **CFL Total Fumbles - 1 and 1 lost.**

Tackles - 26 defensive and 3 special teams with Sacramento in 1993.
CFL Total Tackles - 29 (26 defensive and 3 special teams).

FREEMAN, CORIAN
Born: August 16, 1968
Birthplace: Jacksonville, Florida
Linebacker. 6'3", 225 lbs. Import
Last Amateur Club: Florida State University
Acquired: Selected by the Sacramento Surge in the ninth round (90th overall) in the 1992 WLAF Draft. Signed as a free agent by the Winnipeg Blue Bombers in June, 1993. Claimed on waivers by the Sacramento Gold Miners in September, 1993.

			Scoring				
	Team	GP	TD	C	FG	S	TP
1993	Sac.	5	0	0	0	0	0
	Wpg.	10	2	0	0	0	12
CFL TOTALS		**15**	**2**	**0**	**0**	**0**	**12**

		Interception Returns					Fumble Returns				
	Team	NO	YDS	AVE	LG	TD	NO	YDS	AVE	LG	TD
1993	Sac.	1	15	15.0	15	0	0	0	0.0	0	0
	Wpg.	1	96	96.0	96	1	1	39	39.0	39	1
CFL TOTALS		**2**	**111**	**55.5**	**96**	**1**	**1**	**30**	**39.0**	**30**	**1**

Quarterback Sacks - 1 for 5 yards lost with Sacramento and 2 for 9 yards lost with Winnipeg in 1993. **CFL Total QB Sacks - 3 for 14 yards lost.**

Tackles - 7 defensive with Sacramento and 13 defensive and 1 special teams with Winnipeg in 1993.
CFL Total Tackles - 21 (20 defensive and 1 special teams).

Tackles For Losses - 2 for 6 yards with Sacramento in 1993.
CFL Total Tackles For Losses- 2 for 6 yards.

FRERS, GREG
Born: August 4, 1971
Birthplace: Mississauga, Ontario
Safety. 5'11", 185 lbs. Non-import
Last Amateur Club: Simon Fraser University
Acquired: Selected by the Calgary Stampeders in the second round (14th overall) in the 1993 CFL College Draft.

			Interception Returns					Punt Returns				
	Team	GP	NO	YDS	AVE	LG	TD	NO	YDS	AVE	LG	TD
1993	Cal.	16	2	10	5.0	10	0	1	4	4.0	4	0
CFL TOTALS		**16**	**2**	**10**	**5.0**	**10**	**0**	**1**	**4**	**4.0**	**4**	**0**

Tackles - 2 defensive and 19 special teams with Calgary in 1993.
CFL Total Tackles - 21 (2 defensive and 19 special teams).

Playoffs

Games Played - 2 with Calgary in 1993. **CFL Total Playoff GP - 2.**

Tackles - 4 special teams with Calgary in 1993.
CFL Total Playoff Tackles - 4 (4 special teams).

FRYAR, CHARLES
Born: November 28, 1965
Birthplace: Mount Holly, New Jersey
Defensive Back. 5'10", 175 lbs. Import
Last Amateur Club: University of Nebraska
Acquired: Signed as a free agent by the NFL Pittsburgh Steelers in 1989. Waived by Pittsburgh during their 1989 training camp. Selected by the Barcelona Dragons in the fourth round (34th overall) in the 1991 WLAF Positional Draft. Signed as a free agent by the Sacramento Gold Miners in March, 1993. Released by Sacramento in August, 1993.

Games Played - 1 with Sacramento in 1993. **CFL Total GP - 1.**

Tackles - 2 defensive and 1 special teams with Sacramento in 1993.
CFL Total Tackles - 3 (2 defensive and 1 special teams).

FULLER, JOE
Born: September 25, 1964
Birthplace: Minneapolis, Minnesota
Cornerback. 5'10", 185 lbs. Import
Last Amateur Club: Northern Iowa University
Acquired: Signed as a free agent by the Saskatchewan Roughriders in March, 1986. Granted free agency status in March, 1989. Signed as a free agent by the NFL Minnesota Vikings in March, 1989. Released by Minnesota in September 1989 and was re-signed to their development squad. Released by Minnesota in October, 1989. Signed as a free agent by the NFL San Diego Chargers in February, 1990. Released by San Diego in December, 1990. Signed as a free agent by the NFL Green Bay Packers in April, 1991. Granted free agency status in February, 1992. Signed as a free agent by the Ottawa Rough Riders in April, 1993.

			Punt Returns					Interception Returns				
	Team	GP	NO	YDS	AVE	LG	TD	NO	YDS	AVE	LG	TD
1986	Sask.	7	6	34	5.7	11	0	0	0	0.0	0	0
1987	Sask.	18	52	403	7.8	45	0	5	41	8.2	21	0
1988	Sask.	18	54	426	7.9	89	0	7	131	18.7	49	1
1993	Ott.	14	0	0	0.0	0	0	2	65	32.5	40	1
CFL TOTALS		**57**	**112**	**863**	**7.7**	**89**	**0**	**14**	**237**	**16.9**	**49**	**2**

		Kickoff Returns					Unsuccessful Field Goal Returns				
	Team	NO	YDS	AVE	LG	TD	NO	YDS	AVE	LG	TD
1986	Sask.	5	106	21.2	26	0	0	0	0.0	0	0
1987	Sask.	18	289	16.1	40	0	11	230	20.9	87	0
1988	Sask.	4	55	13.8	25	0	9	185	20.6	45	0
1993	Ott.	10	135	13.5	22	0	0	0	0.0	0	0
CFL TOTALS		**37**	**585**	**15.8**	**40**	**0**	**20**	**415**	**20.8**	**87**	**0**

Fumbles - 2 and 1 lost with Saskatchewan in 1987 and 1 and 1 lost with Ottawa in 1993. **CFL Total Fumbles - 3 and 2 lost.**

Tackles - 43 defensive with Saskatchewan in 1987; 40 defensive in 1988 and 25 defensive and 3 special teams with Ottawa in 1993.
CFL Total Tackles - 111 (108 defensive and 3 special teams).

GABBARD, STEVE
Born: July 19, 1968
Birthplace: Lexington, Kentucky
Offensive Tackle. 6'4", 295 lbs. Import
Last Amateur Club: Florida State University
Acquired: Signed as a free agent by the NFL Philadelphia Eagles in 1989. Was released by Philadelphia during the 1990 pre-season. Selected in the first round (10th overall) by the London Monarchs in the 1991 WLAF Positional Draft. Signed as a free agent by the Sacramento Gold Miners in April, 1993.

Games Played - 14 with Sacramento in 1993. **CFL Total GP - 14.**

Tackles - 2 defensive with Sacramento in 1993. **CFL Total Tackles - 2 (2 defensive).**

GARDERE, PETE
Born: September 28, 1969
Birthplace: Houston, Texas
Quarterback/Punter. 6'0", 190 lbs. Import
Last Amateur Club: University of Texas
Acquired: Signed as a free agent by the NFL Seattle Seahawks in April, 1993. Was released during training camp. Signed as a free agent by the Sacramento Gold Miners in August, 1993.

			Scoring					Punting				
	Team	GP	TD	C	FG	S	TP	NO	YDS	AVE	LK	S
1993	Sac.	10	0	0	0	5	5	77	3246	42.2	63	5
CFL TOTALS		**10**	**0**	**0**	**0**	**5**	**5**	**77**	**3246**	**42.2**	**63**	**5**

Net Punting - 78 for 2779 yards, 35.6 average with Sacramento in 1993.
CFL Total Net Punting - 78 for 2779 yards, 35.6 average.

GARDERE, PETE

Fumbles - 1 and 1 lost with Sacramento in 1993.
CFL Total Fumbles - 1 and 1 lost.

Tackles - 3 special teams with Sacramento in 1993.
CFL Total Tackles - 3 (3 special teams).

GARZA, SAMMY

Born: September 30, 1965
Birthplace: Corpus Christi, Texas
Quarterback. 6'1", 185 lbs. Import
Last Amateur Club: University of Texas-El Paso
Acquired: Eighth round draft choice of Seattle Seahawks in 1987 NFL Draft. Released and signed with the Phoenix Cardinals (NFL) in 1988. Released at the end of training camp and signed as a free agent by Winnipeg Blue Bombers in October, 1988.

			Passing							Rushing				
	Team	GP	ATT	COMP	YDS	PCT	INT	LG	TD	NO	YDS	AVE	LG	TD
1989	Wpg.	5	10	1	20	10.0	2	20	0	0	0	0.0	0	0
1990	Wpg.	8	0	0	0	0.0	0	0	0	0	0	0.0	0	0
1991	Wpg.	18	20	10	192	50.0	2	48	2	3	14	4.7	8	0
1992	Wpg.	18	93	39	580	41.9	3	59	6	11	46	4.2	12	0
1993	Wpg.	13	97	55	829	56.7	3	47	6	4	25	6.3	12	0
CFL TOTALS		**62**	**220**	**105**	**1621**	**47.7**	**10**	**59**	**14**	**18**	**85**	**4.7**	**12**	**0**

2-Pt. Converts - 1 attempt, 0 made with Winnipeg in 1991 and 1 attempt, 0 made in 1992. **CFL Total 2-Pt. Converts - 2 attempts, 0 made.**

Fumbles - 1 and 0 lost with Winnipeg in 1991 and 1 and 0 lost in 1993.
CFL Total Fumbles - 2 and 0 lost.

Playoffs

Games Played - 2 with Winnipeg in 1989; 1 in 1990; 2 in 1991; 1 in 1992 and 1 in 1993. **CFL Total Playoff GP - 7.**

Passing - 23 attempts, 10 complete for 112 yards, 43.5 pct., longest 38 yards and 2 interceptions with Winnipeg in 1991 and 38 attempts, 20 complete for 226 yards, 52.6 pct., longest 44 yards, 1 interception and 1 TD in 1993.
CFL Total Playoff Passing - 61 attempts, 30 complete for 338 yards, 49.2 pct., longest 44 yards, 3 interceptions and 1 TD.

Fumbles - 1 and 0 lost with Winnipeg in 1993.
CFL Total Playoff Fumbles - 1 and 0 lost.

Own Fumbles Recovered - 1 with Winnipeg in 1993.
CFL Total Playoff OFR - 1.

Rushing - 2 for 9 yards, 4.5 average, longest 6 yards with Winnipeg in 1991 and 4 for 3 yards, 0.8 average, longest 4 yards in 1993.
CFL Total Playoff Rushing - 6 for 12 yards, 2.0 average, longest 6 yards.

Grey Cup

Games Played - 1 with Winnipeg in 1990; 1 in 1992 and 1 in 1993.
Total Grey Cup GP - 3.

Scoring - 1 TD for 6 pts. with Winnipeg in 1993.
Total Grey Cup Scoring - 1 TD for 6 pts.

Passing - 4 attempts, 1 complete for 15 yards, 25.0 pct., longest 15 yards and 1 interception with Winnipeg in 1990 and 40 attempts, 23 complete for 322 yards, 57.5 pct, longest 34 yards and 0 interceptions in 1993.
Total Grey Cup Passing - 44 attempts, 24 complete for 337 yards, 54.5 pct., longest 34 yards and 1 interception.

Rushing - 5 for 10 yards, 2.0 average, longest 7 yards and 1 TD with Winnipeg in 1993. **Total Grey Cup Rushing - 5 for 10 yards, 2.0 average, longest 7 yards and 1 TD.**

Fumbles - 1 and 1 lost with Winnipeg in 1993.
Total Grey Cup Fumbles - 1 and 1 lost.

GIFTOPOLOUS, PETER

Born: June 14, 1965
Birthplace: Hamilton, Ontario
Linebacker/Offensive Lineman: 6'3", 240 lbs. Non-import
Last Amateur Club: Penn State University
Acquired: First round selection of the Saskatchewan Roughriders (sixth overall) in the 1988 CFL College Draft. Attended NFL Pittsburgh Steelers training camp as a free agent in 1988 and was released in August, 1988. Released and signed by Saskatchewan. Traded to the Hamilton Tiger-Cats for a first round draft pick in the 1989 CFL College Draft, cornerback Andrew Thomas, and running back Shawn Daniels in August, 1988. Signed by Hamilton in September, 1988. Granted free agency status in February, 1993. Re-signed by Hamilton in May, 1993.

Games Played - 8 with Hamilton in 1988; 18 in 1989; 16 in 1990; 15 in 1991; 11 in 1992 and 18 in 1993. **CFL Total GP - 86.**

Interception Returns - 2 for -1 yards, -0.5 average, longest 1 yard with Hamilton in 1989 and 3 for 28 yards, 9.3 average, longest 19 yards in 1991.
CFL Total Interception Returns - 5 for 27 yards, 5.4 average, longest 19 yards.

Punt Returns - 1 for 5 yards with Hamilton in 1988.
CFL Total Punt Returns - 1 for 5 yards.

Kickoff Returns - 1 for 0 yards with Hamilton in 1989 and 1 for 0 yards in 1991.
CFL Total Kickoff Returns - 2 for 0 yards.

Fumble Returns - 2 for 0 yards with Hamilton in 1990 and 1 for 0 yards in 1992.
CFL Total Fumble Returns - 3 for 0 yards.

Quarterback Sacks - 1 with Hamilton in 1988; 2 in 1989; 3 in 1990 and 1 in 1991.
CFL Total QB Sacks - 7.

Tackles - 1 defensive with Hamilton in 1988; 42 defensive in 1989; 77 defensive in 1990; 62 defensive and 1 special teams in 1991; 15 defensive and 1 special teams in 1992 and 2 defensive and 15 special teams in 1993.
CFL Total Tackles - 216 (199 defensive and 17 special teams).

Tackles for Losses - 6 for 13 yards with Hamilton in 1991 and 1 for 1 yard in 1992.
CFL Total Tackles for Losses - 7 for 14 yards.

Playoffs

Games Played - 1 with Hamilton in 1988; 1 in 1989; 2 in 1992 and 2 in 1993.
CFL Total Playoff GP - 6.

Interception Returns - 1 for 6 yards with Hamilton in 1989.
CFL Total Playoff Interception Returns - 1 for 6 yards.

Tackles - 1 defensive with Hamilton in 1989; 1 defensive in 1992 and 1 defensive and special teams in 1993.
CFL Total Playoff Tackles - 4 (3 defensive and 1 special teams).

Grey Cup

Games Played - 1 with Hamilton in 1989. **Total Grey Cup GP - 1.**

Defensive Tackles - 3 with Hamilton in 1989.
Total Grey Cup Defensive Tackles - 3.

GIOSKOS, CHRIS

Born: December 15, 1967
Birthplace: Hamilton, Ontario
Guard. 6'2", 275 lbs. Non-import
Last Amateur Club: University of Ottawa (OQIFC)
Acquired: Selected in the second round (15th overall) by the Saskatchewan Roughriders in the 1990 CFL College Draft. Saskatchewan acquired the pick from the Hamilton Tiger-Cats in exchange for offensive lineman Bill Henry. Granted free agency status in February, 1992. Signed as a free agent by the B.C. Lions in March, 1993. Traded to the Ottawa Rough Riders in April, 1993 along with offensive lineman Carl Coulter, kicker Wayne Lammle, cornerback Joe Mero and linebacker Mark Scott in exchange for cornerback Less Browne, offensive lineman Rob Smith and linebacker Patrick Wayne.

Games Played - 14 with Saskatchewan in 1990; 18 in 1991; 18 in 1992 and 18 with Ottawa in 1993. **CFL Total GP - 68.**

Own Fumbles Recovered - 1 with Saskatchewan in 1990. **CFL Total OFR - 1.**

Tackles - 1 defensive and 1 special teams with Saskatchewan in 1992.
CFL Total Tackles - 2 (1 defensive and 1 special teams).

Playoffs

Games Played - 1 with Saskatchewan in 1992 and 1 with Ottawa in 1993.
CFL Total Playoff GP - 2.

GOETZ, RON

Born: February 8, 1968
Birthplace: Waconia, Minnesota
Linebacker, 6'2", 234 lbs. Import
Last Amateur Club: University of Minnesota
Acquired: Signed as a free agent by the NFL Philadelphia Eagles in 1992. Signed as a free agent by the Ottawa Rough Riders in March, 1993. Traded to the Saskatchewan Roughriders along with quarterback Tom Burgess, defensive back Anthony Drawhorn and defensive end Paul Yatkowski in exchange for quarterback Kent Austin and offensive lineman Andrew Greene.

Games Played - 17 with Ottawa in 1993. **CFL Total GP - 17.**

Interception Returns - 1 for -2 yards with Ottawa in 1993.
CFL Total Interception Returns - 1 for -2 yards.

Fumble Returns - 1 for 0 yards with Ottawa in 1993.
CFL Total Fumble Returns - 1 for 0 yards.

Quarterback Sacks - 8 for 54 yards lost with Ottawa in 1993.
CFL Total QB Sacks - 8 for 54 yards lost.

Tackles - 54 defensive and 24 special teams with Ottawa in 1993.
CFL Total Tackles - 78 (54 defensive and 24 special teams).

Tackles For Losses - 5 for 13 yards with Ottawa in 1993.
CFL Total Tackles For Losses- 5 for 13 yards.

GOODS, BENNIE

Born: February 20, 1968
Birthplace: Pattison, Mississippi
Linebacker. 6'3", 255 lbs. Import
Last Amateur Club: Alcorn State University
Acquired: Signed as a free agent by the NFL Tampa Bay Buccaneers in 1990 and was released after training camp. Signed as a free agent by the Edmonton Eskimos in October, 1990.

Games Played - 2 with Edmonton in 1990; 12 in 1991; 18 in 1992 and 18 in 1993. **CFL Total GP - 50.**

Scoring - 1 TD for 6 pts. with Edmonton in 1993. **CFL Total Scoring - 1 TD for 6 pts.**

Fumble Returns - 1 for 0 yards with Edmonton in 1991; 1 for 9 yards in 1992 and 3 for 0 yards, 0 average, longest 1 yard in 1993.
CFL Total Fumble Returns - 5 for 9 yards, 1.8 average, longest 9 yards.

Quarterback Sacks - 1 with Edmonton in 1990; 5 in 1991; 10 for 70 yards lost in 1992 and 14 for 135 yards lost in 1993. **CFL Total QB Sacks - 30.**

Defensive Tackles - 1 with Edmonton in 1990; 15 in 1991; 32 in 1992 and 27 in 1993. **CFL Total Defensive Tackles - 75.**

Tackles for Losses - 4 for 20 yards with Edmonton in 1991; 3 for 9 yards in 1992 and 3 for 4 yards in 1993.
CFL Total Tackles for Losses - 10 for 33 yards.

All-Western All-Star in 1993.

Playoffs

Games Played - 1 with Edmonton in 1991; 2 in 1992 and 2 in 1993.
CFL Total Playoff GP - 5.

Quarterback Sacks - 1 for 6 yards lost with Edmonton in 1992.
CFL Total Playoff QB Sacks - 1 for 6 yards lost.

Tackles - 2 defensive with Edmonton in 1991; 2 defensive in 1992 and 4 defensive in 1993. **CFL Total Playoff Tackles - 8 (8 defensive).**

Grey Cup

Games Played - 1 with Edmonton in 1990 and 1 in 1993. **Total Grey Cup GP - 2.**

Fumble Returns - 1 for 0 yards with Edmonton in 1993.
Total Grey Cup Fumble Returns - 1 for 0 yards.

Quarterback Sacks - 1 with Edmonton in 1990 and 1 for 8 yards lost in 1993.
Total Grey Cup QB Sacks - 2.

Defensive Tackles - 2 with Edmonton in 1990 and 3 in 1993.
Total Grey Cup Defensive Tackles - 5.

GORDON, BOB

Born: July 9, 1968
Birthplace: Detroit, Michigan
Wide Receiver. 5'10", 185 lbs. Import
Last Amateur Club: University of Nebraska - Omaha
Acquired: Tried out with the NFL Pittsburgh Steelers in 1990. Signed as a free agent by the Ottawa Rough Riders in April, 1990. Released by Ottawa in October, 1992. Signed as a free agent by the Toronto Argonauts in September, 1993.

		Pass Receiving					
	Team	GP	NO	YDS	AVE	LG	TD
1991	Ott.	8	25	410	16.4	56	1
1992	Ott.	12	28	441	13.3	24	1
1993	Tor.	7	20	266	13.3	24	0
CFL TOTALS		**27**	**73**	**1117**	**15.3**	**56**	**2**

		Punt Returns					Kickoff Returns				
	Team	NO	YDS	AVE	LG	TD	NO	YDS	AVE	LG	TD
1991	Ott.	10	94	9.4	40	0	20	365	18.3	30	0
1992	Ott.	4	-15	-3.8	4	0	7	96	13.7	29	0
1993	Tor.	13	104	8.0	27	0	11	289	26.3	48	0
CFL TOTALS		**27**	**183**	**6.8**	**40**	**0**	**38**	**750**	**19.7**	**48**	**0**

Tackles - 1 special teams with Toronto in 1993.
CFL Total Tackles - 1 (1 special teams).

GORDON, CHARLES

Born: July 30, 1968
Birthplace: East Lansing, Michigan
Defensive Back. 6'0", 190 lbs. Import
Last Amateur Club: Eastern Michigan University
Acquired: Signed as a free agent by the Toronto Argonauts in June, 1991. Released in July, 1991 and signed as a free agent by the Ottawa Rough Riders. Granted free agency status in February, 1993. Re-signed by Ottawa in June, 1993.

Games Played - 17 with Ottawa in 1991; 14 in 1992 and 9 in 1993. **CFL Total GP - 40.**

Scoring - 1 TD for 6 pts. for Ottawa in 1993. **CFL Total Scoring - 1 TD for 6 pts.**

Pass Receiving - 1 for 8 yards with Ottawa in 1991.
CFL Total Pass Receiving - 1 for 8 yards.

Own Kickoffs Recovered - 1 with Ottawa in 1992.
CFL Total Own Kickoffs Recovered - 1.

Fumble Returns - 1 for 0 yards with Ottawa in 1992 and 1 for 0 yards in 1993.
CFL Total Fumble Returns - 2 for 0 yards.

Interception Returns - 1 for 20 yards with Ottawa in 1991; 7 for 82 yards, 11.7 average, longest 37 yards in 1992 and 3 for 51 yards, 17.0 average, longest 51 yards and 1 TD in 1993.
CFL Total Interception Returns - 11 for 153 yards, 13.9 average, longest 51 yards and 1 TD.

Tackles - 39 defensive and 7 special teams with Ottawa in 1991; 51 defensive and 10 special teams in 1992 and 25 defensive and 5 special teams in 1993. **CFL Total Tackles - 137 (115 defensive and 22 special teams).**

Playoffs

Games Played - 1 with Ottawa in 1991; 1 in 1992 and 1 in 1993.
CFL Total Playoff GP - 3.

Punt Returns - 3 for 22 yards, 7.3 average, longest 16 yards with Ottawa in 1993.
CFL Total Playoff Tackles - 3 for 22 yards, 7.3 average, longest 16 yards.

Tackles - 1 defensive with Ottawa in 1991; 4 defensive and 1 special teams in 1992 and 4 defensive in 1993.
CFL Total Playoff Tackles - 10 (9 defensive and 1 special teams).

GORRELL, MILES

Born: October 16, 1955
Birthplace: Calgary, Alberta
Offensive Tackle. 6'8", 290 lbs. Non-import
Last Amateur Club: University of Ottawa (OQIFC)
Acquired: One of Calgary's two Territorial Exemptions in 1978. Traded to Ottawa Rough Riders with Larry James for future considerations. Traded to Montreal Alouettes in September, 1982 for a third round draft choice in 1983 CFL College Draft. Released by Montreal and signed as a free agent by the Hamilton Tiger-Cats in September, 1985. Traded to the Winnipeg Blue Bombers in June, 1993 in exchange for a third round selection, (29th overall) in the 1992 CFL College Draft, tight end Sean Grayson.

Games Played - 16 with Calgary in 1978; 16 in 1979; 16 in 1980; 16 in 1981; 8 in 1982; 2 with Ottawa in 1982; 7 with Montreal in 1982; 16 in 1983; 16 in 1984; 10 in 1985: 1 with Hamilton in 1985; 18 in 1986; 17 in 1987; 18 in 1988; 18 in 1989; 18 in 1990; 18 in 1991; 18 with Winnipeg in 1992 and 18 in 1993.
CFL Total GP - 267.

Fumble Returns - 1 for 0 yards with Calgary in 1979.
CFL Total Fumble Returns - 1 for 0 yards.

Kickoff Returns - 1 for 0 yards with Calgary in 1980.
CFL Total Kickoff Returns - 1 for 0 yards.

Quarterback Sacks - 2 with Calgary in 1981 and 2 in 1982.
CFL Total QB Sacks - 4.

Interception Returns - 1 for 7 yards with Calgary in 1978.
CFL Total Interception Returns - 1 for 7 yards.

Own Fumbles Recovered - 2 with Montreal in 1983; 3 with Hamilton in 1989 and 2 with Winnipeg in 1993. **CFL Total OFR - 7.**

Tackles - 2 defensive with Hamilton in 1987; 2 defensive in 1988; 2 defensive in 1990; 2 defensive and 1 special teams with Winnipeg in 1992 and 3 defensive in 1993. **CFL Total Tackles - 12 (11 defensive and 1 special teams).**

All-Eastern All-Star in 1983; 1984; 1986; 1988 and 1989.
CFL All-Star in 1989.
Winner of the Leo Dandurand Trophy, Most Outstanding Offensive Lineman, Eastern Division in 1986 and 1989.
Runner-up CFL Most Outstanding Offensive Lineman in 1986 and 1989.

Playoffs

Games Played - 2 with Calgary in 1978; 2 in 1979; 1 in 1980; 1 with Montreal in 1984; 2 with Hamilton in 1986; 1 in 1987; 1 in 1988; 1 in 1989; 1 with Winnipeg in 1992 and 1 in 1993. **CFL Total Playoff GP - 13.**

Fumble Returns - 1 for 0 yards with Calgary in 1980.
CFL Total Playoff Fumble Returns - 1 for 0 yards.

Grey Cup

Games Played - 1 with Hamilton in 1986; 1 in 1989; 1 with Winnipeg in 1992 and 1 in 1993. **Total Grey Cup GP - 4.**

GRAVELY, TRACEY

Born: April 24, 1968
Birthplace: Welch, West Virginia
Defensive Back. 6'3" 212 lbs. Import
Last Amateur Club: Concord College
Acquired: Attended the NFL New York Giants' training camp in 1990. Signed as a free agent by the Ottawa Rough Riders in May, 1991. Released by Ottawa in July, 1992. Signed as a free agent by the B.C. Lions in August, 1992. Released by B.C. in August, 1993.

GRAVELY, TRACY

Games Played - 5 with Ottawa in 1991; 8 with B.C. in 1992 and 5 in 1993. **CFL Total GP - 18.**

Interception Returns - 3 for 10 yards, 3.3 average, longest 8 yards with B.C. in 1992 and 1 for 0 yards in 1993. **CFL Total Interception Returns - 4 for 10 yards, 2.5 average, longest 8 yards.**

Fumble Returns - 1 for 0 yards with Ottawa in 1991 and 1 for 4 yards with B.C. in 1992. **CFL Total Fumble Returns - 2 for 4 yards, 2.0 average, longest 4 yards.**

Tackles - 7 defensive and 6 special teams with Ottawa in 1991; 32 defensive and 3 special teams with B.C. in 1992 and 10 defensive and 5 special teams in 1993. **CFL Total Tackles - 63 (49 defensive and 14 special teams).**

Tackles for Losses - 1 for 1 yard with B.C. in 1992. **CFL Total Tackles for Losses - 1 for 1 yard.**

GRAY, MIKE
Born: February 11, 1960
Birthplace: Baltimore, Maryland
Defensive Tackle. 6'4", 255 lbs. Import
Last Amateur Club: University of Oregon
Acquired: Signed as a free agent by the B.C. Lions in November, 1984 following training camps with the NFL's Seattle Seahawks in 1983 and 1984. Selected by Ottawa Rough Riders in the Equalization Draft of February, 1987. Released by Ottawa in June, 1987 and signed as a free agent by Winnipeg Blue Bombers in that same month. Granted free agency status in February, 1993. Re-signed by Winnipeg in June, 1993 and was released in August, 1993.

Games Played - 16 with B.C. in 1985; 17 in 1986; 17 with Winnipeg in 1987; 18 in 1988; 18 in 1989; 17 in 1990; 16 in 1991; 18 in 1992 and 3 in 1993. **CFL Total GP - 140.**

Scoring - 1 TD for 6 points with Winnipeg in 1991. **CFL Total Scoring - 1 TD for 6 points.**

Fumble Returns - 3 with B.C. in 1985; 1 with Winnipeg in 1987; 2 in 1988; 2 in 1989; 1 in 1990; 2 for 26 yards, 13.0 average, longest 26 yards and 1 TD in 1991 and 1 for 0 yards in 1992. **CFL Total Fumble Returns - 12 for 26 yards, 2.2 average, longest 26 yards and 1 TD.**

Interception Returns - 2 for 6 yards, 3.0 average, longest 13 yards with B.C. in 1986. **CFL Total Interception Returns - 2 for 6 yards, 3.0 average, longest 13 yards.**

Quarterback Sacks - 13 with B.C. in 1985; 8 in 1986; 10 with Winnipeg in 1987; 11 in 1988; 11 in 1989; 5 in 1990; 2 in 1991 and 4 for 16 yards lost in 1992. **CFL Total QB Sacks - 64.**

Tackles - 30 defensive with Winnipeg in 1987; 41 defensive in 1988; 44 defensive in 1989; 23 defensive in 1990; 37 defensive and 1 special teams in 1991; 40 defensive in 1992 and 8 defensive in 1993. **CFL Total Tackles - 224 (223 defensive and 1 special teams).**

Tackles for Losses - 2 for 5 yards with Winnipeg in 1991 and 3 for 5 yards in 1992. **CFL Total Tackles for Losses - 5 for 10 yards.**

All-Western All-Star in 1985.
CFL All-Star in 1985.
Jackie Parker Trophy, Most Outstanding Rookie Western Division 1985.
Schenley Most Outstanding Rookie in 1985.
All-Eastern All-Star in 1989.

Playoffs

Games Played - 1 with B.C. in 1985; 2 in 1986; 1 in 1987 with Winnipeg; 2 in 1988; 2 in 1989; 1 in 1990; 2 in 1991 and 1 in 1992. **CFL Total Playoff GP - 12.**

Fumble Returns - 1 for 0 yards with Winnipeg in 1991. **CFL Total Playoff Fumble Returns - 1 for 0 yards.**

Quarterback Sacks - 1 with B.C. in 1985; 1 in 1986; 1 in 1988 with Winnipeg; 2 in 1989; 1 in 1990 and 2 for 14 yards lost in 1992. **CFL Total Playoff QB Sacks - 8.**

Defensive Tackles - 4 with Winnipeg in 1987; 4 in 1988; 3 in 1989; 2 in 1990; 4 in 1991 and 2 in 1992. **CFL Total Playoff Defensive Tackles - 19.**

Tackles for Losses - 1 for 2 yards with Winnipeg in 1991. **CFL Total Playoff Tackles for Losses - 1 for 2 yards.**

Grey Cup

Games Played - 1 with B.C. in 1985; 1 with Winnipeg in 1988; 1 in 1990 and 1 in 1992. **Total Grey Cup GP - 4.**

Fumble Returns - 1 for 0 yards with Winnipeg in 1992. **Total Grey Cup Fumble Returns - 1 for 0 yards.**

Quarterback Sacks - 2 for 13 yards lost with Winnipeg in 1992. **Total Grey Cup QB Sacks - 2.**

Interception Returns - 1 for 0 yards with Winnipeg in 1988. **Total Grey Cup Interception Returns - 1 for 0 yards.**

Defensive Tackles - 3 with Winnipeg in 1988; 2 in 1990 and 2 in 1992. **Total Grey Cup Defensive Tackles - 7.**

GRAYBILL, MICHAEL
Born: November 14, 1966
Birthplace: Washington, D.C.
Offensive Tackle, 6'7", 288 lbs. Import
Last Amateur Club: Boston University
Acquired: Selected by the Cleveland Browns in the seventh round (187th overall) in the 1989 NFL Draft. Released by Cleveland in August, 1990. Awarded on waivers to the NFL Dallas Cowboys in August, 1990. Released by Dallas in September, 1990. Signed as a free agent by the NFL Phoenix Cardinals in November, 1990. Granted unconditional free agency in February, 1991. Signed as a free agent by the NFL Detroit Lions in March, 1991. Released by Detroit. Selected by the Ohio Glory in the second round (12th overall) in the 1992 WLAF Draft. Attended the NFL New Orleans Saints 1992 training camp. Signed as a free agent by the Ottawa Rough Riders in January, 1993.

Games Played - 18 with Ottawa in 1993. **CFL Total GP - 18.**

Fumbles - 2 and 0 lost with Ottawa in 1993. **CFL Total Fumbles - 2 and 0 lost.**

Fumble Returns - 1 for 0 yards with Ottawa in 1993. **CFL Total Fumble Returns - 1 for 0 yards.**

Tackles - 6 defensive and 17 special teams with Ottawa in 1993. **CFL Total Tackles - 23 (6 defensive and 17 special teams).**

All-Eastern All-Star in 1993.

GREEN, CHRIS
Born: March 30, 1968
Birthplace: Kingston, Ontario
Linebacker. 6'6", 305 lbs. Non-import
Last Amateur Club: University of Ottawa (OQIFC)
Acquired: Selected in the second round (13th overall) by the Toronto Argonauts in the 1991 CFL College Draft. Spent the 1991 season on the practice roster. Granted free agency status in February, 1994.

Games Played - 14 with Toronto in 1992 and 18 in 1993. **CFL Total GP - 32.**

Own Fumbles Recovered - 1 with Toronto in 1992. **CFL Total OFR - 1.**

Tackles - 1 defensive with Toronto in 1992 and 1 defensive in 1993. **CFL Total Tackles - 2 (2 defensive).**

GRIER, DEREK
Born: March 4, 1970
Birthplace: Atlanta, Georgia
Cornerback. 6'0", 175 lbs. Import
Last Amateur Club: Marshall University
Acquired: Signed as a free agent by the B.C. Lions in September, 1993.

			Pass Receiving					Interception Returns				
	Team	GP	NO	YDS	AVE	LG	TD	NO	YDS	AVE	LG	TD
1993	B.C.	6	1	12	12.0	12	0	2	6	3.0	6	0
CFL TOTALS		**6**	**1**	**12**	**12.0**	**12**	**0**	**2**	**6**	**3.0**	**6**	**0**

Fumble Returns - 1 for 7 yards with B.C. in 1993. **CFL Total Fumble Returns - 1 for 7 yards.**

Tackles - 12 defensive and 2 special teams with B.C. in 1993. **CFL Total Tackles - 14 (12 defensive and 2 special teams).**

Playoffs

Games Played - 1 with B.C. in 1993. **CFL Total Playoff GP - 1.**

Tackles - 4 defensive with B.C. in 1993. **CFL Total Playoff Tackles - 4 (4 defensive).**

Tackles for Losses - 1 for 4 yards with B.C. in 1993. **CFL Total Playoff Tackles for Losses - 1 for 4 yards.**

GROENEWEGEN, LEO
Born: August 13, 1965
Birthplace: Vancouver, B.C.
Offensive Guard. 6'5", 270 lbs. Non-import
Last Amateur Club: University of British Columbia (WIFL)
Acquired: Selected in first round, (first overall), in the 1987 CFL College Draft by the Ottawa Rough Riders. Traded to B.C. Lions for guard Gerald Roper in September, 1989.

Games Played - 18 with Ottawa in 1987; 18 in 1988; 12 in 1989; 6 with B.C. in 1989; 18 in 1990; 18 in 1991; 18 in 1992 and 18 in 1993. **CFL Total GP - 126.**

GROENEWEGEN, LEO

Own Fumbles Recovered - 1 with Ottawa in 1987; 1 in 1988 and 2 with B.C. in 1990. **CFL Total OFR - 4.**

Defensive Tackles - 3 with Ottawa in 1987; 1 in 1989; 2 with B.C. in 1990 and 2 in 1991. **CFL Total Defensive Tackles - 8.**

All-Western All-Star in 1991.
CFL All-Star in 1991.

Playoffs

Games Played - 1 with B.C. in 1991 and 1 in 1993.
CFL Total Playoff GP - 2.

HAILEY, KEN
Born: July 12, 1961
Birthplace: Oceanside, California
Defensive Back. 5'10", 175 lbs. Import
Last Amateur Club: San Francisco State University
Acquired: Joined Winnipeg Blue Bombers on a 21-day trial, activated for the final five games of the 1983 season. Released in August, 1991. Signed as a free agent by the Ottawa Rough Riders in March, 1992. Traded to the B.C. Lions in June, 1993 in exchange for defensive back Patrick Burke. Released by B.C. in February, 1994.

		Scoring						Interception Returns				
	Team	GP	TD	C	FG	S	TP	NO	YDS	AVE	LG	TD
1983	Wpg.	5	0	0	0	0	0	0	0	0.0	0	0
1984ab	Wpg.	16	1	0	0	0	6	9	240	26.7	74	1
1985ab	Wpg.	16	0	0	0	0	0	2	52	26.0	52	0
1986	Wpg.	18	0	0	0	0	0	2	42	21.0	42	0
1987bc	Wpg.	14	1	0	0	0	6	6	86	14.3	68	1
1988	Wpg.	12	0	0	0	0	0	2	5	2.5	5	0
1989	Wpg.	13	0	0	0	0	0	3	11	3.7	11	0
1990	Wpg.	10	1	0	0	0	6	1	15	15.0	15	0
1991	Wpg.	6	0	0	0	0	0	2	32	16.0	32	0
1992	Ott.	17	0	0	0	0	0	1	5	5.0	5	0
1993	B.C.	7	0	0	0	0	0	0	0	0.0	0	0
CFL TOTALS		**134**	**3**	**0**	**0**	**0**	**18**	**28**	**488**	**17.4**	**74**	**2**

		Punt Returns					Kickoff Returns					QB Sacks
	Team	NO	YDS	AVE	LG	TD	NO	YDS	AVE	LG	TD	NO
1983	Wpg.	0	0	0.0	0	0	6	185	30.8	69	0	0
1984	Wpg.	50	477	9.5	28	0	12	330	27.5	69	0	3
1985	Wpg.	9	101	11.2	21	0	4	61	15.3	29	0	0
1986	Wpg.	0	0	0.0	0	0	2	45	22.5	23	0	3
1987	Wpg.	3	13	4.3	6	0	0	0	0.0	0	0	0
1988	Wpg.	0	0	0.0	0	0	0	0	0.0	0	0	2
1989	Wpg.	1	-4	-4.0	-4	0	0	0	0.0	0	0	0
1990	Wpg.	0	0	0.0	0	0	17	370	21.8	41	0	0
1991	Wpg.	4	32	8.0	9	0	7	126	18.0	23	0	0
1992	Ott.	3	20	6.7	14	0	19	378	19.9	46	0	3
1993	B.C.	0	0	0.0	0	0	11	201	18.3	36	0	0
CFL TOTALS		**70**	**639**	**9.1**	**28**	**0**	**78**	**1696**	**21.7**	**69**	**0**	**11**

Own Kickoffs Recovered - 1 with Winnipeg in 1985.
CFL Total Own Kickoffs Recovered - 1.

Fumble Returns - 2 for 0 yards with Winnipeg in 1985; 1 for 2 yards in 1987 and 2 for 5 yards, 2.5 average, longest 5 yards and 1 TD in 1990; 1 for 0 yards with Ottawa in 1992 and 1 for 0 yards with B.C. in 1993.
CFL Total Fumble Returns - 7 for 7 yards, 1.0 average, longest 5 yards and 1 TD.

Fumbles - 5 and 4 lost with Winnipeg in 1984; 1 and 1 lost with Ottawa in 1992 and 2 and 1 lost with B.C. in 1993. **CFL Total Fumbles - 8 and 6 lost.**

Own Fumbles Recovered - 1 with Winnipeg in 1986 and 1 with B.C. in 1993.
CFL Total OFR - 2.

2-Pt. Converts - 1 attempt, 0 made with Winnipeg in 1991.
CFL Total 2-Pt. Converts - 1 attempt, 0 made.

Unsuccessful Field Goal Returns - 1 for 26 yards with Winnipeg in 1990.
CFL Total Unsuccessful Field Goal Returns - 1 for 26 yards.

Tackles - 60 defensive with Winnipeg in 1987; 19 defensive in 1988; 39 defensive in 1989; 26 defensive in 1990; 17 defensive and 9 special teams in 1991; 25 defensive and 21 special teams with Ottawa in 1992 and 6 defensive and 9 special teams with B.C. in 1993.
CFL Total Tackles - 231 (192 defensive and 39 special teams).

Tackles for Losses - 1 for 1 yard with Winnipeg in 1991 and 2 for 12 yards with Ottawa in 1992. **CFL Total Tackles for Losses - 3 for 13 yards.**

a - All-Western All-Star
b - CFL All-Star
c - All-Eastern All-Star

Playoffs

			Interception Returns					Fumbles	
	Team	GP	NO	YDS	AVE	LG	TD	NO	LOST
1984	Wpg.	2	1	1	1.0	1	0	0	0
1985	Wpg.	2	2	13	6.5	13	0	1	0
1986	Wpg.	1	0	0	0.0	0	0	0	0
1988	Wpg.	2	0	0	0.0	0	0	0	0
1990	Wpg.	1	0	0	0.0	0	0	0	0
1992	Ott.	1	0	0	0.0	0	0	0	0
CFL TOTALS		**9**	**3**	**14**	**4.7**	**13**	**0**	**1**	**0**

Kickoff Returns - 1 for 17 yards with Winnipeg in 1990.
CFL Total Playoff Kickoff Returns - 1 for 17 yards.

Tackles - 2 defensive with Winnipeg in 1990 and 1 defensive and 1 special teams with Ottawa in 1992.
CFL Total Playoff Tackles - 4 (3 defensive and 1 special teams).

Grey Cup

			Interception Returns					Punt Returns				
	Team	GP	NO	YDS	AVE	LG	TD	NO	YDS	AVE	LG	TD
1984	Wpg.	1	1	0	0.0	0	0	1	8	8.0	8	0
1988	Wpg.	1	0	0	0.0	0	0	0	0	0.0	0	0
1990	Wpg.	1	0	0	0.0	0	0	0	0	0.0	0	0
CFL TOTALS		**3**	**1**	**0**	**0.0**	**0**	**0**	**1**	**8**	**8.0**	**8**	**0**

		Kickoff Returns					Fumble Returns				
	Team	NO	YDS	AVE	LG	TD	NO	YDS	AVE	LG	TD
1984	Wpg.	0	0	0.0	0	0	0	0	0.0	0	0
1988	Wpg.	0	0	0.0	0	0	0	0	0.0	0	0
1990	Wpg.	2	55	27.5	35	0	1	0	0.0	0	0
CFL TOTALS		**2**	**55**	**27.5**	**35**	**0**	**1**	**0**	**0.0**	**0**	**0**

Defensive Tackles - 1 with Winnipeg in 1988 and 4 in 1990.
Total Grey Cup Defensive Tackles - 5.

HALLMAN, HAROLD
Born: December 10, 1962
Birthplace: Macon, Georgia
Defensive Tackle. 6'0", 240 lbs. Import
Last Amateur Club: Auburn University
Acquired: Signed as a free agent by the Calgary Stampeders in May, 1986. Traded to Toronto Argonauts for linebacker Doug Landry in September, 1988.

Games Played - 17 with Calgary in 1986; 16 in 1987; 8 in 1988; 7 with Toronto in 1988; 18 in 1989; 18 in 1990; 17 in 1991; 16 in 1992 and 13 in 1993.
CFL Total GP - 130.

Scoring - 1 TD for 6 points with Toronto in 1991.
CFL Total Scoring - 1 TD for 6 points.

Kickoff Returns - 1 for 8 yards with Calgary in 1986.
CFL Total Kickoff Returns - 1 for 8 yards.

Blocked Kicks - 1 field goal with Toronto in 1992.
CFL Total Blocked Kicks - 1 field goal.

Fumble Returns - 1 for 0 yards with Calgary in 1986 and 1 for 0 yards with Toronto in 1988. **CFL Total Fumble Returns - 2 for 0 yards.**

Interception Returns - 1 for 29 yards and 1 TD with Toronto in 1991.
CFL Total Interception Returns - 1 for 29 yards and 1 TD.

Quarterback Sacks - 19 with Calgary in 1986; 15 in 1987; 4 in 1988; 7 with Toronto in 1988; 15 in 1989; 9 in 1990; 7 in 1991; 4 for 18 yards lost in 1992 and 2 for 17 yards lost in 1993.
CFL Total QB Sacks - 82.

Tackles - 34 defensive with Calgary in 1987; 23 defensive in 1988; 16 defensive with Toronto in 1988; 57 defensive in 1989; 43 defensive in 1990; 48 defensive in 1991; 53 defensive in 1992 and 32 defensive and 1 special teams in 1993. **CFL Total Tackles - 307 (306 defensive and 1 special teams).**

Tackles for Losses - 8 for 28 yards with Toronto in 1991; 11 for 27 yards in 1992 and 3 for 8 yards in 1993.
CFL Total Tackles for Losses - 22 for 63 yards.

All-Eastern All-Star in 1989; 1990 and 1991.
All-Western All-Star in 1986 and 1987.
CFL All-Star in 1986; 1989; 1990 and 1991.
Winner of the Jackie Parker Trophy, Most Outstanding Rookie, Western Division, in 1986.
Schenley Most Outstanding Rookie in 1986.

Playoffs

Games Played - 1 with Calgary in 1986; 1 in 1987; 1 with Toronto in 1989; 2 in 1990 and 1 in 1991. **CFL Total Playoff GP - 6.**

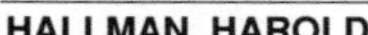

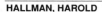

HALLMAN, HAROLD

Fumble Returns - 1 for 0 yards with Calgary in 1986.
CFL Total Playoff Fumble Returns - 1 for 0 yards.

Quarterback Sacks - 1 with Calgary in 1986.
CFL Total Playoff QB Sacks - 1.

Tackles - 3 defensive with Calgary in 1987; 2 defensive with Toronto in 1989; 7 defensive in 1990 and 2 defensive and 1 special teams in 1991.
CFL Total Playoff Tackles - 15 (14 defensive and 1 special teams).

Grey Cup

Games Played - 1 with Toronto in 1991.
Total Grey Cup GP - 1.

Tackles - 2 defensive with Toronto in 1991.
Total Grey Cup Tackles - 2 (2 defensive).

HAM, TRACY
Born: January 5, 1964
Birthplace: High Springs, Florida
Quarterback. 5'10", 190 lbs. Import
Last Amateur Club: Georgia Southern College
Acquired: Signed as a free agent by the Edmonton Eskimos in June, 1987. Traded to the Toronto Argonauts in January, 1993 along with defensive lineman Cameron Brosseau, linebacker John Davis, slotback Craig Ellis, defensive back Enis Jackson, running back Chris Johnstone, defensive back Travis Oliver and wide receiver Ken Winey in exchange for cornerback Ed Berry, wide receiver Eddie Brown, linebacker Bruce Dickson, quarterback Rickey Foggie, slotback J.P. Izquierdo, defensive lineman Leonard Johnson, slotback Darrell K. Smith and defensive back Don Wilson. Granted free agency status in February, 1994. Signed as a free agent by the Baltimore CFL Colts in February, 1994.

		Scoring						Rushing				
	Team	GP	TD	C	FG	S	TP	NO	YDS	AVE	LG	TD
1987	Edm.	5	1	0	0	0	6	9	56	6.2	20	1
1988	Edm.	14	5	0	0	0	30	86	628	7.3	44	5
1989abcde	Edm.	18	10	0	0	0	60	125	1005	8.0	55	10
1990efg	Edm.	18	5	0	0	0	30	136	1096	8.1	32	5
1991h	Edm.	17	7	0	0	0	42	125	998	8.0	42	7
1992g	Edm.	18	5	0	0	0	30	92	655	7.1	45	5
1993	Tor.	18	7	0	0	0	42	72	605	8.4	42	7
CFL TOTALS		**108**	**40**	**0**	**0**	**0**	**240**	**645**	**5043**	**7.8**	**55**	**40**

		Passing							Fumbles		
	Team	ATT	COMP	YDS	PCT	INT	LG	TD	NO	LOST	OFR
1987	Edm.	36	15	231	41.7	3	38	1	0	0	0
1988	Edm.	339	185	2840	54.6	15	85	14	9	5	2
1989	Edm.	517	268	4366	51.8	18	67	30	5	3	1
1990	Edm.	559	285	4286	51.0	24	70	36	9	5	0
1991	Edm.	454	242	3862	53.3	16	66	31	14	10	5
1992	Edm.	428	221	3655	51.6	13	81	30	8	8	0
1993	Tor.	302	146	2147	48.3	11	64	8	5	3	0
CFL TOTALS		**2635**	**1362**	**21387**	**51.7**	**100**	**85**	**150**	**50**	**34**	**8**

Pass Receiving - 1 for -7 yards with Toronto in 1993.
CFL Total Pass Receiving - 1 for -7 yards.

2-Pt. Converts - 1 attempt, 1 complete with Edmonton in 1988; 3 attempts, 0 complete in 1990; 2 attempts, 0 complete in 1991 and 1 attempt, 0 complete with Toronto in 1993.
CFL Total 2-Pt. Converts - 7 attempts, 1 complete.

Defensive Tackles - 1 with Edmonton in 1989; 4 in 1990 and 3 in 1992.
CFL Total Defensive Tackles - 8.

a - Winner of the Jeff Nicklin Trophy, Most Outstanding Player, Western Division
b - CFL Most Outstanding Player Award Winner
c - All-Western All-Star
d - CFL All-Star
e - Set CFL Record for Yards Rushing by a Quarterback in a Season
f - Led CFL with Most Passing TD's
g - Led CFL in Passing Efficiency Rating
h - Set CFL Record for Most Yards Rushing by a Quarterback in One Game (166)

Playoffs

		Scoring						Rushing				
	Team	GP	TD	C	FG	S	TP	NO	YDS	AVE	LG	TD
1988	Edm.	1	0	0	0	0	0	11	85	7.7	32	0
1989	Edm.	1	1	0	0	0	6	9	69	7.7	32	1
1990	Edm.	2	2	0	0	0	12	20	172	8.6	29	2
1991	Edm.	1	0	0	0	0	0	5	34	6.8	27	0
1992	Edm.	2	1	0	0	0	6	20	135	6.8	32	1
CFL TOTALS		**7**	**4**	**0**	**0**	**0**	**24**	**65**	**495**	**7.6**	**32**	**4**

		Passing							Fumbles		
	Team	ATT	COMP	YDS	PCT	INT	LG	TD	NO	LOST	OFR
1988	Edm.	37	17	209	45.9	1	45	1	1	0	0
1989	Edm.	40	17	238	42.5	2	26	0	1	1	0
1990	Edm.	72	42	731	58.3	2	86	5	2	2	0
1991	Edm.	27	16	235	59.3	0	60	3	0	0	0
1992	Edm.	42	24	264	57.1	4	37	2	2	0	2
CFL TOTALS		**218**	**116**	**1677**	**53.2**	**9**	**86**	**11**	**6**	**3**	**2**

Grey Cup

			Passing							Rushing				
	Team	GP	ATT	COMP	YDS	PCT	INT	LG	TD	NO	YDS	AVE	LG	TD
1990	Edm.	1	37	20	253	54.1	3	29	1	11	84	7.6	10	0
CFL TOTALS		**1**	**37**	**20**	**253**	**54.1**	**3**	**29**	**1**	**11**	**84**	**7.6**	**10**	**0**

Fumbles - 2 and 0 lost with Edmonton in 1990.
Total Grey Cup Fumbles - 2 and 0 lost.

Own Fumbles Recovered - 1 with Edmonton in 1990. **Total Grey Cup OFR - 1.**

Defensive Tackles - 1 with Edmonton in 1990.
Total Grey Cup Defensive Tackles - 1.

HAMM, HORACE
Born: December 20, 1969
Birthplace: Jamaica, Wisconsin
Wide Receiver, 5'11", 172 lbs. Import
Last Amateur Club: Clemson University
Acquired: Signed as a free agent by the NFL Atlanta Falcons in 1992 and was later released. Signed as a free agent by the NFL Green Bay Packers and then released. Signed as a free agent by the Sacramento Gold Miners in May, 1993. Released by Sacramento in July, 1993.

			Pass Receiving				
	Team	GP	NO	YDS	AVE	LG	TD
1993	Sac.	2	4	60	15.0	25	0
CFL TOTALS		**2**	**4**	**60**	**15.0**	**25**	**0**

HAMMOND, VANCE
Born: December 4, 1967
Birthplace: Spartanburg, South Carolina
Defensive Tackle. 6'6", 290 lbs. Import
Last Amateur Club: Clemson University
Acquired: Selected by the NFL Phoenix Cardinals in the fifth round (117th overall) in the 1991 NFL Draft. Released by Phoenix during training camp. Signed as a free agent by the NFL Los Angeles Rams in November, 1991 and assigned to their practice squad. Allocated by Los Angeles to the San Antonio Riders of the WLAF prior to the 1992 season. Waived by San Antonio prior to training camp and picked up by the WLAF Sacramento Surge. Signed as a free agent by the Sacramento Gold Miners in February, 1993.

Games Played - 2 with Sacramento in 1993. **CFL Total GP - 2.**

Interception Returns - 1 for 28 yards with Sacramento in 1993.
CFL Total Interception Returns - 1 for 28 yards.

Fumble Returns - 1 for 0 yards with Sacramento in 1993.
CFL Total Fumble Returns - 1 for 0 yards.

Quarterback Sacks - 4 for 25 yards lost with Sacramento in 1993.
CFL Total QB Sacks - 4 for 25 yards lost.

Tackles - 37 defensive with Sacramento in 1993.
CFL Total Tackles - 37 (37 defensive).

Tackles For Losses - 3 for 4 yards with Sacramento in 1993.
CFL Total Tackles For Losses - 3 for 4 yards.

HANSON, RYAN
Born: January 17, 1964
Birthplace: London, England
Running Back. 6'1", 215 lbs. Non-import
Last Amateur Club: Slippery Rock University
Acquired: Selected in the first round (5th overall) by the Winnipeg Blue Bombers in the 1988 CFL College Draft. Traded to Toronto along with wide receiver Jeff Boyd for slotback Jeff Smith and fullback Tony Johns in July, 1988. Traded to B.C. Lions in September, 1990 in exchange for a second round draft choice (running back J.P. Izquierdo) in the 1991 CFL College Draft.

		Scoring						Rushing				
	Team	GP	TD	C	FG	S	TP	NO	YDS	AVE	LG	TD
1988	Tor.	9	1	0	0	0	6	23	121	5.3	39	1
1989	Tor.	18	2	0	0	0	12	14	101	7.2	29	1
1990	Tor.	10	0	0	0	0	0	1	1	1.0	1	0
	B.C.	7	2	0	0	0	12	21	70	3.3	17	0
1991	B.C.	16	1	0	0	0	6	11	102	9.3	23	0
1992	B.C.	15	3	0	0	0	18	32	203	6.3	48	2
1993	B.C.	18	1	0	0	0	6	15	143	9.5	45	1
CFL TOTALS		**93**	**10**	**0**	**0**	**0**	**60**	**117**	**741**	**6.3**	**48**	**5**

		Pass Receiving					Fumble Returns				
	Team	NO	YDS	AVE	LG	TD	NO	YDS	AVE	LG	TD
1988	Tor.	5	54	10.8	24	0	1	0	0.0	0	0
1989	Tor.	4	41	10.3	24	0	1	0	0.0	0	1
1990	Tor.	2	16	8.0	10	0	1	0	0.0	0	0
	B.C.	8	53	6.6	13	2	0	0	0.0	0	0
1991	B.C.	4	68	17.0	27	1	0	0	0.0	0	0
1992	B.C.	15	216	14.4	57	1	1	0	0.0	0	0
1993	B.C.	1	9	9.0	9	0	0	0	0.0	0	0
CFL TOTALS		**39**	**457**	**11.7**	**57**	**4**	**4**	**0**	**0.0**	**0**	**1**

HANSON, RYAN

Kickoff Returns - 1 for 51 yards, 51.0 average, longest 49 yards with Toronto in 1989; 1 for 21 yards with B.C. in 1992 and 6 for 113 yards, 18.8 average, longest 48 yards in 1993.
CFL Total Kickoff Returns - 8 for 185 yards, 23.1 average, longest 49 yards.

Fumbles - 2 and 1 lost with B.C. in 1990; 2 and 2 lost in 1991 and 1 and 1 lost in 1992. **CFL Total Fumbles - 5 and 4 lost.**

Blocked Kicks - 1 punt with Toronto in 1989 and 1 punt with B.C. in 1990.
CFL Total Blocked Kicks - 2 punts.

Tackles - 2 defensive with B.C. in 1990; 11 special teams in 1991; 2 defensive and 10 special teams in 1992 and 2 defensive and 9 special teams in 1993.
CFL Total Tackles - 36 (6 defensive and 30 special teams).

Playoffs

Games Played - 1 with Toronto in 1988; 1 in 1989; 1 with B.C. in 1991 and 1 in 1993.
CFL Total Playoff GP - 4.

Rushing - 1 for 5 yards with Toronto in 1988; 1 for 8 yards in 1989 and 3 for 6 yards, 2.0 average, longest 2 yards with B.C. in 1993.
CFL Total Playoff Rushing - 5 for 19 yards, 3.8 average, longest 8 yards.

HARDING, RODNEY
Born: August 1, 1962
Birthplace: Oklahoma City, Oklahoma
Defensive Tackle. 6'2", 250 lbs. Import
Last Amateur Club: Oklahoma State University
Acquired: Signed by the Toronto Argonauts as a free agent in May, 1985.

			Fumble Returns					Interception Returns				
	Team	GP	NO	YDS	AVE	LG	TD	NO	YDS	AVE	LG	TD
1985	Tor.	14	2	7	3.5	4	0	1	13	13.0	13	0
1986	Tor.	18	1	10	10.0	10	1	0	0	0.0	0	0
1987	Tor.	17	0	0	0.0	0	0	1	70	70.0	70	0
1988	Tor.	18	0	0	0.0	0	0	0	0	0.0	0	0
1989	Tor.	17	2	33	16.5	33	0	1	16	16.0	16	1
1990	Tor.	18	3	0	0.0	0	1	1	16	16.0	16	0
1991	Tor.	11	0	0	0.0	0	0	0	0	0.0	0	0
1992	Tor.	17	3	-10	-3.3	0	0	1	11	11.0	11	0
1993	Tor.	17	1	23	23.0	23	0	0	0	0.0	0	0
CFL TOTALS		**147**	**12**	**63**	**5.3**	**33**	**2**	**5**	**126**	**25.2**	**70**	**1**

Scoring - 1 TD for 6 points with Toronto in 1986; 1 TD for 6 points in 1989 and 1 TD for 6 points in 1990. **CFL Total Scoring - 3 TDs for 18 points.**

Kickoff Returns - 1 for 0 yards with Toronto in 1987.
CFL Total Kickoff Returns - 1 for 0 yards.

Blocked Kicks - 1 punt with Toronto in 1987 and 1 field goal in 1988.
CFL Total Blocked Kicks - 1 punt and 1 field goal.

Quarterback Sacks - 8 with Toronto in 1985; 10 in 1986; 13 in 1987; 12 in 1988; 9 in 1989; 6 in 1990; 3 in 1991; 12 for 72 yards lost in 1992 and 3 for 25 yards in 1993. **CFL Total QB Sacks - 76.**

Defensive Tackles - 26 with Toronto in 1987; 37 in 1988; 29 in 1989; 19 in 1990; 16 in 1991; 31 in 1992 and 29 in 1993. **CFL Total Defensive Tackles - 187.**

Tackles for Losses - 5 for 9 yards with Toronto in 1992 and 7 for 31 yards in 1993. **CFL Total Tackles for Losses - 12 for 40 yards.**

All-Eastern All-Star in 1986, 1987, 1988 and 1992.
CFL All-Star in 1992.

Playoffs

Games Played - 2 with Toronto in 1986; 2 in 1987; 1 in 1988; 2 in 1990 and 1 in 1991. **CFL Total Playoff GP - 8.**

Blocked Kicks - 1 punt with Toronto in 1987.
CFL Total Playoff Blocked Kicks - 1 punt.

Fumble Returns - 1 for 0 yards with Toronto in 1986 and 1 for 0 yards in 1987.
CFL Total Playoff Fumble Returns - 2 for 0 yards.

Interception Returns - 1 for 0 yards with Toronto in 1987.
CFL Total Playoff Interception Returns - 1 for 0 yards.

Quarterback Sacks - 1 with Toronto in 1986. **CFL Total Playoff QB Sacks - 1.**

Defensive Tackles - 4 with Toronto in 1987; 4 in 1988; 2 in 1990 and 2 in 1991.
CFL Total Playoff Defensive Tackles - 12.

Grey Cup

Games Played - 1 with Toronto in 1987 and 1 in 1991. **Total Grey Cup GP - 2.**

Quarterback Sacks - 1 with Toronto in 1987 and 2 in 1991.
Total Grey Cup QB Sacks - 3.

Defensive Tackles - 2 with Toronto in 1987 and 2 in 1991.
Total Grey Cup Defensive Tackles - 4.

HARDY, JOHN
Born: June 11, 1968
Birthplace: Los Angeles, California
Cornerback. 5'10", 175 lbs. Import
Last Amateur Club: University of California
Acquired: Signed as a free agent by the NFL Chicago Bears in April, 1991. Appeared in 2 games prior to being released by Chicago. Spent 1992 WLAF season with Barcelona Dragons. Attended NFL Cleveland Browns' 1992 training camp. Signed as a free agent by the Ottawa Rough Riders in February, 1993. Released by Ottawa in July, 1993 and signed as a free agent by the Toronto Argonauts in October, 1993.

Games Played - 1 with Ottawa and 4 with Toronto in 1993.
CFL Total GP - 5.

Interception Returns - 1 for 0 yards with Toronto in 1993.
CFL Total Interception Returns - 1 for 0 yards.

Tackles - 1 defensive with Ottawa and 15 defensive with Toronto in 1993.
CFL Total Tackles - 16 (16 defensive).

HARDY, ROBERT
Born: September 1, 1967
Birthplace: Gaffney, South Carolina
Running Back, 5'8", 210 lbs. Import
Last Amateur Club: Carson Newman College
Acquired: Signed as a free agent by the NFL Tampa Bay Buccaneers in May, 1991 and released after training camp in 1992. Signed as a free agent by the Edmonton Eskimos in October, 1992. Traded to the Sacramento Gold Miners in March, 1993 in exchange for future considerations. Released by Sacramento in July, 1993.

			Rushing					Fumbles	
	Team	GP	NO	YDS	AVE	LG	TD	NO	LOST
1992	Edm.	3	24	162	6.8	42	0	2	2
1993	Sac.	3	5	12	2.4	4	1	0	0
CFL TOTALS		**6**	**29**	**174**	**4.6**	**42**	**1**	**2**	**2**

Scoring - 1 TD for 6 pts with Sacramento in 1993.
CFL Total Scoring - 1 TD for 6 pts.

Pass Receiving - 3 for 9 yards, 3.0 average, longest 5 yards with Sacramento in 1993.
CFL Total Pass Receiving - 3 for 9 yards, 3.0 average, longest 5 yards.

Tackles - 5 special teams with Edmonton in 1992 and 2 special teams with Sacramento in 1993. **CFL Total Tackles - 7 (7 special teams).**

Playoffs

			Rushing				
	Team	GP	NO	YDS	AVE	LG	TD
1992	Edm.	1	6	9	1.5	5	0
CFL TOTALS		**1**	**6**	**9**	**1.5**	**5**	**0**

HARLE, DARRELL
Born: March 4, 1966
Birthplace: Regina, Saskatchewan
Offensive Guard. 6'2", 270 lbs. Non-import
Last Amateur Club: Eastern Michigan University
Acquired: Selected in the sixth round (42nd overall) by Saskatchewan Roughriders in the 1988 CFL College Draft. Traded to Hamilton Tiger-Cats for defensive lineman Wayne Drinkwalter in July, 1989. Granted free agency status in February, 1993. Signed as a free agent by the Saskatchewan Roughriders in July, 1993. Released by Saskatchewan in July, 1993 and subsequently signed as a free agent by the Toronto Argonauts. Released by Toronto in September, 1993 and signed as a free agent by Hamilton in October, 1993.

Games Played - 16 with Hamilton in 1989; 17 in 1990; 18 in 1991; 12 in 1992 and 8 with Toronto and 5 with Hamilton in 1993.
CFL Total GP - 76.

Fumble Returns - 1 for 0 yards with Hamilton in 1992.
CFL Total Fumble Returns - 1 for 0 yards.

Tackles - 2 defensive with Hamilton in 1990; 4 special teams in 1991 and 2 defensive and 2 special teams in 1992.
CFL Total Tackles - 10 (4 defensive and 6 special teams).

Playoffs

Games Played - 1 with Hamilton in 1989; 2 in 1992 and 2 in 1993.
CFL Total Playoff GP - 5.

Tackles - 2 special teams with Hamilton in 1992 and 2 special teams in 1993.
CFL Total Tackles - 4 (4 special teams).

Grey Cup

Games Played - 1 with Hamilton in 1989. **Total Grey Cup GP - 1.**

HARPER, GLENN

Born: September 12, 1962
Birthplace: Edmonton, Alberta
Punter. 6'0", 173 lbs. Non-import
Last Amateur Club: Washington State University
Acquired: Selected in the fifth round (43rd overall) by the Saskatchewan Roughriders in the 1986 CFL College Draft. Saskatchewan originally acquired the pick from Winnipeg Blue Bombers in return for quarterback Homer Jordan. Released by Saskatchewan and signed as a free agent by the Calgary Stampeders in May, 1986. Granted free agency status in March, 1989. Signed with the San Francisco 49ers (NFL) as a free agent in 1989 and attended training camp. Released and signed as a free agent with Toronto Argonauts in September, 1989. Released by Toronto in October, 1990. Signed as a free agent by Edmonton Eskimos in October, 1991.

		Scoring						Punting					Fumbles		
	Team	GP	TD	C	FG	S	TP	NO	YDS	AVE	LK	S	NO	LOST	OFR
1986	Cal.	18	0	0	0	5	5	156	6487	41.6	83	5	7	6	0
1987ab	Cal.	18	0	0	0	3	3	140	5986	42.8	69	3	5	3	1
1988	Cal.	18	0	0	0	4	4	165	6684	40.5	81	4	2	1	0
1989	Tor.	8	0	0	0	3	3	85	3343	39.3	63	3	1	1	0
1990	Tor.	15	0	0	0	1	1	103	4133	40.1	61	1	1	0	0
1991	Edm.	4	0	0	0	3	3	33	1258	38.1	62	3	1	1	0
1992	Edm.	18	0	x1	0	2	4	130	5261	40.5	74	2	4	2	3
1993b	Edm.	18	0	0	0	7	7	154	6385	41.5	71	7	1	1	0
CFL TOTALS		**117**	**0**	**x1**	**0**	**28**	**30**	**966**	**39537**	**40.9**	**83**	**28**	**22**	**15**	**4**

		Passing							Rushing				
	Team	ATT	COMP	YDS	PCT	INT	LG	TD	NO	YDS	AVE	LG	TD
1986	Cal.	2	2	98	100.0	0	56	1	0	0	0.0	0	0
1987	Cal.	4	3	43	75.0	0	23	0	1	3	3.0	3	0
1988	Cal.	1	0	0	0.0	0	0	0	0	0	0.0	0	0
1989	Tor.	0	0	0	0.0	0	0	0	0	0	0.0	0	0
1990	Tor.	2	1	14	50.0	0	14	0	0	0	0.0	0	0
1991	Edm.	1	1	16	100.0	0	16	0	0	0	0.0	0	0
1992	Edm.	1	0	0	0.0	0	0	0	0	5	0.0	5	0
1993	Edm.	2	2	2	100.0	0	6	1	0	0	0.0	0	0
CFL TOTALS		**13**	**9**	**173**	**69.2**	**0**	**56**	**2**	**1**	**8**	**8.0**	**5**	**0**

Net Punting - 34 for 1096 yards, 32.2 average, with Edmonton in 1991; 132 for 4523 yards, 34.3 average in 1992 and 154 for 5642 yards, 36.6 average in 1993.
CFL Total Net Punting - 320 for 11261 yards, 35.2 average.

Own Punts Recovered - 1 with Calgary in 1987 and 2 in 1988.
CFL Total Own Punts Recovered - 3.

2-Pt. Converts - 1 attempt, 0 made with Calgary in 1987 and 2 attempts, 1 made with Edmonton in 1992. **CFL Total 2-Pt. Converts - 3 attempts, 1 made.**

Fumble Returns - 1 with Calgary in 1987. **CFL Total Fumble Returns - 1.**

Unsuccessful Field Goal Returns - 1 for 15 yards with Calgary in 1987.
CFL Total Unsuccessful Field Goal Returns - 1 for 15 yards.

Tackles - 2 special teams with Edmonton in 1992.
CFL Total Tackles - 2 (2 special teams).

a - Led CFL in punting average.
b - All-Western All-Star.

Playoffs

		Scoring						Punting				
	Team	GP	TD	C	FG	S	TP	NO	YDS	AVE	LK	S
1986	Cal.	1	0	0	0	1	1	7	296	42.3	54	1
1987	Cal.	1	0	0	0	0	0	8	338	42.3	56	0
1989	Tor.	1	0	0	0	0	0	12	429	35.8	50	0
1991	Edm.	1	0	0	0	1	1	7	286	40.9	53	1
1992	Edm.	2	0	0	0	1	1	18	616	34.2	54	1
1993	Edm.	2	0	0	0	1	1	17	608	35.8	51	1
CFL TOTALS		**8**	**0**	**0**	**0**	**4**	**4**	**69**	**2573**	**37.3**	**56**	**4**

Net Punting - 7 for 248 yards, 35.4 average with Edmonton in 1991; 18 for 513 yards, 28.5 average in 1992 and 17 for 478 yards, 28.1 average in 1993.
CFL Total Playoff Net Punting - 42 for 1239 yards, 29.5 average.

Tackles - 1 special teams with Edmonton in 1992.
CFL Total Playoff Tackles - 1 (1 special teams).

Grey Cup

Games Played - 1 with Edmonton in 1993. **Total Grey Cup GP - 1.**

Punting - 6 for 292 yards, 48.7 average, longest 52 yards with Edmonton in 1993.
Total Grey Cup Punting - 6 for 292 yards, 48.7 average, longest 52 yards.

Net Punting - 6 for 276 yards, 46.0 average, with Edmonton in 1993.
Total Grey Cup Net Punting - 6 for 276 yards, 46.0 average.

HARPER, JAMES

Born: September 6, 1966
Birthplace: Jackson, Mississippi
Offensive Guard. 6'2", 285 lbs. Import
Last Amateur Club: Alcorn State University
Acquired: Signed as a free agent by the NFL Minnesota Vikings in 1990. Released by Minnesota. Selected by the San Antonio Riders in the first round (eighth overall) in the 1991 WLAF Positional Draft. Signed as a free agent by the Sacramento Gold Miners in March, 1993.

Games Played - 8 with Sacramento in 1993. **CFL Total GP - 8.**

Own Fumbles Recovered - 1 with Sacramento in 1993. **CFL Total OFR - 1.**

Tackles - 1 defensive with Sacramento in 1993.
CFL Total Tackles - 1 (1 defensive).

HARRIS, ROD

Born: November 14, 1966
Birthplace: Dallas, Texas
Wide Receiver. 5'11", 198 lbs. Import
Last Amateur Club: Texas A & M University
Acquired: Selected in the fourth round (104th overall) by the Houston Oilers in the 1989 NFL Draft. Was released after the pre-season and assigned to New Orleans' developmental squad. Granted unconditional free agency in February, 1990. Signed as a free agent by the NFL Dallas Cowboys in February, 1990. Released by Dallas in November, 1990. Awarded on waivers to the NFL Philadelphia Eagles in December, 1990. Granted unconditional free agency status in February, 1992. Signed as a free agent by the Sacramento Gold Miners in June, 1993.

		Scoring						Pass Receiving				
	Team	GP	TD	C	FG	S	TP	NO	YDS	AVE	LG	TD
1993	Sac.	18	7	0	0	0	42	90	1379	15.3	56	7
CFL TOTALS		**18**	**7**	**0**	**0**	**0**	**42**	**90**	**1379**	**15.3**	**56**	**7**

Punt Returns - 1 for 24 yards with Sacramento in 1993.
CFL Total Punt Returns - 1 for 24 yards.

Kickoff Returns - 1 for 0 yards with Sacramento in 1993.
CFL Total Kickoff Returns - 1 for 0 yards.

Fumbles - 2 and 1 lost with Sacramento in 1993.
CFL Total Fumbles - 2 and 1 lost.

Own Fumbles Recovered - 2 with Sacramento in 1993. **CFL Total OFR - 2.**

Tackles - 1 defensive and 7 special teams with Sacramento in 1993.
CFL Total Tackles - 8 (1 defensive and 7 special teams).

All-Western All-Star in 1993.
CFL All-Star in 1993.

HART, ROY

Born: July 10, 1965
Birthplace: Tifton, Georgia
Defensive Tackle. 6'0", 285 lbs. Import
Last Amateur Club: University of South Carolina
Acquired: Selected in the sixth round (158th overall) by the NFL Seattle Seahawks in the 1988 NFL Draft. Signed by Seattle in June, 1988. Released by Seattle in August, 1990. Selected in the first round (third defensive lineman) by the WLAF London Monarchs in the 1991 WLAF Positional Draft. Signed as a free agent by the NFL Los Angeles Raiders in June, 1991. Granted unconditional free agency in February, 1992. Signed as a free agent by the NFL New York Jets in March, 1992 and was later released during training camp. Signed as a free agent by the Hamilton Tiger-Cats in September, 1992. Released by Hamilton in November, 1993. Signed as a free agent by the Las Vegas Posse in March, 1994.

Games Played - 1 with Hamilton in 1992 and 9 in 1993. **CFL Total GP - 10.**

Quarterback Sacks - 2 for 15 yards with Hamilton in 1993.
CFL Total QB Sacks - 2 for 15 yards.

Tackles - 6 defensive with Hamilton in 1992 and 27 defensive in 1993.
CFL Total Tackles - 33 (33 defensive).

Tackles for Losses - 1 for 3 yards with Hamilton in 1992 and 2 for 3 yards in 1993.
CFL Total Tackles for Losses - 3 for 6 yards.

HASSELBACH, HARALD

Born: September 22, 1967
Birthplace: Amsterdam, Netherlands
Defensive Tackle. 6'4", 260 lbs. Non-import
Last Amateur Club: University of Washington
Acquired: Selected in the fifth round (34th overall) by the Calgary Stampeders in the 1989 CFL College Draft.

Games Played - 3 with Calgary in 1990; 11 in 1991; 18 in 1992 and 18 in 1993.
CFL Total GP - 50.

Interception Returns - 1 for 0 yards with Calgary in 1993.
CFL Total Interception Returns - 1 for 0 yards.

Blocked Kicks - 1 convert with Calgary in 1992 and 1 convert in 1993.
CFL Total Blocked Kicks - 2 (2 converts).

Fumbles - 1 and 0 lost with Calgary in 1993. **CFL Total Fumbles - 1 and 0 lost.**

Fumble Returns - 2 for 0 yards with Calgary in 1992 and 4 for 16 yards, 4.0 average, longest 10 yards in 1993.
CFL Total Fumble Returns - 6 for 16 yards, 2.7 average, longest 10 yards.

HASSELBACH, HARALD

Quarterback Sacks - 3 with Calgary in 1991; 4 for 28 yards lost in 1992 and 7 for 46 yards lost in 1993. **CFL Total QB Sacks - 14.**

Tackles - 7 defensive and 7 special teams with Calgary in 1991; 36 defensive in 1992 and 29 defensive in 1993. **CFL Total Tackles - 79 (72 defensive and 7 special teams).**

Tackles for Losses - 2 for 4 yards with Calgary in 1992 and 2 for 2 yards in 1993. **CFL Total Tackles for Losses - 4 for 6 yards.**

All-Western All-Star in 1993
CFL All-Star in 1993.

Playoffs

Games Played - 1 with Calgary in 1990; 1 in 1991; 1 in 1992 and 2 in 1993. **CFL Total Playoff GP - 5.**

Tackles - 1 defensive with Calgary in 1991; 2 defensive in 1992 and 4 defensive in 1993. **CFL Total Playoff Tackles - 7 (7 defensive).**

Grey Cup

Games Played - 1 with Calgary in 1992. **Total Grey Cup GP - 1.**

Quarterback Sacks - 1 for 7 yards lost with Calgary in 1992. **Total Grey Cup QB Sacks - 1.**

Tackles - 2 defensive with Calgary in 1992. **Total Grey Cup Tackles - 2 (2 defensive).**

HATZIIOANNOU, LEON
Born: March 28, 1965
Birthplace: Toronto, Ontario
Defensive Lineman. 6'2", 265 lbs. Non-import
Last Amateur Club: Simon Fraser University (EVCO)
Acquired: Selected in the third round (22nd overall) by the Ottawa Rough Riders in the 1988 CFL College Draft. Traded to Winnipeg Blue Bombers in October, 1988 for quarterback Roy Dewalt.

Games Played - 5 with Ottawa in 1988; 9 with Winnipeg in 1988; 15 in 1989; 18 in 1990; 18 in 1991; 13 in 1992 and 12 in 1993. **CFL Total GP - 90.**

Fumble Returns - 1 for 0 yards with Ottawa in 1988; 1 for 0 yards with Winnipeg in 1992 and 1 for 0 yards in 1993. **CFL Total Fumble Returns - 3 for 0 yards.**

Quarterback Sacks - 1 with Winnipeg in 1990; 1 in 1991 and 2 for 8 yards lost in 1992. **CFL Total QB Sacks - 4.**

Tackles - 13 defensive with Ottawa in 1988; 3 defensive with Winnipeg in 1988; 11 defensive in 1989; 7 defensive in 1990; 27 defensive and 5 special teams in 1991; 11 defensive and 9 special teams in 1992 and 4 defensive and 12 special teams in 1993.
CFL Total Tackles - 102 (76 defensive and 26 special teams).

Tackles for Losses - 2 for 18 yards with Winnipeg in 1991 and 1 for 1 yard in 1992. **CFL Total Tackles for Losses - 3 for 19 yards.**

Playoffs

Games Played - 2 with Winnipeg in 1988; 2 in 1989; 1 in 1990; 2 in 1991 and 1 in 1993. **CFL Total Playoff GP - 8.**

Tackles - 1 defensive with Winnipeg in 1989; 2 defensive in 1991 and 1 special teams in 1993.
CFL Total Playoff Tackles - 4 (3 defensive and 1 special teams).

Tackles for Losses - 1 for 7 yards with Winnipeg in 1991.
CFL Total Playoff Tackles for Losses - 1 for 7 yards.

Grey Cup

Games Played - 1 with Winnipeg in 1988; 1 in 1990 and 1 in 1993. **Total Grey Cup GP - 3.**

Tackles - 2 defensive with Winnipeg in 1990 and 2 special teams in 1993.
Total Grey Cup Tackles - 4 (2 defensive and 2 special teams).

HAZARD, MANNY
Born: July 22, 1969
Birthplace: Providence, Rhode Island
Slotback. 5'8", 175 lbs. Import
Last Amateur Club: University of Houston
Acquired: Signed as a free agent by the NFL Phoenix Cardinals and was released during their 1991 training camp. Signed as a free agent by the NFL Houston Oilers and was released during their 1992 training camp. Signed as a free agent by the Toronto Argonauts in December, 1992.

		Scoring						Pass Receiving				
	Team	GP	TD	C	FG	S	TP	NO	YDS	AVE	LG	TD
1993	Tor.	14	8	0	0	0	48	61	1033	16.9	61	8
CFL TOTALS		**14**	**8**	**0**	**0**	**0**	**48**	**61**	**1033**	**16.9**	**61**	**8**

Kickoff Returns - 2 for 39 yards, 19.5 average, longest 24 yards with Toronto in 1993. **CFL Total Kickoff Returns - 2 for 39 yards, 19.5 average, longest 24 yards.**

Tackles - 5 defensive and 4 special teams with Toronto in 1993. **CFL Total Tackles - 9 (5 defensive and 4 special teams).**

HENDRICKSON, CRAIG
Born: May 5, 1968
Birthplace: Tucson, Arizona
Tackle. 6'4", 290 lbs. Non-import
Last Amateur Club: University of Minnesota
Acquired: Selected in the third round (21st overall) by the Saskatchewan Roughriders in the 1990 CFL College Draft. Signed by the NFL Buffalo Bills as a free agent in April, 1991. Released by Buffalo in August, 1991. Signed by Saskatchewan in September, 1991. Granted free agency status in February, 1994.

Games Played - 8 with Saskatchewan in 1991; 15 in 1992 and 18 in 1993. **CFL Total GP - 41.**

Tackles - 1 defensive with Saskatchewan in 1992. **CFL Total Tackles - 1 (1 defensive).**

Playoffs

Games Played - 1 with Saskatchewan in 1992 and 1 in 1993. **CFL Total Playoff GP - 2.**

HENDRICKSON, SCOTT
Born: January 25, 1970
Birthplace: Tucson, Arizona
Centre. 6'3", 275 lbs. Non-import
Last Amateur Club: University of Minnesota
Acquired: Selected in the second round (15th overall) by the Saskatchewan Roughriders in the 1992 CFL College Draft. Signed by Saskatchewan in May, 1992.

Games Played - 16 with Saskatchewan in 1992 and 18 in 1993. **CFL Total GP - 34.**

Own Fumbles Recovered - 1 with Saskatchewan in 1993. **CFL Total OFR - 1.**

Tackles - 1 defensive with Saskatchewan in 1992 and 2 defensive in 1993. **CFL Total Tackles - 3 (3 defensive).**

Playoffs

Games Played - 1 with Saskatchewan in 1993. **CFL Total Playoff GP - 1.**

HENNIG, ROGER
Born: October 3, 1966
Birthplace: Penticton, British Columbia
Defensive Back. 6'0", 190 lbs. Non-import
Last Amateur Club: University of British Columbia (CWAA)
Acquired: Selected in the seventh round (49th overall) by the Hamilton Tiger-Cats in the 1991 CFL College Draft. Signed by Hamilton in January, 1992. Granted free agency status in February, 1994. Re-signed by Hamilton in March, 1994.

Games Played - 17 with Hamilton in 1992 and 18 in 1993. **CFL Total GP - 35.**

Rushing - 1 for 6 yards with Hamilton in 1993. **CFL Total Rushing - 1 for 6 yards.**

Fumble Returns - 1 for 3 yards with Hamilton in 1992. **CFL Total Fumble Returns - 1 for 3 yards.**

Quarterback Sacks - 1 for 7 yards lost with Hamilton in 1992. **CFL Total QB Sacks - 1 for 7 yards lost.**

Tackles - 10 defensive and 9 special teams with Hamilton in 1992 and 7 defensive and 12 special teams in 1993.
CFL Total Tackles - 38 (17 defensive and 21 special teams).

Playoffs

Games Played - 2 with Hamilton in 1992 and 2 in 1993. **CFL Total Playoff GP - 4.**

Fumble Returns - 1 for 0 yards with Hamilton in 1993. **CFL Total Playoff Fumble Returns - 1 for 0 yards.**

Tackles - 2 defensive and 2 special teams with Hamilton in 1992 and 1 special teams in 1993.
CFL Total Playoff Tackles - 5 (2 defensive and 3 special teams).

HENRY, MAURICE
Born: March 12, 1967
Birthplace: Starkville, Mississippi
Linebacker. 5'11", 234 lbs. Import
Last Amateur Club: Kansas State University
Acquired: Selected by the San Antonio Riders in the sixth round (38th overall) in the 1992 WLAF Draft. Signed as a free agent by the Ottawa Rough Riders in October, 1993.

Games Played - 1 with Ottawa in 1993. **CFL Total GP - 1.**

Tackles - 5 defensive with Ottawa in 1993.
CFL Total Tackles - 5 (5 defensive).

Playoffs

Games Played - 1 with Ottawa in 1993. **CFL Total Playoff GP - 1.**

Tackles - 2 defensive with Ottawa in 1993.
CFL Total Playoff Tackles - 2 (2 defensive).

HENRY, TOMMY
Born: November 4, 1969
Birthplace: Arcadia, Florida
Cornerback. 6'1", 175 lbs. Import
Last Amateur Club: Florida State University
Acquired: Signed as a free agent by the Sacramento Gold Miners in May, 1993. Released in October, 1993.

Games Played - 9 with Sacramento in 1993. **CFL Total GP - 9.**

Tackles - 12 defensive and 3 special teams with Sacramento in 1993.
CFL Total Tackles - 15 (12 defensive and 3 special teams).

HENRY, WILLIAM
Born: August 31, 1961
Birthplace: Minneapolis, Minnesota
Guard. 6'2", 270 lbs. Non-import
Last Amateur Club: University of British Columbia (WIFL)
Acquired: Selected by Saskatchewan Roughriders in the fifth round (38th overall) of the 1986 CFL College Draft. Traded to Winnipeg Blue Bombers in June, 1987. Released by Winnipeg in July, 1987 and returned to the Richmond Raiders (Jr.) for a year. Signed with Saskatchewan in March, 1988. Traded to Hamilton in August, 1989 for a second round selection in the 1990 CFL College Draft, offensive lineman Chris Gioskos. Released by Hamilton in September, 1990. Signed as a free agent by Calgary Stampeders in January, 1991. Released by Calgary in July, 1992. Signed as a free agent by the B.C. Lions in September, 1992. Traded to the Toronto Argonauts in exchange for a Toronto negotiation list player in June, 1993. Released by Toronto in July, 1993. Signed as a free agent by the Hamilton Tiger-Cats in September, 1993. Released by Hamilton in November, 1993. Signed as a free agent by the Edmonton Eskimos in April, 1994.

Games Played - 18 with Saskatchewan in 1988; 6 in 1989; 12 with Hamilton in 1989; 18 with Calgary in 1991; 1 with B.C. in 1992 and 2 with Toronto and 9 with Hamilton in 1993. **CFL Total GP - 66.**

Own Fumbles Recovered - 3 with Calgary in 1991. **CFL Total OFR - 3.**

Kickoff Returns - 1 for 0 yards with Saskatchewan in 1988.
CFL Total Kickoff Returns - 1 for 0 yards.

Tackles - 1 defensive with Hamilton in 1989 and 1 special teams with Calgary in 1991. **CFL Total Tackles - 2 (1 defensive and 1 special teams).**

Playoffs

Games Played - 1 with Hamilton in 1989; 2 with Calgary in 1991 and 2 with Hamilton in 1993. **CFL Total Playoff GP - 5.**

Tackles - 2 special teams with Hamilton in 1993.
CFL Total Playoff Tackles - 2 (2 special teams).

Grey Cup

Games Played - 1 with Hamilton in 1989 and 1 with Calgary in 1991.
Total Grey Cup GP - 2.

Tackles - 1 defensive with Calgary in 1991.
Total Grey Cup Tackles - 1 (1 defensive).

HILK, BRIAN
Born: April 23, 1969
Birthplace: Pittsburgh, Pennsylvania
Linebacker. 6'1", 230 lbs. Import
Last Amateur Club: University of Akron
Acquired: Signed as a free agent by the Hamilton Tiger-Cats in March, 1991. Released by Hamilton in June, 1992. Signed as a free agent by the Toronto Argonauts in March, 1993. Released by Toronto in August, 1993. Signed as a free agent by the Shreveport Pirates in April, 1994.

Games Played - 7 with Hamilton in 1991 and 1 with Toronto in 1993.
CFL Total GP - 8.

Kickoff Returns - 1 for 0 yards with Hamilton in 1991.
CFL Total Kickoff Returns - 1 for 0 yards.

Fumble Returns - 1 for 0 yards with Hamilton in 1991.
CFL Total Fumble Returns - 1 for 0 yards.

Quarterback Sacks - 1 with Hamilton in 1991. **CFL Total QB Sacks - 1.**

Tackles - 41 defensive and 1 special teams with Hamilton in 1991 and 5 defensive and 2 special teams in 1993.
CFL Total Tackles - 49 (46 defensive and 3 special teams).

Tackles for Losses - 4 for 12 yards with Hamilton in 1991.
CFL Total Tackles for Losses - 4 for 12 yards.

HILL, LONZELL
Born: September 25, 1965
Birthplace: Stockton, California
Wide Receiver. 5'11", 190 lbs. Import
Last Amateur Club: University of Washington
Acquired: Selected in the second round (40th overall) by the NFL New Orleans Saints in the 1987 NFL Draft. Released by New Orleans in 1991. Signed as a free agent by the Ottawa Rough Riders in June, 1992. Released by Ottawa in July, 1992. Signed as a free agent by the Hamilton Tiger-Cats in September, 1992.

		Scoring						Pass Receiving				
	Team	GP	TD	C	FG	S	TP	NO	YDS	AVE	LG	TD
1992	Ham.	7	2	0	0	0	12	23	384	16.7	53	2
1993	Ham.	3	1	0	0	0	6	12	190	15.8	54	1
CFL TOTALS		**10**	**3**	**0**	**0**	**0**	**18**	**35**	**574**	**16.4**	**54**	**3**

		Punt Returns					Rushing				
	Team	NO	YDS	AVE	LG	TD	NO	YDS	AVE	LG	TD
1992	Ham.	4	23	5.8	15	0	1	-5	-5.0	0	0
1993	Ham.	2	7	3.5	5	0	0	0	0.0	0	0
CFL TOTALS		**6**	**30**	**5.0**	**15**	**0**	**1**	**-5**	**-5.0**	**0**	**0**

Tackles - 1 defensive and 1 special teams with Hamilton in 1992 and 1 special teams in 1993.
CFL Total Tackles - 3 (1 defensive and 2 special teams).

Playoffs

			Pass Receiving				
	Team	GP	NO	YDS	AVE	LG	TD
1992	Ham.	2	4	71	17.8	32	0
CFL TOTALS		**2**	**4**	**71**	**17.8**	**32**	**0**

HILL, STEWART
Born: March 16, 1962
Birthplace: Seattle, Washington
Defensive End. 6'1", 230 lbs. Import
Last Amateur Club: University of Washington
Acquired: Signed as a free agent by Edmonton Eskimos for 1984 season. Granted free agency status in February, 1991. Signed as a free agent by the B.C. Lions in May, 1991. Released by B.C. in May, 1993. Signed as a free agent by the Saskatchewan Roughriders in June, 1993.

		Scoring						Pass Receiving				
	Team	GP	TD	C	FG	S	TP	NO	YDS	AVE	LG	TD
1984abcd	Edm.	16	0	0	0	0	0	0	0	0.0	0	0
1985	Edm.	16	0	0	0	0	0	0	0	0.0	0	0
1986a	Edm.	18	3	0	0	0	18	2	28	14.0	24	2
1987	Edm.	17	1	0	0	0	6	1	17	17.0	17	1
1988	Edm.	11	1	0	0	0	6	0	0	0.0	0	0
1989a	Edm.	18	0	0	0	0	0	0	0	0.0	0	0
1990abefg	Edm.	16	0	0	0	0	0	0	0	0.0	0	0
1991a	B.C.	18	1	0	0	0	6	1	5	5.0	5	1
1992	B.C.	16	0	0	0	0	0	0	0	0.0	0	0
1993	Sask.	18	0	0	0	0	0	0	0	0.0	0	0
CFL TOTALS		**164**	**6**	**0**	**0**	**0**	**36**	**4**	**50**	**12.5**	**24**	**4**

		Interception Returns					Fumble Returns					OFR
	Team	NO	YDS	AVE	LG	TD	NO	YDS	AVE	LG	TD	NO
1984	Edm.	0	0	0.0	0	0	0	0	0.0	0	0	0
1985	Edm.	2	24	12.0	18	0	1	0	0.0	0	0	1
1986	Edm.	1	45	45.0	45	1	4	17	4.3	9	0	0
1987	Edm.	0	0	0.0	0	0	0	0	0.0	0	0	0
1988	Edm.	1	11	11.0	11	1	1	0	0.0	0	0	0
1989	Edm.	0	0	0.0	0	0	2	0	0.0	0	0	0
1990	Edm.	1	16	16.0	16	0	2	9	4.5	9	0	0
1991	B.C.	0	0	0.0	0	0	2	0	0.0	0	0	0
1992	B.C.	0	0	0.0	0	0	0	0	0.0	0	0	0
1993	Sask.	0	0	0.0	0	0	0	0	0.0	0	0	0
CFL TOTALS		**5**	**96**	**19.2**	**45**	**2**	**12**	**26**	**2.2**	**9**	**0**	**1**

Quarterback Sacks - 18 with Edmonton in 1984; 8 in 1985; 17 in 1986; 18 in 1987; 11 in 1988; 13 in 1989; 17 in 1990; 8 with B.C. in 1991; 8 for 39 yards lost in 1992 and 8 for 59 yards lost with Saskatchewan in 1993.
CFL Total QB Sacks - 126.

HILL, STEWART

Tackles - 38 defensive with Edmonton in 1987; 13 defensive in 1988; 41 defensive in 1989; 25 defensive in 1990; 47 defensive and 1 special teams with B.C. in 1991; 29 defensive and 1 special teams in 1992 and 36 defensive with Saskatchewan in 1993.
CFL Total Tackles - 231 (229 defensive and 2 special teams).

Tackles for Losses - 10 for 64 yards with B.C. in 1991; 5 for 7 yards in 1992 and 6 for 19 yards with Saskatchewan in 1993.
CFL Total Tackles for Losses - 21 for 90 yards.

a - All-Western All-Star
b - CFL All-Star
c - Winner Jackie Parker Trophy as Outstanding Rookie in Western Division
d - Schenley Award Runner-up Most Outstanding Rookie
e - Winner Norm Fieldgate Trophy as Outstanding Defensive Player in Western Division
f - CFL Most Outstanding Defensive Player Runner-up
g - Led CFL in Quarterback Sacks

Playoffs

			Fumble Returns					Interception Returns				
	Team	GP	NO	YDS	AVE	LG	TD	NO	YDS	AVE	LG	TD
1984	Edm.	1	0	0	0.0	0	0	0	0	0.0	0	0
1985	Edm.	1	1	0	0.0	0	0	0	0	0.0	0	0
1986	Edm.	2	1	3	3.0	3	0	1	3	3.0	3	0
1987	Edm.	2	0	0	0.0	0	0	0	0	0.0	0	0
1988	Edm.	1	0	0	0.0	0	0	0	0	0.0	0	0
1989	Edm.	1	0	0	0.0	0	0	1	8	8.0	8	0
1991	B.C.	1	1	0	0.0	0	0	0	0	0.0	0	0
1993	Sask.	1	0	0	0.0	0	0	0	0	0.0	0	0
CFL TOTALS		**10**	**3**	**3**	**1.0**	**3**	**0**	**2**	**11**	**5.5**	**8**	**0**

Quarterback Sacks - 1 with Edmonton in 1986; 4 in 1987 and 2 with B.C. in 1991.
CFL Total Playoff QB Sacks - 7.

Defensive Tackles - 4 with Edmonton in 1987; 5 in 1988; 4 in 1989; 3 in 1991 and 7 with Saskatchewan in 1993.
CFL Total Playoff Defensive Tackles - 23.

Tackles for Losses - 1 for 1 yard with Saskatchewan in 1993.
CFL Total Playoff Tackles for Losses - 1 for 1 yard.

Grey Cup

Games Played - 1 with Edmonton in 1986 and 1 in 1987. **Total Grey Cup GP - 2.**

Quarterback Sacks - 1 with Edmonton in 1986 and 3 in 1987.
Total Grey Cup QB Sacks - 4.

HINCHCLIFF, WILLIE
Born: September 13, 1968
Birthplace: Trenton, New Jersey
Wide Receiver. 5'11", 195 lbs. Non-import
Last Amateur Club: Auckland Institute (New Zealand)
Acquired: Signed as a free agent by the NFL Los Angeles Raiders in March, 1992 and released after training camp. Signed as a free agent by the B.C. Lions in October, 1992. Released by B.C. in July, 1993 and was subsequently re-signed in October and released again in November.

Games Played - 2 with B.C. in 1992 and 1 in 1993. **CFL Total GP - 3.**

Kickoff Returns - 4 for 65 yards, 16.3 average, longest 24 yards with B.C. in 1992.
CFL Total Kickoff Returns - 4 for 65 yards, 16.3 average, longest 24 yards.

Fumbles - 1 and 0 lost with B.C. in 1992. **CFL Total Fumbles - 1 and 0 lost.**

Fumble Returns - 1 for 2 yards with B.C. in 1992.
CFL Total Fumble Returns - 1 for 2 yards.

HINTON, PATRICK
Born: November 2, 1968
Birthplace: Atlanta, Georgia
Linebacker. 6'2", 230 lbs. Import
Last Amateur Club: University of South Carolina
Acquired: Selected in the 15th round (158th overall) by the San Antonio Riders in the 1992 WLAF Draft. Signed as a free agent by the Winnipeg Blue Bombers in April, 1993. Released by Winnipeg in September, 1993.

Games Played - 4 with Winnipeg in 1993. **CFL Total GP - 4.**

Fumble Returns - 1 for 0 yards with Winnipeg in 1993.
CFL Total Fumble Returns - 1 for 0 yards.

Quarterback Sacks - 1 for 4 yards lost with Winnipeg in 1993.
CFL Total QB Sacks - 1 for 4 yards lost.

Tackles - 11 defensive and 2 special teams with Winnipeg in 1993.
CFL Total Tackles - 13 (11 defensive and 2 special teams).

HOCKING, DOUG
Born: October 16, 1969
Birthplace: Sarnia, Ontario
Linebacker. 6'1", 230 lbs. Non-import
Last Amateur Club: Surrey Rams (BCJFL)
Acquired: Signed as a free agent by the B.C. Lions in July, 1991.

Games Played - 17 with B.C. in 1991; 13 in 1992 and 18 in 1993. **CFL Total GP - 48.**

Own Fumbles Recovered - 1 with B.C. in 1991. **CFL Total OFR - 1.**

Own Kickoffs Recovered - 1 for 2 yards with B.C. in 1993.
CFL Total OKR - 1 for 2 yards.

Tackles - 9 defensive and 9 special teams with B.C. in 1991; 27 defensive and 9 special teams in 1992 and 7 defensive and 17 special teams in 1993.
CFL Total Tackles - 78 (43 defensive and 35 special teams).

Tackles for Losses - 1 for 2 yards with B.C. in 1991 and 1 for 5 yards in 1993.
CFL Total Tackles for Losses - 2 for 7 yards.

Playoffs

Games Played - 1 with B.C. in 1991 and 1 in 1993. **CFL Total Playoff GP - 2.**

Interception Returns - 1 for 12 yards with B.C. in 1991.
CFL Total Playoff Interception Returns - 1 for 12 yards.

Tackles - 2 special teams with B.C. in 1993.
CFL Total Playoff Tackles - 2 (2 special teams).

HOLLAND, ROBERT
Born: July 18, 1965
Birthplace: Sacramento, California
Cornerback. 5'10", 185 lbs. Import
Last Amateur Club: Sacramento State University
Acquired: Selected by the Birmingham Fire in the fourth round (48th overall) in the 1991 WLAF Positional Draft. Signed as a free agent by the Edmonton Eskimos in August, 1993.

			Interception Returns					Punt Returns				
	Team	GP	NO	YDS	AVE	LG	TD	NO	YDS	AVE	LG	TD
1993	Edm.	9	5	56	11.2	34	1	5	41	8.2	13	0
CFL TOTALS		**9**	**5**	**56**	**11.2**	**34**	**1**	**5**	**41**	**8.2**	**13**	**0**

Scoring - 1 TD for 6 points with Edmonton in 1993.
CFL Total Scoring - 1 TD for 6 points.

Tackles - 31 defensive with Edmonton in 1993.
CFL Total Tackles - 31 (31 defensive).

Playoffs

			Punt Returns				
	Team	GP	NO	YDS	AVE	LG	TD
1993	Edm.	2	4	13	3.3	8	0
CFL TOTALS		**2**	**4**	**13**	**3.3**	**8**	**0**

Tackles - 8 defensive with Edmonton in 1993.
CFL Total Playoff Tackles - 8 (8 defensive).

Grey Cup

Games Played - 1 with Edmonton in 1993. **Total Grey Cup GP - 1.**

Tackles - 3 defensive with Edmonton in 1993.
Total Grey Cup Tackles - 3 (3 defensive).

HOOD, JOHN
Born: January 7, 1968
Birthplace: Pontiac, Michigan
Running Back. 6'0", 200 lbs. Import
Last Amateur Club: Central Michigan University
Acquired: Signed as a free agent by the Hamilton Tiger-Cats in May, 1992. Released by Hamilton in August, 1993

			Scoring					Rushing				
	Team	GP	TD	C	FG	S	TP	NO	YDS	AVE	LG	TD
1992	Ham.	5	2	0	0	0	12	70	283	4.0	55	2
1993	Ham.	4	1	0	0	0	6	41	146	3.6	14	1
CFL TOTALS		**9**	**3**	**0**	**0**	**0**	**18**	**111**	**429**	**3.9**	**55**	**3**

		Pass Receiving					Fumbles	
	Team	NO	YDS	AVE	LG	TD	NO	LOST
1992	Ham.	14	151	10.8	44	0	1	1
1993	Ham.	3	21	7.0	13	0	1	0
CFL TOTALS		**17**	**172**	**10.1**	**44**	**0**	**2**	**1**

HOOD, JOHN

Passing - 1 attempt, 0 complete, 1 interception with Hamilton in 1992. **CFL Total Passing - 1 attempt, 0 complete, 1 interception.**

Punt Returns - 1 for 9 yards with Hamilton in 1992. **CFL Total Punt Returns - 1 for 9 yards.**

Kickoff Returns - 2 for 33 yards, 16.5 average, longest 24 yards with Hamilton in 1992. **CFL Total Kickoff Returns - 2 for 33 yards, 16.5 average, longest 24 yards.**

Tackles - 1 defensive with Hamilton in 1992 and 3 defensive and 2 special teams in 1993. **CFL Total Tackles - 6 (4 defensive and 2 special teams).**

HOULDER, MARK

Born: August 22, 1967
Birthplace: San Fernando, Trinidad
Linebacker. 6'1", 230 lbs. Non-import
Last Amateur Club: York University
Acquired: Signed as a free agent by the Toronto Argonauts in November, 1993.

Games Played - 1 with Toronto in 1993. **CFL Total GP - 1.**

HUDSON, WARREN

Born: May 25, 1962
Birthplace: Scarborough, Ontario
Fullback. 6'2", 225 lbs. Non-import
Last Amateur Club: Oshawa Hawkeyes (OJFC)
Acquired: Signed as a free agent by the Toronto Argonauts in July, 1985. Traded to the Winnipeg Blue Bombers in July, 1990 in exchange for defensive back Andrew Thomas and a fifth round draft choice, (40th overall), wide receiver Matt Nealon, in the 1991 CFL College Draft. Traded to Toronto in exchange for running back Chris Johnstone in June, 1993.

		Scoring						Rushing				
	Team	GP	TD	C	FG	S	TP	NO	YDS	AVE	LG	TD
1985	Tor.	7	0	0	0	0	0	0	0	0.0	0	0
1986	Tor.	18	0	0	0	0	0	8	47	5.9	28	0
1987	Tor.	15	1	0	0	0	6	18	74	4.1	11	1
1988	Tor.	18	3	0	0	0	18	37	164	4.4	21	1
1989	Tor.	18	0	0	0	0	0	30	157	5.2	22	0
1990a	Wpg.	16	5	x1	0	0	32	55	270	4.9	21	4
1991	Wpg.	18	2	0	0	0	12	35	178	5.1	18	0
1992a	Wpg.	16	8	0	0	0	48	60	397	6.6	38	6
1993	Tor.	18	4	0	0	0	24	53	220	4.2	28	3
CFL TOTALS		**144**	**23**	**x1**	**0**	**0**	**140**	**296**	**1507**	**5.1**	**38**	**15**

		Pass Receiving					Kickoff Returns				
	Team	NO	YDS	AVE	LG	TD	NO	YDS	AVE	LG	TD
1985	Tor.	0	0	0.0	0	0	2	20	10.0	20	0
1986	Tor.	12	108	9.0	18	0	3	56	18.7	27	0
1987	Tor.	7	66	9.4	21	0	0	0	0.0	0	0
1988	Tor.	31	283	9.1	42	2	1	17	17.0	17	0
1989	Tor.	22	179	8.1	32	0	4	13	3.3	16	0
1990	Wpg.	54	490	9.1	29	1	1	0	0.0	0	0
1991	Wpg.	47	537	11.4	66	2	1	19	19.0	19	0
1992	Wpg.	14	109	7.8	17	2	0	0	0.0	0	0
1993	Tor.	17	179	10.5	24	1	0	0	0.0	0	0
CFL TOTALS		**204**	**1951**	**9.6**	**66**	**8**	**12**	**125**	**10.4**	**27**	**0**

		Fumbles			Fumble Returns				
	Team	NO	LOST	OFR	NO	YDS	AVE	LG	TD
1985	Tor.	0	0	0	0	0	0.0	0	0
1986	Tor.	4	3	0	1	0	0.0	0	0
1987	Tor.	2	2	0	0	0	0.0	0	0
1988	Tor.	3	2	0	1	0	0.0	0	0
1989	Tor.	2	1	1	1	0	0.0	0	0
1990	Wpg.	1	0	1	1	0	0.0	0	0
1991	Wpg.	2	1	1	0	0	0.0	0	0
1992	Wpg.	0	0	1	0	0	0.0	0	0
1993	Tor.	4	2	2	2	0	0.0	0	0
CFL TOTALS		**18**	**11**	**6**	**6**	**0**	**0.0**	**0**	**0**

Passing - 1 attempt, 0 complete with Winnipeg in 1990. **CFL Total Passing - 1 attempt, 0 complete.**

Quarterback Sacks - 1 with Toronto in 1987. **CFL Total QB Sacks - 1.**

Tackles - 3 defensive with Toronto in 1987; 4 defensive in 1988; 7 defensive in 1989; 4 defensive with Winnipeg in 1990; 7 defensive and 1 special teams in 1991; 1 special teams in 1992 and 1 defensive and 1 special teams with Toronto in 1993.
CFL Total Tackles - 29 (26 defensive and 3 special teams).

a - All-Eastern All-Star

Playoffs

			Rushing					Pass Receiving				
	Team	GP	NO	YDS	AVE	LG	TD	NO	YDS	AVE	LG	TD
1986	Tor.	1	2	1	0.5	1	0	1	11	11.0	11	0
1987	Tor.	2	3	22	7.3	17	0	2	10	5.0	9	0
1988	Tor.	1	0	0	0.0	0	0	2	13	6.5	14	0
1989	Tor.	1	2	3	1.5	2	0	3	13	4.3	9	0
1990	Wpg.	1	4	3	0.8	6	0	1	8	8.0	8	0
1991	Wpg.	2	2	8	4.0	6	0	5	44	8.8	18	0
1992	Wpg.	1	5	25	5.0	7	1	1	2	2.0	2	0
CFL TOTALS		**9**	**18**	**62**	**3.4**	**17**	**1**	**15**	**101**	**6.7**	**18**	**0**

Fumbles - 1 and 1 lost with Winnipeg in 1990. **CFL Total Playoff Fumbles - 1 and 1 lost.**

Defensive Tackles - 1 with Winnipeg in 1990 and 1 in 1991. **CFL Total Playoff Defensive Tackles - 2.**

Grey Cup

			Rushing					Pass Receiving				
	Team	GP	NO	YDS	AVE	LG	TD	NO	YDS	AVE	LG	TD
1987	Tor.	1	5	25	5.0	8	0	0	0	0.0	0	0
1990	Wpg.	1	4	7	1.8	2	1	4	66	16.5	23	1
1992	Wpg.	1	0	0	0.0	0	0	1	10	10.0	10	0
CFL TOTALS		**3**	**9**	**32**	**3.6**	**8**	**1**	**5**	**76**	**15.2**	**23**	**1**

Grey Cup Outstanding Canadian - Dick Suderman Trophy in 1990.

HUGHES, DARREN

Born: June 3, 1967
Birthplace: Linwood, California
Defensive Back. 6'1", 180 lbs. Import
Last Amateur Club: Carson-Newman University
Acquired: Signed as a free agent by the Calgary Stampeders in May, 1993. Was subsequently released by Calgary in July, 1993 and signed as a free agent by the Toronto Argonauts later that month.

			Interception Returns					Fumble Returns				
	Team	GP	NO	YDS	AVE	LG	TD	NO	YDS	AVE	LG	TD
1993	Tor.	11	3	19	6.3	16	0	1	0	0.0	0	0
CFL TOTALS		**11**	**3**	**19**	**6.3**	**16**	**0**	**1**	**0**	**0.0**	**0**	**0**

Tackles - 40 defensive and 8 special teams with Toronto in 1993. **CFL Total Tackles - 48 (40 defensive and 8 special teams).**

HUMPHERY, BOBBY

Born: August 23, 1961
Birthplace: Lubbock, Texas
Cornerback. 5'10", 180 lbs. Import
Last Amateur Club: New Mexico State University
Acquired: Selected by the New York Jets in the ninth round (247th overall) in the 1983 NFL Draft. Traded by the Jets to the NFL Los Angeles Rams in exchange for a fifth round pick in the 1990 NFL Draft. Granted unconditional free agency in February, 1991. Signed as a free agent by the NFL San Diego Chargers in March, 1991. Released by San Diego prior to the start of the 1991 sesaon. Selected by the San Antonio Riders in the eleventh round (115th overall) in the 1992 WLAF Draft. Signed as a free agent by the Sacramento Gold Miners in February, 1993.

			Interception Returns					Fumble Returns				
	Team	GP	NO	YDS	AVE	LG	TD	NO	YDS	AVE	LG	TD
1993	Sac.	18	5	54	10.5	30	0	2	0	0.0	0	0
CFL TOTALS		**18**	**5**	**54**	**10.5**	**30**	**0**	**2**	**0**	**0.0**	**0**	**0**

Tackles - 37 defensive and 2 special teams with Sacramento in 1993. **CFL Total Tackles - 39 (37 defensive and 2 special teams).**

Tackles For Losses - 1 for 2 yards with Sacramento in 1993. **CFL Total Tackles For Losses - 1 for 2 yards.**

HUNTER, DANIEL

Born: September 1, 1962
Birthplace: Arkadelphia, Arkansas
Defensive Back. 5'11", 185 lbs. Import
Last Amateur Club: Henderson State University
Acquired: Signed as a free agent by the Los Angeles Express (USFL) in January, 1984. Released in February, 1984 and signed as a free agent by the Dallas Cowboys (NFL) in May, 1984. Released by Dallas in August, 1984. Signed as a free agent by the Denver Broncos (NFL) in February, 1985 and was released in November, 1986. Signed as a free agent by the San Diego Chargers (NFL) in November, 1986. Released by San Diego before 1988 season. Signed as a free agent by the Ottawa Rough Riders in August, 1989. Claimed off waivers by the B.C. Lions in July, 1993. Released by B.C. in November, 1993.

Games Played - 11 with Ottawa in 1989; 9 in 1990; 18 in 1991; 17 in 1992 and 1 with Ottawa and 4 with B.C. in 1993. **CFL Total GP - 60.**

Punt Returns - 1 for 3 yards with Ottawa in 1990. **CFL Total Punt Returns - 1 for 3 yards.**

Kickoff Returns - 3 for 17 yards, 5.7 average, longest 9 yards with Ottawa in 1992. **CFL Total Kickoff Returns - 3 for 17 yards, 5.7 average, longest 9 yards.**

Interception Returns - 2 for 71 yards, 35.5 average, longest 41 yards with Ottawa in 1989; 6 for 13 yards, 2.2 average, longest 10 yards in 1990; 3 for 47 yards, 15.7 average, longest 56 yards in 1991; 3 for 8 yards, 2.7 average, longest 8 yards in 1992 and 1 for 0 yards with Ottawa in 1993. **CFL Total Interception Returns - 15 for 139 yards, 9.3 average, longest 56 yards.**

Own Fumbles Recovered - 1 with Ottawa in 1990 and 1 in 1992. **CFL Total OFR - 2.**

HUNTER, DANIEL

Pass Receiving - 1 for 28 yards with Ottawa in 1991.
CFL Total Pass Receiving - 1 for 28 yards.

Fumble Returns - 3 for 21 yards, 7.0 average, longest 21 yards with Ottawa in 1989.
CFL Total Fumble Returns - 3 for 21 yards, 7.0 average, longest 21 yards.

Fumbles - 1 and 0 lost with Ottawa in 1991 and 1 and 1 lost in 1992.
CFL Total Fumbles - 2 and 1 lost.

Quarterback Sacks - 3 with Ottawa in 1991. **CFL Total QB Sacks - 3.**

Tackles - 44 defensive with Ottawa in 1989; 31 defensive in 1990; 44 defensive and 27 special teams in 1991; 50 defensive and 1 special teams in 1992 and 4 defensive with Ottawa and 9 defensive and 5 special teams with B.C. in 1993. **CFL Total Tackles - 215 (182 defensive and 33 special teams).**

Tackles for Losses - 1 for 2 yards with Ottawa in 1991; 1 for 3 yards in 1992 and 1 for 1 yard with B.C. in 1993. **CFL Total Tackles for Losses - 3 for 6 yards.**

Playoffs

Games Played - 1 with Ottawa in 1990; 1 in 1991 and 1 in 1992.
CFL Total Playoff GP - 3.

Interception Returns - 1 for 2 yards with Ottawa in 1990 and 1 for 13 yards in 1991. **CFL Total Playoff Interception Returns - 2 for 15 yards, 7.5 average, longest 13 yards.**

Own Kickoffs Recovered - 1 for 0 yards with Ottawa in 1991.
CFL Total Playoff Own Kickoffs Recovered - 1 for 0 yards.

Defensive Tackles - 3 with Ottawa in 1990; 2 in 1991 and 1 in 1992.
CFL Total Playoff Defensive Tackles - 6.

HUNTER, MALVIN

Born: November 20, 1969
Birthplace: Harvey, Illinois
Linebacker. 6'3", 230 lbs. Import
Last Amateur Club: University of Wisconsin
Acquired: Selected by the San Antonio Riders in the tenth round (104th overall) of the 1992 WLAF Draft. Signed as a free agent by the Edmonton Eskimos in December, 1992.

Games Played - 18 with Edmonton in 1993. **CFL Total GP - 18.**

Interception Returns - 1 for 9 yards with Edmonton in 1993.
CFL Total Interception Returns - 1 for 9 yards.

Fumble Returns - 1 for 0 yards with Edmonton in 1993.
CFL Total Fumble Returns - 1 for 0 yards.

Quarterback Sacks - 6 for 34 yards lost with Edmonton in 1993.
CFL Total QB Sacks - 6 for 34 yards lost.

Tackles - 49 defensive and 11 special teams with Edmonton in 1993.
CFL Total Tackles - 60 (49 defensive and 11 special teams).

Tackles For Losses - 3 for 8 yards with Edmonton in 1993.
CFL Total Tackles For Losses- 3 for 8 yards.

Playoffs

Games Played - 2 with Edmonton in 1993. **CFL Total Playoff GP - 2.**

Tackles - 2 defensive and 4 special teams with Edmonton in 1993.
CFL Total Playoff Tackles - 6 (2 defensive and 4 special teams).

Grey Cup

Games Played - 1 with Edmonton in 1993. **Total Grey Cup GP - 1.**

Tackles - 1 defensive with Edmonton in 1993.
Total Grey Cup Tackles - 1 (1 defensive).

HUTCHINGS, BRIAN

Born: December 22, 1965
Birthplace: Hamilton, Ontario
Offensive Lineman. 6'5", 265 lbs. Non-import
Last Amateur Club: St. Mary's University (AUAA)
Acquired: Signed as a free agent in May, 1988 by the Hamilton Tiger-Cats. Claimed by the Ottawa Rough Riders on waivers in October, 1989. Traded by Ottawa to Calgary Stampeders in May, 1990 to re-acquire Ottawa's third round draft choice in the 1991 CFL College Draft. Placed on Calgary's suspended list for the 1991 season. Traded to Hamilton in April, 1992 in exchange for future considerations. Released by Hamilton in June, 1992. Signed as a free agent by the Toronto Argonauts in August, 1992. Released by Toronto in December, 1992. Re-signed by Toronto in March, 1993. Released by Toronto in August, 1993.

Games Played - 9 with Hamilton in 1989; 4 with Ottawa in 1989; 9 with Calgary in 1990; 4 with Toronto in 1992 and 2 in 1993. **CFL Total GP - 28.**

Own Fumbles Recovered - 1 with Hamilton in 1989. **CFL Total OFR - 1.**

Defensive Tackles - 1 with Calgary in 1990. **CFL Total Defensive Tackles - 1.**

ILESIC, HANK

Born, September 7, 1959
Birthplace, Edmonton, Alberta
Kicker. 6'1", 210 lbs. Non-import
Last Amateur Club: St. Joseph's High School (Edmonton)
Acquired: Signed by Edmonton Eskimos in 1977. Contract was purchased by the Toronto Argonauts in May, 1983. Released by Toronto in September, 1989 and signed as a free agent by the NFL San Diego Chargers later that month. Granted unconditional free agency in February, 1990 and signed as a free agent by the NFL Los Angeles Rams in March, 1990. Released after training camp and signed as a free agent by Toronto in October, 1990. Released by Toronto in March, 1994.

		Scoring						Punting				
	Team	GP	TD	C	FG	S	TP	NO	YDS	AVE	LK	S
1977	Edm.	10	0	0	0	3	3	77	3469	45.1	87	3
1978abcd	Edm.	16	0	0	0	9	9	132	6240	47.3	87	9
1979cd	Edm.	16	0	1	0	8	9	119	5610	47.1	76	8
1980acd	Edm.	16	0	0	0	7	7	120	5466	45.6	71	7
1981cd	Edm.	16	0	0	0	7	7	115	5252	45.7	88	7
1982	Edm.	14	0	0	0	7	7	115	5297	46.1	81	7
1983e	Tor.	16	0	40	26	30	148	137	6094	44.5	90	11
1984	Tor.	16	0	44	30	25	159	140	6192	44.2	71	8
1985	Tor.	16	0	13	3	24	46	164	7181	43.8	83	17
1986abdfg	Tor.	18	0	0	0	24	24	165	8004	48.5	88	22
1987df	Tor.	18	0	0	0	11	11	147	6268	42.6	71	11
1988a	Tor.	18	0	0	0	10	10	142	6246	44.0	77	9
1989	Tor.	10	0	0	0	6	6	68	2894	42.6	62	6
1990	Tor.	3	0	0	0	0	0	20	784	39.2	52	0
1991adf	Tor.	17	0	0	0	5	5	109	4844	44.4	77	4
1992adf	Tor.	17	0	0	0	5	5	131	5891	45.0	81	5
1993	Tor.	11	0	0	0	2	2	89	3672	41.3	66	2
CFL TOTALS		**248**	**0**	**98**	**59**	**183**	**458**	**1990**	**89404**	**44.9**	**90**	**136**

		Field Goals					Field Goal Attempts				
	Team	T	G	YDS	AVE	LK	NO	YDS	AVE	LK	S
1977	Edm.	0	0	0	0.0	0	0	0	0.0	0	0
1978	Edm.	0	0	0	0.0	0	0	0	0.0	0	0
1979	Edm.	0	0	0	0.0	0	0	0	0.0	0	0
1980	Edm.	0	0	0	0.0	0	0	0	0.0	0	0
1981	Edm.	0	0	0	0.0	0	0	0	0.0	0	0
1982	Edm.	0	0	0	0.0	0	0	0	0.0	0	0
1983	Tor.	39	26	726	27.9	48	13	635	48.8	64	10
1984	Tor.	46	30	931	31.0	53	16	655	40.9	56	10
1985	Tor.	8	3	98	32.7	44	5	210	42.0	48	4
1986	Tor.	0	0	0	0.0	0	0	0	0.0	0	0
1987	Tor.	0	0	0	0.0	0	0	0	0.0	0	0
1988	Tor.	0	0	0	0.0	0	0	0	0.0	0	0
1989	Tor.	0	0	0	0.0	0	0	0	0.0	0	0
1990	Tor.	0	0	0	0.0	0	0	0	0.0	0	0
1991	Tor.	0	0	0	0.0	0	0	0	0.0	0	0
1992	Tor.	0	0	0	0.0	0	0	0	0.0	0	0
1993	Tor.	0	0	0	0.0	0	0	0	0.0	0	0
CFL TOTALS		**93**	**59**	**1755**	**29.7**	**53**	**34**	**1500**	**44.1**	**64**	**24**

		Kickoffs					Rushing				
	Team	NO	YDS	AVE	LK	S	NO	YDS	AVE	LG	TD
1977	Edm.	0	0	0.0	0	0	0	0	0.0	0	0
1978	Edm.	1	55	55.0	55	0	0	0	0.0	0	0
1979	Edm.	2	129	64.5	67	0	0	0	0.0	0	0
1980	Edm.	0	0	0.0	0	0	2	28	14.0	19	0
1981	Edm.	0	0	0.0	0	0	0	0	0.0	0	0
1982	Edm.	0	0	0.0	0	0	0	0	0.0	0	0
1983	Tor.	68	4269	62.8	90	9	2	33	16.5	21	0
1984	Tor.	69	4602	66.7	90	7	2	19	9.5	14	0
1985	Tor.	45	2705	60.1	90	3	0	0	0.0	0	0
1986	Tor.	47	3106	66.1	95	2	0	0	0.0	0	0
1987	Tor.	14	853	60.9	74	0	2	-5	-2.5	-8	0
1988	Tor.	87	5216	60.0	95	1	0	0	0.0	0	0
1989	Tor.	19	1163	61.2	75	0	0	0	0.0	0	0
1990	Tor.	14	925	66.1	80	0	0	0	0.0	0	0
1991	Tor.	64	3891	60.8	78	1	0	0	0.0	0	0
1992	Tor.	61	3655	59.9	70	0	0	0	0.0	0	0
1993	Tor.	23	1401	60.9	95	0	0	0	0.0	0	0
CFL TOTALS		**514**	**31970**	**62.2**	**95**	**23**	**8**	**75**	**9.4**	**21**	**0**

		Passing							Converts		
	Team	ATT	COMP	YDS	PCT	INT	LG	TD	T	G	PCT
1977	Edm.	1	1	14	100.0	0	14	0	0	0	0.0
1978	Edm.	2	2	26	100.0	0	28	0	0	0	0.0
1979	Edm.	1	1	9	100.0	0	9	0	2	1	50.0
1980	Edm.	1	1	11	100.0	0	11	0	0	0	0.0
1981	Edm.	0	0	0	0.0	0	0	0	0	0	0.0
1982	Edm.	0	0	0	0.0	0	0	0	0	0	0.0
1983	Tor.	1	0	0	0.0	0	0	0	41	40	97.5
1984	Tor.	0	0	0	0.0	0	0	0	46	44	95.6
1985	Tor.	1	1	19	100.0	0	19	0	14	13	92.8
1986	Tor.	0	0	0	0.0	0	0	0	0	0	0.0
1987	Tor.	1	0	0	0.0	0	0	0	0	0	0.0
1988	Tor.	0	0	0	0.0	0	0	0	0	0	0.0
1989	Tor.	0	0	0	0.0	0	0	0	0	0	0.0
1990	Tor.	1	1	28	100.0	0	28	0	0	0	0.0
1991	Tor.	0	0	0	0.0	0	0	0	0	0	0.0
1992	Tor.	0	0	0	0.0	0	0	0	0	0	0.0
1993	Tor.	0	0	0	0.0	0	0	0	0	0	0.0
CFL TOTALS		**9**	**7**	**107**	**77.8**	**0**	**28**	**0**	**103**	**98**	**95.1**

ILESIC, HANK

Punt Returns - 1 for 4 yards with Edmonton in 1979; 2 for 31 yards, 15.5 average, longest 19 yards in 1980 and 1 for 20 yards in 1981.
CFL Total Punt Returns - 4 for 55 yards, 13.8 average, longest 20 yards.

Kickoff Returns - 1 for 0 yards with Edmonton in 1981.
CFL Total Kickoff Returns - 1 for 0 yards.

Net Punting - 110 for 3787 yards, 34.4 average, with Toronto in 1991; 132 for 4649 yards, 35.2 average in 1992 and 89 for 3025 yards, 34.0 average in 1993. **CFL Total Net Punting - 331 for 11461 yards, 34.6 average.**

Fumbles - 1 and 1 lost with Edmonton in 1977; 1 and 1 lost in 1981; 2 and 2 lost with Toronto in 1983; 1 and 1 lost in 1984; 2 and 2 lost in 1987; 2 and 2 lost in 1988 and 1 and 1 lost in 1992. **CFL Total Fumbles - 10 and 10 lost.**

Own Fumbles Recovered - 1 with Toronto in 1987. **CFL Total OFR - 1.**

Tackles - 6 special teams with Toronto in 1991; 2 special teams in 1992 and 1 special teams in 1993.
CFL Total Tackles - 9 (9 special teams).

a - Led CFL in punting average.
b - Led CFL in punting yardage.
c - All-Western All-Star Punter.
d - CFL All-Star Punter.
e - Set CFL record for most singles from kickoffs in one season.
f - All-Eastern All-Star.
g - Set single season records for punts and punting yards (the records for most punts and most punting yards in a season have since been surpassed).

Playoffs

		Scoring						Punting				
	Team	GP	TD	C	FG	S	TP	NO	YDS	AVE	LK	S
1977	Edm.	1	0	0	0	0	0	6	234	39.0	49	0
1978	Edm.	1	0	0	0	0	0	9	396	44.0	65	0
1979	Edm.	1	0	0	0	1	1	14	576	41.1	59	1
1980	Edm.	1	0	0	0	0	0	7	308	44.0	57	0
1981	Edm.	1	0	0	0	0	0	9	383	42.6	52	0
1982	Edm.	1	0	0	0	0	0	11	431	39.2	62	0
1983	Tor.	1	0	5	1	3	11	6	308	51.3	77	0
1984	Tor.	1	0	1	1	3	7	17	733	43.1	60	1
1986	Tor.	2	0	0	0	2	2	14	603	43.1	72	2
1987	Tor.	2	0	0	0	5	5	19	876	46.1	73	5
1988	Tor.	1	0	0	0	1	0	11	428	38.9	58	1
1990	Tor.	2	0	0	0	0	0	15	614	40.9	55	0
1991	Tor.	1	0	0	0	2	2	12	499	41.6	65	1
CFL TOTALS		**16**	**0**	**6**	**2**	**17**	**28**	**150**	**6389**	**42.6**	**77**	**11**

		Kickoffs				
	Team	NO	YDS	AVE	LK	S
1977	Edm.	0	0	0.0	0	0
1978	Edm.	0	0	0.0	0	0
1979	Edm.	1	0	0.0	0	0
1980	Edm.	0	0	0.0	0	0
1981	Edm.	0	0	0.0	0	0
1982	Edm.	0	0	0.0	0	0
1983	Tor.	7	422	60.3	81	2
1984	Tor.	4	291	72.8	90	0
1986	Tor.	4	255	63.7	70	0
1987	Tor.	7	398	56.9	67	0
1988	Tor.	1	71	71.0	71	0
1990	Tor.	9	555	61.7	71	0
1991	Tor.	6	369	61.5	78	1
CFL TOTALS		**39**	**2361**	**60.5**	**90**	**3**

Fumbles - 1 and 1 lost with Edmonton in 1980 and 1 with 1 lost with Toronto in 1987. **CFL Total Playoff Fumbles - 2 and 2 lost.**

Field Goals - 2 attempts, 1 good, 17 yards with Toronto in 1983; 3 attempts, 1 good, 40 yards with Toronto in 1984.
CFL Total Playoff Field Goals - 5 attempts, 2 good, 57 yards, 28.5 average, longest 40 yards.

Net Punting - 12 for 465 yards, 38.8 average with Toronto in 1991.
CFL Total Playoff Net Punting - 12 for 465 yards, 38.8 average.

Grey Cup

		Scoring						Punting				
	Team	GP	TD	C	FG	S	TP	NO	YDS	AVE	LK	S
1977	Edm.	1	0	0	0	0	0	9	379	44.1	54	0
1978	Edm.	1	0	0	0	0	0	10	419	41.9	51	0
1979	Edm.	1	0	0	0	0	0	8	323	40.4	57	0
1980	Edm.	1	0	0	0	0	0	2	84	42.0	53	0
1981	Edm.	1	0	0	0	0	0	9	442	49.1	64	0
1982	Edm.	1	0	0	0	0	0	3	138	46.0	57	0
1983	Tor.	1	0	1	1	2	6	8	376	47.0	55	0
1987	Tor.	1	0	0	0	0	0	4	176	44.0	51	0
1991	Tor.	1	0	0	0	2	2	11	398	36.2	44	0
CFL TOTALS		**9**	**0**	**1**	**1**	**2**	**8**	**64**	**2735**	**42.7**	**64**	**0**

		Kickoffs					Field Goals				
	Team	NO	YDS	AVE	LK	S	T	G	YDS	AVE	LK
1977	Edm.	0	0	0.0	0	0	0	0	0	0.0	0
1978	Edm.	0	0	0.0	0	0	0	0	0	0.0	0
1979	Edm.	0	0	0.0	0	0	0	0	0	0.0	0
1980	Edm.	0	0	0.0	0	0	0	0	0	0.0	0
1981	Edm.	0	0	0.0	0	0	0	0	0	0.0	0
1982	Edm.	0	0	0.0	0	0	0	0	0	0.0	0
1983	Tor.	3	204	68.0	74	0	4	1	43	43.0	43
1987	Tor.	7	427	61.0	70	0	0	0	0	0.0	0
1991	Tor.	5	240	48.0	58	0	0	0	0	0.0	0
CFL TOTALS		**15**	**871**	**58.1**	**74**	**0**	**4**	**1**	**43**	**43.0**	**43**

Net Punting - 11 for 350 yards, 31.8 average with Toronto in 1991.
Total Grey Cup Net Punting - 11 for 350 yards, 31.8 average.

Tackles - 1 special teams with Toronto in 1991.
Total Grey Cup Tackles - 1 (1 special teams).

IZQUIERDO, JEAN-PAUL (J.P.)
Born: March 12, 1969
Birthplace: Calgary, Alberta
Slotback. 5'11", 195 lbs. Non-import
Last Amateur Club: University of Calgary (CWAA)
Acquired: Selected in the second round (10th overall) by the Toronto Argonauts in the 1991 CFL College Draft. The pick was obtained from B.C. Lions in exchange for running back Ryan Hanson. Traded to the Edmonton Eskimos in January, 1993 along with cornerback Ed Berry, wide receiver Eddie Brown, linebacker Bruce Dickson, quarterback Rickey Foggie, defensive lineman Leonard Johnson, slotback Darrell K. Smith and defensive back Don Wilson in exchange for defensive lineman Cameron Brosseau, linebacker John Davis, slotback Craig Ellis, quarterback Tracy Ham, defensive back Enis Jackson, running back Chris Johnstone, defensive back Travis Oliver and wide receiver Ken Winey.

		Scoring						Rushing				
	Team	GP	TD	C	FG	S	TP	NO	YDS	AVE	LG	TD
1991	Tor.	18	2	0	0	0	12	13	73	5.6	25	0
1992	Tor.	18	1	0	0	0	6	4	11	2.8	6	0
1993	Edm.	18	1	0	0	0	6	1	4	4.0	4	0
CFL TOTALS		**54**	**4**	**0**	**0**	**0**	**24**	**18**	**88**	**4.9**	**25**	**0**

		Pass Receiving					Kickoff Returns				
	Team	NO	YDS	AVE	LG	TD	NO	YDS	AVE	LG	TD
1991	Tor.	18	187	10.4	23	2	7	42	6.0	26	0
1992	Tor.	3	38	12.7	19	1	2	35	17.5	20	0
1993	Edm.	19	237	12.5	28	1	3	15	5.0	7	0
CFL TOTALS		**40**	**462**	**11.6**	**28**	**4**	**12**	**92**	**7.7**	**26**	**0**

		Fumbles		
	Team	NO	LOST	OFR
1991	Tor.	1	1	1
1992	Tor.	0	0	0
1993	Edm.	2	0	0
CFL TOTALS		**3**	**1**	**1**

Tackles - 25 special teams with Toronto in 1991; 1 defensive and 24 special teams in 1992 and 24 special teams with Edmonton in 1993.
CFL Total Tackles - 74 (1 defensive and 73 special teams).

Playoffs

			Rushing					Pass Receiving				
	Team	GP	NO	YDS	AVE	LG	TD	NO	YDS	AVE	LG	TD
1991	Tor.	1	1	-7	-7.0	-7	0	1	5	5.0	5	0
1993	Edm.	2	0	0	0.0	0	0	0	0	0.0	0	0
CFL TOTALS		**3**	**1**	**-7**	**-7.0**	**-7**	**0**	**1**	**5**	**5.0**	**5**	**0**

Tackles - 2 special teams with Edmonton in 1993.
CFL Total Playoff Tackles - 2 (2 special teams).

Grey Cup

Games Played - 1 with Toronto in 1991 and 1 with Edmonton in 1993.
Total Grey Cup GP - 2.

Tackles - 1 special teams with Toronto in 1991 and 2 special teams with Edmonton in 1993.
Total Grey Cup Tackles - 3 (3 special teams).

JACKSON, ALFRED
Born: July 10, 1967
Birthplace: Tulane, California
Defensive Back/Wide Receiver. 6'0", 185 lbs. Import
Last Amateur Club: San Diego State University
Acquired: Selected by the Los Angeles Rams in the fifth round (135th overall) in the 1989 NFL Draft. Released by Los Angeles in November, 1990. Re-signed by the Rams in February, 1991. Signed as a free agent by the NFL Cleveland Browns in November, 1991. Signed as a free agent by the Winnipeg Blue Bombers in August, 1993.

JACKSON, ALFRED

	Team	Scoring GP	TD	C	FG	S	TP	Pass Receiving NO	YDS	AVE	LG	TD
1993	Wpg.	12	2	0	0	0	12	13	194	14.9	60	2
CFL TOTALS		**12**	**2**	**0**	**0**	**0**	**12**	**13**	**194**	**14.9**	**60**	**2**

	Team	Punt Returns NO	YDS	AVE	LG	TD	Fumbles NO	LOST	OFR
1993	Wpg.	6	32	5.3	12	0	1	0	2
CFL TOTALS		**6**	**32**	**5.3**	**12**	**0**	**1**	**0**	**2**

Blocked Kicks - 1 punt with Winnipeg in 1993.
CFL Total Blocked Kicks - 1 (1 punt).

Tackles - 10 defensive and 5 special teams with Winnipeg in 1993.
CFL Total Tackles - 15 (10 defensive and 5 special teams).

Playoffs

	Team	GP	Pass Receiving NO	YDS	AVE	LG	TD
1993	Wpg.	1	4	55	13.8	18	0
CFL TOTALS		**1**	**4**	**55**	**13.8**	**18**	**0**

Grey Cup

	Team	GP	Pass Receiving NO	YDS	AVE	LG	TD
1993	Wpg.	1	4	57	14.3	21	0
CFL TOTALS		**1**	**4**	**57**	**14.3**	**21**	**0**

JACKSON, BYRON

Born: February 16, 1968
Birthplace: Pittsburgh, Pennsylvania
Wide Receiver. 5'7", 160 lbs. Import
Last Amateur Club: San Jose State University
Acquired: Signed as a free agent by the NFL Kansas City Chiefs in 1992. Released by Kansas City in August, 1992 and was placed on the club's practice roster for the remainder of the season. Re-signed by Kansas City in spring of 1993 and was subsequently released in August, 1993. Signed as a free agent by the Sacramento Gold Miners in August, 1993.

Games Played - 3 with Sacramento in 1993. **CFL Total GP - 3.**

Pass Receiving - 2 for 12 yards, 6.0 average, longest 8 yards with Sacramento in 1993.
CFL Total Pass Receiving - 2 for 12 yards, 6.0 average, longest 8 yards.

Punt Returns - 1 for -7 yards with Sacramento in 1993.
CFL Total Pass Receiving - 1 for -7 yards.

JACKSON, ENIS

Born: May 16, 1963
Birthplace: Helena, Arkansas
Cornerback. 5'9", 175 lbs. Import
Last Amateur Club: Memphis State University
Acquired: Signed as a free agent by the Cleveland Browns (NFL) in 1986. Spent the season on the injury reserve list and was released in 1987 following training camp. Attended the San Diego Chargers (NFL) training camp in 1988. Signed as a free agent with the Edmonton Eskimos in February, 1989. Traded to the Toronto Argonauts in January, 1993 along with defensive lineman Cameron Brosseau, linebacker John Davis, slotback Craig Ellis, quarterback Tracy Ham, running back Chris Johnstone, defensive back Travis Oliver and wide receiver Ken Winey in exchange for cornerback Ed Berry, wide receiver Eddie Brown, linebacker Bruce Dickson, quarterback Rickey Foggie, slotback J.P. Izquierdo, defensive lineman Leonard Johnson, slotback Darrell K. Smith and defensive back Don Wilson.

Games Played - 14 with Edmonton in 1989; 18 in 1990; 13 in 1991; 18 in 1992 and 5 with Toronto in 1993.
CFL Total GP - 68.

Interception Returns - 6 for 99 yards, 16.5 average, longest 45 yards with Edmonton in 1989; 2 for 38 yards, 19.0 average, longest 20 yards in 1990; 4 for 85 yards, 21.3 average, longest 41 yards in 1991 and 3 for 43 yards, 14.3 average, longest 27 yards in 1992.
CFL Total Interception Returns - 15 for 265 yards, 17.7 average, longest 45 yards.

Punt Returns - 1 for 0 yards with Edmonton in 1989.
CFL Total Punt Returns - 1 for 0 yards.

Blocked Kicks - 1 punt with Edmonton in 1989 and 1 punt in 1990.
CFL Total Blocked Kicks - 2 (2 punts).

Fumble Returns - 2 for 11 yards, 5.5 average, longest 11 yards with Edmonton in 1989 and 1 for 6 yards, 6.0 average, longest 6 yards in 1990.
CFL Total Fumble Returns - 3 for 17 yards, 5.7 average, longest 11 yards.

Kickoff Returns - 1 for 0 yards with Edmonton in 1990 and 1 for 52 yards, longest 26 yards in 1991.
CFL Total Kickoff Returns - 2 for 52 yards, 26.0 average, longest 26 yards.

Quarterback Sacks - 1 with Edmonton in 1990 and 1 for 17 yards lost with Toronto in 1993. **CFL Total QB Sacks - 2.**

Tackles - 36 defensive with Edmonton in 1989; 43 defensive in 1990; 27 defensive and 2 special teams in 1991; 54 defensive in 1992 and 20 defensive with Toronto in 1993.
CFL Total Tackles - 182 (180 defensive and 2 special teams).

Tackles for Losses - 1 for 5 yards with Edmonton in 1992.
CFL Total Tackles for Losses - 1 for 5 yards.

All-Western All-Star in 1989, 1991 and 1992.
CFL All-Star in 1989.

Playoffs

Games Played - 2 with Edmonton in 1990; 1 in 1991 and 2 in 1992.
CFL Total Playoff GP - 5.

Interception Returns - 1 for 46 yards with Edmonton in 1990 and 1 for 30 yards in 1992. **CFL Total Playoff Interception Returns - 2 for 76 yards, 38.0 average, longest 46 yards.**

Tackles - 5 defensive with Edmonton in 1990; 3 defensive in 1991 and 6 defensive in 1992. **CFL Total Playoff Tackles - 14 (14 defensive).**

Grey Cup

Games Played - 1 with Edmonton in 1990. **Total Grey Cup GP - 1.**

Defensive Tackles - 3 with Edmonton in 1990.
Total Grey Cup Defensive Tackles - 3.

JACKSON, JEFF

Born: September 10, 1961
Birthplace: Shreveport, Georgia
Linebacker. 6'1", 235 lbs. Import
Last Amateur Club: Auburn University
Acquired: Selected by the Birmingham Stallions in the 1984 USFL Territorial Draft. Selected in the eighth round (206th overall) by the Atlanta Falcons in the 1984 NFL Draft. Signed by Atlanta in June, 1984. Released by Atlanta in August, 1986. Signed as a free agent by the NFL San Diego Chargers in April, 1987. Released by San Diego after training camp in 1989. Signed as a free agent by the Ottawa Rough Riders in April, 1991. Was released by Ottawa in September, 1992. Signed as a free agent by the B.C. Lions in May, 1993.

Games Played - 7 with Ottawa in 1991; 3 in 1992 and 7 with B.C. in 1993.
CFL Total GP - 17.

Interception Returns - 1 for 10 yards with Ottawa in 1991 and 1 for 0 yards with B.C. in 1993.
CFL Total Interception Returns - 2 for 10 yards, 5.0 average, longest 10 yards.

Fumble Returns - 1 for 0 yards with B.C. in 1993.
CFL Total Fumble Returns - 1 for 0 yards.

Tackles - 15 defensive with Ottawa in 1991; 5 defensive and 2 special teams in 1992 and 17 defensive with B.C. in 1993.
CFL Total Tackles - 39 (37 defensive and 2 special teams).

Tackles For Losses - 1 for 2 yards with Ottawa in 1991 and 1 for 4 yards with B.C. in 1993.
CFL Total Tackles For Losses- 2 for 6 yards.

Playoffs

Games Played - 1 with Ottawa in 1993.
CFL Total Playoff GP - 1.

JACKSON, PATRICK

Born: July 8, 1969
Birthplace: Columbus, Ohio
Running Back. 5'9", 175 lbs. Import
Last Amateur Club: Kansas State University
Acquired: Signed as a free agent by the NFL Green Bay Packers in April, 1992. Released by Green Bay in August, 1992. Signed as a free agent by the Toronto Argonauts in January, 1993.

	Team	Scoring GP	TD	C	FG	S	TP	Rushing NO	YDS	AVE	LG	TD
1993	Tor.	5	1	0	0	0	6	13	87	6.7	19	1
CFL TOTALS		**5**	**1**	**0**	**0**	**0**	**6**	**13**	**87**	**6.7**	**19**	**1**

	Team	Pass Receiving NO	YDS	AVE	LG	TD	Punt Returns NO	YDS	AVE	LG	TD
1993	Tor.	4	31	7.8	19	0	5	62	12.4	25	0
CFL TOTALS		**4**	**31**	**7.8**	**19**	**0**	**5**	**62**	**12.4**	**25**	**0**

	Team	Kickoff Returns NO	YDS	AVE	LG	TD	Fumbles NO	LOST	OFR
1993	Tor.	7	146	20.9	30	0	1	1	0
CFL TOTALS		**7**	**146**	**20.9**	**30**	**0**	**1**	**1**	**0**

JACKSON, TIM
Born: November 7, 1965
Birthplace: Dallas, Texas
Defensive Back. 6'0", 190 lbs. Import
Last Amateur Club: University of Nebraska
Acquired: Selected in the ninth round (224th overall) by the Dallas Cowboys in the 1989 NFL Draft. Released by Dallas in November, 1989. Signed to the developmental squad of the NFL Washington Redskins in December, 1989. Released by Washington at the end of the 1989 season. Signed as a free agent by the NFL San Diego Chargers in February, 1990. Released by San Diego during the pre-season. Selected in the third round (27th defensive back) by the Barcelona Dragons in the 1991 WLAF Positional Draft. Signed as a free agent by the Hamilton Tiger-Cats in June, 1991. Granted free agency status in February, 1993. Re-signed by Hamilton in May, 1993.

		Scoring						Interception Returns				
	Team	GP	TD	C	FG	S	TP	NO	YDS	AVE	LG	TD
1991	Ham.	15	1	0	0	0	6	3	47	15.7	39	0
1992	Ham.	17	0	0	0	0	0	0	0	0.0	0	0
1993	Ham.	12	0	0	0	0	0	2	3	1.5	3	0
CFL TOTALS		**44**	**1**	**0**	**0**	**0**	**6**	**5**	**50**	**10.0**	**39**	**0**

Own Kickoffs Recovered - 1 for 0 yards with Hamilton in 1991. **CFL Total Own Kickoffs Recovered - 1 for 0 yards.**

Kickoff Returns - 1 for 0 yards with Hamilton in 1993. **CFL Total Kickoff Returns - 1 for 0 yards.**

Fumble Returns - 2 for 0 yards and 1 TD with Hamilton in 1991 and 2 for 9 yards, 4.5 average, longest 9 yards in 1992. **CFL Total Fumble Returns - 4 for 9 yards, 2.3 average, longest 9 yards and 1 TD.**

Own Fumbles Recovered - 2 with Hamilton in 1991 and 1 in 1992. **CFL Total OFR - 3.**

Tackles - 56 defensive and 10 special teams with Hamilton in 1991; 49 defensive and 1 special teams in 1992 and 46 defensive in 1993. **CFL Total Tackles - 162 (151 defensive and 11 special teams).**

Tackles for Losses - 2 for 9 yards with Hamilton in 1991. **CFL Total Tackles for Losses - 2 for 9 yards.**

Playoffs

Games Played - 2 with Hamilton in 1992 and 2 in 1993. **CFL Total Playoff GP - 4.**

Fumble Returns - 1 for 0 yards with Hamilton in 1992 and 1 for 0 yards in 1993. **CFL Total Playoff Fumble Returns - 2 for 0 yards.**

Tackles - 5 defensive with Hamilton in 1992 and 8 defensive in 1993. **CFL Total Playoff Tackles - 13 (13 defensive).**

JAUCH, JIM
Born: June 25, 1965
Birthplace: Iowa City, Iowa
Defensive Back. 6'1", 180 lbs. Non-import
Last Amateur Club: University of North Carolina
Acquired: Selected in the third round (18th overall) by Saskatchewan Roughriders in the 1988 CFL College Draft. Traded to Calgary Stampeders for a third round draft pick in the 1990 CFL College Draft (offensive lineman Craig Hendrickson). Released by Calgary in July, 1990. Signed as a free agent by Edmonton Eskimos in August, 1990. Released by Edmonton in July, 1991. Signed as a free agent by the Hamilton Tiger-Cats in February, 1992.

Games Played - 17 with Calgary in 1989; 14 with Edmonton in 1990; 11 with Hamilton in 1992 and 11 in 1993. **CFL Total GP - 53.**

Own Kickoffs Recovered - 1 for 5 yards with Calgary in 1989. **CFL Total Own Kickoffs Recovered - 1 for 5 yards.**

Kickoff Returns - 3 for 18 yards, 6.0 average, longest 9 yards with Hamilton in 1992 and 1 for 22 yards in 1993. **CFL Total Kickoff Returns - 4 for 40 yards, 10.0 average, longest 22 yards.**

Interception Returns - 1 for 0 yards with Edmonton in 1990. **CFL Total Interception Returns - 1 for 0 yards.**

Fumbles - 1 and 0 lost with Calgary in 1989. **CFL Total Fumbles - 1 and 0 lost.**

Tackles - 1 defensive with Calgary in 1989; 6 defensive with Edmonton in 1990; 2 defensive and 9 special teams with Hamilton in 1992 and 12 special teams in 1993. **CFL Total Tackles - 30 (9 defensive and 21 special teams).**

Playoffs

Games Played - 1 with Calgary in 1989; 1 with Edmonton in 1990; 2 with Hamilton in 1992 and 2 in 1993. **CFL Total Playoff GP - 6.**

Fumble Returns - 1 for 0 yards with Hamilton in 1992 and 1 for 0 yards in 1993. **CFL Total Playoff Fumble Returns - 2 for 0 yards.**

Kickoff Returns - 2 for 19 yards, 9.5 average, longest 13 yards with Hamilton in 1992. **CFL Total Playoff Kickoff Returns - 2 for 19 yards, 9.5 average, longest 13 yards.**

Fumbles - 1 and 1 lost with Hamilton in 1992. **CFL Total Playoff Fumbles - 1 and 1 lost.**

Tackles - 1 defensive and 4 special teams with Hamilton in 1992 and 1 special teams in 1993. **CFL Total Playoff Tackles - 6 (1 defensive and 5 special teams).**

JAUCH, JOEY
Born: April 25, 1970
Birthplace: Edmonton, Alberta
Slotback. 6'1", 195 lbs. Non-import
Last Amateur Club: University of North Carolina
Acquired: Selected in the second round (ninth overall) by the Hamilton Tiger-Cats in 1992 CFL College Draft. Signed by Hamilton in March, 1992. Granted free agency status in February, 1994. Re-signed by Hamilton in April, 1994.

		Scoring						Pass Receiving				
	Team	GP	TD	C	FG	S	TP	NO	YDS	AVE	LG	TD
1992	Ham.	1	0	0	0	0	0	2	31	15.5	22	0
1993	Ham.	18	1	0	0	0	6	31	512	16.5	41	1
CFL TOTALS		**19**	**1**	**0**	**0**	**0**	**6**	**33**	**543**	**16.5**	**41**	**1**

Rushing - 1 for 25 yards with Hamilton in 1993. **CFL Total Rushing - 1 for 25 yards.**

Tackles - 1 defensive and 4 special teams with Hamilton in 1992 and 4 defensive and 12 special teams. **CFL Total Tackles - 21 (5 defensive and 16 special teams).**

Passing - 1 for 0 yards with Hamilton in 1993. **CFL Total Passing - 1 for 0 yards.**

Kickoff Returns - 0 for 39 yards with Hamilton in 1993. **CFL Total Kickoff Returns - 0 for 39 yards.**

Playoffs

		Scoring						Pass Receiving				
	Team	GP	TD	C	FG	S	TP	NO	YDS	AVE	LG	TD
1992	Ham.	2	0	0	0	0	0	0	0	0.0	0	0
1993	Ham.	2	1	0	0	0	6	8	118	14.8	42	1
CFL TOTAL		**4**	**1**	**0**	**0**	**0**	**6**	**8**	**118**	**14.8**	**42**	**1**

Own Kickoffs Recovered - 1 with Hamilton in 1992. **CFL Total Playoff OKR - 1.**

Tackles - 1 special teams with Hamilton in 1993. **CFL Total Playoff Tackles - 1 (1 special teams).**

JENKINS, KEYVAN
Born: January 6, 1962
Birthplace: Stockton, California
Running Back. 5'10", 185 lbs. Import
Last Amateur Club: University of Nevada-Las Vegas
Acquired: Signed as a free agent by the B.C. Lions prior to the 1984 CFL season. Granted free agency March, 1987 and signed as a free agent by the San Diego Chargers (NFL) in April, 1987. Released by San Diego in October, 1987. Signed as a free agent by the Kansas City Chiefs (NFL) in March, 1988 and was later released. Signed as a free agent by Calgary Stampeders in February, 1990. Released by Calgary in April, 1994.

		Scoring						Rushing				
	Team	GP	TD	C	FG	S	TP	NO	YDS	AVE	LG	TD
1984	B.C.	3	2	0	0	0	12	30	170	5.7	19	2
1985ab	B.C.	14	11	0	0	0	66	193	964	5.0	51	8
1986	B.C.	11	7	0	0	0	42	131	496	3.8	19	7
1987			NFL							NFL		
1988			NFL							NFL		
1990	Cal.	5	3	0	0	0	18	53	238	4.5	23	3
1991	Cal.	15	13	0	0	0	78	166	801	4.8	59	10
1992	Cal.	10	7	0	0	0	42	97	535	5.5	34	5
1993	Cal.	12	2	0	0	0	12	96	435	4.5	26	0
CFL TOTALS		**70**	**45**	**0**	**0**	**0**	**270**	**766**	**3639**	**4.8**	**59**	**35**

		Pass Receiving					Fumbles			Kickoff Returns				
	Team	NO	YDS	AVE	LG	TD	NO	LOST	OFR	NO	YDS	AVE	LG	TD
1984	B.C.	7	56	8.0	18	0	3	3	0	6	173	28.8	43	0
1985	B.C.	51	437	8.6	47	3	5	3	2	35	720	20.6	47	0
1986	B.C.	34	329	9.7	47	0	6	4	0	23	502	21.8	35	0
1987			NFL					NFL			NFL			
1988			NFL					NFL			NFL			
1990	Cal.	8	107	13.4	20	0	1	1	0	7	146	20.9	55	0
1991	Cal.	28	256	9.1	21	3	8	4	1	26	529	20.3	41	0
1992	Cal.	28	376	13.4	45	2	2	1	0	3	69	23.0	26	0
1993	Cal.	32	363	11.3	51	2	3	2	0	10	210	21.0	47	0
CFL TOTALS		**188**	**1924**	**10.2**	**51**	**10**	**28**	**18**	**3**	**110**	**2349**	**21.4**	**55**	**0**

Tackles - 1 defensive with Calgary in 1990; 4 special teams in 1991 and 2 defensive and 2 special teams in 1992. **CFL Total Tackles - 9 (3 defensive and 6 special teams).**

a - All-Western All-Star
b - CFL All-Star

JENKINS, KEYVAN

Playoffs

	Team	Scoring GP	TD	C	FG	S	TP	Rushing NO	YDS	AVE	LG	TD
1984	B.C.	1	0	0	0	0	0	0	0	0.0	0	0
1991	Cal.	2	2	0	0	0	12	11	62	5.6	14	2
1992	Cal.	1	0	0	0	0	0	8	18	2.3	6	0
CFL TOTALS		**4**	**2**	**0**	**0**	**0**	**12**	**19**	**80**	**4.2**	**14**	**2**

	Team	Pass Receiving NO	YDS	AVE	LG	TD	Kickoff Returns NO	YDS	AVE	LG	TD
1984	B.C.	0	0	0.0	0	0	5	112	22.4	35	0
1991	Cal.	2	17	8.5	9	0	3	55	18.3	27	0
1992	Cal.	1	19	19.0	19	0	0	0	0.0	0	0
CFL TOTALS		**3**	**36**	**12.0**	**19**	**0**	**8**	**167**	**20.9**	**35**	**0**

Fumbles - 1 and 1 lost with Calgary in 1991. **CFL Total Playoff Fumbles - 1 and 1 lost.**

Own Fumbles Recovered - 1 with B.C. in 1984 and 1 with Calgary in 1991. **CFL Total Playoff OFR - 2.**

Tackles - 1 defensive with Calgary in 1992. **CFL Total Playoff Tackles - 1 (1 defensive).**

Grey Cup

Games Played - 1 with Calgary in 1991 and 1 in 1992. **Total Grey Cup GP - 2.**

Rushing - 7 for 28 yards, 4.0 average, longest 8 yards with Calgary in 1991 and 9 for 25 yards, 2.8 average, longest 8 yards in 1992. **Total Grey Cup Rushing - 16 for 53 yards, 3.3 average, longest 8 yards.**

Pass Receiving - 2 for 11 yards, 5.5 average, longest 8 yards with Calgary in 1991 and 2 for 9 yards, 4.5 average, longest 6 yards with Calgary in 1992. **Total Grey Cup Pass Receiving - 4 for 20 yards, 5.0 average, longest 8 yards.**

Kickoff Returns - 2 for 29 yards, 14.5 average, longest 31 yards with Calgary in 1991. **Total Grey Cup Kickoff Returns - 2 for 29 yards, 14.5 average, longest 31 yards.**

Fumbles - 1 and 1 lost with Calgary in 1991 and 1 and 1 lost in 1992. **Total Grey Cup Fumbles - 2 and 2 lost.**

JENNINGS, JIM
Born: April 4, 1969
Birthplace: Bellflower, California
Offensive Lineman. 6'3", 285 lbs. Import
Last Amateur Club: San Diego State University
Acquired: Selected by the NFL Kansas City Chiefs in the eighth round (213th overall) of the 1992 NFL Draft. Was released by Kansas City during their 1993 training camp. Signed as a free agent by the Sacramento Gold Miners in August, 1993.

Games Played - 7 with Sacramento in 1993. **CFL Total GP - 7.**

JOELSON, GREG
Born: August 22, 1966
Birthplace: Coos Bay, Oregon
Defensive Tackle/End. 6'3", 265 lbs. Import
Last Amateur Club: Arizona State University
Acquired: Signed as a free agent by the B.C. Lions in August, 1990 and was subsequently released by the club in September, 1990. Signed as a free agent by the NFL San Francisco 49ers in March, 1991. Released by San Francisco in August, 1991 and signed to their practice roster. Granted unconditional free agency in February, 1992. Signed as a free agent by the NFL San Diego Chargers in March, 1992 and was released during their training camp. Signed as a free agent by the Hamilton Tiger-Cats in May, 1993 and was subsequently released in July, 1993. Signed as a free agent by the Sacramento Gold Miners in August, 1993.

	Team	Scoring GP	TD	C	FG	S	TP	Fumble Returns NO	YDS	AVE	LG	TD
1993	Sac.	11	1	0	0	0	6	2	31	15.5	31	1
CFL TOTALS		**11**	**1**	**0**	**0**	**0**	**6**	**2**	**31**	**15.5**	**31**	**1**

Quarterback Sacks - 3 for 19 yards lost with Sacramento in 1993. **CFL Total QB Sacks - 3 for 19 yards lost.**

Tackles - 7 defensive and 6 special teams with Sacramento in 1993. **CFL Total Tackles - 13 (7 defensive and 6 special teams).**

Tackles for Losses - 1 for 1 yard with Sacramento in 1993. **CFL Total Tackles for Losses - 1 for 1 yard.**

JOHNSON, ALONDRA
Born: July 22, 1965
Birthplace: Gardena, California
Linebacker. 5'11", 220 lbs. Import
Last Amateur Club: West Texas State University
Acquired: Signed as a free agent with the B.C. Lions in July, 1989. Granted free agency status in February, 1991. Signed as a free agent by the Calgary Stampeders in February, 1991.

	Team	Scoring GP	TD	C	FG	S	TP	Interception Returns NO	YDS	AVE	LG	TD
1989a	B.C.	18	0	x1	0	0	2	2	10	5.0	8	0
1990	B.C.	14	0	0	0	0	0	1	82	82.0	82	0
1991b	Cal.	16	2	0	0	0	12	4	127	31.8	60	1
1992b	Cal.	18	0	0	0	0	0	0	0	0.0	0	0
1993	Cal.	18	1	0	0	0	6	0	0	0.0	0	0
CFL TOTALS		**84**	**3**	**x1**	**0**	**0**	**20**	**7**	**219**	**31.3**	**82**	**1**

2-pt. Converts - 1 made with B.C. in 1989. **CFL Total 2-Pt. Converts - 1 made.**

Blocked Kicks - 2 punts with B.C. in 1989. **CFL Total Blocked Kicks - 2 punts.**

Fumbles - 1 and 0 lost with Calgary in 1991. **CFL Total Fumbles - 1 and 0 lost.**

Fumble Returns - 0 for 85 yards with B.C. in 1989; 1 for 0 yards in 1990; 4 for 49 yards, 12.3 average, longest 53 yards and 1 TD with Calgary in 1991; 2 for 49 yards, 24.5 average, longest 47 yards in 1992 and 1 for 46 yards in 1993. **CFL Total Fumble Returns - 8 for 229 yards, 26.1 average, longest 85 yards and 2 TDs.**

Quarterback Sacks - 3 with B.C. in 1990; 5 for 45 yards lost with Calgary in 1992 and 6 for 53 yards lost in 1993. **CFL Total QB Sacks - 14.**

Tackles - 115 defensive with B.C. in 1989; 62 defensive in 1990; 89 defensive and 5 special teams with Calgary in 1991; 95 defensive and 10 special teams in 1992 and 78 defensive and 15 special teams in 1993. **CFL Total Tackles - 469 (439 defensive and 30 special teams).**

Tackles for Losses - 2 for 3 yards with Calgary in 1991; 4 for 8 yards in 1992 and 4 for 12 yards in 1993. **CFL Total Tackles for Losses - 10 for 23 yards.**

a - First player to score on a 2-Pt. convert return in CFL history.
b - All-Western All-Star.

Playoffs

Games Played - 2 with Calgary in 1991; 1 in 1992 and 2 in 1993. **CFL Total Playoff GP - 5.**

Tackles - 12 defensive and 1 special teams with Calgary in 1991; 5 defensive in 1992 and 17 defensive and 1 special teams in 1993. **CFL Total Playoff Tackles - 36 (34 defensive and 2 special teams).**

Tackles for Losses - 3 for 3 yards with Calgary in 1991. **CFL Total Playoff Tackles for Losses - 3 for 3 yards.**

Grey Cup

Games Played - 1 with Calgary in 1991 and 1 in 1992. **Total Grey Cup GP - 2.**

Interception Returns - 1 for 0 yards with Calgary in 1992. **Total Grey Cup Interception Returns - 1 for 0 yards.**

Tackles - 3 defensive and 2 special teams with Calgary in 1991 and 4 defensive and 1 special teams in 1992. **Total Grey Cup Tackles - 10 (7 defensive and 3 special teams).**

Tackles for Losses - 2 for 2 yards with Calgary in 1991. **Total Grey Cup Tackles for Losses - 2 for 2 yards.**

JOHNSON, BRET
Born: February 6, 1970
Birthplace: Newport Beach, California
Quarterback. 6'0", 190 lbs. Import
Last Amateur Club: Michigan State University
Acquired: Signed as a free agent by the Toronto Argonauts in April, 1993.

Games Played - 18 with Toronto in 1993. **CFL Total GP - 18.**

Rushing - 2 for 25 yards, 12.5 average, longest 14 yards with Toronto in 1993. **CFL Total Rushing - 2 for 25 yards, 12.5 average, longest 14 yards.**

Passing - 8 attempts, 4 complete for 72 yards, 50.0 percent complete, 1 interception, longest 45 yards with Toronto in 1993. **CFL Total Passing - 8 attempts, 4 complete for 72 yards, 50.0 percent complete, 1 interception, longest 45 yards.**

JOHNSON, ERIC
Born: March 11, 1970
Birthplace: Nacogdoches, Texas
Defensive End. 6'5", 255 lbs. Import
Last Amateur Club: Stephen F. Austin University
Acquired: Signed as a free agent by the NFL Chicago Bears in 1992 and was released by the club during training camp. Signed as a free agent by the Calgary Stampeders in March, 1993.

Games Played - 18 with Calgary in 1993. **CFL Total GP - 18.**

Quarterback Sacks - 6 for 32 yards lost with Calgary in 1993. **CFL Total QB Sacks - 6 for 32 yards lost.**

JOHNSON, ERIC

Tackles - 23 defensive with Calgary in 1993. **CFL Total Tackles - 23 (23 defensive).**

Tackles for Losses - 5 for 11 yards with Calgary in 1993.
CFL Total Tackles for Losses - 5 for 11 yards.

Playoffs

Games Played - 2 with Calgary in 1993. **CFL Total Playoff GP - 2.**

Tackles - 4 defensive with Calgary in 1993.
CFL Total Playoff Tackles - 4 (4 defensive).

JOHNSON, JOE

Born: December 21, 1962
Birthplace: Washington, D.C.
Wide Receiver. 5'8", 170 lbs. Import
Last Amateur Club: University of Notre Dame
Acquired: Signed as a free agent by the NFL Tampa Bay Buccaneers in May, 1985. Released by Tampa Bay in August, 1985. Signed as a free agent by the NFL Buffalo Bills in May, 1986 and was subsequently released in August, 1986. Re-signed by Buffalo in May, 1987 and was released in August, 1987. Re-signed as a replacement player in September, 1987. Spent 1988 season on injured list. Released by Buffalo in August, 1989. Awarded on waivers to the NFL Washington Redskins in August, 1989. Granted unconditional free agency in February, 1992. Assigned by Washington to the Orlando Thunder in the 1992 WLAF enhancement allocation program in February, 1992. Traded by Washington along with DE George Hinkle to the NFL Minnesota Vikings for an undisclosed draft pick in the 1992 NFL Draft in August, 1992. Granted unconditional free agency in March, 1993. Signed as a free agent by the Sacramento Gold Miners in September, 1993.

	Team	Scoring GP	TD	C	FG	S	TP	Rushing NO	YDS	AVE	LG	TD
1993	Sac.	7	6	0	0	0	36	1	16	16.0	16	0
CFL TOTALS		**7**	**6**	**0**	**0**	**0**	**36**	**1**	**16**	**16.0**	**16**	**0**

	Team	Pass Receiving NO	YDS	AVE	LG	TD	Punt Returns NO	YDS	AVE	LG	TD
1993	Sac.	22	421	19.1	39	5	22	205	9.3	63	1
CFL TOTALS		**22**	**421**	**19.1**	**39**	**5**	**22**	**205**	**9.3**	**63**	**1**

	Team	Kickoff Returns NO	YDS	AVE	LG	TD	Unsuccessful Field Goal Returns NO	YDS	AVE	LG	TD
1993	Sac.	1	17	17.0	17	0	1	23	23.0	23	0
CFL TOTALS		**1**	**17**	**17.0**	**17**	**0**	**1**	**23**	**23.0**	**23**	**0**

JOHNSON, LEONARD

Born: May 17, 1963
Birthplace: Savannah, Georgia
Defensive Tackle. 6'6", 255 lbs. Import
Last Amateur Club: Georgia Military College
Acquired: Signed as a free agent by the NFL San Diego Chargers in 1989 and released after training camp. Signed as a free agent by the Ottawa Rough Riders in December, 1990. Traded to the Toronto Argonauts in March, 1991 with kicker Dean Dorsey and linebacker Brian Warren in exchange for quarterback John Congemi. Traded to the Edmonton Eskimos in January, 1993 along with cornerback Ed Berry, wide receiver Eddie Brown, linebacker Bruce Dickson, quarterback Rickey Foggie, slotback J.P. Izquierdo, slotback Darrell K. Smith and defensive back Don Wilson in exchange for defensive lineman Cameron Brosseau, linebacker John Davis, slotback Craig Ellis, quarterback Tracy Ham, defensive back Enis Jackson, running back Chris Johnstone, defensive back Travis Oliver and wide receiver Ken Winey.

Games Played - 8 with Toronto in 1991; 5 in 1992 and 11 with Edmonton in 1993. **CFL Total GP - 24.**

Fumble Returns - 1 for 0 yards with Toronto in 1991 and 1 for 0 yards with Edmonton in 1993. **CFL Total Fumble Returns - 2 for 0 yards.**

Blocked Kicks - 1 convert with Edmonton in 1993.
CFL Total Blocked Kicks - 1 (1 convert).

Quarterback Sacks - 3 with Toronto in 1991; 2 for 18 yards lost in 1992 and 3 for 23 yards lost in 1993. **CFL Total QB Sacks - 8.**

Tackles - 16 defensive and 1 special teams with Toronto in 1991; 5 defensive and 1 special teams in 1992 and 6 defensive and 3 special teams with Edmonton in 1993.
CFL Total Tackles - 32 (27 defensive and 5 special teams).

Tackles for Losses - 1 for 3 yards with Toronto in 1991; 1 for 1 yard in 1992 and 1 for 1 yard with Edmonton in 1993.
CFL Total Tackles for Losses - 3 for 5 yards.

Playoffs

Games Played - 2 with Edmonton in 1993. **CFL Total Playoff GP - 2.**

Grey Cup

Games Played - 1 wth Edmonton in 1993. **Total Grey Cup GP - 1.**

JOHNSON, WILLIAM

Born: December 4, 1964
Birthplace: Munroe, Louisiana
Defensive End. 6'5", 240 lbs. Import
Last Amateur Club: Northeast Louisiana University
Acquired: Fifth round draft pick (138th overall) of the Chicago Bears in the 1987 NFL Draft. Signed by Chicago in July, 1987. Released by Chicago in August, 1988. Signed as a free agent by the New Orleans Saints (NFL) in March, 1989. Attended the New Orleans Saints training camp in 1989. Signed as a free agent by the Calgary Stampeders in August, 1989.

Games Played - 9 with Calgary in 1989; 17 in 1990; 18 in 1991; 17 in 1992 and 18 in 1993. **CFL Total GP - 79.**

Kickoff Returns - 1 for 0 yards with Calgary in 1993.
CFL Total Kickoff Returns - 1 for 0 yards.

Interception Returns - 1 for 18 yards with Calgary in 1990.
CFL Total Interception Returns - 1 for 18 yards.

Fumble Returns - 1 for 0 yards with Calgary in 1989; 2 for 0 yards in 1990 and 3 for 5 yards in 1991.
CFL Total Fumble Returns - 6 for 5 yards, 0.8 average, longest 5 yards.

Quarterback Sacks - 9 with Calgary in 1989; 16 in 1990; 15 in 1991; 10 for 47 yards lost in 1992 and 12 for 50 yards lost in 1993.
CFL Total QB Sacks - 62.

Tackles - 22 defensive with Calgary in 1989; 40 defensive in 1990; 59 defensive in 1991; 45 defensive in 1992 and 27 defensive in 1993.
CFL Total Tackles - 193 (193 defensive).

Tackles for Losses - 13 for 40 yards with Calgary in 1991; 11 for 43 yards in 1992 and 3 for 9 yards in 1993.
CFL Total Tackles for Losses - 27 for 92 yards.

All-Western All-Star in 1990, 1991,1992 and 1993.
CFL All-Star in 1991,1992 and 1993.
Winner of the Norm Fieldgate Trophy as Outstanding Defensive Player, Western Division in 1991.
Runner-up for GMC Most Outstanding Defensive Player in 1991.
Led the League in Quarterback Sacks in 1991.
Led the League in Tackles for Losses in 1991.

Playoffs

Games Played - 1 with Calgary in 1989; 1 in 1990; 2 in 1991; 1 in 1992 and 2 in 1993. **CFL Total Playoff GP - 7.**

Fumbles - 1 and 0 lost with Calgary in 1990.
CFL Total Playoff Fumbles - 1 and 0 lost.

Own Fumbles Recovered - 1 with Calgary in 1990.
CFL Total Playoff OFR - 1.

Fumble Returns - 1 for 4 yards with Calgary in 1990.
CFL Total Playoff Fumble Returns - 1 for 4 yards.

Quarterback Sacks - 1 with Calgary in 1990 and 1 for 17 yards lost in 1992.
CFL Total Playoff QB Sacks - 2.

Tackles - 2 defensive with Calgary in 1990; 5 defensive and 2 special teams in 1991; 3 defensive in 1992 and 7 defensive in 1993.
CFL Total Playoff Tackles - 19 (17 defensive and 2 special teams).

Tackles for Losses - 1 for 1 yard with Calgary in 1991.
CFL Total Playoff Tackles for Losses - 1 for 1 yard.

Grey Cup

Games Played - 1 with Calgary in 1991 and 1 in 1992.
Total Grey Cup GP - 2.

Blocked Kicks - 1 field goal with Calgary in 1992.
Total Grey Cup Blocked Kicks - 1 (1 field goal).

Tackles - 1 defensive with Calgary in 1991 and 1 defensive in 1992.
Total Grey Cup Tackles - 2 (2 defensive).

JOHNSTONE, CHRIS

Born: December 12, 1963
Birthplace: Kingston, Jamaica
Running Back. 6'3", 215 lbs. Non-import
Last Amateur Club: Bakersfield Junior College
Acquired: Signed as a free agent by the Edmonton Eskimos in June, 1986. Traded to the Toronto Argonauts in January, 1993 along with defensive lineman Cameron Brosseau, linebacker John Davis, slotback Craig Ellis, quarterback Tracy Ham, cornerback Enis Jackson, defensive back Travis Oliver and wide receiver Ken Winey in exchange for cornerback Ed Berry, wide receiver Eddie Brown, linebacker Bruce Dickson, quarterback Rickey Foggie, slotback J.P. Izquierdo, defensive lineman Leonard Johnson, slotback Darrell K. Smith and defensive back Don Wilson. Traded to the Winnipeg Blue Bombers in exchange for fullback Warren Hudson in June, 1993. Granted free agency status in February, 1994. Re-signed by Winnipeg in April, 1994.

JOHNSTONE, CHRIS

Year	Team	GP	Scoring TD	C	FG	S	TP	Rushing NO	YDS	AVE	LG	TD
1986	Edm.	17	4	0	0	0	24	71	200	2.8	28	3
1987	Edm.	18	1	0	0	0	6	44	212	4.8	28	1
1988	Edm.	13	3	0	0	0	18	84	346	4.1	17	2
1989	Edm.	14	8	0	0	0	48	63	253	4.0	13	7
1990	Edm.	17	2	0	0	0	12	32	119	3.7	11	2
1991	Edm.	7	0	0	0	0	0	1	-1	-1.0	-1	0
1992	Edm.	16	0	0	0	0	0	2	4	2.0	2	0
1993a	Wpg.	18	5	0	0	0	30	45	196	4.4	24	4
CFL TOTALS		**120**	**23**	**0**	**0**	**0**	**138**	**342**	**1329**	**3.9**	**28**	**19**

Year	Team	Fumbles NO	LOST	OFR	Pass Receiving NO	YDS	AVE	LG	TD
1986	Edm.	2	2	0	11	68	6.2	18	1
1987	Edm.	1	1	0	16	162	10.1	27	0
1988	Edm.	4	4	0	16	124	7.8	24	1
1989	Edm.	0	0	0	10	103	10.3	23	1
1990	Edm.	3	3	0	2	23	11.5	13	0
1991	Edm.	1	0	0	0	0	0.0	0	0
1992	Edm.	1	0	0	0	0	0.0	0	0
1993	Wpg.	2	2	1	18	259	14.4	33	1
CFL TOTALS		**14**	**12**	**1**	**73**	**739**	**10.1**	**33**	**4**

Kickoff Returns - 1 for 0 yards with Edmonton in 1987; 2 for 29 yards in 1990 and 4 for 80 yards, 20.0 average, longest 41 yards in 1992.
CFL Total Kickoff Returns - 7 for 109 yards, 15.6 average, longest 41 yards.

Own Kickoffs Recovered - 1 for 11 yards with Edmonton in 1989.
CFL Total Own Kickoffs Recovered - 1 for 11 yards.

Fumble Returns - 1 for 0 yards with Edmonton in 1992.
CFL Total Fumble Returns - 1 for 0 yards.

Tackles - 1 defensive with Edmonton in 1988; 2 defensive in 1989; 2 defensive in 1990; 4 special teams in 1991; 22 special teams in 1992 and 3 defensive and 1 special teams in 1993.
CFL Total Tackles - 35 (8 defensive and 27 special teams).

a - All-Eastern All-Star Team.

Playoffs

Year	Team	GP	Rushing NO	YDS	AVE	LG	TD	Pass Receiving NO	YDS	AVE	LG	TD	Fumbles NO	LOST
1986	Edm.	2	6	16	2.7	8	0	1	11	11.0	11	0	2	1
1987	Edm.	2	2	9	4.5	5	0	1	5	5.0	5	0	0	0
1988	Edm.	1	4	32	8.0	18	0	2	45	22.5	45	0	0	0
1989	Edm.	1	2	15	7.5	11	0	1	2	2.0	2	0	0	0
1990	Edm.	2	5	28	5.6	12	0	0	0	0.0	0	0	0	0
1992	Edm.	2	0	0	0.0	0	0	0	0	0.0	0	0	0	0
1993	Wpg.	1	1	3	3.0	3	0	1	15	15.0	15	0	0	0
CFL TOTALS		**11**	**20**	**103**	**5.2**	**18**	**0**	**6**	**78**	**13.0**	**45**	**0**	**2**	**1**

Kickoff Returns - 1 for 17 yards with Edmonton in 1990 and 3 for 41 yards, 13.7 average, longest 14 yards in 1992.
CFL Total Playoff Kickoff Returns - 4 for 58 yards, 14.5 average, longest 17 yards.

Tackles - 2 special teams with Edmonton in 1992.
CFL Total Playoff Tackles - 2 (2 special teams).

Grey Cup

Year	Team	GP	Rushing NO	YDS	AVE	LG	TD	Pass Receiving NO	YDS	AVE	LG	TD
1986	Edm.	1	3	14	4.7	10	0	1	20	20.0	20	0
1987	Edm.	1	1	-3	-3.0	-3	0	2	39	19.5	20	0
1990	Edm.	1	1	11	11.0	11	0	0	0	0.0	0	0
1993	Wpg.	1	1	6	6.0	6	0	1	9	9.0	9	0
CFL TOTALS		**4**	**6**	**28**	**4.7**	**11**	**0**	**4**	**68**	**17.0**	**20**	**0**

JONES, CLAUDE

Born: September 12, 1969
Birthplace: Fort Lauderdale, Florida
Offensive Guard. 6'2", 290 lbs. Import
Last Amateur Club: University of Miami
Acquired: Signed as a free agent by the Sacramento Gold Miners in February, 1993. Released by Sacramento in October, 1993. Signed as a free agent by the Las Vegas Posse in March, 1994.

Games Played - 11 with Sacramento in 1993. **CFL Total GP - 11.**

JONES, RICKEY

Born: February 12, 1970
Birthplace: Jackson, Mississippi
Quarterback. 6'1", 200 lbs. Import
Last Amateur Club: Alabama State University
Acquired: Signed as a free agent by the Edmonton Eskimos in April, 1993.

Games Played - 2 with Edmonton in 1993. **CFL Total GP - 2.**

Fumble Returns - 1 for 0 yards with Edmonton in 1993.
CFL Total Fumble Returns - 1 for 0 yards.

JONES, STEPHEN

Born: June 8, 1960
Birthplace: Flint, Michigan
Wide Receiver. 6'0", 190 lbs. Import
Last Amateur Club: Central Michigan University
Acquired: Signed as a free agent by the Saskatchewan Roughriders in October, 1984. Traded to the Ottawa Rough Riders along with running back Robert Reid and linebacker Jeff Roberts for defensive tackle Gary Lewis, defensive back Junior Robinson and wide receiver Daric Zeno in September, 1985. Released by Ottawa in October, 1985 and signed as a free agent by the Edmonton Eskimos in February, 1986. Released by Edmonton in October, 1989. Signed as a free agent by Ottawa in February, 1990.

Year	Team	GP	Scoring TD	C	FG	S	TP	Pass Receiving NO	YDS	AVE	LG	TD
1985	Sask.	8	1	0	0	0	6	18	311	17.3	46	1
1986	Edm.	16	6	0	0	0	36	40	922	23.1	75	5
1987a	Edm.	18	8	0	0	0	48	55	1147	20.9	89	8
1988	Edm.	17	0	0	0	0	0	26	389	15.0	32	0
1989	Edm.	8	1	0	0	0	6	21	374	17.8	67	1
1990bc	Ott.	18	11	0	0	0	66	59	1182	20.0	66	11
1991	Ott.	13	7	0	0	0	42	39	661	16.9	41	7
1992bc	Ott.	18	10	0	0	0	60	75	1400	18.7	55	10
1993b	Ott.	17	6	0	0	0	36	73	1274	17.5	76	6
CFL TOTALS		**133**	**50**	**0**	**0**	**0**	**300**	**406**	**7660**	**18.9**	**89**	**49**

Year	Team	Punt Returns NO	YDS	AVE	LG	TD	Kickoff Returns NO	YDS	AVE	LG	TD
1985	Sask.	7	25	3.6	9	0	3	99	33.0	48	0
1986	Edm.	14	147	10.5	30	0	27	750	27.8	105	1
1987	Edm.	0	0	0.0	0	0	51	957	18.8	48	0
1988	Edm.	0	0	0.0	0	0	31	635	20.5	88	0
1989	Edm.	0	0	0.0	0	0	1	0	0.0	0	0
1990	Ott.	0	0	0.0	0	0	11	175	15.9	28	0
1991	Ott.	0	0	0.0	0	0	5	114	22.8	32	0
1992	Ott.	0	0	0.0	0	0	0	0	0.0	0	0
1993	Ott.	0	0	0.0	0	0	0	0	0.0	0	0
CFL TOTALS		**21**	**172**	**8.2**	**30**	**0**	**129**	**2730**	**21.2**	**105**	**1**

Year	Team	Fumbles NO	LOST	OFR	Passing ATT	COMP	YDS	PCT	INT	LG	TD
1985	Sask.	1	1	0	1	0	0	0.0	0	0	0
1986	Edm.	2	2	0	1	0	0	0.0	0	0	0
1987	Edm.	0	0	2	1	1	52	100.0	0	52	0
1988	Edm.	0	0	0	1	0	0	0.0	0	0	0
1989	Edm.	0	0	0	0	0	0	0.0	0	0	0
1990	Ott.	1	0	1	0	0	0	0.0	0	0	0
1991	Ott.	1	1	0	0	0	0	0.0	0	0	0
1992	Ott.	0	0	0	0	0	0	0.0	0	0	0
1993	Ott.	1	0	1	2	2	92	100.0	0	46	1
CFL TOTALS		**6**	**4**	**4**	**6**	**3**	**144**	**50.0**	**0**	**52**	**1**

Rushing - 3 for 34 yards, 11.3 average, longest 20 yards with Edmonton in 1987; 2 for 22 yards, 11.0 average, longest 18 in 1988; 2 for 5 yards, 2.5 average, longest 18 yards with Ottawa in 1991 and 1 for -14 yards in 1992.
CFL Total Rushing - 8 for 47 yards, 5.9 average, longest 20 yards.

Defensive Tackles - 2 with Edmonton in 1988; 2 with Ottawa in 1992 and 1 in 1993. **CFL Total Defensive Tackles - 5.**

a - Set CFL record, Most Kickoff Returns, One Season - 51. Surpassed by B.C.'s Darrell Wallace in 1989.
b - All-Eastern All-Star
c - CFL All-Star

Playoffs

Year	Team	GP	Scoring TD	C	FG	S	TP	Pass Receiving NO	YDS	AVE	LG	TD
1986	Edm.	1	0	0	0	0	0	3	34	11.3	19	0
1987	Edm.	2	1	0	0	0	6	9	240	26.7	80	1
1988	Edm.	1	0	0	0	0	0	0	0	0.0	0	0
1990	Ott.	1	0	0	0	0	0	2	76	38.0	62	0
1992	Ott.	1	0	0	0	0	0	3	31	10.3	16	0
1993	Ott.	1	1	0	0	0	6	4	109	27.3	75	1
CFL TOTALS		**7**	**2**	**0**	**0**	**0**	**12**	**21**	**490**	**23.3**	**80**	**2**

Rushing - 1 for 14 yards with Edmonton in 1987.
CFL Total Playoff Rushing - 1 for 14 yards.

Kickoff Returns - 3 for 80 yards, 26.7 average, longest 30 yards with Edmonton in 1987 and 3 for 65 yards, 21.7 average, longest 23 yards in 1988.
CFL Total Playoff Kickoff Returns - 6 for 145 yards, 24.2 average, longest 30 yards.

Own Fumbles Recovered - 1 with Ottawa in 1993. **CFL Total Playoff OFR - 1.**

Defensive Tackles - 2 with Edmonton in 1987.
CFL Total Playoff Defensive Tackles - 2.

JONES, STEPHEN

Grey Cup

Games Played - 1 with Edmonton in 1987. **Total Grey Cup GP - 1.**

Pass Receiving - 3 for 41 yards, 13.7 average, longest 20 yards with Edmonton in 1987. **Total Grey Cup Pass Receiving - 3 for 41 yards, 13.7 average, longest 20 yards.**

JONES, TERRENCE
Born: June 18, 1966
Birthplace: New Orleans, Louisiana
Quarterback. 6'1", 210 lbs. Import
Last Amateur Club: Tulane University
Acquired: Selected in the seventh round (195th overall) by the San Diego Chargers in the 1989 NFL Draft. Signed with the Calgary Stampeders as a free agent in May, 1989. Traded to the Ottawa Rough Riders in October, 1991 in exchange for their fourth round draft choice in the 1992 CFL College Draft, slotback Frank Marof. Transferred to the Shreveport Pirates in February, 1994.

		Scoring						Rushing				
	Team	GP	TD	C	FG	S	TP	NO	YDS	AVE	LG	TD
1989	Cal.	13	5	0	0	0	30	28	202	7.2	40	5
1990	Cal.	17	2	0	0	0	12	29	202	7.0	44	2
1991	Cal.	8	0	0	0	0	0	4	22	5.5	10	0
	Ott.	5	0	0	0	0	0	1	7	7.0	7	0
1992	Ott.	18	1	0	0	0	6	7	39	5.6	19	1
1993	Ott.	18	0	0	0	0	0	8	47	5.9	24	0
CFL TOTALS		**79**	**8**	**0**	**0**	**0**	**48**	**77**	**519**	**6.7**	**44**	**8**

		Passing							Fumbles		
	Team	ATT	COMP	YDS	PCT	INT	LG	TD	NO	LOST	OFR
1989	Cal.	92	43	816	46.7	6	55	2	1	1	0
1990	Cal.	130	64	958	49.2	10	56	3	5	4	1
1991	Cal.	17	6	123	35.3	3	54	1	1	1	0
	Ott.	3	2	21	66.7	1	17	0	0	0	0
1992	Ott.	30	13	234	43.3	3	50	1	2	1	1
1993	Ott.	72	29	434	40.3	5	56	1	2	1	1
CFL TOTALS		**344**	**157**	**2586**	**45.6**	**28**	**56**	**8**	**11**	**8**	**3**

2-Pt. Converts - 2 tried, 1 complete with Calgary in 1990 and 1 tried, o complete in 1991. **CFL Total 2-Pt. Converts - 3 tried, 1 complete.**

Defensive Tackles - 1 with Calgary in 1990; 1 with Ottawa in 1991 and 1 in 1993. **CFL Total Defensive Tackles - 3.**

Playoffs

Games Played - 1 with Calgary in 1989; 1 in 1990; 1 with Ottawa in 1991; 1 in 1992 and 1 in 1993. **CFL Total Playoff GP - 5.**

Passing - 8 attempts, 4 completions for 84 yards, 50.0 percent completion rate, 1 interception, longest 36 yards and 1 TD with Calgary in 1989. **CFL Total Playoff Passing - 8 attempts, 4 completions for 84 yards, 50.0 percent completion rate, 1 interception, longest 36 yards and 1 TD.**

JONES, TYRONE
Born: August 3, 1961
Birthplace: St. Mary's, Georgia
Linebacker. 6'0", 220 lbs. Import
Last Amateur Club: Southern University
Acquired: Signed as a free agent by the Winnipeg Blue Bombers in April, 1983. Granted free agency March 1, 1988. Signed as a free agent by Phoenix Cardinals (NFL) in April, 1988. Released at the end of training camp in 1989. Signed as a free agent by Winnipeg Blue Bombers in September, 1989. Traded to the Saskatchewan Roughriders along with future considerations in December, 1991 in exchange for slotback Allen Boyko and a first round draft choice in the 1992 CFL College Draft (acquired in a previous deal from Winnipeg). Transferred to the B.C. Lions in May, 1993. Released by B.C. in November, 1993.

		Scoring						Interception Returns					QB Sacks
	Team	GP	TD	C	FG	S	TP	NO	YDS	AVE	LG	TD	NO
1983	Wpg.	16	0	0	0	0	0	1	22	22.0	22	0	17.5
1984ab	Wpg.	16	0	0	0	0	0	3	10	3.3	10	0	20.5
1985abcd	Wpg.	16	0	0	0	0	0	1	5	5.0	5	0	11.0
1986ab	Wpg.	16	0	0	0	0	0	1	2	2.0	2	0	10.0
1987be	Wpg.	18	2	0	0	0	12	1	0	0.0	0	0	15.0
1988				NFL						NFL			NFL
1989	Wpg.	9	1	0	0	0	6	1	21	21.0	21	1	5.0
1990e	Wpg.	18	0	0	0	0	0	4	14	3.5	11	0	11.0
1991	Wpg.	9	0	0	0	0	0	1	14	14.0	14	0	8.0
1992	Sask.	18	0	0	0	0	0	2	1	0.5	1	0	4.0
1993	B.C.	15	0	0	0	0	0	0	0	0.0	0	0	8.0
CFL TOTALS		**151**	**3**	**0**	**0**	**0**	**18**	**15**	**89**	**5.9**	**22**	**1**	**110.0**

Pass Receiving - 1 for 7 yards with Winnipeg in 1986; 1 for 1 yard and 1 TD in 1987 and 1 for 17 yards in 1991. **CFL Total Pass Receiving - 3 for 25 yards, 8.3 average, longest 17 yards and 1 TD.**

Punt Returns - 1 for 23 yards with Winnipeg in 1984. **CFL Total Punt Returns - 1 for 23 yards.**

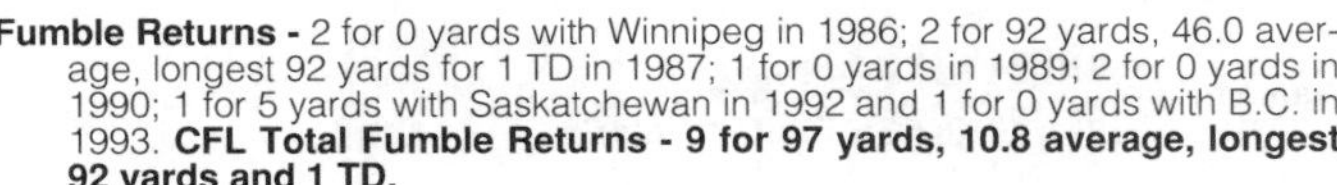

Fumble Returns - 2 for 0 yards with Winnipeg in 1986; 2 for 92 yards, 46.0 average, longest 92 yards for 1 TD in 1987; 1 for 0 yards in 1989; 2 for 0 yards in 1990; 1 for 5 yards with Saskatchewan in 1992 and 1 for 0 yards with B.C. in 1993. **CFL Total Fumble Returns - 9 for 97 yards, 10.8 average, longest 92 yards and 1 TD.**

Blocked Kicks - 1 field goal with Winnipeg in 1983. **CFL Total Blocked Kicks - 1 field goal.**

Own Kickoffs Recovered - 1 with Winnipeg in 1984. **CFL Total Own Kickoffs Recovered - 1.**

Tackles - 36 defensive with Winnipeg in 1987; 33 defensive in 1989; 49 defensive in 1990; 16 defensive and 4 special teams in 1991; 62 defensive and 10 special teams with Saskatchewan in 1992 and 25 defensive with B.C. in 1993. **CFL Total Tackles - 235 (221 defensive and 14 special teams).**

Tackles for Losses - 2 for 7 yards with Winnipeg in 1991; 8 for 25 yards with Saskatchewan in 1992 and 5 for 17 yards with B.C. in 1993. **CFL Total Tackles for Losses - 15 for 49 yards.**

a - All-Western All-Star
b - CFL All-Star
c - Norm Fieldgate Trophy, Most Outstanding Defensive Player, Western Division
d - Schenley Most Outstanding Defensive Player
e - All-Eastern All-Star

Playoffs

			Fumble Returns					QB Sacks
	Team	GP	NO	YDS	AVE	LG	TD	NO
1983	Wpg.	2	0	0	0.0	0	0	2.5
1984	Wpg.	2	1	44	44.0	44	0	2.0
1985	Wpg.	2	0	0	0.0	0	0	0
1986	Wpg.	1	0	0	0.0	0	0	0
1987	Wpg.	1	0	0	0.0	0	0	0
1989	Wpg.	2	0	0	0.0	0	0	0
1990	Wpg.	1	0	0	0.0	0	0	0
1991	Wpg.	2	0	0	0.0	0	0	2.0
1992	Sask.	1	0	0	0.0	0	0	0
1993	B.C.	1	0	0	0.0	0	0	0
CFL TOTALS		**15**	**1**	**44**	**44.0**	**44**	**0**	**6.5**

Interception Returns - 1 for 0 yards with Saskatchewan in 1992. **CFL Total Playoff Interception Returns - 1 for 0 yards.**

Tackles - 6 defensive with Winnipeg in 1989; 2 defensive in 1990; 6 defensive and 3 special teams in 1991; 2 defensive and 2 special teams in 1992 and 2 defensive with B.C. in 1993. **CFL Total Playoff Tackles - 23 (18 defensive and 5 special teams).**

Grey Cup

Games Played - 1 with Winnipeg in 1984 and 1 in 1990. **Total Grey Cup GP - 2.**

Quarterback Sacks - 4 with Winnipeg in 1984 and 1 in 1990. **Total Grey Cup QB Sacks - 5.**

Fumble Returns - 1 for 0 yards with Winnipeg in 1990. **Total Grey Cup Fumble Returns - 1 for 0 yards.**

Defensive Tackles - 1 with Winnipeg in 1990. **Total Grey Cup Defensive Tackles - 1.**

Grey Cup Game Defensive Star in 1984.

JONES, WARREN
Born: September 23, 1966
Birthplace: Dallas, Texas
Quarterback. 6'2", 200 lbs. Import
Last Amateur Club: University of Hawaii
Acquired: Signed as a free agent with Edmonton Eskimos in April, 1989. Spent all of the 1989 season on the injured list. Traded to the Saskatchewan Roughriders in February, 1992 in exchange for a third round draft choice, offensive lineman Simon Taylor and a fourth round draft choice, offensive lineman Terris Chorrey in the 1992 CFL College Draft.

			Rushing					Passing						
	Team	GP	NO	YDS	AVE	LG	TD	ATT	COMP	YDS	PCT	INT	LG	TD
1990	Edm.	14	1	2	2.0	2	0	55	33	390	60.0	2	43	3
1991	Edm.	18	15	51	3.4	22	0	149	83	1113	55.7	4	59	9
1992	Sask.	18	8	60	7.5	13	0	20	6	121	30.0	2	31	1
1993	Sask.	18	24	62	2.6	10	1	55	34	362	61.8	2	56	1
CFL TOTALS		**68**	**48**	**175**	**3.7**	**22**	**1**	**279**	**156**	**1986**	**56.0**	**10**	**59**	**14**

Scoring - 1 TD for 6 points with Saskatchewan in 1993. **CFL Total Scoring - TD for 6 points.**

2-Pt. Converts - 1 tried and 1 complete with Edmonton in 1990. **CFL Total 2-Pt. Converts - 1 tried and 1 complete.**

Fumbles - 5 and 4 lost with Edmonton in 1991 and 1 and 1 lost with Saskatchewan in 1993. **CFL Total Fumbles - 6 and 5 lost.**

JONES, WARREN

Playoffs

Games Played - 2 with Edmonton in 1990; 1 in 1991; 1 with Saskatchewan in 1992 and 1 in 1993. **CFL Total Playoff GP - 5.**

Passing - 2 attempts, 0 completions with Edmonton in 1991 and 4 attempts, 2 completions with Saskatchewan in 1993.
CFL Total Playoff Passing - 6 attempts, 2 completions.

Grey Cup

Games Played - 1 with Edmonton in 1990. **Total Grey Cup GP - 1.**

JOSEPH, DARREN
Born: August 29, 1968
Birthplace: Ottawa, Ontario
Running Back. 6'0", 200 lbs. Non-import
Last Amateur Club: Ottawa Sooners (OJFC)
Acquired: Signed as a free agent by the Ottawa Rough Riders in December, 1990. Released by Ottawa in June, 1991. Signed as a free agent by Ottawa in January, 1992.

		Scoring						Rushing				
	Team	GP	TD	C	FG	S	TP	NO	YDS	AVE	LG	TD
1992	Ott.	18	2	0	0	0	12	119	711	6.0	52	2
1993	Ott.	14	1	0	0	0	6	108	398	3.7	23	1
CFL TOTALS		**32**	**3**	**0**	**0**	**0**	**18**	**227**	**1109**	**4.9**	**52**	**3**

		Pass Receiving					Kickoff Returns				
	Team	NO	YDS	AVE	LG	TD	NO	YDS	AVE	LG	TD
1992	Ott.	15	113	7.5	11	0	7	140	20.0	28	0
1993	Ott.	33	403	12.2	54	0	2	21	10.5	15	0
CFL TOTALS		**48**	**516**	**10.8**	**54**	**0**	**9**	**161**	**17.9**	**28**	**0**

Passing - 1 attempt, 1 complete for 10 yards and 1 TD with Ottawa in 1992.
CFL Total Passing - 1 attempt, 1 complete for 10 yards and 1 TD.

Fumbles - 3 and 3 lost with Ottawa in 1992 and 3 and 2 lost in 1993.
CFL Total Fumbles - 6 and 5 lost.

Own Fumbles Recovered - 1 with Ottawa in 1993. **CFL Total OFR - 1**

Tackles - 2 defensive and 6 special teams with Ottawa in 1992 and 2 defensive and 2 special teams in 1993.
CFL Total Tackles - 12 (4 defensive and 8 special teams).

Playoffs

			Kickoff Returns				
	Team	GP	NO	YDS	AVE	LG	TD
1992	Ott.	1	0	0	0.0	0	0
1993	Ott.	1	2	23	11.5	21	0
CFL TOTALS		**2**	**2**	**23**	**11.5**	**21**	**0**

JOVANOVICH, MIKE
Born: May 11, 1967
Birthplace: Toronto, Ontario
Tackle. 6'5", 290 lbs. Non-import
Last Amateur Club: Boston College
Acquired: Selected in the second round (ninth overall) by the Hamilton Tiger-Cats in the 1991 CFL College Draft. Signed as a free agent by the NFL Seattle Seahawks in April, 1992 and was released after training camp. Signed by Hamilton in September, 1992. Granted free agency status in February, 1994. Signed as a free agent by the Toronto Argonauts in March, 1994.

Games Played - 9 with Hamilton in 1992 and 18 in 1993. **CFL Total GP - 27.**

Fumble Returns - 1 for 0 yards with Hamilton in 1992.
CFL Total Fumble Returns - 1 for 0 yards.

Own Fumbles Recovered - 1 with Hamilton in 1993. **CFL Total OFR - 1**

Tackles - 4 defensive and 6 special teams with Hamilton in 1993.
CFL Total Tackles - 10 (4 defensive and 6 special teams).

Playoffs

Games Played - 2 with Hamilton in 1992. **CFL Total Playoff GP - 2.**

Tackles - 1 defensive with Hamilton in 1992.
CFL Total Playoff Tackles - 1 (1 defensive).

JURASIN, BOBBY
Born: August 26, 1964
Birthplace: Wakefield, Michigan
Defensive End. 6'0", 250 lbs. Import
Last Amateur Club: Northern Michigan University
Acquired: Signed as a free agent by the Saskatchewan Roughriders in March, 1986.

Games Played - 8 with Saskatchewan in 1986; 18 in 1987; 18 in 1988; 17 in 1989; 18 in 1990; 16 in 1991; 14 in 1992 and 17 in 1993.
CFL Total GP - 126.

Scoring - 1 TD for 6 points with Saskatchewan in 1988 and 1 TD for 6 points in 1989. **CFL Total Scoring - 2 TDs for 12 points.**

Pass Receiving - 2 for 27 yards, 13.5 average, longest 24 yards and 1 TD with Saskatchewan in 1988; 1 for 39 yards and 1 TD in 1989 and 1 for 13 yards in 1992.
CFL Total Pass Receiving - 4 for 79 yards, 19.8 average, longest 39 yards and 2 TDs.

Fumble Returns - 1 for 23 yards with Saskatchewan in 1986; 2 for 0 yards in 1987; 3 for 0 yards in 1988; 1 for 0 yards in 1990; 4 for 7 yards, 1.8 average, longest 4 yards in 1991; 3 for 21 yards, 7.0 average, longest 21 yards in 1992 and 1 for 0 yards in 1993.
CFL Total Fumble Returns - 15 for 51 yards, 3.4 average, longest 23 yards.

Interception Returns - 1 for 6 yards with Saskatchewan in 1987.
CFL Total Interception Returns - 1 for 6 yards.

Punt Returns - 1 for 11 yards with Saskatchewan in 1987.
CFL Total Punt Returns - 1 for 11 yards.

Fumbles - 1 and 1 lost with Saskatchewan in 1987. **CFL Total Fumbles - 1 and 1 lost.**

Quarterback Sacks - 3 with Saskatchewan in 1986; 22 in 1987; 16 in 1988; 16 in 1989; 10 in 1990; 10 in 1991; 10 for 78 yards lost in 1992 and 14 for 70 yards lost in 1993. **CFL Total QB Sacks - 101.**

Tackles - 45 defensive with Saskatchewan in 1987; 39 defensive in 1988; 35 defensive in 1989; 51 defensive in 1990; 33 defensive and 1 special teams in 1991; 24 defensive in 1992 and 25 defensive in 1993.
CFL Total Tackles - 253 (252 defensive and 1 special teams).

Tackles for Losses - 3 for 4 yards with Saskatchewan in 1991; 1 for 2 yards in 1992 and 5 for 17 yards in 1993.
CFL Total Tackles for Losses - 9 for 23 yards.

All-Western All-Star in 1987; 1988; 1989 and 1992.
CFL All-Star in 1987; 1988 and 1992.

Playoffs

Games Played - 1 with Saskatchewan in 1988; 2 in 1989; 1 in 1990; 1 in 1992 and 1 in 1993. **CFL Total Playoff GP - 6.**

Interception Returns - 1 for 12 yards with Saskatchewan in 1989.
CFL Total Playoff Interception Returns - 1 for 12 yards.

Quarterback Sacks - 2 with Saskatchewan in 1989; 2 for 7 yards lost in 1992 and 1 for 10 yards lost in 1993.
CFL Total Playoff QB Sacks - 5.

Defensive Tackles - 3 with Saskatchewan in 1988; 2 in 1989; 7 in 1990; 3 in 1992 and 3 in 1993.
CFL Total Playoff Defensive Tackles - 18.

Tackles for Losses - 1 for 1 yard with Saskatchewan in 1992.
CFL Total Playoff Tackles for Losses - 1 for 1 yard.

Grey Cup

Games Played - 1 with Saskatchewan in 1989. **Total Grey Cup GP - 1.**

Defensive Tackles - 2 with Saskatchewan in 1989.
Total Grey Cup Defensive Tackles - 2.

KELSON, DERRICK
Born: May 14, 1968
Birthplace: Warren, Ohio
Cornerback. 6'0", 190 lbs. Import
Last Amateur Club: Purdue University
Acquired: Selected in the 11th round (279th overall) by the New York Jets in the 1990 NFL Draft. Released after training camp in 1990. Signed in October, 1990 to the developmental squad of the NFL San Diego Chargers and spent two seasons with the club. Played for the WLAF Sacramento Surge for the 1992 season. Signed as a free agent by the Hamilton Tiger-Cats in October, 1992. Granted free agency status in February, 1994. Signed as a free agent with the Las Vegas Posse in February, 1994.

Games Played - 1 with Hamilton in 1992 and 7 in 1993. **CFL Total GP - 8.**

Interception Returns - 1 for 0 yards with Hamilton in 1993.
CFL Total Interception Returns - 1 for 0 yards.

Fumble Returns - 1 for 0 yards with Hamilton in 1993.
CFL Total Fumble Returns - 1 for 0 yards.

Tackles - 1 defensive with Hamilton in 1992 and 22 defensive and 1 special teams in 1993. **CFL Total Tackles - 24 (23 defensive and 1 special teams).**

KERRIGAN, MIKE
Born: April 27, 1960
Birthplace: Chicago, Illinois
Quarterback. 6'4", 215 lbs. Import
Last Amateur Club: Northwestern University
Acquired: Signed as a free agent by the NFL New England Patriots in May, 1982. Released by New England in November, 1984. Signed as a free agent by the Hamilton Tiger-Cats in May, 1986 following a 21-day trial with Hamilton in 1985. Granted free agency status in February, 1992. Signed as a free agent by the Toronto Argonauts in June, 1992.

		Scoring						Rushing				
	Team	GP	TD	C	FG	S	TP	NO	YDS	AVE	LG	TD
1986ab	Ham.	18	0	0	0	0	0	25	81	3.2	16	0
1987	Ham.	14	0	0	0	0	0	9	22	2.4	6	0
1988	Ham.	13	1	0	0	0	6	20	59	3.0	12	1
1989a	Ham.	16	0	0	0	0	0	21	17	0.8	12	0
1990	Ham.	18	1	0	0	0	6	24	37	1.5	13	1
1991	Ham.	18	1	0	0	0	6	16	28	1.8	5	1
1992	Tor.	13	1	0	0	0	6	2	4	2.0	2	1
1993	Tor.	7	0	0	0	0	0	4	11	2.8	4	0
CFL TOTALS		**117**	**4**	**0**	**0**	**0**	**24**	**121**	**259**	**2.1**	**16**	**4**

		Passing							Fumbles		
	Team	ATT	COMP	YDS	PCT	INT	LG	TD	NO	LOST	OFR
1986	Ham.	424	242	3193	57.0	19	75	16	5	4	0
1987	Ham.	196	103	1339	52.6	15	75	5	3	1	2
1988	Ham.	342	188	2764	55.0	14	75	16	5	3	1
1989	Ham.	486	248	3635	51.0	28	67	20	6	3	0
1990	Ham.	479	249	3655	52.0	32	75	22	5	4	0
1991	Ham.	311	155	2242	49.8	19	77	13	3	1	2
1992	Tor.	59	31	406	52.5	5	43	3	0	0	0
1993	Tor.	153	86	1323	56.2	5	72	9	1	1	0
CFL TOTALS		**2450**	**1302**	**18557**	**53.1**	**137**	**77**	**104**	**28**	**17**	**5**

2-Pt. Converts - 1 tried with Hamilton in 1987; 1 tried, 1 complete in 1990; 2 tried, 1 complete in 1991; 2 tried, 1 complete with Toronto in 1992 and 1 tried, 1 complete in 1993.
CFL Total 2-Pt. Converts - 7 tried, 4 complete.

Defensive Tackles - 1 with Hamilton in 1987; 1 in 1988; 2 in 1989 and 1 with Toronto in 1993. **CFL Total Defensive Tackles - 5.**

a - All-Eastern All-Star
b - Set CFL Record for completions in a playoff game with 35 against Toronto on November 23, 1986.

Playoffs

			Rushing					Passing						
	Team	GP	NO	YDS	AVE	LG	TD	ATT	COMP	YDS	PCT	INT	LG	TD
1986	Ham.	2	7	19	2.7	9	0	87	58	633	66.7	5	34	4
1989	Ham.	1	2	6	3.0	5	0	19	6	47	31.6	1	13	1
CFL TOTALS		**3**	**9**	**25**	**2.8**	**9**	**0**	**106**	**64**	**680**	**60.4**	**6**	**34**	**5**

Grey Cup

			Rushing					Passing						
	Team	GP	NO	YDS	AVE	LG	TD	ATT	COMP	YDS	PCT	INT	LG	TD
1986	Ham.	1	2	7	3.5	6	0	32	15	304	46.9	2	44	2
1989	Ham.	1	0	0	0.0	0	0	35	23	303	65.7	1	30	3
CFL TOTALS		**2**	**2**	**7**	**3.5**	**6**	**0**	**67**	**38**	**607**	**56.7**	**3**	**44**	**5**

Grey Cup Game Offensive Star 1986.

KING, EMANUEL
Born: August 15, 1963
Birthplace: Leroy, Alabama
Defensive End. 6'4", 270 lbs. Import
Last Amateur Club: University of Alabama
Acquired: Selected by the Birmingham Stallions in the 1985 USFL Territorial Draft. Selected by the Cincinnati Bengals in the first round (25th overall) in the 1985 NFL Draft. Granted unconditional free agency in February, 1989. Signed as a free agent by the NFL Los Angeles Raiders in March, 1989. Released by Los Angeles in August, 1990. Re-signed by Los Angeles in March, 1991. Selected by the Montreal Machine in the first round of the 1992 WLAF Draft. Signed as a free agent by the Ottawa Rough Riders in January, 1993. Released by Ottawa in July, 1993. Signed as a free agent by the Sacramento Gold Miners in October, 1993.

Games Played - 5 with Sacramento in 1993. **CFL Total GP - 5.**

Quarterback Sacks - 2 for 17 yards lost with Sacramento in 1993.
CFL Total QB Sacks - 2 for 17 yards lost.

Tackles - 3 defensive and 1 special teams with Sacramento in 1993.
CFL Total Tackles - 4 (3 defensive and 1 special teams).

KING, LORNE
Born: April 12, 1967
Birthplace: Scarborough, Ontario
Running Back. 6'0", 210 lbs. Non-import
Last Amateur Club: University of Toronto (OUAA)
Acquired: Selected in the first round (fourth overall) by the B.C. Lions in the 1992 CFL College Draft. The pick was acquired from the Winnipeg Blue Bombers in exchange for defensive back Andrew Thomas. Released by B.C. in June, 1993 and was subsequently signed as a free agent by the Toronto Argonauts in August, 1993.

		Scoring						Rushing				
	Team	GP	TD	C	FG	S	TP	NO	YDS	AVE	LG	TD
1992	B.C.	18	3	0	0	0	18	27	125	4.6	57	3
1993	Tor.	10	0	0	0	0	0	6	25	4.2	8	0
CFL TOTALS		**28**	**3**	**0**	**0**	**0**	**18**	**33**	**150**	**4.5**	**57**	**3**

		Pass Receiving					Kickoff Returns				
	Team	NO	YDS	AVE	LG	TD	NO	YDS	AVE	LG	TD
1992	B.C.	6	44	7.3	13	0	1	9	9.0	9	0
1992	Tor.	0	0	0.0	0	0	0	0	0.0	0	0
CFL TOTALS		**6**	**44**	**7.3**	**13**	**0**	**1**	**9**	**9.0**	**9**	**0**

Own Kickoffs Recovered - 1 for 0 yards with B.C. in 1992.
CFL Total OKR - 1 for 0 yards.

Fumbles - 1 and 1 lost with B.C. in 1992. **CFL Total Fumbles - 1 and 1 lost.**

Own Fumbles Recovered - 1 with B.C. in 1992. **CFL Total OFR - 1.**

Tackles - 2 defensive and 20 special teams with B.C. in 1992 and 6 special teams with Toronto in 1993.
CFL Total Tackles - 28 (2 defensive and 26 special teams).

KNIGHT, LEE
Born: February 8, 1965
Birthplace: Wallesey, England
Fullback/Slotback. 6'3", 230 lbs. Non-import
Last Amateur Club: Burlington Tiger-Cats Juniors (OJFC)
Acquired: Signed as a free agent by the Hamilton Tiger-Cats in July, 1987.

		Scoring						Pass Receiving				
	Team	GP	TD	C	FG	S	TP	NO	YDS	AVE	LG	TD
1987	Ham.	12	0	1	1	2	6	7	74	10.6	15	0
1988	Ham.	17	2	0	0	0	12	17	261	15.4	37	2
1989	Ham.	18	1	0	0	0	6	17	238	14.0	28	1
1990	Ham.	18	1	0	0	0	6	41	635	15.5	32	1
1991	Ham.	18	2	0	0	0	12	16	190	11.9	30	1
1992	Ham.	18	4	0	0	0	24	29	296	10.2	29	1
1993	Ham.	17	2	0	0	0	12	30	214	7.1	18	1
CFL TOTALS		**118**	**12**	**1**	**1**	**2**	**78**	**157**	**1908**	**12.2**	**37**	**7**

		Rushing					Kickoffs				
	Team	NO	YDS	AVE	LG	TD	NO	YDS	AVE	LK	S
1987	Ham.	0	0	0.0	0	0	3	131	43.7	48	0
1988	Ham.	0	0	0.0	0	0	0	0	0.0	0	0
1989	Ham.	0	0	0.0	0	0	0	0	0.0	0	0
1990	Ham.	0	0	0.0	0	0	0	0	0.0	0	0
1991	Ham.	15	80	5.3	30	1	0	0	0.0	0	0
1992	Ham.	39	185	4.7	25	3	0	0	0.0	0	0
1993	Ham.	28	108	3.9	22	1	0	0	0.0	0	0
CFL TOTALS		**82**	**373**	**4.5**	**30**	**5**	**3**	**131**	**43.7**	**48**	**0**

		Kickoff Returns					Field Goals				
	Team	NO	YDS	AVE	LG	TD	T	G	YDS	AVE	LK
1987	Ham.	1	6	6.0	6	0	3	1	36	36.0	36
1988	Ham.	0	0	0.0	0	0	0	0	0	0.0	0
1989	Ham.	0	0	0.0	0	0	0	0	0	0.0	0
1990	Ham.	2	13	6.5	13	0	0	0	0	0.0	0
1991	Ham.	0	0	0.0	0	0	0	0	0	0.0	0
1992	Ham.	0	0	0.0	0	0	0	0	0	0.0	0
1993	Ham.	2	9	4.5	8	0	0	0	0	0.0	0
CFL TOTALS		**5**	**28**	**5.6**	**13**	**0**	**3**	**1**	**36**	**36.0**	**36**

		Field Goal Attempts					Converts			Fumbles		
	Team	NO	YDS	AVE	LK	S	T	G	PCT	NO	LOST	OFR
1987	Ham.	2	72	36.0	37	2	1	1	100.0	1	1	0
1988	Ham.	0	0	0.0	0	0	0	0	0.0	0	0	0
1989	Ham.	0	0	0.0	0	0	0	0	0.0	1	1	0
1990	Ham.	0	0	0.0	0	0	0	0	0.0	0	0	0
1991	Ham.	0	0	0.0	0	0	0	0	0.0	1	1	0
1992	Ham.	0	0	0.0	0	0	0	0	0.0	2	1	0
1993	Ham.	0	0	0.0	0	0	0	0	0.0	1	1	0
CFL TOTALS		**2**	**72**	**36.0**	**37**	**2**	**1**	**1**	**100.0**	**6**	**5**	**0**

Punt Returns - 1 for 1 yard with Hamilton in 1987 and 1 for 15 yards in 1993.
CFL Total Punt Returns - 2 for 16 yards, 8.0 average, longest 15 yards.

Passing - 1 attempt, 0 complete with Hamilton in 1993.
CFL Total Passing - 1 attempt, 0 complete.

Tackles - 1 defensive with Hamilton in 1988; 2 defensive in 1989; 6 defensive in 1990; 2 defensive and 16 special teams in 1991; 1 defensive and 11 special teams in 1992 and 1 defensive and 3 special teams in 1993.
CFL Total Tackles - 43 (13 defensive and 30 special teams).

Playoffs

Games Played - 1 with Hamilton in 1987; 1 in 1988; 1 in 1989; 2 in 1992 and 2 in 1993. **CFL Total Playoff GP - 7.**

KNIGHT, LEE

Scoring - 1 TD for 6 points with Hamilton in 1992 and 1 TD for 6 points in 1993. **CFL Total Playoff Scoring - 2 TD for 12 points.**

Rushing - 3 for 5 yards, 1.7 average, longest 5 yards with Hamilton in 1992 and 2 for 0 yards in 1993. **CFL Total Playoff Rushing - 5 for 5 yards, 1.0 average, longest 5 yards.**

Pass Receiving - 7 for 117 yards, 16.7 average, longest 40 yards and 1 TD with Hamilton in 1992 and 7 for 67 yards, 9.6 average, longest 21 yards and 1 TD in 1993. **CFL Total Playoff Pass Receiving - 14 for 184 yards, 13.1 average, longest 40 yards and 2 TDs.**

Tackles - 1 defensive with Hamilton in 1992 and 1 special teams in 1993. **CFL Total Playoff Tackles - 2 (1 defensive and 1 special teams).**

Grey Cup

Games Played - 1 with Hamilton in 1989. **Total Grey Cup GP - 1.**

Pass Receiving - 2 for 34 yards, 17.0 average, longest 18 yards with Hamilton in 1989. **Total Grey Cup Pass Receiving - 2 for 34 yards, 17.0 average, longest 18 yards.**

KNOX, GREG
Born: December 6, 1969
Birthplace: Toronto, Ontario
Defensive Back. 6'0", 180 lbs. Non-import
Last Amateur Club: Wilfrid Laurier University (OUAA)
Acquired: Selected in the sixth round (47th overall) by the Calgary Stampeders in the 1992 CFL College Draft.

Games Played - 18 with Calgary in 1992 and 18 in 1993. **CFL Total GP - 36.**

Interception Returns - 1 for 0 yards with Calgary in 1992 and 3 for 15 yards, 5.0 average, longest 15 yards in 1993. **CFL Total Interception Returns - 4 for 15 yards, 3.8 average, longest 15 yards.**

Fumbles - 1 and 1 lost with Calgary in 1993. **CFL Total Fumbles - 1 and 1 lost.**

Fumble Returns - 1 for 0 yards with Calgary in 1992 and 2 for 0 yards in 1993. **CFL Total Fumble Returns - 3 for 0 yards.**

Quarterback Sacks - 1 for 10 yards lost with Calgary in 1993. **CFL Total QB Sacks - 1 for 10 yards lost.**

Tackles - 24 defensive and 6 special teams with Calgary in 1992 and 32 defensive and 6 special teams in 1993. **CFL Total Tackles - 68 (56 defensive and 12 special teams).**

Tackles for Losses - 1 for 15 yards with Calgary in 1993. **CFL Total Tackles for Losses - 1 for 15 yards.**

Playoffs

Games Played - 1 with Calgary in 1992 and 2 in 1993. **CFL Total Playoff GP - 3.**

Tackles - 1 special teams with Calgary in 1992 and 8 defensive in 1993. **CFL Total Playoff Tackles - 9 (8 defensive and 1 special teams).**

Grey Cup

Games Played - 1 with Calgary in 1992. **Total Grey Cup GP - 1.**

Tackles - 3 special teams with Calgary in 1992. **Total Grey Cup Tackles - 3 (3 special teams).**

KROPKE, JOHN
Born: January 3, 1966
Birthplace: Chicago, Illinois
Defensive Tackle. 6'4", 278 lbs. Import
Last Amateur Club: Illinois State University
Acquired: Signed as a free agent with the Ottawa Rough Riders in October, 1989. Granted free agency status in February, 1992. Re-signed by Ottawa in April, 1992. Granted free agency status in February, 1994. Re-signed by Ottawa in March, 1994.

Games Played - 2 with Ottawa in 1989; 14 in 1990; 18 in 1991; 17 in 1992 and 18 in 1993. **CFL Total GP - 69.**

Scoring - 1 TD for 6 points with Ottawa in 1992 and 1 TD for 6 points in 1993. **CFL Total Scoring - 2 TDs for 12 points.**

Fumble Returns - 1 for 0 yards with Ottawa in 1990; 1 for 3 yards and 1 TD in 1992 and 1 for 29 yards and 1 TD in 1993. **CFL Total Fumble Returns - 3 for 32 yards, 10.7 average, longest 29 yards and 2 TDs.**

Interception Returns - 2 for 38 yards, 19.0 average, longest 38 yards with Ottawa in 1993. **CFL Total Interception Returns - 2 for 38 yards, 19.0 average, longest 38 yards.**

Quarterback Sacks - 1 with Ottawa in 1989; 3 in 1990; 2 in 1991; 7 for 43 yards lost in 1992 and 6 for 31 yards lost in 1993. **CFL Total QB Sacks - 19.**

Tackles - 2 defensive with Ottawa in 1989; 27 defensive in 1990; 46 defensive in 1991; 39 defensive and 1 special teams in 1992 and 31 defensive in 1993. **CFL Total Tackles - 146 (145 defensive and 1 special teams).**

Tackles for Losses - 2 for 4 yards with Ottawa in 1991; 7 for 18 yards in 1992 and 1 for 4 yards in 1993. **CFL Total Tackles for Losses - 10 for 26 yards.**

All-Eastern All-Star in 1992 and 1993.

Playoffs

Games Played - 1 with Ottawa in 1991; 1 in 1992 and 1 in 1993. **CFL Total Playoff GP - 3.**

Scoring - 1 TD for 6 points with Ottawa in 1992. **CFL Total Playoff Scoring - 1 TD for 6 points.**

Fumble Returns - 1 for 23 yards and 1 TD with Ottawa in 1992. **CFL Total Playoff Fumble Returns - 1 for 23 yards and 1 TD.**

Tackles - 3 defensive with Ottawa in 1991; 3 defensive and 1 special teams in 1992 and 2 defensive in 1993. **CFL Total Playoff Tackles - 9 (8 defensive and 1 special teams).**

Tackles for Losses - 1 for 4 yards with Ottawa in 1991. **CFL Total Playoff Tackles for Losses - 1 for 4 yards.**

KRUPEY, STEVE
Born: March 16, 1965
Birthplace: Montreal, Quebec
Guard. 6'3", 265 lbs. Non-import
Last Amateur Club: University of Western Ontario (OUAA)
Acquired: Signed as a free agent by the Edmonton Eskimos in November, 1991.

Games Played - 12 with Edmonton in 1991; 4 in 1992 and 18 in 1993. **CFL Total GP - 34.**

Kickoff Returns - 1 for 13 yards with Edmonton in 1991. **CFL Total Kickoff Returns - 1 for 13 yards.**

Tackles - 1 defensive and 5 special teams with Edmonton in 1991 and 2 defensive in 1993. **CFL Total Tackles - 8 (3 defensive and 5 special teams).**

Playoffs

Games Played - 1 with Edmonton in 1991; 1 in 1992 and 2 in 1993. **CFL Total Playoff GP - 4.**

Grey Cup

Games Played - 1 with Edmonton in 1993. **Total Grey Cup GP - 1**

KULKA, GLENN
Born: March 3, 1964
Birthplace: Edmonton, Alberta
Defensive End. 6'2", 264 lbs. Non-import
Last Amateur Club: Bakersfield College
Acquired: Signed as a free agent by the Edmonton Eskimos in March, 1986. Released by Edmonton and signed by the Montreal Alouettes in September, 1986. Selected by B.C. Lions in first round (sixth overall) of Alouettes Dispersal Draft in June, 1987. Traded in June, 1987 to the Saskatchewan Roughriders along with B.C.'s first round selection in the 1988 CFL College Draft (linebacker Pete Giftopoulos) for defensive tackle Brett Williams. Traded in June, 1987 to the Toronto Argonauts in lieu of Saskatchewan's third round pick in the 1988 CFL College Draft. Signed as a free agent by the Ottawa Rough Riders in March, 1990.

Games Played - 6 with Montreal in 1986; 15 with Toronto in 1987; 18 in 1988; 16 in 1989; 18 with Ottawa in 1990; 15 in 1991; 17 in 1992 and 16 in 1993. **CFL Total GP - 121.**

Fumble Returns - 2 for 9 yards, 4.5 average, longest 9 yards with Toronto in 1987; 2 for 0 yards in 1988; 1 for 0 yards with Ottawa in 1991 and 1 for 0 yards in 1993. **CFL Total Fumble Returns - 6 for 9 yards, 1.5 average, longest 9 yards.**

Quarterback Sacks - 10 with Toronto in 1987; 11 in 1988; 8 in 1989; 7 with Ottawa in 1990; 3 in 1991; 2 for 9 yards lost in 1992 and 2 for 21 yards lost in 1993. **CFL Total QB Sacks - 43.**

Tackles - 23 defensive with Toronto in 1987; 23 defensive in 1988; 32 defensive in 1989; 31 defensive with Ottawa in 1990; 20 defensive in 1991; 19 defensive in 1992 and 12 defensive in 1993. **CFL Total Tackles - 160 (160 defensive).**

Tackles for Losses - 1 for 2 yards with Ottawa in 1991 and 6 for 11 yards in 1992. **CFL Total Tackles for Losses - 7 for 13 yards.**

All-Eastern All-Star in 1988.

KULKA, GLENN

Playoffs

Games Played - 2 with Toronto in 1987; 1 in 1988; 1 in 1989; 1 with Ottawa in 1990; 1 in 1991; 1 in 1992 and 1 in 1993. **CFL Total Playoff GP - 8.**

Quarterback Sacks - 3 with Toronto in 1987 and 1 in 1989. **CFL Total Playoff QB Sacks - 4.**

Tackles - 2 defensive with Toronto in 1987; 2 defensive in 1988; 2 defensive in 1989; 1 defensive with Ottawa in 1990; 4 defensive in 1991; 2 defensive in 1992 and 1 defensive in 1993. **CFL Total Playoff Tackles - 14 (14 defensive).**

Tackles for Losses - 1 for 4 yards with Ottawa in 1991; 1 for 2 yards in 1992 and 1 for 2 yards in 1993. **CFL Total Playoff Tackles for Losses - 3 for 8 yards.**

Grey Cup

Games Played - 1 with Toronto in 1987. **Total Grey Cup GP - 1.**

LAIRD, STUART
Born: July 8, 1960
Birthplace: Assiniboia, Saskatchewan
Defensive Lineman. 6'2", 260 lbs. Non-import
Last Amateur Club: University of Calgary (WIFL)
Acquired: Signed as a free agent by the Saskatchewan Roughriders in January, 1983. Released and signed as a free agent by the Montreal Concordes in June, 1983. Released and signed as a free agent by the Calgary Stampeders in June, 1984.

Games Played - 16 with Calgary in 1985; 14 in 1986; 18 in 1987; 18 in 1988; 5 in 1989; 16 in 1990; 14 in 1991; 10 in 1992 and 14 in 1993. **CFL Total GP - 125.**

Own Fumbles Recovered - 1 with Calgary in 1985 and 1 in 1990. **CFL Total OFR - 2.**

Interception Returns - 1 for 0 yards with Calgary in 1991. **CFL Total Interception Returns - 1 for 0 yards.**

Fumble Returns - 1 for 0 yards with Calgary in 1986; 1 for 0 yards in 1987; 3 for 0 yards in 1988; 3 for 16 yards, 5.3 average, longest 16 yards in 1991; 1 for 0 yards in 1992 and 1 for 0 yards in 1993. **CFL Total Fumble Returns - 10 for 16 yards, 1.6 average, longest 16 yards.**

Blocked Kicks - 1 punt with Calgary in 1989. **CFL Total Blocked Kicks - 1 punt.**

Quarterback Sacks - 2 with Calgary in 1985; 9 in 1986; 7 in 1987; 11 in 1988; 5 in 1990; 5 in 1991; 6 for 49 yards lost in 1992 and 8 for 67 yards lost in 1993. **CFL Total QB Sacks - 53.**

Defensive Tackles - 21 with Calgary in 1987; 54 in 1988; 3 in 1989; 12 in 1990; 34 in 1991; 21 in 1992 and 18 in 1993. **CFL Total Defensive Tackles - 163.**

Tackles for Losses - 3 for 4 yards with Calgary in 1991 and 1 for 2 yards in 1993. **CFL Total Tackles for Losses - 4 for 6 yards.**

Playoffs

Games Played - 1 with Calgary in 1986; 1 in 1987; 1 in 1989; 2 in 1991; 1 in 1992 and 2 in 1993. **CFL Total Playoff GP - 8.**

Quarterback Sacks - 4 with Calgary in 1987. **CFL Total Playoff QB Sacks - 4.**

Defensive Tackles - 4 with Calgary in 1987; 2 in 1989; 3 in 1991; 2 in 1992 and 1 in 1993. **CFL Total Playoff Defensive Tackles - 12.**

Grey Cup

Games Played - 1 with Calgary in 1991 and 1 in 1992. **Total Grey Cup GP - 2.**

Tackles - 3 defensive with Calgary in 1991 and 4 defensive in 1992. **Total Grey Cup Tackles - 7 (7 defensive).**

LAMMLE, WAYNE
Born: April 10, 1969
Birthplace: Vancouver, B.C.
Kicker. 6'4", 220 lbs. Non-import
Last Amateur Club: University of Utah
Acquired: Selected fifth overall by the Toronto Argonauts in the 1991 Supplementary Draft. Signed by Toronto in June, 1991 and released in July, 1991. Signed as a free agent by the Winnipeg Blue Bombers in February, 1992. Released by Winnipeg in July, 1992. Signed as a free agent by the B.C. Lions in July, 1992. Traded to the Ottawa Rough Riders in April, 1993 along with offensive linemen Carl Coulter and Chris Gioskos, cornerback Joe Mero and linebacker Mark Scott in exchange for cornerback Less Browne, offensive tackle Rob Smith and linebacker Patrick Wayne. Claimed on waivers by the Toronto Argonauts in June, 1993.

		Scoring						Field Goals					
	Team	GP	TD	C	FG	S	TP	T	G	YDS	AVE	LK	PCT
1992	B.C.	4	0	8	6	3	29	11	6	173	28.8	45	54.5
1993	Tor.	7	0	0	0	0	0	0	0	0	0.0	0	0.0
CFL TOTALS		**11**	**0**	**8**	**6**	**3**	**29**	**11**	**6**	**173**	**28.8**	**45**	**54.5**

		Converts			Kickoffs				
	Team	T	G	PCT	NO	YDS	AVE	LK	S
1992	B.C.	8	8	100.0	17	871	51.2	69	0
1993	Tor.	0	0	0.0	0	0	0.0	0	0
CFL TOTALS		**8**	**8**	**100.0**	**17**	**871**	**51.2**	**69**	**0**

		Field Goal Attempts					Punting				
	Team	NO	YDS	AVE	LK	S	NO	YDS	AVE	LK	S
1992	B.C.	5	200	40.0	47	3	1	8	8.0	8	0
1993	Tor.	0	0	0.0	0	0	0	0	0.0	0	0
CFL TOTALS		**5**	**200**	**40.0**	**47**	**3**	**1**	**8**	**8.0**	**8**	**0**

Net Punting - 1 for 8 yards with B.C. in 1992. **CFL Total Net Punting - 1 for 8 yards.**

Punt Returns - 1 for 0 yards with B.C. in 1992. **CFL Total Punt Returns - 1 for 0 yards.**

LAMY, MICHEL
Born: June 25, 1967
Birthplace: Tracy, Quebec
Tackle. 6'2", 265 lbs. Non-import
Last Amateur Club: Sequoias Junior College
Acquired: 1989 Territorial exemption of Ottawa Rough Riders.

Games Played - 10 with Ottawa in 1989; 11 in 1990; 15 in 1991; 18 in 1992 and 18 in 1993. **CFL Total GP - 72.**

Fumbles - 1 and 0 lost with Ottawa in 1990. **CFL Total Fumbles - 1 and 0 lost.**

Fumble Returns - 1 for 0 yards with Ottawa in 1990. **CFL Total Fumble Returns - 1 for 0 yards.**

Tackles - 2 defensive with Ottawa in 1989 and 2 defensive and 1 special teams in 1992. **CFL Total Tackles - 5 (4 defensive and 1 special teams).**

Playoffs

Games Played - 1 with Ottawa in 1991; 1 in 1992 and 1 in 1993. **CFL Total Playoff GP - 3.**

Tackles - 1 defensive with Ottawa in 1991 and 1 defensive in 1992. **CFL Total Playoff Tackles - 2 (2 defensive).**

LANCE, CARLTON
Born: October 3, 1970
Birthplace: Queens, New York
Defensive Back. 6'0", 195 lbs. Import
Last Amateur Club: Soutwest State University
Acquired: Signed as a free agent by the NFL Houston Oilers prior to their 1992 training camp and was subsequently released prior to the start of the 1992 season. Signed as a free agent by the Saskatchewan Roughriders in April, 1993.

		Scoring						Interception Returns				
	Team	GP	TD	C	FG	S	TP	NO	YDS	AVE	LG	TD
1993	Sask.	13	2	0	0	0	12	3	40	13.3	31	1
CFL TOTALS		**13**	**2**	**0**	**0**	**0**	**12**	**3**	**40**	**13.3**	**31**	**1**

		Fumble Returns					Fumbles		
	Team	NO	YDS	AVE	LG	TD	NO	LOST	OFR
1993	Sask.	2	30	15.0	21	1	1	0	0
CFL TOTALS		**2**	**30**	**15.0**	**21**	**1**	**1**	**0**	**0**

Kickoff Returns - 1 for 19 yards with Saskatchewan in 1993. **CFL Total Kickoff Returns - 1 for 19 yards.**

Quarterback Sacks - 2 for 18 yards lost with Saskatchewan in 1993. **CFL Total QB Sacks - 2 for 18 yards lost.**

Tackles - 34 defensive and 9 special teams with Saskatchewan in 1993. **CFL Total Tackles - 43 (34 defensive and 9 special teams).**

Playoffs

Games Played - 1 with Saskatchewan in 1993. **CFL Total Playoff GP - 1.**

Tackles - 3 defensive and 1 special teams with Saskatchewan in 1993. **CFL Total Playoff Tackles - 4 (3 defensive and 1 special teams).**

LAZECKI, MICHAEL

Born: February 8, 1965
Birthplace: Regina, Saskatchewan
Kicker. 6'2", 200 lbs. Non-import
Last Amateur Club: University of Saskatchewan (CWUAA)
Acquired: Signed as a free agent by the Saskatchewan Roughriders in March, 1988 and was released in July, 1988. Signed as a free agent by the Calgary Stampeders in June, 1989 and was released that same month. Rights traded by Calgary in March, 1990 to the Ottawa Rough Riders in exchange for a third round draft choice in the 1991 CFL College Draft and future considerations. Traded to Saskatchewan in March, 1990 in exchange for punter Terry Baker, defensive lineman Scott Camper and defensive back Charles McCree. Released by Saskatchewan in December, 1991. Signed as a free agent by the Ottawa Rough Riders in November, 1993. Released by Ottawa in March, 1994.

		Scoring						Punting				
	Team	GP	TD	C	FG	S	TP	NO	YDS	AVE	LK	S
1990	Sask.	18	0	0	0	2	2	111	4174	37.6	65	2
1991	Sask.	18	0	0	0	6	6	140	5471	39.1	78	6
1993	Ott.	1	0	0	0	0	0	8	265	33.1	43	0
CFL TOTALS		**37**	**0**	**0**	**0**	**8**	**8**	**259**	**9910**	**38.3**	**78**	**8**

		Rushing					Kickoffs				
	Team	NO	YDS	AVE	LG	TD	NO	YDS	AVE	LK	S
1990	Sask.	0	0	0.0	0	0	0	0	0.0	0	0
1991	Sask.	2	14	7.0	12	0	0	0	0.0	0	0
1993	Ott.	0	0	0.0	0	0	4	228	57.0	65	0
CFL TOTALS		**2**	**14**	**7.0**	**12**	**0**	**4**	**228**	**57.0**	**65**	**0**

Passing - 2 attempts, 1 complete for 30 yards, 50.0 percent, 1 interception, longest 30 yards with Saskatchewan in 1990 and 1 attempt, 1 complete for 36 yards in 1991.
CFL Total Passing - 3 attempts, 2 complete for 66 yards, 66.7 percent, 1 interception, longest 36 yards.

Net Punting - 142 for 4285 yards, 30.2 average with Saskatchewan in 1991 and 8 for 244 yards, 30.5 average with Ottawa in 1993.
CFL Total Net Punting - 150 for 4529 yards, 30.2 average.

Fumbles - 1 and 1 lost with Saskatchewan in 1990 and 3 and 3 lost in 1991.
CFL Total Fumbles - 4 and 4 lost.

Own Fumbles Recovered - 1 with Ottawa in 1993. **CFL Total OFR - 1.**

Tackles - 1 special teams with Saskatchewan in 1991.
CFL Total Tackles - 1 (1 special teams).

Playoffs

			Punting					Kickoffs				
	Team	GP	NO	YDS	AVE	LK	S	NO	YDS	AVE	LK	S
1990	Sask.	1	7	259	37.0	51	0	0	0	0.0	0	0
1991	Sask.	0	0	0	0.0	0	0	0	0	0.0	0	0
1993	Ott.	1	8	296	37.0	44	0	2	94	47.0	57	0
CFL TOTALS		**2**	**15**	**555**	**37.0**	**51**	**0**	**2**	**94**	**47.0**	**57**	**0**

		Field Goals						Field Goal Attempts				
	Team	T	G	YDS	AVE	LK	PCT	NO	YDS	AVE	LK	S
1990	Sask.	0	0	0	0.0	0	0.0	0	0	0.0	0	0
1991	Sask.	0	0	0	0.0	0	0.0	0	0	0.0	0	0
1993	Ott.	3	1	33	33.0	33	33.3	1	47	47.0	47	0
CFL TOTALS		**3**	**1**	**33**	**33.0**	**33**	**33.3**	**1**	**47**	**47.0**	**47**	**0**

Converts - 1 tried, 1 good with Ottawa in 1993.
CFL Total Playoff Converts - 1 tried, 1 good.

Net Punting - 8 for 285 yards, 35.6 average with Ottawa in 1993.
CFL Total Playoff Net Punting - 8 for 285 yards, 35.6 average.

LEDBETTER, MARK

Born: December 14, 1966
Birthplace: Tacoma, Washington
Defensive End. 6'4", 235 lbs. Import
Last Amateur Club: Washington State University
Acquired: Signed as a free agent by the NFL New Orleans Saints in 1990. Was waived prior to the start of the 1990 season. Selected in the eighth round (79th overall) by the San Antonio Riders in the 1991 WLAF Positional Draft. Signed as a free agent by the Sacramento Gold Miners in March, 1993.

Games Played - 18 with Sacramento in 1993. **CFL Total GP - 18.**

Fumble Returns - 2 for 4 yards, 2.0 average, longest 4 yards with Sacramento in 1993.
CFL Total Fumble Returns - 2 for 4 yards, 2.0 average, longest 4 yards.

Quarterback Sacks - 8 for 39 yards lost with Sacramento in 1993.
CFL Total QB Sacks - 8 for 39 yards lost.

Tackles - 39 defensive and 2 special teams with Sacramento in 1993.
CFL Total Tackles - 41 (39 defensive and 2 special teams).

Tackles For Losses - 3 for 20 yards with Sacramento in 1993.
CFL Total Tackles For Losses- 3 for 20 yards.

LEONARD, KENTON

Born: May 2, 1968
Birthplace: Point Coupee, Louisiana
Cornerback. 5'9", 170 lbs. Import
Last Amateur Club: Nicholls State University
Acquired: Signed as a free agent by the Calgary Stampeders in May, 1991.

			Scoring					Interception Returns				
	Team	GP	TD	C	FG	S	TP	NO	YDS	AVE	LG	TD
1991	Cal.	17	0	0	0	0	0	2	33	16.5	29	0
1992	Cal.	18	1	0	0	0	6	4	44	11.0	36	1
1993	Cal.	15	0	0	0	0	0	1	26	26.0	26	0
CFL TOTALS		**50**	**1**	**0**	**0**	**0**	**6**	**7**	**103**	**14.7**	**36**	**1**

Fumble Returns - 1 for 0 yards with Calgary in 1992.
CFL Total Fumble Returns - 1 for 0 yards.

Blocked Kicks - 1 punt with Calgary in 1992. **CFL Total Blocked Kicks - 1 (1 punt).**

Tackles - 50 defensive and 12 special teams with Calgary in 1991; 39 defensive and 8 special teams in 1992 and 35 defensive and 10 special teams in 1993. **CFL Total Tackles - 154 (124 defensive and 30 special teams).**

Tackles for Losses - 2 for 18 yards with Calgary in 1991 and 4 for 26 yards in 1992. **CFL Total Tackles for Losses - 6 for 44 yards.**

Playoffs

Games Played - 1 with Calgary in 1992 and 2 in 1993. **CFL Total Playoff GP - 3.**

Interceptions - 1 for 0 yards with Calgary in 1993.
CFL Total Playoff Interceptions - 1 for 0 yards.

Tackles - 3 defensive with Calgary in 1992 and 3 in 1993.
CFL Total Playoff Tackles - 6 (6 defensive).

Grey Cup

Games Played - 1 with Calgary in 1992. **Total Grey Cup GP - 1.**

Tackles - 2 defensive and 2 special teams with Calgary in 1992.
Total Grey Cup Tackles - 4 (2 defensive and 2 special teams).

LEVY, NIGEL

Born: February 16, 1969
Birthplace: Scarborough, Ontario
Wide Receiver. 6'3", 190 lbs. Non-import
Last Amateur Club: University of Western Ontario (OUAA)
Acquired: Selected by the Ottawa Rough Riders in the third round (18th overall) in the 1993 CFL College Draft.

Games Played - 1 with Ottawa in 1993. **CFL Total GP - 1.**

LEWIS, GARY

Born: January 14, 1961
Birthplace: Oklahoma City, Oklahoma
Defensive Tackle. 6'3", 270 lbs. Import
Last Amateur Club: Oklahoma State University
Acquired: Selected by the New Orleans Saints in the fourth round (98th overall) in the 1983 NFL Draft. Released and signed as a free agent by the Ottawa Rough Riders in September, 1985. Traded to the Saskatchewan Roughriders in September, 1985 along with wide receiver Daric Zeno and defensive back Junior Robinson for running back Robert Reid, linebacker Jeff Roberts and wide receiver Stephen Jones.

			Fumble Returns					QB Sacks
	Team	GP	NO	YDS	AVE	LG	TD	NO
1985	Ott.	2	0	0	0.0	0	0	0
	Sask.	4	1	0	0.0	0	0	0
1986	Sask.	18	1	0	0.0	0	0	9
1987	Sask.	7	0	0	0.0	0	0	3
1988a	Sask.	18	1	0	0.0	0	1	7
1989	Sask.	18	1	0	0.0	0	0	10
1990	Sask.	18	0	0	0.0	0	0	7
1991a	Sask.	18	0	0	0.0	0	0	11
1992	Sask.	18	2	5	2.5	5	0	6
1993	Sask.	15	0	0	0.0	0	0	5
CFL TOTALS		**136**	**6**	**5**	**0.8**	**5**	**1**	**58**

Scoring - 1 TD for 6 points with Saskatchewan in 1988.
CFL Total Scoring - 1 TD for 6 points.

Defensive Tackles - 25 with Saskatchewan in 1987; 44 in 1988; 31 in 1989; 25 in 1990; 25 in 1991; 30 in 1992 and 31 in 1993. **CFL Total Defensive Tackles - 211.**

Tackles for Losses - 1 for 3 yards with Saskatchewan in 1991; 3 for 18 yards in 1992 and 6 for 22 yards in 1993. **CFL Total Tackles for Losses - 10 for 43 yards.**

a - All-Western All-Star.

LEWIS, GARY

Playoffs

Games Played - 1 with Saskatchewan in 1988; 2 in 1989; 1 in 1990; 1 in 1992 and 1 in 1993. **CFL Total Playoff GP - 6.**

Quarterback Sacks - 2 with Saskatchewan in 1989 and 1 for 12 yards lost in 1992. **CFL Total Playoff QB Sacks - 3.**

Defensive Tackles - 2 with Saskatchewan in 1988; 6 in 1989; 1 in 1990; 2 in 1992 and 1 in 1993. **CFL Total Playoff Defensive Tackles - 12.**

Grey Cup

Games Played - 1 with Saskatchewan in 1989. **Total Grey Cup GP - 1.**

Quarterback Sacks - 1 with Saskatchewan in 1989. **Total Grey Cup QB Sacks - 1.**

Defensive Tackles - 4 with Saskatchewan in 1989. **Total Grey Cup Defensive Tackles - 4.**

LEWIS, KIP
Born: June 2, 1967
Birthplace: East Elmhurst, New York
Slotback. 5'10", 170 lbs. Import
Last Amateur Club: University of Arizona
Acquired: Signed as a free agent by the NFL Detroit Lions in 1990 and was released prior to the 1990 season. Selected by the New York/New Jersey Knights in the second round (fourth overall) in the 1991 WLAF Supplemental Draft. Signed as a free agent by the Toronto Argonauts in May, 1993. Released by Toronto in September, 1993.

	Team	Scoring GP	TD	C	FG	S	TP	Pass Receiving NO	YDS	AVE	LG	TD
1993	Tor.	9	3	x1	0	0	20	29	401	13.8	41	3
CFL TOTALS		**9**	**3**	**x1**	**0**	**0**	**20**	**29**	**401**	**13.8**	**41**	**3**

2-pt. Converts - 1 made with Toronto in 1993. **CFL Total 2-pt. Converts - 1 made.**

Tackles - 3 defensive with Toronto in 1993. **CFL Total Tackles - 3 (3 defensive).**

LEWIS, LOYD
Born: February 23, 1962
Birthplace: Dallas, Texas
Defensive Tackle. 6'3", 265 lbs. Import
Last Amateur Club: Texas A & I University
Acquired: Selected by the USFL's Houston Gamblers in the 1984 Territorial Draft. Selected by the Minnesota Vikings in the seventh round, (196th overall), in the 1984 NFL Draft. Signed by Houston and released following the 1984 season. Signed as a free agent by the Ottawa Rough Riders in July, 1985. Released by Ottawa in June, 1992. Signed as a free agent by the Edmonton Eskimos in June, 1992. Released by Edmonton in July, 1993. Signed as a free agent by the Winnipeg Blue Bombers in July, 1993.

Games Played - 15 with Ottawa in 1985; 17 in 1986; 16 in 1987; 4 in 1988; 18 in 1989; 16 in 1990; 18 in 1991; 18 with Edmonton in 1992 and 16 with Winnipeg in 1993. **CFL Total GP - 138.**

Scoring - 1 TD for 6 pts with Winnipeg in 1993. **CFL Total Scoring - 1 TD for 6 pts.**

Fumble Returns - 1 for 0 yards with Ottawa in 1985; 1 for 1 yard in 1986; 1 for 0 yards in 1987; 1 for 0 yards in 1988; 1 for 0 yards in 1990; 1 for 8 yards in 1991; 1 for 13 yards with Edmonton in 1992 and 1 for 25 yards and 1 TD with Winnipeg in 1993.
CFL Total Fumble Returns - 8 for 47 yards, 5.9 average, longest 25 yards and 1 TD.

Interception Returns - 1 for 3 yards with Winnipeg in 1993.
CFL Total Interception Returns - 1 for 3 yards.

Pass Receiving - 1 for 17 yards with Ottawa in 1987.
CFL Total Pass Receiving - 1 for 17 yards.

Quarterback Sacks - 7 with Ottawa in 1985; 15 in 1986; 13 in 1987; 1 in 1988; 5 in 1989; 5 in 1990; 4 in 1991; 7 for 49 yards lost with Edmonton in 1992 and 7 for 54 yards lost with Winnipeg in 1993.
CFL Total QB Sacks - 64.

Tackles - 33 defensive with Ottawa in 1987; 11 defensive in 1988; 29 defensive in 1989; 30 defensive in 1990; 24 defensive in 1991; 25 defensive and 1 special teams with Edmonton in 1992 and 25 defensive with Winnipeg in 1993.
CFL Total Tackles - 178 (177 defensive and 1 special teams).

Tackles for Losses - 1 for 3 yards with Ottawa in 1991; 7 for 24 yards with Edmonton in 1992 and 6 for 14 yards with Winnipeg in 1993.
CFL Total Tackles for Losses - 14 for 41 yards.

All-Eastern All-Star in 1985; 1990; 1991 and 1993.
All-Western All-Star in 1992.

Playoffs

Games Played - 1 with Ottawa in 1985; 1 in 1990; 1 in 1991; 2 with Edmonton in 1992 and 1 with Winnipeg in 1993.
CFL Total Playoff GP - 6.

Fumble Returns - 1 for 1 yard with Edmonton in 1992.
CFL Total Playoff Fumble Returns - 1 for 1 yard.

Quarterback Sacks - 1 with Ottawa in 1991.
CFL Total Playoff QB Sacks - 1.

Defensive Tackles - 2 with Ottawa in 1990; 3 in 1991; 3 with Edmonton in 1992 and 1 with Winnipeg in 1993.
CFL Total Playoff Defensive Tackles - 9.

Tackles for Losses - 1 for 2 yards with Ottawa in 1991.
CFL Total Playoff Tackles for Losses - 1 for 2 yards.

Grey Cup

Games Played - 1 with Winnipeg in 1993.
Total Grey Cup GP - 1.

Quarterback Sacks - 1 with Winnipeg in 1993.
Total Grey Cup QB Sacks - 1.

Defensive Tackles - 4 with Winnipeg in 1993.
Total Grey Cup Defensive Tackles - 4.

Tackles for Losses - 1 for 12 yards with Winnipeg in 1993.
Total Grey Cup Tackles for Losses - 1 for 12 yards.

LEWIS, TAHAUN
Born: September 29, 1968
Birthplace: Los Angeles, California
Cornerback. 5'10", 175 lbs. Import
Last Amateur Club: University of Nebraska
Acquired: Selected by the Los Angeles Raiders in the ninth round (202nd overall) in the 1988 NFL Draft. Granted unconditional free agency in February, 1989. Signed to the Los Angeles practice squad. Granted unconditional free agency in February, 1992. Signed as a free agent by the NFL Kansas City Chiefs in April, 1992. Released by the Chiefs following the 1992 season. Signed as a free agent by the Toronto Argonauts in August, 1993.

Games Played - 5 with Toronto in 1993. **CFL Total GP - 5.**

Tackles - 17 defensive and 1 special teams with Toronto in 1993.
CFL Total Tackles - 18 (17 defensive and 1 special teams).

Tackles for Losses - 1 for 2 yards with Toronto in 1993.
CFL Total Tackles for Losses - 1 for 2 yards.

LORENZ, TIM
Born: February 12, 1965
Birthplace: Vancouver, British Columbia
Defensive Tackle. 6'2", 240 lbs. Non-import
Last Amateur Club: University of California at Santa Barbara
Acquired: Selected in the second round (11th overall) in the 1988 CFL College Draft by the Hamilton Tiger-Cats. Granted free agency status in February, 1992. Signed as a free agent by the Toronto Argonauts in June, 1992. Released by Toronto in July, 1992. Signed as a free agent by the B.C. Lions in July, 1992.

Games Played - 18 with Hamilton in 1988; 18 in 1989; 8 in 1990; 14 in 1991; 15 with B.C. in 1992 and 10 in 1993. **CFL Total GP - 83.**

Fumble Returns - 1 for 0 yards with Hamilton in 1988; 4 for 4 yards, 1.0 average, longest 3 yards in 1989 and 1 for 0 yards in 1990.
CFL Total Fumble Returns - 6 for 4 yards, 0.7 average, longest 3 yards.

Quarterback Sacks - 2 with Hamilton in 1988; 4 in 1989; 2 in 1991; 1 for 7 yards lost with B.C. in 1992 and 2 for 21 yards lost in 1993.
CFL Total QB Sacks - 11.

Tackles - 13 defensive with Hamilton in 1988; 18 defensive in 1989; 11 defensive in 1990; 1 defensive and 1 special teams in 1991; 7 defensive and 3 special teams with B.C. in 1992 and 6 defensive in 1993.
CFL Total Tackles - 60 (56 defensive and 4 special teams).

Playoffs

Games Played - 1 with Hamilton in 1988; 1 in 1989 and 1 with B.C. in 1993.
CFL Total Playoff GP - 3.

Quarterback Sacks - 1 with Hamilton in 1989.
CFL Total Playoff QB Sacks - 1.

Defensive Tackles - 2 with Hamilton in 1988 and 1 in 1989.
CFL Total Playoff Defensive Tackles - 3.

Grey Cup

Games Played - 1 with Hamilton in 1989.
Total Grey Cup GP - 1.

Defensive Tackles - 2 with Hamilton in 1989.
Total Grey Cup Defensive Tackles - 2.

LYLES, DEL
Born: September 7, 1970
Birthplace: Oakland, California
Linebacker. 6'1", 220 lbs. Import
Last Amateur Club: Utah State University
Acquired: Signed as a free agent by the NFL Minnesota Vikings in 1992 and was released prior to the start of the season. Signed as a free agent by the Winnipeg Blue Bombers in December, 1992. Released by Winnipeg in November, 1993. Re-signed by Winnipeg in March, 1994.

Games Played - 10 with Winnipeg in 1993. **CFL Total GP - 10.**

Quarterback Sacks - 1 for 8 yards lost with Winnipeg in 1993. **CFL Total QB Sacks - 1 for 8 yards lost.**

Tackles - 26 defensive and 8 special teams with Winnipeg in 1993. **CFL Total Tackles - 34 (26 defensive and 8 special teams).**

Tackles For Losses - 2 for 3 yards with Winnipeg in 1993. **CFL Total Tackles For Losses- 2 for 3 yards.**

LYONS, DAMION
Born: April 28, 1968
Birthplace: Berkeley, California
Cornerback. 6'4", 215 lbs. Import
Last Amateur Club: UCLA
Acquired: Signed as a free agent by the Edmonton Eskimos in October, 1991. Granted free agency status in February, 1994.

Games Played - 2 with Edmonton in 1991; 18 in 1992 and 18 in 1993. **CFL Total GP - 38.**

Interception Returns - 8 for 95 yards, 11.9 average, longest 44 yards with Edmonton in 1992 and 3 for 70 yards, 23.3 average, longest 36 yards in 1993. **CFL Total Interception Returns - 11 for 165 yards, 15.0 average, longest 44 yards.**

Fumble Returns - 2 for 9 yards, 4.5 average, longest 5 yards with Edmonton in 1993. **CFL Total Fumble Returns - 2 for 9 yards, 4.5 average, longest 5 yards.**

Tackles - 49 defensive and 5 special teams with Edmonton in 1992 and 35 defensive and 4 special teams in 1993. **CFL Total Tackles - 93 (84 defensive and 9 special teams).**

Tackles for Losses - 1 for 3 yards with Edmonton in 1992. **CFL Total Tackles for Losses - 1 for 3 yards.**

All-Western All-Star in 1992.

Playoffs

Games Played - 2 with Edmonton in 1992 and 2 in 1993. **CFL Total Playoff GP - 4.**

Tackles - 8 defensive with Edmonton in 1992 and 1 defensive in 1993. **CFL Total Playoff Tackles - 9 (9 defensive).**

Grey Cup

Games Played - 1 with Edmonton in 1993. **Total Grey Cup GP - 1.**

Defensive Tackles - 3 with Edmonton in 1993. **Total Grey Cup Defensive Tackles - 3.**

MacCALLUM, TOM
Born: December 22, 1970
Birthplace: Regina, Saskatchewan
Offensive Guard. 6' 3", 270 lbs. Non-import
Last Amateur Club: Regina Rams Juniors
Acquired: Selected by the Saskatchewan Roughriders in the sixth round (42nd overall) in the 1992 CFL College Draft.

Games Played - 18 with Saskatchewan in 1993. **CFL Total GP - 18.**

Playoffs

Games Played - 1 with Saskatchewan in 1993. **CFL Total Playoff GP - 1.**

MacCREADY, DEREK
Born: May 4, 1967
Birthplace: Montreal, Quebec
Defensive Tackle. 6'5", 265 lbs. Non-import
Last Amateur Club: Ohio State University
Acquired: Drafted by the B.C. Lions in the first round (sixth overall) of the 1989 CFL College Draft. B.C. acquired the pick from the Toronto Argonauts in exchange for linebacker Tony Visco. Attended the 1989 training camp of the Detroit Lions (NFL) and was later released. Signed with B.C. in September, 1989. Spent the 1992 season on the Injured List.

Games Played - 2 with B.C. in 1989; 17 in 1990; 18 in 1991 and 18 in 1993. **CFL Total GP - 55.**

Blocked Kicks - 1 field goal with B.C. in 1991. **CFL Total Blocked Kicks - 1 FG.**

Fumble Returns - 1 for 0 yards with B.C. in 1990; 1 for 0 yards in 1991 and 2 for 0 yards in 1993. **CFL Total Fumble Returns - 4 for 0 yards.**

Quarterback Sacks - 4 with B.C. in 1990; 7 in 1991 and 5 for 20 yards lost in 1993. **CFL Total QB Sacks - 16.**

Defensive Tackles - 32 with B.C. in 1990; 35 in 1991 and 22 in 1993. **CFL Total Defensive Tackles - 89.**

Tackles for Losses - 5 for 16 yards with B.C. in 1991 and 3 for 9 yards in 1993. **CFL Total Tackles for Losses - 8 for 25 yards.**

Playoffs

Games Played - 1 with B.C. in 1991 and 1 in 1993. **CFL Total Playoff GP - 2.**

Tackles - 3 defensive with B.C. in 1991 and 4 defensive in 1993. **CFL Total Playoff Tackles - 7 (7 defensive).**

MacDONALD, BOB
Born: October 15, 1967
Birthplace: Hamilton, Ontario
Offensive Lineman. 6'1", 274 lbs. Non-import
Last Amateur Club: McMaster University (OUAA)
Acquired: Selected in the second round (14th overall) by the Edmonton Eskimos in the 1990 CFL College Draft. Traded to the Calgary Stampeders in July, 1990 for future considerations (a fourth round draft pick in the 1991 CFL College Draft, offensive guard Ron Herman). Traded to the Toronto Argonauts in exchange for offensive lineman Pat Mahon in June, 1993. Traded to the Hamilton Tiger-Cats to complete a previous trade in June, 1993. Released by Hamilton in November, 1993.

Games Played - 2 with Calgary in 1991; 18 in 1992 and 12 with Hamilton in 1993. **CFL Total GP - 32.**

Playoffs

Games Played - 1 with Calgary in 1992. **CFL Total Playoff GP - 1.**

Grey Cup

Games Played - 1 with Calgary in 1992. **Total Grey Cup GP - 1.**

MacNEIL, BRETT
Born: November 27, 1967
Birthplace: Nepean, Ontario
Guard. 6'5", 290 lbs. Non-import
Last Amateur Club: Boston University
Acquired: Selected in the first round (seventh overall) of the 1991 CFL College Draft by the Ottawa Rough Riders. Traded to the Winnipeg Blue Bombers in exchange for defensive back Michael Allen in June, 1992.

Games Played - 10 with Winnipeg in 1992 and 18 in 1993. **CFL Total GP - 28.**

Kickoff Returns - 1 for 0 yards with Winnipeg in 1992. **CFL Total Kickoff Returns - 1 for 0 yards.**

Tackles - 1 special teams with Winnipeg in 1992 and 1 defensive in 1993. **CFL Total Tackles - 2 (1 defensive and 1 special teams).**

Playoffs

Games Played - 1 with Winnipeg in 1992 and 1 in 1993. **CFL Total Playoff GP - 2.**

Own Fumbles Recovered - 1 with Winnipeg in 1993. **CFL Total Playoff OFR - 1.**

Tackles - 1 special teams with Winnipeg in 1992 and 2 defensive in 1993. **CFL Total Playoff Tackles - 3 (2 defensive and 1 special teams).**

Grey Cup

Games Played - 1 with Winnipeg in 1992 and 1 in 1993. **Total Grey Cup GP - 2.**

MacNEILL, JOHN
Born: November 15, 1968
Birthplace: Waukesha, Wisconsin
Defensive Tackle. 6'4", 260 lbs. Import
Last Amateur Club: Michigan State University
Acquired: Selected in the 12th round (320th overall) by the Seattle Seahawks in the 1992 NFL Draft. Released by Seattle after training camp. Signed as a free agent by the B.C. Lions in October, 1992.

Games Played - 5 with B.C. in 1992 and 6 in 1993. **CFL Total GP - 11.**

MacNEILL, JOHN

Quarterback Sacks - 3 for 23 yards lost with B.C. in 1992 and 1 for 4 yards lost in 1993. **CFL Total Quarterback Sacks - 4 for 27 yards lost.**

Tackles - 7 defensive with B.C. in 1992 and 9 defensive in 1993. **CFL Total Tackles - 16 (16 defensive).**

Tackles for Losses - 2 for 5 yards with B.C. in 1992 and 1 for 1 yard in 1993. **CFL Total Tackles for Losses - 3 for 6 yards.**

Playoffs

Games Played - 1 with B.C.in 1993. **CFL Total Playoff GP - 1.**

MACORITTI, RAY
Born: January 10, 1966
Birthplace: Hamilton, Ontario
Kicker. 6' 4", 215 lbs. Non-import
Last Amateur Club: University of Western Ontario (OUAA)
Acquired: Signed as a free agent by the Edmonton Eskimos in February, 1990. Released by Edmonton in October, 1991. Signed as a free agent by the Ottawa Rough Riders in October, 1993. Released by Ottawa later that month.

		Scoring						Punting				
	Team	GP	TD	C	FG	S	TP	NO	YDS	AVE	LK	S
1990a	Edm.	18	0	64	36	14	186	134	5765	43.0	87	5
1991	Edm.	12	0	47	23	8	124	72	2775	38.5	65	1
1993	Ott.	3	0	9	5	0	24	36	1256	34.9	47	0
CFL TOTALS		**33**	**0**	**120**	**64**	**22**	**334**	**242**	**9796**	**40.5**	**87**	**6**

		Kickoffs					Field Goals					
	Team	NO	YDS	AVE	LK	S	T	M	YDS	AVE	LK	PCT.
1990	Edm.	95	5037	53.0	66	0	53	36	1133	31.5	47	67.9
1991	Edm.	70	3780	54.0	68	0	37	23	767	33.3	47	62.2
1993	Ott.	16	836	52.3	59	0	5	5	132	26.4	39	100.0
CFL TOTALS		**181**	**9653**	**53.3**	**68**	**0**	**95**	**64**	**2032**	**31.8**	**47**	**67.4**

		Converts			Field Goal Attempts				
	Team	T	G	PCT.	NO	YDS	AVE	LK	S
1990	Edm.	64	64	100.0	17	702	41.3	50	9
1991	Edm.	47	47	100.0	14	649	46.4	63	7
1993	Ott.	9	9	100.0	0	0	0	0	0
CFL TOTALS		**120**	**120**	**100.0**	**31**	**1351**	**43.6**	**63**	**16**

Fumbles - 1 and 0 lost with Edmonton in 1990; 2 and 2 lost in 1991 and 1 and 0 lost with Ottawa in 1993. **CFL Total Fumbles - 4 and 2 lost.**

Net Punting - 73 for 2057 yards, 28.2 average with Edmonton in 1991 and 36 for 1025 yards, 28.5 average with Ottawa in 1993. **CFL Total Net Punting - 109 for 3082 yards, 28.3 average.**

Passing - 1 attempt, 0 complete and 1 interception with Ottawa in 1993. **CFL Total Passing - 1 attempt, 0 complete and 1 interception.**

Tackles - 4 special teams with Edmonton in 1991. **CFL Total Tackles - 4 (4 special teams).**

a - Set CFL Record for Most Points One Season By A First-Year Player

Playoffs

		Scoring						Punting				
	Team	GP	TD	C	FG	S	TP	NO	YDS	AVE	LK	S
1990	Edm.	2	0	10	3	1	20	11	407	37.0	50	0
CFL TOTALS		**2**	**0**	**10**	**3**	**1**	**20**	**11**	**407**	**37.0**	**50**	**0**

		Converts			Kickoffs				
	Team	T	G	PCT	NO	YDS	AVE	LK	S
1990	Edm.	7	7	100.0	15	729	48.6	62	0
CFL TOTALS		**7**	**7**	**100.0**	**15**	**729**	**48.6**	**62**	**0**

		Field Goals						Field Goal Attempts				
	Team	T	G	YDS	AVE	LK	PCT	NO	YDS	AVE	LK	S
1990	Edm.	6	3	107	35.7	42	50.0	3	126	42.0	44	0
CFL TOTALS		**6**	**3**	**107**	**35.7**	**42**	**50.0**	**3**	**126**	**42.0**	**44**	**0**

Fumbles - 1 and 1 lost with Edmonton in 1990. **CFL Total Playoff Fumbles - 1 and 1 lost.**

Grey Cup

Scoring - 1 convert, 1 field goal and 1 single with Edmonton in 1990 for 5 points. **Total Grey Cup Scoring - 1 convert, 1 field goal, and 1 single for 5 points.**

Converts - 1 for 1 with Edmonton in 1990. **Total Grey Cup Converts - 1 for 1.**

Punting - 7 for 314 yards, 44.9 yard average, longest 56 yards with Edmonton in 1990. **Total Grey Cup Punting - 7 for 314 yards, 44.9 average, longest 56 yards.**

Kickoffs - 3 for 157 yards, 52.3 average, longest 57 yards with Edmonton in 1990. **Total Grey Cup Kickoffs - 3 for 157 yards, 52.3 average, longest 57 yards.**

Field Goals - 1 tried and 1 good for 37 yards with Edmonton in 1990. **Total Grey Cup Field Goals - 1 tried and 1 good for 37 yards.**

MAGNUSON, QUINN
Born: March 3, 1971
Birthplace: Saskatoon, Saskatchewan
Offensive Lineman. 6' 5", 270 lbs. Non-import.
Last Amateur Club: Washington State University
Acquired: Selected by the Winnipeg Blue Bombers in the sixth round (45th overall) of the 1993 CFL College Draft.

Games Played - 9 with Winnipeg in 1993. **CFL Total GP - 9.**

Tackles - 4 special teams with Winnipeg in 1993. **CFL Total Tackles - 4 (4 special teams).**

MAHON, PATRICK
Born: August 24, 1968
Birthplace: Kingston, Ontario
Offensive Centre. 6'2", 255 lbs. Non-import
Last Amateur Club: University of Western Ontario
Acquired: Signed as a free agent by the Toronto Argonauts in June, 1992 and was subsequently released in July, 1992. Re-signed as a free agent by the Toronto Argonauts in December, 1992. Traded to the Calgary Stampeders in exchange for offensive lineman Bob MacDonald in June, 1993. Released by Calgary in August, 1993 and signed as a free agent by the Ottawa Rough Riders in October, 1993.

Games Played - 6 with Calgary and 4 with Ottawa in 1993. **CFL Total GP - 10.**

Playoffs

Games Played - 1 with Ottawa in 1993. **CFL Total Playoff GP - 1.**

Fumbles - 1 and 1 lost with Ottawa in 1993. **CFL Total Playoff Fumbles - 1 and 1 lost.**

Tackles - 1 special teams with Ottawa in 1993. **CFL Total Playoff Tackles - 1 (1 special teams).**

MANLEY, DEXTER
Born: February 2, 1959
Birthplace: Houston, Texas
Defensive End. 6'4", 270 lbs. Import
Last Amateur Club: Oklahoma State University
Acquired: Selected by the Washington Redskins in the fifth round (119th overall) in the 1981 NFL Draft. Granted free agency status in February,1986. Released by Washington in November 1990. Awarded on waivers to the NFL Phoenix Cardinals in November, 1990. Released by Phoenix and signed as a free agent by the NFL Tampa Bay Buccaneers in 1991. Released by Tampa Bay and signed as a free agent by the Ottawa Rough Riders in June, 1992. Playing rights were transferred to the Shreveport Pirates on February 15, 1994.

Games Played - 2 with Ottawa in 1993. **CFL Total GP - 2.**

Fumble Returns - 1 for 0 yards with Ottawa in 1993. **CFL Total Fumble Returns - 1 for 0 yards.**

Tackles - 1 defensive with Ottawa in 1993. **CFL Total Tackles - 1 (1 defensive).**

Playoffs

Games Played - 1 with Ottawa in 1993. **CFL Total Playoff GP - 1.**

MAROF, FRANK
Born: September 30, 1968
Birthplace: Hamilton, Ontario
Slotback. 6'0", 190 lbs. Non-import
Last Amateur Club: University of Guelph (OUAA)
Acquired: Selected in the fourth round (27th overall) of the 1992 CFL College Draft by the Calgary Stampeders.

			Pass Receiving				
	Team	GP	NO	YDS	AVE	LG	TD
1992	Cal.	18	2	23	11.5	17	0
1993	Cal.	18	6	49	8.2	13	0
CFL TOTALS		**36**	**8**	**72**	**9.0**	**17**	**0**

2-Pt. Converts - 1 attempt, 0 complete with Calgary in 1993. **CFL Total 2-Pt. Converts - 1 attempt, 0 complete.**

Tackles - 6 special teams with Calgary in 1992 and 14 special teams in 1993. **CFL Total Tackles - 20 (20 special teams)**

Tackles for Losses - 1 for 11 yards with Calgary in 1993. **CFL Total Tackles for Losses - 1 for 11 yards.**

MAROF, FRANK

Playoffs

Games Played - 1 with Calgary in 1992 and 2 in 1993. **CFL Total Playoff GP - 3.**

Fumbles - 1 and 1 lost with Calgary in 1993.
CFL Total Playoff Fumbles - 1 and 1 lost.

Tackles - 1 defensive and 1 special teams with Calgary in 1992 and 1 special teams in 1993..
CFL Total Playoff Tackles - 3 (1 defensive and 2 special teams).

Grey Cup

Games Played - 1 with Calgary in 1992. **Total Grey Cup GP - 1.**

MARSHALL, BLAKE
Born: May 17, 1965
Birthplace: Guelph, Ontario
Fullback. 6'1", 230 lbs. Non-import
Last Amateur Club: University of Western Ontario (OUAA)
Acquired: Selected by the Edmonton Eskimos in the first round (second overall) in the 1987 CFL College Draft. Granted free agency status in February, 1994.

			Scoring					Rushing				
	Team	GP	TD	C	FG	S	TP	NO	YDS	AVE	LG	TD
1987	Edm.	7	1	0	0	0	6	21	87	4.1	12	1
1988	Edm.	12	5	0	0	0	30	69	315	4.6	38	5
1989a	Edm.	18	14	0	0	0	84	65	233	3.6	15	11
1990bcd	Edm.	17	13	0	0	0	78	120	603	5.0	27	12
1991bcefghi	Edm.	16	20	0	0	0	120	125	615	4.9	34	16
1992bc	Edm.	11	9	0	0	0	54	93	495	5.3	50	7
1993	Edm.	7	3	0	0	0	18	30	101	3.4	13	2
CFL TOTALS		**88**	**65**	**0**	**0**	**0**	**390**	**523**	**2449**	**4.7**	**50**	**54**

		Pass Receiving					Kickoff Returns				
	Team	NO	YDS	AVE	LG	TD	NO	YDS	AVE	LG	TD
1987	Edm.	5	58	11.6	15	0	0	0	0.0	0	0
1988	Edm.	10	58	5.8	15	0	4	34	8.5	16	0
1989	Edm.	22	254	11.5	41	3	1	5	5.0	5	0
1990	Edm.	25	252	10.1	62	1	0	0	0.0	0	0
1991	Edm.	50	619	12.4	40	4	0	0	0.0	0	0
1992	Edm.	24	188	7.8	21	2	0	0	0.0	0	0
1993	Edm.	7	38	5.4	10	1	0	0	0.0	0	0
CFL TOTALS		**143**	**1467**	**10.3**	**62**	**11**	**5**	**39**	**7.8**	**16**	**0**

Fumbles - 1 and 1 lost with Edmonton in 1987; 2 and 1 lost in 1989; 4 and 3 lost in 1990; 2 and 1 lost in 1991; 3 and 3 lost in 1992 and 1 and 1 lost in 1993.
CFL Total Fumbles - 13 and 10 lost.

Fumble Returns - 1 for 0 yards with Edmonton in 1989; 1 for 8 yards in 1990 and 1 for 0 yards in 1991.
CFL Total Fumble Returns - 3 for 8 yards, 2.7 average, longest 8 yards.

Punting - 1 for 25 yards with Edmonton in 1992.
CFL Total Punting - 1 for 25 yards.

Own Fumbles Recovered - 2 with Edmonton in 1990. **CFL Total OFR - 2.**

Tackles - 1 defensive with Edmonton in 1988; 2 defensive in 1989; 4 defensive in 1990 and 4 defensive and 4 special teams in 1991.
CFL Total Tackles - 15 (11 defensive and 4 special teams).

a - Tied for CFL Lead in Rushing TDs with Hamilton's Derrick McAdoo.
b - All-Western All-Star.
c - CFL All-Star.
d - Led CFL in Rushing TDs.
e - GMC Most Outstanding Canadian.
f - Dr. Beattie Martin Trophy - Most Outstanding Canadian, Western Division.
g - Tied for CFL lead TDs with B.C.'s Jon Volpe.
h - Tied for CFL lead in rushing TDs with B.C.'s Jon Volpe.
i - Tied CFL record for TDs in a Season.

Playoffs

			Rushing					Pass Receiving				
	Team	GP	NO	YDS	AVE	LG	TD	NO	YDS	AVE	LG	TD
1987	Edm.	2	3	16	5.3	11	1	0	0	0.0	0	0
1988	Edm.	1	8	34	4.2	16	0	0	0	0.0	0	0
1989	Edm.	1	4	21	5.3	11	0	2	17	8.5	11	0
1990	Edm.	2	18	53	2.9	6	3	8	82	10.3	15	0
1991	Edm.	1	18	67	3.7	8	0	5	19	3.8	10	1
1992	Edm.	2	13	56	4.3	20	0	2	2	1.0	3	0
CFL TOTALS		**9**	**64**	**247**	**3.9**	**20**	**4**	**17**	**120**	**7.1**	**15**	**1**

Scoring - 1 TD for 6 points with Edmonton in 1987; 3 TDs for 18 points in 1990 and 1 TD for 6 points in 1991.
CFL Total Playoff Scoring - 5 TDs for 30 points.

Defensive Tackles - 1 with Edmonton in 1990 and 1 in 1992.
CFL Total Playoff Defensive Tackles - 2.

Grey Cup

Games Played - 1 with Edmonton in 1987 and 1 in 1990. **Total Grey Cup GP - 2.**

Rushing - 13 for 54 yards, 4.2 average, longest 9 yards with Edmonton in 1990.
Total Grey Cup Rushing - 13 for 54 yards, 4.2 average, longest 9 yards.

Pass Receiving - 1 for 6 yards with Edmonton in 1990.
Total Grey Cup Pass Receiving - 1 for 6 yards.

Fumbles - 1 and 1 lost with Edmonton in 1990.
Total Grey Cup Fumbles - 1 and 1 lost.

MARTIN, ANDREW
Born: March 31, 1970
Birthplace: Toronto, Ontario
Wide Receiver. 6'1", 200 lbs. Non-import
Last Amateur Club: Cornell University
Acquired: Selected in the fourth round (28th overall) of the 1992 CFL College Draft by the Winnipeg Blue Bombers.

			Pass Receiving					Kickoff Returns				
	Team	GP	NO	YDS	AVE	LG	TD	NO	YDS	AVE	LG	TD
1992	Wpg.	14	3	39	13.0	20	0	3	29	9.7	19	0
1993	Wpg.	5	2	11	5.5	6	0	0	0	0.0	0	0
CFL TOTALS		**19**	**5**	**50**	**10.0**	**20**	**0**	**3**	**29**	**9.7**	**19**	**0**

Fumble Returns - 1 for 0 yards with Winnipeg in 1992 and 1 for 0 yards in 1993. **CFL Total Fumble Returns - 2 for 0 yards.**

Tackles - 1 defensive and 2 special teams with Winnipeg in 1992 and 1 special teams in 1993. **CFL Total Tackles - 4 (1 defensive and 3 special teams).**

Playoffs

Games Played - 1 with Winnipeg in 1992 and 1 in 1993.
CFL Total Playoff GP - 2.

Fumble Returns - 1 for 0 yards with Winnipeg in 1992.
CFL Total Fumble Returns - 1 for 0 yards.

Grey Cup

Games Played - 1 with Winnipeg in 1992. **Total Grey Cup GP - 1.**

MARTIN, ERROL
Born: March 25, 1968
Birthplace: St. Vincent, West Indies
Linebacker. 6'2", 200 lbs. Non-import
Last Amateur Club: University of Louisville
Acquired: Selected by the Edmonton Eskimos in the second round (14th overall) in the 1992 CFL College Draft.

Games Played - 18 with Edmonton in 1993. **CFL Total GP - 18.**

Fumble Returns - 1 for 0 yards with Edmonton in 1993.
CFL Total Fumble Returns - 1 for 0 yards.

Quarterback Sacks - 6 for 53 yards lost with Edmonton in 1993.
CFL Total QB Sacks - 6 for 53 yards lost.

Tackles - 25 defensive and 14 special teams with Edmonton in 1993.
CFL Total Tackles - 39 (25 defensive and 14 special teams).

Playoffs

Games Played - 2 with Edmonton in 1993. **CFL Total Playoff GP - 2.**

Tackles - 1 special teams with Edmonton in 1993.
CFL Total Playoff Tackles - 1 (1 special teams).

Grey Cup

Games Played - 1 with Edmonton in 1993. **Total Grey Cup GP - 1.**

Quarterback Sacks - 1 for 9 yards lost with Edmonton in 1993.
Total Grey Cup QB Sacks - 1 for 9 yards lost.

Tackles - 1 defensive and 1 special teams with Edmonton in 1993.
Total Grey Cup Tackles - 2 (1 defensive and 1 special teams).

MARTIN, P. J.
Born: May 1, 1970
Birthplace: Mississauga, Ontario
Fullback. 6' 0", 229 lbs. Non-import.
Last Amateur Club: Wilfrid Laurier University
Acquired: Selected by the Hamilton Tiger-Cats in the second round (12th overall) in the 1993 CFL College Draft.

MARTIN, P. J.

	Team	GP	Rushing NO	YDS	AVE	LG	TD	Pass Receiving NO	YDS	AVE	LG	TD
1993	Ham.	16	3	21	7.0	14	0	1	11	11.0	11	0
CFL TOTALS		**16**	**3**	**21**	**7.0**	**14**	**0**	**1**	**11**	**11.0**	**11**	**0**

Punt Returns - 1 for 8 yards with Hamilton in 1993.
CFL Total Punt Returns - 1 for 8 yards.

Own Fumbles Recovered - 1 with Hamilton in 1993. **CFL Total OFR - 1.**

Tackles - 1 defensive and 2 special teams with Hamilton in 1993.
CFL Total Tackles - 3 (1 defensive and 2 special teams).

Playoffs

Games Played - 2 with Hamilton in 1993. **CFL Total Playoff GP - 2.**

Tackles - 2 special teams with Hamilton in 1993.
CFL Total Playoff Tackles - 2 (2 special teams).

MARTINO, ANTHONY

Born: June 9, 1966
Birthplace: Kelowna, British Columbia
Kicker. 6'0", 190 lbs. Non-import
Last Amateur Club: Kent State University
Acquired: Selected in the first round (seventh overall) by the B.C. Lions in the 1988 CFL College Draft. Released in August, 1988 and signed by the Ottawa Rough Riders in September, 1988. Released in October, 1988. Re-signed by the B.C. Lions in March, 1989. Released by B.C. in June, 1989. Re-signed by B.C. in December, 1989. Released by B.C. in July, 1990. Signed as a free agent by the Calgary Stampeders in January, 1992.

	Team	GP	Scoring TD	C	FG	S	TP	Punting NO	YDS	AVE	LK	S
1988	B.C.	4	0	11	0	3	14	28	1047	37.4	54	1
	Ott.	2	0	2	1	0	5	0	0	0.0	0	0
1989		Did not play						Did not play				
1990	B.C.	5	0	14	13	4	57	37	1315	35.5	55	1
1992	Cal.	18	0	0	0	7	7	111	4347	39.2	82	7
1993	Cal.	18	0	0	0	3	3	121	4939	40.8	76	2
CFL TOTALS		**47**	**0**	**27**	**14**	**17**	**86**	**297**	**11648**	**39.2**	**82**	**11**

	Team	Kickoffs NO	YDS	AVE	LK	S	Field Goals T	G	YDS	AVE	LK	PCT
1988	B.C.	13	695	53.5	60	0	2	0	0	0.0	0	0.0
	Ott.	0	0	0.0	0	0	2	1	35	35.0	35	50.0
1989		Did not play					Did not play					
1990	B.C.	30	1513	50.4	68	0	18	13	397	30.5	42	72.2
1992	Cal.	0	0	0.0	0	0	0	0	0	0.0	0	0.0
1993	Cal.	22	1291	58.7	81	1	0	0	0	0.0	0	0.0
CFL TOTALS		**65**	**3499**	**53.8**	**81**	**1**	**22**	**14**	**432**	**30.9**	**42**	**63.6**

	Team	Field Goal Attempts NO	YDS	AVE	LK	S	Converts T	G	PCT
1988	B.C.	2	57	28.5	30	2	11	11	100.0
	Ott.	1	16	16.0	16	0	2	2	100.0
1989		Did not play					Did not play		
1990	B.C.	5	211	42.2	47	3	14	14	100.0
1992	Cal.	0	0	0.0	0	0	0	0	0.0
1993	Cal.	0	0	0.0	0	0	0	0	0.0
CFL TOTALS		**8**	**284**	**35.5**	**47**	**5**	**27**	**27**	**100.0**

Passing - 1 attempt, 0 complete with B.C. in 1988 and 2 attempts, 1 complete for 17 yards with B.C. in 1990.
CFL Total Passing - 3 attempts, 1 complete for 17 yards, 33.3 percent.

Rushing - 3 for 49 yards, 16.3 average, longest 22 yards with Calgary in 1992 and 2 for 29 yards, 14.5 average, longest 16 in 1993.
CFL Total Rushing - 5 for 78 yards, 15.6 average, longest 22 yards.

Fumbles - 2 and 2 lost with B.C. in 1988 and 1 and 1 lost with Calgary in 1992.
CFL Total Fumbles - 3 and 3 lost.

Net Punting - 112 for 3660 yards, 32.7 average with Calgary in 1992 and 121 for 4046 yards, 33.4 average in 1993.
CFL Total Net Punting - 233 for 7706 yards, 33.1 average.

Tackles - 2 special teams with Calgary in 1993.
CFL Total Tackles - 2 (2 special teams).

Playoffs

	Team	GP	Punting NO	YDS	AVE	LK	S	Net Punting NO	YDS	AVE
1992	Cal.	1	9	336	37.3	77	1	9	320	35.6
1993	Cal.	2	17	681	40.1	78	0	17	593	34.9
CFL TOTALS		**3**	**26**	**1017**	**39.1**	**78**	**1**	**26**	**913**	**35.1**

Grey Cup

	Team	GP	Punting NO	YDS	AVE	LK	S	Net Punting NO	YDS	AVE
1992	Cal.	1	8	275	34.4	45	0	8	247	30.9
CFL TOTALS		**1**	**8**	**275**	**34.4**	**45**	**0**	**8**	**247**	**30.9**

MASOTTI, PAUL

Born: March 10, 1965
Birthplace: Hamilton, Ontario
Wide Receiver. 6'0", 185 lbs. Non-import
Last Amateur Club: Acadia University (AUAA)
Acquired: Selected in the second round (15th overall) by the Toronto Argonauts in the 1988 CFL College Draft. Attended the NFL Washington Redskins training camp in 1988. Released and signed by Toronto in September, 1988.

	Team	GP	Scoring TD	C	FG	S	TP	Pass Receiving NO	YDS	AVE	LG	TD
1988	Tor.	7	1	0	0	0	6	2	50	25.0	33	1
1989	Tor.	17	4	0	0	0	24	31	443	14.3	55	4
1990	Tor.	18	5	0	0	0	30	37	592	16.0	60	5
1991	Tor.	17	2	0	0	0	12	23	360	15.7	36	2
1992	Tor.	18	3	x1	0	0	20	44	801	18.2	45	2
1993	Tor.	12	3	0	0	0	18	36	606	16.8	72	3
CFL TOTALS		**89**	**18**	**x1**	**0**	**0**	**110**	**173**	**2852**	**16.5**	**72**	**17**

	Team	Punt Returns NO	YDS	AVE	LG	TD	Kickoff Returns NO	YDS	AVE	LG	TD
1988	Tor.	18	127	7.1	39	0	1	25	25.0	25	0
1989	Tor.	0	0	0.0	0	0	0	0	0.0	0	0
1990	Tor.	0	0	0.0	0	0	1	0	0.0	0	0
1991	Tor.	1	5	5.0	5	0	1	4	4.0	6	0
1992	Tor.	0	0	0.0	0	0	1	14	14.0	14	0
1993	Tor.	0	0	0.0	0	0	0	0	0.0	0	0
CFL TOTALS		**19**	**132**	**6.9**	**39**	**0**	**4**	**43**	**10.8**	**25**	**0**

Fumbles - 1 and 1 lost with Toronto in 1989; 2 and 1 lost in 1991; 1 and 1 lost in 1992 and 1 and 0 lost in 1993. **CFL Total Fumbles - 5 and 3 lost.**

Own Fumbles Recovered - 2 with Toronto in 1991; 1 in 1992 and 1 in 1993.
CFL Total OFR - 4.

Punting - 1 for 36 yards with Toronto in 1991.
CFL Total Punting - 1 for 36 yards.

Net Punting - 1 for 29 yards with Toronto in 1991.
CFL Total Net Punting - 1 for 29 yards.

Own Kickoffs Recovered - 1 for 12 yards with Toronto in 1991 and 1 for 0 yards in 1992. **CFL Total Own Kickoffs Recovered - 2 for 12 yards.**

2-Pt. Converts - 2 attempts with Toronto in 1991 and 1 made in 1992.
CFL Total 2-Pt. Converts - 2 attempts, 1 made.

Blocked Kicks - 2 punts with Toronto in 1991 and 1 punt in 1992.
CFL Total Blocked Kicks - 3 punts.

Fumble Returns - 1 for 0 yards with Toronto in 1991; 1 for 0 yards and 1 TD in 1992 and 1 for 0 yards in 1993.
CFL Total Fumble Returns - 3 for 0 yards and 1 TD.

Tackles - 1 defensive with Toronto in 1988; 2 defensive in 1989; 2 defensive in 1990; 5 defensive and 6 special teams in 1991; 4 defensive and 2 special teams in 1992 and 3 defensive and 1 special teams in 1993.
CFL Total Tackles - 26 (17 defensive and 9 special teams).

Tackles for Losses - 1 for 8 yards with Toronto in 1992.
CFL Total Tackles for Losses - 1 for 8 yards.

Playoffs

Games Played - 1 with Toronto in 1988; 1 in 1989; 2 in 1990 and 1 in 1991.
CFL Total Playoff GP - 5.

Pass Receiving - 7 for 120 yards, 17.1 average, longest 28 yards with Toronto in 1989; 1 for 15 yards in 1990 and 3 for 72 yards, 24.0 average, longest 36 yards with Toronto in 1991.
CFL Total Playoff Pass Receiving - 11 for 207 yards, 18.8 average, longest 36 yards.

Own Fumbles Recovered - 1 with Toronto in 1990. **CFL Total Playoff OFR - 1.**

Grey Cup

Games Played - 1 with Toronto in 1991. **Total Grey Cup GP - 1.**

Scoring - 1 TD for 6 points with Toronto in 1991.
Total Grey Cup Scoring - 1 TD for 6 points.

Pass Receiving - 2 for 45 yards, 22.5 average, longest 36 yards and 1 TD with Toronto in 1991. **Total Grey Cup Pass Receiving - 2 for 45 yards, 22.5 average, longest 36 yards and 1 TD.**

MATICH, BRENT

Born: December 5, 1966
Birthplace: Calgary, Alberta
Punter. 6'1", 200 lbs. Non-import
Last Amateur Club: University of Calgary (WIFL)
Acquired: Selected in the sixth round (41st overall) by the Ottawa Rough Riders in the 1988 CFL College Draft. Released prior to the 1988 season. Signed as a free agent by the Calgary Stampeders in December, 1989. Released by Calgary in July, 1992. Signed as a free agent by the Saskatchewan Roughriders in September, 1992.

MATICH, BRENT

	Team	Scoring GP	TD	C	FG	S	TP	Punting NO	YDS	AVE	LK	S
1989ab	Cal.	18	0	0	0	7	7	144	6116	42.5	72	7
1990ab	Cal.	18	0	0	0	5	5	133	5728	43.1	71	5
1991a	Cal.	16	0	0	0	6	6	120	5124	42.7	69	6
1992	Sask.	10	0	0	0	2	2	78	3109	39.9	61	2
1993	Sask.	16	0	0	0	7	7	123	5052	41.1	84	7
CFL TOTALS		**78**	**0**	**0**	**0**	**27**	**27**	**598**	**25129**	**42.0**	**84**	**27**

Net Punting - 121 for 4286 yards, 35.4 average with Calgary in 1991; 80 for 2777 yards, 34.7 average with Saskatchewan in 1992 and 123 for 4586 yards, 37.3 average in 1993.
CFL Total Net Punting - 324 for 11649 yards, 36.0 average.

Rushing - 1 for 25 yards with Calgary in 1989 and 1 for 16 yards in 1993.
CFL Total Rushing - 2 for 41 yards, 20.5 average, longest 25 yards.

Passing - 2 attempts with Calgary in 1989. **CFL Total Passing - 2 attempts.**

Own Punts Recovered - 1 for 27 yards with Calgary in 1989.
CFL Total Own Punts Recovered - 1 for 27 yards.

2-Pt. Converts - 1 tried and 0 made with Calgary in 1989.
CFL Total 2-Pt. Converts - 1 tried and 0 made.

Fumbles - 6 and 4 lost with Calgary in 1989; 4 and 4 lost in 1990; 1 and 1 lost in 1991; 2 and 1 lost with Saskatchewan in 1992 and 1 and 1 lost in 1993.
CFL Total Fumbles - 14 and 11 lost.

Own Fumbles Recovered - 2 with Calgary in 1989 and 1 in 1990.
CFL Total OFR - 3.

Tackles - 2 special teams with Calgary in 1991.
CFL Total Tackles - 2 (2 special teams).

a - All-Western All-Star
b - Led the CFL in Punting Average

Playoffs

Games Played - 1 with Calgary in 1989; 1 in 1990; 1 with Saskatchewan in 1992 and 1 in 1993. **CFL Total Playoff GP - 4.**

Punting - 7 for 294 yards, 42.0 average, longest 53 yards with Calgary in 1989; 8 for 325 yards, 40.6 average, longest 59 yards in 1990; 9 for 355 yards, 39.4 average, longest 53 yards with Saskatchewan in 1992 and 8 for 338 yards, 42.3 average, longest 53 yards in 1993.
CFL Total Playoff Punting - 32 for 1312 yards, 41.0 average, longest 59 yards.

Net Punting - 9 for 208 yards, 23.1 average with Saskatchewan in 1992 and 8 for 309 yards, 38.6 average in 1993.
CFL Total Net Punting - 17 for 517 yards, 30.4 average.

Passing - 1 attempt, 0 complete with Calgary in 1989.
CFL Total Playoff Passing - 1 attempt, 0 complete.

MATTHEWS, KEILAN

Born: December 30, 1967
Birthplace: Sacramento, California
Linebacker. 6'2", 220 lbs. Import
Last Amateur Club: Sacramento State University
Acquired: Signed as a free agent by the Winnipeg Blue Bombers in January 1992 and was released during training camp. Signed as a free agent by the Sacramento Gold Miners in March, 1993. Released by Sacramento in October, 1993. Signed as a free agent by the Las Vegas Posse in March, 1994.

	Team	GP	Interception Returns NO	YDS	AVE	LG	TD	Fumble Returns NO	YDS	AVE	LG	TD
1993a	Sac.	12	1	12	12.0	12	0	6	51	8.5	42	0
CFL TOTALS		**12**	**1**	**12**	**12.0**	**12**	**0**	**6**	**51**	**8.5**	**42**	**0**

Kickoff Returns - 1 for 13 yards with Sacramento in 1993.
CFL Total Kickoff Returns - 1 for 13 yards.

Fumbles - 1 and 0 lost with Sacramento in 1993.
CFL Total Fumbles - 1 and 0 lost.

Quarterback Sacks - 1 for 10 yards lost with Sacramento in 1993.
CFL Total QB Sacks - 1 for 10 yards lost.

Tackles - 47 defensive and 13 special teams with Sacramento in 1993.
CFL Total Tackles - 60 (47 defensive and 13 special teams).

Tackles for Losses - 4 for 12 yards with Sacramento in 1993.
CFL Total Tackles for Losses - 4 for 12 yards.

a - Tied for CFL Lead in Fumble Returns (6).

MAZZOLI, NICK

Born: August 8, 1968
Birthplace: Markham, Ontario
Wide Receiver. 5'11", 180 lbs. Non-import
Last Amateur Club: Simon Fraser University (NAIA CFA)
Acquired: Selected in the first round (first overall) by the Hamilton Tiger-Cats in the 1991 CFL College Draft. Signed by the NFL Seattle Seahawks in July, 1991 and was released during training camp. Signed by Hamilton in August, 1991. Granted free agency status in February, 1994. Signed as a free agent by the Ottawa Rough Riders in March, 1994.

	Team	Scoring GP	TD	C	FG	S	TP	Rushing NO	YDS	AVE	LG	TD
1991	Ham.	12	3	0	0	0	18	2	10	5.0	6	0
1992	Ham.	14	5	0	0	0	30	1	8	8.0	8	0
1993	Ham.	13	0	0	0	0	0	0	0	0.0	0	0
CFL TOTALS		**39**	**8**	**0**	**0**	**0**	**48**	**3**	**18**	**6.0**	**8**	**0**

	Team	Pass Receiving NO	YDS	AVE	LG	TD	Punt Returns NO	YDS	AVE	LG	TD
1991	Ham.	24	339	14.1	33	2	46	557	12.1	74	1
1992	Ham.	41	757	18.5	82	5	17	152	8.9	29	0
1993	Ham.	19	245	12.9	35	0	15	99	6.6	21	0
CFL TOTALS		**84**	**1341**	**16.0**	**82**	**7**	**78**	**808**	**10.4**	**74**	**1**

	Team	Kickoff Returns NO	YDS	AVE	LG	TD	Fumbles NO	LOST	OFR
1991	Ham.	23	519	22.6	37	0	2	2	0
1992	Ham.	11	168	15.3	55	0	1	1	0
1993	Ham.	11	118	10.7	41	0	0	0	0
CFL TOTALS		**45**	**805**	**17.9**	**55**	**0**	**3**	**3**	**0**

Tackles - 4 defensive and 1 special teams with Hamilton in 1991; 3 defensive in 1992 and 1 defensive in 1993.
CFL Total Tackles - 9 (8 defensive and 1 special teams).

Playoffs

	Team	GP	Kickoff Returns NO	YDS	AVE	LG	TD	Punt Returns NO	YDS	AVE	LG	TD
1992	Ham.	2	7	151	21.6	35	0	0	0	0.0	0	0
1993	Ham.	2	1	4	4.0	4	0	2	23	11.5	17	0
CFL TOTALS		**4**	**8**	**155**	**19.4**	**35**	**0**	**2**	**23**	**11.5**	**17**	**0**

McADOO, DERRICK

Born: April 2, 1965
Birthplace: Pensacola, Florida
Running Back, 5' 10", 200 lbs., Import
Last Amateur Club: Baylor University
Acquired: Signed as a free agent with the NFL St. Louis Cardinals in 1987. Acquired by the NFL Tampa Bay Buccaneers on waivers in September, 1988. Released and signed by the NFL Phoenix Cardinals in November, 1988. Signed as a free agent by the Hamilton Tiger-Cats in March, 1989. Released by Hamilton in October, 1991. Signed as a free agent by the Toronto Argonauts in July, 1993. Released by Toronto in August, 1993.

	Team	Scoring GP	TD	C	FG	S	TP	Rushing NO	YDS	AVE	LG	TD
1989abc	Ham.	16	12	0	0	0	72	246	1039	4.2	45	11
1990	Ham.	15	7	0	0	0	42	198	752	3.8	22	5
1991	Ham.	3	1	0	0	0	6	21	107	5.1	20	1
1992		DID NOT PLAY						DID NOT PLAY				
1993	Tor.	4	1	0	0	0	6	13	70	5.4	18	1
CFL TOTALS		**38**	**21**	**0**	**0**	**0**	**126**	**478**	**1968**	**4.1**	**45**	**18**

	Team	Pass Receiving NO	YDS	AVE	LG	TD	Passing ATT	COMP	YDS	PCT	INT	LG	TD
1989	Ham.	57	699	12.3	48	1	1	1	83	100.0	0	83	1
1990	Ham.	65	583	9.0	34	2	6	2	54	33.3	1	36	2
1991	Ham.	4	27	6.8	12	0	0	0	0	0.0	0	0	0
1992		DID NOT PLAY					DID NOT PLAY						
1993	Tor.	7	88	12.6	28	0	0	0	0	0.0	0	0	0
CFL TOTALS		**133**	**1397**	**10.5**	**48**	**3**	**7**	**3**	**137**	**42.9**	**1**	**83**	**3**

	Team	Punt Returns NO	YDS	AVE	LG	TD	Kickoff Returns NO	YDS	AVE	LG	TD
1989	Ham.	12	72	6.0	18	0	18	402	22.3	46	0
1990	Ham.	6	29	4.8	22	0	32	681	21.3	83	0
1991	Ham.	0	0	0	0	0	5	69	13.8	22	0
1992		DID NOT PLAY					DID NOT PLAY				
1993	Tor.	0	0	0	0	0	7	71	10.1	19	0
CFL TOTALS		**18**	**101**	**5.6**	**22**	**0**	**62**	**1223**	**19.7**	**83**	**0**

	Team	Fumbles NO	LOST	OFR
1989	Ham.	13	8	3
1990	Ham.	12	9	1
1991	Ham.	2	2	0
1992		DID NOT PLAY		
1993	Tor.	0	0	1
CFL TOTALS		**27**	**19**	**5**

Tackles - 8 defensive with Hamilton in 1989; 6 defensive in 1990 and 2 defensive and 1 special teams with Toronto in 1993.
CFL Total Tackles - 17 (16 defensive and 1 special teams).

McADOO, DERRICK
a - All-Eastern All-Star.
b - Led CFL in Rushing Attempts.
c - Shared CFL lead for Rushing TDs with Edmonton's Blake Marshall.

Playoffs

			Rushing					Pass Receiving				
	Team	GP	NO	YDS	AVE	LG	TD	NO	YDS	AVE	LG	TD
1989	Ham.	1	17	59	3.5	11	0	1	9	9.0	9	0
CFL TOTALS		**1**	**17**	**59**	**3.5**	**11**	**0**	**1**	**9**	**9.0**	**9**	**0**

Grey Cup

			Scoring					Rushing				
	Team	GP	TD	C	FG	S	TP	NO	YDS	AVE	LG	TD
1989	Ham.	1	2	0		00	12	21	83	4.0	16	1
CFL TOTALS		**1**	**2**	**0**	**0**	**0**	**12**	**21**	**83**	**4.0**	**16**	**1**

		Pass Receiving					Kickoff Returns				
	Team	NO	YDS	AVE	LG	TD	NO	YDS	AVE	LG	TD
1989	Ham.	2	29	14.5	30	1	3	75	25.0	32	0
CFL TOTALS		**2**	**29**	**14.5**	**30**	**1**	**3**	**75**	**25.0**	**32**	**0**

McARTHUR, DANE
Born: August 15, 1968
Birthplace: Prince Albert, Saskatchewan
Running Back. 6'0", 195 lbs. Non-import.
Last Amateur Club: University of Hawaii
Acquired: Selected by the Saskatchewan Roughriders in the first round (eighth overall) in the 1990 CFL College Draft. Placed on the team's suspension list in August, 1994.

			Pass Receiving				
	Team	GP	NO	YDS	AVE	LG	TD
1991	Sask.	10	5	47	9.4	13	0
1992		DID NOT PLAY					
1993	Sask.	2	1	15	15.0	15	0
CFL TOTALS		**12**	**6**	**62**	**10.3**	**15**	**0**

Rushing - 1 for 3 yards, with Saskatchewan in 1991.
CFL Total Rushing - 1 for 3 yards.

McCALLUM, PAUL
Born: January 7, 1970
Birthplace: North Vancouver, British Columbia
Kicker/Punter. 5' 11", 185 lbs. Non-import.
Last Amateur Club: Surrey Juniors.
Acquired: Signed as a free agent by the Hamilton Tiger-Cats in March, 1993. Released by Hamilton in June, 1993. Signed as a free agent by the B.C. Lions in September, 1993 and was released that month. Signed as a free agent by the Ottawa Rough Riders in October, 1993 and was released by Ottawa in November, 1993. Signed as a free agent by the B.C. Lions in December, 1993.

			Scoring					Punting				
	Team	GP	TD	C	FG	S	TP	NO	YDS	AVE	LK	S
1993	B.C.	1	0	1	3	0	10	0	0	0.0	0	0
	Ott.	3	0	5	6	1	24	15	511	34.1	70	0
CFL TOTALS		**4**	**0**	**6**	**9**	**1**	**34**	**15**	**511**	**34.1**	**70**	**0**

		Kickoffs					Field Goals					
	Team	NO	YDS	AVE	LK	S	T	M	YDS	AVE	LK	PCT.
1993	B.C.	2	84	42.0	51	0	4	3	107	35.7	45	75.0
	Ott.	7	341	48.7	61	0	8	6	128	21.3	35	75.0
CFL TOTALS		**9**	**425**	**47.2**	**61**	**0**	**12**	**9**	**235**	**26.1**	**45**	**75.0**

		Field Goal Attempts					Converts		
	Team	NO	YDS	AVE	LK	S	T	G	PCT.
1993	B.C.	1	52	52.0	52	0	1	1	100.0
	Ott.	2	62	31.0	33	1	5	5	100.0
CFL TOTALS		**3**	**114**	**38.0**	**52**	**1**	**6**	**6**	**100.0**

Net Punting - 15 for 484 yards, 32.3 average with Ottawa in 1993.
CFL Total Net Punting - 15 for 484 yards, 32.3 average.

2-pt. Converts - 1 attempt, 0 complete with Ottawa in 1993.
CFL Total 2-pt. Converts - 1 attempt, 0 complete.

Own Fumbles Recovered - 1 with Ottawa in 1993.
CFL Total OFR - 1.

Tackles - 2 special teams with Ottawa in 1993.
CFL Total Tackles - 2 (2 special teams).

McCANT, KEITHEN
Born: March 8, 1969
Birthplace: Grande Prairie, Texas
Quarterback. 6'2", 210 lbs. Import
Last Amateur Club: University of Nebraska
Acquired: Selected by the NFL Cleveland Browns in the twelfth round (316th overall) in the 1992 NFL Draft. Released by the Browns and signed as a free agent by the Winnipeg Blue Bombers in February, 1993.

Games Played - 7 with Winnipeg in 1993. **CFL Total GP - 7.**

Playoffs

Games Played - 1 with Winnipeg in 1993. **CFL Total Playoff GP - 1.**

Grey Cup

Games Played - 1 with Winnipeg in 1993. **Total Grey Cup GP - 1.**

McCURDY, BRIAN
Born: June 11, 1967
Birthplace: Windsor, Ontario
Defensive Back. 6'1", 175 lbs. Non-import.
Last Amateur Club: Northern Arizona University
Acquired: Selected by the Toronto Argonauts in the second round (eighth overall) of the 1993 CFL College Draft.

Games Played - 12 with Toronto in 1993. **CFL Total GP - 12.**

Kickoff Returns - 1 for 5 yards with Toronto in 1993.
CFL Total Kickoff Returns - 1 for 5 yards.

Fumble Returns - 1 for 0 yards with Toronto in 1993.
CFL Total Fumble Returns - 1 for 0 yards.

Blocked Kicks - 1 punt with Toronto in 1993.
CFL Total Blocked Kicks - 1 (1 punt).

Tackles - 5 defensive and 13 special teams with Toronto in 1993.
CFL Total Tackles - 18 (5 defensive and 13 special teams).

Tackles for Losses - 1 for 17 yards with Toronto in 1993.
CFL Total Tackles for Losses - 1 for 17 yards.

McCURTY, GARY
Born: May 29, 1971
Birthplace: Fort Hood, Texas
Running Back. 5'7", 208 lbs. Import.
Last Amateur Club: Puget Sound
Acquired: Signed as a free agent by the Sacramento Gold Miners in August, 1993.

Games Played - 2 with Sacramento in 1993. **CFL Total GP - 2.**

McJULIEN, PAUL
Born: February 24, 1965
Birthplace: Chicago, Illinois
Punter. 5' 10", 210 lbs. Import.
Last Amateur Club: Jackson State University
Acquired: Signed as a free agent by the NFL San Diego Chargers in July, 1988. Released by San Diego in August, 1988. Signed as a free agent by the NFL Seattle Seahawks in 1990 and was released prior to the 1990 season. Signed as a free agent by the NFL Miami Dolphins in June, 1991 and was released during training camp. Signed as a free agent by the NFL San Francisco 49ers in August, 1991 and was released by San Francisco later that month. Signed as free agent by the NFL Green Bay Packers in August, 1991. Released by Green Bay following the 1992 season. Signed as a free agent by the Sacramento Gold Miners in July, 1993. Released by Sacramento in August, 1993.

			Scoring					Punting				
	Team	GP	TD	C	FG	S	TP	NO	YDS	AVE	LK	S
1993	Sac.	4	0	0	0	1	1	27	983	36.4	54	1
CFL TOTALS		**4**	**0**	**0**	**0**	**1**	**1**	**27**	**983**	**36.4**	**54**	**1**

Net Punting - 27 for 814 yards, 30.1 average with Sacramento in 1993.
CFL Total Net Punting - 27 for 814 yards, 30.1 average.

McLENNAN, SPENCER
Born: October 10, 1966
Birthplace: Kelowna, British Columbia
Wide Receiver. 5'10", 190 lbs. Non-import
Last Amateur Club: Okanagan Sun Jrs. (PJFL)
Acquired: Signed as a free agent by the B.C. Lions in July, 1991.

Games Played - 14 with B.C. in 1991; 18 in 1992 and 18 in 1993.
CFL Total GP - 50.

Pass Receiving - 2 for 22 yards, 11.0 average, longest 16 yards with B.C. in 1991 and 9 for 97 yards, 10.8 average, longest 16 yards in 1992.
CFL Total Pass Receiving - 11 for 119 yards, 10.8 average, longest 16 yards.

Own Kickoffs Recovered - 1 for 15 yards with B.C. in 1991 and 1 for 0 yards in 1993. **CFL Total OKR - 2 for 15 yards.**

McLENNAN, SPENCER

Kickoff Returns - 1 for 6 yards with B.C. in 1993.
CFL Total Kickoff Returns - 1 for 6 yards.

Own Fumbles Recovered - 1 with B.C. in 1992. **CFL Total OFR - 1.**

Tackles - 1 defensive and 8 special teams with B.C. in 1991; 4 special teams in 1992 and 2 defensive and 22 special teams in 1993.
CFL Total Tackles - 37 (3 defensive and 34 special teams).

Playoffs

Games Played - 1 with B.C. in 1991 and 1 in 1993. **CFL Total Playoff GP - 2.**

Pass Receiving - 4 for 60 yards, 15.0 average, longest 20 yards with B.C. in 1991 and 2 for 28 yards, 14.0 average, longest 23 yards in 1993.
CFL Total Playoff Pass Receiving - 6 for 88 yards, 14.7 average, longest 23 yards.

Own Fumbles Recovered - 1 with B.C. in 1991. **CFL Total Playoff OFR - 1.**

McLOUGHLIN, MARK
Born: October 26, 1965
Birthplace: Liverpool, England
Kicker. 6'1", 205 lbs. Non-import
Last Amateur Club: University of South Dakota
Acquired: Selected in the third round (20th overall) by the Calgary Stampeders in the 1988 CFL College Draft.

		Scoring						Kickoffs				
	Team	GP	TD	C	FG	S	TP	NO	YDS	AVE	LK	S
1988	Cal.	10	0	17	24	8	97	39	2217	56.8	87	1
1989	Cal.	18	0	43	48	15	202	91	5469	60.1	95	1
1990	Cal.	18	0	56	45	18	209	112	6476	57.8	91	1
1991	Cal.	18	0	57	46	13	208	111	6391	57.6	95	0
1992ab	Cal.	18	0	63	44	13	208	102	5754	56.4	95	1
1993b	Cal.	18	0	63	47	11	215	87	5089	58.5	93	1
CFL TOTALS		**100**	**0**	**299**	**254**	**78**	**1139**	**542**	**31396**	**57.9**	**95**	**5**

		Field Goals						Field Goal Attempts				
	Team	T	G	YDS	AVE	LK	PCT	NO	YDS	AVE	LK	S
1988	Cal.	36	24	792	33.0	58	66.7	12	562	46.8	57	7
1989	Cal.	67	48	1444	30.1	52	71.6	19	854	44.9	63	14
1990	Cal.	69	45	1533	34.1	54	65.2	24	1089	45.4	58	17
1991	Cal.	64	46	1398	30.4	52	71.9	18	852	47.3	59	13
1992	Cal.	64	44	1289	29.3	44	68.8	20	888	44.4	63	12
1993	Cal.	62	47	1391	29.6	51	75.8	15	655	43.7	61	10
CFL TOTALS		**362**	**254**	**7847**	**30.9**	**58**	**70.2**	**108**	**4900**	**45.4**	**63**	**73**

Punting - 1 for 39 yards with Calgary in 1989 and 9 for 318 yards, 35.3 average, longest 48 yards in 1991.
CFL Total Punting - 10 for 357 yards, 35.7 average, longest 48 yards.

Net Punting - 9 for 225 yards, 25.0 average with Calgary in 1991.
CFL Total Net Punting - 9 for 225 yards, 25.0 average.

Converts - 18 attempts, 17 made with Calgary in 1988; 46 attempts, 43 made in 1989; 57 attempts, 56 made in 1990; 57 attempts, 57 made in 1991; 63 attempts, 63 made in 1992 and 63 attempts, 63 made in 1993.
CFL Total Converts - 304 attempts, 299 made, 98.4 percent.

Fumbles - 1 and 1 lost with Calgary in 1988; 1 and 0 lost in 1989; 3 and 3 lost in 1990 and 1 and 1 lost in 1992. **CFL Total Fumbles - 6 and 5 lost.**

Fumble Returns - 1 for 0 yards with Calgary in 1993.
CFL Total Fumble Returns - 1 for 0 yards.

Tackles - 1 special teams with Calgary in 1991.
CFL Total Tackles - 1 (1 special teams).

a - All-Western All-Star
b - Led CFL in Scoring (Kicking)

Playoffs

		Scoring						Kickoffs				
	Team	GP	TD	C	FG	S	TP	NO	YDS	AVE	LK	S
1989	Cal.	1	0	2	4	0	14	4	198	49.5	66	0
1990	Cal.	1	0	1	5	1	17	4	220	55.0	55	1
1991	Cal.	2	0	10	3	2	21	12	717	59.8	70	0
1992	Cal.	1	0	2	2	0	8	4	233	58.3	71	0
1993	Cal.	2	0	3	3	0	12	6	312	52.0	64	0
CFL TOTALS		**7**	**0**	**18**	**17**	**3**	**72**	**30**	**1680**	**56.0**	**71**	**1**

		Field Goals						Field Goal Attempts					Converts		
	Team	T	G	YDS	AVE	LK	PCT	NO	YDS	AVE	LK	S	T	G	PCT
1989	Cal.	4	4	104	26.0	40	100.0	0	0	0.0	0	0	2	2	100.0
1990	Cal.	5	5	173	34.6	47	100.0	0	0	0.0	0	0	1	1	100.0
1991	Cal.	5	3	109	36.3	54	60.0	2	97	48.5	50	2	10	10	100.0
1992	Cal.	2	2	67	33.5	35	100.0	0	0	0.0	0	0	2	2	100.0
1993	Cal.	4	3	83	27.7	39	75.0	1	37	37.0	37	0	3	3	100.0
CFL TOTALS		**20**	**17**	**536**	**31.5**	**54**	**85.0**	**3**	**134**	**44.7**	**87**	**2**	**18**	**18**	**100.0**

Grey Cup

		Scoring						Kickoffs				
	Team	GP	TD	C	FG	S	TP	NO	YDS	AVE	LK	S
1991	Cal.	1	0	2	2	1	9	6	307	51.2	57	0
1992	Cal.	1	0	2	3	1	12	3	168	56.0	57	0
CFL TOTALS		**2**	**0**	**4**	**5**	**2**	**21**	**9**	**475**	**52.8**	**57**	**0**

		Field Goals						Field Goal Attempts					Converts		
	Team	T	G	YDS	AVE	LK	PCT	NO	YDS	AVE	LK	S	T	G	PCT
1991	Cal.	3	2	64	32.0	37	66.7	1	43	43.0	43	1	2	2	100.0
1992	Cal.	5	3	71	23.7	37	60.0	2	66	33.0	52	1	2	2	100.0
CFL TOTALS		**8**	**5**	**135**	**27.0**	**37**	**62.5**	**3**	**109**	**36.3**	**52**	**2**	**4**	**4**	**100.0**

McMANUS, DANNY
Born: June 17, 1965
Birthplace: Dania, Florida
Quarterback. 6'0", 200 lbs. Import
Last Amateur Club: Florida State University
Acquired: Selected in the 11th round (282nd overall) by the Kansas City Chiefs in the 1988 NFL Draft. Signed by Kansas City in July, 1988. Released after the 1989 season. Signed as a free agent by the Winnipeg Blue Bombers in May, 1990. Granted free agency status in February, 1993. Signed as a free agent by the B.C. Lions in June, 1993.

			Rushing					Passing						
	Team	GP	NO	YDS	AVE	LG	TD	ATT	COMP	YDS	PCT	INT	LG	TD
1990	Wpg.	18	3	12	4.0	9	0	130	55	946	42.3	4	73	7
1991	Wpg.	18	0	0	0.0	0	0	119	54	985	45.4	8	47	3
1992	Wpg.	18	4	7	1.8	8	0	122	56	1153	45.9	5	73	6
1993	B.C.	18	12	64	5.3	26	0	223	114	1613	51.1	14	44	10
CFL TOTALS		**72**	**19**	**83**	**4.4**	**26**	**0**	**594**	**279**	**4697**	**47.0**	**31**	**73**	**26**

2-Pt. Converts - 1 tried, 0 complete with Winnipeg in 1990 and 3 tried, 1 complete in 1991. **CFL Total 2-Pt. Converts - 4 tried, 1 complete.**

Fumbles - 2 and 0 lost with Winnipeg in 1990; 2 and 0 lost in 1992 and 4 and 4 lost with B.C. in 1993.
CFL Total Fumbles - 8 and 4 lost.

Own Fumbles Recovered - 1 with Winnipeg in 1992. **CFL Total OFR - 1.**

Tackles - 1 defensive with Winnipeg in 1991 and 1 defensive in 1992.
CFL Total Tackles - 2 (2 defensive).

Playoffs

Games Played - 1 with Winnipeg in 1990; 2 in 1991; 1 in 1992 and 1 with B.C. in 1993. **CFL Total Playoff GP - 5.**

Grey Cup

Games Played - 1 with Winnipeg in 1990 and 1 in 1992.
Total Grey Cup GP - 2.

Passing - 2 attempts, 2 complete for 66 yards, 100.0 percent, longest 56 yards and 1 TD with Winnipeg in 1990 and 18 attempts, 7 complete for 155 yards, 38.9 percent, 1 interception, longest 42 yards and 1 TD in 1992.
Total Grey Cup Passing - 20 attempts, 9 complete for 221 yards, 45.0 percent, 1 interception, longest 56 yards and 2 TDs.

McPHERSON, DON
Born: April 2, 1965
Birthplace: Brooklyn, New York
Quarterback. 6'1", 195 lbs. Import
Last Amateur Club: University of Syracuse
Acquired: Selected in the sixth round (149th overall) by the Philadelphia Eagles in 1988 NFL Draft. Traded to NFL Houston Oilers for conditional pick in 1991 NFL Draft in August, 1990. Released by Houston in October, 1990. Signed as a free agent by NFL Philadelphia Eagles in March, 1991. Released and signed by the Hamilton Tiger-Cats in August, 1991 after rights were traded from Calgary Stampeders in exchange for Hamilton's first round draft pick in the 1992 CFL College Draft (offensive tackle Bruce Covernton). Granted free agency status in February, 1994. Signed as a free agent by the Ottawa Rough Riders in April, 1994.

			Passing							Converts (2-Pt.)		
	Team	GP	ATT	COMP	YDS	PCT	INT	LG	TD	TRIED	COMP	MADE
1991	Ham.	11	52	22	326	42.3	2	37	2	0	0	0
1992	Ham.	18	77	37	680	48.1	5	82	6	1	1	0
1993	Ham.	18	368	152	2242	41.3	21	79	6	1	0	0
CFL TOTALS		**47**	**497**	**211**	**3248**	**42.5**	**28**	**82**	**14**	**2**	**1**	**0**

		Rushing					Fumbles		
	Team	NO	YDS	AVE	LG	TD	NO	LOST	OFR
1991	Ham.	12	75	6.3	23	0	1	0	0
1992	Ham.	5	25	5.0	21	0	2	1	1
1993	Ham.	55	299	5.4	30	2	11	4	5
CFL TOTALS		**72**	**399**	**5.5**	**30**	**2**	**14**	**5**	**6**

McPHERSON, DON

Scoring - 2 TDs for 12 points with Hamilton in 1993.
CFL Total Scoring - 2 TDs for 12 points.

Tackles - 1 defensive with Hamilton in 1993.
CFL Total Tackles - 1 (1 defensive).

Playoffs

	Team	GP	Passing ATT	COMP	YDS	PCT	INT	LG	TD	Fumbles NO	LOST
1992	Ham.	2	22	9	98	40.9	1	23	2	1	0
1993	Ham.	2	0	0	0	0.0	0	0	0	0	0
CFL TOTALS		**4**	**22**	**9**	**98**	**40.9**	**1**	**23**	**2**	**1**	**0**

Rushing - 1 for 8 yards with Hamilton in 1992.
CFL Total Playoff Rushing - 1 for 8 yards.

McVEY, ANDREW
Born: June 6, 1963
Birthplace: Toronto, Ontario
Running Back. 6'1", 210 lbs. Non-import
Last Amateur Club: University of Toronto (OUAA)
Acquired: Selected by the Calgary Stampeders in the second round (14th overall) of the 1987 CFL College Draft.

	Team	GP	Scoring TD	C	FG	S	TP	Rushing NO	YDS	AVE	LG	TD
1987	Cal.	18	1	0	0	0	6	36	209	5.8	16	1
1988	Cal.	18	2	0	0	0	12	47	207	4.4	25	1
1989	Cal.	18	1	0	0	0	6	39	218	5.6	37	1
1990	Cal.	18	5	x1	0	0	32	82	315	3.8	16	3
1991	Cal.	17	2	0	0	0	12	36	158	4.4	19	1
1992	Cal.	18	7	0	0	0	42	59	286	4.8	34	6
1993	Cal.	18	2	0	0	0	12	41	185	4.5	17	2
CFL TOTALS		**125**	**20**	**x1**	**0**	**0**	**122**	**340**	**1578**	**4.6**	**37**	**15**

	Team	Fumbles NO	LOST	OFR	Kickoff Returns NO	YDS	AVE	LG	TD
1987	Cal.	3	1	3	26	534	20.5	82	0
1988	Cal.	2	1	1	13	251	19.3	33	0
1989	Cal.	1	0	0	2	12	6.0	8	0
1990	Cal.	3	3	2	4	33	8.3	22	0
1991	Cal.	4	2	1	3	30	10.0	15	0
1992	Cal.	3	2	0	1	10	10.0	10	0
1993	Cal.	6	2	2	2	20	10.0	20	0
CFL TOTALS		**22**	**11**	**9**	**51**	**890**	**17.5**	**82**	**0**

	Team	Pass Receiving NO	YDS	AVE	LG	TD
1987	Cal.	5	28	5.6	19	0
1988	Cal.	8	92	11.5	30	1
1989	Cal.	11	103	9.4	21	0
1990	Cal.	39	391	10.0	47	2
1991	Cal.	26	266	10.2	25	1
1992	Cal.	11	147	13.4	25	1
1993	Cal.	35	293	8.4	22	0
CFL TOTALS		**135**	**1320**	**9.8**	**47**	**5**

Fumble Returns - 1 for 0 yards with Calgary in 1989.
CFL Total Fumble Returns - 1 for 0 yards.

Own Punts Recovered - 1 for 0 yards with Calgary in 1987.
CFL Total Own Punts Recovered - 1 for 0 yards.

Passing - 1 attempt, 0 complete with Calgary in 1989.
CFL Total Passing - 1 attempt, 0 complete.

Tackles - 3 defensive with Calgary in 1987; 4 defensive in 1990; 1 defensive and 4 special teams in 1991; 9 special teams in 1992 and 2 defensive and 5 special teams in 1993.
CFL Total Tackles - 28 (10 defensive and 18 special teams).

Playoffs

Games Played - 1 with Calgary in 1987; 1 in 1989; 1 in 1990; 2 in 1991; 1 in 1992 and 2 in 1993. **CFL Total Playoff GP - 8.**

Scoring - 1 TD for 6 points with Calgary in 1991.
CFL Total Playoff Scoring - 1 TD for 6 points.

Rushing - 5 for 13 yards, 2.6 average, longest 7 yards with Calgary in 1989; 1 for -1 yard in 1990; 7 for 31 yards, 4.4 average, longest 7 yards in 1991; 3 for 7 yards, 2.3 average, longest 3 yards in 1992 and 8 for 33 yards, 4.1 average, longest 8 yards in 1993.
CFL Total Playoff Rushing - 24 for 83 yards, 3.5 average, longest 8 yards.

Pass Receiving - 2 for 18 yards, 9.0 average, longest 13 yards and 1 TD with Calgary in 1991 and 3 for 35 yards, 11.7 average, longest 18 yards in 1993.
CFL Total Playoff Pass Receiving - 5 for 53 yards, 10.6 average, longest 18 yards and 1 TD.

Kickoff Returns - 1 for 17 yards with Calgary in 1987.
CFL Total Playoff Kickoff Returns - 1 for 17 yards.

Fumbles - 1 and 1 lost with Calgary in 1989 and 1 and 0 lost in 1991.
CFL Total Playoff Fumbles - 2 and 1 lost.

Grey Cup

Games Played - 1 with Calgary in 1991 and 1 in 1992. **Total Grey Cup GP - 2.**

Rushing - 2 for 3 yards, 1.5 average, longest 3 yards with Calgary in 1992.
Total Grey Cup Rushing - 2 for 3 yards, 1.5 average, longest 3 yards.

Tackles - 1 special teams with Calgary in 1991.
Total Grey Cup Tackles - 1 (1 special teams).

MERO, JOE
Born: February 8, 1968
Birthplace: New Orleans, Louisiana
Defensive Back. 5'11", 185 lbs. Import
Last Amateur Club: Louisiana State University
Acquired: Signed as a free agent by the NFL Seattle Seahawks in April, 1992. Released by Seattle after training camp in 1992. Signed as a free agent by the B.C. Lions in September, 1992. Traded to the Ottawa Rough Riders in April, 1993 along with offensive linemen Carl Coulter and Chris Gioskos, kicker Wayne Lammle and linebacker Mark Scott in exchange for cornerback Less Browne, offensive tackle Rob Smith and linebacker Patrick Wayne. Transferred to the Shreveport Pirates in February, 1994.

Games Played - 9 with B.C. in 1992 and 7 with Ottawa in 1993.
CFL Total GP - 16.

Interception Returns - 1 for 0 yards with B.C. in 1992 and 3 for 20 yards, 6.7 average, longest 18 yards with Ottawa in 1993.
CFL Total Interception Returns - 4 for 20 yards, 5.0 average, longest 18 yards.

Tackles - 16 defensive and 2 special teams with B.C. in 1992 and 18 defensive and 4 special teams with Ottawa in 1993.
CFL Total Tackles - 40 (34 defensive and 6 special teams).

MIDDLETON, MIKE
Born: December 4, 1969
Birthplace: Cincinnati, Ohio
Linebacker. 5'11", 205 lbs. Import
Last Amateur Club: Indiana University
Acquired: Signed as a free agent by the Saskatchewan Roughriders in September, 1993 and was released by Saskatchewan in October, 1993.

Games Played - 5 with Saskatchewan in 1993. **CFL Total GP - 5.**

Tackles - 8 defensive and 5 special teams with Saskatchewan in 1993.
CFL Total Tackles - 13 (8 defensive and 5 special teams).

MIKAWOS, STAN
Born: May 11, 1958
Birthplace: Gdansk, Poland
Defensive Tackle. 6'4", 245 lbs. Non-import
Last Amateur Club: University of North Dakota
Acquired: Second Territorial Exemption of the Winnipeg Blue Bombers in 1982.

Games Played - 9 with Winnipeg in 1982; 6 in 1983; 16 in 1984; 16 in 1985; 18 in 1986; 13 in 1987; 15 in 1988; 12 in 1989; 18 in 1990; 8 in 1991; 18 in 1992 and 18 in 1993. **CFL Total GP - 167.**

Interception Returns - 1 for 28 yards with Winnipeg in 1990 and 1 for 0 yards in 1993. **CFL Total Interception Returns - 2 for 28 yards, 14.0 average, longest 28 yards.**

Fumble Returns - 1 for 0 yards with Winnipeg in 1984; 2 for 2 yards, 1.0 average, longest 2 yards in 1986; 1 for 0 yards in 1987; 4 for 2 yards, 0.5 average, longest 2 yards in 1988; 1 for 0 yards in 1989; 1 for 0 yards in 1990; 1 for 0 yards in 1992 and 2 for 0 yards in 1993.
CFL Total Fumble Returns - 13 for 4 yards, 0.3 average, longest 2 yards.

Blocked Kicks - 1 punt with Winnipeg in 1987 and 1 field goal in 1992.
CFL Total Blocked Kicks - 2 (1 punt and 1 field goal).

Quarterback Sacks - 1 with Winnipeg in 1982; 0.5 in 1984; 4 in 1985; 7 in 1986; 3 in 1987; 4 in 1988; 1 in 1989; 2 in 1990; 2 for 5 yards lost in 1992 and 3 for 35 yards lost in 1993. **CFL Total QB Sacks - 27.5.**

Defensive Tackles - 23 with Winnipeg in 1987; 26 in 1988; 14 in 1989; 26 in 1990; 18 in 1991; 30 in 1992 and 35 in 1993.
CFL Total Defensive Tackles - 172.

Tackles for Losses - 2 for 2 yards with Winnipeg in 1992.
CFL Total Tackles for Losses - 2 for 2 yards.

All-Eastern All-Star in 1993.

MIKAWOS, STAN

Playoffs

Games Played - 2 with Winnipeg in 1982; 2 in 1983; 2 in 1984; 2 in 1985; 1 in 1986; 1 in 1987; 2 in 1988; 2 in 1989; 1 in 1990; 2 in 1991; 1 in 1992 and 1 in 1993. **CFL Total Playoff GP - 19.**

Fumble Returns - 3 for 4 yards, 1.3 average, longest 4 yards with Winnipeg in 1985 and 1 for 0 yards in 1993. **CFL Total Playoff Fumble Returns - 4 for 4 yards, 1.0 yards average, longest 4 yards.**

Fumbles - 1 and 1 lost with Winnipeg in 1985.
CFL Total Playoff Fumbles - 1 and 1 lost.

Quarterback Sacks - 2 with Winnipeg in 1986 and 1 for 3 yards lost in 1992.
CFL Total Playoff QB Sacks - 3.

Defensive Tackles - 1 with Winnipeg in 1987; 3 in 1988; 3 in 1989; 2 in 1990; 2 in 1991; 3 in 1992 and 2 in 1993.
CFL Total Playoff Defensive Tackles - 16.

Tackles for Losses - 1 for 4 yards with Winnipeg in 1992.
CFL Total Playoff Tackles for Losses - 1 for 4 yards.

Grey Cup

Games Played - 1 with Winnipeg in 1984; 1 in 1988; 1 in 1990; 1 in 1992 and 1 in 1993. **Total Grey Cup GP - 5.**

Scoring - 1 TD for 6 points with Winnipeg in 1984.
Total Grey Cup Scoring - 1 TD for 6 points.

Fumble Returns - 1 for 22 yards and 1 TD with Winnipeg in 1984.
Total Grey Cup Fumble Returns - 1 for 22 yards and 1 TD.

Defensive Tackles - 1 with Winnipeg in 1988; 1 in 1990; 2 in 1992 and 3 in 1993.
Total Grey Cup Defensive Tackles - 7.

Tackles for Losses - 2 for 3 yards lost with Winnipeg in 1993.
Total Grey Cup Tackles for Losses - 2 for 3 yards lost.

MILBURN, DARRYL

Born: October 25, 1968
Birthplace: Baton Rouge, Louisiana
Defensive End. 6'4", 280 lbs. Import
Last Amateur Club: Grambling State University
Acquired: Selected in the ninth round (231st overall) by the NFL Detroit Lions in the 1991 NFL Draft. Signed by Detroit in July, 1991. Released by Detroit after training camp in 1992. Signed as a free agent by the Toronto Argonauts in October, 1992. Released by Toronto in September, 1993.

Games Played - 1 with Toronto in 1992 and 4 in 1993. **CFL Total GP - 5.**

Quarterback Sacks - 1 for 1 yard lost with Toronto in 1993.
CFL Total QB Sacks - 1 for 1 yard lost.

Tackles - 1 defensive with Toronto in 1992 and 8 defensive in 1993.
CFL Total Tackles - 9 (9 defensive).

Tackles for Losses - 3 for 24 yards with Toronto in 1993.
CFL Total Tackles for Losses - 3 for 24 yards.

MILLER, PETER

Born: June 30, 1968
Birthplace: Montreal, Quebec
Linebacker. 6'2", 215 lbs. Non-import.
Last Amateur Club: University of the Pacific
Acquired: Selected by the Saskatchewan Roughriders in the seventh round (50th overall) in the 1992 CFL College Draft.

Games Played - 10 with Saskatchewan in 1993. **CFL Total GP - 10.**

Quarterback Sacks - 1 for 7 yards lost with Saskatchewan in 1993.
CFL Total QB Sacks - 1 for 7 yards lost.

Tackles - 6 special teams with Saskatchewan in 1993.
CFL Total Tackles - 6 (6 special teams).

Playoffs

Games Played - 1 with Saskatchewan in 1993. **CFL Total Playoff GP - 1.**

MILLINGTON, SEAN

Born: February 1, 1968
Birthplace: Vancouver, B.C.
Running Back. 6'2", 222 lbs. Non-import
Last Amateur Club: Simon Fraser University (NAIA-CFA)
Acquired: Selected in the first round (first overall) by the Edmonton Eskimos in the 1990 CFL College Draft. Pick was acquired from the Ottawa Rough Riders in exchange for running back Chris Skinner. Attended the NFL New York Giants' training camp in 1990. Released and signed by the Edmonton Eskimos. Released in July, 1991 and signed as a free agent by the B.C. Lions in October, 1991.

			Scoring					Rushing					Fumbles		
	Team	GP	TD	C	FG	S	TP	NO	YDS	AVE	LG	TD	NO	LOST	OFR
1991	Edm	2	0	0	0	0	0	0	0	0.0	0	0	0	0	0
	B.C.	4	0	0	0	0	0	2	12	6.0	7	0	0	0	0
1992	B.C.	17	1	0	0	0	6	8	56	7.0	12	1	0	0	0
1993ab	B.C.	18	9	0	0	0	54	52	276	5.3	60	5	3	1	1
CFL TOTALS		**41**	**10**	**0**	**0**	**0**	**60**	**62**	**344**	**5.6**	**60**	**6**	**3**	**1**	**1**

Pass Receiving - 6 for 60 yards, 10.0 average, longest 20 yards with B.C. in 1992 and 38 for 481 yards, 12.7 average, longest 70 yards in 1993.
CFL Total Pass Receiving - 44 for 541 yards, 12.3 average, longest 70 yards.

Fumble Returns - 2 for 38 yards, 19.0 average, longest 25 yards and 1 TD with B.C. in 1993. **CFL Total Fumble Returns - 2 for 38 yards, 19.0 average, longest 25 yards and 1 TD.**

Kickoff Returns - 1 for 0 yards with B.C. in 1992.
CFL Total Kickoff Returns - 1 for 0 yards.

Own Kickoffs Recovered - 1 for 0 yards with B.C. in 1993.
CFL Total Own Kickoffs Recovered - 1 for 0 yards.

Punt Returns - 1 for 5 yards with B.C. in 1991. **CFL Total Punt Returns - 1 for 5 yards.**

Blocked Kicks - 1 punt with B.C. in 1993.
CFL Total Blocked Kicks - 1 (1 punt).

Tackles - 5 special teams with Edmonton and 7 special teams with B.C. in 1991; 17 special teams in 1992 and 5 defensive and 22 special teams in 1993.
CFL Total Tackles - 56 (5 defensive and 51 special teams).

a - All-Western All-Star
b - CFL All-Star

Playoffs

Games Played - 1 with B.C. in 1991 and 1 in 1993. **CFL Total Playoff GP - 2.**

Pass Receiving - 6 for 41 yards, 6.8 average, longest 12 yards with B.C. in 1993.
CFL Total Playoff Pass Receiving 6 for 41 yards, 6.8 average, longest 12 yards.

Rushing - 1 for 6 yards with B.C. in 1993. **CFL Total Playoff Rushing - 1 for 6 yards.**

Tackles - 1 defensive and 4 special teams with B.C. in 1991.
CFL Total Playoff Tackles - 5 (1 defensive and 4 special teams).

MILLS, JAMES

Born: September 24, 1961
Birthplace: Vancouver, B.C.
Offensive Tackle. 6'9", 280 lbs. Non-import
Last Amateur Club: University of Hawaii
Acquired: Selected by the Baltimore Colts in the ninth round (225th overall) of the 1983 NFL College Draft. Signed by Baltimore in May, 1983. Granted free agency in February, 1986; re-signed by the Indianapolis Colts and traded to the Denver Broncos for a draft choice in May, 1986. Released and signed as a free agent by the B.C. Lions in August, 1986. Released by B.C. in February, 1994.

Games Played - 9 with B.C. in 1986; 18 in 1987; 11 in 1988; 17 in 1989; 18 in 1990; 18 in 1991; 18 in 1992 and 18 in 1993. **CFL Total GP - 127.**

Own Fumbles Recovered - 1 with B.C. in 1992 and 1 in 1993.
CFL Total OFR - 2.

Defensive Tackles - 1 with B.C. in 1987; 1 in 1989; 4 in 1990; 1 in 1991 and 1 in 1992. **CFL Total Defensive Tackles - 8.**

All-Western All-Star in 1988; 1990; 1991; 1992 and 1993.
CFL All-Star in 1988; 1990 and 1991.
CFL Outstanding Offensive Lineman Winner in 1990 and 1991.
Winner of the DeMarco-Becket Memorial Trophy in 1990 and 1991 for Most Outstanding Offensive Lineman in Western Division.

Playoffs

Games Played - 2 with B.C. in 1986; 1 in 1987; 1 in 1991 and 1 in 1993.
CFL Total Playoff GP - 5.

MILLS, TROY

Born: July 1, 1966
Birthplace: Glendale, California
Fullback. 6'0", 212 lbs. Import
Last Amateur Club: California State University at Sacramento
Acquired: Signed as a free agent by the Sacramento Gold Miners in July, 1993.

			Scoring					Rushing				
	Team	GP	TD	C	FG	S	TP	NO	YDS	AVE	LG	TD
1993	Sac.	13	1	0	0	0	6	11	40	3.6	18	0
CFL TOTALS		**13**	**1**	**0**	**0**	**0**	**6**	**11**	**40**	**3.6**	**18**	**0**

Pass Receiving - 1 for 4 yards and 1 TD with Sacramento in 1993.
CFL Total Pass Receiving - 1 for 4 yards and 1 TD.

MILLS, TROY

Kickoff Returns - 1 for 0 yards with Sacramento in 1993.
CFL Total Kickoff Returns - 1 for 0 yards.

Fumble Returns - 1 for 0 yards with Sacramento in 1993.
CFL Total Fumble Returns - 1 for 0 yards.

Tackles - 20 special teams with Sacramento in 1993.
CFL Total Tackles - 20 (20 special teams).

MIMBS, ROBERT

Born: August 6, 1964
Birthplace: Kansas City, Missouri
Running Back. 6'0", 195 lbs. Import
Last Amateur Club: Kansas University
Acquired: Signed as a free agent by the NFL New York Jets in April, 1986. Released during training camp and signed as a free agent by the NFL Dallas Cowboys in July, 1986. Released in August, 1986. Signed as a free agent by the NFL Phoenix Cardinals in September, 1987 as a replacement player during the NFL players' strike. Released by Phoenix in October, 1987. Re-signed as a free agent by Phoenix for 1988 training camp. Spent entire 1988 season on injured reserve list. Released by Phoenix after training camp in 1989. Signed as a free agent by the Winnipeg Blue Bombers in May, 1990. Released by Winnipeg in September, 1992. Signed as a free agent by the B.C. Lions in October, 1992. Released by B.C. in November, 1992. Signed as a free agent by the B.C. Lions in June, 1993. Released by B.C. in November, 1993. Signed as a free agent by the Las Vegas Posse in February, 1994.

		Scoring						Rushing				
	Team	GP	TD	C	FG	S	TP	NO	YDS	AVE	LG	TD
1990abcde	Wpg.	18	8	0	0	0	48	285	1341	4.7	32	6
1991abcdefg	Wpg.	18	16	x1	0	0	98	326	1769	5.4	47	15
1992	Wpg.	7	4	0	0	0	24	76	392	5.2	36	4
	B.C.	3	0	0	0	0	0	43	190	4.4	17	0
1993	B.C.	2	2	0	0	0	12	22	130	5.9	28	1
CFL TOTALS		**48**	**30**	**x1**	**0**	**0**	**182**	**752**	**3822**	**5.1**	**47**	**26**

		Pass Receiving					Fumbles		
	Team	NO	YDS	AVE	LG	TD	NO	LOST	OFR
1990	Wpg.	71	538	7.6	32	2	12	11	1
1991	Wpg.	39	438	11.2	33	1	11	9	3
1992	Wpg.	24	202	8.4	28	0	3	3	0
	B.C.	7	115	16.4	41	0	1	1	0
1993	B.C.	4	33	8.3	11	1	1	0	0
CFL TOTALS		**145**	**1326**	**9.1**	**41**	**4**	**28**	**24**	**4**

Kickoff Returns - 1 for 16 yards with Winnipeg in 1990.
CFL Total Kickoff Returns - 1 for 16 yards.

Passing - 1 attempt, 0 complete with Winnipeg in 1991.
CFL Total Passing - 1 attempt, 0 complete.

2-Pt. Converts - 1 attempt, 0 complete, 1 made with Winnipeg in 1991.
CFL Total 2-Pt. Converts - 1 attempt, 0 complete, 1 made.

Tackles - 5 defensive with Winnipeg in 1991 and 2 defensive and 1 special teams in 1992. **CFL Total Tackles - 8 (7 defensive and 1 special teams).**

Tackles for Losses - 1 for 3 yards with Winnipeg in 1991.
CFL Total Tackles for Losses - 1 for 3 yards.

a - All-Eastern All-Star
b - CFL All-Star
c - Led CFL in Yards from Scrimmage (1879 in 1990; 2207 in 1991)
d - Led CFL in Rushing Yards
e - Led CFL in Rushing Carries
f - Jeff Russel Memorial Trophy - Most Outstanding Player, Eastern Division
g - Runner-up CFL Most Outstanding Player Award.

Playoffs

			Rushing					Pass Receiving				
	Team	GP	NO	YDS	AVE	LG	TD	NO	YDS	AVE	LG	TD
1990	Wpg.	1	20	109	5.5	12	0	5	17	3.4	14	0
1991	Wpg.	2	32	131	4.1	25	1	3	38	12.7	24	0
1993	B.C.	1	6	37	6.2	23	0	1	20	20.0	20	0
CFL TOTALS		**4**	**58**	**277**	**4.8**	**25**	**1**	**9**	**75**	**8.3**	**24**	**0**

Scoring - 1 TD for 6 points with Winnipeg in 1991.
CFL Total Playoff Scoring - 1 TD for 6 points.

Fumbles - 1 and 1 lost with Winnipeg in 1991.
CFL Total Playoff Fumbles - 1 and 1 lost.

Defensive Tackles - 1 with Winnipeg in 1990 and 1 in 1991.
CFL Total Playoff Defensive Tackles - 2.

Grey Cup

Games Played - 1 with Winnipeg in 1990. **Total Grey Cup GP - 1.**

Rushing - 11 for 55 yards, 5.0 average, longest 20 yards with Winnipeg in 1990.
CFL Total Grey Cup Rushing - 11 for 55 yards, 5.0 average, longest 20 yards.

Pass Receiving - 1 for 14 yards with Winnipeg in 1990.
Total Grey Cup Pass Receiving - 1 for 14 yards.

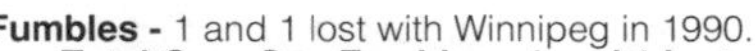

Fumbles - 1 and 1 lost with Winnipeg in 1990.
Total Grey Cup Fumbles - 1 and 1 lost.

Defensive Tackles - 1 with Winnipeg in 1990.
Total Grey Cup Defensive Tackles - 1.

MITCHEL, ERIC

Born: February 13, 1967
Birthplace: Pine Bluff, Arizona
Running Back. 5'11", 205 lbs. Import
Last Amateur Club: University of Oklahoma
Acquired: Selected in the sixth round (165th overall) by the New England Patriots in the 1989 NFL Draft. Released in September, 1989. Attended the Los Angeles Raiders' training camp in 1990. Selected in the second round (17th running back) by the Orlando Thunder in the 1991 WLAF Positional Draft. Attended the Dallas Cowboys' training camp in 1991. Was released and signed as a free agent by the Calgary Stampeders in October, 1991. Claimed on waivers by the Edmonton Eskimos in July, 1993. Transferred to the Las Vegas Posse in February, 1994.

		Scoring						Rushing				
	Team	GP	TD	C	FG	S	TP	NO	YDS	AVE	LG	TD
1991	Cal.	3	2	0	0	0	12	18	83	4.6	28	1
1992	Cal.	8	5	0	0	0	30	73	310	4.2	62	5
1993	Edm.	3	0	0	0	0	0	0	0	0.0	0	0
CFL TOTALS		**14**	**7**	**0**	**0**	**0**	**42**	**91**	**393**	**4.3**	**62**	**6**

		Pass Receiving					Kickoff Returns				
	Team	NO	YDS	AVE	LG	TD	NO	YDS	AVE	LG	TD
1991	Cal.	11	181	16.5	75	1	6	182	30.3	48	0
1992	Cal.	24	258	10.8	49	0	15	352	23.5	62	0
1993	Edm.	0	0	0.0	0	0	8	232	29.0	51	0
CFL TOTALS		**35**	**439**	**12.5**	**75**	**1**	**29**	**766**	**26.4**	**62**	**0**

		Fumbles		
	Team	NO	LOST	OFR
1991	Cal.	3	2	0
1992	Cal.	5	3	1
1993	Edm.	0	0	0
CFL TOTALS		**8**	**5**	**1**

MOEN, DON

Born: April 29, 1960
Birthplace: Swift Current, Saskatchewan
Linebacker. 6'2", 205 lbs. Non-import
Last Amateur Club: University of British Columbia (WIFL)
Acquired: Selected in the second round (14th overall) by the B.C. Lions in the 1982 CFL College Draft. Claimed on waivers from B.C. by the Toronto Argonauts along with defensive lineman Richard Mohr and guard Rob Smith in July, 1982.

			Fumble Returns					QB Sacks
	Team	GP	NO	YDS	AVE	LG	TD	NO
1982	Tor.	16	3	0	0.0	0	0	0.0
1983	Tor.	16	1	0	0.0	0	0	1.0
1984	Tor.	16	1	0	0.0	0	0	5.5
1985	Tor.	16	0	0	0.0	0	0	3.0
1986	Tor.	18	0	0	0.0	0	0	4.0
1987	Tor.	18	1	0	0.0	0	0	5.0
1988a	Tor.	18	2	62	31.0	62	1	2.0
1989	Tor.	18	2	0	0.0	0	0	2.0
1990	Tor.	18	2	4	2.0	4	1	6.0
1991	Tor.	18	2	0	0.0	0	0	3.0
1992	Tor.	18	0	0	0.0	0	0	2.0
1993	Tor.	17	0	0	0	0	0	1.0
CFL TOTALS		**207**	**14**	**66**	**4.7**	**62**	**2**	**34.5**

Scoring - 1 TD for 6 points with Toronto in 1988 and 1 TD for 6 points in 1990.
CFL Total Scoring - 2 TDs for 12 points.

Punt Returns - 1 in 1982 with Toronto. **CFL Total Punt Returns - 1.**

Interception Returns - 1 for 0 yards with Toronto in 1984; 1 for 6 yards in 1985; 1 for 8 yards in 1987; 2 for 4 yards, 2.0 average, longest 11 yards in 1988; 2 for 22 yards, 11.0 average, longest 12 yards in 1990; 2 for 0 yards in 1991 and 1 for 0 yards in 1992. **CFL Total Interception Returns - 10 for 40 yards, 4.0 average, longest 12 yards.**

Tackles - 61 defensive with Toronto in 1987; 57 defensive in 1988; 65 defensive in 1989; 56 defensive in 1990; 71 defensive and 4 special teams in 1991; 84 defensive and 5 special teams in 1992 and 67 defensive and 5 special teams in 1993.
CFL Total Tackles - 475 (461 defensive and 14 special teams).

Tackles for Losses - 2 for 8 yards with Toronto in 1991; 2 for 8 yards in 1992 and 3 for 4 yards in 1993.
CFL Total Tackles for Losses - 7 for 20 yards.

a - All-Eastern All-Star.

Playoffs

Games Played - 1 with Toronto in 1982; 1 in 1983; 1 in 1984; 2 in 1986; 2 in 1987; 1 in 1988; 1 in 1989; 2 in 1990 and 1 in 1991.
CFL Total Playoff GP - 12.

MOEN, DON

Interception Returns - 1 for 0 yards with Toronto in 1987; 1 for 5 yards in 1990 and 1 for 22 yards in 1991. **CFL Total Playoff Interception Returns - 3 for 27 yards, 9.0 average, longest 22 yards.**

Quarterback Sacks - 1 with Toronto in 1990 and 1 in 1991. **CFL Total Playoff QB Sacks - 2.**

Defensive Tackles - 5 with Toronto in 1987; 5 in 1988; 4 in 1989; 13 in 1990 and 2 in 1991. **CFL Total Playoff Defensive Tackles - 29.**

Grey Cup

Games Played - 1 with Toronto in 1982; 1 in 1983; 1 in 1987 and 1 in 1991. **Total Grey Cup GP - 4.**

Own Fumbles Recovered - 1 with Toronto in 1982. **Total Grey Cup OFR - 1.**

Quarterback Sacks - 1 with Toronto in 1991. **Total Grey Cup QB Sacks - 1.**

Tackles - 3 defensive with Toronto in 1987 and 8 defensive and 2 special teams in 1991. **Total Grey Cup Tackles - 13 (11 defensive and 2 special teams).**

MOORE, CURTIS
Born: February 11, 1967
Birthplace: Lincoln, Nebraska
Linebacker. 6'1", 235 lbs. Import
Last Amateur Club: University of Kansas
Acquired: Signed as a free agent by the Sacramento Gold Miners in March, 1993.

Games Played - 18 with Sacramento in 1993. **CFL Total GP - 18.**

Interception Returns - 1 for 8 yards with Sacramento in 1993. **CFL Total Interception Returns - 1 for 8 yards.**

Kickoff Returns - 1 for 0 yards with Sacramento in 1993. **CFL Total Kickoff Returns - 1 for 0 yards.**

Fumble Returns - 2 for 1 yard, 0.5 average, longest 1 yard with Sacramento in 1993. **CFL Total Fumble Returns - 2 for 1 yard, 0.5 average, longest 1 yard.**

Own Kickoffs Recovered - 1 with Sacramento in 1993. **CFL Total Own Kickoffs Recovered - 1.**

Quarterback Sacks - 2 for 27 yards lost with Sacramento in 1993. **CFL Total QB Sacks - 2 for 27 yards lost.**

Tackles - 76 defensive with Sacramento in 1993. **CFL Total Tackles - 76 (76 defensive).**

Tackles for Losses - 6 for 30 yards with Sacramento in 1993. **CFL Total Tackles for Losses - 6 for 30 yards.**

MOORE, KEN
Born: January 27, 1961
Birthplace: Lethbridge, Alberta
Offensive Lineman. 6'5", 255 lbs. Non-import
Last Amateur Club: University of Hawaii
Acquired: First Territorial Exemption of the Calgary Stampeders in 1982. Traded to the Saskatchewan Roughriders with guard Kevin Molle and centre Willie Thomas for centre Bob Poley, tackle Gerry Hornett and fullback Greg Fieger in May, 1985. Traded by Saskatchewan in February, 1991 to Calgary in exchange for Linebacker Wayne Wylie, offensive lineman Brent Pollock and Saskatchewan's second round draft choice in the 1992 CFL College Draft.

			Pass Receiving				
	Team	GP	NO	YDS	AVE	LG	TD
1983	Cal.	2	2	34	17.0	43	0
1984	Cal.	15	1	28	28.0	28	0
1985	Sask.	12	8	61	7.6	15	0
1986	Sask.	11	0	0	0.0	0	0
1987	Sask.	18	0	0	0.0	0	0
1988	Sask.	11	0	0	0.0	0	0
1989	Sask.	18	0	0	0.0	0	0
1990	Sask.	18	0	0	0.0	0	0
1991	Cal.	18	0	0	0.0	0	0
1992	Cal.	18	0	0	0.0	0	0
1993	Cal.	18	0	0	0.0	0	0
CFL TOTALS		**159**	**11**	**123**	**11.2**	**43**	**0**

Fumble Returns - 1 for 0 yards with Calgary in 1984. **CFL Total Fumble Returns - 1 for 0 yards.**

Own Fumbles Recovered - 2 with Calgary in 1991. **CFL Total OFR - 2.**

Kickoff Returns - 1 for 4 yards with Saskatchewan in 1985. **CFL Total Kickoff Returns - 1 for 4 yards.**

Quarterback Sacks - 1.5 with Calgary in 1984 and 2 with Saskatchewan in 1987. **CFL Total QB Sacks - 3.5.**

Tackles - 1 defensive with Saskatchewan in 1987; 1 defensive in 1989; 1 defensive in 1990; 2 defensive with Calgary in 1991 and 3 defensive and 1 special teams in 1992. **CFL Total Tackles - 9 (8 defensive and 1 special teams).**

Playoffs

Games Played - 2 with Saskatchewan in 1989; 1 in 1990; 2 with Calgary in 1991; 1 in 1992 and 2 in 1993. **CFL Total Playoff GP - 8.**

Defensive Tackles - 1 with Saskatchewan in 1989. **CFL Total Playoff Defensive Tackles - 1.**

Grey Cup

Games Played - 1 with Saskatchewan in 1989; 1 with Calgary in 1991 and 1 in 1992. **Total Grey Cup GP - 3.**

MOORE, WILL
Born: February 21, 1970
Birthplace: Dallas, Texas
Wide Receiver. 6'2", 180 lbs. Import
Last Amateur Club: Texas Southern University
Acquired: Signed as a free agent by the Calgary Stampeders in April, 1992.

			Scoring					Pass Receiving					Fumbles		
	Team	GP	TD	C	FG	S	TP	NO	YDS	AVE	LG	TD	NO	LOST	OFR
1992	Cal.	1	0	0	0	0	0	3	38	12.7	16	0	0	0	0
1993	Cal.	18	12	0	0	0	72	73	1083	14.8	55	12	2	1	0
CFL TOTALS		**19**	**12**	**0**	**0**	**0**	**72**	**76**	**1121**	**14.8**	**55**	**12**	**2**	**1**	**0**

Tackles - 3 defensive and 3 special teams with Calgary in 1993. **CFL Total Tackles - 6 (3 defensive and 3 special teams).**

Playoffs

			Scoring					Pass Receiving				
	Team	GP	TD	C	FG	S	TP	NO	YDS	AVE	LG	TD
1993	Cal.	2	1	0	0	0	6	10	113	11.3	26	1
CFL TOTALS		**2**	**1**	**0**	**0**	**0**	**6**	**10**	**113**	**11.3**	**26**	**1**

Own Fumbles Recovered - 1 with Calgary in 1993. **CFL Total Playoff OFR - 1.**

MOREAU, JACQUES
Born: June 9, 1967
Birthplace: Hull, Quebec
Offensive Tackle. 6'3", 265 lbs. Non-import.
Last Amateur Club: Concordia University (OQIFC)
Acquired: Signed as a free agent by the Ottawa Rough Riders in February, 1992.

Games Played - 8 with Ottawa in 1993. **CFL Total GP - 8.**

Tackles - 2 special teams with Ottawa in 1993. **CFL Total Tackles - 2 (2 special teams).**

Playoffs

Games Played - 1 with Ottawa in 1993. **CFL Total Playoff GP - 1.**

MORRIS, CHRIS
Born: September 13, 1968
Birthplace: Scarborough, Ontario
Offensive Tackle, 6'5", 285 lbs., Non-import
Last Amateur Club: University of Toronto (OUAA)
Acquired: Selected in the first round (eighth overall) by the Edmonton Eskimos in the 1992 CFL College Draft. The pick was acquired from the Toronto Argonauts in exchange for wide receiver David Williams.

Games Played - 18 with Edmonton in 1992 and 18 in 1993. **CFL Total GP - 36.**

Own Fumbles Recovered - 1 with Edmonton in 1993. **CFL Total OFR - 1.**

Tackles - 5 defensive with Edmonton in 1992. **CFL Total Tackles - 5 (5 defensive).**

Playoffs

Games Played - 2 with Edmonton in 1992 and 2 in 1993. **CFL Total Playoff GP - 4.**

Grey Cup

Games Played - 1 with Edmonton in 1993. **Total Grey Cup GP - 1.**

MORRIS, GARY
Born: June 26, 1968
Birthplace: Norfolk, Virginia
Wide Receiver. 6'2", 185 lbs. Import.
Last Amateur Club: Norfolk State University
Acquired: Signed as a free agent by the Edmonton Eskimos in December, 1992.

		Scoring						Pass Receiving				
	Team	GP	TD	C	FG	S	TP	NO	YDS	AVE	LG	TD
1993	Edm.	9	2	0	0	0	12	18	233	12.9	38	2
CFL TOTALS		**9**	**2**	**0**	**0**	**0**	**12**	**18**	**233**	**12.9**	**38**	**2**

Kickoff Returns - 1 for 19 yards with Edmonton in 1993. **CFL Total Kickoff Returns - 1 for 19 yards.**

Tackles - 1 defensive with Edmonton in 1993. **CFL Total Tackles - 1 (1 defensive).**

MOTTON, JOHN
Born: June 20, 1967
Birthplace: Columbus, Ohio
Linebacker. 6'1", 235 lbs. Import
Last Amateur Club: University of Akron
Acquired: Signed as a free agent by the Hamilton Tiger-Cats in April, 1991. Granted free agency status in February, 1993. Re-signed by Hamilton in June, 1993.

		Scoring						Interception Returns					QB Sacks
	Team	GP	TD	C	FG	S	TP	NO	YDS	AVE	LG	TD	NO
1991	Ham.	17	2	0	0	0	12	4	137	34.3	47	2	4
1992ab	Ham.	18	0	0	0	0	0	4	67	16.8	42	0	1
1993ab	Ham.	18	0	0	0	0	0	1	15	15.0	15	0	0
CFL TOTALS		**53**	**2**	**0**	**0**	**0**	**12**	**9**	**219**	**24.3**	**47**	**2**	**5**

		Fumble Returns					Fumbles		
	Team	NO	YDS	AVE	LG	TD	NO	LOST	OFR
1991	Ham.	0	0	0.0	0	0	0	0	0
1992	Ham.	4	5	1.3	5	0	1	1	2
1993	Ham.	4	55	13.8	47	0	0	0	0
CFL TOTALS		**8**	**60**	**7.5**	**47**	**0**	**1**	**1**	**2**

Tackles - 68 defensive and 8 special teams with Hamilton in 1991; 95 defensive and 3 special teams in 1992 and 84 defensive and 5 special teams in 1993. **CFL Total Tackles - 263 (247 defensive and 16 special teams).**

Tackles for Losses - 3 for 14 yards with Hamilton in 1991 and 4 for 5 yards in 1992. **CFL Total Tackles for Losses - 7 for 19 yards.**

a - All-Eastern All-Star
b - CFL All-Star

Playoffs

Games Played - 2 with Hamilton in 1992 and 2 in 1993. **CFL Total Playoff GP - 4.**

Tackles - 6 defensive with Hamilton in 1992 and 11 defensive in 1993. **CFL Total Playoff Tackles - 17 (17 defensive).**

Tackles for Losses - 1 for 3 yards with Hamilton in 1992. **CFL Total Playoff Tackles for Losses - 1 for 3 yards.**

MUECKE, TOM
Born: August 20, 1963
Birthplace: Waco, Texas
Quarterback. 6'1", 195 lbs. Import
Last Amateur Club: Baylor University
Acquired: Signed as a free agent by the Winnipeg Blue Bombers in August, 1986. Retired prior to 1989 season. Signed as a free agent by the NFL Houston Oilers in October, 1990. Released by Houston in November, 1990 and signed by the Calgary Stampeders in January, 1991. Released in January and signed as a free agent by the Edmonton Eskimos in September, 1991.

		Passing								Rushing				
	Team	GP	ATT	COMP	YDS	PCT	INT	LG	TD	NO	YDS	AVE	LG	TD
1986	Wpg.	10	2	1	14	50.0	0	14	0	1	0	0.0	0	0
1987	Wpg.	18	37	20	212	54.1	3	42	3	2	0	0.0	-3	0
1988	Wpg.	15	250	124	1892	49.6	11	52	11	25	79	3.2	10	1
1991	Edm.	5	27	15	185	55.6	1	40	2	2	-8	-4.0	-10	0
1992	Edm.	18	157	80	1275	51.0	7	68	11	12	48	4.0	22	1
1993	Edm.	18	54	26	242	48.1	3	28	1	3	15	5.0	12	0
CFL TOTALS		**84**	**527**	**266**	**3820**	**50.5**	**25**	**68**	**28**	**45**	**134**	**3.0**	**22**	**2**

Scoring - 1 TD for 6 points with Winnipeg in 1988 and 1 TD for 6 points with Edmonton in 1992. **CFL Total Scoring - 2 TDs for 12 points.**

2-Pt. Converts - 1 attempt with Winnipeg in 1988. **CFL Total 2-Pt. Converts - 1 attempt.**

Fumbles - 2 and 1 lost with Winnipeg in 1987; 7 and 4 lost in 1988; 1 and 1 lost with Edmonton in 1991 and 2 and 0 lost in 1992. **CFL Total Fumbles - 12 and 6 lost.**

Own Fumbles Recovered - 1 with Winnipeg in 1988 and 1 with Edmonton in 1992. **CFL Total OFR - 2.**

Playoffs

Games Played - 1 with Winnipeg in 1986; 1 in 1987; 1 with Edmonton in 1991; 2 in 1992 and 2 in 1993. **CFL Total Playoff GP -7.**

Grey Cup

Games Played - 1 with Edmonton in 1993. **Total Grey Cup GP - 1.**

MUNFORD, CHRIS
Born: April 26, 1966
Birthplace: Emekuku, Nigeria
Defensive Back. 6'0", 184 lbs. Non-import
Last Amateur Club: Simon Fraser University (EVCO)
Acquired: Selected in the fifth round (39th overall) by the Toronto Argonauts in the 1988 CFL College Draft. Released after the 1988 Training Camp. Signed as a free agent by the Hamilton Tiger-Cats in March, 1989. Released by Hamilton in June, 1990. Signed as a free agent by Toronto in August, 1990. Released by Toronto in December, 1992. Re-signed by Toronto in May, 1993. Released by Toronto in June, 1993. Signed as a free agent by the Saskatchewan Roughriders in August, 1993. Released by Saskatchewan in February, 1994.

Games Played - 7 with Hamilton in 1989; 6 with Toronto in 1990; 15 in 1991; 11 in 1992 and 12 with Saskatchewan in 1993. **CFL Total GP - 51.**

Interception Returns - 2 for 12 yards, 6.0 average, longest 8 yards with Toronto in 1990 and 5 for 59 yards, 11.8 average, longest 23 yards in 1991. **CFL Total Interception Returns - 7 for 71 yards, 10.1 average, longest 23 yards.**

2-Pt. Converts - 1 attempt, 0 made with Toronto in 1991. **CFL Total 2-Pt. Converts - 1 attempt, 0 made.**

Fumbles - 1 and 0 lost with Toronto in 1991. **CFL Total Fumbles - 1 and 0 lost.**

Fumble Returns - 2 for 0 yards with Toronto in 1991. **CFL Total Fumble Returns - 2 for 0 yards.**

Quarterback Sacks - 1 with Toronto in 1990. **CFL Total QB Sacks - 1.**

Tackles - 1 defensive with Hamilton in 1989; 7 defensive with Toronto in 1990; 25 defensive in 1991; 2 defensive and 3 special teams in 1992 and 6 special teams with Saskatchewan in 1993. **CFL Total Tackles - 44 (35 defensive and 9 special teams).**

Playoffs

Games Played - 1 with Saskatchewan in 1993. **CFL Total Playoff GP - 1.**

MURPHY, DAN
Born: August 28, 1968
Birthplace: Ottawa, Ontario
Defensive Back. 6'3", 195 lbs. Non-import
Last Amateur Club: Acadia University (AUAA)
Acquired: Selected in the first round (third overall) by the Edmonton Eskimos in the 1991 CFL College Draft. Pick was acquired along with wide receiver David Williams from the Ottawa Rough Riders in exchange for linebacker Jeff Braswell and Edmonton's first round draft pick (offensive tackle Brett MacNeil). Signed as a free agent by NFL San Diego Chargers in May, 1991. Released during training camp and signed by Edmonton in July, 1991.

Games Played - 16 with Edmonton in 1991; 18 in 1992 and 18 in 1993. **CFL Total GP - 52.**

Interception Returns - 2 for 28 yards, 14.0 average, longest 25 yards with Edmonton in 1991; 1 for 11 yards in 1992 and 5 for 47 yards, 9.4 average, longest 32 yards in 1993. **CFL Total Interception Returns - 8 for 86 yards, 10.8 average, longest 32 yards.**

Kickoff Returns - 1 for 0 yards with Edmonton in 1992. **CFL Total Kickoff Returns - 1 for 0 yards.**

Own Kickoffs Recovered - 1 with Edmonton in 1992. **CFL Total OKR - 1.**

Fumble Returns - 1 for 0 yards with Edmonton in 1991 and 1 for 11 yards in 1992. **CFL Total Fumble Returns - 2 for 11 yards, 5.5 average, longest 11 yards.**

Tackles - 12 defensive and 11 special teams with Edmonton in 1991; 17 defensive and 11 special teams in 1992 and 40 defensive and 12 special teams in 1993. **CFL Total Tackles - 103 (69 defensive and 34 special teams).**

Playoffs

Games Played - 1 with Edmonton in 1991; 2 in 1992 and 2 in 1993. **CFL Total Playoff GP - 5.**

Interception Returns - 1 for 10 yards with Edmonton in 1993. **CFL Total Playoff Interception Returns - 1 for 10 yards.**

MURPHY, DAN

Tackles - 1 defensive and 2 special teams with Edmonton in 1991; 2 special teams in 1992 and 9 defensive and 1 special teams in 1993. **CFL Total Playoff Tackles - 15 (10 defensive and 5 special teams).**

Grey Cup

Games Played - 1 with Edmonton in 1993. **Total Grey Cup GP - 1**

Interception Returns - 1 for 14 yards with Edmonton in 1993. **Total Grey Cup Interception Returns - 1 for 14 yards.**

Tackles - 1 defensive with Edmonton in 1993. **Total Grey Cup Tackles - 1 (1 defensive).**

MURPHY, YO
Born: May 11, 1971
Birthplace: Moscow, Idaho
Wide Receiver. 5'10", 170 lbs. Import.
Last Amateur Club: University of Idaho
Acquired: Signed as a free agent by the B.C. Lions in April, 1993.

Games Played - 1 with B.C. in 1993. **CFL Total GP - 1.**

Tackles - 1 defensive with B.C. in 1993. **CFL Total Tackles - 1 (1 defensive).**

MURRAY, ANDREW
Born: July 15, 1964
Birthplace: Nepean, Ontario
Slotback. 6'3", 200 lbs. Non-import
Last Amateur Club: Carleton University (OQIFC)
Acquired: Selected in the fourth round by the B.C. Lions in the 1987 CFL College Draft. Released and re-signed by B.C. in 1988. Released by B.C. in June, 1990. Signed as a free agent by the Toronto Argonauts in June, 1990. Released by Toronto in December, 1992. Re-signed by Toronto in April, 1993.

		Scoring						Pass Receiving				
	Team	GP	TD	C	FG	S	TP	NO	YDS	AVE	LG	TD
1988	B.C.	18	0	0	0	0	0	36	476	13.2	43	0
1989	B.C.	3	0	0	0	0	0	5	52	10.4	18	0
1990	Tor.	16	3	0	0	0	18	37	629	17.0	47	3
1991	Tor.	10	2	0	0	0	12	15	286	19.1	52	2
1992	Tor.	18	0	0	0	0	0	21	342	16.3	89	0
1993	Tor.	18	0	0	0	0	0	4	57	14.3	27	0
CFL TOTALS		83	5	0	0	0	30	118	1842	15.6	89	5

		Kickoff Returns					Own Fumbles Recovered
	Team	NO	YDS	AVE	LG	TD	NO
1988	B.C.	0	0	0.0	0	0	0
1989	B.C.	0	0	0.0	0	0	0
1990	Tor.	2	16	8.0	11	0	1
1991	Tor.	3	14	4.7	10	0	0
1992	Tor.	0	0	0.0	0	0	0
1993	Tor.	0	0	0.0	0	0	0
CFL TOTALS		5	30	6.0	11	0	1

Rushing - 1 for -6 yards with Toronto in 1993. **CFL Total Rushing - 1 for - 6 yards.**

Punting - 1 for 39 yards with Toronto in 1993. **CFL Total Punting - 1 for 39 yards.**

Tackles - 1 defensive with B.C. in 1988; 2 defensive with Toronto in 1991; 2 defensive and 1 special teams in 1992 and 4 special teams in 1993. **CFL Total Tackles - 10 (5 defensive and 5 special teams).**

Playoffs

			Pass Receiving				
	Team	GP	NO	YDS	AVE	LG	TD
1988	B.C.	2	1	8	8.0	8	0
1990	Tor.	2	3	49	16.3	40	0
1991	Tor.	1	1	13	13.0	13	0
CFL TOTALS		5	5	70	14.0	40	0

Grey Cup

Games Played - 1 with B.C. in 1988 and 1 with Toronto in 1991. **Total Grey Cup GP - 2.**

NARCISSE, DONALD
Born: February 26, 1965
Birthplace: Port Arthur, Texas
Wide Receiver. 5'9", 170 lbs. Import
Last Amateur Club: Texas Southern University
Acquired: Signed as a free agent by the Saskatchewan Roughriders in September, 1987.

		Scoring						Rushing				
	Team	GP	TD	C	FG	S	TP	NO	YDS	AVE	LG	TD
1987	Sask.	8	1	0	0	0	6	1	-2	-2.0	-2	0
1988	Sask.	10	0	0	0	0	0	0	0	0.0	0	0
1989ab	Sask.	18	11	0	0	0	66	1	16	16.0	16	0
1990ab	Sask.	18	9	x1	0	0	56	1	-12	-12.0	-12	0
1991	Sask.	18	7	0	0	0	42	0	0	0.0	0	0
1992	Sask.	18	7	x1	0	0	44	0	0	0.0	0	0
1993a	Sask.	18	9	0	0	0	54	0	0	0.0	0	0
CFL TOTALS		108	44	x2	0	0	268	3	2	0.7	16	0

		Pass Receiving					Kickoff Returns				
	Team	NO	YDS	AVE	LG	TD	NO	YDS	AVE	LG	TD
1987	Sask.	25	319	12.8	43	1	2	45	22.5	24	0
1988	Sask.	21	288	13.7	22	0	0	0	0.0	0	0
1989	Sask.	81	1419	17.5	74	11	5	63	12.6	18	0
1990	Sask.	86	1129	13.1	47	9	0	0	0.0	0	0
1991	Sask.	76	1043	13.7	59	7	0	0	0.0	0	0
1992	Sask.	80	1034	12.9	65	7	0	0	0.0	0	0
1993	Sask.	83	1171	14.1	44	9	0	0	0.0	0	0
CFL TOTALS		452	6403	14.2	74	44	7	108	15.4	24	0

		Fumbles		
	Team	NO	LOST	OFR
1987	Sask.	0	0	1
1988	Sask.	1	1	0
1989	Sask.	0	0	1
1990	Sask.	0	0	0
1991	Sask.	2	2	0
1992	Sask.	0	0	0
1993	Sask.	0	0	0
CFL TOTALS		3	3	2

Own Kickoffs Recovered - 2 for 0 yards with Saskatchewan in 1989. **CFL Total Own Kickoffs Recovered - 2 for 0 yards.**

2-Pt. Converts - 1 made with Saskatchewan in 1992. **CFL Total 2-Pt. Converts - 1 made.**

Punt Returns - 3 for 30 yards, 10.0 average, longest 14 yards with Saskatchewan in 1989. **CFL Total Punt Returns - 3 for 30 yards, 10.0 average, longest 14 yards.**

Defensive Tackles - 1 with Saskatchewan in 1987; 4 in 1989; 3 in 1990; 3 in 1991; 3 in 1992 and 1 in 1993. **CFL Total Defensive Tackles - 15.**

a - All-Western All-Star
b - CFL All-Star

Playoffs

Games Played - 1 with Saskatchewan in 1988; 2 in 1989; 1 in 1990; 1 in 1992 and 1 in 1993. **CFL Total Playoff GP - 6.**

Scoring - 1 TD for 6 points with Saskatchewan in 1992. **CFL Total Playoff Scoring - 1 TD for 6 points.**

Pass Receiving - 9 for 108 yards, 12.0 average, longest 17 yards with Saskatchewan in 1989; 3 for 33 yards, 11.0 average, longest 18 yards in 1990; 10 for 182 yards, 18.2 average, longest 55 yards and 1 TD in 1992 and 6 for 64 yards, 10.7 average, longest 17 yards in 1993. **CFL Total Playoff Pass Receiving - 28 for 387 yards, 13.8 average, longest 55 yards and 1 TD.**

Punt Returns - 1 for 7 yards with Saskatchewan in 1989. **CFL Total Playoff Punt Returns - 1 for 7 yards.**

Fumble Returns - 1 for 0 yards with Saskatchewan in 1989. **CFL Total Playoff Fumble Returns - 1 for 0 yards.**

Fumbles - 2 and 2 lost with Saskatchewan in 1993. **CFL Total Playoff Fumbles - 2 and 2 lost.**

Grey Cup

Games Played - 1 with Saskatchewan in 1989. **Total Grey Cup GP - 1.**

Scoring - 1 TD for 6 points with Saskatchewan in 1989. **Total Grey Cup Scoring - 1 TD for 6 points.**

Pass Receiving - 5 for 98 yards, 19.6 average, longest 52 yards and 1 TD with Saskatchewan in 1989. **Total Grey Cup Pass Receiving - 5 for 98 yards, 19.6 average, longest 52 yards and 1 TD.**

NELSON, LEONARD
Born: November 21, 1969
Birthplace: Sacramento, California
Linebacker. 6'1", 220 lbs. Import
Last Amateur Club: California State University of Sacramento
Acquired: Signed as a free agent by the Sacramento Gold MIners in June, 1993.

Games Played - 10 with Sacramento in 1993. **CFL Total GP - 10.**

NELSON, LEONARD

Fumble Returns - 1 for 0 yards with Sacramento in 1993.
CFL Total Fumble Returns - 1 for 0 yards.

Tackles - 20 defensive and 2 special teams with Sacramento in 1993.
CFL Total Tackles - 22 (20 defensive and 2 special teams).

Tackles for Losses - 1 for 1 yard with Sacramento in 1993.
CFL Total Tackles for Losses - 1 for 1 yard.

NIMAKO, GEORGE
Born: March 9, 1969
Birthplace: Nepean, Ontario
Defensive Back. 5'10", 190 lbs. Non-import
Last Amateur Club: Liberty University
Acquired: Selected by the Toronto Argonauts in the fourth round (24th overall) in the 1993 CFL College Draft.

	Team	GP	Pass Receiving NO	YDS	AVE	LG	TD
1993	Tor.	9	2	29	14.5	27	0
CFL TOTALS		**9**	**2**	**29**	**14.5**	**27**	**0**

Tackles - 10 special teams with Toronto in 1993.
CFL Total Tackles - 10 (10 special teams).

NOEL, DEAN
Born: February 21, 1967
Birthplace: Ottawa, Ontario
Running Back. 5'11", 205 lbs. Non-import
Last Amateur Club: Delaware State University
Acquired: Selected by the Ottawa Rough Riders in the fourth round (26th overall) in the 1993 CFL College Draft.

			Rushing					Kickoff Returns				
	Team	GP	NO	YDS	AVE	LG	TD	NO	YDS	AVE	LG	TD
1993	Ott.	8	2	4	2.0	3	0	3	35	11.7	17	0
CFL TOTALS		**8**	**2**	**4**	**2.0**	**3**	**0**	**3**	**35**	**11.7**	**17**	**0**

Blocked Kicks - 1 punt with Ottawa in 1993.
CFL Total Blocked Kicks - 1 (1 punt).

Tackles - 12 special teams with Ottawa in 1993.
CFL Total Tackles - 12 (12 special teams).

Playoffs

Games Played - 1 with Ottawa in 1993.
CFL Total Playoff GP - 1.

Tackles - 1 special teams with Ottawa in 1993.
CFL Total Playoff Tackles - 1 (1 special teams).

NURSE, RICHARD
Born: March 16, 1967
Birthplace: Trinidad - Tobago
Wide Receiver. 5'11", 185 lbs. Non-import
Last Amateur Club: Canisius College
Acquired: Selected in the third round (23rd overall) by the Hamilton Tiger-Cats in the 1990 CFL College Draft. Granted free agency status in February, 1993 and re-signed by Hamilton later that month.

			Scoring					Pass Receiving				
	Team	GP	TD	C	FG	S	TP	NO	YDS	AVE	LG	TD
1990	Ham.	17	3	0	0	0	18	29	357	12.3	35	3
1991	Ham.	16	1	0	0	0	6	11	142	12.9	34	1
1992	Ham.	18	1	0	0	0	6	5	75	15.0	26	1
1993	Ham.	18	0	0	0	0	0	2	27	13.5	16	0
CFL TOTALS		**69**	**5**	**0**	**0**	**0**	**30**	**47**	**601**	**12.8**	**35**	**5**

		Punt Returns					Kickoff Returns				
	Team	NO	YDS	AVE	LG	TD	NO	YDS	AVE	LG	TD
1990	Ham.	1	12	12.0	12	0	10	130	13.0	28	0
1991	Ham.	1	1	1.0	1	0	5	139	27.8	44	0
1992	Ham.	0	0	0.0	0	0	0	27	0.0	24	0
1993	Ham.	0	0	0.0	0	0	0	0	0.0	0	0
CFL TOTALS		**2**	**13**	**6.5**	**12**	**0**	**15**	**296**	**19.7**	**44**	**0**

Interception Returns - 1 for 41 yards with Hamilton in 1992.
CFL Total Interception Returns - 1 for 41 yards.

Tackles - 1 defensive with Hamilton in 1990; 2 defensive and 8 special teams in 1991; 1 defensive and 9 special teams in 1992 and 15 special teams in 1993. **CFL Total Tackles - 36 (4 defensive and 32 special teams).**

Playoffs

Games Played - 2 with Hamilton in 1992 and 2 in 1993.
CFL Total Playoff GP - 4.

Own Fumbles Recovered - 1 with Hamilton in 1992 and 1 in 1993.
CFL Total Playoff OFR - 2.

Tackles - 1 special teams with Hamilton in 1993.
CFL Total Playoff Tackles - 1 (1 special teams).

OLIPHANT, MIKE
Born: May 19, 1963
Birthplace: Jacksonville, Florida
Running Back. 5'9", 171 lbs. Import
Last Amateur Club: Puget Sound
Acquired: Selected by the Washington Redskins in the third round (66th overall) in the 1988 NFL Draft. Traded by Washington to the NFL Cleveland Browns in exchange for running back Ernest Byner in April, 1989. Granted free agency status in February, 1991. Re-signed by Cleveland in July, 1991. Granted free agency status in February, 1992. Signed as a free agent by the NFL Seattle Seahawks in March, 1992 and was released during training camp. Signed as a free agent by the Sacramento Gold Miners in May, 1993.

			Scoring					Rushing				
	Team	GP	TD	C	FG	S	TP	NO	YDS	AVE	LG	TD
1993ab	Sac.	18	13	0	0	0	78	116	760	6.6	52	8
CFL TOTALS		**18**	**13**	**0**	**0**	**0**	**78**	**116**	**760**	**6.6**	**52**	**8**

		Pass Receiving					Punt Returns				
	Team	NO	YDS	AVE	LG	TD	NO	YDS	AVE	LG	TD
1993	Sac.	47	812	17.3	83	5	2	25	12.5	25	0
CFL TOTALS		**47**	**812**	**17.3**	**83**	**5**	**2**	**25**	**12.5**	**25**	**0**

		Kickoff Returns					Fumbles		
	Team	NO	YDS	AVE	LG	TD	NO	LOST	OFR
1993	Sac.	4	64	16.0	20	0	6	6	1
CFL TOTALS		**4**	**64**	**16.0**	**20**	**0**	**6**	**6**	**1**

Tackles - 2 defensive and 9 special teams with Sacramento in 1993.
CFL Total Tackles - 11 (2 defensive and 9 special teams).

Tackles for Losses - 1 for 3 yards with Sacramento in 1993.
CFL Total Tackles for Losses- 1 for 3 yards.

a - All-Western All-Star
b - Led CFL in Yards from Scrimmage (1572).

OLSACHER, LOUIS
Born: October 12, 1965
Birthplace: Hamilton, Ontario
Tackle. 6'2", 270 lbs. Non-import
Last Amateur Club: St. Mary's University
Acquired: Selected in the fourth round (29th overall) by the Edmonton Eskimos in the 1989 CFL College Draft. Attended Eskimo training camp in 1989 and was released. Signed by Edmonton in April, 1990 and was released in July, 1990. Signed as a free agent by the Toronto Argonauts in February, 1991 and was released in July, 1991. Signed as a free agent by Toronto in January, 1992. Placed on the Toronto Suspended List in August, 1992. Added to the Roster from the Suspended List in January, 1993. Released by Toronto in February, 1994.

Games Played - 5 with Toronto in 1992 and 3 in 1993. **CFL Total GP - 8.**

Tackles - 1 defensive with Toronto in 1993. **CFL Total Tackles - 1 (1 defensive).**

O'SHEA, MICHAEL
Born: September 21, 1970
Birthplace: North Bay, Ontario
Linebacker. 6'3", 223 lbs. Non-import
Last Amateur Club: University of Guelph (OUAA)
Acquired: Selected by the Edmonton Eskimos in the first round (4th overall) in the 1993 CFL College Draft. Traded to the Hamilton Tiger-Cats along with quarterback DeChane Cameron, linebacker DeWayne Odom and a negotiation list player in exchange for quarterback Damon Allen.

Games Played - 18 with Hamilton in 1993. **CFL Total GP - 18.**

Fumble Returns - 1 for 12 yards with Hamilton in 1993.
CFL Total Fumble Returns - 1 for 12 yards.

Quarterback Sacks - 3 for 29 yards lost with Hamilton in 1993.
CFL Total QB Sacks - 3 for 29 yards lost.

Tackles - 75 defensive and 11 special teams with Hamilton in 1993.
CFL Total Tackles - 86 (75 defensive and 11 special teams).

Tackles for Losses - 5 for 14 yards with Hamilton in 1993.
CFL Total Tackles for Losses - 5 for 14 yards.

Winner of Frank M. Gibson Trophy for Outstanding Rookie, Eastern Division in 1993.
CFL Most Outstanding Rookie Award Winner in 1993.

O'SHEA, MICHAEL

Playoffs

Games Played - 2 with Hamilton in 1993.
CFL Total Playoff GP - 2.

Quarterback Sacks - 1 for 3 yards lost with Hamilton in 1993.
CFL Total QB Sacks - 1 for 3 yards lost.

Tackles - 11 defensive and 1 special teams with Hamilton in 1993.
CFL Total Tackles - 12 (11 defensive and 1 special teams).

Tackles for Losses - 2 for 3 yards with Hamilton in 1993.
CFL Total Tackles for Losses - 2 for 3 yards.

OSBALDISTON, PAUL

Born: April 27, 1964
Birthplace: Oldham, England
Punter/Kicker. 6'3", 210 lbs. Non-import
Last Amateur Club: Western Montana University
Acquired: Selected in the seventh round (63rd overall) by the B.C. Lions in the 1986 CFL College Draft. Released by B.C. and signed as a free agent by the Winnipeg Blue Bombers in July, 1986. Released by Winnipeg and signed as a free agent by the Hamilton Tiger-Cats in September, 1986. Granted free agency status in February, 1994. Re-signed by Hamilton later that month.

	Team	Scoring GP	TD	C	FG	S	TP	Rushing NO	YDS	AVE	LG	TD
1986	B.C.	3	0	6	5	4	25	0	0	0.0	0	0
	Wpg.	5	0	17	9	4	48	0	0	0.0	0	0
	Ham.	9	0	16	23	7	92	0	0	0.0	0	0
1987	Ham.	3	0	1	4	5	18	1	7	7.0	7	0
1988	Ham.	18	0	49	36	21	178	1	-3	-3.0	-3	0
1989abc	Ham.	18	0	47	54	24	233	0	0	0.0	0	0
1990ade	Ham.	18	0	41	52	15	212	0	0	0.0	0	0
1991	Ham.	18	0	33	40	19	172	1	30	30.0	30	0
1992	Ham.	18	0	52	41	21	196	0	0	0.0	0	0
1993	Ham.	18	0	28	31	15	136	0	0	0.0	0	0
CFL TOTALS		**128**	**0**	**290**	**295**	**135**	**1310**	**3**	**34**	**11.3**	**30**	**0**

	Team	Field Goals T	G	YDS	AVE	LK	PCT	Field Goal Attempts NO	YDS	AVE	LK	S
1986	B.C.	9	5	177	35.4	45	55.6	4	218	54.5	67	3
	Wpg.	15	9	314	34.9	51	60.0	6	288	48.0	59	4
	Ham.	30	23	743	32.3	51	76.7	7	317	45.3	52	7
1987	Ham.	8	4	167	41.8	54	50.0	4	165	41.3	45	4
1988	Ham.	56	36	1237	34.4	52	64.3	20	967	48.4	62	17
1989	Ham.	74	54	1698	31.4	47	73.0	20	927	46.4	58	16
1990	Ham.	62	52	1853	35.6	57	83.9	10	508	50.8	61	8
1991	Ham.	61	40	1324	33.1	56	65.6	21	1029	49.0	64	10
1992	Ham.	64	41	1312	32.0	55	64.1	23	1136	49.4	75	17
1993	Ham.	48	31	856	27.6	51	64.6	17	799	47.0	60	10
CFL TOTALS		**428**	**295**	**9681**	**32.8**	**57**	**68.9**	**132**	**6354**	**48.1**	**75**	**96**

	Team	Converts T	G	PCT	Punting NO	YDS	AVE	LK	S	Kickoffs NO	YDS	AVE	LK	S
1986	B.C.	6	6	100.0	15	641	42.7	56	1	13	739	56.8	65	0
	Wpg.	17	17	100.0	0	0	0.0	0	0	17	907	53.4	61	0
	Ham.	16	16	100.0	27	1056	39.1	59	0	39	2095	53.7	66	0
1987	Ham.	1	1	100.0	19	675	35.5	68	1	7	326	46.6	66	0
1988	Ham.	49	49	100.0	158	5976	37.8	83	3	87	5130	590	95	1
1989	Ham.	47	47	100.0	151	6056	40.1	73	6	96	5622	58.6	94	2
1990	Ham.	41	41	100.0	128	4983	38.9	74	4	91	5319	58.5	90	3
1991	Ham.	33	33	100.0	146	6105	41.8	77	6	83	4814	58.0	100	3
1992	Ham.	53	52	98.1	149	6032	40.5	79	4	91	5041	55.4	75	0
1993	Ham.	28	28	100.0	164	6648	40.5	84	5	57	3094	54.3	79	0
CFL TOTALS		**291**	**290**	**99.7**	**957**	**38172**	**39.9**	**84**	**30**	**581**	**33087**	**56.9**	**100**	**9**

Passing - 1 attempt, 1 complete for -8 yards, 100.0 percent complete with Winnipeg in 1986 and 1 attempt, 0 complete with Hamilton in 1988.
CFL Total Passing - 2 attempts, 1 complete for -8 yards, 50.0 percent complete.

Own Punts Recovered - 1 with Hamilton in 1992.
CFL Total Own Punts Recovered - 1.

Net Punting - 147 for 4792 yards, 32.6 average with Hamilton in 1991; 150 for 5143 yards, 34.3 average in 1992 and 164 for 5230 yards, 31.9 average in 1993. **CFL Total Net Punting - 461 for 15165 yards, 32.9 average.**

Fumbles - 1 and 1 lost with Hamilton in 1988; 2 and 2 lost in 1989; 2 and 2 lost in 1990; 3 and 3 lost in 1991; 1 and 1 lost in 1992 and 5 and 2 lost in 1993.
CFL Total Fumbles - 14 and 11 lost.

Tackles - 1 defensive with Hamilton in 1989; 2 defensive in 1990; 1 defensive and 4 special teams in 1991 and 1 special teams in 1993.
CFL Total Tackles - 9 (4 defensive and 5 special teams).

a -All-Eastern All-Star
b -Set CFL Record for Most Points One Season since tied by Saskatchewan's Dave Ridgway in 1990
c -Shared CFL Lead for Field Goals with Saskatchewan's Dave Ridgway
d -Most Outstanding Canadian Runner-Up
e -Winner Lew Hayman Trophy, Most Outstanding Canadian, Eastern Division

Playoffs

	Team	Scoring GP	TD	C	FG	S	TP	Converts T	G	PCT
1986	Ham.	2	0	6	5	2	23	6	6	100.0
1988	Ham.	1	0	2	4	2	16	2	2	100.0
1989	Ham.	1	0	1	2	1	8	1	1	100.0
1992	Ham.	2	0	3	4	1	16	3	3	100.0
1993	Ham.	2	0	4	4	0	16	4	4	100.0
CFL TOTALS		**8**	**0**	**16**	**19**	**6**	**79**	**16**	**16**	**100.0**

	Team	Punting NO	YDS	AVE	LK	S	Kickoffs NO	YDS	AVE	LK	S
1986	Ham.	8	293	36.6	41	0	10	550	55.0	63	0
1988	Ham.	4	141	35.3	63	0	4	225	56.3	67	0
1989	Ham.	15	557	37.1	56	0	3	186	62.0	65	0
1992	Ham.	19	701	36.9	50	0	6	278	46.3	60	0
1993	Ham.	17	624	36.7	47	0	6	345	57.5	82	0
CFL TOTALS		**63**	**2316**	**36.7**	**63**	**0**	**29**	**1584**	**54.6**	**82**	**0**

	Team	Field Goals T	G	YDS	AVE	LK	PCT	Field Goal Attempts NO	YDS	AVE	LK	S
1986	Ham.	7	5	180	36.0	58	71.4	2	98	49.0	56	2
1988	Ham.	5	4	114	28.5	48	80.0	1	40	40.0	40	1
1989	Ham.	5	2	64	32.0	37	40.6	3	103	34.3	38	1
1992	Ham.	5	4	149	37.3	46	80.0	1	42	42.0	42	1
1993	Ham.	7	4	150	37.5	43	57.1	3	128	42.7	51	0
CFL TOTALS		**29**	**19**	**657**	**34.6**	**58**	**65.5**	**10**	**411**	**41.1**	**56**	**5**

Net Punting - 19 for 588 yards, 30.9 average with Hamilton in 1992 and 17 for 532 yards, 31.3 average in 1993.
CFL Total Playoff Net Punting - 38 for 1120 yards, 29.5 average.

Grey Cup

	Team	Scoring GP	TD	C	FG	S	TP	Converts T	G	PCT	Punting NO	YDS	AVE	LK	S
1986	Ham.	1	0	3	6	0	21	3	3	100.0	4	147	36.8	41	0
1989	Ham.	1	0	4	4	0	16	4	4	100.0	5	233	46.6	51	0
CFL TOTALS		**2**	**0**	**7**	**10**	**0**	**37**	**7**	**7**	**100.0**	**9**	**380**	**42.2**	**51**	**0**

	Team	Field Goals T	G	YDS	AVE	LK	PCT	Kickoffs NO	YDS	AVE	LK	S	Fumbles NO	LOST
1986	Ham.	6	6	222	37.0	47	100.0	6	328	54.7	58	0	1	1
1989	Ham.	4	4	167	41.8	47	100.0	10	622	62.2	64	0	0	0
CFL TOTALS		**10**	**10**	**389**	**38.9**	**47**	**100.0**	**16**	**950**	**59.4**	**64**	**0**	**1**	**1**

Dick Suderman Trophy as Most Outstanding Canadian in 1986 Grey Cup Game.

PARKER, CARL

Born: February 5, 1965
Birthplace: Columbus, Georgia
Wide Receiver. 6'2", 205 lbs. Import
Last Amateur Club: Vanderbilt University
Acquired: Selected in the 12th round (307th overall) by the NFL Cincinnati Bengals in the 1988 NFL Draft. Signed by Cincinnati in June, 1988. Released by Cincinnati in October, 1989. Awarded on waivers to the NFL New York Jets in October, 1989. Released by New York in August, 1990. Signed as a free agent by the Hamilton Tiger-Cats in September, 1990. Released by Hamilton in October, 1990. Selected in the fourth round of the 1991 WLAF Positional Draft (36th wide receiver overall) by the Sacramento Surge. Signed as a free agent by the NFL Pittsburgh Steelers in June, 1991 and was released after training camp. Played with Sacramento in the 1992 WLAF season. Signed as a free agent by the Sacramento Gold Miners in February, 1993. Released by Sacramento in February, 1994.

	Team	Scoring GP	TD	C	FG	S	TP	Pass Receiving NO	YDS	AVE	LG	TD
1990	Ham.	2	1	0	0	0	6	5	55	11.0	14	1
1993	Sac.	17	5	0	0	0	30	46	684	14.9	43	5
CFL TOTALS		**19**	**1**	**0**	**0**	**0**	**36**	**51**	**739**	**14.5**	**43**	**6**

	Team	Punt Returns NO	YDS	AVE	LG	TD	Kickoff Returns NO	YDS	AVE	LG	TD
1990	Ham.	5	24	4.8	10	0	2	37	18.5	19	0
1993	Sac.	0	0	0.0	0	0	0	0	0.0	0	0
CFL TOTALS		**5**	**24**	**4.8**	**10**	**0**	**2**	**37**	**18.5**	**19**	**0**

Fumbles - 1 and 0 lost with Hamilton in 1990.
CFL Total Fumbles - 1 and 0 lost.

Own Fumbles Recovered - 1 with Sacramento in 1993. **CFL Total OFR - 1.**

Tackles - 1 defensive and 5 special teams with Sacramento in 1993.
CFL Total Tackles - 6 (1 defensive and 5 special teams).

PARRISH, DOUG

Born: February 25, 1968
Birthplace: Tuscaloosa, Alabama
Defensive Back. 6'0", 190 lbs. Import
Last Amateur Club: San Francisco State University
Acquired: Signed as a free agent by the Edmonton Eskimos in March, 1991. Traded to the Sacramento Gold Miners in exchange for defensive back Walter Bailey, in March, 1994.

PARRISH, DOUG

	Team	GP	Interception Returns NO	YDS	AVE	LG	TD	Kickoff Returns NO	YDS	AVE	LG	TD
1991	Edm.	5	2	27	13.5	15	0	2	11	5.5	11	0
1992	Edm.	10	1	0	0.0	0	0	0	0	0.0	0	0
1993	Edm.	13	2	35	17.5	31	0	7	107	15.3	26	0
CFL TOTALS		**28**	**3**	**62**	**20.7**	**31**	**0**	**9**	**118**	**13.1**	**26**	**0**

Scoring - 1 TD for 6 pts with Edmonton in 1993. **CFL Total Scoring - 1 TD for 6 pts.**

Fumbles - 1 and 1 lost with Edmonton in 1993. **CFL Total Fumbles - 1 and 1 lost.**

Fumble Returns - 2 for 32 yards, 16.0 average, longest 32 yards and 1 TD with Edmonton in 1993.
CFL Total Fumble Returns - 2 for 32 yards, 16.0 average, longest 32 yards and 1 TD.

Punt Returns - 1 for -1 yard with Edmonton in 1993.
CFL Total Punt Returns - 1 for -1 yard.

Quarterback Sacks - 1 for 2 yards lost with Edmonton in 1992 and 1 for 13 yards lost in 1993. **CFL Total QB Sacks - 2 for 15 yards lost.**

Tackles - 11 defensive and 1 special teams with Edmonton in 1991; 17 defensive and 6 special teams in 1992 and 45 defensive and 4 special teams in 1993.
CFL Total Tackles - 84 (73 defensive and 11 special teams).

Tackles for Losses - 1 for 4 yards with Edmonton in 1993.
CFL Total Tackles for Losses - 1 for 4 yards.

PARTCHENKO, PETER
Born: June 30, 1970
Birthplace: Toronto, Ontario
Offensive Lineman. 6'4", 300 lbs. Non-import
Last Amateur Club:Michigan State University
Acquired:Selected by the Toronto Argonauts in the sixth round (44th overall) in the 1993 CFL College Draft.

Games Played - 3 with Toronto in 1993. **CFL Total GP - 3.**

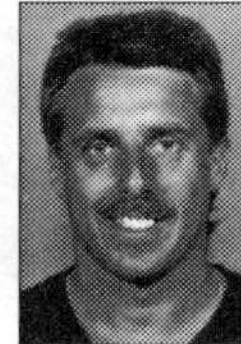

PASSAGLIA, LUI
Born: June 7, 1954
Birthplace: Vancouver, B.C.
Punter/Kicker. 5'11", 180 lbs. Non-import
Last Amateur Club: Simon Fraser University (EVCO)
Acquired: Selected in the first round (fifth overall) by the B.C. Lions in the 1976 CFL College Draft.

	Team	GP	Scoring TD	C	FG	S	TP	Field Goals T	G	YDS	AVE	LK	PCT
1976	B.C.	16	1	28	28	12	130	49	28	821	29.3	50	57.1
1977a	B.C.	16	0	30	40	7	157	53	40	1126	28.2	48	75.5
1978f	B.C.	16	0	30	37	18	159	44	37	1132	30.6	50	84.1
1979abhir	B.C.	16	0	27	32	21	144	45	32	992	31.0	50	71.1
1980a	B.C.	16	0	38	31	16	147	46	31	1023	33.0	54	67.4
1981	B.C.	16	0	42	27	21	144	40	27	859	31.8	45	67.5
1982	B.C.	16	0	45	26	11	134	35	26	733	28.2	48	74.3
1983abcdegij	B.C.	16	0	45	43	17	191	59	43	1260	29.3	52	72.9
1984abcg	B.C.	16	0	46	35	16	167	48	35	1111	31.7	54	72.9
1985kl	B.C.	16	0	49	37	25	185	55	37	1244	33.6	54	67.3
1986	B.C.	15	0	34	39	15	166	56	39	1084	27.8	49	69.6
1987cgmnopq	B.C.	18	0	47	52	11	214	66	52	1566	30.1	49	78.8
1988s	B.C.	12	0	31	13	13	83	20	13	384	29.5	46	65.0
1989t	B.C.	18	0	52	37	12	175	51	37	1155	31.2	53	72.5
1990uv	B.C.	13	0	33	25	8	116	39	25	792	31.7	50	64.1
1991wx	B.C.	18	0	67	44	11	210	59	44	1369	31.1	54	74.6
1992ayz	B.C.	15	0	38	28	9	131	38	28	925	33.0	49	73.7
1993	B.C.	17	0	62	35	9	176	47	35	1007	28.8	52	74.5
CFL TOTALS		**286**	**1**	**744**	**609**	**252**	**2829**	**850**	**609**	**18683**	**30.7**	**54**	**71.6**

	Team	Converts T	G	PCT	Kickoffs NO	YDS	AVE	LK	S
1976	B.C.	28	28	100.0	53	2531	47.8	75	0
1977	B.C.	30	30	100.0	70	4229	60.4	76	1
1978	B.C.	30	30	100.0	68	4148	61.0	88	3
1979	B.C.	27	27	100.0	52	3066	60.0	70	1
1980	B.C.	38	38	100.0	56	3436	61.4	79	2
1981	B.C.	42	42	100.0	66	3994	60.5	90	5
1982	B.C.	45	45	100.0	27	1299	48.1	63	0
1983	B.C.	46	45	97.8	69	3815	55.3	82	1
1984	B.C.	46	46	100.0	70	3834	54.8	70	1
1985	B.C.	49	49	100.0	76	4381	57.6	90	2
1986	B.C.	34	34	100.0	5	253	50.6	57	0
1987	B.C.	47	47	100.0	91	4876	53.6	93	1
1988	B.C.	31	31	100.0	50	2456	49.1	62	0
1989	B.C.	52	52	100.0	100	5202	52.0	81	2
1990	B.C.	33	33	100.0	44	2179	49.5	67	0
1991	B.C.	67	67	100.0	35	1663	47.5	60	0
1992	B.C.	38	38	100.0	58	2790	48.1	72	0
1993	B.C.	62	62	100.0	88	3941	44.8	64	0
CFL TOTALS		**745**	**744**	**99.9**	**1078**	**58093**	**53.9**	**93**	**19**

	Team	Field Goal Attempts NO	YDS	AVE	LK	S	Punting NO	YDS	AVE	LK	S
1976	B.C.	21	845	42.3	59	7	143	5913	41.4	67	5
1977	B.C.	13	567	43.6	54	2	123	5456	44.4	78	4
1978	B.C.	7	332	47.4	54	6	128	5966	46.6	82	9
1979	B.C.	13	577	44.4	54	6	133	6287	47.3	73	14
1980	B.C.	15	591	42.2	64	11	128	5544	43.3	81	3
1981	B.C.	13	584	44.9	57	10	141	6487	46.0	76	6
1982	B.C.	9	365	40.6	46	8	142	5813	40.9	59	3
1983	B.C.	16	710	44.4	59	10	117	5868	50.2	93	6
1984	B.C.	13	568	43.7	54	11	125	5803	46.4	89	4
1985	B.C.	18	782	43.4	48	14	140	6287	44.9	76	9
1986	B.C.	17	736	43.3	61	13	138	5686	41.2	68	2
1987	B.C.	14	566	40.4	58	5	161	6631	41.2	97	5
1988	B.C.	7	304	43.4	57	6	101	4049	40.1	71	7
1989	B.C.	14	541	38.6	47	6	154	6345	41.2	67	4
1990	B.C.	14	572	40.0	57	7	81	3169	39.1	60	1
1991	B.C.	15	641	42.7	54	9	111	4611	41.5	71	2
1992	B.C.	10	441	44.1	58	6	119	4798	40.3	62	3
CFL TOTALS		**229**	**9722**	**42.5**	**64**	**137**	**2185**	**94713**	**43.3**	**97**	**87**

	Team	Passing ATT	COMP	YDS	PCT	INT	LG	TD	Fumbles NO	LOST	OFR
1976	B.C.	2	1	18	50.0	0	18	0	1	1	0
1977	B.C.	2	1	11	50.0	0	11	0	1	1	0
1978	B.C.	2	1	9	50.0	0	9	0	1	1	0
1979	B.C.	0	0	0	0.0	0	0	0	1	0	0
1980	B.C.	2	1	8	50.0	0	8	0	2	1	0
1981	B.C.	0	0	0	0.0	0	0	0	1	1	0
1982	B.C.	1	1	17	100.0	0	17	0	0	0	0
1983	B.C.	2	0	0	0.0	0	0	0	0	0	2
1984	B.C.	2	2	26	100.0	0	14	0	0	0	0
1985	B.C.	0	0	0	0.0	0	0	0	0	0	0
1986	B.C.	2	1	26	50.0	1	26	0	0	0	0
1987	B.C.	4	2	23	50.0	0	15	0	1	1	0
1988	B.C.	0	0	0	0.0	0	0	0	0	0	0
1989	B.C.	4	3	130	75.0	0	89	1	2	2	0
1990	B.C.	1	1	25	100.0	0	25	0	2	2	1
1991	B.C.	1	0	0	0.0	1	0	0	1	1	0
1992	B.C.	2	0	0	0.0	0	0	0	1	1	0
1993	B.C.	1	1	12	100.0	0	12	0	1	1	0
CFL TOTALS		**28**	**15**	**305**	**53.6**	**2**	**89**	**1**	**15**	**13**	**3**

Net Punting - 112 for 3579 yards, 32.0 average with B.C. in 1991 and 120 for 3980 yards, 33.2 average in 1992 and 116 for 4165 yards, 35.9 average in 1993.
CFL Total Net Punting - 232 for 7559 yards, 32.6 average.

Fumble Returns - 1 for 0 yards with B.C. in 1992.
CFL Total Fumble Returns - 1 for 0 yards.

Unsuccessful Field Goal Returns - 1 for 10 yards with B.C. in 1990.
CFL Total Unsuccessful Field Goal Returns - 1 for 10 yards.

Rushing - 1 for 1 yard with B.C. in 1984; 2 for 86 yards, 43.0 average, longest 68 yards in 1985; 2 for 18 yards, 9.0 average, longest 15 yards in 1986; 1 for 12 yards in 1988; 2 for 38 yards, 19.0 average, longest 25 yards in 1989; 2 for 17 yards, 8.5 average, longest 10 yards in 1990; 1 for -13 yards in 1991 and 1 for 16 yards in 1992. **CFL Total Rushing - 12 for 175 yards, 14.6 average, longest 68 yards.**

Pass Receiving - 1 for 10 yards and 1 TD with B.C. in 1976.
CFL Total Pass Receiving - 1 for 10 yards and 1 TD.

Punt Returns - 1 for 2 yards with B.C. in 1979. **CFL Total Punt Returns - 1 for 2 yards.**

Kickoff Returns - 1 for 44 yards, 44.0 average, longest 32 yards with B.C. in 1976. **CFL Total Kickoff Returns - 1 for 44 yards, 44.0 average, longest 32 yards.**

Own Kickoffs Recovered - 1 for 15 yards with B.C. in 1976.
CFL Total Own Kickoffs Recovered - 1 for 15 yards.

Tackles - 3 special teams with B.C. in 1991 and 1 special teams in 1993.
CFL Total Tackles - 4 (4 special teams).

a - All-Western All-Star.
b - CFL All-Star.
c - Led CFL in scoring.
d - Led CFL in converts.
e - Set CFL Record with 246 consecutive converts. Streak began 1976 and ended on July 30, 1983 in Hamilton. Subsequently passed by J.T. Hay.
f - Shared CFL Lead in field goals with Cyril McFall of Calgary.
g - Led CFL in field goals.
h - Led CFL in singles.
i - Led CFL in punting average.
j - Set CFL single season record for punting average.
k - Shared CFL lead in singles with Hamilton's Bernie Ruoff.
l - Shared CFL lead in converts with Edmonton's Tom Dixon.
m- Led CFL in kickoff yards.
n - Shared CFL lead in kickoffs with Winnipeg's Trevor Kennerd.
o - Set CFL record for points in a season (which has since been surpassed).
p - Set CFL record for field goals in a season (which has since been surpassed).
q - All-time leader in number of times punted.
r - Set CFL playoff record for longest punt.
s - All-time leader Most Punting Yardage.

PASSAGLIA, LUI

t - All-Time leader Field Goals.
u - All-Time Leader Most Singles.
v - All-Time Leader in Points.
w - All-Time Leader in Converts.
x - Most Consecutive Converts (398).
y - Most Career Convert Attempts.
z - Most Career Field Goal Attempts.

Playoffs

	Team	Scoring GP	TD	C	FG	S	TP	Punting NO	YDS	AVE	LK	S	Fumbles NO	LOST
1977	B.C.	2	0	2	4	2	16	16	677	42.3	57	0	0	0
1979	B.C.	1	0	0	0	2	2	10	490	49.0	89	2	0	0
1981	B.C.	2	0	2	5	2	19	22	996	45.3	72	1	0	0
1983	B.C.	1	0	5	1	1	9	9	456	50.6	61	0	0	0
1984	B.C.	1	0	1	2	1	8	8	378	54.0	67	0	1	1
1985	B.C.	1	0	5	2	1	12	7	356	44.5	58	1	0	0
1986	B.C.	2	0	2	3	2	13	22	873	39.7	53	0	0	0
1987	B.C.	1	0	0	2	1	7	10	383	38.3	49	0	0	0
1988	B.C.	2	0	9	5	1	25	15	541	36.0	47	0	0	0
1991	B.C.	1	0	4	4	1	17	5	231	46.2	69	1	0	0
1993	B.C.	1	0	0	3	0	9	7	309	44.1	52	0	0	0
CFL TOTALS		**15**	**0**	**30**	**31**	**14**	**137**	**131**	**5690**	**43.4**	**89**	**5**	**1**	**1**

	Team	Kickoffs NO	YDS	AVE	LK	S	Field Goals T	G	YDS	AVE	LK	PCT
1977	B.C.	5	315	63.0	70	0	9	4	94	23.5	30	44.4
1979	B.C.	2	148	74.0	90	0	0	0	0	0.0	0	0.0
1981	B.C.	3	180	60.0	64	0	6	5	177	35.4	48	83.3
1983	B.C.	6	350	58.3	66	0	2	1	43	43.0	43	50.0
1984	B.C.	2	111	55.5	56	0	3	2	88	44.0	47	66.7
1985	B.C.	6	364	60.7	66	0	4	2	44	22.0	22	50.0
1986	B.C.	0	0	0.0	0	0	5	3	95	31.7	39	60.0
1987	B.C.	3	150	50.0	54	0	5	2	50	25.0	33	40.0
1988	B.C.	12	573	47.8	69	0	6	5	196	39.2	49	83.3
1991	B.C.	7	382	54.6	63	0	4	4	156	39.0	43	100.0
1993	B.C.	0	0	0.0	0	0	3	3	74	24.7	34	100.0
CFL TOTALS		**46**	**2573**	**55.9**	**90**	**0**	**47**	**31**	**1017**	**32.8**	**49**	**66.0**

	Team	Converts T	G	PCT	Field Goal Attempts NO	YDS	AVE	LK	S
1977	B.C.	2	2	100.0	5	233	46.6	51	2
1979	B.C.	0	0	0.0	0	0	0.0	0	0
1981	B.C.	2	2	100.0	1	44	44.0	44	1
1983	B.C.	5	5	100.0	1	48	48.0	48	1
1984	B.C.	1	1	100.0	1	45	45.0	45	1
1985	B.C.	5	5	100.0	2	97	48.5	53	0
1986	B.C.	2	2	100.0	2	84	42.0	44	2
1987	B.C.	0	0	0.0	3	130	43.3	45	1
1988	B.C.	9	9	100.0	1	48	48.0	48	1
1991	B.C.	4	4	100.0	0	0	0.0	0	0
1993	B.C.	0	0	0.0	0	0	0.0	0	0
CFL TOTALS		**30**	**30**	**100.0**	**16**	**729**	**45.6**	**53**	**9**

Passing - 1 attempt, 1 completion for 31 yards in 1977; 1 attempt, 1 completion for 20 yards in 1979. **CFL Total Playoff Passing - 2 attempts, 2 completions, 51 yards, 100.0 percent, longest 31 yards.**

Net Punting - 5 for 227 yards, 45.4 average with B.C. in 1991. **CFL Total Playoff Net Punting - 5 for 227 yards, 45.4 average.**

Fumble Returns - 1 for 0 yards with B.C. in 1977. **CFL Total Playoff Fumble Returns - 1 for 0 yards.**

Grey Cup

	Team	Scoring GP	TD	C	FG	S	TP	Punting NO	YDS	AVE	LK	S
1983	B.C.	1	0	2	1	0	5	11	461	41.9	60	0
1985	B.C.	1	0	3	5	1	19	11	457	41.5	51	0
1988	B.C.	1	0	0	1	2	7	9	411	45.7	84	1
CFL TOTALS		**3**	**0**	**5**	**7**	**3**	**31**	**31**	**1329**	**42.9**	**84**	**1**

	Team	Rushing NO	YDS	AVE	LG	TD	Kickoffs NO	YDS	AVE	LK	S
1983	B.C.	0	0	0.0	0	0	3	176	58.6	62	0
1985	B.C.	1	13	13.0	13	0	5	263	52.6	58	0
1988	B.C.	0	0	0.0	0	0	3	187	60.2	73	0
CFL TOTALS		**1**	**13**	**13.0**	**13**	**0**	**11**	**626**	**56.9**	**73**	**0**

	Team	Field Goals T	G	YDS	AVE	LK	PCT	Field Goal Attempts NO	YDS	AVE	LK	S
1983	B.C.	1	1	31	31.0	31	100.0	0	0	0.0	0	0
1985	B.C.	6	5	152	30.4	44	83.3	1	37	37.0	37	1
1988	B.C.	3	1	28	28.0	28	33.3	2	42	21.0	39	1
CFL TOTALS		**10**	**7**	**211**	**30.1**	**44**	**70.0**	**3**	**79**	**26.3**	**39**	**2**

Grey Cup Game Canadian Star (Dick Suderman Trophy) 1985.

PAYNE, DAN
Born: June 7, 1966
Birthplace: Coquitlam, B.C.
Tackle. 6'7", 300 lbs. Non-import
Last Amateur Club: Simon Fraser University (EVCO)
Acquired: Selected in the second round (ninth overall) by the Saskatchewan Roughriders in the 1989 CFL College Draft. Retired from Saskatchewan in June, 1990. Traded by Saskatchewan in September, 1990 to the B.C. Lions in exchange for linebacker Tony Visco. Released by B.C. in July, 1991. Signed as a free agent by the Hamilton Tiger-Cats in March, 1992. Signed as a free agent by the Saskatchewan Roughriders in April, 1993.

Games Played - 7 with Saskatchewan in 1989; 3 with B.C. in 1990; 8 with Hamilton in 1992 and 18 with Saskatchewan in 1993. **CFL Total GP - 36.**

Blocked Kicks - 1 punt with Saskatchewan in 1989. **CFL Total Blocked Kicks - 1 (1 punt).**

Tackles - 3 defensive and 8 special teams with Saskatchewan in 1993. **CFL Total Tackles - 11 (3 defensive and 8 special teams).**

Playoffs

Games Played - 2 with Saskatchewan in 1989 and 1 in 1993. **CFL Total Playoff GP - 2.**

Own Fumbles Recovered - 1 with Saskatchewan in 1993. **CFL Total Playoff OFR - 1.**

Tackles - 2 defensive with Saskatchewan in 1993. **CFL Total Playoff Tackles - 2 (2 defensive).**

Grey Cup

Games Played - 1 with Saskatchewan in 1989. **Total Grey Cup GP - 1.**

PAYTON, ELFRID
Born: September 22, 1967
Birthplace: Gretna, Louisiana
Linebacker. 6'1", 230 lbs. Import
Last Amateur Club: Grambling University
Acquired: Signed as a free agent by the Winnipeg Blue Bombers in January, 1991. Granted free agency status in February, 1994. Signed as a free agent by the Shreveport Pirates in March, 1994.

Games Played - 12 with Winnipeg in 1991; 9 in 1992 and 18 in 1993. **CFL Total GP - 38.**

Interception Returns - 1 for 50 yards with Winnipeg in 1991. **CFL Total Interception Returns - 1 for 50 yards.**

Fumble Returns - 2 for 0 yards with Winnipeg in 1991; 1 for 0 yards in 1992 and 2 for 48 yards, 24.0 average, longest 47 yards and 1 TD in 1993. **CFL Total Fumble Returns - 5 for 48 yards, 9.6 average, longest 47 yards and 1 TD.**

Quarterback Sacks - 6 with Winnipeg in 1991; 6 for 43 yards lost in 1992 and 22 for 150 yards lost in 1993. **CFL Total QB Sacks - 34.**

Tackles - 30 defensive and 7 special teams with Winnipeg in 1991; 26 defensive and 1 special teams in 1992 and 28 defensive and 1 special teams in 1993. **CFL Total Tackles - 93 (84 defensive and 9 special teams).**

Tackles for Losses - 3 for 7 yards with Winnipeg in 1991; 8 for 26 yards in 1992 and 6 for 19 yards in 1993. **CFL Total Tackles for Losses - 17 for 52 yards.**

All-Eastern All-Star in 1993.
CFL All-Star in 1993.
Winner of the James P. McCaffrey Trophy as the Outstanding Defensive Player in the Eastern Division in 1993.
Runner-Up CFL Most Outstanding Player in 1993.
Led CFL in QB Sacks in 1993.

Playoffs

Games Played - 2 with Winnipeg in 1991 and 1 in 1993. **CFL Total Playoff GP - 3.**

Quarterback Sacks - 1 with Winnipeg in 1991. **CFL Total Playoff QB Sacks - 1.**

Tackles - 2 defensive and 3 special teams with Winnipeg in 1991. **CFL Total Playoff Tackles - 5 (2 defensive and 3 special teams).**

Grey Cup

Games Played - 1 with Winnipeg in 1993. **Total Grey Cup GP - 1.**

Quarterback Sacks - 2 for 12 yards lost with Winnipeg in 1993. **Total Grey Cup QB Sacks - 2 for 12 yards lost.**

Tackles - 6 defensive with Winnipeg in 1993. **Total Grey Cup Tackles - 6 (6 defensive).**

PEARCE, MARK
Born: April 10, 1967
Birthplace: Middlesex, England
Defensive Tackle. 6'7", 285 lbs. Non-import
Last Amateur Club: University of Cape Breton (AUAA)
Acquired: Was signed as an Operation Discovery player by the WLAF's Barcelona Dragons in 1991. Selected by the Calgary Stampeders in the first round (sixth overall) of the 1993 CFL College Draft. Released by Calgary in November, 1993. Signed as a free agent by the Shreveport Pirates in April, 1994.

Games Played - 13 with Calgary in 1993. **CFL Total GP - 13.**

Quarterback Sacks - 3 for 27 yards lost with Calgary in 1993. **CFL Total QB Sacks - 3 for 27 yards lost.**

Tackles - 3 defensive and 8 special teams with Calgary in 1993. **CFL Total Tackles - 11 (3 defensive and 8 special teams).**

PEARCE, MATT
Born: April 22, 1967
Birthplace: Cranbrook, British Columbia
Fullback. 6'2", 205 lbs. Non-import
Last Amateur Club: University of British Columbia (WIFL)
Acquired: Selected in the fourth round (32nd overall) by the Winnipeg Blue Bombers in the 1989 CFL College Draft.

		Scoring						Rushing				
	Team	GP	TD	C	FG	S	TP	NO	YDS	AVE	LG	TD
1989	Wpg.	18	0	0	0	0	0	26	96	3.7	17	0
1990	Wpg.	18	1	0	0	0	6	10	38	3.8	7	0
1991	Wpg.	18	0	0	0	0	0	10	24	2.4	5	0
1992	Wpg.	18	0	0	0	0	0	1	8	8.0	8	0
1993	Wpg.	17	1	0	0	0	6	29	145	5.0	15	0
CFL TOTALS		**89**	**2**	**0**	**0**	**0**	**12**	**76**	**311**	**4.1**	**17**	**0**

		Pass Receiving					Punt Returns				
	Team	NO	YDS	AVE	LG	TD	NO	YDS	AVE	LG	TD
1989	Wpg.	5	62	12.4	22	0	3	26	8.7	17	0
1990	Wpg.	10	137	13.7	57	1	9	56	6.2	13	0
1991	Wpg.	1	5	5.0	5	0	18	64	3.6	10	0
1992	Wpg.	0	0	0.0	0	0	15	60	4.0	13	0
1993	Wpg.	4	45	11.3	30	1	1	10	10.0	10	0
CFL TOTALS		**20**	**249**	**12.5**	**57**	**2**	**46**	**216**	**4.7**	**17**	**0**

Kickoff Returns - 8 for 161 yards, 20.1 average, longest 28 yards with Winnipeg in 1989; 8 for 94 yards, 11.8 average, longest 22 yards in 1990; 10 for 109 yards, 10.9 average, longest 23 yards in 1991; 3 for 15 yards, 5.0 average, longest 10 yards in 1992 and 1 for 0 yards in 1993. **CFL Total Kickoff Returns - 30 for 379 yards, 12.6 average, longest 28 yards.**

Fumble Returns - 1 for 0 yards with Winnipeg in 1989. **CFL Total Fumble Returns - 1 for 0 yards.**

Fumbles - 1 and 1 lost with Winnipeg in 1991 and 3 and 2 lost in 1992. **CFL Total Fumbles - 4 and 3 lost.**

Blocked Kicks - 1 punt with Winnipeg in 1990. **CFL Total Blocked Kicks - 1 punt.**

Tackles - 2 defensive with Winnipeg in 1989; 1 defensive in 1990; 2 defensive and 12 special teams in 1991; 1 defensive and 9 special teams in 1992 and 1 defensive and 2 special teams in 1993. **CFL Total Tackles - 30 (7 defensive and 23 special teams).**

Playoffs

Games Played - 2 with Winnipeg in 1989; 1 in 1990; 2 in 1991; 1 in 1992 and 1 in 1993. **CFL Total Playoff GP - 7.**

Scoring - 1 TD for 6 points with Winnipeg in 1992. **CFL Total Playoff Scoring - 1 TD for 6 points.**

Rushing - 3 for 8 yards, 2.7 average, longest 3 yards and 1 TD with Winnipeg in 1992. **CFL Total Playoff Rushing - 3 for 8 yards, 2.7 average, longest 3 yards and 1 TD.**

Pass Receiving - 1 for 4 yards with Winnipeg in 1991. **CFL Total Playoff Pass Receiving - 1 for 4 yards.**

Punt Returns - 7 for 37 yards, 5.3 average, longest 9 yards with Winnipeg in 1991 and 1 for 3 yards in 1993. **CFL Total Playoff Punt Returns - 8 for 40 yards, 5.0 average, longest 9 yards.**

Kickoff Returns - 3 for 44 yards, 14.7 average, longest 17 yards with Winnipeg in 1991. **CFL Total Playoff Kickoff Returns - 3 for 44 yards, 14.7 average, longest 17 yards.**

Fumbles - 1 and 1 lost with Winnipeg in 1991. **CFL Total Playoff Fumbles - 1 and 1 lost.**

Grey Cup

Games Played - 1 with Winnipeg in 1990; 1 in 1992 and 1 in 1993. **Total Grey Cup GP - 3.**

Tackles - 1 special teams with Winnipeg in 1992. **Total Grey Cup Tackles - 1 (1 special teams).**

PERKINS, BRUCE
Born: August 14, 1967
Birthplace: Waterloo, Iowa
Running Back. 6'3", 230 lbs. Import
Last Amateur Club: Arizona State University
Acquired: Signed as a free agent by the NFL Tampa Bay Buccaneers in April, 1990. Released by Tampa Bay in August, 1991. Claimed on waivers by the NFL Indianapolis Colts in August, 1991. Granted unconditional free agency in February, 1992. Signed as a free agent by the NFL Cleveland Browns in March, 1992. Was released by Cleveland prior to the start of the 1992 season. Signed as a free agent by the Hamilton Tiger-Cats in May, 1993.

		Scoring						Rushing				
	Team	GP	TD	C	FG	S	TP	NO	YDS	AVE	LG	TD
1993a	Ham.	14	3	0	0	0	18	173	812	4.7	52	3
CFL TOTALS		**14**	**3**	**0**	**0**	**0**	**18**	**173**	**812**	**4.7**	**52**	**3**

		Pass Receiving					Fumbles		
	Team	NO	YDS	AVE	LG	TD	NO	LOST	OFR
1993	Ham.	20	112	5.6	21	0	4	3	2
CFL TOTALS		**20**	**112**	**5.6**	**21**	**0**	**4**	**3**	**2**

Passing - 1 attempt, 1 complete for 54 yards with Hamilton in 1993. **CFL Total Passing - 1 attempt, 1 complete for 54 yards.**

Kickoff Returns - 1 for 24 yards with Hamilton in 1993. **CFL Total Kickoff Returns - 1 for 24 yards.**

Tackles - 2 defensive and 2 special teams with Hamilton in 1993. **CFL Total Tackles - 4 (2 defensive and 2 special teams).**

a - Led CFL in Rushing Carries

PHILLIPS, KIM
Born: October 28,1966
Birthplace: New Boston, Texas
Defensive Back. 5'10", 190 lbs. Import
Last Amateur Club: University of North Texas
Acquired: Selected in the third round (79th overall) by the New Orleans Saints in the 1989 NFL Draft. Signed by New Orleans in July, 1989. Released by New Orleans in August, 1990. Signed as a free agent by the NFL Buffalo Bills in September, 1990. Released by Buffalo in October, 1990. Signed as a free agent by the NFL Tampa Bay Buccaneers in June, 1991. Released by Tampa Bay in August, 1991. Signed as a free agent by the Winnipeg Blue Bombers in March, 1992.

			Punt Returns					Kickoff Returns				
	Team	GP	NO	YDS	AVE	LG	TD	NO	YDS	AVE	LG	TD
1992	Wpg.	3	4	37	9.3	17	0	2	19	9.5	11	0
1993a	Wpg.	13	1	16	16.0	16	0	2	19	9.5	19	0
CFL TOTALS		**16**	**5**	**53**	**10.6**	**17**	**0**	**4**	**38**	**9.5**	**19**	**0**

Unsuccessful Field Goal Returns - 1 for 0 yards with Winnipeg in 1992. **CFL Total Unsuccessful Field Goal Returns - 1 for 0 yards.**

Interception Returns - 5 for 26 yards, 5.2 average, longest 21 yards with Winnipeg in 1993. **CFL Total Interception Returns - 5 for 26 yards, 5.2 average, longest 21 yards.**

Fumbles - 1 and 0 lost with Winnipeg in 1992. **CFL Total Fumbles - 1 and 0 lost.**

Fumble Returns - 1 for 0 yards with Winnipeg in 1993. **CFL Total Fumble Returns - 1 for 0 yards.**

Tackles - 7 defensive with Winnipeg in 1992 and 33 defensive and 2 special teams in 1993. **CFL Total Tackles - 42 (40 defensive and 2 special teams).**

a - All-Eastern All-Star.

Playoffs

Games Played - 1 with Winnipeg in 1993. **CFL Total Playoff GP - 1**

Interception Returns - 1 for 3 yards with Winnipeg in 1993. **CFL Total Playoff Interception Returns - 1 for 3 yards.**

Tackles - 4 defensive with Winnipeg in 1993. **CFL Total Playoff Tackles - 4 (4 defensive).**

Grey Cup

Games Played - 1 with Winnipeg in 1993. **Total Grey Cup GP - 1.**

Interception Returns - 1 for 10 yards with Winnipeg in 1993. **Total Grey Cup Interception Returns - 1 for 10 yards.**

Tackles - 3 defensive with Winnipeg in 1993. **Total Grey Cup Tackles - 3 (3 defensive).**

PHILPOT, CORY

Born: May 15, 1970
Birthplace: Melbourne, Florida
Running Back. 5'9", 186 lbs. Import
Last Amateur Club: University of Mississippi
Acquired: Signed as a free agent by the B.C. Lions in May, 1993.

	Team	Scoring GP	TD	C	FG	S	TP	Rushing NO	YDS	AVE	LG	TD
1993a	B.C.	11	12	0	0	0	72	66	372	5.6	23	8
CFL TOTALS		**11**	**12**	**0**	**0**	**0**	**72**	**66**	**372**	**5.6**	**23**	**8**

	Team	Pass Receiving NO	YDS	AVE	LG	TD	Punt Returns NO	YDS	AVE	LG	TD
1993	B.C.	20	190	9.5	24	3	9	45	5.0	12	0
CFL TOTALS		**20**	**190**	**9.5**	**24**	**3**	**9**	**45**	**5.0**	**12**	**0**

	Team	Kickoff Returns NO	YDS	AVE	LG	TD	Fumbles NO	LOST	OFR
1993	B.C.	36	1008	28.0	91	1	7	3	2
CFL TOTALS		**36**	**1008**	**28.0**	**91**	**1**	**7**	**3**	**2**

Unsuccessful Field Goal Returns - 1 for 15 yards with B.C. in 1993. **CFL Total Unsuccessful Field Goal Returns - 1 for 15 yards.**

Tackles - 1 special teams with B.C. in 1993. **CFL Total Tackles - 1 (1 special teams).**

a - Led CFL in Kickoff Return Yards

PITCHER, DAVID

Born: January 29, 1967
Birthplace: Port Alberni, B.C.
Slotback. 6'2", 240 lbs. Non-import
Last Amateur Club: Okanagan Sun Juniors (BCJFL)
Acquired: Signed as a free agent by the Saskatchewan Roughriders in April, 1990.

	Team	Scoring GP	TD	C	FG	S	TP	Pass Receiving NO	YDS	AVE	LG	TD
1990	Sask.	10	1	0	0	0	6	6	77	12.8	24	1
1991	Sask.	16	0	0	0	0	0	1	9	9.0	9	0
1992	Sask.	18	1	0	0	0	6	10	84	8.4	16	0
1993	Sask.	18	0	0	0	0	0	1	11	11.0	11	0
CFL TOTALS		**62**	**2**	**0**	**0**	**0**	**12**	**18**	**181**	**10.1**	**24**	**1**

Rushing - 1 for 0 yards with Saskatchewan in 1991; 2 for 26 yards, 13.0 average, longest 19 yards in 1992 and 1 for 9 yards in 1993. **CFL Total Rushing - 4 for 35 yards, 8.8 average, longest 19 yards.**

Punt Returns - 0 for 2 yards with Saskatchewan in 1991. **CFL Total Punt Returns - 0 for 2 yards.**

Kickoff Returns - 2 for 33 yards, 16.5 average, longest 19 yards with Saskatchewan in 1992. **CFL Total Kickoff Returns - 2 for 33 yards, 16.5 average, longest 19 yards.**

Own Fumbles Recovered - 1 with Saskatchewan in 1991. **CFL Total OFR - 1.**

Fumble Returns - 1 for 0 yards with Saskatchewan in 1990 and 2 for 37 yards, 18.5 average, longest 32 yards and 1 TD in 1992. **CFL Total Fumble Returns - 3 for 37 yards, 12.3 average, longest 32 yards and 1 TD.**

Tackles - 1 defensive with Saskatchewan in 1990; 13 special teams in 1991; 15 special teams in 1992 and 1 defensive and 19 special teams in 1993. **CFL Total Tackles - 49 (2 defensive and 47 special teams).**

Playoffs

Games Played - 1 with Saskatchewan in 1990; 1 in 1992 and 1 in 1993. **CFL Total Playoff GP - 3.**

Tackles - 2 special teams with Saskatchewan in 1993. **CFL Total Playoff Tackles - 2 (2 special teams).**

PITTS, ALLEN

Born: June 28, 1963
Birthplace: Tucson, Arizona
Wide Receiver. 6'4", 200 lbs. Import
Last Amateur Club: Cal State University at Fullerton
Acquired: Attended the NFL Los Angeles Rams' training camps in 1986 and 1987. Signed as a free agent by the Calgary Stampeders in May, 1990.

	Team	Scoring GP	TD	C	FG	S	TP	Pass Receiving NO	YDS	AVE	LG	TD
1990	Cal.	18	6	x2	0	0	40	65	1172	18.0	67	6
1991abcde	Cal.	18	15	0	0	0	90	118	1764	14.9	87	15
1992abcdf	Cal.	18	13	0	0	0	78	103	1591	15.4	53	13
1993	Cal.	7	4	0	0	0	24	45	776	17.2	37	4
CFL TOTALS		**61**	**38**	**x2**	**0**	**0**	**232**	**331**	**5303**	**16.0**	**87**	**38**

Rushing - 1 for -5 yards with Calgary in 1990. **CFL Total Rushing - 1 for -5 yards.**

Kickoff Returns - 1 for 0 yards with Calgary in 1991; 1 for 0 yards in 1992 and 1 for 0 yards in 1993. **CFL Total Kickoff Returns - 3 for 0 yards.**

Fumbles - 3 and 2 lost with Calgary in 1990; 3 and 3 lost in 1991; 5 and 3 lost in 1992 and 1 and 1 lost in 1993. **CFL Total Fumbles - 12 and 9 lost.**

Own Fumbles Recovered - 1 with Calgary in 1990; 1 in 1992 and 1 in 1993. **CFL Total OFR - 3.**

Defensive Tackles - 4 with Calgary in 1990; 5 in 1991; 5 in 1992 and 1 in 1993. **CFL Total Defensive Tackles - 15.**

a - All-Western All-Star
b - CFL All-Star
c - Led CFL in Receiving Catches
d - Led CFL in Receiving Yards
e - Set CFL Record for Pass Receptions in a Season
f - Led CFL in Yards from Scrimmage (1591)

Playoffs

	Team	Scoring GP	TD	C	FG	S	TP	Pass Receiving NO	YDS	AVE	LG	TD
1990	Cal.	1	1	0	0	0	6	5	93	18.6	31	1
1991	Cal.	2	2	0	0	0	12	13	245	18.8	61	2
1992	Cal.	1	0	0	0	0	0	5	91	18.2	39	0
CFL TOTALS		**4**	**3**	**0**	**0**	**0**	**18**	**23**	**429**	**18.7**	**61**	**3**

Grey Cup

	Team	Scoring GP	TD	C	FG	S	TP	Pass Receiving NO	YDS	AVE	LG	TD
1991	Cal.	1	1	0	0	0	6	4	66	16.5	31	1
1992	Cal.	1	1	0	0	0	6	7	75	10.7	15	1
CFL TOTALS		**2**	**2**	**0**	**0**	**0**	**12**	**11**	**141**	**12.8**	**31**	**2**

PLEASANT, REGGIE

Born: May 2, 1962
Birthplace: Sumter, South Carolina
Cornerback. 5'9", 175 lbs. Import
Last Amateur Club: Clemson University
Acquired: Selected in the sixth round, (152nd overall) in the 1985 NFL Draft by the Atlanta Falcons. Released in August, 1985 and re-signed in September, 1985. Released in October, 1985 and signed as a free agent by the NFL Tampa Bay Buccaneers in March, 1986. Released and signed as a free agent by the Toronto Argonauts in December, 1986.

	Team	GP	Interception Returns NO	YDS	AVE	LG	TD	Fumble Returns NO	YDS	AVE	LG	TD
1987	Tor.	16	9	182	20.2	39	0	2	0	0.0	0	0
1988ab	Tor.	18	7	107	15.3	29	1	0	0	0.0	0	0
1989a	Tor.	17	9	124	13.8	43	0	4	27	6.8	16	2
1990	Tor.	18	9	171	19.0	63	0	2	6	3.0	6	0
1991a	Tor.	18	4	74	18.5	28	0	2	0	0.0	0	0
1992	Tor.	18	4	68	17.0	31	0	1	5	5.0	5	0
1993	Tor.	18	3	27	9.0	24	0	0	0	0.0	0	0
CFL TOTALS		**123**	**45**	**753**	**16.7**	**63**	**1**	**11**	**38**	**3.5**	**16**	**2**

Scoring - 1 TD for 6 points with Toronto in 1988 and 2 TDs for 12 points in 1989. **CFL Total Scoring - 3 TDs for 18 points.**

Kickoff Returns - 1 for 12 yards with Toronto in 1991 and 1 for 0 yards in 1993. **CFL Total Kickoff Returns - 2 for 12 yards, 6.0 average, longest 12 yards.**

Blocked Kicks - 3 punts with Toronto in 1990. **CFL Total Blocked Kicks - 3 punts.**

Punt Returns - 1 for 0 yards with Toronto in 1988 and 2 for 0 yards in 1989. **CFL Total Punt Returns - 3 for 0 yards.**

Fumbles - 1 and 1 lost with Toronto in 1993. **CFL Total Fumbles - 1 and 1 lost.**

Own Fumbles Recovered - 1 with Toronto in 1991. **CFL Total OFR - 1.**

Quarterback Sacks - 1 for 9 yards with Toronto in 1993. **CFL Total QB Sacks - 1 for 9 yards lost.**

Tackles - 58 defensive with Toronto in 1987; 61 defensive in 1988; 52 defensive in 1989; 57 defensive in 1990; 71 defensive in 1991; 43 defensive and 3 special teams in 1992 and 50 defensive and 2 special teams in 1993. **CFL Total Tackles - 397 (392 defensive and 5 special teams).**

Tackles for Losses - 2 for 3 yards with Toronto in 1991; 1 for 19 yards in 1992 and 1 for 7 yards in 1993. **CFL Total Tackles for Losses - 4 for 29 yards.**

PLEASANT, REGGIE

a - All-Eastern All-Star.
b - CFL All-Star.

Playoffs

Games Played - 2 with Toronto in 1987; 1 in 1988; 1 in 1989; 2 in 1990 and 1 in 1991. **CFL Total Playoff GP - 7.**

Defensive Tackles - 2 with Toronto in 1987; 4 in 1988; 1 in 1989; 5 in 1990 and 2 in 1991. **CFL Total Playoff Defensive Tackles - 14.**

Grey Cup

Games Played - 1 with Toronto in 1987 and 1 in 1991. **Total Grey Cup GP - 2.**

Interception Returns - 2 for 26 yards, 13.0 average, longest 28 yards with Toronto in 1991. **Total Grey Cup Interception Returns - 2 for 26 yards, 13.0 average, longest 28 yards.**

Defensive Tackles - 4 with Toronto in 1987 and 5 in 1991. **Total Grey Cup Defensive Tackles - 9.**

PLESS, WILLIE

Born: February 21, 1964
Birthplace: Anniston, Alabama
Linebacker. 5'11", 210 lbs. Import
Last Amateur Club: University of Kansas
Acquired: Signed as a free agent by the Toronto Argonauts in May, 1986. Attended the New Orleans Saints (NFL) training camp in 1989. Released and re-signed by Toronto in October, 1989. Traded to the B.C. Lions in March, 1990 along with defensive lineman Jearld Baylis, quarterback Rick Johnson, wide receiver Emanuel Tolbert, linebacker Tony Visco and defensive back Todd Wiseman in exchange for quarterback Matt Dunigan. Granted free agency status in February, 1991. Signed as a free agent by the Edmonton Eskimos in February, 1991.

			Interception Returns					Fumble Returns				
	Team	GP	NO	YDS	AVE	LG	TD	NO	YDS	AVE	LG	TD
1986abcd	Tor.	12	3	8	2.7	8	0	3	5	1.7	5	0
1987	Tor.	16	5	22	4.4	17	0	3	0	0.0	0	0
1988ab	Tor.	18	2	22	11.0	11	0	3	20	6.7	20	0
1989	Tor.	5	0	0	0.0	0	0	0	0	0.0	0	0
1990be	B.C.	18	5	83	16.6	51	0	4	0	0.0	0	0
1991be	Edm.	18	6	66	11.0	28	0	2	13	6.5	13	0
1992befghij	Edm.	18	5	59	11.8	40	1	8	20	2.5	10	0
1993be	Edm.	16	1	26	26.0	26	0	3	2	0.7	2	1
CFL TOTALS		**121**	**27**	**286**	**10.6**	**51**	**1**	**26**	**60**	**2.3**	**20**	**1**

Scoring - 1 TD for 6 points with Edmonton in 1992 and 1 TD for 6 points in 1993. **CFL Total Scoring - 2 TDs for 12 points.**

Blocked Kicks - 1 punt with B.C. in 1990. **CFL Total Blocked Kicks - 1 punt.**

Kickoff Returns - 1 for 0 yards with Edmonton in 1992. **CFL Total Kickoff Returns - 1 for 0 yards.**

Own Fumbles Recovered - 1 with B.C. in 1990. **CFL Total OFR - 1.**

Quarterback Sacks - 3 with Toronto in 1986; 7 in 1987; 6 in 1988; 4 with B.C. in 1990; 8 with Edmonton in 1991; 8 for 38 yards lost in 1992 and 9 for 43 yards lost in 1993. **CFL Total QB Sacks - 45.**

Tackles - 93 defensive with Toronto in 1987; 96 defensive in 1988; 30 defensive in 1989; 107 defensive with B.C. in 1990; 84 defensive and 20 special teams with Edmonton in 1991; 110 defensive and 11 special teams in 1992 and 77 defensive and 3 special teams in 1993. **CFL Total Tackles - 631 (597 defensive and 34 special teams).**

Tackles for Losses - 5 for 23 yards with Edmonton in 1991; 5 for 24 yards in 1992 and 4 for 7 yards in 1993. **CFL Total Tackles for Losses - 14 for 54 yards.**

a - All-Eastern All-Star.
b - CFL All-Star.
c - Winner of the Frank M. Gibson Trophy, Most Outstanding Rookie, Eastern Division.
d - Schenley runner-up Most Outstanding Rookie.
e - All-Western All-Star.
f - Winner Norm Fieldgate Trophy as Most Defensive Player, Western Division.
g - Winner CFL Most Outstanding Defensive Player.
h - Led CFL in Combined Tackles (129).
i - Led CFL in Fumble Returns.
j - Set CFL Record for Most Career Defensive Tackles (520).

Playoffs

Games Played - 2 with Toronto in 1986; 2 in 1987; 1 in 1988; 1 in 1989; 1 with Edmonton in 1991; 2 in 1992 and 2 in 1993. **CFL Total Playoff GP - 11.**

Interception Returns - 1 for 27 yards with Toronto in 1986 and 0 for 14 yards in 1987. **CFL Total Playoff Interception Returns - 1 for 41 yards, 41.0 average, longest 27 yards.**

Quarterback Sacks - 1 for 5 yards lost with Edmonton in 1992. **CFL Total Playoff QB Sacks - 1 for 5 yards lost.**

Tackles - 13 defensive with Toronto in 1987; 4 defensive in 1988; 4 defensive in 1989; 3 defensive and 3 special teams with Edmonton in 1991; 12 defensive in 1992 and 13 defensive in 1993. **CFL Total Playoff Tackles - 52 (49 defensive and 3 special teams).**

Tackles for Losses - 1 for 2 yards with Edmonton in 1993. **CFL Total Playoff Tackles for Losses - 1 for 2 yards.**

Grey Cup

Games Played - 1 with Toronto in 1987 and 1 with Edmonton in 1993. **Total Grey Cup GP - 2.**

Fumble Returns - 1 with Toronto in 1987. **Total Grey Cup Fumble Returns - 1.**

Defensive Tackles - 5 with Toronto in 1987 and 5 with Edmonton in 1993. **Total Grey Cup Defensive Tackles - 10.**

PLUMMER, BRUCE

Born: September 1, 1964
Birthplace: Bogalusa, Louisiana
Defensive Back. 6'1", 195 lbs. Import
Last Amateur Club: Mississippi State University
Acquired: Selected in the ninth round (250th overall) by the NFL Denver Broncos in the 1987 NFL Draft. Signed by Denver in July, 1987. Released by Denver in November, 1988. Claimed on waivers by the NFL Miami Dolphins in November, 1988. Granted unconditional free agency in February, 1989. Signed as a free agent by the NFL Indianapolis Colts in March, 1989. Granted unconditional free agency in February, 1990. Signed as a free agent by the NFL San Diego Chargers in February, 1990. Released by San Diego in September, 1990. Signed as a free agent by the NFL Denver Broncos in September, 1990. Released by Denver in November, 1990. Signed as a free agent by the NFL San Francisco 49ers in December, 1990. Released by San Francisco in August, 1991. Signed as a free agent by the NFL Philadelphia Eagles in November, 1991. Granted unconditional free agency in February, 1992. Signed as a free agent by the Winnipeg Blue Bombers in February, 1992. Released by Winnipeg in July, 1993. Signed as a free agent by B.C. Lions in August, 1993. Released by B.C. in September, 1993. Signed as a free agent by the Las Vegas Posse in December, 1993.

			Punt Returns					Kickoff Returns			
	Team	GP	NO	YDS	AVE	LG	TD	NO	YDS	AVE	LG	TD
1992	Wpg	5	9	109	12.1	16	0	4	45	11.3	22	0
1993	B.C.	8	0	0	0.0	0	0	1	6	6.0	6	0
CFL TOTALS		**13**	**9**	**109**	**12.1**	**16**	**0**	**5**	**51**	**10.2**	**22**	**0**

Fumbles - 1 and 0 lost with Winnipeg in 1992. **CFL Total Fumbles - 1 and 0 lost.**

Fumble Returns - 1 for 24 yards with Winnipeg in 1992. **CFL Total Fumble Returns - 1 for 24 yards.**

Own Fumbles Recovered - 1 with Winnipeg in 1992. **CFL Total OFR - 1.**

Interception Returns - 1 for 27 yards with B.C. in 1993. **CFL Total Interception Returns - 1 for 27 yards.**

Tackles - 4 defensive and 14 special teams with Winnipeg in 1992 and 23 defensive and 5 special teams with B.C. in 1993. **CFL Total Tackles - 46 (27 defensive and 19 special teams).**

Tackles for Losses - 1 for 2 yards with Winnipeg in 1992. **CFL Total Tackles for Losses - 1 for 2 yards.**

Playoffs

Games Played - 1 with Winnipeg in 1992. **CFL Total Playoff GP - 1.**

Tackles - 3 special teams with Winnipeg in 1992. **CFL Total Playoff Tackles - 3 (3 special teams).**

Grey Cup

Games Played - 1 with Winnipeg in 1992. **Total Grey Cup GP - 1.**

Tackles - 2 special teams with Winnipeg in 1992. **Total Grey Cup Tackles - 2 (2 special teams).**

POPE, MARVIN

Born: January 18, 1969
Birthplace: Gainesville, Florida
Linebacker. 6'1", 240 lbs. Import
Last Amateur Club: Ohio Central University
Acquired: Signed as a free agent by the Calgary Stampeders in May, 1992.

Games Played - 6 with Calgary in 1992 and 18 in 1993. **CFL Total GP - 24.**

Interception Returns - 1 for 25 yards with Calgary in 1993. **CFL Total Interception Returns - 1 for 25 yards.**

Kickoff Returns - 1 for 0 yards with Calgary in 1993. **CFL Total Kickoff Returns - 1 for 0 yards.**

Quarterback Sacks - 1 for 8 yards lost with Calgary in 1993. **CFL Total QB Sacks - 1 for 8 yards lost.**

Tackles for Losses - 4 for 6 yards with Calgary in 1993. **CFL Total Tackles for Losses - 4 for 6 yards.**

POPE, MARVIN

Tackles - 17 defensive and 7 special teams with Calgary in 1992 and 69 defensive and 4 special teams in 1993.
CFL Total Tackles - 97 (86 defensive and 11 special teams).

All-Western All-Star in 1993.

Playoffs

Games Played - 1 with Calgary in 1992 and 2 in 1993.
CFL Total Playoff GP - 3.

Quarterback Sacks - 1 for 1 yard lost with Calgary in 1993.
CFL Total Playoff QB Sacks - 1 for 1 yard lost.

Tackles - 13 defensive with Calgary in 1992 and 10 defensive in 1993.
CFL Total Playoff Tackles - 23 (23 defensive).

Tackles for Losses - 1 for 1 yard with Calgary in 1993.
CFL Total Playoff Tackles for Losses - 1 for 1 yard.

Grey Cup

Games Played - 1 with Calgary in 1992.
Total Grey Cup GP - 1.

Tackles - 3 defensive with Calgary in 1992.
Total Grey Cup Tackles - 3 (3 defensive).

Set a CFL Playoff Record for Most Defensive Tackles in One Game (13) in 1992.

PORRAS, TOM
Born: March 28, 1958
Birthplace: Oxnard, California
Quarterback. 6'2", 200 lbs. Import
Last Amateur Club: University of Washington
Acquired: Signed as a free agent by the NFL's Oakland Raiders in May, 1980. Released in July, 1980. Signed as a free agent by the Montreal Concordes in March, 1982 and released prior to the start of the 1982 season. Signed as a free agent by the USFL's Chicago Blitz in August, 1982. Chicago became Arizona Wranglers in 1984. Selected by the Portland Breakers in the USFL Dispersal Draft in December, 1984. Released by Portland February, 1985 and re-signed by Arizona Outlaws in March, 1985. Released in July, 1985 and signed as a free agent by the Hamilton Tiger-Cats in September, 1985. Released by Hamilton in May, 1989. Signed as a free agent by the Calgary Stampeders in July, 1989. Released by Calgary in November, 1989. Signed as a free agent by the Toronto Argonauts in January, 1990. Released by Toronto in August, 1990. Re-signed by Calgary in September, 1990 and was subsequently released in October, 1990. Re-signed by Toronto in November, 1990 and subsequently released later that same month. Re-signed by Toronto in October, 1991 and was subsequently released by Toronto in November, 1991. Spent the 1992 season with the Arena Football League's Albany Firebirds. Re-signed by Hamilton in June, 1993. Traded to the Winnipeg Blue Bombers in exchange for the rights to Konrad Pimiskern and a third round draft pick in the 1994 CFL College Draft (Tim Tindale).

		Passing							
	Team	GP	ATT	COMP	YDS	PCT	INT	LG	TD
1985	Ham.	8	17	12	134	70.5	1	28	0
1986	Ham.	18	1	1	16	100.0	0	16	0
1987a	Ham.	15	406	242	3293	59.6	17	81	18
1988	Ham.	8	330	170	2172	51.5	16	62	13
1989	Cal.	11	151	69	1011	45.7	9	63	5
1990	Cal.	3	9	3	52	33.3	0	42	0
	Tor.	5	81	45	650	55.6	5	88	4
1991	Tor.	2	0	0	0	0.0	0	0	0
1992		Arena Football League							
1993a	Wpg.	18	10	6	127	60.0	0	54	1
CFL TOTALS		**88**	**1005**	**548**	**7455**	**54.5**	**48**	**88**	**41**

		Rushing					Fumbles		
	Team	NO	YDS	AVE	LG	TD	NO	LOST	OFR
1985	Ham.	12	27	2.3	11	0	1	1	0
1986	Ham.	1	0	0.0	0	0	0	0	0
1987	Ham.	57	247	4.3	30	1	2	2	0
1988	Ham.	45	169	3.8	15	0	2	1	0
1989	Cal.	8	66	8.3	27	0	1	1	0
1990	Cal.	2	13	6.5	13	0	0	0	0
	Tor.	24	74	3.1	15	0	5	3	1
1991	Tor.	0	0	0.0	0	0	0	0	0
1992		Arena Football League					Arena Football League		
1993	Wpg.	1	-1	-1.0	0	0	0	0	0
CFL TOTALS		**150**	**595**	**4.0**	**30**	**0**	**11**	**8**	**1**

Scoring - 1 for 6 points with Hamilton in 1987.
CFL Total Scoring - 1 for 6 points.

2-Pt. Converts - 3 attempts, 1 complete with Hamilton in 1987.
CFL Total 2-Pt. Converts - 3 attempts, 1 complete.

Tackles - 3 defensive with Hamilton in 1987 and 2 with Toronto in 1990.
CFL Total Tackles - 5 (5 defensive).

a - Led CFL in Passing Efficiency Rating (82.7)

Playoffs

		Passing								Rushing				
	Team	GP	ATT	COMP	YDS	PCT	INT	LG	TD	NO	YDS	AVE	LG	TD
1985	Ham.	1	0	0	0	0.0	0	0	0	0	0	0.0	0	0
1986	Ham.	2	0	0	0	0.0	0	0	0	0	0	0.0	0	0
1987	Ham.	1	27	10	104	37.0	3	38	0	3	11	3.7	9	0
1988	Ham.	1	20	10	108	50.0	1	24	0	1	1	1.0	1	0
1990	Tor.	1	7	3	53	42.9	0	33	0	2	1	0.5	1	1
1993	Wpg.	1	0	0	0	0.0	0	0	0	0	0	0.0	0	0
CFL TOTALS		**7**	**54**	**23**	**265**	**42.6**	**4**	**38**	**0**	**6**	**13**	**2.2**	**9**	**1**

Scoring - 1 for 6 points with Toronto in 1990.
CFL Total Playoff Scoring - 1 for 6 points.

Grey Cup

		Passing							
	Team	GP	ATT	COMP	YDS	PCT	INT	LG	TD
1985	Ham.	1	3	1	10	33.3	1	10	0
1986	Ham.	2	0	0	0	0.0	0	0	0
1993	Wpg.	1	0	0	0	0.0	0	0	0
CFL TOTALS		**4**	**0**	**1**	**10**	**33.3**	**1**	**10**	**0**

POWE, KEITH
Born: June 5, 1969
Birthplace: Biloxi, Mississippi
Linebacker. 6'3", 250 lbs. Import
Last Amateur Club: University of Texas-El Paso
Acquired: Attended the NFL Dallas Cowboys' training camp in 1991. Signed as a free agent by the B.C. Lions in September, 1991. Traded to the Toronto Argonauts along with defensive back Patrick Wayne and the rights to a negotiation list player in exchange for a Toronto negotiation list player. Released by Toronto in November, 1993.

Games Played - 9 with B.C. in 1991; 14 in 1992 and 4 with B.C. and 6 with Toronto in 1993. **CFL Total GP - 33.**

Fumble Returns - 1 for 3 yards with B.C. in 1992 and 1 for 0 yards with Toronto in 1993. **CFL Total Fumble Returns - 2 for 3 yards, 1.5 average, longest 3 yards.**

Quarterback Sacks - 1 with B.C. in 1991; 8 for 63 yards lost in 1992 and 1 for 6 yards lost with B.C. and 2 for 14 yards lost with Toronto in 1993.
CFL Total QB Sacks - 12.

Tackles - 16 defensive with B.C. in 1991; 23 defensive and 5 special teams in 1992 and 4 defensive with B.C. and 5 defensive and 2 special teams with Toronto in 1993.
CFL Total Tackles - 55 (48 defensive and 7 special teams).

Tackles for Losses - 3 for 7 yards with B.C. in 1991; 2 for 15 yards in 1992 and 1 for 2 yards with Toronto in 1993.
CFL Total Tackles for Losses - 6 for 24 yards.

Playoffs

Games Played - 1 with B.C. in 1991. **CFL Total Playoff GP - 1.**

Quarterback Sacks - 1 with B.C. in 1991. **CFL Total Playoff QB Sacks - 1.**

Tackles - 1 defensive with B.C. in 1991.
CFL Total Playoff Tackles - 1 (1 defensive).

PRATT, KHEVIN
Born: May 16, 1970
Birthplace: Los Angeles, California
Wide Receiver. 5'10", 170 lbs. Import
Last Amateur Club: California State University at Chico
Acquired: Signed as a free agent by the Sacramento Gold Miners in June, 1993. Released by Sacramento in August, 1993.

Games Played - 3 with Sacramento in 1993. **CFL Total GP - 3.**

Pass Receiving - 1 for 17 yards with Sacramento in 1993.
CFL Total Pass Receiving - 1 for 17 yards.

PRINGLE, MIKE
Born: October 1, 1967
Birthplace: Los Angeles, California
Running Back. 5'8", 186 lbs. Import
Last Amateur Club: Fullerton State University
Acquired: Selected in the sixth round (139th overall) by the NFL Atlanta Falcons in the 1990 NFL Draft. Signed by Atlanta in July, 1990. Released by Atlanta in 1991. Played with the WLAF Sacramento Surge in the 1992 season. Signed as a free agent by the Edmonton Eskimos in June, 1992. Released by Edmonton in July, 1992. Signed as a free agent by the Sacramento Gold Miners in March, 1993.

PRINGLE, MIKE

	Team	Scoring GP	TD	C	FG	S	TP	Rushing NO	YDS	AVE	LG	TD
1992	Edm.	3	0	0	0	0	0	22	129	5.9	30	0
1993	Sac.	18	5	0	0	0	30	60	366	6.1	44	4
CFL TOTALS		**21**	**5**	**0**	**0**	**0**	**30**	**82**	**495**	**6.0**	**44**	**4**

	Team	Pass Receiving NO	YDS	AVE	LG	TD	Kickoff Returns NO	YDS	AVE	LG	TD
1992	Edm.	4	39	9.8	18	0	6	114	19.0	28	0
1993	Sac.	56	523	9.3	24	1	27	549	20.3	36	0
CFL TOTALS		**60**	**562**	**9.4**	**24**	**1**	**33**	**663**	**20.1**	**36**	**0**

Fumbles - 4 and 2 lost with Sacramento in 1993.
CFL Total Fumbles - 4 and 2 lost.

Own Fumbles Recovered - 1 with Sacramento in 1993. **CFL Total OFR - 1.**

Tackles - 1 defensive and 1 special teams with Edmonton in 1992 and 6 defensive and 30 special teams with Sacramento in 1993.
CFL Total Tackles - 38 (7 defensive and 31 special teams).

Tackles for Losses - 1 for 1 yard with Sacramento in 1993.
CFL Total Tackles for Losses - 1 for 1 yard.

Own Kickoffs Recovered - 1 for 24 yards with Sacramento in 1993.
CFL Total Own Kickoffs Recovered - 1 for 24 yards.

PROCTOR, BASIL
Born: October 6, 1967
Birthplace: Miami, Florida
Linebacker. 6'4", 250 lbs. Import
Last Amateur Club: West Virginia University
Acquired: Selected in the seventh round (168th overall) by the NFL New York Jets in the 1990 NFL Draft. Released by New York after training camp. Signed as a free agent by the NFL San Francisco 49ers in 1991 and released in August, 1991. Signed as a free agent by the Saskatchewan Roughriders in August, 1991. Released by Saskatchewan in November, 1991. Selected by the WLAF Sacramento Surge in the 20th round (211th overall) in the 1992 WLAF Draft and spent the 1992 season with them. Signed as a free agent by the Sacramento Gold Miners in March, 1993. Released by Sacramento in July, 1993. Signed as a free agent by the Las Vegas Posse in February, 1994.

Games Played - 5 with Saskatchewan in 1991 and 3 with Sacramento in 1993.
CFL Total GP - 8.

Quarterback Sacks - 1 for 7 yards lost with Sacramento in 1993.
CFL Total QB Sacks - 1 for 7 yards lost.

Tackles - 8 defensive and 1 special teams with Saskatchewan in 1991 and 4 defensive with Sacramento in 1993.
CFL Total Tackles - 13 (12 defensive and 1 special teams).

Tackles for Losses - 3 for 7 yards with Saskatchewan in 1991 and 1 for 1 yard with Sacramento in 1993.
CFL Total Tackles for Losses - 4 for 8 yards.

PROCTOR, MICHAEL
Born: July 14, 1967
Birthplace: Sylvester, Georgia
Quarterback. 6'2", 200 lbs. Import
Last Amateur Club: Murray State University
Acquired: Signed as a free agent by the Saskatchewan Roughriders in March, 1993. Released by Saskatchewan in February, 1994.

Games Played - 1 with Saskatchewan in 1993. **CFL Total GP - 1.**

Playoffs

Games Played - 1 with Saskatchewan in 1993.
CFL Total Playoff GP - 1.

Rushing - 1 for -2 yards with Saskatchewan in 1993.
CFL Total Playoff Rushing - 1 for -2 yards.

PRUITT, JAMES
Born: January, 24, 1964
Birthplace: Los Angeles California
Wide Receiver. 6'3", 201 lbs. Import
Last Amateur Club: California State University at Fullerton
Acquired: Selected by the Miami Dolphins in the fourth round (107th overall) in the 1986 NFL Draft. Selected by the New Jersey Generals in the first round (fifth overall) in the 1986 USFL Draft. Signed by Miami in July, 1986. Released by Miami in November, 1988. Awarded on waivers to the NFL Indianapolis Colts in November, 1988. Granted free agency status in February, 1990. Re-signed by Indianapolis in September 1990 and was subsequently released later that month. Re-signed by Miami in November, 1990. Granted free agency status in February, 1991. Signed as a free agent by the NFL Minnesota Vikings in March, 1991. Was released by Minnesota prior to the start of the 1991 season. Signed as a free agent by the NFL Cleveland Browns in 1993 and was subsequently released during training camp. Signed as a free agent by the Sacramento Gold Miners in September, 1993.

	Team	Scoring GP	TD	C	FG	S	TP	Pass Receiving NO	YDS	AVE	LG	TD
1993	Sac.	8	2	0	0	0	12	15	260	17.3	46	2
CFL TOTALS		**8**	**2**	**0**	**0**	**0**	**12**	**15**	**260**	**17.3**	**46**	**2**

PULERI, CHARLES
Born: March 1, 1969
Birthplace: Bronx, New York
Quarterback. 6'2", 205 lbs. Import
Last Amateur Club: New Mexico State University
Acquired: Signed as a free agent by the Sacramento Gold Miners in May, 1993.

Games Played - 8 with Sacramento in 1993. **CFL Total GP - 8.**

Passing - 2 attempts, 0 complete with Sacramento in 1993.
CFL Total Passing - 2 attempts, 0 complete.

RABY, MICHEL
Born: December 17, 1968
Birthplace: Hull, Quebec
Defensive Tackle. 6'1", 250 lbs. Non-import
Last Amateur Club: University of Ottawa (OQIFC)
Acquired: Selected by the Ottawa Rough Riders in the 1991 CFL Supplemental Draft.

Games Played - 4 with Ottawa in 1991; 14 in 1992 and 16 in 1993.
CFL Total GP - 34.

Fumble Returns - 1 for 0 yards with Ottawa in 1992 and 1 for 0 yards in 1993.
CFL Total Fumble Returns - 2 for 0 yards.

Quarterback Sacks - 2 for 13 yards lost with Ottawa in 1992.
CFL Total QB Sacks - 2 for 13 yards lost.

Tackles - 1 defensive and 3 special teams with Ottawa in 1991; 11 defensive and 5 special teams in 1992 and 18 defensive and 2 special teams in 1993.
CFL Total Tackles - 40 (30 defensive and 10 special teams).

Tackles for Losses - 4 for 18 yards with Ottawa in 1992 and 2 for 20 yards in 1993.
CFL Total Tackles for Losses - 6 for 38 yards.

Playoffs

Games Played - 1 with Ottawa in 1992. **CFL Total Playoff GP - 1.**

Tackles - 1 defensive with Ottawa in 1992.
CFL Total Playoff Tackles - 1 (1 defensive).

RANDOLPH, PAUL
Born: June 22, 1966
Birthplace: Gainsville, Georgia
Linebacker. 6'0", 235 lbs. Import
Last Amateur Club: University of Tennessee Martin
Acquired: Signed as a free agent by the Winnipeg Blue Bombers in December, 1988.

Games Played - 14 with Winnipeg in 1989; 13 in 1990; 17 in 1991; 18 in 1992 and 18 in 1993. **CFL Total GP - 80.**

Pass Receiving - 1 for 47 yards with Winnipeg in 1991.
CFL Total Pass Receiving - 1 for 47 yards.

Punt Returns - 2 for 4 yards, 2.0 average, longest 4 yards with Winnipeg in 1992.
CFL Total Punt Returns - 2 for 4 yards, 2.0 average, longest 2 yards.

Interception Returns - 1 for 0 yards with Winnipeg in 1990; 1 for 2 yards in 1991; 1 for 27 yards in 1992 and 4 for 74 yards, 18.5 average, longest 37 yards in 1993.
CFL Total Interception Returns - 7 for 103 yards, 14.7 average, longest 37 yards.

Fumble Returns - 1 for 23 yards with Winnipeg in 1989; 1 for 0 yards in 1990; 3 for 4 yards, 1.3 average, longest 3 yards in 1991 and 1 for 3 yards in 1992.
CFL Total Fumble Returns - 6 for 30 yards, 5.0 average, longest 23 yards.

Kickoff Returns - 1 for 8 yards with Winnipeg in 1991.
CFL Total Kickoff Returns - 1 for 8 yards.

Blocked Kicks - 1 field goal with Winnipeg in 1992.
CFL Total Blocked Kicks - 1 field goal.

Quarterback Sacks - 2 with Winnipeg in 1989; 3 in 1990; 6 in 1991; 7 for 39 yards lost in 1992 and 3 for 24 yards lost in 1993. **CFL Total QB Sacks - 21.**

RANDOLPH, PAUL

Tackles - 63 defensive with Winnipeg in 1989; 52 defensive in 1990; 49 defensive and 4 special teams in 1991; 70 defensive and 10 special teams in 1992 and 49 defensive and 10 special teams in 1993. **CFL Total Tackles - 307 (283 defensive and 24 special teams).**

Tackles for Losses - 4 for 15 yards with Winnipeg in 1991; 3 for 9 yards in 1992 and 1 for 3 yards in 1993. **CFL Total Tackles for Losses - 8 for 27 yards.**

Playoffs

Games Played - 2 with Winnipeg in 1989; 1 in 1990; 2 in 1991; 1 in 1992 and 1 in 1993. **CFL Total Playoff GP - 7.**

Fumble Returns - 1 for 0 yards with Winnipeg in 1991 and 1 for 0 yards in 1993. **CFL Total Playoff Fumble Returns - 2 for 0 yards.**

Defensive Tackles - 2 with Winnipeg in 1989; 4 in 1991; 3 in 1992 and 4 in 1993. **CFL Total Playoff Defensive Tackles - 13.**

Tackles for Losses - 1 for 2 yards with Winnipeg in 1991 and 1 for 1 yard in 1992. **CFL Total Playoff Tackles for Losses - 2 for 3 yards.**

Grey Cup

Games Played - 1 with Winnipeg in 1990; 1 in 1992 and 1 in 1993. **Total Grey Cup GP - 3.**

Fumble Returns - 1 for 0 yards with Winnipeg in 1993. **CFL Total Grey Cup Fumble Returns - 1 for 0 yards.**

Tackles - 5 defensive with Winnipeg in 1990; 1 defensive and 1 special teams in 1992 and 2 defensive and 1 special teams in 1993. **Total Grey Cup Tackles - 10 (8 defensive and 2 special teams).**

RASHOVICH, DAN
Born: November 30, 1960
Birthplace: Toronto, Ontario
Linebacker. 6'1", 220 lbs. Non-import
Last Amateur Club: Simon Fraser University (EVCO)
Acquired: Selected in the second round (13th overall) by the Ottawa Rough Riders in the 1984 CFL College Draft. Traded to the Calgary Stampeders with wide receiver Dwight Edwards for quarterback Bernard Quarles and wide receiver Phil Charron in May, 1985. Traded to the Toronto Argonauts in June, 1985 for wide receiver Emanuel Tolbert and linebacker Darrell Nicholson. Transferred to Montreal in the Competitive Balance Plan of February, 1987. Selected by the Saskatchewan Roughriders in the second round (14th overall) of the Alouette's dispersal draft in June, 1987. (The pick was obtained from the B.C. Lions for future considerations.) Granted free agency status in February, 1994. Re-signed by Saskatchewan in April, 1994.

Games Played - 16 with Ottawa in 1984; 16 with Toronto in 1985; 18 in 1986; 15 with Saskatchewan in 1987; 18 in 1988; 10 in 1989; 18 in 1990; 18 in 1991; 18 in 1992 and 11 in 1993. **CFL Total GP - 158.**

Fumble Returns - 2 for 0 yards with Ottawa in 1984; 3 for 0 yards with Saskatchewan in 1990; 2 for -3 yards, -1.5 average, longest -3 yards in 1991 and 1 for 0 yards in 1992. **CFL Total Fumble Returns - 8 for -3 yards, -0.4 average, longest 0 yards.**

Kickoff Returns - 4 for 28 yards, 7.0 average, longest 17 yards with Toronto in 1986 and 1 for 5 yards, 5.0 average, longest 17 yards with Saskatchewan in 1989. **CFL Total Kickoff Returns - 5 for 33 yards, 6.6 average, longest 17 yards.**

Interception Returns - 1 for 3 yards with Saskatchewan in 1989 and 1 for 25 yards in 1990. **CFL Total Interception Returns - 2 for 28 yards, 14.0 average, longest 25 yards.**

Quarterback Sacks - 1 with Saskatchewan in 1988; 1 in 1989; 3 in 1990; 3 in 1991 and 4 for 31 yards lost in 1992. **CFL Total QB Sacks - 12.**

Tackles - 2 defensive with Saskatchewan in 1987; 24 defensive in 1988; 22 defensive in 1989; 80 defensive in 1990; 62 defensive and 22 special teams in 1991; 70 defensive and 20 special teams in 1992 and 4 defensive and 15 special teams in 1993.
CFL Total Tackles - 321 (264 defensive and 57 special teams).

Tackles for Losses - 2 for 8 yards with Saskatchewan in 1991 and 4 for 10 yards in 1992. **CFL Total Tackles for Losses - 6 for 18 yards.**

All-Western All-Star in 1990.

Playoffs

Games Played - 2 with Toronto in 1986; 1 with Saskatchewan in 1988; 2 in 1989; 1 in 1990; 1 in 1992 and 1 in 1993. **CFL Total Playoff GP - 8.**

Quarterback Sacks - 2 with Saskatchewan in 1989 and 1 in 1990. **CFL Total Playoff QB Sacks - 3.**

Tackles - 2 defensive with Saskatchewan in 1988; 5 defensive in 1989; 2 defensive in 1990; 1 special teams in 1992 and 3 defensive and 1 special teams in 1993. **CFL Total Playoff Tackles - 14 (12 defensive and 2 special teams).**

Grey Cup

Games Played - 1 with Saskatchewan in 1989. **Total Grey Cup GP - 1.**

Defensive Tackles - 3 with Saskatchewan in 1989. **Total Grey Cup Defensive Tackles - 3.**

RICHARDS, DWIGHT
Born: July 9, 1969
Birthplace: Kingston, Jamaica
Running Back. 5'10", 200 lbs. Non-import
Last Amateur Club: Weber State University
Acquired: Selected in the second round (10th overall) by the Ottawa Rough Riders in the 1993 CFL College Draft. Claimed on waivers by the Toronto Argonauts in October, 1993.

		Rushing						Pass Receiving				
	Team	GP	NO	YDS	AVE	LG	TD	NO	YDS	AVE	LG	TD
1993	Ott.	12	45	124	2.8	19	0	17	125	7.4	24	0
	Tor.	3	0	0	0.0	0	0	0	0	0.0	0	0
CFL TOTALS		**15**	**45**	**124**	**2.8**	**19**	**0**	**17**	**125**	**7.4**	**24**	**0**

		Punt Returns					Kickoff Returns				
	Team	NO	YDS	AVE	LG	TD	NO	YDS	AVE	LG	TD
1993	Ott.	1	5	5.0	5	0	2	26	13.0	22	0
	Tor.	0	0	0.0	0	0	0	0	0.0	0	0
CFL TOTALS		**1**	**5**	**5.0**	**5**	**0**	**2**	**26**	**13.0**	**22**	**0**

Fumbles - 3 and 2 lost with Ottawa in 1993. **CFL Total Fumbles - 3 and 2 lost.**

Tackles - 5 special teams with Ottawa and 3 special teams with Toronto in 1993. **CFL Total Tackles - 8 (8 special teams).**

RICHARDSON, DAVE
Born: July 1, 1967
Birthplace: Edmonton, Alberta
Tackle. 6'4", 275 lbs. Non-import
Last Amateur Club: Edmonton Wildcats Juniors
Acquired: Signed as a territorial player by the Edmonton Eskimos in July, 1988. Traded by Edmonton in July, 1990 to the Hamilton Tiger-Cats in exchange for a fourth round draft choice in the 1991 CFL College Draft, defensive back Gordon Walker. Granted free agency status in February, 1993. Re-signed with Hamilton in June, 1993.

Games Played - 15 with Edmonton in 1988; 5 in 1989; 7 with Hamilton in 1990; 17 in 1991; 14 in 1992 and 18 in 1993. **CFL Total GP - 76.**

Fumble Returns - 1 for 0 yards with Hamilton in 1993. **CFL Total Fumble Returns - 1 for 0 yards.**

Rushing - 0 for 2 yards with Hamilton in 1993. **CFL Total Rushing - 0 for 2 yards.**

Own Fumbles Recovered - 1 with Edmonton in 1988; 1 with Hamilton in 1991 and 2 in 1993. **CFL Total OFR - 4.**

Tackles - 1 special teams with Hamilton in 1991; 1 defensive in 1992 and 1 defensive in 1993. **CFL Total Tackles - 3 (2 defensive and 1 special teams).**

Playoffs

Games Played - 1 with Edmonton in 1988; 1 in 1989 and 2 with Hamilton in 1992. **CFL Total Playoff GP - 4.**

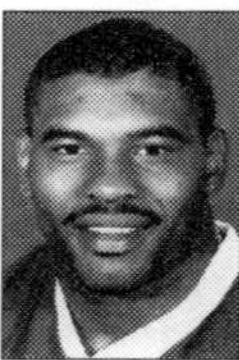

RICHARDSON, MICHAEL
Born: October 13, 1969
Birthplace: Natchez, Louisiana
Running Back. 6'0", 195 lbs. Import
Last Amateur Club: Louisiana Tech University
Acquired: Signed as a free agent by the NFL New York Giants in 1991 and was released after training camp. Signed as a free agent by the Winnipeg Blue Bombers in April, 1992. Granted free agency status in February, 1994. Signed as a free agent by the Ottawa Rough Riders in March, 1994.

		Scoring						Rushing				
	Team	GP	TD	C	FG	S	TP	NO	YDS	AVE	LG	TD
1992abcdef	Wpg.	11	6	0	0	0	36	211	1153	5.5	31	3
1993abd	Wpg.	12	6	0	0	0	36	165	925	5.6	26	4
CFL TOTALS		**23**	**12**	**0**	**0**	**0**	**72**	**376**	**2078**	**5.5**	**31**	**7**

		Pass Receiving					Kickoff Returns				
	Team	NO	YDS	AVE	LG	TD	NO	YDS	AVE	LG	TD
1992	Wpg.	27	263	9.7	41	3	7	172	24.6	38	0
1993	Wpg.	46	378	8.2	26	2	0	0	0.0	0	0
CFL TOTALS		**73**	**641**	**8.8**	**41**	**5**	**7**	**172**	**24.6**	**38**	**0**

		Fumbles		
	Team	NO	LOST	OFR
1992	Wpg.	12	9	2
1992	Wpg.	7	4	0
CFL TOTALS		**19**	**13**	**2**

Tackles - 3 defensive with Winnipeg in 1992. **CFL Total Tackles - 3 (3 defensive).**

a - All-Eastern All-Star
b - CFL All-Star
c - Led CFL in Rushing Carries
d - Led CFL in Rushing Yards
e - Winner Frank M. Gibson Trophy, Most Outstanding Rookie in Eastern Division
f - Winner CFL Most Outstanding Rookie

RICHARDSON, MICHAEL

Playoffs

	Team	GP	TD	C	FG	S	TP		NO	YDS	AVE	LG	TD
		Scoring							Rushing				
1992	Wpg.	1	3	0	0	0	18		33	227	6.9	33	3
1993	Wpg.	1	0	0	0	0	0		27	114	4.2	11	0
CFL TOTALS		**2**	**3**	**0**	**0**	**0**	**18**		**60**	**341**	**5.7**	**33**	**3**

	Team	NO	YDS	AVE	LG	TD		NO	LOST	OFR
		Pass Receiving						Fumbles		
1992	Wpg.	2	20	10.0	15	0		0	0	0
1993	Wpg.	3	26	8.7	11	0		2	1	1
CFL TOTALS		**5**	**46**	**9.2**	**15**	**0**		**2**	**1**	**1**

Grey Cup

	Team	GP	TD	C	FG	S	TP		NO	YDS	AVE	LG	TD
		Scoring							Rushing				
1992	Wpg.	1	0	0	0	0	0		8	27	3.4	13	0
1993	Wpg.	1	1	0	0	0	6		10	26	2.6	8	1
CFL TOTALS		**2**	**1**	**0**	**0**	**0**	**6**		**18**	**53**	**2.9**	**13**	**1**

	Team	NO	YDS	AVE	LG	TD
		Pass Receiving				
1992	Wpg.	3	18	6.0	11	0
1993	Wpg.	4	44	11.0	34	0
CFL TOTALS		**7**	**62**	**8.9**	**34**	**0**

Tackles - 1 defensive with Winnipeg in 1993.
Total Grey Cup Tackles - 1 (1 defensive).

RICKS, MARK

Born: December 16, 1969
Birthplace: Los Angeles, California
Cornerback. 5'9", 160 lbs. Import
Last Amateur Club: Western Michigan University
Acquired: Signed as a free agent by the Saskatchewan Roughriders in April, 1993. Released by Saskatchewan in September, 1993. Signed as a free agent by the Toronto Argonauts in October, 1993 and was subsequently released in November, 1993.

Games Played - 2 with Saskatchewan and 4 with Toronto in 1993.
CFL Total GP - 6.

Interception Returns - 1 for 0 yards with Toronto in 1993.
CFL Total Interception Returns - 1 for 0 yards.

Kickoff Returns - 2 for 31 yards, 15.5 average, longest 19 yards with Saskatchewan in 1993. **CFL Total Kickoff Returns - 2 for 31 yards, 15.5 average, longest 19 yards.**

Fumble Returns - 1 for 5 yards with Toronto in 1993.
CFL Total Fumble Returns - 1 for 5 yards.

Own Kickoffs Recovered - 1 for 9 yards with Toronto in 1993.
CFL Total OKR - 1 for 9 yards.

Tackles - 2 defensive and 2 special teams with Saskatchewan and 18 defensive with Toronto in 1993.
CFL Total Tackles - 22 (20 defensive and 2 special teams).

RIDGWAY, DAVID

Born: April 24, 1959
Birthplace: Stockport, England
Kicker. 6'1", 190 lbs. Non-import
Last Amateur Club: University of Toledo
Acquired: Selected in the seventh round (46th overall) by the Montreal Alouettes in the 1981 CFL College Draft. Released by Montreal in June, 1981. Tried out with the Winnipeg Blue Bombers before signing as a free agent with the Saskatchewan Roughriders in April, 1982. Traded to Edmonton along with Saskatchewan's third round selection in the 1987 CFL College Draft (offensive lineman Todd Storme) for offensive tackle Bryan Illerbrun. Traded to Montreal along with quarterback Brad Taylor and Edmonton's first round selection in the 1987 CFL Draft (offensive lineman Matthew Salo) for offensive tackle Trevor Bowles in February, 1987. Selected by Saskatchewan in the second round, 10th overall, in the Alouettes' Dispersal Draft of June, 1987.

	Team	GP	TD	C	FG	S	TP	T	G	YDS	AVE	LK	PCT
		Scoring						Field Goals					
1982abc	Sask.	16	0	34	38	15	163	51	38	1260	33.2	53	74.5
1983	Sask.	16	0	31	22	14	111	35	22	795	36.1	47	62.9
1984d	Sask.	16	0	30	28	13	127	42	28	935	33.4	55	66.7
1985	Sask.	16	0	25	23	15	109	38	23	785	34.1	52	60.5
1986	Sask.	18	0	34	37	8	153	50	37	1162	31.4	50	74.0
1987abe	Sask.	17	0	23	49	4	174	57	49	1543	31.5	60	86.0
1988abfghij	Sask.	18	0	45	55	5	215	66	55	1934	35.2	53	83.3
1989abk	Sask.	18	0	49	54	5	216	68	54	1586	29.4	53	79.4
1990abfgjl	Sask.	18	0	47	59	9	233	72	59	1905	32.3	53	81.9
1991ag	Sask.	18	0	56	52	4	216	61	52	1680	32.3	52	85.2
1992	Sask.	18	0	50	36	7	165	47	36	1013	28.1	47	76.6
1993abgm	Sask.	18	0	51	48	1	196	53	48	1315	27.4	50	90.6
CFL TOTALS		**207**	**0**	**475**	**501**	**100**	**2078**	**640**	**501**	**15913**	**31.8**	**60**	**78.3**

	Team	T	G	PCT		NO	YDS	AVE	LK	S
		Converts				Field Goal Attempts				
1982	Sask.	34	34	100.0		13	553	42.5	58	9
1983	Sask.	32	31	96.9		13	563	43.3	61	11
1984	Sask.	30	30	100.0		14	665	47.5	58	10
1985	Sask.	25	25	100.0		15	677	45.1	58	9
1986	Sask.	35	34	97.1		13	575	44.2	60	8
1987	Sask.	23	23	100.0		8	358	44.8	50	4
1988	Sask.	45	45	100.0		11	369	33.5	51	5
1989	Sask.	49	49	100.0		14	570	40.7	56	5
1990	Sask.	48	47	97.9		13	617	47.5	67	9
1991	Sask.	56	56	100.0		9	327	36.3	60	3
1992	Sask.	50	50	100.0		11	508	46.2	57	7
1993	Sask.	51	51	100.0		5	229	45.8	53	1
CFL TOTALS		**478**	**475**	**99.4**		**139**	**6011**	**43.2**	**67**	**81**

	Team	NO	YDS	AVE	LK	S		NO	YDS	AVE	LK	S
		Kickoffs						Punting				
1982	Sask.	65	3810	58.6	90	6		0	0	0.0	0	0
1983	Sask.	60	3400	56.7	90	3		0	0	0.0	0	0
1984	Sask.	60	3412	56.9	90	3		10	411	41.1	57	0
1985	Sask.	53	3146	59.4	89	6		0	0	0.0	0	0
1986	Sask.	77	4629	60.1	72	0		0	0	0.0	0	0
1987	Sask.	67	3489	52.1	83	0		0	0	0.0	0	0
1988	Sask.	83	4449	53.6	95	0		0	0	0.0	0	0
1989	Sask.	90	4737	52.6	95	0		0	0	0.0	0	0
1990	Sask.	99	5219	52.7	72	0		0	0	0.0	0	0
1991	Sask.	108	5600	51.9	75	1		0	0	0.0	0	0
1992	Sask.	97	4959	51.1	71	0		0	0	0.0	0	0
1993	Sask.	86	4450	51.7	76	0		0	0	0.0	0	0
CFL TOTALS		**945**	**51300**	**54.3**	**95**	**19**		**10**	**411**	**41.1**	**57**	**0**

Fumble Returns - 1 with Saskatchewan in 1985. **CFL Total Fumble Returns - 1.**

Fumbles - 1 and 0 lost with Saskatchewan in 1984; 1 and 0 lost in 1986; 1 and 0 lost in 1987; 1 and 1 lost in 1988; 1 and 1 lost in 1989; 2 and 1 lost in 1991; 1 and 1 lost in 1992 and 1 and 1 lost in 1993.
CFL Total Fumbles - 9 and 5 lost.

Tackles - 1 special teams with Saskatchewan in 1991 and 2 special teams in 1992. **CFL Total Tackles - 3 (3 special teams).**

a - All-Western All-Star.
b - CFL All-Star.
c - Set CFL Record for the Most Points in one Season by a rookie.
d - Set CFL Record for the Most Field Goals in One Game with 8 against Ottawa at Ottawa on July 29, 1984.
e - Set CFL Record - Longest Field Goal, 60 yards, Saskatchewan vs. Winnipeg, Sept. 6, 1987.
f - Led CFL in Points - Kicking.
g - Led CFL in Field Goals Made.
h - Set CFL Record for Most Points in a Season, since surpassed by Paul Osbaldiston.
i - Equalled CFL Record for the Most Field Goals in One Game (8) against Edmonton at Regina July 23, 1988.
j - Set CFL Record for Most Field Goals in a season.
k - Shared CFL Lead for Field Goals with Hamilton's Paul Osbaldiston.
l - Equalled CFL Record for Most Points in a Season.
m- Set CFL Record for Most Consecutive Field Goals (28)

Playoffs

	Team	GP	TD	C	FG	S	TP		NO	YDS	AVE	LK	S
		Scoring							Kickoffs				
1988	Sask.	1	0	2	1	1	6		5	271	54.2	77	0
1989	Sask.	2	0	7	5	0	22		13	696	53.5	64	0
1990	Sask.	1	0	3	2	0	9		4	201	50.3	74	0
1992	Sask.	1	0	2	2	0	8		4	203	50.8	62	0
1993	Sask.	1	0	1	2	0	7		5	256	51.2	58	0
CFL TOTALS		**6**	**0**	**15**	**12**	**1**	**52**		**31**	**1627**	**52.5**	**77**	**0**

	Team	T	G	YDS	AVE	LK	PCT		NO	YDS	AVE	LK	S
		Field Goals							Field Goal Attempts				
1988	Sask.	3	1	13	13.0	13	33.3		2	101	50.5	61	1
1989	Sask.	7	5	173	34.6	44	71.4		2	23	11.5	23	0
1990	Sask.	3	2	59	29.5	32	66.7		1	42	42.0	42	0
1992	Sask.	2	2	42	21.0	27	100.0		0	0	0.0	0	0
1993	Sask.	2	2	66	33.0	33	100.0		0	0	0.0	0	0
CFL TOTALS		**17**	**12**	**353**	**29.4**	**44**	**70.6**		**5**	**166**	**32.2**	**61**	**1**

Converts - 2 for 2 with Saskatchewan in 1988; 7 for 7 in 1989; 3 for 3 in 1990 and 1 for 1 in 1993. **CFL Total Playoff Converts - 13 for 13.**

Grey Cup

Games Played - 1 with Saskatchewan in 1989. **Total Grey Cup GP - 1.**

Scoring - 4 Converts and 4 Field Goals with Saskatchewan in 1989 for 16 points.
Total Grey Cup Scoring - 16 points.

Converts - 4 for 4 with Saskatchewan in 1989.
Total Grey Cup Converts - 4 for 4.

Kickoffs - 8 for 440 yards, 55.0 average, longest 63 yards with Saskatchewan in 1989. **Total Grey Cup Kickoffs - 8 for 440 yards, 55.0 average, longest 63 yards.**

RIDGWAY, DAVID

Field Goals - 5 tried and 4 good for 114 yards, 28.5 average, longest 35 yards with Saskatchewan in 1989.
Total Grey Cup Field Goals - 5 tried and 4 good for 114 yards, 28.5 average, longest 35 yards.

Field Goal Attempts - 1 for 45 yards with Saskatchewan in 1989.
Total Grey Cup Field Goal Attempts - 1 for 45 yards.

Winner Dick Suderman Trophy (Most Outstanding Canadian - Grey Cup) 1989.

RILEY, JASON

Born: October 4, 1958
Birthplace: Scarborough, Ontario
Guard. 6'4", 270 lbs. Non-import
Last Amateur Club: University of British Columbia (WIFL)
Acquired: Selected in the first round (seventh overall) by the Winnipeg Blue Bombers in the 1982 CFL College Draft. Traded to the Saskatchewan Roughriders in October, 1983 as part of a trade earlier in the month in which Saskatchewan received quarterback Carl (Nickie) Hall, wide receiver Nate Johnson and Winnipeg's fourth round pick in the 1984 CFL College Draft (offensive tackle Angelo Visentin) for quarterback John Hufnagel and defensive end J.C. Pelusi. Released by Saskatchewan in August, 1984 and signed as a free agent by the Hamilton Tiger-Cats in September, 1984. Granted free agency status in February, 1993. Retired in August, 1993.

Games Played - 3 with Winnipeg in 1983; 7 with Saskatchewan in 1984; 6 with Hamilton in 1984; 14 in 1985; 18 in 1986; 18 in 1987; 17 in 1988; 18 in 1989; 16 in 1990; 18 in 1991; 18 in 1992 and 9 in 1993. **CFL Total GP - 162.**

Rushing - 1 for -3 yards with Hamilton in 1992.
CFL Total Rushing - 1 for -3 yards.

Own Fumbles Recovered - 1 with Saskatchewan in 1984; 1 with Hamilton in 1985; 1 in 1988; 1 in 1989; 3 in 1990 and 2 in 1992. **CFL Total OFR - 9.**

Defensive Tackles - 2 with Hamilton in 1989; 1 in 1990; 3 in 1991 and 2 in 1992.
CFL Total Defensive Tackles - 8.

All-Eastern All-Star in 1986, 1988, 1989 and 1992.
CFL All-Star in 1989.

Playoffs

Games Played - 2 with Hamilton in 1984; 1 in 1985; 2 in 1986; 1 in 1988; 1 in 1989 and 2 in 1992.
CFL Total Playoff GP - 9.

Pass Receiving - 1 for 21 yards with Hamilton in 1989.
CFL Total Playoff Pass Receiving - 1 for 21 yards.

Fumbles - 1 and 1 lost with Hamilton in 1989.
CFL Total Playoff Fumbles - 1 and 1 lost.

Grey Cup

Games Played - 1 with Hamilton in 1984; 1 in 1985; 1 in 1986 and 1 in 1989.
Total Grey Cup GP - 4.

RINGOEN, LEIF ERIK

Born: July 1, 1968
Birthplace: Wilmington, Delaware
Linebacker. 6'3", 235 lbs. Import
Last Amateur Club: Hofstra University
Acquired: Selected in the 10th round (266th overall) by the NFL Seattle Seahawks in the 1991 NFL Draft. Released by Seattle in August,1991. Signed as a free agent by the Toronto Argonauts in April, 1992. Released by Toronto in September, 1992. Signed as a free agent by the Baltimore CFL Colts in March, 1994.

Games Played - 2 with Toronto in 1992. **CFL Total GP - 2.**

Tackles - 8 defensive and 1 special teams with Toronto in 1992.
CFL Total Tackles - 9 (8 defensive and 1 special teams).

Tackles for Losses - 1 for 1 yard with Toronto in 1992.
CFL Total Tackles for Losses - 1 for 1 yard.

ROBERTS, JED

Born: November 10, 1967
Birthplace: Grand Prairie, Texas
Linebacker. 6'2", 230 lbs. Non-import
Last Amateur Club: North Colorado State University
Acquired: Signed as a free agent by the Winnipeg Blue Bombers in June, 1990 and released by Winnipeg later that month. Signed as a free agent by the Edmonton Eskimos in September, 1990.

Games Played - 2 with Edmonton in 1990; 18 in 1991; 18 in 1992 and 18 in 1993.
CFL Total GP - 56.

Fumble Returns - 3 for 4 yards, 1.3 average, longest 14 yards with Edmonton in 1992. **CFL Total Fumble Returns - 3 for 4 yards, 1.3 average, longest 14 yards.**

Interception Returns - 1 for 0 yards with Edmonton in 1993.
CFL Total Interception Returns - 1 for 0 yards.

Quarterback Sacks - 2 for 16 yards lost with Edmonton in 1992 and 10 for 69 yards lost in 1993. **CFL Total QB Sacks - 12 for 85 yards lost.**

Tackles - 4 defensive and 23 special teams with Edmonton in 1991; 10 defensive and 20 special teams in 1992 and 17 defensive and 14 special teams in 1993.
CFL Total Tackles - 88 (31 defensive and 57 special teams).

Tackles for Losses - 1 for 3 yards with Edmonton in 1991.
CFL Total Tackles for Losses - 1 for 3 yards.

Playoffs

Games Played - 1 with Edmonton in 1991; 2 in 1992 and 2 in 1993.
CFL Total Playoff GP - 5.

Tackles - 1 defensive and 3 special teams with Edmonton in 1992 and 1 defensive and 3 special teams in 1993.
CFL Total Playoff Tackles - 8 (2 defensive and 6 special teams).

Quarterback Sacks - 1 for 11 yards lost with Edmonton in 1992.
CFL Total Playoff QB Sacks - 1 for 11 yards lost.

Grey Cup

Games Played - 1 with Edmonton in 1993. **Total Grey Cup GP - 1.**

ROBERTS, MARSHALL

Born: August 17, 1969
Birthplace: Abington, Pennsylvania
Cornerback. 5'9", 170 lbs. Import
Last Amateur Club: Rutgers University
Acquired: Signed as a free agent by the Sacramento Gold Miners in May, 1993. Released by Sacramento in August, 1993.

Games Played - 5 with Sacramento in 1993. **CFL Total GP - 5.**

Interception Returns - 1 for 0 yards with Sacramento in 1993.
CFL Total Interception Returns - 1 for 0 yards.

Fumble Returns - 1 for 20 yards with Sacramento in 1993.
CFL Total Fumble Returns - 1 for 20 yards.

Tackles - 5 defensive and 2 special teams with Sacramento in 1993.
CFL Total Tackles - 7 (5 defensive and 2 special teams).

ROBINSON, JUNIOR

Born: February 3, 1968
Birthplace: High Point, North Carolina
Cornerback. 5'9", 181 lbs. Import
Last Amateur Club: East Carolina University
Acquired: Selected by the New England Patriots in the fifth round (110th overall) in the 1990 NFL Draft. Released by New England in August, 1991. Selected by the Sacramento Surge in the fourth round (35th overall) in the 1992 WLAF Draft. Signed as a free agent by the NFL Detroit Lions in June, 1992. Granted unconditional free agency in March, 1993. Signed as a free agent by the Sacramento Gold Miners in September, 1993.

Games Played - 8 with Sacramento in 1993. **CFL Total GP - 8.**

Interception Returns - 1 for 6 yards with Sacramento in 1993.
CFL Total Interception Returns - 1 for 6 yards.

Tackles - 28 defensive and 1 special teams with Sacramento in 1993.
CFL Total Tackles - 29 (28 defensive and 1 special teams).

ROBINSON, LYBRANT

Born: August 31, 1964
Birthplace: Salisbury, Maryland
Defensive End. 6'5", 250 lbs. Import
Last Amateur Club: Delaware State University
Acquired: Selected in the fifth round (139th overall) by the Washington Redskins in the 1989 NFL Draft. Granted unconditional free agency status in February, 1990. Signed by NFL Dallas Cowboys in March, 1990. Released and signed by the Ottawa Rough Riders in December, 1990.

Games Played - 7 with Ottawa in 1991; 15 in 1992 and 16 in 1993.
CFL Total GP - 38.

ROBINSON, LYBRANT

Fumble Returns - 1 for 0 yards with Ottawa in 1991 and 1 for 0 yards in 1992. **CFL Total Fumble Returns - 2 for 0 yards.**

Quarterback Sacks - 2 with Ottawa in 1991; 3 for 7 yards lost in 1992 and 7 for 49 yards lost in 1993. **CFL Total QB Sacks - 12.**

Tackles - 15 defensive with Ottawa in 1991; 39 defensive in 1992 and 26 defensive and 1 special teams in 1993. **CFL Total Tackles - 81 (80 defensive and 1 special teams).**

Tackles for Losses - 2 for 8 yards with Ottawa in 1991; 8 for 23 yards in 1992 and 5 for 16 yards in 1993. **CFL Total Tackles for Losses - 15 for 47 yards.**

Playoffs

Games Played - 1 with Ottawa in 1992 and 1 in 1993. **CFL Total Playoff GP - 2.**

Fumble Returns - 1 for 0 yards with Ottawa in 1992 and 1 for 0 yards in 1993. **CFL Total Playoff Fumble Returns - 2 for 0 yards.**

Tackles - 1 defensive and 1 special teams with Ottawa in 1992 and 4 defensive in 1993. **CFL Total Playoff Tackles - 6 (5 defensive and 1 special teams).**

Tackles for Losses - 2 for 2 yards with Ottawa in 1993. **CFL Total Playoff Tackles for Losses - 2 for 2 yards.**

RODEHUTSKORS, STEVE
Born: November 27, 1963
Birthplace: Calgary, Alberta
Tackle. 6'6", 265 lbs. Non-import
Last Amateur Club: University of Calgary (WIFL)
Acquired: Selected in the third round (22nd overall) by the Winnipeg Blue Bombers in the 1987 CFL College Draft. Granted free agency status in February, 1992. Signed as a free agent by the B.C. Lions in April, 1992. Traded to the Toronto Argonauts in exchange for a first round draft pick in the 1994 CFL College Draft in July, 1993.

Games Played - 18 with Winnipeg in 1987; 18 in 1988; 18 in 1989; 18 in 1990; 18 in 1991; 18 in 1992; 2 with B.C. in 1993 and 12 with Toronto in 1993. **CFL Total GP - 122.**

Fumble Returns - 1 for 5 yards with Winnipeg in 1987. **CFL Total Fumble Returns - 1 for 5 yards.**

Defensive Tackles - 1 with Winnipeg in 1989; 1 in 1991; 2 in 1992; 1 with B.C. in 1993 and 3 with Toronto in 1993. **CFL Total Defensive Tackles - 8.**

Playoffs

Games Played - 1 with Winnipeg in 1987; 2 in 1988; 2 in 1989; 1 in 1990 and 2 in 1991. **CFL Total Playoff GP - 8.**

Grey Cup

Games Played - 1 with Winnipeg in 1988 and 1 in 1990. **Total Grey Cup GP - 2.**

ROGERS, BRENDAN
Born: February 25, 1968
Birthplace: Vancouver, B.C.
Linebacker. 6'1", 235 lbs. Non-import
Last Amateur Club: East Washington University
Acquired: Selected in the fourth round (32nd overall) by the Winnipeg Blue Bombers in the 1991 CFL College Draft.

Games Played - 15 with Winnipeg in 1991; 16 in 1992 and 18 in 1993. **CFL Total GP - 49.**

Pass Receiving - 1 for -10 yards with Winnipeg in 1992. **CFL Total Pass Receiving - 1 for -10 yards.**

Interception Returns - 1 for 0 yards with Winnipeg in 1993. **CFL Total Interception Returns - 1 for 0 yards.**

Punt Returns - 1 for 7 yards with Winnipeg in 1992. **CFL Total Punt Returns - 1 for 7 yards.**

Fumble Returns - 1 for 0 yards with Winnipeg in 1992. **CFL Total Fumble Returns - 1 for 0 yards.**

Own Fumbles Recovered - 1 with Winnipeg in 1993. **CFL Total OFR - 1.**

Kickoff Returns - 2 for 14 yards, 7.0 average, longest 10 yards with Winnipeg in 1992. **CFL Total Kickoff Returns - 2 for 14 yards, 7.0 average, longest 10 yards.**

Quarterback Sacks - 1 with Winnipeg in 1991. **CFL Total QB Sacks - 1.**

Tackles - 4 defensive and 16 special teams with Winnipeg in 1991; 21 special teams in 1992 and 5 defensive and 31 special teams in 1993. **CFL Total Tackles - 77 (9 defensive and 68 special teams).**

Tackles for Losses - 1 for 4 yards with Winnipeg in 1991 and 2 for 3 yards in 1993. **CFL Total Tackles for Losses - 3 for 7 yards.**

Led CFL in Special Teams Tackles in 1993.

Playoffs

Games Played - 2 with Winnipeg in 1991; 1 in 1992 and 1 in 1993. **CFL Total Playoff GP - 4.**

Tackles - 1 special teams with Winnipeg in 1991; 2 special teams in 1992 and 1 defensive and 1 special teams in 1993. **CFL Total Playoff Tackles - 5 (1 defensive and 4 special teams).**

Grey Cup

Games Played - 1 with Winnipeg in 1992 and 1 in 1993. **Total Grey Cup GP - 2.**

Tackles - 1 special teams with Winnipeg in 1992 and 1 special teams in 1993. **Total Grey Cup Tackles - 2 (2 special teams).**

ROGERS, ERNIE
Born: January 3, 1968
Birthplace: Santa Ana, California
Offensive Tackle. 6'5", 290 lbs. Import
Last Amateur Club: California University
Acquired: Selected by the Miami Dolphins in the eleventh round (302nd overall) in the 1991 NFL Draft. Released by Miami during training camp. Selected by the Sacramento Surge in the 1992 WLAF Supplemental Draft. Signed as a free agent by the Sacramento Gold Miners in May, 1993.

Games Played - 2 with Sacramento in 1993. **CFL Total GP - 2.**

ROGERS, GLENN JR.
Born: June 8, 1969
Birthplace: Memphis, Tennessee
Defensive Back. 6'0", 180 lbs. Import
Last Amateur Club: Memphis State University
Acquired: Signed as a free agent by the Edmonton Eskimos in June, 1993.

			Interception Returns					Fumble Returns				
	Team	GP	NO	YDS	AVE	LG	TD	NO	YDS	AVE	LG	TD
1993	Edm.	18	5	7	1.4	6	0	1	15	15.0	15	0
CFL TOTALS		**18**	**5**	**7**	**1.4**	**6**	**0**	**1**	**15**	**15.0**	**15**	**0**

Own Fumbles Recovered - 1 with Edmonton in 1993. **CFL Total OFR - 1.**

Quarterback Sacks - 1 for 12 yards lost with Edmonton in 1993. **CFL Total QB Sacks - 1 for 12 yards lost.**

Tackles - 62 defensive and 3 special teams with Edmonton in 1993. **CFL Total Tackles - 65 (62 defensive and 3 special teams).**

Tackles for Losses - 1 for 3 yards with Edmonton in 1993. **CFL Total Tackles for Losses - 1 for 3 yards.**

a - All-Western All Star

Playoffs

Games Played - 2 with Edmonton in 1993. **CFL Total Playoff GP - 2.**

Fumble Returns - 1 for 13 yards with Edmonton in 1993. **CFL Total Playoff Fumble Returns - 1 for 13 yards.**

Tackles - 4 defensive with Edmonton in 1993. **CFL Total Playoff Tackles - 4 (4 defensive).**

Grey Cup

Games Played - 1 with Edmonton in 1993. **Total Grey Cup GP - 1.**

Tackles - 2 defensive with Edmonton in 1993. **Total Grey Cup Tackles - 2 (2 defensive)**

ROGERS, REGGIE
Born: January 21, 1964
Birthplace: Sacramento, California
Defensive End. 6'6", 285 lbs. Import
Last Amateur Club: University of Washington
Acquired: Selected by the Detroit Lions in the first round (seventh overall) in the 1987 NFL Draft. Granted free agency status in February, 1989. Signed as a free agent by the NFL Buffalo Bills in February, 1991. Released by Buffalo in October, 1991. Signed as a free agent by the NFL Tampa Bay Buccaneers in February, 1992. Released by Tampa Bay later that season and signed as a free agent by the Hamilton Tiger-Cats in April, 1993.

Games Played - 4 with Hamilton in 1993. **CFL Total GP - 4.**

Fumble Returns - 1 for 0 yards with Hamilton in 1993. **CFL Total Fumble Returns - 1 for 0 yards.**

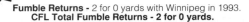

ROGERS, REGGIE

Quarterback Sacks - 4 for 21 yards lost with Hamilton in 1993.
CFL Total QB Sacks - 4 for 21 yards lost.

Tackles - 6 defensive with Hamilton in 1993.
CFL Total Tackles - 6 (6 defensive).

Tackles for Losses - 1 for 1 yard with Hamilton in 1993.
CFL Total Tackles for Losses - 1 for 1 yard.

ROMANO, ROCCO
Born: January 1, 1963
Birthplace: Hamilton, Ontario
Offensive Guard. 6'4", 257 lbs. Non-import
Last Amateur Club: Concordia University (OQIFC)
Acquired: Selected in the first round (fifth overall) by the Calgary Stampeders in the 1987 CFL College Draft. Traded to the Saskatchewan Roughriders for wide receiver Tony Dennis in January, 1988. Released by Saskatchewan in September, 1988 and signed with Toronto Argonauts later that month. Released by Toronto in November, 1988. Signed as a free agent by the Ottawa Rough Riders in April, 1989. Traded to the B.C. Lions in March, 1990 along with offensive lineman Richard McCrory and running back Chris Skinner in exchange for offensive lineman Rob Smith. Traded along with the rights to offensive lineman Jamie Crysdale to Calgary in April, 1992 in exchange for quarterback Danny Barrett.

Games Played - 15 with Calgary in 1987; 5 with Toronto in 1988; 17 with Ottawa in 1989; 18 with B.C. in 1990; 17 in 1991; 18 with Calgary in 1992 and 18 in 1993. **CFL Total GP - 108.**

Own Fumbles Recovered - 1 with B.C. in 1990 and 1 with Calgary in 1992.
CFL Total OFR - 2.

Tackles - 1 defensive and 1 special teams with B.C. in 1991; 1 defensive and 1 special teams with Calgary in 1992 and 2 defensive in 1993.
CFL Total Tackles - 6 (4 defensive and 2 special teams).

All-Western All-Star in 1992 and 1993.
CFL All-Star in 1992.

Playoffs

Games Played - 1 with Calgary in 1987; 1 with B.C. in 1991; 1 with Calgary in 1992 and 2 in 1993. **CFL Total Playoff GP - 5.**

Grey Cup

Games Played - 1 with Calgary in 1992. **Total Grey Cup GP - 1.**

ROYAL, RICKEY
Born: July 26, 1966
Birthplace: Gainsville, Texas
Cornerback. 5'10", 186 lbs. Import
Last Amateur Club: Sam Houston State University
Acquired: Selected in the 10th round (100th defensive back) in the WLAF Positional Draft. Played with the London Monarchs, San Antonio Riders and Team Dallas. Signed as a free agent by the Hamilton Tiger-Cats in June, 1991. Granted free agency status in February, 1993. Re-signed by Hamilton in May, 1993.

Games Played - 8 with Hamilton in 1991; 18 in 1992 and 18 in 1993.
CFL Total GP - 44.

Interception Returns - 2 for 0 yards with Hamilton in 1991.
CFL Total Interception Returns - 2 for 0 yards.

Fumble Returns - 1 for 4 yards with Hamilton in 1993.
CFL Total Fumble Returns - 1 for 4 yards.

Quarterback Sacks - 1 with Hamilton in 1991. **CFL Total QB Sacks - 1.**

Tackles - 14 defensive and 5 special teams with Hamilton in 1991; 20 defensive and 19 special teams in 1992 and 35 defensive and 13 special teams in 1993. **CFL Total Tackles - 106 (69 defensive and 37 special teams).**

Playoffs

Games Played - 2 with Hamilton in 1992 and 2 in 1993. **CFL Total Playoff GP - 4.**

Tackles - 1 defensive and 1 special teams with Hamilton in 1992.
CFL Total Playoff Tackles - 2 (1 defensive and 1 special teams).

RUSH, KEILLY
Born: June 18, 1970
Birthplace: McKeesport, Pennsylvania
Defensive End. 6'7", 255 lbs. Import
Last Amateur Club: Florida State University
Acquired: Signed as a free agent by the Winnipeg Blue Bombers in June, 1993. Released by Winnipeg in November, 1993.

Games Played - 2 with Winnipeg in 1993. **CFL Total GP - 2.**

Fumble Returns - 2 for 0 yards with Winnipeg in 1993.
CFL Total Fumble Returns - 2 for 0 yards.

Quarterback Sacks - 3 for 24 yards lost with Winnipeg in 1993.
CFL Total QB Sacks - 3 for 24 yards lost.

Tackles - 16 defensive with Winnipeg in 1993.
CFL Total Tackles - 16 (16 defensive).

Tackles for Losses - 1 for 8 yards with Winnipeg in 1993.
CFL Total Tackles for Losses - 1 for 8 yards.

SALTZ, LEE
Born: September 25, 1963
Birthplace: Dover, New Jersey
Quarterback. 6'1", 195 lbs. Import
Last Amateur Club: Temple University
Acquired: Signed as a free agent by the NFL Detroit Lions in 1987. Released and signed as a free agent by the Winnipeg Blue Bombers in October, 1988. Traded to the Saskatchewan Roughriders in July, 1990 along with the rights to slotback Allan Boyko and Winnipeg's first round draft choices in 1991 and 1992 CFL College Draft in exchange for quarterback Tom Burgess. Released after training camp in 1990. Signed as a free agent by the NFL New England Patriots in 1991. Was assigned to the WLAF San Antonio Riders by Team Dallas in 1991. Signed as a free agent by the Hamilton Tiger-Cats in June, 1993. Released by Hamilton in March, 1994 and signed as a free agent by the Las Vegas Posse that same month.

		Scoring						Fumbles		
	Team	GP	TD	C	FG	S	TP	NO	LOST	OFR
1988	Wpg.	3	1	0	0	0	6	0	0	0
1989	Wpg.	14	0	0	0	0	0	1	1	0
1993	Ham.	1	0	0	0	0	0	0	0	0
CFL TOTALS		**18**	**1**	**0**	**0**	**0**	**6**	**1**	**1**	**0**

		Passing							Rushing				
	Team	ATT	COMP	YDS	PCT	INT	LG	TD	NO	YDS	AVE	LG	TD
1988	Wpg.	23	11	157	47.8	2	41	1	4	46	11.5	27	1
1989	Wpg.	77	32	398	41.6	5	52	2	17	45	2.6	11	0
1993	Ham.	33	18	281	54.5	2	64	1	2	6	3.0	5	0
CFL TOTALS		**133**	**61**	**836**	**45.8**	**9**	**64**	**4**	**23**	**97**	**4.2**	**27**	**1**

Playoffs

Games Played - 2 with Winnipeg in 1988 and 2 in 1989. **CFL Total Playoff GP - 4.**

Rushing - 12 for 84 yards, 7.0 average, longest 33 yards with Winnipeg in 1989.
CFL Total Playoff Rushing - 12 for 84 yards, 7.0 average, longest 33 yards.

Passing - 71 attempts, 34 completions for 486 yards, 47.9 percent complete, 2 interceptions, longest 87 yards and 3 TDs with Winnipeg in 1989.
CFL Total Playoff Passing - 71 attempts, 34 completions for 486 yards, 47.9 percent complete, 2 interceptions, longest 87 yards and 3 TDs.

Fumbles - 1 and 1 lost with Winnipeg in 1989.
CFL Total Playoff Fumbles - 1 and 1 lost.

Grey Cup

Games Played - 1 with Winnipeg in 1988. **Total Grey Cup GP - 1.**

SAMPSON, DARRYL
Born: September 21, 1963
Birthplace: Scarborough, Ontario
Defensive Back. 6'2", 175 lbs. Non-import
Last Amateur Club: York University (OUAA)
Acquired: Selected in the second round (16th overall) by the Winnipeg Blue Bombers in the 1986 CFL College Draft.

		Scoring						Interception Returns				
	Team	GP	TD	C	FG	S	TP	NO	YDS	AVE	LG	TD
1986	Wpg.	18	0	0	0	0	0	0	0	0.0	0	0
1987	Wpg.	10	1	0	0	0	6	1	53	53.0	53	0
1988	Wpg.	17	1	0	0	0	6	1	21	21.0	21	0
1989	Wpg.	17	0	0	0	0	0	1	8	8.0	8	0
1990	Wpg.	18	0	0	0	0	0	3	57	19.0	31	0
1991	Wpg.	15	1	0	0	0	6	1	38	38.0	38	1
1992	Wpg.	17	0	0	0	0	0	5	51	10.2	28	0
1993ab	Wpg.	18	0	0	0	0	0	6	56	9.3	17	0
CFL TOTALS		**130**	**3**	**0**	**0**	**0**	**18**	**18**	**284**	**15.8**	**53**	**0**

		Punt Returns					Fumbles			QB
	Team	NO	YDS	AVE	LG	TD	NO	LOST	OFR	Sacks
1986	Wpg.	40	428	10.7	28	0	1	0	1	0
1987	Wpg.	29	246	8.5	39	0	2	2	0	0
1988	Wpg.	1	0	0.0	0	0	0	0	1	0
1989	Wpg.	0	0	0.0	0	0	0	0	1	2
1990	Wpg.	0	0	0.0	0	0	0	0	0	0
1991	Wpg.	0	0	0.0	0	0	0	0	0	2
1992	Wpg.	0	0	0.0	0	0	0	0	0	1
1993	Wpg.	0	0	0.0	0	0	0	0	0	0
CFL TOTALS		**70**	**674**	**9.6**	**39**	**0**	**3**	**2**	**3**	**5**

SAMPSON, DARRYL

	Team	Kickoff Returns NO	YDS	AVE	LG	TD	Fumble Returns NO	YDS	AVE	LG	TD
1986	Wpg.	16	348	21.8	35	0	1	0	0.0	0	0
1987	Wpg.	3	45	15.0	25	0	1	39	39.0	39	1
1988	Wpg.	0	0	0.0	0	0	2	0	0.0	0	1
1989	Wpg.	0	0	0.0	0	0	1	0	0.0	0	0
1990	Wpg.	0	0	0.0	0	0	3	11	3.7	8	0
1991	Wpg.	0	0	0.0	0	0	2	15	7.5	15	0
1992	Wpg.	0	0	0.0	0	0	0	0	0.0	0	0
1993	Wpg.	0	0	0.0	0	0	0	0	0.0	0	0
CFL TOTALS		**19**	**393**	**20.7**	**35**	**0**	**10**	**65**	**6.5**	**39**	**2**

Rushing - 1 for 21 yards with Winnipeg in 1986. **CFL Total Rushing - 1 for 21 yards.**

Unsuccessful Field Goal Returns - 1 for 12 yards with Winnipeg in 1987. **CFL Total Unsuccessful Field Goal Returns - 1 for 12 yards.**

Own Punts Recovered - 1 for 3 yards with Winnipeg in 1986. **CFL Total Own Punts Recovered - 1 for 3 yards.**

Tackles - 19 defensive with Winnipeg in 1987; 58 defensive in 1988; 48 defensive in 1989; 76 defensive in 1990; 51 defensive and 6 special teams in 1991; 44 defensive and 1 special teams in 1992 and 54 defensive and 13 special teams in 1993. **CFL Total Tackles - 370 (350 defensive and 20 special teams).**

Tackles for Losses - 1 for 1 yard with Winnipeg in 1991 and 2 for 7 yards in 1992. **CFL Total Tackles for Losses - 3 for 8 yards.**

a - All Eastern All-Star
b - CFL All-Star

Playoffs

	Team	GP	Punt Returns NO	YDS	AVE	LG	TD	Fumbles NO	LOST	OFR
1986	Wpg.	1	0	0	0.0	0	0	0	0	0
1987	Wpg.	1	4	17	4.3	7	0	1	1	0
1988	Wpg.	2	0	0	0.0	0	0	0	0	0
1989	Wpg.	2	0	0	0.0	0	0	0	0	0
1990	Wpg.	1	0	0	0.0	0	0	0	0	0
1991	Wpg.	2	0	0	0.0	0	0	0	0	0
1992	Wpg.	1	0	0	0.0	0	0	0	0	0
1993	Wpg.	1	0	0	0.0	0	0	0	0	0
CFL TOTALS		**11**	**4**	**17**	**4.3**	**7**	**0**	**1**	**1**	**0**

Quarterback Sacks - 1 with Winnipeg in 1991. **CFL Total Playoff QB Sacks - 1.**

Defensive Tackles - 11 with Winnipeg in 1988; 7 in 1989; 2 in 1990; 5 in 1991; 1 in 1992 and 1 in 1993. **CFL Total Playoff Defensive Tackles - 27.**

Grey Cup

Games Played - 1 with Winnipeg in 1988; 1 in 1990; 1 in 1992 and 1 in 1993. **Total Grey Cup GP - 4.**

Defensive Tackles - 5 with Winnipeg in 1988; 5 in 1990; 2 in 1992 and 3 in 1993. **Total Grey Cup Defensive Tackles - 15.**

SANCHEZ, EROS
Born: August 11, 1967
Birthplace: Brooklyn, New York
Quarterback. 5'11", 195 lbs. Import
Last Amateur Club: Virginia Tech University
Acquired: Signed as a free agent by the Hamilton Tiger-Cats in May, 1993. Released by Hamilton in November, 1993. Signed as a free agent by the Shreveport Pirates in April, 1994.

	Team	GP	Passing ATT	COMP	YDS	PCT	INT	LG	TD	Rushing NO	YDS	AVE	LG	TD
1993	Ham.	14	42	18	251	42.9	1	33	1	14	63	4.5	20	0
CFL TOTALS		**14**	**42**	**18**	**251**	**42.9**	**1**	**33**	**1**	**14**	**63**	**4.5**	**20**	**0**

Tackles - 1 defensive and 1 special teams with Hamilton in 1993. **CFL Total Tackles - 2 (1 defensive and 1 special teams).**

SANDERSON, DALE
Born: December 12, 1961
Birthplace: Hamilton, Ontario
Centre. 6'3", 260 lbs. Non-import
Last Amateur Club: University of Tennessee
Acquired: Selected in the fourth round (36th overall) by the Hamilton Tiger-Cats in the 1985 CFL College Draft. Granted free agency status in February, 1993. Re-signed by Hamilton in June, 1993.

Games Played - 2 with Hamilton in 1985; 18 in 1986; 18 in 1987; 18 in 1988; 18 in 1989; 16 in 1990; 18 in 1991; 18 in 1992 and 7 in 1993. **CFL Total GP - 133.**

Fumbles - 1 and 1 lost with Hamilton in 1990; 1 and 1 lost in 1992 and 1 and 1 lost in 1993. **CFL Total Fumbles - 3 and 3 lost.**

Fumble Returns - 1 for 0 yards with Hamilton in 1992. **CFL Total Fumble Returns - 1 for 0 yards.**

Own Fumbles Recovered - 1 with Hamilton in 1992. **CFL Total OFR - 1.**

Tackles - 4 defensive with Hamilton in 1988; 3 defensive in 1989; 2 defensive in 1990; 1 defensive in 1991 and 1 defensive and 1 special teams in 1992. **CFL Total Tackles - 12 (11 defensive and 1 special teams).**

All-Eastern All-Star in 1989.

Playoffs

Games Played - 1 with Hamilton in 1985; 1 in 1986; 1 in 1987; 1 in 1988; 1 in 1989; 1 in 1992 and 2 in 1993. **CFL Total Playoff GP - 8.**

Fumbles - 1 and 0 lost with Hamilton in 1992. **CFL Total Playoff Fumbles - 1 and 0 lost.**

Own Fumbles Recovered - 1 with Hamilton in 1992. **CFL Total Playoff OFR - 1.**

Grey Cup

Games Played - 1 with Hamilton in 1985; 1 in 1986 and 1 in 1989. **Total Grey Cup GP - 3.**

SANDUSKY, JIM
Born: September 9, 1961
Birthplace: Othello, Washington
Wide Receiver. 5'9", 180 lbs. Import
Last Amateur Club: San Diego State University
Acquired: Fourth round pick of the USFL Philadelphia Stars in the 1984 USFL Draft. Signed prior to the NFL Draft with the Detroit Lions. Signed as a free agent with the B.C. Lions in February, 1984. Traded for quarterback Matt Dunigan and future considerations, to the Edmonton Eskimos in June, 1988. The deal was completed in January, 1989 with linebackers Jeff Braswell and Gregg Stumon, running back Reggie Taylor, cornerback Andre Francis and first round draft choice at the 1989 CFL College Draft (Leroy Blugh) going to Edmonton. Signed as a free agent by the NFL Seattle Seahawks in March, 1989. Injured in 1989 and 1990. Released by Seattle and signed as a free agent by Edmonton in May, 1991.

	Team	Scoring GP	TD	C	FG	S	TP	Pass Receiving NO	YDS	AVE	LG	TD
1984	B.C.	9	2	0	0	0	12	27	406	12.6	62	2
1985	B.C.	16	7	0	0	0	42	58	1073	18.5	68	7
1986	B.C.	15	1	0	0	0	6	60	858	14.3	50	1
1987ab	B.C.	18	13	0	0	0	78	80	1437	18.0	75	12
1988	Edm.	17	8	0	0	0	48	55	1089	19.8	59	8
1989					NFL					NFL		
1990					NFL					NFL		
1991a	Edm.	18	10	0	0	0	60	63	1063	16.9	65	10
1992abcd	Edm.	18	15	x1	0	0	92	78	1243	15.9	68	15
1993	Edm.	8	3	0	0	0	18	24	482	20.1	64	3
CFL TOTALS		**119**	**59**	**x1**	**0**	**0**	**356**	**445**	**7651**	**17.2**	**75**	**58**

	Team	Punt Returns NO	YDS	AVE	LG	TD	Fumbles NO	LOST	OFR
1984	B.C.	13	137	10.5	42	0	1	1	0
1985	B.C.	21	210	10.0	33	0	4	2	1
1986	B.C.	42	459	10.9	62	0	0	0	1
1987	B.C.	58	492	8.5	55	1	1	0	0
1988	Edm.	9	82	9.1	38	0	1	0	2
1989				NFL				NFL	
1990				NFL				NFL	
1991	Edm.	3	19	6.3	16	0	1	1	0
1992	Edm.	1	0	0.0	0	0	1	1	0
1993	Edm.	0	0	0.0	0	0	1	1	0
CFL TOTALS		**147**	**1399**	**9.5**	**62**	**1**	**10**	**6**	**4**

	Team	Kickoff Returns NO	YDS	AVE	LG	TD	Passing ATT	COMP	YDS	PCT	INT	LG	TD
1984	B.C.	0	0	0.0	0	0	0	0	0	0.0	0	0	0
1985	B.C.	2	41	20.5	25	0	2	2	42	100.0	0	41	0
1986	B.C.	1	23	23.0	23	0	1	0	0	0.0	0	0	0
1987	B.C.	9	125	13.9	29	0	4	2	65	50.0	0	49	0
1988	Edm.	0	0	0.0	0	0	0	0	0	0.0	0	0	0
1989				NFL						NFL			
1990				NFL						NFL			
1991	Edm.	0	0	0.0	0	0	0	0	0	0.0	0	0	0
1992	Edm.	0	0	0.0	0	0	2	1	18	50.0	0	18	0
1993	Edm.	1	20	20.0	20	0	0	0	0	0.0	0	0	0
CFL TOTALS		**13**	**209**	**16.1**	**29**	**0**	**9**	**5**	**125**	**55.6**	**0**	**49**	**0**

Rushing - 1 for 12 yards with B.C. in 1985 and 1 for 1 yard with Edmonton in 1992. **CFL Total Rushing - 2 for 13 yards, 6.5 average, longest 12 yards.**

2-Pt. Converts - 1 attempt, 1 complete and 1 made with Edmonton in 1992. **CFL Total 2-Pt. Converts - 1 attempt, 1 complete, 1 made.**

Tackles - 2 defensive with B.C. in 1987; 2 defensive in 1988; 3 defensive and 1 special teams with Edmonton in 1991; 2 defensive and 1 special teams in 1992 and 1 defensive in 1993. **CFL Total Tackles - 12 (10 defensive and 2 special teams).**

SANDUSKY, JIM

a - All-Western All-Star
b - CFL All-Star
c - Led CFL in Points (TDs) (Tied with Jon Volpe)
d - Led CFL in Receiving TDs (15)

Playoffs

	Team	Pass Receiving GP	NO	YDS	AVE	LG	TD	Kickoff Returns NO	YDS	AVE	LG	TD
1985	B.C.	1	4	69	17.3	39	0	0	2	0.0	2	0
1986	B.C.	2	6	55	9.2	19	0	3	50	16.7	24	0
1987	B.C.	1	4	41	10.3	31	0	0	0	0.0	0	0
1988	Edm.	1	3	42	14.0	23	0	1	0	0.0	0	0
1991	Edm.	1	2	40	20.0	36	0	0	0	0.0	0	0
1992	Edm.	2	6	103	17.7	37	0	0	0	0.0	0	0
1993	Edm.	2	2	108	54.0	73	2	0	0	0.0	0	0
CFL TOTALS		**10**	**27**	**458**	**17.0**	**73**	**2**	**4**	**52**	**13.0**	**24**	**0**

	Team	Punt Returns NO	YDS	AVE	LG	TD
1985	B.C.	0	0	0.0	0	0
1986	B.C.	0	0	0.0	0	0
1987	B.C.	2	24	12.0	23	0
1988	Edm.	2	4	2.0	3	0
1991	Edm.	0	0	0.0	0	0
1992	Edm.	2	13	6.5	10	0
1993	Edm.	0	0	0	0	0
CFL TOTALS		**6**	**41**	**6.8**	**23**	**0**

Scoring - 2 TDs for 12 points with Edmonton in 1993.
CFL Total Playoff Scoring - 2 TDs for 12 points.

Punting - 1 for 22 yards with Edmonton in 1988.
CFL Total Playoff Punting - 1 for 22 yards.

Grey Cup

	Team	Scoring GP	TD	C	FG	S	TP	Pass Receiving NO	YDS	AVE	LG	TD
1985	B.C.	1	1	0	0	0	6	6	135	22.5	66	1
1993	Edm.	1	1	0	0	0	6	3	36	12.0	19	1
CFL TOTALS		**2**	**2**	**0**	**0**	**0**	**12**	**9**	**171**	**19.0**	**66**	**2**

Tackles - 1 defensive with Edmonton in 1993.
Total Grey Cup Tackles - 1 (1 defensive).

SAPUNJIS, DAVE

Born: September 7, 1967
Birthplace: Toronto, Ontario
Slotback. 6'1", 185 lbs. Non-import
Last Amateur Club: University of Western Ontario (OUAA)
Acquired: Selected in the first round (fifth overall) by the Calgary Stampeders in the 1990 CFL College Draft. Signed by Calgary in April, 1990.

	Team	Scoring GP	TD	C	FG	S	TP	Pass Receiving NO	YDS	AVE	LG	TD
1990	Cal.	18	1	0	0	0	6	21	262	12.5	24	1
1991a	Cal.	18	1	0	0	0	6	9	107	11.9	20	0
1992	Cal.	18	4	0	0	0	24	77	1317	17.1	59	4
1993bcdefgh	Cal.	18	15	0	0	0	90	103	1484	14.4	75	15
CFL TOTALS		**72**	**21**	**0**	**0**	**0**	**126**	**210**	**3170**	**15.1**	**75**	**20**

	Team	Rushing NO	YDS	AVE	LG	TD	Punt Returns NO	YDS	AVE	LG	TD
1990	Cal.	0	0	0.0	0	0	0	0	0.0	0	0
1991	Cal.	2	7	3.5	6	0	10	124	12.4	68	1
1992	Cal.	1	-7	-7.0	-7	0	0	0	0.0	0	0
1993	Cal.	0	24	0.0	24	0	0	0	0.0	0	0
CFL TOTALS		**3**	**24**	**8.0**	**24**	**0**	**10**	**124**	**12.4**	**68**	**1**

Kickoff Returns - 1 for 0 yards with Calgary in 1992.
CFL Total Kickoff Returns - 1 for 0 yards.

Fumble Returns - 1 for 0 yards with Calgary in 1990.
CFL Total Fumble Returns - 1 for 0 yards.

Fumbles - 1 and 1 lost with Calgary in 1993. **CFL Total Fumbles 1 and 1 lost.**

Own Fumbles Recovered - 1 with Calgary in 1993. **CFL Total OFR - 1.**

Tackles - 1 defensive with Calgary in 1990; 1 defensive and 33 special teams in 1991; 4 defensive and 11 special teams in 1992 and 1 defensive and 6 special teams in 1993.
CFL Total Tackles - 57 (7 defensive and 50 special teams).

a - Led CFL in Special Teams Tackles
b - Led CFL in Receiving - Catches
c - Led CFL in Receiving - Yards
d - Tied CFL lead for Receiving TDs
e - All-Western All-Star Team
f - CFL All-Star Team
g - Winner, Dr. Beattie Martin Trophy as Most Outstanding Canadian - Western Division
h - Winner, CFL Most Outstanding Canadian

Playoffs

	Team	Scoring GP	TD	C	FG	S	TP	Pass Receiving NO	YDS	AVE	LG	TD
1990	Cal.	1	0	0	0	0	0	2	13	6.5	8	0
1991	Cal.	2	2	0	0	0	12	4	91	22.8	36	2
1992	Cal.	1	0	0	0	0	0	2	27	13.5	22	0
1993	Cal.	2	0	0	0	0	0	6	85	14.2	29	0
CFL TOTALS		**6**	**2**	**0**	**0**	**0**	**12**	**14**	**216**	**15.4**	**36**	**2**

Passing - 1 attempt, 0 complete with Calgary in 1990.
CFL Total Playoff Passing - 1 attempt, 0 complete.

Rushing - 1 for -3 yards with Calgary in 1991.
CFL Total Playoff Rushing - 1 for -3 yards.

Tackles - 2 special teams with Calgary in 1991; 1 defensive and 1 special teams in 1992 and 1 special teams in 1993.
CFL Total Playoff Tackles - 5 (1 defensive and 4 special teams).

Grey Cup

	Team	Scoring GP	TD	C	FG	S	TP
1991	Cal.	1	0	0	0	0	0
1992	Cal.	1	1	0	0	0	6
CFL TOTALS		**2**	**1**	**0**	**0**	**0**	**6**

	Team	Rushing NO	YDS	AVE	LG	TD	Pass Receiving NO	YDS	AVE	LG	TD
1991	Cal.	2	27	13.5	14	0	4	45	11.3	18	0
1992	Cal.	0	0	0.0	0	0	7	85	12.1	35	1
CFL TOTALS		**2**	**27**	**13.5**	**14**	**0**	**11**	**130**	**11.8**	**35**	**1**

Most Valuable Canadian in 1991 and 1992 Grey Cup Games.

SARDO, JOE

Born: November 7, 1969
Birthplace: Hamilton, Ontario
Linebacker. 6'1", 210 lbs. Import
Last Amateur Club: University of Hawaii
Acquired: Selected in the second round (16th overall) by the Ottawa Rough Riders in the 1992 CFL College Draft. The choice was acquired from the Toronto Argonauts along with quarterback John Congemi in exchange for kicker Dean Dorsey, linebacker Brian Warren and defensive lineman Leonard Johnson. Signed by Ottawa in June, 1992.

Games Played - 18 with Ottawa in 1992 and 18 in 1993. **CFL Total GP - 36.**

Scoring - 1 touchdown for 6 points with Ottawa in 1992.
CFL Total Scoring - 1 TD for 6 points.

Fumble Returns - 1 for 57 yards and 1 TD with Ottawa in 1992 and 2 for 9 yards, 4.5 average, longest 9 yards in 1993.
CFL Total Fumble Returns - 3 for 66 yards 22.0 average, longest 57 yards and 1 TD.

Tackles - 4 defensive and 15 special teams with Ottawa in 1992 and 4 defensive and 20 special teams in 1993.
CFL Total Tackles - 43 (8 defensive and 35 special teams).

Tackles for Losses - 1 for 2 yards with Ottawa in 1992.
CFL Total Tackles for Losses - 1 for 2 yards.

Playoffs

Games Played - 1 with Ottawa in 1992 and 1 in 1993. **CFL Total Playoff GP - 2.**

Tackles - 1 defensive and 1 special teams with Ottawa in 1993.
CFL Total Playoff Tackles - 2 (1 defensive and 1 special teams).

SAUNDERS, MIKE

Born: October 3, 1969
Birthplace: Milton, Wisconsin
Running Back. 5'10", 200 lbs. Import
Last Amateur Club: University of Iowa
Acquired: Selected in the tenth round (262nd overall) by the Pittsburgh Steelers in the 1992 NFL Draft. Released following training camp. Signed as a free agent by the Saskatchewan Roughriders in October, 1992.

	Team	Scoring GP	TD	C	FG	S	TP	Rushing NO	YDS	AVE	LG	TD
1992	Sask.	4	2	x1	0	0	14	21	54	2.6	17	0
1993	Sask.	13	5	0	0	0	30	135	683	5.1	52	4
CFL TOTALS		**17**	**7**	**x1**	**0**	**0**	**44**	**156**	**737**	**4.7**	**52**	**4**

	Team	Pass Receiving NO	YDS	AVE	LG	TD	Punt Returns NO	YDS	AVE	LG	TD
1992	Sask.	20	314	15.7	91	2	11	104	9.5	40	0
1993	Sask.	58	612	10.6	43	1	24	194	8.1	35	0
CFL TOTALS		**78**	**926**	**11.9**	**91**	**3**	**35**	**298**	**8.5**	**40**	**0**

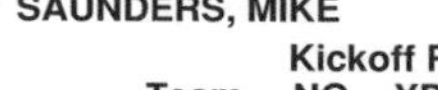

SAUNDERS, MIKE

	Team	Kickoff Returns NO	YDS	AVE	LG	TD	Fumbles NO	LOST	OFR
1992	Sask.	13	267	20.5	34	0	3	2	0
1993	Sask.	17	341	20.1	58	0	10	6	1
CFL TOTALS		**30**	**608**	**20.3**	**58**	**0**	**13**	**8**	**1**

Unsuccessful Field Goal Returns - 1 for 35 yards with Saskatchewan in 1992. **CFL Total Unsuccessful Field Goal Returns - 1 for 35 yards.**

Passing - 2 attempts, 2 complete for 48 yards, 100 percent complete, longest 28 yards with Saskatchewan in 1993. **CFL Total Passing - 2 attempts, 2 complete for 48 yards, 100 percent complete, longest 28 yards.**

Tackles - 1 defensive and 1 special teams with Saskatchewan in 1992 and 2 defensive and 1 special teams in 1993. **CFL Total Tackles - 5 (3 defensive and 2 special teams).**

Playoffs

	Team	GP	Rushing NO	YDS	AVE	LG	TD	Pass Receiving NO	YDS	AVE	LG	TD
1992	Sask.	1	7	27	3.9	11	0	9	77	8.6	13	0
1993	Sask.	1	5	21	4.2	8	0	3	10	3.3	7	0
CFL TOTALS		**2**	**12**	**48**	**4.0**	**11**	**0**	**12**	**87**	**7.3**	**13**	**0**

Punt Returns - 5 for 31 yards, 6.2 average, longest 12 yards with Saskatchewan in 1992 and 4 for 23 yards, 5.8 average, longest 10 yards in 1993. **CFL Total Playoff Punt Returns - 9 for 54 yards, 6.0 average, longest 12 yards.**

Kickoff Returns - 3 for 53 yards, 17.7 average, longest 21 yards with Saskatchewan in 1993. **CFL Total Playoff Kickoff Returns - 3 for 53 yards, 17.7 average, longest 21 yards.**

Tackles - 1 defensive with Saskatchewan in 1992. **CFL Total Playoff Tackles - 1 (1 defensive).**

SCHMIDT, BLAINE

Born: August 23, 1963
Birthplace: Sudbury, Ontario
Centre. 6'4", 260 lbs. Non-import
Last Amateur Club: University of Guelph (OUAA)
Acquired: Selected in the second round, (17th overall), by the Edmonton Eskimos in the 1986 CFL College Draft. Injured in training camp and spent the 1986 season on the injured list. Transferred to the Montreal Alouettes for future considerations in June, 1987 and released later that month. Signed as a free agent by the Toronto Argonauts in August, 1987.

Games Played - 10 with Toronto in 1987; 18 in 1988; 18 in 1989; 18 in 1990; 18 in 1991; 18 in 1992 and 18 in 1993. **CFL Total GP - 118.**

Rushing - 1 for -1 yard with Toronto in 1991. **CFL Total Rushing - 1 for -1 yard.**

Fumble Returns - 1 for 0 yards with Toronto in 1989 and 1 for 0 yards in 1993. **CFL Total Fumble Returns - 2 for 0 yards.**

Fumbles - 1 and 1 lost with Toronto in 1991. **CFL Total Fumbles - 1 and 1 lost.**

Own Fumbles Recovered - 1 with Toronto in 1991. **CFL Total OFR - 1.**

Tackles - 4 defensive with Toronto in 1987; 2 defensive in 1988; 4 defensive in 1990; 2 defensive and 13 special teams in 1991; 4 defensive and 18 special teams in 1992 and 1 defensive and 11 special teams in 1993. **CFL Total Tackles - 59 (17 defensive and 42 special teams).**

Playoffs

Games Played - 2 with Toronto in 1987; 1 in 1988; 1 in 1989; 2 in 1990 and 1 in 1991. **CFL Total Playoff GP - 7.**

Defensive Tackles - 1 with Toronto in 1990. **CFL Total Playoff Defensive Tackles - 1.**

Grey Cup

Games Played - 1 with Toronto in 1987 and 1 in 1991. **Total Grey Cup GP - 2.**

Own Fumbles Recovered - 1 with Toronto in 1991. **Total Grey Cup OFR - 1.**

Tackles - 2 special teams with Toronto in 1991. **Total Grey Cup Tackles - 2 (2 special teams).**

SCHRAMAYR, ERNIE

Born: July 7, 1966
Birthplace: Montreal, Quebec
Fullback. 5'10", 214 lbs. Non-import
Last Amateur Club: Purdue University
Acquired: Selected in the second round (12th overall) by the Hamilton Tiger-Cats in the 1989 CFL College Draft. Released by Hamilton in June, 1993. Signed as a free agent by the Ottawa Rough Riders in July, 1993.

	Team	GP	Scoring TD	C	FG	S	TP	Rushing NO	YDS	AVE	LG	TD
1989	Ham.	3	0	0	0	0	0	0	0	0.0	0	0
1990	Ham.	18	0	0	0	0	0	26	143	5.5	43	0
1991	Ham.	13	1	0	0	0	6	25	92	3.7	12	1
1992	Ham.	13	0	0	0	0	0	3	7	2.3	3	0
1993	Ott.	11	0	0	0	0	0	0	0	0.0	0	0
CFL TOTALS		**58**	**1**	**0**	**0**	**0**	**6**	**54**	**242**	**4.5**	**43**	**1**

	Team	Pass Receiving NO	YDS	AVE	LG	TD	Kickoff Returns NO	YDS	AVE	LG	TD
1989	Ham.	1	36	36.0	36	0	1	7	7.0	7	0
1990	Ham.	7	76	10.9	30	0	5	52	10.4	16	0
1991	Ham.	4	31	7.8	11	0	0	0	0.0	0	0
1993	Ott.	2	23	11.5	14	0	0	0	0.0	0	0
CFL TOTALS		**14**	**166**	**11.9**	**36**	**0**	**6**	**59**	**9.8**	**16**	**0**

Fumbles - 1 and 1 lost with Hamilton in 1989 and 2 and 2 lost in 1990. **CFL Total Fumbles - 3 and 3 lost.**

Fumble Returns - 1 for 0 yards with Hamilton in 1992. **CFL Total Fumble Returns - 1 for 0 yards.**

Punting - 2 for 75 yards, 37.5 average, longest 49 yards with Hamilton in 1990 and 1 for 36 yards in 1991. **CFL Total Punting - 3 for 111 yards, 37.0 average, longest 49 yards.**

Net Punting - 1 for 36 yards with Hamilton in 1991. **CFL Total Net Punting - 1 for 36 yards.**

Tackles - 4 defensive with Hamilton in 1990; 1 defensive and 14 special teams in 1991; 13 special teams in 1992 and 6 special teams with Ottawa in 1993. **CFL Total Tackles - 38 (5 defensive and 33 special teams).**

Playoffs

Games Played - 2 with Hamilton in 1992. **CFL Total Playoff GP - 2.**

Tackles - 1 special teams with Hamilton in 1992. **CFL Total Playoff Tackles - 1 (1 special teams).**

SCHULTZ, CHRIS

Born: February 16, 1960
Birthplace: Burlington, Ontario
Offensive Tackle. 6'8", 288 lbs. Non-import
Last Amateur Club: University of Arizona
Acquired: Selected in the seventh round (189th overall) by the Dallas Cowboys in the 1983 NFL College Draft. Released by Dallas prior to the 1986 season and signed as a free agent by the Toronto Argonauts in September, 1986.

Games Played - 7 with Toronto in 1986; 18 in 1987; 14 in 1988; 16 in 1989; 18 in 1990; 18 in 1991; 17 in 1992 and 1 in 1993. **CFL Total GP - 109.**

Own Fumbles Recovered - 2 with Toronto in 1990. **CFL Total OFR - 2.**

Defensive Tackles - 1 with Toronto in 1987; 1 in 1989; 2 in 1990; 1 in 1991 and 3 in 1992. **CFL Total Defensive Tackles - 8.**

All-Eastern All-Star in 1987; 1988 and 1991.
CFL All-Star in 1987 and 1988.

Playoffs

Games Played - 2 with Toronto in 1986; 2 in 1987; 1 in 1988; 1 in 1989; 2 in 1990 and 1 in 1991. **CFL Total Playoff GP - 9.**

Defensive Tackles - 1 with Toronto in 1988. **CFL Total Playoff Defensive Tackles - 1.**

Grey Cup

Games Played - 1 with Toronto in 1987 and 1 in 1991. **Total Grey Cup GP - 2.**

SCOTT, MARK

Born: December 19, 1968
Birthplace: Kingston, Jamaica
Linebacker. 6'1", 215 lbs. Non- import
Last Amateur Club: Virginia Tech University
Acquired: Drafted by the Saskatchewan Roughriders in the first round (second overall) in the 1992 CFL College Draft. Released by Saskatchewan in August, 1992. Signed as a free agent by the B.C. Lions in 1992. Traded to the Ottawa Rough Riders along with offensive lineman Carl Coulter and Chris Gioskos, kicker Wayne Lammle and cornerback Joe Mero in exchange for cornerback Less Browne, offensive lineman Rob Smith and linebacker Patrick Wayne in April, 1993. Released by Ottawa in July, 1993 and was subsequently signed as a free agent by the Hamilton Tiger-Cats.

Games Played - 11 with B.C. in 1992 and 16 with Hamilton in 1993. **CFL Total GP - 27.**

Fumble Returns - 1 for 0 yards with B.C. in 1992. **CFL Total Fumble Returns - 1 for 0 yards.**

SCOTT, MARK

Kickoff Returns - 2 for 0 yards with B.C. in 1992.
CFL Total Kickoff Returns - 2 for 0 yards.

Tackles - 5 defensive and 12 special teams with B.C. in 1992 and 10 defensive and 8 special teams with Hamilton in 1993.
CFL Total Tackles - 35 (15 defensive and 20 special teams).

Tackles for Losses - 1 for 1 yard with Hamilton in 1993.
CFL Total Tackles for Losses - 1 for 1 yard.

Playoffs

Games Played - 2 with Hamilton in 1993. **CFL Total Playoff GP - 2.**

SCRIVENER, GLEN
Born: July 14, 1967
Birthplace: Winnipeg, Manitoba
Defensive Lineman. 6'4", 275 lbs. Non-import
Last Amateur Club: William Jewell College
Acquired: Selected in the first round (third overall) by the Saskatchewan Roughriders in the 1990 CFL College Draft. Pick was acquired from the Winnipeg Blue Bombers in exchange for the rights to defensive back Andrew Thomas. Traded to the B.C. Lions in July, 1992 in exchange for a third round draft choice in the 1993 CFL College Draft, offensive tackle Kevin Hickey.

Games Played - 18 with Saskatchewan in 1991; 17 with B.C. in 1992 and 18 in 1993. **CFL Total GP - 53.**

Fumble Returns - 3 for 9 yards, 3.0 average, longest 9 yards with Saskatchewan in 1991 and 1 for 0 yards in 1993. **CFL Total Fumble Returns - 4 for 9 yards, 2.3 average, longest 9 yards.**

Quarterback Sacks - 3 with Saskatchewan in 1991; 5 for 39 yards lost with B.C. in 1992 and 10 for 79 yards lost in 1993. **CFL Total QB Sacks - 18.**

Tackles - 16 defensive and 4 special teams with Saskatchewan in 1991; 41 defensive with B.C. in 1992 and 24 defensive in 1993.
CFL Total Tackles - 85 (81 defensive and 4 special teams).

Tackles for Losses - 2 for 7 yards with Saskatchewan in 1991; 5 for 10 yards with B.C. in 1992 and 6 for 12 yards in 1993.
CFL Total Tackles for Losses - 13 for 29 yards.

Playoffs

Games Played - 1 with B.C. in 1993. **CFL Total Playoff GP - 1.**

Quarterback Sacks - 1 for 9 yards lost with B.C. in 1993.
CFL Total Playoff QB Sacks - 1 for 9 yards lost .

Tackles - 2 defensive with B.C. in 1993. **CFL Total Playoff Tackles - 2 (2 defensive).**

Tackles for Losses - 1 for 2 yards with B.C. in 1993. **CFL Total Playoff Tackles for Losses - 1 for 2 yards.**

SHAVERS, TYRONE
Born: February 9, 1968
Birthplace: Texarkana, Texas
Slotback. 6'3", 210 lbs. Import
Last Amateur Club: Lamar University
Acquired: Signed as a free agent by the Ottawa Rough Riders in June, 1993.

Games Played - 5 with Ottawa in 1993. **CFL Total GP - 5.**

Pass Receiving - 7 for 79 yards, 11.3 average, longest 22 yards with Ottawa in 1993. **CFL Total Pass Receiving - 7 for 79 yards, 11.3 average, longest 22 yards.**

Tackles - 1 defensive with Ottawa in 1993. **CFL Total Tackles - 1 (1 defensive).**

SHELTON, DAVID
Born: January 29, 1967
Birthplace: San Jose, California
Defensive Back. 5'11", 200 lbs. Import
Last Amateur Club: Fresno State University
Acquired: Signed as a free agent by the Edmonton Eskimos in April, 1990. Granted free agency status in February, 1993. Re-signed by Edmonton in June, 1993. Granted free agency status in February, 1994.

Games Played - 5 with Edmonton in 1990 and 16 in 1991. **CFL Total GP - 21.**

Kickoff Returns - 4 for 55 yards, 13.8 average, longest 22 yards with Edmonton in 1990. **CFL Total Kickoff Returns - 4 for 55 yards, 13.8 average, longest 22 yards.**

Interception Returns - 4 for 31 yards, 7.8 average, longest 31 yards with Edmonton in 1991. **CFL Total Interception Returns - 4 for 31 yards, 7.8 average, longest 31 yards.**

Fumble Returns - 1 for 0 yards with Edmonton in 1991.
CFL Total Fumble Returns - 1 for 0 yards.

Quarterback Sacks - 1 with Edmonton in 1990. **CFL Total QB Sacks - 1.**

Tackles - 8 defensive with Edmonton in 1990 and 58 defensive and 4 special teams in 1991. **CFL Total Tackles - 70 (66 defensive and 4 special teams).**

Tackles for Losses - 1 for 2 yards with Edmonton in 1991.
CFL Total Tackles for Losses - 1 for 2 yards.

Playoffs

Games Played - 2 with Edmonton in 1990 and 1 in 1991. **CFL Total Playoff GP - 3.**

Kickoff Returns - 1 for 21 yards with Edmonton in 1990.
CFL Total Playoff Kickoff Returns - 1 for 21 yards.

Defensive Tackles - 5 with Edmonton in 1990 and 1 in 1991.
CFL Total Playoff Defensive Tackles - 6.

Grey Cup

Games Played - 1 with Edmonton in 1990. **Total Grey Cup GP - 1.**

Punt Returns - 1 for 2 yards with Edmonton in 1990.
Total Grey Cup Punt Returns - 1 for 2 yards.

Defensive Tackles - 4 with Edmonton in 1990.
Total Grey Cup Defensive Tackles - 4.

SHIPLEY, RON
Born: August 17, 1968
Birthplace: Riverside, California
Offensive Lineman. 6'4", 285 lbs. Import
Last Amateur Club: University of New Mexico
Acquired: Selected by the Kansas City Chiefs in the twelfth round (329th overall) in the 1991 NFL Draft. Released by the Chiefs during training camp. Selected by the London Monarchs in the fifth round (54th overall) in the 1992 WLAF Draft. Signed as a free agent by the Sacramento Gold Miners in May, 1993.

Games Played - 18 with Sacramento in 1993. **CFL Total GP - 18.**

Own Fumbles Recovered - 1 with Sacramento in 1993.
CFL Total OFR - 1.

Tackles - 1 defensive and 1 special teams with Sacramento in 1993.
CFL Total Tackles - 2 (1 defensive and 1 special teams).

SIMS, KELLY
Born: November 10, 1970
Birthplace: St. Petersburgh, Florida
Defensive Back. 5'10", 190 lbs. Import
Last Amateur Club: University of Cincinnati
Acquired: Signed as a free agent by the B.C. Lions in September, 1993.

Games Played - 6 with B.C. in 1993. **CFL Total GP - 6.**

Tackles - 21 defensive and 4 special teams with B.C. in 1993.
CFL Total Tackles - 25 (21 defensive and 4 special teams).

Playoffs

Games Played - 1 with B.C. in 1993. **CFL Total Playoff GP - 1.**

Tackles - 4 defensive with B.C. in 1993.
CFL Total Playoff Tackles - 4 (4 defensive).

SINCLAIR, IAN
Born: July 22, 1960
Birthplace: London, Ontario
Centre. 6'4", 260 lbs. Non-import
Last Amateur Club: University of Miami
Acquired: Selected in the second round (11th overall) by the Montreal Alouettes in the 1984 CFL College Draft. Signed by the B.C. Lions in October, 1985.

Games Played - 5 with B.C. in 1985; 18 in 1986; 18 in 1987; 18 in 1988; 18 in 1989; 18 in 1990; 18 in 1991; 16 in 1992 and 18 in 1993.
CFL Total GP - 147.

Own Fumbles Recovered - 1 with B.C. in 1985; 1 in 1989 and 1 in 1993.
CFL Total OFR - 3.

Fumbles - 1 and 1 lost with B.C. in 1992. **CFL Total Fumbles - 1 and 1 lost.**

Fumble Returns - 1 with B.C. in 1985. **CFL Total Fumble Returns - 1.**

Kickoff Returns - 1 for 12 yards with B.C. in 1986.
CFL Total Kickoff Returns - 1 for 12 yards.

SINCLAIR, IAN

Tackles - 1 defensive with B.C. in 1987; 3 defensive in 1988; 2 defensive in 1989; 2 defensive in 1990; 3 defensive in 1991; 3 defensive and 1 special teams in 1992 and 1 defensive in 1993.
CFL Total Tackles - 16 (15 defensive and 1 special teams).

Playoffs

Games Played - 1 with B.C. in 1985; 2 in 1986; 1 in 1987; 2 in 1988; 1 in 1991 and 1 in 1993. **CFL Total Playoff GP - 8.**

Kickoff Returns - 1 for 14 yards with B.C. in 1986.
CFL Total Kickoff Returns - 1 for 14 yards.

Grey Cup

Games Played - 1 with B.C. in 1985 and 1 in 1988. **Total Grey Cup GP - 2.**

SKINNER, CHRIS
Born: December 18, 1961
Birthplace: Saint John, New Brunswick
Running Back. 6'0", 220 lbs. Non-import
Last Amateur Club: Bishop's University (OQIFC)
Acquired: Selected in the first round (seventh overall) by the Edmonton Eskimos in the 1984 CFL College Draft. Traded to the Ottawa Rough Riders in July, 1989 in exchange for Ottawa's first round choice in the 1990 CFL College Draft, running back Sean Millington. Traded by Ottawa to the B.C. Lions in March, 1990 along with offensive linemen Richard McCrory and Rocco Romano in exchange for offensive lineman Rob Smith. Retired in 1992. Came out of retirement in 1993 to play with the Lions.

		Scoring						Rushing				
	Team	GP	TD	C	FG	S	TP	NO	YDS	AVE	LG	TD
1984	Edm.	13	0	0	0	0	0	14	63	4.5	24	0
1985	Edm.	16	2	0	0	0	12	39	248	6.4	40	1
1986	Edm.	17	4	0	0	0	24	128	605	4.7	58	2
1987	Edm.	18	4	0	0	0	24	84	369	4.4	43	0
1988	Edm.	18	6	0	0	0	36	118	528	4.5	60	4
1989	Ott.	14	4	x1	0	0	26	40	175	4.4	22	3
1990	B.C.	18	1	0	0	0	6	102	603	5.9	36	0
1991	B.C.	18	3	0	0	0	18	45	269	6.0	49	2
1993	B.C.	8	2	0	0	0	12	10	52	5.2	19	2
CFL TOTALS		**140**	**26**	**x1**	**0**	**0**	**158**	**580**	**2912**	**5.0**	**60**	**14**

		Pass Receiving					Fumbles		
	Team	NO	YDS	AVE	LG	TD	NO	LOST	OFR
1984	Edm.	1	11	11.0	11	0	0	0	0
1985	Edm.	13	146	11.2	31	1	2	1	1
1986	Edm.	52	637	12.3	56	2	6	6	0
1987	Edm.	52	518	10.0	43	4	5	4	1
1988	Edm.	31	317	10.2	69	2	6	6	0
1989	Ott.	30	305	10.2	36	1	3	3	1
1990	B.C.	48	415	8.6	23	1	4	4	2
1991	B.C.	51	525	10.3	48	1	2	2	0
1993	B.C.	8	79	9.9	29	0	0	0	0
CFL TOTALS		**286**	**2953**	**10.3**	**69**	**12**	**28**	**26**	**5**

Kickoff Returns - 1 for 0 yards with Edmonton in 1984; 14 for 255 yards, 18.2 average, longest 25 yards in 1985 and 3 for 59 yards, 19.7 average, longest 30 yards in 1986.
CFL Total Kickoff Returns - 19 for 314 yards, 16.5 average, longest 30 yards.

Punt Returns - 1 for 11 yards with Edmonton in 1985.
CFL Total Punt Returns - 1 for 11 yards.

Fumble Returns - 1 for 0 yards with Edmonton in 1985.
CFL Total Fumble Returns - 1 for 0 yards.

Passing - 2 attempts, 2 complete for 40 yards, longest 28 yards and 1 TD with B.C. in 1990. **CFL Total Passing - 2 attempts, 2 complete for 40 yards, longest 28 yards and 1 TD.**

Punting - 1 for 5 yards with Ottawa in 1989.
CFL Total Punting - 1 for 5 yards.

2-Pt. Converts - 1 tried and 1 made good with Ottawa in 1989.
CFL Total 2-Pt. Converts - 1 tried and 1 made good.

Tackles - 4 defensive with Edmonton in 1987; 2 defensive in 1988; 2 defensive with Ottawa in 1989; 3 defensive with B.C. in 1990; 1 defensive and 2 special teams in 1991; 1 special teams with B.C. in 1993.
CFL Total Tackles - 15 (12 defensive and 3 special teams).

Playoffs

			Rushing					Pass Receiving				
	Team	GP	NO	YDS	AVE	LG	TD	NO	YDS	AVE	LG	TD
1984	Edm.	1	1	6	6.0	6	0	1	8	8.0	8	0
1985	Edm.	1	4	29	7.3	15	0	0	0	0.0	0	0
1986	Edm.	2	14	61	4.4	16	0	1	4	4.0	4	0
1987	Edm.	2	11	56	5.1	21	0	1	0	0.0	0	0
1988	Edm.	1	2	6	3.0	4	0	1	3	3.0	3	0
1991	B.C.	1	3	22	7.3	12	0	1	4	4.0	4	0
1993	B.C.	1	0	0	0.0	0	0	0	0	0.0	0	0
CFL TOTALS		**9**	**35**	**180**	**5.1**	**21**	**0**	**5**	**19**	**3.8**	**8**	**0**

Kickoff Returns - 1 for 19 yards with Edmonton in 1985 and 2 for 43 yards, 21.5 average, longest 28 yards in 1986.
CFL Total Playoff Kickoff Returns - 3 for 62 yards, 20.7 average, longest 28 yards.

Fumbles - 2 and 2 lost with Edmonton in 1986.
CFL Total Playoff Fumbles - 2 and 2 lost.

Tackles - 1 defensive with B.C. in 1991.
CFL Total Playoff Tackles - 1 (1 defensive).

Grey Cup

			Rushing					Pass Receiving				
	Team	GP	NO	YDS	AVE	LG	TD	NO	YDS	AVE	LG	TD
1986	Edm.	1	2	2	1.0	2	0	2	31	15.5	17	0
1987	Edm.	1	0	0	0.0	0	0	3	28	9.3	13	0
CFL TOTALS		**2**	**2**	**2**	**1.0**	**2**	**0**	**5**	**59**	**11.8**	**17**	**0**

Fumbles - 1 and 1 lost with Edmonton in 1986.
Total Grey Cup Fumbles - 1 and 1 lost.

SLACK, REGGIE
Born: May 2, 1968
Birthplace: Milton, Florida
Quarterback. 6'2", 220 lbs. Import
Last Amateur Club: Auburn University
Acquired: Selected by the Houston Oilers in the twelfth round (321st overall) in the 1990 NFL Draft. Released by Houston in August, 1990 and was subsequently re-signed to their practice roster in October, 1990. Granted unconditional free agency in February, 1991. Released by Houston in August, 1991 and re-signed to their practice squad later that month. Granted unconditional free agency in February, 1992. Assigned by Houston to the New York/New Jersey Knights in the 1992 WLAF Enhancement Allocation program in February, 1992. Signed as a free agent by the Winnipeg Blue Bombers in December, 1992. Released by Winnipeg in July, 1993. Signed as a free agent by the Toronto Argonauts in August, 1993.

		Scoring						Rushing				
	Team	GP	TD	C	FG	S	TP	NO	YDS	AVE	LG	TD
1993	Tor.	11	2	0	0	0	12	27	172	6.4	31	2
CFL TOTALS		**11**	**2**	**0**	**0**	**0**	**12**	**27**	**172**	**6.4**	**31**	**2**

		Passing							Fumbles		
	Team	ATT	COMP	YDS	PCT	INT	LG	TD	NO	LOST	OFR
1993	Tor.	184	104	1372	56.5	7	61	7	6	5	0
CFL TOTALS		**184**	**104**	**1372**	**56.5**	**7**	**61**	**7**	**6**	**5**	**0**

2-pt. Converts - 3 attempts, 0 complete with Toronto in 1993.
CFL Total 2-pt. Converts - 3 attempts, 0 complete.

Tackles - 1 defensive with Toronto in 1993.
CFL Total Tackles - 1 (1 defensive).

SMITH, DARRELL K.
Born: November 5, 1961
Birthplace: Youngstown, Ohio
Slotback. 6'2", 190 lbs. Import
Last Amateur Club: Central State University (Ohio)
Acquired: Signed as a free agent by the Toronto Argonauts in May, 1986 following brief stints with the NFL's Dallas Cowboys (1984) and Cincinnati Bengals (1985). Traded to the Edmonton Eskimos in January, 1993 along with cornerback Ed Berry, wide receiver Eddie Brown, linebacker Bruce Dickson, quarterback Rickey Foggie, slotback J.P. Izquierdo, defensive lineman Leonard Johnson and defensive back Don Wilson in exchange for defensive lineman Cameron Brosseau, linebacker John Davis, slotback Craig Ellis, quarterback Tracy Ham, cornerback Enis Jackson, running back Chris Johnstone, defensive back Travis Oliver and wide receiver Ken Winey. Released by Edmonton in August, 1993. Signed as a free agent by the Shreveport Pirates in March, 1994.

		Scoring						Pass Receiving				
	Team	GP	TD	C	FG	S	TP	NO	YDS	AVE	LG	TD
1986	Tor.	11	2	0	0	0	12	36	581	16.1	62	2
1987ab	Tor.	17	10	0	0	0	60	79	1392	17.6	54	10
1988a	Tor.	18	7	0	0	0	42	73	1306	17.9	67	7
1989a	Tor.	17	2	0	0	0	12	69	959	13.9	57	2
1990abcdef	Tor.	18	20	0	0	0	120	93	1826	19.6	88	20
1991a	Tor.	18	10	0	0	0	60	73	1399	19.2	89	9
1992	Tor.	13	2	0	0	0	13	42	681	16.2	43	2
1993	Edm.	4	0	0	0	0	0	11	98	8.9	18	0
CFL TOTALS		**116**	**53**	**0**	**0**	**0**	**319**	**476**	**8242**	**17.3**	**89**	**52**

		Fumbles			Rushing				
	Team	NO	LOST	OFR	NO	YDS	AVE	LG	TD
1986	Tor.	3	3	0	2	10	5.0	8	0
1987	Tor.	0	0	0	6	16	2.7	19	0
1988	Tor.	1	1	0	0	0	0.0	0	0
1989	Tor.	2	1	1	1	1	1.0	1	0
1990	Tor.	5	3	0	6	41	6.8	20	0
1991	Tor.	2	1	0	7	33	4.7	16	1
1992	Tor.	1	0	0	0	0	0.0	0	0
1993	Edm.	0	0	0	0	0	0.0	0	0
CFL TOTALS		**14**	**9**	**1**	**22**	**101**	**4.6**	**20**	**1**

SMITH, DARRELL K.

	Team	Punt Returns NO	YDS	AVE	LG	TD	Kickoff Returns NO	YDS	AVE	LG	TD
1986	Tor.	2	-7	-3.5	2	0	12	242	20.2	35	0
1987	Tor.	6	36	6.0	12	0	0	0	0.0	0	0
1988	Tor.	8	108	13.5	51	0	0	0	0.0	0	0
1989	Tor.	6	63	10.5	43	0	6	122	20.3	26	0
1990	Tor.	13	119	9.2	26	0	11	191	174	27	0
1991	Tor.	7	60	8.6	13	0	11	172	15.6	28	0
1992	Tor.	0	0	0.0	0	0	2	23	11.5	23	0
1993	Edm.	0	0	0.0	0	0	1	10	10.0	10	0
CFL TOTALS		**42**	**379**	**9.0**	**51**	**0**	**43**	**760**	**17.7**	**35**	**0**

Passing - 1 attempt, 0 complete and 1 interception with Toronto in 1987.
CFL Total Passing - 1 attempt, 0 complete and 1 interception.

Defensive Tackles - 3 with Toronto in 1987; 6 in 1988; 4 in 1989; 2 in 1990; 4 in 1991; 3 in 1992 and 1 in 1993. **CFL Total Defensive Tackles - 23.**

a - All-Eastern All-Star
b - CFL All-Star
c - Led CFL in Points Scored in TDs.
d - Led CFL in Receiving Yards and TDs
e - Set CFL Record for Most TDs on Pass Receptions in One Season.
f - Tied CFL Record for Most TDs in One Season.

Playoffs

	Team	Scoring GP	TD	C	FG	S	TP	Pass Receiving NO	YDS	AVE	LG	TD
1986	Tor.	2	2	0	0	0	12	7	170	24.3	48	2
1987	Tor.	2	0	0	0	0	0	9	161	17.9	48	0
1988	Tor.	1	0	0	0	0	0	4	31	7.8	11	0
1990	Tor.	2	1	0	0	0	6	8	191	23.9	99	1
1991	Tor.	1	2	0	0	0	12	6	87	14.5	24	2
CFL TOTALS		**8**	**5**	**0**	**0**	**0**	**30**	**34**	**640**	**18.8**	**99**	**5**

	Team	Rushing NO	YDS	AVE	LG	TD	Punt Returns NO	YDS	AVE	LG	TD
1987	Tor.	1	2	2.0	2	0	0	0	0.0	0	0
1988	Tor.	0	0	0.0	0	0	3	10	3.3	9	0
1990	Tor.	1	38	38.0	38	0	0	0	0.0	0	0
1991	Tor.	0	0	0.0	0	0	2	18	9.0	17	0
CFL TOTALS		**2**	**40**	**20.0**	**38**	**0**	**5**	**28**	**5.6**	**17**	**0**

Kickoff Returns - 1 for 31 yards with Toronto in 1991.
CFL Total Playoff Kickoff Returns - 1 for 31 yards.

Defensive Tackles - 1 with Toronto in 1990.
CFL Total Playoff Defensive Tackles - 1.

Grey Cup

	Team	Scoring GP	TD	C	FG	S	TP	Pass Receiving NO	YDS	AVE	LG	TD
1987	Tor.	1	0	0	0	0	0	3	51	17.0	23	0
1991	Tor.	1	1	0	0	0	6	3	62	20.7	48	1
CFL TOTALS		**2**	**1**	**0**	**0**	**0**	**6**	**6**	**113**	**18.8**	**48**	**1**

Kickoff Returns - 1 for 18 yards with Toronto in 1991.
Total Grey Cup Kickoff Returns - 1 for 18 yards.

SMITH, DARYLE
Born: January 18, 1964
Birthplace: Hawkins Court, Tennessee
Offensive Tackle. 6'5", 275 lbs. Import
Last Amateur Club: University of Tennessee
Acquired: Signed as a free agent by the NFL Seattle Seahawks in May, 1987. Released by Seattle in September, 1987. Signed as a replacement player by the NFL Dallas Cowboys in September, 1987. Traded by Dallas to the NFL Seattle Seahawks in July, 1989 in exchange for a ninth-round draft pick in the 1990 NFL Draft. Released by Seattle in August, 1989. Signed as a free agent by the NFL Cleveland Browns in September, 1989. Released by Cleveland in October, 1989. Signed as a free agent by the NFL Philadelphia Eagles in May, 1990. Released by Philadelphia in September, 1990 and was subsequently re-signed in October, 1990. Granted unconditional free agency in February, 1991. Re-signed by Philadelphia in July, 1991. Granted unconditional free agency in February, 1992. Re-signed by Philadelphia in June, 1992. Granted unconditional free agency in March, 1993. Signed as a free agent by the NFL Minnesota Vikings in April, 1993. Released by Minnesota during training camp. Signed as a free agent by the Toronto Argonauts in September, 1993. Released by Toronto in November, 1993.

Games Played - 4 with Toronto in 1993. **CFL Total GP - 4.**

Tackles - 1 defensive with Toronto in 1993.
CFL Total Tackles - 1 (1 defensive).

SMITH, DEMETRIUS (PEE-WEE)
Born: January 3, 1968
Birthplace: Compton, California
Wide Receiver. 6'1", 180 lbs. Import
Last Amateur Club: University of Miami
Acquired: Signed as a free agent by the Calgary Stampeders in September, 1990.

	Team	Scoring GP	TD	C	FG	S	TP	Kickoff Returns NO	YDS	AVE	LG	TD
1990	Cal.	6	0	0	0	0	0	4	72	18.0	32	0
1991	Cal.	14	3	0	0	0	18	29	700	24.1	89	1
1992	Cal.	18	5	0	0	0	30	41	924	22.5	51	0
1993	Cal.	16	2	0	0	0	12	7	161	23.0	41	0
CFL TOTALS		**54**	**10**	**0**	**0**	**0**	**60**	**81**	**1857**	**22.9**	**89**	**1**

	Team	Pass Receiving NO	YDS	AVE	LG	TD	Punt Returns NO	YDS	AVE	LG	TD
1990	Cal.	5	107	21.4	53	0	16	194	12.1	47	0
1991	Cal.	36	467	13.0	48	0	48	713	14.9	87	2
1992	Cal.	30	469	15.6	81	5	81	615	7.6	69	0
1993	Cal.	33	417	12.6	31	1	21	281	13.4	67	1
CFL TOTALS		**104**	**1460**	**14.0**	**81**	**6**	**166**	**1803**	**10.9**	**87**	**3**

Rushing - 1 for -6 yards with Calgary in 1991; 2 for 16 yards, 8.0 average, longest 16 yards in 1992 and 1 for 2 yards in 1993.
CFL Total Rushing - 4 for 12 yards, 3.0 average, longest 16 yards.

Unsuccessful Field Goal Returns - 3 for 27 yards, 9.0 average, longest 20 yards with Calgary in 1991; 8 for 123 yards, 15.4 average, longest 31 yards in 1992 and 3 for 81 yards, 27.0 average, longest 39 yards in 1993.
CFL Total Unsuccessful Field Goal Returns - 14 for 231 yards, 16.5 average, longest 39 yards.

Blocked Kicks - 2 punts with Calgary in 1991. **CFL Total Blocked Kicks - 2 punts.**

Fumbles - 2 and 0 lost with Calgary in 1990; 5 and 2 lost in 1991; 8 and 3 lost in 1992 and 1 and 1 lost in 1993. **CFL Total Fumbles - 16 and 6 lost.**

Own Fumbles Recovered - 3 with Calgary in 1991 and 5 in 1992.
CFL Total OFR - 8.

Tackles - 2 defensive and 1 special teams with Calgary in 1991; 1 defensive and 3 special teams in 1992 and 1 defensive and 9 special teams in 1993.
CFL Total Tackles - 17 (4 defensive and 13 special teams).

Playoffs

	Team	Scoring GP	TD	C	FG	S	TP	Pass Receiving NO	YDS	AVE	LG	TD
1990	Cal.	1	0	0	0	0	0	0	0	0.0	0	0
1991	Cal.	2	2	0	0	0	12	8	201	25.1	67	2
1992	Cal.	1	0	0	0	0	0	1	5	5.0	5	0
1993	Cal.	2	1	0	0	0	6	1	17	17.0	17	0
CFL TOTALS		**6**	**3**	**0**	**0**	**0**	**18**	**10**	**223**	**22.3**	**67**	**2**

	Team	Punt Returns NO	YDS	AVE	LG	TD	Kickoff Returns NO	YDS	AVE	LG	TD
1990	Cal.	0	0	0.0	0	0	0	0	0.0	0	0
1991	Cal.	6	36	6.0	18	0	3	46	15.3	16	0
1992	Cal.	5	18	3.6	8	0	0	0	0.0	0	0
1993	Cal.	2	65	32.5	64	1	0	0	0.0	0	0
CFL TOTALS		**13**	**119**	**9.2**	**64**	**1**	**3**	**46**	**15.3**	**16**	**0**

Fumbles - 2 and 1 lost with Calgary in 1991 and 1 and 0 lost with Calgary in 1992.
CFL Total Playoff Fumbles - 3 and 1 lost.

Tackles - 1 special teams with Calgary in 1991 and 2 special teams in 1993.
CFL Total Playoff Tackles - 3 (3 special teams).

Grey Cup

	Team	Scoring GP	TD	C	FG	S	TP	Pass Receiving NO	YDS	AVE	LG	TD
1991	Cal.	1	0	0	0	0	0	4	39	9.8	23	0
1992	Cal.	1	0	0	0	0	0	3	33	11.0	28	0
CFL TOTALS		**2**	**0**	**0**	**0**	**0**	**0**	**7**	**72**	**10.3**	**28**	**0**

	Team	Punt Returns NO	YDS	AVE	LG	TD	Kickoff Returns NO	YDS	AVE	LG	TD
1991	Cal.	6	46	7.7	17	0	3	36	12.0	21	0
1992	Cal.	1	0	0.0	0	0	1	18	18.0	18	0
CFL TOTALS		**7**	**46**	**6.6**	**17**	**0**	**4**	**54**	**13.5**	**21**	**0**

Unsuccessful Field Goal Returns - 1 for 18 yards with Calgary in 1992.
Total Grey Cup Unsuccessful Field Goal Returns - 1 for 18 yards.

Rushing - 1 for 16 yards with Calgary in 1991.
Total Grey Cup Rushing - 1 for 16 yards.

Fumbles - 1 and 1 lost with Calgary in 1991.
Total Grey Cup Fumbles - 1 and 1 lost.

Tackles - 1 special teams with Calgary in 1991 and 1 special teams with Calgary in 1992. **Total Grey Cup Tackles - 2 (2 special teams).**

SMITH, DONALD
Born: February 21, 1968
Birthplace: Danville, Virginia
Defensive Back. 6'0", 185 lbs. Import
Last Amateur Club: Liberty University
Acquired: Selected by the Minnesota Vikings in the tenth round (271st overall) in the 1990 NFL draft. Released following training camp. Signed as a free agent by the NFL Dallas Cowboys in 1991. Released following training camp. Signed as a free agent by the Winnipeg Blue Bombers in February, 1992.

		Scoring						Interception Returns				
	Team	GP	TD	C	FG	S	TP	NO	YDS	AVE	LG	TD
1992	Wpg.	17	1	0	0	0	6	3	0	0.0	0	0
1993	Wpg.	18	1	0	0	0	6	5	24	4.8	16	0
CFL TOTALS		**35**	**2**	**0**	**0**	**0**	**12**	**8**	**24**	**3.0**	**16**	**0**

		Punt Returns					Kickoff Returns				
	Team	NO	YDS	AVE	LG	TD	NO	YDS	AVE	LG	TD
1992	Wpg.	23	208	9.0	71	1	11	165	15.0	40	0
1993	Wpg.	6	50	8.3	25	1	5	142	28.4	73	0
CFL TOTALS		**29**	**258**	**8.9**	**71**	**2**	**16**	**307**	**19.2**	**73**	**0**

Unsuccessful Field Goal Returns - 1 for 5 yards, 5.0 average, longest 5 yards with Winnipeg in 1992. **CFL Total Unsuccessful Field Goal Returns - 1 for 5 yards, 5.0 average, longest 5 yards.**

Fumbles - 1 and 1 lost with Winnipeg in 1992. **CFL Total Fumbles - 1 and 1 lost.**

Fumble Returns - 2 for 0 yards with Winnipeg in 1993.
CFL Total Fumble Returns - 2 for 0 yards.

Own Fumbles Recovered - 1 with Winnipeg in 1992 and 1 in 1993.
CFL Total OFR - 2.

Tackles - 67 defensive and 24 special teams with Winnipeg in 1992 and 51 defensive and 10 special teams.
CFL Total Tackles - 152 (118 defensive and 34 special teams).

All Eastern All-Star in 1993.

Playoffs

Games Played - 1 with Winnipeg in 1992 and 1 in 1993. **CFL Total Playoff GP - 2.**

Tackles - 2 defensive and 1 special teams with Winnipeg in 1992 and 8 defensive and 1 special teams in 1993.
CFL Total Playoff Tackles - 12 (10 defensive and 2 special teams).

Grey Cup

Games Played - 1 with Winnipeg in 1992 and 1 in 1993. **Total Grey Cup GP - 2.**

Tackles - 6 defensive and 3 special teams with Winnipeg in 1992 and 3 defensive in 1993.
Total Grey Cup Tackles - 12 (9 defensive and 3 special teams).

SMITH, LEROY
Born: January 6, 1969
Birthplace: El Paso, Texas
Defensive End. 6'2", 225 lbs. Import
Last Amateur Club: University of Iowa
Acquired: Signed as a free agent by the Toronto Argonauts in October, 1993. Released by Toronto in March, 1994.

Games Played - 2 with Toronto in 1993**. CFL Total GP - 2.**

Tackles - 1 special teams with Toronto in 1993.
CFL Total Tackles - 1 (1 special teams).

SMITH, ROBERT (ROB)
Born: October 3, 1958
Birthplace: New Westminster, B.C.
Tackle. 6'4", 270 lbs. Non-import
Last Amateur Club: Utah State University
Acquired: First Territorial Exemption of the B.C. Lions in 1981. Waived to the Toronto Argonauts along with linebacker Don Moen and defensive lineman Richard Mohr in July, 1982. Played one game and then loaned to the Montreal Concordes. Recalled by Toronto at the end of the 1982 CFL season and then traded to Montreal in June, 1983 for wide receiver Kevin Neiles. Traded to the Calgary Stampeders in May, 1986 for defensive back Darrell Moir. Traded to B.C. Lions in October, 1988 for guard Leo Blanchard. Traded to the Ottawa Rough Riders in March, 1990 in exchange for offensive linemen Richard McCrory and Rocco Romano and running back Chris Skinner. Traded to the B.C. Lions in April, 1993 along with cornerback Less Browne and linebacker Patrick Wayne in exchange for offensive linemen Carl Coulter and Chris Gioskos, kicker Wayne Lammle, cornerback Joe Mero and linebacker Mark Scott.

Games Played - 1 with B.C. in 1981; 1 with Toronto in 1982; 13 with Montreal in 1982; 16 in 1983; 16 in 1984; 16 in 1985; 18 with Calgary in 1986; 18 in 1987; 13 in 1988; 5 with B.C. in 1988; 18 in 1989; 18 with Ottawa in 1990; 18 in 1991; 18 in 1992 and 18 with B.C. in 1993.
CFL Total GP - 207.

Own Fumbles Recovered - 2 in 1984 with Montreal; 1 in 1985; 1 with Calgary in 1987; 1 with B.C. in 1989; 1 with Ottawa in 1990 and 1 with B.C. in 1993.
CFL Total OFR - 7.

Fumble Returns - 1 for 0 yards with Calgary in 1986.
CFL Total Fumble Returns - 1 for 0 yards.

Tackles - 1 defensive with Calgary in 1987; 2 defensive in 1988; 2 defensive with Ottawa in 1990; 1 defensive in 1991; 3 defensive and 1 special teams in 1992 and 2 defensive with B.C. in 1993.
CFL Total Tackles - 12 (11 defensive and 1 special teams).

All-Eastern All-Star in 1990 and 1992.
All-Western All-Star in 1993.
CFL All-Star in 1992 and 1993.
Winner Leo Dandurand Trophy for Outstanding Offensive Lineman in Eastern Division in 1992.
Winner CFL Most Outstanding Offensive Lineman in 1992.

Playoffs

Games Played - 1 with Montreal in 1984; 2 in 1985; 1 with Calgary in 1986; 1 in 1987; 2 with B.C. in 1988; 1 with Ottawa in 1990; 1 in 1991; 1 in 1992 and 1 in 1993. **CFL Total Playoff GP - 11.**

Grey Cup

Games Played - 1 with B.C. in 1988. **Total Grey Cup GP - 1.**

SNIPES, ANGELO
Born: November 1, 1963
Birthplace: Atlanta, Georgia
Linebacker. 6'1", 235 lbs. Import
Last Amateur Club: West Georgia College
Acquired: Selected in the 14th round (196th overall) in the 1985 USFL Draft by the Oakland Invaders. Traded to Memphis Showboats in February, 1986 for past considerations. Granted free agency when USFL suspended operations. Signed as a free agent by the NFL Washington Redskins in August, 1986. Released by Washington in November, 1986 and awarded on waivers to San Diego Chargers. Released by San Diego in October, 1987. Signed as a free agent by the Kansas City Chiefs in December, 1987. Released in 1990 and signed as a free agent by the Ottawa Rough Riders in May, 1991. Released by Ottawa in November, 1992. Re-signed by Ottawa in June, 1993.

Games Played - 15 with Ottawa in 1991; 18 in 1992 and 18 in 1993.
CFL Total GP - 51.

Scoring - 1 TD for 6 points with Ottawa in 1991.
CFL Total Scoring - 1 TD for 6 points.

Interception Returns - 1 for 89 yards and 1 TD with Ottawa in 1991 and 1 for 10 yards in 1992. **CFL Total Interception Returns - 2 for 99 yards, 49.5 average, longest 89 yards and 1 TD.**

Fumble Returns - 1 for 2 yards with Ottawa in 1991; 1 for 0 yards in 1992 and 1 for 3 yards in 1993.
CFL Total Fumble Returns - 3 for 5 yards, 1.7 average, longest 3 yards.

Quarterback Sacks - 5 with Ottawa in 1991; 20 for 146 yards lost in 1992 and 14 for 128 yards lost in 1993. **CFL Total QB Sacks - 39.**

Tackles - 52 defensive and 4 special teams with Ottawa in 1991; 43 defensive and 3 special teams in 1992 and 32 defensive and 1 special teams in 1993.
CFL Total Tackles - 135 (127 defensive and 8 special teams).

Tackles for Losses - 7 for 12 yards with Ottawa in 1992 and 3 for 5 yards in 1993. **CFL Total Tackles for Losses - 10 for 17 yards.**

All-Eastern All-Star in 1992 and 1993.
CFL All-Star in 1992.
Led CFL in Quarterback Sacks in 1992.
Winner, Jeff Russel Memorial Trophy - Most Outstanding Player, Eastern Division in 1992.
Winner, James P. McCaffrey Trophy - Most Outstanding Defensive Player, Eastern Division in 1992.
Runner-up CFL Most Outstanding Player in 1992.
Runner-up CFL Most Outstanding Defensive Player in 1992.

Playoffs

Games Played - 1 with Ottawa in 1991; 1 in 1992 and 1 in 1993.
CFL Total Playoff GP - 3.

Quarterback Sacks - 1 for 8 yards lost with Ottawa in 1993.
CFL Total Playoff QB Sacks - 1 for 8 yards lost.

Tackles - 3 defensive and 1 special teams with Ottawa in 1991; 2 defensive with Ottawa in 1992 and 2 defensive in 1993.
CFL Total Playoff Tackles - 8 (7 defensive and 1 special teams).

SOLES, MICHAEL
Born: November 8, 1966
Birthplace: Point Claire,Quebec
Running Back. 6'1", 215 lbs. Non-import
Last Amateur Club: McGill University (OQIFC)
Acquired: Selected in the first round (fifth overall) by the Edmonton Eskimos in the 1989 CFL College Draft.

SOLES, MICHAEL

	Team	Scoring GP	TD	C	FG	S	TP	Rushing NO	YDS	AVE	LG	TD
1989	Edm.	18	2	0	0	0	12	33	215	6.5	31	2
1990	Edm.	18	2	x1	0	0	14	52	394	7.6	45	0
1991	Edm.	16	3	0	0	0	18	45	302	6.7	49	1
1992	Edm.	18	4	0	0	0	24	115	656	5.7	51	4
1993	Edm.	18	3	0	0	0	18	79	334	4.2	18	3
CFL TOTALS		**88**	**14**	**x1**	**0**	**0**	**86**	**324**	**1901**	**5.9**	**51**	**10**

	Team	Pass Receiving NO	YDS	AVE	LG	TD	Kickoff Returns NO	YDS	AVE	LG	TD
1989	Edm.	3	17	5.7	9	0	2	20	10.0	14	0
1990	Edm.	16	158	9.9	29	2	1	12	12.0	12	0
1991	Edm.	16	135	8.4	16	2	2	3	1.5	3	0
1992	Edm.	25	285	11.4	39	0	1	0	0.0	0	0
1993	Edm.	26	263	10.1	25	0	1	0	0.0	0	0
CFL TOTALS		**86**	**858**	**10.0**	**39**	**4**	**7**	**35**	**5.0**	**14**	**0**

Fumble Returns - 2 for 0 yards with Edmonton in 1989.
CFL Total Fumble Returns - 2 for 0 yards.

Passing - 1 attempt, 0 complete and 1 interception with Edmonton in 1992.
CFL Total Passing - 1 attempt, 0 made and 1 interception.

Fumbles - 2 and 2 lost with Edmonton in 1990; 1 and 1 lost in 1991 and 1 and 1 lost in 1993. **CFL Total Fumbles - 4 and 4 lost.**

Own Fumbles Recovered - 1 with Edmonton in 1989; 1 in 1991; 3 in 1992 and 2 in 1993. **CFL Total OFR - 7.**

Tackles - 3 defensive with Edmonton in 1989; 2 defensive in 1990; 2 defensive and 17 special teams in 1991; 3 defensive and 9 special teams in 1992 and 3 defensive and 6 special teams in 1993.
CFL Total Tackles - 45 (13 defensive and 32 special teams).

Playoffs

	Team	GP	Rushing NO	YDS	AVE	LG	TD	Pass Receiving NO	YDS	AVE	LG	TD
1989	Edm.	1	1	4	4.0	4	0	0	0	0.0	0	0
1990	Edm.	2	5	18	3.6	7	0	3	26	8.7	11	0
1991	Edm.	1	1	29	29.0	29	0	0	0	0.0	0	0
1992	Edm.	2	26	151	5.8	21	1	5	29	5.8	10	0
1993	Edm.	2	4	18	4.5	9	0	6	53	8.8	11	0
CFL TOTALS		**8**	**37**	**220**	**6.0**	**29**	**1**	**14**	**108**	**7.7**	**11**	**0**

Kickoff Returns - 2 for 9 yards, 4.5 average, longest 6 yards with Edmonton in 1989 and 1 for 9 yards in 1990.
CFL Total Playoff Kickoff Returns - 3 for 18 yards, 6.0 average, longest 9 yards.

Fumbles - 1 and 1 lost with Edmonton in 1990.
CFL Total Playoff Fumbles - 1 and 1 lost.

Fumble Returns - 1 for 0 yards with Edmonton in 1990.
CFL Total Playoff Fumble Returns - 1 for 0 yards.

Tackles - 2 special teams with Edmonton in 1991.
CFL Total Playoff Tackles - 2 (2 special teams).

Grey Cup

Games Played - 1 with Edmonton in 1990 and 1 in 1993. **Total Grey Cup GP - 2.**

Rushing - 1 for 8 yards with Edmonton in 1990 and 5 for 4 yards, 0.8 average, longest 6 yards in 1993.
Total Grey Cup Rushing - 6 for 12 yards, 2.0 average, longest 8 yards.

Pass Receiving - 2 for 17 yards, 8.5 average, longest 13 yards with Edmonton in 1990 and 4 for 46 yards, 11.5 average, longest 18 yards in 1993.
Total Grey Cup Pass Receiving - 6 for 63 yards, 10.5 average, longest 18 yards.

STANLEY, WALTER

Born: November 5, 1962
Birthplace: Chicago, Illinois
Wide Receiver. 5'10", 180 lbs. Import
Last Amateur Club: Mesa College
Acquired: Selected by the Memphis Showboats in the fourth round (54th overall) in the 1985 USFL Draft. Selected by the NFL Green Bay Packers in September, 1989. Granted unconditional free agency in February, 1990. Signed as a free agent by the NFL Washington Redskins in March, 1990. Signed as a free agent by the Ottawa Rough Riders in September, 1993.

	Team	Scoring GP	TD	C	FG	S	TP	Rushing NO	YDS	AVE	LG	TD
1993	Ott.	4	1	0	0	0	6	11	302	27.5	57	1
CFL TOTALS		**4**	**1**	**0**	**0**	**0**	**6**	**11**	**302**	**27.5**	**57**	**1**

	Team	Punt Returns NO	YDS	AVE	LG	TD	Kickoff Returns NO	YDS	AVE	LG	TD
1993	Ott.	32	175	5.5	44	0	8	110	13.8	21	0
CFL TOTALS		**32**	**175**	**5.5**	**44**	**0**	**8**	**110**	**13.8**	**21**	**0**

Fumbles - 1 and 1 lost with Ottawa in 1993. **CFL Total Fumbles - 1 and 1 lost.**

STEVENSON, VICTOR

Born: September 22, 1960
Birthplace: New Westminster, B.C.
Tackle. 6'4", 255 lbs. Non-import
Last Amateur Club: University of Calgary (WIFL)
Acquired: Selected in the fifth round (37th overall) by the Saskatchewan Roughriders in the 1981 CFL College Draft. Released by Saskatchewan in March, 1993. Signed as a free agent by the B.C. Lions in June, 1993.

Games Played - INJURED with Saskatchewan in 1982; 10 in 1983; 16 in 1984; 16 in 1985; 12 in 1986; 18 in 1987; 18 in 1988; 18 in 1989; 18 in 1990; 18 in 1991; 18 in 1992 and 18 with B.C. in 1993. **CFL Total GP - 180.**

Fumble Returns - 1 for 8 yards with Saskatchewan in 1984.
CFL Total Fumble Returns - 1 for 8 yards.

Rushing - 0 for 2 yards, longest 2 yards with Saskatchewan in 1985.
CFL Total Rushing - 0 for 2 yards, longest 2 yards.

Own Fumbles Recovered - 1 with Saskatchewan in 1985 and 1 in 1987.
CFL Total OFR - 2.

Defensive Tackles - 1 with Saskatchewan in 1988; 1 in 1989 and 1 in 1991.
CFL Total Defensive Tackles - 3.

All-Western All-Star in 1991 and 1992.
CFL All-Star in 1992.
Winner DeMarco-Becket Memorial Trophy for Most Outstanding Offensive Lineman in Western Division in 1992.
Runner-up CFL Most Outstanding Offensive Lineman in 1992.

Playoffs

Games Played - 1 with Saskatchewan in 1988; 2 in 1989; 1 in 1990; 1 in 1992 and 1 with B.C. in 1993. **CFL Total Playoff GP - 6.**

Own Fumbles Recovered - 1 with B.C. in 1993. **CFL Total OFR - 1**.

Grey Cup

Games Played - 1 with Saskatchewan in 1989. **Total Grey Cup GP - 1.**

STEWART, ANDREW

Born: November 20, 1965
Birthplace: Kingston, Jamaica
Defensive Tackle. 6'3", 275 lbs. Non-import
Last Amateur Club: University of Cincinnati
Acquired: Signed as a free agent by the Ottawa Rough Riders in October, 1993.

Games Played - 6 with Ottawa in 1993. **CFL Total GP - 6.**

Fumble Returns - 1 for 0 yards with Ottawa in 1993.
CFL Total Fumble Returns - 1 for 0 yards.

Tackles - 11 defensive and 1 special teams with Ottawa in 1993.
CFL Total Tackles - 12 (11 defensive and 1 special teams).

Tackles for Losses - 1 for 1 yard with Ottawa in 1993.
CFL Total Tackles for Losses - 1 for 1 yard.

Playoffs

Games Played - 1 with Ottawa in 1993. **CFL Total Playoff GP - 1.**

Fumble Returns - 1 for 0 yards with Ottawa in 1993.
CFL Total Playoff Fumble Returns - 1 for 0 yards.

STEWART, TONY

Born: January 30, 1968
Birthplace: Chester, South Carolina
Running Back. 6'1", 206 lbs. Import
Last Amateur Club: University of Iowa
Acquired: Selected by the Seattle Seahawks in the tenth round (297th overall) in the 1991 NFL Draft. Signed as a free agent by the Calgary Stampeders in January, 1993.

	Team	Scoring GP	TD	C	FG	S	TP	Rushing NO	YDS	AVE	LG	TD
1993	Cal.	6	1	0	0	0	6	53	196	3.7	17	1
CFL TOTALS		**6**	**1**	**0**	**0**	**0**	**6**	**53**	**196**	**3.7**	**17**	**1**

	Team	Pass Receiving NO	YDS	AVE	LG	TD	Fumbles NO	LOST	OFR
1993	Cal.	8	87	10.9	20	0	3	2	1
CFL TOTALS		**8**	**87**	**10.9**	**20**	**0**	**3**	**2**	**1**

Tackles - 1 defensive and 1 special teams with Calgary in 1993.
CFL Total Tackles - 2 (1 defensive and 1 special teams).

STORME, TODD
Born: October 16, 1964
Birthplace: Red Deer, Alberta
Offensive Tackle. 6'5", 275 lbs. Non-import
Last Amateur Club: Utah State University
Acquired: Selected in the first round (third overall) by the Edmonton Eskimos in the 1987 CFL College Draft. Released by Edmonton in August, 1991. Signed as a free agent by the Calgary Stampeders in February, 1992.

Games Played - 18 with Calgary in 1993. **CFL Total GP - 18.**

Tackles - 1 defensive with Calgary in 1993. **CFL Total Tackles - 1 (1 defensive).**

Playoffs

Games Played - 2 with Calgary in 1993. **CFL Total Playoff GP - 2.**

STUMON, GREGG
Born: May 26, 1963
Birthplace: Plain Dealing, Louisiana
Defensive End. 6'0", 235 lbs. Import
Last Amateur Club: University of Southern Arkansas
Acquired: Signed as a free agent by the B.C. Lions prior to the 1986 season. Traded to the Edmonton Eskimos in January, 1989 along with linebacker Jeff Braswell, wide receiver Jim Sandusky, running back Reggie Taylor, defensive back Andre Francis and a first round draft choice in the 1989 CFL College Draft (linebacker Leroy Blugh) to complete a trade for quarterback Matt Dunigan. Granted free agent status in March, 1990. Signed as a free agent by the Ottawa Rough Riders in June, 1990. Transferred to the Shreveport Pirates in February, 1994.

			Scoring					Fumble Returns				
	Team	GP	TD	C	FG	S	TP	NO	YDS	AVE	LG	TD
1986	B.C.	1	0	0	0	0	0	0	11	0.0	11	0
1987abcde	B.C.	17	0	0	0	0	0	0	0	0.0	0	0
1988de	B.C.	18	0	0	0	1	1	4	11	2.8	11	0
1989	Edm.	18	0	0	0	0	0	2	0	0.0	0	0
1990ef	Ott.	18	1	0	0	0	6	2	0	0.0	0	0
1991	Ott.	18	0	0	0	0	0	1	0	0.0	0	0
1992f	Ott.	17	0	0	0	0	0	3	33	11.0	21	0
1993	Ott.	18	0	0	0	0	0	2	0	0.0	0	0
CFL TOTALS		**125**	**1**	**0**	**0**	**1**	**7**	**14**	**55**	**3.9**	**21**	**0**

Interception Returns - 1 for 20 yards with B.C. in 1988 and 1 for 21 yards and 1 TD with Ottawa in 1990. **CFL Total Interception Returns - 2 for 41 yards, 20.5 average, longest 21 yards and 1 TD.**

Rushing - 1 for 5 yards with Ottawa in 1992 and 1 for 3 yards in 1993. **CFL Total Rushing - 2 for 8 yards, 4.0 average, longest 5 yards.**

Kickoff Returns - 1 for 0 yards with Ottawa in 1991 and 1 for 0 yards in 1993. **CFL Total Kickoff Returns - 2 for 0 yards.**

Fumbles - 1 and 0 lost with Ottawa in 1992. **CFL Total Fumbles - 1 and 0 lost.**

Punting - 1 for 20 yards and 1 single with B.C. in 1988. **CFL Total Punting - 1 for 20 yards and 1 single.**

Own Fumbles Recovered - 1 with Ottawa in 1991. **CFL Total OFR - 1.**

Quarterback Sacks - 23 with B.C. in 1987; 8 in 1988; 8 with Edmonton in 1989; 13 with Ottawa in 1990; 9 in 1991; 11 for 74 yards lost in 1992 and 8 for 58 yards lost in 1993. **CFL Total QB Sacks - 80.**

Tackles - 34 defensive with B.C. in 1987; 61 defensive in 1988; 25 defensive with Edmonton in 1989; 59 defensive with Ottawa in 1990; 49 defensive and 4 special teams in 1991; 29 defensive and 10 special teams in 1992 and 31 defensive and 10 special teams in 1993. **CFL Total Tackles - 312 (288 defensive and 24 special teams).**

Tackles for Losses - 6 for 23 yards with Ottawa in 1991; 4 for 17 yards in 1992 and 4 for 14 yards in 1993. **CFL Total Tackles for Losses - 14 for 54 yards.**

a - Schenley Most Outstanding Defensive Player.
b - Winner of the Norm Fieldgate Trophy as Most Outstanding Defensive Player, Western Division.
c - Led CFL in Quarterback Sacks.
d - All-Western All-Star.
e - CFL All-Star.
f - All-Eastern All-Star.

Playoffs

Games Played - 1 with B.C. in 1986; 1 in 1987; 2 in 1988; 1 with Edmonton in 1989; 1 with Ottawa in 1990; 1 in 1991; 1 in 1992 and 1 in 1993. **CFL Total Playoff GP - 9.**

Fumble Returns - 1 for 0 yards with B.C. in 1987 and 1 for 26 yards with Ottawa in 1990. **CFL Total Playoff Fumble Returns - 2 for 26 yards, 13.0 average, longest 26 yards.**

Quarterback Sacks - 1 with B.C. in 1988; 2 with Ottawa in 1990 and 1 for 3 yards lost in 1993. **CFL Total Playoff QB Sacks - 4.**

Defensive Tackles - 6 with B.C. in 1988; 4 with Edmonton in 1989; 1 with Ottawa in 1990; 4 in 1991; 1 in 1992 and 6 in 1993. **CFL Total Playoff Defensive Tackles - 22.**

Tackles for Losses - 1 for 2 yards with Ottawa in 1991. **CFL Total Playoff Tackles for Losses - 1 for 2 yards.**

Grey Cup

Games Played - 1 with B.C. in 1988. **Total Grey Cup GP - 1.**

Quarterback Sacks - 1 with B.C. in 1988. **Total Grey Cup QB Sacks - 1.**

Defensive Tackles - 2 with B.C. in 1988. **Total Grey Cup Defensive Tackles - 2.**

SUBIS, NICK
Born: December 24, 1967
Birthplace: Inglewood, California
Offensive Tackle. 6'4", 278 lbs. Import
Last Amateur Club: San Diego State University
Acquired: Selected by the Denver Broncos in the sixth round (142nd overall) in the 1991 NFL Draft. Released by Denver in August, 1992. Signed as a free agent by the NFL Los Angeles Rams in April, 1993. Signed as a free agent by the Sacramento Gold Miners in August, 1993. Released by Sacramento in October, 1993.

Games Played - 4 with Sacramento in 1993. **CFL Total GP - 4.**

SUITOR, GLEN
Born: November 24, 1962
Birthplace: Sidney, B.C.
Defensive Back. 6'0", 190 lbs. Non-import
Last Amateur Club: Simon Fraser University (EVCO)
Acquired: Selected in the second round (10th overall) by the Saskatchewan Roughriders in the 1984 CFL College Draft.

			Scoring					Interception Returns				
	Team	GP	TD	C	FG	S	TP	NO	YDS	AVE	LG	TD
1984	Sask.	16	0	0	0	0	0	4	67	16.8	33	0
1985	Sask.	16	0	0	0	0	0	5	50	10.0	24	0
1986	Sask.	18	0	0	0	0	0	1	0	0.0	0	0
1987	Sask.	18	3	0	0	0	18	7	112	16.0	56	2
1988	Sask.	18	0	0	0	0	0	2	80	40.0	75	0
1989a	Sask.	18	0	0	0	0	0	5	49	9.8	17	0
1990	Sask.	18	0	0	0	0	0	3	33	11.0	31	0
1991ab	Sask.	18	0	0	0	0	0	8	145	18.1	42	0
1992ab	Sask.	18	0	0	0	0	0	6	30	5.0	31	0
1993ab	Sask.	18	0	0	0	0	0	5	72	14.4	26	0
CFL TOTALS		**176**	**3**	**0**	**0**	**0**	**18**	**46**	**638**	**13.9**	**75**	**2**

		Fumble Returns					Fumbles		
	Team	NO	YDS	AVE	LG	TD	NO	LOST	OFR
1984	Sask.	1	0	0.0	0	0	1	1	0
1985	Sask.	0	0	0.0	0	0	0	0	0
1986	Sask.	4	4	1.0	4	0	1	1	1
1987	Sask.	1	0	0.0	0	0	0	0	1
1988	Sask.	1	0	0.0	0	0	2	2	0
1989	Sask.	1	0	0.0	0	0	1	0	1
1990	Sask.	1	29	29.0	29	0	0	0	0
1991	Sask.	3	0	0.0	0	0	1	1	2
1992	Sask.	1	0	0.0	0	0	1	0	1
1993	Sask.	0	0	0.0	0	0	0	0	1
CFL TOTALS		**13**	**33**	**2.5**	**29**	**0**	**7**	**5**	**7**

Passing - 1 attempt with Saskatchewan in 1986. **CFL Total Passing - 1 attempt.**

Rushing - 1 for -1 yard with Saskatchewan in 1986 and 1 for 12 yards and 1 TD in 1987. **CFL Total Rushing - 2 for 11 yards, 5.5 average, longest 12 yards and 1 TD.**

Unsuccessful Field Goal Returns - 1 for 5 yards with Saskatchewan in 1992. **CFL Total Unsuccessful Field Goal Returns - 1 for 5 yards.**

Punt Returns - 5 for 25 yards, 5.0 average, longest 8 yards with Saskatchewan in 1984; 1 for 0 yards in 1986 and 1 for 2 yards in 1992. **CFL Total Punt Returns - 7 for 27 yards, 3.9 average, longest 8 yards.**

Punting - 1 for 41 yards with Saskatchewan in 1991. **CFL Total Punting - 1 for 41 yards.**

Quarterback Sacks - 1 with Saskatchewan in 1988; 2 in 1989 and 1 in 1990. **CFL Total QB Sacks - 4.**

2-Pt. Converts - 2 attempts with Saskatchewan in 1988. **CFL Total 2-Pt. Converts - 2 attempts.**

SUITOR, GLEN

Tackles - 50 defensive with Saskatchewan in 1987; 28 defensive in 1988; 38 defensive in 1989; 27 defensive in 1990; 54 defensive and 7 special teams in 1991; 59 defensive and 4 special teams in 1992 and 44 defensive in 1993. **CFL Total Tackles - 311 (300 defensive and 11 special teams).**

Tackles for Losses - 2 for 2 yards with Saskatchewan in 1992 and 1 for 4 yards in 1993. **CFL Total Tackles for Losses - 3 for 6 yards.**

a - All-Western All-Star
b - CFL All-Star

Playoffs

Games Played - 2 with Saskatchewan in 1989; 1 in 1990; 1 in 1992 and 1 in 1993. **CFL Total Playoff GP - 5.**

Tackles - 4 defensive with Saskatchewan in 1992 and 4 defensive in 1993. **CFL Total Playoff Tackles - 8 (8 defensive).**

Interception Returns - 1 for 9 yards with Saskatchewan in 1989. **CFL Total Playoff Interception Returns - 1 for 9 yards.**

Quarterback Sacks - 1 with Saskatchewan in 1989. **CFL Total Playoff QB Sacks - 1.**

Defensive Tackles - 6 with Saskatchewan in 1989; 3 in 1990 and 4 in 1993. **CFL Total Playoff Defensive Tackles - 13.**

Grey Cup

Games Played - 1 with Saskatchewan in 1989. **Total Grey Cup GP - 1.**

Interception Returns - 1 for 18 yards with Saskatchewan in 1989. **Total Grey Cup Interception Returns - 1 for 18 yards.**

Defensive Tackles - 1 with Saskatchewan in 1989. **Total Grey Cup Defensive Tackles - 1.**

TARAS, JAMIE
Born: January 31, 1966
Birthplace: Acton, Ontario
Running Back/Offensive Guard. 6'3", 240 lbs. Non-import
Last Amateur Club: University of Western Ontario (OUAA)
Acquired: Selected in the third round (25th overall) by the B.C. Lions in the 1987 CFL College Draft.

			Pass Receiving					Rushing				
	Team	GP	NO	YDS	AVE	LG	TD	NO	YDS	AVE	LG	TD
1987	B.C.	10	5	22	4.4	6	0	4	4	1.0	4	0
1988	B.C.	13	2	25	12.5	13	0	2	8	4.0	4	0
1989	B.C.	18	13	185	14.2	34	0	5	11	2.2	3	0
1990	B.C.	16	3	15	5.0	8	0	1	0	0.0	0	0
1991	B.C.	16	0	0	0.0	0	0	0	0	0.0	0	0
1992	B.C.	17	0	0	0.0	0	0	0	0	0.0	0	0
1993	B.C.	16	0	0	0.0	0	0	0	0	0.0	0	0
CFL TOTALS		**106**	**23**	**247**	**10.7**	**34**	**0**	**12**	**23**	**1.9**	**4**	**0**

Scoring - 1 TD for 6 points with B.C. in 1990. **CFL Total Scoring - 1 TD for 6 points.**

Fumble Returns - 1 for 0 yards with B.C. in 1987 and 2 for 25 yards, 12.5 average, longest 25 yards and 1 TD in 1990. **CFL Total Fumble Returns - 3 for 25 yards, 8.3 average, longest 25 yards and 1 TD.**

Fumbles - 1 and 0 lost with B.C. in 1987. **CFL Total Fumbles - 1 and 0 lost.**

Own Fumbles Recovered - 1 with B.C. in 1991. **CFL Total OFR - 1.**

Tackles - 1 defensive with B.C. in 1987; 2 defensive in 1989; 2 special teams in 1991 and 1 defensive in 1993. **CFL Total Tackles - 6 (4 defensive and 2 special teams).**

Playoffs

Games Played - 1 with B.C. in 1987; 2 in 1988; 1 in 1991 and 1 in 1993. **CFL Total Playoff GP - 5.**

Rushing - 1 for 4 yards with B.C. in 1988. **CFL Total Playoff Rushing - 1 for 4 yards.**

Grey Cup

Games Played - 1 with B.C. in 1988. **Total Grey Cup GP - 1.**

TAYLOR, EDDIE
Born: October 12, 1968
Birthplace: Miltipas, California
Defensive Back. 5'11", 180 lbs. Import
Last Amateur Club: San Jose State University
Acquired: Signed as a free agent by the Winnipeg Blue Bombers in February, 1991. Released by Winnipeg in August, 1992. Signed as a free agent by the B.C. Lions in February, 1993. Released by B.C. in November, 1993.

			Punt Returns					Kickoff Returns				
	Team	GP	NO	YDS	AVE	LG	TD	NO	YDS	AVE	LG	TD
1991	Wpg.	3	2	1	0.5	4	0	3	65	21.7	32	0
1992	Wpg.	4	7	29	4.1	12	0	7	140	20.0	30	0
1993	B.C.	14	1	-6	-6.0	0	0	0	0	0.0	0	0
CFL TOTALS		**21**	**10**	**24**	**2.4**	**12**	**0**	**10**	**205**	**20.5**	**32**	**0**

Interception Returns - 1 for 46 yards with Winnipeg in 1992 and 2 for 21 yards, 10.5 average, longest 19 yards with B.C. in 1993. **CFL Total Interception Returns - 3 for 67 yards, 22.3 average, longest 46 yards.**

Unsuccessful Field Goal Returns - 1 for 20 yards with Winnipeg in 1992. **CFL Total Unsuccessful Field Goal Returns - 1 for 20 yards.**

Fumbles - 1 and 1 lost with B.C. in 1993. **CFL Total Fumbles - 1 and 1 lost.**

Fumble Returns - 2 for 19 yards, 9.5 average, longest 14 yards with B.C. in 1993. **CFL Total Fumble Returns - 2 for 19 yards, 9.5 average, longest 14 yards.**

Tackles - 6 defensive and 1 special teams with Winnipeg in 1991; 16 defensive in 1992 and 48 defensive and 1 special teams with B.C. in 1993. **CFL Total Tackles - 72 (70 defensive and 2 special teams).**

TAYLOR, STEVE
Born: January 7, 1967
Birthplace: Fresno, California
Quarterback. 6'0", 205 lbs. Import
Last Amateur Club: University of Nebraska
Acquired: Signed as a free agent by Edmonton Eskimos in February, 1989. Released by Edmonton and signed by the Calgary Stampeders in July, 1991.

			Rushing					Passing						
	Team	GP	NO	YDS	AVE	LG	TD	ATT	COMP	YDS	PCT	INT	LG	TD
1989	Edm.	2	4	21	5.3	11	0	10	3	35	30.0	0	14	0
1990	Edm.	12	17	169	9.9	26	1	49	29	367	59.2	4	49	4
1991	Cal.	18	38	263	6.9	22	0	127	69	980	54.3	8	87	7
1992	Cal.	18	10	88	8.8	22	0	36	23	285	63.9	0	29	2
1993	Cal.	18	23	155	6.7	32	2	56	28	402	50.0	1	54	5
CFL TOTALS		**68**	**92**	**696**	**7.6**	**32**	**3**	**278**	**152**	**2069**	**54.7**	**13**	**87**	**18**

Scoring - 2 TDs for 12 points with Calgary in 1993. **CFL Total Scoring - 2 TDs for 12 points.**

Fumbles - 2 and 0 lost with Edmonton in 1989; 1 and 0 lost in 1990; 2 and 2 lost with Calgary in 1991 and 1 and 0 lost in 1992. **CFL Total Fumbles - 6 and 2 lost.**

2-Pt. Converts - 1 tried and 0 complete with Edmonton in 1990; 3 tried and 1 complete with Calgary in 1991 and 1 tried and 0 complete in 1992. **CFL Total 2-Pt. Converts - 5 tried and 1 complete.**

Own Fumbles Recovered - 1 with Calgary in 1992. **CFL Total OFR - 1.**

Tackles - 1 defensive with Calgary in 1992. **CFL Total Tackles - 1 (1 defensive).**

Playoffs

			Rushing					Passing						
	Team	GP	NO	YDS	AVE	LG	TD	ATT	COMP	YDS	PCT	INT	LG	TD
1990	Edm.	2	0	0	0.0	0	0	0	0	0	0.0	0	0	0
1991	Cal.	2	1	9	9.0	9	0	4	1	7	0.3	1	7	0
1992	Cal.	1	0	0	0.0	0	0	0	0	0	0.0	0	0	0
1993	Cal.	2	0	0	0.0	0	0	1	0	0	0.0	0	0	0
CFL TOTALS		**7**	**1**	**9**	**9.0**	**9**	**0**	**5**	**1**	**7**	**0.2**	**1**	**7**	**0**

Grey Cup

Games Played - 1 with Edmonton in 1990; 1 with Calgary in 1991 and 1 in 1992. **Total Grey Cup GP - 3.**

TEXADA, KIP
Born: January 15, 1968
Birthplace: Port Arthur, Texas
Cornerback. 5'9", 180 lbs. Import
Last Amateur Club: McNeese State University
Acquired: Selected by the Montreal Machine in the 14th round (147th overall) in the 1992 WLAF Draft. Signed as a free agent by the Sacramento Gold Miners in May, 1993.

Games Played - 17 with Sacramento in 1993. **CFL Total GP - 17.**

Interception Returns - 5 for 61 yards, 12.2 average, longest 27 yards with Sacramento in 1993. **CFL Total Interception Returns - 5 for 61 yards, 12.2 average, longest 27 yards.**

Fumble Returns - 1 for 9 yards with Sacramento in 1993. **CFL Total Fumble Returns - 1 for 9 yards.**

TEXADA, KIP

Own Fumbles Recovered - 1 with Sacramento in 1993. **CFL Total OFR - 1.**

Tackles - 37 defensive and 4 special teams with Sacramento in 1993.
CFL Total Tackles - 41 (37 defensive and 4 special teams).

THIENEMAN, CHRIS
Born: May 6, 1965
Birthplace: Louisville, Kentucky
Defensive Tackle. 6'5", 285 lbs. Import
Last Amateur Club: University of Louisville
Acquired: Signed as a free agent by the NFL Dallas Cowboys in 1988. Released by Dallas prior to the start of the 1988 season. Selected by the San Antonio Riders in the eighteenth round (191st overall) in the 1992 WLAF Draft. Signed as a free agent by the Sacramento Gold Miners in September, 1993.

Games Played - 7 with Sacramento in 1993. **CFL Total GP - 7.**

Quarterback Sacks - 1 for 7 yards lost with Sacramento in 1993.
CFL Total QB Sacks - 1 for 7 yards lost.

Tackles - 3 defensive with Sacramento in 1993.
CFL Total Tackles - 3 (3 defensive).

Tackles for Losses - 1 for 6 yards with Sacramento in 1993.
CFL Total Tackles for Losses - 1 for 6 yards.

THOMAS, ANDREW
Born: October 5, 1966
Birthplace: Kingston, Jamaica
Defensive Back. 5'11", 185 lbs. Non-import
Last Amateur Club: University of Massachusetts
Acquired: Selected in the first round (third overall) by the Saskatchewan Roughriders in the 1989 CFL College Draft. Saskatchewan originally acquired the pick in August, 1988 from Hamilton along with the rights to fullback Shawn Daniels for linebacker Pete Giftopolous. Traded to Winnipeg Blue Bombers in 1989 for their first round pick in the 1990 CFL College Draft, defensive lineman Glen Scrivener. Traded to Toronto in July, 1990 along with Winnipeg's fifth round draft choice in the 1991 CFL College Draft in exchange for fullback Warren Hudson. Traded to B.C. in 1990 for third round choice in the 1991 CFL College Draft, linebacker Bruce Dickson. Traded to Winnipeg in October, 1991 in exchange for a first round draft choice in the 1992 CFL Draft, running back Lorne King. Granted free agency status in February, 1993. Signed as a free agent by the Toronto Argonauts in June, 1993.

Games Played - 3 with B.C. in 1990; 13 in 1991; 4 with Winnipeg in 1991; 14 in 1992 and 16 with Toronto in 1993. **CFL Total GP - 50.**

Own Kickoffs Recovered - 1 for 0 yards with B.C. in 1991.
CFL Total OKR - 1 for 0 yards.

Interception Returns - 2 for 27 yards, 13.5 average, longest 27 yards with Winnipeg in 1992 and 1 for 9 yards with Toronto in 1993. **CFL Total Interception Returns - 3 for 36 yards, 12.0 average, longest 27 yards.**

Punt Returns - 0 for 3 yards with Winnipeg in 1992.
CFL Total Punt Returns - 0 for 3 yards.

Fumble Returns - 1 for 6 yards with Winnipeg in 1992.
CFL Total Fumble Returns - 1 for 6 yards.

Own Fumbles Recovered - 1 with Winnipeg in 1992. **CFL Total OFR - 1.**

Unsuccessful Field Goal Returns - 1 for 0 yards with B.C. in 1991 and 2 for 17 yards, 8.5 average, longest 17 yards with Winnipeg in 1992.
CFL Total Unsuccessful Field Goal Returns - 3 for 17 yards, 5.7 average, longest 17 yards.

Quarterback Sacks - 1 for 7 yards lost with Toronto in 1993.
CFL Total QB Sacks - 1 for 7 yards lost.

Tackles - 8 defensive with B.C. in 1990; 27 defensive and 12 special teams with B.C. and 3 defensive and 4 special teams with Winnipeg in 1991; 24 defensive and 5 special teams in 1992 and 24 defensive and 7 special teams with Toronto in 1993.
CFL Total Tackles - 114 (86 defensive and 28 special teams).

Tackles for Losses - 1 for 2 yards with B.C. in 1991.
CFL Total Tackles for Losses - 1 for 2 yards.

Playoffs

Games Played - 2 with Winnipeg in 1991 and 1 in 1992. **CFL Total Playoff GP - 3.**

Interception Returns - 1 for 6 yards with Winnipeg in 1992.
CFL Total Playoff Interception Returns - 1 for 6 yards.

Tackles - 1 defensive and 5 special teams with Winnipeg in 1991.
CFL Total Playoff Tackles - 6 (1 defensive and 5 special teams).

Grey Cup

Games Played - 1 with Winnipeg in 1992. **Total Grey Cup GP - 1.**

Tackles - 4 defensive with Winnipeg in 1992.
Total Grey Cup Tackles - 4 (4 defensive).

THOMAS, JEFF
Born: January 31, 1966
Birthplace: London, Ontario
Offensive Tackle. 6'8", 305 lbs. Non-import
Last Amateur Club: Taft College
Acquired: Signed as a free agent by the Edmonton Eskimos in March, 1993.

Games Played - 5 with Edmonton in 1993. **CFL Total GP - 5.**

THOMPSON, CHARLES
Born: May 28, 1968
Birthplace: Lawton, Oklahoma
Running Back. 5'9", 180 lbs. Import
Last Amateur Club: Central State (Ohio) University
Acquired: Signed as a free agent by the Sacramento Gold Miners in April, 1993. Claimed on waivers by the Shreveport Pirates in April, 1994.

	Team	Pass Receiving GP	NO	YDS	AVE	LG	TD	Rushing NO	YDS	AVE	LG	TD
1993	Sac.	11	12	143	11.9	27	0	1	-15	-15.0	0	0
CFL TOTALS		**11**	**12**	**143**	**11.9**	**27**	**0**	**1**	**-15**	**-15.0**	**0**	**0**

	Team	Punt Returns NO	YDS	AVE	LG	TD	Kickoff Returns NO	YDS	AVE	LG	TD
1993	Sac.	14	120	8.6	22	0	20	425	21.3	62	0
CFL TOTALS		**14**	**120**	**8.6**	**22**	**0**	**20**	**425**	**21.3**	**62**	**0**

Fumbles - 1 and 1 lost with Sacramento in 1993. **CFL Total Fumbles - 1 and 1 lost.**

Tackles - 2 defensive and 9 special teams with Sacramento in 1993.
CFL Total Tackles - 11 (2 defensive and 9 special teams).

THORNTON, RANDY
Born: December 23, 1964
Birthplace: New Orleans, Louisiana
Defensive End. 6'5", 260 lbs. Import
Last Amateur Club: Houston University
Acquired: Signed as a free agent by the NFL Denver Broncos in 1988. Signed as a free agent by the NFL New York Giants in 1990 but was subsequently released prior to training camp. Was San Antonio Riders' fourth choice in the 1992 WLAF Supplemental Draft. Released by San Antonio prior to the beginning of the season and was subsequently signed as a free agent by WLAF Team Dallas. Signed as a free agent by the Sacramento Gold Miners in February, 1993.

Games Played - 7 with Sacramento in 1993. **CFL Total GP - 7.**

Quarterback Sacks - 1 for 24 yards lost with Sacramento in 1993.
CFL Total QB Sacks - 1 for 24 yards lost.

Tackles - 3 defensive and 1 special teams with Sacramento in 1993.
CFL Total Tackles - 4 (3 defensive and 1 special teams).

Tackles for Losses - 1 for 3 yards with Sacramento in 1993.
CFL Total Tackles for Losses - 1 for 3 yards.

THURMAN, ULYSES (JUNIOR)
Born: September 8, 1964
Birthplace: Santa Monica, California
Cornerback. 6'0", 185 lbs. Import
Last Amateur Club: University of Southern California
Acquired: Signed as a free agent by New Orleans Saints (NFL) in 1987. Released and attended Phoenix Cardinals (NFL) training camp in 1988 and was released prior to the regular season. Signed as a free agent by Calgary Stampeders in March, 1989.

	Team	Scoring GP	TD	C	FG	S	TP	Interception Returns NO	YDS	AVE	LG	TD
1989	Cal.	16	1	0	0	0	6	1	0	0.0	0	0
1990	Cal.	18	0	0	0	0	0	2	4	2.0	2	0
1991abc	Cal.	18	2	0	0	0	12	5	13	2.6	6	0
1992bc	Cal.	17	0	0	0	0	0	2	45	22.5	31	0
1993	Cal.	8	0	0	0	0	0	2	44	22.0	27	0
CFL TOTALS		**77**	**3**	**0**	**0**	**0**	**18**	**12**	**106**	**8.8**	**31**	**0**

	Team	Fumble Returns NO	YDS	AVE	LG	TD	Punt Returns NO	YDS	AVE	LG	TD
1989	Cal.	2	1	0.5	1	1	0	0	0.0	0	0
1990	Cal.	1	4	4.0	4	0	0	0	0.0	0	0
1991	Cal.	1	114	114.0	62	2	1	7	7.0	7	0
1992	Cal.	2	15	7.5	15	0	1	3	3.0	3	0
1993	Cal.	0	0	0	0	0	0	0	0.0	0	0
CFL TOTALS		**6**	**134**	**22.3**	**62**	**3**	**2**	**10**	**5.0**	**7**	**0**

THURMAN, ULYSES (JUNIOR)

Blocked Kicks - 1 punt with Calgary in 1989. **CFL Total Blocked Kicks - 1 punt.**

Own Fumbles Recovered - 1 with Calgary in 1991. **CFL Total OFR - 1.**

Quarterback Sacks - 1 with Calgary in 1990. **CFL Total QB Sacks - 1.**

Tackles - 54 defensive with Calgary in 1989; 51 defensive in 1990; 55 defensive and 6 special teams in 1991; 49 defensive and 4 special teams in 1992 and 29 defensive and 2 special teams in 1993.
CFL Total Tackles - 250 (238 defensive and 12 special teams).

Tackles for Losses - 2 for 11 yards with Calgary in 1991.
CFL Total Tackles for Losses - 2 for 11 yards.

a - Led CFL in Fumble Return Yards
b - All-Western All-Star
c - CFL All-Star

Playoffs

Games Played - 1 with Calgary in 1989; 1 in 1990; 2 in 1991 and 1 in 1992.
CFL Total Playoff GP - 5.

Interception Returns - 1 for 51 yards with Calgary in 1989.
CFL Total Playoff Interception Returns - 1 for 51 yards.

Fumble Returns - 1 for 0 yards with Calgary in 1991.
CFL Total Playoff Fumble Returns - 1 for 0 yards.

Defensive Tackles - 4 with Calgary in 1989; 2 in 1990; 9 in 1991 and 1 in 1992.
CFL Total Playoff Defensive Tackles - 16.

Grey Cup

Games Played - 1 with Calgary in 1991 and 1 in 1992. **Total Grey Cup GP - 2.**

Fumble Returns - 1 for 17 yards with Calgary in 1992.
Total Grey Cup Fumble Returns - 1 for 17 yards.

Tackles - 1 defensive with Calgary in 1991. **Total Grey Cup Tackles - 1 (1 defensive).**

TIERNEY, BRAD
Born: May 6, 1965
Birthplace: Wolfville, Nova Scotia
Tackle. 6'4", 265 lbs. Non-import
Last Amateur Club: Acadia University (AUAA)
Acquired: Selected in the fourth round (25th overall) by the Winnipeg Blue Bombers in the 1988 CFL College Draft. Traded to the Ottawa Rough Riders in August, 1989 with defensive end Willie Fears for guard Nick Benjamin. Granted free agency status in February, 1993. Re-signed by Ottawa in March, 1994.

Games Played - 14 with Winnipeg in 1988; 1 with Winnipeg; 13 with Ottawa in 1989; 15 in 1990; 18 in 1991 and 17 in 1992. **CFL Total GP - 78.**

Kickoff Returns - 1 for 0 yards with Winnipeg in 1988.
CFL Total Kickoff Returns - 1 for 0 yards.

Own Fumbles Recovered - 1 with Ottawa in 1989 and 1 in 1992.
CFL Total OFR - 2.

Tackles - 1 defensive with Ottawa in 1992. **CFL Total Tackles - 1 (1 defensive).**

Playoffs

Games Played - 1 with Winnipeg in 1988; 1 with Ottawa in 1990; 1 in 1991 and 1 in 1992. **CFL Total Playoff GP - 4.**

Grey Cup

Games Played - 1 with Winnipeg in 1988. **Total Grey Cup GP - 1.**

TORRANCE, BOB
Born: June 4, 1968
Birthplace: Calgary, Alberta
Quarterback. 6'1", 205 lbs. Non-import
Last Amateur Club: University of Calgary (CWAA)
Acquired: Selected in the third round (22nd overall) by the Calgary Stampeders in the 1991 CFL College Draft. Released by Calgary in July, 1993. Signed as a free agent by the Hamilton Tiger-Cats in August, 1993.

			Passing								Fumbles		
	Team	GP	ATT	COMP	YDS	PCT	INT	LG	TD		NO	LOST	OFR
1991	Cal.	6	0	0	0	0.0	0	0	0		0	0	0
1992	Cal.	18	4	3	33	75.0	0	12	0		1	0	1
1993	Ham.	11	152	78	837	51.3	12	47	3		0	0	0
CFL TOTALS		**35**	**156**	**81**	**870**	**51.9**	**12**	**47**	**3**		**1**	**0**	**1**

Rushing - 2 for -2 yards, -1.0 average, longest 2 yards with Calgary in 1992 and 12 for 71 yards, 5.9 average, longest 32 yards with Hamilton in 1993.
CFL Total Rushing - 14 for 69 yards, 4.9 average, longest 32 yards.

Punting - 1 for 57 yards with Hamilton in 1993.
CFL Total Punting - 1 for 57 yards.

Net Punting - 1 for 57 yards with Hamilton in 1993.
CFL Total Net Punting - 1 for 57 yards.

Fumble Returns - 1 for 0 yards with Hamilton in 1993.
CFL Total Fumble Returns - 1 for 0 yards.

Playoffs

Games Played - 1 with Calgary in 1992 and 2 with Hamilton in 1993.
CFL Total Playoff GP - 3.

Grey Cup

Games Played - 1 with Calgary in 1992. **Total Grey Cup GP - 1.**

TREVATHAN, MIKE
Born: March 26, 1968
Birthplace: Thousand Oaks, California
Wide Receiver. 6'1", 205 lbs. Import
Last Amateur Club: University of Montana
Acquired: Signed as a free agent by the B.C. Lions in April, 1991.

		Scoring						Rushing				
	Team	GP	TD	C	FG	S	TP	NO	YDS	AVE	LG	TD
1991	B.C.	14	1	0	0	0	6	2	14	7.0	8	0
1992	B.C.	16	5	0	0	0	30	2	5	2.5	5	0
1993	B.C.	17	12	0	0	0	72	0	0	0.0	0	0
CFL TOTALS		**47**	**18**	**0**	**0**	**0**	**108**	**4**	**19**	**4.8**	**8**	**0**

		Pass Receiving					Punt Returns				
	Team	NO	YDS	AVE	LG	TD	NO	YDS	AVE	LG	TD
1991	B.C.	45	579	12.9	51	1	10	69	6.9	23	0
1992	B.C.	71	1004	14.1	50	5	3	26	8.7	13	0
1993	B.C.	64	965	15.1	44	12	12	64	5.3	11	0
CFL TOTALS		**180**	**2548**	**14.2**	**51**	**18**	**25**	**159**	**6.4**	**23**	**0**

		Fumbles			Fumble Returns				
	Team	NO	LOST	OFR	NO	YDS	AVE	LG	TD
1991	B.C.	2	2	1	0	0	0.0	0	0
1992	B.C.	3	1	1	0	0	0.0	0	0
1993	B.C.	0	0	1	2	4	2.0	4	0
CFL TOTALS		**5**	**3**	**3**	**2**	**4**	**2.0**	**4**	**0**

Kickoff Returns - 1 for 0 yards with B.C. in 1992.
CFL Total Kickoff Returns - 1 for 0 yards.

Own Kickoffs Recovered - 1 with B.C. in 1991.
CFL Total Own Kickoffs Recovered - 1.

Blocked Kicks - 1 punt with B.C. in 1991. **CFL Total Blocked Kicks - 1 punt.**

Tackles - 3 defensive and 1 special teams with B.C. in 1991; 4 defensive and 1 special teams in 1992 and 4 defensive in 1993.
CFL Total Tackles - 13 (11 defensive and 2 special teams).

Playoffs

			Pass Receiving					Punt Returns				
	Team	GP	NO	YDS	AVE	LG	TD	NO	YDS	AVE	LG	TD
1991	B.C.	1	2	31	15.5	22	0	0	0	0.0	0	0
1993	B.C.	1	3	64	21.3	39	0	4	32	8.0	20	0
CFL TOTALS		**2**	**5**	**95**	**19.0**	**39**	**0**	**4**	**32**	**8.0**	**20**	**0**

TRITHART, KELLY
Born: June 13, 1967
Birthplace: Weyburn, Saskatchewan
Linebacker. 5'11", 205 lbs. Non-import
Last Amateur Club: Regina Rams Jr. (PJFC)
Acquired: Selected in the seventh round (52nd overall) by the Saskatchewan Roughriders in the 1989 CFL College Draft. Released by Saskatchewan in August,1991. Re-signed by Saskatchewan in May, 1992. Released by Saskatchewan in August, 1993.

Games Played - 1 with Saskatchewan in 1989; 4 in 1990; 1 in 1991; 4 in 1992 and 1 in 1993. **CFL Total GP - 11.**

Tackles - 2 special teams with Saskatchewan in 1991; 1 defensive and 4 special teams in 1992 and 1 special teams in 1993.
CFL Total Tackles - 8 (1 defensive and 7 special teams).

TRUDEL, REMI
Born: October 23, 1968
Birthplace: Prince George, B.C.
Defensive Back. 5'9", 175 lbs. Non-import
Last Amateur Club: Simon Fraser University (EVCO)
Acquired: Signed as a free agent by the B.C. Lions in June, 1990. Released by B.C. in July, 1993. Signed as a free agent by the Ottawa Rough Riders in August, 1993.

Games Played - 9 with B.C. in 1990; 8 in 1991; 18 in 1992 and 13 with Ottawa in 1993. **CFL Total GP - 48.**

Interception Returns - 3 for 45 yards, 15.0 average, longest 30 yards with B.C. in 1992 and 6 for 61 yards, 10.2 average, longest 18 yards with Ottawa in 1993. **CFL Total Interception Returns - 9 for 106 yards, 11.8 average, longest 30 yards.**

Fumble Returns - 1 for 0 yards with B.C. in 1992 and 1 for 0 yards with Ottawa in 1993. **CFL Total Fumble Returns - 2 for 0 yards.**

Punt Returns - 0 for -3 yards with B.C. in 1990 and 2 for 6 yards, 3.0 average, longest 6 yards with Ottawa in 1993. **CFL Total Punt Returns - 2 for 3 yards, 1.5 average, longest 6 yards.**

Kickoff Returns - 0 for 8 yards with B.C. in 1990.
CFL Total Kickoff Returns - 0 for 8 yards.

Fumbles - 1 and 1 lost with Ottawa in 1993. **CFL Total Fumbles - 1 and 1 lost.**

Tackles - 17 defensive with B.C. in 1990; 3 special teams in 1991; 21 defensive and 11 special teams in 1992 and 31 defensive and 6 special teams with Ottawa in 1993.
CFL Total Tackles - 89 (69 defensive and 20 special teams).

Tackles for Losses - 1 for 5 yards with Ottawa in 1993.
CFL Total Tackles for Losses - 1 for 5 yards.

All-Eastern All-Star in 1993.

Playoffs

Games Played - 1 with B.C. in 1991 and 1 with Ottawa in 1993.
CFL Total Playoff GP - 2.

Tackles - 2 special teams with B.C. in 1991 and 1 defensive with Ottawa in 1993.
CFL Total Playoff Tackles - 3 (1 defensive and 2 special teams).

TSANGARIS, CHRIS
Born: July 20, 1968
Birthplace: Montreal, Quebec
Linebacker. 6'2", 240 lbs. Non-import
Last Amateur Club: Long Beach State University
Acquired: Selected in the second round (12th overall) by the Winnipeg Blue Bombers in the 1992 CFL College Draft.

Games Played - 10 with Winnipeg in 1992 and 18 in 1993. **CFL Total GP - 28.**

Fumble Returns - 1 for 19 yards with Winnipeg in 1993.
CFL Total Fumble Returns - 1 for 19 yards.

Kickoff Returns - 2 for 11 yards, 5.5 average, longest 9 yards with Winnipeg in 1993.
CFL Total Kickoff Returns - 2 for 11 yards, 5.5 average, longest 9 yards.

Tackles - 10 defensive and 12 special teams with Winnipeg in 1992 and 1 defensive and 30 special teams in 1993.
CFL Total Tackles - 53 (11 defensive and 42 special teams).

Tackles for Losses - 2 for 4 yards with Winnipeg in 1993.
CFL Total Tackles for Losses - 2 for 4 yards.

Playoffs

Games Played - 1 with Winnipeg in 1992 and 1 in 1993. **CFL Total Playoff GP - 2.**

Tackles - 1 special teams with Winnipeg in 1992 and 1 special teams in 1993.
CFL Total Playoff Tackles - 2 (2 special teams).

Grey Cup

Games Played - 1 with Winnipeg in 1992 and 1 in 1993. **Total Grey Cup GP - 2.**

Tackles - 3 special teams with Winnipeg in 1993.
Total Grey Cup Tackles - 3 (3 special teams).

TURNER, LONNIE
Born: August 31, 1960
Birthplace: Los Angeles, California
Wide Receiver. 5'7", 160 lbs. Import
Last Amateur Club: Cal Poly Pomona
Acquired: Was selected by the New York/New Jersey Knights in the fifth round (second selection) of the 1991 WLAF Supplemental Draft. Signed as a free agent by the B.C. Lions in July, 1993.

		Scoring						Rushing				
	Team	GP	TD	C	FG	S	TP	NO	YDS	AVE	LG	TD
1993	B.C.	10	2	0	0	0	12	4	25	6.3	16	0
CFL TOTALS		**10**	**2**	**0**	**0**	**0**	**12**	**4**	**25**	**6.3**	**16**	**0**

		Pass Receiving					Punt Returns				
	Team	NO	YDS	AVE	LG	TD	NO	YDS	AVE	LG	TD
1993	B.C.	27	420	15.6	50	2	38	270	7.1	43	0
CFL TOTALS		**27**	**420**	**15.6**	**50**	**2**	**38**	**270**	**7.1**	**43**	**0**

		Kickoff Returns					Unsuccessful Field Goal Returns				
	Team	NO	YDS	AVE	LG	TD	NO	YDS	AVE	LG	TD
1993	B.C.	11	196	17.8	45	0	6	95	15.8	44	0
CFL TOTALS		**11**	**196**	**17.8**	**45**	**0**	**6**	**95**	**15.8**	**44**	**0**

Fumbles - 3 and 3 lost with B.C. in 1993. **CFL Total Fumbles - 3 and 3 lost.**

Tackles - 3 defensive with B.C. in 1993. **CFL Total Tackles - 3 (3 defensive).**

ULMER, TERRYL
Born: March 3, 1971
Birthplace: Laural, Mississippi
Cornerback. 5'10", 170 lbs. Import
Last Amateur Club: University of Southern Mississippi
Acquired: Signed as a free agent by the Saskatchewan Roughriders in May, 1993. Released by Saskatchewan in November, 1993.

			Punt Returns					Kickoff Returns				
	Team	GP	NO	YDS	AVE	LG	TD	NO	YDS	AVE	LG	TD
1993	Sask.	9	22	118	5.4	13	0	12	230	19.2	47	0
CFL TOTALS		**9**	**22**	**118**	**5.4**	**13**	**0**	**12**	**230**	**19.2**	**47**	**0**

		Unsuccessful Field Goal Returns					Fumbles		
	Team	NO	YDS	AVE	LG	TD	NO	LOST	OFR
1993	Sask.	3	169	56.3	96	0	2	2	0
CFL TOTALS		**3**	**169**	**56.3**	**96**	**0**	**2**	**2**	**0**

Blocked Kicks - 1 punt with Saskatchewan in 1993.
CFL Total Blocked Kicks - 1 (1 punt).

Tackles - 12 defensive and 5 special teams with Saskatchewan in 1993.
CFL Total Tackles - 17 (12 defensive and 5 special teams).

VAJDA, PAUL
Born: July 27, 1966
Birthplace: Montreal, Quebec
Guard. 6'2", 265 lbs. Non-import
Last Amateur Club: Concordia University (OQIFC)
Acquired: Selected in the first round (fifth overall) by the Saskatchewan Roughriders in the 1991 CFL College Draft. Choice was earlier acquired from Toronto Argonauts in exchange for running back Kevin Smellie.

Games Played - 18 with Saskatchewan in 1991; 5 in 1992 and 18 in 1993.
CFL Total GP - 41.

Own Fumbles Recovered - 1 with Saskatchewan in 1993. **CFL Total OFR - 1.**

Tackles - 2 defensive with Saskatchewan in 1991.
CFL Total Tackles - 2 (2 defensive).

Playoffs

Games Played - 1 with Saskatchewan in 1992 and 1 in 1993.
CFL Total Playoff GP - 2.

VAN BELLEGHEM, DAVE
Born: March 20, 1967
Birthplace: Kingston, Ontario
Defensive Back. 5'11", 185 lbs. Non-import
Last Amateur Club: University of Calgary (WIFL)
Acquired: Selected in the fourth round (28th overall) by the Toronto Argonauts in the 1990 CFL College Draft. Released by Toronto in April, 1994.

VAN BELLEGHEM, DAVE

	Team	GP	Interception Returns NO	YDS	AVE	LG	TD	Fumble Returns NO	YDS	AVE	LG	TD
1990	Tor.	17	2	42	21.0	24	0	1	0	0.0	0	0
1991	Tor.	12	0	0	0.0	0	0	1	15	15.0	15	1
1992	Tor.	16	2	19	9.5	10	0	1	0	0.0	0	0
1993	Tor.	17	3	38	12.7	30	0	1	0	0.0	0	0
CFL TOTALS		**62**	**7**	**99**	**14.1**	**30**	**0**	**4**	**15**	**3.8**	**15**	**1**

Scoring - 1 TD for 6 points with Toronto in 1991. **CFL Total Scoring - 1 TD for 6 points.**

Blocked Kicks - 1 punt with Toronto in 1991. **CFL Total Blocked Kicks - 1 punt.**

Kickoff Returns - 1 for 7 yards with Toronto in 1990 and 1 for 0 yards in 1991. **CFL Total Kickoff Returns - 2 for 7 yards, 3.5 average longest 7 yards.**

Own Fumbles Recovered - 1 with Toronto in 1990. **CFL Total OFR - 1.**

Tackles - 21 defensive with Toronto in 1990; 9 defensive and 9 special teams in 1991; 28 defensive and 10 special teams in 1992 and 36 defensive and 17 special teams in 1993. **CFL Total Tackles - 130 (94 defensive and 36 special teams).**

Playoffs

Games Played - 2 with Toronto in 1990 and 1 in 1991. **CFL Total Playoff GP - 3.**

Tackles - 6 defensive with Toronto in 1990 and 1 special teams in 1991. **CFL Total Playoff Tackles - 7 (6 defensive and 1 special teams).**

Grey Cup

Games Played - 1 with Toronto in 1991. **Total Grey Cup GP - 1.**

VANDERJAGT, MIKE

Born: March 24, 1970
Birthplace: Oakville, Ontario
Punter. 6'5", 210 lbs. Non-import
Last Amateur Club: West Virginia University
Acquired: Selected by the Saskatchewan Roughriders in the eighth round (58th overall) of the 1992 CFL College Draft. Released by Saskatchewan in July, 1993. Signed as a free agent by the Toronto Argonauts in February, 1994.

	Team	GP	Punting NO	YDS	AVE	LK	S	Kickoffs NO	YDS	AVE	LK	S
1993	Sask.	2	17	672	39.5	59	0	2	109	54.5	57	0
CFL TOTALS		**2**	**17**	**672**	**39.5**	**59**	**0**	**2**	**109**	**54.5**	**57**	**0**

Net Punting - 18 for 577 yards, 32.1 average with Saskatchewan in 1993. **CFL Total Net Punting - 18 for 577 yards, 32.1 average.**

Rushing - 1 for -8 yards with Saskatchewan in 1993. **CFL Total Rushing - 1 for -8 yards.**

Passing - 1 attempt, 0 complete with Saskatchewan in 1993. **CFL Total Passing - 1 attempt, 0 complete.**

Fumbles - 1 and 1 lost with Saskatchewan in 1993. **CFL Total Fumbles - 1 and 1 lost.**

Tackles - 1 defensive with Saskatchewan in 1993. **CFL Total Tackles - 1 (1 defensive).**

VANKOUGHNETT, DAVE

Born: April 1, 1966
Birthplace: Kamloops, British Columbia
Offensive Lineman. 6'4", 240 lbs. Non-import
Last Amateur Club: Boise State University
Acquired: Second round draft choice (14th overall) by B.C. Lions in 1988 CFL College Draft. Released and signed as a free agent by Saskatchewan Roughriders in May, 1989. Traded to Winnipeg Blue Bombers in June, 1989 for future considerations.

Games Played - 1 with Winnipeg in 1989; 16 in 1991; 18 in 1992 and 18 in 1993. **CFL Total GP - 53.**

Punt Returns - 1 for 2 yards with Winnipeg in 1992. **CFL Total Punt Returns - 1 for 2 yards.**

Fumbles - 1 and 0 lost with Winnipeg in 1992. **CFL Total Fumbles - 1 and 0 lost.**

Own Fumbles Recovered - 2 with Winnipeg in 1992 and 1 in 1993. **CFL Total OFR - 3.**

Tackles - 1 defensive with Winnipeg in 1992. **CFL Total Tackles - 1 (1 defensive).**

All-Eastern All-Star in 1993.

Playoffs

Games Played - 2 with Winnipeg in 1991; 1 in 1992 and 1 in 1993. **CFL Total Playoff GP - 4.**

Grey Cup

Games Played - 1 with Winnipeg in 1992 and 1 in 1993. **Total Grey Cup GP - 2.**

Tackles - 1 defensive with Winnipeg in 1992. **Total Grey Cup Tackles - 1 (1 defensive).**

VAUGHN, GERALD

Born: April 8, 1970
Birthplace: Abbeville, Mississippi
Defensive Back. 6'3", 195 lbs. Import
Last Amateur Club: University of Mississippi
Acquired: Signed as a free agent by the Calgary Stampeders in June, 1993.

Games Played - 18 with Calgary in 1993. **CFL Total GP - 18.**

Interception Returns - 4 for 24 yards, 6.0 average, longest 24 yards with Calgary in 1993. **CFL Total Interception Returns - 4 for 24 yards, 6.0 average, longest 24 yards.**

Fumble Returns - 3 for 2 yards, 0.7 average, longest 2 yards with Calgary in 1993. **CFL Total Fumble Returns - 3 for 2 yards, 0.7 average, longest 2 yards.**

Tackles - 38 defensive and 14 special teams with Calgary in 1993. **CFL Total Tackles - 52 (38 defensive and 14 special teams).**

Playoffs

Games Played - 2 with Calgary in 1993. **CFL Total Playoff GP - 2.**

Tackles - 3 defensive and 1 special teams with Calgary in 1993. **CFL Total Playoff Tackles - 4 (3 defensive and 1 special teams).**

VERCHEVAL, PIERRE

Born: November 22, 1964
Birthplace: Quebec City, Quebec
Offensive Guard. 6'1", 275 lbs. Non-import
Last Amateur Club: University of Western Ontario (OUAA)
Acquired: Selected in the second round (17th overall) by the Edmonton Eskimos in the 1987 CFL College Draft. Attended the NFL New England Patriots training camp in 1988. Released and signed by the Edmonton Eskimos in September, 1988. Granted free agency status in February, 1993. Signed as a free agent by the Toronto Argonauts in August, 1993.

Games Played - 10 with Edmonton in 1988; 18 in 1989; 18 in 1990; 14 in 1991; 17 in 1992 and 3 with Toronto in 1993. **CFL Total GP - 80.**

Own Fumbles Recovered - 2 with Edmonton in 1989 and 2 in 1990. **CFL Total OFR - 4.**

Fumbles - 1 and 0 lost with Edmonton in 1990. **CFL Total Fumbles - 1 and 0 lost.**

Fumble Returns - 1 for 0 yards with Edmonton in 1990. **CFL Total Fumble Returns - 1 for 0 yards.**

Tackles - 2 defensive with Edmonton in 1988; 1 defensive in 1989; 2 defensive in 1990; 2 defensive and 2 special teams in 1991 and 3 special teams in 1992. **CFL Total Tackles - 12 (7 defensive and 5 special teams).**

All-Western All-Star in 1992.
CFL All-Star in 1992.

Playoffs

Games Played - 1 with Edmonton in 1988; 1 in 1989; 1 in 1990; 1 in 1991 and 2 in 1992. **CFL Total Playoff GP - 6.**

Grey Cup

Games Played - 1 with Edmonton in 1990. **Total Grey Cup GP - 1.**

VERDUZCO, JASON

Born: April 3, 1970
Birthplace: Walnut Creek, California
Quarterback. 5'9", 190 lbs. Import
Last Amateur Club: University of Illinois
Acquired: Signed as a free agent by the B.C. Lions in March, 1993. Released by B.C. in November, 1993. Signed as a free agent by the Las Vegas Posse in December, 1993.

Games Played - 12 with B.C. in 1993. **CFL Total GP - 12.**

VOLPE, JON
Born: April 17, 1968
Birthplace: Kincheloe, Michigan
Running Back. 5'7", 195 lbs. Import
Last Amateur Club: Stanford University
Acquired: Signed as a free agent by the B.C. Lions in April, 1991. Released by B.C. in November, 1993.

	Team	GP	Scoring TD	C	FG	S	TP	Rushing NO	YDS	AVE	LG	TD
1991abcdefghi	B.C.	17	20	0	0	0	120	239	1395	5.8	44	16
1992gjk	B.C.	14	15	x1	0	0	92	184	941	5.1	27	13
1993	B.C.	5	4	0	0	0	24	45	136	3.0	13	4
CFL TOTALS		**36**	**39**	**x1**	**0**	**0**	**236**	**468**	**2472**	**5.3**	**44**	**33**

	Team	Pass Receiving NO	YDS	AVE	LG	TD	Kickoff Returns NO	YDS	AVE	LG	TD
1991	B.C.	53	459	8.7	37	4	7	118	16.9	24	0
1992	B.C.	36	303	8.4	28	2	2	32	16.0	21	0
1993	B.C.	10	117	11.7	25	0	4	134	33.5	24	0
CFL TOTALS		**99**	**879**	**8.9**	**37**	**6**	**13**	**284**	**21.9**	**24**	**0**

Passing - 1 attempt, 0 complete with B.C. in 1992.
CFL Total Passing - 1 attempt, 0 complete.

2-Pt. Converts - 1 made with B.C. in 1992. **CFL Total 2-Pt. Converts - 1 made.**

Fumbles - 11 and 7 lost with B.C. in 1991; 5 and 4 lost in 1992 and 1 and 0 lost in 1993. **CFL Total Fumbles - 17 and 11 lost.**

Own Fumbles Recovered - 2 with B.C. in 1991 and 1 in 1992. **CFL Total OFR - 3.**

Tackles - 4 defensive with B.C. in 1991 and 1 special teams in 1993.
CFL Total Tackles - 5 (4 defensive and 1 special teams).

a - Winner of Jackie Parker Trophy for Outstanding Rookie, Western Division.
b - Winner of GMC Award as Most Outstanding Rookie.
c - Tied for the League lead in touchdowns with Edmonton's Blake Marshall.
d - Tied for the League lead in rushing touchdowns with Edmonton's Blake Marshall.
e - Tied League record for touchdowns in a season.
f - Set League record for touchdowns by a first-year player.
g - All-Western All-Star.
h - CFL All-Star.
i - Set League record for rushing yards by a first-year player.
j - Led CFL in Scoring TDs.
k - Led CFL in Rushing TDs (13).

Playoffs

	Team	GP	Scoring TD	C	FG	S	TP	Rushing NO	YDS	AVE	LG	TD
1991	B.C.	1	3	0	0	0	18	17	93	5.5	28	3
CFL TOTALS		**1**	**3**	**0**	**0**	**0**	**18**	**17**	**93**	**5.5**	**28**	**3**

Fumbles - 1 and 1 lost with B.C. in 1991. **CFL Total Playoff Fumbles - 1 and 1 lost.**

WALBY, CHRIS
Born: October 23, 1956
Birthplace: Winnipeg, Manitoba
Tackle. 6'7", 290 lbs. Non-import
Last Amateur Club: Dickinson State University
Acquired: Selected in the first round (fourth overall) by the Montreal Alouettes in the 1981 CFL College Draft. Released after five games by Montreal and signed as a free agent by the Winnipeg Blue Bombers.

Games Played - 5 with Montreal in 1981; 2 with Winnipeg in 1981; 16 in 1982; 13 in 1983; 16 in 1984; 16 in 1985; 18 in 1986; 18 in 1987; 18 in 1988; 17 in 1989; 14 in 1990; 18 in 1991; 14 in 1992 and 18 in 1993.
CFL Total GP - 203.

Scoring - 1 TD for 6 points with Winnipeg in 1981.
CFL Total Scoring - 1 TD for 6 points.

Fumble Returns - 1 for 0 yards and 1 TD in 1981 with Winnipeg.
CFL Total Fumble Returns - 1 for 0 yards and 1 TD.

Own Fumbles Recovered - 1 with Winnipeg in 1983; 1 in 1984; 1 in 1986; 2 in 1988 and 1 in 1993. **CFL Total OFR - 6.**

Defensive Tackles - 3 with Winnipeg in 1989; 1 in 1990; 1 in 1991 and 1 in 1993.
CFL Total Defensive Tackles - 6.

All-Western All-Star in 1984, 1985 and 1986.
CFL All-Star in 1984, 1985, 1986, 1987, 1989, 1990, 1991 and 1993.
All-Eastern All-Star in 1987, 1989, 1990, 1991, 1992 and 1993.
Winner, CFL Most Outstanding Offensive Lineman in 1987 and 1993.
Leo Dandurand Trophy - Outstanding Offensive Lineman, Eastern Division in 1987, 1990, 1991 and 1993.
Runner-up, CFL Most Outstanding Offensive Lineman in 1990 and 1991.

Playoffs

Games Played - 2 with Winnipeg in 1982; 2 in 1983; 2 in 1984; 1 in 1985; 1 in 1986; 1 in 1987; 1 in 1988; 2 in 1989; 1 in 1990; 2 in 1991; 1 in 1992 and 1 in 1993. **CFL Total Playoff GP - 17.**

Defensive Tackles - 1 with Winnipeg in 1989.
CFL Total Playoff Defensive Tackles - 1.

Grey Cup

Games Played - 1 with Winnipeg in 1984; 1 in 1990; 1 in 1992 and 1 in 1993.
Total Grey Cup GP - 4.

WALCOTT, KEN
Born: May 1, 1969
Birthplace: Sydney, Nova Scotia
Defensive Back. 6'0", 205 lbs. Non-import
Last Amateur Club: St. Mary's University
Acquired: Selected in the second round (11th overall) by the Ottawa Rough Riders in the 1992 CFL College Draft.

Games Played - 4 with Ottawa in 1992 and 15 in 1993. **CFL Total GP - 19.**

Own Fumbles Recovered - 1 with Ottawa in 1992. **CFL Total OFR - 1.**

Kickoff Returns - 1 for 0 yards with Ottawa in 1993.
CFL Total Kickoff Returns - 1 for 0 yards.

Tackles - 2 special teams with Ottawa in 1992 and 12 defensive and 4 special teams in 1993.
CFL Total Tackles - 18 (12 defensive and 6 special teams).

WALKER, SCOTT
Born: November 6, 1967
Birthplace: Fayette County, Alabama
Wide Receiver. 5'7", 180 lbs. Import
Last Amateur Club: Lenoir-Rhyne College
Acquired: Signed as a free agent by the NFL Houston Oilers in 1991. Released following training camp. Signed as a free agent by the Hamilton Tiger-Cats in January, 1992. Released by Hamilton in August, 1993.

	Team	GP	Scoring TD	C	FG	S	TP	Pass Receiving NO	YDS	AVE	LG	TD
1992	Ham.	2	1	0	0	0	6	6	92	15.3	34	0
1993	Ham.	6	1	0	0	0	6	11	245	22.3	56	1
CFL TOTALS		**8**	**2**	**0**	**0**	**0**	**12**	**17**	**337**	**19.8**	**56**	**1**

	Team	Punt Returns NO	YDS	AVE	LG	TD	Kickoff Returns NO	YDS	AVE	LG	TD
1992	Ham.	5	102	20.4	62	1	2	67	33.5	55	0
1993	Ham.	25	186	7.4	23	0	16	281	17.6	51	0
CFL TOTALS		**30**	**288**	**9.6**	**62**	**1**	**18**	**348**	**19.3**	**55**	**0**

Fumbles - 4 and 2 lost with Hamilton in 1993. **CFL Total Fumbles - 4 and 2 lost.**

Own Fumbles Recovered - 1 with Hamilton in 1993. **CFL Total OFR - 1.**

Playoffs

	Team	GP	Punt Returns NO	YDS	AVE	LG	TD	Kickoff Returns NO	YDS	AVE	LG	TD
1992	Ham.	2	10	91	9.1	27	0	2	48	24.0	28	0
CFL TOTALS		**2**	**10**	**91**	**9.1**	**27**	**0**	**2**	**48**	**24.0**	**28**	**0**

Unsuccessful Field Goal Returns - 1 for 18 yards with Hamilton in 1992.
CFL Total Playoff Unsuccessful Field Goal Returns - 1 for 18 yards.

WALKER, WAYNE
Born: December 27, 1966
Birthplace: Waco, Texas
Wide Receiver. 5'8", 165 lbs. Import
Last Amateur Club: Texas Tech University
Acquired: Signed as a free agent by the NFL San Diego Chargers in May, 1989. Released in February, 1991. Signed as a free agent by the NFL Minnesota Vikings in March, 1991. Released following Training Camp. Selected in the second round (14th overall) by the WLAF San Antonio Riders in the 1992 World League of American Football Draft. Signed as a free agent by the NFL Buffalo Bills in June, 1992. Released following training camp. Signed as a free agent in September, 1992 by the Ottawa Rough Riders. Transferred to the Shreveport Pirates in February, 1994.

WALKER, WAYNE

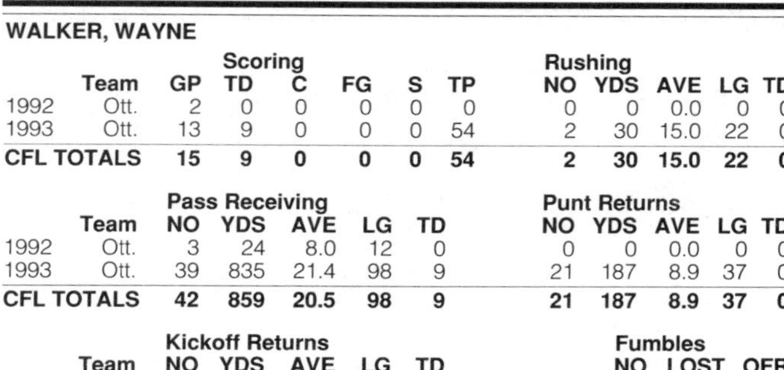

		Scoring						Rushing				
	Team	GP	TD	C	FG	S	TP	NO	YDS	AVE	LG	TD
1992	Ott.	2	0	0	0	0	0	0	0	0.0	0	0
1993	Ott.	13	9	0	0	0	54	2	30	15.0	22	0
CFL TOTALS		**15**	**9**	**0**	**0**	**0**	**54**	**2**	**30**	**15.0**	**22**	**0**

		Pass Receiving					Punt Returns				
	Team	NO	YDS	AVE	LG	TD	NO	YDS	AVE	LG	TD
1992	Ott.	3	24	8.0	12	0	0	0	0.0	0	0
1993	Ott.	39	835	21.4	98	9	21	187	8.9	37	0
CFL TOTALS		**42**	**859**	**20.5**	**98**	**9**	**21**	**187**	**8.9**	**37**	**0**

		Kickoff Returns					Fumbles		
	Team	NO	YDS	AVE	LG	TD	NO	LOST	OFR
1992	Ott.	5	126	25.2	39	0	1	0	1
1993	Ott.	20	268	13.4	24	0	2	2	0
CFL TOTALS		**25**	**394**	**15.8**	**39**	**0**	**3**	**2**	**1**

Tackles - 2 defensive with Ottawa in 1993. **CFL Total Tackles - 2 (2 defensive).**

Playoffs

			Pass Receiving					Kickoff Returns				
	Team	GP	NO	YDS	AVE	LG	TD	NO	YDS	AVE	LG	TD
1992	Ott.	1	3	63	21.0	43	0	1	20	20.0	20	0
1993	Ott.	1	0	0	0.0	0	0	0	0	0.0	0	0
CFL TOTALS		**2**	**3**	**63**	**21.0**	**43**	**0**	**1**	**20**	**20.0**	**20**	**0**

Punt Returns - 3 for 12 yards, 4.0 average, longest 15 yards with Ottawa in 1993.
CFL Total Punt Returns - 3 for 12 yards, 4.0 average, longest 15 yards.

WALLACE, DARRELL

Born: September 27, 1965
Birthplace: St. Louis, Missouri
Running Back. 5'9", 180 lbs. Import
Last Amateur Club: University of Missouri
Acquired: Signed as a free agent by the B.C. Lions in December, 1988. Released by B.C. in August, 1990. Signed as a free agent by the Calgary Stampeders in August, 1990. Released by Calgary in October, 1990. Signed as a free agent by the Saskatchewan Roughriders in October, 1993.

		Scoring						Rushing				
	Team	GP	TD	C	FG	S	TP	NO	YDS	AVE	LG	TD
1989abcdef								75	382	5.1	61	2
	B.C.	17	5	0	0	0	30	5	13	2.6	5	1
1990	Cal.	5	2	0	0	0	12	55	290	5.3	33	1
1993	Sask.	3	3	0	0	0	18	36	156	4.3	26	3
CFL TOTALS		**25**	**10**	**0**	**0**	**0**	**60**	**171**	**841**	**4.9**	**61**	**7**

		Pass Receiving					Punt Returns				
	Team	NO	YDS	AVE	LG	TD	NO	YDS	AVE	LG	TD
1989	B.C.	18	115	6.4	20	1	83	780	9.4	93	1
1990	B.C.	5	19	3.8	12	0	16	59	3.7	21	0
	Cal.	13	89	6.8	25	1	7	31	4.4	21	0
1993	Sask.	15	181	12.1	35	0	11	55	5.0	16	0
CFL TOTALS		**51**	**300**	**5.9**	**35**	**2**	**117**	**925**	**7.9**	**93**	**1**

		Kickoff Returns					Fumbles		
	Team	NO	YDS	AVE	LG	TD	NO	LOST	OFR
1989	B.C.	57	1255	21.5	91	1	3	1	1
1990	B.C.	10	163	16.3	29	0	1	1	1
	Cal.	4	84	21.0	33	0	2	2	0
1993	Sask.	7	122	17.4	25	0	2	0	0
CFL TOTALS		**78**	**1624**	**20.8**	**91**	**1**	**8**	**4**	**2**

Defensive Tackles - 2 with Calgary in 1990.
CFL Total Defensive Tackles - 2

a - Winner of the Jackie Parker Trophy Most Outstanding Western Division Rookie
b - Set CFL Record for Kickoff Returns
c - Set CFL Record for Kickoff Return Yardage
d - Runner-up CFL Most Outstanding Rookie
e - Led CFL in Kickoff Returns
f - Led CFL in Kickoff Return Yards

WALLACE, JASON

Born: August 28, 1969
Birthplace: Hampton, Virginia
Cornerback. 5'10", 170 lbs. Import
Last Amateur Club: University of Virginia
Acquired: Signed as a free agent by the NFL Indianapolis Colts in 1991 and was subsequently released prior to training camp. Selected by the Ohio Glory in the third round (23rd overall) of the 1992 WLAF Draft. Signed as a free agent by the Sacramento Gold Miners in April, 1993.

Games Played - 9 with Sacramento in 1993. **CFL Total GP - 9.**

Interception Returns - 1 for 26 yards with Sacramento in 1993.
CFL Total Interception Returns - 1 for 26 yards.

Fumble Returns - 1 for 10 yards with Sacramento in 1993.
CFL Total Fumble Returns - 1 for 10 yards.

Tackles - 40 defensive with Sacramento in 1993.
CFL Total Tackles - 40 (40 defensive).

Tackles for Losses - 2 for 3 yards with Sacramento in 1993.
CFL Total Tackles for Losses - 2 for 3 yards.

WALLING, BRIAN

Born: September 16, 1963
Birthplace: Toronto, Ontario
Running Back. 5'8", 187 lbs. Non-import
Last Amateur Club: Acadia University (AUAA)
Acquired: Signed as a free agent in April, 1986 by the Toronto Argonauts. Selected by the Saskatchewan Roughriders in the Equalization Draft of March, 1988. Released by Saskatchewan in July, 1988. Signed as a free agent by the Edmonton Eskimos in August, 1988. Released and signed as a free agent by Saskatchewan in October, 1989. Traded to Edmonton in December, 1989 in exchange for future considerations.

		Scoring						Rushing				
	Team	GP	TD	C	FG	S	TP	NO	YDS	AVE	LG	TD
1987	Tor.	4	0	0	0	0	0	0	0	0.0	0	0
1988	Edm.	12	2	0	0	0	12	29	148	5.1	22	1
1989	Edm.	10	0	0	0	0	0	14	49	3.5	16	0
	Sask.	3	0	0	0	0	0	7	15	2.1	6	0
1990	Edm.	15	3	0	0	0	18	29	162	5.6	31	0
1991	Edm.	18	0	0	0	0	0	9	59	6.6	13	0
1992	Edm.	9	0	0	0	0	0	43	218	5.1	24	0
1993	Edm.	18	0	0	0	0	0	35	161	4.6	17	0
CFL TOTALS		**89**	**5**	**0**	**0**	**0**	**30**	**166**	**812**	**4.9**	**31**	**1**

		Pass Receiving					Fumble Returns				
	Team	NO	YDS	AVE	LG	TD	NO	YDS	AVE	LG	TD
1987	Tor.	0	0	0.0	0	0	0	0	0.0	0	0
1988	Edm.	3	7	2.3	6	1	1	0	0.0	0	0
1989	Edm.	0	0	0.0	0	0	1	0	0.0	0	0
	Sask.	2	18	9.0	12	0	0	0	0.0	0	0
1990	Edm.	13	80	6.2	15	3	0	0	0.0	0	0
1991	Edm.	2	0	0.0	3	0	1	0	0.0	0	0
1992	Edm.	0	0	0.0	0	0	0	0	0.0	0	0
1993	Edm.	7	65	9.3	15	0	0	0	0.0	0	0
CFL TOTALS		**27**	**170**	**6.3**	**15**	**4**	**3**	**0**	**0**	**0**	**0**

		Kickoff Returns					Fumbles		
	Team	NO	YDS	AVE	LG	TD	NO	LOST	OFR
1987	Tor.	3	35	11.7	20	0	0	0	0
1988	Edm.	0	0	0.0	0	0	1	1	0
1989	Edm.	1	9	9.0	9	0	1	1	0
	Sask.	0	0	0.0	0	0	0	0	0
1990	Edm.	0	0	0.0	0	0	3	2	2
1991	Edm.	0	0	0.0	0	0	3	3	0
1992	Edm.	0	0	0.0	0	0	1	1	0
1993	Edm.	0	0	0.0	0	0	1	1	0
CFL TOTALS		**4**	**44**	**11.0**	**20**	**0**	**10**	**9**	**2**

Punt Returns - 1 for 11 yards with Edmonton in 1989; 1 for 6 yards with Saskatchewan in 1989 and 1 for -1 yard with Edmonton in 1993.
CFL Total Punt Returns - 3 for 16 yards, 5.3 average, longest 11 yards.

Tackles - 2 defensive with Edmonton in 1990; 21 special teams in 1991; 1 defensive and 3 special teams in 1992 and 3 defensive and 17 special teams in 1993. **CFL Total Tackles - 47 (6 defensive and 41 special teams).**

Playoffs

			Rushing					Pass Receiving				
	Team	GP	NO	YDS	AVE	LG	TD	NO	YDS	AVE	LG	TD
1988	Edm.	1	0	0	0.0	0	0	0	0	0.0	0	0
1989	Sask.	2	3	65	21.7	50	1	0	0	0.0	0	0
1990	Edm.	1	10	87	8.7	20	0	5	74	14.8	43	0
1991	Edm.	1	1	3	3.0	3	1	0	0	0.0	0	0
1992	Edm.	2	5	27	5.4	7	0	0	0	0.0	0	0
1993	Edm.	2	5	45	9.0	18	1	0	0	0.0	0	0
CFL TOTALS		**9**	**24**	**227**	**9.5**	**50**	**3**	**5**	**74**	**14.8**	**43**	**0**

Scoring - 1 TD for 6 points with Saskatchewan in 1989; 1 TD for 6 points with Edmonton in 1991 and 1 TD for 6 points in 1993.
CFL Total Playoff Scoring - 3 TDs for 18 points.

Kickoff Returns - 1 for 15 yards with Saskatchewan in 1989.
CFL Total Playoff Kickoff Returns - 1 for 15 yards.

Tackles - 1 defensive with Saskatchewan in 1989; 1 special teams with Edmonton in 1992 and 3 special teams in 1993.
CFL Total Playoff Tackles - 5 (1 defensive and 4 special teams).

WALLING, BRIAN

Grey Cup

Games Played - 1 with Saskatchewan in 1989; 1 with Edmonton in 1990 and 1 in 1993. **Total Grey Cup GP - 3.**

Rushing - 1 for -1 yard with Edmonton in 1990.
Total Grey Cup Rushing - 1 for -1 yard.

Pass Receiving - 1 for 10 yards with Edmonton in 1990.
Total Grey Cup Pass Receiving - 1 for 10 yards.

Kickoff Returns - 1 for 6 yards with Edmonton in 1990.
Total Grey Cup Kickoff Returns - 1 for 6 yards.

Tackles - 1 special teams with Edmonton in 1993.
Total Grey Cup Tackles - 1 (1 special teams).

WARNOCK, KENT
Born: June 3, 1964
Birthplace: Saint John, New Brunswick
Defensive End. 6'7", 270 lbs. Non-import
Last Amateur Club: University of Calgary (WIFL)
Acquired: Selected in the first round (first overall) by the Calgary Stampeders in the 1986 CFL College Draft. Tried out with the NFL Pittsburgh Steelers in 1986 and signed with Calgary in September, 1986. Released by Calgary in May, 1993. Signed as a free agent by the B.C. Lions in June, 1993.

Games Played - 8 with Calgary in 1987; 13 in 1988; 17 in 1989; 18 in 1990; 15 in 1991; 14 in 1992 and 17 with B.C. in 1993. **CFL Total GP - 102.**

Fumble Returns - 1 for 0 yards with Calgary in 1987; 3 for 0 yards in 1989; 4 for 0 yards in 1990; 1 for 0 yards in 1992 and 2 for 0 yards with B.C. in 1993.
CFL Total Fumble Returns - 11 for 0 yards.

Quarterback Sacks - 14 with Calgary in 1989; 16 in 1990; 4 in 1991; 4 for 31 yards lost in 1992 and 4 for 32 yards lost with B.C. in 1993.
CFL Total QB Sacks - 42.

Defensive Tackles - 10 with Calgary in 1987; 28 in 1988; 31 in 1989; 55 in 1990; 27 in 1991; 17 in 1992 and 23 with B.C. in 1993.
CFL Total Defensive Tackles - 191.

Tackles for Losses - 4 for 23 yards with Calgary in 1991; 3 for 4 yards in 1992 and 2 for 5 yards with B.C. in 1993.
CFL Total Tackles for Losses - 9 for 32 yards.

All-Western All-Star in 1990.
CFL All-Star in 1990.

Playoffs

Games Played - 1 with Calgary in 1987; 1 in 1989; 1 in 1990; 2 in 1991 and 1 in 1992.
CFL Total Playoff GP - 6.

Fumble Returns - 1 for 0 yards with Calgary in 1991.
CFL Total Playoff Fumble Returns - 1 for 0 yards.

Quarterback Sacks - 1 with Calgary in 1989 and 1 in 1991.
CFL Total Playoff QB Sacks - 2.

Defensive Tackles - 2 with Calgary in 1989; 3 in 1990; 4 in 1991 and 5 in 1992.
CFL Total Playoff Defensive Tackles - 14.

Grey Cup

Games Played - 1 with Calgary in 1991 and 1 in 1992. **Total Grey Cup GP - 2.**

Quarterback Sacks - 1 with Calgary in 1991 and 1 for 10 yards lost in 1992.
Total Grey Cup QB Sacks - 2.

Tackles - 1 defensive with Calgary in 1991 and 1 defensive in 1992.
Total Grey Cup Tackles - 2 (2 defensive).

WARREN, BRIAN
Born: July 25, 1962
Birthplace: Phoenix, Arizona
Linebacker. 6'2", 230 lbs. Import
Last Amateur Club: University of Arizona
Acquired: Signed as a free agent with the USFL Arizona Outlaws in 1985 and was subsequently released. Signed as a free agent with the Edmonton Eskimos in September, 1986. Granted free agent status in March, 1990. Signed as a free agent by the B.C. Lions in May, 1990. Released by B.C. in August, 1990. Signed as a free agent by the Ottawa Rough Riders in September, 1990. Traded to Toronto Argonauts in March, 1991 along with kicker Dean Dorsey and defensive lineman Leonard Johnson in exchange for quarterback John Congemi. Released by Toronto in February, 1994.

			Interception Returns						QB Sacks	
	Team	GP	NO	YDS	AVE	LG	TD		NO	YDS LOST
1987	Edm.	13	1	22	22.0	22	0		4	–
1988	Edm.	18	1	14	14.0	14	0		4	–
1989	Edm.	8	0	0	0.0	0	0		1	–
1990	B.C.	3	0	0	0.0	0	0		0	–
	Ott.	2	0	0	0.0	0	0		1	–
1991a	Tor.	18	0	0	0.0	0	0		10	–
1992	Tor.	17	0	0	0.0	0	0		9	61
1993	Tor.	15	0	0	0.0	0	0		4	61
CFL TOTALS		**94**	**2**	**36**	**18.0**	**22**	**0**		**33**	**122**

2-Pt. Converts - 1 attempt, 0 made with Toronto in 1991.
CFL Total 2-Pt. Converts - 1 attempt, 0 made.

Pass Receiving - 1 for 5 yards with Toronto in 1992.
CFL Total Pass Receiving - 1 for 5 yards.

Fumbles - 1 and 0 lost with Toronto in 1991. **CFL Total Fumbles - 1 and 0 lost.**

Fumble Returns - 2 for 45 yards, 22.5 average, longest 36 yards with Toronto in 1991 and 1 for 0 yards in 1992.
CFL Total Fumble Returns - 3 for 45 yards, 15.0 average, longest 36 yards.

Punt Returns - 1 for 1 yard with Edmonton in 1987.
CFL Total Punt Returns - 1 for 1 yard.

Own Fumbles Recovered - 1 with Edmonton in 1989. **CFL Total OFR - 1.**

Tackles - 33 defensive with Edmonton in 1987; 43 defensive in 1988; 7 defensive in 1989; 7 defensive with B.C. and 7 defensive with Ottawa in 1990; 38 defensive and 2 special teams with Toronto in 1991; 34 defensive in 1992 and 20 defensive and 1 special teams in 1993.
CFL Total Tackles - 192 (189 defensive and 3 special teams).

Tackles for Losses - 1 for 3 yards with Toronto in 1991; 1 for 1 yard in 1992 and 1 for 10 yards in 1993.
CFL Total Tackles for Losses - 3 for 14 yards.

a - All-Eastern All-Star

Playoffs

Games Played - 2 with Edmonton in 1987; 1 in 1988; 1 with Ottawa in 1990 and 1 with Toronto in 1991. **CFL Total Playoff GP - 5.**

Fumble Returns - 1 for 0 yards with Ottawa in 1990.
CFL Total Playoff Fumble Returns - 1 for 0 yards.

Quarterback Sacks - 1 with Toronto in 1991.
CFL Total Playoff QB Sacks - 1.

Defensive Tackles - 2 with Edmonton in 1987; 4 with Ottawa in 1990 and 2 in 1991. **CFL Total Playoff Defensive Tackles - 8.**

Grey Cup

Games Played - 1 with Edmonton in 1987 and 1 with Toronto in 1991.
Total Grey Cup GP - 2.

Defensive Tackles - 1 with Edmonton in 1987 and 3 with Toronto in 1991.
Total Grey Cup Defensive Tackles - 4.

WATSON, KEN
Born: November 10, 1966
Birthplace: Docena, Alabama
Defensive Back. 6'1", 190 lbs. Import
Last Amateur Club: Livingston University
Acquired: Signed as a free agent by the B.C. Lions in September, 1989. Granted free agent status in February, 1991. Selected in the second round (15th overall) by the San Antonio Riders in the 1991 WLAF Supplemental Draft. Signed as a free agent by B.C. in July, 1991. Released by B.C. in September, 1991. Signed as a free agent by the Calgary Stampeders in October, 1991. Granted free agency status in February, 1994. Signed as a free agent by the Baltimore CFL Colts in April, 1994.

Games Played - 8 with B.C. in 1989; 17 in 1990; 9 with B.C. and 3 with Calgary in 1991; 10 in 1992 and 17 in 1993. **CFL Total GP - 64.**

Interception Returns - 4 for 72 yards, 18.0 average, longest 47 yards and 1 TD with B.C. in 1989; 3 for 17 yards, 5.7 average, longest 15 yards in 1990; 1 for 19 yards in 1991 and 1 for 7 yards with Calgary in 1993.
CFL Total Interception Returns - 9 for 115 yards, 12.8 average, longest 47 yards and 1 TD.

Kickoff Returns - 1 for 6 yards with Calgary in 1991 and 3 for 14 yards, 4.7 average, longest 10 yards in 1993.
CFL Total Kickoff Returns - 4 for 20 yards, 5.0 average, longest 10 yards.

Fumble Returns - 1 for 0 yards with B.C. in 1989; 1 for 0 yards with Calgary in 1992 and 1 for 10 yards in 1993. **CFL Total Fumble Returns - 3 for 10 yards, 3.3 average, longest 10 yards.**

Own Fumbles Recovered - 1 with Calgary in 1992. **CFL Total OFR - 1.**

Tackles - 31 defensive with B.C. in 1989; 56 defensive in 1990; 30 defensive and 5 special teams in 1991; 6 defensive and 1 special teams with Calgary in 1991; 19 defensive and 11 special teams in 1992 and 38 defensive and 10 special teams in 1993.
CFL Total Tackles - 207 (180 defensive and 27 special teams).

WATSON, KEN

Playoffs

Games Played - 1 with Calgary in 1991; 1 in 1992 and 2 in 1993. **CFL Total Playoff GP - 4.**

Interception Returns - 1 for 22 yards with Calgary in 1991. **CFL Total Playoff Interception Returns - 1 for 22 yards.**

Tackles - 2 defensive with Calgary in 1991; 1 defensive and 1 special teams in 1992 and 4 special teams in 1993. **CFL Total Playoff Tackles - 8 (3 defensive and 5 special teams).**

Grey Cup

Games Played - 1 with Calgary in 1991 and 1 in 1992. **Total Grey Cup GP - 2.**

Tackles - 1 defensive and 2 special teams with Calgary in 1991. **Total Grey Cup Tackles - 3 (1 defensive and 2 special teams).**

WAYNE, PATRICK

Born: February 22, 1964
Birthplace: Toronto, Ontario
Linebacker. 6'3", 225 lbs. Non-import
Last Amateur Club: Simon Fraser University (EVCO)
Acquired: Selected in the second round (12th overall) by the Ottawa Rough Riders in the 1987 CFL College Draft. Traded to the B.C. Lions in March, 1993 along with cornerback Less Browne and tackle Robert Smith in exchange for offensive linemen Carl Coulter and Chris Gioskos, kicker Wayne Lammle, cornerback Joe Mero and linebacker Mark Scott. Traded to the Toronto Argonauts along with defensive lineman Keith Powe and the rights to a negotiation list player in exchange for future considerations and the rights to a negotiation list player in September, 1993. Released by Toronto in April, 1994.

Games Played - 13 with Ottawa in 1987; 18 in 1988; 18 in 1989; 18 in 1990; 17 in 1991; 17 in 1992; 1 with B.C. and 5 with Toronto in 1993. **CFL Total GP - 107.**

Pass Receiving - 1 for 9 yards with Ottawa in 1987 and 0 for -3 yards in 1989. **CFL Total Pass Receiving - 1 for 6 yards.**

Kickoff Returns - 1 for 14 yards with Ottawa in 1987; 2 for 29 yards, 14.5 average, longest 15 yards in 1988 and 1 for 0 yards in 1992. **CFL Total Kickoff Returns - 4 for 43 yards, 10.8 average, longest 15 yards.**

Fumbles - 1 and 0 lost with Ottawa in 1992. **CFL Total Fumbles - 1 and 0 lost.**

Fumble Returns - 1 for 0 yards with Ottawa in 1987; 2 for 5 yards 2.5 average, longest 5 yards in 1988; 2 for 0 yards in 1989; 1 for 0 yards in 1991 and 3 for 0 yards in 1992. **CFL Total Fumble Returns - 9 for 5 yards, 0.6 average, longest 5 yards.**

Interception Returns - 1 for 14 yards with Ottawa in 1989 and 1 for 4 yards in 1992. **CFL Total Interception Returns - 2 for 18 yards, 9.0 average, longest 14 yards.**

2-Pt. Converts - 1 attempt with Ottawa in 1988. **CFL Total 2-Pt. Converts - 1 attempt.**

Quarterback Sacks - 1 with Ottawa in 1987; 3 in 1989; 8 in 1990; 4 in 1991 and 4 for 36 yards lost in 1992. **CFL Total QB Sacks - 20.**

Tackles - 27 defensive with Ottawa in 1987; 26 defensive in 1988; 64 defensive in 1989; 57 defensive in 1990; 51 defensive and 12 special teams in 1991; 63 defensive and 2 special teams in 1992 and 3 defensive and 3 special teams with Toronto in 1993. **CFL Total Tackles - 308 (291 defensive and 17 special teams).**

Tackles for Losses - 3 for 5 yards with Ottawa in 1991 and 2 for 4 yards in 1992. **CFL Total Tackles for Losses - 5 for 9 yards.**

Playoffs

Games Played - 1 with Ottawa in 1990; 1 in 1991 and 1 in 1992. **CFL Total Playoff GP - 3.**

Tackles - 4 defensive with Ottawa in 1990; 4 defensive and 1 special teams in 1991 and 3 defensive and 1 special teams in 1992. **CFL Total Playoff Tackles - 13 (11 defensive and 2 special teams).**

Tackles for Losses - 1 for 3 yards with Ottawa in 1992. **CFL Total Playoff Tackles for Losses - 1 for 3 yards.**

WEBER, GORDON

Born: February 12, 1965
Birthplace: Ottawa, Ontario
Linebacker. 6'3", 210 lbs. Non-import
Last Amateur Club: University of Ottawa (OQIFC)
Acquired: Selected in the seventh round (49th overall) by the Ottawa Rough Riders in the 1989 CFL College Draft. Signed by Ottawa in February, 1990.

Games Played - 4 with Ottawa in 1990; 18 in 1991; 18 in 1992 and 11 in 1993. **CFL Total GP - 51.**

Interception Returns - 1 for 7 yards with Ottawa in 1992. **CFL Total Interception Returns - 1 for 7 yards.**

Own Fumbles Recovered - 1 with Ottawa in 1991. **CFL Total OFR - 1.**

Fumble Returns - 1 for 0 yards with Ottawa in 1992. **CFL Total Fumble Returns - 1 for 0 yards.**

Quarterback Sacks - 1 with Ottawa in 1991 and 1 for 8 yards lost in 1992. **CFL Total QB Sacks - 2.**

Tackles - 5 defensive and 12 special teams with Ottawa in 1991; 7 defensive and 26 special teams in 1992 and 10 defensive and 11 special teams in 1993. **CFL Total Tackles - 71 (22 defensive and 49 special teams).**

Tackles for Losses - 1 for 6 yards with Ottawa in 1993. **CFL Tackles for Losses - 1 for 6 yards.**

Playoffs

Games Played - 1 with Ottawa in 1991 and 1 in 1992. **CFL Total Playoff GP - 2.**

Interception Returns - 1 for 54 yards with Ottawa in 1992. **CFL Total Playoff Interception Returns - 1 for 54 yards.**

Tackles - 1 defensive with Ottawa in 1991 and 1 defensive and 1 special teams in 1992. **CFL Total Playoff Tackles - 3 (2 defensive and 1 special teams).**

Tackles for Losses - 1 for 5 yards with Ottawa in 1992. **CFL Total Playoff Tackles for Losses - 1 for 5 yards.**

WEST, JAMES

Born: December 19, 1956
Birthplace: Fort Worth, Texas
Linebacker. 6'2", 220 lbs. Import
Last Amateur Club: Texas Southern University
Acquired: Signed as a free agent by the NFL's Oakland Raiders in 1980 and released following pre-season. Signed as a free agent by the Calgary Stampeders in May, 1982. Signed as a free agent by the USFL Houston Gamblers in the spring of 1985. Signed as a free agent by the Winnipeg Blue Bombers in September, 1985. Traded to the B.C. Lions in exchange for defensive lineman Leo Brown in June, 1993.

			Scoring					Interception Returns				
	Team	GP	TD	C	FG	S	TP	NO	YDS	AVE	LG	TD
1982	Cal.	9	0	0	0	0	0	0	0	0.0	0	0
1983a	Cal.	15	0	0	0	0	0	2	61	30.5	36	0
1984	Cal.	13	1	0	0	0	6	2	31	15.5	25	1
1985	Wpg.	5	0	0	0	0	0	0	0	0.0	0	0
1986	Wpg.	18	1	0	0	0	6	2	3	1.5	3	1
1987bcde	Wpg.	18	0	0	0	0	0	0	0	0.0	0	0
1988b	Wpg.	17	0	0	0	0	0	3	63	21.0	40	0
1989bc	Wpg.	12	0	0	0	0	0	3	64	21.3	35	0
1990	Wpg.	8	0	0	0	0	0	4	25	6.3	17	0
1991	Wpg.	16	0	0	0	0	0	2	0	0.0	0	0
1992	Wpg.	16	1	0	0	0	6	1	49	49.0	32	0
1993	B.C.	17	0	0	0	0	0	2	5	2.5	5	0
CFL TOTALS		**164**	**3**	**0**	**0**	**0**	**18**	**21**	**301**	**14.3**	**40**	**2**

Fumble Returns - 2 for 0 yards with Calgary in 1982; 3 for 0 yards in 1983; 1 for 5 yards in 1984; 1 for 0 yards with Winnipeg in 1986; 1 for 0 yards in 1987; 4 for 0 yards in 1988; 1 for 11 yards in 1990; 1 for 10 yards in 1991; 4 for 0 yards and 1 TD in 1992 and 1 for 0 yards with B.C. in 1993. **CFL Total Fumble Returns - 19 for 26 yards, 1.4 average, longest 11 yards and 1 TD.**

Blocked Kicks - 1 punt with Calgary in 1983. **CFL Total Blocked Kicks - 1 punt.**

Quarterback Sacks - 1 with Calgary in 1982; 8.5 in 1983; 4 in 1984; 4 with Winnipeg in 1986; 7 in 1987; 8 in 1988; 5 in 1989; 2 in 1990; 3 in 1991; 5 for 38 yards lost in 1992 and 4 for 39 yards with B.C. in 1993. **CFL Total QB Sacks - 51.5**

Own Fumbles Recovered - 1 with Winnipeg in 1986. **CFL Total OFR - 1.**

Tackles - 75 defensive with Winnipeg in 1987; 76 defensive in 1988; 69 defensive in 1989; 37 defensive in 1990; 65 defensive and 16 special teams in 1991; 56 defensive and 6 special teams in 1992 and 79 defensive and 2 special teams with B.C. in 1993. **CFL Total Tackles - 481 (457 defensive and 24 special teams).**

Tackles for Losses - 4 for 15 yards with Winnipeg in 1991; 3 for 12 yards in 1992 and 5 for 14 yards with B.C. in 1993. **CFL Total Tackles for Losses - 12 for 41 yards.**

a - All-Western All-Star
b - All-Eastern All-Star
c - CFL All-Star
d - Runner-up Schenley Most Outstanding Defensive Player
e - James P. McCaffrey Trophy Most Outstanding Defensive Player - Eastern Division

Playoffs

Games Played - 1 with Calgary in 1982; 2 with Winnipeg in 1985; 1 in 1986; 1 in 1987; 2 in 1988; 2 in 1989; 1 in 1990; 2 in 1991; 1 in 1992 and 1 with B.C. in 1993. **CFL Total Playoff GP - 14.**

Rushing - 17 for 62 yards, 3.7 average, longest 10 yards with Calgary in 1982. **CFL Total Playoff Rushing - 17 for 62 yards, 3.7 average, longest 10 yards.**

WEST, JAMES

Pass Receiving - 2 for 14 yards, 7.0 average, longest 13 yards with Calgary in 1982. **CFL Total Playoff Pass Receiving - 2 for 14 yards, 7.0 average, longest 13 yards.**

Quarterback Sacks - 1 with Winnipeg in 1987; 1 in 1988; 1 in 1989; 1 in 1991 and 3 for 19 yards lost in 1992. **CFL Total Playoff QB Sacks - 7.**

Interception Returns - 1 for 25 yards with Winnipeg in 1989. **CFL Total Playoff Interception Returns - 1 for 25 yards.**

Tackles - 5 defensive with Winnipeg in 1987; 12 defensive in 1988; 10 defensive in 1989; 7 defensive and 1 special teams in 1991; 2 defensive and 2 special teams in 1992 and 6 defensive with B.C. in 1993. **CFL Total Playoff Tackles - 45 (42 defensive and 3 special teams).**

Tackles for Losses - 2 for 17 yards with Winnipeg in 1991. **CFL Total Playoff Tackles for Losses - 2 for 17 yards.**

Grey Cup

Games Played - 1 with Winnipeg in 1988; 1 in 1990 and 1 in 1992. **Total Grey Cup GP - 3.**

Quarterback Sacks - 1 with Winnipeg in 1990. **Total Grey Cup QB Sacks - 1.**

Tackles - 2 defensive with Winnipeg in 1988; 5 defensive in 1990 and 3 defensive and 2 special teams in 1992. **Total Grey Cup Tackles - 12 (10 defensive and 2 special teams).**

WESTERBROOKS, DAVID
Born: March 23, 1968
Birthplace: Miami, Florida
Defensive End. 6'4", 265 lbs. Import
Last Amateur Club: Howard University
Acquired: Signed as a free agent by the NFL Chicago Bears in 1990 and was subsequently waived by Chicago during training camp. Signed as a free agent by the NFL Minnesota Vikings in November, 1990. Was released by Minnesota in 1991. Selected by the Sacramento Surge in the 21st round (222nd overall) of 1992 WLAF Draft. Signed as a free agent by the Sacramento Gold Miners in March, 1993.

Games Played - 9 with Sacramento in 1993. **CFL Total GP - 9.**

Tackles - 3 defensive with Sacramento in 1993. **CFL Total Tackles - 3 (3 defensive).**

WESTWOOD, TROY
Born: March 21, 1967
Birthplace: Selkirk, Manitoba
Kicker. 5'10", 165 lbs. Non-import
Last Amateur Club: Augustana College
Acquired: Selected in the sixth round (48th overall) by the Winnipeg Blue Bombers in the 1991 CFL College Draft. Granted free agency status in February, 1994.

		Scoring						Field Goals					
	Team	GP	TD	C	FG	S	TP	T	G	YDS	AVE	LK	PCT
1991	Wpg.	8	0	21	16	6	75	22	16	517	32.3	47	72.7
1992abc	Wpg.	18	0	47	47	11	199	62	47	1483	31.6	55	75.8
1993a	Wpg.	18	0	68	45	6	209	56	45	1477	32.8	50	80.4
CFL TOTALS		**44**	**0**	**136**	**108**	**23**	**483**	**140**	**108**	**3477**	**32.2**	**55**	**77.1**

		Field Goal Attempts					Converts			Kickoffs				
	Team	NO	YDS	AVE	LK	S	T	G	PCT	NO	YDS	AVE	LK	S
1991	Wpg.	6	286	47.7	55	6	21	21	100.0	42	2266	54.0	76	0
1992	Wpg.	15	663	44.2	56	7	48	47	97.9	89	5176	58.2	86	4
1993	Wpg.	11	501	45.5	63	6	69	68	98.6	105	5990	57.0	95	0
CFL TOTALS		**32**	**1450**	**45.3**	**63**	**19**	**138**	**136**	**98.6**	**236**	**13432**	**56.9**	**95**	**4**

Passing - 1 attempt, 1 complete for -10 yards with Winnipeg in 1992. **CFL Total Passing - 1 attempt, 1 complete for -10 yards.**

Fumbles - 2 and 2 lost with Winnipeg in 1993. **CFL Total Fumbles - 2 and 2 lost.**

2-Pt. Converts - 1 tried, 1 complete with Winnipeg in 1992. **CFL Total 2-Pt. Converts - 1 tried, 1 complete.**

Unsuccessful Field Goal Returns - 1 for 4 yards with Winnipeg in 1993. **CFL Total Unsuccessful Field Goal Returns - 1 for 4 yards.**

Tackles - 1 special teams with Winnipeg in 1992 and 1 defensive in 1993. **CFL Total Tackles - 2 (1 defensive and 1 special teams).**

a - All-Eastern All-Star
b - CFL All-Star
c - Led CFL in Field Goals Made

Playoffs

		Scoring						Field Goals					
	Team	GP	TD	C	FG	S	TP	T	G	YDS	AVE	LK	PCT
1991	Wpg.	2	0	2	5	0	17	5	5	155	31.0	42	100.0
1992	Wpg.	1	0	6	5	2	23	7	5	175	35.0	45	71.4
1993	Wpg.	1	0	1	4	0	13	4	4	122	30.5	42	100.0
CFL TOTALS		**4**	**0**	**9**	**14**	**2**	**53**	**16**	**14**	**452**	**32.3**	**45**	**87.5**

		Field Goal Attempts					Converts			Kickoffs				
	Team	NO	YDS	AVE	LK	S	T	G	PCT	NO	YDS	AVE	LK	S
1991	Wpg.	0	0	0.0	0	0	2	2	100.0	7	388	55.4	66	0
1992	Wpg.	2	108	54.0	61	1	6	6	100.0	7	397	56.7	86	1
1993	Wpg.	0	0	0.0	0	0	1	1	100.0	2	102	51.0	66	0
CFL TOTALS		**2**	**108**	**54.0**	**61**	**1**	**9**	**9**	**100.0**	**16**	**887**	**55.4**	**86**	**1**

Grey Cup

		Scoring						Field Goals					
	Team	GP	TD	C	FG	S	TP	T	G	YDS	AVE	LK	PCT
1992	Wpg.	1	0	1	1	0	4	2	1	46	46.0	46	50.0
1993	Wpg.	1	0	2	3	0	11	3	3	112	37.3	48	100.0
CFL TOTALS		**2**	**0**	**3**	**4**	**0**	**15**	**5**	**4**	**158**	**39.5**	**48**	**80.0**

		Field Goal Attempts					Converts			Kickoffs				
	Team	NO	YDS	AVE	LK	S	T	G	PCT	NO	YDS	AVE	LK	S
1992	Wpg.	1	44	44.0	44	0	1	1	100.0	2	102	51.0	58	0
1993	Wpg.	0	0	0.0	0	0	2	2	100.0	4	249	62.3	67	0
CFL TOTALS		**1**	**44**	**44.0**	**44**	**0**	**3**	**3**	**100.0**	**6**	**351**	**56.6**	**67**	**0**

WETMORE, ALAN
Born: May 17, 1970
Birthplace: Halifax, Nova Scotia
Linebacker/Full Back. 6'3", 225 lbs. Non-import
Last Amateur Club: Acadia University
Acquired: Selected by the Winnipeg Blue Bombers in the first round (sixth overall) in the 1993 CFL College Draft.

Games Played - 2 with Winnipeg in 1993. **CFL Total GP - 2.**

WETMORE, PAUL
Born: October 10, 1966
Birthplace: Halifax, Nova Scotia
Linebacker. 6'3", 225 lbs. Non-import
Last Amateur Club: Acadia University (AUAA)
Acquired: Selected in the second round (15th overall) by the B.C. Lions in the 1989 CFL College Draft. Granted free agency status in February, 1993. Signed as a free agent by the Toronto Argonauts in June, 1993 and was released later that month. Signed as a free agent by the Saskatchewan Roughriders in August, 1993 and was subsequently released in September, 1993. Signed as a free agent by the Ottawa Rough Riders in September, 1993.

Games Played - 18 with B.C. in 1989; 17 in 1990; 18 in 1991; 17 in 1992 and 3 with Saskatchewan and 3 with Ottawa in 1993. **CFL Total GP - 76.**

Own Kickoffs Recovered - 1 for 4 yards with B.C. in 1989. **CFL Total Own Kickoffs Recovered - 1 for 4 yards.**

Fumble Returns - 3 for 13 yards, 4.3 average, longest 12 yards with B.C. in 1991 and 2 for 14 yards, 7.0 average, longest 14 yards in 1992. **CFL Total Fumble Returns - 5 for 27 yards, 5.4 average, longest 14 yards.**

Quarterback Sacks - 1 with B.C. in 1990; 4 in 1991 and 4 for 41 yards lost in 1992. **CFL Total QB Sacks - 9.**

Tackles - 7 defensive with B.C. in 1989; 7 defensive in 1990; 42 defensive and 9 special teams in 1991; 43 defensive and 10 special teams in 1992; 3 defensive and 2 special teams with Saskatchewan and 4 special teams with Ottawa in 1993. **CFL Total Tackles - 127 (102 defensive and 25 special teams).**

Tackles for Losses - 4 for 14 yards with B.C. in 1991. **CFL Total Tackles for Losses - 4 for 14 yards.**

Playoffs

Games Played - 1 with B.C. in 1991 and 1 with Ottawa in 1993. **CFL Total Playoff GP - 2.**

Tackles - 2 special teams with B.C. in 1991. **CFL Total Playoff Tackles - 2 (2 special teams).**

WHITE, BRENT
Born: February 28, 1967
Birthplace: Wichita Falls, Texas
Defensive End. 6'5", 273 lbs. Import
Last Amateur Club: University of Michigan
Acquired: Selected by the Chicago Bears in the eleventh round (284th overall) in the 1990 NFL Draft. Was released by Chicago prior to the start of the regular season. Selected by the Barcelona Dragons in the first round (ninth overall) in the 1991 WLAF Positional Draft. Signed as a free agent by the NFL Kansas City Chiefs in June, 1992. Released by Kansas City during training camp. Signed as a free agent by the Sacramento Gold Miners in April, 1993.

WHITE, BRENT

Games Played - 17 with Sacramento in 1993.
CFL Total GP - 17.

Fumble Returns - 1 for 0 yards with Sacramento in 1993.
CFL Total Fumble Returns - 1 for 0 yards.

Tackles - 29 defensive and 3 special teams with Sacramento in 1993.
CFL Total Tackles - 32 (29 defensive and 3 special teams).

Tackles for Losses - 3 for 7 yards with Sacramento in 1993.
CFL Total Tackles for Losses - 3 for 7 yards.

WHITE, ROBB
Born: May 26, 1965
Birthplace: Aberdeen, South Dakota
Defensive Tackle. 6'5", 280 lbs. Import
Last Amateur Club: University of South Dakota
Acquired: Signed as a free agent by the NFL Washington Redskins in May, 1988. Released by Washington in November, 1988. Awarded on waivers to the NFL New York Giants in November, 1988. Granted free agency status in February, 1990. Signed as a free agent by the NFL Denver Broncos in March, 1990. Released by Denver in August, 1990. Signed as a free agent by the NFL New York Giants in September, 1990 and was subsequently released later that month. Signed as a free agent by the NFL Tampa Bay Buccaneers in November, 1990. Waived by Tampa Bay prior to the start of the 1991 season. Spent the 1992 season with the WLAF San Antonio Riders. Signed as a free agent by the Sacramento Gold Miners in May, 1993.

Games Played - 18 with Sacramento in 1993. **CFL Total GP - 18.**

Quarterback Sacks - 2 for 12 yards lost with Sacramento in 1993.
CFL Total QB Sacks - 2 for 12 yards lost.

Tackles - 31 defensive and 2 special teams with Sacramento in 1993.
CFL Total Tackles - 33 (31 defensive and 2 special teams).

Tackles for Losses - 3 for 11 yards with Sacramento in 1993.
CFL Total Tackles for Losses - 3 for 11 yards.

WHITLEY, KEVIN
Born: February 26, 1970
Birthplace: Greenville, North Carolina
Defensive back. 5'10", 190 lbs. Import
Last Amateur Club: Georgia Southern University
Acquired: Signed as a free agent by the NFL New England Patriots in May, 1992 and was subsequently released prior to the start of the season. Signed as a free agent by the Toronto Argonauts in December, 1992.

Games Played - 13 with Toronto in 1993. **CFL Total GP - 13.**

Kickoff Returns - 1 for 12 yards with Toronto in 1993.
CFL Total Kickoff Returns - 1 for 12 yards.

Fumble Returns - 2 for 4 yards, 2.0 average, longest 4 yards with Toronto in 1993.
CFL Total Fumble Returns - 2 for 4 yards, 2.0 average, longest 4 yards.

Tackles - 35 defensive and 2 special teams with Toronto in 1993.
CFL Total Tackles - 37 (35 defensive and 2 special teams).

WIGGINS, BRIAN
Born: June 14, 1968
Birthplace: New Rochelle, New York
Wide Receiver. 5'11", 183 lbs. Import
Last Amateur Club: Texas Southern University
Acquired: Signed as a free agent by the NFL New England Patriots in 1991 and was subsequently released during training camp. Spent the 1992 season with the Arena Football League's New Orleans Knights. Signed as a free agent by the Calgary Stampeders in December, 1992.

		Scoring						Pass Receiving				
	Team	GP	TD	C	FG	S	TP	NO	YDS	AVE	LG	TD
1993ab	Cal.	11	5	x1	0	0	32	47	881	18.7	52	5
CFL TOTALS		**11**	**5**	**x1**	**0**	**0**	**32**	**47**	**881**	**18.7**	**52**	**5**

		Punt Returns					Kickoff Returns				
	Team	NO	YDS	AVE	LG	TD	NO	YDS	AVE	LG	TD
1993	Cal.	27	254	9.4	29	0	24	510	21.3	46	0
CFL TOTALS		**27**	**254**	**9.4**	**29**	**0**	**24**	**510**	**21.3**	**46**	**0**

		Fumbles		
	Team	NO	LOST	OFR
1993	Cal.	1	1	1
CFL TOTALS		**1**	**1**	**1**

2-pt. Converts - 1 attempt, 1 complete and 1 made with Calgary in 1993.
CFL Total 2-pt. Converts - 1 attempt, 1 complete and 1 made.

Tackles - 3 defensive with Calgary in 1993.
CFL Total Tackles - 3 (3 defensive).

a - Winner, Jackie Parker Trophy, Most Outstanding Rookie in Western Division.
b - Runner-Up, CFL Most Outstanding Rookie.

Playoffs

		Pass Receiving						Punt Returns				
	Team	GP	NO	YDS	AVE	LG	TD	NO	YDS	AVE	LG	TD
1993	Cal.	2	4	15	3.8	10	0	7	30	4.3	8	0
CFL TOTALS		**2**	**4**	**15**	**3.8**	**10**	**0**	**7**	**30**	**4.3**	**8**	**0**

		Kickoff Returns					Rushing				
	Team	NO	YDS	AVE	LG	TD	NO	YDS	AVE	LG	TD
1993	Cal.	2	33	16.5	17	0	1	4	4.0	4	0
CFL TOTALS		**2**	**33**	**16.5**	**17**	**0**	**1**	**4**	**4.0**	**4**	**0**

WILBURN, BARRY
Born: December 19, 1963
Birthplace: Memphis, Tennessee
Cornerback. 6'3", 186 lbs. Import
Last Amateur Club: University of Mississippi
Acquired: Selected by the NFL Washington Redskins in the eighth round (219th overall) in the 1985 NFL Draft. Released by Washington in May, 1990. Signed as a free agent by the Cleveland Browns in April, 1992. Was released by Cleveland in October, 1992. Signed as a free agent by the Saskatchewan Roughriders in June, 1993. Released by Saskatchewan in November, 1993.

Games Played - 16 with Saskatchewan in 1993. **CFL Total GP - 16.**

Interception Returns - 2 for 21 yards, 10.5 average, longest 18 yards with Saskatchewan in 1993. **CFL Total Interception Returns - 2 for 21 yards, 10.5 average, longest 18 yards.**

Kickoff Returns - 1 for 0 yards with Saskatchewan in 1993.
CFL Total Kickoff Returns - 1 for 0 yards.

Own Fumbles Recovered - 1 with Saskatchewan in 1993. **CFL Total OFR - 1.**

Tackles - 29 defensive and 2 special teams with Saskatchewan in 1993.
CFL Total Tackles - 31 (29 defensive and 2 special teams).

All-Western All-Star in 1993.
CFL All-Star in 1993.

WILCOX, GERALD
Born: July 8, 1966
Birthplace: London, England
Slotback. 6'2", 215 lbs. Non-import
Last Amateur Club: Weber State University
Acquired: Selected in the first round (first overall) by the Ottawa Rough Riders in the 1989 CFL College Draft. Traded to the Winnipeg Blue Bombers in June, 1992 in exchange for cornerback Less Browne.

		Scoring						Pass Receiving				
	Team	GP	TD	C	FG	S	TP	NO	YDS	AVE	LG	TD
1989	Ott.	15	3	0	0	0	18	24	331	13.8	36	3
1990	Ott.	3	0	0	0	0	0	6	71	11.8	33	0
1991	Ott.	18	3	0	0	0	18	26	455	17.5	61	3
1992	Wpg.	4	1	0	0	0	6	20	352	17.6	48	1
1993abc	Wpg.	16	10	0	0	0	60	79	1340	17.0	75	10
CFL TOTALS		**56**	**17**	**0**	**0**	**0**	**102**	**155**	**2549**	**16.5**	**75**	**17**

Own Fumbles Recovered - 2 with Ottawa in 1991. **CFL Total OFR - 2.**

Fumbles - 1 and 1 lost with Ottawa in 1989. **CFL Total Fumbles - 1 and 1 lost.**

Tackles - 1 defensive with Ottawa in 1989; 2 defensive in 1990; 6 defensive and 2 special teams in 1991; 1 defensive with Winnipeg in 1992 and 3 defensive in 1993. **CFL Total Tackles - 15 (13 defensive and 2 special teams).**

a - All-Eastern All-Star
b - Winner, Lew Hayman Award as Most Outstanding Canadian in the Eastern Division.
c - Runner-up, CFL Most Outstanding Canadian.

Playoffs

Games Played - 1 with Ottawa in 1991 and 1 with Winnipeg in 1993.
CFL Total Playoff GP - 2.

Scoring - 1 TD for 6 points with Winnipeg in 1993.
CFL Total Playoff Scoring - 1 TD for 6 points.

Pass Receiving - 2 for 19 yards, 9.5 average, longest 12 yards with Ottawa in 1991 and 7 for 43 yards, 6.1 average, longest 16 yards and 1 TD with Winnipeg in 1993. **CFL Total Playoff Pass Receiving - 9 for 62 yards, 6.9 average, longest 16 yards and 1 TD.**

WILCOX, GERALD

Fumbles - 1 and 0 lost with Winnipeg in 1993.
CFL Total Playoff Fumbles - 1 and 0 lost.

Grey Cup

Games Played - 1 with Winnipeg in 1993. **Total Grey Cup GP - 1.**

Pass Receiving - 4 for 39 yards, 9.8 average, longest 15 yards with Winnipeg in 1993. **Total Grey Cup Pass Receiving - 4 for 39 yards, 9.8 average, longest 15 yards.**

WILEY, JOHN
Born: August 8, 1969
Birthplace: Tuskegee, Alabama
Defensive Back. 6'0", 195 lbs. Import
Last Amateur Club: Auburn University
Acquired: Attended training camp with the NFL Chicago Bears in 1991 and 1992 and was subsequently released prior to the start of both seasons. Signed as a free agent by the Sacramento Gold Miners in May, 1993. Transferred to the Shreveport Pirates in March, 1994.

Games Played - 18 with Sacramento in 1993. **CFL Total GP - 18.**

Interception Returns - 4 for 46 yards, 11.5 average, longest 18 yards with Sacramento in 1993. **CFL Total Interception Returns - 4 for 46 yards, 11.5 average, longest 18 yards.**

Fumble Returns - 1 for 15 yards with Sacramento in 1993.
CFL Total Fumble Returns - 1 for 15 yards.

Tackles - 80 defensive and 2 special teams with Sacramento in 1993.
CFL Total Tackles - 82 (80 defensive and 2 special teams).

Tackles for Losses - 2 for 18 yards with Sacramento in 1993.
CFL Total Tackles for Losses - 2 for 18 yards.

WILKERSON, GARY
Born: October 11, 1965
Birthplace: Sutherland, Virginia
Cornerback. 6'0", 180 lbs. Import
Last Amateur Club: Penn State University
Acquired: Selected in the sixth round (160th overall) by the Cleveland Browns in the 1989 NFL Draft. Spent 1989 season on injured reserve and was released before training camp. Signed as a free agent by the Hamilton Tiger-Cats in May, 1990. Granted free agency status in February, 1992. Signed as a free agent by the NFL Cleveland Browns and released in August, 1992. Re-signed as a free agent by Hamilton in August, 1992.

		Scoring						Interception Returns				
	Team	GP	TD	C	FG	S	TP	NO	YDS	AVE	LG	TD
1990	Ham.	18	2	0	0	0	12	7	111	15.9	51	1
1991	Ham.	13	1	0	0	0	6	3	74	24.7	59	1
1992	Ham.	11	1	0	0	0	6	1	51	51.0	51	0
1993	Ham.	11	2	0	0	0	12	3	73	24.3	45	2
CFL TOTALS		**53**	**6**	**0**	**0**	**0**	**36**	**14**	**309**	**22.1**	**59**	**4**

Punt Returns - 0 for 3 yards with Hamilton in 1992 and 1 for 29 yards in 1993.
CFL Total Punt Returns - 1 for 32 yards.

Fumble Returns - 2 for 28 yards, 14.0 average, longest 28 yards and 1 TD with Hamilton in 1990 and 1 for 30 yards and 1 TD in 1992.
CFL Total Fumble Returns - 3 for 58 yards, 19.3 average, longest 28 yards and 2 TDs.

Own Fumbles Recovered - 1 with Hamilton in 1992. **CFL Total OFR - 1.**

Blocked Kicks - 1 field goal with Hamilton in 1991.
CFL Total Blocked Kicks - 1 field goal.

Tackles - 51 defensive with Hamilton in 1990; 46 defensive and 1 special teams in 1991; 35 defensive and 3 special teams in 1992 and 43 defensive in 1993.
CFL Total Tackles - 179 (175 defensive and 4 special teams).

Tackles for Losses - 1 for 27 yards with Hamilton in 1993.
CFL Total Tackles for Losses - 1 for 27 yards.

Playoffs

Games Played - 2 with Hamilton in 1992 and 2 in 1993.
CFL Total Playoff GP - 4.

Kickoff Returns - 1 for 0 yards with Hamilton in 1993.
CFL Total Kickoff Returns - 1 for 0 yards.

Tackles - 4 defensive with Hamilton in 1992 and 5 defensive in 1993.
CFL Total Playoff Tackles - 9 (9 defensive).

Fumble Returns - 1 for 0 yards with Hamilton in 1992.
CFL Total Playoff Fumble Returns - 1 for 0 yards.

WILLIAMS, ARNIE
Born: August 14, 1970
Birthplace: Bay Minette, Alabama
Linebacker. 6'2", 235 lbs. Import
Last Amateur Club: Southern Mississippi University
Acquired: Signed as a free agent by the NFL Chicago Bears in 1992 and was subsequently released during training camp. Signed as a free agent with the Toronto Argonauts in April, 1993. Released by Toronto in September, 1993. Signed as a free agent by the B.C. Lions in November, 1993.

Games Played - 7 with Toronto in 1993. **CFL Total GP - 7.**

Quarterback Sacks - 1 for 12 yards lost with Toronto in 1993.
CFL Total QB Sacks - 1 for 12 yards.

Tackles - 27 defensive and 3 special teams with Toronto in 1993.
CFL Total Tackles - 30 (27 defensive and 3 special teams).

WILLIAMS, BRETT
Born: May 23, 1958
Birthplace: Norfolk, Virgina
Defensive End. 6'3", 260 lbs. Import
Last Amateur Club: Austin Peay University
Acquired: Selected in the 12th round by the Minnesota Vikings in the 1981 NFL Draft. Released in August, 1981 and signed as a free agent by the New England Patriots (NFL) in March, 1982. Released in November, 1982 and signed as a free agent by the Baltimore Colts (NFL) in May, 1983. Released in August, 1983 and signed as a free agent by the USFL's Houston Gamblers in September, 1983. Released in January, 1984 and signed as a free agent by the Oakland Invaders (USFL) in March, 1984. Released and signed as a free agent by the Montreal Concordes in August, 1985. Selected by the Saskatchewan Roughriders in the first round (second overall) of the Alouettes Dispersal Draft in June, 1987 and transferred to the B.C. Lions for their first round selection in the 1988 CFL College Draft (linebacker Pete Giftopolous). Traded to the Edmonton Eskimos for offensive lineman Leo Blanchard in March, 1988. Granted free agency status in February, 1992. Signed as a free agent by the Hamilton Tiger-Cats in July, 1992.

			Fumble Returns					Kickoff Returns				
	Team	GP	NO	YDS	AVE	LG	TD	NO	YDS	AVE	LG	TD
1985	Mtl.	11	1	0	0.0	0	0	0	0	0.0	0	0
1986ab	Mtl.	18	2	6	3.0	3	0	4	41	10.3	18	0
1987	B.C.	14	0	0	0.0	0	0	0	0	0.0	0	0
1988bc	Edm.	18	0	0	0.0	0	0	5	28	5.6	15	0
1989c	Edm.	17	3	0	0.0	0	0	2	21	10.5	15	0
1990c	Edm.	18	3	0	0.0	0	0	2	22	11.0	12	0
1991bc	Edm.	17	1	3	3.0	3	0	0	0	0.0	0	0
1992	Ham.	11	0	0	0.0	0	0	0	0	0.0	0	0
1993	Ham.	10	1	0	3.0	0	0	0	0	0.0	0	0
CFL TOTALS		**134**	**11**	**9**	**9.0**	**3**	**0**	**13**	**112**	**8.6**	**18**	**0**

Pass Receiving - 1 for 7 yards with Edmonton in 1988.
CFL Total Pass Receiving 1 for 7 yards.

Fumbles - 1 with Edmonton in 1988. **CFL Total Fumbles - 1**

Own Fumbles Recovered - 1 with Edmonton in 1988. **CFL Total OFR - 1.**

Interception Returns - 1 for 16 yards with Montreal in 1986 and 1 for 0 yards with Edmonton in 1991. **CFL Total Interception Returns - 2 for 16 yards, 8.0 average, longest 16 yards.**

Quarterback Sacks - 3 with Montreal in 1985; 21 in 1986; 10 with B.C. in 1987; 12 with Edmonton in 1988; 9 in 1989; 9 in 1990; 11 in 1991; 9 with Hamilton in 1992 and 5 for 26 yards lost in 1993. **CFL Total QB Sacks - 89.**

Blocked Kicks - 1 field goal with Edmonton in 1988.
CFL Total Blocked Kicks - 1 field goal.

Tackles - 28 defensive with B.C. in 1987; 40 defensive with Edmonton in 1988; 27 defensive in 1989; 37 defensive in 1990; 28 defensive and 2 special teams in 1991; 26 defensive with Hamilton in 1992 and 20 defensive in 1993. **CFL Total Tackles - 208 (206 defensive and 2 special teams).**

Tackles for Losses - 3 for 4 yards with Edmonton in 1991; 3 for 5 yards with Hamilton in 1992 and 1 for 2 yards in 1993.
CFL Total Tackles for Losses - 7 for 11 yards.

a - All-Eastern All-Star
b - CFL All-Star
c - All-Western All-Star

Playoffs

Games Played - 2 with Montreal in 1985; 1 with B.C. in 1987; 1 with Edmonton in 1988. 1 in 1989; 2 in 1990; 1 in 1991 and 2 with Hamilton in 1992.
CFL Total Playoff GP - 8.

Scoring - 1 TD for 6 points with Edmonton in 1988.
CFL Total Playoff Scoring - 1 TD for 6 points.

Pass Receiving - 1 for 4 yards and 1 TD with Edmonton in 1988.
CFL Total Playoff Pass Receiving - 1 for 4 yards and 1 TD.

Punt Returns - 1 for 0 yards with Edmonton in 1990.
CFL Total Playoff Punt Returns - 1 for 0 yards.

WILLIAMS, BRETT

Kickoff Returns - 2 for 18 yards, 9.0 average, longest 14 yards with Edmonton in 1988 and 1 for 0 yards in 1990. **CFL Total Playoff Kickoff Returns - 3 for 18 yards, 6.0 average, longest 14 yards.**

Quarterback Sacks - 2 with Montreal in 1985 and 2 with Edmonton in 1990. **CFL Total Playoff QB Sacks - 4.**

Defensive Tackles - 3 with B.C. in 1987; 3 with Edmonton in 1988; 4 in 1989 and 11 with Hamilton in 1992. **CFL Total Playoff Defensive Tackles - 21**

Tackles for Losses - 1 for 1 yard with Hamilton in 1992. **CFL Total Tackles for Losses - 1 for 1 yard.**

Grey Cup

Games Played - 1 with Edmonton in 1990. **Total Grey Cup GP - 1.**

Defensive Tackles - 5 with Edmonton in 1990. **Total Grey Cup Defensive Tackles - 5.**

WILLIAMS, BYRON

Born: October 30, 1960
Birthplace: Texarkana, Texas
Wide Receiver. 6'2", 185 lbs. Import
Last Amateur Club: Texas-Arlington University
Acquired: Selected in the twenty-first round (249th overall) by Denver in the 1983 USFL Draft. Selected in the tenth round (253rd overall) by the NFL Green Bay Packers in the 1983 Draft. Released in August, 1983. Signed as a free agent by the NFL Philadelphia Eagles in September, 1983. Released later that month. Signed as a free agent by the NFL New York Giants in October, 1983. Released in August, 1986. Signed as a free agent by the NFL Indianapolis Colts in May, 1987. Released in August, 1987. Signed as a free agent by the B.C. Lions in September, 1987. Released in September, 1988. Signed as a free agent by the Edmonton Eskimos in April, 1989. Released in July, 1989. Picked up on waivers by the Ottawa Rough Riders in July, 1989. Released in September, 1989. Signed as a free agent by the NFL Detroit Lions in March, 1990. Released in June, 1990. Selected in the third round (26th overall) by the WLAF Orlando Thunder in the 1991 Supplemental Draft. Signed as a free agent by the Saskatchewan Roughriders in August, 1991. Released in October, 1991. Re-signed as a free agent by Saskatchewan in September, 1992. Released by Saskatchewan in April, 1994.

	Team	Scoring GP	TD	C	FG	S	TP	Fumbles NO	LOST	OFR
1987	Sask.	9	1	0	0	0	6	1	0	1
1988	B.C.	4	1	0	0	0	6	0	0	0
1989	Ott.	10	2	0	0	0	12	1	1	0
1991	Sask.	7	3	0	0	0	18	1	1	0
1992	Sask.	10	4	x1	0	0	26	0	0	0
1993	Sask.	12	1	0	0	0	6	1	0	0
CFL TOTALS		**52**	**12**	**x1**	**0**	**0**	**74**	**4**	**2**	**1**

	Team	Pass Receiving NO	YDS	AVG	LG	TD	Kickoff Returns NO	YDS	AVE	LG	TD
1987	Sask.	29	494	17.0	57	1	0	0	0.0	0	0
1988	B.C.	10	187	18.7	57	1	0	0	0.0	0	0
1989	Ott.	37	666	18.0	64	2	0	0	0.0	0	0
1991	Sask.	24	463	19.3	85	3	0	0	0.0	0	0
1992	Sask.	32	596	18.6	83	4	8	123	15.4	31	0
1993	Sask.	37	545	14.7	59	1	1	0	0.0	0	0
CFL TOTALS		**169**	**2951**	**17.5**	**85**	**12**	**9**	**123**	**13.7**	**31**	**0**

Rushing - 1 for -4 yards with Saskatchewan in 1993. **CFL Total Rushing - 1 for -4 yards.**

2-Pt. converts - 1 made good with Saskatchewan in 1992. **CFL Total 2-Pt. Converts - 1 made good.**

Fumble Returns - 1 for 0 yards with Saskatchewan in 1993. **CFL Total Fumble Returns - 1 for 0 yards.**

Tackles - 1 defensive with B.C. in 1987; 3 defensive with Ottawa in 1989; 1 defensive with Saskatchewan in 1991; 1 defensive in 1992 and 3 defensive in 1993. **CFL Total Tackles - 9 (9 defensive).**

Playoffs

	Team	Scoring GP	TD	C	FG	S	TP	Pass Receiving NO	YDS	AVE	LG	TD
1987	B.C.	1	0	0	0	0	0	2	11	5.5	8	0
1992	Sask.	1	1	0	0	0	6	1	22	22.0	22	0
1993	Sask.	1	0	0	0	0	0	1	8	8.0	8	0
CFL TOTALS		**3**	**1**	**0**	**0**	**0**	**6**	**4**	**41**	**10.3**	**22**	**0**

	Team	Kickoff Returns NO	YDS	AVE	LG	TD
1992	Sask.	2	35	11.7	14	0
1993	Sask.	0	0	0.0	0	0
CFL TOTALS		**2**	**35**	**11.7**	**14**	**0**

WILLIAMS, DAVID

Born: June 1, 1964
Birthplace: Los Angeles, California
Wide Receiver. 6'4", 195 lbs. Import
Last Amateur Club: University of Illinois
Acquired: Drafted in the sixth round by the NFL Chicago Bears in 1986. Later tried out with the NFL Tampa Bay Buccaneers and Los Angeles Raiders before signing as a free agent with the B.C. Lions prior to the start of the 1988 CFL season. Signed as a free agent by the Ottawa Rough Riders in March, 1990. Traded to the Edmonton Eskimos in February, 1991 along with Ottawa's first round draft choice in the 1991 CFL College Draft, defensive back Dan Murphy, in exchange for linebacker Jeff Braswell and Edmonton's first round draft choice in the 1991 CFL College Draft, offensive lineman Brett MacNeil. Traded to the Toronto Argonauts in September, 1991 in exchange for a first round pick in the 1992 CFL College Draft, offensive lineman Chris Morris. Granted free agency status in February, 1992. Re-signed by Toronto in June, 1992. Released by Toronto in October, 1992. Signed as a free agent by the Winnipeg Blue Bombers in May, 1993.

	Team	Scoring GP	TD	C	FG	S	TP	Pass Receiving NO	YDS	AVE	LG	TD
1988abcdefgh	B.C.	18	18	x1	0	0	110	83	1468	17.7	77	18
1989e	B.C.	17	14	0	0	0	84	79	1446	18.3	71	14
1990	Ott.	17	12	0	0	0	72	61	895	14.7	55	12
1991ij	Edm.	11	9	0	0	0	54	37	597	16.1	46	9
	Tor.	7	7	0	0	0	36	29	552	19.0	68	6
1992	Tor.	9	1	0	0	0	6	30	444	14.8	39	1
1993hijk	Wpg.	16	15	0	0	0	90	84	1144	13.6	44	15
CFL TOTALS		**95**	**76**	**x1**	**0**	**0**	**452**	**403**	**6546**	**16.2**	**77**	**75**

	Team	Rushing NO	YDS	AVE	LG	TD	Fumbles NO	LOST	OFR
1988	B.C.	1	4	4.0	4	0	1	1	0
1989	B.C.	0	0	0	0	0	1	0	1
1990	Ott.	0	0	0	0	0	0	0	2
1991	Edm.	0	0	0	0	0	0	0	0
	Tor.	0	0	0	0	0	2	1	0
1992	Tor.	0	0	0	0	0	2	2	0
1993	Wpg.	1	-14.	-14.0	0	0	3	2	1
CFL TOTALS		**2**	**-10**	**-5.0**	**4**	**0**	**9**	**6**	**4**

Kickoff Returns - 1 for 20 yards with B.C. in 1988 and 1 for 21 yards in 1989. **CFL Total Kickoff Returns - 2 for 41 yards, 20.5 average, longest 21 yards.**

Defensive Tackles - 3 with B.C. in 1988; 1 in 1989; 3 with Ottawa in 1990; 4 with Toronto in 1992 and 5 defensive with Winnipeg in 1993. **CFL Total Defensive Tackles - 16.**

a - Jeff Nicklin Memorial Trophy Western Division Outstanding Player
b - Led CFL in Pass Receiving Catches and Yards
c - Led CFL in Combined Yards from Scrimmage
d - Led CFL in Touchdown Points and Pass Receiving Touchdowns
e - All-Western All-Star
f - Schenley Award Most Outstanding Player
g - Tied CFL Record for Most TD Catches in a Season
h - CFL All-Star
i - All-Eastern All-Star
j - Tied for CFL Lead - Most Receiving TDs
k - Tied for CFL Lead - Most Points (TDs)

Playoffs

	Team	Scoring GP	TD	C	FG	S	TP	Pass Receiving NO	YDS	AVE	LG	TD
1988	B.C.	2	1	0	0	0	6	12	112	9.3	30	1
1990	Ott.	1	0	0	0	0	0	2	64	32.0	56	0
1991	Tor.	1	1	0	0	0	6	6	51	8.5	15	1
1993	Wpg.	1	0	0	0	0	0	3	63	21.0	44	0
CFL TOTALS		**5**	**2**	**0**	**0**	**0**	**12**	**23**	**290**	**12.6**	**56**	**2**

Tackles - 1 defensive with Toronto in 1991 and 1 defensive with Winnipeg in 1993. **CFL Total Playoff Tackles - 2 (2 defensive).**

Grey Cup

	Team	Pass Receiving GP	NO	YDS	AVE	LG	TD
1988	B.C.	1	3	78	26.0	41	1
1991	Tor.	1	3	14	4.7	8	0
1993	Wpg.	1	7	118	16.9	29	0
CFL TOTALS		**3**	**13**	**210**	**16.2**	**41**	**1**

Fumbles - 1 and 1 lost with Winnipeg in 1993. **Total Grey Cup Fumbles - 1 and 1 lost.**

Tackles - 1 defensive with Toronto in 1991 and 1 defensive with Winnipeg in 1993. **Total Grey Cup Tackles - 2 (2 defensive).**

WILLIAMS, HENRY (GIZMO)

Born: May 31, 1963
Birthplace: Memphis, Tennessee
Specialty Teams/Wide Receiver. 5'6", 185 lbs. Import
Last Amateur Club: University of East Carolina
Acquired: Signed as a free agent by the Edmonton Eskimos in September, 1986 following a stint with the USFL Memphis Showboats in 1985. Signed as a free agent by the NFL Philadelphia Eagles in March, 1989. Was released midway through the season. Re-signed as a free agent by Edmonton Eskimos in April, 1990.

WILLIAMS, HENRY (GIZMO)

	Team	GP	TD	C	FG	S	TP	NO	YDS	AVE	LG	TD
		Scoring						Rushing				
1986	Edm.	8	2	0	0	0	12	2	49	24.5	36	1
1987abcdefghijkl	Edm.	16	5	0	0	0	30	0	0	0.0	0	0
1988a	Edm.	17	7	0	0	0	42	3	-1	-0.3	-9	0
1989		NFL						NFL				
1990m	Edm.	16	4	0	0	0	24	2	-1	0.5	-15	0
1991abegnopqr	Edm.	18	6	0	0	0	36	1	1	1.0	1	0
1992abe	Edm.	18	9	0	0	0	54	6	57	9.5	26	0
1992abes	Edm.	18	10	0	0	0	60	2	-3	-1.5	9	0
CFL TOTALS		**111**	**43**	**0**	**0**	**0**	**258**	**16**	**102**	**6.4**	**36**	**1**

	Team	NO	YDS	AVE	LG	TD	NO	YDS	AVE	LG	TD
		Pass Receiving					Punt Returns				
1986	Edm.	3	79	26.3	56	0	37	423	11.4	74	1
1987	Edm.	4	48	12.0	21	0	80	951	11.9	91	4
1988	Edm.	25	515	20.6	85	5	96	964	10.0	100	2
1989			NFL						NFL		
1990	Edm.	15	260	17.3	48	0	90	987	11.0	81	2
1991	Edm.	13	233	17.9	35	1	98	1440	14.7	88	5
1992	Edm.	41	948	23.1	81	6	92	1124	12.2	104	3
1993	Edm.	52	950	18.3	102	6	83	1077	13.0	104	4
CFL TOTALS		**153**	**3033**	**19.8**	**102**	**18**	**576**	**6966**	**12.1**	**104**	**21**

	Team	NO	YDS	AVE	LG	TD	NO	LOST	OFR
		Kickoff Returns					Fumbles		
1986	Edm.	9	210	23.3	35	0	0	0	0
1987	Edm.	26	623	24.0	43	0	2	0	1
1988	Edm.	15	379	25.3	34	0	4	2	1
1989			NFL					NFL	
1990	Edm.	31	743	24.0	92	1	6	6	1
1991	Edm.	32	593	18.5	51	0	5	3	1
1992	Edm.	24	441	18.4	34	0	0	0	0
1993	Edm.	21	381	18.1	28	0	5	2	1
CFL TOTALS		**158**	**3370**	**21.3**	**92**	**1**	**22**	**13**	**5**

Unsuccessful Field Goal Returns - 5 for 212 yards, 42.4 average, longest 111 yards and 1 TD with Edmonton in 1987; 5 for 90 yards, 18.0 average, longest 22 yards in 1988; 5 for 229 yards, 45.8 average, longest 110 yards and 1 TD in 1990; 6 for 169 yards, 28.2 average, longest 51 yards in 1991; 7 for 197 yards, 28.1 average, longest 70 yards in 1992 and 4 for 118 yards, 29.5 average, longest 42 yards in 1993.
CFL Total Unsuccessful Field Goal Returns - 32 for 1015 yards, 31.7 average, longest 111 yards and 2 TDs.

Defensive Tackles - 3 with Edmonton in 1988; 2 in 1990; 1 in 1991; 1 in 1992 and 1 in 1993. **CFL Total Defensive Tackles - 8.**

a - All-Western All-Star.
b - CFL All-Star.
c - Set CFL record Most Punt Return Yardage One Game (221).
d - Set CFL record Most Punt Return TDs One Season (four).
e - Led CFL in Punt Return Yards.
f - Tied CFL record Most Punt Return Touchdowns all-time (five).
g - Tied CFL record Most Punt Return Touchdowns One Game (two).
h - Set CFL record Most Punt Return Touchdowns in One Quarter (two).
i - Set CFL record for Longest Unsuccessful Field Goal Return, Regular Season.
j - Set Grey Cup record for Longest Unsuccessful Field Goal Return.
k - Scored first Unsuccessful Field Goal Return TD in Regular Season.
l - Scored first Grey Cup Unsuccessful Field Goal Return TD.
m- All-Time Leader in Punt Return Touchdowns.
n - Set CFL record Most Punt Return Yards One Season.
o - Set CFL record Most Punt Return Yardage One Game (232).
p - Tied CFL record Most 100-yard Punt Return Games (five).
q - Set CFL record Most Punt Return TDs One Season (five).
r - Tied own CFL record Most Punt Return TDs in One Quarter (two).
s - Led CFL in Combined Yards.

Playoffs

	Team	GP	NO	YDS	AVE	LG	TD	NO	YDS	AVE	LG	TD
			Pass Receiving					Punt Returns				
1986	Edm.	1	1	3	3.0	3	0	3	3	1.0	2	0
1987	Edm.	2	0	0	0	0	0	12	49	4.1	23	0
1988	Edm.	1	3	32	10.7	15	0	2	55	27.5	43	0
1990	Edm.	2	0	0	0.0	0	0	7	95	136	39	0
1991	Edm.	1	1	8	8.0	8	0	2	10	5.0	5	0
1992	Edm.	2	1	10	10.0	10	1	8	150	18.6	103	1
1993	Edm.	2	2	76	38.0	39	1	5	58	11.6	31	0
CFL TOTALS		**11**	**8**	**129**	**16.1**	**39**	**2**	**39**	**420**	**10.8**	**103**	**1**

	Team	NO	LOST	OFR	NO	YDS	AVE	LG	TD
		Fumbles			Kickoff Returns				
1986	Edm.	2	1	1	2	19	9.5	19	0
1987	Edm.	0	0	0	4	83	20.7	24	0
1988	Edm.	0	0	0	1	39	39.0	39	0
1990	Edm.	0	0	0	0	37	0.0	23	0
1991	Edm.	0	0	0	1	17	17.0	17	0
1992	Edm.	1	1	0	5	103	20.6	33	0
1993	Edm.	0	0	0	2	52	26.0	27	0
CFL TOTALS		**3**	**2**	**1**	**15**	**350**	**23.3**	**39**	**0**

Scoring - 1 TD for 6 points with Edmonton in 1993.
CFL Total Playoff Scoring - 1 TD for 6 points.

Unsuccessful Field Goal Returns - 3 for 88 yards, 29.3 average, longest 59 yards with Edmonton in 1987 and 1 for 57 yards in 1990.
CFL Total Playoff Unsuccessful Field Goal Returns - 4 for 145 yards, 36.3 average, longest 59 yards.

Rushing - 1 for -15 yards with Edmonton in 1988.
CFL Total Playoff Rushing - 1 for -15 yards.

Grey Cup

	Team	GP	TD	C	FG	S	TP	NO	YDS	AVE	LG	TD
			Scoring					Punt Returns				
1987	Edm.	1	1	0	0	0	6	3	14	4.7	6	0
1990	Edm.	1	0	0	0	0	0	6	24	4.0	9	0
1993	Edm.	1	0	0	0	0	0	5	4	0.8	9	0
CFL TOTALS		**3**	**1**	**0**	**0**	**0**	**6**	**14**	**42**	**3.0**	**9**	**0**

	Team	NO	YDS	AVE	LG	TD	NO	YDS	AVE	LG	TD
		Kickoff Returns					Unsuccessful Field Goal Returns				
1987	Edm.	1	23	23.0	23	0	2	143	71.5	115	1
1990	Edm.	3	78	26.0	26	0	0	0	0.0	0	0
1993	Edm.	0	0	0.0	0	0	0	0	0.0	0	0
CFL TOTALS		**4**	**101**	**25.3**	**26**	**0**	**2**	**143**	**71.5**	**115**	**1**

Fumbles - 1 and 1 lost with Edmonton in 1990.
Total Grey Cup Fumbles - 1 and 1 lost.

WILLIS, LARRY

Born: July 13, 1963
Birthplace: Santa Monica, California
Wide Receiver. 5'11", 170 lbs. Import
Last Amateur Club: Fresno State University
Acquired: Signed as a free agent by the NFL Denver Broncos in May, 1985 despite being selected by Oakland in the 1985 USFL Territorial Draft. Released by Denver following the 1985 season and signed as a free agent by the Calgary Stampeders in October, 1986. Signed as a free agent by the B.C. Lions in April, 1990. Traded to the Edmonton Eskimos in October, 1990 in exchange for wide receiver Darrell Colbert. Released by Edmonton in March, 1991. Signed as a free agent by the Winnipeg Blue Bombers in June, 1991. Released by Winnipeg in May, 1993. Signed as a free agent by the Toronto Argonauts in July, 1993. Released by Toronto in August ,1993.

	Team	GP	TD	C	FG	S	TP	NO	YDS	AVE	LG	TD
			Scoring					Pass Receiving				
1986	Cal.	1	0	0	0	0	0	0	0	0.0	0	0
1987	Cal.	18	10	0	0	0	60	74	1477	20.0	86	10
1988a	Cal.	18	9	x1	0	0	56	73	1328	18.2	72	9
1989	Cal.	18	10	0	0	0	60	73	1451	19.9	80	10
1990	B.C.	12	6	0	0	0	36	49	837	17.1	48	6
	Edm.	4	0	0	0	0	0	14	193	13.8	45	0
1991	Wpg.	11	3	0	0	0	18	36	741	20.6	104	3
1992	Wpg.	4	1	0	0	0	6	22	291	13.2	56	1
1993	Tor.	3	1	0	0	0	6	11	195	17.7	54	1
CFL TOTALS		**89**	**40**	**x1**	**0**	**0**	**242**	**352**	**6513**	**18.5**	**104**	**40**

	Team	NO	YDS	AVE	LG	TD	NO	LOST	OFR
		Punt Returns					Fumbles		
1986	Cal.	4	25	6.3	23	0	1	1	0
1987	Cal.	12	55	4.6	17	0	4	1	2
1988	Cal.	3	17	5.7	10	0	2	0	2
1989	Cal.	0	0	0.0	0	0	2	2	1
1990	B.C.	0	0	0.0	0	0	1	0	0
	Edm.	0	0	0.0	0	0	3	3	0
1991	Wpg.	3	8	2.7	5	0	0	0	0
1992	Wpg.	0	0	0.0	0	0	0	0	0
1993	Tor.	0	0	0.0	0	0	0	0	0
CFL TOTALS		**22**	**105**	**4.8**	**23**	**0**	**13**	**7**	**5**

Rushing - 6 for 72 yards, 12.0 average, longest 20 yards with Calgary in 1986 and 4 for 15 yards, 3.8 average, longest 13 yards with B.C. in 1990.
CFL Total Rushing - 10 for 87 yards, 8.7 average, longest 20 yards.

Kickoff Returns - 1 for 20 yards with Calgary in 1987.
CFL Total Kickoff Returns - 1 for 20 yards.

Passing - 1 attempt, 0 complete with Winnipeg in 1991.
CFL Total Passing - 1 attempt, 0 complete.

Fumble Returns - 1 for 0 yards with Calgary in 1987.
CFL Total Fumble Returns - 1 for 0 yards.

Tackles - 3 defensive with Calgary in 1987; 1 defensive in 1988; 3 defensive in 1989; 1 defensive with B.C. and 1 defensive with Edmonton in 1990; 5 defensive and 2 special teams with Winnipeg in 1991; 1 defensive and 2 special teams in 1992 and 1 special teams with Toronto in 1993.
CFL Total Tackles - 20 (15 defensive and 5 special teams).

a - All-Western All-Star

WILLIS, LARRY

Playoffs

	Team	GP	Rushing NO	YDS	AVE	LG	TD	Pass Receiving NO	YDS	AVE	LG	TD
1986	Cal.	1	1	-1	-1.0	-1	0	2	22	11.0	13	0
1987	Cal.	1	0	0	0.0	0	0	7	96	13.7	21	0
1989	Cal.	1	0	0	0.0	0	0	3	126	42.0	58	0
1990	Edm.	2	0	0	0.0	0	0	3	59	19.7	27	1
1991	Wpg.	2	0	0	0.0	0	0	6	75	12.5	26	0
CFL TOTALS		**7**	**1**	**-1**	**-1.0**	**-1**	**0**	**21**	**378**	**18.0**	**58**	**1**

Punt Returns - 2 for 24 yards, 12.0 average, longest 17 yards with Calgary in 1986. **CFL Total Playoff Punt Returns - 2 for 24 yards, 12.0 average, longest 17 yards.**

Tackles - 2 defensive with Winnipeg in 1991. **CFL Total Playoff Tackles - 2 (2 defensive).**

Grey Cup

	Team	GP	Scoring TD	C	FG	S	TP	Pass Receiving NO	YDS	AVE	LG	TD
1990	Edm.	1	1	0	0	0	6	4	46	11.5	20	1
CFL TOTALS		**1**	**1**	**0**	**0**	**0**	**6**	**4**	**46**	**11.5**	**20**	**1**

WILSON, DON
Born: July 21, 1961
Birthplace: Washington, D.C.
Defensive Back. 6'2", 195 lbs. Import
Last Amateur Club: North Carolina State University
Acquired: Signed as a free agent with NFL Buffalo Bills in 1984 and released after 1986 season. Signed as a free agent by the Montreal Alouettes in March, 1987. Selected by the Winnipeg Blue Bombers in the third round, (21st overall) in the Alouettes Dispersal Draft in June, 1987. Released later that same month and signed as a free agent by the Edmonton Eskimos in July, 1987. Released by Edmonton in June, 1990. Signed as a free agent by the Toronto Argonauts in July, 1990. Traded to the Edmonton Eskimos in January, 1993 along with cornerback Ed Berry, wide receiver Eddie Brown, linebacker Bruce Dickson, quarterback Rickey Foggie, slotback J.P. Izquierdo, defensive lineman Leonard Johnson and slotback Darrell K. Smith in exchange for defensive lineman Cameron Brosseau, linebacker John Davis, slotback Craig Ellis, quarterback Tracy Ham, cornerback Enis Jackson, running back Chris Johnstone, defensive back Travis Oliver and wide receiver Ken Winey.

	Team	GP	Scoring TD	C	FG	S	TP	Interception Returns NO	YDS	AVE	LG	TD
1987	Edm.	15	1	0	0	0	6	7	127	18.1	47	1
1988a	Edm.	18	0	0	0	0	0	7	68	9.7	23	0
1989ab	Edm.	18	1	0	0	0	6	4	35	8.8	18	0
1990bc	Tor.	18	1	0	0	0	6	6	134	22.3	65	1
1991bc	Tor.	18	1	0	0	0	6	7	184	26.3	73	0
1992c	Tor.	18	2	0	0	0	12	6	162	27.0	94	1
1993ab	Edm.	18	1	0	0	0	6	7	68	9.7	34	1
CFL TOTALS		**123**	**7**	**0**	**0**	**0**	**42**	**42**	**778**	**18.5**	**94**	**4**

	Team	Punt Returns NO	YDS	AVE	LG	TD	Fumble Returns NO	YDS	AVE	LG	TD
1987	Edm.	10	83	8.3	16	0	2	9	4.5	9	0
1988	Edm.	4	5	1.3	4	0	2	4	2.0	4	0
1989	Edm.	8	124	15.5	37	0	2	20	10.0	20	1
1990	Tor.	0	0	0.0	0	0	2	14	7.0	14	0
1991	Tor.	0	0	0.0	0	0	1	101	101.0	101	1
1992	Tor.	0	0	0.0	0	0	1	45	45.0	45	1
1993	Edm.	0	0	0.0	0	0	1	4	4.0	4	0
CFL TOTALS		**22**	**212**	**9.6**	**37**	**0**	**11**	**197**	**17.9**	**105**	**3**

	Team	Fumbles NO	LOST	OFR	Kickoff Returns NO	YDS	AVE	LG	TD
1987	Edm.	1	1	0	0	0	0.0	0	0
1988	Edm.	0	0	0	2	44	22.0	23	0
1989	Edm.	0	0	0	0	0	0.0	0	0
1990	Tor.	0	0	0	0	0	0.0	0	0
1991	Tor.	0	0	0	0	0	0.0	0	0
1992	Tor.	2	1	0	3	39	13.0	25	0
1993	Edm.	0	0	0	0	0	0.0	0	0
CFL TOTALS		**3**	**2**	**0**	**5**	**83**	**16.6**	**25**	**0**

Unsuccessful Field Goal Returns - 1 for 6 yards with Edmonton in 1993. **CFL Total Unsuccessful Field Goal Returns - 1 for 6 yards.**

Blocked Kicks - 1 field goal with Edmonton in 1989; 1 punt with Toronto in 1991; 1 punt in 1992 and 1 punt with Edmonton in 1993. **CFL Total Blocked Kicks - 4 (1 field goal and 3 punts).**

Pass Receiving - 1 for 28 yards with Toronto in 1990. **CFL Total Pass Receiving - 1 for 28 yards.**

Quarterback Sacks - 1 with Edmonton in 1987; 1 in 1988; 4 in 1989; 2 for 9 yards lost with Toronto in 1992 and 2 for 15 yards lost with Edmonton in 1993. **CFL Total QB Sacks - 10.**

Tackles - 69 defensive with Edmonton in 1987; 54 defensive in 1988; 57 defensive in 1989; 64 defensive with Toronto in 1990; 56 defensive and 10 special teams in 1991; 51 defensive and 4 special teams in 1992 and 68 defensive and 4 special teams with Edmonton in 1993. **CFL Total Tackles - 437 (419 defensive and 18 special teams).**

Tackles for Losses - 1 for 3 yards with Toronto in 1991; 2 for 2 yards in 1992 and 5 for 21 yards with Edmonton in 1993. **CFL Total Tackles for Losses - 8 for 26 yards.**

a - All-Western All-Star
b - CFL All-Star
c - All-Eastern All-Star

Playoffs

Games Played - 2 with Edmonton in 1987; 1 in 1988; 1 in 1989; 2 with Toronto in 1990; 1 in 1991 and 2 with Edmonton in 1993. **CFL Total Playoff GP - 9.**

Scoring - 1 TD for 6 points with Toronto in 1990. **CFL Total Playoff Scoring - 1 TD for 6 points.**

Interception Returns - 1 for 0 yards with Edmonton in 1987; 1 for 0 yards in 1988; 1 for 73 yards and 1 TD with Toronto in 1990 and 1 for 20 yards in 1991. **CFL Total Playoff Interception Returns - 4 for 93 yards, 23.3 average, longest 73 yards and 1 TD.**

Tackles - 7 defensive with Edmonton in 1987; 8 defensive in 1988; 3 defensive in 1989; 4 defensive with Toronto in 1990; 3 defensive in 1991 and 8 defensive and 1 special teams with Edmonton in 1993. **CFL Total Playoff Tackles - 34 (33 defensive and 1 special teams).**

Tackles for Losses - 1 for 1 yard with Toronto in 1991 and 1 for 1 yard with Edmonton in 1993. **CFL Total Playoff Tackles for Losses - 2 for 2 yards.**

Grey Cup

Games Played - 1 with Edmonton in 1987; 1 with Toronto in 1991 and 1 with Edmonton in 1993. **Total Grey Cup GP - 3.**

Tackles - 4 defensive with Toronto in 1991 and 2 defensive with Edmonton in 1993. **Total Grey Cup Tackles - 6 (6 defensive).**

WILSON, JOHNATHAN
Born: December 27, 1970
Birthplace: Hampton, Virginia
Defensive Back. 6'2", 215 lbs. Import
Last Amateur Club: Hampton University
Acquired: Signed as a free agent by the Toronto Argonauts in May, 1992. Released by Toronto in September, 1993.

	Team	GP	Punt Returns NO	YDS	AVE	LG	TD	Kickoff Returns NO	YDS	AVE	LG	TD
1992	Tor.	11	9	29	3.2	14	0	9	183	20.3	40	0
1993	Tor.	9	0	0	0.0	0	0	0	0	0.0	0	0
CFL TOTALS		**20**	**9**	**29**	**3.2**	**14**	**0**	**9**	**183**	**20.3**	**40**	**0**

	Team	Interception Returns NO	YDS	AVE	LG	TD	Fumbles NO	LOST	OFR
1992	Tor.	1	0	0.0	0	0	4	4	0
1993	Tor.	1	16	16.0	16	0	0	0	1
CFL TOTALS		**2**	**16**	**8.0**	**16**	**0**	**4**	**4**	**1**

Punting - 1 for 51 yards with Toronto in 1992. **CFL Total Punting - 1 for 51 yards.**

Blocked Kicks - 1 convert with Toronto in 1992. **CFL Total Blocked Kicks - 1 convert.**

Fumble Returns - 1 for 5 yards with Toronto in 1992. **CFL Total Fumble Returns - 1 for 5 yards.**

Quarterback Sacks - 2 for 21 yards lost with Toronto in 1992 and 1 for 1 yard lost in 1993. **CFL Total QB Sacks - 3 for 22 yards lost.**

Tackles - 13 defensive and 5 special teams with Toronto in 1992 and 15 defensive and 8 special teams in 1993. **CFL Total Tackles - 41 (28 defensive and 13 special teams).**

Tackles for Losses - 2 for 2 yards lost with Toronto in 1992. **CFL Total Tackles for Losses - 2 for 2 yards lost.**

WINEY, KEN
Born: September 17, 1962
Birthplace: Lake Charles, Louisiana
Wide Receiver. 5'11", 180 lbs. Non-import
Last Amateur Club: Southern University
Acquired: Signed as a free agent by the Winnipeg Blue Bombers in February, 1986. Released in June, 1986 and re-signed in March, 1987. Traded to the Edmonton Eskimos in June, 1992 in exchange for future considerations. Traded to the Toronto Argonauts in January, 1993 along with defensive lineman Cameron Brosseau, linebacker John Davis, slotback Craig Ellis, quarterback Tracy Ham, cornerback Enis Jackson, running back Chris Johnstone, and defensive back Travis Oliver in exchange for cornerback Ed Berry, wide receiver Eddie Brown, linebacker Bruce Dickson, quarterback Rickey Foggie, slotback J.P. Izquierdo, defensive lineman Leonard Johnson, slotback Darrell K. Smith and defensive back Don Wilson. Granted free agency status in February, 1993. Signed as a free agent by the Toronto Argonauts in May, 1993. Released by Toronto in September, 1993.

WINEY, KEN

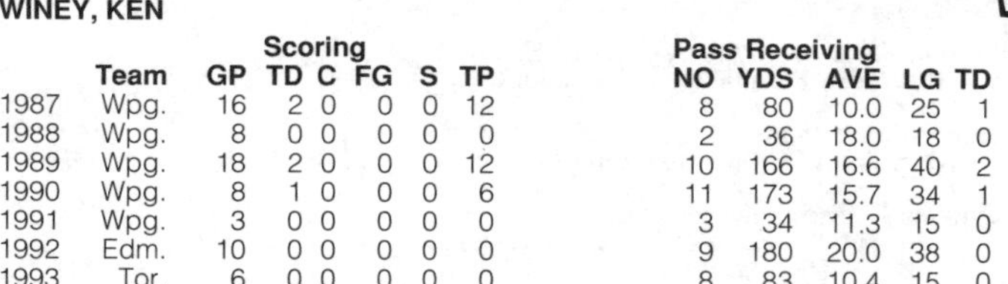

	Team	Scoring GP	TD	C	FG	S	TP	Pass Receiving NO	YDS	AVE	LG	TD
1987	Wpg.	16	2	0	0	0	12	8	80	10.0	25	1
1988	Wpg.	8	0	0	0	0	0	2	36	18.0	18	0
1989	Wpg.	18	2	0	0	0	12	10	166	16.6	40	2
1990	Wpg.	8	1	0	0	0	6	11	173	15.7	34	1
1991	Wpg.	3	0	0	0	0	0	3	34	11.3	15	0
1992	Edm.	10	0	0	0	0	0	9	180	20.0	38	0
1993	Tor.	6	0	0	0	0	0	8	83	10.4	15	0
CFL TOTALS		**69**	**5**	**0**	**0**	**0**	**30**	**51**	**752**	**14.8**	**40**	**4**

	Team	Punt Returns NO	YDS	AVE	LG	TD	Kickoff Returns NO	YDS	AVE	LG	TD
1987	Wpg.	33	211	6.4	40	0	28	552	19.7	93	1
1988	Wpg.	1	8	8.0	8	0	4	36	9.0	15	0
1989	Wpg.	31	213	6.9	38	0	27	421	15.6	27	0
1990	Wpg.	26	246	9.5	43	0	11	170	15.5	29	0
1991	Wpg.	8	132	16.5	63	0	4	79	19.8	45	0
1992	Wpg.	3	2	0.7	3	0	1	7	7.0	7	0
1993	Tor.	4	40	10.0	31	0	3	36	12.0	17	0
CFL TOTALS		**106**	**852**	**8.0**	**63**	**0**	**78**	**1301**	**16.7**	**93**	**1**

	Team	Fumbles NO	LOST	OFR	Unsuccessful Field Goal Returns NO	YDS	AVE	LG	TD
1987	Wpg.	3	2	0	0	0	0.0	0	0
1988	Wpg.	0	0	0	0	0	0.0	0	0
1989	Wpg.	1	0	1	0	0	0.0	0	0
1990	Wpg.	2	1	0	5	93	18.6	28	0
1991	Wpg.	0	0	0	0	0	0.0	0	0
1992	Edm.	0	0	0	0	0	0.0	0	0
1993	Tor.	1	1	0	0	0	0.0	0	0
CFL TOTALS		**7**	**4**	**1**	**5**	**93**	**18.6**	**28**	**0**

Tackles - 1 defensive with Edmonton in 1992 and 2 defensive and 2 special teams with Toronto in 1993.
CFL Total Tackles - 5 (3 defensive and 2 special teams).

Playoffs

	Team	GP	Pass Receiving NO	YDS	AVE	LG	TD	Kickoff Returns NO	YDS	AVE	LG	TD
1988	Wpg.	2	7	75	10.7	14	0	0	0	0.0	0	0
1989	Wpg.	2	0	0	0.0	0	0	3	82	27.3	38	0
1990	Wpg.	1	0	0	0.0	0	0	2	29	14.5	18	0
CFL TOTALS		**5**	**7**	**75**	**10.7**	**14**	**0**	**5**	**111**	**22.2**	**38**	**0**

	Team	Punt Returns NO	YDS	AVE	LG	TD	Unsuccessful Field Goal Returns NO	YDS	AVE	LG	TD
1988	Wpg.	0	0	0.0	0	0	0	0	0.0	0	0
1989	Wpg.	12	54	4.5	8	0	2	29	14.5	30	0
1990	Wpg.	0	0	0.0	0	0	0	0	0.0	0	0
CFL TOTALS		**12**	**54**	**4.5**	**8**	**0**	**2**	**29**	**14.5**	**30**	**0**

Fumbles - 1 and 0 lost with Winnipeg in 1989.
CFL Total Playoff Fumbles - 1 and 0 lost.

Own Fumbles Recovered - 1 with Winnipeg in 1989. **CFL Total Playoff OFR - 1.**

Grey Cup

	Team	GP	Pass Receiving NO	YDS	AVE	LG	TD	Punt Returns NO	YDS	AVE	LG	TD
1988	Wpg.	1	1	16	16.0	16	0	0	0	0.0	0	0
1990	Wpg.	1	3	67	22.3	34	0	4	83	20.8	40	0
CFL TOTALS		**2**	**4**	**83**	**20.8**	**34**	**0**	**4**	**83**	**20.8**	**40**	**0**

Kickoff Returns - 1 for 10 yards with Winnipeg in 1990.
Total Grey Cup Kickoff Returns - 1 for 10 yards.

Defensive Tackles - 1 with Winnipeg in 1990.
Total Grey Cup Defensive Tackles - 1.

WINFIELD, EARL

Born: August 6, 1961
Birthplace: Petersburg, Virginia
Wide Receiver. 5'11", 185 lbs. Import
Last Amateur Club: University of North Carolina
Acquired: Tried out with the NFL Seattle Seahawks in 1986 and signed as a free agent with the Hamilton Tiger-Cats in February, 1987. Attended the San Francisco 49ers (NFL) training camp in 1989 and was later released. Signed with Hamilton in August, 1989.

	Team	Scoring GP	TD	C	FG	S	TP	Pass Receiving NO	YDS	AVE	LG	TD
1987	Ham.	11	3	0	0	0	18	38	746	19.6	81	2
1988abcde	Ham.	18	13	0	0	0	78	60	1213	20.2	73	8
1989	Ham.	9	4	0	0	0	24	15	324	21.6	56	3
1990b	Ham.	13	13	0	0	0	78	62	1054	17.0	75	13
1991	Ham.	10	4	0	0	0	24	45	874	19.4	77	4
1992	Ham.	12	11	0	0	0	66	52	880	16.9	80	9
1993f	Ham.	15	8	0	0	0	48	61	1076	17.6	79	5
CFL TOTALS		**88**	**56**	**0**	**0**	**0**	**336**	**333**	**6167**	**18.5**	**81**	**44**

	Team	Punt Returns NO	YDS	AVE	LG	TD	Kickoff Returns NO	YDS	AVE	LG	TD
1987	Ham.	22	256	11.6	71	1	18	347	19.3	34	0
1988	Ham.	74	865	11.7	101	4	20	538	26.6	100	1
1989	Ham.	36	361	10.0	77	1	10	226	22.6	43	0
1990	Ham.	24	102	4.3	19	0	8	164	20.5	34	0
1991	Ham.	2	15	7.5	15	0	1	20	20.0	20	0
1992	Ham.	22	291	13.2	77	2	1	20	20.0	20	0
1993	Ham.	41	530	12.9	71	3	13	282	21.7	44	0
CFL TOTALS		**221**	**2420**	**11.0**	**101**	**11**	**71**	**1597**	**22.5**	**100**	**1**

	Team	Fumbles NO	LOST	OFR	Rushing NO	YDS	AVE	LG	TD
1987	Ham.	5	4	0	0	0	0.0	0	0
1988	Ham.	7	5	2	1	2	2.0	2	0
1989	Ham.	2	1	0	2	18	9.0	10	0
1990	Ham.	2	2	0	0	0	0.0	0	0
1991	Ham.	1	1	0	2	5	2.5	13	0
1992	Ham.	3	2	0	1	7	7.0	7	0
1993	Ham.	3	2	2	1	-8	-8.0	0	0
CFL TOTALS		**23**	**17**	**4**	**7**	**24**	**3.4**	**13**	**0**

Passing - 1 attempt and 0 complete with Hamilton in 1990.
CFL Total Passing - 1 attempt and 0 complete.

Fumble Returns - 1 for 0 yards with Hamilton in 1993.
CFL Total Fumble Returns - 1 for 0 yards.

Unsuccessful Field Goal Returns - 1 for 15 yards with Hamilton in 1990; 2 for 5 yards, 2.5 average, longest 5 yards in 1992 and 1 for 61 yards in 1993.
CFL Total Unsuccessful Field Goal Returns - 4 for 81 yards, 20.3 average, longest 15 yards.

Tackles - 2 defensive with Hamilton in 1987; 2 defensive in 1988; 5 defensive in 1990; 3 defensive and 1 special teams in 1991; 5 defensive in 1992 and 7 defensive in 1993.
CFL Total Tackles - 25 (24 defensive and 1 special teams).

a - Jeff Russel Memorial East Division Outstanding Player Trophy
b - All-Eastern All-Star
c - All-Eastern All-Star Specialty Teams
d - Runner-up Schenley Most Outstanding Player
e - CFL All-Star Special Teams
f - Tied CFL Record for Most Punt Return TDs in One Game (2)

Playoffs

	Team	GP	Pass Receiving NO	YDS	AVE	LG	TD	Punt Returns NO	YDS	AVE	LG	TD
1988	Ham.	1	3	31	10.3	14	0	2	91	45.5	91	0
1989	Ham.	1	0	0	0.0	0	0	9	43	4.8	15	0
1992	Ham.	2	10	127	12.7	22	1	0	0	0.0	0	0
1993	Ham.	2	11	100	9.1	18	0	3	9	3.0	9	0
CFL TOTALS		**6**	**24**	**258**	**10.8**	**22**	**0**	**14**	**143**	**10.2**	**91**	**0**

Fumbles - 1 and 0 lost with Hamilton in 1989.
CFL Total Playoff Fumbles - 1 and 0 lost.

Own Fumbles Recovered - 1 with Hamilton in 1993. **CFL Total Playoff OFR - 1.**

Unsuccessful Field Goal Returns - 1 for 14 yards with Hamilton in 1993.
CFL Total Playoff Unsuccessful Field Goal Returns - 1 for 14 yards.

Tackles - 1 defensive with Hamilton in 1992 and 1 defensive in 1993.
CFL Total Playoff Tackles - 2 (2 defensive).

Grey Cup

Games Played - 1 with Hamilton in 1989. **Total Grey Cup GP - 1.**

Pass Receiving - 2 for 34 yards, 17.0 average, longest 19 yards with Hamilton in 1989. **Total Grey Cup Pass Receiving - 2 for 34 yards, 17.0 average, longest 19 yards.**

Punt Returns - 2 for 25 yards, 12.5 average, longest 20 yards with Hamilton in 1989. **Total Grey Cup Punt Returns - 2 for 25 yards, 12.5 average, longest 20 yards.**

Fumbles - 1 and 0 lost with Hamilton in 1989.
Total Grey Cup Fumbles - 1 and 0 lost.

Own Fumbles Recovered - 1 with Hamilton in 1989.
Total Grey Cup OFR - 1.

Defensive Tackles - 1 with Hamilton in 1989.
Total Grey Cup Defensive Tackles - 1.

WISE, MYRON

Born: June 26, 1972
Birthplace: Brenham, Texas
Wide Receiver. 6'1", 170 lbs. Import
Last Amateur Club: Palomar Junior College
Acquired: Signed as a free agent by the Sacramento Gold Miners in March, 1993.

Games Played - 2 with Sacramento in 1993. **CFL Total GP - 2.**

WISEMAN, TODD

Born: May 26, 1965
Birthplace: Dunnville, Ontario
Defensive Back. 5'11", 185 lbs. Non-import
Last Amateur Club: Simon Fraser University (EVCO)
Acquired: Selected in the second round (13th overall) by the B.C. Lions in the 1987 CFL College Draft. Traded to Toronto Argos in June, 1989 in exchange for a second round choice in the 1990 CFL College Draft, running back Keith Kelly. Traded to B.C. Lions in March, 1990 along with linebackers Willie Pless and Tony Visco, defensive lineman Jearld Baylis, wide receiver Emanuel Tolbert and quarterback Richard Johnson in exchange for quarterback Matt Dunigan. Released by B.C. in June, 1990. Signed as a free agent by the Hamilton Tiger-Cats in May, 1991.

		Scoring						Punt Returns				
	Team	GP	TD	C	FG	S	TP	NO	YDS	AVE	LG	TD
1987	B.C.	18	1	0	0	0	6	1	0	0.0	0	0
1988	B.C.	17	0	0	0	0	0	3	9	3.0	8	0
1989	Tor.	17	0	0	0	0	0	0	0	0.0	0	0
1990		Did not play						Did not play				
1991	Ham.	18	0	0	0	0	0	7	46	6.6	10	0
1992a	Ham.	18	0	0	0	0	0	0	0	0.0	0	0
1993	Ham.	18	0	0	0	0	0	0	0	0.0	0	0
CFL TOTALS		**106**	**1**	**0**	**0**	**0**	**6**	**11**	**55**	**5.0**	**10**	**0**

		Interception Returns					Fumble Returns				
	Team	NO	YDS	AVE	LG	TD	NO	YDS	AVE	LG	TD
1987	B.C.	1	23	23.0	23	0	2	42	21.0	42	1
1988	B.C.	0	0	0.0	0	0	0	0	0.0	0	0
1989	Tor.	1	26	26.0	26	0	1	0	0.0	0	0
1990		Did not play					Did not play				
1991	Ham.	3	87	29.0	48	0	2	0	0.0	0	0
1992	Ham.	5	105	21.0	47	0	2	0	0.0	0	0
1993	Ham.	2	46	23.0	27	0	0	0	0.0	0	0
CFL TOTALS		**12**	**287**	**23.9**	**48**	**0**	**7**	**42**	**6.0**	**42**	**1**

Unsuccessful Field Goal Returns - 5 for 63 yards, 12.6 average, longest 22 yards with Hamilton in 1991; 4 for 20 yards, 5.0 average, longest 19 yards in 1992 and 1 for 20 yards in 1993.
CFL Total Unsuccessful Field Goal Returns - 10 for 103 yards, 10.3 average, longest 22 yards.

Fumbles - 1 and 1 lost with Hamilton in 1991. **CFL Total Fumbles - 1 and 1 lost.**

Own Fumbles Recovered - 1 with Hamilton in 1992. **CFL Total OFR - 1.**

Quarterback Sacks - 1 with Toronto in 1989 and 1 with Hamilton in 1991.
CFL Total QB Sacks - 2.

Punting - 1 for 48 yards with Hamilton in 1992. **CFL Total Punting - 1 for 48 yards.**

Tackles - 3 defensive with B.C. in 1987; 6 defensive in 1988; 15 defensive with Toronto in 1989; 75 defensive and 4 special teams with Hamilton in 1991; 52 defensive and 1 special teams in 1992 and 26 defensive and 4 special teams in 1993.
CFL Total Tackles - 186 (177 defensive and 9 special teams).

Tackles for Losses - 1 for 1 yard with Hamilton in 1991.
CFL Total Tackles for Losses - 1 for 1 yard.

a - All-Eastern All-Star

Playoffs

Games Played - 1 with B.C. in 1987; 2 in 1988; 1 with Toronto in 1989; 2 with Hamilton in 1992 and 2 in 1993. **CFL Total Playoff GP - 8.**

Interception Returns - 1 for 11 yards with Hamilton in 1993.
CFL Total Playoff Interception Returns - 1 for 11 yards.

Tackles - 1 defensive with B.C. in 1987; 2 defensive in 1988; 1 defensive with Toronto in 1989; 8 defensive with Hamilton in 1992 and 5 defensive and 1 special teams in 1993.
CFL Total Playoff Tackles - 18 (17 defensive and 1 special teams).

Grey Cup

			Punt Returns				
	Team	GP	NO	YDS	AVE	LG	TD
1988	B.C.	1	2	1	0.5	5	0
CFL TOTALS		**1**	**2**	**1**	**0.5**	**5**	**0**

WOODS, (CLINTON) TONY

Born: March 19, 1966
Birthplace: Fort Lee, Virginia
Defensive End. 6'4", 270 lbs. Import
Last Amateur Club: University of Oklahoma
Acquired: Signed as a free agent by the Edmonton Eskimos in February, 1993.

Games Played - 2 with Edmonton in 1993. **CFL Total GP - 2.**

Fumble Returns - 2 for 0 yards with Edmonton in 1993.
CFL Total Fumble Returns - 2 for 0 yards.

Quarterback Sacks - 8 for 45 yards lost with Edmonton in 1993.
CFL Total QB Sacks - 8 for 45 yards.

Tackles - 25 defensive with Edmonton in 1993.
CFL Total Tackles - 25 (25 defensive).

Tackles for Losses - 4 for 8 yards with Edmonton in 1993.
CFL Total Tackles for Losses - 4 for 8 yards.

Playoffs

Games Played - 2 with Edmonton in 1993. **CFL Total Playoff GP - 2.**

Fumble Returns - 1 for 0 yards with Edmonton in 1993.
CFL Total Playoff Fumble Returns - 1 for 0 yards.

Tackles - 3 defensive with Edmonton in 1993.
CFL Total Playoff Tackles - 3 (3 defensive).

Grey Cup

Games Played - 1 with Edmonton in 1993. **Total Grey Cup GP - 1.**

Fumble Returns - 1 for 0 yards with Edmonton in 1993.
Total Grey Cup Fumble Returns - 1 for 0 yards.

Tackles - 1 defensive with Edmonton in 1993.
Total Grey Cup Tackles - 1 (1 defensive).

Tackles for Losses - 1 for 4 yards with Edmonton in 1993.
Total Grey Cup Tackles for Losses - 1 for 4 yards.

WORTHMAN, ANTOINE

Born: June 20, 1970
Birthplace: Gary, Indiana
Defensive Back. 5'10", 195 lbs. Import
Last Amateur Club: Illinois State University
Acquired: Signed as a free agent by the Toronto Argonauts in May 1992. Released by Toronto in July, 1993. Signed as a free agent by the Shreveport Pirates in April, 1994.

Games Played - 7 with Toronto in 1992 and 1 in 1993. **CFL Total GP - 8.**

Kickoff Returns - 3 for 6 yards, 2.0 average, longest 3 yards with Toronto in 1992.
CFL Total Kickoff Returns - 3 for 6 yards, 2.0 average, longest 3 yards.

Fumble Returns - 1 for 0 yards with Toronto in 1993.
CFL Total Fumble Returns - 1 for 0 yards.

Quarterback Sacks - 1 for 12 yards lost with Toronto in 1992.
CFL Total QB Sacks - 1 for 12 yards lost.

Tackles - 3 defensive and 6 special teams with Toronto in 1992 and 1 defensive and 2 special teams in 1993.
CFL Total Tackles - 12 (4 defensive and 8 special teams).

Tackles For Losses - 1 for 4 yards with Toronto in 1992.
CFL Total Tackles for Losses - 1 for 4 yards.

WRIGHT, CHARLES

Born: April 5, 1965
Birthplace: Carthage, Missouri
Cornerback. 5'9", 180 lbs. Import
Last Amateur Club: University of Tulsa
Acquired: Selected by the St. Louis Cardinals in the 10th round (257th overall) of the 1987 NFL draft. Released by St. Louis in November, 1987. Signed as a free agent by the NFL Dallas Cowboys in February, 1988. Released by Dallas in September, 1988. Signed as a free agent by the NFL Tampa Bay Buccaneers in November, 1988. Released by Tampa Bay in December, 1988. Signed as a free agent by the NFL Cleveland Browns in March, 1990. Released by Cleveland in August, 1990. Signed as a free agent by the Ottawa Rough Riders in October, 1990. Granted free agency status in February, 1994.

Games Played - 5 with Ottawa in 1990; 9 in 1991; 7 in 1992 and 8 in 1993.
CFL Total GP - 29.

Interception Returns - 4 for 51 yards, 12.8 average, longest 29 yards with Ottawa in 1990; 1 for 0 yards in 1992 and 3 for 12 yards, 4.0 average, longest 9 yards in 1993.
CFL Total Interception Returns - 8 for 63 yards, 7.9 average, longest 29 yards.

Punt Returns - 1 for 0 yards with Ottawa in 1992 and 1 for 10 yards in 1993.
CFL Total Punt Returns - 2 for 10 yards, 5.0 average, longest 10 yards.

Fumble Returns - 1 for 0 yards with Ottawa in 1990 and 1 for 0 yards in 1991.
CFL Total Fumble Returns - 2 for 0 yards.

Tackles - 14 defensive with Ottawa in 1990; 13 defensive and 3 special teams in 1991; 16 defensive and 2 special teams in 1992 and 21 defensive and 1 special teams in 1993.
CFL Total Tackles - 70 (64 defensive and 6 special teams).

WRIGHT, CHARLES

Playoffs

Games Played - 1 with Ottawa in 1990; 1 in 1991 and 1 in 1993.
CFL Total Playoff GP - 3.

Punt Returns - 4 for 21 yards, 5.3 average, longest 9 yards with Ottawa in 1990.
CFL Total Playoff Punt Returns - 4 for 21 yards, 5.3 average, longest 9 yards.

Quarterback Sacks - 2 with Ottawa in 1991. **CFL Total Playoff QB Sacks - 2.**

Tackles - 1 defensive with Ottawa in 1991.
CFL Total Playoff Tackles - 1 (1 defensive).

WRIGHT, DONOVAN

Born: October 16, 1966
Birthplace: Markham, Ontario
Linebacker. 6'3", 200 lbs. Non-import
Last Amateur Club: Slippery Rock University
Acquired: Selected in the first round (fourth overall) by the Saskatchewan Roughriders in the 1989 CFL College Draft. Released by Saskatchewan in July, 1990. Signed as a free agent by the Toronto Argonauts in November, 1990. Released by Toronto in September, 1991. Signed as a free agent by the B.C. Lions in February, 1992.

Games Played - 12 with Saskatchewan in 1989; 6 with Toronto in 1991; 18 with B.C. in 1992 and 18 in 1993. **CFL Total GP - 54.**

Scoring - 1 TD for 6 points with B.C. in 1992. **CFL Total Scoring - 1 TD for 6 points.**

Interception Returns - 1 for 5 yards with Saskatchewan in 1989; 1 for 34 yards with Toronto in 1991 and 1 for 66 yards and 1 TD with B.C. in 1992.
CFL Total Interception Returns - 3 for 105 yards, 35.0 average, longest 66 yards and 1 TD.

Kickoff Returns - 2 for 18 yards, 9.0 average, longest 10 yards with Saskatchewan in 1989; 1 for 0 yards with Toronto in 1991 and 1 for 0 yards with B.C. in 1993. **CFL Total Kickoff Returns - 4 for 18 yards, 4.5 average, longest 10 yards.**

Fumble Returns - 3 for 0 yards with B.C. in 1992 and 1 for 2 yards in 1993.
CFL Total Fumble Returns - 4 for 2 yards, 0.5 average, longest 2 yards.

Quarterback Sacks - 1 for 10 yards lost with B.C. in 1992.
CFL Total QB Sacks - 1 for 10 yards.

Tackles - 7 defensive with Saskatchewan in 1989; 1 defensive and 6 special teams with Toronto in 1991; 46 defensive and 18 special teams with B.C. in 1992 and 5 defensive and 15 special teams in 1993.
CFL Total Tackles - 98 (59 defensive and 39 special teams).

Tackles for Losses - 4 for 15 yards with B.C. in 1992 and 2 for 4 yards in 1993.
CFL Total Tackles for Losses - 6 for 19 yards.

Playoffs

Games Played - 1 with Toronto in 1990 and 1 with B.C. in 1993.
CFL Total Playoff GP - 2.

WRIGHT, TERRY

Born: July 17, 1965
Birthplace: Phoenix, Arizona
Cornerback. 6'0", 195 lbs. Import
Last Amateur Club: Temple University
Acquired: Signed as a free agent by the NFL Cleveland Browns in May, 1987 and released in August, 1987. Signed as a replacement player during the NFL players strike by the Indianapolis Colts in September, 1987. Released by Indianapolis after the 1988 season. Signed as a free agent by the Hamilton Tiger-Cats in April, 1991. Granted free agency status in February, 1993. Re-signed by Hamilton in May, 1993.

			Interception Returns					Fumble Returns				
	Team	GP	NO	YDS	AVE	LG	TD	NO	YDS	AVE	LG	TD
1991	Ham.	12	3	53	17.7	30	0	4	53	13.3	49	0
1992	Ham.	16	4	94	23.5	47	1	6	56	9.3	31	1
1993	Ham.	18	0	0	0.0	0	0	0	0	0.0	0	0
CFL TOTALS		**46**	**7**	**147**	**21.0**	**47**	**1**	**10**	**109**	**10.9**	**49**	**1**

		Kickoff Returns					Unsuccessful Field Goal Returns				
	Team	NO	YDS	AVE	LG	TD	NO	YDS	AVE	LG	TD
1991	Ham.	5	76	15.2	23	0	1	49	49.0	49	0
1992	Ham.	7	30	4.3	10	0	0	0	0.0	0	0
1992	Ham.	1	0	0.0	0	0	0	0	0.0	0	0
CFL TOTALS		**13**	**106**	**8.2**	**23**	**0**	**1**	**49**	**49.0**	**49**	**0**

Scoring - 2 TDs for 12 points with Hamilton in 1992.
CFL Total Scoring - 2 TDs for 12 points.

Punt Returns - 1 for 5 yards with Hamilton in 1991.
CFL Total Punt Returns - 1 for 5 yards.

Fumbles - 2 and 2 lost with Hamilton in 1991 and 2 and 2 lost in 1992.
CFL Total Fumbles - 4 and 4 lost.

Quarterback Sacks - 3 for 20 yards lost with Hamilton in 1992 and 3 for 25 yards lost in 1993. **CFL Total QB Sacks - 6 for 45 yards lost.**

Tackles - 29 defensive and 11 special teams with Hamilton in 1991; 62 defensive and 10 special teams in 1992 and 82 defensive and 2 special teams in 1993.
CFL Total Tackles - 196 (173 defensive and 23 special teams).

Tackles for Losses - 1 for 1 yard with Hamilton in 1991; 4 for 18 yards in 1992 and 3 for 4 yards in 1993.
CFL Total Tackles for Losses - 8 for 23 yards.

Playoffs

Games Played - 2 with Hamilton in 1992 and 2 in 1993. **CFL Total Playoff GP - 4.**

Fumble Returns - 1 for 10 yards with Hamilton in 1993.
CFL Total Playoff Fumble Returns - 1 for 10 yards.

Tackles - 9 defensive and 3 special teams with Hamilton in 1992 and 2 defensive and 2 special teams in 1993.
CFL Total Playoff Tackles - 16 (11 defensive and 5 special teams).

WRUCK, LARRY

Born: October 29, 1962
Birthplace: Saskatoon, Saskatchewan
Linebacker. 6'0", 220 lbs. Non-import
Last Amateur Club: Saskatoon Hilltops Jrs. (PJFC)
Acquired: Signed as a free agent by the Edmonton Eskimos in March, 1985.

			Scoring					Fumble Returns					QB Sacks
	Team	GP	TD	C	FG	S	TP	NO	YDS	AVE	LG	TD	NO
1985	Edm.	16	1	0	0	0	6	2	9	4.5	9	1	1
1986	Edm.	18	0	0	0	0	0	3	0	0.0	0	0	0
1987	Edm.	18	0	0	0	0	0	0	0	0.0	0	0	0
1988	Edm.	18	0	0	0	0	0	1	0	0.0	0	0	3
1989a	Edm.	18	0	0	0	0	0	0	0	0.0	0	0	8
1990	Edm.	18	0	0	0	0	0	3	0	0.0	0	0	1
1991	Edm.	18	0	0	0	0	0	1	0	0.0	0	0	5
1992	Edm.	18	0	0	0	0	0	0	0	0.0	0	0	5
1993	Edm.	17	0	0	0	0	0	0	0	0.0	0	0	5
CFL TOTALS		**159**	**1**	**0**	**0**	**0**	**6**	**10**	**9**	**0.9**	**9**	**1**	**23**

Blocked Kicks - 1 with Edmonton in 1986. **CFL Total Blocked Kicks - 1.**

Punt Returns - 1 for -1 yard with Edmonton in 1989 and 2 for 6 yards, 3.0 average, longest 6 yards in 1990.
CFL Total Punt Returns - 3 for 5 yards, 1.7 average, longest 6 yards.

Kickoff Returns - 1 for 11 yards with Edmonton in 1992.
CFL Total Kickoff Returns - 1 for 11 yards.

Interception Returns - 1 for 0 yards with Edmonton in 1987; 1 for 0 yards in 1988; 2 for 3 yards, 1.5 average, longest 3 yards in 1989; 1 for 6 yards in 1992 and 1 for 4 yards in 1993. **CFL Total Interception Returns - 6 for 13 yards, 2.2 average, longest 4 yards.**

Tackles - 70 defensive with Edmonton in 1987; 44 defensive in 1988; 51 defensive in 1989; 74 defensive in 1990; 51 defensive and 8 special teams in 1991; 94 defensive and 9 special teams in 1992 and 59 defensive and 7 special teams in 1993.
CFL Total Tackles - 467 (443 defensive and 24 special teams).

Tackles for Losses - 3 for 18 yards with Edmonton in 1991; 10 for 35 yards in 1992 and 3 for 4 yards in 1993. **CFL Total Tackles for Losses - 16 for 57 yards.**

a - All-Western All-Star

Playoffs

Games Played - 1 with Edmonton in 1985; 2 in 1986; 2 in 1987; 1 in 1988; 1 in 1989; 2 in 1990; 1 in 1991; 2 in 1992 and 2 in 1993. **CFL Total Playoff GP - 14.**

Interception Returns - 1 for 1 yard with Edmonton in 1992.
CFL Total Playoff Interception Returns - 1 for 1 yard.

Fumble Returns - 1 for 1 yard with Edmonton in 1993.
CFL Total Playoff Fumble Returns - 1 for 1 yard.

Tackles - 9 defensive with Edmonton in 1987; 2 defensive in 1988; 6 defensive in 1989; 6 defensive and 1 special teams in 1991; 9 defensive and 1 special teams in 1992 and 8 defensive and 1 special teams in 1993.
CFL Total Playoff Tackles - 43 (40 defensive and 3 special teams).

Tackles for Losses - 2 for 5 yards with Edmonton in 1992.
CFL Total Playoff Tackles for Losses - 2 for 5 yards.

WRUCK, LARRY

Grey Cup

Games Played - 1 with Edmonton in 1986; 1 in 1987; 1 in 1990 and 1 in 1993. **Total Grey Cup GP - 4.**

Interception Returns - 1 for 7 yards with Edmonton in 1990 and 1 for 6 yards in 1993. **Total Grey Cup Interception Returns - 2 for 13 yards, 6.5 average, longest 7 yards.**

Defensive Tackles - 2 with Edmonton in 1987; 2 in 1990 and 4 in 1993. **Total Grey Cup Defensive Tackles - 8.**

Tackles for Losses - 1 for 3 yards with Edmonton in 1993. **Total Grey Cup Tackles for Losses - 1 for 3 yards.**

YLI-RENKO, KARI
Born: November 17, 1959
Birthplace: Sudbury, Ontario
Tackle. 6'5", 270 lbs. Non-import
Last Amateur Club: University of Cincinnati
Acquired: Selected in the eighth round, (222nd overall) of the 1982 NFL Draft by the Cincinnati Bengals. Released in September, 1982 and signed as a free agent by the USFL's Chicago Blitz in November, 1982. Traded to the New Jersey Generals (USFL) along with a draft choice in May, 1983 for quarterback Bobby Scott. Released and signed by the Hamilton Tiger-Cats in July, 1985 (he was Hamilton's territorial exemption in the 1982 CFL College Draft). Released and signed as a free agent by the Calgary Stampeders in September, 1985. Selected by the Ottawa Rough Riders in the Equalization Draft of March, 1988. Released by Ottawa in June, 1993. Signed as a free agent by the Toronto Argonauts in July, 1993.

Games Played - 10 with Hamilton in 1985; 4 with Calgary in 1985; 18 in 1986; 18 in 1987; 18 with Ottawa in 1988; 15 in 1989; 18 in 1990; 18 in 1991; 14 in 1992 and 18 with Toronto in 1993. **CFL Total GP - 151.**

Fumble Returns - 1 for 0 yards with Ottawa in 1992. **CFL Total Fumble Returns - 1 for 0 yards.**

Own Fumbles Recovered - 1 with Ottawa in 1988 and 1 in 1990. **CFL Total OFR - 2.**

Defensive Tackles - 1 with Calgary in 1987; 1 with Ottawa in 1991 and 1 with Toronto in 1993. **CFL Total Defensive Tackles - 3.**

Playoffs

Games Played - 1 with Calgary in 1986; 1 in 1987; 1 with Ottawa in 1990; 1 in 1991 and 1 in 1992. **CFL Total Playoff GP - 5.**

YOUNG, BRETT
Born: April 3, 1967
Birthplace: Carson, California
Cornerback. 5'10", 180 lbs. Import
Last Amateur Club: University of Oregon
Acquired: Signed as a free agent by the Ottawa Rough Riders in August, 1989. Granted free agency status in February, 1991. Signed as a free agent by the Buffalo Bills (NFL) in February, 1991. Released following training camp. Signed as a free agent by the Ottawa Rough Riders in August, 1992. Traded to B.C. for future considerations in August, 1992. Traded to Ottawa in December, 1992 in exchange for future considerations.

			Interception Returns					Fumble Returns				
	Team	GP	NO	YDS	AVE	LG	TD	NO	YDS	AVE	LG	TD
1989	Ott.	10	2	22	11.0	13	0	2	33	16.5	33	1
1990	Ott.	14	5	28	5.6	23	0	1	0	1.0	0	0
1991			Did not play					Did not play				
1992	Ott.	1	0	0	0.0	0	0	0	0	0.0	0	0
	B.C.	11	0	9	0.0	9	0	0	0	0.0	0	0
1993	Ott.	13	1	0	0.0	0	0	1	0	0.0	0	0
CFL TOTALS		**49**	**8**	**59**	**7.4**	**23**	**0**	**4**	**33**	**8.3**	**33**	**1**

Quarterback Sacks - 1 for 10 yards lost with Ottawa in 1993. **CFL Total QB Sacks - 1 for 10 yards lost.**

Own Fumbles Recovered - 1 with B.C. in 1992. **CFL Total OFR - 1.**

Tackles - 34 defensive with Ottawa in 1989; 44 defensive in 1990; 1 defensive and 1 special teams with Ottawa and 41 defensive and 2 special teams with B.C. in 1992 and 29 defensive and 8 special teams with Ottawa in 1993. **CFL Total Tackles - 160 (149 defensive and 11 special teams).**

Tackles for Losses - 1 for 7 yards with B.C. in 1992 and 2 for 18 yards with Ottawa in 1993. **CFL Total Tackles for Losses - 3 for 25 yards.**

Playoffs

Games Played - 1 with Ottawa in 1990 and 1 in 1993. **CFL Total Playoff GP - 2.**

Fumble Returns - 1 for 0 yards with Ottawa in 1993. **CFL Total Playoff Fumble Returns - 1 for 0 yards.**

Defensive Tackles - 5 with Ottawa in 1990 and 5 in 1993. **CFL Total Playoff Defensive Tackles - 10.**

ZAJDEL, JOHN
Born: March 31, 1967
Birthplace: Toronto, Ontario
Linebacker. 6'3", 235 lbs. Non-import
Last Amateur Club: Vancouver Meralomas Juniors (BCJFL)
Acquired: Selected by the Toronto Argonauts in the 1990 Supplementary Draft. Released by Toronto in July, 1990. Signed as a free agent by the Hamilton Tiger-Cats in August, 1990. Released by Hamilton in June, 1993. Signed as a free agent by the Toronto Argonauts in August, 1993. Released by Toronto in September, 1993.

Games Played - 2 with Toronto and 7 with Hamilton in 1990; 18 in 1991; 18 in 1992 and 2 with Toronto in 1993. **CFL Total GP - 47.**

Scoring - 1 TD for 6 points with Hamilton in 1992. **CFL Total Scoring - 1 TD for 6 points.**

Rushing - 0 for 1 yard and 1 TD with Hamilton in 1992. **CFL Total Rushing - 0 for 1 yard and 1 TD.**

Own Fumbles Recovered - 1 with Hamilton in 1992. **CFL Total OFR - 1.**

Interception Returns - 1 for 23 yards with Toronto in 1990. **CFL Total Interception Returns - 1 for 23 yards.**

Fumble Returns - 1 for 11 yards with Hamilton in 1991 and 1 for 0 yards in 1992. **CFL Total Fumble Returns - 2 for 11 yards, 5.5 average, longest 11 yards.**

Tackles - 4 defensive with Toronto and 2 defensive with Hamilton in 1990; 2 defensive and 20 special teams in 1991; 5 defensive and 24 special teams in 1992 and 1 special teams with Toronto in 1993. **CFL Total Tackles - 58 (13 defensive and 45 special teams).**

Tackles for Losses - 1 for 1 yard with Hamilton in 1992. **CFL Total Tackles for Losses - 1 for 1 yard.**

Playoffs

Games Played - 2 with Hamilton in 1992. **CFL Total Playoff GP - 2.**

Tackles - 1 special teams with Hamilton in 1992. **CFL Total Playoff Tackles - 1 (1 special teams).**

ZATYLNY, WALLY
Born: March 25, 1964
Birthplace: Montreal, Quebec
Wide Receiver. 5'9", 177 lbs. Non-import
Last Amateur Club: Bishop's University (OQIFC)
Acquired: Selected in the fourth round (28th overall) by the Calgary Stampeders in the 1988 CFL College Draft. Traded to the Hamilton Tiger-Cats for defensive lineman Mike Rodriguez in July, 1988. Granted free agency status in February, 1993. Signed as a free agent by the Toronto Argonauts in May, 1993. Traded to Hamilton by Toronto in exchange for future considerations in March, 1994.

			Scoring					Pass Receiving				
	Team	GP	TD	C	FG	S	TD	NO	YDS	AVE	LG	TD
1988	Ham.	18	2	0	0	0	12	7	153	21.9	62	1
1989a	Ham.	15	4	0	0	0	24	16	279	17.4	67	2
1990	Ham.	11	3	0	0	0	18	15	325	21.7	57	2
1991	Ham.	18	2	0	0	0	12	16	241	15.1	75	2
1992	Ham.	17	2	0	0	0	12	11	153	13.9	29	2
1993	Tor.	16	1	0	0	0	6	34	464	13.6	41	1
CFL TOTALS		**95**	**14**	**0**	**0**	**0**	**84**	**99**	**1615**	**16.3**	**75**	**10**

		Punt Returns					Kickoff Returns				
	Team	NO	YDS	AVE	LG	TD	NO	YDS	AVE	LG	TD
1988	Ham.	39	187	4.8	47	1	39	785	20.1	44	0
1989	Ham.	58	523	9.0	66	2	40	793	19.8	56	0
1990	Ham.	47	445	9.5	42	0	33	687	20.8	93	1
1991	Ham.	28	259	9.3	30	0	23	366	15.9	33	0
1992	Ham.	20	201	10.1	46	0	8	156	19.5	48	0
1993	Tor.	5	30	6.0	11	0	23	361	15.7	32	0
CFL TOTALS		**197**	**1645**	**8.4**	**66**	**3**	**166**	**3148**	**19.0**	**93**	**1**

Rushing - 1 for -4 yards with Hamilton in 1989; 1 for -2 yards in 1990 and 1 for -12 yards in 1992. **CFL Total Rushing - 3 for -18 yards, -6.0 average, longest 0 yards.**

Fumbles - 4 and 3 lost with Hamilton in 1988; 2 and 1 lost in 1989; 1 and 1 lost in 1990; 1 and 1 lost in 1991; 2 and 2 lost in 1992 and 2 and 2 lost with Toronto in 1993. **CFL Total Fumbles - 12 and 10 lost.**

Unsuccessful Field Goal Returns - 3 for 25 yards, 8.3 average, longest 18 yards with Hamilton in 1989; 2 for 28 yards, 14.0 average, longest 18 yards in 1990 and 4 for 49 yards, 12.3 average, longest 46 yards in 1991. **CFL Total Unsuccessful Field Goal Returns - 9 for 102 yards, 11.3 average, longest 46 yards.**

Net Punting - 1 for 35 yards with Toronto in 1993. **CFL Total Net Punting - 1 for 35 yards.**

Own Fumbles Recovered - 1 with Hamilton in 1988 and 1 in 1989. **CFL Total OFR - 2.**

ZATYLNY, WALLY

Tackles - 3 defensive with Hamilton in 1989; 1 defensive in 1990; 2 defensive and 5 special teams in 1991; 2 defensive and 11 special teams in 1992 and 1 special teams with Toronto in 1993.
CFL Total Tackles - 25 (8 defensive and 17 special teams).

a - All-Eastern All-Star

Playoffs

Games Played - 1 with Hamilton in 1989. **CFL Total Playoff GP - 1.**

Pass Receiving - 1 for 9 yards and 1 TD with Hamilton in 1989.
CFL Total Playoff Pass Receiving - 1 for 9 yards and 1 TD.

Punt Returns - 6 for 30 yards, 5.0 average, longest 12 yards with Hamilton in 1989. **CFL Total Playoff Punt Returns - 6 for 30 yards, 5.0 average, longest 12 yards.**

Fumbles - 1 and 1 lost with Hamilton in 1989.
CFL Total Playoff Fumbles - 1 and 1 lost.

Grey Cup

Games Played - 1 with Hamilton in 1989. **Total Grey Cup GP - 1.**

Pass Receiving - 1 for 13 yards with Hamilton in 1989.
Total Grey Cup Pass Receiving - 1 for 13 yards.

Punt Returns - 1 for 10 yards with Hamilton in 1989.
Total Grey Cup Punt Returns - 1 for 10 yards.

Unsuccessful Field Goal Returns - 1 for 14 yards with Hamilton in 1989.
Total Grey Cup Unsuccessful Field Goal Returns - 1 for 14 yards.

Kickoff Returns - 3 for 53 yards, 17.7 average, longest 25 yards with Hamilton in 1989. **Total Grey Cup Kickoff Returns - 3 for 53 yards, 17.7 average, longest 25 yards.**

ZERR, BLAIR
Born: November 22, 1966
Birthplace: Regina, Saskatchewan
Fullback. 6'0", 200 lbs. Non-import
Last Amateur Club: San Jose State University
Acquired: Selected in the seventh round (54th overall) by the Calgary Stampeders in the 1991 CFL CFL College Draft. Signed by Calgary in April, 1992.

Games Played - 15 with Calgary in 1992 and 18 in 1993. **CFL Total GP - 33.**

Rushing - 2 for 3 yards, 1.5 average, longest 2 yards with Calgary in 1993.
CFL Total Rushing - 2 for 3 yards, 1.5 average, longest 2 yards.

Pass Receiving - 3 for 38 yards, 12.7 average, longest 19 yards with Calgary in 1993. **CFL Total Pass Receiving - 3 for 38 yards, 12.7 average, longest 19 yards.**

Blocked Kicks - 1 punt with Calgary in 1992. **CFL Total Blocked Kicks - 1 punt.**

Tackles - 24 special teams with Calgary in 1992 and 1 defensive and 15 special teams in 1993. **CFL Total Tackles - 40 (1 defensive and 39 special teams).**

Tackles for Losses - 1 for 6 yards with Calgary in 1992.
CFL Total Tackles for Losses - 1 for 6 yards.

Playoffs

Games Played - 1 with Calgary in 1992 and 2 in 1993. **CFL Total Playoff GP - 3.**

Tackles - 1 special teams with Calgary in 1992 and 1 special teams in 1993.
CFL Total Playoff Tackles - 2 (2 special teams).

Grey Cup

Games Played - 1 with Calgary in 1992. **Total Grey Cup GP - 1.**

ZIZAKOVIC, LUBO
Born: February 28, 1968
Birthplace: Weston, Ontario
Defensive Tackle. 6'8", 270 lbs. Non-import
Last Amateur Club: University of Maryland
Acquired: Selected in the third round (17th overall) by the Hamilton Tiger-Cats in the 1991 CFL College Draft. Signed by Hamilton in September, 1992. Traded to the Calgary Stampeders in exchange for offensive lineman Lou Cafazzo in April, 1994.

Games Played - 8 with Hamilton in 1992 and 18 in 1993. **CFL Total GP - 26.**

Own Kickoffs Recovered - 1 for 0 yards with Hamilton in 1992.
CFL Total Own Kickoffs Recovered - 1 for 0 yards.

Fumble Returns - 1 for 0 yards with Hamilton in 1992.
CFL Total Fumble Returns - 1 for 0 yards.

Quarterback Sacks - 3 for 17 yards lost with Hamilton in 1993.
CFL Total QB Sacks - 3 for 17 yards lost.

Blocked Kicks - 2 converts with Hamilton in 1993.
CFL Total Blocked Kicks - 2 (2 converts).

Tackles - 10 defensive and 1 special teams with Hamilton in 1992 and 12 defensive and 3 special teams in 1993.
CFL Total Tackles - 26 (22 defensive and 4 special teams).

Tackles for Losses - 1 for 1 yard with Hamilton in 1993.
CFL Total Tackles for Losses - 1 for 1 yard.

Playoffs

Games Played - 2 with Hamilton in 1992 and 2 in 1993. **CFL Total Playoff GP - 2.**

Tackles - 3 defensive with Hamilton in 1992.
CFL Total Playoff Tackles - 3 (3 defensive).

ZIZAKOVIC, SRECKO
Born: August 13, 1966
Birthplace: Weston, Ontario
Defensive End. 6'5", 255 lbs. Non-import
Last Amateur Club: Ohio State University
Acquired: Selected in the fourth round (26th overall) by the Calgary Stampeders in the 1989 CFL College Draft.

Games Played - 2 with Calgary in 1990; 15 in 1991; 15 in 1992 and 13 in 1993.
CFL Total GP - 45.

Scoring - 1 TD for 6 points with Calgary in 1991.
CFL Total Scoring - 1 TD for 6 points.

Interception Returns - 1 for 21 yards with Calgary in 1993.
CFL Total Interception Returns - 1 for 21 yards.

Rushing - 0 carries and 1 TD with Calgary in 1991.
CFL Total Rushing - 0 carries and 1 TD.

Kickoff Returns - 1 for 8 yards with Calgary in 1992.
CFL Total Kickoff Returns - 1 for 8 yards.

Blocked Kicks - 1 field goal with Calgary in 1991.
CFL Total Blocked Kicks - 1 field goal.

Fumble Returns - 2 for 16 yards, 8.0 average, longest 16 yards with Calgary in 1991. **CFL Total Fumble Returns - 2 for 16 yards, 8.0 average, longest 16 yards.**

Own Fumbles Recovered - 1 with Calgary in 1991. **CFL Total OFR - 1.**

Quarterback Sacks - 5 with Calgary in 1991; 6 for 22 yards lost in 1992 and 3 for 17 yards lost in 1993. **CFL Total QB Sacks - 14.**

Tackles - 34 defensive with Calgary in 1991; 19 defensive in 1992 and 22 defensive in 1993. **CFL Total Tackles - 75 (75 defensive).**

Tackles for Losses - 3 for 7 yards with Calgary in 1991; 1 for 4 yards in 1992 and 2 for 2 yards in 1993. **CFL Total Tackles for Losses - 6 for 13 yards.**

Playoffs

Games Played - 1 with Calgary in 1991; 1 in 1992 and 2 in 1993.
CFL Total Playoff GP - 4.

Scoring - 1 TD for 6 points with Calgary in 1993.
CFL Total Playoff Scoring 1 TD for 6 points.

Quarterback Sacks - 1 for 8 yards lost with Calgary in 1992.
CFL Total Playoff QB Sacks - 1 for 8 yards lost.

Interception Returns - 1 for 6 yards and 1 TD with Calgary in 1993.
CFL Total Playoff Interception Returns - 1 for 6 yards and 1 TD.

Tackles - 3 defensive with Calgary in 1993.
CFL Total Playoff Tackles - 3 (3 defensive).

Grey Cup

Games Played - 1 with Calgary in 1991 and 1 in 1992. **Total Grey Cup GP - 2.**

Tackles - 2 defensive with Calgary in 1991. **Total Grey Cup Tackles - 2 (2 defensive).**

Tackles for Losses - 1 for 2 yards with Calgary in 1991.
Total Grey Cup Tackles for Losses - 1 for 2 yards

'93 CFL Statistical Highlights

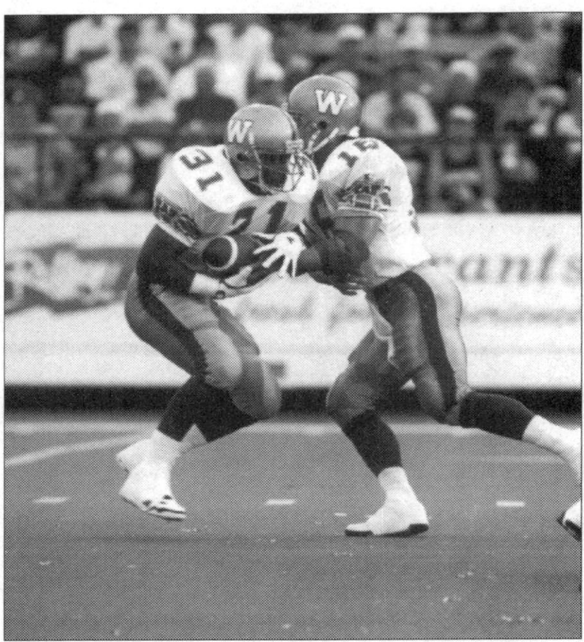

#31 RB Mike Richardson - Winnipeg
Led CFL in Rushing Yards (925)

#1 CB Andre Francis - B.C.
Led CFL in Interceptions (8) and Interception Yards (153)

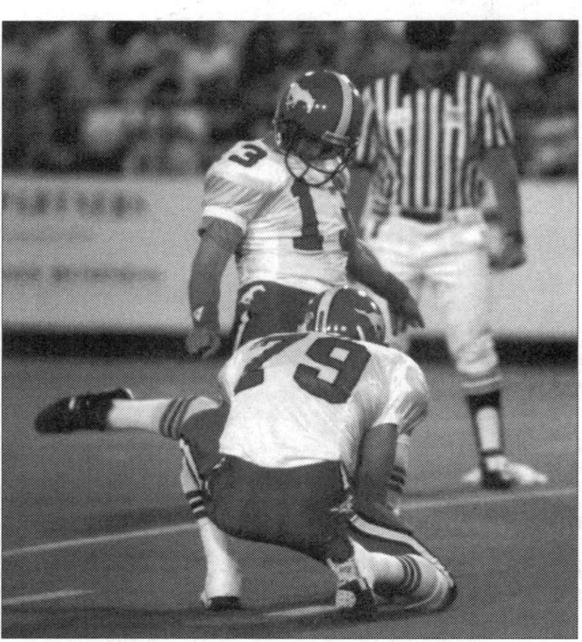

#13 K Mark McLoughlin - Calgary
Led CFL in Points (215)

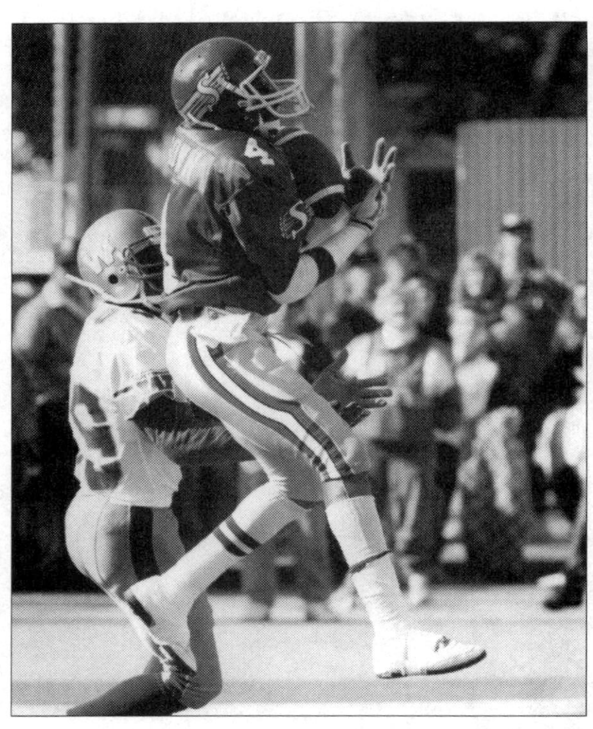

#4 CB Albert Brown - Saskatchewan
Longest Unsuccessful Field Goal Return (108 yards)

1993 FINAL STANDINGS

EASTERN DIVISION	W	L	T	F	A	PTS.	PCT
Winnipeg Blue Bombers	14	4	0	646	421	28	0.778
Hamilton Tiger-Cats	6	12	0	316	567	12	0.333
Ottawa Rough Riders	4	14	0	387	517	8	0.222
Toronto Argonauts	3	15	0	390	593	6	0.167

WESTERN DIVISION	W	L	T	F	A	PTS.	PCT
Calgary Stampeders	15	3	0	646	418	30	0.833
Edmonton Eskimos	12	6	0	507	372	24	0.667
Saskatchewan Roughriders	11	7	0	511	495	22	0.611
B.C. Lions	10	8	0	574	583	20	0.556
Sacramento Gold Miners	6	12	0	498	509	12	0.333

HOME RECORDS	W	L	T	F	A	PTS.	PCT
Calgary Stampeders	9	0	0	323	170	18	1.000
Winnipeg Blue Bombers	8	1	0	327	163	16	0.889
Edmonton Eskimos	7	2	0	256	160	14	0.778
Saskatchewan Roughriders	7	2	0	290	240	14	0.778
Sacramento Gold Miners	5	4	0	310	247	10	0.556
B.C. Lions	5	4	0	292	287	10	0.556
Hamilton Tiger-Cats	4	5	0	193	236	8	0.444
Toronto Argonauts	3	6	0	194	294	6	0.333
Ottawa Rough Riders	2	7	0	225	268	4	0.222

AWAY RECORDS	W	L	T	F	A	PTS.	PCT
Calgary Stampeders	6	3	0	323	248	12	0.667
Winnipeg Blue Bombers	6	3	0	319	258	12	0.667
Edmonton Eskimos	5	4	0	251	212	10	0.556
B.C. Lions	5	4	0	282	296	10	0.556
Saskatchewan Roughriders	4	5	0	221	255	8	0.444
Hamilton Tiger-Cats	2	7	0	123	331	4	0.222
Ottawa Rough Riders	2	7	0	162	249	4	0.222
Sacramento Gold Miners	1	8	0	188	262	2	0.111
Toronto Argonauts	0	9	0	196	299	0	0.000

EAST VERSUS EAST	W	L	T	F	A	PTS.	PCT
Winnipeg Blue Bombers	7	1	0	279	149	14	0.875
Hamilton Tiger-Cats	4	4	0	155	233	8	0.500
Ottawa Rough Riders	3	5	0	191	216	6	0.375
Toronto Argonauts	2	6	0	159	186	4	0.250

WEST VERSUS WEST	W	L	T	F	A	PTS.	PCT
Edmonton Eskimos	7	3	0	305	185	14	0.700
Calgary Stampeders	7	3	0	337	262	14	0.700
Saskatchewan Roughriders	5	5	0	256	315	10	0.500
Sacramento Gold Miners	3	7	0	251	298	6	0.300
B.C. Lions	3	7	0	273	362	6	0.300

EAST VERSUS WEST	W	L	T	F	A	PTS.	PCT
Winnipeg Blue Bombers	7	3	0	367	272	14	0.700
Hamilton Tiger-Cats	2	8	0	161	334	4	0.200
Ottawa Rough Riders	1	9	0	196	301	2	0.100
Toronto Argonauts	1	9	0	231	407	2	0.100

WEST VERSUS EAST	W	L	T	F	A	PTS.	PCT
Calgary Stampeders	8	0	0	309	156	16	1.000
B.C. Lions	7	1	0	301	221	14	0.875
Saskatchewan Roughriders	6	2	0	255	180	12	0.750
Edmonton Eskimos	5	3	0	202	187	10	0.625
Sacramento Gold Miners	3	5	0	247	211	6	0.375

1993 FINAL SCORES - PRE-SEASON

Date		Visiting Team		Home Team	
JUNE	17	Sacramento	21	Winnipeg	15
	18	Saskatchewan	11	Calgary	21
	21	Toronto	25	Ottawa	30
	25	Ottawa (Hall of Fame Game)	15	Hamilton	19
		Winnipeg	40	Saskatchewan	17
		Calgary	22	Edmonton	8
JUNE	26	B.C.	20	Sacramento	39
	29	Hamilton	39	Toronto	25-OT
	30	Edmonton	27	B.C.	20

1993 FINAL SCORES - REGULAR SEASON

Date		Visiting Team		Home Team	
JULY	6	Winnipeg	34	Calgary	54
	7	Sacramento	23	Ottawa	32
	9	Saskatchewan	26	B.C.	33-OT
	10	Sacramento	14	Hamilton	30
		Toronto	8	Edmonton	38
	14	B.C.	40	Toronto	27
	15	Edmonton	22	Saskatchewan	23
	16	Hamilton	21	Ottawa	20
	17	B.C.	14	Winnipeg	36
		Calgary	38	Sacramento	36
	21	Saskatchewan	3	Edmonton	35
	22	Hamilton	25	Toronto	9
	23	Ottawa	18	Winnipeg	21
	24	Calgary	34	B.C.	20
		Saskatchewan	26	Sacramento	37
	28	Toronto	36	Calgary	39
	29	Winnipeg	40	Hamilton	11
	30	Ottawa	24	B.C.	28
	31	Toronto	17	Saskatchewan	36
		Edmonton	43	Sacramento	11
AUGUST	3	Calgary	40	Winnipeg	35
	5	Sacramento	35	Toronto	37
	6	Saskatchewan	37	Hamilton	10
		Calgary	47	Ottawa	22
	7	B.C.	39	Edmonton	23
	11	Ottawa	28	Saskatchewan	45
	12	Toronto	38	B.C.	55
	13	Edmonton	11	Winnipeg	53
	14	Ottawa	7	Calgary	21
		Hamilton	10	Sacramento	46
	18	Edmonton	45	Toronto	14
		Winnipeg	28	B.C.	48
	19	Saskatchewan	27	Ottawa	26
	20	Calgary	31	Hamilton	12
	21	Winnipeg	30	Sacramento	18
	25	Hamilton	8	Edmonton	46
	26	Ottawa	26	Toronto	25
	27	Sacramento	23	Saskatchewan	26
		B.C.	30	Calgary	35
	28	Hamilton	11	Winnipeg	35
SEPTEMBER	2	Sacramento	12	Edmonton	13
	4	B.C.	25	Ottawa	24
	5	Winnipeg	25	Saskatchewan	24
	6	Edmonton	13	Calgary	33
		Toronto	21	Hamilton	23
	10	Calgary	16	Edmonton	29
	11	Hamilton	25	B.C.	55
		Ottawa	15	Sacramento	47
	12	Saskatchewan	23	Winnipeg	41
	17	Edmonton	10	Hamilton	34
	18	B.C.	21	Calgary	40
	19	Winnipeg	26	Toronto	35
		Sacramento	20	Saskatchewan	27
	24	Hamilton	3	Calgary	26
	25	Toronto	22	Ottawa	30
		Saskatchewan	31	B.C.	16
	26	Winnipeg	52	Edmonton	14
OCTOBER	1	B.C.	50	Saskatchewan	28
	2	Hamilton	10	Winnipeg	61
		Edmonton	34	Sacramento	13
	3	Ottawa	16	Toronto	17
	8	Sacramento	27	B.C.	23
	9	Winnipeg	48	Ottawa	38
	10	Saskatchewan	18	Calgary	34
	11	Toronto	20	Hamilton	28
	15	Sacramento	26	Winnipeg	33
	16	Ottawa	1	Edmonton	19
	17	Hamilton	10	Saskatchewan	33
	18	Calgary	51	Toronto	7
	22	Edmonton	19	Ottawa	17
	23	Calgary	45	Saskatchewan	48
		Toronto	24	Sacramento	38
	24	B.C.	36	Hamilton	19
	29	Edmonton	54	B.C.	14
	30	Winnipeg	36	Ottawa	16
		Sacramento	8	Calgary	41
	31	Saskatchewan	30	Toronto	23
NOVEMBER	6	B.C.	27	Sacramento	64
	7	Ottawa	27	Hamilton	26
		Toronto	10	Winnipeg	12
		Calgary	21	Edmonton	39

1993 PLAYOFFS

DIVISIONAL SEMI-FINALS

Date	Visiting Team		Home Team	
NOVEMBER 14	Ottawa	10	Hamilton	21
	B.C.	9	Calgary	17
	Saskatchewan	13	Edmonton	51

DIVISIONAL FINALS

Date	Visiting Team		Home Team	
NOVEMBER 21	Hamilton	19	Winnipeg	20
	Edmonton	29	Calgary	15

1993 GREY CUP CHAMPIONSHIP

Date					
NOVEMBER	28	Winnipeg	23	Edmonton	33

(Played at McMahon Stadium, Calgary)

1993 TEAM STATISTICS

Rank	Most Points Scored		Most Touchdowns Scored		Most Touchdowns Rushing		Most Touchdowns Passing		Most Field Goals		Most 1-point Converts		Most Singles	
1	WP	646	WP	71	BC	25	CG	49	SK	48	WP	68	SC	22
2	CG	646	CG	70	WP	20	WP	43	CG	47	CG	63	ED	17
3	BC	574	BC	64	CG	16	SC	37	WP	45	BC	63	HM	15
4	SK	511	SC	56	TO	15	BC	34	BC	38	SC	56	OT	14
5	ED	507	ED	55	SK	15	OT	32	ED	34	ED	54	CG	14
6	SC	498	SK	51	ED	15	SK	32	HM	31	SK	51	TO	13
7	TO	390	OT	41	SC	15	ED	31	TO	30	OT	38	WP	11
8	OT	387	TO	41	HM	9	TO	24	OT	29	TO	35	BC	9
9	HM	316	HM	29	OT	6	HM	12	SC	28	HM	28	SK	8

Rank	Average Points Scored Per Game		Most Plays From Scrimmage		Most Kickoff Return Yards		Most First Downs		Most First Downs Rushing		Most First Downs Passing		Most Yards Total Offence	
1	WP	35.9	WP	1622	BC	2331	CG	421	WP	151	CG	289	CG	7605
2	CG	35.9	CG	1534	SC	1720	WP	417	ED	120	BC	274	WP	7442
3	BC	31.9	OT	1512	TO	1702	SC	407	SK	108	SC	269	SC	7179
4	SK	28.4	SK	1505	HM	1409	BC	404	HM	103	SK	257	SK	7056
5	ED	28.2	BC	1457	CG	1377	SK	402	CG	103	TO	232	BC	6882
6	SC	27.7	TO	1441	WP	1223	OT	363	SC	98	WP	229	OT	6318
7	TO	21.7	ED	1426	ED	1209	TO	358	OT	97	OT	228	ED	5891
8	OT	21.5	SC	1419	SK	1138	ED	326	TO	97	ED	172	TO	5826
9	HM	17.6	HM	1417	OT	1110	HM	305	BC	89	HM	169	HM	5050

Rank	Average Yards Offence Per Game		Fewest First Downs Vs		Fewest First Downs Rushing Vs		Fewest First Downs Passing Vs		Fewest Yards Total Offence Vs		Average Yards Offence Per Game Vs		Most Yards Net Rushing	
1	CG	422.5	WP	314	CG	87	WP	190	WP	5595	WP	310.8	WP	2118
2	WP	413.4	CG	345	WP	95	OT	199	CG	6034	CG	335.2	ED	2006
3	SC	398.8	OT	353	TO	99	CG	219	OT	6343	OT	352.4	HM	1751
4	SK	392.0	SK	373	OT	105	SK	238	ED	6346	ED	352.6	TO	1706
5	BC	382.3	ED	380	SK	106	ED	240	SK	6454	SK	358.6	SC	1479
6	OT	351.0	TO	398	SC	107	HM	245	HM	6539	HM	363.3	OT	1436
7	ED	327.3	HM	400	ED	115	BC	247	SC	7231	SC	401.7	CG	1421
8	TO	323.7	SC	419	BC	125	SC	270	TO	7233	TO	401.8	BC	1360
9	HM	280.6	BC	421	HM	127	TO	271	BC	7474	BC	415.2	SK	1200

Rank	Average Yards Rushing Per Game		Most Time Rushed		Average Gain Per Rush		Average Gain Per Pass		Fewest Yards Net Rushing Vs		Average Yards Rushing Per Game Vs		Fewest Times Rushed Vs	
1	WP	117.7	WP	395	TO	6.0	CG	8.6	CG	1233	CG	68.5	CG	280
2	ED	111.4	ED	366	SC	5.7	SC	8.6	TO	1418	TO	78.8	WP	294
3	HM	97.3	HM	363	ED	5.5	OT	8.3	WP	1446	WP	80.3	OT	303
4	TO	94.8	OT	340	WP	5.4	WP	8.0	OT	1618	OT	89.9	TO	310
5	SC	82.2	CG	296	BC	5.1	SK	8.0	SK	1623	SK	90.2	ED	324
6	OT	79.8	TO	285	HM	4.8	ED	7.9	SC	1644	SC	91.3	BC	328
7	CG	78.9	SK	278	CG	4.8	BC	7.8	ED	1809	ED	100.5	SC	330
8	BC	75.6	BC	268	SK	4.3	TO	7.6	BC	1835	BC	101.9	SK	334
9	SK	66.7	SC	258	OT	4.2	HM	6.2	HM	1851	HM	102.8	HM	346

Rank	Average Gain Per Rush Vs		Average Gain Per Pass Vs		Most Yards Net Passing		Average Yards Passing Per Game		Most Passes Attempted		Most Passes Completed		Highest % Pass Completions	
1	CG	4.4	WP	6.8	CG	6494	CG	360.8	SK	773	CG	444	CG	58.5
2	TO	4.6	ED	7.1	SC	6319	SC	351.1	CG	759	SK	441	SC	57.7
3	WP	4.9	HM	7.4	SK	6164	SK	342.4	BC	740	SC	425	SK	57.1
4	SK	4.9	CG	7.6	BC	5764	BC	320.2	SC	737	BC	409	WP	55.9
5	SC	5.0	SK	7.8	WP	5666	WP	314.8	WP	708	WP	396	BC	55.3
6	OT	5.3	OT	8.3	OT	5596	OT	310.9	OT	671	OT	362	OT	53.9
7	HM	5.3	SC	8.4	TO	4914	TO	273.0	TO	648	TO	340	TO	52.5
8	ED	5.6	TO	8.8	ED	4376	ED	243.1	HM	620	ED	284	ED	51.4
9	BC	5.6	BC	9.0	HM	3857	HM	214.3	ED	552	HM	281	HM	45.3

Rank	Fewest Yards Net Passing Vs		Average Yards Passing Per Game Vs		Fewest Passes Attempted Vs		Fewest Passes Completed Vs		Lowest % Passes Completed Vs		Most Times Punted		Highest Punting Average	
1	WP	4632	WP	257.3	OT	640	OT	307	WP	45.9	HM	166	WP	42.0
2	ED	5109	ED	283.8	WP	677	WP	311	OT	48.0	OT	165	ED	41.5
3	CG	5251	CG	291.7	BC	679	ED	385	ED	53.6	ED	154	SK	40.9
4	SK	5286	SK	293.7	SK	681	CG	386	CG	55.8	TO	143	CG	40.8
5	OT	5334	OT	296.3	CG	692	SK	390	SC	56.3	WP	141	HM	40.6
6	HM	5344	HM	296.9	SC	700	BC	390	HM	56.7	SK	140	OT	40.5
7	SC	5912	SC	328.4	TO	701	SC	394	SK	57.3	SC	138	TO	40.0
8	TO	6140	TO	341.1	ED	718	HM	408	BC	57.4	BC	124	BC	39.9
9	BC	6142	BC	341.2	HM	720	TO	411	TO	58.6	CG	121	SC	39.5

Rank	Most Punt Return Yards		Passes Intercepted		Fewest Interception Return Yards Vs		Most Interceptions		Most Interception Return Yards		Fewest Plays From Scrimmage Vs		Fewest Field Goals Vs	
1	ED	1315	ED	17	ED	124	WP	37	CG	490	CG	1418	CG	27
2	CG	1128	CG	18	CG	132	ED	34	SC	424	SC	1444	WP	29
3	HM	1000	WP	21	WP	218	SC	28	WP	418	WP	1459	ED	30
4	TO	963	TO	24	TO	318	OT	27	BC	387	OT	1465	BC	35
5	SC	778	SC	24	SC	358	CG	27	ED	370	ED	1478	OT	39
6	WP	769	BC	26	BC	376	BC	24	OT	279	SK	1480	HM	41
7	OT	717	SK	27	HM	402	SK	19	HM	203	TO	1486	TO	42
8	SK	669	OT	32	OT	421	HM	16	SK	163	BC	1517	SK	42
9	BC	585	HM	37	SK	500	TO	14	TO	115	HM	1586	SC	45

Rank	Average Points Per Game Vs		Fewest Times Fumbled		Fewest Fumbles Lost		Fewest Times Penalized		Fewest Yards Penalized		Fewest Quarterback Sacks Vs		Most Quarterback Sacks	
1	ED	20.7	CG	28	HM	18	HM	165	HM	1257	WP	20	ED	69
2	CG	23.2	ED	28	CG	18	CG	188	SC	1497	SK	22	BC	58
3	WP	23.4	SK	31	OT	20	SC	193	WP	1530	BC	27	OT	57
4	SK	27.5	TO	33	ED	20	TO	198	TO	1561	CG	29	HM	53
5	SC	28.3	SC	33	SC	20	WP	198	ED	1592	ED	44	WP	50
6	OT	28.7	BC	34	WP	22	ED	202	CG	1646	HM	59	SK	49
7	HM	31.5	HM	35	SK	22	OT	214	BC	1740	SC	73	CG	48
8	BC	32.4	OT	37	BC	22	BC	223	OT	1770	OT	77	TO	31
9	TO	32.9	WP	37	TO	24	SK	230	SK	1780	TO	93	SC	29

Rank	Fewest Touchdowns Passing Vs		Fewest Touchdowns Rushing Vs		Fewest Touchdowns Vs		Fewest Points Vs	
1	ED	22	SC	10	ED	38	ED	372
2	WP	25	ED	11	WP	45	CG	418
3	CG	29	SK	13	CG	45	WP	421
4	SK	31	CG	13	SK	51	SK	495
5	OT	35	WP	14	SC	52	SC	509
6	HM	36	OT	15	OT	54	OT	517
7	BC	37	TO	19	HM	62	HM	567
8	SC	39	HM	19	TO	65	BC	583
9	TO	40	BC	22	BC	66	TO	593

CLUB TEAM PASSING

	A	C	PCT	YDS	AVE GAIN	TD	PCT TD	LG	INT	PCT INT	RATING
Calgary	759	444	58.5	6494	8.6	49	6.5	75	18	2.4	98.1
Winnipeg	708	396	55.9	5666	8.0	43	6.1	75	21	3.0	89.8
Sacramento	737	425	57.7	6319	8.6	37	5.0	90	24	3.3	88.8
Edmonton	552	284	51.4	4376	7.9	31	5.6	102	17	3.1	83.8
Saskatchewan	773	441	57.1	6164	8.0	32	4.1	78	27	3.5	81.9
B.C.	740	409	55.3	5764	7.8	34	4.6	70	26	3.5	81.3
Ottawa	671	362	53.9	5596	8.3	32	4.8	98	32	4.8	77.8
Toronto	648	340	52.5	4914	7.6	24	3.7	72	24	3.7	74.3
Hamilton	620	281	45.3	3857	6.2	12	1.9	79	37	6.0	47.0

TAKEAWAYS GIVEAWAYS

CLUB	TAKEAWAYS Int.	Fumbles	Downs	Total	GIVEAWAYS Int.	Fumbles	Downs	Total	+/-
Edmonton	34	25	14	73	17	20	9	46	+27
Calgary	27	20	19	66	18	18	4	40	+26
Winnipeg	37	17	6	60	21	22	9	52	+ 8
B.C.	24	23	12	59	26	22	7	55	+ 4
Sacramento	28	25	6	59	24	20	12	56	+ 3
Saskatchewan	19	23	10	52	27	22	9	58	- 6
Ottawa	27	17	11	55	32	20	13	65	-10
Hamilton	16	20	8	44	37	18	13	68	-24
Toronto	14	16	2	32	24	24	12	60	-28

INDIVIDUAL LEADERS

Points - TDs

David Williams	WP	90
David Sapunjis	CG	90
Eddie Brown	ED	90

Rushing - TDs

Matt Dunigan	WP	11
Doug Flutie	CG	11
Cory Philpot	BC	8
Mike Oliphant	SC	8

Receiving - TDs

David Williams	WP	15
David Sapunjis	CG	15
Eddie Brown	ED	15

Passing - TDs

Doug Flutie	CG	44
Matt Dunigan	WP	36
David Archer	SC	35

Interception Returns

Andre Francis	BC	8
Don Wilson	ED	7
3	tied with 6 each	

Interception Returns - Yards

Andre Francis	BC	153
Karl Anthony	CG	145
Less Browne	BC	140

Points - Kicking

Mark McLoughlin	CG	215
Troy Westwood	WP	209
David Ridgway	SK	196

Rushing - Carries

Bruce Perkins	HM	173
Mike Richardson	WP	165
Mike Saunders	SK	135

Receiving - Catches

David Sapunjis	CG	103
Rod Harris	SC	90
Ray Elgaard	SK	89

Passing - Completions

Doug Flutie	CG	416
Kent Austin	SK	405
David Archer	SC	403

Fumble Returns

Kelian Matthews	SC	6
Charles Anthony	SK	6
3	tied with 4 each	

Fumble Returns - Yards

Charles Anthony	SK	137
Less Browne	BC	85
Greg Eaglin	HM/CG	75

Yards From Scrimmage

Mike Oliphant	SC	1572
David Sapunjis	CG	1508
Ray Elgaard	SK	1412

Rushing - Yards

Mike Richardson	WP	925
Damon Allen	ED	920
Bruce Perkins	HM	812

Receiving - Yards

David Sapunjis	CG	1484
Ray Elgaard	SK	1393
Jeff Fairholm	SK	1391

Passing - Yards

Doug Flutie	CG	6092
David Archer	SC	6023
Kent Austin	SK	5754

Passing Efficiency Rating

Doug Flutie	CG	98.5
Damon Allen	ED	92.6
Danny Barrett	BC	89.0

Passing - Attempts

Kent Austin	SK	715
Doug Flutie	CG	703
David Archer	SC	701

Field Goals - Made

David Ridgway	SK	48
Mark McLoughlin	CG	47
Troy Westwood	WP	45

Kickoff Return - Yards

Cory Philpot	BC	1008
Mike Clemons	TO	604
Titus Dixon	SC	602

Punt Return - Yards

Henry Williams	ED	1157
Mike Clemons	TO	716
Derrick Crawford	CG	589

QB Sacks

Elfrid Payton	WP	22
O.J. Brigance	BC	20
Tim Colfield	HM	18

Punters - Average

Terry Baker	OT	45.5
Bob Cameron	WP	42.0
Glenn Harper	ED	41.5

Combined Tackles

Ken Benson	TO	103
Ray Bernard	SK	99
Alondra Johnson	CG	99

1993 INDIVIDUAL STATISTICS

SCORING – TOUCHDOWNS

PLAYER		TOTAL TDS	RUSHING TDS	RECEIVING TDS	TDS BY RETURN	OTHER POINTS	TOTAL POINTS
Williams David	WP	15	0	15	0	0	90
Sapunjis David	CG	15	0	15	0	0	90
Brown Eddie	ED	15	0	15	0	0	90
Oliphant Mike	SC	13	8	5	0	0	78
Philpot Cory	BC	12	8	3	1	0	72
Trevathan Mike	BC	12	0	12	0	0	72
Moore Will	CG	12	0	12	0	0	72
Crawford Derrick	CG	11	0	10	1	4	70
Climie Jock	OT	11	0	11	0	1	67
Dunigan Matt	WP	11	11	0	0	0	66
Flutie Doug	CG	11	11	0	0	0	66
Wilcox Gerald	WP	10	0	10	0	0	60
Williams Henry	ED	10	0	6	4	0	60
Millington Sean	BC	9	5	3	1	0	54
Walker Wayne	OT	9	0	9	0	0	54
Narcisse Donald	SK	9	0	9	0	0	54
Fairholm Jeff	SK	9	0	9	0	0	54
Hazard Manny	TO	8	0	8	0	0	48
Elgaard Ray	SK	8	0	8	0	0	48
Winfield Earl	HM	8	0	5	3	0	48
Austin Kent	SK	7	7	0	0	0	42
Ham Tracy	TO	7	7	0	0	0	42
Harris Rod	SC	7	0	7	0	0	42
Clemons Mike	TO	6	1	3	2	2	38
Allen Damon	ED	6	6	0	0	0	36
Richardson Mike	WP	6	4	2	0	0	36
Jones Stephen	OT	6	0	6	0	0	36
Johnson Joe	SC	6	0	5	1	0	36
Bolton Nathaniel	WP	6	0	5	1	0	36
Wiggins Brian	CG	5	0	5	0	2	32
Saunders Mike	SK	5	4	1	0	0	30
Johnstone Chris	WP	5	4	1	0	0	30
Pringle Mike	SC	5	4	1	0	0	30
Dixon Titus	SC	5	0	5	0	0	30
Flutie Darren	BC	5	0	5	0	0	30
Parker Carl	SC	5	0	5	0	0	30
Volpe Jon	BC	4	4	0	0	0	24
Barrett Danny	BC	4	4	0	0	0	24
Hudson Warren	TO	4	3	1	0	0	24
Floyd Lucius	ED	4	2	2	0	0	24
Pitts Allen	CG	4	0	4	0	0	24
Alexander Ray	BC	4	0	4	0	0	24
Alphin Gerald	WP	4	0	4	0	0	24
Clark Matt	BC	4	0	4	0	0	24
Baysinger Freeman	SC	4	0	3	1	0	24
	BC	0	0	0	0	0	0
Total		4	0	3	1	0	24
Lewis Kip	TO	3	0	3	0	2	20
Wallace Darrell	SK	3	3	0	0	0	18
Perkins Bruce	HM	3	3	0	0	0	18
Burgess Tom	OT	3	3	0	0	0	18
Soles Michael	ED	3	3	0	0	0	18
Marshall Blake	ED	3	2	1	0	0	18
Daniels Shawn	OT	3	2	1	0	0	18
Sandusky Jim	ED	3	0	3	0	0	18
Masotti Paul	TO	3	0	3	0	0	18
Burbage Cornell	HM	3	0	3	0	0	18
Clark Robert	TO	3	0	3	0	0	18
Boyko Allen	WP	3	0	3	0	0	18
Crifo Rob	WP	0	0	0	0	2	2
	OT	2	0	2	0	0	12
Total		2	0	2	0	2	14
Skinner Chris	BC	2	2	0	0	0	12
Slack Reggie	TO	2	2	0	0	0	12
McPherson Don	HM	2	2	0	0	0	12
McVey Andrew	CG	2	2	0	0	0	12
Taylor Steve	CG	2	2	0	0	0	12
Foggie Rickey	ED	2	2	0	0	0	12
Archer David	SC	2	2	0	0	0	12
Mimbs Robert	BC	2	1	1	0	0	12
Knight Lee	HM	2	1	1	0	0	12
Dinnall Dave	HM	2	1	0	1	0	12
Bouyer Willie	SC	2	0	2	0	0	12
Everett Tre	SK	1	0	1	0	0	6
	SC	1	0	1	0	0	6
Total		2	0	2	0	0	12
Pruitt James	SC	2	0	2	0	0	12
Morris Gary	ED	2	0	2	0	0	12
Turner Lonnie	BC	2	0	2	0	0	12
Jackson Alfred	WP	2	0	2	0	0	12
Jenkins Keyvan	CG	2	0	2	0	0	12
Ellingson James	OT	2	0	2	0	0	12
Boyko Bruce	SK	2	0	2	0	0	12
Smith Peewee	CG	2	0	1	1	0	12
Wilkerson Gary	HM	2	0	0	2	0	12
Lance Carlton	SK	2	0	0	2	0	12
Freeman Corian	WP	2	0	0	2	0	12
Total		2	0	0	2	0	12
Battle Greg	WP	2	0	0	2	0	12
Browne Less	BC	2	0	0	2	0	12
Hardy Robert	SC	1	1	0	0	0	6
McAdoo Derrick	TO	1	1	0	0	0	6
Hood John	HM	1	1	0	0	0	6
Jackson Patrick	TO	1	1	0	0	0	6
Stewart Tony	CG	1	1	0	0	0	6
Bryant Blaise	SK	0	0	0	0	0	0
	WP	1	1	0	0	0	6
Total		1	1	0	0	0	6
Joseph Darren	OT	1	1	0	0	0	6
Bushey Paul	HM	1	1	0	0	0	6
Jones Warren	SK	1	1	0	0	0	6
Hanson Ryan	BC	1	1	0	0	0	6
Willis Larry	TO	1	0	1	0	0	6
Hill Lonzell	HM	1	0	1	0	0	6
Culpepper Willie	SK	1	0	1	0	0	6
Walker Scott	HM	1	0	1	0	0	6
Dunn Kasey	ED	1	0	1	0	0	6
Stanley Walter	OT	1	0	1	0	0	6
Brown Andre	OT	0	0	0	0	0	0
	TO	1	0	1	0	0	6
Total		1	0	1	0	0	6
Williams Byron	SK	1	0	1	0	0	6
Mills Troy	SC	1	0	1	0	0	6
Zatylny Walter	TO	1	0	1	0	0	6
Pearce Matt	WP	1	0	1	0	0	6
Jauch Joey	HM	1	0	1	0	0	6
Izquierdo J.P.	ED	1	0	1	0	0	6
Craft Doug	CG	1	0	0	1	0	6
Gordon Charles	OT	1	0	0	1	0	6
Holland Robert	ED	1	0	0	1	0	6
Dawson Bobby	HM	1	0	0	1	0	6
Joelson Greg	SC	1	0	0	1	0	6
Parrish Doug	ED	1	0	0	1	0	6
Fuller Joe	OT	1	0	0	1	0	6
Eaglin Greg	HM	1	0	0	1	0	6
Total		1	0	0	1	0	6
Lewis Loyd	WP	1	0	0	1	0	6
Pless Willie	ED	1	0	0	1	0	6
Francis Andre	BC	1	0	0	1	0	6
Kropke John	OT	1	0	0	1	0	6
Payton Elfrid	WP	1	0	0	1	0	6
Smith Donald	WP	1	0	0	1	0	6
Brown Albert	SK	1	0	0	1	0	6
Anthony Charles	SK	1	0	0	1	0	6
Johnson Alondra	CG	1	0	0	1	0	6
Anthony Karl	CG	1	0	0	1	0	6
Wilson Don	ED	1	0	0	1	0	6
Goods Bennie	ED	1	0	0	1	0	6
Davis Paschall	SC	1	0	0	1	0	6

SCORING – KICKING

PLAYER		CONVERTS TRIED	CONVERTS GOOD	FIELD GOALS TRIED	FIELD GOALS GOOD	PCT GOOD	AVERAGE	LONGEST	SINGLES	OTHER POINTS	TOTAL POINTS
McLoughlin Mark	CG	63	63	62	47	75.8	29.6	51	11	0	215
Westwood Troy	WP	69	68	56	45	80.4	32.8	50	6	0	209
Ridgway David	SK	51	51	53	48	90.6	27.4	50	1	0	196
Passaglia Lui	BC	62	62	47	35	74.5	28.8	52	9	0	176
Fleming Sean	ED	54	54	48	34	70.8	33.3	58	10	0	166
Crouch Jim	SC	56	56	45	28	62.2	25.4	42	16	0	156
Osbaldiston Paul	HM	28	28	48	31	64.6	27.6	51	15	0	136
Chomyc Lance	TO	35	35	44	30	68.2	32.8	52	10	0	135
Baker Terry	OT	24	24	30	18	60.0	30.9	50	11	0	89
MacCallum Paul	BC	1	1	4	3	75.0	35.7	45	0	0	10
	OT	5	5	8	6	75.0	21.3	35	1	0	24
Total		6	6	12	9	75.0	26.1	45	1	0	34
Macoritti Ray	OT	9	9	5	5	100.0	26.4	39	0	0	24
Matich Brent	SK	0	0	0	0	0.0	0.0	0	7	0	7
Harper Glenn	ED	0	0	0	0	0.0	0.0	0	7	0	7
Gardere Pete	SC	0	0	0	0	0.0	0.0	0	5	0	5
Cameron Bob	WP	0	0	0	0	0.0	0.0	0	5	0	5
Martino Tony	CG	0	0	0	0	0.0	0.0	0	3	0	3
Ilesic Hank	TO	0	0	0	0	0.0	0.0	0	2	0	2
Climie Jock	OT	0	0	0	0	0.0	0.0	0	1	66	67
Duncan Greg	OT	0	0	1	0	0.0	0.0	0	1	0	1
McJulien Paul	SC	0	0	0	0	0.0	0.0	0	1	0	1
Lammle Wayne	TO	0	0	0	0	0.0	0.0	0	1	0	1

PASSING

		ATT	COMP	YDS	PCT	I/C	LG	TD
Flutie Doug	CG	703	416	6092	59.2	17	75	44
Archer David	SC	701	403	6023	57.5	23	90	35
Austin Kent	SK	715	405	5754	56.6	25	78	31
Burgess Tom	OT	591	329	5063	55.7	25	98	30
Dunigan Matt	WP	600	334	4682	55.7	18	75	36
Barrett Danny	BC	513	293	4097	57.1	12	70	24
Allen Damon	ED	400	214	3394	53.5	10	102	25
McPherson Don	HM	368	152	2242	41.3	21	79	6
Ham Tracy	TO	302	146	2147	48.3	11	64	8
McManus Danny	BC	223	114	1613	51.1	14	44	10
Slack Reggie	TO	184	104	1372	56.5	7	61	7
Kerrigan Mike	TO	153	86	1323	56.2	5	72	9
Torrance Bob	HM	152	78	837	51.3	12	47	3
Garza Sammy	WP	97	55	829	56.7	3	47	6
Foggie Rickey	ED	96	42	738	43.8	4	64	4
Jones Terrence	OT	72	29	434	40.3	5	56	1
Taylor Steve	CG	56	28	402	50.0	1	54	5
Jones Warren	SK	55	34	362	61.8	2	56	1
Bell Kerwin	SC	34	22	296	64.7	1	58	2
Saltz Lee	HM	33	18	281	54.5	2	64	1

		ATT	COMP	YDS	PCT	I/C	LG	TD
Sanchez Eros	HM	42	18	251	42.9	1	33	1
Muecke Tom	ED	54	26	242	48.1	3	28	1
Dillon Todd	HM	22	14	192	63.6	1	46	1
Porras Tom	WP	10	6	127	60.0	0	54	1
Jones Stephen	OT	2	2	92	100.0	0	46	1
Johnson Bret	TO	8	4	72	50.0	1	45	0
Perkins Bruce	HM	1	1	54	100.0	0	54	0
Saunders Mike	SK	2	2	48	100.0	0	28	0
Flutie Darren	BC	3	1	42	33.3	0	42	0
Alphin Gerald	WP	1	1	28	100.0	0	28	0
Passaglia Lui	BC	1	1	12	100.0	0	12	0
Fleetwood Marquel	OT	5	2	7	40.0	1	5	0
Harper Glenn	ED	2	2	2	100.0	0	6	1
Vanderjagt Mike	SK	1	0	0	0.0	0	0	0
Macoritti Ray	OT	1	0	0	0.0	1	0	0
Puleri Charles	SC	2	0	0	0.0	0	0	0
Knight Lee	HM	1	0	0	0.0	0	0	0
Clemons Mike	TO	1	0	0	0.0	0	0	0
Jauch Joey	HM	1	0	0	0.0	0	0	0

RUSHING

PLAYER		NO	YDS	AVE	LG	TD
Richardson Mike	WP	165	925	5.6	26	4
Allen Damon	ED	120	920	7.7	43	6
Perkins Bruce	HM	173	812	4.7	52	3
Oliphant Mike	SC	116	760	6.6	52	8
Saunders Mike	SK	135	683	5.1	52	4
Ham Tracy	TO	72	605	8.4	42	7
Dunigan Matt	WP	84	517	6.2	37	11
Clemons Mike	TO	89	481	5.4	32	1
Jenkins Keyvan	CG	96	435	4.5	26	0
Floyd Lucius	ED	81	423	5.2	35	2
Bryant Blaise	SK	24	100	4.2	25	0
	WP	62	313	5.0	68	1
Total		86	413	4.8	68	1
Joseph Darren	OT	108	398	3.7	23	1
Flutie Doug	CG	74	373	5.0	50	11
Philpot Cory	BC	66	372	5.6	23	8
Pringle Mike	SC	60	366	6.1	44	4
Burgess Tom	OT	75	347	4.6	18	3
Soles Michael	ED	79	334	4.2	18	3
McPherson Don	HM	55	299	5.4	30	2
Archer David	SC	60	287	4.8	18	2
Millington Sean	BC	52	276	5.3	60	5
Daniels Shawn	OT	52	238	4.6	20	2
Barnes Reggie	OT	45	233	5.2	28	0
Hudson Warren	TO	53	220	4.2	28	3
Johnstone Chris	WP	45	196	4.4	24	4
Stewart Tony	CG	53	196	3.7	17	1
McVey Andrew	CG	41	185	4.5	17	2
Slack Reggie	TO	27	172	6.4	31	2
Barrett Danny	BC	42	162	3.9	15	4
Walling Brian	ED	35	161	4.6	17	0
Wallace Darrell	SK	36	156	4.3	26	3
Taylor Steve	CG	23	155	6.7	32	2
Hood John	HM	41	146	3.6	14	1
Pearce Matt	WP	29	145	5.0	15	0
Hanson Ryan	BC	15	143	9.5	45	1
Volpe Jon	BC	45	136	3.0	13	4
Mimbs Robert	BC	22	130	5.9	28	1
Richards Dwight	OT	45	124	2.8	19	0
	TO	0	0	0.0	0	0
Total		45	124	2.8	19	0
Dinnall Dave	HM	12	117	9.8	63	1
Knight Lee	HM	28	108	3.9	22	1
Marshall Blake	ED	30	101	3.4	13	2
Austin Kent	SK	32	88	2.8	21	7
Jackson Patrick	TO	13	87	6.7	19	1
Boyko Bruce	SK	20	72	3.6	10	0
Torrance Bob	HM	12	71	5.9	32	0
McAdoo Derrick	TO	13	70	5.4	18	1
McManus Danny	BC	12	64	5.3	26	0
Sanchez Eros	HM	14	63	4.5	20	0

PLAYER		NO	YDS	AVE	LG	TD
Jones Warren	SK	24	62	2.6	10	1
Bushey Paul	HM	15	60	4.0	12	1
Skinner Chris	BC	10	52	5.2	19	2
Jones Terrence	OT	8	47	5.9	24	0
Mills Troy	SC	11	40	3.6	18	0
Foggie Rickey	ED	12	32	2.7	14	2
Walker Wayne	OT	2	30	15.0	22	0
Martino Tony	CG	2	29	14.5	16	0
Jauch Joey	HM	1	25	25.0	25	0
Johnson Bret	TO	2	25	12.5	14	0
Turner Lonnie	BC	4	25	6.3	16	0
Garza Sammy	WP	4	25	6.3	12	0
King Lorne	TO	6	25	4.2	8	0
Sapunjis David	CG	0	24	0.0	24	0
Dillon Todd	HM	5	23	4.6	11	0
Martin P.J.	HM	3	21	7.0	14	0
Brown Eddie	ED	3	19	6.3	21	0
Crawford Derrick	CG	4	19	4.8	7	0
Elgaard Ray	SK	0	19	0.0	19	0
Johnson Joe	SC	1	16	16.0	16	0
Matich Brent	SK	1	16	16.0	16	0
Muecke Tom	ED	3	15	5.0	12	0
Bell Kerwin	SC	4	13	3.3	8	0
Hardy Robert	SC	5	12	2.4	4	1
Kerrigan Mike	TO	4	11	2.8	4	0
Dickey Terry	TO	3	10	3.3	4	0
Pitcher David	SK	1	9	9.0	9	0
Baker Terry	OT	1	7	7.0	7	0
Fairholm Jeff	SK	3	7	2.3	7	0
Hennig Roger	HM	1	6	6.0	6	0
Saltz Lee	HM	2	6	3.0	5	0
Bolton Nathaniel	WP	2	6	3.0	17	0
Forde Duane	WP	2	6	3.0	5	0
Fleetwood Marquel	OT	1	5	5.0	5	0
Hadnot Butch	TO	1	4	4.0	4	0
Izquierdo J.P.	ED	1	4	4.0	4	0
Noel Dean	OT	2	4	2.0	3	0
Stumon Gregg	OT	1	3	3.0	3	0
Zerr Blair	CG	2	3	1.5	2	0
Croonen Jeff	TO	1	2	2.0	2	0
Smith Peewee	CG	1	2	2.0	2	0
Richardson Dave	HM	0	2	0.0	2	0
Porras Tom	WP	1	-1	-1.0	0	0
Williams Henry	ED	2	-3	-1.5	9	0
Williams Byron	SK	1	-4	-4.0	0	0
Murray Andrew	TO	1	-6	-6.0	0	0
Vanderjagt Mike	SK	1	-8	-8.0	0	0
Winfield Earl	HM	1	-8	-8.0	0	0
Williams David	WP	1	-14	-14.0	0	0
Thompson Charles	SC	1	-15	-15.0	0	0

PASS RECEIVING

PLAYER		NO	YDS	AVE	LG	TD
Sapunjis David	CG	103	1484	14.4	75	15
Elgaard Ray	SK	89	1393	15.7	64	8
Fairholm Jeff	SK	72	1391	19.3	78	9
Harris Rod	SC	90	1379	15.3	56	7
Brown Eddie	ED	67	1378	20.6	75	15
Wilcox Gerald	WP	76	1340	17.6	75	10
Alexander Ray	BC	77	1300	16.9	43	4
Climie Jock	OT	67	1281	19.1	89	11
Jones Stephen	OT	74	1279	17.3	76	6
Narcisse Donald	SK	83	1171	14.1	44	9
Williams David	WP	84	1144	13.6	44	15
Moore Will	CG	73	1083	14.8	55	12
Winfield Earl	HM	61	1076	17.6	79	5
Dixon Titus	SC	61	1074	17.6	90	5
Flutie Darren	BC	79	1068	13.5	45	5
Alphin Gerald	WP	55	1052	19.1	54	4
Hazard Manny	TO	61	1033	16.9	61	8
Crawford Derrick	CG	57	1007	17.7	75	10
Clark Matt	BC	74	970	13.1	55	4
Trevathan Mike	BC	64	965	15.1	44	12
Williams Henry	ED	52	950	18.3	102	6
Clark Robert	TO	50	900	18.0	64	3
Wiggins Brian	CG	47	881	18.7	52	5
Baysinger Freeman	SC	48	736	15.3	83	3
	BC	5	97	19.4	42	0
Total		53	833	15.7	83	3

PLAYER		NO	YDS	AVE	LG	TD
Walker Wayne	OT	38	830	21.8	98	9
Oliphant Mike	SC	47	812	17.3	83	5
Pitts Allen	CG	45	776	17.2	37	4
Bolton Nathaniel	WP	42	730	17.4	57	5
Parker Carl	SC	46	684	14.9	43	5
Evraire Ken	HM	41	679	16.6	64	0
Saunders Mike	SK	58	612	10.6	43	1
Masotti Paul	TO	36	606	16.8	72	3
Williams Byron	SK	37	545	14.7	59	1
Pringle Mike	SC	56	523	9.3	24	1
Jauch Joey	HM	31	512	16.5	41	1
Sandusky Jim	ED	24	482	20.1	64	3
Millington Sean	BC	38	481	12.7	70	3
Zatylny Walter	TO	34	464	13.6	41	1
Johnson Joe	SC	22	421	19.1	39	5
Turner Lonnie	BC	27	420	15.6	50	2
Smith Peewee	CG	33	417	12.6	31	1
Joseph Darren	OT	33	403	12.2	54	0
Lewis Kip	TO	29	401	13.8	41	3
Bryant Blaise	SK	16	132	8.3	35	0
	WP	31	252	8.1	31	0
Total		47	384	8.2	35	0
Richardson Mike	WP	46	378	8.2	26	2
Brown Andre	OT	19	287	15.1	31	0
	TO	5	84	16.8	35	1
Total		24	371	15.5	35	1

PASS RECEIVING (Cont'd)

PLAYER		NO	YDS	AVE	LG	TD
Burbage Cornell	HM	31	367	11.8	31	3
Jenkins Keyvan	CG	32	363	11.3	51	2
Daniels Shawn	OT	43	326	7.6	28	1
Clemons Mike	TO	32	313	9.8	31	3
Stanley Walter	OT	11	302	27.5	57	1
Boyko Bruce	SK	30	299	10.0	28	2
McVey Andrew	CG	35	293	8.4	22	0
Ellingson James	OT	25	281	11.2	23	2
Christensen Jay	ED	16	273	17.1	38	0
Crifo Rob	WP	2	21	10.5	11	0
	OT	15	252	16.8	39	2
Total		17	273	16.1	39	2
Gordon Bob	TO	20	266	13.3	24	0
Soles Michael	ED	26	263	10.1	25	0
Floyd Lucius	ED	29	262	9.0	25	2
Pruitt James	SC	15	260	17.3	46	2
Johnstone Chris	WP	18	259	14.4	33	1
Walker Scott	HM	11	245	22.3	56	1
Mazzoli Nick	HM	19	245	12.9	35	0
Izquierdo J.P.	ED	19	237	12.5	28	1
Morris Gary	ED	18	233	12.9	38	2
Knight Lee	HM	30	214	7.1	18	1
Willis Larry	TO	11	195	17.7	54	1
Jackson Alfred	WP	13	194	14.9	60	2
Farthing Dan	SK	22	192	8.7	25	0
Hill Lonzell	HM	12	190	15.8	54	1
Philpot Cory	BC	20	190	9.5	24	3
Wallace Darrell	SK	15	181	12.1	35	0
Hudson Warren	TO	17	179	10.5	24	1
Bouyer Willie	SC	15	175	11.7	31	2
Thompson Charles	SC	12	143	11.9	27	0
Everett Tre	SK	11	127	11.5	44	1
	SC	2	10	5.0	13	1
Total		13	137	10.5	44	2
Dickey Terry	TO	16	136	8.5	24	0
Bushey Paul	HM	18	135	7.5	30	0
Barnes Reggie	OT	11	128	11.6	40	0
Richards Dwight	OT	17	125	7.4	24	0
	TO	0	0	0.0	0	0
Total		17	125	7.4	24	0
Volpe Jon	BC	10	117	11.7	25	0
Perkins Bruce	HM	20	112	5.6	21	0
Boyko Allen	WP	7	108	15.4	27	3
Bellamy Mike	WP	12	104	8.7	17	0

PLAYER		NO	YDS	AVE	LG	TD
Smith Darrell K.	ED	11	98	8.9	18	0
Culpepper Willie	SK	6	95	15.8	34	1
Dunn Kasey	ED	7	90	12.9	28	1
McAdoo Derrick	TO	7	88	12.6	28	0
Stewart Tony	CG	8	87	10.9	20	0
Winey Ken	TO	8	83	10.4	15	0
Shavers Tyrone	OT	7	79	11.3	22	0
Skinner Chris	BC	8	79	9.9	29	0
Walling Brian	ED	7	65	9.3	15	0
Hamm Horace	SC	4	60	15.0	25	0
Murray Andrew	TO	4	57	14.3	27	0
Ellis Craig	TO	2	51	25.5	38	0
Marof Frank	CG	6	49	8.2	13	0
Pearce Matt	WP	4	45	11.3	30	1
Brownlee Vincent	BC	2	41	20.5	36	0
Zerr Blair	CG	3	38	12.7	19	0
Marshall Blake	ED	7	38	5.4	10	1
Mimbs Robert	BC	4	33	8.3	11	1
Jackson Patrick	TO	4	31	7.8	19	0
Nimako George	TO	2	29	14.5	27	0
Dunigan Matt	WP	1	28	28.0	28	0
Britton Eddie	CG	1	27	27.0	27	0
Nurse Richard	HM	2	27	13.5	16	0
Schramayr Ernie	OT	2	23	11.5	14	0
Dinnall Dave	HM	2	23	11.5	14	0
Hood John	HM	3	21	7.0	13	0
Pratt Khevin	SC	1	17	17.0	17	0
McArthur Dane	SK	1	15	15.0	15	0
Grier Derek	BC	1	12	12.0	12	0
Jackson Byron	SC	2	12	6.0	8	0
Martin P.J.	HM	1	11	11.0	11	0
Pitcher David	SK	1	11	11.0	11	0
Martin Andrew	WP	2	11	5.5	6	0
Hanson Ryan	BC	1	9	9.0	9	0
Hardy Robert	SC	3	9	3.0	5	0
Butler Wayde	ED	1	7	7.0	7	0
Davies Doug	CG	0	5	0.0	5	0
Covernton Bruce	CG	0	5	0.0	5	0
Castello Keith	TO	1	5	5.0	5	0
Mills Troy	SC	1	4	4.0	4	1
Moore Ken	CG	0	0	0.0	0	0
Ham Tracy	TO	1	-7	-7.0	0	0
Flutie Doug	CG	1	-11	-11.0	0	0

PUNTING

(100 punts required to qualify for average title)

PLAYER		NO	BLOCKED	YDS	AVE	LK	S
Torrance Bob	HM	1	0	57	57.0	57	0
Baker Terry	OT	91	1	4142	45.5	68	2
Gardere Pete	SC	77	1	3246	42.2	63	5
Cameron Bob	WP	141	2	5916	42.0	70	5
Harper Glenn	ED	154	1	6385	41.5	71	7
Caravatta Giulio	BC	8	0	331	41.4	49	0
Ilesic Hank	TO	89	0	3672	41.3	66	2
Matich Brent	SK	123	0	5052	41.1	84	7
Martino Tony	CG	121	0	4939	40.8	76	2
Osbaldiston Paul	HM	164	4	6648	40.5	84	5
Bushey Paul	HM	1	0	40	40.0	40	0
Passaglia Lui	BC	116	1	4616	39.8	71	2
Vanderjagt Mike	SK	17	1	672	39.5	59	0
Murray Andrew	TO	1	0	39	39.0	39	0
Lammle Wayne	TO	49	1	1901	38.8	61	1
McJulien Paul	SC	27	0	983	36.4	54	1
Crouch Jim	SC	34	0	1220	35.9	58	0
Macoritti Ray	OT	36	0	1256	34.9	47	0
MacCallum Paul	BC	0	0	0	0.0	0	0
	OT	15	0	511	34.1	70	0
Total		15	0	511	34.1	70	0
Climie Jock	OT	15	1	506	33.7	55	1
Lazecki Michael	OT	8	0	265	33.1	43	0
Clemons Mike	TO	1	0	28	28.0	28	0
Chomyc Lance	TO	3	0	77	25.7	34	0

NET PUNTING

(100 punts required to qualify for average title)

PLAYER		ATT	NET	AVE
Torrance Bob	HM	1	57	57.0
Caravatta Giulio	BC	8	302	37.8
Matich Brent	SK	123	4586	37.3
Harper Glenn	ED	154	5642	36.6
Baker Terry	OT	92	3340	36.3
Passaglia Lui	BC	116	4165	35.9
Gardere Pete	SC	78	2779	35.6
Cameron Bob	WP	142	5026	35.4
Zatylny Walter	TO	1	35	35.0
Ilesic Hank	TO	89	3025	34.0
Bushey Paul	HM	1	34	34.0
Lammle Wayne	TO	50	1683	33.7
Martino Tony	CG	121	4046	33.4
* MacCallum Paul	BC	0	0	0.0
	OT	15	484	32.3
Total		15	484	32.3
Vanderjagt Mike	SK	18	577	32.1
Osbaldiston Paul	HM	164	5230	31.9
Lazecki Michael	OT	8	244	30.5
Crouch Jim	SC	34	1025	30.1
McJulien Paul	SC	27	814	30.1
Barrett Danny	BC	1	29	29.0
Macoritti Ray	OT	36	1025	28.5
Climie Jock	OT	15	424	28.3
Chomyc Lance	TO	3	68	22.7

UNSUCCESSFUL FIELD GOALS

PLAYER		NUMBER	TOTAL YARDS	AVG. YDS / ATTEMPT	LONGEST KICK	SINGLES SCORED
Osbaldiston Paul	HM	17	799	47.0	60	10
Crouch Jim	SC	17	775	45.6	59	13
Fleming Sean	ED	14	690	49.3	63	10
McLoughlin Mark	CG	15	655	43.7	61	10
Chomyc Lance	TO	14	595	42.5	55	10
Baker Terry	OT	12	559	46.6	54	8
Passaglia Lui	BC	12	553	46.1	61	7

PLAYER		NUMBER	TOTAL YARDS	AVG. YDS / ATTEMPT	LONGEST KICK	SINGLES SCORED
Westwood Troy	WP	11	501	45.5	63	6
Ridgway David	SK	5	229	45.8	53	1
MacCallum Paul	BC	1	52	52.0	52	0
	OT	2	62	31.0	33	1
Total		3	114	38.0	52	1
Duncan Greg	OT	1	38	38.0	38	1

UNSUCCESSFUL FIELD GOAL RETURNS

PLAYER		NO. OF RETURNS	TOTAL YARDS	AVERAGE RETURN	LONGEST RETURN	NUMBER TD
Ulmer Terryl	SK	3	169	56.3	96	0
Brown Albert	SK	3	169	56.3	108*	1
Crawford Derrick	CG	4	136	34.0	51	0
Williams Henry	ED	4	118	29.5	42	0
* Baysinger Freeman	SC	4	114	28.5	63	0
	BC	0	0	0.0	0	0
Total		4	114	28.5	63	0
Turner Lonnie	BC	6	95	15.8	44	0
Smith Peewee	CG	3	81	27.0	39	0
Drawhorn Anthony	OT	8	70	8.8	29	0
Winfield Earl	HM	1	61	61.0	61	0
Europe Tom	BC	3	35	11.7	35	0

PLAYER		NO. OF RETURNS	TOTAL YARDS	AVERAGE RETURN	LONGEST RETURN	NUMBER TD
Clemons Mike	TO	3	31	10.3	14	0
Johnson Joe	SC	1	23	23.0	23	0
Culpepper Willie	SK	1	21	21.0	21	0
Wiseman Todd	HM	1	20	20.0	20	0
Cartwright Ricardo	SK	2	19	9.5	19	0
Philpot Cory	BC	1	15	15.0	15	0
Wilson Don	ED	1	6	6.0	6	0
Burbage Cornell	HM	1	4	4.0	4	0
Westwood Troy	WP	1	4	4.0	4	0
Brownlee Vincent	BC	1	0	0.0	0	0
Flutie Darren	BC	1	0	0.0	0	0
Evans Bobby	WP	1	0	0.0	0	0

KICKOFFS

PLAYER		NO	YDS	AVE	LK	S
Westwood Troy	WP	105	5990	57.0	95	0
McLoughlin Mark	CG	87	5089	58.5	93	1
Fleming Sean	ED	82	4908	59.9	74	0
Ridgway David	SK	86	4450	51.7	76	0
Crouch Jim	SC	78	4441	56.9	95	3
Passaglia Lui	BC	88	3941	44.8	64	0
Osbaldiston Paul	HM	57	3094	54.3	79	0
Baker Terry	OT	44	2491	56.6	86	1
Ilesic Hank	TO	23	1401	60.9	95	0
Lammle Wayne	TO	24	1356	56.5	69	0
Chomyc Lance	TO	24	1311	54.6	80	0
Martino Tony	CG	22	1291	58.7	81	1
Macoritti Ray	OT	16	836	52.3	59	0
* MacCallum Paul	BC	2	84	42.0	51	0
	OT	7	341	48.7	61	0
Total		9	425	47.2	61	0
Lazecki Michael	OT	4	228	57.0	65	0
Vanderjagt Mike	SK	2	109	54.5	57	0
Duncan Greg	OT	1	49	49.0	49	0

FIELD GOALS

		TRIED	GOOD	YDS	AVE	LG	PCT
Macoritti Ray	OT	5	5	132	26.4	39	100.0
Ridgway David	SK	53	48	1315	27.4	50	90.6
Westwood Troy	WP	56	45	1477	32.8	50	80.4
McLoughlin Mark	CG	62	47	1391	29.6	51	75.8
* MacCallum Paul	BC	4	3	107	35.7	45	75.0
	OT	8	6	128	21.3	35	75.0
Total		12	9	235	26.1	45	75.0
Passaglia Lui	BC	47	35	1007	28.8	52	74.5
Fleming Sean	ED	48	34	1132	33.3	58	70.8
Chomyc Lance	TO	44	30	984	32.8	52	68.2
Osbaldiston Paul	HM	48	31	856	27.6	51	64.6
Crouch Jim	SC	45	28	711	25.4	42	62.2
Baker Terry	OT	30	18	556	30.9	50	60.0
Duncan Greg	OT	1	0	0	0.0	0	0.0

FIELD GOAL RANGE

		ATTEMPTS 1 - 19 Yds	MADE GOOD 1 - 19 Yds	ATTEMPTS 20-29 Yds	MADE GOOD 20-29 Yds	ATTEMPTS 30-39 Yds	MADE GOOD 30-39 Yds	ATTEMPTS 40-49 Yds	MADE GOOD 40-49 Yds	ATTEMPTS 50+ Yds	MADE GOOD 50+ Yds
Chomyc Lance	TO	5	5	8	8	12	7	14	9	5	2
Osbaldiston Paul	HM	10	10	10	9	6	5	16	6	5	1
Westwood Troy	WP	7	6	12	12	17	13	14	12	4	2
Ridgway David	SK	16	16	10	10	15	13	11	8	1	1
McLoughlin Mark	CG	7	7	20	18	17	14	15	7	3	1
Fleming Sean	ED	7	7	6	5	17	11	13	10	4	1
Crouch Jim	SC	8	8	11	11	12	8	14	1	0	0
Passaglia Lui	BC	12	12	9	9	6	4	19	9	1	1
Baker Terry	OT	3	3	6	5	11	5	9	4	1	1
MacCallum Paul	BC	0	0	1	1	1	1	2	1	0	0
	OT	3	3	2	2	3	1	0	0	0	0
Total		3	3	3	3	4	2	2	1	0	0
Macoritti Ray	OT	1	1	3	3	1	1	0	0	0	0
Duncan Greg	OT	0	0	1	1	0	0	0	0	0	0

KICKOFF RETURNS

PLAYER		NO	YDS	AVE	LG	TD
Philpot Cory	BC	36	1008	28.0	91	1
Clemons Mike	TO	30	604	20.1	41	0
Dixon Titus	SC	31	602	19.4	42	0
Burbage Cornell	HM	35	597	17.1	43	0
Pringle Mike	SC	27	549	20.3	36	0
Wiggins Brian	CG	24	510	21.3	46	0
Bolton Nathaniel	WP	20	494	24.7	55	0
Crawford Derrick	CG	24	462	19.3	40	0
Boyko Allen	WP	27	446	16.5	43	0
Thompson Charles	SC	20	425	21.3	62	0
Burke Patrick	OT	27	415	15.4	30	0
Baysinger Freeman	SC	0	0	0.0	0	0
	BC	18	385	21.4	47	0
Total		18	385	21.4	47	0
Williams Henry	ED	21	381	18.1	28	0
Zatylny Walter	TO	23	361	15.7	32	0
Floyd Lucius	ED	17	360	21.2	44	0
Saunders Mike	SK	17	341	20.1	58	0
Gordon Bob	TO	11	289	26.3	48	0
Winfield Earl	HM	13	282	21.7	44	0
Walker Scott	HM	16	281	17.6	51	0
Walker Wayne	OT	20	268	13.4	24	0
Mitchel Eric	ED	8	232	29.0	51	0
Ulmer Terryl	SK	12	230	19.2	47	0
Jenkins Keyvan	CG	10	210	21.0	47	0
Hailey Ken	BC	11	201	18.3	36	0
Turner Lonnie	BC	11	196	17.8	45	0
Smith Peewee	CG	7	161	23.0	41	0
Brownlee Vincent	BC	9	160	17.8	36	0
Brown Errol	SK	8	144	18.0	26	0
	WP	1	12	12.0	12	0
Total		9	156	17.3	26	0
Jackson Patrick	TO	7	146	20.9	30	0
Smith Donald	WP	5	142	28.4	73	0
Fuller Joe	OT	10	135	13.5	22	0
Volpe Jon	BC	4	134	33.5	45	0
Wallace Darrell	SK	7	122	17.4	25	0
Flutie Darren	BC	11	122	11.1	26	0
Bryant Blaise	SK	4	88	22.0	28	0
	WP	1	31	31.0	31	0
Total		5	119	23.8	31	0
Mazzoli Nick	HM	11	118	10.7	41	0
Hanson Ryan	BC	6	113	18.8	48	0
Stanley Walter	OT	8	110	13.8	21	0
Parrish Doug	ED	7	107	15.3	26	0
Drawhorn Anthony	OT	6	100	16.7	26	0
Dickey Terry	TO	9	98	10.9	20	0
McAdoo Derrick	TO	7	71	10.1	19	0
Miles Lee	ED	3	65	21.7	34	0
Oliphant Mike	SC	4	64	16.0	20	0
Farthing Dan	SK	5	54	10.8	21	0
Culpepper Willie	SK	2	42	21.0	24	0
Branch Darrick	TO	2	41	20.5	31	0
Hazard Manny	TO	2	39	19.5	24	0
Jauch Joey	HM	0	39	0.0	39	0
Bailey Walter	SC	1	37	37.0	37	0
Cartwright Ricardo	SK	3	36	12.0	20	0
Winey Ken	TO	3	36	12.0	17	0
Battle Greg	WP	3	36	12.0	19	0
Noel Dean	OT	3	35	11.7	17	0
Bellamy Mike	WP	1	32	32.0	32	0
Ricks Mark	SK	2	31	15.5	19	0
	TO	0	0	0.0	0	0
Total		2	31	15.5	19	0
Everett Tre	SK	2	29	14.5	17	0
	SC	0	0	0.0	0	0
Total		2	29	14.5	17	0
Richards Dwight	OT	2	26	13.0	22	0
	TO	0	0	0.0	0	0
Total		2	26	13.0	22	0
Perkins Bruce	HM	1	24	24.0	24	0
Bushey Paul	HM	2	23	11.5	13	0
Jauch Jim	HM	1	22	22.0	22	0
Joseph Darren	OT	2	21	10.5	15	0
Sandusky Jim	ED	1	20	20.0	20	0
McVey Andrew	CG	2	20	10.0	20	0
Morris Gary	ED	1	19	19.0	19	0
Lance Carlton	SK	1	19	19.0	19	0
Phillips Kim	WP	2	19	9.5	19	0
Johnson Joe	SC	1	17	17.0	17	0
Dinnall Dave	HM	1	16	16.0	16	0
Izquierdo J.P.	ED	3	15	5.0	7	0
Watson Ken	CG	3	14	4.7	10	0
Matthews Kelian	SC	1	13	13.0	13	0
Davis Paschall	SC	1	13	13.0	13	0
Whitley Kevin	TO	1	12	12.0	12	0
Tsangaris Chris	WP	2	11	5.5	9	0
Smith Darrell K.	ED	1	10	10.0	10	0
Knight Lee	HM	2	9	4.5	8	0
Plummer Bruce	BC	1	6	6.0	6	0
McLennan Spencer	BC	1	6	6.0	6	0
McCurdy Brian	TO	1	5	5.0	5	0
Crum Maurice	SK	1	1	1.0	1	0
Boyko Bruce	SK	2	1	0.5	1	0

Davidson Rob - WP, Pitts Allen, CG, Jackson Tim - HM, Williams Byron - SK, Mills Troy - SC, Walcott Ken - OT, Dickson Bruce - ED, Alphin Gerald - WP, Wilburn Barry - SK, Pearce Matt - WP, Stumon Gregg - OT, Pleasant Reggie - TO, Wright Terry - HM, Johnson Will - CG, Pope Marvin - CG, Soles Michael - ED, Wright Donovan - BC, Harris Rod - SC, Moore Curtis - SC: **Each have 1 Kickoff Return for 0 yards**

Evraire, Ken - HM **1 Kickoff Return for -2.0 yards.**

PUNT RETURNS

PLAYER		NO	YDS	AVE	LG	TD
Williams Henry	ED	83	1157	13.9	104	4
Clemons Mike	TO	77	716	9.3	79	2
Crawford Derrick	CG	65	589	9.1	70	1
Winfield Earl	HM	41	530	12.9	71	3
Baysinger Freeman	SC	52	405	7.8	59	1
	BC	12	99	8.3	20	0
Total		64	504	7.9	59	1
Drawhorn Anthony	OT	52	334	6.4	28	0

PUNT RETURNS (Con't)

PLAYER		NO	YDS	AVE	LG	TD
Bolton Nathaniel	WP	49	325	6.6	71	1
Boyko Allen	WP	63	299	4.7	20	0
Smith Peewee	CG	21	281	13.4	67	1
Turner Lonnie	BC	38	270	7.1	43	0
Wiggins Brian	CG	27	254	9.4	29	0
Johnson Joe	SC	22	205	9.3	63	1
Saunders Mike	SK	24	194	8.1	35	0
Walker Wayne	OT	21	187	8.9	37	0
Walker Scott	HM	25	186	7.4	23	0
Brown Errol	SK	22	158	7.2	26	0
	WP	5	23	4.6	16	0
Total		27	181	6.7	26	0
Stanley Walter	OT	32	175	5.5	44	0
Burbage Cornell	HM	16	126	7.9	45	0
Thompson Charles	SC	14	120	8.6	22	0
Brown Eddie	ED	15	119	7.9	49	0
Ulmer Terryl	SK	22	118	5.4	13	0
Gordon Bob	TO	13	104	8.0	27	0
Mazzoli Nick	HM	15	99	6.6	21	0
Flutie Darren	BC	11	84	7.6	25	0
Trevathan Mike	BC	12	64	5.3	11	0
Jackson Patrick	TO	5	62	12.4	25	0
Wallace Darrell	SK	11	55	5.0	16	0
Smith Donald	WP	6	50	8.3	25	1
Philpot Cory	BC	9	45	5.0	12	0
Everett Tre	SK	6	44	7.3	13	0
	SC	0	0	0.0	0	0
Total		6	44	7.3	13	0
Farthing Dan	SK	5	43	8.6	12	0
Holland Robert	ED	5	41	8.2	13	0

PLAYER		NO	YDS	AVE	LG	TD
Winey Ken	TO	4	40	10.0	31	0
Jackson Alfred	WP	6	32	5.3	12	0
Zatylny Walter	TO	5	30	6.0	11	0
Wilkerson Gary	HM	1	29	29.0	29	0
Brownlee Vincent	BC	5	29	5.8	21	0
Oliphant Mike	SC	2	25	12.5	25	0
Harris Rod	SC	1	24	24.0	24	0
Brown Albert	SK	5	23	4.6	8	0
Cartwright Ricardo	SK	4	18	4.5	10	0
Phillips Kim	WP	1	16	16.0	16	0
Culpepper Willie	SK	2	16	8.0	14	0
Knight Lee	HM	1	15	15.0	15	0
Bellamy Mike	WP	3	13	4.3	8	0
Dickey Terry	TO	2	11	5.5	9	0
Wright Charles	OT	1	10	10.0	10	0
Pearce Matt	WP	1	10	10.0	10	0
Martin P.J.	HM	1	8	8.0	8	0
Hill Lonzell	HM	2	7	3.5	5	0
Trudel Remi	OT	2	6	3.0	6	0
Dixon Titus	SC	3	6	2.0	6	0
Richards Dwight	OT	1	5	5.0	5	0
	TO	0	0	0.0	0	0
Total		1	5	5.0	5	0
Frers Greg	CG	1	4	4.0	4	0
Dzikowicz Jason	WP	1	1	1.0	1	0
Browne Less	BC	1	0	0.0	0	0
Parrish Doug	ED	1	-1	-1.0	0	0
Walling Brian	ED	1	-1	-1.0	0	0
Taylor Eddie	BC	1	-6	-6.0	0	0
Jackson Byron	SC	1	-7	-7.0	0	0

COMBINED YARDAGE: RUSH/REC/PR/KOR/UFGR (100+ YARDS)

PLAYER		NO	YDS	AVE	LG	TD
Williams Henry	ED	162	2603	16.1	104	10
Crawford Derrick	CG	154	2213	14.4	75	11
Clemons Mike	TO	231	2145	9.3	79	6
Winfield Earl	HM	117	1941	16.6	79	8
Baysinger Freeman	SC	104	1255	12.1	83	4
	BC	35	581	16.6	47	0
Total		139	1836	13.2	83	4
Saunders Mike	SK	234	1830	7.8	58	5
Dixon Titus	SC	95	1682	17.7	90	5
Oliphant Mike	SC	169	1661	9.8	83	13
Wiggins Brian	CG	98	1645	16.8	52	5
Philpot Cory	BC	132	1630	12.3	91	12
Bolton Nathaniel	WP	113	1555	13.8	71	6
Brown Eddie	ED	85	1516	17.8	75	15
Sapunjis David	CG	103	1508	14.6	75	15
Pringle Mike	SC	143	1438	10.1	44	5
Elgaard Ray	SK	89	1412	15.9	64	8
Harris Rod	SC	92	1403	15.3	56	7
Fairholm Jeff	SK	75	1398	18.6	78	9
Wilcox Gerald	WP	76	1340	17.6	75	10
Walker Wayne	OT	81	1315	16.2	98	9
Richardson Mike	WP	211	1303	6.2	26	6
Alexander Ray	BC	77	1300	16.9	43	4
Climie Jock	OT	67	1281	19.1	89	11
Jones Stephen	OT	74	1279	17.3	76	6
Flutie Darren	BC	102	1274	12.5	45	5
Narcisse Donald	SK	83	1171	14.1	44	9
Williams David	WP	85	1130	13.3	44	15
Burbage Cornell	HM	83	1094	13.2	45	3
Moore Will	CG	73	1083	14.8	55	12
Hazard Manny	TO	63	1072	17.0	61	8
Alphin Gerald	WP	56	1052	18.8	54	4
Floyd Lucius	ED	127	1045	8.2	44	4
Trevathan Mike	BC	76	1029	13.5	44	12
Jenkins Keyvan	CG	138	1008	7.3	51	2
Turner Lonnie	BC	86	1006	11.7	50	2
Clark Matt	BC	74	970	13.1	55	4
Perkins Bruce	HM	194	948	4.9	52	3
Smith Peewee	CG	65	942	14.5	67	2
Allen Damon	ED	120	920	7.7	43	6
Bryant Blaise	SK	44	320	7.3	35	0
	WP	94	596	6.3	68	1
Total		138	916	6.6	68	1
Clark Robert	TO	50	900	18.0	64	3
Zatylny Walter	TO	62	855	13.8	41	1
Boyko Allen	WP	97	853	8.8	43	3
Joseph Darren	OT	143	822	5.7	54	1
Pitts Allen	CG	46	776	16.9	37	4
Millington Sean	BC	90	757	8.4	70	8
Walker Scott	HM	52	712	13.7	56	1
Parker Carl	SC	46	684	14.9	43	5
Johnson Joe	SC	47	682	14.5	63	6
Evraire Ken	HM	42	677	16.1	64	0
Thompson Charles	SC	47	673	14.3	62	0
Gordon Bob	TO	44	659	15.0	48	0
Masotti Paul	TO	36	606	16.8	72	3
Ham Tracy	TO	73	598	8.2	42	7
Soles Michael	ED	106	597	5.6	25	3
Stanley Walter	OT	51	587	11.5	57	1
Jauch Joey	HM	32	576	18.0	41	1
Daniels Shawn	OT	95	564	5.9	28	3
Dunigan Matt	WP	85	545	6.4	37	11
Williams Byron	SK	39	541	13.9	59	1
Ulmer Terryl	SK	37	517	14.0	96	0
Wallace Darrell	SK	69	514	7.4	35	3
Drawhorn Anthony	OT	66	504	7.6	29	0

PLAYER		NO	YDS	AVE	LG	TD
Sandusky Jim	ED	25	502	20.1	64	3
McVey Andrew	CG	78	498	6.4	22	2
Mazzoli Nick	HM	45	462	10.3	41	0
Johnstone Chris	WP	63	455	7.2	33	5
Burke Patrick	OT	27	415	15.4	30	0
Lewis Kip	TO	29	401	13.8	41	3
Hudson Warren	TO	70	399	5.7	28	4
Volpe Jon	BC	59	387	6.6	45	4
Boyko Bruce	SK	52	372	7.2	28	2
Brown Andre	OT	19	287	15.1	31	0
	TO	5	84	16.8	35	1
Total		24	371	15.5	35	1
Flutie Doug	CG	75	362	4.8	50	11
Barnes Reggie	OT	56	361	6.4	40	0
Burgess Tom	OT	75	347	4.6	18	3
Knight Lee	HM	61	346	5.7	22	2
Brown Errol	SK	30	302	10.1	26	0
	WP	6	35	5.8	16	0
Total		36	337	9.4	26	0
Jackson Patrick	TO	29	326	11.2	30	1
McPherson Don	HM	55	299	5.4	30	2
Farthing Dan	SK	32	289	9.0	25	0
Archer David	SC	60	287	4.8	18	2
Stewart Tony	CG	61	283	4.6	20	1
Ellingson James	OT	25	281	11.2	23	2
Richards Dwight	OT	65	280	4.3	24	0
Total		65	280	4.3	24	0
Christensen Jay	ED	16	273	17.1	38	0
Crifo Rob	WP	2	21	10.5	11	0
	OT	15	252	16.8	39	2
Total		17	273	16.1	39	2
Hanson Ryan	BC	22	265	12.0	48	1
Pruitt James	SC	15	260	17.3	46	2
Izquierdo J.P.	ED	23	256	11.1	28	1
Dickey Terry	TO	30	255	8.5	24	0
Morris Gary	ED	19	252	13.3	38	2
Mitchel Eric	ED	8	232	29.0	51	0
Brownlee Vincent	BC	17	230	13.5	36	0
McAdoo Derrick	TO	27	229	8.5	28	1
Jackson Alfred	WP	19	226	11.9	60	2
Walling Brian	ED	43	225	5.2	17	0
Bushey Paul	HM	35	218	6.2	30	1
Everett Tre	SK	19	200	10.5	44	1
	SC	2	10	5.0	13	1
Total		21	210	10.0	44	2
Hailey Ken	BC	11	201	18.3	36	0
Pearce Matt	WP	35	200	5.7	30	1
Hill Lonzell	HM	14	197	14.1	54	1
Willis Larry	TO	11	195	17.7	54	1
Brown Albert	SK	8	192	24.0	108	1
Smith Donald	WP	11	192	17.5	73	1
Bouyer Willie	SC	15	175	11.7	31	2
Culpepper Willie	SK	11	174	15.8	34	1
Slack Reggie	TO	27	172	6.4	31	2
Hood John	HM	44	167	3.8	14	1
Mimbs Robert	BC	26	163	6.3	28	2
Barrett Danny	BC	42	162	3.9	15	4
Winey Ken	TO	15	159	10.6	31	0
Dinnall Dave	HM	15	156	10.4	63	1
Taylor Steve	CG	23	155	6.7	32	2
Bellamy Mike	WP	16	149	9.3	32	0
Marshall Blake	ED	37	139	3.8	13	3
Fuller Joe	OT	10	135	13.5	22	0
Skinner Chris	BC	18	131	7.3	29	2
Smith Darrell K.	ED	12	108	9.0	18	0
Parrish Doug	ED	8	106	13.3	26	0

FUMBLES

PLAYER		TOTAL FUMBLES	FUMBLES LOST	PER CENT LOST
McPherson Don	HM	11	4	36.4
Burgess Tom	OT	11	2	18.2
Saunders Mike	SK	10	6	60.0
Allen Damon	ED	8	4	50.0
Archer David	SC	8	3	37.5
Richardson Mike	WP	7	4	57.1
Dunigan Matt	WP	7	4	57.1
Philpot Cory	BC	7	3	42.9
Oliphant Mike	SC	6	6	100.0
Slack Reggie	TO	6	5	83.3
Clemons Mike	TO	6	5	83.3
McVey Andrew	CG	6	2	33.3
Bryant Blaise	SK	2	2	100.0
	WP	3	3	100.0
Total		5	5	100.0
Flutie Doug	CG	5	5	100.0
Ham Tracy	TO	5	3	60.0
Osbaldiston Paul	HM	5	2	40.0
Williams Henry	ED	5	2	40.0
Barrett Danny	BC	5	2	40.0
Floyd Lucius	ED	4	4	100.0
McManus Danny	BC	4	4	100.0

PLAYER		TOTAL FUMBLES	FUMBLES LOST	PER CENT LOST
Perkins Bruce	HM	4	3	75.0
Drawhorn Anthony	OT	4	3	75.0
Walker Scott	HM	4	2	50.0
Hudson Warren	TO	4	2	50.0
Pringle Mike	SC	4	2	50.0
Turner Lonnie	BC	3	3	100.0
Baysinger Freeman	SC	1	1	100.0
	BC	2	2	100.0
Total		3	3	100.0
Brown Eddie	ED	3	3	100.0
Stewart Tony	CG	3	2	66.7
Jenkins Keyvan	CG	3	2	66.7
Joseph Darren	OT	3	2	66.7
Richards Dwight	OT	3	2	66.7
	TO	0	0	0.0
Total		3	2	66.7
Winfield Earl	HM	3	2	66.7
Williams David	WP	3	2	66.7
Austin Kent	SK	3	2	66.7
Chomyc Lance	TO	3	2	66.7
Crouch Jim	SC	3	2	66.7
Dixon Titus	SC	3	1	33.3

PLAYER		TOTAL FUMBLES	FUMBLES LOST	PER CENT LOST
Cameron Bob	WP	3	1	33.3
Crawford Derrick	CG	3	1	33.3
Millington Sean	BC	3	1	33.3
Ulmer Terryl	SK	2	2	100.0
Walker Wayne	OT	2	2	100.0
Zatylny Walter	TO	2	2	100.0
Alphin Gerald	WP	2	2	100.0
Clark Matt	BC	2	2	100.0
Daniels Shawn	OT	2	2	100.0
Climie Jock	OT	2	2	100.0
Johnstone Chris	WP	2	2	100.0
Westwood Troy	WP	2	2	100.0
Boyko Bruce	SK	2	2	100.0
Hailey Ken	BC	2	1	50.0
Jones Terrence	OT	2	1	50.0
Moore Will	CG	2	1	50.0
Harris Rod	SC	2	1	50.0
Wallace Darrell	SK	2	0	0.0
Benjamin Nick	WP	2	0	0.0
Graybill Michael	OT	2	0	0.0

Todd Dillon - HM, Mike Vanderjagt - SK, Vincent Brownlee - BC, Willie Culpepper - SK, Patrick Jackson - TO, Ken Winey - TO, Willie Bouyer - SC, Mike Kerrigan - TO, Wayne Lammle - TO, Dale Sanderson - HM, Allen Pitts - CG, Blake Marshall - ED, Tre Everett - SK/SC, Walter Stanley - OT, Jim Sandusky - ED, Charles Franks - SC, Pete Gardere - SC, Terry Baker - OT, Brian Wiggins - CG, Charles Thompson - SC, Remi Trudel - OT, Doug Parrish - ED, Joe Fuller - OT, Eddie Taylor - BC, Paul Bushey - HM, Dave Dinnall - HM, Greg Battle - WP, Brent Matich - SK, Peewee Smith - CG, Andre Francis - BC, Lee Knight - HM, Lui Passaglia - BC, Reggie Pleasant - TO, Bobby Evans - WP, Ray Elgaard - SK, David Ridgway - SK, Jeff Fairholm - SK, Warren Jones - SK, David Sapunjis - CG, Greg Knox - CG, Glenn Harper - ED, Brian Walling - ED, Rickey Foggie - ED, Michael Soles - ED: **Each have 1 Fumble, 1 Lost, 100.0 percent.**

Robert Mimbs - BC, Ray Macoritti - OT, John Hood - HM, Jon Volpe - BC, Terry Dickey - TO, Rob Davidson - WP, Paul Masotti - TO, Cornell Burbage - HM,Nathaniel Bolton - WP, Alfred Jackson - WP, Byron Williams - SK, Kelian Matthews - SC, Sammy Garza - WP, Carlton Lance - SK, Ken Evraire - HM, Bruce Dickson - ED, Walter Bailey - SC, Stephen Jones - OT, Harold Hasselbach - CG: **Each have 1 Fumble, 0 Lost, 0.0 percent.**

OWN FUMBLES RECOVERED

PLAYER		NO
Burgess Tom	OT	6
McPherson Don	HM	5
Cameron Bob	WP	4
Clemons Mike	TO	3
Philpot Cory	BC	2
Jackson Alfred	WP	2
Perkins Bruce	HM	2
Winfield Earl	HM	2
Chronopoulos Denny	OT	2
Hudson Warren	TO	2
Richardson Dave	HM	2
Gorrell Miles	WP	2
Boyko Bruce	SK	2
McVey Andrew	CG	2
Soles Michael	ED	2
Barrett Danny	BC	2
Archer David	SC	2
Harris Rod	SC	2

Michael Lazecki - OT, Ray Macoritti - OT, Paul MacCallum - BC/OT, Derrick McAdoo - TO, Scott Walker - HM, Tony Stewart - CG, Darrell Beavers - HM, Allen Pitts - CG, Ken Hailey - BC, James Harper - SC, Jonathan Wilson - TO, Andre Brown - OT/TO, Brian Wiggins - CG, Paul Masotti - TO, Cornell Burbage - HM, Mike Saunders - SK, Randy Ambrosie - ED, Darren Joseph - OT, Bruce Dickson - ED, Ray Alexander - BC, Titus Dixon - SC, Walter Bailey - SC, P.J. Martin - HM, Matt Dunigan - WP, David Williams - WP, Barry Wilburn - SK, Stephen Jones - OT, Mike Trevathan - BC, Darren Flutie - BC, Carl Parker - SC, Kip Texada - SC, Anthony Drawhorn - OT, Terrence Jones - OT, Jock Climie - OT, Lance Chomyc - TO, Mike Jovanovich - HM, Chris Johnstone - WP, Chris Walby - WP, Dave Vankoughnett - WP, Brendan Rogers - WP, Donald Smith - WP, Mike Anderson - SK, Mike Anderson - SK, Glen Suitor - SK, Paul Vajda - SK, Dan Farhing - SK, Scott Hendrickson - SK, David Sapunjis - CG, Derrick Crawford - CG, Doug Flutie - CG, Karl Anthony - CG, Bruce Covernton - CG, Damon Allen - ED, Henry Williams - ED, Chris Morris - ED, Glenn Rogers Jr. - ED, Ian Sinclair - BC, Rob Smith - BC, Jim Mills - BC, Sean Millington - BC, Jim Crouch - SC, Mike Pringle - SC, Mike Oliphant - SC, Ron Shipley - SC: **Each have 1 Own Fumble Recovered.**

INTERCEPTION RETURNS

PLAYER		NO	YDS	AVE	LG	TD
Francis Andre	BC	8	153	19.1	71	1
Wilson Don	ED	7	68	9.7	34	1
Anthony Karl	CG	6	145	24.2	115	1
Trudel Remi	OT	6	61	10.2	18	0
Sampson Darryl	WP	6	56	9.3	17	0
Browne Less	BC	5	140	28.0	52	1
Suitor Glen	SK	5	72	14.4	26	0
Texada Kip	SC	5	61	12.2	27	0
Holland Robert	ED	5	56	11.2	34	1
Humphrey Bobby	SC	5	54	10.8	30	0
Murphy Dan	ED	5	47	9.4	32	0
Evans Bobby	WP	5	43	8.6	32	0
Phillips Kim	WP	5	26	5.2	21	0
Smith Donald	WP	5	24	4.8	16	0
Anthony Charles	SK	5	10	2.0	6	0
Rogers Glenn Jr	ED	5	7	1.4	6	0
Randolph Paul	WP	4	74	18.5	37	0
Battle Greg	WP	4	53	13.3	34	1
Wiley John	SC	4	46	11.5	18	0
Vaughn Gerald	CG	4	24	6.0	24	0
Franks Charles	SC	3	93	31.0	53	0
Wilkerson Gary	HM	3	73	24.3	45	2
Lyons Damion	ED	3	70	23.3	36	0
Gordon Charles	OT	3	51	17.0	51	1
Lance Carlton	SK	3	40	13.3	31	1
Van Belleghem Dave	TO	3	38	12.7	30	0
Ervin Corris	TO	0	0	0.0	0	0
	HM	3	31	10.3	16	0
Total		3	31	10.3	16	0
Drawhorn Anthony	OT	3	28	9.3	28	0
Pleasant Reggie	TO	3	27	9.0	24	0
Mero Joe	OT	3	20	6.7	18	0
Brown Albert	SK	3	20	6.7	20	0
Hughes Darren	TO	3	19	6.3	16	0
Knox Greg	CG	3	15	5.0	15	0
Wright Charles	OT	3	12	4.0	9	0
Freeman Corian	WP	1	96	96.0	96	1
	SC	1	15	15.0	15	0
Total		2	111	55.5	96	1
Craft Doug	CG	2	104	52.0	64	1
Fuller Joe	OT	2	65	32.5	40	1
Davis Paschall	SC	2	46	23.0	39	1
Wiseman Todd	HM	2	46	23.0	27	0
Thurman Junior	CG	2	44	22.0	27	0
Kropke John	OT	2	38	19.0	38	0
Dawson Bobby	HM	2	35	17.5	29	1
Parrish Doug	ED	2	35	17.5	31	0
Europe Tom	BC	2	35	17.5	23	0
Bailey Walter	SC	2	29	14.5	29	0
Berry Ed	ED	2	26	13.0	16	0

PLAYER		NO	YDS	AVE	LG	TD
Taylor Eddie	BC	2	21	10.5	19	0
Wilburn Barry	SK	2	21	10.5	18	0
Dzikowicz Jason	WP	2	20	10.0	19	0
Frers Greg	CG	2	10	5.0	10	0
Grier Derek	BC	2	6	3.0	6	0
West James	BC	2	5	2.5	5	0
Jackson Tim	HM	2	3	1.5	3	0
Finch Lonnie	HM	2	0	0.0	0	0
Boyko Allen	WP	1	30	30.0	30	0
Finlay Matt	CG	1	29	29.0	29	0
Hammond Vance	SC	1	28	28.0	28	0
Plummer Bruce	BC	1	27	27.0	27	0
Wallace Jason	SC	1	26	26.0	26	0
Leonard Kenton	CG	1	26	26.0	26	0
Pless Willie	ED	1	26	26.0	26	0
Biggs Raymond	CG	1	26	26.0	26	0
Pope Marvin	CG	1	25	25.0	25	0
Dickson Bruce	ED	1	22	22.0	22	0
Zizakovic Srecko	CG	1	21	21.0	21	0
Wilson Jonathan	TO	1	16	16.0	16	0
Motton John	HM	1	15	15.0	15	0
Eaglin Greg	HM	0	0	0.0	0	0
	CG	1	14	14.0	14	0
Total		1	14	14.0	14	0
Matthews Kelian	SC	1	12	12.0	12	0
Thomas Andrew	TO	1	9	9.0	9	0
Hunter Malvin	ED	1	9	9.0	9	0
Moore Curtis	SC	1	8	8.0	8	0
Watson Ken	CG	1	7	7.0	7	0
Robinson Junior	SC	1	6	6.0	6	0
Cummings Burt	OT	1	6	6.0	6	0
Hardy John	OT	0	0	0.0	0	0
	TO	1	4	4.0	4	0
Total		1	4	4.0	4	0
Wruck Larry	ED	1	4	4.0	4	0
Lewis Loyd	WP	1	3	3.0	3	0
Benson Ken	TO	1	2	2.0	2	0
Hunter Daniel	OT	1	0	0.0	0	0
	BC	0	0	0.0	0	0
Total		1	0	0.0	0	0
Gravely Tracey	BC	1	0	0.0	0	0
Roberts Marshall	SC	1	0	0.0	0	0
Ricks Mark	SK	0	0	0.0	0	0
	TO	1	0	0.0	0	0
Total		1	0	0.0	0	0
Kelson Derrick	HM	1	0	0.0	0	0
Jackson Jeff	BC	1	0	0.0	0	0
Young Brett	OT	1	0	0.0	0	0
Burke Patrick	OT	1	0	0.0	0	0
Mikawos Stan	WP	1	0	0.0	0	0

INTERCEPTION RETURNS (Cont'd)

PLAYER		NO	YDS	AVE	LG	TD
Rogers Brendan	WP	1	0	0.0	0	0
Crum Maurice	SK	1	0	0.0	0	0
Hasselbach Harold	CG	1	0	0.0	0	0
Roberts Jed	ED	1	0	0.0	0	0
Goetz Ron	OT	1	-2	-2.0	0	0
Bary Ousmane	WP	1	-7	-7.0	0	0

FUMBLE RETURNS

PLAYER		NO	YDS	LG	TD
Anthony Charles	SK	6	137	92	1
Matthews Kelian	SC	6	51	42	0
Motton John	HM	4	55	47	0
Hasselbach Harold	CG	4	16	10	0
Baylis Jearld	SK	4	1	1	0
Biggs Raymond	CG	3	21	15	0
Pless Willie	ED	3	2	2	1
Vaughn Gerald	CG	3	2	2	0
Bernard Ray	SK	3	0	0	0
Goods Bennie	ED	3	0	0	1
Eaglin Greg	HM	2	75	75	1
	CG	0	0	0	0
Total		2	75	75	1
Payton Elfrid	WP	2	48	47	1
Battle Greg	WP	2	41	41	1
Millington Sean	BC	2	38	25	1
Parrish Doug	ED	2	32	32	1
Joelson Greg	SC	2	31	31	1
Lance Carlton	SK	2	30	21	1
Blugh Leroy	ED	2	30	30	0
Taylor Eddie	BC	2	19	14	0
Sardo Joe	OT	2	9	9	0
Lyons Damion	ED	2	9	5	0
Whitley Kevin	TO	2	4	4	0
Trevathan Mike	BC	2	4	4	0
Ledbetter Mark	SC	2	4	4	0
Bailey David	HM	2	1	1	0
Moore Curtis	SC	2	1	1	0
Rush Keilly	WP	2	0	0	0
Foudy Sean	BC	2	0	0	0
Woods Tony	ED	2	0	0	0
MacCready Derek	BC	2	0	0	0
Warnock Kent	BC	2	0	0	0
Stumon Gregg	OT	2	0	0	0
Hudson Warren	TO	2	0	0	0
Benson Ken	TO	2	0	0	0
Cofield Tim	HM	2	0	0	0
Mikawos Stan	WP	2	0	0	0
Smith Donald	WP	2	0	0	0
Knox Greg	CG	2	0	0	0
Izquierdo J.P.	ED	2	0	0	0
Humphrey Bobby	SC	2	0	0	0
Browne Less	BC	1	85	85	1
Crum Maurice	SK	1	65	65	0
Boyko Bruce	SK	1	54	54	0
Johnson Alondra	CG	1	46	46	1
Freeman Corian	WP	1	39	39	1
	SC	0	0	0	0
Total		1	39	39	1
Brigance O.J.	BC	1	27	27	0
Lewis Loyd	WP	1	25	25	1
Harding Rodney	TO	1	23	23	0
Finlay Matt	CG	1	21	21	0
Roberts Marshall	SC	1	20	20	0
Dinnall Dave	HM	1	20	20	1
Tsangaris Chris	WP	1	19	19	0
Rogers Glenn Jr	ED	1	15	15	0
Wiley John	SC	1	15	15	0
OShea Mike	HM	1	12	12	0
Wallace Jason	SC	1	10	10	0
Watson Ken	CG	1	10	10	0
Texada Kip	SC	1	9	9	0
Fields Jeff	HM	1	8	8	0
Grier Derek	BC	1	7	7	0
Ricks Mark	SK	0	0	0	0
	TO	1	5	5	0
Total		1	5	5	0
Elliott Bruce	TO	1	5	5	0
Cummings Burt	OT	1	4	4	0
Royal Rickey	HM	1	4	4	0
Wilson Don	ED	1	4	4	0
Snipes Angelo	OT	1	3	3	0
Berry Ed	ED	1	2	2	0
Wright Donovan	BC	1	2	2	0
Allen Zock	BC	1	1	1	0

Antoine Worthman - TO, Dexter Manley - OT, Rickey Jones - ED, Reggie Rogers - HM, Patrick Hinton -WP, Andrew Martin - WP, Andrew Stewart - OT, Derrick Kelson - HM, Ken Hailey - BC, Jeff Jackson - BC, Doug Craft - CG, Charles Gordon - OT, Keith Powe - BC/TO, Brett Williams - HM, Leonard Nelson - SC, Darren Hughes - TO, Bob Torrance -HM, Leonard Johnson - ED, Brian McCurdy - TO, Leon Hatziioannou - WP, Byron Williams - SK, Lou Cafazzo, CG, Brett Young - OT, Remi Trudel - OT, Dave Chaytors - OT, Kim Phillips - WP, Troy Mills - SC, Stu Laird - CG, Earl Winfield - HM, Bruce Dickson - ED, Tyrone Jones - BC, Walter Bailey - SC, Glenn Kulka - OT, Michael Raby - OT, Ron Goetz - OT, Dave Van Belleghem - TO, Bobby Jurasin - SK/OT, Michel Bourgeau - ED, James West, BC, Brent White - SC, Michael Graybill - OT, Blaine Schmidt - TO, Mike Clemons - TO, Dave Richardson - HM, Ray Elgaard - SK, Mark McLoughlin - CG, Karl Anthony - CG, Errol Martin - ED, Malvin Hunter - ED, Glen Scrivener - BC, Tom Europe - BC, Jim Crouch - SC, Vance Hammond - SC, Paschall Davis - SC: **Each have 1 Fumble Return, 0 yards.**

OWN KICKOFFS RECOVERED

PLAYER		NO	YDS	AVE	LG	TD
Pruitt James	SC	1	24	24.0	24	0
Ricks Mark	SK	0	0	0.0	0	0
	TO	1	9	9.0	9	0
Total		1	9	9.0	9	0
Hocking Doug	BC	1	2	2.0	2	0
Brown Errol	SK	1	0	0.0	0	0
	WP	0	0	0.0	0	0
Total		1	0	0.0	0	0
McLennan Spencer	BC	1	0	0.0	0	0
Millington Sean	BC	1	0	0.0	0	0
Moore Curtis	SC	1	0	0.0	0	0

QUARTERBACK SACKS

PLAYER		SACKS	YDS LOST
Payton Elfrid	WP	22	150
Brigance O.J.	BC	20	131
Cofield Tim	HM	18	148
Goods Bennie	ED	14	135
Snipes Angelo	OT	14	128
Jurasin Bobby	SK	14	70
Johnson Will	CG	12	50
Baylis Jearld	SK	11	79
Scrivener Glen	BC	10	79
Roberts Jed	ED	10	69
Pless Willie	ED	9	43
Jones Tyrone	BC	8	71
Laird Stu	CG	8	67
Hill Stewart	SK	8	59
Stumon Gregg	OT	8	58
Goetz Ron	OT	8	54
Bailey David	HM	8	53
Woods Tony	ED	8	45
Ledbetter Mark	SC	8	39
Lewis Loyd	WP	7	54
Robinson Lybrant	OT	7	49
Hasselbach Harold	CG	7	46
Blugh Leroy	ED	7	41
Benefield Daved	OT	6	63
Johnson Alondra	CG	6	53
Martin Errol	ED	6	53
Hunter Malvin	ED	6	34
Johnson Eric	CG	6	32
Kropke John	OT	6	31
Lewis Gary	SK	5	43
Benson Ken	TO	5	30
Williams Brett	HM	5	26
Campbell Mike	TO	5	21
MacCready Derek	BC	5	20
Warren Brian	TO	4	61
West James	BC	4	39
Warnock Kent	BC	4	32
Hammond Vance	SC	4	25
Rogers Reggie	HM	4	21
Bonner Brian	SK	1	8
	OT	3	12
Total		4	20
Booker Vaughn	WP	4	16
Mikawos Stan	WP	3	35
OShea Mike	HM	3	29
Pearce Mark	CG	3	27
Harding Rodney	TO	3	25
Wright Terry	HM	3	25
Rush Keilly	WP	3	24
Randolph Paul	WP	3	24
Johnson Leonard	ED	3	23
Powe Keith	BC	1	6
	TO	2	14
Total		3	20
Joelson Greg	SC	3	19
Zizakovic Srecko	CG	3	17
Freeman Corian	WP	2	9
	SC	1	5
Total		3	14
Team - Saskatchewan	SK	2	31
Moore Curtis	SC	2	27
Bailey Walter	SC	2	25
Lorenz Tim	BC	2	21
Kulka Glenn	OT	2	21
Lance Carlton	SK	2	18
King Emanuel	SC	2	17
Hallman Harold	TO	2	17
Hart Roy	HM	2	15
Zizakovic Lubo	HM	2	15
Wilson Don	ED	2	15
Fields Jeff	HM	2	13
Team - Ottawa	OT	2	12
White Robb	SC	2	12
Allen Zock	BC	2	11
Elliott Bruce	TO	2	9
Battle Greg	WP	2	8
Thornton Randy	SC	1	24
Jackson Enis	TO	1	17
Parrish Doug	ED	1	13
Williams Arnie	TO	1	12
Rogers Glenn Jr	ED	1	12
Matthews Kelian	SC	1	10
Young Brett	OT	1	10
Bernard Ray	SK	1	10
Knox Greg	CG	1	10
Moen Don	TO	1	9
Team - Toronto	TO	1	9
Pleasant Reggie	TO	1	9
Evans Bobby	WP	1	9
Crum Maurice	SK	1	9
Lyles Del	WP	1	8
Pope Marvin	CG	1	8
Brantley Sean	SK	1	7
Proctor Basil	SC	1	7
Thieneman Chris	SC	1	7
Miller Peter	SK	1	7
Thomas Andrew	TO	1	7
Brown Trent	ED	1	7
Drinkwalter Wayne	SK	1	7
Brown Hurlie	SC	1	6
Dickson Bruce	ED	1	6
Team - Hamilton	HM	1	5
Bates Steve	HM	1	4
Hinton Patrick	WP	1	4
MacNeil John	BC	1	4
Donelson Ventson	SK	1	4
Team - B.C.	BC	1	4
Clark Greg	WP	1	2
Team - Calgary	CG	1	2
Milburn Darryl	TO	1	1
Wilson Jonathan	TO	1	1

DEFENSIVE TACKLES

PLAYER		DEFENSIVE TACKLES
Bernard Ray	SK	92
Motton John	HM	84
Wright Terry	HM	82
Benson Ken	TO	80
Crum Maurice	SK	80
Wiley John	SC	80
West James	BC	79
Johnson Alondra	CG	78
Pless Willie	ED	77
Moore Curtis	SC	76
O'Shea Mike	HM	75
Pope Marvin	CG	69
Wilson Don	ED	68
Moen Don	TO	67
Anthony Karl	CG	64
Rogers Glenn Jr	ED	62
Finlay Matt	CG	61
Evans Bobby	WP	60
Allen Zock	BC	59
Bonner Brian	SK	39
	OT	20
Total		59
Wruck Larry	ED	59
Baylis Jearld	SK	56
Goetz Ron	OT	54
Sampson Darryl	WP	54
Drawhorn Anthony	OT	52
Smith Donald	WP	51
Pleasant Reggie	TO	50
Browne Less	BC	49
Hunter Malvin	ED	49
Randolph Paul	WP	49
Ervin Corris	TO	25
	HM	24
Total		49
Anthony Charles	SK	48
Taylor Eddie	BC	48
Matthews Kelian	SC	47
Blugh Leroy	ED	46
Brigance O.J.	BC	46
Jackson Tim	HM	46
Battle Greg	WP	45
Parrish Doug	ED	45
Berry Ed	ED	44
Europe Tom	BC	44
Suitor Glen	SK	44
Wilkerson Gary	HM	43
Eaglin Greg	HM	33
	CG	8
Total		41
Hughes Darren	TO	40
Murphy Dan	ED	40
Wallace Jason	SC	40
Brown Albert	SK	39
Ledbetter Mark	SC	39
Vaughn Gerald	CG	38
Watson Ken	CG	38
Francis Andre	BC	37
Hammond Vance	SC	37
Humphrey Bobby	SC	37
Texada Kip	SC	37
Burke Patrick	OT	36
Hill Stewart	SK	36
Van Belleghem Dave	TO	36
Donelson Ventson	SK	35
Leonard Kenton	CG	35
Lyons Damion	ED	35
Mikawos Stan	WP	35
Royal Rickey	HM	35
Whitley Kevin	TO	35
Lance Carlton	SK	34
Dawson Bobby	HM	33
Phillips Kim	WP	33
Hallman Harold	TO	32
Knox Greg	CG	32
Snipes Angelo	OT	32
Holland Robert	ED	31
Kropke John	OT	31
Lewis Gary	SK	31
Stumon Gregg	OT	31
Trudel Remi	OT	31
White Robb	SC	31
Castello Keith	TO	30
Cofield Tim	HM	30
Harding Rodney	TO	29
Hasselbach Harold	CG	29
Thurman Junior	CG	29
White Brent	SC	29
Wilburn Barry	SK	29
Young Brett	OT	29
Craft Doug	CG	28
Payton Elfrid	WP	28
Robinson Junior	SC	28
Davis Darrick	SC	27
Goods Bennie	ED	27
Hart Roy	HM	27
Johnson Will	CG	27
Williams Arnie	TO	27
Foudy Sean	BC	26
Franks Charles	SC	26
Lyles Del	WP	26
Robinson Lybrant	OT	26
Wiseman Todd	HM	26
Fuller Joe	OT	25
Gordon Charles	OT	25
Jones Tyrone	BC	25
Jurasin Bobby	SK	25
Lewis Loyd	WP	25
Martin Errol	ED	25
Woods Tony	ED	25
Dzikowicz Jason	WP	24
Scrivener Glen	BC	24
Thomas Andrew	TO	24
Johnson Eric	CG	23
Plummer Bruce	BC	23
Warnock Kent	BC	23
Kelson Derrick	HM	22
MacCready Derek	BC	22
Zizakovic Srecko	CG	22
Campbell Mike	TO	21
Sims Kelly	BC	21
Wright Charles	OT	21
Jackson Enis	TO	20
Nelson Leonard	SC	20
Ricks Mark	SK	2
	TO	18
Total		20
Freeman Corian	WP	13
	SC	7
Total		20
Warren Brian	TO	20
Williams Brett	HM	20
Booker Vaughn	WP	18
Finch Lonnie	HM	18
Laird Stu	CG	18
Mero Joe	OT	18
Raby Michael	OT	18
Bailey Walter	SC	17
Jackson Jeff	BC	17
Lewis Tahaun	TO	17
Roberts Jed	ED	17
Bailey David	HM	16
Fields Jeff	HM	16
Rush Keilly	WP	16
Hardy John	OT	1
	TO	15
Total		16
Wilson Jonathan	TO	15
Davis Paschall	SC	13
Allen Michael	OT	9
	BC	4
Total		13
Hunter Daniel	OT	4
	BC	9
Total		13
Clark Greg	WP	12
Grier Derek	BC	12
Henry Tommy	SC	12
Kulka Glenn	OT	12
Ulmer Terryl	SK	12
Walcott Ken	OT	12
Zizakovic Lubo	HM	12
Andrews Romel	HM	11
Bary Ousmane	WP	11
Biggs Raymond	CG	11
Colar Heshimu	SC	11
Hinton Patrick	WP	11
Stewart Andrew	OT	11
Gravely Tracey	BC	10
Jackson Alfred	WP	10
Scott Mark	HM	10
Weber Gord	OT	10
MacNeil John	BC	9
Powe Keith	BC	4
	TO	5
Total		9
Benefield Daved	OT	8
Brown Trent	ED	8
Chaytors Dave	OT	8
Francis Ron	BC	8
Gray Michael	WP	8
Middleton Mike	SK	8
Milburn Darryl	TO	8
Bates Steve	HM	7
Brantley Sean	SK	7
Hennig Roger	HM	7
Hocking Doug	BC	7
Joelson Greg	SC	7
Winfield Earl	HM	7
Dickson Bruce	ED	6
Graybill Michael	OT	6
Hailey Ken	BC	6
Johnson Leonard	ED	6
Lorenz Tim	BC	6
Pringle Mike	SC	6
Rogers Reggie	HM	6
Brown Errol	SK	4
	WP	2
Total		6
Beavers Darrell	HM	5
Burbage Cornell	HM	5
Cummings Burt	OT	5
Dunigan Matt	WP	5
Elliott Bruce	TO	5
Hazard Manny	TO	5
Henry Maurice	OT	5
Hilk Brian	TO	5
McCurdy Brian	TO	5
Millington Sean	BC	5
Roberts Marshall	SC	5
Rogers Brendan	WP	5
Williams David	WP	5
Wright Donovan	BC	5
Bourgeau Michel	ED	4
Brown Hurlie	SC	4
Cartwright Ricardo	SK	4
Daymond Irv	OT	4
Evraire Ken	HM	4
Fairholm Jeff	SK	4
Hatziioannou Leon	WP	4
Jauch Joey	HM	4
Jovanovich Mike	HM	4
Proctor Basil	SC	4
Rashovich Dan	SK	4
Sardo Joe	OT	4
Rodehutskors Steven	BC	1
	TO	3
Total		4
Trevathan Mike	BC	4

Allen Boyko - WP, Eddie Brown - ED, Reggie Clark - TO, Robert Clark - TO, Mike Clemons - TO, Anthony Florence - WP, Miles Gorrell - WP, John Hood - HM, Chris Johnstone - WP, Emanuel King - SC, Kip Lewis - TO, Paul Masotti - TO, Will Moore - CG, Dan Payne - SK, Mark Pearce - CG, Michael Soles - ED, Chris Thieneman - SC, RandyThornton - SC, Paul Wetmore - SK, OT, Lonnie Turner - BC, Brian Walling - ED, Patrick Wayne - TO, David Westerbrooks - SC, Brian Wiggins - CG, Gerald Wilcox - WP, Byron Williams - SK: **Each have 3 Defensive Tackles.**

Gerald Alphin - WP, Nick Benjamin - WP, David Black - WP, Nathaniel Bolton - WP, Willie Bouyer - SC, Tom Burgess - OT, Rod Connop - ED, Rob Crifo - WP, OT, Shawn Daniels - OT, Mark Dennis - HM, Dave Dinnall - HM, Titus Dixon - SC, Tre Everett - SK, SC, Lucius Floyd - ED, Darren Flutie - BC, Greg Frers - CG, Charles Fryar - SC, Steve Gabbard - SC, Pete Giftopoulos - HM, Ryan Hanson - BC, Scott Hendrickson - SK, Darren Joseph - OT, Steve Krupey - ED, Derrick McAdoo - TO, Spencer McLennan - BC, Andrew McVey - CG, Mike Oliphant - SC, Bruce Perkins - HM, Rocco Romano - CG, Mike Saunders - SK, Rob Smith - BC, Charles Thompson - SC, Freeman Baysinger - SC, BC, Wayne Walker - OT, Ken Winey - TO: **Each have 2 Defensive Tackles.**

Damon Allen - ED, Mike Anderson - SK, Kent Austin - SK, Terry Baker - OT, Danny Barrett - BC, Paul Bushey - HM, Wayde Butler - ED, Lou Cafazzo - CG, Jay Christensen - ED, Denny Chronopoulos - OT, Matt Clark - BC, Matt Clarke - BC, Jock Climie - OT, Derrick Crawford - CG, Rob Davidson - WP, Terry Dickey - TO, Wayne Drinkwalter - SK, Marc Dube - CG, Mike Dumaresq - ED, Ray Elgaard - SK, James Ellingson - OT, Dan Farthing - SK, Doug Flutie - CG, Chris Green - TO, James Harper - SC, Warren Hudson - TO, Shawn Jones - BC, Stephen Jones - OT, Terrence Jones - OT, Mike Kerrigan - TO, Lee Knight - HM, Dexter Manley - OT, P.J. Martin - HM, Nick Mazzoli - HM, Brett McNeil - WP, Don, McPherson - HM, Maurice Miller - SC, Gary Morris - ED, Yo Murphy - BC, Donald Narcisse - SK, Lou Olsacher - TO, Carl Parker - SC, Matt Pearce - WP, David Pitcher - SK, Allen Pitts - CG, Dave Richardson - HM, Eros Sanchez - HM, Jim Sandusky - ED, David Sapunjis - CG, Blaine Schmidt - TO, Tyrone Shavers - OT, Ron Shipley - SC, Ian Sinclair - BC, Reggie Slack - TO, Darrell K. Smith - ED, Daryle Smith - TO, Peewee Smith - CG, Derek Steele - TO, Tony Stewart - CG, Todd Storme - CG, Jamie Taras - BC, Rod Harris - SC, Andre Brown - OT, TO, Blaise Bryant - SK, WP, Chris Tsangaris - WP, Mike Vanderjagt - SK, Chris Walby - WP, Troy Westwood - WP, Henry Williams - ED, Antoine Worthman - TO, Kari Yli-Renko - TO, Blair Zerr - CG: **Each have 1 Defensive Tackle.**

SPECIAL TEAMS TACKLES

Brendan Rogers - WP: **31 Special Teams Tackles.**

Chris Tsangaris - WP, Mike Pringle - SC: **30 Special Teams Tackles each.**

Ron Goetz - OT, J.P. Izquierdo - ED: **24 Special Teams Tackles each.**

Spencer McLennan - BC, Sean Millington, BC: **22 Special Teams Tackles each.**

Troy Mills - SC, Bruce Dickson - ED, Trent Brown - ED, Joe Sardo - OT: **20 Special Teams Tackles each.**

Paul Bushey - HM, Greg Frers - CG, David Pitcher - SK: **19 Special Teams Tackles each.**

Ken Benson - TO: **18 Special Teams Tackles.**

Dave Van Belleghem - TO, Michael Graybill - OT, Brooks Findlay - SK, Raymond Biggs - CG, Brian Walling - ED, Doug Hocking - BC: **17 Special Teams Tackles each.**

Bruce Elliott - TO: **16 Special Teams Tackles.**

Dan Rashovich - SK, Pete Giftopoulos - HM, Richard Nurse - HM, Alondra Johnson, CG - Blair Zerr, CG - 15, Donovan Wright - BC, Paschall Davis - SC: **15 Special Teams Tackles each.**

Frank Marof - CG, Gerald Vaughn - CG, Jed Roberts - ED, Errol Martin - ED: **14 Special Teams Tackles each.**

Marc Dube - CG, Brian McCurdy - TO, Kelian Matthews - SC, Dave Dinnall - HM, Rickey Royal - HM, Darryl Sampson - WP, Bobby Evans - WP, Bruce Boyko - SK, O.J. Brigance - BC: **13 Special Teams Tackles each.**

Dean Noel - OT, Jim Jauch - HM, Leon Hatziioannou - WP, Walter Bailey - SC, Jason Dzikowicz - WP, Roger Hennig - HM, Joey Jauch - HM, Dan Murphy - ED: **12 Special Teams Tackles each.**

Gord Weber - OT, Blaine Schmidt - TO, Mike O'Shea - HM, Malvin Hunter - ED: **11 Special Teams Tackles each.**

George Nimako - TO, Greg Eaglin - HM, CG, Kenton Leonard - CG, Ken Watson - CG, Michel Bourgeau - ED, Gregg Stumon - OT, Paul Randolph - WP, Donald Smith - WP, Tom Europe - BC: **10 Special Teams Tackles each.**

Ken Hailey - BC, Charles Thompson - SC, Carlton Lance - SK, Peewee Smith - CG, Keith Castello - TO, Wayne Drinkwalter - SK, Ryan Hanson - BC, Mike Oliphant - SC: **9 Special Teams Tackles each.**

SPECIAL TEAMS TACKLES (Cont'd.)

Doug Craft - CG, Jonathan Wilson - TO, Del Lyles - WP, Darren Hughes - TO, Brett Young - OT, Mark Pearce - CG, Ventson Donelson - SK, Dwight Richards - OT/TO, Zock Allen - BC, Mark Scott - HM, Brian Bonner - SK/OT, Patrick Burke - OT, Charles Anthony - SK, Sean Fleming - ED: **8 Special Teams Tackles each.**

Andrew Thomas - TO, Allen Boyko - WP, Larry Wruck - ED, Ray Elgaard - SK, Dan Farthing - SK, Maurice Crum - SK, Rod Harris - SC: **7 Special Teams Tackles each.**

Lorne King - TO, Peter Miller - SK, Terry Baker - OT, Ernie Schramayr - OT, Daved Benefield - OT, Greg Joelson - SC, Chris Munford - SK, Remi Trudel - OT, Duane Forde - WP, Michael Allen - OT/BC, Jock Climie - OT, Mike Jovanovich - HM, Ray Bernard - SK, David Sapunjis - CG, Greg Knox - CG, Michael Soles - ED: **6 Special Teams Tackles each.**

Mike Middleton - SK, Daniel Hunter - OT/BC, Tracey Gravely - BC, Darrell Beavers - HM, Bruce Plummer - BC, Charles Gordon - OT, Terryl Ulmer - SK, Nick Benjamin - WP, Alfred Jackson - WP, Don Moen - TO, Carl Parker - SC, John Motton - HM, Andrew McVey - CG, Karl Anthony - CG: **5 Special Teams Tackles each.**

Kelly Sims - BC, Joe Mero - OT, Quinn Magnuson - WP, Doug Parrish - ED, Manny Hazard - TO, Ken Walcott - OT, Errol Brown - SK/WP, Kip Texada - SC, Andrew Murray - TO, Todd Wiseman - HM, Marvin Pope - CG, Don Wilson - ED, Damion Lyons - ED: **4 Special Teams Tackles each.**

Jeff Croonen - TO, Patrick Wayne - TO, Heshimu Colar - SC, Arnie Williams - TO, Burt Cummings - OT, Jay Christensen - ED, Sean Foudy - BC, Tommy Henry - SC, Charles Franks - SC, Pete Gardere - SC, Leonard Johnson - ED, Joe Fuller - OT, Ed Berry - ED, Willie Pless - ED, Lee Knight - HM, Brent White - SC, Shawn Daniels - OT, Lubo Zizakovic - HM, Will Moore - CG, Glenn Rogers Jr. - ED: **3 Special Teams Tackles each.**

Brian Hilk - TO, Antoine Worthman - TO, Robert Hardy - SC, Paul MacCallum - BC/OT, John Hood - HM, Patrick Hinton - WP, Marshall Roberts - SC, Ken Winey - TO, Mark Ricks - SK/TO, Rob Davidson - WP, Derek Grier - BC, Jacques Moreau - OT, Junior Thurman - CG, Keith Powe - BC/TO, Leonard Nelson - SC, Bill Henry - HM, Ousmane Bary - WP, Kevin Whitley - TO, Kim Phillips - WP, Darren Joseph - OT, Bruce Perkins - HM, Michael Raby - OT, P.J. Martin - HM, Greg Battle - WP, Barry Wilburn - SK, Matt Pearce - WP, James West - BC, Reggie Pleasant - TO, Terry Wright - HM, Bob Cameron - WP, Albert Brown - SK, Doug Davies - CG, Tony Martino - CG, Matt Clarke - BC, John Wiley - SC, Bobby Humphrey - SC, Robb White - SC, Mark Ledbetter - SC: **2 Special Teams Tackles each.**

Carl Coulter - OT, Butch Hadnot - TO, Kelly Trithart - SK, Paul Cranmer - SK, Shawn Jones - BC, Charles Fryar - SC, Maurice Miller - SC, John Zajdel - TO, Reggie Clark - TO, Leroy Smith - TO, Ricardo Cartwright - SK, Larry Willis - TO, Lonzell Hill - HM, Derrick McAdoo - TO, Tahaun Lewis - TO, Andrew Martin - WP, Jon Volpe - BC, Emanuel King - SC, Andrew Stewart - OT, Tony Stewart - CG, Bob Gordon - TO, Wayne Lammle - TO, Derrick Kelson - HM, Kasey Dunn - ED, Randy Thornton - SC, Tre Everett - SK/SC, Charles Wright - OT, Chris Skinner - BC, Junior Robinson - SC, Darrick Davis - SC, Andre Brown - OT/TO, Hank Ilesic - TO, Bobby Dawson - HM, Cory Philpot - BC, Paul Masotti - TO, Cornell Burbage - HM, Nathaniel Bolton - WP, Dave Chaytors - OT, Harold Hallman - TO, Mike Saunders - SK, Eros Sanchez - HM, Eddie Taylor - BC, Brian Warren - TO, Corian Freeman - WP/SC, Lybrant Robinson - OT, Walter Zatylny - TO, Lui Passaglia - BC, Anthony Drawhorn - OT, Angelo Snipes - OT, Warren Hudson - TO, Paul Osbaldiston - HM, Chris Johnstone - WP, Elfrid Payton - WP, Jearld Baylis - SK, Leroy Blugh - ED, Jim Crouch - SC, Ron Shipley - SC: **1 Special Teams Tackle each.**

COMBINED TACKLES (20+)

PLAYER		DEFENSIVE TACKLES	SPECIAL TEAMS	SACKS	TOTAL
Benson Ken	TO	80	18	5	103
Johnson Alondra	CG	78	15	6	99
Bernard Ray	SK	92	6	1	99
Pless Willie	ED	77	3	9	89
OShea Mike	HM	75	11	3	89
Motton John	HM	84	5	0	89
Crum Maurice	SK	80	7	1	88
Wright Terry	HM	82	2	3	87
Goetz Ron	OT	54	24	8	86
West James	BC	79	2	4	85
Wiley John	SC	80	2	0	82
Brigance O.J.	BC	46	13	20	79
Moore Curtis	SC	76	0	2	78
Wilson Don	ED	68	4	2	74
Pope Marvin	CG	69	4	1	74
Evans Bobby	WP	60	13	1	74
Moon Don	TO	67	5	1	73
Bonner Brian	SK	39	1	1	41
	OT	20	7	3	30
Total		59	8	4	71
Allen Zock	BC	59	8	2	69
Anthony Karl	CG	64	5	0	69
Baylis Jearld	SK	56	1	11	68
Sampson Darryl	WP	54	13	0	67
Hunter Malvin	ED	49	11	6	66
Rogers Glenn Jr	ED	62	3	1	66
Wruck Larry	ED	59	7	0	66
Randolph Paul	WP	49	10	3	62
Matthews Kelian	SC	47	13	1	61
Finlay Matt	CG	61	0	0	61
Smith Donald	WP	51	10	0	61
Anthony Charles	SK	48	8	0	56
Blugh Leroy	ED	46	1	7	54
Europe Tom	BC	44	10	0	54
Pleasant Reggie	TO	50	2	1	53
Drawhorn Anthony	OT	52	1	0	53
Van Belleghem Dave	TO	36	17	0	53
Murphy Dan	ED	40	12	0	52
Vaughn Gerald	CG	38	14	0	52
Payton Elfrid	WP	28	1	22	51
Eaglin Greg	HM	33	2	0	35
	CG	8	8	0	16
Total		41	10	0	51
Parrish Doug	ED	45	4	1	50
Ledbetter Mark	SC	39	2	8	49
Stumon Gregg	OT	31	10	8	49
Battle Greg	WP	45	2	2	49
Ervin Corris	TO	25	0	0	25
	HM	24	0	0	24
Total		49	0	0	49
Browne Less	BC	49	0	0	49
Taylor Eddie	BC	48	1	0	49
Cofield Tim	HM	30	0	18	48
Hughes Darren	TO	40	8	0	48
Watson Ken	CG	38	10	0	48
Royal Rickey	HM	35	13	0	48
Snipes Angelo	OT	32	1	14	47
Berry Ed	ED	44	3	0	47
Jackson Tim	HM	46	0	0	46
Martin Errol	ED	25	14	6	45
Lance Carlton	SK	34	9	2	45
Leonard Kenton	CG	35	10	0	45
Hill Stewart	SK	36	0	8	44
Donelson Ventson	SK	35	8	1	44
Suitor Glen	SK	44	0	0	44
Burke Patrick	OT	36	8	0	44
Wilkerson Gary	HM	43	0	0	43
Goods Bennie	ED	27	0	14	41
Roberts Jed	ED	17	14	10	41
Hammond Vance	SC	37	0	4	41
Brown Albert	SK	39	2	0	41
Texada Kip	SC	37	4	0	41
Wallace Jason	SC	40	0	0	40
Jurasin Bobby	SK	25	0	14	39
Johnson Will	CG	27	0	12	39

PLAYER		DEFENSIVE TACKLES	SPECIAL TEAMS	SACKS	TOTAL
Knox Greg	CG	32	6	1	39
Humphrey Bobby	SC	37	2	0	39
Lyons Damion	ED	35	4	0	39
Castello Keith	TO	30	9	0	39
Mikawos Stan	WP	35	0	3	38
Young Brett	OT	29	8	1	38
Kropke John	OT	31	0	6	37
Francis Andre	BC	37	0	0	37
Whitley Kevin	TO	35	2	0	37
Trudel Remi	OT	31	6	0	37
Hasselbach Harold	CG	29	0	7	36
Lewis Gary	SK	31	0	5	36
Craft Doug	CG	28	8	0	36
Dzikowicz Jason	WP	24	12	0	36
Pringle Mike	SC	6	30	0	36
Rogers Brendan	WP	5	31	0	36
Hallman Harold	TO	32	1	2	35
White Robb	SC	31	2	2	35
Lyles Del	WP	26	8	1	35
Phillips Kim	WP	33	2	0	35
Scrivener Glen	BC	24	0	10	34
Robinson Lybrant	OT	26	1	7	34
Dawson Bobby	HM	33	1	0	34
Woods Tony	ED	25	0	8	33
Jones Tyrone	BC	25	0	8	33
Lewis Loyd	WP	25	0	7	32
Harding Rodney	TO	29	0	3	32
Thomas Andrew	TO	24	7	1	32
White Brent	SC	29	3	0	32
Bailey Walter	SC	17	12	2	31
Williams Arnie	TO	27	3	1	31
Holland Robert	ED	31	0	0	31
Thurman Junior	CG	29	2	0	31
Wilburn Barry	SK	29	2	0	31
Tsangaris Chris	WP	1	30	0	31
Wiseman Todd	HM	26	4	0	30
Gordon Charles	OT	25	5	0	30
Johnson Eric	CG	23	0	6	29
Hart Roy	HM	27	0	2	29
Brown Trent	ED	8	20	1	29
Robinson Junior	SC	28	1	0	29
Foudy Sean	BC	26	3	0	29
Franks Charles	SC	26	3	0	29
Davis Darrick	SC	27	1	0	28
Fuller Joe	OT	25	3	0	28
Plummer Bruce	BC	23	5	0	28
Davis Paschall	SC	13	15	0	28
Biggs Raymond	CG	11	17	0	28
MacCready Derek	BC	22	0	5	27
Warnock Kent	BC	23	0	4	27
Dickson Bruce	ED	6	20	1	27
Millington Sean	BC	5	22	0	27
Laird Stu	CG	18	0	8	26
Campbell Mike	TO	21	0	5	26
Williams Brett	HM	20	0	5	25
Warren Brian	TO	20	1	4	25
Zizakovic Srecko	CG	22	0	3	25
Sims Kelly	BC	21	4	0	25
Bailey David	HM	16	0	8	24
Freeman Corian	WP	13	1	2	16
	SC	7	0	1	8
Total		20	1	3	24
Wilson Jonathan	TO	15	8	1	24
Hocking Doug	BC	7	17	0	24
Sardo Joe	OT	4	20	0	24
McLennan Spencer	BC	2	22	0	24
Izquierdo J.P.	ED	0	24	0	24
Elliott Bruce	TO	5	16	2	23
Kelson Derrick	HM	22	1	0	23
Graybill Michael	OT	6	17	0	23
Booker Vaughn	WP	18	0	4	22
Wright Charles	OT	21	1	0	22
Ricks Mark	SK	2	2	0	4
	TO	18	0	0	18
Total		20	2	0	22

COMBINED TACKLES (20+) (Cont'd.)

PLAYER		DEFENSIVE TACKLES	SPECIAL TEAMS	SACKS	TOTAL
Nelson Leonard	SC	20	2	0	22
Mero Joe	OT	18	4	0	22
Jackson Enis	TO	20	0	1	21
Weber Gord	OT	10	11	0	21
Frers Greg	CG	2	19	0	21
Benefield Daved	OT	8	6	6	20
Raby Michael	OT	18	2	0	20
Wright Donovan	BC	5	15	0	20
Walling Brian	ED	3	17	0	20
Bushey Paul	HM	1	19	0	20
Pitcher David	SK	1	19	0	20
Mills Troy	SC	0	20	0	20

TACKLES FOR LOSSES

PLAYER		NO	YDS
Baylis Jearld	SK	18	36
Brigance O.J.	BC	10	32
Harding Rodney	TO	7	31
Crum Maurice	SK	7	16
Moore Curtis	SC	6	30
Lewis Gary	SK	6	22
Payton Elfrid	WP	6	19
Lewis Loyd	WP	6	14
Scrivener Glen	BC	6	12
Wilson Don	ED	5	21
Jones Tyrone	BC	5	17
Jurasin Bobby	SK	5	17
Robinson Lybrant	OT	5	16
West James	BC	5	14
OShea Mike	HM	5	14
Goetz Ron	OT	5	13
Hill Stewart	SK	5	13
Allen Zock	BC	5	11
Johnson Eric	CG	5	11
Castello Keith	TO	5	9
Stumon Gregg	OT	4	14
Matthews Kelian	SC	4	12
Johnson Alondra	CG	4	12
Benson Ken	TO	4	11
Woods Tony	ED	4	8
Pless Willie	ED	4	7
Pope Marvin	CG	4	6
Cofield Tim	HM	3	26
Milburn Darryl	TO	3	24
Ledbetter Mark	SC	3	20
White Robb	SC	3	11
MacCready Derek	BC	3	9
Johnson Will	CG	3	9
Brantley Sean	SK	3	8
Hallman Harold	TO	3	8
Hunter Malvin	ED	3	8
Fields Jeff	HM	3	7
White Brent	SC	3	7
Blugh Leroy	ED	3	6
Snipes Angelo	OT	3	5
Evans Bobby	WP	3	5
Moen Don	TO	3	4
Wruck Larry	ED	3	4
Wright Terry	HM	3	4
Goods Bennie	ED	3	4
Hammond Vance	SC	3	4
Raby Michael	OT	2	20
Young Brett	OT	2	18
Wiley John	SC	2	18
Booker Vaughn	WP	2	15
Browne Less	BC	2	15
Campbell Mike	TO	2	7
Freeman Corian	WP	0	0
	SC	2	6
Total		2	6
Bailey David	HM	2	5
Warnock Kent	BC	2	5
Tsangaris Chris	WP	2	4
Wright Donovan	BC	2	4
Hart Roy	HM	2	3
Wallace Jason	SC	2	3
Lyles Del	WP	2	3
Battle Greg	WP	2	3
Zizakovic Lubo	HM	2	3
Rogers Brendan	WP	2	3
Bernard Ray	SK	2	3
Zizakovic Srecko	CG	2	2
Finlay Matt	CG	2	2
Bonner Brian	SK	2	2
	OT	0	0
Total		2	2
Hasselbach Harold	CG	2	2
Eaglin Greg	HM	1	36
	CG	0	0
Total		1	36
Wilkerson Gary	HM	1	27
McCurdy Brian	TO	1	17
Knox Greg	CG	1	15
Marof Frank	CG	1	11
Warren Brian	TO	1	10
Rush Keilly	WP	1	8
Pleasant Reggie	TO	1	7
Thieneman Chris	SC	1	6
Weber Gord	OT	1	6
Burke Patrick	OT	1	6
Trudel Remi	OT	1	5
Hocking Doug	BC	1	5
Jackson Jeff	BC	1	4
Parrish Doug	ED	1	4
Kropke John	OT	1	4
Suitor Glen	SK	1	4

Randy Thornton - SC, Romel Andrews - HM, Paul Randolph - WP, Dan Payne - SK, Raymond Biggs - CG, Glenn Rogers Jr. - ED, Mike Oliphant - SC: **1 for 3 yards each.**

Tahaun Lewis - TO, Sean Foudy, BC, Keith Powe - BC/TO, Brett Williams - HM, Ventson Donelson - SK, Stu Laird - CG, Bobby Humphrey - SC, Paschall Davis - SC: **1 for 2 yards each.**

Basil Proctor - SC, Reggie Rogers - HM, Daniel Hunter - OT/BC, Andrew Stewart - OT, John MacNeil - BC, Leonard Nelson - SC, Greg Joelson - SC, Mark Scott - HM, Andre Francis - BC, Anthony Drawhorn - OT, Charles Anthony - SK, Mike Pringle - SC: **1 for 1 yard each.**

CONVERT (1 POINT)

PLAYER		TRIED	MADE GOOD	PER CENT MADE
McLoughlin Mark	CG	63	63	100.0
Passaglia Lui	BC	62	62	100.0
Crouch Jim	SC	56	56	100.0
Fleming Sean	ED	54	54	100.0
Ridgway David	SK	51	51	100.0
Chomyc Lance	TO	35	35	100.0
Osbaldiston Paul	HM	28	28	100.0
Baker Terry	OT	24	24	100.0
Macoritti Ray	OT	9	9	100.0
MacCallum Paul	BC	1	1	100.0
	OT	5	5	100.0
Total		6	6	100.0
Westwood Troy	WP	69	68	98.6

CONVERTS (2 POINTS)

PLAYER		TRIED	COMP	MADE GOOD
Crawford Derrick	CG	0	1	2
Lewis Kip	TO	0	0	1
Crifo Rob	WP	0	0	1
	OT	0	0	0
Total		0	0	1
Wiggins Brian	CG	1	1	1
Clemons Mike	TO	1	0	1
MacCallum Paul	BC	0	0	0
	OT	1	0	0
Total		1	0	0
Kerrigan Mike	TO	1	1	0
Slack Reggie	TO	3	0	0
Bolton Nathaniel	WP	0	0	0
Walker Wayne	OT	0	0	0
Clark Robert	TO	0	0	0
Hazard Manny	TO	0	0	0
Perkins Bruce	HM	0	0	0
Dunigan Matt	WP	2	1	0
Clark Matt	BC	0	0	0
Burgess Tom	OT	1	0	0
Ham Tracy	TO	1	0	0
McPherson Don	HM	1	0	0
Flutie Doug	CG	5	1	0
Marof Frank	CG	1	0	0
Foggie Rickey	ED	1	0	0
Barrett Danny	BC	1	0	0

BLOCKED KICKS

PLAYER		TOTAL BLOCKED	CONVERTS	PUNTS	FIELD GOALS
Zizakovic Lubo	HM	2	0	0	2
Anthony Charles	SK	2	0	0	2
Crum Maurice	SK	2	0	0	2
Noel Dean	OT	1	0	1	0
Ulmer Terryl	SK	1	0	1	0
Foudy Sean	BC	1	0	1	0
Benefield Daved	OT	1	0	1	0
Johnson Leonard	ED	1	0	0	1
McCurdy Brian	TO	1	0	1	0
Jackson Alfred	WP	1	0	1	0
Cafazzo Lou	CG	1	0	1	0
Dickson Bruce	ED	1	0	1	0
Alexander Ray	BC	1	0	0	1
Finlay Matt	CG	1	0	1	0
Elliott Bruce	TO	1	0	1	0
Drinkwalter Wayne	SK	1	0	0	1
Hasselbach Harold	CG	1	0	0	1
Anthony Karl	CG	1	0	1	0
Wilson Don	ED	1	0	1	0
Millington Sean	BC	1	0	1	0

BEST SINGLE GAME PERFORMANCES IN 1993

* - new CFL Record
** - ties CFL Record

SCORING

INDIVIDUAL:
MOST POINTS: 24 - Sean Fleming, Edm., Edm. at B.C., October 29 (6 FGs, 5 1-Point converts and 1 Single)
MOST TOUCHDOWNS: 3 - Doug Flutie, Cal., Wpg. at Cal., July 6, Eddie Brown, Edm., Sask. at Edm., July 21, Derrick Crawford, Cal., Cal. at Wpg., Aug. 6, Tracy Ham, Tor., Tor. at B.C., Aug. 12, Matt Dunigan, Wpg., Edm. at Wpg., Aug. 13, Eddie Brown, Edm., Edm. at Tor., Aug. 18, Cory Philpot, B.C., Ham. at B.C., Sept. 11, Matt Dunigan, Wpg., Sask. at Wpg., Sept. 12, Earl Winfield, Ham., Edm. at Ham., Sept. 17, Eddie Brown, Edm., Edm. at Sac., Oct. 2, David Williams, Wpg., Sac. at Wpg., Oct. 15, Kent Austin, Sask., Cal. at Sask., Oct. 23, Brian Wiggins, Cal., Cal. at Sask., Oct. 23, Carl Parker, Sac., B.C. at Sac., Nov. 6
MOST FIELD GOALS: 6 - Sean Fleming, Edm., Edm. at B.C., October 29
MOST CONVERTS: 9 - Jim Crouch, Sac., B.C. at Sac., Nov. 6**
TEAM:
MOST POINTS, ONE TEAM: 64 - Sacramento, B.C. at Sac., Nov. 6
MOST POINTS, BOTH TEAMS ONE GAME: 93 - Toronto (38) at B.C. (55), Aug. 12, Calgary (45) at Saskatchewan (48), Oct. 23
MOST TOUCHDOWNS, ONE TEAM: 9 - Sacramento, B.C. at Sac., Nov. 6
MOST TOUCHDOWNS, BOTH TEAMS: 12 - Tor. (5 at B.C. (7), Aug. 12, Cal. (6) at Sask. (6), Oct. 23, B.C. (3) at Sac. (9), Nov. 6

RUSHING

INDIVIDUAL:
MOST TIMES CARRIED: 24 - Mike Richardson, Wpg., Sask. at Wpg., Sept 12
MOST TIMES RUSHED: 181 - Mike Richardson, Wpg., Sask. at Wpg., Sept. 12
MOST TOUCHDOWNS: 3 - Doug Flutie, Cal., Wpg. at Cal., July 6, Tracy Ham, Tor., Tor at B.C., Aug. 12, Matt Dunigan, Wpg., Edm. at Wpg., Aug. 13, Cory Philpot, B.C., Ham. at B.C., Sept. 11, Matt Dunigan, Wpg., Sask. at Wpg., Sept. 12
TEAM:
MOST TIMES CARRIED ONE TEAM: 34 - Wpg., Sask. at Wpg., Sept. 12
MOST TIMES CARRIED BOTH TEAMS: 52 - Edm. (27) at Ott. (25), Oct. 22
MOST YARDS RUSHED ONE TEAM: 302 - Edm. Edm. at B.C., Oct. 29
MOST YARDS RUSHED BOTH TEAMS: 412 - Edm. (302) at B.C. (110), Oct. 29
MOST TOUCHDOWNS ONE TEAM: 5 - B.C., Ham. at B.C., Sept. 11
MOST TOUCHDOWNS BOTH TEAMS: 7 - Ham. (2) at B.C. (5), Sept. 11

PASS RECEIVING

MOST PASSES CAUGHT: 16 - Brian Wiggins, Cal., Cal. at Sask., Oct. 23, (230 yards)
MOST YARDS GAINED: 230 - Brian Wiggins, Cal., Cal. at Sask., Oct. 23, (16 receptions)
MOST TOUCHDOWNS: 3 - Eddie Brown, Edm., Sask. at Edm., July 21, Derrick Crawford, Cal., Cal. at Wpg., Aug. 3, Eddie Brown, Edm., Edm. at Tor., Aug. 18, Manny Hazard, Tor., Ott. at Tor., Aug. 26, Eddie Brown, Edm., Edm. at Sac., Oct. 2, David Williams, Wpg., Sac. at Wpg., Oct. 15, Brian Wiggins, Cal., Cal. at Sask., Oct. 23, Carl Parker, Sac., B.C. at Sac., Nov. 6
AVERAGE GAIN (Min. 10 catches): 22.7 - Manny Hazard, Tor., Ott. at Tor., Aug. 26

PASSING

INDIVIDUAL:
MOST PASSES THROWN: 56 - Kent Austin, Sask., Sask. at Ham., Aug. 6, Doug Flutie, Cal., Cal. at Sask., Oct. 23
MOST COMPLETIONS: 41 - Kent Austin, Sask., Sask. at Tor., Oct. 31**
MOST YARDS PASSING: 601 - Danny Barrett, B.C., Tor. at B.C., Aug. 12 (30 Completions)*
MOST TOUCHDOWNS PASSING: 5 - Doug Flutie,Cal., Cal. at Ott., Aug. 7, Kent Austin, Sask., Ott. at Sask., Aug. 11, Danny Barrett, B.C., Tor. at B.C., Aug.12
BEST PASSING PERCENTAGE (Min 20 Passes): 78.6 - Kent Austin, Sask., Cal. at Sask., Oct. 23
TEAM:
MOST PASSES THROWN ONE TEAM: 56 - Saskatchewan, Sask. at Ham., Aug. 6, Calgary, Cal. at Sask., Oct. 23
MOST PASSES THROWN BOTH TEAMS: 101 - Sask. (54) at B.C. (47), July 9
MOST COMPLETIONS ONE TEAM: 37 - Calgary, Cal. at Sask., Oct. 23
MOST COMPLETIONS TWO TEAMS: 70 - Calgary (37) at Saskatchewan (33), Oct. 23*
MOST YARDS PASSING ONE TEAM: 601 - B.C., Tor. at B.C., Aug.12
MOST YARDS PASSING BOTH TEAMS: 1,093, Cal. (547) at Sask. (546), Oct.23*

PUNTING

MOST PUNTS: 15 - Glenn Harper, Edm., Edm. at Ham., Sept. 17
MOST YARDS: 612 - Glenn Harper, Edm., Edm. at Ham., Sept. 17
BEST PUNTING AVERAGE (Min 5 Punts): 52.9 - Brent Matich, Sask., Sask. at Cal., Oct. 10

PUNT RETURNS

MOST PUNTS RETURNED: 10 - Errol Brown, Sask., Edm. at Sask., July 15
MOST YARDS: 208 - Henry Williams, Edm., Edm. at Cal., Nov. 7

KICKOFF RETURNS

MOST KICKOFFS RETURNED: 9 - Freeman Baysinger, B.C., Edm. at B.C., Oct. 29 (163 yards)
MOST YARDS: 206 - Cory Philpot, B.C. at Cal., Sept. 18

INTERCEPTION RETURNS

MOST INTERCEPTIONS: 3 - Remi Trudel, Ott., B.C. at Ott., Sept. 4
MOST YARDS: 115 - Karl Anthony, Cal., Sask. at Cal., Oct. 10

MISCELLANEOUS

MOST QUARTERBACK SACKS: 5 - Tim Cofield, Ham., Tor. at Ham., Sept. 6**
MOST COMBINED TACKLES: 12 - Maurice Crum, Sask., Sask. at Ham., July 21, Ray Bernard, Sask., Sask. at Sac., July 24
MOST YARDS TOTAL OFFENCE, ONE TEAM: 615 - Calgary, Cal. at Ott., Aug. 6, B.C., Tor. at B.C., Aug. 12
MOST YARDS TOTAL OFFENCE, BOTH TEAMS: 1,174 - Calgary (603) at Sasktachewan (571), Oct. 23

BEST SINGLE PLAY PERFORMANCES

LONGEST RUN FROM SCRIMMAGE: 68 - Blaise Bryant, Wpg., Wpg. at B.C., July 17
LONGEST COMPLETED PASS: 102 - Damon Allen, Edm., Ott. at Edm., Oct. 16 (to Henry Williams)
LONGEST FIELD GOAL: 58 - Sean Fleming, Edm., Edm. at Sac., July 31
LONGEST PUNT: 84 - Brent Matich, Sask., Tor. at Sask., July 31
LONGEST KICKOFF: 95 - Hank Ilesic, Tor., Tor. at Cal., July 28, Hank Ilesic, Tor., Tor. at Sask., July 31, Jim Crouch, Sac., Edm. at Sac., Oct.2
LONGEST PUNT RETURN: 104 - Henry Williams, Edm., Sask. at Edm., July 21
LONGEST UNSUCCESSFUL FIELD GOAL RETURN: 108 - Albert Brown, Sask., B.C. at Sask., Oct. 1
LONGEST INTERCEPTION RETURN: 115 - Karl Anthony, Cal., Sask. at C[illegible]

CFL RECORDS SE

- CLUB RECORDS -

MOST PASSES COMPLETED BOTH TEAMS ONE GAM
70 - Calgary 37, at Saskatchewan 33, Oct. 23, 1993
MOST YARDS PASSING ONE TEAM ONE GAME:
601 - B.C., Tor. at B.C., Aug. 12, 1993
MOST PENTALTIES ONE SEASON (tied):
230 - Saskatchewan, 1993
- Saskatchewan, 1992
MOST QUARTERBACK SACKS ONE GAME:
13 - Edmonton, Edm. at Tor., Aug. 18, 1993
MOST QUARTERBACK SACKS AGAINST ONE GAME:
13 - Toronto, Edm. at Tor., Aug. 18, 1993
MOST ONE-POINT CONVERTS ONE TEAM, ONE GAME: (Tied)
9 - Sacramento, B.C. at Sac., Nov. 6, 1993
- Montreal, Ham. at Mtl., Oct. 20, 1956
- Winnipeg, Ott. at Wpg., Sept. 7, 1984
- Toronto, Cal. at Tor., Sept. 20, 1990

- INDIVIDUAL RECORDS -

ALL-TIME PASS RECEPTION YARDAGE LEADER:
11,253 - Ray Elgaard, Saskatchewan
MOST PASS RECEPTIONS ONE GAME (Tied):
16 - Brian Wiggins, Calgary, Cal. at Sask., Oct. 23, 1993
- Terry Greer, Toronto, Tor. at Ott., Aug. 19, 1983
MOST 1000-YARD PASS RECEIVING SEASONS:
7 - Ray Elgaard, Saskatchewan
MOST PASSES COMPLETED ONE GAME: (Tied)
41 - Kent Austin, Sask., Sask. at Tor., Oct. 31, 1993
- Dieter Brock, Wpg., Wpg. at Ott., Oct. 3, 1981
MOST YARDS RUSHING ONE GAME BY A QUARTERBACK:
170 - Damon Allen, Edm., Oct. 29, 1993 vs. B.C. (15 carries)
MOST YARDS PASSED ONE GAME:
601 - Danny Barrett, B.C., Tor. at B.C., Aug. 12, 1993
MOST TOUCHDOWN PASSES ONE SEASON:
44 - Doug Flutie, Calgary, 1993
MOST CONVERTS ONE GAME (Tied):
9 - Jim Crouch, Sac., B.C. at Sac., Nov. 6, 1993
- Bill Bewley, Mtl., Ham. at Mtl., Oct. 20, 1956
- Trevor Kennerd, Wpg., Ott. at JWpg., Sept. 7, 1984
- Lance Chomyc, Tor., Cal. at Tor., Sept. 20, 1990
MOST CONSECUTIVE FIELD GOALS:
28 - Dave Ridgway, Sask. Streak covered 9 games, starting July 24, 1993 and ending Sept. 19, 1993
ALL-TIME LEADERS PUNT RETURN YARDAGE:
7,046 - Henry Williams, Edmonton
MOST TOUCHDOWNS ON PUNT RETURNS IN ONE GAME (Tied):
2 - Earl Winfield, Ham. , Edm. at Ham. , Sept 17, 1993
- Henry Williams, Edm., Cal. at Edm., Nov. 7, 1993
- Ron Howell, Ham., Ham. at Tor., Sept. 20, 1959
- Henry Williams, Edm., Cal. at Edm., June 27, 1987
- Henry Williams, Edm , Cal. at Edm., Sept. 6, 1991
MOST QUARTERBACK SACKS ONE GAME (Tied):
5 - Tim Cofield, Ham., September 6, 1993, Tor. at Ham.
- Rodney Harding, Tor., September 25, 1988, Edm. at Tor.
- Mack Moore, B.C., September 3, 1962, B.C. at Ott.

1993 WEEKLY GAME-BY-GAME REVIEWS

WEEK #1

Tuesday, July 6 - Winnipeg Blue Bombers 34 @ Calgary Stampeders 54 - 25,486
A rematch of the 1992 Grey Cup Final opened the 1993 CFL season with the champion Calgary Stampeders defeating the Winnipeg Blue Bombers by a lopsided score of 54-34. CFL Most Outstanding Player and Grey Cup MVP QB Doug Flutie was outstanding running, for 76 yds. and 3 TDs while completing 16-of-30 passes for 192 yds. and 2 TD tosses. A 67-yard punt return by Calgary's Peewee Smith opened the scoring just 2:42 into the game. Flutie proceeded to score his 1st TD of the game from the 1-yd. line. Winnipeg QB Matt Dunigan finally got down to business picking apart the Stampeder defence, marching his team 83 yds. down the field and hooking up with David Williams from 4 yds. out (converted by Troy Westwood) for his first TD pass of the night. Flutie then connected with Grey Cup Outstanding Canadian Dave Sapunjis to make the score 20-7 after 15 minutes of play. Winnipeg retaliated with 8 points of its own on a Bob Cameron punt and a 10-yd. TD pass from Dunigan to Gerald Wilcox. After 2 Mark McLoughlin FGs (28 & 42 yds.), Winnipeg conceded 2 points and on the following series, Flutie ran down the field himself on a quarterback sneak from the 50-yd. line to put his team up 34-17 with 8 seconds left in the half. Flutie continued to show his magic in the second half as he ran in for a 6-yd. TD and then set up McLoughlin for his 3rd FG of the night. Dunigan found Gerald Alphin down the lane for a 13-yd. major and Williams once again, while Westwood kicked 2 more FGs, but it was too little, too late as the Stamps put the game out of reach with McLoughlin's 4th FG and a Flutie pass to Derrick Crawford to win their season opener in front of 25,486 fans at McMahon Stadium.

Wednesday, July 7 - Sacramento Gold Miners 23 @ Ottawa Rough Riders 32 - 23,916
The first-ever CFL regular season game to be played by a team based outside of Canada was seen by 23,916 fans at the newly-renamed Frank Clair Stadium in Ottawa. The Rough Riders, who finished third in the East last season, demonstrated that they would be a team to contend with this year as the defence reached QB David Archer seven times throughout the night and picked him off twice to close down the visiting team's offence. Ottawa QB Tom Burgess was outstanding as he completed 21-of-41 attempts for 373 yds. and 3 TDs, including an 11-yd. toss to Stephen Jones, a 61-yarder to Jock Climie in the first half and a 44-yd. throw to W. Walker at the start of the third quarter. The Gold Miners could not get things rolling until the end of the 2nd frame when Archer found Mike Oliphant open from 8 yds. out for the team's first points of the night. Oliphant then opened the second half scoring with his second major, an 8-yd. run. An 18-yd. toss from Archer to Bouyer made the score 28-22 for the home team before Miner K Jim Crouch added a single on a 47-yd. missed FG attempt for a single. Ottawa kicker Terry Baker completed the Otttawa scoring with a FG and a single while Crouch missed his 3rd FG try of the night for another single but it was all Ottawa as they spoiled Sacramento's initiation into the League on this history-making night.

Friday, July 9 - Saskatchewan Roughriders 26 @ B.C. Lions 32 (OT) - 25,849
An outstanding performance by the B.C. Lion defence was the major contributor to the team's victory at B.C. Place Stadium as 25,849 spectators watched their home team defeat the 'Riders in overtime. A total of 24 of the 33 B.C. points were scored as a result of turnovers as the Lions intercepted one pass (Tracy Gravely), knocked down 6 passes, blocked a punt and recovered the ball (Sean Millington), and sacked Saskatchewan QB Kent Austin 6 times throughout the night. Leo pivot Danny Barrett showed his stuff as he completed 28 of 47 passes for 368 yds. and 2 TDs, including a 20-yd. pass to Ray Alexander in the 1st O/T period after rookie punter Mike Vanderjagt was tackled on 3rd down by veteran Less Browne to give up the ball on his own 39-yd. line. Barrett opened the scoring by tossing a 12-yarder to Matt Clark and 18-year veteran K Lui Passaglia counted his first 3-pointer of the night to make the score 10-0 after the 1st quarter. Saskatchewan K Dave Ridgway connected on a boot from 36 yds. out and one from 17 yds. to give his team their first points in the 2nd period while B.C. RB Chris Skinner completed a 25-yd. drive with a 1-yd. TD to give the Lions a 17-6 edge at the half. After exchanging FGs in the 3rd quarter, Passaglia scored his 3rd FG on the night, before Jeff Fairhold caught a spectacular pass from Austin for a 75-yd. major. Another exchange of FGs brougth the score to 26-19. With less than 2 minutes left in the game, Austin again found his receiver, this time CFL Outstanding Canadian Ray Elgaard, to send the game into extra time. Over 900 yards of offence contributed to a wide open contest as the Lions got off to a better start than expected after their 3-15 record of last season.

Saturday, July 10 - Sacramento Gold Miners 14 @ Hamilton Tiger-Cats 30 - 20,307
In anticipation of making history by being the first American team to win a CFL game, the Sacramento Gold Miners were stiffled by the Tiger-Cat defence at Ivor Wynne Stadium. 20,307 spectators watched as their home team's defensive unit showed that they were products of that Steel City mentality, sacking Miner QB David Archer 5 times and picking off 3 of his passes, including a 55-yd. TD return by Gary Wilkerson (who later set up another TD after an interception) to increase Hamilton's lead by 17 points in the last quarter. After playing their first game in Ottawa less than 72 hours before, the Gold Miners were unable to get things going until the second quarter, when K Jim Crouch missed his 4th FG attempt in a row (3 vs. Ottawa) for a single and then finally connected from 17 yds. out to make the score 7-4. Ti-Cat K Paul Osbaldiston booted his first of 3 FGs just before the 2 teams headed for the half-time break. The 3rd quarter only saw Wilkerson's major while a 56-yd. TD pass from QB Don McPherson to Scott Walker put the game out of reach for the visitors. Ozzie's 2nd and 3rd FGs sandwiched Sacramento's only TD, a 4-yd. toss by Archer to Rod Harris to wrap up the win for the Tabbies.

Saturday, July 10 - Toronto Argonauts 8 @ Edmonton Eskimos 38 - 26,336
In a game loaded with errors, the Edmonton Eskimos seemed to have benefitted the most from the biggest trade in CFL history from last January as they trounced the visiting team 38-8 in front of a crowd of 26,336 at Commonwealth Stadium. Former Argonaut QB Rickey Foggie connected with 3 of his receivers while former Tiger-Cat pivot Damon Allen threw 1 TD pass as the Eskimos took a 17-1 lead to the dressing room at half-time. Allen had found Jim Sandusky to open the scoring at 9:34 of the first frame with an 25-yd. toss, while K Sean Fleming booted the convert and then a FG before Lance Chomyc missed on a 35-yd. FG attempt in the 2nd quarter to put the Argonauts on the board. Sandusky then caught an 11-yd. pass from Foggie at 13:07 of the second for his 2nd major of the night. Foggie again connected in the 3rd, as he threw a 46-yd. pass to Henry "Gizmo" Williams and then a 29-yd. strike to Eddie Brown (also a member of the trade). It seemed like Toronto came out ready to play the game in the third quarter as Warren Hudson, the former Winnipeg FB, scrambled into the end zone from the 1-yd. line to get Toronto's first TD of the night after a long 72-yd. drive up the field led by QB Tracy Ham. But that would be all of their scoring as the Eskies took over, racking up their 3 TDs in a row, making the count 38-8 with no points being scored in the final period.

WEEK #2

Wednesday, July 14 - B.C. Lions 40 @ Toronto Argonauts 27 - 26,759
This night saw the Toronto Argonauts open their 1993 home schedule vs. the B.C. Lions in front of 26,759 fans at SkyDome. However, the party was short lived as the Lions came away with a 40-27 victory to run their 1993 record to 2-0 and drop Toronto's record to 0-2. Lions' kicker Lui Passaglia opened the scoring 5 minutes into the first quarter with a single. A Mike Trevathan TD and a Passaglia convert and FG made the score 11-0 after one period. Jon Volpe, in his first game of the year, was the Lions' leading rusher with 17 carries for 89 yds. and got the Lions jump-started in the second frame.He turned the corner on a 12-yd. TD run to make the score 18-0 Lions early in the second quarter. Argonaut pivot Tracy Ham got the Boatmen on the scoreboard with a 9-yd. TD run. Volpe plunged in from 3 yds. out while Chomyc added a 19-yd. FG making the score B.C. 25, Toronto 10 at the half. The B.C. offence picked up where it left off early in the third quarter as Danny Barrett, who was 19-of-33 for 231 yds. on the day, hooked up with Ray Alexander for a 7-yd. TD pass to give the Lions a 32-10 lead. Chomyc added a 27-yd. FG to close the gap to 32-13 after 3 periods. After a Passaglia single, fullback Warren Hudson hooked up with QB Mike Kerrigan, who replaced an injured Tracy Ham in the second quarter, for an 11-yd. TD. Toronto's defence was tough and got them the ball back and they capitalized as Mike Clemons hauled in a 12-yd. Kerrigan pass for the major, The comeback fell short however as a costly Illegal Substitution penalty vs Toronto gave the Lions a 1st down on the Argo 43. 5 plays later the Lions' Chris Skinner put the game out of reach with a 13-yd. TD run.

Thursday, July 15 - Saskatchewan Roughriders 23 @ Edmonton Eskimos 22 - 17,566
The Sakatchewan Roughriders sent 17,566 opening night fans home happy on "Roger Aldag Night" in Regina, as they defeated the Edmonton Eskimos by a score of 23-22. The hometown 'Riders, on the heels of 17 second half points edged the visiting Edmonton Eskimos 23-22. The only points of the first quarter came off the foot of Saskatchewan's Dave Ridgway as he booted a 43-yd. FG to give them the early 3-0 lead. Ridgway picked up where he left off in the second quarter by kicking a 25-yd. FG just 10 seconds into the 2nd frame. Edmonton's Blake Marshall pulled the Eskimos even as he plunged in from 1-yd. out. Sean Fleming added the extra point to give Edmonton a 7-6 half-time lead. Willie Pless, the 1992 Most Outstanding Defensive Player, got the Eskimos on the board early as he recovered a loose ball in the Saskatchewan endzone for the TD. The Fleming convert made the score 14-6 in favour of the Eskimos. Jeff Fairholm, who was the Roughriders' leading pass catcher on the evening with 3 catches for 109 yds., hauled in his only major of the game, a 64-yd. pass from Austin. Ridgway added the convert to pull the 'Riders to within 1 after 3 periods. The Roughriders took the lead just 0:26 into the 4th quarter as Byron Williams was on the receiving end of Austin's 2nd TD pass of the game, this one a 25-yarder. Ridway's convert attempt was good to give Saskatchewan a 20-14 advantage. Rickey Foggie who was in in relief of starter Damon Allen, tied the game with a 14-yd. TD run and Fleming gave them the lead with the extra point at 3:07 of the 4th quarter. Ridgway connected on a 50-yd. FG to give Saskatchewan a 23-21 lead with just 2:31 remaining to play. Fleming had an opportunity to win the game for the Esks but his 52-yd FG attempt was short, and good for a single only.

Friday, July 16 - Hamilton Tiger-Cats 23 @ Ottawa Rough Riders 22 - 20,016
For the Ottawa Rough Riders the game against the Hamilton Tiger-Cats was a replay of a game they would rather forget. Paul Osbaldiston, as he did last November in the Eastern Semi-Final, booted a 27-yd. FG with no time on the clock to give the visiting Tiger-Cats a 23-22 win over the hometown Rough Riders in front of 20,016 fans at Frank Clair Stadium. The only scoring in the first quarter was a result of a 41-yd. pass by Don McPherson to Joey Jauch for a TD. The Rough Riders responded in the second quarter by scoring 13 unanswered points as Terry Baker booted 2 FGs and added a convert. Tom Burgess then hooked up with James Ellingson for a 3-yd. TD. Hamilton took the lead late in the quarter as Don MacPherson threw a 7-yd. TD strike to Earl Winfield and Osbaldiston added the convert to make the half-time score 14-13 in favour of the Tabbies. "Ozzy" increased Hamilton's lead to 4 early in the 3rd quarter, connecting on a 16-yd. FG. The lead was short-lived as Wayne Walker ran under a Burgess pass for a 15-yd. TD. The Baker convert made the score 20-17 in favour of the Rough Riders at the end of 3 periods. Osbaldistion had a chance to tie the game with 0:53 remaining on the clock but his 39-yd. FG attempt was wide. The Hamilton defence held tough and the offence put together a last second drive, culminating in an Osbaldistion FG from 27 yds. out with no time left on the clock to give the Tabbies a 21-20 victory.

Saturday, July 17 - B.C. Lions 36 @ Winnipeg Blue Bombers 14 - 20,665
The Winnipeg Blue Bombers scored 23 first-half points and went on to defeat the visiting B.C. Lions 36-14 in front of 20,665 home town fans in Winnipeg. The Bombers opened the scoring as Troy Westwood connected on a 45-yd. and a 19-yd. FG to give the Bombers an early 6-0 lead. Sean Millington gave the Lions their only lead of the game as he returned a fumble 25 yds. for a TD making the score 7-6 in favour of the Lions after one frame. The Bombers' offence got jump started in the second half as they put 17 unanswered points on the board. Chris Johnstone opened the scoring with a 1-yd. TD run with Westwood adding the convert before Matt Dunigan hooked up with Nathaniel Bolton for a 57-yd. major. Westwood then added the convert and then chipped in with a 47-yd. FG to give the Bombers a 23-7 half-time lead. Rookie sensation Blaise Bryant galloped 68 yds. for a TD to open the third quarter scoring while Westwood added the convert and a 45-yd. FG to give them a 33-7 lead after three frames. Mike Trevathan opened up the fourth quarter scoring hauling in an 18-yd. pass from Danny McManus. The Lui Passaglia convert made the score 33-14. Westwood added a 50-yd. FG to make the final score 36-14 in favour of the Bombers.

Saturday, July 17 - Calgary Stampeders 38 @ Sacramento Gold Miners 36 - 20,082
The defending Grey Cup champion Calgary Stampeders and the newly-formed Sacramento Gold Miners made CFL history as they hooked up in the first ever CFL regular season game to be played between an American and a Canadian team on American soil. The game, witnessed by 20,082 enthusiastic Sacamento fans, was a shootout between the 1992 CFL Most Outstanding Player, Doug Flutie and Gold Miners' QB David Archer, who combined, passed for almost 900 yds.. The Gold Miners jumped into the lead following a Mark McLoughlin single, as Robert Hardy ran in from 1-yd. out. Jim Crouch added the convert and then recorded a single and then added a 27-yd. FG to give the Miners' a short-lived lead. McLoughlin closed the gap by booting a 20-yd. FG to make the score 14-10 in favour of the Gold Miners at the end of the first-half. It was all Calgary in the third quarter as they got on the board early and appeared to be running away with the game as Allen Pitts was on the receiving end of a 37-yd. pass from Flutie. Flutie then found Will Moore and Dave Sapunjis, who both ran into the end zone to give the Stamps a commanding 31-14 lead. However, the Gold Miners rebounded with Rod Harris catching a 13-yd. TD pass from Archer with Crouch adding the convert to close the gap to 10 points after 3 quarters. Mike Oliphant opened up the fourth quarter scoring 8-yd. TD and Willie Bouyer then hooked up with Archer for a 12-yd. TD pass. Calgary regained the lead as Flutie ran in from 3-yds. out, with the McLoughlin convert, the Stamps led 38-35 with 3:09 left to play. The Gold Miners had an opportunity to tie the game late in the final quarter but a 40-yd. FG attempt was wide and Sacramento's comeback bid fell short giving the Stampeders a 38-36 victory.

WEEK #3

Wednesday, July 21 - Saskatchewan Roughriders 3 @ Edmonton Eskimos 35 - 27,894
Edmonton's Eddie Brown scored 3 TDs while teammate Henry "Gizmo" Williams chipped in with 2 more as the hometown Edmonton Eskimos upped their record to 2-1 with a 35-3 victory over the Saskatchewan Roughriders. Williams got the Esks on the board early in the 1st quarter hooking up with QB Damon Allen for a 20-yd. TD strike. Allen then caught Brown in the open for his 1st TD of the game, a 14-yd. pass to make the score 14-0 in favour of the Eskimos after 1 period. The "Giz" electrified the fans 12:08 into the 2nd frame as he took a Brent Matich punt back 89 yds. for the TD. Saskatchewan kicker Dave Ridgway added the 'Riders' only points of the game with a 17-yd. FG on the last play of the half to make the score 21-3 in favour of the Eskimos at the half. Eddie Brown accounted for the only scoring of the second half hooking up with Allen on passes of 35 and 9 yds. to send the 27,894 in attendance at Commonwealth Stadium home happy.

Thursday, July 22 - Hamilton Tiger-Cats 25 @ Toronto Argonauts 9- 27,373
The 2-0 Hamilton Tiger-Cats travelled down the highway to meet their longtime rivals the Toronto Argonauts. The Argonauts, however came up on the short end of a 25-9 decision in front of 27,373 fans at SkyDome. The 2 teams traded FGs in the 1st quarter as Hamilton kicker Paul Osbaldiston got the Tabbies on the board first, connecting on a 38 yarder, while his Toronto counterpart, Lance Chomyc, was good from 45 yds. out. The "Osbaldiston Factor" accounted for all of the scoring in the 2nd quarter as he connected on FGs from 17 and 20 yds. out while chipping in with a single to make the score 10-3 in favour of Hamilton at half-time. Ozzy opened up the 2nd-half scoring with a single off a 40-yd. FG attempt which gave the 'Cats an 11-3 lead. Lubo Zizakovic and rookie Greg Eaglin teamed up to put the game out of reach as Zizakovic blocked a Chomyc FG attempt and Eaglin scooped it up and scampered 75 yds. for the major. Toronto scored their only TD of the game on a 27-yd. TD pass by Tracy Ham to Robert Clark. John Hood sealed the victory with just 37 seconds left as he ran in from 8 yds. out to make the final score 25-9 in favour of the Tiger-Cats.

Friday, July 23 - Ottawa Rough Riders 18 @ Winnipeg Blue Bombers 21 - 19,030
The Winnipeg Blue Bombers scored 14 4th quarter points to complete their comeback and defeat the visiting Ottawa Rough Riders 21-18 in front of 19,030 damp spectators at Winnipeg Stadium. Winnipeg kicker Troy Westwood opened the scoring with a 32-yd. FG which was all of the scoring in the 1st quarter. Westwood gave the Bombers an early 4-0 lead in the second quarter as he booted a 47-yd. single. Rough Rider kicker Terry Baker got them on the scoreboard with a 21-yd. FG to close the gap to one but Westwood added another FG, this time from 43 yds. out, to give the Bombers a 7-3 lead. Baker added a single off a 48-yd. punt to make the score at the half 7-4 in favour of the Bombers. Baker opened the second-half scoring with 7 points, a 28-yd. single off a missed FG, a 35-yd. FG and a 11-yd. FG to give the Riders an 11-7 edge after 3 frames. Ottawa increased their lead 10:06 into the 4th quarter as WR Wayne Walker hooked up with QB Tom Burgess for a 26-yd. TD, but the Bombers stormed back as LB Greg Battle made a spectacular one-handed interception and returned it 34 yds. for the major. With the missed convert the Bombers trailed by just 4 with 8:12 remaining to play. Winnipeg completed the comeback as Allen Boyko ran under a 27-yd. Matt Dunigan pass with just 4 seconds on the clock to make the final score 21-18.

Saturday, July 24 - Calgary Stampeders 34 @ B.C. Lions 20 - 31,199
The Lions scored first on a 47-yd. FG by Lui Passaglia, but that was all the points B.C. could manage as Calgary built up a 23-3 lead by half-time. Mark McLoughlin scored 3 FGs (22, 29 and 12 yds.), and Doug Flutie threw 2 TDs passes, to Dave Sapunjis (40 yds.) and Allen Pitts (23 yds.). Early in the 3rd quarter Flutie hit Sapunjis for his 2nd TD of the game from 12 yds. out to make the score 30-3, before B.C. began their comeback bid. Passaglia connected on a 21-yd. FG and QB Danny Barrett passed 32 yds. to Mike Trevathan for a major. McLoughlin added a single and a 36-yd. FG, before Barrett again hit Trevathan (2 yds.) for a TD to round out the scoring on the night. A crowd of 31,199 was on hand at B.C. Place Stadium to see the game. Flutie was good on 25-of-40 for 413 yds. and 3 TDs.

Saturday, July 24 - Saskatchewan Rough Riders 26 @ Sacramento Gold Miners 37 - 17,319
There were 17,319 spectators at Hornet Field to witness the first regular-season win for the Gold Miners. Sacramento built up an early lead as QB David Archer connected with Mike Oliphant (33 yds.), Carl Parker (8 yds.) and Titus Dixon (90 yds.), and Jim Crouch added a 37-yd. FG to give the home squad a 24-0 advantage early in the 2nd quarter. The first two Miner TDs came after Saskatchewan QB Kent Austin was intercepted. The Roughriders fought back as Austin hit Jeff Fairholm with a 36-yd. pass and then took the ball in himself from the 1-yd. line for the TD. The teams traded FGs to end the quarter and at half-time the score read Sacramento 27, Saskatchewan 17. Dave Ridgway booted 3 FGs in the 2nd half (24, 14 and 32 yds.), but Crouch connected from 34 yds. out and Mike Pringle dashed 25 yds. for a major to seal the win for Sacramento. Archer ended the evening good on 25-of-41 for 394 yds. and 3 TDs, while Austin completed 24-of-49 for 385 yds., 3 interceptions and 1 TD.

WEEK #4

Wednesday, July 28 - Toronto Argonauts 36 @ Calgary Stampeders 39 - 25,510
In front of 25,510 fans at McMahon Stadium, Keyvan Jenkins scored his 2nd TD of the night on a 21-yd. play where he dove into the end zone with less than a minute to play to tie the game, setting up K Mark McLoughlin up for a 38-yd. FG to steal the victory away from Toronto. McLoughlin opened and closed the scoring for the 1st half on a missed 47-yd. FG before the 3:00 mark of the 1st quarter but then was good on a 42-yarder just before heading into the dressing room. Argo K Lance Chomyc replied with a successful 40-yd. boot for 3 points and a convert on a TD by starting QB Tracy Ham to Larry Willis (a 54-yd. toss) gave the Argos 10 points. With Calgary leading 21-11 in the 3rd quarter on TDs by Keyvan Jenkins (11-yd. pass from Doug Flutie) and an 18-yarder thrown to David Sapunjis, Toronto's Mike Kerrigan came in to replace Ham and got the ball rolling, hooking up with Paul Masotti on a 72-yd. pass and run play. Calgary answered that with a 15-yd. FG by McLoughlin and a 20-yd. pass to Allen Pitts. Kerrigan then found Mike "Pinball" Clemons (10-yd. throw) and Kip Lewis (41-yd. pass), who also caught a 2-point convert pass on Clemons' TD, in the fourth quarter to close the gap and then put his team ahead of the Grey Cup Champions. But the Stamps were determined to not let this one get away and Flutie made sure of that with his accuracy to Jenkins for his 2nd TD out of 9 catches for a total of 121 yds. on the night. Several others had key games as Pitts was good for 183 yds. on 10 catches and a TD, Sapunjis contributed 90 yds. on 7 receptions and 1 TD while for Toronto, Masotti caught 6 passes for 170 and 1 TD and Willis caught 3 throws for 89 yds. and a major. Flutie racked up a total of 477 yds. on 34-of-52 attempts for 4 TD passes while in a quarter and a half, Kerrigan was good on 13-of-20 for 279 yds. and 3 TDs.

Thursday, July 29 - Winnipeg Blue Bombers 40 @ Hamilton Tiger-Cats 11 - 16,198
On a wet and overcast night at Ivor Wynne Stadium, 16,198 fans watched as their team was overcome by a strong Blue Bomber squad. Matt Dunigan got his team going as teammate Keilly Rush scooped up 2 fumbles by Hamilton QB Don McPherson in the opening quarter. Dunigan passed a 26-yd. TD to Michael Richardson, who was playing in his 1st game of the year, and just over five minutes later, ran in himself from the 1-yd. line to put his team up 14-0 after the 1st quarter. P Bob Cameron added a single on a 51-yd. punt and K Troy Westwood booted a 50-yd. FG to add to his 2 converts before Hamilton K Paul Osbaldiston answered to that with a 43-yd. punt single and a 12-yd. FG of his own to close the gap to 18-4 at the half. Tiger-Cat WR Earl Winfield returned a punt 71 yds. for a major at 2:52 of the 3rd quarter for the only scoring of that period but after Richardson rushed in untouched from 4 yds. out at the start of the final frame, McPherson was replaced by rookie Eros Sanchez. However, Sanchez was unable to generate much more offence as he faced a stiff wind. Winnipeg's Donald Smith scored a TD for his team as he ran back a blocked punt 20 yds. before Westwood's single from 46 yds. made it 33-11 with less than 2 minutes remaining in the game. Chris Johnstone added the final score as he carried the ball from 6 yds. out and Westwood converted it for a 40-11 final. Dunigan completed the evening with a record of 23-of-37 attempts for 257 yds., no ints., 1 TD pass and 1 rushing TD as he carried the ball himself 7 times for 17 yds..

Friday, July 30 - Ottawa Rough Riders 24 @ B.C. Lions 28 - 22,667
A 39-yd. TD pass by Lion QB Danny Barrett to newcomer Lonnie Turner in the 3rd quarter may have been the turning point for B.C. as they defeated the visiting Rough Riders in front of a hometown crowd of 22,667 fans at B.C. Place. Veteran K Lui Passaglia capped off a 26-yd. drive with a 48-yd. FG at 9:24 of the opening quarter. Ottawa K Terry Baker had problems connecting as he missed his first of 4 FG attempts at 13:34 for a single, making the score 3-1 to end the first period. B.C. rookie Cory Philpot scored on a 10-yd. TD pass from Barrett to begin the second period before Ottawa responded with a Tom Burgess 1-yd. TD run to close the gap to 2 points. Passaglia added a 15-yd. FG while Ottawa countered with a Terry Baker 38-yd. single to make the score at the half 13-9 in favour of the Lions. Ottawa got on the board first in the 2nd half as James Ellingson hooked up with Burgess for an 8-yd. TD strike to give the Rough Riders their first lead of the game. However, the lead was short-lived as the Lions stormed back with Barrett connecting with Turner for a 39-yd. TD. The see-saw battle continued though as Jock Climie hauled in a Tom Burgess pass for a 22-yd. TD giving the Riders a 23-20 lead. Philpot electrified the B.C. Place crowd on the ensuing kickoff, returning it 91 yds. for the major to put the Lions in the lead to stay. The two teams traded 4th quarter singles to make the final B.C. 28-Ottawa 24.

Saturday, July 31 - Toronto Argonauts 17 @ Saskatchewan Roughriders 36 - 18,212
The Toronto Argonauts continued their Western road swing with a game against the Saskatchewan Roughriders at Taylor Field in Regina. The Argonauts on the heels of a solid effort, albeit in a losing cause, two nights earlier in Calgary, not only had fatigue against them but also a gusting 59 km/h prairie wind. It was all Saskatchewan in the first quarter as they put 12 points on the board with the wind at their backs. Brent Matich opened the scoring with an 84-yd. single, while the defence came up strong and forced the Argos to give up a 2-point safety rather than attempting the punt. Saskatchewan kicker Dave Ridgway later connected on a 25-yd. FG and Kent Austin plunged in from 1-yd. out to make the score 12-0 in favour of the Roughriders after 1 period of play. Lance Chomyc got Toronto on the scoreboard early in the 2nd quarter with a 55-yd. single. Ridgway then added his 2nd FG of the contest, this one coming from 27 yds. out. Toronto QB Mike Kerrigan, who was making his first start of the year, hooked up with Kip Lewis for their only major of the game at 9:47 of the 2nd frame. Austin then took it in himself from 2 yds. out for his second TD of the game to make the score at the half 23-8 in favour of the Green Riders. Lance Chomyc accounted for the only scoring of the 3rd quarter, connecting from 19, 52 and 50 yds. out. Jeff Fairholm hooked up with Austin 8 seconds into the fourth quarter to scuttle any thought of an Argonaut comeback. Ridgway closed out the scoring with 2 FG's to make the final 37-17 Saskatchewan.

Saturday, July 31 - Edmonton Eskimos 43 @ Sacramento Gold Miners 11 - 17,827
The Sacramento Gold Miners, hot off their first-ever CFL win over Saskatchewan, entertained the Edmonton Eskimos in front of 17,827 fans at Sacramento's Hornet Field. The Eskimos showed no mercy however, putting up 23 2nd quarter points to lead them to a convincing 43-11 win over the 1-4 Gold Miners. It didn't take long for Edmonton to get on the board as Sean Fleming, who booted 5 FGs on the evening, connected on a 34-yd. attempt. Sacramento's Jim Crouch evened the score at 3 as he made good on a 26-yd. attempt. However, this was as close as the 'Miners would get as the Edmonton offence got its wheels in motion with 3 Fleming FGs (19, 45 and 58 yds.) and fullback Blake Marshall added 2 TDs, the second coming off a fake FG attempt, to put the Eskimos up by 20, 23-3 at the half. Crouch opened up the 3rd quarter scoring with a single off a 43-yd. missed FG. Bennie Goods was "Johnny on the spot" recovering a loose ball in the end-zone for Edmonton's 3rd TD of the game. Sacramento opened the 4th quarter with their only TD of the game as Rod Harris hooked up with Archer for an 8-yd. TD strike. Fleming added his 5th FG, this one from 19 yds. and Eddie Brown rounded out the scoring running under a 59-yd. Damon Allen pass to make the final count 43-1 for the Esks.

WEEK #5

Tuesday, August 3 - Calgary Stampeders 40 @ Winnipeg Blue Bombers 35 - 23,869
Once again, it was an outstanding demonstration by QB Doug Flutie which gave his team their 5th straight victory of the season over the Blue Bombers in front of 23,869 fans at Winnipeg Stadium. Flutie passed for 481 yds. and 5 TDs completing 31-of-51 passes and ran for over 100 yds.. Winnipeg opened the scoring as they capped off their opening drive of 68 yds. in 10 plays with a 20-yd. TD pass from QB Matt Dunigan to SB Gerald Wilcox. Just 1:24 later, Winnipeg LB Corian Freeman stripped the ball from Flutie and ran it back 39 yds. for a score putting his team up 14-0. A 65-yd. drive was completed with a 23-yd. TD toss from Flutie to Peewee Smith and followed up by a single point by Bomber P Bob Cameron to make the score 15-7 after 1 quarter. Calgary K Mark McLoughlin booted a 28-yd. FG in the 2nd quarter to bring the Stamps within 5 points but Dunigan led his team downfield as the Stampeders were penalized twice, enabling the Bomber pivot to run in from the 1-yd. line for the TD closing out the 1st half scoring at 22-10. The visiting team came out flying in the 2nd half as Flutie tossed the 1st of 3 TDs to Derrick Crawford, a 21-yd. pass to end a 69-yd. drive. Dunigan replied to that with a 23-yd. TD pass to David Williams to put his team up by 12 points before Flutie found Crawford again, this time for 11 yds.. McLoughlin, who converted all 5 TDs, was wide on a 46-yd. FG attempt for a single while Westwood was able to connect on a 23-yarder to put the Bombers up 32-25 with 14:48 remaining in the game. A 73-yd., 7-play drive was highlighted by a 6-yd. TD pass from Flutie to Crawford, giving him his 3rd TD on 9 catches for 123 yds. on the evening, followed by a 24-yd. major pass to Allen Pitts, who caught 5 passes for 100 yds.. Winnipeg then tried to recover but could only manage a 27-yd. FG by Westwood with 4:53 left with the Stamps still leading by 4 points. McLoughlin ended the scoring with a single on a 32-yd. FG attempt to make the final count 40-35. Will Moore also had a great night as he connected with Flutie for 150 yds. on 6 catches while Winnipeg's leading receiver was Wilcox with 94 yds. and 1 TD on 5 receptions. Dunigan finished the evening with 20-of-41 passes for 276 yds. and 2 TDs and ran 5 times for 36 yds. and 1 TD.

Thursday, August 5 - Sacramento Gold Miners 35 @ Toronto Argonauts 37 - 28,612
It took the Toronto Argonauts 6 games but they finally notched a win defeating the Sacramento Gold Miners by a 37-35 margin. The Argonauts got on the scoreboard first as WR Paul Masotti hooked up with QB Mike Kerrigan for a 32-yd. TD. However, the Gold Miners wasted no time in catching up as RB Mike Oliphant broke loose for a 52-yd. TD run. Toronto regained the lead as kicker Lance Chomyc connected from 24 yds. out to put the Argos up 10-7 after 1 period of play. The Argonauts' run-and-shoot offence came out gunning in the second quarter, as Kerrigan hooked up with Kip Lewis for a 7-yd. TD and then connected with Masotti on a 15-yd. pass for his second TD of the game. Sacramento kicker Jim Crouch added a single off a missed FG to make the score 24-8 at the half. Newcomer Derrick McAdoo plunged in from 1-yd. out to open the second half scoring. With 1:54 left in the 3rd quarter Crouch added a 29-yd. FG to pull the 'Miners to within 20 after 3 frames. Chomyc, who was good on all three of his FG attempts in this game, opened up the fourth quarter scoring with an 18-yd. FG. It was at 3:22 into the final frame that the Gold Miners came alive as Crouch booted a 37-yd. FG to get the ball rolling for the Miners. Freeman Baysinger then took a Lance Chomyc punt back 59 yds. for Sacramento's second TD of the game. Oliphant, who carried the ball 5 times for 73 yds., picked up his second TD of the game turning the corner from 4 yds. out. Chomyc added another FG, this one from 32 yds. out to hinder the Sacramento comeback bid. Rod Harris hooked up with Archer from 2 yds. out with 1 second on the clock but the Argonauts hung on to win 37-35 in front of 28,612 fans at SkyDome.

Friday, August 6 - Saskatchewan Roughriders 37 @ Hamilton Tiger-Cats 10 - 16,061
Dave Ridgway booted 5 FGs and Ray Elgaard caught 2 TD passes leading the Saskatchewan Roughriders to a 37-10 victory over the hometown Hamilton Tiger-Cats. It didn't take long for the "Big Green Offensive Machine" to strike as quarterback Kent Austin, who was good on 28-of-56 passes for 462 yds. and 2 TDs, hooked up with Ray Elgaard for a 25-yd. TD to give the 'Riders a lead that they would never relinquish. Hamilton kicker, Paul Osbaldiston booted a 37-yd. FG accounting for the only Hamilton scoring of the half. Saskatchewan punter Brent Matich was credited with a 49-yd. single and Mike Saunders scored from 3 yds. out to make the score 24-3 in favour of the Roughriders at the half. Ridgway accounted for all of the Green Riders' points in the 2nd quarter as he was good from 10, 45 and 15 yds. out. Hamilton running back Bruce Perkins scored the Tabbies' only TD of the game taking it in from 11 yds. out to narrow the gap to 24-10 after 3 periods of play. Ridgway added two more FGs to open up the 4th quarter connecting from 34 and 20 yds. out. Elgaard ran under a 43-yd. Austin pass to make the final score 37-10. Elgaard was on the receiving end of 21 passes for 210 yds. (LG-43) and 2 TDs, checking in as the 'Riders top receiver on the day.

Friday, August 6 - Calgary Stampeders 47 @ Ottawa Rough Riders 22 - 27,341
The Calgary Stampeders upped their record to 6-0 defeating the Ottawa Rough Riders 47-22 in front of 27,341 Rider faithful at Frank Clair Stadium. Calgary quarterback Doug Fluite set a Calgary team passing record completing 24-of-38 passes for 556 yds. with 1 INT and 3 TD throws. Ottawa actually got on the board first as quarterback Tom Burgess ran in from 1-yd. out giving the Riders an early 7-0 lead. It took the Stamps approximately 9 minutes to tie the game up as Flutie hooked up with Will Moore for a 55-yd. pass and run to even the score at 7. The Riders re-captured the lead at 10:46 into the opening frame as Burgess hooked up with Wayne Walker for a 75-yd. TD. The Stampeders rounded out the first quarter scoring as Mark McLoughlin booted a 29-yd. FG and Flutie found Dave Sapunjis, who ranked second amongst Calgary pass receivers with 5 receptions for 108 yds., for a 66-yd. TD to make the score 16-14 in favour of the defending Grey Cup champions. The second quarter belonged to the Stamps as they put up 17 unanswered points. McLoughlin, who was good on all 4 of his FG attempts, connected from 41, 39 and 22 yds. out. LB Alondra Johnson scooped up a fumble and scampered 46 yds. for the TD put the Stampeders up 33-14 at the half. Ottawa kicker Terry Baker opened up the 3rd quarter scoring with a 56-yd. single. Flutie continued his great game by hooking up with Crawford for a 75-yd. TD to close out the 3rd quarter scoring. Wayne Walker scored his second TD of the game 31 seconds into the 4th quarter and was on the receiving end of an 11-yd. Burgess toss. Flutie then added the icing on the cake however, as he took it in himself from 4 yds. out to make the final 47-22.

Saturday, August 7 - B.C. Lions 39 @ Edmonton Eskimos 23 - 25,236
The B.C. Lions, who are clearly the most improved team in the CFL this season, came into Commonwealth Stadium and accomplished something a number of teams have not been able to do: come away with a victory. The Lions scored 24 second quarter points and added another 15 in the second half to come away with a 39-23 victory and sole possesion of second place in the Western Division. The only scoring in the first quarter was a Sean Fleming single at 10:49 of the first quarter. It didn't take long for the Lions to reply as Lui Passaglia connected on a 25-yd. FG to give B.C. a 3-1 lead. The Eskimos went ahead for the only time in the game as Kasey Dunn was on the receiving end of a 28-yd. Damon Allen pass. B.C. pivot Danny McManus, who was making his first start of the season hooked up with Cory Philpot for an 11-yd. TD strike to give the Lions a 10-8 lead. This tandem joined forces again, this time from 17 yds. out putting the Lions up 17-8. The Eskimos climbed back to within 2 as Rickey Foggie, who was in in relief of starter Damon Allen, took it in himself from 1-yd. out. McManus found WR Ray Alexander in the open for a 14-yd. TD pass to send the Lions into the locker room with a 24-15 lead at the half. B.C. opened up the 2nd half scoring as Passaglia connected from 13 yds. out then Bruce Plummer caught Eddie Brown in the end zone for a safety giving the Lions a 29-15 lead. The Eskimos replied with a 3-yd. TD run by Damon Allen to narrow the gap to 7 after 3 periods of play. Mike Trevathan opened up the 4th quarter scoring as McManus spotted him in the open for a 28-yd. TD. The kickers rounded out the scoring as Glenn Harper added a single while Passaglia connected on his 3rd FG of the day to make the final 39-23 in front of 25,236 fans at B.C. Place.

WEEK #6

Wednesday, August 11 - Ottawa Rough Riders 28 @ Saskatchewan Roughriders 45 - 20,254
The Saskatchewan Roughriders sent the 20,254 in attendance at Taylor Field home satisfied as they handed the visiting Ottawa Rough Riders a 45-28 loss. The win upped the Western "Riders' record to 4-3, good for sole possession of 3rd place in the Western Division. The Green 'Riders scored first as the CFL's leading rusher, Mike Saunders, carried it in from 4 yds. out to give them a lead that they would never relinquish. Less than a minute later, SB Jeff Fairholm hooked up with Kent Austin for a 23-yd. TD strike to put Saskatchewan out in front by 14 early in the 1st quarter. At 8:03 into the opening frame they struck again, this time it was Willie Culpepper running under an Austin pass for a 23-yd. TD. Ottawa kicker Terry Baker got them on the board on the final play of the 1st quarter by booting a 28-yd. FG to make the score 21-3 in favour of the Western 'Riders after 1. Saskatchewan wasted little time in the 2nd quarter as Saunders hooked up with Austin for a 30-yd. TD, giving him 2 in the game. After an Ottawa safety, Don Narcisse ran under an 8-yd. Austin attempt for their second major of the 2nd quarter. Ottawa WR Jock Climie finally got them into the TD column as he ran under a 25-yd. Tom Burgess toss for the TD. Baker added a single at 13:04 of the 2nd frame to close out the 1st half scoring with Saskatchewan on top with a 35-13 lead. Baker added yet another single 3:25 into the 3rd frame and then Ottawa DB Charles Gordon stepped in front of an Austin pass and took it back 51 yds. for the major to narrow the gap to 35-21 at the end of 3 quarters of play. Saskatchewan negated any thoughts of an Ottawa comeback 43 seconds into the final frame as Narcisse hooked up with Austin for the 2nd time, this one a 10-yd. TD catch, putting them up 42-21. Saskatchewan K Dave "Robo Kicker" Ridgway added a 17-yd. FG to close out the Green 'Riders' scoring but this was all they would need as Ottawa's Stephen Jones hauled in a 13-yd. Terrence Jones pass with just 5 seconds left to make the final 45-28 in favour of Saskatchewan.

Thursday, August 12 - Toronto Argonauts 38 @ B.C. Lions 55 - 24,691
The Toronto Argonauts travelled into B.C Place in search of their 1st road victory in 12 tries. There to greet them however was one Danny Barrett, who single-handedly put to rest any chances the Argonauts had of winning this contest. Barrett led the Lions to a 55-38 win over Toronto and in the mean time set a new CFL record for Most Passing Yd.s in One Game as he threw for 601 yds.. It did not take long for the Lions' offence to get on track as on the 3rd play of the game, Sean Millington grabbed a little dump pass and scampered 70 yds. for the TD then Cory Philpot plunged in from 1 yd. out. With the Argonauts' starting QB Mike Kerrigan on the sidelines with a broken collar bone, it was up to Tracy Ham to come in and lead the Argos down the field. He then took the ball in himself from 7 yds. out to get Toronto on the scoreboard. Mike Trevathan scooped up a ball fumbled by Millington and continued on into the end-zone to put the Lions up by 14 at the end of the 1st quarter. Toronto K Lance Chomyc and his B.C. counterpart, Lui Passaglia, traded FGs to round out the 2nd quarter. Ham once again took matters into his own hands and ran it in from 15 yds. out for his second major of the game. Millington then hooked up with Barrett for a 15-yd. TD strike before Ham and WR Manny Hazard countered with a 46-yd. pass and run for the TD making the score 31-24 in favour of the Lions at the half. Toronto scored the only points of the 3rd period as Robert Clark hooked up with Ham for a 19-yd. TD to tie the game at 31 each after 3 periods of play. Passaglia put the Lions out in front 8 seconds into the 4th quarter with an 18-yd. FG but the Argos stormed back with Tracy Ham running in from 11 yds. out for his 3rd major of the game. Barrett put the Lions up once again, this time for good, running it in himself from 1-yd. out. The Lions put the game out of reach as Trevathan hooked up with Barrett for a 29-yd. TD to make the score 48-38 in favour of the Lions. SB Matt Clark added a little more insurance at 10:57 as he ran under a 55-yd. Barrett toss to make the final 55-38 B.C. in front of 24,691 at B.C. Place.

Friday, August 13 - Edmonton Eskimos 11 @ Winnipeg Blue Bombers 53 - 25,786
Winnipeg quarterback Matt Dunigan ran for 3 TDs and added another 3 passing, leading the Blue Bombers to a convincing 53-11 win over the Edmonton Eskimos before 25,786 spectators at Winnipeg Stadium. Dunigan got the Bombers on the scoreboard 3:32 into the opening frame as he scored the 1st of his 3 TDs, this one a 1-yd. run giving Winnipeg a lead that they would not relinquish on this night. Blue Bomber kicker Troy Westwood, who was good on 1-of-2 FG attempts and all 7 of his convert attempts, increased the Bomber lead to 8 with a single off a 50-yd. missed FG attempt to close out the 1st quarter scoring. Dunigan then ran in from 2 yds. out for his 2nd TD of the game and then hooked up with David Williams for an 18-yd. major to round out the 1st half scoring with the Bombers on top 22-0. The Eskimos finally got on the board as kicker Sean Fleming booted a 46-yd. FG and added a single off a 39-yd. attempt. Westwood added a 40-yarder to make the score 25-4 Winnipeg after 3 periods of play. The 4th quarter belonged to the Blue Bombers as they put up 28 points. Dunigan got his team going again as he ran in himself from 2 yds. out for his 3rd major of the game. Winnipeg's Nathaniel Bolton padded the Bomber lead as he was on the receiving end of a 17-yd. Dunigan toss. Fullback Chris Johnstone plunged in from 1-yd. out 9:16 into the 4th quarter to put the Bombers up by 46-4 margin. Edmonton slotback J.P. Izquierdo hooked up with Tom Muecke for an 18-yd. pass and run to account for the only Edmonton TD of the game, with less than 3 minutes left to play before Winnipeg's David Williams rounded out the scoring by hauling in a 25-yd. pass from Sammy Garza to make the final 53-11 in favour of the Blue Bombers.

Saturday, August 14 - Ottawa Rough Riders 7 @ Calgary Stampeders 21 - 24,153
The Calgary Stampeders stretched their record to 7-0 with their 21-7 victory over the visiting Ottawa Rough Riders which was seen by 24,153 Stampeder faithful in Calgary. The Stampeders, who are just 4 games shy of setting a new CFL record for Most Wins at the Start of a Season, tallied the only points of the 1st half as Mark McLoughlin booted a 30-yd. FG and added a single to send the Stampeders into the locker room with a slim 4-0 lead. It wasn't until 11:57 into the 3rd quarter that the first TD of the game was scored as Calgary quarterback Doug Flutie hooked up with slotback Dave Sapunjis for a 20-yd. TD strike. This gave the Stampeders a 11-0 lead after 3 periods of play. The Stamps increased their lead to 18 points as Flutie scampered into the end-zone from 11 yds. out. Ottawa quarterback Terrence Jones was then trapped in the end-zone to give Calgary the safety and a 20-0 lead. The Rough Riders finally got on the board as QB Tom Burgess hooked up with Jock Climie for a 60-yd. TD narrowing the gap to 20-7. Mark McLoughlin added another single with just 18 seconds left giving the Stamps a 21-7 victory. On the day Flutie was 28-of-46 for 322 yds. with 1 interception and 1 TD pass while Allen Pitts had a very impressive day, adding to his League-leading pass receiving totals.

Saturday, August 14 - Hamilton Tiger-Cats 10 @ Sacramento Gold Miners 46 - 14,656
The Sacramento Gold Miners scored 31 1st-half points and went on to defeat the visiting Tiger-Cats before 14,656 fans at Hornet Field. Sacramento QB David Archer had another outstanding day, completing 22-of-38 passes for 370 yds. with 3 TDs. Carl Parker was the Gold Miners' leading pass catcher as he hauled in 6 passes for 121 yds. and 1 TD. The Gold Miners got on the board 3:22 into the 1st quarter as WR Freeman Baysinger capped off a 6-play drive hauling in an Archer pass for a 31-yd. TD. Carl Parker made it 14-0 as he grabbed a 24-yd. strike from Archer. After a Sacramento single, Hamilton's Paul Osbaldiston booted a 20-yd. FG to close out the 1st quarter scoring with the Gold Miners on top 15-3. Jim Crouch booted a 25-yarder to put the Miners up by 15 then Sacramento LB Paschell Davis stepped in front of a Don McPherson toss and returned it 39 yds. for the TD. Crouch then added a 13-yd. and 31-yd. FGs to round out the 1st half scoring putting the Gold Miners on top 31-3. Crouch opened up the 3rd quarter scoring with a single and then it was Baysinger hauling in a 30-yd. pass from Archer for his 2nd major of the game. Mike Oliphant capped off a 9-play drive by running it in from 4 yds. out making the score 46-3 in favour of Sacramento after 3 periods. Hamilton scored the only points of the 4th quarter as WR Earl Winfield hooked up with Eros Sanchez for a 15-yd. TD on the final play of the game making the final 46-10 for the Miners.

WEEK #7

Wednesday, August 18 - Edmonton Eskimos 45 @ Toronto Argonauts 14 - 20,563
The Toronto Argonauts could not prevent the strong Eskimo defense from attacking their trio of quarterbacks as a record 13 sacks were counted in a 45-14 loss at SkyDome before a crowd of 20,563. It was slow going as Edmonton K Sean Fleming kicked an 11-yd. FG on the first drive of the game after Mike "Pinball" Clemons fumbled the opening kickoff. QB Damon Allen ran in from the 1-yd. line to cap off a 36-yd. drive for the only other scoring of the quarter. Toronto finally got on the board at 1:53 of the second when Warren Hudson charged in from 1 yd. out to put his team within 3 points but the Eskimos came right back as Fleming got a single off a missed 53-yd. FG attempt and Michael Soles carried the ball for a 9-yd. major to make the count 18-7 at inter-

mission time. Toronto came out flying as Clemons made up for his first punt return goof by returning a punt 79 yds. for the score less than 2 minutes into the 3rd quarter (converted by K Lance Chomyc), but that would be all the scoring for the home town team as a new CFL record for most sacks versus one team was set. Fleming booted another 2 FGs (46 and 34 yds. out) and Allen passed for 3 TDs in the final frame, connecting with Eddie Brown on all three (11, 22 and 45 yds.) to put the game way out of reach for the Argonauts. Toronto QB Tracy Ham, who was sacked 7 times in the first half, started the game, but was replaced in the third period by Reggie Slack, who was then replaced after he completed 4-of-9 passes for 81 yds. and 1 interception, by Bret Johnson, who could not make either of his 2 passes, having one of them picked off along the way.

Wednesday, August 18 - Winnipeg Blue Bombers 28 @ B.C. Lions 48 - 28,541
The B.C. Lions upped their record to 6-2 with a 48-28 victory over the visiting Winnipeg Blue Bombers in front of 28,541 fans at B.C. Place. The Lions jumped out to a 14-0 1st quarter lead when Ray Alexander blocked a Troy Westwood FG attempt which was scooped up by Less Browne who returned it 85 yds. for the major. Robert Mimbs then hooked up with Danny Barrett for an 8-yd. pass and run to give the Lions a 14-0 lead after 15 minutes of play. B.C. added to their lead as Danny Barrett ran it in from 1-yd. out to make it 21-0. Winnipeg QB Matt Dunigan finally got the Bombers on the scoreboard, plunging over from 1-yd. out to narrow the gap to just 14. Winnipeg scored its second major of the 2nd quarter as David Williams ran under a Dunigan pass for a 10-yd. score to make the score 21-14 with 52 seconds left to play in the half. Lui Passaglia added a late FG to make the score 24-14 at half-time. Barrett got the Lions on the board first in the 3rd quarter scoring his 2nd TD of the game from 1-yd. out to make it 31-14 in favour of the Lions. Barrett kept the Lions' offensive machine rolling as he hooked up with Mike Trevathan for a 22-yd. TD to make the tally 38-14 after 3 periods of play. A Passaglia 16-yd. FG opened up the 4th quarter scoring before Bomber DB Corian Freeman stepped in front of a Barrett attempt and ran it back 96-yds. for the score, cutting the lead to 20. Winnipeg continued to chip away at the lead as Alfred Jackson capped off a 6-play drive with a 60-yd. TD catch to narrow the margin to 13 with just under 5 minutes left. The Lions then put together a time consuming drive which was capped off by a Mimbs 2-yd. TD run to put the game out of reach. The Passaglia convert made the final 48-28 for the Lions.

Thursday, August 19 - Saskatchewan Roughriders 27 @ Ottawa Rough Riders 26 - 23,463
Dave Ridgway booted a 38-yd. FG with 1:23 left on the clock to give the Saskatchewan Roughriders a 27-26 victory over the hometown Ottawa Rough Riders in front of 23,463 faithful at Frank Clair Stadium. The win upped the Green 'Riders' record to 5-3 and dropped Ottawa's record to 1-7. Ottawa got on the board first as quarterback Tom Burgess hooked up with slotback Jock Climie for a 51-yd. TD 2:14 into the opening frame. Saskatchewan tied the score at 7 as Kent Austin hooked up with longtime favourite receiver, Ray Elgaard, for a 14-yd. major. Ottawa closed out the 1st quarter scoring with Burgess finding Wayne Walker in the open for a 98-yd. TD, making the score 14-7 in favour of Ottawa after 1 period of play. Saskatchewan kicker Dave Ridgway opened up the 2nd quarter scoring with a 42-yd. FG to narrow the gap to just 4. The Green 'Riders' Carlton Lance then pounced on a loose ball and took it in 9-yds. for the major to give Saskatchewan their first lead of the game. Ottawa kicker Terry Baker then connected from 21 yds. out to tie the score at 17. The Western Riders re-captured the lead as Austin hooked up with Don Narcisse for a 36-yd. TD giving them a 24-17 lead. Baker closed out the 2nd quarter scoring by booting a 42-yd. FG to make it 24-20 in favour of the Green Riders at the half. Baker's 11-yd. chip shot accounted for all of the 3rd quarter scoring making the score 24-23 for Saskatchewan after 3 quarters of play. Baker gave the Eastern Riders a 26-24 lead with a 43-yd. FG with 5:11 left to play in the game. This lead was short lived however as "Robo Kicker" Ridgway connected from 38 yds. out to give Saskatchewan a 27-26 lead with 1:21 remaining. Ottawa was unable to mount a comeback giving Saskatchewan a 27-26 victory.

Friday, August 20 - Calgary Stampeders 31 @ Hamilton Tiger-Cats 12 - 19,402
The Calgary Stampeders, on the strength of 24 1st quarter points, won their 8th straight game of the 1993 season with a 31-12 win over the Hamilton Tiger-Cats, in front of 19,402 fans at Ivor Wynne Stadium. It didn't take long for the Stampeder offensive machine to get rolling as quarterback Doug Flutie hooked up with Will Moore for a 16-yd. TD 1:29 into the opening frame. This pair hooked up again 1:59 later this time Moore grabbed an 8-yd. Flutie pass, set up by a Greg Knox blocked Paul Osbaldiston punt, for his second major of the game. The Stampeders quickly put the game out of reach as Derrick Crawford returned an Osbaldiston punt at his own 40-yd. line and ran it back 70 yds. for the TD. The Tiger-Cats finally got on the board after a Mark McLoughlin FG as Bruce Perkins plunged in from 1-yd. out on the final play of the quarter to make the score 24-6 after the 1st frame. Osbaldiston added the convert on the first play of the 2nd quarter narrowing the margin to 17. McLoughlin, who booted 3 FGs on the night, added his second of the contest, this one coming from 23 yds. out. Osbaldiston then connected from 28 yds. out and the Stamps conceded a safety to make the score 27-12 at the half. A Tony Martino 76-yd. single accounted for all of the 3rd quarter scoring and McLoughlin added his 3rd FG of the game, this one from 20 yds. out to make the final score 31-12 in favour of the Stamps.

Saturday, August 21 - Winnipeg Blue Bombers 30 @ Sacramento Gold Miners 18 - 15,509
The Blue Bombers completed their Western swing in Sacramento, coming away with a 30-18 win over the hometown Gold Miners, avenging their loss 48-28 loss earlier in the week at the hands of the B.C. Lions. 15,509 spectators watched as the Blue Bombers got on the board first when kicker Troy Westwood booted 2 FGs, the 1st from 12 yds. out and the other coming from 22 yds. away. Westwood added his 3rd FG of the game to open up the 2nd quarter scoring. The Bombers increased their lead to 16-0 as QB Matt Dunigan hooked up with slotback Gerald Wilcox for a 13-yd. TD. The Miners then got on the board putting up 11 straight points as kicker Jim Crouch added a 58-yd. single off a missed FG, then added a FG from 12-yds. out to make the score 17-4. Mike Oliphant capped off a 2-play drive hooking up with quarterback David Archer for a 78-yd. TD with 30 seconds remaining in the half. The Bombers got the ball back with 30-seconds left in the half and quickly went to work with a 3-play and 1 penalty drive capped off by a 11-yd. pass from Dunigan to David Williams to make the score 23-11 at the half. The Bombers opened up the 4th quarter scoring, after a scoreless 3rd quarter, as Williams ran under a 34-yd. Dunigan pass for the major giving the Winnipeg a 30-11 lead. Sacramento attempted to make a comeback as Oliphant teamed up with Archer for his 2nd pass receiving TD of the game, this one a 69-yd. pass. This however, was the end of the comeback for the 'Miners as the Bombers held on for a 30-18 victory.

WEEK #8

Wednesday, August 25 - Hamilton Tiger-Cats 8 @ Edmonton Eskimos 46 - 24,356
The Edmonton Eskimos, on the strength of 28 first half points, defeated the Hamilton Tiger-Cats by a score of 46-8 in front of 24,356 fans at Commonwealth Stadium. Edmonton's "Gizmo" Williams opened the scoring in the sixth minute of play as he caught a 20-yd. TD pass from QB Damon Allen. Less than a minute after a Hamilton field goal attempt went wide, Edmonton counted its second major of the first quarter as Eddie Brown hauled in a 75-yd. TD bomb from Allen to close out the first quarter. Hamilton then accounted for the rest of its scores with Paul Osbaldiston responsible for them all as he kicked a punt single, followed by 2 FGs. From then on, it was all Edmonton as Eddie Brown grabbed his 2nd TD catch of the day with a 23-yd. reception and Doug Parrish scooped up a fumble and rumbled 32 yds. into the end zone. The second half was all Edmonton as they counted another 18 points, 17 of which came in the fourth quarter. Sean Fleming booted a 47-yd. field goal which was followed by Williams' second TD reception of the day, a 28 yd. pass which made the score 39-8. Don Wilson picked off the ball and returned it for 34 yds. for the TD with just under 5 minutes leftto make the final score 46-8 for the Esks.

Wednesday, August 25 - Ottawa Rough Riders 26 @ Toronto Argonauts 25 - 21,327
In what was unofficially the battle for sole possession of 3rd place in the CFL East, Toronto was defeated in front of a home crowd of 21,327 by the Ottawa Rough Riders by a score of 26-25. Ottawa started off the scoring in the first minute of the first quarter when John Kropke returned a Toronto fumble 29 yds. for the TD. The Riders' struck again in the 2nd quarter when Terry Baker banged a 15-yd. field goal to make the score 10-0 in the early going. Toronto then scored their first points of the game when SB Manny Hazard and QB Reggie Slack connected on a 25-yd. pass play. However, Ottawa came back and closed out the first quarter with another Baker field goal, this time from 50 yds.. To open up the 2nd half, Toronto found new life and tallied 10 points on the strength of a TD reception again from the duo of Hazard and Slack, this time from 25 yds. out. Lance Chomyc then fired a 15-yd. FG to give Toronto 10 consecutive points. Ottawa countered with 2 FGs of its own when Baker hit for 2 consecutive 37 yarders. The Slack-Hazard connection then hooked up for a third time for a 61-yd. TD bomb to make the score 25-19 with under a minute to play. The Riders got the better of the Argo defensive corps and hit for a 56-yd. TD when Tom Burgess found Stephen Jones flying solo down the sidelines. The convert made the score 26-25 for the Ottawa Rough Riders and gave them 3rd place alone in the CFL East.

Friday, August 27 - Sacramento Gold Miners 23 @ Saskatchewan Roughriders 26 - 33,032
In front of a home crowd of 33,032, the largest in Roughrider history, Saskatchewan came from behind to beat the Sacramento Gold Miners by a score of 26-23 at Taylor Field. Although the 1st quarter was scoreless, Sacramento seemed to find its groove in the 2nd when QB David Archer hit Rod Harris with a 14-yd. pass for a TD and then Mike Oliphant for another just under 3 minutes later. Sacramento padded its lead with a pair of singles by Jim Crouch before Dave "Robo Kicker" Ridgway put Saskatchewan on the board with a 48-yd. field goal to close out the half.To open the second half, Saskatchewan's Ray Elgaard brought down a 27-yd. pass from QB Kent Austin to bring the score to 16-10 for the Miners. Jim Crouch then countered for Sacramento by booting a single and two field goals of 22 and 21 yds. respectively. The 4th quarter belonged completely to the Rough Riders however as they put 1 TD and 3 FGs on the board to erase Sacramento's lead and put them in front to stay. Don Narcisse was on the receiving end of Kent Austin's 2nd TD pass of the day which came from 19 yds. out, and Dave Ridgway put the finishing touches on with kicks of 23, 46 and 50 yds. - the last with no time showing on the clock and giving Saskatchewan a 26-23 victory.

Friday, August 27 - B.C. Lions 30 @ Calgary Stampeders 35 - 27,011
This game matched the top two teams in the West against each other before 27,011 spectators at McMahon Stadium, and in the end, the home team remained the best in the League with 9 consecutive victories. After a scoreless first period, K Lui Passaglia booted a 60-yd. single into the Calgary endzone. With QB Doug Flutie displaying his magical talents once again, the Stampeders were able to get on the board as Derrick Crawford pulled in a 9-yd. toss for 6 points. The Lions, led by QB Danny Barrett, were unable to get going once they got the ball back and were forced to punt. Crawford returned the ball for 12 yds.,setting up Flutie for the 2nd TD of the night, this time a 31-yd. pass to Dave Sapunjis for a 14-1 lead. The Stamps would score again in the first half, a 9-yd. TD throw to Sapunjis, but not before Passaglia kicked a 17-yarder for 3 points. It was all B.C. in the third quarter, as the Lions closed in on a 21-4 Stampeder lead. Passaglia scored another single off a 71-yd. punt as well as connecting on a 47-yd. FG attempt, while Cory Philpot ran in from the 4-yd. line to put his team within 6 points of the Stamps. The Lions then went ahead in the fourth as Barrett found Darren Flutie for a 7-yd. TD score but Calgary did not stop as Flutie ran in himself from the 1-yd. line and then completed a 2-point convert to Crawford to make the count 29-22 with less than 11 minutes to go. Passaglia went wide on a 44-yd. FG attempt, counting only one point before K Mark McLoughlin was successful from 17 and 39 yds. out. B.C. made one final attempt to catch up as Barrett once again found Flutie, this time for a 4-yd. toss, but it would be too little too late, as the Grey Cup Champions hung on to win and to bump their record to 9-0 on the season.

Saturday, August 28 - Hamilton Tiger-Cats 11 @ Winnipeg Blue Bombers 35 - 24,475
For the 6th game in a row, the Tiger-Cats were unable to put enough points on the scoreboard to give them 2 points in the win column as they were beat 35-11 by the Blue Bombers before 24,475 fans at Winnipeg Stadium. Bomber QB Matt Dunigan got the game going as he took his team down the field on a 55-yd. drive which ended with a 14-yd. TD throw to Gerald Alphin at 8:57 of the opening frame. Hamilton K Paul Osbaldiston kicked a single on a missed FG from 44 yds. out a couple of minutes later before Bob Torrance, a Canadian QB starting his 2nd game in the CFL, passed for his 1st career TD, a 15-yd. pass to Cornell Burbage after Earl Winfield was able to return a punt 42 yds. to the Winnipeg 19-yd. line. Osbaldiston made the convert to give the Cats an 8-7 lead. But that was short-lived as Winnipeg came back with a 45-yd. drive, which included a 23-yd. run by Michael Richardson and a 15-yd. pass to David Williams from Dunigan, and was capped off by a 2-yd. TD rush by Richardson. Dunigan continued on a roll as he connected on some key passes, including a 9-yd. throw for the major to Allen Boyko with three and a half minutes left in the 2nd quarter. It was the kickers' quarter in the 3rd as K Troy Westwood added to his team's 21-8 lead, kicking a 39-yd. FG, followed by a 47-yarder off the foot of Osbaldiston. Westwood came back with a 16-yd. FG to complete a 66-yd. drive, giving Winnipeg a 27-11 edge going into the final period. The Bombers would score another 8 points (a single off the toe of P Bob Cameron and a 10-yd. TD run by Richardson) for a final count of 35-11 as Winnipeg pads its lead in the Eastern Division to 6 points ahead of the Cats, who remain in 2nd place over Ottawa and Toronto.

WEEK #9

Thursday, September 2 - Sacramento Gold Miners 12 @ Edmonton Eskimos 13 - 37,042
In front of the largest crowd of the year at Commonwealth Stadium, the Eskimos squeezed past the visiting Sacramento Gold Miners by one point to win 13-12. 37,042 fans sat through the first quarter as Edmonton struck for 10 points on the strength of a TD and field goal by Damon Allen and Sean Fleming respectively. Allen took the ball in himself on a 2-yd. rush while Fleming punched it through the uprights from 14 yds. out. Sacramento got on the board late in the second quarter when Pete Gardere hit a 63-yd. punt for a single and Jim Crouch followed just over a minute later with a 42-yd. field goal. In the second half, after a scoreless third quarter, Fleming counted a field goal from 37 yds. out to make the score 13-4 with just over 6 minutes to play. Sacramento then waited until close to the last minute to score their only TD of the day, a 1-yd. pass from QB David Archer to Rod Harris and Crouch closed out the scoring for the Gold Miners by hitting an 85-yd. kickoff for a single to make the final score 13-12 for Edmonton. In this game, Henry "Gizmo" Williams broke the all-time record for Punt Return Yd.s as he ran back 7 for 113 yds., giving him a total of 6,427 to surpass Paul Bennett's previous mark of 6,350 career yds..

Saturday, September 4 - B.C. Lions 25 @ Ottawa Rough Riders 24 - 21,567
In another 1-point affair, the Lions travelled to Ottawa to take on the Rough Riders at Frank Clair Stadium in front of 21,567 and came out victorious 25-24. The Lions opened the scoring at the 15-minute mark of the first quarter when Sean Millington barreled in from 15 yds. out for his first of two majors on the day. Ottawa then followed with a 5-yd. TD pass from Tom Burgess to Wayne Walker who had 5 catches for 125 yds. in the game. Millington then went in for his 2nd TD on a run from 3 yds. out to put B.C. back out in front. Ottawa followed with a 28-yd. field goal from Terry Baker and a single from Jock Climie to come within 3 pts. at the half. In the third quarter they regained the lead on a 44-yd. field goal and single on a wide field goal, both by Baker who had another of 22 yds. to start off the 4th and give Ottawa an 18-14 lead. Ottawa RB Darren Joseph was then tackled in the end zone by Tyrone Jones for a safety touch to give B.C. 2 points and the ball back. B.C. then added a 25 yd. field goal by Lui Passaglia to give them a 19-18 lead with just under half the quarter remaining. With less than a minute and a half remaining, Ottawa seemed to take control when Jones rambled in from 1 yd. out. An attempted 2-point convert and failed so it was up to the defense. The B.C. offense proved to be too strong in the remaining minute and marched down the field for a TD of their own when Danny Barrett took it in from 1 yd. out to make the final score 25-24 for the Lions.

Sunday, September 5 - Winnipeg Blue Bombers 25 @ Saskatchewan Roughriders 24 - 30,216
The Labour Day weekend had yet another 1 point differential in the matchup between the Winnipeg Blue Bombers and the Saskatchewan Rough Riders in a battle that had Winnipeg winning in front of the second consecutive sold-out crowd at Taylor Field. Winnipeg's defensive unit accounted for the first points scored when Loyd Lewis recovered a fumble and took it 25 yds. for a TD. K Troy Westwood then increased Winnipeg's lead to 10-0 when he kicked one from 37 yds. out, but Saskatchewan K Dave Ridgway hit for 2 successive FGs of his own to cut the lead to 10-6 for Winnipeg. In the second quarter, Winnipeg came back with 5 points on the basis of a safety touch and another Westwood FG, this one from 24 yds.. The 3rd quarter was all Saskatchewan though,as they found their groove and hit for two TDs; Warren Jones went in from 1 yd. out and was followed by a 34-yd. TD pass from Kent Austin to Don Narcisse which made the score 20-15 for Saskatchewan. In the 4th quarter, Saskatchewan padded its lead by hammering a single from Brent Matich and a field goal from Ridgway from 33 yds. out before Winnipeg started its comeback. The Bombers started with a 19-yd. TD pass from Matt Dunigan to Alfred Jackson and added a 37-yd. FG by Westwood with just 4 seconds remaining to win the game 25-24.

Monday, September 6 - Edmonton Eskimos 13 @ Calgary Stampeders 33 - 38,205
The Stampeders continued their undefeated streak in the CFL this season when they hosted and proceeded to roll over the Eskimos 33-13 in front of a sold out crowd of 38,205 at McMahon Stadium. The Stampeders began the rout as they opened the game with a 38 yd. Mark McLoughlin field goal and two singles before Edmonton countered with a single of their own. Calgary then put the 1st major of the day on the board when Doug Flutie and Will Moore hooked up for a 13-yd. TD pass, their first of 2 TD connections on the day. Edmonton followed with a 47-yd. FG by Sean Fleming at the 14-minute mark of the 2nd quarter which was then matched by McLoughlin to close the half and leave the score at 15-4 in favour of the Stampeders. The only score of the 3rd came when Fleming hit for another FG, this time from 40 yds. away and Calgary came right back to answer with 2 TDs. The first was from the Flutie-Moore connection and while the second arrived in the hands of Dave Sapunjis from Flutie. Edmonton got their 1st TD with just under 3 minutes to go when Gary Morris grabbed a Ricky Foggie pass 3 yds. out which Calgary followed by scoring a single and a 24-yd. field goal by McLoughlin to make the score 33-13 for Calgary and put them at 10-0 for the season.

Monday, September 6 - Toronto Argonauts 21 @ Hamilton Tiger-Cats 23 - 21,762
An old rivalry between the Hamilton Tiger-Cats and the Toronto Argonauts found itself at work again at Ivor Wynne Stadium in the final matchup of the holiday weekend in front of 21,762 fans as the Tiger-Cats downed the Argos 23-21. The first half was all Hamilton as Toronto failed to put any points on the board and Hamilton was able to rack up 11 points, on the strength of a field goal, a TD and a single. The field goal was a 12-yarder by K Paul Osbaldiston who was also responsible for the single which followed a Hamilton TD scored by Don McPherson on a 14-yd. rush. In the 3rd quarter, Toronto finally put some points up and cut into Hamilton's lead by scoring a field goal which Lance Chomyc put through the uprights from 32 yds. away and Mike Clemons scored a TD on a 44-yd. punt return. Toronto continued to put points up when QB Reggie Slack took the ball in from 3 yds. away which made the score 15-11 for Toronto. Hamilton countered with an Osbaldiston field goal from 21 yds. away and then the defense scored with a 29 yd. interception return which Bobby Dawson took all the way for the major. Toronto looked to be in control as they punched in the ball from 2 yds. away when Slack took it in again with less than 1 minute remaining, however the Argo defense couldn't hold off the Tiger-Cats and Osbaldiston put through a 42-yd. field goal with 5 seconds left to make the final 23-21 in Hamilton's favour.

WEEK #10

Friday, September 10 - Calgary Stampeders 16 @ Edmonton Eskimos 29 - 54,324
For the 2nd week in a row Edmonton has set seasonal highs in attendance at Commonwealth Stadium with a crowd of 54,324 fans who watched the Eskimos defeat the previously unbeaten Calgary Stampeders by a score of 29-16. Edmonton opened the scoring with a single that came off a 50-yd. punt from P Glenn Harper and followed up on that with a field goal from 44 yds. out from K Sean Fleming. Calgary didn't get on the board until late in the 2nd quarter when WR Derrick Crawford hauled in a 16-yd. pass from QB Doug Flutie and less than 2 minutes later, K Mark McLoughlin booted a 28-yd. field goal through the uprights to make the score 10-4 at the half. The third quarter however was all Edmonton as they struck for 11 of their 18 unanswered points and Calgary seemed to fall apart. Fleming hit for another field goal, this time from 32 yds. out while RB Michael Soles rumbled in from 14 yds. out at just past the halfway point of the 3rd. Harper then kicked another single, this time from 60 yds. while RB Lucius Floyd grabbed an 11-yd. TD pass from QB Damon Allen to complete the string of continuous points. Calgary just never seemed to be in the game in the second half and this is perhaps most evident by the fact that Flutie went 16-of-34 with 3 interceptions, for only 124 yds. and 1 TD pass. The Stamps got their only points of the 2nd half when RB Andy McVey carried the ball in from 6 yds. out to make the score 22-17 but that was all the scoring of the evening for Calgary and Edmonton finished them off when Floyd grabbed his 2nd TD pass of the half, to make the final 29-16 for the Eskimos.

Saturday, September 11 - Hamilton Tiger-Cats 25 @ B.C. Lions 55 - 24,789
In a game played in front of 24,789 fans at B.C. Place, the Hamilton Tiger-Cats were just not able to keep pace with the high scoring B.C. Lions as they were defeated 55-25. Hamilton scored first on 2 plays from the leg of K Paul Osbaldiston as he kicked a single and then followed it with a 14-yd. field goal but B.C. came on strong to close out the 1st quarter. Cory Philpot carried the ball in from 3 yds. out to start what would be a great day for the Lion RB, for the first of his 3 TDs in the game. Philpot then scored again to open the 2nd quarter from 3 yds. away while his counterpart in the backfield, Sean Millington went in from 5 yds. out to make the score 21-4 at just over the halfway mark of the 2nd quarter, before Hamilton was able to answer when RB Dave Dinall broke free for a 20-yd. TD rush. However, WR Matt Clark caught a 9-yd. TD pass from QB Danny Barrett late in the half to make the score 28-11 for the Lions. To begin the 3rd quarter, K Lui Passaglia of the Lions hit two consecutive field goals from 12 yds. away to increase the Lions' lead. Hamilton pivot Don MacPherson countered with a TD rush from 1 yd. out but the Lions came right back when Clark brought down his 2nd TD catch, and Philpot scored his 3rd TD of the day , in addition to his 4 kickoff returns for 164 yds. with a long of 61. Hamilton scored their final TD of the day when Dinall scored his 2nd of the game. The Lions then came back with one of their own when Ryan Hanson rushed in to finish the scoring and the Tiger-Cats and make the score 55-25 in favour of the Leos.

Saturday, September 11- Ottawa Rough Riders 15 @ Sacramento Gold Miners 47 - 16,510
At Hornet Field in Sacramento, the Gold Miners put on a victorious show for the 16,510 fans as they thumped the Ottawa Rough Riders by a score of 47-15. Sacramento got on the board as Mike Pringle went into the end zone from 1 yd. out but Ottawa was able to drive right back and score a TD of their own when Shawn Daniels grabbed a 6-yd. pass to even the score. Sacramento continued the see-saw nature of the first half though, following up with a field goal at the close of the 1st quarter and a TD to open the 2nd as they went up by a score of 17-7. Ottawa answered by coming back with a TD when QB Tom Burgess took the ball in himself from 5 yds. out and then Terry Baker missed a FG which accounted for a single. In the 2nd half, the game turned out to be all Sacramento as they scored 23 points and the Miners' defense shut out the Rough Riders' offense. The Miners started off when K Jim Crouch kicked a 10-yd. FG and then Mike Oliphant rumbled in from 14 yds. away to increase Sacramento's lead. Crouch hit another FG, this one from 21 yds. and another from 14 yds. before James Pruitt closed out the scoring for the day when he hauled in a 15-yd. throw to make the final score 47-15 for Sacramento.

Sunday, September 12 - Saskatchewan Roughriders 23 @ Winnipeg Blue Bombers 41 - 35,959
In this matchup at Winnipeg Stadium, the Rough Riders put up a strong fight in the first half and came closer in the 3rd quarter, but in the end were outscored by the Bombers 41-23. Winnipeg opened the game by scoring early when K Troy Westwood hit a field goal from 45 yds. out with under a minute played in the game. Saskatchewan went ahead though when SB Jeff Fairholm caught a 27-yd. TD pass from QB Kent Austin and K Dave Rigway hit from 30 yds. out on the Roughriders' next possesion. Winnipeg mirrored the scoring of Saskatchewan as Westwood hit for another field goal of his own, this time from 48 yds. and Nathaniel Bolton caught a 38-yd. pass from QB Matt Dunigan. They also added a TD when Dunigan carried in himself from 1 yd. away to make the score 20-10 for Winnipeg. Saskatchewan closed to within a field goal when Mike Saunders had a 1-yd. rush for a TD, but again Winnipeg matched the 'Riders as Dunigan went in for his 2nd of 3 rushing TDs on the day with a short rush of 2 yds.. Ridway gave Saskatchewan another 6 points as he booted 2 consecutive field goals from 41 and 17 yds. respectively to put them within 4 points going into the final quarter where Winnipeg took command. Bolton grabbed his 2nd TD catch of the day from 14 yds. away and Dunigan rushed for his 3rd and longest TD run on the day when he took it in from 17 yds. away to close out the scoring as Saskatchewan was shut out in the final period. The final was 41-23 for Winnipeg over Saskatchewan before an overcapacity crowd of 35,959 at Winnipeg Stadium, largest in Blue Bombers' history.

WEEK #11

Friday, September 17 - Edmonton Eskimos 10 @ Hamilton Tiger-Cats 34 - 17,102
The Hamilton Tiger-Cats were able to overcome the many concerns about their team being on the verge of folding to defeat the visiting Eskimos in front of 17,102 faithfuls at Ivor Wynne Stadium. Led by QB Don MacPherson, the 'Cats got on the board when K Paul Osbaldiston punted a 61-yarder for a single and a 17-yd. FG in the opening quarter while Edmonton squeezed a 48-yd. FG by Sean Fleming in between the 2 scores. Hamilton receiver Earl Winfield was at his best once again as he returned his 1st of 2 punt return TDs on the night, a 65-yarder (converted by Osbaldiston) to give the 'Cats an 11-3 lead. Edmonton was unable to do much throughout the 1st half, scoring a single off the foot of P Glenn Harper at 9:13 of the 2nd period. Winfield displayed his magic once again, this time capping off a 4-play drive originating at the Hamilton 20 with a 79-yd. pass-and-run play for his 2nd score of the evening. The 2 teams exchanged FGs before halftime, making the count 21-7 going into the dressing rooms. The 3rd quarter was a kicking competition, as Osbaldistion sandwiched a 37-yd boot by Fleming with a 27-yarder and a 17-yarder of his own to increase his team's lead to 27-10 after 3 quarters. The final frame saw Winfield return another punt for a major score, this time a 46-yd. return, giving him a total of 232 yds and 3 TDs in receiving and returns on the night. The Hamilton defense was also pretty stingy throughout the game, sacking Edmonton QBs 6 times while allowing only 162 yds. in total offence, including no TDs.

Saturday, September 18 - B.C. Lions 21 @ Calgary Stampeders 40 - 29,110
At McMahon Stadium, the Calgary Stampeders hosted the B.C. Lions in a game that saw one of the league's premier receivers return to form in front of a crowd of 29,110. Calgary slotback Dave Sapunjis had an outstanding game as he pulled down 10 catches for 187 yds. after 2 games in which he was held to a total of just 5 catches for 33 yds.. Calgary hit for two TDs in the first quarter as WR Will Moore and WR Derrick Crawford both caught passes from QB Doug Flutie in a span of just under 3 minutes. The Moore reception was a 10-yarder while Crawford's came from 13 yds. out. Following the Calgary assault, the Lions came back and hit for 10 consecutive points to close out the first quarter and open the second on the strength of a 5-yd. TD catch from QB Danny Barrett to RB Sean Millington and a 20-yd. field goal from K Lui Passaglia. However, Calgary wasn't finished, as they answered with 10 points of their own on a 1 yd. TD run from Doug Flutie and a 39-yd. field goal off the foot of K Mark McLoughlin. With halftime sandwiched in between, the Stamps came right back out in the 2nd half as they opened the scoring with another FG, this one from 13 yds. out. B.C. followed up with a FG when Passaglia booted a 22-yarder through the uprights to make the score 27-14 with the 4th yet to be played. The Lions looked to be on the right track as Barrett hit WR Mike Trevathan from 16 yds. to bring B.C. closer, but the Stamps put the game out of reach when Flutie hit Sapunjis for an 18-yd TD and then threw a 5-yd. strike to Moore, his 2nd of the day to make the final, 40-21 in favour of the Stampeders.

Sunday, September 19 - Winnipeg Blue Bombers 26 @ Toronto Argonauts 35 - 29,915
In front of a season high crowd of 28,915 at SkyDome in Toronto, the Argonauts greeted their new head coach Bob O'Billovich with a win over the Winnipeg Blue Bombers. The Argos seemed to be piecing their game together in the first quarter as Winnipeg K Troy Westwood hit for 2 field goals of 35, and 37 yds. to give the Blue Bombers the early lead. Toronto finally found their groove as they scored 11 consecutive points on the basis of a single, a 35-yd. Lance Chomyc field goal and a 16-yd. TD rush from QB Tracy Ham who was inserted in the first quarter when QB Reggie Slack went down after being hit on the left knee. Winnipeg came back to close out the second quarter by scoring a TD when Nathaniel Bolton pulled in a 41-yd. pass from QB Matt Dunigan, who was 18-for-33 for 230 yds. with 2 TDs and an interception. The 3rd quarter

belonged to Toronto as they hit for 14 points on two TDs, one on a rush of 10 yds. from RB Mike "Pinball" Clemons and the other on a 61-yd. pass reception from Ham to WR Robert Clark. Winnipeg came back to open the 4th with a 2 yd. Dunigan rush yet Toronto responded to that by hitting for a 20-yd. Chomyc field goal and another Ham TD, this one on a 9-yd. carry. Winnipeg scored one last time, when Dunigan hit SB Gerald Wilcox for a 29-yd. major but it wasn't enough as Toronto held on to win 35-26.

Sunday, September 19 - Sacramento Gold Miners 20 @ Saskatchewan Roughriders 27 - 25,367
In Saskatchewan, the Rough Riders held off a late attack by the visiting Gold Miners to win 27-20 in front of a crowd of 27,367. The Rough Riders opened the scoring just over midway through the 1st quarter when QB Kent Austin hit WR Tre Everett on a 12-yd. TD pass and continued their run as they struck for another 13 points as they held Sacramento scoreless. The remainder of the points came from a Dave Ridgway field goal from 30 yds. out, a 1-yd. TD run by RB Mike Saunders and another FG from Rigdway, this one from 10 yds. out. Sacramento finally got on the board in the 3rd quarter, when QB David Archer hit RB Troy Mills with a 4-yd. pass and then followed up by hitting WR Freeman Baysinger with an 83-yd. pass play to bring the Gold Miners to 20-14. K Jim Crouch brought Sacramento to a tie when he booted two consecutive field goals from 34 and 12 yds. respectively. However Austin took Saskatchewan back down the field and hit SB Jeff Fairholm for a 12-yd. TD reception to make the final 27-20 for the Rough Riders. Of note is the fact that Dave Ridgway's consecutive field goal streak continues as he was 2-for-2 on the day.

WEEK #12

Friday, September 24 - Hamilton Tiger-Cats 3 @ Calgary Stampeders 26 - 29,817
In Calgary, the Stampeders played host to Hamilton in a game that saw the Stampeders run over the Tiger-Cats by a score of 26-3 in front of 29,817 fans at McMahon Stadium. The game was dominated by Calgary the whole way through and their defense held the Tiger-Cats scoreless until the 4th quarter. Calgary got on the board when K Mark McLoughlin kicked a 34-yd. field goal through the uprights and followed that up when FB Andy McVey rumbled in from 1 yd. out to make the score 10-0 in the early going. To close out the 1st, McLoughlin hit his 2nd of 4 FGs on the day, this time from 51 yds. away; he then hit again for the only score of the 2nd frame when he hit a 30-yarder to put the Stamps up 16-0 at the half. Calgary opened the scoring in the second half when McLoughlin hit for a 33-yd. effort which RB Tony Stewart backed up when he plunged through from 2 yds. away to make the count 26-0 after 3 quarters. Hamilton scored their only points when K Paul Osbaldiston prevented the shutout by kicking a 43-yd. field goal of his own with just under 3 minutes remaining to make the final 26-3 for the Stampeders and improve their record to 12-1 for the season.

Saturday, September 25 - Toronto Argonauts 22 @ Ottawa Rough Riders 30 - 24,631
In the battle for sole possession of 3rd place in the CFL Eastern Division, the Toronto Argonauts and Ottawa Rough Riders met at Frank Clair Stadium in front of 24,631 fans. After a scoreless 1st quarter, both teams seemed to find their offensive grooves in the 2nd as they struck for 30 points combined. Ottawa opened the 2nd quarter by striking for the day's first major as QB Tom Burgess found SB Jock Climie on a 23-yd. throw but Toronto had an answer in mind when QB Tracy Ham hooked up with SB Wally Zatylny for a 29-yd. effort of their own. Ottawa followed up by sending K Ray Macoritti out to fire a 21-yd. blast through the posts and Burgess decided to add insult to the injury by finding Climie for his 2nd major of the evening on an 89-yd. bomb which left the Toronto secondary way behind the action. Toronto scored with 5 seconds left in the half as Ham hit SB Manny Hazard with a 3-yd. pass to make the score 16-14 in favour of Ottawa at the half. The 3rd half opened with Toronto scoring a single and hitting for another major when RB Pat Jackson rushed in from 7 yds. out. However, the Ottawa defense was able to close out the Argonauts in the 4th quarter while the offense scored 14 points of its own as FB Shawn Daniels took it in from 1 yd. out and WR Stephen Jones was on the receiving end of a 76-yd. passfrom Burgess. The final was 30-22 in favour of the Rough Riders and gave them sole hold on 3rd place in the CFL Eastern Division.

Saturday, September 25 - Saskatchewan Roughriders 31 @ B.C. Lions 16 - 31,888
In a game that saw a CFL record come to an end, the Saskatchewan Roughriders downed the B.C. Lions in front of a crowd of 31,888 at B.C. Place Stadium. Early in the 1st quarter, B.C. got on the board when RB Cory Philpot scrambled in from 10 yds. away to give the Lions an early 7-0 lead. B.C. struck again as K Paul MacCallum booted a 25-yd. field goal but then Saskatchewan got on track when DB Charles Anthony returned a fumble for a TD which QB Kent Austin then followed by going in from 1 yd. out. Saskatchewan was up by a score of 14-10 at the half and they opened the scoring in the 3rd when WR Don Narcisse hauled in a 20-yd. catch on a pass from Austin. The Lions came back again and hit for a FG early in the 4th to make the score 21-13 with just over 14 minutes to play. But the Green 'Riders began to close the door as Narcisse brought down an 18-yd. reception which B.C. answered by kicking a FG off the foot of MacCallum from 45 yds. out. However, Saskatchewan's K Dave Ridgway hit his only FG of the day from 30 yds., thus ending his CFL record for consecutive FGs at 28. After Ridway's kick, the score was 31-16 in Saskatchewan's favour.

Sunday, September 26 - Winnipeg Blue Bombers 52 @ Edmonton Eskimos 14 - 30,972
In a game that was dominated by Winnipeg on both sides of the ball, the Blue Bombers decimated the Edmonton Eskimos 52-14, in front of 30,972 hometown fans who saw the Eskimos go down for the 2nd week in a row. Winnipeg showed what kind of game they were going to play early as they scored 15 points in the 1st quarter and kept Edmonton off the board. RB Chris Johnstone crashed through to the end zone from 2 yds. away, and SB Gerald Wilcox was on the receiving end of a 40-yd. pass from QB Matt Dunigan while K Troy Westwood sandwiched a single from a missed FG attempt in between. Winnipeg continued its assault on the Eskimo defense in the 2nd quarter when Westwood hit from 30 yds., WR Nat Bolton returned a punt 71 yds. for a major, and Westwood hit for another FG before Edmonton even got on the board. When they did, with only 3 seconds left in the half, it was RB Lucius Floyd who went in on a 1-yd. rush. In the 2nd half, the Bombers continued their dominance as WR David Williams hauled in a 7-yd. TD pass from Dunigan, 1 of 3 on the day for the Winnipeg QB who was 26-of-43 for 429 yds. with 2 interceptions. SB Allan Boyko then caught another Dunigan pass for a 13-yd. TD before Edmonton put their only other points on the board for the day when WR Gary Morris caught a 38-yd. TD pass. Winnipeg put the nails in the coffin in the final frame when Westwood hit his 3rd FG and LB Greg Battle returned a fumble 42 yds. for a TD to make the final score 52-14 for Winnipeg.

WEEK #13

Friday, October 1 - B.C. Lions 50 @ Saskatchewan Roughriders 28 - 22,103
In a game at Taylor Field, the Roughriders met up with the Lions in a game that would give the winner sole possession of second place in the CFL Western Division. The Lions opened the scoring early in front of the crowd of 22,103 when WR Mike Trevathan caught a 44-yd. pass from QB Danny McManu., K Lui Passaglia followed that with a 52-yd. FG to give B.C. an early 10-0 lead. Saskatchewan got on the board later in the quarter when SB Bruce Boyko was on the receiving end of a 28-yd. pass from QB Kent Austin which cut the Lion lead to 3. Saskatchewan then found its groove when, after another Passaglia FG, they scored 17 consecutive points from the offence, the defense and the special teams. The offense got its share when K Dave Ridgway hit from 34 yds. away, which CB Albert Brown followed with a 108-yd return following an unsuccessful field goal attempt from 45 yds. out by Passaglia for a TD and CB Carlton Lance put in his share when he returned an interception 31 yds. for another TD. To close out the half, Passaglia hit for another FG, a 41-yarder. RB Jon Volpe took it in from 6 yds in the 3rd to bring the score to 24-23 for Saskatchewan. Ridgway countered with an 18-yarder which Passaglia replied to with 2 of his own. Going into the 4th, B.C. led 29-27 and continued to build its lead after all Saskatchewan could manage was a single to open the quarter's scoring. Trevathan hauled in his 2nd of the day from 46 yds. out, Volpe ran in for his 2nd from 3 yds, CB Andre Francis took an interception back 71 yds to close out the scoring at 50-28 in favour of the Lions.

Saturday, October 2 - Hamilton Tiger-Cats 10 @ Winnipeg Blue Bombers 61 - 26,386
The matchup at Winnipeg Stadium saw the first place team meet the second place in front of a crowd of 26,386. The Hamilton Tiger-Cats were in town to meet the Winnipeg Blue Bombers and unfortunately, the Tabbies came out on the wrong end of a blowout. The Bombers opened the scoring in the 1st quarter when RB Chris Johnstone grabbed an 11-yd. pass from QB Matt Dunigan which K Troy Westwood followed up with a 45-yd. boot to make the score 10-0 in the early going. Hamilton answered by striking for a TD of their own when SB Lee Knight ran it in from 1 yd. out to bring the 'Cats back to within 3 points. But Winnipeg countered by hitting for a TD when SB Gerald Wilcox brought in a 23-yd. pass from Dunigan and Westwood again followed up by kicking another FG from 38 -yds. away. Hamilton came back with a safety, but Westwood hit a 33-yarder for another 3 points to close out the scoring for the half at 23-9. The Bombers continued the assault on the Tiger-Cat defense when WR David Williams was on the receiving end of a 37-yd. pass from Dunigan and Wilcox caught his 2nd from 34 yds. away from Dunigan within the 1st six minutes of the 2nd half. LB Elfrid Payton even got into the act by returning a fumble 47 yds. for a major before Hamilton put their only point of the second half on the board when K Paul Osbaldiston hit for a single. Winnipeg continued their romp in the 4th quarter as SB Gerald Alphin grabbed a 28 yd. TD pass from QB Sammy Garza, Westwood hit a 27-yarder and Alphin grabbed his 2nd of the quarter from 19 yds away off the arm of QB Tom Porras to make the final 61-10 for Winnipeg.

Saturday, October 2 - Edmonton Eskimos 34 @ Sacramento Gold Miners 13 - 15,914
At Hornet Field in Sacramento, the Edmonton Eskimos visited the Sacramento Gold Miners in front of 15,914 fans and dashed their hopes of making CFL history by being the 1st U.S. team in League history to make the playoffs. Edmonton opened the scoring early in the first quarter when WR Trent Brown hauled in a 58-yd. pass from QB Damon Allen. But Sacramento came back to answer when WR Titus Dixon was on the receiving end of a 9-yd. pass from QB David Archer. In the 2nd quarter, Edmonton K Sean Fleming hit for a single off a 49-yd. missed field goal attempt and Sacramento K Jim Crouch hit a FG from 18 yds. to give the Gold Miners a 10-8 lead at the half. After the half though it was all Edmonton as they struck for 17 consecutive points on the strength of a 45-yd. Fleming FG, a 71-yd. TD pass from Allen to WR Eddie Brown, and a 37-yd. TD pass to WR "Gizmo" Williams before Crouch ended the streak by kicking a 22-yarder for a FG. In the 4th, it was again all Edmonton as they hit for another Brown TD from 11 yds. on a toss from Allen, and also scored a safety with less than a minute to play to make the score 34-13 for Edmonton.

Sunday, October 3 - Ottawa Rough Riders 16 @ Toronto Argonauts 17 - 24,089
In a rematch of the previous week's game between these teams in Ottawa, the Ottawa Rough Riders visited the Toronto Argonauts at SkyDome in front of 24,089 fans. The game was important for Toronto if they were to keep their playoff hopes alive and would tie them with Ottawa in the Eastern Division if they could manage a victory. At the end of the 1st quarter, Toronto had an early lead as they struck for a FG from K Lance Chomyc from 25 yds. away and also had a major score as FB Warren Hudson rumbled in from 1 yd. to give Toronto a 10-point lead. In the 2nd quarter though, Ottawa came right back as K Ray Macoritti hit a 29-yarder for a FG, and WR Stephen Jones caught a 46-yd. pass from QB Tom Burgess before Toronto regained the lead for a short period as Chomyc booted a 47-yarder before Macoritti countered with a 39-yd. effort of his own to make the score even at 13-13 going into the second half. In the 3rd quarter, Toronto hit for a Chomyc FG from 26 yds. away and also scored what would prove to be the game winning point as he sailed a missed FG attempt through the end zone for a single. In the 4th quarter, Ottawa could only manage a FG halfway through the period but couldn't manage another score as they fell 17-16 to the Argos and back into a tie for third place in the CFL Eastern Division.

WEEK #14

Friday, October 8 - Sacramento Gold Miners 27 @ B.C. Lions 23 - 30,615
In a game at B.C. Place Stadium, the Sacramento Gold Miners beat the B.C. Lions in front of 30,615 fans for their 1st-ever victory away from home. It didn't take the Lions long to open the scoring as they struck at the 2 minute mark of the first quarter for their 1st major of the day on a 34-yd. interception return by CB Less Browne. They added to their lead when K Lui Passaglia hit for 2 field goals, from 19 and 16 yds., before Sacramento got on the board with a single to close out the quarter. In the 2nd quarter, K Jim Crouch hit a 32-yd. field goal for Sacramento to cut the lead to 13-4 but B.C. came right back to score a TD of its own when WR Lonnie Turner caught a 15-yd. pass from QB Danny Barrett. But Sacramento answered quickly as QB David Archer found WR Joe Johnson on a 17-yd. pass play for a major to bring the score to 20-11 at the half. In the 3rd quarter, Passaglia booted a 40-yarder while K Pete Gardere of the Miners hit for a single. Sacramento found its groove in the 4th though as they hit for 15 unanswered points when Crouch kicked a single, WR Titus Dixon caught a 33-yd. Archer pass and Johnson added his 2nd of the day when he hauled in a 26-yd. pass for a TD. That final outburst by the Gold Miners made the final 27-23 in Sacramento's favour.

Saturday, October 9 - Winnipeg Blue Bombers 48 @ Ottawa Rough Riders 38 - 18,486
At Frank Clair Stadium the Winnipeg Blue Bombers paid a visit to the Ottawa Rough Riders in front of 18,486 fans, who were hoping the Rough Riders could take sole possession of 3rd in the Eastern Division with a win but that would not be the case. The Blue Bombers opened the scoring early in the 1st when QB Matt Dunigan found WR Gerald Wilcox with a 55-yd. TD pass and RB Mike Richardson ran in from 3 yds. out before FB Shawn Daniels went into the end zone from 2 yds. out to cut the Winnipeg lead to 14-7 at the close of the 1st quarter. To open the 2nd, Ottawa struck for another TD when CB Joe Fuller ran back an interception 40 yds. for a major. Winnipeg came right back to answer with a TD, a 75-yd. pass from Dunigan to Wilcox, his 2nd of the day to go along with his 180 yds. receiving on 6 catches. But Ottawa would not let up, following up with two consecutive scoring drives which resulted in a 16-yd. FG from K Ray Macoritti and a TD from QB Tom Burgess to Rob Crifo to make the score 24-21 at the half. In the 3rd, the teams again traded scores as Winnipeg's Troy Westwood hit for two field goals from 35 and 36 yds. before Ottawa countered with a TD when Burgess hit WR Stephen Jones on a 19-yd. recep-

tion. Dunigan then drove the Bombers down the field again and ended up with a TD when he hit WR David Williams with a 5-yd. pass, however the Rough Riders countered as Burgess hit SB Jock Climie with a 49-yd. pass to make the score 38-34 for Ottawa. The 4th turned out to be all Winnipeg as they managed 14 points while holding the 'Riders scoreless. FB Matt Pearce pulled down a 30-yd. TD pass from Dunigan, who then scored one of his own to make the final 48-38 for the Bombers.

Sunday, October 10 - Saskatchewan Roughriders 18 @ Calgary Stampeders 34 - 28,210
In Calgary the Stampeders were hoping to put a lock on their hold on 1st place in the Western Division by winning over Saskatchewan in front of 28,210 fans. The Stampeders opened the scoring when K Mark McLoughlin kicked a 48-yd. field goal which was followed up by a 54-yd. TD pass from QB Doug Flutie to WR Derrick Crawford. Saskatchewan didn't get on the board until the 2nd quarter when QB Warren Jones hit SB Jeff Fairholm on a 9-yd. TD pass which was followed up by a 40-yd field goal by K Dave Ridgway, a single by P Brent Matich and another FG by Ridgway. Calgary managed a 39-yd. McLoughlin FG to close out the half at 14-13 in Saskatchewan's favour. In the 2nd half, the Roughriders got off track as Calgary scored 21 points while Saskatchewan could only manage 4. The Stamps opened the 2nd half when McLoughlin hit a single from 47 yds. which Saskatchewan answered to when Matich kicked one of his own. Calgary then hit for a TD when CB Douglas Craft returned an interception 64 yds.. Saskatchewan finished off when Ridgway hit from 20 yds out for another FG but McLoughlin kicked another of his own before DB Charles Anthony ran back an interception 115 yds for the TD and McLoughlin closed the scoring with his final FG of the day, a 45-yd. effort to make the final 34-18 for the Stamps, who clinched 1st place in the West on a big game by the defense.

Monday, October 11 - Toronto Argonauts 20 @ Hamilton Tiger-Cats 28 - 18,425
Owners of 15 consecutive road losses, the Argonauts desperately needed a win, taking Ottawa's loss into consideration in order to make up ground for a playoff spot as the Hamilton Tiger-Cats played host to the Argos at Ivor Wynne Stadium in front of 18,425 fans. Toronto got off to a solid start as they opened the scoring with 2 FGs from K Lance Chomyc before Hamilton was able to manage a single from K Paul Osbaldiston in the 2nd quarter. The Tiger-Cats continued their run as QB Lee Saltz hit WR Lonzell Hill on a 10-yd. pass and FB Paul Bushey ran it in from 1 yd. out before Chomyc kicked a 39-yarder to close out the half with the score 15-9 for the Tiger-Cats. In the 2nd half, Osbaldiston kicked a 22-yarder before Toronto came back with a TD from QB Reggie Slack to WR Manny Hazard on a 48-yd. pass. Chomyc added a 33-yd. FG and P Hank Ilesic kicked a single before Osbaldiston kicked a 14-yarder of his own to make the score 21-20 with Toronto having the ball. However, with less than 1 minute remaining, Hamilton CB Gary Wilkerson intercepted a Slack pass and returned it 20 yds. for a TD to make the score 28-20. The Argos tried a last second Hail Mary but the pass was knocked out of the receiver's hands in the endzone and Hamilton prevailed 28-20 over their neighbouring rivals.

WEEK #15

Friday, October 15 - Sacramento Gold Miners 26 @ Winnipeg Blue Bombers 33 - 27,451
In Winnipeg the Sacramento Gold Miners came to pay the Blue Bombers a visit and hoped to salvage what is left of their inaugural CFL season in front of the 27,451 fans. Sacramento got on the board first but were only able to manage 2 singles which came off 2 punts by P Pete Gardere. However Winnipeg came back at the end of the first quarter when WR David Williams caught a 15-yd. TD pass from QB Matt Dunigan to make the score 7-2 for the Bombers. In the 2nd quarter, Winnipeg scored again this time when K Troy Westwood kicked 2 FGs before the Miners' special teams managed to score a TD when WR Joe Howard Johnson returned a punt 63 yds. for the major. In the second half, Sacramento came out and opened the scoring when K Jim Crouch kicked a 28-yd. field goal to cut Winnipeg's lead to 13-12. But Winnipeg came back and hit for a TD when Williams grabbed his 2nd of the evening from Dunigan on a 32-yd. pass before Sacramento decided to answer when WR Titus Dixon hauled in a 20-yd. pass from QB David Archer to bring the score to 20-19 with the 4th quarter remaining. In the last quarter, Winnipeg came out on a tear as they struck for an 18-yd. Westwood FG, another Williams TD from 44 yds. away on a pass from backup QB Sammy Garza who had entered the game when Dunigan was injured with suspected achilles tendon damage. They continued their scoring streak on another Westwood FG from 27 yds. before Sacramento was able to put their only points of the 4th on the board with a 17-yd. pass from Archer to Dixon with 32 seconds left in the game.

Saturday, October 16 - Ottawa Rough Riders 1 @ Edmonton Eskimos 19 - 25,140
At Commonwealth Stadium the Ottawa Rough Riders came out to visit the Edmonton Eskimos and hoped to put some distance between themselves and the Toronto Argonauts, who are chasing the Rough Riders for a playoff position in the Eastern Division. The game turned out to be all Edmonton right from the start as they opened with a single from K Sean Fleming, and a TD from QB Damon Allen to WR Eddie Brown on a 71-yd. pass to give the Esks an 8-0 lead after the 1st quarter. In the 2nd, Edmonton added to their lead when Allen hit WR "Gizmo" Williams for a 102 yd. TD pass before Ottawa scored their only points of the day when K Greg Duncan kicked for a single. In the second half, Edmonton scored a single and a field goal from Fleming on his 29-yd. FG to make the final 19-1 in favour of the Eskimos.

Sunday, October 17 - Hamilton Tiger-Cats 10 @ Saskatchewan Roughriders 33 - 21,772
The Hamilton Tiger-Cats arrived at Taylor Field hoping to follow their winning ways after the team's victory over Toronto last Monday, however the Roughriders put those thoughts to rest in a 33-10 romp before 21,772 fans. The game was all Saskatchewan from the beginning as they hit for 8 points on a single from P Brent Matich and a TD from RB Darrell Wallace on a 2-yd. run in the 1st quarter. In the 2nd quarter, QB Ken Austin hit SB Ray Elgaard for a TD from 22 yds. away, and Wallace added his 2nd of the day on a 1-yd. plunge into the end zone before Hamilton finally got on the board with a 42-yd. field goal from K Paul Osbaldiston to make the score 22-3 for the Roughriders. Saskatchewan continued its scoring run in the 2nd half when K Dave Ridgway kicked a 34-yarder through the uprights and Austin hit WR Don Narcisse on a 10-yd. pass. The 4th quarter saw Matich kick for another single and Hamilton scored their only major as WR Cornell Burbage caught a 22-yd. pass from QB Don McPherson to make the final score 33-10 for Saskatchewan.

Monday, October 18 - Calgary Stampeders 51 @ Toronto Argonauts 7 - 21,023
The CFL's best team, the Calgary Stampeders, appeared at SkyDome to take on the Toronto Argonauts, who in their previous encounter gave the Stampeders a tough battle. The Argos started the evening off well as K Lance Chomyc kicked a 46-yd. field goal midway through the 1st quarter. But Calgary, led by QB Doug Flutie who was 16-of -25 for 292 yds. and 4 TDs, didn't take long to strike back as Flutie hit SB Dave Sapunjis, the CFL's leading receiver for a TD on a 17-yd. pass. Toronto came back to tie the game as Chomyc hit another FG and also scored a single in the 2nd quarter. That was all the offense that the Argos would manage to put together for the day however as the Stampeders shut them out for the remainder of the day. Following Chomyc's single, Sapunjis grabbed his 2nd TD of the day from Flutie on a 24-yd. pass. Calgary WR Will Moore got into the act as he caught a 6-yd. Flutie TD pass to make the score 20-7 at the end of the 2nd quarter. In the 3rd, Flutie took it into the end zone himself from 3 yds. away and also managed to find WR Alan Wiggins with a 28-yd. TD pass. Backup QB Steve Taylor entered the game in the 4th quarter, after a brief appearance in the 1st half, and picked up where Flutie left off. He hit WR Derrick Crawford on a 54-yd. TD pass and also found Moore on a 14-yd. reception, both for their 2nd TDs of the day, before K Mark McLoughlin came in and put Calgary over the 50 point mark when he kicked a FG with under 2 minutes to go.

WEEK #16

Friday, October 22 - Edmonton Eskimos 19 @ Ottawa Rough Riders 17 - 19,580
The Rough Riders welcomed the Eskimos and were hoping to be able to improve their playoff hopes with a win in front of the 19,580 fans. Edmonton's K Sean Fleming was responsible for 4 of Edmonton's first 5 scores as he kicked a single followed by FGs of 48, 35 and 35 yards to give the Eskimos a 12-0 lead. In between Fleming's kicking, the Edmonton defence got into the act and tackled Ottawa QB Tom Burgess in the end zone for a safety before the Rough Riders got on the board. Ottawa then scored a TD on a 57-yard pass play when Burgess hit WR Walter Stanley. K Paul McCallum added to that count when he kicked a 24-yard FG to cut the Eskimo lead to 13-10 at the half. In the 3rd quarter, the only scoring took place when McCallum added another FG to tie the game with just under 20 minutes to play. In the 4th, Ottawa hit for another FG from 13 yards out to take the lead for the first time, however, it was short-lived as Edmonton came back with FGs of their own when Fleming hit from 30 and 23 yards to give Edmonton a 3-point lead with less than 50 seconds remaining. The Riders came back though and had a chance to win on a last second FG from 33 yards but McCallum was wide and the Eskimos squeaked out a victory 19-17.

Saturday, October 23 - Calgary Stampeders 45 @ Saskatchewan Roughriders 48 - 26,137
In a game that featured 2 of the CFL's top QBs, the defenses were put to work as the Stampeders and Roughriders combined for 93 points and 1,174 passing yards for a new CFL record for Most Yards Passing by Both Teams in One Game, in a shootout at Taylor Field on Saturday as 26,137 fans watched on. In the first half, the game was definitely in Saskatchewan's hands as they controlled the ball and the scoring, putting up 31 points in the opening half. QB Kent Austin opened the scoring as he ran the ball in from 1 yard out to give Saskatchewan the early lead and then added to it when SB Jeff Fairholm caught a 28-yd. pass for a TD before QB Doug Flutie put Calgary on the scoreboard when he ran the ball in himself from 18 yards to cut the Roughrider lead to 7 points. But the 'Riders answered back when Austin scored a TD from 1 yd. out and then mirrored the same play again one minute later to put his team up 28-7. He then added to what appeared to be a blowout when he hit SB Bruce Boyko for a 9-yd TD pass before Calgary K Mark McLoughlin kicked a FG with no time left in the 2nd quarter from 32 yards away to make the score 35-10 at the half. To open the 3rd, Flutie ran it in from 2 yds out and then SB Ray Elgaard caught a 15-yd. Austin pass for a TD to add to his record-breaking day in which he broke the CFL record for most yards receiving, by catching 10 passes for 154 yds. After Elgaard's TD, the Stampeders offense broke loose as SB Dave Sapunjis went 75 yds on a Flutie pass and WR Brian Wiggins caught 2 consecutive TD passes from 10 and 42 yds and suddenly the score was 42-37 for the 'Riders with just over half a quarter left to play. K Dave Ridgway hit an 8-yd FG, and then Flutie threw a 5-yd. TD pass to Wiggins, his 3rd of the day and followed WR Derrick Crawford's 2-pt convert. With 1 second on the clock, Ridgway kicked a 34-yarder for the win.

Saturday, October 23 - Toronto Argonauts 24 @ Sacramento Gold Miners 38 - 16,242
For the 3rd consecutive week, the Argonauts had a chance to move ahead of the Rough Riders in the Eastern Division as Ottawa had lost earlier and Sacramento had already been eliminated from a post-season appearance in the West. Toronto started the game on a positive note as QB Tracy Ham ran the ball in from 21 yards out and K Lance Chomyc kicked 52-yd single to put Toronto up 8-0. But Sacramento came back late in the quarter to score a TD as QB David Archer hit WR James Pruitt from 46 yards to cut into the Toronto lead. In the 2nd, Toronto again got on the board when Chomyc missed a FG for a single and RB Mike Clemons grabbed an 11-yard TD pass from Ham. Sacramento found their gear and scored 2 more TDs before the half as Archer threw TD passes of 17 and 20 yards to WR Rod Harris and WR Joe Howard Johnson to put the Miners up 21-16 at the intermission. In the 3rd, Sacramento got a 30-yd FG from K Jim Crouch and Archer ran one in himself and then hit Johnson for his 2nd of the day from 7 yards out. Toronto managed one last score as WR Manny Hazard caught a 17-yd. pass and Clemons ran the ball in for a 2-pt convert but that would not be enough as the Miners won their 5th game of the year.

Sunday, October 24 - B.C. Lions 36 @ Hamilton Tiger-Cats 19 - 11,574
The B.C. Lions visited the Tiger-Cats and were hoping to keep pace with the Eskimos and the Roughriders, who both had notched their tenth victories of the year earlier in the weekend. K Lui Passaglia opened the scoring early in the 1st quarter when he kicked a 45-yard FG and then later in the quarter, WR Darren Flutie caught an 11-yd TD from QB Danny Barrett to give the Lions an early 10-0 lead. In the 2nd, Hamilton put a single on the board and later scored a TD on a 5-yd. pass to WR Cornell Burbage from QB Bob Torrance while in between, Passaglia kicked a single for the Lions. The 3rd quarter saw B.C. get another TD from Flutie, then Passaglia kicked a single and a 13-yd FG and WR Mike Trevathan caught a 17-yd TD catch to increase the Lions' lead to 29-9. The Cats scored a TD in the 4th when SB Lee Knight caught a 6-yd toss and K Paul Osbaldiston kicked a 51-yd. FG before B.C. closed out the scoring with a 60-yd. run from RB Sean Millionton to give the Lions the win and a share of second place in the West.

WEEK #17

Friday, October 29 - Edmonton Eskimos 54 @ B.C. Lions 14 - 35,674
The 2teams tied for 2nd place in the CFL Western Division met as the Lions played host to the Eskimos in front of 35,654 fans at B.C. Place. The winner of the game would move into another tie if Saskatchewan won their game against Toronto. Edmonton opened with two scores in the 1st quarter as K Sean Fleming kicked a FG and WR Eddie Brown caught a 14-yd. pass from QB Damon Allen to give the Eskimos a 10-0 lead after the 1st quarter. In the 2nd quarter, B.C. got on the board when RB Cory Philpot scored on a 2-yd. rush to cut the Edmonton lead to 10-7 but then the Eskimos went on a scoring tear as they put another 20 points on the board before the half. Fleming kicked another FG and Allen scored a major as he went into the end zone on a 1-yd. effort. Following Allen's TD, the Eskimos struck again when Allen hit WR Jim Sandusky for a score on a 16-yd. pass to put Edmonton up 27-7 which Fleming added to when he kicked a 33-yd. FG. In the 2nd half, Fleming hit a 23-yarder and then added a single before B.C. put their 2nd score of the day on the board as Cory Philpot took in a 4-yd. rush for his 2nd of the day. The 4th quarter was all Edmonton as they scored 2 TDs and a FG when Allen ran 32 yds. for one TD while CB John Holland had an interception return for another and Fleming kicked his 6th FG of the day, this one from 38 yds. to make the final score 54—14 for the

Saturday, October 30 - Winnipeg Blue Bombers 36 @ Ottawa Rough Riders 16 - 19,240
The Blue Bombers paid a visit to the confines of Frank Clair Stadium to take on the Rough Riders

in a meeting of Eastern division rivals before 19, 240 people. Winnipeg opened the scoring midway through the 1st quarter when QB Sammy Garza hit WR David Williams on a 12-yd. pass to give the Bombers an early lead. However, Ottawa was able to strike back as they put together two consecutive FGs of 27 and 35 yds. from Paul McCallum to cut into Winnipeg's lead. But the Bombers then managed to put together a sustained string of drives and scored 3 consecutive FGs to go up 16-6. The teams again traded FGs to make the score 19-9 at the half. To open the 3rd quarter, the Bombers scored a major as Garza found WR Gerald Wilcox on a 35-yd. pass play to widen the lead, but Ottawa managed to come right back and score a TD of their own as QB Tom Burgess hit SB Jock Climie for a 28-yd. passing TD. Winnipeg put the game out of reach when they hit for a FG midway through the 3rd and then midway through the 4th, Garza found RB Mike Richardson with a 15-yd. TD pass to give the Bombers a 36-16 victory.

Saturday, October 30 - Sacramento Gold Miners 8 @ Calgary Stampeders 41 - 26,015
The Calgary Stampeder welcomed the Gold Miners to McMahon Stadium and ended up giving the hometown crowd of 26,015 a performance that was entered into the record books. Calgary got off to a fast start as K Mark McLoughlin scored a single off the opening kickoff, which was then followed up by a 19-yd. TD pass from QB Doug Flutie to WR Will Moore. Sacramento managed a single on a 61-yd. punt by P Pete Gardere before Flutie hit SB Dave Sapunjis for a 33-yd. TD. In the 2nd quarter, with QB Steve Taylor in at quarterback, the new QB took it in himself from a yd. out. Sacramento added a TD when QB David Archer hit RB Mike Pringle with a 1-yd. pass to cut the Stamps' lead to 22-8 at the half. The second half was all Calgary as McLoughlin booted 2 FGs of 28 and 33 yds. and in a record-setting catch, Sapunjis made his 100th reception of the season, the first Canadian ever to do so. In the 4th quarter, Taylor hit Will Moore for his 2nd of the day from 10 yds. away, and McLoughlin added another 2 FGs from 23 and 16 yds. away to make the final 41-8 for the Stamps.

Sunday, October 31 - Saskatchewan Roughriders 30 @ Toronto Argonauts 23 - 29,348
At SkyDome on Halloween, the Argonauts were hoping to scare a win out of the Roughriders and get a hold of sole possession of 3rd place in the Eastern Division and a possible playoff berth. The 29,348 fans in attendance saw Toronto get on the board less than a minute into the game as WR Manny Hazard hauled in a 46-yd. pass from QB Reggie Slack. But the Roughriders were able to counter with 2 FGs from K Dave Ridgway to cut the Argo lead to 1 point. In the 2nd quarter, SB Ray Elgaard grabbed a 9-yd. pass from QB Ken Austin to give Saskatchewan its first lead of the day. However, the Argos got a FG from K Lance Chomyc of 27-yds. and a TD when Slack hit Andre Brown for a TD. The Roughriders scored another TD when WR Don Narcisse grabbed a 20-yd. pass from Austin which the Argos countered with a 45-yd. Chomyc FG to even the score at 20-20 at the half. In the 2nd half, the 'Riders were able to score a FG in the 3rd quarter and then in the 4th they scored a TD when Darrell Wallace ran into the end zone from 11 yds. to give Saskatchewan a 10 point lead with just over 14 minutes to play. Unfortunately the Argos could only manage a FG and were not able to cap off another drive near the end of the game as Sasktchewan prevailed with a 30-23 count. Austin went 41-of-55 for 507 yds. to tie the League record for the Most Pass Completions in One Game, held by Dieter Brock, while Narcisse became the first player to catch for over 1,000 yds. in five consecutive seasons as he racked up 15 catches for 199 yds. and 1 TD.

WEEK #18

Saturday, November 6 - B.C. Lions 27 @ Sacramento Gold Miners 64 - 18,748
The Sacramento Gold Miners thrashed the B.C. Lions 64-27 in front of 18,748 fans at Hornet Field in their last game of the year. QB David Archer was outstanding as he threw for 375 yds. and 4 TDs, making him only the 3rd pivot to pass for over 6,000 yds. in a season. The Miners took an early lead as Mike Oliphant capped off an 80-yd. drive with a 5-yd. run for the score. Two B.C. turnovers led to two more TDs for the home team as FB Mike Pringle ran in from the 44-yd. line following a fumble by Sean Millington to put his team up 14-0. On the following kickoff, former Miner Freeman Baysinger fumbled when he was hit by Bobby Humphrey. The ball was recovered at the Lions' 48-yd. line. Four plays later, Archer scored from the 1-yd. line. B.C. finally put some points on the board when K Lui Passaglia made 2 FGs (Sacramento K Jim Crouch missed one from the 42 for a single in between), Miner WR Carl Parker caught a 20-yd. toss to put his team up 29-6 before half-time. Sacramento continued their romp in the third as Greg Joelson returned a fumble 31 yds. for the major and then Archer passed for 2 more TDs while Lions QB Danny Barrett found Ray Alexander for a 22-yd. toss and a one-yd. throw to Darren Flutie to make the count 49-20 after 3 periods. The final quarter saw Archer pass a 3rd TD to Parker and had Pringle run from the 3-yd. line before Millington ran one in for his team as the Gold Miners won their 6th game of the year. Crouch tied a CFL record in that game for Most Converts in One Game with 9.

Sunday, November 7 - Ottawa Rough Riders 27 @ Hamilton Tiger-Cats 26 - 17,032
It came down to the last weekend of the season, but finally the Ottawa Rough Riders were able to take a win and claim a playoff spot ahead of the Argonauts as they defeated the Tiger-Cats at Ivor Wynne Stadium in Hamilton before 17,032 fans. Hamilton opened the scoring at 6:57 of the first quarter with a 28-yd. FG by K Paul Osbaldiston. Bruce Perkins then ran in from the 1-yd. line as the gun sounded to end the 1st period to put his team up 10-0. Ottawa managed to put some points on the board when QB Tom Burgess found Rob Crifo for a 15-yd. TD catch, which was followed by a missed 2-point convert attempt. The 'Cats came back 3 minutes later as QB Todd Dillon, back with his former team after a one-year layoff, threw a 13-yd. TD to Earl Winfield. Down 20-6 (Osbaldiston added another FG before the end of the half and a team safety was added), the Riders began their comeback, scoring 2 TDs by SB Jock Climie (24-yd. and 17-yd. catches). Hamilton kept its lead as Osbaldiston booted another FG but things started to go Ottawa's way when Dexter Manley and Maurice Henry teamed up to knock the ball out of Dillon's hands to cause the fumble, recovered by Manley. That led to another Rider TD, to make the count 27-25 with less than 5 minutes to go. Hamilton could have gone ahead again but a 51-yd. FG attempt by Osbaldiston went wide, and Ottawa held on to win their fourth game of the season and assure themselves of an additional game against the Tiger-Cats next week in the Eastern Semi-Final.

Sunday, November 7 - Toronto Argonauts 10 @ Winnipeg Blue Bombers 12 - 22,287
It was a kickers' contest on a chilly day at Winnipeg Stadium as neither the Argonauts nor the Blue Bombers scored a TD on the day. Troy Westwood scored the only points by either team in the opening frame as he booted a 29-yd. FG to put the home squad up 3-0. In the 2nd, Lance Chomyc put Toronto on the board with a single on a missed FG. Westwood added to his totals with a 31-yd. FG and a single on a missed FG. At 12:06 Chomyc connected from 41 yds. out to pull the Argonauts to within three points at the half. Leading 7-4 heading into the 3rd quarter, Westwood hoofed a 40-yd. FG and Chomyc replied with a single, missing another attempt, this one from 39 yds. out. In the final quarter, Westwood recorded a single and Chomyc connected from 38 yds. out for a FG, before P Bob Cameron of Winnipeg rounded out the scoring by notching a single and conceded a safety with just 43 seconds to go in the contest. The Blue Bombers now have a bye and await the winner of the Eastern Semi-Final game. The Toronto Argonauts miss the playoffs for the second consecutive season.

Sunday, November 7 - Calgary Stampeders 21 @ Edmonton Eskimos 39 - 23,536
The Eskimos ran up a 29-0 lead in the first half and coasted to their second win over the Stampeders this season. Edmonton P Glenn Harper opened the scoring with a single just 1:36 into the contest. Henry "Gizmo" Williams then electrified the crowd with a 104-yd. punt return before QB Damon Allen took the ball in himself to put the Esks ahead 15-0 at the end of the first quarter. In the 2nd, Lucius Floyd rushed 13 yds. for a TD, before Williams had the crowd on their feet again, this time with an 83-yd. punt return for a TD. Down 29-0 heading into the 3rd, Calgary finally got on track as QB Steve Taylor plunged 1 yd. for their first TD. K Mark McLoughlin added to his league-leading point totals with 2 FGs (22 yds. and 25 yds.) to make the score 29-13 at the end of the 3rd. The Eskimos racked up 10 more points to start the 4th as K Sean Fleming connected on a 21-yd. FG and Michael Soles carried the ball 1 yd. for the major. At 12:46 Taylor hooked up with Brian Wiggins for a 13-yd. TD, and Wiggins also caught the 2-point convert. The Eskimos will host the Saskatchewan Roughriders in one Western Semi-Final, while the Stampeders return home to face the B.C. Lions in the other Semi-Final game.

PLAYOFF WEEK #1

Sunday, November 14 - Ottawa Rough Riders 10 @ Hamilton Tiger-Cats 21 - 18,781
The Rough Riders were hoping to begin a "new" season and repeat the outcome of their last visit as they returned to Hamilton following their win over the Tiger-Cats last weekend that enabled them to enter the post-season. However, a whole Tiger-Cat team was determined not to let that happen as they got on the board first as SB Lee Knight caught an 11-yd. pass from QB Todd Dillon to give the Ti-Cats an early 7-0 lead. Ottawa got on the board late in the 2nd quarter as K Mike Lazecki kicked a 33-yd. FG to cut into the Hamilton lead 7-3 at the half. In the 3rd period, the Tiger-Cats increased their lead as SB Joey Jauch hauled in a 10-yd. TD catch from Dillon to give Hamilton a 14-3 lead before Ottawa WR Stephen Jones came down with a 75-yd. bomb from QB Tom Burgess to put Ottawa within 4 points with over 17 minutes to play. In the 4th quarter however, Hamilton RB Dave Dinall took off on a 34-yd. rush for a TD that put Hamilton up by 11 points with just under 10 minutes to go. However, Ottawa just couldn't seem to mount a scoring drive and failed to put any more points on the board. As the final gun sounded, the score was 21-10 for the Tiger-Cats, who will now meet Winnipeg in this weekend's Eastern Division final.

Sunday, November 14 - Saskatchewan Roughriders 13 @ Edmonton Eskimos 51 - 26,397
This past weekend's matchup featured the Saskatchewan Roughriders visiting Commonwealth Stadium to meet the Eskimos in front of 26,397 fans. The Esks opened the scoring as K Sean Fleming hit a 30-yd. field goal to give Edmonton an early 3-0 lead but it was short lived as Saskatchewan's K Dave Ridgway countered with a 33-yd. effort of his own to tie the game. From that point on, the Eskimos seemed to find their groove as they began to find holes in the Roughrider defense. RB Lucius Floyd ran the ball in from 3 yds. for the TD and was a force in the game running for 121 yds. on 22 carries. Ridgway managed another FG and the Riders were still within striking distance. Floyd then ran for his 2nd major of the day from 15 yds. away while Saskatchewan's SB Bruce Boyko caught a 13-yd. pass to make the score 24-13 for the Esks before Fleming hit a FG from 34 yds. to increase the lead to 14 points at the half. The second half was all Edmonton as they shut out the Roughriders and scored 24 points. They opened the 3rd quarter with Fleming hitting for another FG and closed the quarter with 2 TDs as WR Eddie Brown caught a 9-yd. pass and Henry "Gizmo" Williams hauled in a 39-yd. reception for the score. The 4th quarter saw RB Bruce Walling take the ball in from 18 yds. out to hit for the major and close out the scoring. The final was 51-13 in favour of the Eskimos who advance to the Western Final against the defending Grey Cup Champion CalgaryStampeders.

Sunday, November 14 - B.C. Lions 9 @ Calgary Stampeders 17 - 15,407
The B.C. Lions entered McMahon Stadium to face the defending Grey Cup Champions, the Calgary Stampeders before 15,407 fans. In what turned out to be one of the key plays of the game, DT Srecko Zizakovic intercepted an errant pass as B.C. QB Danny Barrett was hit by DE Harold Hasselbach and he returned it 6 yds. for a TD at 12:24 of the opening frame. B.C. K Lui Passaglia put the Lions on the board in the second quarter as he kicked a 25-yd. field goal to cut into the Stampeder lead. Yet Calgary came right back and scored as WR Will Moore caught a 10-yd. pass from QB Doug Flutie and K Mark McLoughlin kicked a 22-yd. FG to give the Stamps a 17-3 lead at the half. In the 3rd quarter, B.C. appeared to start a comeback as they scored 2 FGs from 15 and 34 yds. off the foot of Passaglia, but thanks to some super punting by Calgary K Tony Martino who had a 46.6 yd. average on 9 punts on a windy day in Calgary, the Lions could do no more damage. The final score was 17-9 for the Stampeders who will host Edmonton in next weekend's Western Division final.

PLAYOFF WEEK #2

Sunday, November 21 - Hamilton Tiger-Cats 19 @ Winnipeg Blue Bombers 20 - 23,332
The Hamilton Tiger-Cats visited Winnipeg Stadium for the Eastern title with the intention of making amends for last year's 59-11 loss in the Division Final. The Blue Bombers opened the scoring early when K Troy Westwood connected on a 32-yd. FG 2:43 into the game. But the Ti-Cats answered back midway through the first quarter with K Paul Osbaldiston's 26-yd. FG. Winnipeg then scrimmaged from their own 35-yd. line and promptly drove down the field and scored on a third-down play as QB Sammy Garza hit SB Gerald Wilcox for a 3-yd. TD to put Winnipeg ahead 10-3. Following another Bomber FG, Hamilton dominated the second quarter, scoring on a 4-yd. TD run by RB Dave Dinnall and three Paul Osbaldiston FGs of 42, 39 and 43 yds. to take a 19-13 halftime lead. After a scoreless third quarter, the Bombers scored a single on a 68-yd. punt by P Bob Cameron and then added a 42-yd. Troy Westwood field goal to move to within two points of the Cats. Late in the fourth quarter, Winnipeg took possession of the ball on its own 50-yd. line and moved the ball downfield to set up the game-winning FG by Westwood with 21 seconds left in regulation time. Hamilton still managed to move the ball into Winnipeg territory to set up a 44-yd. FG attempt. But Osbaldiston's kick into the wind fell just short as time ran out and Winnipeg advanced to the Grey Cup Championship Game.

Sunday, November 21 - Edmonton Eskimos 29 @ Calgary Stampeders 15 - 20,218
The defending Grey Cup Champion Stampeders were hoping to advance to the Grey Cup Game again this year and it looked good for them early as Peewee Smith returned a punt 64 yds. for a TD three minutes into the game on a snow-covered field. Calgary added a FG by K Mark McLoughlin about midway through the quarter and the Stampeders were ahead 10-0. But Edmonton answered back in the 2nd as QB Damon Allen connected with WR Jim Sandusky on a 73-yd. TD pass. Mark McLoughlin would add another FG to give the Stamps a 13-8 halftime lead. The 2nd half was all Edmonton as Allen again connected with Sandusky to put the Esks up 15-13. Allen was at it again early in the 4th quarter when he hit Eddie Brown with a 32-yd. TD pass and the Esks never looked back. They would add one more TD when Allen hit Jay Christensen on a 16-yd. pass to seal the victory 29-15 and send the Eskimos to the Grey Cup Championship against the Winnipeg Blue Bombers.

1993 GAME PARTICIPATION

OTTAWA ROUGH RIDERS

18 Games - Tom Burgess, Patrick Burke, Denny Chronopoulos, Jock Climie, Shawn Daniels, Anthony Drawhorn, James Ellingson, Chris Gioskos, Michael Graybill, Terrence Jones, John Kropke, Michel Lamy, Joe Sardo, Angelo Snipes, Gregg Stumon.

17 Games or Fewer - Michael Allen (5), Terry Baker (11), Reggie Barnes (4), Bruce Beaton (16), Daved Benefield (11), Brian Bonner (7) , Dave Chaytors (13), Carl Coulter (1), Rob Crifo (7), Burtland Cummings (6), Irv Daymond (12), Greg Duncan (1), Marquel Fleetwood (14), Joe Fuller (14), Ron Goetz (17), Charles Gordon (9), John Hardy (1), Maurice Henry (1), Daniel Hunter (1), Stephen Jones (17), Darren Joseph (14), Glen Kulka (16), Michael Lazecki (1), Nigel Levy (1), Ray Macoritti (3), Pat Mahon (4), Dexter Manley (2), Paul McCallum (3), Joe Mero (7), Jacques Moreau (8), Dean Noel (8), Michel Raby (16), Dwight Richards (12), Lybrant Robinson (16), Ernie Schramayr (11), Mark Scott (0), Tyrone Shavers (5), Walter Stanley (8), Andrew Stewart (6), Remi Trudel (13), Ken Walcott (15), Wayne Walker (13), Gordon Weber (10), Paul Wetmore (3), Charles Wright (8), Brett Young (13).

TORONTO ARGONAUTS

18 Games - Ken Benson, Keith Castello, Lance Chomyc, Mike Clemons, Tracy Ham, Chris Green, Warren Hudson, Bret Johnson, Andrew Murray, Reggie Pleasant, Blaine Schmidt.

17 Games or Fewer - Francois Belanger (12), Derrick Branch (2), Michael Campbell (17), Reggie Clark (2), Robert Clark (14), Jeff Croonen (3), Terry Dickey (6), Bruce Elliott (17), Craig Ellis (1), Corris Ervin (6), Robert Gordon (7), Derek Hadnot (1), Harold Hallman (13), Rodney Harding (17), John Hardy (4), Darrell Harle (8), Manny Hazard (14), William Henry (2), Brian Hilk (1), Mark Houlder (1), Darren Hughes (11), Brian Hutchings(2), Hank Ilesic (11), Enis Jackson (5), Pat Jackson (5), Mike Kerrigan (7), Lorne King (10), Wayne Lammle (7), Hugh Lawson (2), Orville Lee (0), Sherman Lewis (9), Tahaun Lewis (5), Paul Masotti (12), Derrick McAdoo (4), Brian McCurdy (12), Darryl Milburn (4), Don Moen (17), George Nimako (9), Lou Olsacher (3), Peter Partchenko (8), Keith Powe (6), Dwight Richards (3), Mark Ricks (4), Steve Rodehutskors (12), Chris Schultz (1), Reggie Slack (11), Daryle Smith (4), Leroy Smith (1), Derek Steele (2), Andrew Thomas (16), Dave Van Belleghem (17), Pierre Vercheval (3), Brian Warren (15), Patrick Wayne (5), Kevin Whitley (13), Ken Whitney (10), Arnie Williams (7), Larry Willis (3), Jonathan Wilson (9), Ken Winey (6), Antoine Worthman (1), John Zajdel (2), Wally Zatylny (16).

HAMILTON TIGER-CATS

18 Games - Tim Cofield, Scott Douglas, Pete Giftopoulos, Roger Henning, Joey Jauch, Mike Jovanovich, John Motton, Don McPherson, Richard Nurse, Paul Osbaldiston, Mike O'Shea, Dave Richardson, Rickey Royal, Todd Wiseman, Terry Wright, Lubo Zizakovic.

17 Games or Fewer - Romel Andrews (11), David Bailey (13), Stephen Bates (2), Darrell Beavers (7), Cornell Burbage (12), Paul Bushey (15), Bobby Dawson (11), Mark Dennis (1), Todd Dillon (1), David Dinnall (15), Greg Eaglin (9), Corris Ervin (7), Ken Evraire (15), Jeff Fields (5), Lonnie Finch (8), Darrell Harle (5), Roy Hart (9), William Henry (9), Lonzell Hill (3), John Hood (4), Tim Jackson (12), James Jauch (11), Derrick Kelson (7), Lee Knight (17), Robert MacDonald (12), P.J. Martin (16), Nick Mazzoli (13), Bruce Perkins (14), Jason Riley (9), Reggie Rogers (4), Lee Saltz (1), Eros Sanchez (14), Dale Sanderson (7), Mark Scott (16), Robert Torrance (11), Lance Trumble (1), Scott Walker (6), Rob Wallow (0), Gary Wilkerson (11), Brett Williams (10), Earl Winfield (15).

WINNIPEG BLUE BOMBERS

18 Games - David Black, Bob Cameron, Bobby Evans, Miles Gorrell, Chris Johnstone, Stan Mikowas, Brett MacNeil, Elfrid Payton, Tom Porras, Paul Randlolph, Brendan Rogers, Darryl Sampson, Donald Smith, Chris Tsangaris, Dave Vankoughnett, Chris Walby, Troy Westwood.

17 Games or Fewer - Gerald Alphin (16), Ousmane Bary (12), Greg Battle (16), Michael Bellamy (7), Nick Benjamin (12), George Bethune (1), Nathaniel Bolton (12), Vaughn Booker (9), Allan Boyko (17), Errol Brown (2), Blaise Bryant (8), Greg Clark (4), Robert Crifo (4), Rob Davidson (6), Matt Dunigan (16), Jayson Dzikowicz (16), Anthony Florence (3), Duane Forde (13), Corian Freeman (10), Sammy Garza (13), Steve Grant (0), Michael Gray (3), Leon Hatziioannou (12), Patrick Hinton (4), Alfred Jackson (12), Loyd Lewis (16), Quinn Magnuson (9), Andrew Martin (5), Keithen McCant (7), Matt Pearce (17), Kim Phillips (13), Mike Richardson (12), Keilly Rush (8), Alan Wetmore (2), Gerald Wilcox (16), David Williams (16).

SASKATCHEWAN ROUGHRIDERS

18 Games - Michael Anderson, Charles Anthony, Jerald Baylis, Ray Bernard, Bruce Boyko, Albert Brown, Maurice Crum, Wayne Drinkwalter, Ray Elgaard, Jeff Fairholm, Dan Farthing, Brooks Findlay, Craig Hendrickson, Scott Hendrickson, Stewart Hill, Warren Jones, Tom MacCallum, Don Narcisse, Dan Payne, David Pitcher, Dave Ridgway, Glen Suitor, Paul Vajda.

17 Games or Fewer - Kent Austin (17), Brian Bonner (10), Sean Brantley (3), Errol Brown (14), Blaise Bryant (2), Ricardo Cartwright (2), Lance Cook (1), Paul Cranmer (1), Willie Culpepper (3), Ventson Donelson (14), Tre Everett (4), Bobby Jurasin (17), Carlton Lance (13), Gary Lewis (15), Brent Matich (16), Dane McArthur (2), Mike Middleton (5), Peter Miller (10), Chris Munford (12), Michael Proctor (3), Dan Rashovich (11), Mark Ricks (2), Mike Saunders (13), Kelly Trithart (1), Terryl Ulmer (9), Mike Vanderjagt (2), Darrell Wallace (3), Paul Wetmore (3), Barry Wilburn (16), Byron Williams (12).

CALGARY STAMPEDERS

18 Games - Karl Anthony, Raymond Biggs, Derrick Crawford, Bruce Covernton, Doug Davies, Doug Flutie, Harald Hasselbach, Alondra Johnson, Eric Johnson, William Johnson, Greg Knox, Frank Marof, Tony Martino, Ken Moore, Will Moore, Mark McLoughlin, Andy McVey, Marvin Pope, Rocco Romano, David Sapunjis, Todd Storme, Steve Taylor, Gerald Vaughn, Blair Zerr.

17 Games or Fewer - Eddie Britton (2), Lui Cafazzo (12), Douglas Craft (8), Jamie Crysdale (7), Duane Dmytryshyn (1), Marc Dube (10), Greg Eaglin (6), Matt Finlay (16), Greg Frers (16), Keyvan Jenkins (12), Stuart Laird (14), Kenton Leonard (15), Patrick Mahon (6), Eric Mitchel (0), Mark Pearce (13), Allen Pitts (7), PeeWee Smith (16), Tony Stewart (6), Ulyses Thurman (8), Ken Watson (17), Brian Wiggins (11), Srecko Zizakovic (13).

EDMONTON ESKIMOS

18 Games - Damon Allen, Leroy Blugh, Eddie Brown, Rod Connop, Blake Dermott, Mike Dumaresq, Sean Fleming, Rickey Foggie, Benny Goods, Glenn Harper, Malvin Hunter, J.P. Izquierdo, Steve Krupey, Damion Lyons, Errol Martin, Tom Muecke, Chris Morris, Dan Murphy, Jed Roberts, Glenn Rogers, Henry Williams, Don Wilson, Michael Sloles, Brian Walling.

17 Games or Fewer - Randy Ambrosie (13), Ed Berry (14), Michel Bourgeau (17), Trent Brown (16), Wayde Butler (3), Terris Chorney (9), Jay Christensen (9), Bruce Dickson (15), Kasey Dunn (7), Lucius Floyd (8), John R. Holland (9), Leonard Johnson (11), Rickey Jones (2), Michael Kerr (1), Morris Lolar (0), Blake Marshall (7), Lee Miles (2), Eric Mitchel (3), Doug Parrish (13), Willie Pless (16), Jim Sandusky (8), David Shelton (0), Darrell K. Smith (4), Jeff Thomas (5), Clinton Woods (16), Larry Wruck (17).

B.C. LIONS

18 Games - Danny Barrett, O.J. Brigance, Less Browne, Matt Clarke, Tom Europe, Leo Groenwegen, Ryan Hanson, Doug Hocking, Sean Millington, Jim Mills, Spencer McLennan, Danny McManus, Glen Scrivener, Ian Sinclair, Rob Smith, Vic Stevenson, Donovan Wright.

17 Games or Fewer - Ray Alexander (15), Michael Allen (9), Zock Allen (15), Freeman Baysinger (3), Vincent Brownlee (2), Giulio Caravatta (6), Matt Clark (16), Burtland Cummings (3), Darren Flutie (17), Sean Foudy (9), Andre Francis (16), Ron Francis (2), Todd Furdyk (0), Tracy Gravely (5), Derek Grier (6), Ken Hailey (7), Willie Hinchcliff (1), Daniel Hunter (4), Jeff Jackson (7), Shawn Jones (1), Tyrone Jones (15), Tim Lorenz (10), Darek MacCready (16), John MacNeill (6), Corey Mantyka (0), Paul McCallum (1), Robert Mimbs (2), Yo Murphy (1), Lui Passaglia (17), Cory Philpot (11), Bruce Plummer (8), Keith Powe (4), Steve Rodehutskors (2), Kelly Sims (6), Chris Skinner (8), Jamie Taras (16), Eddie Taylor (14), Mike Trevathan (17), Lonnie Turner (10), Jason Verduzco (12), Jon Volpe (5), Kent Warnock (17), Patrick Wayne (1), James West (17), Arnie Williams (0).

SACRAMENTO GOLD MINERS

18 Games - David Archer, Kerwin Bell, Jim Crouch, Paschall Davis, Vance Hammond, Rod Harris, Bobby Humphery, Michael Kiselak, Mark Ledbetter, Curtis Moore, Mike Oliphant, Mike Pringle, Ron Shipley, Robb White, John Wiley.

17 Games or Fewer - Walter Bailey (15), Freeman Baysinger (13), Willie Bouyer (6), Hurlie Brown (1), Heshimu Colar (6), David Diaz-Infante (8), Titus Dixon (15), Robert Dressel (5), Chris Dyko (16), Garry Frank (4), Charles Franks (10), Corrian Freeman (5), Charles Fryar (1), Steve Gabbard (14), Jon Garber (1), Peter Gardere (10), Horace Hamm (2), Robert Hardy (3), James Harper (8), Tommy Henry (9), Byron Jackson (3), Jim Jennings (7), Greg Joelson (11), Joe Howard Johnson (7), Claude Jones (11), Emanuel King (5), Keilan Matthews (12), Matt McCall (2), Gary McCurty (2), Paul McJulien (4), Maurice Miller (1), Troy Mills (13), Leonard Nelson (10), Carl Parker (17), Khevin Pratt (3), Basil Proctor (3), James Pruitt (8), Charles Puleri (8), Marshall Roberts (5), Calvin Schexnayder (2), Nick Subis (4), Kip Texada (17), Chris Thieneman (7), Charles Thompson (11), Randy Thornton (7), Jason Wallace (11), Larry Wallace (2), David Westerbrooks (9), Brent White (17), Myron Wise (2).

CFL ATTENDANCE 1966-93

	Pre-Season	Regular Season	Playoff Games	Grey Cup	TOTAL
1966	-	1,413,942	105,537	36,553	1,556,032
1967	-	1,365,607	135,754	31,358	1,532,719
1968	-	1,396,292	148,705	32,655	1,577,652
1969	-	1,413,440	151,945	33,172	1,598,557
1970	308,659	1,585,096	171,277	32,669	2,097,701
1971	330,324	1,625,541	145,600	34,484	2,135,949
1972	345,618	1,584,408	104,300	33,993	2,068,319
1973	351,327	1,674,589	80,582	36,653	2,143,151
1974	311,018	1,677,017	80,808	34,450	2,103,293
1975	354,043	1,826,950	94,105	32,454	2,307,552
1976	388,335	2,029,586	99,569	53,467	2,570,957
1977	387,937	2,254,144	132,707	68,318	2,843,106
1978	429,320	2,291,834	138,538	54,695	2,914,387
1979	446,759	2,236,918	135,130	65,113	2,883,920
1980	433,777	2,117,150	123,226	54,661	2,728,814

	Pre-Season	Regular Season	Playoff Games	Grey Cup	TOTAL
1981	417,869	2,122,870	131,455	52,478	2,724,672
1982	404,415	2,115,167	135,524	54,471	2,709,577
1983	428,912	2,194,056	173,842	59,345	2,856,155
1984	397,254	1,976,118	156,126	60,081	2,589,579
1985	377,005	1,907,802	124,464	56,723	2,465,994
1986	198,209	2,097,070	152,102	59,621	2,507,002
1987	172,417	1,871,278	125,479	59,478	2,228,652
1988	161,822	1,744,430	91,585	50,604	2,048,441
1989	190,498	1,837,644	94,545	54,088	2,176,775
1990	168,431	1,919,890	108,548	46,968	2,243,837
1991	199,598	2,001,858	118,921	51,985	2,372,362
1992	172,564	1,827,099	102,110	45,863	2,147,636
1993	201,200	1,961,642	104,225	50,035	2,317,102
TOTALS	**7,592,673**	**52,069,438**	**3,466,709**	**1,336,435**	**64,465,255**

Note: The 1993 attendance consisted of: 9 pre-season, 81 regular season, 5 playoff and the Grey Cup games.
The 1989 and 1992 attendances consisted of: 9 pre-season, 72 regular season, 4 playoff and the Grey Cup games.
The 1987, 1988, 1990 and 1991 attendances consisted of: 8 pre-season, 72 regular season, 4 playoff and the Grey Cup games.
The 1986 attendance consisted of: 10 pre-season, 81 regular season, 5 playoff and the Grey Cup games.
The 1985 attendance consisted of: 18 pre-season, 72 regular season, 4 playoff and the Grey Cup games.

CFL OUTSTANDING PLAYER AWARDS

'93 WINNERS

The Canadian Football League Outstanding Player Awards were presented on Friday, November 26th, 1993 at the Corral in Calgary, Alberta. For the third year in a row, quarterback Doug Flutie of the Calgary Stampeders was selected as the Most Outstanding Player in the CFL. He became the first player in CFL history to accomplish this feat. The show, a Rodeo-style Awards Show, featured players from four of the nine CFL teams, demonstrating excellent competition throughout the League in 1993. Other winners included the Most Outstanding Canadian, Calgary slotback David Sapunjis, Winnipeg tackle Chris Walby as the Most Outstanding Offensive Lineman, defensive tackle Jearld Baylis of Saskatchewan as the Most Outstanding Defensive Player and Michael O'Shea, a linebacker with Hamilton as the Most Outstanding Rookie.

MOST OUTSTANDING PLAYER

Year-By-Year Team Nominees

*denotes runner-up

	BRITISH COLUMBIA LIONS	EDMONTON ESKIMOS	CALGARY STAMPEDERS	SASKATCHEWAN ROUGHRIDERS	WINNIPEG BLUE BOMBERS
1993	Danny Barrett	Willie Pless	**Doug Flutie**	Jearld Baylis	**Matt Dunigan***
1992	Jon Volpe	Henry Williams	**Doug Flutie**	Kent Austin	Larry Thompson
1991	**Doug Flutie**	Blake Marshall	Allen Pitts	Kent Austin	**Robert Mimbs***
1990	Willie Pless	**Craig Ellis***	Derrick Crawford	Kent Austin	Robert Mimbs
1989	Matt Dunigan	**Tracy Ham**	Doug Landry	Tim McCray	Greg Battle
1988	**David Williams**	Danny Bass	Emanuel Tolbert	Ray Elgaard	James Murphy
1987	Jim Sandusky	**Brian Kelly***	Larry Willis	David Ridgway	**Tom Clements**
1986	James Parker	Stewart Hill	Rick Johnson	Bobby Johnson	**James Murphy**
1985	**Merv Fernandez**	Matt Dunigan	Larry Hogue	Eddie Lowe	Jeff Boyd
1984	Merv Fernandez	Matt Dunigan	Lewis Walker	Craig Ellis	**Willard Reaves**
1983	Roy Dewalt	**Warren Moon**	Danny Bass	Vince Goldsmith	Willard Reaves
1982	Roy Dewalt	**Tom Scott***	Danny Bass	Joey Walters	Dieter Brock
1981	Larry Key	Warren Moon	James Sykes	Joey Walters	**Dieter Brock**
1980	John Henry White	Warren Moon	James Sykes	Ken McEachern	**Dieter Brock**
1979	John Henry White	**Waddell Smith***	Ed McAleney	Ken McEachern	John Helton
1978	Larry Key	**Tom Wilkinson***	James Sykes	Mike Strickland	Dieter Brock
1977	**Jerry Tagge***	Larry Highbaugh	Willie Burden	Ron Lancaster	Jim Washington
1976	Bill Baker	George McGowan	Tom Forzani	**Ron Lancaster**	Jim Washington
1975	Bill Baker	George McGowan	**Willie Burden**	Tom Campana	Steve Beaird
1974	Lou Harris	**Tom Wilkinson**	John Helton	George Reed	Paul Williams
1973	John Musso	**George McGowan**	Rudy Linterman	Ron Lancaster	Don Jonas
1972	Jim Young	George McGowan	Gerry Shaw	Ron Lancaster	**Mack Herron***
1971	Jim Evenson	Dick Dupuis	Wayne Harris	George Reed	**Don Jonas**
1970	Jim Evenson	Terry Swarn	Wayne Harris	**Ron Lancaster**	Bill Frank
1969	Jim Young	John Lagrone	Jerry Keeling	**George Reed***	Phil Minnick
1968	Jim Evenson	Jim Thomas	Herm Harrison	**George Reed***	Dave Raimey
1967	Jim Young	Jim Thomas	**Peter Liske**	George Reed	Ken Neilsen
1966	Larry Eilmes	Jim Thomas	Don Luzzi	**Ron Lancaster***	Dave Raimey
1965	Joe Kapp	Tommy Joe Coffey	Lovell Coleman	**George Reed**	Leo Lewis
1964	Tom Brown	Tommy Joe Coffey	**Lovell Coleman**	Ed Buchanan	Ken Ploen
1963	**Joe Kapp***	Al Ecuyer	Lovell Coleman	Bob Ptacek	Farrell Funston
1962	Nub Beamer	**Tommy Joe Coffey***	Eagle Day	Ray Purdin	Leo Lewis
1961	Willie Flemming	**Jackie Parker***	Earl Lunsford	Bob Ptacek	Leo Lewis
1960	Willie Flemming	**Jackie Parker**	Earl Lunsford	Clair Branch	Leo Lewis
1959	Tom Hinton	**Johnny Bright**	Joe Kapp	Don Allard	Jim Van Pelt
1958	Paul Cameron	**Jackie Parker**	Don Luzzi	Frank Tripucka	Leo Lewis
1957	Paul Cameron	**Jackie Parker**	Dick Huffman	Frank Tripucka	Kenny Ploen
1956	Ed Vereb	**Jackie Parker***	Earl Lunsford	Ken Carpenter	Bob McNamara
1955		Jackie Parker		Ken Carpenter	
1954		Jackie Parker		Martin Ruby	Dick Huffman
		Rollie Miles		Harry Lampman	Gerry James
1953		**Billy Vessels**	John Henry Johnson		

	HAMILTON TIGER-CATS	TORONTO ARGONAUTS	OTTAWA ROUGH RIDERS	MONTREAL ALOUETTES
1993	Earl Winfield	Manny Hazard	Stephen Jones	—
1992	John Motton	Rodney Harding	**Angelo Snipes***	—
1991	Paul Osbaldiston	Raghib Ismail	Reggie Barnes	—
1990	Earl Winfield	**Mike Clemons**	Reggie Barnes	—
1989	**Tony Champion***	Gill Fenerty	Gerald Alphin	—
1988	**Earl Winfield***	Gilbert Renfroe	Gerald Alphin	—
1987	Steve Stapler	Darrell Smith	Marc Lewis	—
1986	Less Browne	Lance Chomyc	Loyd Lewis	**James Hood***
1985	**Ken Hobart***	Carl Brazley	Loyd Lewis	Mike McTague
1984	**Rufus Crawford***	Joe Barnes	Rick Barden	Nick Arakgi
1983	Johnny Shepherd	**Terry Greer***	Skip Walker	Delbert Fowler
1982	Tom Clements	**Condredge Holloway**	Skip Walker	Nick Arakgi
1981	**Tom Clements***	Paul Pearson	Tony Gabriel	James Scott
1980	Jerry Anderson	Bob Gaddis	Richard Crump	**Gerry Dattilio***
1979	Tom Clements	Terry Metcalfe	Mike Nelms	**David Green**
1978	Ray Nettles	Jim Corrigall	**Tony Gabriel**	Randy Rhino
1977	**Jimmy Edwards**	Ray Nettles	Tony Gabriel	Glen Weir
1976	**Jimmy Edwards***	Granny Liggins	Tom Clements	Peter Dalla Riva
1975	Garney Henley	Jim Corrigall	Art Green	**Johnny Rodgers***
1974	Andy Hopkins	Peter Muller	Rhome Nixon	**Johnny Rodgers***
1973	Andy Hopkins	Joe Theismann	Gerry Organ	**John Harvey***
1972	**Garney Henley**	Eric Allen	Dick Adams	Ed George
1971	Garney Henley	**Leon McQuay***	Marshall Shirk	Mark Kosmos
1970	**Tommy Joe Coffey***	Marv Luster	Hugh Oldham	Moses Denson
1969	Tommy Joe Coffey	Bill Symons	Russ Jackson	Sonny Wade
1968	Tommy Joe Coffey	**Bill Symons**	Vic Washington	Dave Lewis
1967	**Tommy Joe Coffey***	Jim Dillard	Russ Jackson	Phil Brady
1966	Garney Henley	Marv Luster	**Russ Jackson**	Don Lisbon
1965	**Garney Henley***	Jackie Parker	Russ Jackson	Bernie Faloney
1964	Tommy Grant	**Dick Shatto***	Ron Stewart	Ted Elsby
1963	Garney Henley	Dick Shatto	**Russ Jackson**	George Dixon
1962	Hal Patterson	Dick Shatto	Ernie White	George Dixon
1961	**Bernie Faloney**	Jim Rountree	Gerry Nesbitt	Don Clark
1960	John Barrow	**Cookie Gilchrist***	Ron Stewart	Sam Etcheverry
1959	**Bernie Faloney***	Dick Shatto	Dave Thelen	Sam Etcheverry

OVERALL WINNER

Doug Flutie, Calgary - 1993
Doug Flutie, Calgary - 1992
Doug Flutie, B.C. - 1991
Mike Clemons, Toronto - 1990
Tracy Ham, Edmonton - 1989
David Williams, B.C. - 1988
Tom Clements, Winnipeg - 1987
James Murphy, Winnipeg - 1986
Merv Fernandez, B.C. - 1985
Willard Reaves, Winnipeg - 1984
Warren Moon, Edmonton - 1983
Condredge Holloway, Toronto - 1982
Dieter Brock, Winnipeg - 1981
Dieter Brock, Winnipeg - 1980
David Green, Montreal - 1979
Tony Gabriel, Ottawa - 1978
Jimmy Edwards, Hamilton - 1977
Ron Lancaster, Saskatchewan - 1976
Willie Burden, Calgary - 1975
Tom Wilkinson, Edmonton - 1974
George McGowan, Edmonton - 1973
Garney Henley, Hamilton - 1972
Don Jonas, Winnipeg - 1971
Ron Lancaster, Saskatchewan - 1970
Russ Jackson, Ottawa - 1969
Bill Symons, Toronto - 1968
Peter Liske, Calgary - 1967
Russ Jackson, Ottawa - 1966
George Reed, Saskatchewan - 1965
Lovell Coleman, Calgary - 1964
Russ Jackson, Ottawa - 1963
George Dixon, Montreal - 1962
Bernie Faloney, Hamilton - 1961
Jackie Parker, Edmonton - 1960
Johnny Bright, Edmonton - 1959

1958	Bernie Faloney	**Dick Shatto***	Bill Sowalski	Sam Etcheverry	**Jackie Parker, Edmonton - 1958**
1957	Cookie Gilchrist	Dick Shatto	Kaye Vaughan	**Hal Patterson***	**Jackie Parker, Edmonton - 1957**
1956	Cookie Gilchrist		Bob Simpson	**Hal Patterson**	**Hal Patterson, Montreal - 1956**
1955		Dick Shatto		Sam Etcheverry	**Pat Abbruzzi, Montreal - 1955**
				Pat Abbruzzi	
1954	Tip Logan			**Sam Etcheverry**	
	Bernie Custis			Alex Webster	**Sam Etcheverry, Montreal - 1954**
				Doug McNichol	**Billy Vessels, Edmonton - 1953**
1953			'Choo Choo' Roberts	Tex Coulter	

MOST OUTSTANDING ROOKIE
Year-By-Year Team Nominees

	BRITISH COLUMBIA	EDMONTON	CALGARY	SASKATCHEWAN	WINNIPEG
1993	Cory Philpot	Errol Martin	**Brian Wiggins***	Carlton Lance	Nathaniel Bolton
1992	Lorne King	Chris Morris	**Bruce Covernton***	Ray Bernard	**Michael Richardson**
1991	**Jon Volpe**	Eddie Thomas	Kenton Leonard	Paul Vajda	Elfrid Payton
1990	Deatrich Wise	Ray Macoritti	Darryl Hall	**Lucius Floyd***	Dave Bovell
1989	**Darrell Wallace***	Enis Jackson	Brent Matich	Tuineau Alipate	Paul Randolph
1988	Anthony Drawhorn	Dave Richardson	Mark McLoughlin	**Jeff Fairholm***	Dan Wicklum
1987	Kevin Dixon	**Stanley Blair***	David McCrary	Terry Cochrane	Ken Pettway
1986	Scott Lecky	Tom Richards	**Harold Hallman**	Bobby Jurasin	Bennie Thompson
1985	**Michael Gray**	Tom Dixon	Randy Ambrosie	Mark Urness	Roy Bennett
1984	Darnell Clash	**Stewart Hill***	Mel Jenkins	Billy Jackson	Kevin Neiles
1983	Sammy Greene	Paul Hickie	Bernard Quarles	Karl Morgan	**Willard Reaves***
1982	**Merv Fernandez***	Rod Connop	Larry Barker	Dave Ridgway	Milson Jones
1981	Mack Moore	Gary Hayes	Norm Hopely	**Vince Goldsmith**	Pete Catan
1980	Roy Dewalt	Mike McLeod	Ron Paggett	Lester Brown	**William Miller**
1979	Joe Paopao	**Brian Kelly**	Mike McTague	Neil Quilter	Walt Passaglia
1978	Larry Key	Warren Moon	James Sykes	Eary Jones	**Joe Poplawski**
1977	**Leon Bright**	Jim Germany	Willie Thomas	Joey Walters	Lyall Woznesensky
1976	**John Sciarra**	Joe Hollimon	Tom Higgins	Randy Graham	Chuck Wills
1975	**Larry Cameron***	Pete Lavorato	Vernon Roberson	Jesse O'Neil	Steve Beaird
1974	Elton Brown	Stu Lang	Harold Holton	Ken McEachern	**Tom Scott***
1973	Bud Magrum	Sam Britts	Tom Forzani	**Lorne Richardson***	John Bledsoe
1972	Ray Nettles	Tyrone Walls	Gary Kerr	**Tom Campana***	Mike Kuhn

	HAMILTON	TORONTO	OTTAWA	MONTREAL	OVERALL WINNER
1993	**Michael O'Shea**	Kevin Whitley	Patrick Burke	—	**Michael O'Shea, Hamilton - 1993**
1992	David Lucas	Ken Benson	Treamelle Taylor	—	**Michael Richardson, Winnipeg - 1992**
1991	John Motton	**Raghib Ismail***	Charles Gordon	—	**Jon Volpe, B.C. - 1991**
1990	Bobby Dawson	Darryl Ford	**Reggie Barnes**	—	**Reggie Barnes, Ottawa - 1990**
1989	**Stephen Jordan**	Reg Berry	Tyrone Thurman	—	**Stephen Jordan, Hamilton - 1989**
1988	Darrell Corbin	Pernell Moore	**Orville Lee**	—	**Orville Lee, Ottawa - 1988**
1987	Johnnie Jones	**Gill Fenerty**	Leo Groenewegen	—	**Gill Fenerty, Toronto - 1987**
1986	Paul Osbaldiston	**Willie Pless***	Gilbert Renfroe	David Daniels	**Harold Hallman, Calgary - 1986**
1985	Mike Derks	Kerry Taylor	**Nick Benjamin***	Tony Johns	**Michael Gray, B.C. - 1985**
1984	Rod Skillman	Dennis Clay	Tim McCray	**Dwaine Wilson**	**Dwaine Wilson, Montreal - 1984**
1983	**Johnny Shepherd**	Darrell Nicholson	Junior Robinson	Jeff Patterson	**Johnny Shepherd, Hamilton - 1983**
1982	Jeff Arp	Bob Bronk	**Chris Isaac**	Mark Young	**Chris Isaac, Ottawa - 1982**
1981	Howard Fields	**Cedric Minter***	Eric Manns	David Overstreet	**Vince Goldsmith, Sask. - 1981**
1980	Jim Muller	**Dave Newman***	Jordan Case	Alvin 'Skip' Walker	**William Miller, Winnipeg - 1980**
1979	Jim Reid	Mike McArthur	**Martin Cox***	Tom Cousineau	**Brian Kelly, Edmonton - 1979**
1978	**Ben Zambiasi***	Dwight Edwards	J.T. Hay	Jerry Friesen	**Joe Poplawski, Winnipeg - 1978**
1977	John Martini	Paul Bennett	**Mike Murphy***	John O'Leary	**Leon Bright, B.C. - 1977**
1976	Allan Moffat	**Neil Lumsden***	John Palazetti	Charles McCann	**John Sciarra, B.C. - 1976**
1975	Angelo Santucci	L.J. Clayton	**Tom Clements**	Joe Petty	**Tom Clements, Ottawa - 1975**
1974	George Campbell	**Sam Cvijanovich**	Peter Crepin	Ian Mofford	**Sam Cvijanovich, Toronto - 1974**
1973	Louis Clare	Peter Muller	Donn Smith	**Johnny Rodgers**	**Johnny Rodgers, Montreal - 1973**
1972	**Chuck Ealey**	Eric Allen	Dick Adams	Dickie Harris	**Chuck Ealey, Hamilton - 1972**

MOST OUTSTANDING CANADIAN
Year-By-Year Team Nominees

	BRITISH COLUMBIA	EDMONTON	CALGARY	SASKATCHEWAN	WINNIPEG
1993	Matt Clark	Larry Wruck	**Dave Sapunjis**	Ray Elgaard	**Gerald Wilcox***
1992	Glen Scrivener	Larry Wruck	Dave Sapunjis	**Ray Elgaard**	Troy Westwood
1991	Matt Clark	**Blake Marshall**	Matt Finlay	Ray Elgaard	Rick House
1990	Jay Christensen	Blake Marshall	Kent Warnock	**Ray Elgaard**	Rick House
1989	Lui Passaglia	Larry Wruck	Eugene Belliveau	**Jeff Fairholm***	Chris Walby
1988	Kevin Konar	Tom Richards	Tim Petros	**Ray Elgaard**	Bob Cameron
1987	**Nelson Martin***	Marco Cyncar	Bernie Morrison	David Ridgway	**Scott Flagel**
1986	Glen Jackson	Chris Skinner	Bernie Morrison	Tony Dennis	**Joe Poplawski**
1985	Lui Passaglia	Milson Jones	Eugene Belliveau	Roger Aldag	**Joe Poplawski***
1984	Kevin Konar	Laurent DesLauriers	Lyall Woznesensky	Ray Elgaard	**Joe Poplawski***
1983	Lui Passaglia	Brian Fryer	Bernie Morrison	Roger Aldag	**Paul Bennett**
1982	Glen Jackson	Brian Fryer	Doug Battershill	Dave Ridgway	**Rick House***
1981	Glen Jackson	Dale Potter	J.T. Hay	Lyall Woznesensky	**Joe Poplawski**
1980	Al Wilson	**Dave Fennell***	Lloyd Fairbanks	Ken McEachern	Joe Poplawski
1979	Lui Passaglia	**Dave Fennell**	Tom Forzani	Ken McEachern	Bernie Ruoff
1978	Al Charuk	Dave Fennell	John Palazeti	Bob Macoritti	**Joe Poplawski***
1977	Lui Passaglia	Dave Fennell	Tom Forzani	Steve Molnar	**Gord Paterson***
1976	**Bill Baker***	Dave Fennell	Tom Forzani	Steve Molnar	Jim Heighton
1975	Bill Baker	John Konihowski	**Tom Forzani***	Ted Dushinski	Bob Swift
1974	Slade Wilis	Gary Lefebvre	**Rudy Linterman***	Lorne Richardson	Jim Heighton
1973	Larry Hendrickson	**Dave Cutler***	Rudy Linterman	Bill Baker	Gene Lakusiak
1972	**Jim Young**	Bayne Norrie	Gerry Shaw	Bill Baker	Bob Swift
1971	Jim Young	**Dick Dupuis***	Larry Robinson	Wayne Shaw	Bob Larose
1970	**Jim Young**	Ron Forwick	Dave Cranmer	Alan Ford	Paul Brule
1969	**Jim Young***	John Wydareny	Larry Robinson	William Baker	Ken Neilsen
1968	Ted Gerela	Roy Shatzko	Dave Cranmer	Alan Ford	**Ken Neilsen**
1967	Jim Young	Frank Cosentino	**Terry Evanshen**	Wayne Shaw	Ken Neilsen
1966	Mike Cacic	Ron Brewer	**Terry Evanshen***	Ted Urness	Ken Neilsen
1965	Norm Fieldgate	Ron Forwick	**Larry Robinson***	Ted Urness	Bill Cooper
1964	Pat Claridge	Bill Mitchell	**Larry Robinson***	Wayne Shaw	Bill Cooper
1963	Norm Fieldgate	Oscar Kruger	Harvey Wylie	**Dale West***	Henry Janzen

1962	Norm Fieldgate	Mike Lashuk	**Harvey Wylie**	Len Legault	Roger Savoie
1961	Norm Fieldgate	Mike Lashuk	**Tony Pajaczkowski**	Bill Clarke	Norm Rauhaus
1960	Norm Fieldgate	Bill Smith	**Tony Pajaczkowski***	Ron Atchison	Gerry James
1959	Don Lord	**Don Getty***	Tony Pajaczkowski	Ron Atchison	Steve Patrick
1958	Norm Fieldgate	**Normie Kwong**	Harry Langford	Ron Atchison	**Gord Rowland***
1957	Ted Hunt	Don Getty	Al Valdez	Harry Lunn	**Gerry James**
1956	Lorne Reid	**Normie Kwong**	Harry Langford	Bill Clarke	Roger Savoie
1955		Normie Kwong			Gerry James
1954				Harry Lampman	**Gerry James**

	HAMILTON	TORONTO	OTTAWA	MONTREAL	OVERALL WINNER
1993	Michael O'Shea	Don Moen	Jock Climie	—	**Dave Sapunjis, Calgary - 1993**
1992	**Ken Evraire***	Don Moen	Patrick Wayne	—	**Ray Elgaard, Saskatchewan - 1992**
1991	Paul Osbaldiston	**Lance Chomyc***	Scott Flagel	—	**Blake Marshall, Edmonton - 1991**
1990	**Paul Osbaldiston***	Don Moen	Patrick Wayne	—	**Ray Elgaard, Saskatchewan - 1990**
1989	**Rocky DiPietro**	Don Moen	Patrick Wayne	—	**Rocky DiPietro, Hamilton - 1989**
1988	Rocky DiPietro	Don Moen	**Orville Lee***	—	**Ray Elgaard, Saskatchewan - 1988**
1987	Rocky DiPietro	Don Moen	Dean Dorsey	—	**Scott Flagel, Winnipeg - 1987**
1986	**Rocky DiPietro***	Lance Chomyc	Ken Clark	Rick Ryan	**Joe Poplawski, Winnipeg - 1986**
1985	**Paul Bennett**	Bob Bronk	Jim Reid	Mike McTague	**Paul Bennett, Hamilton - 1985**
1984	Bernie Ruoff	Paul Pearson	Ken Clark	**Nick Arakgi**	**Nick Arakgi, Montreal - 1984**
1983	Benie Ruoff	Paul Pearson	Mark Seale	**Denny Ferdinand***	**Paul Bennett, Winnipeg - 1983**
1982	**Rocky DiPietro**	Paul Pearson	Bruce Walker	Nick Arakgi	**Rocky DiPietro, Hamilton - 1982**
1981	Rocky DiPietro	Paul Pearson	**Tony Gabriel***	Doug Scott	**Joe Poplawski, Winnipeg - 1981**
1980	Rocky DiPietro	Zenon Andrusyshyn	Rick Sowieta	**Gerry Dattilio**	**Gerry Dattilio, Montreal - 1980**
1979	**Leif Pettersen***	Peter Muller	Tony Gabriel	Ray Watrin	**Dave Fennell, Edmonton - 1979**
1978	Neil Lumsden	Jim Corrigall	**Tony Gabriel**	Gerry Dattilio	**Tony Gabriel, Ottawa - 1978**
1977	Ken Clark	Paul Bennett	**Tony Gabriel**	Glen Weir	**Tony Gabriel, Ottawa - 1977**
1976	Ken Clark	Neil Lumsden	**Tony Gabriel**	Peter Dalla Riva	**Tony Gabriel, Ottawa - 1976**
1975	Terry Evanshen	Jim Corrigall	**Jim Foley**	Peter Dalla Riva	**Jim Foley, Ottawa - 1975**
1974	**Tony Gabriel**	Peter Muller	Jim Foley	Larry Smith	**Tony Gabriel, Hamilton - 1974**
1973	Tony Gabriel	Mike Eben	**Gerry Organ**	Gord Judges	**Gerry Organ, Ottawa - 1973**
1972	Tony Gabriel	Mike Eben	**Gerry Organ***	Gord Judges	**Jim Young, B.C. - 1972**
1971	Bill Danychuk	Mike Eben	Wayne Giardino	**Terry Evanshen**	**Terry Evanshen, Montreal - 1971**
1970	Bill Danychuk	Tony Moro	Billy Cooper	**Al Phaneuf***	**Jim Young, B.C. - 1970**
1969	Bill Danychuk	Bobby Taylor	**Russ Jackson**	Larry Fairholm	**Russ Jackson, Ottawa - 1969**
1968	Bill Danychuk	Bobby Taylor	**Whit Tucker***	Larry Fairholm	**Ken Nielsen, Winnipeg - 1968**
1967	Gene Cepetelli	Bobby Taylor	**Russ Jackson***	Larry Fairholm	**Terry Evanshen. Calgary - 1967**
1966	Bob Kuntz	Bobby Taylor	**Russ Jackson**	Ed Learn	**Russ Jackson, Ottawa - 1966**
1965	**Zeno Karcz**	Ron Brewer	Russ Jackson	Terry Evanshen	**Zeno Karcz, Hamilton - 1965**
1964	**Tommy Grant**	Ron Brewer	Ron Stewart	Ted Elsby	**Tommy Grant, Hamilton - 1964**
1963	Tommy Grant	John Wydareny	**Russ Jackson**	Ted Elsby	**Russ Jackson, Ottawa - 1963**
1962	Pete Neumann	Doug McNichol	**Russ Jackson***	Ed Learn	**Harvey Wylie, Calgary - 1962**
1961	Pete Neumann	**Bob Kuntz***	Ron Stewart	Ed Learn	**Tony Pajaczkowski, Calgary - 1961**
1960	Tommy Grant	Bill Mitchell	**Ron Stewart**	Bill Bewley	**Ron Stewart, Ottawa - 1960**
1959	**Ron Howell**	Bob Kuntz	**Russ Jackson**	Doug McNichol	**Russ Jackson, Ottawa - 1959**
1958	Ron Howell	Bob Kuntz	Bill Sowalski	Doug McNichol	**Ron Howell, Hamilton - 1958**
1957	Pete Neumann	**Bob Kuntz***	Bob Simpson	Ted Elsby	**Gerry James, Winnipeg - 1957**
1956	Ray Truant	Bob Kuntz	Bob Simpson*	Tom Moran	**Normie Kwong, Edmonton - 1956**
1955			**Bob Simpson**	Joey Pal	**Normie Kwong, Edmonton - 1955**
1954	Tip Logan			Doug McNichol	**Gerry James, Winnipeg - 1954**

MOST OUTSTANDING DEFENSIVE PLAYER
Year-By-Year Team Nominees

	BRITISH COLUMBIA	EDMONTON	CALGARY	SASKATCHEWAN	WINNIPEG
1993	O.J. Brigance	Willie Pless	Marvin Pope	**Jearld Baylis**	**Elfrid Payton***
1992	Brian Smith	**Willie Pless**	Darryl Hall	Jearld Baylis	Greg Battle
1991	O.J. Brigance	Willie Pless	**Will Johnson***	Eddie Lowe	**Greg Battle**
1990	Willie Pless	**Stewart Hill***	Kent Warnock	Dan Rashovich	**Greg Battle**
1989	Alondra Johnson	**Danny Bass**	Doug Landry	James Curry	**Greg Battle***
1988	Greg Stumon	**Danny Bass***	Ken Ford	Richie Hall	Bennie Thompson
1987	**Greg Stumon**	Danny Bass	Ron Hopkins	Bobby Jurasin	**James West***
1986	**James Parker**	Stewart Hill	Harold Hallman	Billy Jackson	Darrell Patterson
1985	Michael Gray	James Zachery	Larry Hogue	Eddie Lowe	**Tyrone Jones**
1984	**James Parker**	Stewart Hill	Lyall Woznesensky	Terry Irvin	Aaron Brown
1983	Larry Crawford	Joe Hollimon	**Danny Bass***	Vince Goldsmith	Aaron Brown
1982	Glen Jackson	**James Parker**	Danny Bass	Mike Samples	Paul Bennett
1981	Glen Jackson	**Dan Kepley**	Ed McAleney	Lyall Woznesensky	James Reed
1980	Joe Fourqurean	**Dan Kepley**	Ed McAleney	Ken McEachern	John Helton
1979	Glen Jackson	Dan Kepley	Ed McAleney	Ken McEachern	**John Helton***
1978	Sam Britts	**Dave Fennell**	John Helton	Cleveland Vann	Vince Phason
1977	Grady Cavness	**Dan Kepley**	Al Burleson	Roger Goree	Brian Herosian
1976	**Bill Baker**	Dave Fennell	John Helton	Cleveland Vann	Harry Walters
1975	**Bill Baker***	Ron Estay	John Helton	Tim Roth	Brian Herosian
1974	Garrett Hunsperger	John Lagrone	**John Helton**	George Wells	Jim Heighton

	HAMILTON	TORONTO	OTTAWA	MONTREAL	OVERALL WINNER
1993	Tim Cofield	Ken Benson	John Kropke	—	**Jearld Baylis, Saskatchewan - 1993**
1992	John Motton	Rodney Harding	**Angelo Snipes***	—	**Willie Pless, Edmonton - 1992**
1991	Peter Giftopoulos	Darryl Ford	Brian Bonner	—	**Greg Battle, Winnipeg - 1991**
1990	Gary Wilkerson	Reggie Pleasant	Greg Stumon	—	**Greg Battle, Winnipeg - 1990**
1989	Lance Shields	Harold Hallman	Loyd Lewis	—	**Danny Bass, Edmonton - 1989**
1988	**Grover Covington**	Willie Pless	Troy Wilson	—	**Grover Covington, Hamilton - 1988**
1987	Frank Robinson	Willie Pless	Loyd Lewis	—	**Greg Stumon, B.C. - 1987**
1986	Less Browne	David Marshall	Loyd Lewis	**Brett Williams***	**James Parker, B.C. - 1986**
1985	**Paul Bennett***	Carl Brazley	Loyd Lewis	Paul Gray	**Tyrone Jones, Winnipeg - 1985**
1984	Ben Zambiasi	William Mitchell	Rick Barden	**Harry Skipper***	**James Parker, B.C. - 1984**
1983	Ben Zambiasi	Rick Mohr	**Greg Marshall**	Delbert Fowler	**Greg Marshall, Ottawa - 1983**
1982	Ben Zambiasi	**Zac Henderson***	Greg Marshall	Doug Scott	**James Parker, Edmonton - 1982**
1981	**Ben Zambiasi***	Danny Bass	Greg Marshall	Doug Scott	**Dan Kepley, Edmonton - 1981**
1980	Jerry Anderson	Billy Hardee	Mike Raines	**Tom Cousineau***	**Dan Kepley, Edmonton - 1980**
1979	**Ben Zambiasi**	Bruce Smith	Mike Raines	Dickie Harris	**Ben Zambiasi, Hamilton - 1979**
1978	Ray Nettles	Jim Corrigall	Ken Downing	**Randy Rhino***	**Dave Fennell, Edmonton - 1978**
1977	Mike Samples	Ray Nettles	Jim Piaskoski	**Glen Weir***	**Dan Kepley, Edmonton - 1977**
1976	Joe Harris	**Granny Liggins***	Mark Kosmos	Chuck Zapiec	**Bill Baker, B.C. - 1976**

1975	Mike Samples	**Jim Corrigall**	Rod Woodward	Glen Weir	**Jim Corrigall, Toronto - 1975**
1974	Fred Grambau	Sam Cvijanovich	**Wayne Smith***	Mike Widger	**John Helton, Calgary - 1974**

MOST OUTSTANDING OFFENSIVE LINEMAN
Year-By-Year Team Nominees

	BRITISH COLUMBIA	EDMONTON	CALGARY	SASKATCHEWAN	WINNIPEG
1993	Robert Smith	Rod Connop	**Bruce Covernton***	Craig Hendrickson	**Chris Walby**
1992	Jim Mills	Pierre Vercheval	Ken Moore	**Vic Stevenson***	Chris Walby
1991	**Jim Mills**	Rod Connop	Lloyd Fairbanks	Vic Stevenson	**Chris Walby***
1990	**Jim Mills**	Blake Dermott	Lloyd Fairbanks	Roger Aldag	**Chris Walby***
1989	Jim Mills	**Rod Connop**	Dan Ferrone	Roger Aldag	Chris Walby
1988	Gerald Roper	Blake Dermott	Tom Spoletini	**Roger Aldag**	Lyle Bauer
1987	Gerald Roper	Rod Connop	**Bob Poley***	Roger Aldag	**Chris Walby**
1986	John Blain	Leo Blanchard	Bob Poley	**Roger Aldag**	Chris Walby
1985	John Blain	Leo Blanchard	Dave Kirzinger	Roger Aldag	**Nick Bastaja**
1984	John Blain	Leo Blanchard	Dave Kirzinger	Roger Aldag	**John Bonk**
1983	John Blain	Leo Blanchard	Dave Kirzinger	Roger Aldag	**John Bonk***
1982	John Blain	Leo Blanchard	**Lloyd Fairbanks***	Don Swafford	John Bonk
1981	Al Wilson	Hector Pothier	Lloyd Fairbanks	Don Swafford	**Larry Butler**
1980	Al Wilson	**Mike Wilson**	Lloyd Fairbanks	Roger Aldag	Butch Norman
1979	Al Wilson	**Mike Wilson**	Lloyd Fairbanks	Curtis Wester	John Bonk
1978	**Al Wilson***	Bill Stevenson	Lloyd Fairbanks	Joe Miller	Butch Norman
1977	**Al Wilson**	Charlie Turner	Harold Holton	Ralph Galloway	Bob Swift
1976	**Al Wilson***	Bob Howes	Lloyd Fairbanks	Mike Dirks	Butch Norman
1975	Layne McDowell	**Charlie Turner**	Max Huber	Gary Brandt	Bill Frank
1974	**Curtis Wester***	Larry Watkins	Harold Holton	Ralph Galloway	Bob Swift

	HAMILTON	TORONTO	OTTAWA	MONTREAL	OVERALL WINNER
1993	Dave Richardson	Blaine Schmidt	Mike Graybill	—	**Chris Walby, Winnipeg - 1993**
1992	Jason Riley	Dan Ferrone	**Robert Smith**	—	**Robert Smith, Ottawa - 1992**
1991	Dale Sanderson	Dan Ferrone	Robert Smith	—	**Jim Mills, B.C. - 1991**
1990	Miles Gorrell	Dan Ferrone	Robert Smith	—	**Jim Mills, B.C. - 1990**
1989	**Miles Gorrell***	Chris Schultz	Kari Yli-Renko	—	**Rod Connop, Edmonton - 1989**
1988	Dale Sanderson	**Ian Beckstead***	Marv Allemang	—	**Roger Aldag, Saskatchewan - 1988**
1987	Miles Gorrell	Chris Schultz	Kevin Powell	—	**Chris Walby, Winnipeg - 1987**
1986	Miles Gorrell*	Dan Ferrone	Bill Kidd	Lloyd Fairbanks	**Roger Aldag, Saskatchewan - 1986**
1985	Marv Allemang	**Dan Ferrone***	Kevin Powell	Lloyd Fairbanks	**Nick Bastaja, Winnipeg - 1985**
1984	Henry Waszczuk	**Dan Ferrone***	Rudy Phillips	Lloyd Fairbanks	**John Bonk, Winnipeg - 1984**
1983	Ross Francis	Dan Ferrone	**Rudy Phillips**	Miles Gorrell	**Rudy Phillips, Ottawa - 1983**
1982	Ed Fulton	Roland Mangold	**Rudy Phillips**	Doug Payton	**Rudy Phillips, Ottawa - 1982**
1981	Henry Waszczuk	Dan Ferrone	**Val Belcher***	Doug Payton	**Larry Butler, Winnipeg - 1981**
1980	Henry Waszczuk	Mike Obrovac	**Val Belcher***	Doug Payton	**Mike Wilson, Edmonton - 1980**
1979	Larry Butler	Nick Bastaja	Val Belcher	**Ray Watrin***	**Mike Wilson, Edmonton - 1979**
1978	Larry Butler	Nick Bastaja	**Jim Coode**	Dan Yochum	**Jim Coode, Ottawa - 1978**
1977	Larry Butler	**Mike Wilson***	Donn Smith	Dan Yochum	**Al Wilson, B.C. - 1977**
1976	Larry Butler	Wally Highsmith	Donn Smith	**Dan Yochum**	**Dan Yochum, Montreal - 1976**
1975	Ed Chalupka	Terry Shelsta	Tom Schuette	**Dave Braggins***	**Charlie Turner, Edmonton - 1975**
1974	Ed Chalupka	Noah Jackson	Charlie Brandon	**Ed George**	**Ed George, Montreal - 1974**

MOST OUTSTANDING LINEMAN
IN 1974 THIS CATEGORY BECAME THE OFFENSIVE LINEMAN AND THE MOST OUTSTANDING DEFENSIVE PLAYER
Year-By-Year Team Nominees

	BRITISH COLUMBIA	EDMONTON	CALGARY	SASKATCHEWAN	WINNIPEG
1973	**Ray Nettles**	Bob Howes	John Helton	Bill Baker	Bill Frank
1972	Ray Nettles	Charlie Turner	**John Helton**	Bill Baker	Mike Doyle
1971	Garrett Hunsperger	John Lagrone	**Wayne Harris**	Ed McQuarters	Bill Frank
1970	Ken Sugarman	Greg Pipes	**Wayne Harris**	Jack Abendschan	Bill Frank
1969	Ken Sugarman	**John Lagrone**	Granville Liggins	Ed McQuarters	Phil Minnick
1968	Greg Findlay	John Lagrone	Wayne Harris	**Ted Urness***	Phil Minnick
1967	Dwayne Czupka	John Lagrone	Wayne Harris	**Ed McQuarters**	Bill Whistler
1966	Mike Cacic	E.A. Sims	**Wayne Harris**	Al Benecick	Phil Minnick
1965	Dick Fouts	E.A. Sims	**Wayne Harris**	Al Benecick	Al Miller
1964	**Tom Brown**	Al Ecuyer	Don Luzzi	Al Benecick	Bill Whistler
1963	**Tom Brown**	Al Ecuyer	Wayne Harris	Garner Ekstran	Herb Gray
1962	Tom Brown	Al Ecuyer	**Wayne Harris***	Len Legault	Dave Burkholder
1961	Ed Sullivan	Don Stephenson	Wayne Harris	Garner Ekstran	**Frank Rigney**
1960	Ralph Hinton	Roger Nelson	Tony Pajaczkowski	Bill Burrell	**Herb Gray**
1959	Tom Hinton	**Roger Nelson**	Opie Bandy	Neil Habig	Herb Gray
1958	Tom Hinton	Roger Nelson	**Don Luzzi**	Kurt Burris	Steve Patrick
1957	Ed Sharkey	**Art Walker***	Dick Huffman	Galen Wahlmeir	Herb Gray
1956	Steve Palmer	Frankie Anderson	Dick Huffman	Martin Ruby	**Bud Alliston***
1955		Dale Meinert		Matin Ruby	

	HAMILTON	TORONTO	OTTAWA	MONTREAL	OVERALL WINNERS
1973	Ed Chalupka	Jim Stillwagon	Charlie Brandon	**Ed George***	**Ray Nettles, B.C. - 1973**
1972	Ed Chalupka	**Jim Stillwagon***	Wayne Smith	Ed George	**John Helton, Calgary - 1972**
1971	Bill Danychuk	Jim Stillwagon	Marshall Shirk	**Mark Kosmos***	**Wayne Harris, Calgary - 1971**
1970	**Angelo Mosca***	Charlie Bray	Marshall Shirk	Charlie Collins	**Wayne Harris, Calgary - 1970**
1969	Henry Sorrell	Danny Nykoluk	**Billy Joe Booth***	Harry Olszewski	**John Lagrone, Edmonton - 1969**
1968	Billy Ray Locklin	Ed Harrington	**Ken Lehmann**	Charlie Parker	**Ken Lehmann, Ottawa - 1968**
1967	**John Barrow***	Bill Frank	Bob Brown	John Baker	**Ed McQuarters, Saskatchewan - 1967**
1966	Billy Ray Locklin	Bill Frank	**Ken Lehmann***	Roger Lalonde	**Wayne Harris, Calgary - 1966**
1965	**John Barrow***	Billy Shipp	Ken Lehmann	Bob Minihane	**Wayne Harris, Calgary - 1965**
1964	**John Barrow***	Billy Shipp	John Kenerson	Ted Elsby	**Tom Brown, B.C. - 1964**
1963	**Angelo Mosca***	John Autry	Billy Joe Booth	Ed Nickla	**Tom Brown, B.C. - 1963**
1962	**John Barrow**	Gerry Patrick	Kaye Vaughan	Ed Nickla	**John Barrow, Hamilton - 1962**
1961	**John Barrow***	Jim Adreotti	Kaye Vaughan	Bobby J. Oliver	**Frank Rigney, Winnipeg - 1961**
1960	John Barrow	Dick Fouts	**Kaye Vaughan***	Bill Hudson	**Herb Gray, Winnipeg - 1960**
1959	**John Barrow***	Bob Oliver	Larry Hayes	Billy Shipp	**Roger Nelson, Edmonton - 1959**
1958	John Barrow	Dick Fouts	Hardiman Cureton	**Jackie Simpson***	**Don Luzzi, Calgary - 1958**
1957	John Barrow	John Weldon	**Kaye Vaughan**	Tom Hugo	**Kaye Vaughan, Ottawa - 1957**
1956	Vince Scott	Bill Albright	**Kaye Vaughan**	Jim Stratton	**Kaye Vaughan, Ottawa - 1956**
1955	Vince Scott			**Tex Coulter**	**Tex Coulter, Montreal - 1955**

ANNIS STUKUS TROPHY — COACH OF THE YEAR

Presented annually by the Edmonton Eskimo Alumni Association to the Coach of the Year as selected by Members of The Football Reporters of Canada

1993	Wally Buono, Calgary	1976	Bob Shaw, Hamilton
1992	Wally Buono, Calgary	1975	George Brancato, Ottawa
1991	Adam Rita, Toronto	1974	Marv Levy, Montreal
1990	Mike Riley, Winnipeg	1973	Jack Gotta, Ottawa
1989	John Gregory, Saskatchewan	1972	Jack Gotta, Ottawa
1988	Mike Riley, Winnipeg	1971	Leo Cahill, Toronto
1987	Bob O'Billovich, Toronto	1970	Ray Jauch, Edmonton
1986	Al Bruno, Hamilton	1969	Frank Clair, Ottawa
1985	Don Matthews, B.C.	1968	Eagle Keys, Saskatchewan
1984	Cal Murphy, Winnipeg	1967	Jerry Williams, Calgary
1983	Cal Murphy, Winnipeg	1966	Frank Clair, Ottawa
1982	Bob O'Billovich, Toronto	1965	Bud Grant, Winnipeg
1981	Joe Faragalli, Saskatchewan	1964	Ralph Sazio, Hamilton
1980	Ray Jauch, Winnipeg	1963	Dave Skrien, B.C.
1979	Hugh Campbell, Edmonton	1962	Steve Owen, Saskatchewan
1978	Jack Gotta, Calgary	1961	Jim Trimble, Hamilton
1977	Vic Rapp, B.C.		

JEFF NICKLIN MEMORIAL TROPHY

Awarded annually to the player in the Western Division considered to be the most valuable to his team. Donated in 1946 by the first Canadian Paratroop Battalion in memory of its commanding officer, Lt.-Col. Jeff Nicklin, killed in action March 24, 1945. He had been an outstanding end with Winnipeg. Since 1973 the award has gone to the Most Outstanding Player in the Western Division.

1993	Doug Flutie, Calgary	1969	Ron Lancaster, Saskatchewan
1992	Doug Flutie, Calgary	1968	Ron Lancaster, Saskatchewan
1991	Doug Flutie, B.C.	1967	Peter Liske, Calgary
1990	Craig Ellis, Edmonton	1966	Ron Lancaster, Saskatchewan
1989	Tracy Ham, Edmonton	1965	George Reed, Saskatchewan
1988	David Williams, B.C.	1964	Tom Brown, B.C.
1987	Brian Kelly, Edmonton	1963	Joe Kapp, B.C.
1986	James Murphy, Winnipeg	1962	Eagle Day, Calgary
1985	Mervyn Fernandez, B.C.	1961	Jackie Parker, Edmonton
1984	Willard Reaves, Winnipeg	1960	Jackie Parker, Edmonton
1983	Warren Moon, Edmonton	1959	Jackie Parker, Edmonton
1982	Tom Scott, Edmonton	1958	Jackie Parker, Edmonton
1981	Dieter Brock, Winnipeg	1957	Jackie Parker, Edmonton
1980	Dieter Brock, Winnipeg	1956	Jackie Parker, Edmonton
1979	Waddell Smith, Edmonton	1955	Ken Carpenter, Saskatchewan
1978	Tom Wilkinson, Edmonton	1954	Jackie Parker, Edmonton
1977	Jerry Tagge, B.C.	1953	John Henry Johnson, Calgary
1976	Ron Lancaster, Saskatchewan	1952	Jack Jacobs, Winnipeg
1975	Willie Burden, Calgary	1951	Glen Dobbs, Saskatchewan
1974	Tom Wilkinson, Edmonton	1950	Lindy Berry, Edmonton
1973	George McGowan, Edmonton	1949	Keith Spaith, Calgary
1972	Mack Herron, Winnipeg	1948	Keith Spaith, Calgary
1971	Don Jonas, Winnipeg	1947	Bob Sandberg, Winnipeg
1970	Ron Lancaster, Saskatchewan	1946	Bill Wusyk, Calgary

JEFF RUSSEL MEMORIAL TROPHY

Awarded annually to the player in the Eastern Division possessing the highest qualities of courage, fair play and sportsmanship. Originally donated in 1928 to commemorate an outstanding Montreal player who in 1926 had been killed while repairing lines for the Montreal Power Company, Since 1973, the award has gone to the Most Outstanding Player in the Eastern Division.

1993	Matt Dunigan, Winnipeg	1966	Gene Gaines, Ottawa
1992	Angelo Snipes, Ottawa	1965	Bernie Faloney, Montreal
1991	Robert Mimbs, Winnipeg	1964	Dick Shatto, Toronto
1990	Michael Clemons, Toronto	1963	Garney Henley, Hamilton
1989	Tony Champion, Hamilton	1962	George Dixon, Montreal
1988	Earl Winfield, Hamilton	1961	Bob-Jack Oliver, Montreal
1987	Tom Clements, Winnipeg	1960	Ron Stewart, Ottawa
1986	James Hood, Montreal	1959	Russ Jackson, Ottawa
1985	Ken Hobart, Hamilton	1958	Sam Etcheverry, Montreal
1984	Rufus Crawford, Hamilton	1957	Dick Shatto, Toronto
1983	Terry Greer, Toronto	1956	Hal Patterson, Montreal
1982	Condredge Holloway, Toronto	1955	Avatus Stone, Ottawa
1981	Tom Clements, Hamilton	1954	Sam Etcheverry, Montreal
1980	Gerry Dattilio, Montreal	1953	Bob Cunningham, Ottawa
1979	David Green, Montreal	1952	Vince Mazza, Hamilton
1978	Tony Gabriel, Ottawa	1951	Bruce Cummings, Ottawa
1977	Jimmy Edwards, Hamilton	1950	Don Loney, Ottawa
1976	Jimmy Edwards, Hamilton	1949	Royal Copeland, Toronto
1975	Johnny Rodgers, Montreal	1948	Eric Chipper, Ottawa
1974	Johnny Rodgers, Montreal	1947	Virgil Wagner, Montreal
1973	John Harvey, Montreal	1946	Joe Krol, Toronto
1972	Garney Henley, Hamilton	1945	George Fraser, Ottawa
1971	Mel Profit, Toronto	1941	Tony Golab, Ottawa
1970	Bill Symons, Toronto	1940	Andy Tommy, Ottawa
1969	Russ Jackson, Ottawa	1939	Bill Davies, Montreal
1968	Larry Fairholm, Montreal	1938	Wes Cutler, Toronto
1967	Ron Stewart, Ottawa	1937	Ted Morris, Toronto
1936	Arnie Morrison, Ottawa	1931	Gordie Perry, Montreal
1935	Abe Eliowitz, Ottawa	1930	Frank Turville, Toronto
1934	Ab Box, Toronto	1929	Red Wilson, Toronto
1933	Huck Welch, Montreal	1928	Ernie Cox, Hamilton
1932	Alex Denman, Hamilton		

NORM FIELDGATE TROPHY

Awarded annually to the Outstanding Defensive Player in the Western Division. Prior to 1978, the award was the Western Conference Trophy.

1993	Jearld Baylis, Saskatchewan	1983	Danny Bass, Calgary
1992	Willie Pless, Edmonton	1982	James Parker, Edmonton
1991	Will Johnson, Calgary	1981	Dan Kepley, Edmonton
1990	Stewart Hill, Edmonton	1980	Dan Kepley, Edmonton
1989	Danny Bass, Edmonton	1979	John Helton, Winnipeg
1988	Danny Bass, Edmonton	1978	Dave Fennell, Edmonton
1987	Greg Stumon, B.C.	1977	Dan Kepley, Edmonton
1986	James Parker, B.C.	1976	Bill Baker, B.C.
1985	Tyrone Jones, Winnipeg	1975	Bill Baker, B.C.
1984	James Parker, B.C.	1974	John Helton, Calgary

JAMES P. McCAFFREY TROPHY

Awarded annually to the Outstanding Defensive Player in the Eastern Division.

1993	Elfrid Payton, Winnipeg	1983	Greg Marshall, Ottawa
1992	Angelo Snipes, Ottawa	1982	Zac Henderson, Toronto
1991	Greg Battle, Winnipeg	1981	Ben Zambiasi, Hamilton
1990	Greg Battle, Winnipeg	1980	Tom Cousineau, Montreal
1989	Greg Battle, Winnipeg	1979	Ben Zambiasi, Hamilton
1988	Grover Covington, Hamilton	1978	Randy Rhino, Montreal
1987	James West, Winnipeg	1977	Glen Weir, Montreal
1986	Brett Williams, Montreal	1976	Granville Liggins, Toronto
1985	Paul Bennett, Hamilton	1975	Jim Corrigall, Toronto
1984	Harry Skipper, Montreal		

JACKIE PARKER TROPHY

Awarded annually to the Western Division Rookie-of-the-Year. Prior to 1974, the top rookie award was the Dr. Beattie Martin Trophy.

1993	Brian Wiggins, Calgary	1983	Willard Reaves, Winnipeg
1992	Bruce Covernton, Calgary	1982	Mervyn Fernandez, B.C.
1991	Jon Volpe, B.C.	1981	Vince Goldsmith, Saskatchewan
1990	Lucius Floyd, Saskatchewan	1980	William Miller, Winnipeg
1989	Darrell Wallace, B.C.	1979	Brian Kelly, Edmonton
1988	Jeff Fairholm, Saskatchewan	1978	Joe Poplawski, Winnipeg
1987	Stanley Blair, Edmonton	1977	Leon Bright, B.C.
1986	Harold Hallman, Calgary	1976	John Sciarra, B.C.
1985	Michael Gray, B.C.	1975	Larry Cameron, B.C.
1984	Stewart Hill, Edmonton	1974	Tom Scott, Winnipeg

FRANK M. GIBSON TROPHY

Awarded annually to the Outstanding Rookie in the Eastern Division.

1993	Michael O'Shea	1983	Johnny Shepherd, Hamilton
1992	Michael Richardson, Winnipeg	1982	Chris Isaac, Ottawa
1991	Raghib Ismail, Toronto	1981	Cedric Minter, Toronto
1990	Reggie Barnes, Ottawa	1980	Dave Newman, Toronto
1989	Stephen Jordan, Hamilton	1979	Martin Cox, Ottawa
1988	Orville Lee, Ottawa	1978	Ben Zambiasi, Hamilton
1987	Gill Fenerty, Toronto	1977	Mike Murphy, Ottawa
1986	Willie Pless, Toronto	1976	Neil Lumsden, Toronto
1985	Nick Benjamin, Ottawa	1975	Tom Clements, Ottawa
1984	Dwaine Wilson, Montreal		

DeMARCO-BECKET MEMORIAL TROPHY

Awarded originally to the player selected as the outstanding lineman in the Western Division. Donated by the families of Mel Becket and Mario DeMarco,two prominent Saskatchewan players who were victims of the Mount Slesse aircraft disaster on December 9, 1956. Since 1974 this trophy has been awarded to the Most Outstanding Offensive Lineman in the Western Division.

1993	Bruce Covernton, Calgary	1982	Lloyd Fairbanks, Calgary
1992	Vic Stevenson, Saskatchewan	1981	Larry Butler, Winnipeg
1991	Jim Mills, B.C.	1980	Mike Wilson, Edmonton
1990	Jim Mills, B.C.	1979	Mike Wilson, Edmonton
1989	Rod Connop, Edmonton	1978	Al Wilson, B.C.
1988	Roger Aldag, Saskatchewan	1977	Al Wilson, B.C.
1987	Bob Poley, Calgary	1976	Al Wilson, B.C.
1986	Roger Aldag, Saskatchewan	1975	Charlie Turner, Edmonton
1985	Nick Bastaja, Winnipeg	1974	Curtis Wester, B.C.
1984	John Bonk, Winnipeg	1973	Ray Nettles, B.C.
1983	John Bonk, Winnipeg	1972	John Helton, Calgary

DeMarco - Becket Memorial Trophy (Cont'd)

1971	Wayne Harris, Calgary	1963	Tom Brown, B.C.
1970	Greg Pipes, Edmonton	1962	Tom Brown, B.C.
1969	Ed McQuarters, Saskatchewan	1961	Frank Rigney, Winnipeg
1968	Ed McQuarters, Saskatchewan	1960	Frank Rigney, Winnipeg
1967	John LaGrone, Edmonton	1959	Art Walker, Edmonton
1966	Wayne Harris, Calgary	1958	Don Luzzi, Calgary
1965	Dick Fouts, B.C.	1957	Art Walker, Edmonton
1964	Tom Brown, B.C.		

LEO DANDURAND TROPHY

Awarded annually to the Outstanding Offensive Lineman in the Eastern Division.

1993	Chris Walby, Winnipeg	1983	Rudy Phillips, Ottawa
1992	Rob Smith, Ottawa	1982	Rudy Phillips, Ottawa
1991	Chris Walby, Winnipeg	1981	Val Belcher, Ottawa
1990	Chris Walby, Winnipeg	1980	Val Belcher, Ottawa
1989	Miles Gorrell, Hamilton	1979	Ray Watrin, Montreal
1988	Ian Beckstead, Toronto	1978	Jim Coode, Ottawa
1987	Chris Walby, Winnipeg	1977	Mike Wilson, Toronto
1986	Miles Gorrell, Hamilton	1976	Dan Yochum, Montreal
1985	Dan Ferrone, Toronto	1975	Dave Braggins, Montreal
1984	Dan Ferrone, Toronto		

Dr. BEATTIE MARTIN TROPHY

Awarded annually to the Outstanding Canadian Player in the Western Division. Dr. Martin was a former President of the Saskatchewan Roughriders. Prior to 1971 this award went to the Outstanding Canadian Rookie Player in the Western Conference.

1993	David Sapunjis, Calgary	1971	Bob Kraemer, Winnipeg
1992	Ray Elgaard, Saskatchewan	1970	John Senst, Winnipeg
1991	Blake Marshall, Edmonton	1969	Dave Easley, B.C.
1990	Ray Elgaard, Saskatchewan	1968	Dave Cranmer, Calgary
1989	Jeff Fairholm, Saskatchewan	1967	Ted Gerela, B.C.
1988	Ray Elgaard, Saskatchewan	1966	Garry Lefebvre, Edmonton
1987	Nelson Martin, B.C.	1965	Ron Forwick, Edmonton
1986	Joe Poplawski, Winnipeg	1964	Billy Cooper, Winnipeg
1985	Joe Poplawski, Winnipeg	1963	Peter Kempf, B.C.
1984	Joe Poplawski, Winnipeg	1962	Ted Frechette, Edmonton
1983	Paul Bennett, Winnipeg	1961	Larry Robinson, Calgary
1982	Rick House, Winnipeg	1960	Neal Beaumont, B.C.
1981	Joe Poplawski, Winnipeg	1959	Henry Janzen, Winnipeg
1980	Dave Fennell, Edmonton	1958	Walt Radzick, Calgary
1979	Dave Fennell, Edmonton	1957	Mike Lashuk, Edmonton
1978	Joe Poplawski, Winnipeg	1956	Norm Rauhaus, Winnipeg
1977	Gordon Paterson, Winnipeg	1955	Jarry Lunn, Saskatchewan
1976	Bill Baker, B.C.	1954	Lynn Bottoms, Calgary
1975	Tom Forzani, Calgary	1953	Gordon Sturtridge, Sask.
1974	Rudy Linterman, Calgary	1952	Lorne Benson, Winnipeg
1973	Lorne Richardson, Sask.	1951	Jim Chambers, Edmonton
1972	Walt McKee, Winnipeg	1950	Gordon Brown, Calgary
		1949	John Stroppa, Winnipeg

LEW HAYMAN TROPHY

Awarded annually to the Outstanding Canadian Player in the Eastern Division.

1993	Gerald Wilcox, Winnipeg	1983	Denny Ferdinand, Montreal
1992	Ken Evraire, Hamilton	1982	Rocky DiPietro, Hamilton
1991	Lance Chomyc, Toronto	1981	Tony Gabriel, Ottawa
1990	Paul Osbaldiston, Hamilton	1980	Gerry Dattilio, Montreal
1989	Rocky DiPietro, Hamilton	1979	Leif Pettersen, Hamilton
1988	Orville Lee, Ottawa	1978	Tony Gabriel, Ottawa
1987	Scott Flagel, Winnipeg	1977	Tony Gabriel, Ottawa
1986	Rocky DiPietro, Hamilton	1976	Tony Gabriel, Ottawa
1985	Paul Bennett, Hamilton	1975	Jim Foley, Ottawa
1984	Nick Arakgi, Montreal		

DAVE DRYBURGH MEMORIAL TROPHY

The Dave Dryburgh Memorial Trophy is presented annually to the player finishing first in scoring in the Western Division of the Canadian Football League. The trophy is named in honour of Dryburgh, a well-respected sports editor of the Regina Leader-Post who died in 1947.

	Winner	Pts.
1993	Mark McLoughlin, Calgary	215
1992	Mark McLoughlin, Calgary	208
1991	David Ridgway, Saskatchewan	216
1990	David Ridgway, Saskatchewan	233
1989	Jerry Kauric, Edmonton	224
1988	David Ridgway, Saskatchewan	215
1987	Lui Passaglia, B.C.	214
1986	Tom Dixon, Edmonton	190
1985	Trevor Kennerd, Winnipeg	198
1984	Lui Passaglia, B.C.	167
1983	Lui Passaglia, B.C.	191
1982	Dave Cutler, Edmonton	170
1981	Trevor Kennerd, Winnipeg	185
1980	Dave Cutler, Edmonton	158
1979	Bernie Ruoff, Winnipeg	151
1978	Dave Cutler, Edmonton	167
1977	Dave Cutler, Edmonton	195
1976	Bernie Ruoff, Winnipeg	152
1975	Dave Cutler, Edmonton	169
1974	Dave Cutler, Edmonton	144
1973	Dave Cutler, Edmonton	133
1972	Dave Cutler, Edmonton	126
1971	Don Jonas, Winnipeg	121
1970	Jack Abendschan, Saskatchewan	116
1969	Jack Abendschan, Saskatchewan	116
1968	Ted Gerela, B.C.	115
1967	Terry Evanshen, Calgary	102
1966	Hugh Campbell, Saskatchewan	102
1965	Larry Robinson, Calgary	95
1964	Larry Robinson, Calgary	106
1963	George Fleming, Winnipeg	135
1962	Tommy Joe Coffey, Edmonton	129
1961	Jackie Parker, Edmonton	104
1960	Gerry James, Winnipeg	114
1959	Jackie Parker, Edmonton	109
1958	Jack Hill, Saskatchewan	145
1957	Gerry James, Winnipeg	131
1956	Buddy Leake, Winnipeg	103
1955	Ken Carpenter, Saskatchewan	90
1954	Joe Aguirre, Saskatchewan	85
1953	Bud Korchak, Winnipeg	66
1952	Bob Shaw, Calgary	110
1951	Bob Shaw, Calgary	61
1950	Joe Aguirre, Winnipeg	57
1949	Vern Graham, Calgary	58
1948	Paul Rowe, Calgary	35

EDDIE JAMES MEMORIAL TROPHY

The Eddie James Memorial Trophy is presented annually to the leading rusher in the Western Division of the Canadian Football League. The award is named in honour of the Saskatchewan all-time great running back who played for the Roughriders during the 1930's.

	Winner	Yards
1993	Damon Allen, Edmonton	920
1992	Jon Volpe, B.C.	941
1991	Jon Volpe, B.C.	1395
1990	Tracy Ham, Edmonton	1096
1989	Reggie Taylor, Edmonton	1503
1988	Anthony Cherry, B.C.	889
1987	Gary Allen, Calgary	857
1986	Gary Allen, Calgary	1153
1985	Willard Reaves, Winnipeg	1323
1984	Willard Reaves, Winnipeg	1733
1983	Willard Reaves, Winnipeg	898
1982	William Miller, Winnipeg	1076
1981	Jimmy Sykes, Calgary	1107
1980	Jimmy Sykes, Calgary	1263
1979	Jim Germany, Edmonton	1324
1978	Mike Strickland, Saskatchewan	1306
1977	Jim Washington, Winnipeg	1262
1976	Jim Washington, Winnipeg	1277
1975	Willie Burden, Calgary	1896
1974	George Reed, Saskatchewan	1447
1973	Roy Bell, Edmonton	1455
1972	Mack Herron, Winnipeg	1527
1971	Jim Evenson, B.C.	1237
1970	Hugh McKinnis, Calgary	1135
1969	George Reed, Saskatchewan	1353
1968	George Reed, Saskatchewan	1222
1967	George Reed, Saskatchewan	1471
1966	George Reed, Saskatchewan	1409
1965	George Reed, Saskatchewan	1768
1964	Lovell Coleman, Calgary	1629
1963	Lovell Coleman, Calgary	1343
1962	Nub Beamer, B.C.	1161
1961	Earl Lunsford, Calgary	1794
1960	Earl Lunsford, Calgary	1343\
1959	Johnny Bright, Edmonton	1340
1958	Johnny Bright, Edmonton	1722
1957	Johnny Bright, Edmonton	1679
1966	Normie Kwong, Edmonton	1437
1955	Normie Kwong, Edmonton	1250
1954	Howard Waugh, Calgary	1043
1953	Billy Vessels, Edmonton	926
1952	Johnny Bright, Calgary	815
1951	Normie Kwong, Edmonton	933
1950	Tom Casey, Winnipeg	637

1993 CFL/JOSTENS PLAYERS OF THE WEEK

(as chosen by CFL judges Ellison Kelly and Peter Muller)

Week	Offensive	Defensive	Lineman
1.	Doug Flutie, Cal.	Gary Wilkerson, Ham.	Gregg Stumon, Ott.
2.	Earl Winfield, Ham.	O.J. Brigance, B.C.	Rob Smith, B.C.
3.	David Sapunjis, Cal.	Willie Pless, Edm.	Tim Cofield, Ham.
4.	Allen Pitts, Cal.	Willie Pless, Edm.	Keilly Rush, Wpg.
5.	Doug Flutie, Cal.	Alondra Johnson, Cal.	Jearld Baylis, Sask.
6.	Danny Barrett, B.C.	Kip Texada, Sac.	David Black, Wpg.
7.	Damon Allen, Edm.	Less Browne, B.C.	Elfrid Payton, Wpg.
8.	Manny Hazard, Tor.	Greg Battle, Wpg.	Rocco Romano, Cal.
9.	Doug Flutie, Cal.	O.J. Brigance, B.C.	Tim Cofield, Ham.
10.	Corey Philpot, B.C.	Glenn Rogers Jr., Edm.	Bennie Goods, Edm.
11.	Earl Winfield, Ham.	Carlton Lance, Sask.	Tim Cofield, Ham.
12.	Tom Burgess, Ott.	Marvin Pope, Cal.	Harald Hasselbach, Cal.
13.	Eddie Brown, Edm.	O.J. Brigance, B.C.	Jim Mills, B.C.
14.	Gerald Wilcox, Wpg.	Mark Ledbetter, Sac.	Harald Hasselbach, Cal
15.	David Williams, Wpg.	Charles Anthony, Sask.	Stew Hill, Sask.
16.	Kent Austin, Sask.	Don Wilson, Edm.	Mike Anderson, Sask.
17.	Damon Allen, Edm.	Charles Anthony, Sask.	Bennie Goods, Edm.
18.	David Archer, Sac.	Bobby Humphery, Sac.	Mark Ledbetter, Sac.
Playoffs - Week 1	Damon Allen, Edm.	Bobby Dawson, Ham.	Harald Hasselbach, Cal.
Week 2	Damon Allen, Edm.	Willie Pless, Edm.	Chris Walby, Wpg.

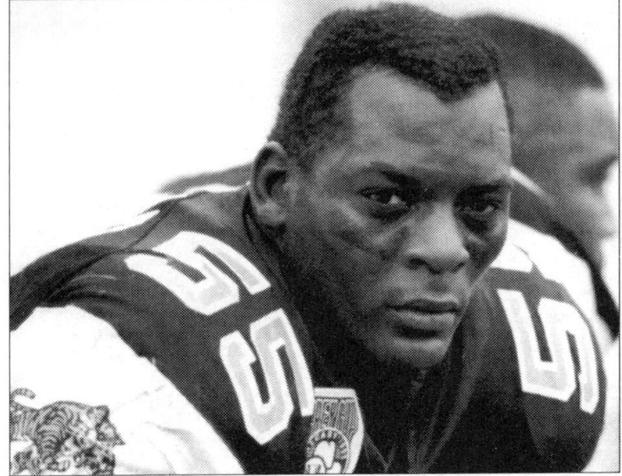

#55 DE Tim Cofield, Hamilton

CFL ALL-STAR TEAMS

Also known as All-Canadian All-Star Teams
(The Canadian Press initially voted for All-Star Teams. Voting for the CFL, All-Eastern and All-Western All-Star Teams, is currently done by the Football Reporters of Canada.)
**denotes unanimous selection (information regarding unanimous selections not available prior to 1982) *denotes tie

1993 CFL ALL-STAR TEAM

OFFENCE

Quarterback - Doug Flutie, Calgary**
Fullback - Sean Millington, B.C.
Running Back - Michael Richardson, Winnipeg
Slotback - Ray Elgaard, Saskatchewan
Slotback - David Sapunjis, Calgary
Wide Receiver - David Williams, Winnipeg
Wide Receiver - Rod Harris, Sacramento
Centre - Rod Connop, Edmonton
Guard - David Black, Winnipeg
Guard - Rob Smith, B.C.
Tackle - Bruce Covernton, Calgary
Tackle - Chris Walby, Winnipeg
Punter - Bob Cameron, Winnipeg
Kicker - David Ridgway, Saskatchewan

DEFENCE

Tackle - Jearld Baylis, Saskatchewan **
Tackle - Harald Hasselbach, Calgary
End - Will Johnson, Calgary
End - Tim Cofield, Hamilton
Linebacker - Elfrid Payton, Winnipeg
Linebacker - Willie Pless, Edmonton
Middle Linebacker - John Motton, Hamilton
Cornerback - Karl Anthony, Calgary
Cornerback - Barry Wilburn, Saskatchewan
Halfback - Don Wilson, Edmonton
Halfback - Darryl Sampson, Winnipeg
Safety - Glen Suitor, Saskatchewan

Special Teams - Henry Williams, Edmonton**

1992

OFFENCE

Quarterback - Doug Flutie, Calgary**
Fullback - Blake Marshall, Edmonton
Running Back - Michael Richardson, Winnipeg
Slotback - Ray Elgaard, Saskatchewan
Slotback - Allen Pitts, Calgary
Wide Receiver - Stephen Jones, Ottawa
Wide Receiver - Jim Sandusky, Edmonton
Centre - Rod Connop, Edmonton
Guard - Pierre Vercheval, Edmonton
Guard - Rocco Romano, Calgary
Tackle - Rob Smith, Ottawa
Tackle - Vic Stevenson, Saskatchewan
Punter - Hank Ilesic, Toronto
Kicker - Troy Westwood, Winnipeg

DEFENCE

Tackle - Rodney Harding, Toronto
Tackle - Jearld Baylis, Saskatchewan
End - Will Johnson, Calgary
End - Bobby Jurasin, Saskatchewan
Linebacker - Angelo Snipes, Ottawa
Linebacker - Willie Pless, Edmonton
Middle Linebacker - John Motton, Hamilton
Cornerback - Less Browne, Ottawa
Cornerback - Junior Thurman, Calgary
Halfback - Anthony Drawhorn, Ottawa
Halfback - Darryl Hall, Calgary
Safety - Glen Suitor, Saskatchewan

Special Teams - Henry Williams, Edmonton

1991

OFFENCE

Quarterback - Doug Flutie, B.C.**
Fullback - Blake Marshall, Edmonton**
Running Back - Robert Mimbs, Winnipeg
Slotback - Matt Clark, B.C.
Slotback - Allen Pitts, Calgary
Wide Receiver - Ray Alexander, B.C.**
Wide Receiver - Raghib Ismail, Toronto
Centre - Rod Connop, Edmonton
Guard - Leo Groenewegen, B.C.
Guard, Dan Ferrone, Toronto
Tackle - Jim Mills, B.C.
Tackle - Chris Walby, Winnipeg
Punter - Hank Ilesic, Toronto
Kicker - Lance Chomyc, Toronto

DEFENCE

Tackle - Harold Hallman, Toronto
Tackle - Brett Williams, Edmonton
End - Will Johnson, Calgary**
End - Mike Campbell, Toronto
Linebacker - Willie Pless, Edmonton
Linebacker - Darryl Ford, Toronto
Middle Linebacker - Greg Battle, Winnipeg
Cornerback - Less Browne, Winnipeg
Cornerback - Junior Thurman, Calgary
Halfback - Darryl Hall, Calgary
Halfback - Don Wilson, Toronto
Safety - Glen Suitor, Saskatchewan

Special Teams - Henry Williams, Edmonton

1990

OFFENCE

Quarterback - Kent Austin, Saskatchewan
Fullback - Blake Marshall, Edmonton
Running Back - Robert Mimbs, Winnipeg
Slotback - Darrell Smith, Toronto
Slotback - Craig Ellis, Edmonton
Wide Receiver - Stephen Jones, Ottawa
Wide Receiver - Don Narcisse, Saskatchewan
Centre - Rod Connop, Edmonton
Guard - Dan Ferrone, Toronto
Guard - Roger Aldag, Saskatchewan
Tackle - Jim Mills, B.C.
Tackle - Chris Walby, Winnipeg
Punter - Bob Cameron, Winnipeg
Kicker - Dave Ridgway, Saskatchewan

DEFENCE

Tackle - Kent Warnock, Calgary
Tackle - Harold Hallman, Toronto
End - Stewart Hill, Edmonton
End - Greg Stumon, Ottawa
Middle Linebacker - Dan Bass, Edmonton
Outside Linebacker - Willie Pless, B.C.
Outside Linebacker - Greg Battle, Winnipeg
Cornerback - Less Browne, Winnipeg
Cornerback - Rod Hill, Winnipeg
Halfback - Troy Wilson, Ottawa
Halfback - Don Wilson, Toronto
Safety - Greg Peterson, Calgary

Special Teams - Mike Clemons, Toronto

1989

OFFENCE
Quarterback - Tracy Ham, Edmonton**
Running Back - Tim McCray,Saskatchewan
Running Back - Reggie Taylor, Edmonton
Slotback - Rocky DiPietro, Hamilton
Slotback - Craig Ellis, Edmonton
Wide Receiver - Tony Champion, Hamilton**
Wide Receiver - Donald Narcisse, Saskatchewan
Centre - Rod Connop, Edmonton
Guard - Jason Riley, Hamilton
Guard - Roger Aldag, Saskatchewan
Tackle - Miles Gorrell, Hamilton
Tackle - Chris Walby, Winnipeg
Punter - Bob Cameron, Winnipeg
Kicker - Dave Ridgway, Saskatchewan

DEFENCE
Tackle - Harold Hallman, Toronto
Tackle - Mike Walker, Hamilton
End - Grover Covington, Hamilton
End - Stewart Hill, Edmonton
Middle Linebacker - Dan Bass, Edmonton
Outside Linebacker - Eddie Lowe, Saskatchewan
Outside Linebacker - James West, Hamilton
Cornerback - Stanley Blair, Edmonton
Cornerback - Rod Hill, Winnipeg
Halfback - Don Wilson, Edmonton
Halfback - Enis Jackson, Edmonton
Safety - Scott Flagel, Ottawa
Special Teams - Anthony Hunter, Edmonton

1988

OFFENCE
Quarterback - Matt Dunigan, B.C.
Running Back - Anthony Cherry, B.C.
Running Back - Gill Fenerty, Toronto
Slotback - Ray Elgaard, Saskatchewan
Slotback - Emanuel Tolbert, Calgary
Wide Receiver - David Williams, B.C.
Wide Receiver - James Murphy, Winnipeg
Centre - Ian Beckstead, Toronto
Guard - Roger Aldag, Saskatchewan
Guard - Gerald Roper, B.C.
Tackle - Chris Schultz, Toronto**
Tackle - Jim Mills, B.C.
Punter - Bob Cameron, Winnipeg
Kicker - Dave Ridgway, Saskatchewan
Special Teams - Earl Winfield, Hamilton

DEFENCE
Tackle - Mike Walker, Hamilton
Tackle - Brett Williams, Edmonton
End - Grover Covington, Hamilton
End - Bobby Jurasin, Saskatchewan
Middle Linebacker - Dan Bass, Edmonton
Outside Linebacker - Greg Stumon, B.C.
Outside Linebacker - Willie Pless, Toronto
Cornerback - Stanley Blair, Edmonton
Cornerback - Reggie Pleasant, Toronto
Halfback - Selwyn Drain, Toronto
Halfback - Howard Fields, Hamilton
Safety - Bennie Thompson, Winnipeg

1987

OFFENCE
Quarterback - Tom Clements, Winnipeg**
Running Back - Willard Reaves, Winnipeg
Running Back - Gill Fenerty, Toronto
Slotback - Darrell Smith, Toronto
Slotback - Perry Tuttle, Winnipeg
Wide Receiver - Brian Kelly, Edmonton
Wide Receiver - Jim Sandusky, B.C.
Centre - Rod Connop, Edmonton
Guard - Roger Aldag, Saskatchewan
Guard - Dan Ferrone, Toronto
Tackle - Chris Walby, Winnipeg
Tackle - Chris Schultz, Toronto
Punter - Hank Ilesic, Toronto
Kicker - David Ridgway, Saskatchewan
Special Teams - Henry Williams, Edmonton**

DEFENCE
Tackle - Mike Walker, Hamilton
Tackle - Jearld Baylis, Toronto
End - Greg Stumon, B.C.
End - Bobby Jurasin, Saskatchewan
Middle Linebacker - James West, Winnipeg
Outside Linebacker - Tyrone Jones, Winnipeg
Outside Linebacker - Kevin Konar, B.C.
Cornerback - Roy Bennett, Winnipeg
Cornerback - James Jefferson, Winnipeg
Defensive Back - Larry Crawford, B.C.
Defensive Back - Ken Hailey, Winnipeg
Safety - Scott Flagel, Winnipeg

1986

OFFENCE
Quarterback - Rick Johnson, Calgary
Running Back - Gary Allen, Calgary
Running Back - Bobby Johnson, Saskatchewan
Slotback - Joe Poplawski, Winnipeg
Slotback - Rocky DiPietro, Hamilton
Wide Receiver - James Murphy, Winnipeg**
Wide Receiver - James Hood, Montreal
Centre - Bob Poley, Calgary
Guard - Roger Aldag, Saskatchewan
Guard - Leo Blanchard, Edmonton
Tackle - Chris Walby, Winnipeg
Tackle - Rudy Phillips, Edmonton
Punter - Hank Ilesic, Toronto
Kicker - Lance Chomyc, Toronto
Special Teams - Gary Allen, Calgary

DEFENCE
Tackle - Harold Hallman, Calgary
Tackle - Brett Williams, Montreal
End - James Parker, B.C.**
End - Grover Covington, Hamilton
Middle Linebacker - Dan Bass, Edmonton
Outside Linebacker - Tyrone Jones, Winnipeg
Outside Linebacker - Willie Pless, Toronto
Cornerback - Roy Bennett, Winnipeg
Cornerback - Less Browne, Hamilton
Defensive Back - Larry Crawford, B.C.
Defensive Back - Mark Streeter, Hamilton
Safety - Scott Flagel, Winnipeg

1985

OFFENCE
Quarterback - Matt Dunigan, Edmonton
Running Back - Willard Reaves, Winnipeg
Running Back - Keyvan Jenkins, B.C.
Slotback - Joe Poplawski, Winnipeg
Tight End - Ray Elgaard, Saskatchewan
Wide Receiver - Mervyn Fernandez, B.C.
Wide Receiver - Jeff Boyd, Winnipeg
Centre - John Bonk, Winnipeg
Guard - Dan Ferrone, Toronto
Guard - Nick Bastaja, Winnipeg
Tackle - John Blain, B.C.
Tackle - Chris Walby, Winnipeg
Punter - Ken Clark, Ottawa
Kicker - Trevor Kennerd, Winnipeg

DEFENCE
Tackle - Mike Gray, B.C.
Tackle - James Curry, Toronto
End - Grover Covington, Hamilton
End - James Parker, B.C.
Middle Linebacker - Ben Zambiasi, Hamilton
Outside Linebacker - Tyrone Jones, Winnipeg
Outside Linebacker - Kevin Konar, B.C.
Defensive Back - Darnell Clash, B.C.
Defensive Back - Less Browne, Hamilton
Defensive Back - Ken Hailey, Winnipeg
Defensive Back - Howard Fields, Hamilton
Defensive Back - Paul Bennett, Hamilton

1984

OFFENCE
Quarterback - Tom Clements, Winnipeg
Running Back - Willard Reaves, Winnipeg
Running Back - Dwaine Wilson, Montreal
Slotback - Nick Arakgi, Montreal
Slotback - Joe Poplawski, Winnipeg
Wide Receiver - Brian Kelly, Edmonton
Wide Receiver - Mervyn Fernandez, B.C.
Centre - John Bonk, Winnipeg
Guard - Nick Bastaja, Winnipeg
Guard - Dan Ferrone, Toronto
Tackle - Chris Walby, Winnipeg
Tackle - John Blain, B.C.
Punter - Bernie Ruoff, Hamilton
Kicker - Lui Passaglia, B.C.

DEFENCE
Tackle - James Curry, Toronto
Tackle - Mack Moore, B.C.
End - Steve Raquet, Montreal
End - James Parker, B.C.
Middle Linebacker - Aaron Brown, Winnipeg
Outside Linebacker - Tyrone Jones, Winnipeg
Outside Linebacker - Stewart Hill, Edmonton
Defensive Back - David Shaw, Winnipeg
Defensive Back - Harry Skipper, Montreal
Defensive Back - Ken Hailey, Winnipeg
Defensive Back - Larry Crawford, B.C.
Defensive Back - Laurent DesLauriers, Edmonton

1983

OFFENCE
Quarterback - Warren Moon, Edmonton
Running Back - Alvin (Skip) Walker, Ottawa
Running Back - Johnny Shepherd, Hamilton
Slotback - Tom Scott, Edmonton
Slotback - Ron Robinson, Montreal
Wide Receiver - Brian Kelly, Edmonton
Wide Receiver - Terry Greer, Toronto
Centre - John Bonk, Winnipeg
Guard - Leo Blanchard, Edmonton
Guard - Rudy Phillips, Ottawa
Tackle - John Blain, B.C.
Tackle - Kevin Powell, Ottawa
Punter/Kicker - Lui Passaglia, B.C.

DEFENCE
Tackle - Mack Moore, B.C.
Tackle - Garry Dulin, Ottawa
End - Greg Marshall, Ottawa
End - Rick Mohr, Toronto
Middle Linebacker - Dan Bass, Calgary
Outside Linebacker - Delbert Fowler, Montreal
Outside Linebacker - Vince Goldsmith, Saskatchewan
Defensive Back - Harry Skipper, Montreal
Defensive Back - Kerry Parker, B.C.
Defensive Back - Larry Crawford, B.C.
Defensive Back - Richard Hall, Calgary*
Defensive Back - Carl Brazley, Toronto*
Defensive Back - Paul Bennett, Winnipeg

1982

OFFENCE
Quarterback - Condredge Holloway, Toronto
Running Back - Alvin (Skip) Walker, Ottawa**
Running Back - William Miller, Winnipeg
Slotback - Tom Scott, Edmonton
Slotback - Joey Walters, Saskatchewan
Wide Receiver - Terry Greer, Toronto**
Wide Receiver - Keith Baker, Hamilton
Centre - John Bonk, Winnipeg
Guard - Val Belcher, Ottawa
Guard - Rudy Phillips, Ottawa
Tackle - Bobby Thompson, Winnipeg
Tackle - Lloyd Fairbanks, Calgary
Punter - Ken Clark, Saskatchewan
Kicker - Dave Ridgway, Saskatchewan

DEFENCE
Tackle - Mike Samples, Saskatchewan
Tackle - John Helton, Winnipeg
End - Nick Hebeler, B.C.
End - Pete Catan, Winnipeg
Middle Linebacker - Dan Bass, Calgary
Outside Linebacker - James Parker, Edmonton
Outside Linebacker - Ben Zambiasi, Hamilton
Defensive Back - David Shaw, Hamilton
Defensive Back - Ray Odums, Calgary
Defensive Back - Vince Phason, Winnipeg
Defensive Back - Fran McDermott, Saskatchewan
Defensive Back - Zac Henderson, Toronto

1981

OFFENCE
Quarterback - Dieter Brock, Winnipeg
Running Back - Larry Key, B.C.
Running Back - Jim Germany, Edmonton
Slotback - Joe Poplawski, Winnipeg
Slotback - Joey Walters, Saskatchewan
Wide Receiver - Brian Kelly, Edmonton
Wide Receiver - James Scott, Montreal
Centre - Al Wilson, B.C.
Guard - Val Belcher, Ottawa
Guard - Larry Butler, Winnipeg
Tackle - Bill Stevenson, Edmonton
Tackle - Hector Pothier, Edmonton
Punter - Hank Ilesic, Edmonton
Kicker - Trevor Kennerd, Winnipeg

DEFENCE
Tackle - Dave Fennell, Edmonton
Tackle - Mike Raines, Ottawa
End - David Boone, Edmonton
End - Greg Marshall, Ottawa
Middle Linebacker - Dan Kepley, Edmonton
Outside Linebacker - Ben Zambiasi, Hamilton
Outside Linebacker - James Parker, Edmonton
Defensive Back - Ray Odums, Calgary
Defensive Back - David Shaw, Hamilton
Defensive Back - Harold Woods, Hamilton
Defensive Back - Ed Jones, Edmonton
Defensive Back - Randy Rhino, Ottawa

1980

OFFENCE
Quarterback - Dieter Brock, Winnipeg
Running Back - James Sykes, Calgary
Running Back - William Miller, Winnipeg
Slotback - Tom Scott, Edmonton
Tight End - Tony Gabriel, Ottawa
Wide Receiver - Brian Kelly, Edmonton
Wide Receiver - Mike Holmes, Winnipeg
Centre - Al Wilson, B.C.
Guard - Larry Butler, Winnipeg
Guard - Val Belcher, Ottawa
Tackle - Mike Wilson, Edmonton
Tackle - Butch Norman, Winnipeg
Punter - Hank Ilesic, Edmonton
Kicker - Bernie Ruoff, Hamilton

DEFENCE
Tackle - Dave Fennell, Edmonton
Tackle - Bruce Clark, Toronto
End - Ron Estay, Edmonton
End - Reggie Lewis, Calgary
Middle Linebacker - Dan Kepley, Edmonton
Outside Linebacker - Ben Zambiasi, Hamilton
Outside Linebacker - Dale Potter, Edmonton
Defensive Back - Ray Odums, Calgary
Defensive Back - Dickie Harris, Montreal*
Defensive Back - David Shaw, Hamilton*
Defensive Back - Ed Jones, Edmonton
Defensive Back - Greg Butler, Edmonton
Defensive Back - Ken McEachern, Saskatchewan

1979

OFFENCE
Quarterback - Tom Wilkinson, Edmonton
Running Back - David Green, Montreal
Running Back - Larry Key, B.C.
Slotback - Willie Armstead, Calgary
Tight End - Tony Gabriel, Ottawa
Wide Receiver - Waddell Smith, Edmonton
Wide Receiver - Brian Kelly, Edmonton
Centre - Al Wilson, B.C.
Guard - Ray Watrin, Montreal
Guard - Larry Butler, Hamilton
Tackle - Mike Wilson, Edmonton
Tackle - Lloyd Fairbanks, Calgary
Punter - Hank Ilesic, Edmonton
Kicker - Lui Passaglia, B.C.

DEFENCE
Tackle - Dave Fennell, Edmonton
Tackle - John Helton, Winnipeg
End - Junior Ah You, Montreal
End - Reggie Lewis, Calgary
Middle Linebacker - Dan Kepley, Edmonton
Outside Linebacker - Ben Zambiasi, Hamilton
Outside Linebacker - Ron Foxx, Ottawa
Defensive Back - Dickie Harris, Montreal
Defensive Back - Mike Nelms, Ottawa
Defensive Back - Greg Butler, Edmonton
Defensive Back - Ed Jones, Edmonton
Defensive Back - Al Burleson, Calgary

1978

OFFENCE
Quarterback - Tom Wilkinson, Edmonton
Running Back - James Sykes, Calgary
Running Back - Mike Strickland, Saskatchewan
Slotback - Tom Scott, Edmonton
Tight End - Tony Gabriel, Ottawa
Wide Receiver - Joe Poplawski, Winnipeg
Wide Receiver - Bob Gaddis, Montreal
Centre - Al Wilson, B.C.
Guard - Harold Holton, Calgary
Guard - Bill Stevenson, Edmonton
Tackle - Jim Coode - Ottawa
Tackle - Dan Yochum, Montreal
Punter - Hank Ilesic, Edmonton
Kicker - Dave Cutler, Edmonton

DEFENCE
Tackle - Dave Fennell, Edmonton
Tackle - John Helton, Calgary
End - Mike Fanucci, Ottawa
End - Reggie Lewis, Calgary
Middle Linebacker - Dan Kepley, Edmonton
Outside Linebacker - Ben Zambiasi, Hamilton
Outside Linebacker - Chuck Zapiec, Montreal
Defensive Back - Joe Hollimon, Edmonton
Defensive Back - Dickie Harris, Montreal
Defensive Back - Larry Brune, Ottawa
Defensive Back - Greg Butler, Edmonton
Defensive Back - Randy Rhino, Montreal

1977

OFFENCE
Quarterback - Jerry Tagge, B.C.
Running Back - Jimmy Edwards, Hamilton
Running Back - Jim Washington, Winnipeg
Slotback - Tom Scott, Winnipeg
Tight End - Tony Gabriel, Ottawa
Wide Receiver - Tom Forzani, Calgary
Wide Receiver - Leon Bright, B.C.
Centre - Al Wilson, B.C.
Guard - Jeff Turcotte, Ottawa
Guard - Ralph Galloway, Saskatchewan
Tackle - Mike Wilson, Toronto
Tackle - Dan Yochum, Montreal
Punter - Ken Clark, Hamilton
Kicker - Dave Cutler, Edmonton

DEFENCE
Tackle - Glen Weir, Montreal
Tackle - Dave Fennell, Edmonton
End - Jim Corrigall, Toronto
End - Ron Estay, Edmonton
Middle Linebacker - Dan Kepley, Edmonton
Outside Linebacker - Mike Widger, Ottawa
Outside Linebacker - Chuck Zapiec, Montreal
Defensive Back - Dickie Harris, Montreal
Defensive Back - Larry Highbaugh, Edmonton
Defensive Back - Paul Bennett, Toronto
Defensive Back - Pete Lavorato, Edmonton
Defensive Back - Randy Rhino, Montreal

1976

OFFENCE
Quarterback - Ron Lancaster, Saskatchewan
Running Back - Jimmy Edwards, Hamilton
Running Back - Jim Washington, Winnipeg
Running Back - Art Green, Ottawa
Tight End - Tony Gabriel, Ottawa
Wide Receiver - Rhett Dawson, Saskatchewan
Wide Receiver - George McGowan, Edmonton
Centre - Al Wilson, B.C.
Guard - Ralph Galloway, Saskatchewan
Guard - Dave Braggins, Montreal
Tackle - Dan Yochum, Montreal
Tackle - Butch Norman, Winnipeg

DEFENCE
Tackle - Granville Liggins, Toronto
Tackle - John Helton, Calgary
End - Bill Baker, B.C.
End - Junior Ah You, Montreal
Middle Linebacker - Harry Walters, Winnipeg
Outside Linebacker - Mark Kosmos, Ottawa
Outside Linebacker - Roger Goree, Saskatchewan
Defensive Back - Lorne Richardson, Saskatchewan
Defensive Back - Brian Herosian, Winnipeg
Defensive Back - Dickie Harris, Montreal
Defensive Back - David Shaw, Hamilton
Defensive Back - Paul Williams, Saskatchewan*
Defensive Back - Lewis Porter, Hamilton*

1975

OFFENCE
Quarterback - Ron Lancaster, Saskatchewan
Running Back - Willie Burden, Calgary
Running Back - Art Green, Ottawa
Running Back - Johnny Rodgers, Montreal
Tight End - Peter Dalla Riva, Montreal
Tight End - Tony Gabriel, Ottawa
Wide Receiver - George McGowan, Edmonton
Centre - Wayne Conrad, Montreal*
Centre - Al Wilson, B.C.*
Guard - Dave Braggins, Montreal
Guard - Willie Martin, Edmonton
Tackle - Charlie Turner, Edmonton
Tackle - Dan Yochum, Montreal

DEFENCE
Tackle - John Helton, Calgary
Tackle - Glen Weir, Montreal
End - Jim Corrigall, Toronto
End - Bill Baker, B.C.
Middle Linebacker - Jerry Campbell, Ottawa
Outside Linebacker - Larry Cameron, B.C.
Outside Linebacker - Mike Widger, Montreal
Defensive Back - Rod Woodward, Ottawa
Defensive Back - Dick Adams, Ottawa
Defensive Back - Lorne Richardson, Saskatchewan
Defensive Back - Vern Roberson, Calgary
Defensive Back - Dickie Harris, Montreal

1974

OFFENCE
Quarterback - Tom Wilkinson, Edmonton
Running Back - George Reed, Saskatchewan
Running Back - Lou Harris, B.C.
Running Back - Roy Bell, Edmonton
Tight End - Tony Gabriel, Hamilton
Wide Receiver - Johnny Rodgers, Montreal
Wide Receiver - Rhome Nixon, Ottawa
Centre - Bob Swift, Winnipeg
Guard - Ed George, Montreal
Guard - Curtis Wester, B.C.
Tackle - Charlie Turner, Edmonton
Tackle - Larry Watkins, Edmonton

1974 (Cont'd)

DEFENCE
Tackle - John Helton, Calgary
Tackle - Jim Stillwagon, Toronto
End - Wayne Smith, Ottawa
End - George Wells, Saskatchewan
Middle Linebacker - Jerry Campbell, Ottawa
Outside Linebacker - Mike Widger, Montreal
Outside Linebacker - Roger Goree, Calgary
Defensive Back - Al Marcelin, Ottawa
Defensive Back - Dick Adams, Ottawa
Defensive Back - Larry Highbaugh, Edmonton
Defensive Back - Paul Williams, Winnipeg
Defensive Back - Lorne Richardson, Saskatchewan*
Defensive Back - Dickie Harris, Montreal*

1973

OFFENCE
Quarterback - Ron Lancaster, Saskatchewan
Running Back - George Reed, Saskatchewan
Running Back - Roy Bell, Edmonton
Running Back - John Harvey, Montreal
Tight End - Peter Dalla Riva, Montreal
Wide Receiver - George McGowan, Edmonton
Wide Receiver - Johnny Rodgers, Montreal
Centre - Paul Desjardins, Toronto
Guard - Jack Abendschan, Saskatchewan
Guard - Ed George, Montreal
Tackle - Bill Frank, Winnipeg
Tackle - Charlie Turner, Edmonton

DEFENCE
Tackle - John Helton, Calgary
Tackle - Rudy Sims, Ottawa
End - Bill Baker, Saskatchewan
End - Jim Corrigall, Toronto
Linebacker - Jerry Campbell, Ottawa
Linebacker - Ray Nettles, B.C.
Linebacker - Mike Widger, Montreal
Defensive Back - Lorne Richardson, Saskatchewan
Defensive Back - Larry Highbaugh, Edmonton
Defensive Back - Al Marcelin, Ottawa
Defensive Back - Lewis Porter, Hamilton
Defensive Back - Dick Adams, Ottawa

1972

OFFENCE
Quarterback - Don Jonas, Winnipeg
Running Back - George Reed, Saskatchewan
Running Back - Mack Herron, Winnipeg
Running Back - Dave Buchanan, Hamilton
Tight End - Peter Dalla Riva, Montreal
Tight End - Tony Gabriel, Hamilton
Wide Receiver - Garney Henley, Hamilton
Wide Receiver - Jim Young, B.C.
Centre - Bob Swift, Winnipeg
Guard - Bob Lueck, Winnipeg
Guard - Jack Abendschan, Saskatchewan
Tackle - Bill Frank, Winnipeg
Tackle - Ed George, Montreal

DEFENCE
Tackle - Jim Stillwagon, Toronto
Tackle - John Helton, Calgary
End - Bill Baker, Saskatchewan
End - Wayne Smith, Ottawa
Linebacker - Dave Gasser, Edmonton
Linebacker - Ray Nettles, B.C.
Linebacker - Jerry Campbell, Ottawa
Defensive Back - Al Brenner, Hamilton
Defensive Back - Johnny Williams, Hamilton
Defensive Back - Grady Cavness, Winnipeg
Defensive Back - Dick Adams, Ottawa
Defensive Back - Marv Luster, Toronto

1971

OFFENCE
Quarterback - Don Jonas, Winnipeg
Running Back - George Reed, Saskatchewan
Running Back - Jim Evenson, B.C.
Running Back - Leon McQuay, Toronto
Tight End - Mel Profit, Toronto
Split End - Jim Thorpe, Winnipeg
Wide Receiver - Bob LaRose, Winnipeg
Centre - Bob Swift, Winnipeg
Guard - Jack Abendschan, Saskatchewan
Guard - Granville Liggins, Calgary
Tackle - Bill Frank, Winnipeg
Tackle - Ed George, Montreal

DEFENCE
Tackle - John Helton, Calgary
Tackle - Jim Stillwagon, Toronto
End - Jim Corrigall, Toronto
End - Craig Koinzan, Calgary
Linebacker - Wayne Harris, Calgary
Linebacker - Mark Kosmos, Montreal
Linebacker - Jerry Campbell, Ottawa
Defensive Back - Dick Dupuis, Edmonton
Defensive Back - Frank Andruski, Calgary
Defensive Back - Garney Henley, Hamilton
Defensive Back - Marv Luster, Toronto
Defensive Back - Dick Thornton, Toronto

1970

OFFENCE
Quarterback - Ron Lancaster, Saskatchewan
Running Back - Bill Symons, Toronto
Running Back - Hugh McKinnis, Calgary
Running Back - Jim Evenson, B.C.
Tight End - Herman Harrison, Calgary
Spilt End - Tommy Joe Coffey, Hamilton
Flanker - Jim Thorpe, Toronto
Centre - Ted Urness, Saskatchewan
Guard - Charlie Bray, Toronto
Guard - Bill Danychuk, Hamilton
Guard - Ken Sugarman, B.C.
Tackle - Bill Frank, Winnipeg
Tackle - Ellison Kelly, Hamilton

DEFENCE
Tackle - Angelo Mosca, Hamilton
Tackle - Greg Pipes, Edmonton
End - Steve Smear, Montreal
End - Ed Harrington, Toronto
Linebacker - Wayne Harris, Calgary
Linebacker - Jerry Campbell, Ottawa
Linebacker - Greg Findlay, B.C.
Defensive Back - John Wydareny, Edmonton
Defensive Back - Garney Henley, Hamilton
Defensive Back - Al Phaneuf, Montreal
Defensive Back - Al Marcelin, Ottawa
Defensive Back - Marv Luster, Toronto

1969

OFFENCE
Quarterback - Russ Jackson, Ottawa
Running Back - George Reed, Saskatchewan
Running Back - Vic Washington, Ottawa
Running Back - Dave Raimey, Toronto
Tight End - Herman Harrison, Calgary
Split End - Margene Adkins, Ottawa
Flanker - Ken Nielsen, Winnipeg
Centre - Ted Urness, Saskatchewan
Guard - Jack Abendschan, Saskatchewan
Guard - Charlie Bray, Toronto
Tackle - Clyde Brock, Saskatchewan
Tackle - Ellison Kelly, Hamilton

DEFENCE
Tackle - John LaGrone, Edmonton
Tackle - Ed McQuarters, Saskatchewan
End - Billy Joe Booth, Ottawa
End - Ed Harrington, Toronto
Linebacker - Ken Lehmann, Ottawa
Linebacker - Jerry Campbell, Ottawa
Linebacker - Phil Minnick, Winnipeg
Defensive Back - John Wydarney, Edmonton
Defensive Back - Marv Luster, Toronto
Defensive Back - Bruce Bennett, Saskatchewan
Defensive Back - Don Sutherin, Ottawa
Defensive Back - Garney Henley, Hamilton
Defensive Back - Larry Fairholm, Montreal

1968

OFFENCE
Quarterback - Russ Jackson, Ottawa
Running Back - George Reed, Saskatchewan
Running Back - Bill Symons, Toronto
Running Back - Vic Washington, Ottawa
End - Tommy Joe Coffey, Hamilton
End - Herman Harrison, Calgary
Flanker - Ken Nielsen, Winnipeg
Centre - Ted Urness, Saskatchewan
Guard - Charlie Parker, Montreal
Guard - Bill Danychuk, Hamilton
Tackle - Bill Frank, Toronto
Tackle - Clyde Brock, Saskatchewan

DEFENCE
Tackle - Ed McQuarters, Saskatchewan
Tackle - John LaGrone, Edmonton
End - Billy Ray Locklin, Hamilton
End - Ed Harrington, Toronto
Linebacker - Wayne Harris, Calgary
Linebacker - Wally Dempsey, Saskatchewan
Linebacker - Ken Lehmann, Ottawa
Defensive Back - Frank Andruski, Calgary
Defensive Back - Bob Kosid, Saskatchewan
Defensive Back - Garney Henley, Hamilton
Defensive Back - Ed Learn, Toronto
Defensive Back - Marv Luster, Toronto

1967

OFFENCE
Quarterback - Peter Liske, Calgary
Running Back - George Reed, Saskatchewan
Running Back - Bo Scott, Ottawa
Running Back - Jim Thomas, Edmonton
End - Terry Evanshen, Calgary
End - Tommy Joe Coffey, Hamilton
Flanker - Whit Tucker, Ottawa
Centre - Ted Urness, Saskatchewan
Guard - Jack Abendschan, Saskatchewan
Guard - Roger Perdrix, Ottawa
Tackle - Clyde Brock, Saskatchewan
Tackle - Bill Frank, Winnipeg

1967 (Cont')

DEFENCE
Tackle - John Barrow, Hamilton
Tackle - Ed McQuarters, Saskatchewan
End - E.A. Sims, Edmonton
End - John Baker, Montreal
Linebacker - Wayne Harris, Calgary
Linebacker - Garner Ekstran, Saskatchewan
Linebacker - Wayne Shaw, Saskatchewan
Defensive Back - Jerry Keeling, Calgary
Defensive Back - Phil Brady, Montreal
Defensive Back - Gene Gaines, Ottawa
Defensive Back - Garney Henley, Hamilton
Defensive Back - Frank Andruski, Calgary

1966

OFFENCE
Quarterback - Russ Jackson, Ottawa
Running Back - George Reed, Saskatchewan
Running Back - Jim Thomas, Edmonton
Running Back - Dave Raimey, Winnipeg
End - Jim Worden, Saskatchewan
End - Tommy Joe Coffey, Edmonton
Flanker - Hugh Campbell, Saskatchewan
Centre - Ted Urness - Saskatchewan
Guard - Al Benecick, Saskatchewan
Guard - Chuck Walton, Hamilton
Tackle - Bill Frank, Toronto
Tackle - Frank Rigney, Winnipeg
Tackle - Clyde Brock, Saskatchewan

DEFENCE
Tackle - John Barrow, Hamilton
Tackle - Don Luzzi, Calgary
End - Billy Ray Locklin, Hamilton
End - E.A. Sims, Edmonton
Linebacker - Wayne Harris, Calgary
Linebacker - Phil Minnick, Winnipeg
Linebacker - Ken Lehmann, Ottawa
Linebacker - Jim Conroy, Ottawa
Defensive Back - Gene Gaines, Ottawa
Defensive Back - Garney Henley, Hamilton
Defensive Back - Marv Luster, Toronto
Defensive Back - Ed Ulmer, Winnipeg
Defensive Back - Joe Poirier, Ottawa

1965

OFFENCE
Quarterback - Ken Ploen, Winnipeg
Running Back - George Reed, Saskatchewan
Running Back - Bo Scott, Ottawa
Running Back - Lovell Coleman, Calgary
End - Tommy Joe Coffey, Edmonton
End - Ted Watkins, Ottawa
Flanker - Hugh Campbell, Saskatchewan
Centre - Ted Urness, Saskatchewan
Guard - Al Benecick, Saskatchewan
Guard - Tony Pajaczkowski, Calgary
Tackle - Frank Rigney, Winnipeg
Tackle - Bronko Nagurski, Hamilton

DEFENCE
Tackle - John Barrow, Hamilton
Tackle - Pat Holmes, Calgary
End - Billy Ray Locklin, Hamilton
End - Dick Fouts, B.C.
Linebacker - Wayne Harris, Calgary
Linebacker - Ken Lehmann, Ottawa
Linebacker - Zeno Karcz, Hamilton
Defensive Back - Garney Henley, Hamilton
Defensive Back - Billy Wayte, Hamilton
Defensive Back - Dick Thornton, Winnipeg
Defensive Back - Jerry Keeling, Calgary
Defensive Back - Gene Gaines, Ottawa

1964

OFFENCE
Quarterback - Joe Kapp, B.C.
Running Back - Lovell Coleman, Calgary
Running Back - Dick Shatto, Toronto
Running Back - Ed Buchanan, Saskatchewan
End - Tommy Joe Coffey, Edmonton
End - Hal Patterson, Hamilton
Flanker - Tommy Grant, Hamilton
Centre - Chet Miksza, Hamilton
Guard - Tony Pajaczkowski, Calgary
Guard - Ellison Kelly, Hamilton
Guard - Al Benecick, Saskatchewan
Tackle - Roger Kramer, Ottawa
Tackle - Lonnie Dennis, B.C.

1964 (Cont'd)

DEFENCE
Tackle - John Barrow, Hamilton
Tackle - Mike Cacic, B.C.
End - Dick Fouts, B.C.
End - Peter Neumann, Hamilton
Middle Guard - Tom Brown, B.C.
Linebacker - Wayne Hams, Calgary
Linebacker - Ron Brewer, Toronto
Linebacker - Bobby Kuntz, Hamilton
Defensive Back - Garney Henley, Hamilton
Defensive Back - Don Sutherin, Hamilton
Defensive Back - Bill Munsey, B.C.
Defensive Back - Jerry Keeling - Calgary
Defensive Back - Bob Ptacek, Saskatchewan

1963

OFFENCE
Quarterback - Joe Kapp, B.C.
Running Back - Dick Shatto, Toronto
Ruuning Back - Willie Fleming, B.C.
Running Back - George Dixon, Montreal
Running Back - Lovell Coleman, Calgary
End - Hal Patterson, Hamilton
End - Pete Manning, Calgary
Centre - Milt Crain, Montreal
Guard - Tony Pajaczkowski, Calgary
Guard - Tom Hinton, B.C.
Tackle - Roger Kramer, Ottawa
Tackle - Lonnie Dennis, B.C.

DEFENCE
Tackle - Don Luzzi, Calgary
Tackle - Angelo Mosca, Hamilton
End - Garner Ekstran, Saskatchewan
End - Dick Fouts, B.C.
Middle Guard - John Barrow, Hamilton
Linebacker - Tom Brown, B.C.
Linebacker - Jim Andreotti, Montreal
Linebacker - Jim Conroy, Ottawa
Linebacker - Norm Fieldgate, B.C.
Defensive Back - Garney Henley, Hamilton
Defensive Back - Harvey Wylie, Calgary
Defensive Back - Dick Thornton, Winnipeg

1962

OFFENCE
Quarterback - Eagle Day,Calgary
Running Back - Earl Lunsford, Calgary
Running Back - George Dixon, Montreal
Running Back - Leo Lewis, Winnipeg
Running Back - Ray Purdin, Saskatchewan
End - Hal Patterson, Hamilton
End - Tommy Joe Coffey, Edmonton
Centre - Neil Habig, Saskatchewan
Guard - Tony Pajaczkowski, Calgary
Guard - Gerry Patrick, Toronto
Tackle - Frank Rigney, Winnipeg
Tackle - Bronko Nagurski, Hamilton

DEFENCE
Tackle - Don Luzzi, Calgary
Tackle - John Barrow, Hamilton
End - Garner Ekstran, Saskatchewan
End - Herb Gray, Winnipeg
Middle Guard - Kaye Vaughan, Ottawa
Linebacker - Wayne Harris, Calgary
Linebacker - Tom Brown, B.C.
Linebacker - Gord Rowland, Winnipeg
Linebacker - Jim Conroy, Ottawa
Defensive Back - Harvey Wylie, Calgary
Defensive Back - Jim Rountree, Toronto
Defensive Back - Don Sutherin, Hamilton

ALL-TIME EASTERN AND WESTERN ALL-STAR TEAMS

1993 ALL-EASTERN ALL-STARS

OFFENCE
Quarterback - Matt Dunigan, Winnipeg**
Fullback - Chris Johnstone, Winnipeg
Running Back - Michael Richardson, Winnipeg
Slotback - Gerald Wilcox, Winnipeg**
Slotback - Jock Climie, Ottawa
Wide Receiver - Stephen Jones, Ottawa **
Wide Receiver - David Williams, Winnipeg Hamilton
Centre - Dave Vankoughnett, Winnipeg
Guard - Denny Chronopoulos, Ottawa
Guard - David Black, Winnipeg
Tackle - Mike Graybill, Ottawa
Tackle - Chris Walby, Winnipeg**
Punter - Bob Cameron, Winnipeg
Kicker - Troy Westwood, Winnipeg

DEFENCE
Tackle - Stan Mikawos, Winnipeg
Tackle - John Kropke, Ottawa
End - Tim Cofield, Hamilton **
End - Loyd Lewis, Winnipeg
Linebacker - Angelo Snipes, Ottawa
Linebacker - Elfrid Payton, Winnipeg **
Middle Linebacker - John Motton,
Cornerback - Donald Smith, Winnipeg
Cornerback - Kim Phillips, Winnipeg
Halfback - Bobby Evans, Winnipeg
Halfback - Darryl Sampson, Winnipeg
Safety - Remi Trudel, Ottawa
Special Teams - Mike Clemons, Toronto

* unanimous selection

1993 ALL-WESTERN ALL-STARS

OFFENCE
Quarterback - Doug Flutie, Calgary**
Fullback - Sean Millington, B.C.
Running Back - Mike Oliphant, Sacramento
Slotback - Ray Elgaard, Saskatchewan
Slotback - David Sapunjis, Calgary
Wide Receiver - Don Narcisse, Saskatchewan
Wide Receiver - Rod Harris, Sacramento
Calgary
Centre - Rod Connop, Edmonton
Guard - Rocco Romano, Calgary
Saskatchewan
Guard - Rob Smith, B.C.
Tackle - Bruce Covernton, Calgary
Tackle - Jim Mills, B.C.
Punter - Glenn Harper, Edmonton
Edmonton
Kicker - David Ridgway, Saskatchewan

DEFENCE
Tackle - Jearld Baylis, Saskatchewan
Tackle - Harald Hasselbach, Calgary
End - Will Johnson, Calgary
End - Bennie Goods, Edmonton
Linebacker - O.J. Brigance, B.C.
Linebacker - Willie Pless, Edmonton
Middle Linebacker - Marvin Pope,
Cornerback - Karl Anthony, Calgary
Cornerback - Barry Wilburn,
Halfback - Don Wilson, Edmonton
Halfback - Glenn Rogers, Jr., Edmonton
Safety - Glen Suitor, Saskatchewan
Special Teams - Henry Williams,

ALL-EASTERN/ALL-WESTERN ALL-STAR TEAM MEMBERS

The following list is in alphabetical order, the names of All-Eastern/All-Western All-Starts throughout the years with their positions and years of All-Star honours:

* unanimous selection

- A -

Abbruzzi, Pat - Montreal, Running Back, '55, '56
Abendschan, Jack - Saskatchewan, Guard, '66, '67, '69, '70, '71, '73
Adams, Bert - Montreal, Guard, '33
Adams, Dick - Ottawa, Defensive Back, '72, '73, '74, '75
Adams, Steaky - Calgary, Guard, '46, '47
Adkins, Margene - Ottawa, Offensive End, '67, '69
Aguirre, Joe - Winnipeg, Offensive End, '50
Aguirre, Johnny - Calgary, Tackle, '48, '49
Ah You, Junior - Montreal, Defensive End, '74, '75, '76, '79, '80
Albright, Bill - Toronto, Guard, '55; Offensive Tackle, '56; Defensive Tackle '56
Aldag, Roger - Saskatchewan, Guard, '82, '83, '86, '87, '88, '89, '90, '91
Alexander, Ray - Calgary, Wide Receiver, '86; B.C., Wide Receiver, '90, '91
Allemang, Marvin - Hamilton, Centre, '85, '86
Allen, Damon - Ottawa, Quarterback, '91
Allen, Eric - Toronto, Wide Receiver, '72, '73
Allen, Gary - Calgary, Running Back, '86, '87; Special Teams, '86
Allison, Buddy - Winnipeg, Guard, '56
Alphin, Gerald - Ottawa, Slotback, '88
Anderson, Chuck - Calgary, Centre, '48
Anderson, Ezzret - Calgary, End, '49; Defensive End, '53
Anderson, Jerry - Hamilton, Defensive Back, '80
Anderson, Mike - Saskatchewan, Centre, '88
Anderson, Tim - Toronto, Defensive Back, '73
Andreotti, Jim - Toronto, Linebacker, '60, '61, '62; Montreal, Linebacker, '63
Andrew, Bud - Ottawa, Flying Wing, '33
Andrews, Rupe - Edmonton, Defensive Back, '55
Andruski, Frank - Calgary, Defensive Back, '67, '68, '69, '71, '72, '73
Andrusyshyn, Zenon - Toronto, Punter, '80, '81
Anthony, Karl - Calgary, Cornerback, '93
Anthony, Matt - Ottawa, End, '47
Arakgi, Nick - Montreal, Tight End, '82, '84, '85
Armstead, Willie - Calgary, Tight End/Slotback, '78, '79, '82
Armstrong, Neill - Winnipeg, Offensive End, '51; Defensive Back, '53
Arnold, Claude - Edmonton, Quarterback, '53
Ascott, Les - Toronto, Tackle, '45
Atamian, John - Saskatchewan, Guard, '68
Atchison, Ron - Saskatchewan, Middle Guard, '56, '60, '61, '62, '63; Defensive Tackle, '64
Austin, Kent - Saskatchewan, Quarterback, '90
Autry, John - Toronto, Defensive End, '63
Avery, Jeff - Ottawa, Wide Receiver, '77, '78
Aynsley, Brock - Montreal, Wide Receiver, '77, '78

- B -

Bailey, By - B.C., Running Back, '57
Bailey, Morris - Edmonton, Offensive End, '50
Baker, Bill - Saskatchewan, Defensive End, '71, '72, '73; B.C., Defensive End, '75, '76
Baker, John - Montreal, Defensive End, '65, '67
Baker, Keith - Montreal, Wide Receiver, '80, '81; Hamilton, Wide Receiver, '82, '83
Bandiera, Dean - Winnipeg, Defensive Guard, '53
Barden, Ricky - Ottawa, Defensive Back, '84, '85
Bark, Basil - Montreal, Centre, '68, '69; Calgary, Centre, '71, '73
Barnes, Joe - Toronto, Quarterback, '84
Barousse, Mark - Ottawa, Slotback, '86
Barrow, John - Hamilton, Offensive Tackle, '57, '58, '59, '60; Defensive Tackle, '57, '58, '59, '60, '61, '62, '65, '66, '67, '69; Middle Guard, '63, '64
Bass, Billy - Toronto, Running Back, '51
Bass, Dan - Calgary, Linebacker, '82, '83; Edmonton, Linebacker, '85, '86, '87, '88,'89, '90
Bastaja, Nick - Toronto, Offensive Tackle, '79; Winnipeg, Guard, '81, '82, '84, '85, '87, '88
Battle, Greg - Winnipeg, Linebacker, '89, '90; Middle Linebacker, '91
Bauer, Lyle - Winnipeg, Centre, '90
Baylis, Jearld - Toronto, Defensive Tackle, '87; Saskatchewan, Defensive Tackle, '92, '93
Baysinger, Hal - Montreal, Quarterback, '32
Beaird, Steve - Winnipeg, Running Back, '76
Beamer, Nub - B.C., Running Back, '62, '63
Beaumont, Neal - B.C., Defensive Back, '64
Becket, Mel - Saskatchewan, Centre, '56
Beckstead, Ian - Toronto, Centre, '87, '88
Belcher, Val - Ottawa, Guard, '80, '81, '82
Bell, Eddie - Hamilton, Linebacker, '59
Bell, Johhny - Regina, End, '46, '47, '48
Bell, Roy - Edmonton, Running Back, '73, '74
Bender, Walter - Hamilton, Running Back, '86; Saskatchewan, Running Back, '87
Benecick, Al - Saskatchewan, Offensive Tackle, '63; Guard, '64, '65, '66
Bennett, Bruce - Saskatchewan, Defensive Back, '67, '68, '69, '70, '71, '72
Bennett, Paul - Toronto, Defensive Back, '77; Winnipeg, Defensive Back, '82, '83, Hamilton, Defensive Back, '85
Bennett, Roy - Winnipeg, Cornerback, '86, '87
Berry, Ed - Toronto, Defensive Halfback, '89
Bethea, Willie - Hamilton, Running Back, '67
Bevan, Eddie - Hamilton, Guard, '51, '52; Defensive Guard, '53, '54, '55
Blackburn, Bill - Calgary, Centre, '52
Black, David - Winnipeg, Guard, '89, '93
Blanchard, Leo - Edmonton, Guard, '82, '83, '84, '85, '86; Calgary, Guard, '90
Blain, John - B.C., Offensive Tackle, '83, '84, '85, '87
Blair, Stanley - Edmonton, Cornerback, '88, '89
Blum, Mike - Ottawa, Linebacker, '67; Hamilton, Linebacker, '71
Bodine, Al - Saskatchewan, Running Back, '50
Boleski, Lanny - Calgary, Offensive Tackle, '69, '70
Bonk, John - Winnipeg, Centre, '82, '83, '84, '85
Bonner, Brian - Ottawa, Linebacker, '91
Boone, David - Edmonton, Defensive End, '77, '79, '81
Booras, Steve - Montreal, Defensive End, '70
Booth, Billy Joe - Ottawa, Defensive End, '63, '64, '66, '69
Boyd, Jeff - Winnipeg, Wide Receiver, '85
Bradley, Ed - Montreal, Guard, '53
Bradley, Jerry - B.C., Defensive Back, '69
Brady, Phil - Montreal, Defensive Back, '67
Braggins, Dave - Montreal, Guard, '75, '76
Brancato, George - Ottawa, Defensive Back, '61
Bray, Charlie - Toronto, Guard, '69, '70, '71
Brazley, Carl - Ottawa, Defensive Back, '82; Toronto, Defensive Back, '83, '84, '85, '86
Brenner, Al - Hamilton, Defensive Back, '72, '74
Brewer, Ron - Montreal, Linebacker, '61; Toronto, Linebacker, '64, '65
Brigance, O.J. - B.C., Linebacker, '91, '93
Bright, Johnny - Calgary, Running Back, '52; Edmonton, Running Back, '57, '58, '59, '60, '61
Bright, Leon - B.C., Wide Receiver, '77
Brito, Phil - Calgary, Defensive End, '54
Britts, Sam - Edmonton, Linebacker, '73
Brock, Clyde - Saskatchewan, Offensive Tackle, '65, '66, '67, '68, '69
Brock, Dieter - Winnipeg, Quarterback, '80, '81, '82
Bronk, Bob - Toronto, Running Back, '85
Brown, Aaron - Winnipeg, Linebacker, '84
Brown, Bob - Ottawa, Defensive End, '67
Brown, Buddy - Winnipeg, Guard, '76, '77
Brown, Dick - Hamilton, Defensive Back, '53
Brown, Gordon - Calgary, Defensive Guard, '53
Brown, Ike - Montreal, Running Back, '72
Brown, John - Winnipeg, Centre, '50
Brown, Lester - Toronto, Running Back, '84; Ottawa, Running Back, '85
Brown, Tom - B.C., Linebacker, '62, '63; Middle Guard, '64
Browne, Less - Hamilton, Defensive Back, '85; Cornerback, '86; Winnipeg, Cornerback, '90, '91; Ottawa, Cornerback, '92
Bruce, Lou - Ottawa, Defensive End, '60
Brule, Paul - Winnipeg, Defensive Back, '70
Brune, Larry - Ottawa, Defensive Back, '78, '81
Bruno, Al - Toronto, End, '52

All-Eastern/All-Western All-Star Team Members

Buchanan, Dave - Hamilton, Running Back, '72
Buchanan, Ed - Saskatchewan, Running Back, '64
Burden, Willie - Calgary, Running Back, '75, '77
Burgess, Tom - Winnipeg, Quarterback, '90, '92
Burkholder, Dave - Winnipeg, Linebacker, '58, '60, '61
Burleson, Al - Calgary, Defensive Back, '78, '79
Burley, Ecomet - Toronto, Defensive Tackle, '77; Hamilton, Defensive Tackle, '81
Burns, Tommy - Toronto, Tackle, '33, '35; Montreal, Tackle, '37
Burrell, Bill - Saskatchewan, Linebacker, '60, '62
Burris, Kent - Edmonton, Centre, '55; Linebacker, '55
Burrow, Jim - Montreal, Defensive Back, '78, '79
Burton, Eddie - Montreal, End, '40
Butler, Greg - Edmonton, Defensive Back, '78, '79, '80
Butler, Larry - Hamilton, Guard, '76, '77, '78, '79; Winnipeg, Guard, '80, '81
Byrd, Melvin - B.C., Defensive Back, '85, '87

- C -

Cacic, Mike - B.C., Defensive Tackle, '64, '65, '66
Cameron, Bob - Winnipeg, Punter, '84, '88, '89, '90, '93
Cameron, Larry - Ottawa, Linebacker, '76
Cameron, Paul - B.C., Defensive Back, '56
Campana, Tom - Saskatchewan, Running Back, '72
Campbell, Hugh - Saskatchewan, Flanker, '64, '65, '66, '69
Campbell, Jerry - Ottawa, Linebacker, '68, '69, '70, '72, '73, '74, '75
Campbell, Mike - Toronto, Defensive End, '91, '92
Canale, Justin - Montreal, Guard, '71
Capraru, Dan - Saskatchewan, Running Back, '41
Carpenter, Jack - Hamilton, Tackle, '51
Carpenter, Ken - Saskatchewan, Running Back, '55, '56; Offensive End, '58
Carteri, Carmelo - Hamilton, Linebacker, '81
Casey, Tom - Winnipeg, Running Back, '50, '51, '52; Winnipeg, Defensive Back, '53, '54, '55
Cassidy, Mike - Saskatchewan, Tackle, '48, '49; Guard, '53; Defensive Guard, '54
Catan, Pete - Winnipeg, Defensive End, '82
Cattelan, Roger - Ottawa, Offensive Tackle, '85
Cavness, Grady - Winnipeg, Defensive Back, '72; B.C., Defensive Back, '77
Ceppetelli, Gene - Hamilton, Centre, '67, '70
Ceretti, Bill - Winnipeg, Guard, '38, '40, '46
Chalupka, Ed - Hamilton, Guard, '72, '73, '74
Champion, Tony - Hamilton, Wide Receiver, '86, '89
Charlton, Ken - Saskatchewan, Flying Wing, '41; Ottawa, Flying Wing, '45, '46; Saskatchewan, Running Back, '48, '49
Chepesuik, Mike - Toronto, Guard, '34
Cherry, Anthony - B.C., Running Back, '88
Chipper, Eric - Ottawa, Tackle, '45
Chomyc, Lance - Toronto, Kicker, '86, '88, '91
Christman, Hank - Ottawa, Tackle, '46, '47
Chronopolous, Denny - Ottawa, Guard, '93
Cicia, Ray - Montreal, Guard, '50, '51; Offensive Guard, '54
Claridge, Pat - B.C., Offensive End, '64
Clark, Bob - Toronto, Quarterback, '34
Clark, Bruce - Toronto, Defensive Tackle, '80
Clark, Don - Montreal, Running Back, '61
Clark, Ken - Hamilton, Punter, '77; Toronto, Punter, '78; Saskatchewan, Punter, '82; Ottawa, Punter, '85
Clark, Matt - B.C., Slotback, '91
Clarke, Bill - Saskatchewan, Defensive Tackle, '61, '63
Clash, Darnell - B.C., Defensive Back, '85; Toronto, Special Teams, '87
Clements, Tom - Ottawa, Quarterback, '75, '76, '77, '79; Hamilton, Quarterback, '81; Winnipeg, Quarterback, '84, '87
Clemons, Michael - Toronto, Special Teams, '90, '93
Cleveland, Howard - Saskatchewan, Running Back, '39
Climie, Jock - Ottawa, Slotback, '93
Coffey, Tommy Joe - Edmonton, Offensive End, '62, '64, '65; Hamilton, Offensive End, '67, '68, '69, '70
Cofield, Tim - Hamilton, Defensive End, '93
Coleman, Lovell - Calgary, Running Back, '63, '64, '65
Collins, Charlie - Montreal, Linebacker, '70
Connop, Rod - Edmonton, Centre, '87, '89, '90, '91, '92, '93
Conrad, David - Ottawa, Fullback, '91
Conrad, Wayne - Montreal, Centre, '75
Conroy, Jim - Ottawa, Linebacker, '62, '63, '66
Coode, Jim - Ottawa, Offensive Tackle, '76, '78
Copeland, Royal - Toronto, Running Back, '45, '46, '47, '49
Corrigall, Jim - Toronto, Defensive End, '71, '72, '73, '75, '77, '78, '79, '80
Cousineau, Tom - Montreal, Linebacker, '80
Coulter, Bobby - Toronto, Quarterback, '36, '40
Coulter, Tex - Montreal, Offensive Tackle, '53, '54, '55; Defensive Tackle, '53, '54, '55
Covernton, Bruce - Calgary, Offensive Tackle, '93
Covington, Grover - Hamilton, Defensive End, '81, '85, '86, '87, '88, '89, '90
Cox, Martin - Ottawa, Wide Receiver, '79
Crain, Milt - Montreal, Offensive Tackle, '61; Centre, '63
Crawford, Derrick - Calgary, Special Teams, '90
Crawford, Larry - B.C., Defensive Back, '83, '84, '86, '87, '88
Crawford, Rufus - Hamilton, Running Back, '81
Crennel, Carl - Montreal, Defensive End, '73; Linebacker, '78, '79
Crifo, Rob - Winnipeg, Slotback, '91, '92
Crisson, Stan - Hamilton, Offensive End, '65
Critchlow, Joe - Winnipeg, Defensive Tackle, '72
Cross, Billy - Toronto, Defensive Back, '54
Crouse, Ray - Calgary, Running Back, '83
Crump, Richard - Ottawa, Running Back, '80
Cummings, Bruce - Ottawa, Flying Wing, '51
Curcillo, Tony - Hamilton, Linebacker, '57, '58
Cureton, Hardiman - Toronto, Defensive Guard, '56; Ottawa, Offensive Guard, '58; Hamilton, Linebacker, '61; Hamilton, Offensive Guard, '62; Hamilton, Offensive Tackle, '63
Curry, James - Toronto, Defensive Tackle, '84, '85; Saskatchewan, Defensive Tackle, '87, '89
Curtis, Uly - Toronto, Running Back, '50, '51, '52
Custis, Bernie - Hamilton, Quarterback, '51; Running Back, '54
Cutler, Dave - Edmonton, Kicker, '77, '78, '80
Cutler, Wes - Toronto, End, '33, '34, '35, '36, '37, '38

- D -

Dalla Riva, Peter - Montreal, Tight End, '72, '75, '76
Danaher, Leo - Saskatchewan, Running Back, '38
Danjean, Ernie - Hamilton, Linebacker, '59
Danychuk, Bill - Hamilton, Guard, '67, '68, '70; Offensive Tackle, '72, '73
Dattilio, Gerry - Montreal, Quarterback, '80
Davies, Bill - Montreal, Flying Wing, '38
Dawson, Rhett - Saskatchewan, Wide Receiver, '75, '76
Day, Eagle - Calgary, Quarterback, '62
Daymond, Irv - Ottawa, Centre, '91, '92
DeFrance, Chris - Saskatchewan, Slotback, '83, '84
Dekker, Paul - Hamilton, Offensive End, '58, '59, '60, '61
DeMarco, Mario - Edmonton, Guard, '51, '52; Saskatchewan, Guard, '54
Dempsey, Frank - Ottawa, Linebacker, '55
Dempsey, Wally - Saskatchewan, Linebacker, '68, '69
Denman, Alex - Hamilton, Guard, '32
Dennis, Lonnie - B.C., Offensive Tackle, '62, '63, '64
Dennis, Steve - Toronto, Defensive Back, '76
Denson, Moses - Montreal, Running Back, '70, '72
Dermott, Blake - Edmonton, Offensive Tackle, '89
DesLauriers, Laurent - Edmonton, Defensive Back, '84
Dewalt, Roy - B.C., Quarterback, '87
Dillard, Jim - Calgary, Running Back, '63, Ottawa, Running Back, '65; Toronto, Running Back, '66
DiPietro, Rocky - Hamilton, Slotback, '81, '82, '86, '89
Dixon, George - Montreal, Running Back, '62, '63
Dixon, Tom - Edmonton, Punter, '85, '86
Dobbs, Glenn - Saskatchewan, Quarterback, '51
Dobler, Walter - Winnipeg, Quarterback, '46
Dorsey, Dean - Ottawa, Kicker, '85, '87
Doyle, Mickey - Winnipeg, Linebacker, '72
Drain, Selwyn - Toronto, Defensive Back, '88
Drawhorn, Anthony - Ottawa, Defensive Halfback, '91, '92
Drew, Doug - Saskatchewan, Guard, '47
Druen, Max - Saskatchewan, Offensive Guard, '50
Druxman, George - Winnipeg, Centre, '56
Dulin, Gary - Ottawa, Defensive Tackle, '82, '83
Duncan, Dennis - Montreal, Running Back, '69; Ottawa, Running Back, '71
Dunigan Matt - Edmonton, Quarterback, '85; B.C., Quarterback, '88; Winnipeg, Quarterback, '93
Dunlap, Frank - Ottawa, Quarterback, '46
Dupuis, Dick - Edmonton, Defensive Back, '71, '72
Dushinski, Ted - Saskatchewan, Defensive Back, '70, '75

- E -

Ealey, Chuck - Hamilton, Quarterback, '72
Eben, Mike - Edmonton, Flanker, '70; Toronto, Flanker, '71
Ecuyer, Al - Edmonton, Linebacker, '59
Edberg, Rollie - Saskatchewan, End, '39
Edwards, Dan - B.C., Offensive End, '56
Edwards, Jimmy - Hamilton, Running Back, '76, '77, '78
Ekstran, Garner - Saskatchewan, Defensive End, '62, '63, '66, '67
Elgaard, Ray - Saskatchewan, Tight End, '85; Slotback, '87, '88, '90, '92, '93
Eliowitz, Abe - Ottawa, Flying Wing, '34; Running Back, '35; Montreal, Flying Wing, '36; Running Back, '37
Ellis, Craig - Saskatchewan, Running Back, '84; Edmonton, Slotback, '89, '90
Elsby, Ted - Montreal, Defensive Tackle, '64
Estay, Ron - Edmonton, Defensive End, '73, '77, '78, '80
Etcheverry, Sam - Montreal, Quarterback, '53, '54, '55, '56, '57, '60
Ettinger, Red - Saskatchewan, Centre, '51; Toronto, Centre, '52; Linebacker, '53; Hamilton, Linebacker, '54
Evans, Bobby - Winnipeg, Halfback, '93
Evanshen, Terry - Montreal, Wide Receiver, '65, '71; Calgary, Wide Receiver, '66, '67, '68, '69; Hamilton, Wide Receiver, '75
Evenson, Jim - Ottawa, Running Back, '73
Evraire, Ken - Hamilton, Slotback, '92
Exelby, Clare - Calgary, Defensive Back, '60
Ezerins, Leo - Hamilton, Linebacker, '86

- F -

Fairbanks, Lloyd - Calgary, Offensive Tackle, '78, '79, '82; Montreal, Guard, '84, '85; Offensive Tackle, '86; Calgary, Offensive Tackle, '90
Fairholm, Jeff - Saskatchewan, Slotback, '89
Fairholm, Larry - Montreal, Defensive Back, '68
Faloney, Bernie - Hamilton, Quarterback, '58, '59, '61, '64; Montreal, Quarterback, '65
Fanucci, Mike - Ottawa, Defensive End, '78
Fedosoff, John - Hamilton, Defensive Back, '55
Fenerty, Gill - Toronto, Running Back, '87, '88, '89
Fennell, Dave - Edmonton, Defensive Tackle, '77, '78, '79, '80, '81
Fernandez, Mervyn, B.C., Wide Receiver, '82, '83, '84, '85
Ferrero, Johnny - Montreal, Flying Wing, '37
Ferrone, Dan - Toronto, Guard, '83, '84, '85, '86, '87; Calgary, Guard, '89; Toronto, Guard, '90, '91, '92
Ferrughelli, Steve - Montreal, Running Back, '74
Fieldgate, Norm - B.C., Linebacker, '59, '60, '63
Fields, Howard - Hamilton, Defensive Back, '82, '83, '85, '87, '88
Fields, Jeff - Hamilton, Defensive Tackle, '92
Filchock, Frank - Hamilton, Quarterback, '47; Montreal, Quarterback, '49, '50
Filipski, Gene - Calgary, Running Back, '69
Findlay, Greg - B.C., Linebacker, '68, '70
Finlay, Matt - Calgary, Linebacker, '92
Flagel, Scott - Winnipeg, Defensive Back, '85; Safety, '86, '87; Ottawa, Safety, '89, '90, '91

All-Eastern/All-Western All-Star Team Members

Fleming, Dave - Hamilton, Running Back, '70
Fleming, Willie - B.C., Running Back, '60, '61, '63
Flowers, Bernie - Ottawa, Offensive End, '53
Flutie, Darren - B.C., Wide Receiver, '92
Flutie, Doug - B.C., Quarterback, '91; Calgary, Quarterback, '92, '93
Ford, Darryl - Toronto, Linebacker, '91
Ford, Ken - Calgary, Linebacker, '88
Forwick, Ron - Edmonton, Defensive End, '70
Forzani, Joe - Calgary, Linebacker, '75
Forzani, Tom - Calgary, Wide Receiver, '73, '74, '77
Fourqurean, Joe - B.C., Defensive Back, '77
Fouts, Dick - B.C., Defensive End, '63, '64, '65
Fowler, Delbert - Montreal, Linebacker, '83
Foxx, Ron - Ottawa, Linebacker, '79, '80
Francis, Andre - Edmonton, Cornerback, '89, '90
Frank, Bill - Toronto, Offensive Tackle, '66, '67, '68; Winnipeg, '70, '71, '72, '73
Fraser, George - Ottawa, Guard, '38, '40, '45
Frith, Ken - Saskatchewan, Defensive End, '70
Fritz, Bob - Winnipeg, Quarterback, '37
Fulton, Ed - Hamilton, Offensive Tackle, '81, '82
Funston, Farrell - Winnipeg, Offensive End, '61, '63
Furey, Jim - Calgary, Centre, '58
Furlong, Jim - Calgary, Linebacker, '65

- G -

Gabriel, Tony - Hamilton, Tight End, '72, '73, '74; Ottawa, Tight End, '75, '76, '78, '79, '80, '81
Gaddis, Bob - Montreal, Wide Receiver, '78, '79; Toronto, Wide Receiver, '80
Gain, Bob - Ottawa, Tackle, '51
Gaines, Gene - Ottawa, Linebacker, '63; Defensive Back, '65, '66, '67; Montreal, Defensive Back, '71
Gainor, Martin - Winnipeg, Tackle, '37, '38, '39, '46
Galloway, Ralph - Saskatchewan, Guard, '73, '74, '75, '76, '77
Garbarino, Henry - Montreal, End, '32
Gasser, Dave - Edmonton, Linebacker, '70, '71, '72
Gelhaye, Gordon - Edmonton, Tackle, '39; Calgary, Tackle, '40; B.C., Tackle, '41
George, Ed - Montreal, Offensive Tackle, '70, '71, '72; Guard, '73, '74
Germany, Jim - Edmonton, Running Back, '79, '81
Gilchrist, Cookie - Hamilton, Running Back, '56, '57; Saskatchewan, Running Back, '58; Toronto, Running Back, '59, '60; Toronto, Linebacker, '60
Glasser, Sully - Saskatchewan, Running Back, '46
Golab, Tony - Ottawa, Running Back, '39, '40, '45; Flying Wing, '47, '48
Goldsmith, Vince - Saskatchewan, Linebacker, '81, '83; End, '88
Goldston, Ralph - Hamilton, Defensive Back, '56, '57, '58, '59
Gooch, Keith - B.C., Cornerback, '87; Edmonton, Cornerback, '90
Goodlow, Eugene - Winnipeg, Wide Receiver, '81
Goods, Bennie - Edmonton, Defensive End, '93
Gordon, Andy - Ottawa, Quarterback, '49
Goree, Roger - Calgary, Linebacker, '73, '74; Saskatchewan, Linebacker, '76, '77
Gorrell, Miles - Montreal, Offensive Tackle, '83, '84; Hamilton, Offensive Tackle, '86, '88
Gotta, Jack - Calgary, Offensive End, '57, '61; Defensive Back, '57, '58
Graham, Milt - Ottawa, Offensive Tackle, '58
Graham, Vern - Calgary, Running Back, '49
Grant, Bud - Winnipeg, Offensive End, '53, '54, '56
Grant, Tommy - Hamilton, Running Back, '63; Flanker, '64
Gray, Ed - Edmonton, Defensive End, '59, '60
Gray, Herb - Winnipeg, Defensive End, '57, '58, '59, '60, '61, '62; Guard, '65
Gray, Mike - B.C., Defensive Tackle, '85; Winnipeg, Defensive End, '89
Gray, Tyron - B.C., Wide Receiver, '81
Graybill, Mike - Ottawa, Offensive Tackle, '93
Green, Art - Ottawa, Running Back, '74, '75
Green, David - Montreal, Running Back, '79
Greer, Terry - Toronto, Wide Receiver, '82, '83, '84, '85
Gregus, Bill - Hamilton, Running Back, '50
Griffin, Murray - Ottawa, Running Back, '38
Griffing, Dean - Saskatchewan, Centre, '37, '38, '40
Groenewegen, Leo - B.C., Guard, '91
Groom, Dick - Hamilton, End, '45, '46

- H -

Habig, Neil - Saskatchewan, Centre, '59, '60, '61, '62, '63, '64
Haigh, Bert - Ottawa, End, '46, '47, '48
Hailey, Ken - Winnipeg, Defensive Back, '84, '85, '87
Hall, Darryl - Calgary, Defensive Halfback, '91, '92
Hall, Richard - Calgary, Defensive Back, '83, '86; Saskatchewan, Defensive Halfback, '88, '90
Hallman, Harold - Calgary, Defensive Tackle, '86, '87; Toronto, Defensive Tackle, '89, '90, '91
Ham, Tracy - Edmonton, Quarterback, '89
Hampton, William - Montreal, Linebacker, '82
Hanson, Fritz - Winnipeg, Running Back, '37, '38, '39, '40, '41
Hardee, Billy - Toronto, Defensive Back, '79, '80
Harding, Rodney - Toronto, Defensive End, '86, '87; Defensive Tackle, '88, '92
Harper, Glenn - Calgary, Punter, '87; Edmonton, Punter, '93
Harrington, Ed - Toronto, Defensive End, '64, '68, '69, '70
Harraway, Floyd - Winnipeg, Defensive Guard, '55
Harris, Dickie - Montreal, Defensive Back, '73, '74, '75, '76, '77, '78, '79
Harris, Eric - Toronto, Defensive Back, '77, '78, '80
Harris, Lou - B.C., Running Back, '74, '75
Harris, Rod - Sacramento, Wide Receiver, '93
Harris, Wayne - Calgary, Linebacker, '61, '62, '63, '64, '65, '66, '67, '68, '69, '70, '71
Harrison, Herman - Calgary, Offensive End, '65, '67, '68, '69, '70, '71
Harvey, John - Montreal, Running Back, '73
Hasselbach, Harold - Calgary, Defensive Tackle, '93
Hay, John T. - Calgary, Kicker, '86
Hayes, Larry - Ottawa, Offensive Guard, '56, '57; Defensive Guard, '57; Linebacker, '59
Haynes, Larry - Calgary, Centre, '37, '40; B.C., Centre, '41
Hebeler, Nick - B.C., Defensive End, '82
Heighton, Jim - Winnipeg, Defensive End, '72, '74
Helton, John - Calgary, Defensive End, '69; Defensive Tackle, '70, '71, '72, '73, '74, '75, '76, '78; Winnipeg, Defensive Tackle, '79, '81, '82
Henderson, Zac - Toronto, Defensive Back, '82
Hendrickson, Lefty - B.C., Tight End, '73
Henke, Ed - Calgary, Linebacker, '54
Henley, Garney - Hamilton, Defensive Back, '63, '64, '65, '66, '67, '68, '69, '70, '71; Wide Receiver, '72
Henry, Urban - B.C., Defensive Tackle, '59, '60
Herman, Tiny - Ottawa, Guard, '36, '37, '38, '39
Herosian, Brian - Winnipeg, Defensive Back, '75, '76
Herron, Mack - Winnipeg, Running Back, '71, '72
Highbaugh, Larry - Edmonton, Defensive Back, '73, '74, '75, '77
Hill, Jack - Saskatchewan, Running Back, '58
Hill, Rod - Winnipeg, Cornerback, '89, '90, '92
Hill, Stewart - Edmonton, Linebacker, '84; Defensive End, '86, '89, '90; B.C., Defensive End, '91
Hiney, Don - Winnipeg, Running Back, '48
Hinton, Tom - B.C., Guard, '58, '59, '63, '64, '66
Hirsch, Ed - Toronto, Centre, '50, '51
Hobart, Ken - Hamilton, Quarterback, '85
Hohman, Jon - Hamilton, Guard, '72
Hollimon, Joe - Edmonton, Defensive Back, '76, '78, '82
Holloway, Condredge - Ottawa, Quarterback, '78; Toronto, Quarterback, '82, '83
Holmes, Bruce - Ottawa, Middle Linebacker, '90
Holmes, Mike - Winnipeg, Wide Receiver, '78, '80
Holmes, Pat - Calgary, Defensive Tackle, '65
Holmes, Richard - Ottawa, Running Back, '77
Holt, Harry - B.C., Tight End, '79, '80
Holton, Harold - Calgary, Guard, '78
Hood, James - Montreal, Wide Receiver, '86
Hood, Robert - Hamilton, End, '49
Hopkins, Andy - Hamilton, Running Back, '73, '74; Montreal, Running Back, '76
Hoptowit, Al - Calgary, Guard, '38
House, Rick - Winnipeg, Slotback, '90
Howell, Ron - Hamilton, Flying Wing, '58; Hamilton, Flanker, '59
Howes, Bob - Edmonton, Centre, '73
Hudson, Bill - Montreal, Offensive Tackle, '60
Hudson, Warren - Winnipeg, Fullback, '90, '92
Huffman, Dick - Winnipeg, Offensive Tackle, '52, '54; Winnipeg, Defensive Tackle, '53, '54, '55; Calgary, Defensive Tackle, '56, '57; Calgary, Offensive Tackle, '57
Hugo, Tommy - Montreal, Centre, '53, '54, '55, '56, '57, '58, '59; Montreal, Linebacker, '54, '55, '56, '57, '58
Hunsperger, Garrett - B.C., Defensive Tackle, '74
Hunter, Tony - Edmonton, Special Teams, '89
Hurd, Howard - Calgary, Guard, '37
Hutton, Len - Montreal, End, '35

- I -

Iannone, Bert - Winnipeg, Guard, '47; Calgary, Guard, '48; Saskatchewan, Guard, '51
Ilesic, Hank - Edmonton, Punter, '78, '79, '80, '81; Toronto, Punter, '86, '87, '91, '92
Irvin, Terry - Calgary, Defensive Back, '78, '79; Saskatchewan, Defensive Back, '84; Montreal, Cornerback, '86
Irving, Bud - Winnipeg, Guard, '48
Isbell, Larry - Saskatchewan, Defensive Back, '56, '57, '58
Isbister, Bob - Toronto, Running Back, '38; Hamilton, Running Back, '39
Ismail, Raghib - Toronto, Wide Receiver, '91, Special Teams, '91, '92

- J -

Jackson, Billy - Saskatchewan, Linebacker, '86
Jackson, Enis - Edmonton, Defensive Halfback, '89, '91, '92
Jackson, Glen - B.C., Linebacker, '77, '78, '79, '82, '85, '87
Jackson, Noah - Toronto, Offensive Tackle, '74
Jackson, Russ - Ottawa, Quarterback, '62, '63, '66, '67, '68, '69
Jacobs, Jack - Winnipeg, Quarterback, '50, '52
James, Gerry - Winnipeg, Running Back, '55, '57
Janzen, Henry - Winnipeg, Defensive Back, '65
Jefferson, James - Winnipeg, Cornerback, '87, '88
Jenkins, Keyvan - B.C., Running Back, '85
Jenkins, Mel - Calgary, Cornerback, '86
Jenson, Roy - Calgary, Guard, '54
Jessup, Bill - B.C., Defensive Back, '59
Johnson, Alondra - Calgary, Middle Linebacker, '91, '92
Johnson, Bobby - Saskatchewan, Running Back, '86
Johnson, Glenn - Winnipeg, Offensive Tackle, '50
Johnson, Rick - Calgary, Quarterback, '86
Johnson, Ron - Hamilton, Wide Receiver, '84
Johnson, Will - Calgary, Defensive End, '90, '91, '92, '93
Johnstone, Chris - Winnipeg, Fullback, '93
Jonas, Don - Winnipeg, Quarterback, '71, '72
Jones, Ed - Edmonton, Defensive Back, '78, '79, '80, '81
Jones, Edgar - Hamilton, Running Back, '50
Jones, Jimmy - Montreal, Quarterback, '74
Jones, Phil - Montreal, Defensive Back, '84
Jones, Stephen - Ottawa, Wide Receiver, '90, '92, '93
Jones, Tom - Ottawa, Offensive Tackle, '61
Jones, Tyrone - Winnipeg, Linebacker, '84, '85, '86, '87, '90
Jordan, Stephen - Hamilton, Defensive Back, '89; Ottawa, Wide Receiver, '90
Jotkus, Pete - Montreal, Guard, '32; Tackle, '33, '34, '35, '36
Judges, Gordon - Montreal, Defensive Tackle, '73
Jurasin, Bobby - Saskatchewan, Defensive End, '87, '88, '89, '92

- K -

Kabat, Greg - Winnipeg, Flying Wing, '38; Guard, '39; Quarterback, '40
Kapp, Joe - B.C., Quarterback, '63, '64
Karcz, Zeno - Hamilton, Linebacker, '62, '65
Kauric, Jerry - Edmonton, Punter, '88

All-Eastern/All-Western All-Star Team Members

Keeling, Jerry - Calgary, Defensive Back, '64, '65, '66, '67, '68
Keith, Jimmy - Toronto, End, '32
Kelly, Brian - Edmonton, Wide Receiver, '79, '80, '81, '83, '84, '87
Kelly, Ellison - Hamilton, Guard, '61, '62, '63, '64; Offensive Tackle, '68, '69, '70; Toronto, Offensive Tackle, '71
Kennerd, Trevor - Winnipeg, Kicker, '81, '83, '85
Kepley, Dan - Edmonton, Linebacker, '77, '78, '79, '80, '81
Kerrigan, Mike - Hamilton, Quarterback, '86, '89
Key, Larry - B.C., Running Back, '79, '81
Keys, Eagle - Edmonton, Centre, '53, '54
King, Franklin - Toronto, Defensive Tackle, '83
King, Mike - Edmonton, Running Back, '50, '51
Kirzinger, Dave - Calgary, Offensive Tackle, '83
Kissell, Mike - Winnipeg, Guard, '49
Klassen, Rick - B.C., Defensive Tackle, '85
Kmech, Mike - Edmonton, Guard, '61
Koinzan, Craig - Calgary, Defensive End, '71
Konar, Kevin - B.C., Linebacker, '85, '87
Korchak, Bud - Winnipeg, Flying Wing, '52, '53
Kosid, Bob - Saskatchewan, Defensive Back, '66, '68
Kosmos, Mark - Montreal, Linebacker, '71; Ottawa, Linebacker, '75, '76
Kotowich, Ed - Winnipeg, Guard, '59
Kramer, Roger - Ottawa, Offensive Tackle, '63, '64; Calgary, Offensive Tackle, '67
Krol, Joe - Toronto, Running Back, '45, '46, '47, '48
Kropke, John - Ottawa, Defensive End, '92, '93
Krouse, Bob - Hamilton, Linebacker, '67
Kruger, Oscar - Edmonton, Defensive Back, '57, '58, '61, '62
Kulka, Glen - Toronto, Defensive End, '88
Kuntz, Bobby - Toronto, Defensive Back, '57; Hamilton, Running Back, '62; Hamilton, Linebacker, '64
Kusserow, Lou - Hamilton, Defensive Back, '53, '54, '55; Running Back, '55
Kwong, Normie - Edmonton, Running Back, '51, '53, '55, '56

- L -

LaGrone, John - Edmonton, Defensive Tackle, '67, '68, '69, '71, '72, '73
Lakusiak, Gene - Winnipeg, Defensive Back, '72, '73
Lancaster, Ron - Saskatchewan, Quarterback, '66, '68, '69, '70, '73, '75, '76
Lander, Jim - Saskatchewan, Running Back, '41
Landy, Frank - B.C., Defensive Tackle, '77
Langford, Harry - Calgary, Guard, '55, '56, '57, '58
Laputka, Tom - Ottawa, Defensive End, '71
LaRose, Bob - Winnipeg, Flanker, '71
Lavorato, Pete - Edmonton, Defensive Back, '77
Lear, Les - Winnipeg, Guard, '41
Learn, Ed - Montreal, Defensive Back, '64, '66; Toronto, Defensive Back, '68, '69
Lee, Orville - Ottawa, Running Back, '88
Lehmann, Ken - Ottawa, Linebacker, '65, '66, '67, '68, '69
Levantis, Steve - Toronto, Tackle, '45
Levenhagen, Bob - B.C., Defensive Guard, '54, '55
Lewis, Gary - Saskatchewan, Defensive Tackle, '88, '91
Lewis, Leo - Winnipeg, Running Back, '55, '58, '60, '61, '62, '64
Lewis, Loyd - Ottawa, Defensive End, '85, Defensive Tackle, '90, '91; Edmonton, Defensive Tackle, '92; Winnipeg, Defensive End, '93
Lewis, Reggie - Calgary, Defensive End, '78, '79, '80
Liggins, Granville - Calgary, Guard, '72; Toronto, Defensive Tackle, '75, '76
Lindley, Earl - Edmonton, Linebacker, '56
Linterman, Rudy - Calgary, Wide Receiver, '74
Lisbon, Don - Montreal, Running Back, '66
Liske, Peter - Calgary, Quarterback, '67
Locklin, Billy Ray - Montreal, Defensive End, '61, '62; Hamilton, Defensive End, '65, '66, '68
Loney, Don - Toronto, Centre, '46; Ottawa, Centre, '47, '48, '49
Long, Rocky - B.C., Defensive Back, '77
Lowe, Eddie - Saskatchewan, Linebacker, '89
Lueck, Bob - Calgary, Guard, '67, '68; Winnipeg, Guard, '71, '72
Lunsford, Earl - Calgary, Running Back, '60, '61, '62
Luster, Marv - Montreal, Offensive End, '61, '62; Toronto, Defensive Back, '66, '67, '68, '69, '70, '71,'72
Luzzi, Don - Calgary, Offensive Tackle, '58, '61; Defensive Tackle, '58, '60, '62, '63, '66
Lyons, Damion - Edmonton, Cornerback, '92

- M -

Machinsky, Francis - Toronto, Guard, '56
Mack, Gene - Toronto, Linebacker, '72, '73
Mackrides, Bill - Hamilton, Quarterback, '52
Macon, Ed - Calgary, Running Back, '54; Hamilton, Defensive Back, '58
Major, Chris - Calgary, Cornerback, '88
Malinosky, John - Toronto, Offensive Tackle, '84
Manchuk, Bill - Saskatchewan, Defensive Back, '76
Manley, Leon - Edmonton, Offensive Tackle, '53
Mann, Dave - Toronto, Flanker, '60, '61
Manning, Pete - Calgary, Offensive End, '62, '63, '64
Marcelin, Al - Ottawa, Defensive Back, '70, '73, '74
Marlow, Bobby - Saskatchewan, Running Back, '53, '54, '55; Linebacker, '56, '57
Marquardt, Bud - Winnipeg, End, '37, '39, '40
Marshall, Blake - Edmonton, Fullback, '90, '91, '92
Marshall, Greg - Ottawa, Defensive End, '81, '82, '83, '84
Marshall, Jim - Saskatchewan, Defensive Back, '75
Martin, Nelson - B.C., Safety, '87
Martin, Willie - Edmonton, Guard, '75; Hamilton, Offensive Tackle, '80
Martinello, Marty - Toronto, Middle Guard, '60, '61
Masters, Wally - Ottawa, Running Back, '32
Matheson, Riley - Calgary, Guard, '49, '50
Matich, Brent - Calgary, Punter, '89, '90, '91
Mazza, Vince - Hamilton, End, '50, '51; Tackle, '52; Defensive Tackle, '53; Offensive Tackle, '53, '54
McAleney, Ed - Calgary, Defensive Tackle, '80
McCance, Ches - Winnipeg, End, '40, '41
McCarthy, Tony - Ottawa, End, '38, '39
McCrary, David - Calgary, Defensive Halfback, '90
McDermott, Fran - Saskatchewan, Defensive Back, '82
McDougall, Gerry - Hamilton, Running Back, '57, '58
McDowell, Layne - B.C., Offensive Tackle, '75, '76, '77
McEachern, Ken - Saskatchewan, Defensive Back, '76, '80, '81; Toronto, Defensive Back, '83
McFarlane, Bill - Toronto, Defensive Back, '54
McGowan, George - Edmonton, Wide Receiver, '73, '75, '76
McKee, Johnny - Calgary, Centre, '39
McKeown, Bob - Ottawa, Centre, '74
McKinnie, Silas - Saskatchewan, Running Back, '70
McKinnis, Hugh - Calgary, Running Back, '70
McLaren, Bob - Winnipeg, Linebacker, '71
McLoughlin, Mark - Calgary, Kicker, '92
McNamara, Bob - Winnipeg, Running Back, '56
McNichol, Doug - Montreal, Defensive End, '53, '54, '55, '58, '59
McPherson, Jim - Winnipeg, Guard, '52
McQuarters, Ed - Saskatchewan, Defensive Tackle, '67, '68, '69
McQuay, Leon - Toronto, Running Back, '71
McTague, Mike - Montreal, Slotback, '85
Meiers, Buddy - Ottawa, Centre, '35
Meinert, Dale - Edmonton, Offensive Tackle, '55
Metcalf, Terry - Toronto, Running Back, '79
Michaels, Eddie - Ottawa, Guard, '48, '49
Mikawos, Stan - Winnipeg, Defensive Tackle, '93
Miksza, Chet - Hamilton, Centre, '64
Miles, Rollie - Edmonton, Running Back, '52, '53, '54; Defensive Back, '54, '55, '56; Linebacker, '58, '59
Miller, Al - Winnipeg, Linebacker, '65
Miller, Jim - Montreal, Defensive End, '56
Miller, William - Winnipeg, Running Back, '80, '82
Millington, Sean - B.C., Fullback, '93
Mills, Jim - B.C., Offensive Tackle, '88, '90, '91, '92, '93
Mimbs, Robert - Winnipeg, Running Back, '90, '91
Minihane, Bob - Montreal, Defensive Tackle, '67
Minnick, Phil - Winnipeg, Linebacker, '66, '68
Minter, Cedric - Toronto, Running Back, '81, '82
Mitchell, William - Toronto, Linebacker, '83, '84, '85
Moen, Don - Toronto, Linebacker, '88
Moffatt, Alan - Hamilton, Guard, '80
Mogul, Lou - Winnipeg, Guard, '37; Tackle, '41
Mohr, Rick - Toronto, Defensive End, '83
Momsen, Tony - Calgary, Linebacker, '53
Moon, Warren - Edmonton, Quarterback, '83
Moore, Mack - B.C., Defensive Tackle, '83, '84
Morris, Ted - Toronto, Running Back, '33, '34, '36; Flying Wing, '35, '38
Morrison, Arnie - Ottawa, Quarterback, '37
Mosca, Angelo - Ottawa, Defensive Tackle, '60; Hamilton, Defensive Tackle, '63, '65, '66, '70
Motton, John - Hamilton, Middle Linebacker, '92, '93
Moynahan, Curly - Ottawa, Centre, '38, '45
Mullin, Andy - Toronto, Quarterback, '35
Munsey, Bill - B.C., Defensive Back, '64
Murphy, James - Winnipeg, Wide Receiver, '86, '87, '88, '89
Murphy, Mike - Ottawa, Running Back, '78
Musso, Johnny - B.C., Running Back, '73
Myers, Billy - Toronto, Quarterback, '45

- N -

Nagurski, Bronko - Hamilton, Offensive Tackle, '62, '64, '65
Nagy, Andy - Saskatchewan, Tackle, '46
Narcisse, Donald - Saskatchewan, Wide Receiver, '89, '90, '93
Nelms, Mike - Ottawa, Defensive Back, '79
Nelson, Roger - Edmonton, Offensive Tackle, '57, '58, '59, '60
Nesbitt, Gerry - Ottawa, Linebacker, '60, '61
Nettles, Ray - B.C., Linebacker, '72, '73, '74; Toronto, Linebacker, '77
Neumann, Pete - Hamilton, Defensive End, '53, '54, '55, '56, '57, '58, '59, '61, '64
Newman, Dave - Toronto, Slotback, '80
Newton, Lou - Montreal, Centre, '32, '33, '34
Nicholson, Darrell - Toronto, Linebacker, '83
Nickla, Ed - Montreal, Linebacker, '62; Defensive Tackle, '63
Nicklin, Jeff - Winnipeg, End, '37, '38; Flying Wing, '39, '40
Nielsen, Ken - Winnipeg, Flanker, '67, '68, '69
Nixon, Rhome - Ottawa, Wide Receiver, '74
Noel, Red - Saskatchewan, End, '47
Norman, Haywood Butch - Winnipeg, Offensive Tackle, '76, '78, '80
Norman, Tony - Winnipeg, Defensive End, '83, '84, '85
Noseworthy, Gordon - Montreal, Running Back, '40
Nykoluk, Danny - Toronto, Offensive Tackle, '67, '69

- O -

O'Billovich, Bob - Ottawa, Defensive Back, '65
O'Brien, Eddie - Edmonton, End, '38
Odums, Ray - Calgary, Defensive Back, '79, '80, '81, '82
Oliphant, Mike - Sacramento, Running Back, '93
Oliver, Bobby Jack - Montreal, Defensive Tackle, '61, '62
O'Neill, Stan - Ottawa, Running Back, '37
O'Quinn, Red - Montreal, End, '52; Offensive End, '53, '54, '55, '58
Orange, Doyle - Toronto, Running Back, '75
Ordway, Bill - Winnipeg, Running Back, '46
Organ, Gerry - Ottawa, Kicker, '82
Osbaldiston, Paul - Hamilton, Kicker, '89, '90

- P -

Paffrath, Bob - Ottawa, Quarterback, '48; Flying Wing, '49; Edmonton, Running Back, '50; Flying Wing, '51

All-Eastern/All-Western All-Star Team Members

Pajaczkowski, Tony - Calgary, Guard, '60, '62, '63, '64, '65; Defensive End, '61; Montreal, Guard, '66
Pal, Joe - Montreal, Running Back, '54, '55, '56
Palmer, Jim - Toronto, Guard, '33, '34, '35, '37
Pantages, Rod - Montreal, Flying Wing, '50
Parker, Charlie - Montreal, Guard, '68, '69
Parker, Anthony - B.C., Running Back, '88
Parker, Jackie - Edmonton, Running Back, '54, '57, '59; Quarterback, '55, '56, '58, '60, '61
Parker, James - Edmonton, Linebacker, '81, '82; Defensive End, '83; B.C., Defensive End, '84, '85,'86
Parker, Kerry - B.C., Defensive Back, '83
Passaglia, Lui - B.C., Kicker, '79, '80, '83, '84; Punter, '77, '83, '92
Paterson, Gord - Winnipeg, Tight End, '77
Patrick, Steve - Winnipeg, Middle Guard, '58, '59
Patterson, Gabe - Saskatchewan, Running Back, '47, '48
Patterson, Hal - Montreal, Defensive Back, '54, '55, '56, '57, '58; Offensive End, '56, '57, '60; - Hamilton, Offensive End, '62, '63, '64, '65
Paul, Leroy - Hamilton, Defensive Back, '81; Toronto, Defensive Back, '83
Payton, Doug - Montreal, Offensive Tackle, '80, '81, '82
Payton, Elfrid - Winnipeg, Linebacker, '93
Pearson, Paul - Toronto, Slotback, '84
Pentecost, John - Ottawa, Guard, '65
Perdrix, Roger - Ottawa, Guard, '67
Perina, Carl - Montreal, Quarterback, '33
Perry, Gordon - Montreal, Running Back, '32
Peterson, Greg - Calgary, Safety, '90
Petterson, Leif - Hamilton, Slotback, '79
Pfeifer, Al - Toronto, Offensive End, '55
Phaneuf, Al - Montreal, Defensive Back, '70
Phason, Vince - Winnipeg, Defensive Back, '82
Phillips, Kim - Winnipeg, Cornerback, '93
Phillips, Rudy - Ottawa, Guard, '82, '83; Edmonton, Offensive Guard, '86
Piaskoski, Jim - Ottawa, Defensive End, '77
Pierce, Ralph - Saskatchewan, Running Back, '37
Pierce, Sammy - Saskatchewan, Running Back, '49
Pigeon, George - Montreal, Guard, '34, '35, '36
Pinhey, Don - Ottawa, Defensive Back, '56
Piper, Cornell - Winnipeg, Guard, '60, '61
Pipes, Greg - Edmonton, Defensive Tackle, '70
Pitts, Allen - Calgary, Slotback, '91, '92
Pitts, Ernie - Winnipeg, Offensive End, '57, '60; Defensive Back, '59, '65, '68
Pleasant, Reggie - Toronto, Cornerback, '88, '89, '91
Pless, Willie - Toronto, Linebacker, '86, '88; B.C., Linebacker, '90; Edmonton, Linebacker, '91, '92, '93
Ploen, Ken - Winnipeg, Quarterback, '57, '65; Defensive Back, '59
Pointer, John - Toronto, Linebacker, '82
Poirier, Joe - Ottawa, Defensive Back, '60, '62, '63, '64, '66
Poley, Bob - Calgary, Centre, '86
Pope, Marvin - Calgary, Middle Linebacker, '93
Poplawski, Joe - Winnipeg, Slotback, '81, '84, '85, '86; Wide Receiver, '78
Porter, Lewis - Hamilton, Defensive Back, '73, '76
Pothier, Hector - Edmonton, Offensive Tackle, '81, '87, '88, '89
Potter, Dale - Edmonton, Linebacker, '80
Powell, Kevin - Ottawa, Offensive Tackle, '83, '85
Prather, Rollin - Edmonton, Offensive End, '52
Price, Phil - Montreal, Defensive Back, '74, '76
Priestner, John - Hamilton, Linebacker, '81
Profit, Mel - Toronto, Offensive End, '68; Tight End, '69, '70, '71
Proudfoot, Tony - Montreal, Defensive Back, '77, '79
Provost, Ted - Saskatchewan, Defensive Back, '73, '74
Ptacek, Bob - Saskatchewan, Linebacker, '61; Defensive Back, '64
Pullar, Bill - Calgary, Tackle, '47
Purdin, Ray - Saskatchewan, Running Back, '62

- Q -

Quandamatteo, Jim - Edmonton, Guard, '53

- R -

Racine, Moe - Ottawa, Offensive Tackle, '62, '65, '66
Raimey, Dave - Winnipeg, Running Back, '65, '66, '67, '68; Toronto, Running Back, '69
Raines, Mike - Ottawa, Defensive Tackle, '78, '79, '80, '81
Ramsey, Ray - Hamilton, Offensive End, '54
Raquet, Steve - Montreal, Defensive End, '84
Rashovich, Dan - Saskatchewan, Linebacker, '90
Rauhaus, Norm - Winnipeg, Defensive Back, '61
Reaves, Willard - Winnipeg, Running Back, '83, '84, '85, '87
Redell, Bill - Edmonton, Defensive Back, '66
Reed, George - Saskatchewan, Running Back, '65, '66, '67, '68, '69, '71, '72, '73, '74, '75
Reed, Ken - Saskatchewan, Defensive End, '69
Reese, Lloyd - Montreal, Guard, '48
Reid, Jim - Ottawa, Running Back, '86
Remegis, Eddie - Hamilton, Guard, '45, '47
Renfroe, Gilbert - Toronto, Quarterback, '88
Reynolds, Jim - Montreal, Linebacker, '63
Rhino, Randy - Montreal, Defensive Back, '77, '78; Ottawa, Defensive Back, '81
Richardson, Bob - Saskatchewan, Tight End, '76
Richardson, Lorne - Saskatchewan, Defensive Back, '73, '74, '75, '76
Richardson, Michael - Winnipeg, Running Back, '92, '93
Ridgway, Dave - Saskatchewan, Kicker, '82, '87, '88, '89, '90, '91, '93
Rigney, Frank - Winnipeg, Offensive Tackle, '59, '60, '61, '62, '64, '65, '66
Riley, Jason - Hamilton, Guard, '86, '88, '89, '92
Roberson, Vernon - Calgary, Defensive Back, '75
Roberts, Gene - Ottawa, Running Back, '52, '53
Roberts, Willie - Calgary, Offensive End, '55
Robinson, Frank - Hamilton, Linebacker, '87, '89
Robinson, Larry - Calgary, Defensive Back, '65, '71, '72
Robinson, Rick - B.C., Defensive Back, '69
Robinson, Ron - Montreal, Slotback, '83
Rodgers, Johnny - Montreal, Wide Receiver, '73, '74, '76; Running Back, '75
Rogers, Glenn Jr. - Edmonton, Defensive Halfback, '93
Romano, Rocco - Calgary, Offensive Guard, '92, '93
Roper, Gerald - B.C., Guard, '87, '88; Ottawa, Guard, '90, '91
Rorvig, Ed - Calgary, Running Back, '37
Roth, Tim - Saskatchewan, Offensive Tackle, '75; Defensive Tackle, '76
Rountree, Jim - Toronto, Defensive Back, '59, '60, '61, '62, '63, '64, '67
Rowe, Paul - Calgary, Running Back, '39, '40, '46, '47, '48
Rowland, Gordon - Winnipeg, Linebacker, '57, '58, '60, '61, '62
Ruby, Martin - Saskatchewan, Offensive Tackle, '51, '53, '54, '56; Defensive Tackle, '53, '54, '56
Ruoff, Bernie - Hamilton, Kicker, '80, '81, '83, '84, '85; Punter, '82, '83, '84
Russell, Jack - Saskatchewan, Offensive End, '51
Ryan, Dave - Montreal, Centre, '37
Ryan, Pat - Montreal, Running Back, '35
Ryan, Rick - Montreal, Safety, '86

- S -

Samples, Mike - Hamilton, Defensive End, '76; Saskatchewan, Defensive Tackle, '81, '82
Sampson, Darryl - Winnipeg, Halfback, '93
Sandberg, Bob - Winnipeg, Running Back, '47
Sanderson, Dale - Hamilton, Centre, '89
Sandusky, Jim - B.C., Wide Receiver, '87; Edmonton, Wide Receiver, '91, '92
Sapunjis, Dave - Calgary, Slotback, '93
Savoie, Roger - Winnipeg, Defensive Tackle, '62
Sazio, Ralph - Hamilton, Tackle, '50
Schrieder, Gary - Ottawa, Linebacker, '60
Schriewer, Menan - Toronto, Offensive End, '57
Schuette, Tom - Ottawa, Guard, '75
Schultz, Chris - Toronto, Offensive Tackle, '87, '88, '91
Scott, Bo - Ottawa, Running Back, '65, '66, '67, '68
Scott, Doug - Montreal, Defensive Tackle, '82, '84, '85
Scott, James - Montreal, Wide Receiver, '81
Scott, Tom - Winnipeg, Slotback, '77; Edmonton, Slotback, '78, '80, '82, '83
Scott, Vince - Hamilton, Guard, '49, '50, '52; Defensive Guard, '53, '54, '55, '56, '57, '58; Middle Guard, '59
Scott, Wilbert - Montreal, Linebacker, '66
Scudero, Joe - Toronto, Running Back, '53
Semenko, Mel - Ottawa, Defensive End, '62
Sharkey, Ed - B.C., Guard, '57; Linebacker, '57
Shatto, Dick - Toronto, Running Back, '56, '57, '58, '59, '61, '62, '63, '64
Shaw, Bob - Calgary, Offensive End, '52
Shaw, David - Hamilton, Defensive Back, '76, '80, '81, '82; Winnipeg, Defensive Back, '83, '84,'85
Shaw, Gerry - Calgary, Wide Receiver, '72
Shaw, Rick - Winnipeg, Split End, '70
Shaw, Wayne - Saskatchewan, Linebacker, '63, '64, '66, '67, '69, '71
Sheley, Wayne - Winnipeg, Quarterback, '39
Shepard, Charlie - Winnipeg, Running Back, '59
Shepherd, Johnny - Hamilton, Running Back, '83
Shipp, Billy - Toronto, Offensive Tackle, '55; Defensive Tackle, '55, '64; Montreal, Offensive Tackle, '59
Shirk, Marshall - Ottawa, Defensive Tackle, '68, '69, '70
Shore, Nate - Winnipeg, End, '46
Simpson, Bob - Ottawa, End, '51; Flying Wing, '52, '53; Offensive End, '56, '59; Running Back, '57; Defensive Back, '57, '58
Simpson, Jackie - Montreal, Defensive Guard, '58; Guard, '58, '60
Simpson, Jim - Hamilton, End, '37
Sims, E.A. - Edmonton, Defensive End, '65, '66
Sims, Rudy - Ottawa, Defensive Tackle, '71, '72, '73, '74
Skipper, Harry - Montreal, Defensive Back, '83, '84; Saskatchewan, Cornerback, '87
Sluman, Ken - Calgary, End, '47
Smear, Steve - Montreal, Defensive End, '70; Linebacker, '71
Smith, Bill - Edmonton, Defensive Back, '60
Smith, Bob - Winnipeg, Tackle, '47
Smith, Darrell - Toronto, Slotback, '87, '88, '89, '90, '91
Smith, Don - Ottawa, Centre, '76, '77, '78
Smith, Donald - Winnipeg, Cornerback, '93
Smith, Doug - Montreal, Centre, '79
Smith, Robert - Ottawa, Offensive Tackle, '90, '92; B.C., Offensive Guard, '93
Smith, Waddell - Edmonton, Wide Receiver, '79
Smith, Wayne - Ottawa, Defensive End, '72, '74
Snipes, Angelo - Ottawa, Linebacker, '92, '93
Sorrell, Henry - Hamilton, Linebacker, '69
Sowalski, Bill - Ottawa, Linebacker, '59
Sowieta, Rick - Ottawa, Linebacker, '80, '83, '85
Spaith, Keith - Calgary, Quarterback, '48, '49
Specht, Doug - Ottawa, Centre, '66
Speedie, Mac - Saskatchewan, Offensive End, '53, '54
Sprague, Dave - Hamilton, Tackle, '32; Ottawa, Tackle, '36, '37, '38, '39, '40
Springstein, Toar - Saskatchewan, Tackle, '40
Stanton, Bill - Ottawa, End, '50
Staton, Jim - Montreal, Tackle, '52; Defensive Tackle, '54
Stapler, Steve - Hamilton, Wide Receiver, '85, '87
Staughton, Len - Toronto, Guard, '39, '40
Steck, Benny - Montreal, Guard, '46
Stevenson, Art - Winnipeg, Running Back, '37, '40; Quarterback, '38, '41
Stevenson, Bill - Edmonton, Guard, '78, '79; Offensive Tackle, '81
Stevenson, Vic - Saskatchewan, Offensive Tackle, '91, '92
Stewart, Ron - Ottawa, Running Back, '60, '61, '64
Stillwagon, Jim - Toronto, Defensive Tackle, '71, '72, '74
Stone, Avatus - Ottawa, Running Back, '53; Defensive Back, '55
Stoneburgh, Norm - Toronto, Centre, '58, '60, '61, '65
Storey, Red - Toronto, Running Back, '38
Streeter, Mark - Hamilton, Defensive Back, '86

All-Eastern/All-Western All-Star Team Members

Strickland, Mike - B.C., Running Back, '76; Saskatchewan, Running Back, '78
Strode, Woody - Calgary, End, '48, '49
Stukus, Annis - Toronto, Quarterback, '38
Stukus, Bill - Toronto, Quarterback, '39
Stumon, Greg - B.C., Defensive End, '87; Linebacker, '88; Ottawa, Defensive End, '90; Linebacker, '92
Sturtridge, Gordon - Saskatchewan, Defensive End, '55, '56
Suderman, Dick - Calgary, Defensive End, '67, '68, '71
Sugarman, Ken - B.C., Offensive Tackle, '68, '71; Guard, '69, '70
Suitor, Glen - Saskatchewan, Safety, '89, '91, '92, '93
Sullivan, Johnny Mike - Calgary, Running Back, '38
Suminski, Dave - Hamilton, Guard, '57, '59
Sunter, Ian - Toronto, Punter, '79
Sutherin, Don - Hamilton, Defensive Back, '61, '62, '64, '65; Ottawa, Defensive Back, '68, '69
Sward, Sammy - Ottawa, Running Back, '40
Sweet, Don - Montreal, Kicker, '77, '78, '79
Swift, Bob - Winnipeg, Centre, '71, '72, '73, '74
Sykes, James - Calgary, Running Back, '78, '80, '82
Symons, Bill - Toronto, Running Back, '68, '70

- T -

Tagge, Jerry - B.C., Quarterback, '77
Taylor, Bobby - Toronto, Flanker, '69
Taylor, Jack - Toronto, Running Back, '33
Taylor, Reggie - Edmonton, Running Back, '89, '90
Theismann, Joe - Toronto, Quarterback, '71, '73
Thelen, Dave - Ottawa, Running Back, '59, '60, '63, '64; Toronto, Running Back, '65, '66
Thomas, Eddie - Edmonton, Cornerback, '91
Thomas, Jim - Edmonton, Running Back, '65, '66, '67
Thompson, Bennie - Winnipeg, Safety, '88
Thompson, Bobby - Winnipeg, Offensive Tackle, '82
Thompson, Larry - Winnipeg, Wide Receiver, '92
Thornton, Bernie - Toronto, End, '38, '39, '40
Thornton, Dick - Winnipeg, Defensive Back, '62, '63, '65; Toronto, Defensive Back, '69, '71
Thorpe, Jim - Toronto, Flanker, '70; Winnipeg, Split End, '71; Wide Receiver, '72
Thorson, Sherwyn - Winnipeg, Guard, '62
Thurman, Junior - Calgary, Cornerback, '91, '92
Timmis, Brian - Hamilton, Tackle, '32, '34
Tinsley, Buddy - Winnipeg, Offensive Tackle, '50, '51, '52, '55, '56; Defensive Tackle, '57, '58
Tittley, Larry - Ottawa, Centre, '83
Tolbert, Emanuel - Toronto, Slotback, '83; Calgary, Slotback, '86, '87, '88
Tomlin, Jim - Toronto, Defensive Back, '70
Tomlinson, Dave - Calgary, Guard, '48
Tommy, Andy - Ottawa, Running Back, '36; Flying Wing, '40
Toogood, Teddy - Toronto, Defensive Back, '53
Toohy, Ralph - Montreal, End, '48, '49; Hamilton, Linebacker, '53
Tosh, Wayne - Ottawa, Defensive Back, '75
Towns, Tom - Edmonton, Linebacker, '78, '79, '80
Tracy, Tom - Ottawa, Running Back, '55
Trautman, Randy - Calgary, Defensive Tackle, '83, '84
Trawick, Herb - Montreal, Tackle, '46, '47, '48, '49, '50; Guard, '54, '55
Treftlin, Jeff - Montreal, Special Teams, '86
Tripucka, Frank - Saskatchewan, Quarterback, '54
Truant, Ray - Hamilton, Defensive Back, '56
Trudel, Remi - Ottawa, Safety, '93
Tucker, Whit - Ottawa, Flanker, '66, '67, '68
Tully, Ted - Edmonton, Linebacker, '55, '56, '57, '58
Turcotte, Jeff - Ottawa, Offensive Tackle, '75, '77
Turner, Charlie - Edmonton, Offensive Tackle, '72, '73, '74, '75, '77
Turner, Doug - Hamilton, Centre, '40
Turner, Howie - Ottawa, Running Back, '48, '49; Defensive Back, '53
Turner, Wylie - Winnipeg, Defensive Back, '85
Turville, Frank - Toronto, Running Back, '32; Hamilton, Running Back, '34
Tuttle, Perry - Winnipeg, Slotback, '87

- U -

Ulmer, Ed - Winnipeg, Defensive Back, '66
Upton, Eric - Edmonton, Guard, '79
Urness, Ted - Saskatchewan, Centre, '65, '66, '67, '68, '69, '70
Uteck, Larry - Toronto, Defensive Back, '75, '76

- V -

Vankoughnett, Dave - Winnipeg, Centre, '93
Van Ness, Bruce - Montreal, Running Back, '71
Van Pelt, Jim - Winnipeg, Quarterback, '59
Vargo, Ken - Ottawa, Linebacker, '56
Vaughan, Kaye - Ottawa, Offensive Guard, '53, '59, '60, '61; Offensive Tackle, '56, '57; Defensive Tackle, '56, '57, '59; Middle Guard, '62
Vercheval, Pierre - Edmonton, Offensive Guard, '92
Vereb, Ed - B.C., Running Back, '56
Vessels, Billy - Edmonton, Running Back, '53
Volpe, Jon - B.C., Running Back, '91, '92

- W -

Wadsworth, Bunny - Ottawa, Tackle, '38, '39, '40
Wadsworth, Mike - Toronto, Defensive Tackle, '68
Waggoner, Hal - Hamilton, Running Back, '51, '52
Wagner, Virgil - Montreal, Running Back, '46, '47, '48, '49
Wagoner, John - Ottawa, Tackle, '48, '49
Wahlmeier, Galen - Saskatchewan, Centre, '57
Walby, Chris - Winnipeg, Offensive Tackle, '84, '85, '86, '87, '89, '90, '91, '92, '93
Walker, Alvin Skip - Montreal, Running Back, '80; Ottawa, Running Back, '82, '83
Walker, Bob - Saskatchewan, Tackle, '37, '38
Walker, Merv - Calgary, Defensive Back, '81
Walker, Mike - Hamilton, Defensive Tackle, '86, '87, '88, '89
Wallace, Stan - Toronto, Defensive Back, '60
Walls, Tyrone - Edmonton, Tight End, '72, '74, '75
Walters, Harry - Winnipeg, Linebacker, '75, '76
Walters, Joey - Saskatchewan, Slotback/Tight End, '81, '82
Walton, Chuck - Montreal, Guard, '63; Hamilton, Guard, '65, '66
Wardien, Del - Saskatchewan, Running Back, '47, '49
Warlick, Ernie - Calgary, Offensive End, '58, '59, '60
Warnock, Kent - Calgary, Defensive Tackle, '90
Warren, Brian - Toronto, Defensive End, '91
Warren, Gar - Winnipeg, Linebacker, '59
Washington, Al - Ottawa, Linebacker, '84
Washington, Jim - Winnipeg, Running Back, '76, '77
Washington, Vic - Ottawa, Running Back, '68, '69
Waszczuk, Henry - Hamilton, Centre, '80, '81, '82, '84
Watkins, Larry - Edmonton, Guard, '72; Offensive Tackle, '74
Watkins, Ted - Ottawa, Offensive End, '63, '64, '65, '66
Watrin, Ray - Montreal, Guard, '79
Watton, Ron - Hamilton, Centre, '62
Waugh, Howard - Calgary, Running Back, '54
Wayte, Billy - Hamilton, Defensive Back, '65
Webster, Alex - Montreal, Running Back, '54
Wedley, Jack - Toronto, End, '45
Weir, Glen - Montreal, Defensive Tackle, '75, '76, '77, '78, '79, '82
Welch, Huck - Montreal, Running Back, '33, '34; Hamilton, Running Back, '35, '36, '37
Wells, George - Hamilton, Defensive End, '72; Saskatchewan, Defensive End, '74, '75, '76
Wells, Joel - Montreal, Running Back, '58
Welton, John - Toronto, Defensive End, '57
West, Art - Toronto, Running Back, '38
West, Dale - Saskatchewan, Defensive Back, '63, '64, '65
West, James - Calgary, Linebacker, '83; Winnipeg, Linebacker, '87, '88, '89
Wester, Curtis - B.C., Guard, '74
Westwood, Troy - Winnipeg, Kicker, '92, '93
Whisler, Bill - Winnipeg, Defensive End, '64, '67, '68, '69
White, Ernie - Ottawa, Running Back, '62
Widger, Mike - Montreal, Linebacker, '70, '72, '73, '74, '75; Ottawa, Linebacker, '77
Wigle, Fred - Montreal, Centre. '36
Wilburn, Barry - Saskatchewan, Cornerback, '93
Wilcox, Gerald - Winnipeg, Slotback, '93
Wile, Russ - Edmonton, Guard, '39
Wilkinson, Tom - Edmonton, Quarterback, '74, '78, '79
Williams, Brett - Montreal, Defensive Tackle, '86; Edmonton, Defensive Tackle, '88, '89, '90, '91
Williams, Charles - Winnipeg, Defensive Back, '80, '81
Williams, David - B.C., Wide Receiver, '88, '89; Toronto, Wide Receiver, '91; Winnipeg, Wide Receiver, '93
Williams, Henry - Edmonton, Special Teams, '87, '88, '91, '92, '93
Williams, John - Hamilton, Defensive Back, '71, '72
Williams, Maurice - Saskatchewan, Guard, '40, '41
Williams, Paul - Winnipeg, Defensive Back, '74; Saskatchewan, Defensive Back, '76, '77
Williams, Stan - Saskatchewan, Defensive Back, '54; Offensive End, '55
Willis, George - Toronto, Centre, '39
Willis, Larry - Calgary, Wide Receiver, '88
Wills, Chuck - Winnipeg, Defensive Back, '77
Willsey, Ray - Edmonton, Defensive Back, '53
Wilson, A. Michael - Toronto, Offensive Tackle, '77
Wilson, Al - B.C., Centre, '75, '76, '77, '78, '79, '80, '81
Wilson, Darrell - Toronto, Defensive Back, '83
Wilson, Don - Edmonton, Safety, '88; Defensive Halfback, '89; Toronto, Defensive Halfback, '90, '91, '92; Edmonton, Defensive Halfback, '93
Wilson, Dwaine - Montreal, Running Back, '84
Wilson, Gene - Toronto, Running Back, '54
Wilson, Michael D. - Edmonton, Offensive Tackle, '79, '80
Wilson, Mel - Winnipeg, Centre, '41, '46, '47; Calgary, '49
Wilson, Seymour - Hamilton, End, '33, '34, '35
Wilson, Troy - Ottawa, Halfback, '90
Winfield, Earl - Hamilton, Wide Receiver, Special Teams, '88, Wide Receiver, '90
Wiseman, Todd - Hamilton, Safety, '92
Wood, Duane - Hamilton, Defensive Back, '59
Wood, Gary - Ottawa, Quarterback, '70
Woods, Harold - Hamilton, Defensive Back, '80, '81
Woodward, Rod - Ottawa, Defensive Back, '72, '74, '75
Worden, Jim - Saskatchewan, Offensive End, '66
Woznesensky, Lyall - Saskatchewan, Defensive End, '81
Wozniak, John - Saskatchewan, Linebacker, '53, '54, '56
Wright, Felix - Hamilton, Defensive Back, '84
Wright, Mike - Winnipeg, Defensive Tackle, '61
Wruck, Larry - Edmonton, Linebacker, '89
Wusyk, Bill - Calgary, Flying Wing, '46
Wydareny, John - Edmonton, Defensive Back, '67, '69, '70
Wylie, Harvey - Calgary, Defensive Back, '59, '60, '61, '62, '63
Wysocki, Pete - Saskatchewan, Linebacker, '74

- Y -

Yochum, Dan - Montreal, Offensive Tackle, '73, '74, '75, '76
Young, Jim - B.C., Running Back, '69; Wide Receiver, '72
Young, Mark - Montreal, Defensive Back, '82

- Z -

Zachery, James - Edmonton, Defensive Tackle, '86
Zambiasi, Ben - Hamilton, Linebacker, '78, '79, '80, '81, '82, '84, '85, '86
Zapiec, Chuck - Montreal, Linebacker, '74, '76, '77, '78
Zatylny, Wally - Hamilton, Special Teams, '89
Zock, Bill - Toronto, Guard, '46, '47

ALL-STAR GAME REVIEW

There have been 14 All-Star Games played in the professional era of Canadian football, the first of which occurred in 1955 and the last in 1988.

Six of the All-Star Games pitted the Grey Cup champion against the All-Stars, while the rest were played under the East-West format.

Based on the weather problems which plagued the first four All-Star Games, the 1983 Game provided quite a contrast since it was played under the dome at B.C. Place.

Following the initial schedule which saw the first four All-Star Games take place a week after the Grey Cup Game, the All-Star Games were revived and held in late spring or early summer from 1970 to 1978 (excluding 1975 when no Game took place).

The 1983 All-Star Game in Vancouver was played one week after the Grey Cup Game which also took place at B.C. Place.

The 1988 All-Star Game opened the season, as it was played in June at Commonwealth Stadium in Edmonton.

The scoreboard for East-West All-Star Games reads West 5, East 2 with one game tied. Under the Grey Cup champion-All-Star format, the All-Stars have four victories while Calgary in 1972 and Ottawa in 1974 came through with wins.

The following is the recap of All-Star Games:

1955 (Attendance 15,088)

Played at Varsity Stadium, Toronto, Dec. 3, 1955
East 6 – West 6
Scoring - East - Hal Patterson, TD; Hal Patterson, convert.
West - Gord Sturtridge, TD; Jim Heydenfeldt, single.

1956 (Attendance 13,546)

Played at Empire Stadium, Vancouver, Dec. 8, 1956
West 35 – East 0
Scoring - West - Bud Grant, 2 TDs; Jack Parker, TD; Normie Kwong, TD; By Bailey, TD; Reg Whitehouse, 5 converts.
East - No scoring.

1957 (Attendance approx. 5,000)

Played at McGill Stadium, Montreal, Dec. 7, 1957
East 20 – West 2
Scoring - East - Gerry McDougall, 2 TDs; Cookie Gilchrist, TD; Bill Bewley, 1 convert; Cam Fraser, 1 single.
West - Vic Chapman, 2 singles.

1958 (Attendance approx. 7,000)

Played at Civic Stadium, Hamilton, Dec. 6, 1958
West 9 – East 3
Scoring - West - Kenny Ploen, TD; Vic Chapman, 3 singles.
East - Safety touch; Cam Fraser, 1 single.

1970 (Attendance 23,094)

Played at Lansdowne Park, Ottawa, July 2, 1970
All-Stars 35 – Ottawa 14
Scoring - All-Stars - Bill Symons, TD; Dennis Duncan, TD; Jim Young, TD; George Reed, TD; Ted Gerela, 2 field goals, 3 converts; Safety touch.
Ottawa - Whit Tucker, TD; Bill Van Burkleo, TD; Don Sutherin, 2 converts.
Most Valuable Player – Ron Lancaster, Sask.

1971 (Attendance approx. 9,000)

Played at Autostade, Montreal, June 29, 1971
All-Stars 30 – Montreal 13
Scoring - All-Stars - Tommy Joe Coffey, TD; Gary Wood, TD; Hugh McKinnis, TD; Jack Abendschan, 2 field goals, 3 converts, 3 singles.
Montreal - Sonny Wade, TD; George Springate, 2 field goals, 1 convert.
Most Valuable Player - Bill Symons, Tor.

1972 (Attendance 23,616)

Played at McMahon Stadium, Calgary, June 28, 1972
Calgary 23 – All-Stars 22
Scoring - Calgary - John Helton, TD; Herman Harrison, TD; Jesse Mims, TD; Larry Robinson, field goal, 2 converts.
All-Stars - Jim Young, TD; Peter Dalla Riva, TD; Terry Evanshen, TD; Ken Phillips, field goal; Joe Theismann, single.

1973 (Attendance 24,765)

Played at Ivor Wynne Stadium, Hamilton, June 27, 1973
All-Stars 22 – Hamilton 11
Scoring - All-Stars - Jim Young, TD; Peter Dalla Riva, TD; Gerry Organ, field goal, 2 converts, single; 2 Safety touches.
Hamilton - Tony Gabriel, TD; Ian Sunter, field goal, convert, single.
Most Valuable Player – Peter Dalla Riva, Mtl.

1974 (Attendance 15,102)

Played at Lansdowne Park, Ottawa, June 26, 1974
Ottawa 25 – All-Stars 22
Scoring - Ottawa - Rhome Nixon, 2 TDs; Gerry Organ, 3 field goals, 2 converts; Dick Adams, 2 singles.
All-Stars - Jim Young, TD; Terry Evanshen, TD; Dave Cutler, 2 field goals, 2 converts, 1 single; Zenon Andrusyshyn, 1 single.
Most Valuable Player – Rhome Nixon, Ott.

1976 (Attendance 21,762)

Played at Clarke Stadium, Edmonton, May 29, 1976
West 27 – East 16
Scoring - West - Tom Campana, 2 TDs; Larry Highbaugh, TD; Dave Cutler, 3 FGs.
East - Art Green, TD; Don Sweet, 3 FGs and 1 convert.

1977 (Attendance 7,500)

Played at Exhibition Stadium, Toronto, June 4, 1977
East 20 – West 19
Scoring - East - Tony Gabriel, TD; Terry Evanshen, TD; Zenon Andrusyshyn, 2 FGs and 2 converts.
West - Ron Lancaster, TD; Tom Forzani, TD; Bernie Ruoff, 2 FGs and 1 convert.
Most Valuable Player – Offence - Jimmie Jones, Ham.
Defence - Chuck Zapiec, Mtl.

1978 (Attendance approx. 21,000)

Played at McMahon Stadium, Calgary, June 3, 1978
West 24 – East 12
Scoring - West - Ray Odums, 2 TDs; Dave Cutler, 2 FGs, 4 singles, 2 converts.
East - Tony Gabriel, TD; Lawrie Skolrood, 2 pt. convert; Don Sweet, FG, single.
Most Valuable Player – Offence - Brock Aynsley, Mtl.; Tom Scott, Edm.
Defence - Ray Odums, Cal.; Granny Liggins, Tor.

1983 (Attendance approx. 14,000)

Played at B.C. Place, Vancouver, December 3, 1983
West 25 – East 15
Scoring - West - Ray Crouse, TD; Dave Kirzinger, TD; Trevor Kennerd, 2 converts, 1 FG and 1 single; Lui Passaglia, 1 FG. Team Safety.
East - Terry Greer, 1 TD and 1 (2 pt.) convert; Ron Johnson, TD; Bernie Ruoff, 1 convert.
Most Valuable Player – Offence - Roy Dewalt, B.C.
Defence - Dave Fennell, Edm.

1988 (Attendance 27,573)

Played at Commonwealth Stadium, Edmonton, June 23, 1988
All-Stars 15 – Edmonton 4
Scoring - Edmonton - Jerry Kauric, 1 FG, 1 single.
All-Stars - Will Lewis, TD; Dave Ridgway, 2 FGs, 1 convert, 1 single; 1 Team Safety.
Most Valuable Player – Larry Willis, Cal.

REGULAR SEASON
TEAM RECORDS

CLUB-BY-CLUB STREAKS

Streaks listed from the time they began to the time they ended.

LONGEST WINNING STREAKS

22 - Calgary (Aug. 25, 1948 to Oct. 22, 1949)
14 - Edmonton (Oct. 16, 1954 to Oct. 1, 1955)
11 - Winnipeg (Oct. 26, 1959 to Sept. 26, 1960)
- Saskatchewan (Sept. 20, 1969 to Aug. 17, 1970)
- Calgary (Nov. 8, 1992 to Sept. 10, 1993)
10 - Hamilton (Aug. 24, 1972 to Aug. 1, 1973)
9 - Edmonton, 2 times, (Sept. 13, 1981 to July 25, 1982 & Sept. 24, 1989 to July 18, 1990)
- Calgary (Oct. 21, 1990 to Aug. 22, 1991)
8 - Ottawa (Oct. 30, 1948 to Oct. 8, 1949)
- Montreal (Nov. 6, 1976 to Aug. 30, 1977)
- B.C., 2 times, (Oct. 9, 1978 to Aug. 7, 1979 & Oct. 13, 1984 to Aug. 17, 1985)

LONGEST HOME WINNING STREAKS

20 - Montreal (Nov. 8, 1953 to Nov. 3, 1956)
17 - Edmonton (Oct. 4, 1954 to Oct. 1, 1956)
16 - Winnipeg (Oct. 23, 1983 to Oct. 18, 1985)
- Edmonton (Nov. 6, 1988 to Sept. 21, 1990)
14 - Hamilton (Oct. 12, 1957 to Oct. 3, 1959)
- Calgary (Sept. 20, 1992 to Nov. 7, 1993)
13 - Ottawa (Aug. 15, 1963 to Oct. 17, 1964)
- Saskatchewan (Oct. 29, 1967 to Sept. 14, 1969)
- Toronto (Oct. 20, 1990 to July 27, 1992)
12 - B.C. (Nov. 4, 1962 to Sept. 8, 1964)
11 - Calgary (Sept. 29, 1964 to Oct. 27, 1965)

LONGEST ROAD WINNING STREAKS

20 - Winnipeg (Aug. 11, 1960 to Sept. 24, 1962)
13 - Calgary (Sept. 3, 1948 to Aug. 26, 1950)
9 - Saskatchewan (Sept. 10, 1969 to Sept. 12, 1970)
8 - Ottawa (Nov. 6, 1948 to Sept. 23, 1950)
- B.C. (Sept. 28, 1984 to Oct. 6, 1985)
7 - Edmonton, 2 times, (Oct. 18, 1954 to Oct. 1, 1955 and Sept. 19, 1982 to Sept. 5, 1983)
- Calgary (Sept. 30, 1990 to Aug. 27, 1991)
6 - Toronto (Aug. 19, 1983 to July 8, 1984)
5 - Montreal, 3 times, (Sept. 10, 1949 to Sept. 2, 1950; July 23, 1975 to Sept. 23, 1975 and July 13, 1977 to Sept. 18, 1977)
- Hamilton, 2 times, (Aug. 24, 1972 to Aug. 7, 1973 and Aug. 16, 1981 to July 10, 1982)
- B.C. (Sept. 8, 1991 to Oct. 27, 1991)
- Calgary (July 17, 1993 to Sept. 10, 1993)

LONGEST UNBEATEN STREAKS

22 - Calgary (22-0-0, Aug. 25, 1948 to Oct. 22, 1949)
15 - Edmonton (14-0-1, July 26, 1981 to July 25, 1982)
14 - Edmonton (14-0-0, Oct. 16, 1954 to Oct. 1, 1955)
11 - Winnipeg (11-0-0, Oct. 26, 1959 to Sept. 26, 1960)
- B.C. (8-0-3, Nov. 3, 1963 to Oct. 5, 1964)
- Hamilton (10-0-1, Sept. 20, 1964 to Aug. 28, 1965)
- Saskatchewan (11-0-0, Sept. 20, 1969 to Aug. 17, 1970)
- Calgary (11-0-0, Nov. 8, 1992 to Sept. 10, 1993)
10 - Ottawa, 2 times, (9-0-1, Sept. 24, 1967 to Aug. 22, 1968; 9-0-1, Sept. 28, 1968 to Sept. 1, 1969)
- Hamilton (10-0-0, Aug. 24, 1972 to Aug. 1, 1973)
9 - Edmonton (9-0-0, Sept. 24, 1989 to July 18, 1990)
- Calgary (9-0-0, Oct. 21, 1990 to Aug. 22, 1991)

LONGEST HOME UNBEATEN STREAKS

20 - Montreal (20-0-0, Nov. 8, 1953 to Nov. 3, 1956)
18 - B.C. (16-0-2, Nov. 4, 1962 to Aug. 16, 1965)
17 - Edmonton (17-0-0, Oct. 4, 1954 to Oct. 1, 1956)
16 - Winnipeg (16-0-0, Oct. 23, 1983 to Oct. 18, 1985)
- Edmonton (16-0-0, Nov. 6, 1988 to Sept. 21, 1990)
14 - Hamilton (14-0-0, Oct. 12, 1957 to Oct. 9, 1959)
- Ottawa (13-0-1, Oct. 20, 1962 to Oct. 17, 1964)
- Calgary (14-0-0, Sept. 20, 1992 to Nov. 7, 1993)
13 - Saskatchewan (13-0-0, Oct. 29, 1967 to Sept. 14, 1969)
- Toronto (13-0-0, Oct. 20, 1990 to July 27, 1992)
11 - Calgary (11-0-0, Sept. 29, 1964 to Oct. 27, 1965)

LONGEST ROAD UNBEATEN STREAKS

20 - Winnipeg (20-0-0, Aug. 11, 1960 to Sept. 24, 1962)
13 - Calgary (13-0-0, Sept. 3, 1948 to Aug. 26, 1950)
9 - Saskatchewan (9-0-0, Sept. 10, 1969 to Sept. 12, 1970)
- Edmonton (8-0-1, Oct. 16, 1977 to Nov. 4, 1978)
8 - Ottawa (8-0-0, Nov. 6, 1948 to Sept. 23, 1950)
- B.C. (8-0-0, Sept. 28, 1984 to Oct. 6, 1985)
7 - Edmonton, 2 times, (7-0-0, Oct. 18, 1954 to Oct.1, 1955 and 7-0-0, Sept. 19, 1982 to Sept. 5, 1983)
- Hamilton (6-0-1, Aug. 27, 1964 to Aug. 28, 1965)
- Calgary (7-0-0, Sept. 30, 1990 to Aug. 27, 1991)
6 - Toronto (6-0-0, Aug. 19, 1983 to July 8, 1984)

LONGEST WINLESS STREAKS

20 - Hamilton (0-19-1, Sept. 28, 1948 to Sept. 2, 1950)
16 - Montreal (0-12-4, Sept. 15, 1968 to Sept. 21, 1969)
13 - B.C. (0-13-0, Oct. 19, 1957 to Oct. 6, 1958)
- Saskatchewan (0-12-1, Oct. 10, 1959 to Sept. 26, 1960)
- Edmonton (0-13-0, Sept. 21, 1963 to Sept. 4, 1964)
- Winnipeg (0-13-0, Aug. 18, 1964 to July 30, 1965)
- Ottawa (0-13-0, July 19, 1987 to Oct. 30, 1987)
12 - Saskatchewan (0-12-0, July 11, 1979 to Oct. 14, 1979)
- Toronto (0-12-0, Nov. 2, 1980 to Sept. 27, 1981)
11 - Calgary (0-10-1, July 20, 1976 to Oct. 9, 1976)
- Hamilton (0-11-0, Oct. 21, 1990 to Sept. 2, 1991)

LONGEST HOME WINLESS STREAKS

14 - Ottawa (0-14-0, July 11, 1987 to Oct. 22, 1988)
12 - Saskatchewan (0-11-1, Aug. 14, 1959 to Sept. 26, 1960)
10 - Hamilton (0-9-1, Oct. 2, 1948 to Sept. 4, 1950)
- Montreal (0-8-2, Sept. 15, 1968 to Oct. 26, 1969)
9 - Saskatchewan (0-9-0, Aug. 25, 1952 to Sept. 7, 1953)
8 - Winnipeg (0-8-0, Sept. 2, 1970 to Sept. 1, 1971)
7 - Toronto, 2 times (0-7-0, Sept. 22, 1956 to Oct. 5,1957 and 0-7-0, Oct. 17, 1971 to Oct. 8, 1972)
- B.C., 2 times, (0-7-0, Oct. 19, 1957 to Oct. 6, 1958 and 0-6-1, Nov. 4, 1967 to Oct. 19, 1968)
- Ottawa, 2 times, (0-6-1, July 10, 1986 to Nov. 1, 1986 and 0-7-0, July 19, 1987 to Nov. 7, 1987)
6 - Calgary, 2 times, (0-5-1, Sept. 14, 1953 to Aug. 28, 1954 and 0-6-0, Sept. 29, 1984 to Sept. 14, 1985)
- Edmonton (0-6-0, Sept. 8, 1962 to Aug. 16, 1963)

LONGEST ROAD WINLESS STREAKS

26 - Hamilton (0-24-2, Oct. 6, 1945 to Sept. 2, 1950)
22 - Montreal (0-22-0, Oct. 5, 1980 to Sept. 10, 1983)
18 - Toronto (July 9, 1992 to Nov. 7, 1993)
12 - Calgary (0-12-0, Sept. 10, 1955 to Oct. 20, 1956)
- B.C. (0-11-1, Sept. 19, 1960 to Aug. 20, 1962)
- Toronto, 2 times, (0-12-0, Oct. 21, 1962 to Sept. 27, 1964 and 0-12-0, Sept. 27, 1980 to July 30, 1982)
11 - Winnipeg, 2 times, (0-11-0, Sept. 13, 1948 to Sept. 9, 1950 and 0-10-1, Aug. 14, 1969 to Oct. 3, 1970)
- Ottawa (0-11-0, Oct. 3, 1986 to Oct. 30, 1987)
10 - Edmonton (0-10-0, Aug. 12, 1963 to Sept. 11, 1964)
- Saskatchewan (0-10-0, July 17, 1979 to July 30, 1980)
- Hamilton (0-10-0, Oct. 28, 1990 to Nov. 2, 1991)

LONGEST LOSING STREAKS

16 - Hamilton (Oct. 17, 1948 to Sept. 2, 1950)
13 - B.C. (Oct. 19, 1957 to Oct. 6, 1958)
- Edmonton (Sept. 21, 1963 to Sept. 4, 1964)
- Winnipeg (Aug. 18, 1964 to July 30, 1965)
- Ottawa (July 19, 1987 to Oct. 30, 1987)
12 - Saskatchewan (July 11, 1979 to Oct. 14, 1979)
- Toronto (Nov. 2, 1980 to Sept. 27, 1981)
11 - Montreal (Sept. 16, 1967 to Aug. 22, 1968)
9 - Calgary (Aug. 3, 1976 to Oct. 9, 1976)

LONGEST HOME LOSING STREAK

14 - Ottawa (July 19, 1987 to Oct. 22, 1988)
9 - Saskatchewan (Aug. 25, 1952 to Sept. 7, 1953)
8 - Hamilton (Oct. 23, 1948 to Oct. 22, 1949)
- Winnipeg (Sept. 2, 1970 to Aug. 19, 1971)
7 - Toronto, 2 times, (Sept. 22, 1956 to Sept. 21, 1957 and Oct. 17, 1971 to Sept. 30, 1972)
- B.C. (Oct. 19, 1957 to Sept. 29, 1958)
6 - Edmonton (Sept. 8, 1962 to Aug. 5, 1963)
- Calgary (Sept. 29, 1984 to Sept. 14, 1985)
5 - Montreal, 2 times, (Sept. 16, 1967 to July 31, 1968 and Oct. 10, 1971 to Sept. 4, 1972)
- Hamilton (Oct. 20, 1990 to Sept. 2, 1991)

LONGEST ROAD LOSING STREAK

22 - Montreal (Oct. 5, 1980 to Sept. 10, 1983)
18 - Toronto (July 9, 1992 to Nov. 7, 1993)
12 - Hamilton (Sept. 4, 1948 to Sept. 26, 1950)
- Calgary (Sept. 10, 1955 to Oct. 20, 1956)
- Toronto, 2 times, (Oct. 21, 1962 to Sept. 27, 1964 and Sept. 27, 1980 to July 30, 1982)
11 - Winnipeg (Sept. 13, 1948 to Sept. 9, 1950)
- Ottawa (Oct. 3, 1986 to Oct. 30, 1987)
10 - Edmonton (Aug. 12, 1963 to Sept. 11, 1964)
- Saskatchewan (July 17, 1979 to July 30, 1980)
- Hamilton (Oct. 28, 1990 to Nov. 2, 1991)
9 - B.C. (Sept. 4, 1954 to Sept. 3, 1955)
- Toronto (July 9, 1992 to Oct. 31, 1992)

MOST CONSECUTIVE WINNING SEASONS

11 - Edmonton, 2 times (1951 to 1961 and 1972 to 1982)
10 - B.C. (1979 to 1988)
9 - Edmonton (1984 to 1992)

MOST POINTS IN STANDINGS ONE SEASON (minimum 12 games):

32 - Edmonton, 1989 (16-2-0)
30 - Calgary, 1993 (15-3-0)
29 - Edmonton, 1981 (14-1-1)
28 - Edmonton, 1955 (14-2-0)
- Edmonton, 1957 (14-2-0)
28 - Winnipeg, 1960 (14-2-0)
- Saskatchewan, 1970 (14-2-0)
- Toronto, 1988 (14-4-0)
- Winnipeg, 1993 (14-4-0)

FEWEST POINTS IN STANDINGS ONE SEASON (minimum 12 games):

0 - Hamilton, 1949 (0-12-0)
2 - Hamilton, 1946 (0-10-2)
- B.C., 1954 (1-15-0)
2 - Saskatchewan, 1959 (1-15-0)
3 - Hamilton, 1948 (1-10-1)
- Winnipeg, 1964 (1-14-1)

HIGHEST SHUTOUT:

56-0 Winnipeg, Sask. at Wpg., July 5, 1986
55-0 Edmonton, Sask. at Edm., Aug. 24, 1959
53-0 Toronto, Wpg. at Tor., Oct 8, 1967

MOST SHUTOUTS ONE SEASON:

3 - Calgary (1967, 1954, 1948, 1946)
- Edmonton (1957, 1955)
- Saskatchewan (1949)
2 - Winnipeg (1965, 1956, 1955, 1950, 1946)
- Calgary (1970, 1949)
- Edmonton (1959, 1956)
- Toronto (1958, 1947)
- Hamilton (1956)

MOST TIMES SHUTOUT ONE SEASON:

4	- B.C. (1954)	2	-	Calgary (1956, 1950)
	- Saskatchewan (1946)		-	Toronto (1965)
3	- Winnipeg (1949)		-	Ottawa (1958)
2	- Winnipeg (1967, 1948)		-	Montreal (1952)
	- Edmonton (1967, 1949)		-	Hamilton (1946)
	- Saskatchewan (1960, 1959)			

CFL AVERAGE POINTS PER GAME

64.2	- 1991	51.8	-	1982
61.9	- 1990	51.6	-	1983
57.4	- 1992	50.7	-	1984
54.6	- 1989	50.3	-	1988
53.1	- 1987	48.6	-	1981

AVERAGE POINTS SCORED PER SEASON

38.3	- Toronto	1990	35.8	- Edmonton	1989
37.3	- Edmonton	1991	34.3	- Edmonton	1987
36.7	- B.C.	1991	34.1	- Montreal	1956
36.0	- Edmonton	1981	34.0	- Edmonton	1982
35.9	- Toronto	1991		- Edmonton	1990

MOST POINTS SCORED ONE SEASON:

689	- Toronto	1990	647	- Toronto	1991
671	- Edmonton	1991	644	- Edmonton	1989
661	- B.C.	1991			

FEWEST POINTS AGAINST ONE SEASON (minimum 14 games):

77	- Calgary	1949	142	- Edmonton	1957
102	- Saskatchewan	1949	148	- Montreal	1954
117	- Edmonton	1955			

MOST POINTS SCORED AGAINST ONE SEASON:

710	- Saskatchewan	1991	628	- Hamilton	1990
667	- B.C.	1992	620	- B.C.	1990
630	- Ottawa	1989			

MOST POINTS ONE TEAM ONE GAME:

82 - Montreal, Oct. 20, 1956, 82-14 over Hamilton at Montreal
70 - Toronto, Sept. 20, 1990, 70-18 over Calgary at Toronto
68 - Toronto, Sept. 1, 1990, 68-43 over B.C. at Toronto
- Winnipeg, Oct. 19, 1991, 68-14 over Hamilton at Winnipeg
67 - Hamilton, Oct. 15, 1962, 67-21 over Saskatchewan at Hamilton
65 - Winnipeg, Sept. 7, 1984, 65-25 over Ottawa at Winnipeg

MOST POINTS BOTH TEAMS ONE GAME:

111	- Toronto	68	B.C.	43,	at Toronto, Sept. 1, 1990
103	- Calgary	55	Hamilton	48,	at Calgary, Oct. 17, 1982
99	- Toronto	60	Hamilton	39,	at Toronto, Sept. 29, 1990
96	- Montreal	82	Hamilton	14,	at Montreal, Oct. 20, 1956
	- Ottawa	50	Edmonton	46,	at Ottawa, July 26, 1990
	- Saskatchewan	49	B.C.	47,	at B.C., Sept. 21, 1991
	- Winnipeg	49	Ottawa	47,	at Ottawa, October 12, 1992

MOST POINTS SCORED IN ONE QUARTER ONE TEAM:

38 - Edmonton against Montreal, Sept. 26, 1981, 2nd quarter
- Hamilton at Toronto, Nov. 8, 1992, 2nd quarter
35 - B.C. at Saskatchewan, Oct. 19, 1959, 4th quarter
- Toronto against Montreal, Oct. 30, 1960, 4th quarter
34 - Winnipeg at Saskatchewan, Aug. 29, 1959, 2nd quarter
- Montreal against Hamilton, Oct. 20, 1956, 2nd quarter

MOST POINTS SCORED IN ONE QUARTER BOTH TEAMS:

50 - Toronto against B.C., Sept. 1, 1990, 2nd quarter (Toronto 27 points, B.C. 23 points)
43 - Hamilton against Saskatchewan, Oct. 14, 1985, 4th quarter (Hamilton 29 points, Saskatchewan 14 points)
41 - Montreal against Hamilton, Oct. 20, 1956, 2nd quarter (Montreal 34 points, Hamilton 7 points)
- Toronto against Montreal, Oct. 30, 1960, 4th quarter (Toronto 35 points, Montreal 6 points)
- Hamilton against Montreal, Sept. 21, 1969, 4th quarter (Hamilton 21 points, Montreal 20 points)

MOST TOUCHDOWNS ONE SEASON:

81	- Toronto	1990	70	- Edmonton	1987
77	- Edmonton	1991		- Edmonton	1989
74	- B.C.	1991		- Edmonton	1990
71	- Winnipeg	1993		- Calgary	1993

MOST TOUCHDOWNS ONE TEAM ONE GAME:

12 - Montreal, Ham. at Mtl., Oct. 20, 1956
10 - Hamilton, Sask. at Ham., Oct. 15, 1962
- Toronto, Cal. at Tor., Sept. 20, 1990
9 - Winnipeg, Wpg. at Sask., Aug. 29, 1959
- Toronto, Mtl. at Tor., Oct. 30, 1960
- Winnipeg, Ott. at Wpg., Sept. 7, 1984

MOST ONE-POINT CONVERTS ONE SEASON:

77	- Toronto	1990	69	- Edmonton	1987
75	- Edmonton	1991	67	- B.C.	1991
70	- Edmonton	1989			

MOST ONE-POINT CONVERTS ONE TEAM ONE GAME

9 - Montreal, Ham. at Mtl., Oct. 20, 1956
- Winnipeg, Ott. at Wpg., Sept. 7, 1984
- Toronto, Cal. at Tor., Sept. 20, 1990
- Sacramento, B.C. at Sac., Nov 6, 1993
8 - Toronto, Mtl. at Tor., Oct. 30, 1960
- Ottawa, Ham. at Ott., Sept. 7, 1975

MOST ONE-POINT CONVERTS ONE TEAM ONE GAME (Cont'd)

8 - Hamilton, Tor. at Ham., July 25, 1981
- Edmonton, Mtl. at Edm., Sept. 26, 1981
- Edmonton, Tor. at Edm., Oct. 24, 1981
- Winnipeg, Ham. at Wpg., Oct. 19, 1991
7 - Edmonton, Sask. at Edm., Aug. 24, 1959
- Hamilton, Sask. at Ham., Oct. 15, 1962
- Winnipeg, Sask. at Wpg., July 5, 1986
- Toronto, B.C. at Tor., Sept. 1, 1990
- Toronto, B.C. at Tor., July 16, 1992
- Winnipeg, Wpg. at Ott., October 12, 1992

MOST FIELD GOALS TRIED ONE SEASON

74	- Hamilton	1989	69	- Edmonton	1975
73	- Edmonton	1977		- Calgary	1990
72	- Saskatchewan	1990	68	- Saskatchewan	1989

MOST FIELD GOALS MADE ONE SEASON

59	- Saskatchewan	1990	52	- B.C.	1987
55	- Saskatchewan	1988		- Hamilton	1990
	- Toronto	1991		- Saskatchewan	1991
54	- Hamilton	1989	51	- Saskatchewan	1987
	- Saskatchewan	1989			

MOST SINGLES ONE SEASON

33	- Toronto	1985	30	- Toronto	1983
	- Edmonton	1986		- Winnipeg	1985
32	- Toronto	1986	27	- Hamilton	1976
31	- Edmonton	1983		- Winnipeg	1982
30	- Winnipeg	1950		- Edmonton	1990

MOST SAFETY TOUCHES ONE SEASON

8	- Calgary	1971	5	- Saskatchewan	1953
6	- Hamilton	1965		- Saskatchewan	1981
	- Saskatchewan	1966		- Saskatchewan	1991

MOST FIRST DOWNS ONE SEASON:

508	- B.C.	1991	455	- Edmonton	1990
482	- Edmonton	1991	454	- Saskatchewan	1990
478	- Edmonton	1989			

MOST FIRST DOWNS ONE TEAM ONE GAME:

46 - Saskatchewan, Sask. at B.C., Aug. 13, 1992
44 - Edmonton, Ham. at Edm., Sept. 11, 1983
42 - Montreal, Ham. at Mtl., Oct. 20, 1956
- Ottawa, Tor. at Ott., Aug. 19, 1958
- Calgary, Sask. at Cal., Oct. 10, 1959
- Hamilton, Ham. at Tor., Aug. 21, 1987

MOST YARDS GAINED ONE SEASON:

9117	- B.C.	1991	7894	- Calgary	1992
8015	- Edmonton	1991	7707	- Edmonton	1990
7951	- Edmonton	1989			

MOST YARDS TOTAL OFFENCE ONE TEAM ONE GAME:

799 - Montreal, Ham. at Mtl., Oct. 20, 1956
796 - Montreal, Mtl. at Tor., Oct. 22, 1955
740 - Montreal, Ham. at Mtl., Sept. 22, 1956

MOST YARDS TOTAL OFFENCE BOTH TEAMS ONE GAME:

1248 - B.C. 724, Edmonton 524 at B.C., Oct. 12, 1991
1236 - Montreal 796, Toronto 440 at Toronto, Oct. 22, 1955
1193 - B.C. 645, Calgary 548 at B.C., Nov. 4, 1989

MOST RUSHING ATTEMPTS ONE SEASON

738	- Edmonton	1958	685	- Winnipeg	1957
726	- Winnipeg	1958	670	- Winnipeg	1960
722	- Edmonton	1957			

MOST RUSHING ATTEMPTS ONE TEAM ONE GAME:

67 - Edmonton, Edm. at Wpg., Aug. 25, 1951
65 - Hamilton, Ott. at Ham., Oct. 15, 1955
- Winnipeg, Edm. at Wpg., Oct. 6, 1956
64 - Ottawa, Tor. at Ott., Sept. 14, 1960

MOST YARDS RUSHING ONE SEASON:

4345	- Edmonton	1957	3744	- Winnipeg	1957
3972	- Winnipeg	1960	3722	- Edmonton	1958
3957	- Winnipeg	1958			

MOST YARDS RUSHING ONE TEAM ONE GAME:

468 - Ottawa, Ott. at Mtl., Oct. 10, 1960
445 - Ottawa, Tor. at Ott., Aug. 19, 1958
441 - Edmonton, Edm. at Cal., Sept. 15, 1951

MOST TOUCHDOWNS RUSHING ONE SEASON:

46	- Edmonton	1957	34	- Montreal	1956
36	- Ottawa	1960		- B.C.	1991
35	- Edmonton	1951	33	- Hamilton	1955

MOST TOUCHDOWNS RUSHING ONE TEAM ONE GAME:

7 - Ottawa, Ott. at Mtl., Oct. 10, 1960
6 - Hamilton, Tor. at Ham., Sept. 5, 1955
- Edmonton, B.C. at Edm., Oct. 22, 1956
5 - Edmonton, Sask. at Edm., Aug. 24, 1959
- Calgary, Edm. at Cal., Sept. 3, 1962
- Calgary, Sask. at Cal., July 23, 1980
- Calgary, Cal. at Ham., Oct. 21, 1990
- Toronto, Sask. at Tor., Aug. 15, 1991
- B.C., B.C. at Ott., Sept. 8, 1991

MOST PASSES THROWN ONE SEASON:
793 - Saskatchewan 1990
792 - Saskatchewan 1992
782 - Saskatchewan 1991
766 - Ottawa 1987
743 - B.C. 1992

MOST PASSES THROWN ONE TEAM ONE GAME:
65 - Saskatchewan, Edm. at Sask., Sept. 15, 1991
63 - Calgary, Cal. at Sask., Aug. 7, 1992
62 - Saskatchewan, Tor. at Sask., July 29, 1983
- Saskatchewan, B.C. at Sask., Aug. 13, 1992
60 - Calgary, Wpg. at Cal., July 16, 1987
- Saskatchewan, Sask. at Edm., July 15, 1992
59 - Saskatchewan, Ham. at Sask., Oct. 14, 1984
- B.C., B.C. at Ott., Aug 28, 1990

MOST PASSES THROWN BOTH TEAMS ONE GAME:
108 - Saskatchewan 56, at Winnipeg 52, Sept. 8, 1991
103 - Saskatchewan 53, at B.C. 50, Aug. 21, 1991
99 - Calgary 63 at Saskatchewan 36, Aug. 7, 1992

MOST PASSES COMPLETED ONE SEASON:
470 - B.C. 1991
465 - Saskatchewan 1992
450 - Saskatchewan 1990
444 - Calgary 1993
441 - Saskatchewan 1993

MOST PASSES COMPLETED ONE TEAM ONE GAME:
41 - Winnipeg, Wpg. at Tor., Oct. 3, 1981
40 - Sask., Sask. at B.C., Aug. 13, 1992
37 - B.C., B.C. at Sask., Aug. 21, 1991
36 - Hamilton, Ham. at Tor., Aug. 21, 1987
32 - B.C., Sask. at B.C., July 18, 1989
- B.C., B.C., at Ott., Aug. 28, 1990

MOST PASSES COMPLETED BOTH TEAMS ONE GAME:
70 - Calgary 37, at Saskatchewan 33, Oct.. 23, 1993
67 - B.C. 37, at Saskatchewan 30, Aug. 21, 1991
62 - Calgary 23, at Saskatchewan 39, July 8, 1992

MOST YARDS PASSING ONE SEASON:
6714 - B.C. 1991
6494 - Calgary 1993
6346 - Saskatchewan 1992
6319 - Sacramento 1993
6263 - Calgary 1992

MOST YARDS PASSING ONE TEAM ONE GAME:
601 - B.C., Tor. at B.C., Aug. 12, 1993
586 - Montreal, Ham. at Mtl., Oct. 16, 1954
582 - B.C., Edm. at B.C., Oct. 12, 1991

MOST YARDS PASSING BOTH TEAMS ONE GAME:
1093 - Calgary 547, at Saskatchewan 546, Oct. 23, 1993
1021 - Toronto 420, at B.C. 601, Aug. 12, 1993
988 - Edmonton 406, at B.C. 582, Oct. 12, 1991

MOST TOUCHDOWNS PASSING ONE SEASON:
50 - Toronto 1990
49 - Calgary 1993
43 - Edmonton 1990
- Winnipeg 1993
42 - Edmonton 1991
41 - Calgary 1967
- Saskatchewan 1991
- Edmonton 1992

MOST TOUCHDOWNS PASSING ONE TEAM ONE GAME:
10 - Hamilton, Sask. at Ham., Oct. 15, 1962
8 - Winnipeg, Wpg. at Sask., Aug. 29, 1959

MOST OWN PASSES INTERCEPTED ONE SEASON:
45 - Saskatchewan 1959
- Calgary 1972
- Hamilton 1990
43 - Saskatchewan 1990
42 - Edmonton 1970
- Montreal 1986
- Ottawa 1986

MOST OWN PASSES INTERCEPTED ONE TEAM ONE GAME:
8 - Saskatchewan, Sask. at Ott., Sept. 22, 1974
7 - Several clubs, 21 times
6 - Several clubs, 37 times

MOST INTERCEPTIONS BY ONE SEASON:
48 - Winnipeg 1990
46 - Hamilton 1985
44 - B.C. 1986
43 - Hamilton 1986
42 - B.C. 1983
- Toronto 1990

MOST PASSES INTERCEPTED BY ONE TEAM ONE GAME:
8 - Ottawa, Sask. at Ott., Sept. 22, 1974
7 - Several clubs, 21 times
6 - Several clubs, 37 times

MOST PASSES INTERCEPTED BY BOTH TEAMS ONE GAME:
11 - Calgary at Toronto, July 8, 1982
10 - Hamilton at Toronto, Oct. 13, 1958
- Calgary at Winnipeg, Sept. 1, 1971
- Montreal at Calgary, Sept. 24, 1972
- Edmonton at Hamilton, Aug. 12, 1988
- Toronto at Winnipeg, July 20, 1990
9 - Ottawa at Toronto, Sept. 22, 1956
- Montreal at Toronto, Oct. 18, 1970
- Saskatchewan at Ottawa, Sept. 22, 1974
- Toronto at Saskatchewan, Aug. 26, 1988

MOST YARDS ON INTERCEPTION RETURNS ONE SEASON:
786 - Hamilton 1985
733 - Toronto 1990
723 - B.C. 1983
692 - Winnipeg 1991
669 - B.C. 1986

MOST YARDS ON INTERCEPTION RETURNS ONE TEAM ONE GAME:
291 - Saskatchewan, Cal. at Sask., Aug. 27, 1972
205 - Calgary, Cal. at Wpg., Sept. 1, 1971
195 - Saskatchewan, Cal. at Sask., Sept. 15, 1958

MOST FUMBLES ONE SEASON:
62 - Hamilton 1957
56 - Ottawa 1957
55 - Hamilton 1955
- Toronto 1957

MOST FUMBLES LOST ONE SEASON:
36 - B.C. 1956
34 - B.C. 1960
- Edmonton 1991
33 - Calgary 1955
33 - Calgary 1956
- Hamilton 1957
- Toronto 1961

MOST FUMBLES LOST ONE TEAM ONE GAME:
8 - Ottawa, Ott. at Ham., Oct. 23, 1971
6 - Calgary, Cal. at Sask., Oct. 8, 1951
- Montreal, Mtl. at Ham., Sept. 22, 1956
- Edmonton, Edm. at Cal., Aug. 24, 1957
- Toronto, Tor. at Mtl., Sept. 14, 1957
6 - Calgary, Cal. vs Wpg., Aug. 15, 1960
- Calgary, Cal. vs Sask., Sept. 20, 1969
- Edmonton, Edm. vs Mtl., Oct 13, 1969
- Montreal, Mtl. at Ott., Sept. 6, 1971
- Toronto, Tor. at Ott., Aug. 3, 1977

MOST FUMBLES LOST BOTH TEAMS ONE GAME:
10 - Saskatchewan at Calgary, Oct. 1, 1951
- Winnipeg at Calgary, Aug. 15, 1960
- Ottawa at Hamilton, Oct. 23, 1971
9 - Hamilton at Montreal, Sept. 22, 1956
- B.C. at Edmonton, Sept. 19, 1960

MOST OPPOSITION FUMBLES RECOVERED ONE SEASON:
41 - Hamilton 1992
36 - Saskatchewan 1956
34 - Hamilton 1971
- Winnipeg 1988
34 - Toronto 1989
- Ottawa 1990
- Saskatchewan 1991

BEST TAKEAWAY-GIVEAWAY DIFFERENTIAL ONE SEASON:
(interceptions, fumbles and downs)
+41 - Edmonton, 1981 [72 takeaways (39 int, 16 fum, 17 dwn) - 31 giveaways (18 int, 11 fumb, 2 dwn)]
+40 - Edmonton, 1989 [84 takeaways (37 int, 28 fumb, 19 dwn) - 44 giveaways (24 int, 15 fumb, 5 dwn)]
+31 - Hamilton, 1972 [64 takeaways (39 int, 16 fum, 9 dwn) - 33 giveaways (12 int, 15 fumb, 6 dwn)]
+29 - Winnipeg, 1987 [82 takeaways (39 int, 24 fum, 19 dwn) - 53 giveaways (33 int, 14 fumb, 9 dwn)]
+27 - Winnipeg, 1981 [58 takeaways (28 int, 17 fum, 13 dwn) - 31 giveaways (15 int, 11 fumb, 5 dwn)]
- Edmonton, 1993 [73 takeaways (34 int, 25 fum, 14 dwn) - 46 giveaways (17 int, 20 fumb, 9 dwn)]

MOST PENALTIES ONE SEASON:
230 - Saskatchewan 1992
- Saskatchewan 1993
223 - B.C. 1993
216 - Winnipeg 1991
216 - B.C. 1992
214 - Ottawa 1993
213 - Calgary 1991

MOST PENALTIES ONE TEAM ONE GAME:
27 - Hamilton, Wpg. at Ham., July 9, 1992
23 - Edmonton, Sask. at Edm., July 15, 1992
22 - Calgary, Edm. at Cal., Sept. 2, 1991

MOST PENALTIES BOTH TEAMS ONE GAME:
46 - Winnipeg (19) at Hamilton (27), July 9, 1992
40 - Edmonton (18) at Calgary (22), Sept. 2, 1991
- Saskatchewan (23) at Edmonton (17), July 15, 1992
39 - Ottawa (20) at Toronto (19), July 27, 1977

MOST YARDS PENALIZED ONE SEASON:
1974 - Saskatchewan 1992
1884 - Winnipeg 1992
1881 - Edmonton 1992
1853 - B.C. 1992
1822 - Winnipeg 1991

MOST YARDS PENALIZED ONE TEAM ONE GAME:
265 - Hamilton, Wpg. at Ham., July 9, 1992
238 - Hamilton, Tor. at Ham., Oct. 10, 1977
216 - Calgary, Edm. at Cal., Sept. 2, 1991

MOST YARDS PENALIZED BOTH TEAMS ONE GAME:
445 - Winnipeg (180) at Hamilton (265), July 9, 1992
389 - Edmonton (173) at Calgary (216), September 2, 1991
376 - Toronto (138) at Hamilton (238), October 10, 1977

MOST PUNTS ONE SEASON:
188 - Winnipeg 1988
175 - Calgary 1970
175 - Winnipeg 1989
174 - Hamilton 1986

MOST PUNTS ONE TEAM ONE GAME:
17 - Hamilton, Mtl. at Ham., Nov. 5, 1955
15 - Montreal, Ott. at Mtl., Aug. 30, 1958
- Saskatchewan, Sask. at B.C., Oct. 31, 1981
- B.C., Sask. at B.C., Oct. 31, 1981
- Montreal, Mtl. at Edm., Aug. 15, 1982
- Saskatchewan, B.C. at Sask., Oct. 30, 1983
- Montreal, Mtl. at Wpg., Sept. 13, 1985

MOST PUNTS, ONE TEAM, ONE GAME (Cont'd)
15 - Toronto, Ott. at Tor., Aug. 22, 1985
- Winnipeg, Wpg. at Ham., Aug. 14, 1987
- Ottawa, B.C. at Ott., Sept. 27, 1992

MOST PUNTS, BOTH TEAMS, ONE GAME:
30 - Saskatchewan 15, at B.C. 15, Oct. 31, 1981

MOST YARDS PUNTED ONE SEASON:

8214	- Winnipeg	1988	7708	- Saskatchewan	1983
8004	- Toronto	1986	7700	- Hamilton	1971
7729	- Hamilton	1984			

MOST YARDS PUNTED ONE TEAM ONE GAME:
785 - Hamilton, Ham. at Ott., Sept. 14, 1958
759 - Saskatchewan, B.C. at Sask., Oct. 30, 1983
721 - Edmonton, Edm. at B.C., Sept. 19, 1986

BEST PUNTING AVERAGE ONE SEASON:

49.5	- B.C.	1983	47.5	- Hamilton	1971
48.5	- Toronto	1986		- Edmonton	1978
47.8	- Toronto	1961	47.4	- Hamilton	1955
47.5	- Hamilton	1968			

MOST PUNT RETURNS ONE SEASON:

186	- B.C.	1964	151	- Ottawa	1974
168	- Calgary	1970	149	- Edmonton	1982
154	- Calgary	1968			

MOST PUNT RETURNS ONE TEAM ONE GAME:
17 - Saskatchewan, Edm. at Sask., Aug. 27, 1951
- Calgary, Sask. at Cal., Sept. 14, 1963
16 - Hamilton, Ham. at Ott., Oct. 30, 1954
- Winnipeg, Sask. at Wpg., Sept. 12, 1955
- Montreal, Mtl. at Ham., Nov. 5, 1955
- Saskatchewan, Sask. at B.C., Oct. 31, 1981
15 - Saskatchewan, Cal. at Sask., Aug. 25, 1951
- B.C., B.C. at Wpg., Oct. 11, 1958
- Calgary, Cal. at Edm., Aug. 28, 1968
- Calgary, Ham. at Cal., July 20, 1984

MOST YARDS ON PUNT RETURNS ONE SEASON:

1606	- Montreal	1975	1557	- B.C.	1986
1583	- B.C.	1980	1491	- B.C.	1984
1568	- Montreal	1976			

MOST YARDS ON PUNT RETURNS ONE TEAM ONE GAME:
269 - Edmonton, Cal. at Edm., June 27, 1987
236 - Montreal, Tor. at Mtl., Aug. 23, 1976
232 - Edmonton, Ott. at Edm., July 17, 1991

MOST KICKOFFS, ONE TEAM, ONE GAME:
12 - Toronto, B.C. at Tor., Sept. 1, 1990
- Toronto, B.C. at Tor., July 16, 1992
11 - Montreal, Ham. at Mtl., Oct. 20, 1956
- Hamilton, Sask. at Ham., Oct. 15, 1962
- Toronto, Cal. at Tor., Sept. 20, 1990
- B.C., Tor. at B.C., Aug. 1, 1991
- Toronto, Sask. at Tor., Aug. 15, 1991
- Winnipeg, Ham. at Wpg., Oct. 19, 1991
10 - Winnipeg, Wpg. at Sask., Aug. 29, 1959
- Toronto, Mtl. at Tor., Oct. 30, 1960
- Saskatchewan, Ott. at Sask., Aug. 7, 1989
- Edmonton, Edm. at Ott., July 26, 1990
- Edmonton, Sask. at Edm., Aug. 7, 1990
- Edmonton, Tor. at Edm., Aug. 14, 1990
- Toronto, Sask. at Tor., Oct. 20, 1990
- Saskatchewan, B.C. at Sask., Aug. 21, 1991
- Toronto, Ham. at Tor., Sept. 7, 1991
- Winnipeg, Sask. at Wpg., Sept. 8, 1991
- Edmonton, Edm. at B.C., Oct. 12, 1991
- Saskatchewan, Sask. at B.C., Aug. 13, 1992

MOST YARDS ON KICKOFFS ONE TEAM ONE GAME:
749 - Toronto, B.C. at Tor., July 16, 1992
675 - Toronto, B.C. at Tor., Sept. 1, 1990
662 - Toronto, Mtl. at Tor., Oct. 30, 1960
- B.C., B.C. at Cal., July 31, 1981

MOST KICKOFF RETURNS ONE SEASON:

128	- B.C.	1992	116	- Saskatchewan	1990
126	- B.C.	1991	113	- Calgary	1990
118	- B.C.	1989			

MOST KICKOFF RETURNS ONE TEAM ONE GAME:
11 - Hamilton, Ham. at Mtl., Oct. 20, 1956
- Saskatchewan, Sask. at Ham., Oct. 15, 1962
10 - Saskatchewan, Wpg. at Sask., Oct. 29, 1959
- Montreal, Mtl. at Tor., Oct. 20, 1960
- B.C., B.C. at Cal., Oct. 14, 1989
- Saskatchewan, Cal. at Sask., July 27, 1990
- Saskatchewan, Sask. at Edm., Aug. 7, 1990
- Saskatchewan, Sask. at Tor., Oct. 20, 1990
- B.C., B.C. at Sask., Aug. 21, 1991

MOST KICKOFF RETURN YARDAGE ONE SEASON:

2761	- Calgary	1990	2331	- B.C.	1993
2591	- B.C.	1991	2297	- Calgary	1991
2529	- B.C.	1989			

MOST YARDS ON KICKOFF RETURNS ONE TEAM ONE GAME:
287 - Calgary, Wpg. at Cal., Oct. 4, 1952
279 - Montreal, Mtl. at Tor., Oct. 30, 1960
261 - Calgary, Cal. at Edm., Sept. 20, 1952

MOST BLOCKED KICKS ONE SEASON:

8	- Edmonton	1986	6	- Winnipeg	1974
6	- Saskatchewan	1967		- Winnipeg	1988
	- Edmonton	1967			

MOST BLOCKED KICKS ONE GAME:
3 - Winnipeg, Sask. at Wpg., Sept. 13, 1992
2 - Ottawa, Ott. at Ham., Aug. 23, 1967
- Toronto, Tor. at Sask., Aug. 25, 1968
- Hamilton, Ham. at B.C., Sept. 23, 1970
- Hamilton, Ham. at Wpg., Aug. 30, 1977
- Edmonton, Cal. at Edm., Oct. 19, 1986
2 - Winnipeg, Wpg. at Cal., July 16, 1987
- Saskatchewan, Ott. at Sask., Oct. 30, 1987
- Winnipeg, Wpg. at Ott., July 12, 1990
- Calgary, Sask. at Cal., July 18, 1991

MOST BLOCKED KICKS AGAINST ONE GAME:
3 - Saskatchewan, Sask. at Wpg., Sept. 13, 1992
2 - Hamilton, Ott. at Ham., Aug. 23, 1967
- Saskatchewan, Tor. at Sask., Aug. 25, 1968
- B.C., Ham. at B.C., Sept. 23, 1970
- Winnipeg, Ham. at Wpg., Aug. 30, 1977
- Calgary, Cal. at Edm., Oct. 19, 1986
- Calgary, Wpg. at Cal., July 16, 1987
- Ottawa, Ott. at Sask., Oct. 30, 1987
- Ottawa, Wpg. at Ott., July 12, 1990
- Saskatchewan, Sask. at Cal., July 18, 1991

MOST QUARTERBACK SACKS ONE SEASON:

85	- Calgary	1986	80	- Hamilton	1988
82	- B.C.	1987			

FEWEST QUARTERBACK SACKS AGAINST ONE SEASON:

13	- Calgary	1980	26	- Winnipeg	1990
20	- Winnipeg	1993	28	- Saskatchewan	1982
23	- Saskatchewan	1993			

MOST QUARTERBACK SACKS AGAINST ONE SEASON:

103	- Toronto	1986	79	- Ottawa	1984
82	- Ottawa	1988		- Ottawa	1987

MOST QUARTERBACK SACKS ONE GAME:
13 - Edmonton, Edm. at Tor., Aug. 18, 1993
11 - Calgary, Tor. at Cal., Oct. 13, 1986
- Calgary, Edm. at Cal., June 24, 1986
- Ottawa, Ott. at Ham., Oct. 25, 1992
- Montreal, B.C. at Mtl., Oct. 10, 1986
10 - Edmonton, Edm. at Ham., Oct. 7, 1984
- Saskatchewan, Sask. at Ott., July 29, 1984
- Edmonton, Sask. at Edm., Aug. 7, 1990

MOST QUARTERBACK SACKS AGAINST ONE GAME:
13 - Toronto, Edm. at Tor., Aug. 18, 1993
11 - Toronto, Tor. at Cal., Oct. 13, 1986
- Edmonton, Edm. at Cal., June 24, 1986
- Hamilton, Ott. at Ham., Oct. 25, 1992
- B.C., B.C. at Mtl., Oct. 5, 1986
- Hamilton, Edm. at Ham., Oct. 7, 1984
10 - Ottawa, Sask. at Ott., July 29, 1984
- Saskatchewan, Sask. at Edm., Aug. 7, 1990

INDIVIDUAL RECORDS

Games and Season totals are based upon available game participation sheets.

MOST GAMES PLAYED

No.		Player
288	-	Ron Lancaster, Ottawa-Saskatchewan (1960-1978)
286	-	Lui Passaglia, B.C. (1976-1993)
271	-	Roger Aldag, Saskatchewan (1976-1992)
267	-	Miles Gorrell, Calgary-Ottawa-Montreal-Hamilton-Winnipeg (1978-1993)
257	-	Lloyd Fairbanks, Calgary-Montreal-Hamilton (1975-1991)
254	-	Dave Cutler, Edmonton (1969-1984)
248	-	Hank Ilesic, Edmonton-Toronto (1977-1993)
239	-	Bob Cameron, Winnipeg (1980-1993)
236	-	Bob Poley, Saskatchewan-Calgary (1978-1992)
233	-	Al Wilson, B.C. (1972-1986)
229	-	Jerry Keeling, Calgary-Ottawa-Hamilton (1961-1975)
224	-	Larry Robinson, Calgary (1961-1974)
223	-	Norm Fieldgate, B.C. (1954-1967)
219	-	John Helton, Calgary-Winnipeg (1969-1982)
217	-	Gene Gaines, Montreal-Ottawa (1961-1976)
216	-	Garney Henley, Hamilton (1960-1975)
	-	Bryan Illerbrun, Saskatchewan-B.C.-Ottawa (1978-1991)
215	-	Bob Howes, B.C.-Edmonton (1968-1981)
	-	Lawrie Skolrood, Hamilton-Saskatchewan (1974-1987)
212	-	Nick Bastaja, Ottawa-Hamilton-Winnipeg (1975-1988)
209	-	Marv Allemang, Hamilton-Ottawa (1975-1988)
207	-	Bob Swift, B.C.-Toronto-Winnipeg (1964-1977)
	-	Don Moen, Toronto (1982-1993)
	-	Dave Ridgway, Saskatchewan (1982-1993)
	-	Rob Smith, B.C., Toronto-Montreal-Calgary-Ottawa (1981-1993)
206	-	John Bonk, Winnipeg (1972-1985)
204	-	Danny Nykoluk, Toronto (1955-1971)
204	-	Rocky DiPietro, Hamilton (1978-1991)
203	-	George Reed, Saskatchewan (1963-1975)
	-	Chris Walby, Montreal, Winnipeg (1981-1993)

MOST GAMES PLAYED (Cont'd)

No.		Player
202	-	Glen Weir, Montreal (1972-1984)
	-	Leo Blanchard, Edmonton-B.C.-Calgary (1979-1991)
201	-	Moe Racine, Ottawa (1958-1974)

MOST CONSECUTIVE GAMES PLAYED

No.		Player
253	-	Dave Cutler, Edmonton (1969-1984)
250	-	Roger Aldag, Saskatchewan (1976-1991)
234	-	Bob Cameron, Winnipeg (1980-1993)
224	-	Larry Robinson, Calgary (1966-1977)
207	-	Dave Ridgway, Saskatchewan (1982-1993)
206	-	Rob Smith, Toronto-Montreal-Calgary-B.C.-Ottawa-B.C. (1982-1993)
205	-	Bob Howes, B.C.-Edmonton (1968-1980)
191	-	John Bonk, Winnipeg (1973-1985)
198	-	Don Moen, Toronto (1982-1993)
186	-	Gerry Organ, Ottawa (1971-1983)
184	-	Basil Bark, Montreal (1966-1977)
179	-	Alan Ford, Saskatchewan (1965-1976)
177	-	Danny Nykoluk, Toronto (1958-1970)
	-	Ron Lancaster, Ottawa-Saskatchewan (1966-1977)
176	-	Norm Fieldgate, B.C. (1956-1967)
175	-	Ellison Kelly, Hamilton-Toronto (1960-1972)
172	-	John T. Hay, Ottawa-Calgary (1978-1988)
170	-	John Blain, B.C. (1977-1987)
168	-	Joe Poirier, Ottawa (1959-1970)
	-	Bob Swift, B.C.-Toronto (1967-1977)
167	-	Alan Wilson, B.C. (1972-1982)
163	-	Bill Stevenson, Edmonton (1975-1985)
162	-	Bernie Ruoff, Winnipeg-Hamilton-B.C. (1975-1985)
161	-	Gene Gaines, Montreal-Ottawa (1961-1973)
	-	Gary Brandt, Montreal (1967-1977)

MOST SEASONS PLAYED

No.		Player
22	-	Eddie Emerson, Ottawa (1911-1937)
19	-	Ron Lancaster, Ottawa-Saskatchewan (1960-1978)
18	-	Lui Passaglia, B.C. (1976-1993)
17	-	Ron Atchison, Saskatchewan (1952-1968)
	-	Moe Racine, Ottawa (1958-1974)
	-	Roger Aldag, Saskatchewan (1976-1992)
	-	Lloyd Fairbanks, Calgary-Montreal-Hamilton (1975-1991)
	-	Hank Ilesic, Edmonton-Toronto (1977-1993)
16	-	Chet Miksza, Hamilton-Montreal (1952-1968)
	-	Danny Nykoluk, Toronto (1955-1971)
	-	Garney Henley, Hamilton (1960-1975)
	-	Gene Gaines, Montreal-Ottawa (1961-1976)
	-	Dave Cutler, Edmonton (1969-1984)
	-	Miles Gorrell, Calgary-Ottawa-Montreal-Hamilton-Winnipeg (1978-1993)
15	-	Annis Stukus, Toronto-Edmonton (1935-1951)
	-	Roger Savoie, Winnipeg (1951-1965)
	-	Reg Whitehouse, Saskatchewan (1952-1966)
	-	Angelo Mosca, Hamilton-Ottawa-Montreal (1958-1972)
	-	Jerry Keeling, Calgary-Ottawa-Hamilton (1961-1975)
	-	Bill Frank, B.C.-Toronto-Winnipeg (1962-1976)
	-	Tom Wilkinson, Toronto-B.C.-Edmonton (1967-1981)
	-	Gordon Judges, Toronto-Montreal (1968-1982)
	-	Al Wilson, B.C. (1972-1986)

MOST CONSECUTIVE SEASONS PLAYED

No.		Player
19	-	Ron Lancaster, Ottawa-Saskatchewan (1960-1978)
18	-	Lui Passaglia, B.C. (1976-1993)
17	-	Eddie Emerson, Ottawa (1919-1935)
	-	Ron Atchison, Saskatchewan (1952-1968)
	-	Moe Racine, Ottawa (1958-1974)
	-	Roger Aldag, Saskatchewan (1976-1992)
	-	Lloyd Fairbanks, Calgary-Montreal-Hamilton (1975-1991)
	-	Hank Ilesic, Edmonton-Toronto (1977-1993)
16	-	Garney Henley, Hamilton (1960-1975)
	-	Gene Gaines, Montreal-Ottawa (1961-1976)
	-	Dave Cutler, Edmonton (1969-1984)
	-	Miles Gorrell, Calgary-Ottawa-Montreal-Hamilton-Winnipeg (1978-1993)

ALL-TIME POINT LEADERS
(Note: Prior to 1956, a touchdown was worth five points)

	Seasons	TDs.	Cons.	FGs.	Sing.	Points
Lui Passaglia, B.C.	18	1	744	609	252	2829
Dave Cutler, Edm.	16	0	627	464	218	2237
Dave Ridgway, Sask.	12	0	475	501	100	2058
Trevor Kennerd, Wpg.	12	0	509	394	149	1840
Bernie Ruoff, Wpg.-Ham.-B.C.	14	0	401	384	219	1772
Lance Chomyc, Tor.	9	0	412	337	75	1498
Gerry Organ, Ott.	12	2	391	318	105	1462
John T. Hay, Ott.-Cal.	11	0	363	308	124	1411
Don Sweet, Mtl.-Ham.	14	0	327	314	73	1342
Paul Osbaldiston, B.C.-Wpg.-Ham.	8	0	290	295	135	1310
Mark McLoughlin, Cal.	6	0	299	254	78	1139
Larry Robinson, Cal.	14	9	362	171	101	1030
Zenon Andrusyshyn, Tor.-Ham.-Edm.-Mtl.	12	0	222	215	143	1010
Tommy Joe Coffey, Edm.-Ham.-Tor.	14	65	204	108	53	971
Dean Dorsey, Tor.-Ott.-Edm.	8	0	244	219	50	951
Jack Abendschan, Sask.	11	0	312	159	74	863
George Reed, Sask.	13	137	0	0	1	823
Jackie Parker, Edm.-Tor.-B.C.	13	88	103	40	19	750
Don Sutherin, Ham.-Ott.-Tor.	12	4	270	114	78	714
Gerry James, Wpg.-Sask.	11	63	143	40	21	645
Ian Sunter, Ham-Tor.	6	0	155	135	66	626
Brian Kelly, Edm.	9	97	X2	0	0	586
Cyril McFall, Cal.	5	0	131	134	45	578
Jerry Kauric, Edm.-Cal.	4	0	170	118	53	577
Bob Macoritti, Wpg.-Sask.	6	0	145	122	65	576

X - Two point converts

MOST POINTS ONE SEASON:

No.		Player	Year	TDs.	Con.	FGs.	Sing.
236	-	Lance Chomyc, Tor.	1991	0	64	55	7
233	-	Paul Osbaldiston, Ham.	1989	0	47	54	24
	-	Dave Ridgway, Sask.	1990	0	47	59	9
224	-	Jerry Kauric, Edm.	1989	0	70	45	19
216	-	Dave Ridgway, Sask.	1989	0	49	54	5
	-	Dave Ridgway, Sask.	1991	0	56	52	4
215	-	Dave Ridgway, Sask.	1988	0	45	55	5
	-	Mark McLoughlin, Cal.	1993	0	56	28	16

MOST POINTS ONE SEASON BY A FIRST-YEAR PLAYER:

No.		Player	Year	TDs.	Con.	FGs.	Sing.
186	-	Ray Macoritti, Edm.	1990	0	64	36	14
165	-	Paul Osbaldiston, B.C.-Wpg.-Ham.	1986	0	39	37	15
164	-	Sean Fleming, Edm.	1992	0	60	30	14
163	-	Dave Ridgway, Sask.	1982	0	34	38	15
156	-	Jim Crouch, Sac.	1993	0	56	28	16

MOST POINTS ONE GAME:

No.		Player
36	-	Bob McNamara, Wpg., Wpg. at B.C., Oct. 13,1956
30	-	Ernie Pitts, Wpg., Wpg. at Sask., Aug. 29, 1959
	-	Ferd Burket, Sask., Sask. at Wpg., Oct. 26, 1959
	-	Earl Lunsford, Cal., Edm. at Cal., Sept. 2, 1962
29	-	Sean Fleming, Edm., Edm. at B.C., Oct. 29, 1993
28	-	Dave Ridgway, Sask., Sask. at Ott., July 29, 1984
25	-	Lance Chomyc, Tor., Ott. at Tor., Oct. 14, 1988
	-	Dave Ridgway, Sask., Edm. at Sask., Aug. 19, 1990

YEAR-BY-YEAR SCORING LEADERS

	East	Pts.	West	Pts.
1993	Troy Westwood, Wpg.	209	Mark McLoughlin, Cal.	215
1992	Troy Westwood, Wpg.	199	Mark McLoughlin, Cal.	208
1991	Lance Chomyc, Tor.	236	Dave Ridgway, Sask.	216
1990	Paul Osbaldiston, Ham.	212	Dave Ridgway, Sask.	233
1989	Paul Osbaldiston, Ham.	233	Jerry Kauric, Edm.	224
1988	Lance Chomyc, Tor.	207	Dave Ridgway, Sask.	215
1987	Lance Chomyc, Tor.	193	Lui Passaglia, B.C.	214
*1986	Lance Chomyc, Tor.	157	Tom Dixon, Edm.	190
1985	Bernie Ruoff, Ham.	154	Trevor Kennerd, Wpg.	198
1984	Hank Ilesic, Tor.	159	Lui Passaglia, B.C.	167
1983	Bernie Ruoff, Ham.	149	Lui Passaglia, B.C.	191
1982	Bernie Ruoff, Ham.	142	Dave Cutler, Edm.	170
1981	Bernie Ruoff, Ham.	152	Trevor Kennerd, Wpg.	185
1980	Zenon Andrusyshyn, Tor.	136	Dave Cutler, Edm.	158
	Bernie Ruoff, Ham.	136		
1979	Don Sweet, Mtl.	111	Bernie Ruoff, Wpg.	151
1978	John (J.T.) Hay, Ott.	136	Dave Cutler, Edm.	167
1977	Don Sweet, Mtl.	136	Dave Cutler, Edm.	195
1976	Don Sweet, Mtl.	141	Bernie Ruoff, Wpg.	152
1975	Gerry Organ, Ott.	124	Dave Cutler, Edm.	169
1974	Ian Sunter, Ham.	141	Dave Cutler, Edm.	144
1973	Gerry Organ, Ott.	123	Dave Cutler, Edm.	133
1972	Gerry Organ, Ott.	131	Dave Cutler, Edm.	126
1971	Gerry Organ, Ott.	92	Don Jonas, Wpg.	121
1970	Tommy Joe Coffey, Ham.	113	Jack Abendschan, Sask.	116
1969	Tommy Joe Coffey, Ham.	148	Jack Abendschan, Sask.	116
1968	Don Sutherin, Ott.	112	Ted Gerela, B.C.	115
1967	Tommy Joe Coffey, Ham.	107	Terry Evanshen, Cal.	102
1966	Moe Racine, Ott.	71	Hugh Campbell, Sask.	102
1965	Don Sutherin, Ham.	82	Larry Robinson, Cal.	95
1964	Don Sutherin, Ham.	94	Larry Robinson, Cal.	106
1963	Dick Shatto, Tor.	81	George Fleming, Wpg.	135
1962	George Dixon, Mtl.	90	Tommy Joe Coffey, Edm.	129
1961	Don Sutherin, Ham.	69	Jackie Parker, Edm.	104
1960	Cookie Gilchrist, Tor.	115	Gerry James, Wpg.	114
1959	Cookie Gilchrist, Tor.	75	Jackie Parker, Edm.	109
1958	Bill Bewley, Mtl.	62	Jack Hill, Sask.	145
1957	Hal Patterson, Mtl.	78	Gerry James, Wpg.	131
1956	Pat Abbruzzi, Mtl.	120	Buddy Leake, Wpg.	103
1955	Al Pfeifer, Tor.	98	Ken Carpenter, Sask.	90
1954	Alex Webster, Mtl.	80	Joe Aguirre, Sask.	85
1953	Gene Roberts, Ott.	88	Bud Korchak, Wpg.	66
1952	Ulysses Curtis, Tor.	80	Bob Shaw, Cal.	110
1951	John (Tip) Logan, Ham.	51	Bob Shaw, Cal.	61
1950	Edgar Jones, Ham.	108	Joe Aguirre, Wpg.	57
1949	Virgil Wagner, Mtl.	77	Vern Graham, Cal.	58
1948	Virgil Wagner, Mtl.	60	Paul Rowe, Cal.	35
1947	Virgil Wagner, Mtl.	71	Gabe Patterson, Sask.	36
1946	Joe Krol, Tor.	65	Bill Wusyk, Cal.	32
	Virgil Wagner, Mtl.	65		
1945	Royal Copeland, Tor.	40		
1941			Art Stevenson, Wpg.	29
1940	Scotty Wright, Ham.	21	Art Stevenson, Wpg.	26
			Andy Bieber, Wpg.	26
1939	Red Storey, Tor.	25	Paul Rowe, Cal.	61
1938	Annis Stukus, Tor.	32	Fritz Hanson, Wpg.	31
1937	Tiny Herman, Ott.	22	Paul Kirk, Regina	19
1936	Huck Welch, Ham.	37		
1935	Abe Eliowitz, Ott.	62		
1934	Frank Turville, Ham.	27		
1933	Huck Welch, Mtl.	29		
1932	Frank Turville, Ham.	52		
1931	Frank Turville, Tor.	26		
1930	Brian Timmis, Ham.	35		

*Paul Osbaldiston of Hamilton finished the 1986 season with 165 points, however, he scored 92 of those points with Hamilton, 48 with Winnipeg and 25 with B.C.

ALL-TIME TOUCHDOWN LEADERS

No.		Player	Seasons	Earliest	Latest
137	-	George Reed, Sask.	13	1963	1975
97	-	Brian Kelly, Edm.	9	1979	1987
91	-	Dick Shatto, Tor.	12	1954	1965
	-	Tom Scott, Wpg.-Edm.-Cal.	11	1974	1984
88	-	Jackie Parker, Edm.-Tor.-B.C.	13	1954	1968
	-	Craig Ellis, Wpg.-Cal.-Sask.-Tor.-Edm.	10	1982	1993
86	-	Willie Fleming, B.C.	8	1959	1968
83	-	Normie Kwong, Cal.-Edm.	13	1948	1960
80	-	Terry Evanshen, Mtl.-Cal.-Ham.-Tor.	14	1965	1978
79	-	Virgil Wagner, Mtl.	9	1946	1954
	-	Leo Lewis, Wpg.	12	1955	1966
	-	Hal Patterson, Mtl.-Ham.	14	1954	1967

ALL-TIME TOUCHDOWN LEADERS (Cont'd)

72 -	Tony Gabriel, Ham.-Ott.	11	1971	1981
71 -	Johnny Bright, Cal.-Edm.	13	1952	1964
-	Jim Germany, Edm.	7	1977	1983
70 -	Bob Simpson, Ott.	13	1950	1962
-	Jeff Boyd, Wpg.-Tor.	9	1983	1991
68 -	Jim Young, B.C.	13	1967	1979
67 -	Ron Stewart, Ott.	12	1959	1970
65 -	Tommy Joe Coffey, Edm.-Ham.-Tor.	14	1959	1973
63 -	Gerry James, Wpg.-Sask.	11	1952	1964
-	Milson Jones, Wpg.-Edm.-Sask.	11	1982	1992
62 -	Lovell Coleman, Cal.-Ott.-B.C.	10	1960	1970
-	Tom Forzani, Cal.	11	1973	1983
-	James Murphy, Wpg.	8	1983	1990

MOST TOUCHDOWNS ONE SEASON:

20 -	Pat Abbruzzi, Mtl.	1956	18 -	Ken Carpenter, Sask.	1955
-	Darrell K. Smith, Tor.	1990	-	Willie Fleming, B.C.	1960
-	Blake Marshall, Edm.	1991	-	George Dixon, Mtl.	1960
-	Jon Volpe, B.C.	1991	-	Alvin (Skip) Walker, Ott.	1982
19 -	Pat Abbruzzi, Mtl.	1955	-	Lester Brown, Tor.	1984
-	Gerry James, Wpg.	1957	-	Brian Kelly, Edm.	1984
-	Jim Germany, Edm.	1981	-	Willard Reaves, Wpg.	1984
-	Larry Key, B.C.	1981	-	David Williams, B.C.	1988

MOST TOUCHDOWNS ONE GAME:

6 - Bob McNamara, Wpg., Wpg. at B.C., Oct 13, 1956
- Eddie James, Wpg., Wpg. St. Johns at Wpg. Garrison, Sept. 28, 1932
5 - Ernie Pitts, Wpg., Wpg. at Sask., Aug. 29, 1959
- Ferd Burket, Sask., Sask. at Wpg., Oct 26, 1959
- Earl Lunsford, Cal., Edm. at Cal., Sept. 3, 1962

MOST TOUCHDOWNS ONE SEASON BY A FIRST-YEAR PLAYER:

20 -	Jon Volpe, B.C.	1991	15 -	Gill Fenerty, Tor.	1987
19 -	Pat Abbruzzi, Mtl.	1955	-	Derrick Crawford, Cal.	1990
15 -	James Sykes, Cal.	1978			

ALL-TIME RUSHING LEADERS

	Seasons	No.	Yds.	Ave.	Long.	TDs.
George Reed, Sask.	13	3243	16116	5.0	71	134
Johnny Bright, Cal.-Edm.	13	1969	10909	5.5	90	69
Normie Kwong, Cal.-Edm.	13	1745	9022	5.2	60	78
Leo Lewis, Wpg.	11	1351	8861	6.5	92	48
Dave Thelen, Ott.-Tor.	9	1530	8463	5.5	77	47
Jim Evenson, B.C.-Ott.	7	1460	7060	4.8	68	37
Earl Lunsford, Cal.	6	1199	6994	5.8	85	55
Dick Shatto, Tor.	12	1322	6958	5.3	67	39
Lovell Coleman,Cal.-Ott.-B.C.	10	1135	6566	5.8	85	42
Willie Burden, Cal.	8	1242	6234	5.0	71	32

MOST YARDS RUSHING ONE SEASON:

1896 -	Willie Burden, Cal.	1975
1794 -	Earl Lunsford, Cal.	1961
1769 -	Robert Mimbs, Wpg.	1991

MOST YARDS RUSHING ONE SEASON BY A FIRST-YEAR PLAYER:

1395 -	Jon Volpe, B.C.	1991
1341 -	Robert Mimbs, Wpg.	1990
1283 -	Earl Lunsford, Cal.	1956

MOST YARDS RUSHING ONE GAME:

287 - Ron Stewart, Ott. (15 carries), Ott. at Mtl., Oct. 10, 1960
268 - George Reed, Sask. (30 carries), Sask. at B.C., Oct. 24, 1965
238 - Lovell Coleman, Cal. (25 carries), Cal. at Ham., Sept. 15, 1964
- Willie Burden, Cal. (34 carries), Wpg. at Cal., Nov. 2, 1975

ALL-TIME QUARTERBACK RUSHING LEADERS:

5241 - Damon Allen, Edm.-Ott.-Ham.
5210 - Jackie Parker, Edm.-Tor.-B.C.
5070 - Tracy Ham, Edm.-Tor.
5045 - Russ Jackson, Ott.
4434 - Matt Dunigan, Edm.-B.C.-Tor.-Wpg.
3984 - Chuck Ealey, Ham.-Wpg.-Tor.
3167 - Condredge Holloway, Ott.-Tor.-B.C.
3001 - Kenny Ploen, Wpg.
2806 - Bernie Faloney, Edm.-Ham.-B.C.-Mtl.
2784 - Joe Kapp, Cal.-B.C.

MOST YARDS RUSHING ONE SEASON BY A QUARTERBACK:

1096 -	Tracy Ham, Edm.,	1990	1005 -	Tracy Ham, Edm.,	1989
1036 -	Damon Allen, Ott.,	1991			

MOST YARDS RUSHING ONE GAME BY A QUARTERBACK:

Damon Allen, Edm.	170 (15 carries)	Oct. 29, 1993 vs. B.C.
Tracy Ham, Edm.	166 (13 carries)	Aug. 15, 1991 at Ott.
Tracy Ham, Edm.	150 (9 carries)	Sept. 29, 1989 at Ham.
Kenny Ploen, Wpg.	148 (12 carries)	Aug. 28, 1958 vs. B.C.

LONGEST RUSHING PLAYS:

109 - George Dixon, Mtl., Ott. at Mtl., Sept. 2, 1963
- Willie Fleming, B.C., B.C. at Edm., Oct. 17, 1964
106 - Don Clark, Mtl., Wpg. at Mtl., Aug. 11, 1961
104 - Jim Thomas, Edm., B.C. at Edm., Oct. 9, 1965

ALL-TIME LEADERS TIMES CARRIED:

		Years
3243 -	George Reed, Saskatchewan	1963-75
1969 -	Johnny Bright, Calgary-Edmonton	1952-64
1745 -	Normie Kwong, Calgary-Edmonton	1948-60
1530 -	Dave Thelen, Ottawa-Toronto	1958-66
1460 -	Jim Evenson, B.C.-Ottawa	1968-74
1351 -	Leo Lewis, Winnipeg	1955-66
1322 -	Dick Shatto, Toronto	1954-65
1242 -	Willie Burden, Calgary	1974-81
1206 -	Jim Washington, Winnipeg-Saskatchewan	1974-80
1199 -	Earl Lunsford, Calgary	1956-63

MOST CARRIES ONE SEASON:

332 -	Willie Burden, Cal.,	1975	323 -	George Reed, Sask.,	1975
326 -	Robert Mimbs, Wpg.,	1991			

MOST CARRIES ONE GAME:

37 - Doyle Orange, Tor. (175 yards), Ham. at Tor., Aug. 13, 1975
36 - Lovell Coleman, Cal. (156 yards), Cal. at Wpg., Aug. 12, 1963
34 - George Reed, Sask. (199 yards), Sask. at Ham., Aug. 8, 1970
- George Reed, Sask. (150 yards), Sask. at Wpg., Oct. 12, 1975
- Willie Burden, Cal. (230 yards), Wpg. at Cal., Nov. 2, 1975

YEAR-BY-YEAR LEADING RUSHERS:

	East	Yds.	West	Yds.
1993 -	Mike Richardson, Wpg.	925	Damon Allen, Edm.	920
1992 -	Mike Richardson, Wpg.	1153	Jon Volpe, B.C.	941
1991 -	Robert Mimbs, Wpg.	1769	Jon Volpe, B.C.	1395
1990 -	Robert Mimbs, Wpg.	1341	Tracy Ham, Edm.	1096
1989 -	Gill Fenerty, Tor.	1247	Reggie Taylor, Edm.	1503
1988 -	Orville Lee, Ott.	1075	Tony Cherry, B.C.	889
1987 -	Willard Reaves, Wpg.	1471	Gary Allen, Cal.	857
1986 -	Walter Bender, Ham.	618	Gary Allen, Cal.	1153
1985 -	Ken Hobart, Ham.	928	Willard Reaves, Wpg.	1323
1984 -	Dwaine Wilson, Mtl.	1083	Willard Reaves, Wpg.	1733
1983 -	Alvin (Skip) Walker, Ott.	1431	Willard Reaves, Wpg.	898
1982 -	Alvin (Skip) Walker, Ott.	1141	William Miller, Wpg.	1076
1981 -	David Overstreet, Mtl.	952	Jimmy Sykes, Cal.	1107
1980 -	Richard Crump, Ott.	1074	Jimmy Sykes, Cal.	1263
1979 -	David Green, Mtl.	1678	Jim Germany, Edm.	1324
1978 -	Jimmy Edwards, Ham.	840	Mike Strickland, Sask.	1306
1977 -	Jimmy Edwards, Ham.	1581	Jim Washington, Wpg.	1262
1976 -	Art Green, Ott.	1257	Jim Washington, Wpg.	1277
1975 -	Art Green, Ott.	1188	Willie Burden, Cal.	1896
1974 -	Steve Ferrughelli, Mtl.	1134	George Reed, Sask.	1447
1973 -	Andy Hopkins, Ham.	1223	Roy Bell, Edm.	1455
1972 -	Dave Buchanan, Ham.	1163	Mack Herron, Wpg.	1527
1971 -	Leon McQuay, Tor.	977	Jim Evenson, B.C.	1237
1970 -	Bill Symons, Tor.	908	Hugh McKinnis, Cal.	1135
1969 -	Dennis Duncan, Mtl.	1037	George Reed, Sask.	1353
1968 -	Bill Symons, Tor.	1107	George Reed, Sask.	1222
1967 -	Bo Scott, Ott.	762	George Reed, Sask.	1471
1966 -	Don Lisbon, Mtl.	1007	George Reed, Sask.	1409
1965 -	Dave Thelen, Ott.	801	George Reed, Sask.	1768
1964 -	Ron Stewart, Ott.	867	Lovell Coleman, Cal.	1629
1963 -	George Dixon, Mtl.	1270	Lovell Coleman, Cal.	1343
1962 -	George Dixon, Mtl.	1520	Nub Beamer, B.C.	1161
1961 -	Don Clark, Mtl.	1143	Earl Lunsford, Cal.	1794
1960 -	Dave Thelen, Ott.	1407	Earl Lunsford, Cal.	1343
1959 -	Dave Thelen, Ott.	1339	Johnny Bright, Edm.	1340
1958 -	Gerry McDougall, Ham.	1109	Johnny Bright, Edm.	1722
1957 -	Gerry McDougall, Ham.	1053	Johnny Bright, Edm.	1679
1956 -	Pat Abbruzzi, Mtl.	1062	Normie Kwong, Edm.	1437
1955 -	Pat Abbruzzi, Mtl.	1248	Normie Kwong, Edm.	1250
1954 -	Alex Webster, Mtl.	984	Howard Waugh, Cal.	1043
1953 -			Billy Vessels, Edm.	926
1952 -			Johnny Bright, Cal.	815
1951 -			Normie Kwong, Edm.	933
1950 -			Tom Casey, Wpg.	637

THE THOUSAND YARD CLUB

			Carries	Yds.	Ave.	Long.	TDs.
1993	-	none.					
1992	-	Mike Richardson, Wpg.	211	1153	5.5	31	3
1991	-	Robert Mimbs, Wpg.	326	1769	5.4	47	15
	-	Reggie Barnes, Ott.	291	1486	5.1	57	10
	-	Jon Volpe, B.C.	239	1395	5.8	44	16
	-	Reggie Taylor, Edm.	198	1293	6.5	69	4
	-	Damon Allen, Ott.	129	1036	8.0	42	8
1990	-	Robert Mimbs, Wpg.	285	1341	4.7	32	6
	-	Reggie Barnes, Ott.	211	1260	6.0	58	5
	-	Tracy Ham, Edm.	136	1096	8.1	32	5
1989	-	Reggie Taylor, Edm.	237	1503	6.3	49	2
	-	Tim McCray, Sask.	218	1285	5.9	44	2
	-	Gill Fenerty, Tor.	245	1247	5.1	60	10
	-	Derrick McAdoo, Ham.	246	1039	4.2	45	11
	-	Tracy Ham, Edm.	125	1005	8.0	55	10
1988	-	Orville Lee, Ott.	232	1075	4.6	61	2
1987	-	Willard Reaves, Wpg.	271	1471	5.4	69	9
1986	-	Gary Allen, Cal.	205	1153	5.6	38	4
1985	-	Willard Reaves, Wpg.	267	1323	5.0	68	9
1984	-	Willard Reaves, Wpg.	304	1733	5.7	68	14
	-	Dwaine Wilson, Mtl.	226	1083	4.8	36	4
1983	-	Alvin (Skip) Walker, Ott.	238	1431	6.0	56	10
	-	Johnny Shepherd, Ham.	197	1069	5.4	62	1
1982	-	Alvin (Skip) Walker, Ott.	210	1141	5.4	35	13
	-	William Miller, Wpg.	202	1076	5.3	54	7
	-	Jimmy Sykes, Cal.	193	1046	5.4	84	11
1981	-	Jimmy Sykes, Cal.	240	1107	4.6	68	6
	-	Larry Key, B.C.	204	1098	5.4	60	17
1980	-	Jimmy Sykes, Cal.	222	1263	5.7	75	10
	-	Richard Crump, Ott.	228	1074	4.7	54	9
	-	William Miller, Wpg.	218	1053	4.8	53	4
	-	Jim Germany, Edm.	181	1019	5.6	51	10
1979	-	David Green, Mtl.	287	1678	5.8	51	11
	-	Jim Germany, Edm.	238	1324	5.6	40	9
	-	Larry Key, B.C.	204	1060	5.2	71	9
1978	-	Mike Strickland, Sask.	284	1306	4.6	37	7
	-	Larry Key, B.C.	215	1054	4.9	66	7
	-	Jim Washington, Wpg.	200	1032	5.2	31	6
	-	Jimmy Sykes, Cal.	204	1020	5.0	31	13
1977	-	Jimmy Edwards, Ham.	250	1581	6.3	69	6
	-	Jim Washington, Wpg.	252	1262	5.0	54	5
	-	Willie Burden, Cal.	220	1032	4.7	47	3
	-	Richard Holmes, Tor.-Ott.	178	1016	5.7	72	10
	-	Jim Germany, Edm.	211	1004	4.8	96	8
1976	-	Jim Washington, Wpg.	219	1277	5.8	68	12
	-	Art Green, Ott.	234	1257	5.4	69	13
	-	Mike Strickland, B.C.	223	1119	5.0	49	10
	-	Andy Hopkins, Mtl.	219	1075	4.9	41	3
	-	Jimmy Edwards, Ham.	194	1046	5.4	87	7
1975	-	Willie Burden, Cal.	332	1896	5.7	40	10
	-	George Reed, Sask.	323	1454	4.5	22	11
	-	Art Green, Ott.	258	1188	4.6	47	11

THE THOUSAND YARD CLUB (Cont'd)

Year		Player					
1975	-	Doyle Orange, Tor.	205	1055	5.1	56	5
1975	-	Roy Bell, Edm.	232	1006	4.3	33	5
1974	-	George Reed, Sask.	288	1447	5.0	26	5
	-	Roy Bell, Edm.	286	1341	4.7	70	4
	-	Lou Harris, B.C.	222	1239	5.6	62	8
	-	Monroe Eley, B.C.	191	1176	6.2	63	3
	-	Steve Ferrughelli, Mtl.	228	1134	5.0	26	3
1973	-	Roy Bell, Edm.	254	1455	5.7	76	5
	-	Andy Hopkins, Ham.	223	1223	5.5	97	5
	-	George Reed, Sask.	256	1193	4.7	23	12
	-	Johnny Musso, B.C.	220	1029	4.7	25	10
	-	John Harvey, Mtl.	137	1024	7.5	66	2
1972	-	Mack Herron, Wpg.	258	1527	5.9	65	11
	-	Dave Buchanan, Ham.	263	1163	4.4	52	4
	-	George Reed, Sask.	224	1069	4.8	59	13
1971	-	Jim Evenson, B.C.	260	1237	4.8	22	8
	-	George Reed, Sask.	218	1146	5.3	56	12
1970	-	Hugh McKinnis, Cal.	205	1135	5.5	37	9
	-	Jim Evenson, B.C.	204	1003	4.9	42	8
1969	-	George Reed, Sask.	273	1353	5.0	29	12
	-	Jim Evenson, B.C.	255	1287	5.0	63	4
	-	Dennis Duncan, Mtl.	199	1037	5.2	46	9
1968	-	George Reed, Sask.	268	1222	4.6	69	16
	-	Jim Evenson, B.C.	248	1220	4.9	32	4
	-	Bill Symons, Tor.	164	1107	6.8	75	9
1967	-	George Reed, Sask.	302	1471	4.9	50	15
	-	Jim Thomas, Edm.	172	1006	5.8	71	6
1966	-	George Reed, Sask.	266	1409	5.3	71	6
	-	Dave Raimey, Wpg.	188	1223	6.5	100	3
	-	Don Lisbon, Mtl.	199	1007	5.1	31	5
1965	-	George Reed, Sask.	274	1768	6.5	46	12
	-	Lovell Coleman, Cal.	249	1509	6.1	69	8
	-	Dave Raimey, Wpg.	130	1052	8.1	45	4
1964	-	Lovell Coleman, Cal.	260	1629	6.3	85	10
	-	Ed Buchanan, Sask.	179	1390	7.8	93	7
	-	Bob Swift, B.C.	229	1054	4.6	24	11
	-	George Reed, Sask.	185	1012	5.5	55	10
1963	-	Lovell Coleman, Cal.	237	1343	5.7	51	13
	-	George Dixon, Mtl.	189	1270	6.7	109	10
	-	Willie Fleming, B.C.	127	1234	9.7	97	5
1962	-	George Dixon, Mtl.	216	1520	7.0	75	11
	-	Nub Beamer, B.C.	208	1161	5.6	40	7
	-	Earl Lunsford, Cal.	180	1016	5.6	64	8
1961	-	Earl Lunsford, Cal.	296	1794	6.1	62	10
	-	Johnny Bright, Edm.	236	1350	5.7	81	11
	-	Don Clark, Mtl.	200	1143	5.7	106	5
	-	Leo Lewis, Wpg.	146	1035	7.1	63	8
	-	Dave Thelen, Ott.	180	1032	5.7	47	3
1960	-	Dave Thelen, Ott.	245	1407	5.7	52	3
	-	Earl Lunsford, Cal.	214	1343	6.3	85	13
	-	Johnny Bright, Edm.	251	1268	5.1	28	13
	-	Willie Fleming, B.C.	125	1051	8.4	98	10
	-	Ron Stewart, Ott.	139	1020	7.3	59	15
1959	-	Johnny Bright, Edm.	231	1340	5.8	53	11
	-	Dave Thelen, Ott.	228	1339	5.9	59	10
	-	Charlie Shepard, Wpg.	174	1076	6.2	45	6
	-	Earl Lunsford, Cal.	184	1027	5.6	22	10
	-	Gerry McDougall, Ham.	230	1010	4.4	70	7
1958	-	Johnny Bright, Edm.	296	1722	5.8	90	8
	-	Cookie Gilchrist, Sask.	235	1254	5.3	73	5
	-	Leo Lewis, Wpg.	167	1160	7.0	47	8
	-	Gerry McDougall, Ham.	212	1109	5.2	88	7
	-	Normie Kwong, Edm.	232	1033	4.5	23	10
1957	-	Johnny Bright, Edm.	259	1679	6.5	27	16
	-	Gerry James, Wpg.	197	1192	6.1	74	18
	-	Gerry McDougall, Ham.	177	1053	6.0	44	8
	-	Normie Kwong, Edm.	204	1050	5.1	22	15
1956	-	Normie Kwong, Edm.	232	1437	6.2	26	5
	-	Earl Lunsford, Cal.	216	1283	5.9	57	7
	-	Bob McNamara, Wpg.	178	1101	6.2	30	13
	-	Pat Abbruzzi, Mtl.	207	1062	5.1	30	17
1955	-	Normie Kwong, Edm.	241	1250	5.2	39	10
	-	Pat Abbruzzi, Mtl.	182	1248	6.9	63	17
	-	Gerry James, Wpg.	189	1205	6.4	60	7
1954	-	Howard Waugh, Cal.	166	1043	6.3	43	7

MOST 1000-YARD RUSHING SEASONS:

11 - George Reed, Sask.
5 - Johnny Bright, Edm.
- Earl Lunsford, Cal.
4 - Normie Kwong, Edm.
- Jim Evenson, B.C.
- Jimmy Sykes, Cal.

MOST CONSECUTIVE 1000-YARD RUSHING SEASONS:

6 - George Reed, Sask.
5 - George Reed, Sask.
- Johnny Bright, Edm.
4 - Normie Kwong, Edm.
- Earl Lunsford, Cal.
- Jim Evenson, B.C.

ALL-TIME LEADERS 100-YARD RUSHING GAMES:

66 - George Reed, Sask.
36 - Johnny Bright, Edm.
30 - Dave Thelen, Ott.-Tor.
28 - Earl Lunsford, Cal.
26 - Willard Reaves, Wpg.
- Lovell Coleman, Cal.
24 - George Dixon, Mtl.
22 - Willie Burden, Cal.
20 - Leo Lewis, Wpg.
19 - Normie Kwong, Cal.-Edm.
- James Sykes, Cal.-Wpg.

MOST 100-YARD RUSHING GAMES ONE SEASON:

10 - Willie Burden, Cal. 1975
- Willard Reaves, Wpg. 1984
- Robert Mimbs, Wpg. 1991
9 - Johnny Bright, Edm. 1957
- George Reed, Sask. 1965
8 - Johnny Bright, Edm. 1958
- Dave Thelen, Ott. 1960
- Earl Lunsford, Cal. 1961
- George Dixon, Mtl. 1962
8 - George Reed, Sask. 1974
- George Reed, Sask. 1975
- David Green, Mtl. 1979
- Pat Abbruzzi, Mtl. 1955
- Normie Kwong, Edm. 1956
- Lovell Coleman, Cal. 1964
- Jimmy Edwards, Ham. 1977
- Alvin (Skip) Walker, Ott. 1983

MOST 100-YARD RUSHING GAMES BY A QUARTERBACK ONE SEASON:

4 - Rickey Foggie, Tor. 1990
3 - Chuck Ealey, Ham. 1973
- Tracy Ham, Edm. 1990
2 - Matt Dunigan, Edm. 1984
- Tracy Ham, Edm. 1991
- Rickey Foggie, Tor. 1991

MOST CONSECUTIVE 100-YARD RUSHING GAMES:

8 - Johnny Bright, Edm. 1957
- Willard Reaves, Wpg. 1984
5 - Willie Burden, Cal. 1975
4 - Normie Kwong, Edm. 1956
- Earl Lunsford, Cal. 1961
- Lovell Coleman, Cal. 1964
4 - Lovell Coleman, Cal. 1965
- Bill Symons, Tor. 1968
- George Reed, Sask. 1969
- Willie Burden, Cal. 1974
- Mike Strickland, Sask. 1978
- David Green, Mtl. 1979

MOST CONSECUTIVE 100-YARD RUSHING GAMES BY A QUARTERBACK:

2 - Chuck Ealey, Ham. 1973
- Matt Dunigan, Edm. 1984

ALL-TIME LEADERS TOUCHDOWNS SCORED RUSHING:

134 - George Reed, Sask 1963-75
78 - Normie Kwong, Cal.-Edm. 1948-60
69 - Johnny Bright, Cal.-Edm. 1952-64
68 - Jackie Parker, Edm.-Tor.-B.C. 1954-68
65 - Jim Germany, Edm. 1977-83
- Matt Dunigan, Edm.-B.C.-Tor.-Wpg. 1983-93
57 - Gerry James, Wpg.-Sask. 1952-64
55 - Earl Lunsford, Cal. 1956-73
54 - Russ Jackson, Ott. 1958-69
- Blake Marshall, Edm. 1987-93

MOST TOUCHDOWNS SCORED RUSHING ONE SEASON:

18 - Gerry James, Wpg. 1957
- Jim Germany, Edm. 1981
17 - Pat Abbruzzi, Mtl. 1955
- Pat Abbruzzi, Mtl. 1956
- Larry Key, B.C. 1981
16 - Johnny Bright, Edm. 1957
- George Reed, Sask. 1968
- Blake Marshall, Edm. 1991
- Jon Volpe, B.C. 1991

MOST TOUCHDOWNS SCORED RUSHING ONE GAME:

5 - Earl Lunsford, Cal., Edm. at Cal., Sept. 3, 1962
4 - Pat Abbruzzi, Mtl., Mtl. at Tor., Oct. 22, 1955
- Bob McNamara, Wpg., Wpg. at B.C., Oct 13, 1956
- Dave Thelen, Ott., Tor. at Ott., Sept. 16, 1959
- Ferd Burket, Sask., Sask. at Wpg., Oct. 26, 1959
- Ron Stewart, Ott., Ott. at Mtl., Oct 10, 1960
- George Reed, Sask., Edm. at Reg., Oct 30, 1968
- Art Green, Ott., Ham. at Ott., Sept. 7, 1975
- Larry Key, B.C., B.C. at Cal., July 31, 1981
- Jim Germany, Edm., Ham. at Edm., Aug 1, 1981
- Willard Reaves, Wpg., Ham at Wpg., Sept. 15, 1984
- Milson Jones, Sask., Sask. at Wpg., Aug. 31, 1988
- Tim Jessie, Wpg., Wpg. at Ott., July 25, 1989

ALL-TIME PASS RECEPTION YARDAGE LEADERS:

	Seasons	C	Yds.	Ave.	LG.	TDs.
Ray Elgaard, Sask.	11	694	11,253	16.2	81	69
Brian Kelly, Edm.	9	575	11,169	19.4	97	97
Tom Scott, Wpg.-Edm.-Cal.	11	649	10,837	16.7	98	88
Tommy Joe Coffey, Edm.-Ham.-Tor.	14	650	10,320	15.9	83	63
Tony Gabriel, Ham.-Ott.	11	614	9,832	16.0	80	69
Rocky DiPietro, Ham.	14	706	9,762	13.8	80	45
Terry Evanshen, Mtl.-Cal.-Ham.-Tor.	14	600	9,697	16.2	109	80
Hal Patterson, Mtl.-Ham.	14	460	9,473	20.6	109	64
Jim Young, B.C.	13	522	9,248	17.7	87	65
James Murphy, Wpg.	8	573	9,036	15.8	86	61
Joe Poplawski, Wpg.	9	549	8,341	15.2	68	48

MOST PASS RECEPTION YARDAGE ONE SEASON:

2003 - Terry Greer, Tor. 1983
1914 - Hal Patterson, Mtl. 1956
1826 - Darrell K. Smith, Tor. 1990

MOST PASS RECEPTION YARDAGE ONE SEASON BY A FIRST-YEAR PLAYER:

1530 - Matt Clark, B.C. 1991
1300 - Raghib Ismail, Tor. 1991
1098 - Brian Kelly, Edm. 1979

MOST PASS RECEPTION YARDAGE ONE GAME:

338 - Hal Patterson, Mtl. (11 catches), Mtl. at Ham., Sept. 29, 1956
270 - Tyron Gray, B.C. (9 catches), B.C. at Edm., Sept. 13, 1981
266 - Brian Kelly, Edm. (13 catches), Mtl. at Edm., Oct. 15, 1983

ALL-TIME LEADERS PASS RECEPTIONS:

			Seasons	Earliest	Latest
706	-	Rocky DiPietro, Ham.	14	1978	1991
694	-	Ray Elgaard, Sask.	11	1983	1993
650	-	Tommy Joe Coffey, Edm.-Ham.-Tor.	14	1959	1973
649	-	Tom Scott, Wpg.-Edm.-Cal.	11	1974	1984
614	-	Tony Gabriel, Ham.-Ott.	11	1971	1981
600	-	Terry Evanshen, Mtl.-Cal.-Ham.-Tor.	14	1965	1978
580	-	Craig Ellis, Wpg.-Cal.-Sask.-Tor.-Edm.	10	1982	1993
575	-	Brian Kelly, Edm.	9	1979	1987
573	-	James Murphy, Wpg.	8	1983	1990
553	-	Tom Forzani, Cal.	11	1973	1983

MOST PASS RECEPTIONS ONE SEASON:

118 - Allen Pitts, Cal. 1991
116 - James Murphy, Wpg. 1986
113 - Terry Greer, Tor. 1983

MOST PASS RECEPTIONS ONE SEASON BY A FIRST-YEAR PLAYER:

79 - Matt Clark, B.C. 1991
75 - Joe Poplawski, Wpg. 1978
67 - Morris Bailey, Edm. 1950

MOST PASS RECEPTIONS ONE GAME:

16 - Terry Greer, Tor. (230 yards), Tor. at Ott., Aug. 19, 1983
- Brian Wiggins, Cal. (230 yards), Cal at Sask., Oct. 23, 1993

MOST PASS RECEPTIONS ONE GAME (Cont'd)

15 - George McGowan, Edm. (249 yards), Edm. at Sask., Sept. 3, 1973
- Eugene Goodlow, Wpg. (184 yards), Cal. at Wpg., Nov. 1, 1981
- Terry Greer, Tor. (206 yards), Tor. at Wpg., Oct. 11, 1982

14 - Joey Walters, Sask. (191 yards), Sask. at Wpg., Oct. 21, 1979
- Mike Levenseller, Cal. (138 yards), Sask. at Cal., Aug. 19, 1984
- Eric Streater, B.C. (234 yards), Ham. at B.C., Oct. 6, 1989
- Lorenzo Graham, B.C. (132 yards), Sask. at B.C., Aug. 2, 1990
- Ray Alexander, B.C. (222 yards), B.C. at Sask., Aug. 21, 1991

YEAR-BY-YEAR PASS RECEPTION LEADERS:

	East	No.	West	No.
1993 -	David Williams, Wpg.	84	David Sapunjis, Cal.	103
1992 -	Stephen Jones, Ott.	75	Allen Pitts, Cal.	103
1991 -	Darrell K. Smith, Tor.	73	Allen Pitts, Cal.	118
1990 -	Darrell K. Smith, Tor.	93	Craig Ellis, Edm.	106
1989 -	Tony Champion, Ham.	95	Donald Narcisse, Sask.	81
1988 -	James Murphy, Wpg.	76	David Williams, B.C.	83
1987 -	Marc Lewis, Ott.	94	Jim Sandusky, B.C.	80
1986 -	James Hood, Mtl.	95	James Murphy, Wpg.	116
1985 -	Terry Greer, Tor.	78	Craig Ellis, Sask.	102
1984 -	Rocky DiPietro, Ham.	71	Craig Ellis, Sask.	91
-	Paul Pearson, Tor.	71		
1983 -	Terry Greer, Tor.	113	Brian Kelly, Edm.	104
1982 -	Nick Arakgi, Mtl.	89	Joey Walters, Sask.	102
1981 -	James Scott, Mtl.	81	Eugene Goodlow, Wpg.	100
1980 -	Bob Gaddis, Tor.	68	Mike Holmes, Wpg.	79
1979 -	Leif Pettersen, Ham.	56	Waddell Smith, Edm.	74
1978 -	Tony Gabriel, Ott.	67	Joe Poplawski, Wpg.	75
1977 -	Tony Gabriel, Ott.	65	Molly McGee, Sask.	68
1976 -	Tony Gabriel, Ott.	72	Rhett Dawson, Sask.	65
1975 -	Tony Gabriel, Ott.	65	George McGowan, Edm.	98
1974 -	Tony Gabriel, Ham.	61	Rudy Linterman, Cal.	64
1973 -	Johnny Rodgers, Mtl.	41	George McGowan, Edm.	81
1972 -	Eric Allen, Tor.	53	Jim Thorpe, Wpg.	70
1971 -	Terry Evanshen, Mtl.	50	Jim Thorpe, Wpg.	70
			Herman Harrison, Cal.	70
1970 -	Dave Fleming, Ham.	56	Herman Harrison, Cal.	70
1969 -	Tommy Joe Coffey, Ham.	71	Herman Harrison, Cal.	68
1968 -	Bobby Taylor, Tor.	56	Ken Nielsen, Wpg.	68
1967 -	Bobby Taylor, Tor.	53	Terry Evanshen, Cal.	96
1966 -	Bobby Taylor, Tor.	56	Terry Evanshen, Cal.	67
1965 -	Terry Evanshen, Mtl.	37	Tommy Joe Coffey, Edm.	81
1964 -	Dick Shatto, Tor.	53	Tommy Joe Coffey, Edm.	81
1963 -	Dick Shatto, Tor.	67	Bobby Taylor, Cal.	74
1962 -	Dick Shatto, Tor.	47	Tommy Joe Coffey, Edm.	65
1961 -	Dave Mann, Tor.	53	Farrell Funston, Wpg.	47
1960 -	Dave Mann, Tor.	61	Gene Filipski, Cal.	47
-	Hal Patterson, Mtl.	61		
1959 -	Red O'Quinn, Mtl.	53	Ernie Pitts, Wpg.	68
1958 -	Red O'Quinn, Mtl.	65	Jack Hill Sask.	60
1957 -	Red O'Quinn, Mtl.	61	Jack Gotta, Cal.	39
1956 -	Hal Patterson, Mtl.	88	Bud Grant, Wpg.	63
1955 -	Red O'Quinn, Mtl.	78	Willie Roberts, Cal.	59
1954 -	Al Pfeifer, Tor.	68	Bud Grant, Wpg.	49
1953 -			Bud Grant, Wpg.	68
1952 -			Paul Salata, Cal.	65
1951 -			Bob Shaw, Cal.	61
1950 -			Morris Bailey, Edm.	67

MOST GAMES CATCHING PASSES:

181 - Terry Evanshen, Mtl.-Cal.-Ham.-Tor.
173 - Tommy Joe Coffey, Edm.-Ham.-Tor.
164 - Peter Dalla Riva, Mtl.

MOST CONSECUTIVE GAMES CATCHING PASSES:

137 - Tony Gabriel, Ham.-Ott. (1973-81)
119 - Craig Ellis, Wpg.-Cal.-Sask.-Tor.-Edm. (1983-1992)
116 - Tom Scott, Wpg.-Edm.-Cal. (1977-84)

MOST CONSECUTIVE SEASONS CATCHING PASSES:

16 - Garney Henley, Ham. (1960-75)

14 - Hal Patterson, Mtl.-Ham. (1954-67)
- Tommy Grant, Ham.-Wpg. (1956-69)
- Terry Evanshen, Mtl.-Cal.-Ham.-Tor. (1965-78)
- Peter Dalla Riva, Mtl. (1968-81)

13 - Johnny Bright, Cal.-Edm. (1952-64)
- Ron Stewart, Ott. (1958-70)
- Bobby Taylor, Cal.-Tor.-Ham.-Edm. (1962-74)
- George Reed, Sask. (1963-75)
- Jim Young, B.C. (1967-79)

MOST SEASONS CATCHING PASSES ALL GAMES:

8 - Craig Ellis, Wpg.-Cal.-Sask.-Tor.-Edm. (1983-92)
7 - Tony Gabriel, Ham.-Ott. (1973-81)
6 - Bobby Taylor, Cal.-Tor.-Ham.-Edm. (1962-74)
- Tom Scott, Wpg.-Edm.-Cal. (1974-84)

AVERAGE GAIN PASS RECEIVING:

Career (200 or more catches)

Ave.		Seasons	Catches	Yds.	Earliest	Latest
22.4 -	Whit Tucker, Ott.	9	272	6092	1962	1970
22.0 -	Bob Simpson, Ott.	9	274	6034	1954	1962
20.6 -	Hal Patterson, Mtl.-Ham.	14	460	9473	1954	1967
19.9 -	Tommy Grant, Ham.-Wpg.	14	329	6542	1956	1969
19.6 -	Jim Thorpe, Tor.-Wpg.	4	209	4091	1969	1972

AVERAGE GAIN PASS RECEIVING ONE SEASON:

(44 or more catches)

Ave.		Catches	Yds.	Season
25.0 -	Margene Adkins, Ott.	56	1402	1969
23.9 -	Brian Kelly, Edm.	68	1626	1987
23.4 -	Tommy Grant, Ham.	44	1029	1964

AVERAGE GAIN PASS RECEIVING ONE GAME:

(3 or more catches)

72.0 - Bob Shaw, Cal. (3 for 216 yards), Cal. at Edm., Oct. 11, 1952
65.3 - Bob Simpson, Ott. (3 for 196 yards), Ott. at Tor., Sept. 17, 1955
57.7 - Jim Thorpe, Tor. (3 for 173 yards), Tor. at Mtl., Aug. 5, 1969

THE THOUSAND YARD CLUB

		C	Yds.	Ave.	LG.	TDs.
1993	- David Sapunjis, Cal	103	1484	14.4	75	15
	- Ray Elgaard, Sask.	89	1393	15.7	64	8
	- Jeff Fairholm, Sask.	72	1391	19.3	78	9
	- Rod Harris, Sac.	90	1379	15.3	56	7
	- Eddie Brown, Edm.	67	1378	20.6	75	15
	- Gerald Wilcox, Wpg.	79	1340	17.0	75	10
	- Ray Alexander, B.C.	77	1300	16.9	43	4
	- Jock Climie, Ott.	67	1281	19.1	89	11
	- Stephen Jones, Ott.	74	1279	17.3	76	6
	- Donald Narcisse, Sask.	83	1171	14.1	44	9
	- David Williams, Wpg.	84	1144	13.6	44	15
	- Will Moore, Cal.	73	1083	14.8	55	12
	- Earl Winfield, Ham.	61	1076	17.6	79	5
	- Titus Dixon, Sac.	61	1074	17.6	90	5
	- Darren Flutie, B.C.	79	1068	13.5	45	5
	- Gerald Alphin, Wpg.	55	1052	19.1	54	4
	- Manny Hazard, Tor.	61	1033	16.9	61	8
	- Derrick Crawford, Cal.	57	1007	17.7	75	10
1992	- Allen Pitts, Cal.	103	1591	15.4	53	13
	- Ray Elgaard, Sask.	91	1444	15.9	51	11
	- Stephen Jones, Ott.	75	1400	18.7	55	10
	- Jeff Fairholm, Sask.	74	1344	18.2	76	6
	- Darren Flutie, B.C.	90	1336	14.8	76	4
	- David Sapunjis, Cal.	77	1317	17.1	59	4
	- Jim Sandusky, Edm.	78	1243	15.9	68	15
	- Larry Thompson, Wpg.	61	1192	19.5	62	10
	- Ken Evraire, Ham.	61	1081	17.7	53	3
	- Carl Bland, Cal.	72	1052	14.6	79	4
	- Donald Narcisse, Sask.	80	1034	12.9	65	7
	- Craig Ellis, Edm.	62	1018	16.4	41	10
	- Mike Trevathan, B.C.	71	1004	14.1	50	5
1991	- Allen Pitts, Cal.	118	1764	14.9	87	15
	- Ray Alexander, B.C.	104	1605	15.4	31	3
	- Matt Clark, B.C.	79	1530	19.4	89	10
	- Darrell K. Smith, Tor.	73	1399	19.2	89	9
	- Raghib Ismail, Tor.	64	1300	20.3	87	9
	- Jeff Fairholm, Sask.	70	1239	17.7	99	13
	- David Williams, Edm.-Tor.	66	1149	17.4	68	15
	- Craig Ellis, Edm.	66	1133	17.2	52	10
	- Ray Elgaard, Sask.	62	1069	17.2	59	11
	- Jim Sandusky, Edm.	63	1063	16.9	65	10
	- Donald Narcisse, Sask.	76	1043	13.7	59	7
1990	- Darrell K. Smith, Tor.	93	1826	19.6	88	20
	- Craig Ellis, Edm.	106	1654	15.6	63	17
	- Ray Elgaard, Sask.	94	1494	15.9	81	11
	- Stephen Jones, Ott.	59	1182	20.0	66	11
	- Allen Pitts, Cal.	65	1172	18.0	67	6
	- Donald Narcisse, Sask.	86	1129	13.1	47	9
	- Ray Alexander, B.C.	65	1120	17.2	44	9
	- Derrick Crawford, Cal.	57	1096	19.2	58	11
	- Earl Winfield, Ham.	62	1054	17.0	75	13
	- Jeff Boyd, Tor.	59	1053	17.8	76	8
	- Jay Christensen, B.C.	62	1036	16.7	48	8
	- Larry Willis, B.C.-Edm.	63	1030	16.3	48	6
1989	- Tony Champion, Ham.	95	1656	17.4	83	15
	- Gerald Alphin, Ott.	68	1471	21.6	78	10
	- Larry Willis, Cal.	73	1451	19.9	80	10
	- David Williams, B.C.	79	1446	18.3	71	14
	- Donald Narcisse, Sask.	81	1419	17.5	74	11
	- Craig Ellis, Edm.	80	1264	15.8	59	9
	- Tom Richards, Edm.	60	1239	20.7	63	7
	- James Murphy, Wpg.	68	1150	16.9	58	8
	- Eric Streater, B.C.	76	1091	14.4	83	6
1988	- David Williams, B.C.	83	1468	17.7	77	18
	- James Murphy, Wpg.	76	1409	18.5	72	10
	- Emanuel Tolbert, Cal.	67	1328	19.8	61	7
	- Larry Willis, Cal.	73	1328	18.2	72	9
	- Gerald Alphin, Ott.	64	1307	20.4	61	5
	- Darrell K. Smith, Tor.	73	1306	17.9	67	7
	- Ray Elgaard, Sask.	69	1290	18.7	75	6
	- Earl Winfield, Ham.	60	1213	20.2	73	8
	- Jeff Boyd, Tor.	65	1159	17.8	78	11
	- Jim Sandusky, Edm.	55	1089	19.8	59	8
1987	- Brian Kelly, Edm.	68	1626	23.9	97	13
	- Steve Stapler, Ham.	85	1516	17.8	81	13
	- Larry Willis, Cal.	74	1477	20.0	86	10
	- Jim Sandusky, B.C.	80	1437	18.0	75	12
	- Darrell K. Smith, Tor.	79	1392	17.6	54	10
	- Perry Tuttle, Wpg.	75	1310	17.5	72	8
	- Marc Lewis, Ott.	94	1195	12.7	38	3
	- Stephen Jones, Edm.	55	1147	20.9	89	8
	- James Murphy, Wpg.	84	1130	13.5	61	10
	- Jeff Boyd, Wpg.	57	1039	18.2	67	9
	- Gerald Alphin, Ott.	67	1029	15.4	57	8
	- Emanuel Tolbert, Cal.	57	1014	17.8	62	6
1986	- James Murphy, Wpg.	116	1746	15.1	82	12
	- Ray Alexander, Cal.	88	1590	18.1	59	10
	- James Hood, Mtl.	95	1411	14.9	58	2
	- Perry Tuttle, Wpg.	83	1373	16.5	85	8
	- Emanuel Tolbert, Cal.	69	1286	18.6	51	11
	- Tony Champion, Ham.	74	1216	16.4	75	6
	- Marc Lewis, Ott.	71	1197	16.9	72	4
	- Chris Woods, Tor.	61	1163	19.1	54	6
	- Rocky DiPietro, Ham.	86	1087	12.6	47	4
	- Joe Poplawski, Wpg.	74	1075	14.5	65	8
	- Ray Elgaard, Sask.	55	1003	18.2	59	4
1985	- Mervyn Fernandez, B.C.	95	1727	18.2	90	15
	- Jeff Boyd, Wpg.	76	1372	18.1	105	14
	- Terry Greer, Tor.	78	1323	17.0	65	9
	- Joe Poplawski, Wpg.	75	1271	16.9	47	6
	- Ray Elgaard, Sask.	79	1193	15.1	44	4
	- Emanuel Tolbert, Cal.	67	1124	16.8	70	6
	- Jim Sandusky, B.C.	58	1073	18.5	68	7
	- Brian Kelly, Edm.	59	1034	17.5	54	6
1984	- Mervyn Fernandez, B.C.	89	1486	16.7	78	17
	- Brian Kelly, Edm.	66	1310	19.8	85	18

THE THOUSAND YARD CLUB (Cont'd)

Year		Player					
1984	-	James Murphy, Wpg.	70	1220	17.4	86	12
	-	Terry Greer, Tor.	70	1189	17.0	61	14
	-	Jeff Boyd, Wpg.	65	1106	17.0	79	11
	-	Nick Arakgi, Mtl.	67	1078	16.1	82	10
	-	Rocky DiPietro, Ham.	71	1063	15.0	80	5
	-	Ron Robinson, Mtl.-B.C.	55	1016	18.5	75	6
1983	-	Terry Greer, Tor.	113	2003	17.7	72	8
	-	Brian Kelly, Edm.	104	1812	17.4	48	11
	-	Ron Robinson, Sask.-Mtl.	73	1379	18.9	60	14
	-	Mervyn Fernandez, B.C.	78	1284	16.5	74	10
	-	Tom Scott, Edm.	80	1234	15.4	48	9
	-	Emanuel Tolbert, Tor.	70	1225	17.5	80	11
	-	Chris DeFrance, Sask.	71	1165	16.4	88	9
	-	James Murphy, Wpg.	61	1126	18.5	82	4
1982	-	Joey Walters, Sask.	102	1692	16.6	72	7
	-	Tom Scott, Edm.	91	1518	16.7	49	13
	-	Terry Greer, Tor.	85	1466	17.2	61	11
	-	Keith Baker, Ham.	80	1282	16.0	75	8
	-	Rocky DiPietro, Ham.	85	1160	13.6	49	5
	-	Willie Armstead, Cal.	61	1081	17.7	74	5
	-	Chris DeFrance, Sask.	78	1062	13.6	44	2
	-	Nick Arakgi, Mtl.	89	1062	11.9	46	6
	-	Mervyn Fernandez, B.C.	64	1046	16.3	84	8
	-	Rick House, Wpg.	63	1020	16.2	49	6
1981	-	Joey Walters, Sask.	91	1715	18.8	72	14
	-	Brian Kelly, Edm.	74	1665	22.5	91	11
	-	Eugene Goodlow, Wpg.	100	1494	14.9	85	14
	-	Tyrone Gray, B.C.	63	1428	22.7	91	9
	-	James Scott, Mtl.	81	1422	17.6	77	6
	-	Joe Poplawski, Wpg.	84	1271	15.1	55	8
	-	Tom Scott, Edm.	73	1240	17.0	46	8
	-	Keith Baker, Ham.	68	1218	17.9	81	11
	-	Chris DeFrance, Sask.	64	1195	18.7	100	5
	-	Rick House, Wpg.	61	1102	18.1	81	10
	-	Waddell Smith, Edm.	65	1077	16.6	50	9
	-	Billy Johnson, Mtl.	65	1060	16.3	54	5
	-	John Holland, Cal.	56	1017	18.2	81	4
	-	Tony Gabriel, Ott.	73	1006	13.8	46	5
1980	-	Tom Scott, Edm.	73	1245	17.1	46	13
	-	Bob Gaddis, Tor.	68	1112	16.4	68	3
	-	Mike Holmes, Wpg.	79	1092	13.8	47	10
1979	-	Waddell Smith, Edm.	74	1214	16.4	77	13
	-	Brian Kelly, Edm.	61	1098	18.0	80	11
	-	Mike Holmes, Wpg.	60	1034	17.2	75	10
1978	-	Tom Scott, Edm.	67	1091	16.3	46	10
	-	Tony Gabriel, Ott.	67	1070	16.0	80	11
1977	-	Tony Gabriel, Ott.	65	1362	21.0	75	8
	-	Tom Scott, Wpg.	66	1079	16.3	98	10
1976	-	Tony Gabriel, Ott.	72	1320	18.3	62	14
1975	-	George McGowan, Edm.	98	1472	15.0	55	8
	-	Rhett Dawson, Sask.	69	1191	17.3	85	10
	-	Tony Gabriel, Ott.	65	1115	17.2	46	10
1974	-	Johnny Rodgers, Mtl.	60	1024	17.1	70	7
1973	-	George McGowan, Edm.	81	1123	13.9	44	9
1972	-	Jimmy Young, B.C.	63	1362	21.6	73	11
	-	Jim Thorpe, Wpg.	70	1260	18.0	97	11
	-	Eric Allen, Tor.	53	1067	20.0	62	8
	-	George McGowan, Edm.	54	1015	18.8	61	11
	-	Gerry Shaw, Cal.	65	1002	15.4	70	12
1971	-	Jim Thorpe, Wpg.	70	1436	20.5	94	9
	-	Bob LaRose, Wpg.	58	1080	18.6	70	7
1970	-	Hugh Oldham, Ott.	45	1043	23.2	73	13
	-	Jimmy Young, B.C.	54	1041	19.3	80	6
	-	Herman Harrison, Cal.	70	1024	14.6	47	12
1969	-	Margene Adkins, Ott.	56	1402	25.0	74	9
	-	Bobby Taylor, Tor.	59	1183	20.1	79	5
	-	Tommy Joe Coffey, Ham.	71	1110	15.6	68	11
	-	Herman Harrison, Cal.	68	1043	15.3	43	4
1968	-	Herman Harrison, Cal.	67	1306	19.5	48	7
	-	Ken Nielsen, Wpg.	68	1031	15.2	72	5
	-	Terry Evanshen, Cal.	63	1002	15.9	43	9
1967	-	Terry Evanshen, Cal.	96	1662	17.3	63	17
	-	Whit Tucker, Ott.	52	1171	22.5	94	9
	-	Ken Nielsen, Wpg.	76	1121	14.8	49	9
1966	-	Terry Evanshen, Cal.	67	1200	17.9	109	9
	-	Hugh Campbell, Sask.	66	1109	16.8	73	17
1965	-	Hugh Campbell, Sask.	73	1329	18.2	53	10
	-	Tommy Joe Coffey, Edm.	81	1286	15.8	65	2
1964	-	Tommy Joe Coffey, Edm.	81	1142	14.1	72	6
	-	Tommy Grant, Ham.	44	1029	23.4	66	7
	-	Hugh Campbell, Sask.	65	1000	15.3	35	11
1963	-	Tommy Joe Coffey, Edm.	61	1104	18.1	79	5
	-	Bobby Taylor, Cal.	74	1057	14.2	60	6
1960	-	Dave Mann, Tor.	61	1382	22.6	103	13
	-	Hal Patterson, Mtl.	61	1121	18.4	98	7
1959	-	Ernie Pitts, Wpg.	68	1126	16.5	65	16
	-	Joe Bob Smith, Edm.	62	1108	17.8	80	8
1958	-	Jack Hill, Sask.	60	1065	17.7	91	14
1957	-	Red O'Quinn, Mtl.	61	1006	16.5	54	4
1956	-	Hal Patterson, Mtl.	88	1914	21.8	109	12
	-	Bob Simpson, Ott.	47	1030	21.9	58	7
1955	-	Al Pfeifer, Tor.	75	1342	17.9	54	15
	-	Red O'Quinn, Mtl.	78	1097	14.1	38	3
	-	Willie Roberts, Cal.	59	1091	18.4	76	5
1954	-	Al Pfeifer, Tor.	68	1142	16.8	63	6
	-	Red O'Quinn, Mtl.	62	1024	16.5	89	6
1952	-	Bob Shaw, Cal.	51	1094	21.4	82	9
	-	Paul Salata, Cal.	65	1088	16.7	67	11
1951	-	Neill Armstrong, Wpg.	56	1024	18.3	85	10
1950	-	Morris Bailey, Edm.	67	1060	15.8	51	4

MOST 1000-YARD PASS RECEIVING SEASONS:

7 - Ray Elgaard, Sask.
6 - Tom Scott, Wpg.-Edm.-Cal.
- Brian Kelly, Edm.
- James Murphy, Wpg.
5 - Tony Gabriel, Ham.-Ott.
- Emanuel Tolbert, Sask.-Tor.-Cal.-B.C.
- Donald Narcisse, Sask.
4 - Tommy Joe Coffey, Edm.-Ham.-Tor.
- Mervyn Fernandez, B.C.
- Ray Alexander, Calgary-B.C.
- Stephen Jones, Sask.-Edm.-Ott.
- Terry Greer, Tor.
- Larry Willis, Cal.-B.C.-Edm.-Wpg.
4 - Jeff Boyd, Wpg.-Tor.
- James Murphy, Wpg.
- Jim Sandusky, B.C.-Edm.
- Don Narcisse, Sask.
4 - Darrell K. Smith, Tor.
- Craig Ellis, Wpg.-Cal.-Sask.-Tor.-Edm.

MOST 100-YARD PASS RECEIVING GAMES:

41 - Brian Kelly, Edm.
40 - Tommy Scott, Wpg.-Edm.-Cal.
34 - Hal Patterson, Mtl.-Ham.

MOST 100-YARD PASS RECEIVING GAMES ONE SEASON:

11	-	Terry Greer, Tor.	1983
	-	Hal Patterson, Mtl.	1956
	-	Joey Walters, Sask.	1981
9	-	Joey Walters, Sask.	1982
	-	Brian Kelly, Edm.	1981
	-	Darrell K. Smith, Tor.	1990
	-	Matt Clark, B.C.	1991
	-	Allen Pitts, Cal.	1991
8	-	Al Pfeifer, Tor.	1955
	-	Terry Evanshen, Cal.	1967
8	-	James Scott, Mtl.	1981
	-	Brian Kelly, Edm.	1983
	-	Jeff Boyd, Wpg.	1985
	-	Ray Alexander, Cal.	1986
	-	James Murphy, Wpg.	1986
	-	Tony Champion, Ham.	1989
	-	David Williams, B.C.	1989
	-	Gerald Alphin, Ott.	1989
	-	Ray Alexander, B.C.	1991

CONSECUTIVE 100-YARD PASS RECEIVING GAMES:

8	-	Hal Patterson, Mtl.	1956
	-	Terry Greer, Tor.	1983
5	-	Joey Walters, Sask. (twice)	1981
	-	Tom Scott, Edm.	1982
	-	Brian Kelly, Edm.	1983
4	-	Red O'Quinn, Mtl.	1955
	-	Whit Tucker, Ott.	1967
	-	Joey Walters, Sask. (twice)	1982
4	-	Margene Adkins, Ott.	1969
	-	Brian DeRoo, Mtl.	1982
	-	Tony Gabriel, Ott.	1977
	-	Ron Robinson, Sask.-Mtl.	1983
	-	Terry Greer, Tor.	1984
	-	Ray Alexander, Cal.	1986
	-	Gerald Alphin, Ott.	1989
	-	Craig Ellis, Edm.	1990

ALL-TIME TOUCHDOWN LEADERS ON PASS RECEPTIONS:

No.			Seasons	Earliest	Latest
97	-	Brian Kelly, Edm.	9	1979	1987
88	-	Tom Scott, Wpg.-Edm.-Cal.	11	1974	1984
80	-	Terry Evanshen, Mtl.-Cal.-Ham.-Tor.	14	1965	1978
69	-	Tony Gabriel, Ham.-Ott.	11	1971	1981
	-	Jeff Boyd, Wpg.-Tor.	9	1983	1991
	-	Ray Elgaard, Sask.	11	1983	1993
65	-	Bob Simpson, Ott.	13	1950	1962
	-	Jim Young, B.C.	13	1967	1979
64	-	Hal Patterson, Mtl.-Ham.	14	1954	1967
63	-	Tommy Joe Coffey, Edm.-Ham.-Tor.	14	1959	1973
62	-	Tom Forzani, Cal.	11	1973	1983

MOST TOUCHDOWNS ON PASS RECEPTIONS ONE SEASON:

20	-	Darrell K. Smith, Tor.	1990
18	-	Brian Kelly, Edm.	1984
	-	David Williams, B.C.	1988
17	-	Hugh Campbell, Sask.	1966
17	-	Terry Evanshen, Cal.	1967
	-	Mervyn Fernandez, B.C.	1984
	-	Craig Ellis, Edm.	1990

MOST TOUCHDOWNS ON PASS RECEPTIONS ONE GAME:

5 - Ernie Pitts, Wpg., Wpg. at Sask., Aug. 29, 1959
4 - Royal Copeland, Tor., Tor. at Mtl., Oct. 27, 1945
- Garney Henley, Ham., Sask. at Ham., Oct. 15, 1962
- Herman Harrison, Cal., Cal. at Wpg., Sept. 2, 1970
- Terry Evanshen, Ham., Ham. at Ott., Sept. 7, 1975
- Brian Kelly, Edm., Ott. at Edm., June 30, 1984
- Mervyn Fernandez, B.C., Edm. at B.C., July 6, 1984
- Mervyn Fernandez, B.C., B.C. at Ott., Oct. 13, 1984
- Mervyn Fernandez, B.C., Cal. at B.C., Aug. 17, 1985
- David Williams, B.C., Edm. at B.C., Oct. 29, 1988
- Darrell K. Smith, Tor., Ham. at Tor., Sept. 29, 1990

MOST GAMES CATCHING TOUCHDOWN PASSES:

71 - Brian Kelly, Edm.
70 - Tommy Scott, Wpg.-Edm.-Cal.
61 - Terry Evanshen, Mtl.-Cal.-Ham.-Tor.

MOST CONSECUTIVE GAMES CATCHING TOUCHDOWN PASSES:

10 - Terry Evanshen, Cal. (1967-68)
7 - Tony Gabriel, Ott. (1978)
6 - Al Pfeifer, Tor. (1954-56)
- Joe Pal, Mtl. (1955)
6 - Ron Howell, Ham. (1959)
- Ken Nielsen, Wpg. (1966-67)
- Hugh Campbell, Sask. (1969)
- Tommy Scott, Edm. (1982)

ALL-TIME PASSING LEADERS

No.			Seasons	Earliest	Latest
6233	-	Ron Lancaster, Ott.-Sask.	19	1960	1978
4657	-	Tom Clements, Ott.-Sask.-Ham.-Wpg.	12	1975	1987
4535	-	Dieter Brock, Wpg.-Ham.	11	1974	1984
4191	-	Matt Dunigan, Edm-B.C.-Tor.-Wpg.	11	1983	1993
3413	-	Kent Austin, Sask.	7	1987	1993
3316	-	Tom Burgess, Ott.-Sask.-Wpg.	8	1986	1993
3130	-	Roy Dewalt, B.C.-Wpg.-Ott.	9	1980	1988
3121	-	Damon Allen, Edm.	9	1985	1993
3013	-	Condredge Holloway, Ott.-Tor.-B.C.	13	1975	1987
3008	-	Joe Paopao, B.C.-Sask.-Ott.	11	1978	1990
2876	-	Bernie Faloney, Edm.-Ham.-Mtl.-B.C.	12	1954	1967
2829	-	Sam Etcheverry, Mtl.	7	1954	1960

MOST PASSES THROWN ONE SEASON:

770	-	Kent Austin, Sask.	1992
730	-	Doug Flutie, B.C.	1991
715	-	Kent Austin, Sask.	1993
703	-	Doug Flutie, Cal.	1993
701	-	David Archer, Sac.	1993

MOST PASSES THROWN ONE GAME:

65 - Kent Austin, Sask., Edm. at Sask., Sept.15, 1991
63 - Doug Flutie, Cal., Sask. at Cal., Aug. 7, 1992
62 - Joe Adams, Sask., Tor. at Sask., July 29, 1983
- Kent Austin, Sask., B.C. at Sask., Aug. 13, 1992

ALL-TIME PASS COMPLETION LEADERS:

No.			Seasons	Earliest	Latest
3384	-	Ron Lancaster, Ott.-Sask.	19	1960	1978
2807	-	Tom Clements, Ott.-Sask.-Ham.-Wpg.	12	1975	1987
2602	-	Dieter Brock, Wpg.-Ham.	11	1974	1984

LOOK AT LEADING PASSERS (Ranked in Yardage)

	Seasons	Att.	Comp.	Yds.	Pct.	Ave.	I/C	LG	TDs.
Ron Lancaster, Ott.-Sask.	19	6233	3384	50535	54.3	14.9	396	102	333
Tom Clements, Ott.-Sask.-Ham.-Wpg.	12	4657	2807	39041	60.3	13.9	214	105	252
Dieter Brock, Wpg-Ham.	11	4535	2602	34830	57.4	13.4	158	98	210
Matt Dunigan, Edm.-B.C.-Tor.-Wpg.	11	4191	2329	33256	55.6	14.3	175	89	226
Sam Etcheverry, Mtl.	7	2829	1630	25582	57.6	15.7	163	109	183
Condredge Holloway, Ott.-Tor.-B.C.	13	3013	1710	25193	56.8	14.7	94	80	155
Russ Jackson, Ott.	12	2530	1356	24592	53.6	18.1	125	107	185
Bernie Faloney, Edm.-Ham.-Mtl.-B.C.	12	2876	1493	24264	51.9	16.3	201	96	151
Roy Dewalt, B.C.-Wpg.-Ott.	9	3130	1803	24147	57.6	13.4	96	90	132
Joe Kapp, Cal.-B.C.	8	2709	1476	22725	54.5	15.4	130	106	136
Tom Wilkinson, Tor.-B.C.-Edm.	15	2662	1613	22579	60.6	14.0	126	87	154
Joe Paopao, B.C.-Sask.-Ott.	11	3008	1721	22474	57.2	13.1	157	94	117
John Hufnagel, Cal.-Sask.-Wpg.-Sask.	12	2694	1495	21594	55.5	14.4	131	85	127
Peter Liske, Tor.-Cal.-B.C.	7	2571	1449	21266	56.4	14.7	133	104	130
Warren Moon, Edm.	6	2382	1369	21228	57.5	15.5	77	91	144
Kent Austin, Sask.	7	3413	1964	26626	57.5	13.6	134	107	152
Tom Burgess, Ott.-Sask.-Wpg.	8	3316	1739	25264	52.4	14.5	163	104	164
Damon Allen, Edm.-Ott.-Ham.	9	3121	1588	24021	50.9	18.1	125	102	151
Doug Flutie, B.C.-Cal.	4	2513	1485	21616	59.1	14.6	90	89	130
Tracy Ham, Edm.-Tor.	7	2635	1362	21387	51.7	15.7	100	85	150
Mike Kerrigan, Ham.-Tor.	8	2450	1302	18557	53.1	14.3	137	77	106
Joe Barnes, Mtl.-Sask.-Tor.-Cal.	11	2454	1350	18491	55.0	13.7	117	100	94
Jerry Keeling, Cal.-Ott.-Ham.	15	2477	1302	18239	52.6	14.0	158	109	119
Jackie Parker, Edm.-Tor.-B.C.	13	2061	1089	16476	52.8	15.1	123	85	88
Kenny Ploen, Wpg.	11	1916	1084	16470	56.6	15.2	106	96	119
Danny Barrett, Cal.-Tor.-B.C.	10	2267	1220	17388	53.8	14.3	67	83	96

ALL-TIME PASS COMPLETION LEADERS (Cont'd)

2329	Matt Dunigan, Edm.-B.C.-Tor.	11	1983	1993
1964	Kent Austin, Sask.	7	1987	1993
1803	Roy Dewalt, B.C.-Wpg.-Ott.	9	1980	1988
1721	Joe Paopao, B.C.-Sask.-Ott.	11	1978	1990
1710	Condredge Holloway, Ott.-Tor.-B.C.	13	1975	1987
1739	Tom Burgess, Ott.-Sask.-Wpg.	8	1986	1993
1630	Sam Etcheverry, Mtl.	7	1954	1960
1613	Tom Wilkinson, Tor.-B.C.-Edm.	15	1967	1981

MOST PASSES COMPLETED ONE SEASON:

466 - Doug Flutie, B.C., 1991
459 - Kent Austin, Sask., 1992
416 - Doug Flutie, Cal., 1993
405 - Kent Austin, Sask., 1993
- David Archer, Sac., 1993
396 - Doug Flutie, Cal., 1992

MOST PASSES COMPLETED ONE GAME:

41 - Dieter Brock, Wpg., Wpg. at Ott., Oct. 3, 1981
- Kent Austin, Sask., Sask. at Tor., Oct. 31, 1993
40 - Kent Austin, Sask., Sask. at B.C., Aug. 13, 1992
39 - Kent Austin, Sask., Sask. at Cal., July 8, 1992

MOST CONSECUTIVE PASS COMPLETIONS:

18 - Joe Paopao, B.C., Tor. at B.C. Sept. 22, 1979
17 - Mike Rae, Tor., Mtl. at Mtl., Aug. 27, 1975
16 - Dieter Brock, Wpg., Ott. at Ott., Oct. 3, 1981

THE LONGEST COMPLETED PASSES:

109 - Sam Etcheverry to Hal Patterson, Mtl., Ham. at Mtl., Sept. 22, 1956
- Jerry Keeling to Terry Evanshen, Cal., Cal. at Wpg., Sept. 27, 1966
108 - Tobin Rote to Jim Rountree, Tor., Sask. at Tor., Sept. 10, 1961
- Joe Zuger to Dave Fleming, Ham., Tor. at Ham., Sept. 6, 1971
107 - Jim Van Pelt to Ernie Pitts, Wpg., Cal. at Wpg., Oct. 25, 1958
- Russ Jackson to Ted Watkins, Ott., Ott. at Mtl., Sept. 19, 1964
- Kent Austin to Jeff Fairholm, Sask., Wpg. at Sask., Sept. 2, 1990

ALL-TIME PASSING YARDAGE LEADERS:

Yds.		Seasons	Earliest	Latest
50535	Ron Lancaster, Ott.-Sask.	19	1960	1978
39041	Tom Clements, Ott.-Sask.-Ham.-Wpg.	12	1975	1987
34830	Dieter Brock, Wpg.-Ham.	11	1974	1984
33256	Matt Dunigan, Edm.-B.C.-Tor.-Wpg.	11	1983	1993
26626	Kent Austin, Sask.	7	1987	1993
25582	Sam Etcheverry, Mtl.	7	1954	1960
25264	Tom Burgess, Sask.-Wpg.-Ott.	8	1986	1993
25193	Condredge Holloway, Ott.-Tor.-B.C.	13	1975	1987
24592	Russ Jackson, Ott.	12	1958	1969
24264	Bernie Faloney, Edm.-Ham.-Mtl.-B.C.	12	1954	1967
24147	Roy Dewalt, B.C.-Wpg.-Ott.	9	1980	1988
24021	Damon Allen, Edm.-Ott.-Ham.	9	1985	1993
22725	Joe Kapp, Cal.-B.C.	8	1959	1966

MOST YARDS PASSED ONE SEASON:

6619 - Doug Flutie, B.C., 1991
6225 - Kent Austin, Sask., 1992
6092 - Doug Flutie, Cal., 1993
6023 - David Archer, Sac., 1993
5945 - Doug Flutie, Cal., 1992

MOST YARDS PASSED ONE GAME:

601 - Danny Barrett, B.C., Tor. at B.C., Aug. 12, 1993
586 - Sam Etcheverry, Mtl., Ham. at Mtl., Oct. 16, 1954
582 - Doug Flutie, B.C., Edm. at B.C., Oct. 12, 1991
561 - Sam Etcheverry, Mtl., Ham. at Mtl. Sept. 29, 1956

ALL-TIME LEADERS PASSING AVERAGE (min. 1000 attempts)

Pct.		Seasons	Earliest	Latest
60.6	Tom Wilkinson, Tor.-B.C.-Edm.	15	1967	1981
60.3	Tom Clements, Ott.-Sask.-Ham.-Wpg.	12	1975	1987
59.0	Doug Flutie, B.C.-Cal.	4	1990	1993
57.9	Eagle Day, Wpg.-Cal.-Tor.	7	1956	1966
57.5	Kent Austin, Sask.	7	1987	1993
57.6	Sam Etcheverry, Mtl.	7	1954	1960
-	Roy Dewalt, B.C.-Wpg.-Ott.	9	1980	1988
57.5	Warren Moon, Edm.	6	1978	1983
-	Ken Johnson, Cal.-Mtl.	4	1978	1962
57.4	Dieter Brock, Wpg.-Ham.	11	1974	1984

BEST PASSING AVERAGE ONE SEASON:

Pct.		Attempts	Completions	Year
67.58	Tom Clements, Wpg.	256	173	1986
66.19	Condredge Holloway, Tor.	210	139	1985
66.04	Tom Wilkinson, Edm.	268	177	1972

BEST PASSING AVERAGE ONE GAME:

(Minimum 20 passes)
90.5 (19-21) Tom Wilkinson, Edm., Ott. at Edm., Aug. 19, 1974
87.5 (21-24) Joe Paopao, B.C., Tor. at Van., Sept. 22, 1979
87.2 (41-47) Dieter Brock, Wpg.,Wpg. at Ott., Oct. 3, 1981

HIGHEST PASSING EFFICIENCY RATING ONE SEASON:

108.3 - Warren Moon, Edm. 1981
107.9 - Russ Jackson, Ott. 1967
107.5 - Jack Jacobs, Wpg. 1951

ALL-TIME TOUCHDOWN PASS LEADERS

No.		Seasons	Earliest	Latest
333	Ron Lancaster, Ott.-Sask.	19	1960	1978
252	Tom Clements, Ott.-Sask.-Ham.-Wpg.	12	1975	1987
210	Dieter Brock, Wpg.-Ham.	11	1974	1984
226	Matt Dunigan, Edm.-B.C.-Tor.-Wpg.	11	1983	1993
185	Russ Jackson, Ott.	12	1958	1969
183	Sam Etcheverry, Mtl.	7	1954	1960
164	Tom Burgess, Sask.-Wpg.-Ott	8	1986	1993
155	Condredge Holloway, Ott.-Tor.-B.C.	13	1975	1987
154	Tom Wilkinson, Tor.-B.C.-Edm.	15	1967	1981
152	Kent Austin, Sask.	7	1987	1993
151	Bernie Faloney, Edm.-Ham.-Mtl.-B.C.	12	1954	1967
-	Damon Allen, Edm.-Ott.-Ham	9	1985	1993
150	Tracy Ham, Edm.-Tor.	7	1987	1993
144	Warren Moon, Edm.	6	1978	1983

MOST TOUCHDOWN PASSES ONE SEASON:

44 - Doug Flutie, Cal., 1993
40 - Peter Liske, Cal., 1967
38 - Tobin Rote, Tor., 1960
38 - Doug Flutie, B.C., 1991
36 - Warren Moon, Edm., 1982
- Tracy Ham, Edm., 1990

MOST TOUCHDOWN PASSES ONE GAME:

8 - Joe Zuger, Ham., Sask. at Ham., Oct. 15, 1962
7 - Jim Van Pelt, Wpg., Wpg. at Sask., Aug. 29, 1959
- Tobin Rote, Tor., Mtl. at Tor., Oct. 1, 1960
- Tobin Rote, Tor., Mtl. at Tor., Oct. 30, 1960
- Rickey Foggie, Tor., Ham. at Tor., Sept. 29, 1990
6 - Jack Jacobs, Wpg., Wpg. at Cal., Oct. 4, 1952
- Sam Etcheverry, Mtl., Tor. at Mtl., Oct. 30, 1954
- Sam Etcheverry, Mtl., Ham. at Mtl., Oct. 20, 1956
- Joe Kapp, B.C., B.C. at Edm., Sept. 29, 1962
- Peter Liske, Cal., Wpg. at Cal., Oct. 15, 1967
- Joe Barnes, Tor., Edm. at Tor., July 22, 1984
- Sean Salisbury, Wpg., B.C. at Wpg., Sept. 10, 1989
- Kent Austin, Sask., Sask. at B.C., Sept. 21, 1991

MOST CONSECUTIVE GAMES THROWING TOUCHDOWN PASSES:

34 - Sam Etcheverry, Mtl. 1954-56
15 - Joe Kapp, B.C. 1962-63
14 - Russ Jackson, Ott. 1966-67

ALL-TIME PASSES INTERCEPTED LEADERS:

No.		Seasons	Earliest	Latest
396	Ron Lancaster, Ott.-Sask.	19	1960	1978
214	Tom Clements, Ott.-Sask.-Ham.-Wpg.	12	1975	1987
201	Bernie Faloney, Edm.-Ham.-Mtl.-B.C.	12	1954	1967
175	Matt Dunigan, Edm.-B.C.-Tor.-Wpg.	10	1983	1992
169	Sonny Wade, Mtl.	10	1969	1978
163	Sam Etcheverry, Mtl.	7	1954	1960
-	Tom Burgess, Ott.-Sask.-Wpg.	7	1986	1992
158	Jerry Keeling, Cal.-Ott.-Ham.	15	1961	1975
-	Dieter Brock, Wpg.-Ham.	11	1974	1984
157	Joe Paopao, B.C.-Sask.-Ott.	11	1978	1990
137	Mike Kerrigan, Ham.-Tor.	8	1986	1993

MOST PASSES INTERCEPTED ONE SEASON:

34 - Tom Dublinski, Tor., 1955
33 - Carroll Williams, Mtl., 1968
33 - Paul Brothers, B.C., 1969
32 - Mike Kerrigan, Ham., 1990

MOST PASSES INTERCEPTED ONE GAME:

7 - Sonny Wade, Mtl., Mtl. at Cal., Sept 24, 1972
- Bernie Faloney, Ham., Ham. at Tor., Oct. 13, 1958
- Al Dorow, B.C., B.C. at Edm., Oct. 25, 1958
6 - Lindy Berry, Edm., Wpg. at Edm., Sept. 9, 1950

MOST PASSES INTERCEPTED ONE GAME

- Sam Etcheverry, Mtl., Mtl. at Ott., Sept. 5, 1955

6 - Tom Dublinski, Tor., Ott. at Tor., Sept. 17, 1955

- Arnold Galiffa, Tor., Ott. at Tor., Sept. 22, 1956
- Tom Maudlin, Edm., Sask. at Edm., Sept. 7, 1963
- Ron Lancaster, Sask., Ham. at Reg., Aug. 31, 1965
- Charlie Fulton, Edm., Edm. at Ott., Sept. 27, 1969
- John Eckman, Ham., Ham. at Tor., Oct. 19, 1969
- John Eckman, Ham., Ham. at Mtl., Oct. 26, 1969
- John Eckman, Ham., Ham. at Edm., Sept. 26, 1970
- Sonny Wade, Mtl., Mtl. at Tor., Oct. 18, 1970
- Sonny Wade, Mtl., Mtl. at Ott., Sept. 11, 1976
- Gerry Dattilio, Cal., Cal. at Tor., July 8, 1982
- Tracy Ham, Edm., Edm. at Ham., Aug. 12, 1988
- Erik Kramer, Cal., Edm. at Cal., Oct. 16, 1988
- Tracy Ham, Edm., Edm. at Tor., July 27, 1989
- Doug Flutie, Cal., Edm. at Cal., Sept. 7, 1992

YEAR-BY-YEAR PASSING ATTEMPT - PASSING COMPLETION LEADERS

	East	Att-Comp.	West	Att-Comp.
1993 -	Matt Dunigan, Wpg.	600-334	Kent Austin, Sask.	715-405
1992 -	Damon Allen, Ham.	523-266	Kent Austin, Sask.	770-459
1991 -	Damon Allen, Ott.	546-282	Doug Flutie, B.C.	730-466
1990 -	Tom Burgess, Wpg.	574-330	Kent Austin, Sask.	618-360
1989 -	Sean Salisbury, Wpg.	595-293	Matt Dunigan, B.C.	597-331
1988 -	Gilbert Renfroe, Tor.	527-290	Matt Dunigan, B.C.	471-268
1987 -	Tom Clements, Wpg.	592-336	Roy Dewalt, B.C.	531-303
1986 -	Brian Ransom, Mtl.	494-247	Rick Johnson, Cal.	604-314
			Roy Dewalt, B.C.	604-314
1985 -	Joe Barnes, Mtl.	453-265	Roy Dewalt, B.C.	476-301
1984 -	Dieter Brock, Ham.	561-320	Joe Paopao, Sask.	453-279
			Tom Clements Moon, Wpg.	453-279
1983 -	Dieter Brock, Wpg.-Ham.	420-229	Warren Moon, Edm.	664-380
1982 -	Tom Clements, Ham.	546-356	Warren Moon, Edm.	562-333
1981 -	Tom Clements, Ham.	523-301	Dieter Brock, Wpg.	566-354
1980 -	Mark Jackson, Tor.	404-231	Dieter Brock, Wpg.	514-304
1979 -	Tony Adams, Tor.	394-241	Dieter Brock, Wpg.	354-194
1978 -	Jimmy Jones, Ham.	269-158	Dieter Brock, Wpg.	486-294
1977 -	Jimmy Jones, Ham.	302-182	Ron Lancaster, Sask.	449-255
	Tom Clements, Ott.	302-182		
1976 -	Sonny Wade, Mtl.	382-205	Ron Lancaster, Sask.	494-297
1975 -	Jerry Keeling, Ott.-Ham.	274-149	Ron Lancaster, Sask.	441-239
			Peter Liske, Cal.-B.C.	-228
1974 -	Mike Rae, Tor.	352-171	Ron Lancaster, Sask.	395-222
1973 -	Chuck Ealey, Ham.	309-181	Ron Lancaster, Sask.	464-263
1972 -	Rick Cassata, Ott.	357-179	Don Jonas, Wpg.	447-252
1971 -	Sonny Wade, Mtl.	338-155	Don Jonas, Wpg.	485-253
1970 -	Gary Wood, Ott.	340-174	Don Trull, Edm.	364-185
1969 -	Russ Jackson, Ott.	358-193	Jerry Keeling, Cal.	411-229
1968 -	Wally Gabler, Tor.	365-205	Peter Liske, Cal.	438-271
1967 -	Russ Jackson, Ott.	323-189	Peter Liske, Cal.	508-303
1966 -	Russ Jackson, Ott.	276-142	Joe Kapp, B.C.	363-211
1965 -	Bernie Faloney, Mtl.	275-148	Joe Kapp, B.C.	423-219
1964 -	Jackie Parker, Tor.	233-137	Joe Kapp, B.C.	329-194
1963 -	Bernie Faloney, Ham.	273-152	Joe Kapp, B.C.	374-228
-	Russ Jackson, Ott.	273-152		
1962 -	Tobin Rote, Tor.	348-187	Joe Kapp, B.C.	359-197
1961 -	Tobin Rote, Tor.	389-220	Joe Kapp, Cal.-B.C.	231-106
			Eagle Day, Cal.	231-106
1960 -	Tobin Rote, Tor.	450-255	Joe Kapp, Cal.	337-182
1959 -	Sam Etcheverry, Mtl.	402-231	Joe Kapp, Cal.	328-196
1958 -	Sam Etcheverry, Mtl.	423-247	Frank Tripucka, Sask.	338-189
1957 -	Sam Etcheverry, Mtl.	408-215	Frank Tripucka, Sask.	343-172
1956 -	Sam Etcheverry, Mtl.	446-276	Frank Tripucka, Sask.	383-216
1955 -	Sam Etcheverry, Mtl.	400-227	Don Klosterman, Cal.	279-258
			Frank Tripucka, Sask.	279-158
1954 -	Sam Etcheverry, Mtl.	372-206	Frank Tripucka, Sask.	259-152
1953 -			Jack Jacobs, Wpg.	252-146
1952 -			Jack Jacobs, Wpg.	286-147
1951 -			Jack Jacobs, Wpg.	355-204
1950 -			Keith Spaith, Cal.	263-129
			Lindy Berry, Edm.	263-129

YEAR-BY-YEAR PASSING YARDAGE LEADERS:

	East		West	
1993 -	Tom Burgess, Ott.	5063	Doug Flutie, Cal.	6092
1992 -	Tom Burgess, Ott.	4026	Kent Austin, Sask.	6225
1991 -	Damon Allen, Ott.	4275	Doug Flutie, B.C.	6619
1990 -	Tom Burgess, Wpg.	3958	Kent Austin, Sask.	4604
1989 -	Sean Salisbury, Wpg.	4049	Matt Dunigan, B.C.	4509
1988 -	Gilbert Renfroe, Tor.	4113	Matt Dunigan, B.C.	3776
1987 -	Tom Clements, Wpg.	4686	Roy Dewalt, B.C.	3855
1986 -	Brian Ransom, Mtl.	3204	Rick Johnson, Cal.	4379
1985 -	Joe Barnes, Mtl.	3432	Roy Dewalt, B.C.	4237
1984 -	Dieter Brock, Ham.	3966	Tom Clements, Wpg.	3845
1983 -	Condredge Holloway, Tor.	3184	Warren Moon, Edm.	5648
1982 -	Tom Clements, Ham.	4706	Warren Moon, Edm.	5000
1981 -	Tom Clements, Ham.	4536	Dieter Brock, Wpg.	4796
1980 -	Mark Jackson, Tor.	3041	Dieter Brock, Wpg.	4252
1979 -	Tony Adams, Tor.	2692	Dieter Brock, Wpg.	2383
1978 -	Jimmy Jones, Ham.	2060	Dieter Brock, Wpg.	3755
1977 -	Tom Clements, Ott.	2804	Ron Lancaster, Sask.	3072
1976 -	Tom Clements, Ott.	2856	Ron Lancaster, Sask.	3869
1975 -	Tom Clements, Ott.	2013	Ron Lancaster, Sask.	3545
1974 -	Mike Rae, Tor.	2501	Peter Liske, Cal.-B.C.	3259
1973 -	Joe Theismann, Tor.	2496	Ron Lancaster, Sask.	3767
1972 -	Chuck Ealey, Ham.	2573	Don Jonas, Wpg.	3583
1971 -	Joe Theismann, Tor.	2440	Don Jonas, Wpg.	4036
1970 -	Gary Wood, Ott.	2759	Ron Lancaster, Sask.	2779
1969 -	Russ Jackson, Ott.	3641	Jerry Keeling, Cal.	3179
1968 -	Wally Gabler, Tor.	3242	Peter Liske, Cal.	4333
1967 -	Russ Jackson, Ott.	3332	Peter Liske, Cal.	4479
1966 -	Russ Jackson, Ott.	2400	Ron Lancaster, Sask.	2976
1965 -	Russ Jackson, Ott.	2303	Joe Kapp, B.C.	2961
1964 -	Russ Jackson, Ott.	2156	Joe Kapp, B.C.	2816
1963 -	Russ Jackson, Ott.	2910	Joe Kapp, B.C.	3126
1962 -	Tobin Rote, Tor.	2532	Joe Kapp, B.C.	3279
1961 -	Tobin Rote, Tor.	3093	Eagle Day, Cal.	1800
1960 -	Tobin Rote, Tor.	4247	Joe Kapp, Cal.	3060
1959 -	Sam Etcheverry, Mtl.	3133	Joe Kapp, Cal.	2990
1958 -	Sam Etcheverry, Mtl.	3548	Frank Tripucka, Sask.	2766
1957 -	Sam Etcheverry, Mtl.	3341	Frank Tripucka, Sask.	2589
1956 -	Sam Etcheverry, Mtl.	4723	Frank Tripucka, Sask.	3274
1955 -	Sam Etcheverry, Mtl.	3657	Don Klosterman, Cal.	2405
1954 -	Sam Etcheverry, Mtl.	3610	Frank Tripucka, Sask.	2003
1953 -			Jack Jacobs, Wpg.	1924
1952 -			Jack Jacobs, Wpg.	2586
1951 -			Jack Jacobs, Wpg.	3248
1950 -			Lindy Berry, Edm.	2201

ALL-TIME CONVERT ATTEMPT LEADERS:

		Seasons	Earliest	Latest
745 -	Lui Passaglia, B.C.	18	1976	1993
650 -	Dave Cutler, Edm.	16	1969	1984
511 -	Trevor Kennerd, Wpg.	12	1980	1991
478 -	Dave Ridgway, Sask.	12	1982	1993
421 -	Larry Robinson, Cal.	14	1961	1974
414 -	Lance Chomyc, Tor.	9	1985	1993
408 -	Bernie Ruoff, Wpg.-Ham.-B.C.	14	1975	1988
395 -	Gerry Organ, Ott.	12	1971	1983
363 -	John T. Hay, Ott.-Cal.	11	1978	1988
348 -	Jack Abendschan, Sask.	11	1965	1975

ALL-TIME CONVERT LEADERS:

		Seasons	Earliest	Latest
744 -	Lui Passaglia, B.C.	18	1976	1993
627 -	Dave Cutler, Edm.	16	1969	1984
509 -	Trevor Kennerd, Wpg.	12	1980	1991
478 -	Dave Ridgway, Sask.	12	1982	1993
412 -	Lance Chomyc, Tor.	9	1985	1993
401 -	Bernie Ruoff, Wpg.-Ham.-B.C.	14	1975	1988
391 -	Gerry Organ, Ott.	12	1971	1983
363 -	John T. Hay, Ott.-Cal.	11	1978	1988
362 -	Larry Robinson, Cal.	14	1961	1974
327 -	Don Sweet, Mtl.-Ham.	14	1972	1985

MOST CONVERTS ONE SEASON:

76 -	Lance Chomyc, Tor.,	1990
70 -	Jerry Kauric, Edm.,	1989
67 -	Lui Passaglia, B.C.,	1991

MOST CONVERTS ONE GAME:

9 - Bill Bewley, Mtl., Ham. at Mtl., Oct. 20, 1956

- Trevor Kennerd, Wpg., Ott. at Wpg., Sept. 7, 1984
- Lance Chomyc, Tor., Cal. at Tor., Sept. 20, 1990
- Jim Crouch, Sac., B.C. at Sac., Nov. 6, 1993

8 - Cookie Gilchrist, Tor., Mtl. at Tor., Oct. 30, 1960

- Gerry Organ, Ott., Ham. at Ott., Sept. 7, 1975
- Bernie Ruoff, Ham., Tor. at Ham., July 25, 1981
- Dave Cutler, Edm., Mtl. at Edm., Sept. 26, 1981
- Dave Cutler, Edm., Tor. at Edm., Oct. 24, 1981
- Troy Westwood, Wpg., Ham. at Wpg., Oct. 19, 1991

MOST CONSECUTIVE CONVERTS:

498 - Lui Passaglia, B.C. (1983-93)
363 - John T. Hay, Ott.-Cal. (1978-87)
251 - Trevor Kennerd, Wpg. (1983-88)

ALL-TIME TWO-POINT CONVERT LEADERS:

		Seasons	Earliest	Latest
5 -	Peter Dalla Riva, Mtl.	14	1968	1981
-	Nick Arakgi, Mtl.-Wpg.-Ott.	9	1979	1988
4 -	Willie Armstead, Cal.	7	1976	1982
-	Cedric Minter, Tor.-Ott.	5	1981	1987
3 -	Tom Forzani, Cal.	11	1973	1983
-	Todd Brown, Mtl.-Sask.	5	1983	1988
-	Steve Stapler, Ham.	4	1981	1988
-	Lawrie Skolrood, Ham.-Sask.	14	1974	1987
-	Joe Barnes, Mtl.-Sask.-Tor.-Cal.	11	1976	1986
-	Jimmy Edwards, Ham.	3	1976	1978
-	Bruce Walker, Ott.	6	1979	1984
-	Bob LaRose, Wpg.	7	1970	1976

MOST TWO-POINT CONVERTS ONE SEASON:

4 -	Peter Dalla Riva, Mtl.	1975	3 -	Bob LaRose, Wpg.	1975
-	Nick Arakgi, Mtl.	1984	-	Lawrie Skolrood, Ham.	1978

MOST TWO-POINT CONVERTS ONE GAME:

2 - Jim McMillan, Ham., Mtl. at Ham., July 23, 1975

- Tyrone Walls, Edm., Edm. at Ott., Sept. 17, 1975
- Bob LaRose, Wpg., Wpg. at Edm., Oct. 26, 1975
- Mike Murphy, Ott., Ott. at Edm., Aug. 26, 1980
- Darrell Smith, Cal., Cal. at Edm., Sept. 26, 1982
- Nick Arakgi, Mtl., Ham. at Mtl., June 30, 1984
- Jay Christensen, B.C., B.C. at Tor., Sept. 1, 1990

ALL-TIME FIELD GOAL ATTEMPT LEADERS:

		Seasons	Earliest	Latest
850 -	Lui Passaglia, B.C.	18	1976	1993
790 -	Dave Cutler, Edm.	16	1969	1984
640 -	Dave Ridgway, Sask.	12	1982	1993
595 -	Bernie Ruoff, Wpg.-Ham.-B.C.	14	1975	1988
592 -	Trevor Kennerd, Wpg.	12	1980	1991
502 -	Gerry Organ, Ott.	12	1971	1984
457 -	Don Sweet, Mtl.-Ham.	14	1972	1985
-	Lance Chomyc, Tor.	9	1985	1993
445 -	John T. Hay, Ott.-Cal.	11	1978	1988
427 -	Paul Osbaldiston, B.C.-Wpg.-Ham.	8	1986	1993

ALL-TIME FIELD GOAL LEADERS:

		Seasons	Earliest	Latest
609 -	Lui Passaglia, B.C.	18	1976	1993
501 -	Dave Ridgway, Sask.	12	1982	1993
464 -	Dave Cutler, Edm.	16	1969	1984
394 -	Trevor Kennerd, Wpg.	12	1980	1991
384 -	Bernie Ruoff, Wpg.-Ham.-B.C.	14	1975	1988
337 -	Lance Chomyc, Tor.	9	1985	1993
318 -	Gerry Organ, Ott.	12	1971	1983
314 -	Don Sweet, Mtl.-Ham.	14	1972	1985
308 -	John T. Hay, Ott.-Cal.	11	1978	1988
295 -	Paul Osbaldiston, B.C.-Wpg.-Ham.	8	1986	1993

ALL-TIME FIELD GOAL ACCURACY LEADERS (min. 100 attempts)

Pct.	Player	Tried	Good	Seasons	Earliest	Latest
78.28 -	Dave Ridgway, Sask.	640	501	12	1982	1993
75.52 -	Dean Dorsey, Tor.-Ott.-Edm.	290	219	8	1982	1991
73.71 -	Lance Chomyc, Tor.	457	337	9	1985	1993
71.64 -	Lui Passaglia, B.C.	850	609	18	1976	1993
70.74 -	Terry Baker, Sask.-Ott.	147	104	7	1987	1993
69.08 -	Paul Osbaldiston, B.C.-Wpg.-Ham.	427	295	8	1986	1993
69.21 -	J.T. Hay, Ott.-Cal.	445	308	11	1978	1988
68.83 -	Mark McLoughlin, Cal.	369	254	6	1988	1993
68.71 -	Don Sweet, Mtl.-Ham.	457	314	14	1972	1985
68.21 -	Jerry Kauric, Edm.-Cal.	173	118	5	1987	1991

MOST FIELD GOALS ONE SEASON:

59 - Dave Ridgway, Sask. 1990
55 - Dave Ridgway, Sask. 1988
- Lance Chomyc, Tor. 1991
54 - Dave Ridgway, Sask. 1989
- Paul Osbaldiston, Ham. 1989

MOST FIELD GOALS ONE GAME:

8 - Dave Ridgway, Sask., Sask. at Ott., July 29, 1984
- Dave Ridgway, Sask., Edm. at Sask., July 23, 1988
7 - Bob Macoritti, Sask., Tor. at Sask., Aug. 27, 1978
- Trevor Kennerd, Wpg., Tor. at Wpg., Oct. 11, 1981
- Lui Passaglia, B.C., Tor. at B.C., Sept. 6, 1985
- Dave Ridgway, Sask., B.C. at Sask., Sept. 27, 1987
- Lance Chomyc, Tor., Tor at Cal., Sept. 30, 1988
- Lance Chomyc, Tor., Ott. at Tor., Oct. 14, 1988
- Dean Dorsey, Ott., Sask. at Ott., Sept. 24, 1989
- Dave Ridgway, Sask., Sask. at B.C., Aug. 2, 1990
- Dave Ridgway, Sask., Edm. at Sask., Aug. 19, 1990
6 - Dave Cutler, Edm., Sask. at Edm., Oct. 22, 1972
- Gerry Organ, Ott., Edm. at Ott., Sept. 22, 1973
- Lui Passaglia, B.C., Mtl. at B.C., Oct. 15, 1977
- Lui Passaglia, B.C., B.C. at Wpg., Sept. 24, 1978
- Bernie Ruoff, Wpg., Ott. at Wpg., Sept. 15, 1979
- Gerry Organ, Ott., Mtl. at Ott., Aug. 18, 1980
- John T. Hay, Cal., B.C. at Cal., Oct. 31, 1982
- Trevor Kennerd, Wpg., Edm. at Wpg., Oct. 23, 1983
- Lui Passaglia, B.C., Ott. at B.C., Nov. 5, 1984
- Lui Passaglia, B.C., Sask. at B.C., Sept. 28, 1985
- Lance Chomyc, Tor., Edm. at Tor., Aug. 23, 1986
- Trevor Kennerd, Wpg., Tor. at Wpg., Oct. 5, 1986
- Trevor Kennerd, Wpg., Edm. at Wpg., Oct. 25, 1986
- Bernie Ruoff, Ham., Tor. at Ham., Sept. 7, 1987
- Dave Ridgway, Sask., Wpg. at Sask., July 29, 1988
- Trevor Kennerd, Wpg., B.C. at Wpg., Sept. 11, 1988
- Dave Ridgway, Sask., Cal. at Sask., Oct. 9, 1988
- Jerry Kauric, Edm., B.C. at Edm., July 13, 1989
- Paul Osbaldiston, Ham., Wpg. at Ham., July 20, 1989
- Dean Dorsey, Ott., Ott. at Ham., July 19, 1990
- Dave Ridgway, Sask., Sask. at Cal., July 19, 1990
- Mark McLoughlin, Cal., Cal. at B.C., July 11, 1991
- Lui Passaglia, B.C., B.C. at Wpg., July 19, 1991
- Lance Chomyc, Tor., Tor. at Ham., Oct. 27, 1991
- Dave Ridgway, Sask., Sask. at B.C., Aug. 13, 1992

LONGEST FIELD GOALS:

60 - Dave Ridgway, Sask., Wpg. at Sask., Sept. 6, 1987
59 - Dave Cutler, Edm., Edm. at Sask., Oct. 28, 1970
- Paul Watson, Sask., Wpg. at Sask., July 12, 1981
58 - Bill Mitchell, Edm., Edm. at Cal., Aug. 17, 1964
- Bernie Ruoff, Wpg., Wpg. at Cal., Aug. 12, 1975
- Dave Cutler, Edm., Edm. at Ham., Sept. 24, 1973
- Mark McLoughlin, Cal., Cal. at Sask., Oct. 9, 1988
- Sean Fleming, Edm., Edm. at Sac., July 31, 1993

MOST FIELD GOALS IN ONE QUARTER:

4 - Gerry Organ, Ott., Edm. at Ott., Sept. 22, 1973
(In 10 minute, 22 second span of 1st quarter)
- Dave Cutler, Edm., Edm. at Wpg., July 27, 1977
(In 11 minute, 3 second span of 2nd quarter)
- Don Sweet, Mtl., Mtl. at Sask., Sept. 6, 1981
(In 11 minute, 24 second span of 2nd quarter)
- John T. Hay, Cal., B.C. at Cal., Oct. 31, 1982
(In 10 minute, 37 second span of 4th quarter)
- Dave Ridgway, Sask., Cal. at Sask., Oct. 9, 1988
(In 10 minute, 10 second span of 1st quarter)
- Lance Chomyc, Tor., Ott. at Tor., Oct. 14, 1988
(In 10 minute, 23 second span of 2nd quarter)

MOST CONSECUTIVE FIELD GOALS:

28 - Dave Ridgway, Sask., Streak covered 9 games, starting July 24, 1993, ending Sept.19, 1993.
23 - Dean Dorsey, Ott., Streak covered 8 games, starting Nov. 1, 1986, ending Aug. 9, 1987.
21 - Don Sweet, Mtl., Streak covered 7 games, starting Aug. 16, 1976, ending Oct. 3, 1976.
- Dave Ridgway, Sask., Streak covered 8 games, starting Sept. 29, 1991, ending July 15, 1992.
18 - Don Sweet, Mtl., Streak covered 7 games, starting July 28, 1984, ending Sept. 22, 1984.

LONGEST UNSUCCESSFUL FIELD GOAL RETURN:

Yds.	Player		Game	Date
128 -	Ron Hopkins, Cal.	(TD)	Wpg. at Cal.	Sept. 14, 1990
111 -	Henry Williams, Edm.	(TD)	Wpg. at Edm.	Oct. 25, 1987
110 -	Henry Williams, Edm.	(TD)	Tor. at Edm.	Aug. 27, 1990

ALL-TIME SINGLES LEADERS:

No.	Player	Seasons	Earliest	Latest
252 -	Lui Passaglia, B.C.	18	1976	1993
219 -	Bernie Ruoff, Wpg.-Ham.-B.C.	14	1975	1988
218 -	Dave Cutler, Edm.	16	1969	1984
183 -	Hank Ilesic, Edm.-Tor.	17	1977	1993
149 -	Trevor Kennerd, Wpg.	12	1980	1991
143 -	Zenon Andrusyshyn, Tor-Ham.-Edm.-Mtl.	12	1971	1986
135 -	Paul Osbaldiston, B.C.-Wpg.-Ham.	8	1986	1993
124 -	John T. Hay, Cal.	11	1978	1988
123 -	Huck Welch, Mtl.-Ham.	10	1928	1937
116 -	Frank Turville, Tor-Ham.	8	1928	1935

MOST SINGLES ONE SEASON:

33 - Lionel Conacher, Tor. 1922
- Tom Dixon, Edm. 1986
32 - Ben Simpson, Ham. 1909
30 - Hank Ilesic, Tor. 1983

MOST SINGLES ONE GAME:

No.	Player	Opponent	Date
11 -	Bert Simpson, Ham.	Mtl.	Oct. 29, 1910
10 -	Bill Dobbie, Cal.	Edm.	Oct. 28, 1911
-	Fred Wilson, Reg.	Sask.	Oct. 4, 1913
-	Billy Mallett, Ham.	Ott.	Nov. 14, 1914
9 -	Ben Simpson, Ham.	Tor.	Nov. 13, 1909
-	Billy Mallett, Ham.	Ott.	Oct. 5, 1912
-	Vern Bradburn, Wpg.-Vic.	Wpg. T.T.	Sept. 25, 1920
-	Bert Gibbs, Ham.	Mtl.	Oct. 2, 1926

ALL-TIME PUNTING YARDAGE LEADERS:

Player	Seasons	Punts	Yds.	Ave.	Long.	Singl.
Lui Passaglia, B.C.	18	2301	99,329	43.2	97	89
Hank Ilesic, Edm.-Tor.	17	1990	89,404	41.4	90	136
Bob Cameron, Wpg.	14	1965	84,567	43.0	95	95
Ken Clark, Ham.-Tor.-Sask.-Ott.	12	1592	72,520	45.6	101	90
Bernie Ruoff, Wpg.-Ham.-B.C.	14	1600	71,801	44.9	96	64
Zenon Andrusyshyn, Tor.-Ham.-Edm.-Mtl.	12	1367	61,342	44.9	108	61
Dave Mann, Tor.	12	1261	55,745	44.2	102	87
Joe Zuger, Ham.	10	1075	48,930	45.5	85	68
Mike McTague, Cal.-Mtl.-Sask.	9	1040	44,885	43.2	92	62
Cam Fraser, Ham.-Mtl.	12	987	44,287	44.9	84	76

MOST PUNTING YARDAGE ONE SEASON:

8214 - Bob Cameron, Wpg. 1988
8004 - Hank Ilesic, Tor. 1986
7425 - Bob Cameron, Wpg. 1989

MOST PUNTING YARDAGE ONE GAME:

Yds.	Player	Game	Date
814 -	Martin Fabi, Sask.	Sask. at Cal.,	Sept. 14, 1963
785 -	Cam Fraser, Ham.	Ott. at Phila.,	Sept. 14, 1958
781 -	Cam Fraser, Ham.	Tor. at Ham.,	Nov. 13, 1954

ALL-TIME PUNTING LEADERS:

No.	Player	Seasons	Earliest	Latest
2361 -	Lui Passaglia, B.C.	18	1976	1993
1990 -	Hank Ilesic, Edm.-Tor.	17	1977	1993
1965 -	Bob Cameron, Wpg.	14	1980	1993
1600 -	Bernie Ruoff, Wpg.-Ham.-B.C.	14	1975	1988
1592 -	Ken Clark, Ham.-Tor.-Sask.-Ott.	12	1976	1987
1367 -	Zenon Andrusyshyn, Tor.-Ham.-Edm.-Mtl.	12	1971	1986
1261 -	Dave Mann, Tor.	12	1958	1970
1075 -	Joe Zuger, Ham.	10	1962	1971
1041 -	Alan Ford, Sask.	11	1965	1975
1040 -	Mike McTague, Cal.-Mtl.-Sask.	9	1979	1987

MOST PUNTS ONE SEASON:

188 - Bob Cameron, Wpg. 1988
175 - Bob Cameron, Wpg. 1989
168 - Ken Clark, Ott. 1987
- Tom Dixon, Ott. 1988

MOST PUNTS ONE GAME:

No.	Player	Game	Date
18 -	Martin Fabi, Sask.	Sask. at Cal.	Sept. 14, 1963
17 -	Larry Isbell, Sask.	Sask. at Wpg.	Sept. 12, 1955
-	Cam Fraser, Ham.	Mtl. at Ham.	Nov. 5, 1955
16 -	Avantus Stone, Ott.	Ott. at Mtl.	Sept. 4, 1954
-	Avantus Stone, Ott.	Ham. at Ott.	Oct. 30, 1954
-	Ron Quillan, Ott.	Ott. at Ham.	Nov. 9, 1957
-	Roger Kettlewell, Edm.	Edm. at B.C.	Sept. 17, 1969

LONGEST PUNTS:

Yds.	Player	Game	Date
108 -	Zenon Andrusyshyn, Tor.	Tor. at Edm.	Oct. 23, 1977
102 -	Dave Mann, Tor.	Sask. at Reg.	Sept. 18, 1966
101 -	Ken Clark, Sask.	Wpg. at Sask.	Sept. 3, 1983
-	Dean Dorsey, Tor.	Tor. at Wpg.	Oct. 11, 1982

ALL-TIME PUNTING AVERAGE LEADERS:

Ave.	Player	Seasons	Earliest	Latest
45.6 -	Ken Clark, Ham.-Tor.-Sask.-Ott.	12	1975	1987
45.5 -	Joe Zuger, Ham.	10	1962	1971
44.9 -	Bernie Ruoff, Wpg.-Ham.-B.C.	14	1975	1988
-	Zenon Andrusyshyn, Tor.-Ham.-Edm.-Mtl.	12	1971	1986
-	Cam Fraser, Ham.-Mtl.	12	1951	1962
44.2 -	Dave Mann, Tor.	12	1958	1970
44.1 -	Charlie Shepard, Wpg.	6	1957	1962
43.2 -	Lui Passaglia, B.C.	18	1976	1993
43.0 -	Bob Cameron, Wpg.	14	1980	1993

BEST PUNTING AVERAGE ONE SEASON:

50.2 - Lui Passaglia, B.C. 1983
48.5 - Joe Zuger, Ham. 1971
48.5 - Hank Ilesic, Tor. 1986
48.4 - Joe Zuger, Ham. 1968

BEST PUNTING AVERAGE ONE GAME:

Ave.	Player	Game	Date
60.2 -	Ken Clark, Sask.	Cal. at Reg.	Aug. 14, 1981
58.8 -	Butch Avinger, Sask.	Edm. at Reg.	Aug. 23, 1952
58.6 -	Jack Delveaux, Wpg.	Wpg. at Reg.	Sept. 2, 1963

YEAR-BY-YEAR PUNTING AVERAGE LEADERS:

Year	East		West	
1993	Terry Baker, Ottawa	45.5	Pete Gardere, Sacramento	42.2
1992	Hank Ilesic, Toronto	45.0	Glenn Harper, Edmonton	40.5
1991	Hank Ilesic, Toronto	44.4	Brent Matich, Calgary	42.7
1990	Bob Cameron, Winnipeg	42.0	Brent Matich, Calgary	43.1
1989	Bob Cameron, Winnipeg	42.4	Brent Matich, Calgary	42.5
1988	Bob Cameron, Winnipeg	44.0	Jerry Kauric, Edmonton	43.6
1987	Hank Ilesic, Toronto	42.6	Glenn Harper, Calgary	42.8
1986	Hank Ilesic, Toronto	48.5	Tom Dixon, Edmonton	45.3
1985	Ken Clark, Ottawa	47.0	Tom Dixon, Edmonton	45.5
1984	Bernie Ruoff, Hamilton	46.8	Lui Passaglia, B.C.	46.4
	Ken Clark, Ottawa	46.8		
1983	Bernie Ruoff, Hamilton	47.4	Lui Passaglia, B.C.	50.2
1982	Bernie Ruoff, Hamilton	45.3	Ken Clark, Saskatchewan	47.3
1981	Zenon Andrusyshyn, Toronto	47.2	Lui Passaglia, B.C.	46.0
1980	Zenon Andrusyshyn, Toronto	45.3	Hank Ilesic, Edmonton	45.6
1979	Ian Sunter, Toronto	41.7	Lui Passaglia, B.C.	47.3
1978	Ken Clark, Hamilton-Toronto	45.1	Hank Ilesic, Edmonton	47.3
1977	Ken Clark, Hamilton	46.8	Hank Ilesic, Edmonton	45.1

YEAR-BY-YEAR PUNTING AVERAGE LEADERS

1976	Ken Clark, Hamilton	47.0	Bernie Ruoff, Winnipeg	45.1
1975	Ken Clark, Hamilton	43.8	Gerald Kunyk, Calgary	45.9
1974	Zenon Andrusyshyn, Toronto	46.9	Walt McKee, Winnipeg	41.8
1973	Zenon Andrusyshyn, Toronto	45.6	Walt McKee, Winnipeg	44.2
1972	Zenon Andrusyshyn, Toronto	45.0	Eric Guthrie, B.C.	42.2
1971	Joe Zuger, Hamilton	48.5	Ken Phillips, B.C.	42.6
1970	Dave Mann, Toronto	44.8	Ken Phillips, B.C.	44.6
1969	Joe Zuger, Hamilton	48.2	Ed Ulmer, Winnipeg	40.8
1968	Joe Zuger, Hamilton	48.4	Ed Ulmer, Winnipeg	43.0
1967	Dave Mann, Toronto	46.8	Jim Furlong, Calgary	44.5
1966	Joe Zuger, Hamilton	44.0	Randy Kerbow, Edmonton	42.9
1965	Joe Zuger, Hamilton	44.7	Martin Fabi, Saskatchewan	42.5
1964	Gino Berretta, Montreal	42.4	Neal Beaumont, B.C.	42.1
1963	Dave Mann, Toronto	41.7	Martin Fabi, Saskatchewan	44.0
1962	Dave Mann, Toronto	43.7	Ferd Burket, Saskatchewan	45.2
1961	Dave Mann, Toronto	48.0	Bobby Walden, Edmonton	46.8
1960	Dave Mann, Toronto	43.9	Charlie Shepard, Winnipeg	44.7
1959	Cam Fraser, Hamilton	45.1	Charlie Shepard, Winnipeg	43.1
1958	Cam Fraser, Hamilton	45.6	Charlie Shepard, Winnipeg	44.2
1957	Cam Fraser, Hamilton	46.0	Vic Chapman, B.C.	42.4
1956	Cam Fraser, Hamilton	46.0	Larry Isbell, Saskatchewan	44.2
1955	Cam Fraser, Hamilton	47.4	Bob Heydenfeldt, Edmonton	43.3
1954	Cam Fraser, Hamilton	43.1	Larry Isbell, Saskatchewan	46.3
1953			Rod Pantages, Edmonton	44.4
1952			Butch Avinger, Saskatchewan	44.7
1951			Glen Dobbs, Saskatchewan	44.2
1950			Keith Spaith, Calgary	41.5

ALL-TIME LEADERS PUNT RETURN YARDAGE:

	Seasons	No.	Yds.	Ave.	Long.	TD
Henry Williams, Edm.	7	576	7046	12.2	104	21
Paul Bennett, Tor.-Wpg.-Ham.	11	659	6358	9.6	99	1
Larry Crawford, B.C.-Tor.	9	405	4159	10.3	82	3
Darnell Clash, B.C.-Tor.	4	340	3407	10.0	83	3
Randy Rhino, Mtl.-Ott.	7	296	3367	11.4	64	0
Gene Wlasiuk, Wpg.-Sask.	10	553	3333	6.0	67	1
Richie Hall, Cal.-Sask.	9	334	3215	9.6	74	1
Dickie Harris, Mtl.	10	271	3107	11.5	102	4
Dick Dupuis, Cal.-Edm.	11	410	3092	7.5	32	0
Ed Learn, Mtl.-Tor.	12	506	3091	6.1	31	0

MOST PUNT RETURN YARDAGE ONE SEASON:

1440	-	Henry Williams, Edm.	1991	1157	-	Henry Williams, Edm.	1993
1181	-	Anthony Hunter, Edm.	1989				

MOST PUNT RETURN YARDAGE ONE GAME:

232	-	Henry Williams, Edm.,	Ott. at Edm.,	July 17, 1991
221	-	Henry Williams, Edm.	Cal. at Edm.	June 27, 1987
208	-	Moody Jackson, Ott.	Ott. at Tor.	Aug. 11, 1976
	-	Henry Williams, Edm.	Cal. at Edm.	Nov. 7, 1993

MOST 100-YARD PUNT RETURN GAMES ONE SEASON:

5	-	Larry Crawford, B.C.	1988	3	-	Dickie Harris, Mtl.	1979
	-	Anthony Hunter, Edm.	1989		-	Mike Nelms, Ott.	1979
	-	Henry Williams, Edm.	1991		-	Randy Rhino, Mtl.	1981
4	-	Darnell Clash, B.C.	1986		-	Mike Clemons, Tor.	1990
	-	Willis Jacox, Sask.	1991		-	Nick Mazzoli, Ham.	1991
	-	Henry Williams, Edm.	1992		-	Willis Jacox, Sask-B.C.	1992
3	-	Rufus Crawford, Ham.	1984		-	Treamelle Taylor, Ott.	1992
	-	Tyrone Thurman, Ott.	1989		-	Henry Williams, Edm.	1993
	-	Henry Williams, Edm.	1990				

MOST CONSECUTIVE 100-YARD PUNT RETURN GAMES:

4	-	Larry Crawford, B.C.	October 7 - October 29, 1988
	-	Darnell Clash, B.C.	July 19 - August 9, 1986
3	-	Henry Williams, Edm.	August 6 - August 20, 1992
2	-	Randy Rhino, Mtl.	September 5 - September 10, 1978
	-	Randy Rhino, Mtl.	August 20 - August 29, 1979
	-	Dickie Harris, Mtl.	October 27 - November 4, 1979
	-	Randy Rhino, Mtl.	September 4 - September 13, 1981
	-	Mike Clemons, Tor.	September 15 - September 20, 1990
	-	Raghib Ismail, Tor.	October 18 - October 25, 1992

ALL-TIME PUNT RETURN LEADERS:

			Seasons	Earliest	Latest
659	-	Paul Bennett, Tor.-Wpg.-Ham.	11	1977	1987
576	-	Henry Williams, Edm.	7	1986	1993
553	-	Gene Wlasiuk, Wpg.-Sask.	10	1958	1967
506	-	Ed Learn, Mtl.-Tor.	12	1958	1969
471	-	Ron Latourelle, Wpg.	10	1955	1964
458	-	Ron Howell, Ham.-B.C.-Tor.-Mtl.	13	1954	1966
430	-	Lynn Bottoms, Cal.-Tor.	10	1954	1963
422	-	Jim Copeland, Mtl.-Sask.-Tor.	9	1960	1968
410	-	Dick Dupuis, Cal.-Edm.	11	1965	1976
405	-	Larry Crawford, B.C.-Tor.	9	1981	1989

MOST PUNT RETURNS ONE SEASON:

123	-	Jim Silye, Cal.	1970	112	-	Rudy Linterman, Cal.	1968
118	-	Anthony Hunter, Edm.	1989				

MOST PUNT RETURNS ONE GAME:

14	-	Rudy Linterman, Cal.	Cal. at Edm.	Aug. 28, 1968
	-	Jim Copeland, Tor.	Ham. at Ham.	Oct. 29, 1966
	-	Rufus Crawford, Ham.	Mtl. at Ham.	Sept. 3, 1984
	-	Will Lewis, Ott.	Ham. at Ott.	Oct. 24, 1987
13	-	Will Lewis, Ott.	Wpg. at Ott.	Sept. 24, 1988
12	-	Jerry Bradley, B.C.	Sask. at B.C.	Nov. 2, 1968
	-	Jim Walter, Sask.	Sask. at B.C.	Sept. 18, 1970
	-	Jim Silye, Cal.	Cal. at Reg.	Oct. 18, 1970
	-	Dick Adams, Ott.	Ham. at Ott.	Sept. 7, 1974
	-	Dickie Harris, Mtl.	Ott. at Mtl.	Oct. 27, 1979
	-	Glenn Steele, Wpg.	Wpg. at Sask.	Sept. 1, 1985
	-	Anthony Hunter, Edm.	B.C. at Edm.	Sept. 24, 1989
	-	Tyrone Thurman, Ott.	Ott. at Wpg.	Oct. 29, 1989

LONGEST PUNT RETURN:

131	-	Boyd Carter (15), Tor.		
	-	Dave Mann (116), Tor.	Mtl. at Tor.	Aug. 22, 1958
130	-	Ken Hinton, B.C.	Edm. at B.C.	Sept. 24, 1977
116	-	Larry Highbaugh, Edm.	Wpg. at Edm.	Oct. 26, 1975

ALL-TIME LEADERS MOST TOUCHDOWNS ON PUNT RETURNS:

			Seasons	Earliest	Latest
21	-	Henry Williams, Edm.	7	1986	1993
11	-	Earl Winfield, Ham.	7	1987	1993
5	-	Ron Howell, Ham.-B.C.-Tor.-Mtl.	13	1954	1966
	-	Mike Clemons, Tor.	5	1989	1993

MOST TOUCHDOWNS ON PUNT RETURNS ONE SEASON:

5	-	Henry Williams, Edm.	1991	3	-	Larry Crawford, B.C.	1987
4	-	Earl Winfield, Ham.	1988		-	Derrick Crawford, Cal.	1990
	-	Henry Williams, Edm.	1987		-	Willis Jacox, Sask.	1991
	-	Henry Williams, Edm.	1993		-	Henry Williams, Edm.	1992
3	-	Dickie Harris, Mtl.	1979				

MOST TOUCHDOWNS ON PUNT RETURNS IN ONE GAME:

2	-	Ron Howell, Ham.	Ham. at Tor.	Sept 20, 1959
	-	Henry Williams, Edm.	Cal. at Edm.	June 27, 1987
	-	Henry Williams, Edm.	Cal. at Edm.	Sept 6, 1991
	-	Earl Winfield, Ham.	Edm. at Ham.	Sept. 17, 1993
	-	Henry Williams, Edm.	Cal. at Edm.	Nov. 7, 1993

MOST TOUCHDOWNS ON PUNT RETURNS IN ONE QUARTER:

2	-	Henry Williams, Edm. (3rd quarter)	Cal. at Edm.	June 27, 1987
	-	Henry Williams, Edm. (2nd quarter)	Cal. at Edm.	Sept 6, 1991

ALL-TIME LEADERS, SINGLES ON KICKOFFS:

30	-	Dave Cutler, Edm.	1969-1984
24	-	Bernie Ruoff, Wpg.-Ham.-B.C.	1975-1988
23	-	Hank Ilesic, Edm.-Tor.	1977-1993
19	-	John T. Hay, Ott.-Cal.	1978-1988
	-	Lui Passaglia, B.C.	1976-1993
	-	Dave Ridgway, Sask.	1982-1993
18	-	Trevor Kennerd, Wpg.	1980-1991

MOST SINGLES ON KICKOFFS ONE SEASON:

9	-	Hank Ilesic, Tor.	1983	6	-	Dave Ridgway, Sask.	1982
7	-	Hank Ilesic, Tor.	1984				

ALL-TIME LEADERS KICKOFF RETURN YARDAGE:

	Seas.	No.	Yds.	Ave.	Long.	TD
Leo Lewis, Wpg.	11	187	5444	29.1	91	1
Dwight Edwards, Tor.-Sask.-Ott.-Mtl.-Tor.	11	247	5384	21.8	89	0
Ron Hopkins, Cal.	9	226	5238	23.2	100	2
Larry Highbaugh, B.C.-Edm.	13	141	4966	35.2	118	3
Harvey Wylie, Cal.	9	151	4293	28.4	110	5
Dave Raimey, Wpg.-Tor.	10	140	3722	26.6	105	2
Vince Phason, Edm.-B.C.-Wpg.-Mtl.	11	144	3715	25.8	80	0
Joe Hollimon, Edm.	10	130	3283	25.3	82	0
Paul Williams, Wpg.-Sask.	8	126	3134	24.9	109	1
Byron Bailey, B.C.	11	128	3114	24.3	96	1
Henry Williams, Edm.	7	158	3370	21.3	92	1

MOST YARDS ON KICKOFF RETURNS ONE SEASON:

1307	-	Stacey Dawsey, Ott.	1990	1231	-	Willis Jacox, Sask.	1991
1287	-	Ron Hopkins, Cal.	1990				

MOST YARDS ON KICKOFF RETURNS ONE GAME:

257	-	Anthony Cherry, B.C.	B.C. at Ham.	Aug. 4, 1989
239	-	Joe Hollimon, Edm.	Cal. at Cal.	Sept. 6, 1976
228	-	Stephen Jones, Edm.	Tor. at Edm.	Aug. 1, 1986

ALL-TIME KICKOFF RETURN LEADERS:

			Seasons	Earliest	Latest
247	-	Dwight Edwards, Tor.-Sask.-Ott.-Mtl.-Tor.	11	1978	1988
226	-	Ron Hopkins, Cal.	9	1983	1991
187	-	Leo Lewis, Wpg.	11	1955	1966
151	-	Harvey Wylie, Cal.	9	1956	1964
144	-	Vince Phason, Edm.-B.C.-Wpg.-Mtl.	11	1975	1985
141	-	Larry Highbaugh, B.C.-Edm.	13	1971	1983
140	-	Dave Raimey, Wpg.-Tor.	10	1965	1974
158	-	Henry Williams, Edm.	7	1986	1993
131	-	Craig Ellis, Wpg.-Cal.-Sask.-Tor.-Edm.	10	1982	1993
130	-	Joe Hollimon, Edm.	10	1976	1985

MOST KICKOFF RETURNS ONE SEASON:

59	-	Stacey Dawsey, Ott.	1990	57	-	Darrell Wallace, B.C.	1989
58	-	Willis Jacox, Sask.	1991				

MOST KICKOFF RETURNS ONE GAME:

9	-	Anthony Cherry, B.C.	B.C. at Ham.	Aug. 4, 1989
	-	Lee Hull, Wpg.	Cal. at Wpg.	Aug. 28, 1990
	-	Lorenzo Graham, B.C.	B.C. at Tor.	Sept. 1, 1990
8	-	Joe Hollimon, Edm.	Cal. at Edm.	Oct. 31, 1976
	-	Bruce Walker, Ott.	B.C. at Ott.	Sept. 3, 1982
	-	Cedric Minter, Ott.	Ott. at Wpg.	July 3, 1987
	-	Lorenzo Graham, B.C.	B.C. vs. Cal.	Aug. 15, 1991
	-	Mike Clemons, Tor.	Tor. at Edm.	Aug. 21, 1991
	-	Maurice Smith, B.C.	Edm. at Sask.	Oct. 12, 1991

LONGEST KICKOFF RETURN:

120	-	Lovell Coleman, Cal.	Edm. at Cal.	Aug. 17, 1964
	-	Mack Herron, Wpg.	Edm. at Wpg.	Aug. 30, 1972
118	-	Larry Highbaugh, Edm.	Edm. at Wpg.	Oct. 17, 1976
115	-	Bobby Thompson, Sask.	B.C. at Reg.	Oct. 24, 1971

ALL-TIME LEADERS TOUCHDOWNS ON KICKOFF RETURNS:

			Seasons	Earliest	Latest
5	-	Harvey Wylie, Cal.	9	1956	1964
3	-	Hal Patterson, Mtl.-Ham.	14	1954	1967
	-	Larry Highbaugh, B.C.-Edm.	13	1971	1983

ALL-TIME MOST BLOCKED KICKS:

			Seasons	Earliest	Latest
8	-	Rod Hill, Wpg.	5	1988	1992
7	-	James Zachery, Edm.	8	1980	1987
	-	Scott Flagel, Wpg.-Cal.-Ham.-Ott.	10	1982	1991
6	-	Junior Ah You, Mtl.	10	1972	1981
	-	Frank Andruski, Cal.	8	1966	1973
	-	Harry Skipper, Sask.-Mtl.	7	1983	1989
	-	Less Browne, Ham.-Wpg.-Ott.-B.C.	10	1984	1993

MOST BLOCKED KICKS ONE SEASON:

5	-	James Zachery, Edm.	1986
3	-	Mark Philp, Ott.	1980
	-	Merv Walker, Wpg.	1974
	-	Scott Flagel, Cal.-Ham.	1988
	-	Paul Clatney, Wpg.	1988
	-	Reggie Pleasant, Tor.	1990
	-	Less Browne, Ott.	1992

MOST BLOCKED KICKS ONE GAME:

2	-	Ken Lehmann, Ott.	Aug. 23, 1967
	-	Allan Ray Aldridge, Tor.	Aug. 25, 1968
	-	John Vilunas, Ham.	Sept. 23, 1970
	-	Donnie Thomas, Ham.	Aug. 30, 1977

ALL-TIME LEADERS YARDAGE ON FUMBLE RETURNS:

			Seasons	Earliest	Latest
241	-	Greg Battle, Wpg.	7	1987	1993
234	-	Wayne Giardino, Ott.	9	1967	1975
219	-	Larry Robinson, Cal.	14	1961	1974

MOST YARDS ON FUMBLE RETURNS ONE SEASON:

146	-	Wayne Giardino, Ott.	1972
	-	Al Washington, Ott.	1984
139	-	Jim Reynolds, Ott.	1961

LONGEST FUMBLE RETURNS:

104	-	Al Washington, Ott.	Cal. at Ott.	July 7, 1984
102	-	Jerry Keeling, Cal.	B.C. at Cal.	Sept. 22, 1964
101	-	Don Wilson, Tor.	Tor. at Edm.	Aug. 21, 1991

ALL-TIME LEADERS TOUCHDOWNS ON FUMBLE RETURNS:

5	-	Michael Allen, Wpg.	1988-93
4	-	Jim Reynolds, Ott.-Mtl.	1961-63
	-	Vince Goldsmith, Sask.-Tor.-Cal.-Sask.	1981-89

ALL-TIME LEADERS INTERCEPTIONS:

			Seasons	Earliest	Latest
76	-	Less Browne, Ham.-Wpg.-Ott.	10	1984	1993
66	-	Larry Highbaugh, B.C.-Edm.	13	1971	1983
62	-	Terry Irvin, Cal.-Sask.-Mtl.	10	1977	1986
59	-	Garney Henley, Ham.	16	1960	1975
58	-	Don Sutherin, Ham.-Ott.-Tor.	13	1958	1970
52	-	John Wydareny, Tor.-Edm.	10	1963	1972
	-	Larry Crawford, B.C.-Tor.	9	1981	1989
51	-	Ed Learn, Mtl.-Tor.	12	1958	1969
50	-	Larry Robinson, Cal.	14	1961	1974
47	-	Joe Poirier, Ott.	11	1960	1970
	-	Harry Skipper, Mtl.-Sask.	7	1983	1989
	-	Rod Hill, Wpg.	5	1988	1992
5	-	Harry Skipper, Mtl.-Sask.	7	1983	1989
	-	Keith Gooch, B.C.	7	1984	1990
4	-	Gordie Rowland, Wpg.	10	1954	1963
	-	Earl Lindley, Edm.	3	1954	1956
	-	Bill Wayte, Mtl.-Ham.	6	1961	1966
	-	Frank Andruski, Cal.	8	1966	1973
	-	Larry Highbaugh, B.C.-Edm.	13	1971	1983
	-	Ken McEachern, Sask.-Tor.	11	1974	1984
	-	Ray Odums, Wpg.-Sask.-Cal.	10	1975	1984
	-	Darrell Moir, Cal.	8	1979	1986
	-	Terry Irvin, Cal.-Sask.-Mtl.- Cal.	11	1977	1987
	-	Larry Crawford, B.C.	9	1981	1989
	-	Ben Zambiasi, Ham.-Tor.	11	1978	1988

MOST INTERCEPTIONS ONE SEASON:

15	-	Al Brenner, Ham.	1972
14	-	Less Browne, Wpg.	1990
13	-	Roy Bennett, Wpg.	1987

MOST INTERCEPTIONS ONE SEASON BY A FIRST-YEAR PLAYER:

10	-	Bill McFarlane, Tor.	1954
	-	Dale West, Sask.	1963
	-	Harry Skipper, Mtl.	1983
9	-	Al Marcelin, Ott.	1970
	-	Laurent DesLauriers, Edm.	1984
	-	Reggie Pleasant, Tor.	1987

MOST INTERCEPTIONS ONE GAME:

5	-	Rod Hill, Wpg.	Ham. at Wpg.	Sept. 9, 1990
4	-	Don Sutherin, Ham.	Edm. at Ham.	Sept. 11, 1961
	-	Art Johnson, Tor.	Tor. at Mtl.	Oct. 7, 1961
	-	Peter Ribbins, Wpg.	Wpg. at B.C.	Aug. 17, 1972
	-	Al Brenner, Ham.	Tor. at Ham.	Nov. 5, 1972
	-	Chris Sigler, Ott.	Mtl. at Ott.	June 27, 1986
	-	Less Browne, Ham.	Ham. at Mtl.	Aug. 21, 1986
	-	Terry Irvin, Mtl.	Mtl. at Tor.	Nov. 2, 1986

MOST INTERCEPTIONS ONE GAME BY A FIRST-YEAR PLAYER:

3	-	Bill McFarlane, Tor.	Tor. at Ott.	Sept. 18, 1954
	-	Dale West, Sask.	Sask. at Ham.	Aug. 15, 1963
	-	Harry Skipper, Cal.	Cal. at Mtl.	Oct. 22, 1983
	-	Laurent DesLauriers, Edm.	Ott. at Edm.	June 30, 1984

ALL-TIME LEADERS YARDS ON INTERCEPTION RETURNS:

			Seasons	Earliest	Latest
1385	-	Less Browne, Ham.-Wpg.-Ott.-B.C.	10	1984	1993
1067	-	Harry Skipper, Mtl.-Sask.	7	1983	1989
1004	-	Paul Bennett, Tor.-Wpg.-Ham.	11	1977	1987
916	-	Garney Henley, Ham.	16	1960	1975
847	-	Dick Thornton, Wpg.-Tor.	12	1961	1972
837	-	Ken McEachern, Sask.-Tor.	11	1974	1984
810	-	Larry Crawford, B.C.-Tor.	9	1981	1989
770	-	Larry Highbaugh, B.C.-Edm.	13	1971	1983
747	-	John Wydarney, Tor.-Edm.	10	1963	1972
740	-	David Shaw, Ham.-Wpg.	12	1975	1986

MOST YARDS INTERCEPTION RETURNS ONE SEASON:

273	-	Less Browne, Wpg.	1990
267	-	Less Browne, Wpg.	1991
259	-	Less Browne, Ott.	1992

MOST YARDS ON INTERCEPTION RETURNS ONE GAME:

172	-	Barry Ardern, Ott.	Ott. at Ham.	Nov. 1, 1969
135	-	Lewis Cook, Sask.	Cal. at Reg.	Aug. 27, 1972
129	-	Melvin Byrd, B.C.	Ott. at B.C.	Aug. 11, 1984

LONGEST INTERCEPTION RETURN:

120	-	Neal Beaumont, B.C.	Sask. at Van.	Oct. 12, 1963
119	-	Lewis Porter, Ham.	Ott. at Ham.	Oct. 8, 1973
118	-	Dickie Harris, Mtl.	Ott. at Mtl.	Aug. 10, 1972

ALL-TIME LEADERS TOUCHDOWNS ON INTERCEPTION RETURNS:

			Seasons	Earliest	Latest
8	-	Dick Thornton, Wpg.-Tor.	12	1961	1972
5	-	Garney Henley, Ham.	16	1960	1975
	-	Joe Hollimon, Edm.	9	1976	1984
	-	Cliff Toney, Edm.	5	1984	1988

MOST TOUCHDOWNS ON INTERCEPTION RETURNS ONE SEASON:

4	-	Joe Hollimon, Edm.	1978
3	-	Dick Thornton, Wpg.	1963
3	-	Ed Jones, Edm.	1980
	-	Keith Gooch, B.C.	1989

MOST TOUCHDOWNS ON INTERCEPTION RETURNS ONE GAME:

2	-	Dick Thornton, Wpg.	Wpg. at Edm.	Aug. 23, 1963
	-	Ed Jones, Edm.	Ham. at Edm.	Sept. 7, 1980
	-	James Jefferson, Wpg.	Ham. at Wpg.	Oct. 4, 1987

ALL-TIME COMBINED YARDAGE LEADERS:
(Includes: Rushing, Pass Receiving and Punt and Kickoff Return Yards.)

20051	-	George Reed, Saskatchewan (1963-75)
18576	-	Leo Lewis, Winnipeg (1955-66)
18174	-	Rufus Crawford, Hamilton (1979-85)
15725	-	Dick Shatto, Toronto (1954-65)
14095	-	Tom Scott, Winnipeg-Edmonton-Calgary (1974-84)
13669	-	Henry Williams, Edmonton (1986-88 and 1989-93)
13245	-	Hal Patterson, Montreal-Hamilton (1954-67)
13225	-	Johnny Bright, Calgary-Edmonton (1952-64)
12828	-	Craig Ellis, Wpg.-Cal.-Sask.-Tor.-Edm. (1982-1993)
12465	-	Willie Fleming, B.C. (1959-68)
11546	-	Dwight Edwards, Tor.-Sask.-Ott.-Cal.-Mtl. (1978-88)

MOST COMBINED YARDAGE ONE SEASON:

3300	-	Mike Clemons, Toronto	1990
3049	-	Raghib Ismail, Toronto	1991
2896	-	Rufus Crawford, Hamilton	1984

MOST COMBINED YARDAGE ONE GAME:

401	-	Raghib Ismail, Tor.	Tor. at Ott.	July 9, 1992
400	-	Earl Winfield, Ham.	Tor. at Ham.	Sept. 5, 1988
381	-	Hal Patterson, Mtl.	Mtl. at Ham.	Sept. 29, 1956

ALL-TIME YARDS FROM SCRIMMAGE LEADERS:
(Includes Rushing and Pass Receiving.)

			Seasons	Earliest	Latest
18888	-	George Reed, Sask.	13	1963	1975
13423	-	Dick Shatto, Tor.	12	1954	1965
13107	-	Leo Lewis, Wpg.	11	1955	1966
12735	-	Johnny Bright, Cal.-Edm.	13	1952	1964
11248	-	Tom Scott, Wpg.-Edm.-Cal.	11	1974	1984

MOST YARDS FROM SCRIMMAGE ONE SEASON:

2207	-	Robert Mimbs, Wpg.	1991
2140	-	Willard Reaves, Wpg.	1984
2127	-	Willie Burden, Cal.	1975

MOST YARDS FROM SCRIMMAGE ONE GAME:

338	-	Hal Patterson, Mtl.	Mtl. at Ham.	Sept. 29, 1956
319	-	Dick Smith, Mtl.	Tor. at Mtl.	Sept. 30, 1969
299	-	Ed Buchanan, Sask.	Sask. at Edm.	Aug. 28, 1964

ALL-TIME QUARTERBACK SACK LEADERS:

			Seasons	Earliest	Latest
157.0	-	Grover Covington, Ham.	11	1981	1991
139.5	-	James Parker, B.C.-Edm.-Tor.	12	1980	1991
130.5	-	Vince Goldsmith, Cal.-Tor.-Sask.-Cal.	10	1981	1990
126.0	-	Stewart Hill, Edm.-B.C.	10	1984	1993
	-	Tyrone Jones, Wpg.-Sask.	11	1983	1993

MOST QUARTERBACK SACKS ONE SEASON:

26.5	-	James Parker, B.C.	1984
25	-	Grover Covington, Ham.	1988
23	-	Gregg Stumon, B.C.	1987
22	-	James Curry, Toronto	1984
	-	James Parker, B.C.	1986
22	-	Elfrid Payton, Winnipg	1993
	-	Bobby Jurasin, Sask.	1987
21	-	Mike Walker, Ham.	1986
	-	Brett Williams, Mtl.	1986

MOST QUARTERBACK SACKS ONE GAME:

5	-	Rodney Harding, Tor.	Sept. 25, 1988	Edm. at Tor.
	-	Mack Moore, B.C.	Sept. 3, 1982	B.C. at Ott.
	-	Tim Cofield, Hamilton	Sept. 6, 1993	Tor. at Ham.
4.5	-	Tyrone Jones, Winnipeg	July 22, 1984	B.C. at Wpg.
	-	James Curry, Toronto	Aug. 31, 1984	Tor. at Ott.

ALL-TIME MOST DEFENSIVE TACKLES:
(Defensive Tackles recorded since 1987)

597	-	Willie Pless, Tor.-B.C.-Edm.	1986-93
505	-	Greg Battle, Wpg.	1987-93
465	-	Dan Bass, Tor.-Cal.-Edm.	1980-91
461	-	Don Moen, Tor.	1982-93
457	-	James West, Cal.-Wpg.	1982-93
443	-	Larry Wruck, Edm.	1985-93
439	-	Alondra Johnson, B.C.-Cal.	1989-93
435	-	Matt Finlay, Mtl.-Tor.-Cal.	1986-93
428	-	Eddie Lowe, Sask.	1983-91
373	-	David Albright, Sask.	1986-91

MOST DEFENSIVE TACKLES ONE SEASON:
(Defensive Tackles recorded since 1987)

127	-	Bruce Holmes, Ott.	1990
122	-	Doug Landry, Cal.	1989
118	-	David Albright, Sask.	1987

MOST DEFENSIVE TACKLES ONE GAME:
(Defensive Tackles recorded since 1987)

14 -	Bruce Holmes, Ott.	Ott. at Edm.	Oct. 15, 1989
-	Jeff Braswell, Tor.	Tor. at Ott.	Oct. 31, 1992
13 -	Jearld Baylis, Tor.	Tor. at Sask.	July 4, 1987
-	Willie Pless, Tor.	Cal. at Tor.	July 22, 1987
-	Ken Hailey, Wpg.	Wpg. at Ham.	Aug. 14, 1987
-	Greg Peterson, Cal.	Cal. at Wpg.	Sept.13, 1987
-	Darrell Patterson, Ham.	Ham. at Ott.	Aug. 9, 1990
-	Chris Gaines, Tor.	Wpg. at Tor.	Aug. 22, 1990
-	Greg Battle, Wpg.	Sask. at Wpg.	Sept. 23, 1990
-	Tracy Gravely, B.C.	Sask. at B.C.	Aug. 13, 1992
-	Don Moen, Tor.	Tor. at Wpg.	Oct. 25, 1992
12 -	Bruce Holmes, Ott.	Wpg. at Ott.	July 12, 1990
-	Bruce Holmes, Ott.	Ott. at Edm.	Sept. 21, 1990
-	Darryl Ford, Tor.	Tor. at Ott.	July 11, 1991
-	O.J. Brigance, B.C.	B.C. at Cal.	Aug. 8, 1991
-	James King, Sask.	Sask. at Wpg.	Sept. 8, 1991
-	Eddie Lowe, Sask.	Sask. at Wpg.	Sept. 8, 1991
-	Willie Pless, Edm.	Edm. at B.C.	Oct 12, 1991
-	Eddie Lowe, Sask.	Ott. at Sask.	Oct 20, 1991

MOST SPECIAL TEAMS TACKLES ONE GAME:
(Special Team Tackles recorded since 1991)

7 -	Paul Clatney, Cal.	B.C. at Cal.	July 11, 1991
-	Terry Wright, Ham.	Ott. at Ham.	Sept. 14, 1991
6 -	Daniel Hunter, Ott.	Cal. at Ott.	July 24, 1991
-	Paul Bushey, Ham.	Ham. at Edm.	Oct. 4, 1991
5 -	Paul Bushey, Sask.	Cal. at Sask.	July 18, 1991
-	Sean Foudy, Ott.	Wpg. at Ott.	Aug. 8, 1991
-	Lance Trumble, Ham.	Ott. at Ham.	Aug. 24, 1991
-	Gord Weber, Ott.	Tor. at Ott.	July 9, 1992
-	Paul Bushey, Ham.	Sask. at Ham.	July 30, 1992
-	Bruce Plummer, Wpg.	Wpg. at B.C.	Oct. 31, 1992

MOST TACKLES FOR LOSSES ONE GAME:
(Tackles for Losses recorded since 1991)

4 (12 yards) -	Brian Hilk, Ham.	Ott. at Ham.	Sept. 14, 1991
3 (22 yards) -	Stewart Hill, B.C.	Edm. at B.C.	July 25, 1991
3 (6 yards) -	Angelo Snipes, Ott.	Ott. at Edm.	Aug. 6, 1992
3 (9 yards) -	Larry Wruck, Edm.	Edm. at Cal.	Sept. 7, 1992
3 (9 yards) -	Larry Wruck, Edm.	B.C. at Edm.	Sept. 11, 1992
3 (5 yards) -	Lee Johnson, B.C.	Cal. at B.C.	Oct. 10, 1992
3 (8 yards) -	Matt Finlay, Cal.	Cal. at B.C.	Oct. 10, 1992

1993 CFL Record Holders

#8 QB Danny Barrett - Set a new CFL Record for Most Yards Passed One Game on Aug. 12/93 vs. Toronto when he threw for 601 yards.

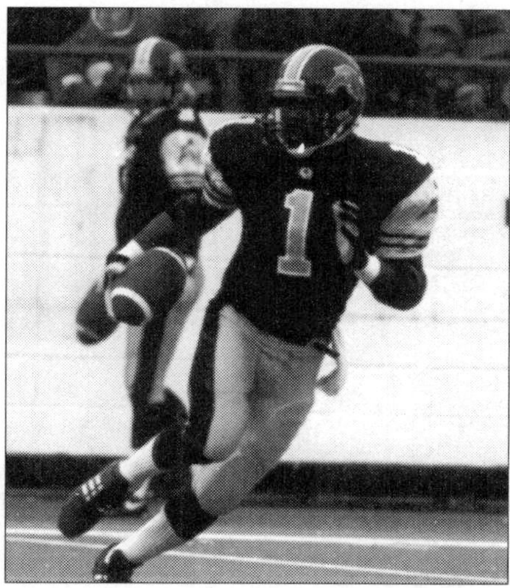

#1 WR Earl Winfield tied a CFL Record when he returned two punts for touchdowns on Sept. 17/93 vs. Edmonton.

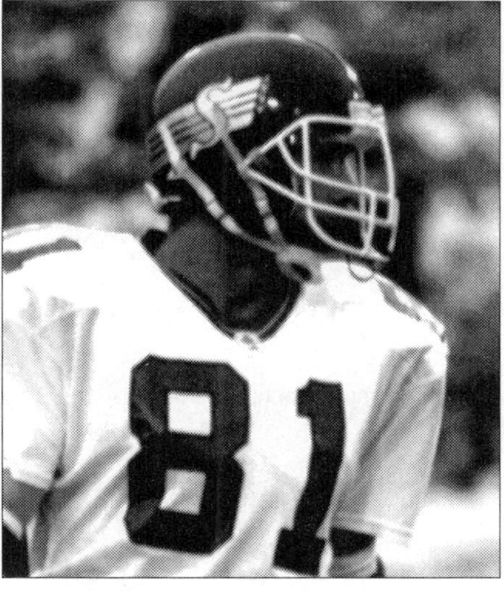

#81 SB Ray Elgaard caught for over 1,000 yards for the 7th time in his career to become the All-Time Leader in Reception Yards with 11,253.

PLAYOFF TEAM RECORDS

MOST PLAYOFF YEARS PLAYED:

39	-	Hamilton
38	-	Edmonton
37	-	Winnipeg

MOST PLAYOFF GAMES PLAYED:

81	-	Winnipeg
75	-	Edmonton
70	-	Hamilton

MOST CONSECUTIVE YEARS IN PLAYOFFS:

22	-	Edmonton,	1972-93
15	-	Saskatchewan,	1962-76
14	-	Ottawa,	1956-69
14	-	Winnipeg	1980-93

MOST CONSECUTIVE PLAYOFF GAMES:

16	-	Edmonton,	1950-53
14	-	Winnipeg,	1953-55
	-	Edmonton,	1958-60
12	-	Calgary,	1968-71
	-	Saskatchewan,	1971-76

MOST GAMES PLAYED ONE SEASON:

5	-	Edmonton,	'52, '58, '60
	-	Winnipeg,	'53, '54, '57
	-	Saskatchewan,	'56, '63
	-	Calgary,	'62, '64

ALL-TIME MOST WINS:

44	-	Edmonton
42	-	Winnipeg
33	-	Hamilton
31	-	Ottawa

MOST WINS ONE SEASON:

4	-	Edmonton,	1960
3	-	several teams	

ALL-TIME MOST LOSSES:

37	-	Winnipeg
36	-	Hamilton
35	-	Ottawa

MOST LOSSES ONE SEASON:

3	-	Saskatchewan,	1956, 1963
	-	Calgary,	1961, 1964
	-	Hamilton,	1951
	-	Winnipeg,	1955

ALL-TIME MOST TIES:

3	-	Calgary
2	-	Winnipeg
	-	Saskatchewan

MOST UNDEFEATED SEASONS:

14	-	Edmonton
10	-	Montreal
9	-	Hamilton

MOST WINLESS SEASONS:

16	-	Ottawa
14	-	Hamilton
13	-	Montreal

HIGHEST ATTENDANCE:

59,478	- Wpg. 22 at B.C. 42, Division Final	Nov. 17, 1985
59,421	- Wpg. 31 at B.C. 14, Division Final	Nov. 11, 1984
59,409	- Wpg. 21 at B.C. 39, Division Final	Nov. 20, 1983
55,400	- Ott. 18 at Mtl. 21, Division Final	Nov. 19, 1977
54,530	- Ham. 36 at Tor. 41, Division Final	Nov. 20, 1983

ALL-TIME MOST POINTS SCORED:

1527	-	Edmonton
1477	-	Winnipeg
1443	-	Hamilton

ALL-TIME MOST POINTS AGAINST:

1352	-	Hamilton
1322	-	Saskatchewan
1308	-	Ottawa
1285	-	Winnipeg

MOST POINTS ONE TEAM ONE GAME:

59	-	Wpg. vs. Ham.,	Nov. 22, 1992
55	-	Wpg. vs. Edm.,	Nov. 4, 1984
51	-	Edm. vs. Sask.,	Nov. 17, 1956
	-	Cal. vs. Sask.,	Nov. 9, 1964
	-	Edm. vs. Sask.	Nov. 14, 1993
50	-	Ham. vs. Mtl.,	Nov. 17, 1985

MOST POINTS BOTH TEAMS ONE GAME:

89	-	Mtl. 48 vs. Ham. 41,	Nov. 17, 1956
84	-	Cal. 43 vs. B.C. 41,	Nov. 10, 1991
77	-	Tor. 41 vs. Ham. 36,	Nov. 20, 1983
76	-	Ham. 50 vs. Mtl. 26,	Nov. 17, 1985

FEWEST POINTS BOTH TEAMS ONE GAME:

3	-	Tor. 3 vs. Ott. 0,	1947
5	-	Edm. 4 vs. Wpg. 1,	Oct. 27, 1951
6	-	Edm. 4 vs. Wpg. 2,	Nov. 19, 1960
8	-	Cal. 4 vs. Sask. 4,	Nov. 6, 1948

MOST TIMES SHUTOUT:

4	-	Ottawa,	1947 (2), 1963, 1967
3	-	Montreal,	1959, 1964, 1976
2	-	Hamilton Tigers,	1948, 1949
	-	Saskatchewan,	1962, 1968

HIGHEST SHUTOUT:

45-0	-	Ham. at Ott.,	Nov. 16, 1963
43-0	-	Ott. vs. Mtl.,	Nov. 7, 1959
40-0	-	Mtl. vs. Ham.,	Nov. 19, 1949

MOST TOUCHDOWNS ONE TEAM ONE GAME:

7	-	Ham. vs. Queen's,	Nov. 23, 1935
	-	Mtl. vs. Ham.,	Nov. 19, 1949
	-	Tor. vs. Balmy Beach,	1950
	-	Ott. vs. Sarnia,	1951
	-	Wpg. vs. Sask.,	Oct. 28, 1953
	-	Mtl. vs. Ham.,	Nov. 17, 1956
	-	Edm. vs. Sask.,	Nov. 17, 1956
	-	Wpg. vs. Edm.,	Nov. 4, 1984
	-	Ham. vs. Mtl.,	Nov. 17, 1985
6	-	Edm. vs. Kitchener,	Nov. 20, 1954
	-	Tor. at Mtl.,	Nov. 19, 1955
	-	Sask. vs. Wpg.,	Nov. 3, 1956
	-	Wpg. vs. Edm.,	Nov. 13, 1983
	-	Edm. vs. Sask.,	Nov. 11, 1990
	-	Cal. vs. B.C.,	Nov. 10, 1991
	-	Wpg. vs. Ham.,	Nov. 22, 1992
	-	Edm. vs. Sask.,	Nov. 14, 1993

MOST CONVERTS ONE TEAM ONE GAME:

7	-	Tor. vs. Balmy Beach,	1950
	-	Ott. vs. Sarnia,	1951
	-	Wpg. vs. Sask.,	Oct. 28, 1953
	-	Wpg. vs. Edm.,	Nov. 4, 1984
	-	Ham. vs. Mtl.,	Nov. 17, 1985
6	-	Mtl. vs. Ham.,	1953
	-	Edm. vs. Kitchener,	Nov. 20, 1954
	-	Edm. vs. Sask.,	Nov. 17, 1956
	-	Mtl. vs. Ham.,	Nov. 17, 1956
	-	Ham. at Mtl.,	Nov. 17, 1956
	-	Wpg. vs. Edm.,	Nov. 13, 1983
	-	Edm. vs. Sask.,	Nov. 11, 1990
	-	Cal. vs. B.C.,	Nov. 10, 1991
	-	Wpg. vs. Ham.,	Nov. 22, 1992
	-	Edm. vs. Sask.,	Nov. 14, 1993

MOST FIELD GOALS ONE TEAM ONE GAME:

6	-	Edm. vs. Sask.,	Nov. 18, 1973
	-	Ott. vs. Ham.,	Nov. 11, 1979
	-	Tor. vs. Ham.,	Nov. 15, 1987
5	-	Ham. vs. Ott.,	Nov. 26, 1972
	-	Edm. vs. Cal.,	Nov. 15, 1987
	-	Cal. vs. Edm.,	Nov. 18, 1990
	-	Wpg. vs. Ham.,	Nov. 22, 1992

MOST SINGLES ONE TEAM ONE GAME:

9	-	Ott. vs. Ham.,	1909
	-	Tor. vs. Ham.,	1911
	-	Ham. vs. Tor.,	1914
8	-	Ham. vs. Ham. R.C.,	1923

MOST TOUCHDOWNS RUSHING ONE TEAM ONE GAME:

7	-	Wpg. vs. Sask.,	Oct. 28, 1953
5	-	Ham. vs. Ott.,	Nov. 7, 1956
	-	Ott. at Ham.,	Nov. 24, 1963
4	-	Ham. at Ott.,	Nov. 16, 1963
	-	B.C. at Cal.,	Nov. 10, 1991
	-	Wpg. vs. Ham.,	Nov. 22, 1992

MOST TOUCHDOWN PASSES ONE TEAM ONE GAME:

6	-	Ott. vs. Ham. at Mtl.,	Nov. 19, 1966
5	-	Ham. at Mtl.,	Nov. 17, 1956
	-	Ham. vs. Tor.,	Nov. 25, 1961
	-	Sask. vs. Cal.,	Nov. 11, 1963
	-	Ham. vs. Mtl.,	Nov. 17, 1985
	-	Cal. vs. B.C.,	Nov. 10, 1991

MOST TOTAL YARDS ONE TEAM ONE GAME:

746	-	Ham. at Mtl.,	Nov. 17, 1956
648	-	Ham. vs. Tor.,	Nov. 26, 1961
607	-	Sask. at Wpg.,	Nov. 3, 1956

MOST TOTAL YARDS BOTH TEAMS ONE GAME:

1,151	-	Ham. at Mtl.,	Nov. 17, 1956
1,069	-	Mtl. at Ham.,	Nov. 10, 1956
1,011	-	Ott. vs. Mtl.,	Nov. 13, 1957

MOST POINTS IN ONE QUARTER ONE TEAM:

29	-	Calgary, B.C. at Cal.,	Nov. 10, 1979
28	-	Calgary, B.C. at Cal.,	Nov. 10, 1991
26	-	Saskatchewan, Cal. at Sask.,	Nov. 7, 1964
25	-	Saskatchewan, Wpg. at Sask.,	Nov. 8, 1975
24	-	Toronto, Tor. at Mtl.,	Nov. 19, 1955
	-	Edmonton, Edm. at Cal.,	Nov. 18, 1990

MOST POINTS IN ONE QUARTER BOTH TEAMS:

32	-	Winnipeg (7) at Saskatchewan (25),	Nov. 8, 1975
31	-	Edmonton (14) at Saskatchewan (17),	Nov. 10, 1956
	-	B.C. (3) at Calgary (28),	Nov. 10, 1991
30	-	Winnipeg (24) at Edmonton (6),	Nov. 14, 1953

MOST FIRST DOWNS ONE TEAM ONE GAME:

37	-	Hamilton, Tor. at Ham.,	Nov. 26, 1961
35	-	Hamilton, Ham. at Tor.,	Nov. 23, 1986
34	-	Edmonton, Edm. at Cal.,	Nov. 5, 1960
	-	Calgary, Sask. at Cal.,	Nov. 9, 1963
33	-	Hamilton, Ott. at Ham.,	Nov. 7, 1956
	-	Edmonton, Edm. at Sask.,	Nov. 8, 1958

MOST RUSHING ATTEMPTS ONE TEAM ONE GAME:

63	-	Winnipeg, Edm. at Wpg.,	Nov. 22, 1958
	-	Montreal, Mtl. at Tor.,	Nov. 11, 1973
59	-	Edmonton, Wpg. at Edm.,	Nov. 23, 1957
58	-	Edmonton, Edm. at Wpg.,	Nov. 11, 1955
57	-	Ottawa, Mtl. at Ott.,	Nov. 5, 1960

MOST RUSHING ATTEMPTS BOTH TEAMS ONE GAME:

104	-	Montreal (63) at Toronto (41),	Nov. 11, 1973
98	-	Montreal (41) at Ottawa (57),	Nov. 5, 1960
96	-	Edmonton (58) at Winnipeg (38),	Nov. 11, 1955
	-	Winnipeg (37) at Edmonton (59),	Nov. 23, 1957
95	-	Ottawa (41) at Hamilton (54),	Nov. 7, 1956

MOST YARDS RUSHING ONE TEAM ONE GAME:

413	-	Hamilton, Mtl. at Ham.,	Nov. 23, 1957
412	-	Edmonton, Sask. at Edm.,	Nov. 3, 1951
391	-	Montreal, Mtl. at Ott.,	Nov. 13, 1957
340	-	Ottawa, Tor. at Ott.,	Nov. 12, 1960
338	-	Edmonton, Edm. at Sask.,	Nov. 8, 1958

MOST YARDS RUSHING BOTH TEAMS ONE GAME:

696	-	Montreal (391) at Ottawa (305),	Nov. 13, 1957
557	-	Montreal (264) at Ottawa (293),	Nov. 10, 1962
555	-	Montreal (242) at Ottawa (313),	Nov. 5, 1960
	-	Hamilton (225) at Toronto (330),	Nov. 9, 1968
527	-	Winnipeg (215) at Edmonton (312),	Nov. 23, 1957

MOST PASSES THROWN ONE TEAM ONE GAME:

50	-	Toronto, Ott. at Tor.,	Nov. 20, 1960
	-	Toronto, Ham. at Tor.,	Nov. 11, 1984
49	-	Hamilton, Ham. at Mtl.,	Nov. 20, 1954
	-	Saskatchewan, Cal. at Sask.,	Nov. 11, 1963
	-	Hamilton, Ham. at Tor.,	Nov. 11, 1984
48	-	Calgary, Cal. at Edm.,	Nov. 18, 1979
	-	Calgary, Edm. at Cal.,	Nov. 21, 1993

MOST PASSES THROWN BOTH TEAMS ONE GAME:

99	-	Hamilton (49) at Toronto (50),	Nov. 11, 1984
84	-	Toronto (42) at Hamilton (42),	Nov. 26, 1961
83	-	Saskatchewan (37) at Calgary (46),	Nov. 20, 1968
81	-	Hamilton (49) at Montreal (32),	Nov. 20, 1954
80	-	Ottawa (39) at Hamilton (41),	Nov. 15, 1981
	-	Toronto (35) at Hamilton (45),	Nov. 16, 1986

MOST PASSES COMPLETED ONE TEAM ONE GAME:

35	-	Hamilton, Ham. at Tor.,	Nov. 23, 1986
32	-	Saskatchewan, Sask. at Edm.,	Nov. 15, 1992
29	-	Saskatchewan, Sask. at Edm.,	Nov. 14, 1993
28	-	Calgary, B.C. at Cal.,	Nov. 10, 1979
	-	Hamilton, Ham. at Ott.,	Nov. 13, 1983
	-	Toronto, Ham. at Tor.,	Nov. 11, 1984
	-	Montreal, Ott. at Mtl.,	Nov. 10, 1985
27	-	Hamilton, Ham. at Mtl.,	Nov. 11, 1978
	-	Hamilton, Ham. at Mtl.,	Nov. 9, 1975
	-	Hamilton, Ham. at Ott.,	Nov. 10, 1974

MOST PASSES COMPLETED BOTH TEAMS ONE GAME:

53	-	Hamilton (35) at Toronto (18),	Nov. 23, 1986
49	-	Saskatchewan (32) at Edmonton (17),	Nov. 15, 1992
51	-	Hamilton (23) at Toronto (28),	Nov. 11, 1984
48	-	Ottawa (25) at Hamilton (23),	Nov. 14, 1993
47	-	Hamilton (27) at Montreal (20),	Nov. 9, 1975
	-	Hamilton (23) at Toronto (24),	Nov. 20, 1983

MOST YARDS PASSED ONE TEAM ONE GAME:

540	-	Hamilton, Ham. at Mtl.,	Nov. 17, 1956
492	-	Saskatchewan, Cal. at Sask.,	Nov. 11, 1963
468	-	Saskatchewan, Sask. at Edm.,	Nov. 15, 1992
467	-	Calgary, B.C. at Cal.,	Nov. 10, 1979
	-	Winnipeg, Edm. at Wpg.,	Nov. 13, 1983
461	-	Toronto, Ott. at Tor.,	Nov. 21, 1982

MOST YARDS PASSED BOTH TEAMS ONE GAME:

876	-	Hamilton (540) at Montreal (336),	Nov. 17, 1956
788	-	Edmonton (321) at Winnipeg (467),	Nov. 13, 1983
715	-	Hamilton (341) at Toronto (374),	Nov. 20, 1983
691	-	Hamilton (264) at Montreal (427),	Nov. 20, 1954
686	-	Toronto (454) at Hamilton (232),	Nov. 14, 1955

MOST INTERCEPTIONS BY ONE TEAM ONE GAME

8	-	Wpg. vs. Sask.,	Oct. 28, 1953
	-	Ott. vs. Ham. at Mtl.,	Nov. 19, 1966
6	-	Ott. vs. Mtl.,	Nov. 7, 1964
5	-	Sask. at Wpg.,	Oct. 30, 1954
	-	Edm. vs. B.C.,	Nov. 4, 1959
	-	B.C. vs. Sask.,	Nov. 20, 1963
	-	Cal. vs. Sask.,	Nov. 9, 1964
	-	Ott. vs. Tor.,	Nov. 12, 1967
	-	Cal. vs. Sask.,	Nov. 20, 1968
	-	Mtl. at Ham.,	Nov. 21, 1970
	-	B.C. vs. Wpg.,	Nov. 17, 1985
	-	Tor. at Ham.,	Nov. 16, 1986

MOST INTERCEPTIONS BY BOTH TEAMS ONE GAME

9	-	Sask. at Wpg.,	Oct. 28, 1953
	-	Tor. at Ham.,	Nov. 16, 1986
8	-	Ott. vs. Ham. at Mtl.,	Nov. 19, 1966
	-	Sask. at Cal.,	Nov. 20, 1968
7	-	Tor. at Mtl.,	Nov. 19, 1955
	-	Sask. at B.C.,	Nov. 20, 1963
	-	Mtl. at Ott.,	Nov. 7, 1964
	-	Ham. vs. Ott.,	Nov. 26, 1972
	-	Sask. at Cal.,	Nov. 12, 1989

MOST QUARTERBACK SACKS ONE TEAM ONE GAME

9	-	Ham. vs. Mtl.,	Nov. 17, 1985
	-	Wpg. vs. Ham.,	Nov. 22, 1992
6	-	Wpg. vs. Edm.,	Nov. 4, 1984
	-	Wpg. at B.C.,	Nov. 11, 1984
	-	Ham. at Tor.,	Nov. 11, 1984
	-	Tor. vs. Ham.,	Nov. 11, 1984
	-	Wpg. at B.C.,	Nov. 15, 1986
	-	Sask. at Cal.,	Nov. 12, 1989
	-	Ham. vs. Wpg.,	Nov. 19, 1989
5	-	Wpg. at Edm.,	Nov. 21, 1982
	-	Wpg. vs. Edm.,	Nov. 13, 1983
	-	Wpg. at B.C.,	Nov. 17, 1985
	-	B.C. at Edm.,	Nov. 23, 1986
	-	Edm. vs. Cal.,	Nov. 16, 1986
	-	B.C. at Edm.,	Nov. 20, 1988
	-	Wpg. at Tor.,	Nov. 12, 1989
	-	Tor. vs. Wpg.,	Nov. 17, 1991

MOST QUARTERBACK SACKS BOTH TEAMS ONE GAME

12	-	Ham. (6) at Tor. (6),	Nov. 11, 1984
11	-	Ham. (9) vs. Mtl. (1),	Nov. 17, 1985
9	-	Wpg. (5) at Edm. (4),	Nov. 21, 1982
	-	Wpg. (6) at B.C. (3),	Nov. 11, 1984
	-	Wpg. (5) at Tor. (4),	Nov. 12, 1989
8	-	Tor. (4) vs. Ott. (4),	Nov. 21, 1982
	-	Wpg. (5) vs. Edm. (3),	Nov. 13, 1983
	-	B.C. (5) at Edm. (3),	Nov. 23, 1986
	-	Wpg. (6) at B.C. (2),	Nov. 15, 1986
	-	Sask. (6) at Cal. (2),	Nov. 12, 1989
	-	Edm. (4) vs. Sask. (4),	Nov. 19, 1989
	-	Tor. (5) vs. Wpg. (3),	Nov. 17, 1991

MOST DEFENSIVE TACKLES ONE TEAM ONE GAME
(Defensive Tackles recorded since 1987)

55	-	Tor. (at Wpg.),	Nov. 18, 1990
54	-	Ham (at Wpg.),	Nov. 22, 1992
53	-	Cal. vs. (Sask.),	Nov. 12, 1989
	-	Tor. vs. (Ott.),	Nov. 11, 1990
52	-	Ham. vs. (Ott.),	Nov. 15, 1992
51	-	Ham. at (Wpg.),	Nov. 13, 1988
	-	Ham. (at Wpg.),	Nov. 21, 1993
50	-	Sask.(at Edm.),	Nov. 14, 1993
49	-	Ham. at (Tor.),	Nov. 15, 1987
	-	Sask. at (Edm.),	Nov. 11, 1990
48	-	Cal. at (Edm.),	Nov. 17, 1991

MOST DEFENSIVE TACKLES BOTH TEAMS ONE GAME
(Defensive Tackles recorded since 1987)

97	-	Tor. (53) vs. Ott. (44),	Nov. 11, 1990
96	-	Sask. (49) at Edm. (47),	Nov. 11, 1990
92	-	Sask. (48) at Edm. (44),	Nov. 15, 1992
90	-	Wpg. (39) vs. Ham. (51),	Nov. 21, 1993
89	-	Ott. (37) at Ham. (52),	Nov. 15, 1992
86	-	Ham. (51) at Wpg. (35),	Nov. 13, 1988
	-	Cal. (45) vs. B.C. (41)	Nov. 14, 1993
	-	Edm. (36) vs. Sask. (50)	Nov. 14, 1993
85	-	Tor. (55) at Wpg. (30),	Nov. 18, 1990
84	-	Cal. (53) vs. Sask. (31),	Nov. 12, 1989
	-	Cal. (44) vs. B.C. (40),	Nov. 10, 1991

MOST SPECIAL TEAMS TACKLES ONE TEAM ONE GAME
(Special Teams Tackles recorded since 1991)

14	-	Cal. (vs. B.C.),	Nov. 10, 1991
	-	Edm. (at Cal.)	Nov. 21, 1993
	-	Ham. (vs. Ott.)	Nov. 14, 1993
13	-	Tor. (vs. Wpg.),	Nov. 17, 1991
12	-	Edm. (vs. Cal.),	Nov. 17, 1991
	-	Cal. (vs. B.C.),	Nov. 14, 1993
	-	Edm. (vs. Sask.),	Nov. 14, 1993
	-	Sask. (at Edm.),	Nov. 14, 1993
11	-	Ott. (at Ham.),	Nov. 15, 1992
	-	Wpg. (vs. Ham.),	Nov. 22, 1992
10	-	Cal. (at Edm.),	Nov. 17, 1991
	-	Sask. (at Edm.),	Nov. 15, 1992
	-	Edm. (at Cal.),	Nov. 22, 1992
	-	Ham. (at Wpg.),	Nov. 21, 1993

MOST SPECIAL TEAMS TACKLES BOTH TEAMS ONE GAME
(Special Teams Tackles recorded since 1991)

24	-	Edm. (12)vs. Sask. (12),	Nov. 14, 1993
23	-	Cal.(14) vs. B.C. (9),	Nov. 10, 1991
22	-	Edm. (12) vs. Cal. (10),	Nov. 17, 1991
	-	Tor. (13) vs. Wpg. (9),	Nov. 17, 1991
	-	Cal. (8) vs. Edm. (14)	Nov. 21, 1993

PLAYOFF INDIVIDUAL RECORDS

ALL-TIME MOST GAMES PLAYED:

36	-	Gerry James, Wpg.-Sask.	1952-64
34	-	Larry Robinson, Cal.	1961-74
31	-	Ron Atchison, Sask.	1952-68
30	-	George Reed, Sask.	1963-75
29	-	Johnny Bright, Cal.-Edm.	1952-64
28	-	Jackie Parker, Edm.-Tor.-B.C.	1954-68
25	-	John Barrow, Ham.	1957-70
	-	Jack Abendschan, Sask.	1965-75
22	-	Don Sutherin, Ham.-Ott.-Tor.	1958-70
	-	Tommy Joe Coffey, Edm.-Ham.-Tor.	1959-73

ALL-TIME MOST POINTS:

196	-	Larry Robinson, Cal.	1961-74
154	-	Trevor Kennerd, Wpg.	1980-90
149	-	Jack Abendschan, Sask.	1965-75
148	-	Dave Cutler, Edm.	1969-84
137	-	Lui Passaglia, B.C.	1976-93
123	-	Don Sutherin, Ham.-Ott.	1958-69
114	-	George Reed, Sask.	1963-75
107	-	Johnny Bright, Cal.-Edm.	1952-64
	-	Bernie Ruoff, Wpg.-Ham.-B.C.	1975-90
102	-	Jackie Parker, Edm.	1954-62
96	-	Gerry James, Wpg.-Sask.	1952-63

MOST POINTS ONE SEASON:

40	-	Larry Robinson, Cal.	1964
34	-	Larry Robinson, Cal.	1962
32	-	Tom Dixon, Edm.	1986

MOST POINTS ONE GAME:

30	-	Lorne Benson, Wpg.	1953
24	-	Ron Morris, Tor.	1961
23	-	Troy Westwood, Wpg.	1992
20	-	Jackie Parker, Edm.	1956

ALL-TIME MOST GAMES SCORING POINTS:

27	-	Larry Robinson, Cal.	1961-74
22	-	Jack Abendschan, Sask.	1965-75
19	-	Gerry James, Wpg.	1952-63
	-	Gerry Organ, Ott.	1971-77, 1979-83
18	-	Don Sutherin, Ham.-Ott.-Tor.	1958-70
	-	Trevor Kennerd, Wpg.	1980-91
17	-	Jackie Parker, Edm.	1954-62

MOST GAMES SCORING POINTS ONE SEASON:

6	-	Bud Korchak, Wpg.	1953
5	-	Wilbur Snyder, Edm.	1952
	-	Charlie Shepard, Wpg.	1957
	-	Larry Robinson, Cal.	1962
	-	Larry Robinson, Cal.	1964
	-	Bill Rogers, Wpg.	1954
	-	Joe Mobra, Edm.	1958

ALL-TIME MOST TOUCHDOWNS:

19	-	Johnny Bright, Cal.-Edm.	1952-64
	-	George Reed, Sask.	1963-75
14	-	Rollie Miles, Edm.	1951-61
12	-	Jackie Parker, Edm.	1954-62
	-	Terry Evanshen, Mtl.-Cal.-Ham.	1965-77
11	-	Jim Dillard, Cal.-Ott.-Tor.	1962-68
10	-	Russ Jackson, Ott.	1958-69
	-	Normie Kwong, Cal.-Edm.	1948-60
9	-	Lorne Benson, Wpg.	1951-55
	-	Gerry McDougall, Ham.-Tor.-Edm.	1957-67
	-	Leo Lewis, Wpg.	1955-66
	-	Dave Thelen, Ott.-Tor.	1958-66
	-	James Murphy, Wpg.	1983-90

MOST TOUCHDOWNS ONE SEASON:

6	-	Lorne Benson, Wpg.	1953
5	-	Ken Carpenter, Sask.	1956
	-	Joe Kelly, Ott.	1960
	-	George Reed, Sask.	1971
4	-	Mike King, Edm.	1950
	-	Cookie Gilchrist, Ham.	1956
	-	Hal Waggoner, Ham.	1956
	-	Gerry McDougall, Ham.	1957
	-	John Varone, Wpg.	1958
	-	Ron Morris, Tor.	1961
	-	Tobin Rote, Tor.	1961
	-	Jim Dillard, Ott.	1966
	-	Johnny Shepherd, Ham.	1983
	-	Tony Cherry, B.C.	1988

MOST TOUCHDOWNS ONE GAME:

6	-	Lorne Benson, Wpg.	1953
4	-	Ron Morris, Tor.	1961
3	-	Johnny Bright, Cal.	1952
	-	Ron Howell, Ham.	1955
	-	Cookie Gilchrist, Ham.	1956
	-	Ken Carpenter, Sask.	1956
	-	Hal Waggoner, Ham.	1956
	-	Pat Abbruzzi, Mtl.	1956
	-	Jackie Parker, Edm.	1956
	-	Gerry McDougall, Ham.	1957
	-	Jim Dillard, Ott.	1966
	-	Wayne Giardino, Ott.	1969
	-	David Green, Mtl.	1978
	-	John Holland, Ham.	1979
	-	Mervyn Fernandez, B.C.	1983
	-	Johnny Shepherd, Ham.	1983
	-	Steve Stapler, Ham.	1985
	-	Tony Cherry, B.C.	1988
	-	Jon Volpe, B.C.	1991
	-	Michael Richardson, Wpg.	1992

ALL-TIME MOST CONVERTS:

51	-	Larry Robinson, Cal.	1961-74
44	-	Trevor Kennerd, Wpg.	1980-91
43	-	Don Sutherin, Ham.-Ott.-Tor.	1958-70
42	-	Jack Abendschan, Sask.	1965-75
30	-	Lui Passaglia, B.C.	1977-93
29	-	Dave Cutler, Edm.	1969-84

MOST CONVERTS ONE SEASON:

19	-	Bud Korchak, Wpg.	1953
14	-	Wilbur Snyder, Edm.	1952
12	-	Steve Oneschuk, Ham.	1956

MOST CONVERTS ONE GAME:

7	-	Nick Volpe, Tor.	1950
	-	Bob Gain, Ott.	1951
	-	Bud Korchak, Wpg.	1953
	-	Trevor Kennerd, Wpg.	1984
	-	Bernie Ruoff, Ham.	1985
6	-	Bob Dean, Edm.	1954
	-	Bill Bewley, Mtl.	1956
	-	Joe Mobra, Edm.	1956
	-	Gary Schreider, Ott.	1959
	-	Bill Mitchell, Tor.	1961
	-	Don Sutherin, Ham.	1961
	-	Trevor Kennerd, Wpg.	1983
	-	Ray Macoritti, Edm.	1990
	-	Mark McLoughlin, Cal.	1991
	-	Sean Fleming, Edm.	1993

5- Al Pfeifer, Tor. (twice): Moe Racine, Ott. (twice); Lui Passaglia, B.C. (3 times); Steve Oneschuk, Ham. (twice); Bob Shaw, Cal.; Wilbur Snyder, Edm.; Bud Korchak, Mtl.; Tommy Joe Coffey, Edm.; Don Sutherin, Ham.; Cyril McFall, Cal.; Larry Robinson, Cal.; Don Sweet, Mtl.; Jack Abendschan, Sask.; Jackie Parker; Edm.; Gerry James, Wpg.; Hank Ilesic, Tor.; Paul Osbaldiston, Ham.; Lance Chomyc, Tor.

ALL-TIME MOST FIELD GOALS:

37	-	Dave Cutler, Edm.	1969-84
35	-	Larry Robinson, Cal.	1961-74
32	-	Trevor Kennerd, Wpg.	1980-91
31	-	Jack Abendschan, Sask.	1965-75
	-	Lui Passaglia, B.C.	1976-93
30	-	Gerry Organ, Ott.	1971-83
21	-	Don Sutherin, Ham.-Ott.-Tor.	1958-70
19	-	Bernie Ruoff, Wpg.-Ham.	1975-87
18	-	Lance Chomyc, Tor.	1985-93
17	-	Don Sweet, Mtl.	1972-83

MOST FIELD GOALS ONE SEASON:

8	-	Larry Robinson, Cal.	1964
	-	Tom Dixon, Edm.	1986
	-	Trevor Kennerd, Wpg.	1988
7	-	Gerry Organ, Ott.	1979
	-	Roy Kurtz, Mtl.	1985
	-	Lance Chomyc, Tor.	1987
6	-	Peter Kempf, B.C.	1963
	-	Dave Mann, Tor.	1969
	-	Larry Robinson, Cal.	1970
	-	Dave Cutler, Edm.	1973
	-	Dave Cutler, Edm.	1976
	-	Jerry Kauric, Edm.	1987

MOST FIELD GOALS ONE GAME:

6	-	Dave Cutler, Edm.	1973
	-	Lance Chomyc, Tor.	1987
5	-	Ian Sunter, Ham.	1972
	-	Gerry Organ, Ott.	1979
	-	Dave Cutler, Edm.	1981
	-	Jerry Kauric, Edm.	1987
	-	Mark McLoughlin, Cal.	1990
	-	Troy Westwood, Wpg.	1992
4	-	Dave Mann, Tor.	1968
	-	Dave Cutler, Edm.	1976
	-	Lui Passaglia, B.C.	1977
	-	Dave Cutler, Edm.	1978
	-	Gerry McGrath, Mtl.	1980
	-	Dave Cutler, Edm.	1980
	-	Bernie Ruoff, Ham.	1982
	-	Roy Kurtz, Mtl.	1985
	-	Tom Dixon, Edm.	(twice) 1986
	-	Trevor Kennerd, Wpg.	(twice) 1988
	-	Paul Osbaldiston, Ham.	1988
	-	Mark McLoughlin, Cal.	1989
	-	Dave Ridgway, Sask.	1989
	-	Lance Chomyc, Tor.	1990
	-	Trevor Kennerd, Wpg.	1990
	-	Troy Westwood, Wpg.	1991
	-	Lui Passaglia, B.C.	1991
	-	Troy Westwood, Wpg.,	1993
	-	Paul Osbaldiston, Ham.	1993

LONGEST FIELD GOALS:

56	-	Bernie Ruoff, Ham.	1984
54	-	Mark McLouglin, Cal.	1991
53	-	Dave Cutler, Edm.	1976
	-	Dave Cutler, Edm.	1970

LONGEST FIELD GOALS (Cont'd)

52 - Bernie Ruoff, Wpg. 1978
- Gerry Organ, Ott. 1972
- Bernie Ruoff, Ham. 1987

ALL-TIME MOST SINGLES:

30 - Fred Wilson, Reg. 1911-16, 1919-21, 1925-30
28 - Larry Robinson, Cal. 1961-74
23 - Joe Krol, Tor. 1945-55
- Bernie Ruoff, Wpg.-Ham.-B.C. 1975-90
22 - Huck Welch, Ham.-Mtl. 1928-37
20 - Charlie Shepard, Wpg. 1957-62

MOST SINGLES ONE SEASON:

13 - Bill Mallett, Ham. 1914
10 - Jack Williams, Ott. 1909
9 - Matt Gonter, Tor. 1914

MOST SINGLES ONE GAME:

9 - Jack Williams, Ott. 1908
- Bill Mallett, Ham. 1914
8 - Bert Gibb, Ham. 1923
- Bob Hall, Cal. 1931
7 - George McGuicken, Ott. 1898
- Ben Simpson, Ham. 1906

ALL-TIME MOST RUSHES:

577 - George Reed, Sask. 1963-75
408 - Normie Kwong, Edm. 1951-60
372 - Johnny Bright, Cal.-Edm. 1952-64
247 - Dave Thelen, Ott. 1958-64
208 - Lovell Coleman, Cal.-Ott. 1960-68
204 - Leo Lewis, Wpg. 1955-66
202 - Gerry James, Wpg. 1952-63
186 - Jim Dillard, Cal.-Ott.-Tor. 1962-68
170 - Jackie Parker, Edm. 1954-62
160 - Charlie Shepard, Wpg. 1957-62

MOST TIMES RUSHING ONE SEASON:

105 - George Reed, Sask. 1967
74 - Johnny Bright, Edm. 1959
73 - Lovell Coleman, Cal. 1964

MOST TIMES RUSHING ONE GAME:

37 - George Reed, Sask. 1967
33 - Michael Richardson, Wpg. 1992
31 - George Reed, Sask. 1971
- Reggie Barnes, Ott. 1992
30 - Skip Walker, Ott. 1982

MOST PLAYOFF GAMES RUSHING:

34 - Normie Kwong, Edm.
32 - George Reed, Sask.
29 - Rollie Miles, Edm.
26 - Jackie Parker, Edm.
- Russ Jackson, Ott.
25 - Johnny Bright, Cal.-Edm.
- Gerry James, Wpg.

MOST PLAYOFF SEASONS RUSHING:

13 - George Reed, Sask.
12 - Russ Jackson, Ott.
11 - Ron Stewart, Ott.
10 - Normie Kwong, Edm.
- Rollie Miles, Edm.
- Tom Clements, Ott.-Ham.-Wpg.
9 - Ed Buchanan, Cal.-Sask.-Ham.

MOST PLAYOFF GAMES RUSHING ONE SEASON:

6 - Andy Sokol, Winnipeg, 1953

ALL-TIME MOST YARDS RUSHING:

2584 - George Reed, Sask. 1963-75
1967 - Normie Kwong, Edm. 1951-60
1962 - Johnny Bright, Cal.-Edm. 1952-64
1429 - Dave Thelen, Ott. 1958-64
1122 - Leo Lewis, Wpg. 1955-66
1007 - Lovell Coleman, Cal.-Ott. 1960-68
903 - Jim Dillard, Cal.-Ott.-Tor. 1962-68
900 - Russ Jackson, Ott. 1958-69
892 - Jackie Parker, Edm. 1954-62
827 - Gerry McDougall, Ham. 1957-61, 1965-66

MOST YARDS RUSHING ONE SEASON:

529 - George Reed, Sask. 1967
399 - Dave Thelen, Ott. 1960
364 - Cookie Gilchrist, Ham. 1956

MOST YARDS RUSHING ONE GAME:

253 - Skip Walker, Ott. 1982
227 - Michael Richardson, Wpg. 1992
204 - George Reed, Sask. 1967
192 - Dave Thelen, Ott. 1962

LONGEST RUSHING PLAY:

100 - Bill Symons, Tor. 1968
83 - Ted Woods, Cal. 1964
80 - Leo Lewis, Wpg. 1955

ALL-TIME MOST TOUCHDOWNS RUSHING:

18 - George Reed, Sask. 1963-75
14 - Johnny Bright, Cal.-Edm. 1952-64
11 - Russ Jackson, Ott. 1958-69
9 - Normie Kwong, Edm. 1951-60
- Lorne Benson, Wpg. 1951-55
8 - Brian Timmis Jr., Reg. 1953
- Bobby Marlow, Sask. 1953-60
- Earl Lunsford, Cal. 1956-63
- Dave Thelen, Ott. 1958-64

MOST TOUCHDOWNS RUSHING ONE SEASON:

6 - Lorne Benson, Wpg. 1953
4 - John Varone, Wpg. 1958
- Tobin Rote, Tor. 1961
- George Reed, Sask. 1971
- Mike King, Edm. 1950
3 - Several Players

MOST TOUCHDOWNS RUSHING ONE GAME:

6 - Lorne Benson, Wpg. 1953
3 - Cookie Gilchrist, Ham. 1956
- Wayne Giardino, Ott. 1969
- David Green, Mtl. 1978
- Tony Cherry, B.C. 1988
- Jon Volpe, B.C. 1991
- Michael Richardson, Wpg. 1992

MOST 100-YARD RUSHING GAMES:

9 - George Reed, Sask.
7 - Johnny Bright, Edm.
6 - Dave Thelen, Ott.
5 - Gerry McDougall, Ham.
- Cookie Gilchrist, Ham.
- Normie Kwong, Edm.
4 - Lovell Coleman, Cal.

MOST 100-YARD RUSHING GAMES ONE SEASON:

3 - Cookie Gilchrist, Ham. 1956
2 - Normie Kwong, Edm. 1954
- Johnny Bright, Edm. 1955
- Pat Abbruzzi, Mtl. 1957
- Johnny Bright, Edm. 1957
- Gerry McDougall, Ham. 1957
- Gerry McDougall, Ham. 1958
- Dave Thelen, Ott. 1960
- Bobby Kuntz, Ham. 1962
- Dave Thelen, Ott. 1963
- Lovell Coleman, Cal. 1965
- George Reed, Sask. 1967
- Jim Dillard, Tor. 1968
- George Reed, Sask. 1973
- James Sykes, Wpg. 1983
- Lucius Floyd, Edm., 1993

ALL-TIME MOST PASS RECEPTIONS:

70 - Rollie Miles, Edm. 1951-61
- Rick House, Wpg.-Edm. 1979-91
69 - George Reed, Sask. 1963-75
66 - Herman Harrison, Cal. 1964-72
- Terry Evanshen, Mtl.-Cal.-Ham. 1965-77
60 - Jim Dillard, Cal.-Ott.-Tor. 1962-68
59 - Tony Gabriel, Ham.-Ott. 1971-81
- James Murphy, Wpg. 1983-90
56 - Bobby Taylor, Cal.-Tor.-Edm. 1961-74
55 - Rollin Prather, Edm. 1950-54
49 - Hugh Campbell, Sask. 1963-69

MOST PASS RECEPTIONS ONE SEASON:

33 - Rollin Prather, Edm. 1952
21 - Hugh Campbell, Sask. 1963
20 - Jim Dillard, Cal. 1964
- Morris Bailey, Edm. 1950

MOST PASS RECEPTIONS ONE GAME:

15 - Rollin Prather, Edm. 1952
- Tony Gabriel, Ham. 1974
11 - Red O'Quinn, Mtl. 1956
10 - Willie Armstead, Cal. 1979
- Cedric Minter, Tor. 1983
- Donald Narcisse, Sask. 1992
- Reggie Barnes, Ott. 1993

ALL-TIME MOST GAMES CATCHING PASSES:

26 - George Reed, Sask. 1963-75
23 - Rollie Miles, Edm. 1951-61
22 - Herman Harrison, Cal. 1964-72
19 - Normie Kwong, Edm. 1951-60
- Bobby Taylor, Cal.-Tor.-Edm. 1961-74
- Rick House, Wpg.-Edm. 1979-91
18 - Jim Dillard, Cal.-Ott.-Tor. 1962-68

MOST SEASONS CATCHING PASSES:

13 - George Reed, Sask. 1963-75
11 - Rick House, Wpg.-Edm. 1979-91
10 - Ron Stewart, Ott. 1958-70
- Tony Gabriel, Ham.-Ott. 1971-81
- Peter Dalla Riva, Mtl. 1968-81
9 - Hal Patterson, Ham.-Mtl. 1954-57
- Johnny Bright, Cal.-Edm. 1952-64
- Rollie Miles, Edm. 1951-61
- Alan Ford, Sask. 1965-76
- Terry Evanshen, Mtl.-Cal.-Ham. 1965-77
- Gordon Barwell, Sask. 1964-73
- Tommy Scott, Wpg.-Edm. 1974-83
- Rocky DiPietro, Ham. 1978-90

MOST GAMES CATCHING PASSES ONE SEASON:

5 - Jim Dillard, Peter Manning, Bobby Taylor - Calgary, 1964; Hugh Campbell, Ray Purdin, Jack Gotta - Saskatchewan, 1963; Neill Armstrong, Andy Sokol - Winnipeg, 1953; Tom Casey, Pete Thodos - Winnipeg, 1954; Jim Letcavits - Edmonton, 1958; Ernie Pitts - Winnipeg, 1957; Ken Carpenter - Saskatchewan, 1956; Rollie Miles, Rollin Prather - Edmonton, 1952.

ALL-TIME MOST YARDS ON PASS RECEPTIONS:

1241 - Rollie Miles, Edm. 1951-61
1101 - Herman Harrison, Cal. 1964-72
1040 - Terry Evanshen, Mtl.-Cal. Ham. 1965-77
991 - Rollin Prather, Edm. 1950-54
981 - Rick House, Wpg.-Edm. 1979-91
956 - Bobby Taylor, Cal.-Tor.-Edm. 1961-74
917 - James Murphy, Wpg. 1983-90
835 - Brian Kelly, Edm. 1979-88
809 - Jim Dillard, Cal.-Ott.-Tor. 1962-68
771 - George Reed, Sask. 1963-75

MOST YARDS ON PASS RECEPTIONS ONE SEASON:

589 - Rollin Prather, Edm. 1952
341 - Rollie Miles, Edm. 1953
318 - Jim Letcavits, Edm. 1958

MOST YARDS ON PASS RECEPTIONS ONE GAME:

270 - Rollin Prather, Edm. 1952
260 - Mervyn Fernandez, B.C. 1983
251 - Hal Waggoner, Ham. 1956

ALL-TIME MOST TOUCHDOWNS ON PASS RECEPTIONS:

12 - Terry Evanshen, Mtl.-Cal. Ham. 1965-77
11 - Rollie Miles, Edm. 1951-61
9 - James Murphy, Wpg. 1983-90
8 - Jim Dillard, Cal.-Ott.-Tor. 1962-68
7 - Brian Kelly, Edm. 1979-88
- Rick House, Edm.-Wpg. 1979-91

MOST TOUCHDOWNS ON PASS RECEPTIONS ONE SEASON:

4 - Hal Waggoner, Ham. 1956
- Ron Morris, Tor. 1961
- Jim Dillard, Ott. 1966
3 - Rollin Prather, Edm. 1952
- Jackie Parker, Edm. 1956
- Rollie Miles, Edm. 1953
- Dick Cohee, Sask. 1963
- Terry Evanshen, Ham. 1976
- John Holland, Ham. 1979
- Mervyn Fernandez, B.C. 1983
- James Murphy, Wpg. 1984
- Steve Stapler, Ham. 1985
- James Murphy, Wpg. 1985
- Eddie Brown, Edm. 1993

MOST TOUCHDOWNS ON PASS RECEPTIONS ONE GAME:

4 - Ron Morris, Tor. 1961
3 - Jackie Parker, Edm. 1956
- Hal Waggoner, Ham. 1956
- Jim Dillard, Ott. 1966
- John Holland, Ham. 1979
- Mervyn Fernandez, B.C. 1983
- Steve Stapler, Ham. 1985
2 - several players

ALL-TIME MOST 100-YARD PASS RECEIVING GAMES

4 - Rollie Miles, Edm. 1951-61
- Brian Kelly, Edm. 1979-88
3 - Herman Harrison, Cal. 1964-72
- Hal Patterson, Mtl.-Ham. 1954-67
- Terry Evanshen, Mtl.-Ham. 1965-77
- James Murphy, Wpg. 1983-90
2 - Dave West, Cal.-Ham. 1951-56
- Red O'Quinn, Mtl. 1952-59
- George Reed, Sask. 1963-75
- Whit Tucker, Ott. 1962-70
- Gerry Shaw, Cal. 1965-74
- Bob McCarthy, Cal. 1967-70
- Tony Gabriel, Ham.-Ott. 1971-81
- Tommy Grant, Ham. 1956-68
- Bobby Taylor, Tor.-Edm. 1966-74
- Mervyn Fernandez, B.C. 1982-86

MOST 100-YARD PASS RECEIVING GAMES ONE SEASON:

2 - Morris Bailey, Edm. 1950
- Rollin Prather, Edm. 1952
- Rollie Miles, Edm. 1953
- Dave Mann, Tor. 1960
- Ray Purdin, Sask. 1963
- Willie Armstead, Cal. 1979
- Jeff Boyd, Wpg. 1984
- James Murphy, Wpg. 1988

LONGEST PASS-COMPLETION PLAYS:

109 - Ken Nielsen (from Kenny Ploen) Winnipeg Nov. 20, 1965
102 - Alex Webster (from Sam Etcheverry) Montreal Nov. 20, 1954
- Pat Stoqua (from J.C. Watts) Ottawa Nov. 15, 1981
99 - Darrell K. Smith (from Willie Gillus) Toronto Nov. 11, 1990

MOST PLAYOFF GAMES THROWING PASSES:

35 - Ron Lancaster, Sask. 1960-78
28 - Russ Jackson, Ott. 1958-69
23 - Ken Ploen, Wpg. 1957-67

MOST PLAYOFF SEASONS THROWING PASSES:

16 - Ron Lancaster, Sask. 1968-78
12 - Russ Jackson, Ott. 1958-69
- Jerry Keeling, Cal.-Ott.-Ham. 1961-75
11 - Tom Clements, Ott-Ham.-Wpg. 1975-87
10 - Tom Wilkinson, Tor.-B.C.-Edm. 1967-81
9 - Condredge Holloway, Ott.-Tor.-B.C. 1975-87

ALL-TIME MOST PASSES THROWN:

886 - Ron Lancaster, Ott.-Sask. 1960-78
449 - Eagle Day, Wpg.-Cal.-Tor. 1956-66
435 - Russ Jackson, Ott. 1958-69
432 - Tom Clements, Ott-Ham.-Wpg. 1978-87
399 - Dieter Brock, Wpg.-Ham. 1974-84
350 - Jerry Keeling, Cal.-Ott.-Ham. 1961-75
326 - Jack Jacobs, Wpg. 1950-54
298 - Ken Ploen, Wpg. 1957-67
273 - Bernie Faloney, Edm.-Ham.-Mtl. 1954-66
246 - Sam Etcheverry, Mtl. 1952-60

MOST PASSES THROWN ONE SEASON:

182 - Ron Lancaster, Sask. 1963
125 - Eagle Day, Cal. 1964
120 - Claude Arnold, Edm. 1952

MOST PASSES THROWN ONE GAME:

50 - Tobin Rote, Tor. 1960
49 - Ed Songin, Ham. 1954
- Dieter Brock, Ham. 1984
48 - Ron Lancaster, Sask. 1963
- Ken Johnson, Cal. 1979

ALL-TIME MOST PASSES COMPLETED:

453 - Ron Lancaster, Ott.-Sask. 1960-78
266 - Tom Clements, Ott.-Ham.-Wpg. 1975-87
226 - Eagle Day, Wpg.-Cal.-Tor. 1956-66
218 - Dieter Brock, Wpg.-Ham. 1974-84
208 - Russ Jackson, Ott. 1958-69
186 - Jerry Keeling, Cal.-Ott.-Ham. 1961-75
168 - Jack Jacobs, Wpg. 1950-54
143 - Ken Ploen, Wpg. 1957-67
139 - Matt Dunigan, Edm.-B.C.-Tor.-Wpg. 1983-93
134 - Sam Etcheverry, Mtl. 1952-60

MOST PASSES COMPLETED ONE SEASON:

87 - Ron Lancaster, Sask. 1963
71 - Tobin Rote, Tor. 1961
62 - Eagle Day, Cal. 1964
- Peter Liske, Cal. 1968

MOST PASSES COMPLETED ONE GAME:

35 - Mike Kerrigan, Ham. 1986
32 - Kent Austin, Sask. 1992
28 - Ron Lancaster, Sask. 1964
- Ken Johnson, Cal. 1979
- Dieter Brock, Ham. 1983
- Joe Barnes, Mtl. 1985

ALL-TIME MOST YARDS PASSED:

6676 - Ron Lancaster, Ott.-Sask. 1960-78
3581 - Tom Clements, Ott.-Ham.-Wpg. 1975-87
3173 - Russ Jackson, Ott. 1958-69
3132 - Eagle Day, Wpg.-Cal.-Tor. 1956-66
2790 - Dieter Brock, Wpg.-Ham. 1974-84
2785 - Jerry Keeling, Cal.-Ott.-Ham. 1961-75
2592 - Jack Jacobs, Wpg. 1950-54
2354 - Ken Ploen, Wpg. 1957-67
2322 - Bernie Faloney, Edm.-Ham. 1954-66
2207 - Matt Dunigan, Edm.-B.C.-Tor.-Wpg. 1983-93
1942 - Sam Etcheverry, Mtl. 1952-60

MOST YARDS PASSED ONE SEASON:

1273 - Ron Lancaster, Sask. 1963
1074 - Claude Arnold, Edm. 1952
1046 - Tony Curcillo, Ham. 1956

MOST YARDS PASSED ONE GAME:

518 - Tony Curcillo, Ham. 1956
492 - Ron Lancaster, Sask. 1963
468 - Kent Austin, Sask. 1992

ALL-TIME MOST TOUCHDOWN PASSES:

40 - Ron Lancaster, Ott.-Sask. 1960-78
25 - Russ Jackson, Ott. 1958-69
24 - Tom Clements, Ott.-Ham.-Wpg. 1975-87
18 - Bernie Faloney, Edm.-Ham.-Mtl. 1954-66
15 - Jerry Keeling, Cal.-Ott.-Ham. 1961-75
- Matt Dunigan, Edm.-B.C.-Tor.-Wpg. 1983-93
14 - Dieter Brock, Wpg.-Ham. 1974-84
13 - Jackie Parker, Edm. 1954-62
12 - Kenny Ploen, Wpg. 1957-67
- Don Getty, Edm. 1955-64
- Sam Etcheverry, Mtl. 1952-60
- Jack Jacobs, Wpg. 1950-54

MOST TOUCHDOWN PASSES ONE SEASON:

8 - Claude Arnold, Edm. 1952
- Tony Curcillo, Ham. 1956
- Ron Lancaster, Sask. 1963
7 - Tom Dublinski, Tor. 1955
- Tom Clements, Wpg. 1984
- Danny Barrett, Cal. 1991
- Damon Allen, Edm. 1993
6 - Jack Jacobs, Wpg. 1953
- Tobin Rote, Tor. 1961
- Russ Jackson, Ott. 1966

MOST TOUCHDOWN PASSES ONE GAME:

5 Tony Curcillo, Ham. 1956
- Bernie Faloney, Ham. 1961
- Ron Lancaster, Sask. 1963
- Ken Hobart, Ham. 1985
- Danny Barrett, Cal. 1991
4 - Joe Krol, Tor. 1945
- Keith Spaith, Cal. 1952
4 - Jack Jacobs, Wpg. 1953
- Tom Dublinski, Tor. 1955
- Joe Kapp, B.C. 1964
- Russ Jackson, Ott. 1966
- Russ Jackson, Ott. 1967
- Ron Lancaster, Sask. 1975
- Sam Etcheverry, Mtl. 1956
- Don Getty, Edm. 1956
- Tobin Rote, Tor. 1961
- Ron Lancaster, Sask. 1964
- Damon Allen, Edm., 1993

ALL-TIME MOST PASSES INTERCEPTED:

65 - Ron Lancaster, Ott.-Sask. 1960-78
27 - Jack Jacobs, Wpg. 1950-54
25 - Russ Jackson, Ott. 1958-69
- Tom Clements, Ott.-Ham.-Wpg. 1975-87
20 - Jerry Keeling, Cal.-Ott.-Ham. 1961-75
- Frank Tripucka, Sask.-Ott. 1953-63
19 - Tom Wilkinson, Tor.-B.C.-Edm. 1967-81

MOST PASSES INTERCEPTED ONE SEASON:

19 - Ron Lancaster, Sask. 1963
10 - Claude Arnold, Edm. 1953
- Jack Jacobs, Wpg. 1954
- Frank Tripucka, Sask. 1956
9 - Peter Liske, Cal. 1967

MOST TIMES INTERCEPTED ONE GAME:

5 - Glenn Dobbs, Sask. 1953
- Jack Jacobs, Wpg. 1954
- Tony Curcillo, Ham. 1956
- Ron Lancaster, Sask. 1963
- Ron Lancaster, Sask. 1964

ALL-TIME MOST GAMES PUNTED:

23 - Alan Ford, Sask. 1965-76
- Jim Furlong, Cal. 1962-74
22 - Bob Cameron, Wpg. 1980-92
18 - Charlie Shepard, Wpg. 1957-62
16 - Joe Zuger, Ham. 1962-71
- Hank Ilesic, Tor. 1983-92
15 - Jack Jacobs, Wpg. 1950-54
14 - Cam Fraser, Ham.-Mtl. 1951-69
- Dave Mann, Tor. 1958, 1960-70

ALL-TIME MOST TIMES PUNTED:

203 - Alan Ford, Sask. 1965-76
187 - Jim Furlong, Cal. 1962-74
193 - Bob Cameron, Wpg. 1980-92
151 - Charlie Shepard, Wpg. 1957-62
150 - Hank Ilesic, Edm.-Tor. 1977-91
143 - Joe Zuger, Ham. 1962-71
142 - Dave Mann, Tor. 1958-70
139 - Cam Fraser, Ham.-Mtl. 1951-69
130 - Ed Ulmer, Ott.-Wpg. 1963-71
125 - Bernie Ruoff, Wpg.-Ham. 1975-87

MOST TIMES PUNTED ONE SEASON:

46 - Larry Isbell, Sask. 1956
- Ron Stewart, Cal. 1970
45 - Ed Ulmer, Wpg. 1965
44 - Charlie Shepard, Wpg. 1957

MOST TIMES PUNTED ONE GAME:

22 - Bernie Ruoff, Ham. 1984
19 - Bernie Ruoff, Ham. 1984
17 - Hank Ilesic, Tor. 1984
- Bob Cameron, Wpg. 1989

ALL-TIME MOST YARDS PUNTING:

7924 - Bob Cameron, Wpg. 1980-93
7503 - Alan Ford, Sask. 1965-76
7306 - Jim Furlong, Cal. 1962-74
6620 - Charlie Shepard, Wpg. 1957-62
6389 - Hank Ilesic, Edm.-Tor. 1977-92
6093 - Cam Fraser, Ham.-Mtl. 1951-69
6010 - Joe Zuger, Ham. 1962-71
5967 - Dave Mann, Tor. 1958-70
5690 - Lui Passaglia, B.C. 1976-93
5493 - Bernie Ruoff, Wpg.-Ham. 1975-87

MOST YARDS PUNTING ONE SEASON:

2089 - Larry Isbell, Sask. 1956
1996 - Bernie Ruoff, Ham. 1984
1916 - Charlie Shepard, Wpg. 1957

MOST YARDS PUNTING ONE GAME:

1054 - Bernie Ruoff, Ham. 1984
942 - Bernie Ruoff, Ham. 1984
779 - Glenn Dobbs, Sask. 1951

LONGEST PUNT:

89 - Lui Passaglia, B.C. 1979
83 - Larry Isbell, Sask. 1956
- Paul Hickie, Edm. 1983
82 - Charlie Shepard, Wpg. 1961
- Joe Zuger, Ham. 1966

BEST PUNTING AVERAGE ONE SEASON:

54.0 - Lui Passaglia, B.C. 1984
50.7 - Lui Passaglia, B.C. 1983
48.7 - Bernie Ruoff, Ham. 1984

BEST PUNTING AVERAGE ONE GAME:

54.0 - Lui Passaglia, B.C. 1984
53.1 - Rod Pantages, Edm. 1953
51.3 - Hank Ilesic, Tor. 1983

ALL TIME MOST PUNT RETURNS:

93 - Rollie Miles, Edm. 1951-61
73 - Gene Wlasiuk, Wpg.-Sask. 1957-67
65 - Gordie Rowland, Wpg. 1954-63
62 - Jim Copeland, Sask.-Tor. 1961-68
60 - Jim Silye, Cal. 1969-75

MOST PUNT RETURNS ONE SEASON:

29 - Leigh McMillan, Edm. 1958
- Jim Silye, Cal. 1970
28 - Jim Copeland, Sask. 1963
26 - Gene Wlasiuk, Sask. 1967

MOST PUNT RETURNS ONE GAME:

12 - Gene Wlasiuk
Sask. at Cal., Nov. 26, 1967
11 - Leigh McMillan
Edm. vs. Sask., Nov. 11, 1958
- Ron Howell
Ham. vs. Tor., Nov. 26, 1961
- Larry Robinson
Cal. vs. Sask., Nov. 20, 1968
10 - Gene Wlasiuk
Sask. vs. Wpg., Nov. 13, 1966
- Jim Copeland
Tor. vs. Ham., Nov. 9, 1968

ALL-TIME MOST PUNT RETURN YARDS:

608 - Rollie Miles, Edm. 1951-61
487 - Gordie Rowland, Wpg. 1954-63
420 - Henry Williams, Edm., 1987-93
412 - Gene Wlasiuk, Wpg.-Sask. 1957-67
328 - Garney Henley, Ham. 1960-75
314 - Harry Lunn, Sask.-Ott. 1955-59

MOST PUNT RETURN YARDS ONE SEASON:

190 - Gordie Rowland, Wpg. 1954
177 - Jim MacRae, Edm. 1951
163 - Bill Miller, Cal. 1962

MOST PUNT RETURN YARDS ONE GAME:

157 - Johnny Rodgers
Mtl. at Ott., Nov. 15, 1975
147 - Henry Williams
Edm. vs. Sask., Nov. 15, 1992
127 - Johnny Rodgers
Mtl. at Ham., Nov. 13, 1976

LONGEST PUNT RETURN:

103 - Henry Williams
Edm. vs. Sask., Nov. 15, 1992
95 - Johnny Rodgers
Mtl. at Ott., Nov. 15, 1975
75 - Raghib Ismail
Tor. vs. Wpg., Nov. 17, 1991
63 - Jim Silye
Cal. at Sask., Nov. 22, 1970
57 - Dick Thorton
Wpg. at Cal., Nov. 13, 1965

ALL-TIME MOST PUNT RETURN TOUCHDOWNS:

1 - Several Players

ALL-TIME MOST KICKOFF RETURNS:

32 - Rollie Miles, Edm. 1951-61
25 - Gerry James, Wpg. 1952-63
16 - Peter Thodos, Cal.-Mtl. 1948-53
- Bill Symons, Tor. 1967-73
15 - Harry Lunn, Sask.-Ott. 1955-59
- Leo Lewis, Wpg. 1955-66
- Henry Williams, Edm., 1987-93

MOST KICKOFF RETURNS ONE SEASON:

9 - Peter Thodos, Cal. 1956
8 - Gerry James, Wpg. 1953
- Nellie Green, Sask. 1953
- Silas McKinnie, Sask. 1971
- Erroll Tucker, Cal. 1991
7 - Gerry James, Wpg. 1954
- Willie Bethea, Ham. 1966

MOST KICKOFF RETURNS ONE GAME:

6 - Ed Ulmer, Ott. vs. Ham., Nov. 16, 1963
5 - Nellie Green, Sask. at Wpg., Oct. 28, 1953
- By Bailey, B.C. at Edm., Nov. 4, 1959
- Willie Bethea, Ham. vs. Ott. at Mtl., Nov. 19, 1966
- Mike Clemons, Tor. vs. Ott., Nov. 11, 1990
- Erroll Tucker, Cal. vs. B.C., Nov. 10, 1991
- Maurice Smith, B.C. at Cal., Nov. 10, 1991
- Lucious Floyd, Edm. vs. Sask., Nov. 14, 1993
4 - Keeper McWhinney, Edm. at Cal., Oct. 22, 1952
- Gerry James, Wpg. at Edm., Nov. 14, 1953
- Kennard Martin, Cal. vs. Sask., Nov. 12, 1989
- Anthony Stafford, Ott. at Tor., Nov. 11, 1990
- Paul Bushey, Sask. at Edm., Nov. 11, 1990
- Kevin Smellie, Tor. at Wpg., Nov. 18, 1990
- Ron Hopkins, Cal. vs. Edm., Nov. 18, 1990
- Nick Mazzoli, Ham. at Wpg., Nov. 22, 1992
- Derrick Crawford, Cal. vs. Edm., Nov. 21, 1993

ALL-TIME MOST KICKOFF RETURN YARDS:

805	-	Gerry James, Wpg.	1952-63
782	-	Rollie Miles, Edm.	1951-61
429	-	Gene Gaines, Ott.	1962-69
400	-	Leo Lewis, Wpg.	1955-66
397	-	Bill Symons, Tor.	1967-73

MOST KICKOFF RETURN YARDS ONE SEASON:

263	-	Gerry James, Wpg.	1953
237	-	Gene Gaines, Ott.	1964
233	-	Gerry James, Wpg.	1957
217	-	Gerry James, Wpg.	1954
205	-	Ed Buchanan, Sask.	1967

MOST KICKOFF RETURN YARDS ONE GAME:

185	-	Angelo Santucci Ham. at Mtl.	Nov. 9, 1975
176	-	Gene Gaines Ott. vs. Ham.	Nov. 14, 1964
144	-	Willie Bethea Ham. vs. Ott. at Mtl.	Nov. 19, 1966

LONGEST KICKOFF RETURN:

128	-	Gene Gaines Ott. vs. Ham.	Nov. 14, 1964
101	-	Gerry James Wpg. vs. Edm.	Nov. 16, 1957
98	-	Ron Howell Ham. vs. Tor.	Nov. 12, 1955

ALL-TIME MOST KICKOFF RETURN TOUCHDOWNS:

3	-	Gerry James, Wpg.	1952-63
1	-	Several Players	

MOST KICKOFF RETURN TOUCHDOWNS ONE GAME:

1	-	Several Players	

ALL-TIME MOST FUMBLE RETURNS:

6	-	Buddy Tinsley, Wpg.	1950-60
5	-	Roger Savoie, Wpg.	1951-65
	-	Gene Gaines, Mtl.-Ott.	1962-69
4	-	Sugarfoot Anderson, Cal.	1949-54
	-	Bill Briggs, Tor.-Edm.	1945-57
	-	Ben Zambiasi, Ham.-Tor.	1978-88

MOST FUMBLE RETURNS ONE SEASON:

3	-	Roger Savoie, Wpg.	1955
	-	Gord Sturtridge, Sask.	1956
	-	Dave Burkholder, Wpg.	1959
	-	Wayne Harris, Sr., Cal.	1962
	-	Bob Ptacek, Sask.	1963

MOST FUMBLE RETURNS ONE GAME:

2	-	Frank Anderson, Edm. Edm. at Wpg.	Nov. 8, 1952
	-	Mike Cassidy, Sask. Sask. at Wpg.	Nov. 7, 1955
	-	Roger Savoie, Wpg. Wpg. at Edm.	Nov. 16, 1955
	-	Gord Sturtridge, Sask. Sask. at Wpg.	Nov. 5, 1956
	-	Frank Rigney, Wpg. Edm. at Wpg.	Nov. 22, 1958
	-	David Albright Sask. at Edm.,	Nov. 11, 1990

ALL-TIME MOST FUMBLE RETURN YARDS:

140	-	Ed McQuarters, Sask.	1966-74
118	-	Ben Zambiasi, Ham.-Tor.	1978-88
55	-	Dave Burkholder, Wpg.	1958-64
54	-	Tom Casey, Wpg.	1950-56
42	-	Dick Cohee, Mtl.-Ott.-Sask.-Ham.	1960-68

MOST FUMBLE RETURN YARDS ONE SEASON:

102	-	Ben Zambiasi, Ham.	1978
80	-	Ed McQuarters, Sask.	1970
60	-	Ed McQuarters, Sask.	1966

MOST FUMBLE RETURN YARDS ONE GAME:

102	-	Ben Zambiasi, Ham. Ham. at Mtl.	Nov. 11, 1978
80	-	Ed McQuarters, Sask. Sask. at Cal.	Nov. 18, 1970
60	-	Ed McQuarters, Sask. Sask. at Wpg.	Nov. 16, 1966

LONGEST FUMBLE RECOVERY:

102	-	Ben Zambiasi, Ham. Ham at Mtl.	Nov. 11, 1978
82	-	Vince Phason, Wpg. Wpg. at B.C.	Nov. 12, 1977
80	-	Ed McQuarters, Sask. Sask. at Cal.	Nov. 18, 1970

ALL-TIME MOST INTERCEPTIONS:

12	-	Don Sutherin, Ham.-Ott.-Tor.	1958-70
9	-	Bob Kosid, Sask.	1964-72
	-	Garney Henley, Ham.	1960-75
	-	Oscar Kruger, Edm.	1954-63
8	-	Rollie Miles, Edm.	1951-61
	-	Bud Grant, Wpg.	1953-56

MOST INTERCEPTIONS ONE SEASON:

7	-	Bud Grant, Wpg.	1953
6	-	Oscar Kruger, Edm.	1959
4	-	Al Romine, Ott.	1959
	-	Don Sutherin, Ham.	1961
	-	Art Johnson, Cal.	1963
	-	Bob Kosid, Sask.	1967
	-	Felix Wright, Ham.	1984

MOST INTERCEPTIONS ONE GAME:

5	-	Bud Grant, Wpg., Sask. at Wpg.	Oct. 28, 1953
4	-	Felix Wright, Ham., Tor. at Tor.	Nov. 11, 1984
3	-	Keith Pearce, Wpg., Edm. at Wpg.	Nov. 11, 1954
	-	Oscar Kruger, Edm., B.C. at Edm	Nov. 4, 1959
	-	Art Johnson, Cal., Sask. at Cal.	Nov. 9, 1963
	-	Darrell Moir, Tor., Tor. at Ham.	Nov. 16, 1986

ALL-TIME MOST YARDS ON INTERCEPTION RETURNS:

157	-	Harvey Wylie, Cal.	1956-64
151	-	Gene Gaines, Mtl.-Ott.	1961-76
147	-	Don Sutherin, Ham.-Ott.-Tor.	1958-70
144	-	Bob Kosid, Sask.	1964-72
115	-	Larry Highbaugh, B.C.-Edm.	1971-83

MOST YARDS ON INTERCEPTION RETURNS ONE SEASON:

107	-	Tom Casey, Wpg.	1953
106	-	Greg Peterson, Cal.	1987
102	-	Harry Skipper, Sask.	1984
90	-	Tom Moran, Mtl.	1956
83	-	Reggie Holmes, Cal.	1971

MOST YARDS ON INTERCEPTION RETURNS ONE GAME:

106	-	Greg Peterson, Cal. Cal. at Edm.	Nov. 15, 1987
102	-	Harry Skipper, Sask. Sask. at Cal.	Nov. 12, 1989
90	-	Tom Moran, Mtl. Ham. at Mtl.	Nov. 17, 1956

LONGEST INTERCEPTION RETURN:

106	-	Greg Peterson, Cal. Cal. at Edm.	Nov. 15, 1987
102	-	Harry Skipper, Sask. Sask. at Cal.	Nov. 12, 1989
90	-	Tom Moran, Mtl. Ham. at Mtl.	Nov. 17, 1956

ALL-TIME MOST QUARTERBACK SACKS:

11.0	-	Tony Norman, Wpg.	1980-86
9.5	-	Grover Covington, Ham.	1981-90
8.0	-	Michael Gray, B.C.-Wpg.	1985-92
8.5	-	James Parker, Edm.-B.C.-Tor.	1980-90
7.0	-	Rod Skillman, Ham.	1984-90
	-	Mitchell Price, Ham.-Cal.	1983-87
	-	James West, Cal.-Wpg.-B.C.	1982-93

MOST QUARTERBACK SACKS ONE GAME:

4	-	Tony Norman, Wpg., Wpg. at B.C., Nov. 11, 1984
	-	Grover Covington, Ham., Mtl. at Ham., Nov. 17, 1985
	-	Stu Laird, Cal., Cal. at Edm., Nov. 15, 1987
3.5	-	James Curry, Tor., Ham. at Tor., Nov. 11, 1984
3	-	several players

ALL-TIME DEFENSIVE TACKLES:
(Defensive Tackles recorded since 1987)

52	-	Willie Pless, Tor.-B.C.-Edm.	1986-93
42	-	Dan Bass, Tor.-Cal.-Edm.	1980-91
39	-	Greg Battle, Wpg.	1987-93
42	-	James West, Cal.-Wpg.-B.C.	1982-93
41	-	Larry Wruck, Edm.	1985-93

MOST DEFENSIVE TACKLES ONE SEASON:
(Defensive Tackles recorded since 1987)

18	-	Keith Castello, Tor.	1990
16	-	Jeff Fields, Ham.	1992
15	-	Dan Bass, Edm.	1990
	-	Darryl Ford, Tor.	1990
14	-	Dan Bass, Edm.	1987
13	-	Willie Pless, Tor.	1987
	-	Anthony Drawhorn, B.C.	1988
	-	Don Moen, Tor.	1990
	-	Tim Cofield, Cal.	1991
	-	Marvin Pope, Cal.	1992
	-	Willie Pless, Edm.	1993

MOST DEFENSIVE TACKLES ONE GAME:
(Defensive Tackles recorded since 1987)

13	-	Marvin Pope, Cal.	vs. Edm., Nov. 22, 1992
12	-	Doug Landry, Cal.	vs. Sask., Nov. 12, 1989
11	-	Dan Bass, Edm.	vs. Sask., Nov. 11, 1990
	-	Alondra Johnson, Cal.	vs. B.C., Nov. 14, 1993
10	-	Dan Bass, Edm.	vs. B.C., Nov. 27, 1987
	-	Keith Castello, Tor.	vs. Ott., Nov. 11, 1990
	-	David Albright, Sask.	at Edm., Nov. 11, 1990
	-	Jeff Fields, Ham.	at Wpg., Nov. 22, 1992
	-	Willie Pless, Edm.	at Cal., Nov. 21, 1993

MOST SPECIAL TEAMS TACKLES ONE GAME
(Special Teams Tackles recorded since 1991)

5	-	Paul Nastasiuk, Tor. Wpg. at Tor.,	Nov. 17, 1991
	-	Paul Bushey, Ham.,Ham. at Wpg.,	Nov. 21, 1993
4	-	Sean Millington, B.C., B.C. at Cal.,	Nov. 10, 1991
	-	Bruce Boyko, Sask, .Sask. at Edm.,	Nov. 15, 1992
5	-	Paul Bushey, Ham., Ham at Wpg.,	Nov. 21, 1993

#39 LB Willie Pless - Recorded 77 tackles during the '93 season, increasing his CFL Record Total for All-Time Defensive Tackles to 597.

1993 GREY CUP CHAMPIONSHIP

Edmonton Eskimos 33 **Winnipeg Blue Bombers 23**

Played at McMahon Stadium in Calgary, Alberta on Sunday, November 28, 1993. The temperature for the first game played in Calgary since 1975 was 6° C with SE winds blowing at 13 km/h. The artificial turf was dry under sunny skies.

OFFICIALS: Referee: Dave Yule (#64); Umpire: Dave Hutton (#41); Head Linesman: Bill Hagans (#24); Line Judge: Ron Artelle (#76); Field Judge: Al McColman (#54); Side Judge: Turk Trtany (#31); Back Judge: Don Ellis (#70).

Alternate Referee: Ken Lazaruk (53)
Alternate Official: Bernie Prusko (79)

Edmonton Eskimos

RECEIVERS: 2 Henry Williams, 7 Jim Sandusky, 87 Jay Christensen, 4 Eddie Brown, 23 J.P. Izquierdo.
RUNNING BACKS: 32 Michael Soles, 33 Lucius Floyd, 34 Brian Walling.
QUARTERBACKS: 9 Damon Allen, 16 Rickey Foggie, 15 Tom Muecke.
KICKERS: 3 Sean Fleming, 18 Glenn Harper.
OFFENSIVE LINE: 50 Blake Dermott, 53 Mike DuMaresq, 67 Rod Connop, 57 Randy Ambrosie, 60 Chris Morris, 56 Steve Krupey.
DEFENSIVE LINE: 43 Jed Roberts, 91 Clinton Woods, 40 Bennie Goods, 90 Leonard Johnson, 63 Michel Bourgeau.
LINEBACKERS: 46 Malvin Hunter, 47 Larry Wruck, 39 Willie Pless, 89 Leroy Blugh, 38 Errol Martin, 36 Bruce Dickson.
DEFENSIVE BACKS: 10 Damion Lyons, 26 Glenn Rogers Jr., 24 Dan Murphy, 20 Don Wilson, 25 Morris Lolar, 17 Robert Holland, 28 Trent Brown.

Winnipeg Blue Bombers

RECEIVERS: 2 David Williams, 7 Alfred Jackson, 21 Blaise Bryant, 86 Gerald Alphin, 87 Gerald Wilcox.
RUNNING BACKS: 31 Michael Richardson, 25 Chris Johnstone, 37 Duane Forde, 32 Matt Pearce.
QUARTERBACKS: 9 Sammy Garza, 8 Tom Porras, 15 Keithen McCant.
KICKERS: 74 Troy Westwood, 6 Bob Cameron.
OFFENSIVE LINE: 66 Miles Gorrell, 57 Brett MacNeil, 60 Dave Vankoughnett, 51 David Black, 63 Chris Walby, 68 Nick Benjamin.
DEFENSIVE LINE: 76 Loyd Lewis, 77 Stan Mikawos, 99 Vaughn Booker, 44/94 Leon Hatziioannou.
LINEBACKERS: 56 Elfrid Payton, 58 Greg Clark, 34 Greg Battle, 36 Paul Randolph, 92 Chris Tsangaris, 35 Brendan Rogers
DEFENSIVE BACKS: 19 Donald Smith, 33 Bobby Evans, 20 Jayson Dzikowicz, 30 Darryl Sampson, 26 Kim Phillips, 3 Errol Brown, 17 Allan Boyko.

SCORING SUMMARY

	Time	Team	Scoring Play	Edm.	Wpg
1	7:10	Edm	TD-Floyd-4-yd. run	6	
	7:20	Edm	Convert-Fleming	1	
	10:10	Edm	TD-Sandusky-2-yd. pass from Allen	6	
	10:27	Edm	Convert-Fleming	1	
	12:07	Edm	FG-Fleming-41 yds.	3	
2	3:36	Edm	Single-Fleming-59 yds.-MFG	1	
	7:11	Edm	FG-Fleming-26 yds.	3	
	12:14	Wpg	TD-Richardson-2-yd. run		6
	12:18	Wpg	Convert-Westwood		1
	14:47	Edm	FG-Fleming-45 yds.	3	
	15:00	Wpg	FG-Westwood-48 yds.		3
3	12:49	Wpg	TD-Garza-1-yd. run		6
	13:04	Wpg	Convert-Westwood		1
4	4:19	Wpg	FG-Westwood-32 yds.		3
	7:40	Edm	FG-Fleming-36 yds.	3	
	9:53	Edm	FG-Fleming-15 yds.	3	
	12:16	Wpg	FG-Westwood-32 yds.		3
	14:54	Edm	FG-Fleming-19 yds.	3	
				33	23

INDIVIDUAL STATISTICS

EDMONTON **WINNIPEG**

PASSING

	ATT	COMP	YDS	I/C	LG	TD
Allen	28	16	238	1	52	1
TOTALS	28	16	238	1	52	1

	ATT	COMP	YDS	I/C	LG	TD
Garza	40	23	322	2	34	0
TOTALS	40	23	322	2	34	0

RUSHING

	NO	YDS	AVE	LG	TD
Allen	14	90	6.4	21	0
Floyd	15	41	2.7	10	1
Soles	5	4	0.8	6	0
TOTALS	34	135	4.0	21	1

	NO	YDS	AVE	LG	TD
Richardson	10	26	2.6	8	1
Garza	5	10	2.0	7	1
Johnstone	1	6	6.0	6	0
TOTALS	16	42	2.6	8	2

PASS RECEIVING

	NO	YDS	AVE	LG	TD
Brown, E.	4	114	28.5	52	0
Soles	4	46	11.5	18	0
Sandusky	3	36	12.0	19	1
Christensen	2	25	12.5	19	0
Floyd	3	17	5.7	14	0
TOTALS	16	238	14.9	52	1

	NO	YDS	AVE	LG	TD
Williams, D.	7	118	16.9	29	0
Jackson	4	57	14.3	21	0
Alphin	3	55	18.3	24	0
Richardson	4	44	11.0	34	0
Wilcox	4	39	9.8	15	0
Johnstone	1	9	9.0	9	0
TOTALS	23	322	14.0	34	0

PUNTING

	NO	YDS	AVE	LK	S
Harper	6	292	48.7	52	0
TOTALS	6	292	48.7	52	0

	NO	YDS	AVE	LK	S
Cameron	7	317	45.3	57	0
TOTALS	7	317	45.3	57	0

PUNT RETURNS

	NO	YDS	AVE	LG	TD
Williams	5	4	0.8	9	0
TOTALS	5	4	0.8	9	0

	NO	YDS	AVE	LG	TD
Boyko	5	16	3.2	8	0
TOTALS	5	16	3.2	8	0

KICKOFFS

	NO	YDS	AVE	LK	S
Fleming	3	167	55.7	62	0
TOTALS	3	167	55.7	62	0

	NO	YDS	AVE	LK	S
Westwood	4	249	62.3	67	0
TOTALS	4	249	62.3	67	0

KICKOFF RETURNS

	NO	YDS	AVE	LG	TD
Floyd	4	94	23.5	28	0
TOTALS	4	94	23.5	28	0

	NO	YDS	AVE	LG	TD
Bryant	2	22	11.0	12	0
Boyko	1	9	9.0	9	0
TOTALS	3	31	10.3	12	0

FIELD GOALS

	TRIED	MADE	YDS	LK
Fleming	7	6	182	45
TOTALS	7	6	182	45

	TRIED	MADE	YDS	LK
Westwood	3	3	112	48
TOTALS	3	3	112	48

UNSUCCESSFUL FIELD GOALS

	NO	YDS	LK	S
Fleming	1	59	59	1
TOTALS	1	59	59	1

BLOCKED KICKS

	NO	FG	P	C
Dickson	1	0	1	0
TOTALS	1	0	1	0

FUMBLE RETURNS

	NO	YDS	AVE	LG	TD
Lolar	1	17	17.0	17	0
Brown, T.	1	0	0.0	0	0
Dickson	1	0	0.0	0	0
Woods	1	0	0.0	0	0
Goods	1	0	0.0	0	0
TOTALS	5	17	3.4	17	0

	NO	YDS	AVE	LG	TD
Clark	1	3	3.0	3	0
Randolph	1	0	0.0	0	0
TOTALS	2	3	1.5	3	0

INTERCEPTION RETURNS

	NO	YDS	AVE	LG	TD
Murphy	1	14	14.0	14	0
Wruck	1	6	6.0	6	0
TOTALS	2	20	10.0	14	0

	NO	YDS	AVE	LG	TD
Phillips	1	10	10.0	10	0
TOTALS	1	10	10.0	10	0

QUARTERBACK SACKS

	NO	YDS LOST
Goods	1	8
Martin	1	9
TOTALS	2	17

	NO	YDS LOST
Battle	2	6
Payton	2	12
Lewis	1	12
TOTALS	5	30

THE GREY CUP

In 1909, Earl Grey, the Governor-General of Canada, donated a trophy for the Rugby Football Championship of Canada. The trophy, which subsequently became known as The Grey Cup, was originally open to competition only for teams which were registered with the Canada Rugby Union. Since 1954 only the teams of the CFL have challenged for the Grey Cup.

Grey Cup Results

Year	Date	Site		Score		Score	Winning Coach	Losing Coach	Attendance
1993	Nov. 28	Calgary	Edmonton	33	Winnipeg	23	Ron Lancaster	Cal Murphy	50,035
1992	Nov. 29	Toronto	Calgary	24	Winnipeg	10	Wally Buono	Urban Bowman	45,863
1991	Nov. 24	Winnipeg	Toronto	36	Calgary	21	Adam Rita	Wally Buono	51,985
1990	Nov. 25	Vancouver	Winnipeg	50	Edmonton	11	Mike Riley	Joe Faragalli	46,968
1989	Nov. 26	Toronto	Saskatchewan	43	Hamilton	40	John Gregory	Al Bruno	54,088
1988	Nov. 27	Ottawa	Winnipeg	22	B.C.	21	Mike Riley	Larry Donovan	50,604
1987	Nov. 29	Vancouver	Edmonton	38	Toronto	36	Joe Faragalli	Bob O'Billovich	59,478
1986	Nov. 30	Vancouver	Hamilton	39	Edmonton	15	Al Bruno	Jack Parker	59,621
1985	Nov. 24	Montreal	B.C.	37	Hamilton	24	Don Matthews	Al Bruno	56,723
1984	Nov. 18	Edmonton	Winnipeg	47	Hamilton	17	Cal Murphy	Al Bruno	60,081
1983	Nov. 27	Vancouver	Toronto	18	B.C.	17	Bob O'Billovich	Don Matthews	59,345
1982	Nov. 28	Toronto	Edmonton	32	Toronto	16	Hugh Campbell	Bob O'Billovich	54,741
1981	Nov. 22	Montreal	Edmonton	26	Ottawa	23	Hugh Campbell	George Brancato	52,478
1980	Nov. 23	Toronto	Edmonton	48	Hamilton	10	Hugh Campbell	John Payne	54,661
1979	Nov. 25	Montreal	Edmonton	17	Montreal	9	Hugh Campbell	Joe Scannella	65,113
1978	Nov. 26	Toronto	Edmonton	20	Montreal	13	Hugh Campbell	Joe Scannella	54,695
1977	Nov. 27	Montreal	Montreal	41	Edmonton	6	Marv Levy	Hugh Campbell	68,318
1976	Nov. 28	Toronto	Ottawa	23	Saskatchewan	20	George Brancato	John Payne	53,467
1975	Nov. 23	Calgary	Edmonton	9	Montreal	8	Ray Jauch	Marv Levy	32,454
1974	Nov. 24	Vancouver	Montreal	20	Edmonton	7	Marv Levy	Ray Jauch	34,450
1973	Nov. 25	Toronto	Ottawa	22	Edmonton	18	Jack Gotta	Ray Jauch	36,653
1972	Dec. 3	Hamilton	Hamilton	13	Saskatchewan	10	Jerry Williams	Dave Skrien	33,993
1971	Nov. 28	Vancouver	Calgary	14	Toronto	11	Jim Duncan	Leo Cahill	34,484
1970	Nov. 28	Toronto	Montreal	23	Calgary	10	Sam Etcheverry	Jim Duncan	32,669
1969	Nov. 30	Montreal	Ottawa	29	Saskatchewan	11	Frank Clair	Eagle Keys	33,172
1968	Nov. 30	Toronto	Ottawa	24	Calgary	21	Frank Clair	Jerry Williams	32,655
1967	Dec. 2	Ottawa	Hamilton	24	Saskatchewan	1	Ralph Sazio	Eagle Keys	31,358
1966	Nov. 26	Vancouver	Saskatchewan	29	Ottawa	14	Eagle Keys	Frank Clair	36,553
1965	Nov. 27	Toronto	Hamilton	22	Winnipeg	16	Ralph Sazio	Bud Grant	32,655
1964	Nov. 28	Toronto	B.C.	34	Hamilton	24	Dave Skrien	Ralph Sazio	32,655
1963	Nov. 30	Vancouver	Hamilton	21	B.C.	10	Ralph Sazio	Dave Skrien	36,545
1962	Dec. 1-2*	Toronto	Winnipeg	28	Hamilton	27	Bud Grant	Jim Trimble	32,655
1961	Dec. 2**	Toronto	Winnipeg	21	Hamilton	14	Bud Grant	Jim Trimble	32,651
1960	Nov. 26	Vancouver	Ottawa	16	Edmonton	6	Frank Clair	Eagle Keys	38,102
1959	Nov. 28	Toronto	Winnipeg	21	Hamilton	7	Bud Grant	Jim Trimble	33,133
1958	Nov. 29	Vancouver	Winnipeg	35	Hamilton	28	Bud Grant	Jim Trimble	36,567
1957	Nov. 30	Toronto	Hamilton	32	Winnipeg	7	Jim Trimble	Bud Grant	27,051
1956	Nov. 24	Toronto	Edmonton	50	Montreal	27	Frank Ivy	Doug Walker	27,425
1955	Nov. 26	Vancouver	Edmonton	34	Montreal	19	Frank Ivy	Doug Walker	39,417
1954	Nov. 27	Toronto	Edmonton	26	Montreal	25	Frank Ivy	Doug Walker	27,321
1953	Nov. 28	Toronto	Ham. Ticats	12	Winnipeg	6	Carl Voyles	George Trafton	27,313
1952	Nov. 29	Toronto	Toronto	21	Edmonton	11	Frank Clair	Frank Filchok	27,391
1951	Nov. 24	Toronto	Ottawa	21	Saskatchewan	14	Clem Crowe	Harry Smith	27,341
1950	Nov. 25	Toronto	Toronto	13	Winnipeg	0	Frank Clair	Frank Larson	27,101
1949	Nov. 26	Toronto	Mtl. Als.	28	Calgary	15	Lew Hayman	Les Lear	20,087
1948	Nov. 27	Toronto	Calgary	12	Ottawa	7	Les Lear	Wally Masters	20,013
1947	Nov. 29	Toronto	Toronto	10	Winnipeg	9	Ted Morris	Jack West	18,885
1946	Nov. 30	Toronto	Toronto	28	Winnipeg	6	Ted Morris	Jack West	18,960
1945	Dec. 1	Toronto	Toronto	35	Winnipeg	0	Ted Morris	Bert Warwick	18,660
1944	Nov. 25	Hamilton	Mtl. St. H-D. Navy	7	Ham. F. Wild	6	Glen Brown	Eddie McLean	3,871
1943	Nov. 27	Toronto	Ham. F. Wild	23	Win R.C.A.F.	14	Brian Timmis	Reg Threlfall	16,423
1942	Dec. 5	Toronto	Tor. R.C.A.F.	8	Win R.C.A.F.	5	Lew Hayman	Reg Threlfall	12,455
1941	Nov. 29	Toronto	Winnipeg	18	Ottawa	16	Reg Threlfall	Ross Trimble	19,065
1940	Nov. 30	Toronto	Ottawa	8	Balmy Beach	2	Ross Trimble	Alex Ponton	4,998
	Dec. 7	Ottawa	Ottawa	12	Balmy Beach	5	Ross Trimble	Alex Ponton	1,700
1939	Dec. 9	Ottawa	Winnipeg	8	Ottawa	7	Reg Threlfall	Ross Trimble	11,738
1938	Dec. 10	Toronto	Toronto	30	Winnipeg	7	Lew Hayman	Reg Threlfall	18,778
1937	Dec. 11	Toronto	Toronto	4	Winnipeg	3	Lew Hayman	Bob Fritz	11,522
1936	Dec. 5	Toronto	Sarnia	26	Ott. R.R.	20	Art Massucci	Billy Hughes	5,883
1935	Dec. 7	Hamilton	Winnipeg	18	Ham. Tigers	12	Bib Fritz	Fred Veale	6,405
1934	Nov. 24	Toronto	Sarnia	20	Regina	12	Art Massucci	Greg Grassick	8,900
1933	Dec. 9	Sarnia	Toronto	4	Sarnia	3	Lew Hayman	Pat Ouellette	2,751
1932	Dec. 3	Hamilton	Ham. Tigers	25	Regina	6	Billy Hughes	Al Ritchie	4,806
1931	Dec. 5	Montreal	Mtl. A.A.A.	22	Regina	0	Clary Foran	Al Ritchie	5,112
1930	Dec. 6	Toronto	Balmy Beach	11	Regina	6	Alex Ponton	Al Ritchie	3,914
1929	Nov. 30	Hamilton	Ham. Tigers	14	Regina	3	Mike Rodden	Al Ritchie	1,906
1928	Dec. 1	Hamilton	Ham. Tigers	30	Regina	0	Mike Rodden	Howie Milne	4,767
1927	Nov. 26	Toronto	Balmy Beach	9	Ham. Tigers	6	Dr. H. Hobbs	Mike Rodden	13,676
1926	Dec. 4	Toronto	Ott. Senators	10	Toronto U	7	Dave McCann	Ron McPherson	8,276
1925	Dec. 5	Ottawa	Ott. Senators	24	Winnipeg	1	Dave McCann	Harold Roth	6,900
1924	Nov. 29	Toronto	Queen's U	11	Balmy Beach	3	Billy Hughes	M. Rodden-A. Buett	5,978
1923	Dec. 1	Toronto	Queen's U	54	Regina	0	Billy Hughes	Jack Eddis	8,629
1922	Dec. 2	Kingston	Queen's U	13	Edmonton	1	Billy Hughes	Deacon White	4,700
1921	Dec. 3	Toronto	Toronto	23	Edmonton	0	Sinc McEvenue	Deacon White	9,558
1920	Dec. 4	Toronto	U. of Toronto	16	Toronto	3	Laddie Cassels	Mike Rodden	10,088
1916-18 - No Game, War 1919 No Playoff Games									
1915	Nov. 20	Toronto	Ham. Tigers	13	Tor. R.A.A.	7	Liz Marriott	Ed Livingstone	2,808
1914	Dec. 5	Toronto	Toronto	14	U. of Toronto	2	Billy Foulds	Hugh Gall	10,500
1913	Nov. 29	Hamilton	Ham. Tigers	44	Parkdale	2	Liz Marriott	Ed Livingstone	2,100
1912	Nov. 30	Hamilton	Ham. Alerts	11	Toronto	4	Liz Marriott	Jack Newton	5,337
1911	Nov. 25	Toronto	U. of Toronto	14	Toronto	7	Dr. A.B. Wright	Billy Foulds	13,687
1910	Nov. 26	Hamilton	U. of Toronto	16	Ham. Tigers	7	Harry Griffith	Seppi DuMoulin	12,000
1909	Dec. 4	Toronto	U. of Toronto	26	Parkdale	6	Harry Griffith	Ed Livingston	3,807

* - Halted by fog on Dec. 1. Final 9 minutes and 29 seconds were played on Dec. 2. ** - Overtime

GREY CUP CHAMPIONSHIP SCORING SUMMARIES

1993 at Calgary McMahon Stadium, November 28, 1993
Edmonton (33) - TDs, Lucius Floyd, Jim Sandusky; FGs, Sean Fleming (6); cons., Fleming (2); single, Fleming.
Winnipeg (23) - TDs, Michael Richardson, Sammy Garza; FGs, Troy Westwood (3); cons., Westwood (2).

1992 at Toronto SkyDome, Sunday, Nov. 29
CALGARY (24) - TDs, David Sapunjis, Allen Pitts; FGs, Mark McLoughlin (3); cons., McLoughlin (2); single, McLoughlin.
WINNIPEG (10) - TDs, Gerald Alphin; FGs, Troy Westwood; con., Westwood.

1991 at Winnipeg Stadium, Sunday, Nov. 24
TORONTO (36) - TDs, Ed Berry, Darrell K. Smith, Raghib Ismail, Paul Masotti; FGs, Lance Chomyc (2); cons., Chomyc (4); singles, Chomyc (2).
CALGARY (21) - TDs, Danny Barrett, Allen Pitts; FGs, Mark McLoughlin (2); cons., McLoughlin (2); single, McLoughlin.

1990 at Vancouver B.C. Place, Sunday, Nov. 25
WINNIPEG (50) - TDs, Warren Hudson (2), Lee Hull, Greg Battle, Perry Tuttle, Rick House; FGs, Trevor Kennerd (2); cons., Kennerd (6), safety touch.
EDMONTON (11) - TD, Larry Willis; FG, Ray Macoritti; con., Macoritti; single, Macoritti.

1989 at Toronto SkyDome, Sunday, Nov. 26
SASKATCHEWAN (43) - TDs, Ray Elgaard, Jeff Fairholm, Donald Narcisse, Tim McCray; FGs, David Ridgway (4); cons., Ridgway (4); single, Terry Baker; safety touch.
HAMILTON (40) - TDs, Tony Champion (2), Derrick McAdoo (2); FGs, Paul Osbaldiston (4); cons., Osbaldiston (4).

1988 at Ottawa Lansdowne Park, Sunday, Nov. 27
WINNIPEG (22) - TD, James Murphy; FGs, Trevor Kennerd (4); con., Kennerd; singles, Kennerd, Bob Cameron (2).
B.C. (21) - TDs, Anthony Cherry, David Williams; FG, Lui Passaglia; cons., Passaglia (2); singles, Passaglia (2); safety touch.

1987 at Vancouver B.C. Place Stadium, Sunday, Nov. 29
EDMONTON (38) - TDs, Henry Williams, Marco Cyncar, Brian Kelly, Damon Allen; FGs, Jerry Kauric (3); cons., Kauric (4); single, Kauric.
TORONTO (36) - TDs, Gill Fenerty (2), Doug Landry, Danny Barrett; FGs, Lance Chomyc (3); cons., Chomyc (3).

1986 at Vancouver B.C. Place Stadium, Sunday, Nov. 30
HAMILTON (39) - TDs, Steve Stapler, James Rockford, Ron Ingram; FGs, Paul Osbaldiston (6); cons., Osbaldiston (3).
EDMONTON (15) - TDs, Damon Allen, Brian Kelly; 2 pt-con., Allen; con., Tom Dixon.

1985 at Montreal Olympic Stadium, Sunday, Nov. 24
B.C. (37) - TDs, Ned Armour (2), Jim Sandusky; FGs, Lui Passaglia (5); cons., Passaglia (3); single, Passaglia.
HAMILTON (24) - TDs, Ron Ingram, Johnny Shepherd, Steve Stapler; FG, Bernie Ruoff; cons., Ruoff (3).

1984 at Edmonton Commonwealth Stadium, Sunday, Nov. 18
WINNIPEG (47) - TDs, Willard Reaves (2), Joe Poplawski, Stan Mikawos, Jeff Boyd; FGs, Trevor Kennerd (4), cons., Kennerd (5).
HAMILTON (17) - TDs, Dieter Brock, Rocky DiPietro; FG, Bernie Ruoff; cons., Ruoff (2).

1983 at Vancouver B.C. Place Stadium, Sunday, Nov. 27
TORONTO (18) - TDs, Jan Carinci, Cedric Minter; FG, Hank Ilesic; con., Ilesic; singles, Ilesic (2).
B.C. (17) - TDs, Mervyn Fernandez, John Henry White; FG, Lui Passaglia; cons., Passaglia (2).

1982 at Toronto Exhibition Stadium, Sunday, Nov. 28
EDMONTON (32) - TDs, Brian Kelly (2), Neil Lumsden; FGs, Dave Cutler (4); cons., Cutler (2).
TORONTO (16) - TDs, Emanuel Tolbert, Terry Greer; cons., Dean Dorsey (2); safety touch.

1981 at Montreal Olympic Stadium, Sunday, Nov.22
EDMONTON (26) - TDs, Warren Moon (2), Jim Germany; FG, Dave Cutler; 2 pt-con., Marco Cyncar; cons., Cutler (2); single, Cutler.
OTTAWA (23) - TDs, Jim Reid, Sam Platt; FGs, Gerry Organ (3); cons., Organ (2).

1980 at Toronto Exhibition Stadium, Sunday, Nov. 23
EDMONTON (48) - TDs, Tom Scott (3), Jim Germany (2), Brian Kelly; FGs, Dave Cutler (2); cons., Cutler (6).
HAMILTON (10) - FGs, Bernie Ruoff (3); single, Ruoff.

1979 at Montreal Olympic Stadium, Sunday, Nov. 25
EDMONTON (17) - TDs, Waddell Smith, Tom Scott; FG, Dave Cutler; cons., Cutler (2).
MONTREAL (9) - FGs, Don Sweet (3).

1978 at Toronto Exhibition Stadium, Sunday, Nov. 26
EDMONTON (20) - TD, Jim Germany; FGs, Dave Cutler (4); con., Cutler; single, Cutler.
MONTREAL (13) - TD, Joe Barnes; FGs; Don Sweet (2); con., Sweet.

1977 at Montreal Olympic Stadium, Sunday, Nov. 27
MONTREAL (41) - TDs, Peter Dalla Riva, John O'Leary, Bob Gaddis; FGs, Don Sweet (6); cons., Sweet (3); singles, Sweet (2).
EDMONTON (6) - FGs, Dave Cutler (2).

1976 at Toronto Exhibition Stadium, Sunday, Nov. 28
OTTAWA (23) - TDs, Bill Hatanaka, Tony Gabriel; FGs, Gerry Organ (3); cons., Organ (2).
SASKATCHEWAN (20) - TDs, Steve Mazurak, Bob Richardson; FGs, Bob Macoritti (2); con., Macoritti (2).

1975 at Calgary McMahon Stadium, Sunday, Nov. 23
EDMONTON (9) - FGs, Dave Cutler (3).
MONTREAL (8) - FGs, Don Sweet (2); singles, Sweet (2).

1974 at Vancouver Empire Stadium, Sunday, Nov. 24
MONTREAL (20) - TD, Larry Sherrer; FGs; Don Sweet (4); con., Sweet; single, Sweet.
EDMONTON (7) - TD, Calvin Harrell; con., Dave Cutler.

1973 at Toronto C.N.E. Stadium, Sunday, Nov. 25
OTTAWA (22) - TDs, Rhome Nixon, Jim Evenson; FGs, Gerry Organ (2); cons., Organ (2); safety touch.
EDMONTON (18) - TDs, Roy Bell, Garry Lefebvre, FG, Dave Cutler; con., Cutler (2); single, Lefebvre.

1972 at Hamilton Ivor Wynne Stadium, Sunday, Dec. 3
HAMILTON (13) - TD, Dave Fleming; FGs, Ian Sunter (2); con., Sunter.
SASKATCHEWAN (10) - TD, Tom Campana; FG, Jack Abendschan; con., Abendschan.

1971 at Vancouver Empire Stadium, Sunday, Nov. 28
CALGARY (14) - TDs, Herman Harrison, Jesse Mims; cons., Larry Robinson (2).
TORONTO (11) - TD, Roger Scales; FG, Ivan MacMillan; con., Macmillan; single, MacMillan.

1970 at Toronto C.N.E. Stadium, Saturday, Nov. 28
MONTREAL (23) - TDs, Ted Alflen, Tom Pullen, Garry Lefebvre; FG, George Springate; cons., Springate (2).
CALGARY (10) - TD, Hugh McKinnis, FG, Larry Robinson; con., Robinson.

1969 at Montreal Autostade, Sunday, Nov. 30
OTTAWA (29) - TDs, Ron Stewart (2), Jim Mankins, Jay Roberts; cons., Don Sutherin (4); single, Sutherin.
SASKATCHEWAN (11) - TD, Alan Ford; con., Jack Abendschan; singles, Ford, Abendschan; safety touch.

1968 at Toronto C.N.E. Stadium, Saturday, Nov. 30
OTTAWA (24) - TDs, Russ Jackson, Vic Washington, Margene Adkins; FG, Don Sutherin; cons., Sutherin (2); single, Wayne Giardino.
CALGARY (21) - TDs, Terry Evanshen (2), Peter Liske; cons., Larry Robinson (3).

1967 at Ottawa Lansdowne Park, Saturday, Dec. 2
HAMILTON (24) - TDs, Joe Zuger, Ted Watkins, Billy Ray Locklin; cons., Tommy Joe Coffey (2); singles, Zuger (3), Coffey.
SASKATCHEWAN (1) - Single, Alan Ford.

1966 at Vancouver Empire Stadium, Saturday, Nov. 26.
SASKATCHEWAN (29) - TDs, Jim Worden, Alan Ford, Hugh Campbell, George Reed, cons., Jack Abendschan (4); single, Ford.
OTTAWA (14) - TDs, Whit Tucker (2); con., Moe Racine; single, Bill Cline.

1965 at Toronto C.N.E. Stadium, Saturday, Nov. 27
HAMILTON (22) - TDs, Dick Cohee, Willie Bethea; cons., Don Sutherin (2); singles, Sutherin, Joe Zuger; safety touches (3).
WINNIPEG (16) - TDs, Art Perkins, Leo Lewis; FG, Norm Winton; con., Winton.

1964 at Toronto C.N.E. Stadium, Saturday, Nov. 28
B.C. LIONS (34) - TDs, Bill Munsey (2), Jim Carphin, Bob Swift, Willie Fleming; cons., Peter Kempf (4).
HAMILTON (24) - TDs, Johnny Counts, Stan Crisson, Tommy Grant; cons., Don Sutherin (2); singles, Joe Zuger (2); safety touch.

1963 at Vancouver Empire Stadium, Saturday, Nov. 30
HAMILTON (21) - TDs, Willie Bethea, Hal Patterson, Art Baker, cons., Don Sutherin (3).
B.C. LIONS (10) - TD, Mack Burton; FG, Peter Kempf; con., Kempf.

1962 at Toronto C.N.E. Stadium, Sat & Sun., Dec. 1-2
WINNIPEG (28) - TDs, Leo Lewis (2), Charlie Shepard (2); cons., Gerry James (4).
HAMILTON (27) - TDs, Garney Henley (2); Bobby Kuntz, Dave Viti; cons., Don Sutherin (2); single, Sutherin.

1961 at Toronto C.N.E Stadium, Saturday, Dec. 2
WINNIPEG (21) - TDs, Gerry James, Ken Ploen (in overtime); FGs, James (2); cons., James (2); single, Jack Delveaux.
HAMILTON (14) - TDs, Paul Dekker, Ralph Goldston; cons., Don Sutherin (2).

1960 at Vancouver Empire Stadium, Saturday, Nov 26
OTTAWA (16) - TDs, Bill Sowalski, Kaye Vaughan; FG, Gary Schreider; con., Schreider.
EDMONTON (6) - TD, Jim Letcavits.

1959 at Toronto C.N.E. Stadium, Saturday, Nov. 28
WINNIPEG (21) - TDs, Charlie Shepard, Ernie Pitts; FG, Gerry James; cons., James (2); singles, Shepard (4).
HAMILTON (7) - FGs, Steve Oneschuk (2); single, Vince Scott.

1958 at Vancouver Empire Stadium, Saturday, Nov. 29
WINNIPEG (35) - TDs, Jim Van Pelt (2), Norm Rauhaus, Charlie Shepard; FGs, Van Pelt (2); cons., Van Pelt (4); single, Shepard.
HAMILTON (28) - TDs, Ron Howell (2), Ralph Goldston, Gerry McDougall; cons., Steve Oneschuk (4).

1957 at Toronto Varsity Stadium, Saturday, Nov. 30
HAMILTON (32) - TDs, Ray Bawel, Bernie Faloney, Gerry McDougall, Cookie Gilchrist (2); cons., Steve Oneschuk (2).
WINNIPEG (7) - TD, Dennis Mendyk; con., Ken Ploen.

1956 at Toronto Varsity Stadium, Saturday, Nov. 24
EDMONTON (50) - TDs, Jackie Parker (3), Don Getty (2), Johnny Bright (2); FG, Joe Mobra; cons., Mobra (4); single, Parker.
MONTREAL (27) - TDs, Hal Patterson (2), Sam Etcheverry, Pat Abbruzzi; cons., Bill Bewley (3).

1955 at Vancouver Empire Stadium, Saturday, Nov. 26
EDMONTON (34) - TDs, Normie Kwong (2), Johnny Bright (2), Bob Heydenfeldt; FG, Bob Dean; cons., Dean (5); single, Dean.
MONTREAL (19) - TDs, Hal Patterson (2), Pat Abbruzzi; cons., Bud Korchak (3); single, Korchak.

1954 at Toronto Varsity Stadium, Saturday, Nov. 27
EDMONTON (26) - TDs, Earl Lindley, Bernie Faloney, Glenn Lippman, Jackie Parker; FG, Bob Dean; cons., Dean (3).
MONTREAL (25) - TDs, Red O'Quinn (2); Chuck Hunsinger, Joey Pal; cons., Jim Poole (4); single, Poole.

1953 at Toronto Varsity Stadium, Saturday, Nov. 28
HAMILTON TIGER CATS (12) - TDs, Vito Ragazzo, Ed Songin; cons., Tip Logan (2).
WINNIPEG BLUE BOMBERS (6) - TD, Gerry James; con., Bud Korchak.

1952 at Toronto Varsity Stadium, Saturday, Nov. 29
ARGONAUTS (21) - TDs, Nobby Wirkowski, Billy Bass, Zeke O'Connor; cons., Red Ettinger (3); FG, Ettinger.
EDMONTON ESKIMOS (11) - TDs, Normie Kwong (2); con., Wilbur Snyder.

1951 at Toronto Varsity Stadium, Saturday, Nov. 24
OTTAWA ROUGH RIDERS (21) - TDs, Benny MacDonnel, Pete Karpuk, Alton Baldwin; cons., Bob Gain (3); singles, Bruce Cummings (2), Tom O'Malley.
SASKATCHEWAN ROUGHRIDERS (14) - TDs, Jack Nix, Sully Glasser; cons., Red Ettinger (2); singles, Glenn Dobbs (2).

1950 at Toronto Varsity Stadium, Saturday, Nov. 25
ARGONAUTS (13) - TD, Al Dekdebrun; FGs, Nick Volpe (2); singles, Joe Krol (2).
WINNIPEG BLUE BOMBERS (0).

1949 at Toronto Varsity Stadium, Saturday, Nov. 26
MONTREAL ALOUETTES (28) - TDs, Virgil Wagner (2), Bob Cunningham, Herb Trawick; cons., Ches McCance (3); FG, McCance; singles, McCance; Fred Kijek.
CALGARY STAMPEDERS (15) - TDs, Harry Hood, Sugarfoot Anderson; cons., Vern Graham (2); single, Keith Spaith; safety touch.

1948 at Toronto Varsity Stadium, Saturday, Nov. 27
CALGARY STAMPEDERS (12) - TDs, Normie Hill, Pete Thodos; cons., Fred Wilmot (2).
OTTAWA ROUGH RIDERS (7) - TD, Bob Paffrath; con., Eric Chipper; single, Tony Golab.

1947 at Toronto Varsity Stadium, Saturday, Nov. 29
ARGONAUTS (10) - TD, Royal Copeland, con., Joe Krol; singles, Krol (4).
WINNIPEG BLUE BOMBERS (9) - TD, Bob Sandberg; con., Don Hiney; FG, Hiney.

1946 at Toronto Varsity Stadium, Saturday, Nov. 30
ARGONAUTS (28) - TDs, Royal Copeland, Joe Krol, Rod Smylie, Byron Karrys, Boris Tipoff; cons., Krol (3).
WINNIPEG BLUE BOMBERS (6) - TD, Wally Dobler; con., Dobler.

1945 at Toronto Varsity Stadium, Saturday, Dec. 1
ARGONAUTS (35) - TDs, Doug Smylie (2); Billy Myers (2), Royal Copeland, Joe Krol; cons., Krol (2), Smylie, Frank Hickey; single, Art Skidmore.
WINNIPEG BLUE BOMBERS (0).

1944 at Hamilton Civic Stadium, Saturday, Nov. 25
ST. HYACINTHE-DONNACONA NAVY (7) - TD, Johnny Taylor; singles, Dutch Davey (2).
HAMILTON WILDCATS (6) - TD, Paul Miocinovich; con., Joe Krol.

1943 at Toronto Varsity Stadium, Saturday, Nov. 27
HAMILTON FLYING WILDCATS (23) - TDs, Doug Smith, Jimmy Fumio, Mel Lawson; cons., Joe Krol (3); FG, Krol; singles, Krol, Smith.
WINNIPEG R.C.A.F. BOMBERS (14) - TDs, Garney Smith, Dave Berry, cons., Ches McCance (2); singles, Brian Quinn (2).

1942 at Toronto Varsity Stadium, Saturday, Dec. 5
TORONTO R.C.A.F. HURRICANES (8) - TD, John Poplowski; singles, Fred Kijek (2), Don Crowe (1).
WINNIPEG R.C.A.F. BOMBERS (5) - TD, Lloyd Boivin.

1941 at Toronto Varsity Stadium, Saturday, Nov. 29
WINNIPEG BLUE BOMBERS (18) - TDs, Mel Wilson, Bud Marquardt; cons., Ches McCance (2); FGs, McCance (2).
OTTAWA ROUGH RIDERS (16) - TD, Tony Golab; con., George Fraser; FGs, Fraser (3); single, Fraser.

1940 at Ottawa Lansdowne Park, Saturday, Dec. 7
OTTAWA ROUGH RIDERS (12) - TD, Tommy Daley; con., Tiny Herman; singles, Sammy Sward (5), Herman.
TORONTO BALMY BEACH (5) - TD, Bobby Porter.

1940 at Toronto Varsity Stadium, Saturday, Nov. 30
OTTAWA ROUGH RIDERS (8) - TD, Dave Sprague; con., Rick Perley; singles, Sammy Sward (2).
TORONTO BALMY BEACH (2) - Singles, Bobby Porter (2).

1939 at Ottawa Lansdowne Park, Saturday, Dec. 9
WINNIPEG BLUE BOMBERS (8) - TD, Andy Bieber; singles, Greg Kabat (2), Art Stevenson.
OTTAWA ROUGH RIDERS (7) - TD, Andy Tommy; con., Tiny Herman; single, Herman.

1938 at Toronto Varsity Stadium, Saturday, Dec. 10
TORONTO ARGONAUTS (30) - TDs, Red Storey (3), Art West, Bernie Thornton; cons., Bill Stukus (2), Annis Stukus (2); single, Annis Stukus.
WINNIPEG BLUE BOMBERS (7) - FGs, Greg Kabat (2); single, Art Stevenson.

1937 at Toronto Varsity Stadium, Saturday, Dec. 11
ARGONAUTS (4) - FG, Earl Selkirk; single, Bob Isbister.
WINNIPEG BLUE BOMBERS (3) - Singles, Steve Olander (2), Greg Kabat.

1936 at Toronto Varsity Stadium, Saturday, Dec. 5
SARNIA IMPERIALS (26) - TDs, Ormond Beach (2), Mike Hedgewick (2); cons., Alex Hayes (4); singles, Bummer Stirling (2).
OTTAWA ROUGH RIDERS (20) - TDs, Andy Tommy, Bunny Wadsworth, Arnie Morrison; cons., Tiny Herman (2); singles, Morrison (2), Jack Leore.

1935 at Hamilton A.A.A. Grounds, Saturday, Dec. 7
WINNIPEG (18) - TDs, Bud Marquardt, Greg Kabat, Fritz Hanson; cons., Russ Rebholz (2); single, Kabat.
HAMILTON TIGERS (12) - TD, Wilf Patterson; FG, Frank Turville; singles, Turville (2); safety touch.

1934 at Toronto Varsity Stadium, Saturday, Nov. 24
SARNIA IMPERIALS (20) - TDs, Gordon Paterson, Johnny Manore; cons., Alex Hayes (2); FG, Hayes; singles, Bummer Stirling (5).
REGINA ROUGHRIDERS (12) - TDs, Ted Olson, Steve Adkins; con., Paul Kirk; single, Olson.

1933 at Sarnia Davis Field, Saturday, Dec. 9
TORONTO ARGONAUTS (4) - FG, Tommy Burns; single, Ab Box.
SARNIA IMPERIALS (3) - Singles, Bummer Stirling (3).

1932 at Hamilton A.A.A. Grounds, Saturday, Dec. 3
HAMILTON TIGERS (25) - TDs, Dinny Gardner, Beano Wright, Jimmy Simpson; cons., Gardner (2), Frank Turville; singles, Turville, Ray Boadway; FG, Gardner, safety touch.
REGINA ROUGHRIDERS (6) - TD, Austin DeFrate; con., Curt Schave.

1931 at Montreal Molson Stadium, Saturday, Dec. 5
MONTREAL AAA WINGED WHEELERS (22) - TDs, Pete Jotkus, Kenny Grant, Wally Whitty; FG, Huck Welch; cons., Welch, Warren Stevens; singles, Welch (2).
REGINA ROUGHRIDERS (0).

1930 at Toronto Varsity Stadium, Saturday, Dec. 6
TORONTO BALMY BEACH (11) - TD, Bobby Reid; singles, Claude Harris (3), Ab Box (3).
REGINA ROUGHRIDERS (6) - TD, Fred Brown; single, Sol Bloomfield.

1929 at Hamilton A.A.A. Grounds, Saturday, Nov. 30
HAMILTON TIGERS (14) - TD, Jimmy Simpson; singles, Pep Leadlay (3), Huck Welch (6).
REGINA ROUGHRIDERS (3) - Singles, Sol Bloomfield (2), Jerry Erskine.

1928 at Hamilton A.A.A. Grounds, Saturday, Dec. 1
HAMILTON TIGERS (30) - TDs, Jimmy Simpson (2), Brian Timmis (2), Ken Walker; cons., Pep Leadlay (3); singles, Huck Welch (2).
REGINA ROUGHRIDERS (0).

1927 at Toronto Varsity Stadium, Saturday Nov. 26
TORONTO BALMY BEACH (9) - TD, Alex Ponton Sr.; singles, Yip Foster (3), Ernie Crowhurst.
HAMILTON TIGERS (6) - TD, Tebor McKelvey; single, Pep Leadlay.

1926 at Toronto Varsity Stadium, Saturday, Dec. 4
OTTAWA SENATORS (10) - TD, Charlie Lynch; singles, Joe Miller (5).
U. of TORONTO (7) - Singles, Trimble (5), Snyder (2).

1925 at Ottawa Lansdowne Park, Saturday, Dec. 5
OTTAWA SENATORS (24) - TDs, Charlie Connell (2), Edgar Mulroney, Don Young; singles, Charlie Lynch (4).
WINNIPEG TAMMANY TIGERS (1) - Single, Eddie Grant.

1924 at Toronto Varsity Stadium, Saturday, Nov. 29
QUEEN'S (11) - TDs, James Wright; con., Pep Leadlay; singles, Leadlay (3); safety touch.
TORONTO BALMY BEACH (3) - Singles, Morris Hughes (3).

1923 at Toronto Varsity Stadium, Saturday, Dec. 1
QUEEN'S (54) - TDs, Harry Batstone (2); Bill Campbell (2), Johhny Evans (2), N.L. Walker, Carl Quinn, Roy Reynolds; cons., Pep Leadlay (4), Batstone (2); singles, Leadlay (3).
REGINA ROUGHRIDERS (0).

1922 at Kingston Richardson Stadium, Saturday, Dec. 2
QUEEN'S (13) - TDs, Charlie Mundell, Dave Harding; con., Pep Leadlay; singles, Leadlay (2).
EDMONTON ELKS (1) - Single, Jack Fraser.

1921 at Toronto Varsity Stadium, Saturday, Dec. 3
ARGONAUTS (23) - TDs, Lionel Conacher (2), Shrimp Cochrane; con., Harry Batstone; FG, Conacher; singles, Conacher (2), Glenn Sullivan (2).
EDMONTON ESKIMOS (0).

1920 at Toronto Varsity Stadium, Saturday, Dec. 4
U. of TORONTO (16) - TDs, Warren Snyder, Jo-Jo Stirrett, Red Mackenzie; con., Mackenzie.
ARGONAUTS (3) - Singles, Dunc Munro (3).

(No Competition 1916-17-18-19)

1915 at Toronto Varsity Stadium, Saturday, Nov. 20
HAMILTON TIGERS (13) - TDs, Jack Erskine, Chicken McKelvey; con., Sam Manson; singles, Manson (2).
TORONTO ROWING (7) - FG, George Bickle; singles, Hal DeGruchy (2), Bickle (2).

1914 at Varsity Stadium, Toronto, Saturday, Dec. 5
ARGONAUTS (14) - TDs, Glad Murphy, Freddie Mills; con., Jack O'Connor, FG, O'Connor.
U. of TORONTO (2) - Singles, J.W. MacKenzie, L. Saunders.

1913 at Hamilton Cricket Grounds, Saturday, Nov. 29
HAMILTON TIGERS (44) - TDs, Ross Craig (3), Art Wilson, Norm Clark, Sam Manson, Hary Glassford; cons., Manson (4); singles, Manson (4), Billy Mallett.
TORONTO PARKDALE (2) - Singles, Hughie Gall (2).

1912 at Hamilton Cricket Grounds, Saturday, Nov. 30
HAMILTON ALERTS (11) - TD, Ross Craig; con., Craig; singles, Tout Leckie (5).
ARGONAUTS (4) - Singles, Crossen Clarke (2); safety touch.

1911 at Toronto Varsity Stadium, Saturday, Nov. 25
U. of TORONTO (14) - TDs, Allan Ramsay, Frank Knight; cons., Jack Maynard (2); singles, Maynard (2).
ARGONAUTS (7) - FG, Ross Binkley; singles, Binkley (3), Bill Mallett.

1910 at Hamilton Cricket Grounds, Saturday, Nov. 26
U. of TORONTO (16) - TDs, Red Dixon, Jack Maynard; con., Maynard; singles, Hughie Gall (2); Dixon (2), Maynard.
HAMILTON TIGERS (7) - FG, Kid Smith; singles, Ben Simpson (3), Smith.

1909 at Toronto Rosedale Field, Saturday, Dec. 4
U. of TORONTO (26) - TDs, Hughie Gall, Murray Thomson, Smirle Lawson; con., Bill Ritchie; singles, Gall (8), Lawson (2).
TORONTO PARKDALE (6) - TD, Tom Meighan; single, Percy Killaly.

GREY CUP WINNERS

By City	By Team
19 - TORONTO	ARGONAUTS (12) - 1914, 1921, 1933, 1937, 1938, 1945, 1946, 1947, 1950, 1952, 1983, 1991 BALMY BEACH (2) - 1927, 1930 U. OF TORONTO (4) - 1909, 1910, 1911, 1920 RCAF HURRICANES (1) - 1942
14 - HAMILTON	ALERTS (1) - 1912 TIGERS (5) - 1913, 1915, 1928, 1929, 1932 FLYING WILDCATS (1) - 1943 TIGER-CATS (7) - 1953, 1957, 1963, 1965, 1967, 1972, 1986
11 - EDMONTON	ESKIMOS - 1954, 1955, 1956, 1975, 1978, 1979, 1980, 1981, 1982, 1987, 1993
9 - OTTAWA	SENATORS (2) - 1925, 1926 ROUGH RIDERS (7) - 1940, 1951, 1960, 1968, 1969, 1973, 1976
10 - WINNIPEG	WINNIPEGS (1) - 1935 BLUE BOMBERS (9) - 1939, 1941, 1958, 1959, 1961, 1962, 1984, 1988, 1990
6 - MONTREAL	M.A.A.A. (1) - 1931 HMCS ST. HYACINTHE-DONNACONA (1) - 1944 ALOUETTES (4) - 1949, 1970, 1974, 1977
3 - CALGARY	STAMPEDERS - 1948, 1971, 1992
3 - KINGSTON	QUEEN'S UNIVERSITY - 1922, 1923, 1924
2 - SARNIA	IMPERIALS - 1934, 1936
2 - VANCOUVER	BRITISH COLUMBIA LIONS - 1964, 1985
2 - REGINA	SASKATCHEWAN ROUGHRIDERS - 1966, 1989
81 - TOTAL	

ALLEN AND FLEMING - GREY CUP MVPs

In 1991, an old standard for selecting the Grey Cup Game Stars was reintroduced to the Canadian Football League. For almost two decades, three outstanding players (Offensive, Defensive and Canadian) were selected by the Football Reporters of Canada. Three years ago, it was decided that the awards would go to the Most Valuable Player and to the Most Valuable Canadian of the Game. The 1993 Grey Cup Most Valuable Player was Edmonton Eskimo pivot Damon Allen while teammate Sean Fleming, was recognized as the Canadian MVP. Allen, who won this same honour for his efforts in the 1987 Championship Game, quarterbacked his team to a Grey Cup victory for the first time in six years as they defeated the Winnipeg Blue Bombers 33-23. A second-year kicker, Fleming was a determining factor in his team's outcome in the game. For their performances, Allen was presented with the keys to a new Dodge Ram truck while Fleming received a Sony Entertainment Package.

1993- Most Valuable Player, Damon Allen, QB, Edmonton; Most Valuable Canadian, Sean Fleming, K, Edmonton.
1992 - Most Valuable Player, Doug Flutie, QB, Calgary; Most Valuable Canadian, David Sapunjis, SB, Calgary.
1991 - Most Valuable Player, Raghib Ismail, WR, Toronto; Most Valuable Canadian, David Sapunjis, SB, Calgary.
1990 - Offence, Tom Burgess, QB, Winnipeg; Defence, Greg Battle, LB, Winnipeg; Canadian, Warren Hudson, FB, Winnipeg.
1989 - Offence, Kent Austin, QB, Saskatchewan; Defence, Chuck Klingbeil, DT, Saskatchewan; Canadian, David Ridgway, K, Saskatchewan
1988 - Offence, James Murphy, WR, Winnipeg; Defence, Michael Gray, DT, Winnipeg; Canadian, Bob Cameron, P, Winnipeg
1987 - Offence, Damon Allen, QB, Edmonton; Defence, Stewart Hill, DE, Edmonton; Canadian, Milson Jones, RB, Edmonton
1986 - Offence, Mike Kerrigan, QB, Hamilton; Defence, Grover Covington, DE, Hamilton; Canadian, Paul Osbaldiston, K/P, Hamilton
1985 - Offence, Roy Dewalt, QB, B.C.; Defence, James Parker, DE, B.C.; Canadian, Lui Passaglia, P/K, B.C.
1984 - Offence, Tom Clements, QB, Winnipeg; Defence, Tyrone Jones, LB, Winnipeg; Canadian, Sean Kehoe, RB, Winnipeg
1983 - Offence, Joe Barnes, QB, Toronto; Defence, Carl Brazley, DB, Toronto; Canadian Rick Klassen, DT, B.C.
1982 - Offence, Warren Moon, QB, Edmonton; Defence, Dave Fennell, DT, Edmonton; Canadian, Dave Fennell, DT, Edmonton
1981 - Offence, J.C. Watts, QB, Ottawa; Defence, John Glassford, LB, Ottawa; Canadian, Neil Lumsden, RB, Edmonton
1980 - Offence, Warren Moon, QB, Edmonton; Defence, Dale Potter, LB, Edmonton; Canadian, Dale Potter, LB, Edmonton
1979 - Offence, David Green, RB, Montreal; Defence, Tom Cousineau, LB, Montreal; Canadian, Don Sweet, K, Montreal
1978 - Offence, Tom Wilkinson, QB, Edmonton; Defence, Dave Fennell, DT, Edmonton; Canadian, Angelo Santucci, RB, Edmonton
1977 - Offence, Sonny Wade, QB, Montreal; Defence, Glen Weir, DT, Montreal; Canadian Don Sweet, K, Montreal
1976 - Offence, Tom Clements, QB, Ottawa; Defence, Cleveland Vann, LB, Saskatchewan; Canadian, Tony Gabriel, TE, Ottawa
1975 - Offence, Steve Ferrughelli, RB, Montreal; Defence, Lewis Cook, DB, Montreal; Canadian, Dave Cutler, K, Edmonton
1974 - Offence, Sonny Wade, QB, Montreal; Defence, Junior Ah You, DE, Montreal; Canadian, Don Sweet, K, Montreal
1973 - Most Valuable Player, Charlie Brandon, DE, Ottawa; Canadian, Garry Lefebvre, DB, Edmonton
1972 - Most Valuable Player, Chuck Ealey, QB, Hamilton; Canadian, Ian Sunter, K, Hamilton
1971 - Most Valuable Player, Wayne Harris, LB, Calgary; Canadian, Dick Suderman, DE, Calgary
1970 - Most Valuable Player, Sonny Wade, QB, Montreal
1969 - Most Valuable Player, Russ Jackson, QB, Ottawa
1968 - Most Valuable Player, Vic Washington, RB, Ottawa
1967 - Most Valuable Player, Joe Zuger, QB, Hamilton
1962 - Most Valuable Player, Leo Lewis, RB, Winnipeg
1961 - Most Valuable Player, Ken Ploen, QB, Winnipeg
1960 - Most Valuable Player, Ron Stewart, RB, Ottawa
1959 - Most Valuable Player, Charlie Shepard, RB, Winnipeg

GREY CUP TEAM RECORDS

(Scoring and appearance records date from 1909; all other records date from 1953.)

MOST GREY CUP GAMES PLAYED:
32 - Toronto
27 - Hamilton
24 - Winnipeg
20 - Edmonton
15 - Ottawa
14 - Saskatchewan
12 - Montreal

MOST WINS:
19 - Toronto
14 - Hamilton
11 - Edmonton
- Winnipeg
9 - Ottawa
6 - Montreal

MOST LOSSES:
14 - Winnipeg
13 - Toronto
- Hamilton
12 - Saskatchewan
9 - Edmonton
6 - Montreal
- Ottawa

HIGHEST ATTENDANCE:
68,318 - Mtl. 41 vs. Edm. 6 (at Montreal) Nov. 27, 1977
65,113 - Edm. 17 vs. Mtl. 9 (at Montreal) Nov. 25, 1979
60,081 - Wpg. 47 vs. Ham. 17 (at Edmonton) Nov. 18, 1984
59,621 - Ham. 39 vs. Edm. 15 (at Vancouver) Nov. 30, 1986
59,478 - Edm. 38 vs. Tor. 36 (at Vancouver) Nov. 29, 1987

ALL-TIME MOST POINTS SCORED:
545 - Hamilton
447 - Toronto
408 - Edmonton
375 - Winnipeg
276 - Ottawa

ALL-TIME MOST POINTS AGAINST:
465 - Hamilton
458 - Winnipeg
454 - Edmonton
382 - Toronto
340 - Saskatchewan

MOST POINTS ONE TEAM ONE GAME:
54 - Queens Un. vs. Reg., Dec. 1, 1923
50 - Edm. vs. Mtl., Nov. 24, 1956
- Wpg. vs. Edm., Nov. 25, 1990
48 - Edm. vs. Ham., Nov. 23, 1980

MOST POINTS BOTH TEAMS ONE GAME:
83 - Sask. vs. Ham., Nov. 26, 1989
77 - Edm. vs. Mtl., Nov. 24, 1956
74 - Edm. vs. Tor., Nov. 29, 1987

MOST POINTS ONE TEAM ONE QUARTER:
28 - Wpg. vs. Edm. (3rd quarter), Nov. 25, 1990
27 - Wpg. vs. Ham. (2nd quarter), Nov. 18, 1984
24 - Tor. vs. Wpg. (4th quarter), Dec. 10, 1938

MOST POINTS ONE TEAM FIRST QUARTER:
18 - Ham. vs. Wpg., Nov. 27, 1943
17 - Ham. vs. Edm., Nov. 30, 1986
Edm. vs. Wpg., Nov. 28, 1993
14 - Ham. vs. Wpg., Nov. 29, 1958
- Ham. vs. Wpg., Nov. 18, 1984

MOST POINTS ONE TEAM SECOND QUARTER:
27 - Wpg. vs. Ham., Nov. 18, 1984
21 - Wpg. vs. Ham., Dec. 1, 1962
- Tor. vs. Edm., Nov. 29, 1987
- Sask. vs. Ham., Nov. 26, 1989
17 - Sask. vs. Ott., Nov. 28, 1976
- Edm. vs. Tor., Nov. 28, 1982

MOST POINTS ONE TEAM THIRD QUARTER:
28 - Wpg. vs. Edm., Nov. 25, 1990
20 - Mtl. vs. Edm., Nov, 27, 1977
18 - Edm. vs. Mtl., Nov. 24, 1956

MOST POINTS ONE TEAM FOURTH QUARTER:
24 - Tor. vs. Wpg., Dec. 10, 1938
19 - Ham. vs. Wpg., Nov. 30, 1957
18 - Wpg. vs. Ham., Nov. 28, 1959

FEWEST POINTS WINNING TEAM:
4 - Tor. vs. Sarnia Dec. 9, 1933
- Tor. vs. Wpg., Dec. 11, 1937
7 - Mtl. vs. Ham., Nov. 25, 1944

FEWEST POINTS BOTH TEAMS ONE GAME:
7 - Tor.-Sarnia, Dec. 9, 1933
- Tor.-Winnipeg, Dec. 11, 1937
10 - Ott.-Balmy Beach, Nov. 30, 1940
13 - Tor. RCAF-Wpg. RCAF, Dec. 5, 1942
- Mtl. Navy-Ham. Wildcats, Nov. 23, 1944
- Tor.-Wpg., Nov. 25, 1950

HIGHEST SHUTOUT:
54-0 - Queen's vs. Reg., Dec. 1, 1923
35-0 - Tor. vs. Wpg., Dec. 1, 1945
30-0 - Ham. vs. Reg., Dec. 1, 1928

ALL-TIME MOST TOUCHDOWNS:
66 - Hamilton
54 - Toronto
46 - Edmonton
42 - Winnipeg
33 - Ottawa
26 - Montreal
18 - Saskatchewan
14 - Calgary
13 - B.C.

MOST TOUCHDOWNS ONE TEAM ONE GAME:
9 - Queen's vs. Reg., Dec. 1, 1923
7 - Ham. vs. Tor., Nov. 29, 1913
- Edm. vs. Mtl., Nov. 24, 1956
6 - Tor. vs. Wpg., Dec. 1, 1945
- Edm. vs. Ham., Nov. 23, 1980
- Wpg. vs. Edm., Nov. 25, 1990

MOST TOUCHDOWNS BOTH TEAMS ONE GAME:
11 - Edm.-Mtl., Nov. 24, 1956
9 - Queen's-Reg., Dec. 1, 1923
8 - Edm.-Mtl., Nov. 27, 1954
- Edm.-Mtl., Nov. 26, 1955
- Wpg.-Ham., Nov. 29, 1958
- Wpg.-Ham., Dec. 1-2, 1962
- B.C.-Ham., Nov. 28, 1964
- Edm.-Tor., Nov. 29, 1987
- Sask.-Ham., Nov. 26, 1989

ALL-TIME MOST CONVERTS:
50 - Hamilton
39 - Edmonton
37 - Winnipeg
34 - Toronto

MOST CONVERTS ONE TEAM ONE GAME:
7 - Queen's vs. Reg., Dec. 1, 1923
6 - Edm. vs. Ham., Nov. 23, 1980
- Wpg. vs. Edm., Nov. 25, 1990
5 - Edm. vs. Mtl., Nov. 26, 1955
- Wpg. vs. Ham., Nov. 18, 1984

MOST CONVERTS BOTH TEAMS ONE GAME:
8 - Edm.-Mtl., Nov. 26, 1955
- Wpg.-Ham., Nov. 29, 1958
- Sask.-Ham., Nov. 26, 1989
7 - Queen's vs. Reg., Dec. 1, 1923
- Edm.-Mtl., Nov. 27, 1954
- Edm.-Mtl., Nov. 24, 1956
- Wpg.-Ham., Nov. 18, 1984
- Edm.-Tor., Nov. 29, 1987
- Wpg.-Edm., Nov. 25, 1990

ALL-TIME MOST FIELD GOALS:
31 - Edmonton
22 - Hamilton
23 - Winnipeg
19 - Montreal

MOST FIELD GOALS ONE TEAM ONE GAME:
6 - Mtl. vs. Edm., Nov. 27, 1977
- Ham. vs. Edm., Nov. 30, 1986
Edm. vs. Wpg., Nov. 28, 1993
5 - B.C. vs. Ham., Nov. 24, 1985
4 - Mtl. vs. Edm., Nov. 24, 1974
- Edm. vs. Mtl., Nov. 26, 1978
- Edm. vs. Tor., Nov. 28, 1982
- Wpg. vs. Ham., Nov. 18, 1984
- Edm. vs. Tor., Nov. 29, 1987
- Wpg. vs. B.C., Nov. 27, 1988
- Sask. vs. Ham., Nov. 26, 1989
- Ham. vs. Sask., Nov. 26, 1989

MOST FIELD GOALS BOTH TEAMS ONE GAME:
9 Edm.-Wpg. Nov. 28, 1993
8 - Mtl.-Edm., Nov. 27, 1977
- Sask.-Ham., Nov. 26, 1989
6 - Edm.-Mtl., Nov. 26, 1978
- B.C.-Ham., Nov. 24, 1985
- Ham.-Edm., Nov. 30, 1986
- Edm.-Tor., Nov. 29, 1987
5 - Wpg.-Ott., Nov. 29, 1941
- Edm.-Mtl., Nov. 23, 1975
- Ott.-Sask., Nov. 28, 1976
- Edm.-Ham., Nov. 23, 1980
- Wpg.-Ham., Nov. 18, 1984
- Wpg.-B.C., Nov. 27, 1988

ALL-TIME MOST SINGLES:
79 - Toronto
46 - Hamilton
29 - Ottawa

MOST SINGLES ONE TEAM ONE GAME:
10 - U. of Tor. vs. Tor. Parkdale, Dec. 4, 1909
9 - Ham. vs. Reg., Nov. 30, 1929
7 - U. of Tor. vs. Ott., Dec. 4, 1926

MOST SINGLES BOTH TEAMS ONE GAME:
12 - Ott.-U. of Tor., Dec. 4, 1926
- Ham.-Reg., Nov. 30, 1929
11 - U. of Tor.-Parkdale, Dec. 4, 1909
9 - U. of Tor.-Ham., Nov. 26, 1910

ALL-TIME MOST SAFETY TOUCHES:
6 - Hamilton

MOST SAFETY TOUCHES ONE TEAM ONE GAME:
3 - Ham. vs. Wpg., Nov. 27, 1965

MOST FIRST DOWNS ONE TEAM ONE GAME:
36 - Edm. vs. Mtl., Nov. 24, 1956
34 - Mtl. vs. Edm., Nov. 27, 1954
- Edm. vs. Mtl., Nov. 26, 1955
32 - Edm. vs. Tor., Nov. 28, 1982

FEWEST FIRST DOWNS ONE TEAM ONE GAME:
7 - Ham. vs. Wpg., Nov. 27, 1965
- Tor. vs. Cal., Nov. 24, 1991
8 - Cal. vs. Tor., Nov. 28, 1971
- Edm. vs. Mtl., Nov. 24, 1974
9 - Ham. vs. Sask., Dec. 2, 1967
- Edm. vs. Mtl., Nov. 27, 1977

MOST FIRST DOWNS RUSHING ONE TEAM ONE GAME:
32 - Edm. vs. Mtl., Nov. 24, 1956
28 - Edm. vs. Mtl., Nov. 25, 1955
15 - Edm. vs. Mtl., Nov. 27, 1954

FEWEST FIRST DOWNS RUSHING ONE TEAM ONE GAME:
1 - Edm. vs. Mtl., Nov. 24, 1974
- Wpg. vs. B.C., Nov. 27, 1988
- Wpg. vs. Cal., Nov. 29, 1992
2 - Edm. vs. Ott., Nov. 26, 1960
- Tor. vs. Cal., Nov. 28, 1971
- Edm. vs. Mtl., Nov. 23, 1975
- Ham. vs. Wpg., Nov. 18, 1984
- Sask. vs. Ham., Nov. 26, 1989
3 - Ham. vs. Wpg., Dec. 2, 1961
- Sask. vs. Ham., Dec. 2, 1967
- Sask. vs. Ott., Nov. 30, 1969

MOST FIRST DOWNS PASSING ONE TEAM ONE GAME:
24 - Sask. vs. Ham., Nov. 26, 1989
23 - Mtl. vs. Edm., Nov. 26, 1955
21 - Cal. vs. Wpg., Nov. 29, 1992
20 - Wpg. vs. Ham., Nov. 28, 1953

FEWEST FIRST DOWNS PASSING ONE TEAM ONE GAME:
1 - Ham. vs. Wpg., Nov. 27, 1965
2 - Edm. vs. Mtl., Nov. 27, 1977
3 - Ham. vs. Wpg., Nov. 30, 1957
- Ott. vs. Sask., Nov. 26, 1966
- Tor. vs. Cal., Nov. 24, 1991

MOST FIRST DOWNS VIA PENALTIES ONE GAME:
5 - B.C. vs. Wpg., Nov. 27, 1988
3 - Edmonton (4 times); Montreal, Winnipeg, Saskatchewan, Calgary and Toronto once each.

ALL-TIME MOST PLAYS FROM SCRIMMAGE:
1283 - Edmonton
1105 - Hamilton
961 - Winnipeg

MOST PLAYS ONE TEAM ONE GAME:
121 - Edm. vs. Mtl., Nov. 24, 1956
105 - Wpg. vs. Ham., Dec. 2, 1961
100 - Cal. vs. Tor., Nov. 24, 1991

MOST PLAYS BOTH TEAMS ONE GAME:
216 - Edm.-Mtl., Nov. 24, 1956
179 - Wpg.-Ham., Dec. 2, 1961
175 - Mtl.-Edm., Nov. 27, 1977

ALL-TIME MOST TOTAL YARDS:
6118 - Edmonton
4761 - Hamilton
4609 - Winnipeg

MOST TOTAL YARDS ONE TEAM ONE GAME:
656 - Mtl. vs. Edm., Nov. 27, 1954
606 - Edm. vs. Ham., Nov. 23, 1980
566 - Edm. vs. Mtl., Nov. 26, 1955

MOST TOTAL YARDS BOTH TEAMS ONE GAME:
1115 - Edm.-Mtl., Nov. 26, 1955
1090 - Edm.-Mtl., Nov. 27, 1954
1018 - Edm.-Mtl., Nov. 24, 1956

FEWEST TOTAL YARDS ONE TEAM ONE GAME:
102 - Edm. vs. Mtl., Nov. 27, 1977
155 - Edm. vs. Mtl., Nov. 24, 1974
171 - Ham. vs. Wpg., Nov. 28, 1959

FEWEST TOTAL YARDS BOTH TEAMS ONE GAME:
376 - Wpg.-Ham., Nov. 18, 1984
389 - Edm.-Mtl., Nov. 24, 1974
391 - Wpg.-Ham., Nov. 27, 1965
- Edm.-Mtl., Nov. 26, 1978

ALL-TIME MOST TIMES RUSHING:
546 - Edmonton
529 - Hamilton
383 - Winnipeg

MOST TIMES RUSHING ONE TEAM ONE GAME:
83 - Edm. vs. Mtl., Nov. 24, 1956
62 - Edm. vs. Mtl., Nov. 26, 1955
56 - Wpg. vs. Ham., Dec. 2, 1961

FEWEST TIMES RUSHING ONE TEAM ONE GAME:
8 - Tor. vs. Edm., Nov. 28, 1982
9 - Ham. vs. Wpg., Nov. 18, 1984
10 - B.C. vs. Tor., Nov. 27, 1983
- Wpg. vs. Cal., Nov. 29, 1992

ALL-TIME MOST YARDS RUSHING:
2667 - Edmonton
1901 - Hamilton
1596 - Winnipeg

MOST YARDS RUSHING ONE TEAM ONE GAME:
456 - Edm. vs. Mtl., Nov. 24, 1956
438 - Edm. vs. Mtl., Nov. 26, 1955
295 - Wpg. vs. Ham., Dec. 2, 1961

FEWEST YARDS RUSHING ONE TEAM ONE GAME:
24 - Ham. vs. Wpg., Nov. 18, 1984
36 - Wpg. vs. Cal., Nov. 29, 1992
41 - Mtl. vs. Edm., Nov. 26, 1955
- Sask. vs. Ham. Nov. 26, 1989

ALL-TIME MOST TOUCHDOWNS RUSHING:
21 - Edmonton
16 - Hamilton
15 - Winnipeg

MOST TOUCHDOWNS RUSHING ONE TEAM ONE GAME:
4 - Edm. vs. Mtl., Nov. 26, 1955
- Edm. vs. Mtl., Nov. 24, 1956
- Ham. vs. Wpg., Nov. 30, 1957

ALL-TIME MOST PASSES ATTEMPTED:
502 - Edmonton
454 - Hamilton
350 - Winnipeg

MOST PASSES ATTEMPTED ONE TEAM ONE GAME:
56 - Cal. vs. Tor., Nov. 24, 1991
49 - Cal. vs. Wpg., Nov. 29, 1992
48 - Wpg. vs. Ham., Nov. 28, 1953

FEWEST PASSES ATTEMPTED ONE TEAM ONE GAME:
5 - Ham. vs. Wpg., Nov. 27, 1965
12 - Wpg. vs. Ham., Nov. 28, 1959
13 - Wpg. vs. Ham., Nov. 27, 1965

ALL-TIME MOST PASSES COMPLETED:
273 - Edmonton
217 - Hamilton
192 - Winnipeg

MOST PASSES COMPLETED ONE TEAM ONE GAME:
34 - Cal. vs. Tor., Nov. 24, 1991
33 - Cal. vs. Wpg., Nov. 29, 1992
31 - Wpg. vs. Ham., Nov. 28, 1953

FEWEST PASSES COMPLETED ONE TEAM ONE GAME:
2 - Ham. vs. Wpg., Nov. 27, 1965
5 - Wpg. vs. Ham., Nov. 28, 1959
6 - Ham. vs. Wpg., Nov. 30, 1957
- Ott.vs. Edm., Nov. 26, 1960
- Ott. vs. Sask., Nov. 26, 1966

ALL-TIME MOST YARDS PASSING:
3629 - Edmonton
3375 - Hamilton
2810 - Winnipeg

MOST YARDS PASSING ONE TEAM ONE GAME:
508 - Mtl. vs. Edm., Nov. 26, 1955
480 - Cal. vs. Wpg., Nov. 29, 1992
474 - Sask. vs. Ham., Nov. 26, 1989

FEWEST YARDS PASSING ONE TEAM ONE GAME:
68 - Wpg. vs. Ham., Nov. 27, 1965
71 - Ham. vs. Wpg., Nov. 27, 1965
83 - Ham. vs. Wpg., Nov. 30, 1957

ALL-TIME MOST TOUCHDOWNS PASSING:
21 - Hamilton
19 - Edmonton
13 - Winnipeg
11 - Ottawa
- Montreal
10 - Saskatchewan

MOST TOUCHDOWNS PASSING ONE TEAM ONE GAME:
4 - Ott. vs. Sask., Nov. 30, 1969
- Edm. vs. Ham., Nov. 23, 1980
- Wpg. vs. Edm., Nov. 25, 1990
3 - Mtl. vs. Edm., Nov. 27, 1954
- Sask. vs. Ott., Nov. 26, 1966
- Mtl. vs. Edm., Nov. 27, 1977
- B.C. vs. Ham., Nov. 24, 1985
- Sask. vs. Ham., Nov. 26, 1989
- Ham. vs. Sask., Nov. 26, 1989

ALL-TIME MOST TURNOVERS:
79 - Edmonton
47 - Hamilton
42 - Montreal

MOST TURNOVERS ONE TEAM ONE GAME:
10 - Wpg. vs. Ham., Nov. 30, 1957
(6 fumb. 2 int. 2 lost poss.)
- Edm. vs. Mtl., Nov. 27, 1977
(4 fumb. 4 int. 2 lost poss.)
- Edm.vs. Ham., Nov. 30, 1986
(6 fumb. 2 int. 2 lost poss.)
8 - Mtl. vs. Edm., Nov. 27, 1954
(6 fumb. 2 int.)
7 - Cal. vs. Tor., Nov. 24, 1991
(2 fumb. 3 int. 2 lost poss.)
Wpg. vs. Edm., Nov. 28, 1993
(5 fumb. 2 int)
6 - Mtl. vs. Edm., Nov. 24, 1956
(3 fumb. 4 int. 1 lost poss.)
- Edm. vs. Wpg., Nov. 25, 1990
(4 fumb. 3 int. 1 lost poss.)

MOST FUMBLES ONE TEAM ONE GAME:
7 - Edm. vs. Ham., Nov. 30, 1986
6 - Mtl. vs. Edm., Nov. 27, 1954
- Wpg. vs. Ham., Nov. 30, 1957
- Edm. vs. Wpg. Nov. 25, 1990
5 - Wpg. vs. Ham., Dec. 2, 1961
- Ham. vs. Wpg., Nov. 27, 1965
- Edm. vs. Ott., Nov. 25, 1973
- Edm. vs. Mtl., Nov. 27, 1977
- Tor. vs. Cal., Nov. 24, 1991
Wpg. vs. Edm. Nov. 28, 1993

MOST FUMBLES LOST ONE TEAM ONE GAME:
6 - Mtl. vs. Edm., Nov. 27, 1954
- Wpg. vs. Ham., Nov. 30, 1957
- Edm. vs. Ham., Nov. 30, 1986
5 - Ham. vs. Wpg., Nov. 27, 1965
Wpg. vs. Edm. Nov. 28, 1993

MOST FUMBLES BOTH TEAMS ONE GAME:
10 - Edm.-Mtl., Nov. 27, 1954
- Wpg.-Ham., Nov. 30, 1957
9 - Ham.-Edm., Nov. 30, 1986
- Edm.-Wpg. Nov. 25, 1990
8 - Edm.-Mtl., Nov. 27, 1977
- Tor.-Cal., Nov. 24, 1991

ALL-TIME MOST INTERCEPTIONS:
28 - Edmonton
21 - Hamilton
16 - Montreal

MOST INTERCEPTIONS ONE TEAM ONE GAME:
4 - Edm. vs. Mtl., Nov. 24, 1956
- Mtl. vs. Edm., Nov. 27, 1977
- Edm. vs. Ham., Nov. 23, 1980
3 - Ham. vs. Sask., Dec. 2, 1967
- Cal. vs. Mtl., Nov. 28, 1970
- Tor. vs. Cal., Nov. 28, 1971
- Sask. vs. Ott., Nov. 28, 1976
- Ott. vs. Edm., Nov. 22, 1981
- Edm. vs. Ott., Nov. 22, 1981
- Edm. vs. Ham., Nov. 30, 1986
- Wpg. vs. Edm., Nov. 25, 1990
- Tor. vs. Cal., Nov. 24, 1991

MOST INTERCEPTIONS BOTH TEAMS ONE GAME:
6 - Edm.-Mtl., Nov. 24, 1956
- Ott.-Edm., Nov. 22, 1981
5 - Cal.-Mtl., Nov. 28, 1970
- Mtl.-Edm., Nov. 27, 1977
- Edm.-Ham., Nov. 23, 1980
- Edm.-Ham., Nov. 30, 1986

ALL-TIME MOST PUNTS:
177 - Hamilton
143 - Edmonton
116 - Winnipeg

MOST PUNTS ONE TEAM ONE GAME:
18 - Ham. vs. Wpg., Nov. 28, 1959
- Ham. vs. Sask., Dec. 2, 1967
17 - Wpg. vs. Ham., Nov. 28, 1959
- Ham. vs. Wpg., Dec. 2, 1961

MOST PUNTS BOTH TEAMS ONE GAME:
33 - Ham.-Wpg., Nov. 28, 1959
32 - Ham.-Sask., Dec. 2, 1967
31 - Wpg.-Ham., Dec. 2, 1961

ALL-TIME MOST YARDS PUNTED:
6760 - Hamilton
5851 - Edmonton
4740 - Winnipeg

MOST YARDS PUNTED ONE TEAM ONE GAME:
818 - Ham. vs. Sask., Dec. 2, 1967
782 - Wpg. vs. Ham., Nov. 28, 1959
703 - Ham. vs. Wpg., Dec 2, 1963

MOST YARDS PUNTED BOTH TEAMS ONE GAME:
1417 - Ham.-Wpg., Nov. 28, 1959
1353 - Ham.-Sask., Dec. 2, 1967
1316 - Wpg.-Ham., Dec. 2, 1961

ALL-TIME MOST PUNT RETURNS:
127 - Hamilton
126 - Edmonton
112 - Winnipeg

MOST PUNT RETURNS ONE TEAM ONE GAME:
17 - Wpg. vs. Ham., Dec. 2, 1961
15 - Wpg. vs. Ham., Nov. 28, 1959
- Sask. vs. Ham., Dec. 2, 1967
- Mtl. vs. Cal., Nov. 28, 1970

MOST PUNT RETURNS BOTH TEAMS ONE GAME:
28 - Sask.-Ham., Dec. 2, 1967
27 - Wpg.-Ham., Nov. 28, 1959
- Wpg.-Ham., Dec. 2, 1961
- Mtl.-Cal., Nov. 28, 1970

ALL-TIME MOST YARDS ON PUNT RETURNS:
765 - Hamilton
746 - Winnipeg
661 - Edmonton

MOST YARDS ON PUNT RETURNS ONE TEAM ONE GAME:
128 - Ott. vs. Sask., Nov. 28, 1976
117 - Mtl. vs. Edm., Nov. 27, 1977
105 - B.C. vs. Ham., Nov. 24, 1985

MOST YARDS ON PUNT RETURNS BOTH TEAMS ONE GAME:
167 - Wpg.-Ham., Dec. 2, 1961
161 - Ott.-Sask., Nov. 28, 1976
156 - Wpg.-Ham., Nov. 28, 1959

ALL-TIME KICKOFFS:
67 - Edmonton
59 - Hamilton
53 - Winnipeg

MOST KICKOFFS ONE TEAM ONE GAME:

10 -	Wpg. vs. Ham.,	Nov. 18, 1984
-	Ham. vs. Sask.,	Nov. 26, 1989
8 -	B.C. vs. Ham.,	Nov. 28, 1964
-	Mtl. vs. Edm.,	Nov. 27, 1977
-	Sask. vs. Ham.,	Nov. 26, 1989
7 -	Edm. vs. Mtl.,	Nov. 24, 1956
-	Edm. vs. Ham.,	Nov. 23, 1980
-	Wpg. vs. Edm.,	Nov. 25, 1990

MOST KICKOFFS BOTH TEAMS ONE GAME:

18 -	Sask.-Ham.	Nov. 26, 1989
15 -	Edm.-Tor.,	Nov. 29, 1987
13 -	Wpg.-Ham.,	Nov. 18, 1984

ALL-TIME MOST YARDS ON KICKOFFS:
3445 - Edmonton
3179 - Hamilton
2813 - Winnipeg
1811 - Montreal

MOST YARDS ON KICKOFFS ONE TEAM ONE GAME:

622 -	Ham. vs. Sask.,	Nov. 26, 1989
551 -	Wpg. vs. Ham.,	Nov. 18, 1984
440 -	Sask. vs. Ham.,	Nov. 26, 1989

MOST YARDS ON KICKOFFS BOTH TEAMS ONE GAME:

1062 -	Sask.-Ham.,	Nov. 26, 1989
860 -	Edm.-Tor.,	Nov. 29, 1987
671 -	Wpg.-Ham.,	Nov. 18, 1984

ALL-TIME MOST KICKOFF RETURNS:
70 - Hamilton
65 - Edmonton
41 - Winnipeg
29 - Montreal

MOST KICKOFF RETURNS ONE TEAM ONE GAME:

10 -	Ham. vs. B.C.,	Nov. 28, 1964
-	Ham. vs. Wpg.,	Nov. 18, 1984
-	Sask. vs. Ham.,	Nov. 26, 1989
8 -	Tor. vs. Edm.,	Nov. 29, 1987
-	Ham. vs. Sask.,	Nov. 26, 1989
7 -	Mtl. vs. Edm.,	Nov. 24, 1956
-	Edm. vs. Mtl.,	Nov. 27, 1977
-	Ham. vs. Edm.,	Nov. 23, 1980
-	Edm. vs. Tor.,	Nov. 29, 1987
-	Edm. vs. Wpg.,	Nov. 25, 1990

MOST KICKOFF RETURNS BOTH TEAMS ONE GAME:

18 -	Sask.-Ham.,	Nov. 26, 1989
15 -	Edm.-Tor.,	Nov. 29, 1987
13 -	Wpg.-Ham.,	Nov. 18, 1984

ALL-TIME MOST YARDS ON KICKOFF RETURNS:
1192 - Hamilton
1279 - Edmonton
757 - Winnipeg

MOST YARDS ON KICKOFF RETURNS ONE TEAM ONE GAME:

296 -	Sask. vs. Ham.,	Nov. 26, 1989
244 -	Tor. vs. Cal.,	Nov. 24, 1991
178 -	Edm. vs. Mtl.,	Nov. 27, 1977

MOST YARDS ON KICKOFF RETURNS BOTH TEAMS ONE GAME:

439 -	Sask.-Ham.,	Nov. 26, 1989
309 -	Tor.-Cal.,	Nov. 24, 1991
263 -	Edm.-Tor.,	Nov. 29, 1987

ALL-TIME MOST UNSUCCESSFUL FIELD GOAL RETURNS:
2 - Edmonton
1 - Calgary

MOST UNSUCCESSFUL FIELD GOAL RETURNS ONE TEAM ONE GAME:

2 -	Edm. vs. Tor.	Nov. 29, 1987
1 -	Cal. vs. Wpg.	Nov. 29, 1992

MOST UNSUCCESSFUL FIELD GOAL RETURNS BOTH TEAMS ONE GAME:

3 -	Edm. vs. Tor.,	Nov. 29, 1987

ALL-TIME MOST PENALTIES:
98 - Edmonton
87 - Hamilton
69 - Montreal

MOST PENALTIES ONE TEAM ONE GAME:

19 -	Mtl. vs. Edm.,	Nov. 27, 1977
15 -	Mtl. vs. Edm.,	Nov. 25, 1979
14 -	Ott. vs. Sask.,	Nov. 28, 1976

MOST PENALTIES BOTH TEAMS ONE GAME:

27 -	Mtl.-Edm.,	Nov. 27, 1977
23 -	Wpg.-B.C.,	Nov. 27, 1988
20 -	Mtl.-Edm.,	Nov. 25, 1979

ALL-TIME MOST YARDS PENALIZED:
712 - Hamilton
583 - Montreal
589 - Edmonton

MOST YARDS PENALIZED ONE TEAM ONE GAME:

157 -	Mtl. vs. Edm.,	Nov. 27, 1977
145 -	Mtl. vs. Edm.,	Nov. 25, 1979
116 -	Cal. vs. Wpg.,	Nov. 29, 1992

MOST YARDS PENALIZED BOTH TEAMS ONE GAME:

181 -	Wpg.-B.C.,	Nov. 27, 1988
172 -	Mtl.-Edm.,	Nov. 27, 1977
170 -	Mtl.-Edm.,	Nov. 25, 1979

ALL-TIME MOST QUARTERBACK SACKS:
17 - Edmonton
16 - Winnipeg
15 - B.C.
- Hamilton
14 - Toronto
13 - Saskatchewan
12 - Ottawa

MOST QUARTERBACK SACKS ONE TEAM ONE GAME:

10 -	Ham. vs. Edm.,	Nov. 30, 1986
7 -	Edm. vs. Tor.,	Nov. 28, 1982
-	B.C. vs. Tor.,	Nov. 27, 1983
6 -	Tor. vs. Cal.,	Nov. 24, 1991

MOST QUARTERBACK SACKS BOTH TEAMS ONE GAME:

12 -	Ham. vs. Edm.,	Nov. 30, 1986
9 -	Tor. vs. B.C.,	Nov. 27, 1983
8 -	Edm. vs. Tor.,	Nov. 28, 1982
-	Edm. vs. Tor.,	Nov. 29, 1987

ALL-TIME MOST DEFENSIVE TACKLES:
191 - Winnipeg
110 - Edmonton
87 - Toronto
41 - Saskatchewan
38 - Hamilton

MOST DEFENSIVE TACKLES ONE TEAM ONE GAME:

50 -	Wpg. vs. B.C.,	Nov. 27, 1988
48 -	Tor. vs. Cal.,	Nov. 24, 1991
46 -	Wpg. vs. Edm.,	Nov. 25, 1990

MOST DEFENSIVE TACKLES BOTH TEAMS ONE GAME:

86 -	Wpg. vs. Edm.,	Nov. 25, 1990
79 -	Wpg. vs. B.C.,	Nov. 27, 1988
-	Sask. vs. Ham.,	Nov. 26, 1989
75 -	Tor. vs. Cal.,	Nov. 24, 1991

MOST SPECIAL TEAMS TACKLES ONE TEAM ONE GAME:

14 -	Cal. vs. Wpg.,	Nov. 29, 1992
13 -	Tor. vs. Cal.,	Nov. 24, 1991

MOST SPECIAL TEAMS TACKLES BOTH TEAMS ONE GAME:

24 -	Tor. (13) vs. Cal. (11),	Nov. 24, 1991
-	Cal. (14) vs. Wpg. (10),	Nov. 29, 1992

GREY CUP INDIVIDUAL RECORDS

ALL-TIME MOST GAMES PLAYED:

9 - Tommy Grant, Ham.; John Barrow, Ham.; Angelo Mosca, Ott./Ham.; Dave Cutler, Edm.; Larry Highbaugh, Edm.; Hank Ilesic, Edm.-Tor.

8 - Jack Wedley, Tor., Bert Iannone, Wpg.-Cal.-Sask.; Mel Wilson, Wpg.-Cal.; Ches McCance, Wpg.-Mtl.,; Hal Patterson, Ham.; Pete Neuman, Ham.; Zeno Karcz, Ham.; Don Sutherin, Ham.-Ott.; Ron Estay, Edm.; Dave Fennell, Edm.; Bob Howes, Edm.; Dale Potter, Edm.; Bill Stevenson, Edm.; Tom Wilkinson, Edm.

7 - Joe Krol, Ham.-Tor.; Frank Morris, Tor.-Edm.; Normie Kwong, Cal.-Edm.; Dan Kepley, Edm.; Tom Towns, Edm.; Stu Lang, Edm.; Ellison Kelly, Ham.

ALL-TIME MOST GAMES WON:

7 - Jack Wedley, Tor.-Mtl. St. Hyacinthe-Donnacona "Combines"; Bill Stevenson, Edm.; Hank Ilesic, Edm.-Tor.

6 - Joe Krol, Ham.-Tor.; Frank Morris, Tor.-Edm.; Dave Fennell, Edm.; Dave Cutler, Edm.; Larry Highbaugh, Edm.; Dan Kepley, Edm.; Hector Pothier, Edm.; Dale Potter, Edm.; Tom Towns, Edm.

5 - Tom Scott, Edm.; Angelo Mosca, Ott.-Ham.; Pep Leadley, Queen's-Ham.; Leo Blanchard, Edm.; Brian Kelly, Edm.; David Boone, Edm.; Jim Germany, Edm.; Joe Holliman, Edm.; Ed Jones, Edm.; Warren Moon, Edm.; Ted Milian, Edm.; Eric Upton, Edm.; Ron Estay, Edm.; Bob Howes, Edm.

ALL-TIME MOST POINTS:

72 -	Dave Cutler, Edm.	1969-84
61 -	Don Sweet, Mtl.-Ham.	1972-85
43 -	Trevor Kennerd, Wpg.	1980-91
37 -	Paul Osbaldiston, Ham.	1986-93
31 -	Lui Passaglia, B.C.	1976-91
30 -	Gerry Organ, Ott.	1971-83
-	Joe Krol, Ham.-Tor.	1945-55
29 -	Charlie Shepard, Wpg.	1957-62
28 -	Gerry James, Wpg.	1952-63
-	Hal Patterson, Mtl.-Ham.	1954-67

MOST POINTS ONE GAME:

23 -	Don Sweet,	Mtl. vs. Edm.,	Nov. 27, 1977
22 -	Jim Van Pelt,	Wpg. vs. Ham.,	Nov. 29, 1958
21 -	Paul Osbaldiston,	Ham. vs. Edm.,	Nov. 30, 1986
	Sean Fleming	Edm. vs. Wpg.,	Nov. 28, 1993

ALL-TIME MOST TOUCHDOWNS:

5 -	Hal Patterson, Mtl.-Ham.	1954-67
-	Brian Kelly, Edm.	1979-87
4 -	Normie Kwong, Edm.	1951-60
-	Jimmy Simpson, Ham.	
-	Johnny Bright, Edm.	1954-64
4 -	Charlie Shepard, Wpg.	1957-62
-	Tommy Scott, Edm.	1978-83
-	Jackie Parker, Edm.	1954-62
-	Ross Craig, Ham.	
-	Jim Germany, Edm.	1977-83

MOST TOUCHDOWNS ONE GAME:

3 -	Ross Craig,	Ham. vs. Tor.,	Nov. 29, 1913
-	Red Storey,	Tor. vs. Wpg.,	Dec. 10, 1938
-	Jackie Parker,	Edm. vs. Mtl.,	Nov. 24, 1956
-	Tommy Scott,	Edm. vs. Ham.,	Nov. 23, 1980

ALL-TIME MOST CONVERTS:

17 -	Don Sutherin, Ham.-Ott.-Tor.	1958-70
16 -	Dave Cutler, Edm.	1969-84
12 -	Pep Leadlay, Queens-Ham.	1925-29
-	Trevor Kennerd, Wpg.	1980-91

MOST CONVERTS ONE GAME:

6 -	Dave Cutler,	Edm. vs. Ham.,	Nov. 23, 1980
-	Trevor Kennerd,	Wpg. vs. Edm.,	Nov. 25, 1990
5 -	Bob Dean,	Edm. vs. Mtl.,	Nov. 26, 1955
-	Trevor Kennerd,	Wpg. vs. Ham.,	Nov. 18, 1984

ALL-TIME MOST FIELD GOALS:

18 -	Dave Cutler, Edm.	1969-84
17 -	Don Sweet, Mtl.-Ham.	1972-85
10 -	Paul Osbaldiston, Ham.	1986-93
10 -	Trevor Kennerd, Wpg.	1980-91
8 -	Gerry Organ, Ott.	1971-83
7 -	Lui Passaglia, B.C.	1976-93

MOST FIELD GOALS ONE GAME:

6 -	Don Sweet,	Mtl. vs. Edm.,	Nov. 27, 1977
-	Paul Osbaldiston,	Ham. vs. Edm.,	Nov. 30, 1986
	Sean Fleming	Edm. vs. Wpg.,	Nov. 28, 1993
5 -	Lui Passaglia,	B.C. vs. Ham.,	Nov. 24, 1985
4 -	Don Sweet,	Mtl. vs. Edm.,	Nov. 24, 1974
-	Dave Cutler,	Edm. vs. Mtl.,	Nov. 26, 1978
-	Dave Cutler,	Edm. vs. Tor.,	Nov. 28, 1982
-	Trevor Kennerd,	Wpg. vs. Ham.,	Nov. 18, 1984
-	Trevor Kennerd,	Wpg. vs. B.C.,	Nov. 27, 1988
-	Dave Ridgway,	Sask. vs. Ham.,	Nov. 26, 1989
-	Paul Osbaldiston,	Ham. vs. Sask.	Nov. 26, 1989

LONGEST FIELD GOALS:

52 -	Dave Cutler,	Edm. vs. Mtl.,	Nov. 23, 1975
51 -	Bob Macoritti,	Sask. vs. Ott.,	Nov. 28, 1976
50 -	Lance Chomyc,	Tor. vs. Edm.,	Nov. 29, 1987

ALL-TIME MOST SINGLES:

12 -	Hugh Gall, U. of T. Parkdale	1908-12
11 -	Pep Leadlay, Queens-Ham.	1925-29
10 -	Huck Welch, Ham.-Mtl.	1928-37
-	Bummer Stirling, Sarnia	1931-37

MOST SINGLES ONE GAME:

8 -	Hugh Gall,	U. of T. vs. Tor.-Parkdale	Dec. 4, 1909
6 -	Huck Welch,	Ham. vs. Regina,	Nov. 30, 1929
5 -	Tout Leckie,	Ham. Alerts vs. Tor.,	Nov. 30, 1912
-	Joe Miller,	Ott. vs. U. of T.,	Dec. 4, 1926
-	Charles Trimble,	U. of T. vs. Ott.,	Dec. 4, 1926
-	Bummer Stirling,	Sarnia vs. Regina	Nov. 24, 1934
-	Sammy Sward,	Ott. vs. Balmy Beach,	Dec. 7, 1940

ALL-TIME MOST TIMES RUSHED:

77 -	George Reed, Sask.	1963-75
72 -	Normie Kwong, Edm.	1951-60
-	Leo Lewis, Wpg.	1955-66
69 -	Jim Germany, Edm.	1977-83
53 -	Gerry McDougall, Ham.-Tor.	1957-66

MOST TIMES RUSHED ONE GAME:

30 -	Normie Kwong,	Edm. vs. Mtl.,	Nov. 26, 1955	(145 yds.)
28 -	Johnny Bright,	Edm. vs. Mtl.,	Nov. 24, 1956	(171 yds.)
23 -	George Reed,	Sask. vs. Ott.,	Nov. 26, 1966	(133 yds.)
-	Tony Cherry,	B.C. vs. Wpg.,	Nov. 27, 1988	(133 yds.)

ALL-TIME MOST YARDS RUSHED:

359 -	Leo Lewis, Wpg.	1955-66
346 -	George Reed, Sask.	1963-75
318 -	Normie Kwong, Edm.	1951-60

MOST YARDS RUSHED ONE GAME:

171 -	Johnny Bright,	Edm. vs. Mtl.,	Nov. 24, 1956	(28 rushes)
145 -	Normie Kwong,	Edm.vs. Mtl.,	Nov. 26, 1955	(30 rushes)
142 -	David Green,	Mtl. vs. Edm.,	Nov. 25, 1979	(21 rushes)

LONGEST RUN:

80 -	Vic Washington,	Ott. vs. Cal.,	Nov. 30, 1968 (TD)
74 -	Garney Henley,	Ham. vs. Wpg.,	Dec. 1-2, 1962 (TD)
58 -	Bernie Faloney (1); Johnny Counts (57)	Ham. vs. B.C.,	Nov. 28, 1964 (TD)

ALL-TIME MOST TOUCHDOWNS RUSHING:

4 -	Ross Craig, Ham.	
-	Johnny Bright, Edm.	1954-64
-	Normie Kwong, Edm.	1951-60
4 -	Jim Germany, Edm.	1977-83
3 -	Red Storey, Tor.	1936-41
-	Charlie Shepard, Wpg.	1957-62

MOST TOUCHDOWNS RUSHING ONE GAME:

3 -	Ross Craig,	Ham. vs. Tor.-Parkdale	Nov. 29, 1913
-	Red Storey,	Tor. vs. Wpg.,	Dec. 10, 1938

ALL-TIME MOST PASS RECEPTIONS:

29 -	Hal Patterson, Mtl.-Ham.	1954-67
26 -	Tommy Scott, Edm.	1978-83
22 -	Red O'Quinn, Mtl.	1952-59
-	Brian Kelly, Edm.	1979-87
21 -	George McGowan, Edm.	1971-78
20 -	Ernie Pitts, Wpg.	1957-69
18 -	Tommy Grant, Ham.	1956-68
16 -	Tony Gabriel, Ham.-Ott.	1971-81
15 -	Garney Henley, Ham.	1960-75
-	Rick House, Wpg.-Edm.	1979-90
14 -	Gerry McDougall, Ham.-Tor.	1957-66
-	John O'Leary, Mtl.	1977-79
13 -	Cedric Minter, Tor.	1981-85

ALL-TIME MOST PASS RECEPTIONS (Cont'd):

13 -	Rocky DiPietro, Ham.	1978-90
-	Marco Cyncar, Ham.-Edm.	1979-90

MOST PASS RECEPTIONS ONE GAME:

13 -	Red O'Quinn,	Mtl. vs. Edm.,	Nov. 27, 1954	(316 yds.)
12 -	Tommy Scott,	Edm. vs. Ham.,	Nov. 23, 1980	(174 yds.)
11 -	Carl Bland,	Cal. vs. Tor.,	Nov. 24, 1991	(136 yds.)

ALL-TIME MOST YARDS ON PASS RECEPTIONS:

580 -	Hal Patterson, Mtl.-Ham.	1954-67
441 -	Red O'Quinn, Mtl.	1952-59
400 -	Tommy Scott, Edm.	1978-83
384 -	Brian Kelly, Edm.	1979-87
345 -	Ernie Pitts, Wpg.	1957-69
292 -	Rick House, Wpg.-Edm.	1979-90
267 -	Garney Henley, Ham.	1960-75
259 -	Tommy Grant, Ham.	1956-68
254 -	Tony Gabriel, Ham.-Ott.	1971-81
-	George McGowan, Edm.	1971-78

MOST YARDS ON PASS RECEPTIONS ONE GAME:

316 -	Red O'Quinn,	Mtl. vs. Edm.,	Nov. 27, 1954	(13 rec.)
174 -	Whit Tucker,	Ott. vs. Sask.,	Nov. 26, 1966	(4 rec.)
-	Tommy Scott,	Edm. vs. Ham.,	Nov. 23, 1980	(12 rec.)
165 -	James Murphy,	Wpg. vs. B.C.,	Nov. 27, 1988	(5 rec.)

LONGEST COMPLETED PASS:

90 -	Red O'Quinn	(Etcheverry),	Mtl. vs. Edm.,	Nov. 27, 1954 (TD)
-	Paul Dekker	(Faloney),	Ham. vs. Wpg.,	Dec. 2, 1961 (TD)
85 -	Whit Tucker	(Jackson),	Ott. vs. Sask.,	Nov. 26, 1966 (TD)
84 -	Emanuel Tolbert	(Holloway)	Tor. vs. Edm.,	Nov. 28, 1982 (TD)
-	Ned Armour	(Dewalt)	B.C. vs. Ham.,	Nov. 24, 1985 (TD)

ALL-TIME MOST TOUCHDOWNS ON PASS RECEPTIONS:

5 -	Brian Kelly, Edm.	1979-87
4 -	Hal Patterson, Mtl.-Ham.	1954-67
-	Tommy Scott, Edm.	1978-83

MOST TOUCHDOWNS ON PASS RECEPTIONS ONE GAME:

3 -	Tommy Scott,	Edm. vs. Ham.,	Nov. 23, 1980
2 -	Red O'Quinn,	Mtl. vs. Edm.,	Nov. 27, 1954
-	Hal Patterson,	Mtl. vs. Edm.,	Nov. 26, 1955
-	Ron Howell,	Ham. vs. Wpg.,	Nov. 29, 1958
-	Whit Tucker,	Ott. vs. Sask.,	Nov. 26, 1966
-	Terry Evanshen,	Cal. vs. Ott.,	Nov. 30, 1968
-	Ron Stewart,	Ott. vs. Sask.,	Nov. 30, 1969
-	Brian Kelly,	Edm. vs. Tor.,	Nov. 28, 1982
-	Ned Armour,	B.C. vs. Ham.,	Nov. 24, 1985
-	Tony Champion,	Ham. vs. Sask.,	Nov. 26, 1989

ALL-TIME MOST PASSES:

169 -	Bernie Faloney, Edm.-Ham.-Mtl.-B.C.	1954-67
139 -	Ron Lancaster, Ott.-Sask.	1960-78
119 -	Sonny Wade, Mtl.	1969-78
118 -	Matt Dunigan, Edm.-B.C.-Tor.-Wpg.	1983-92
116 -	Tom Wilkinson, Tor.-B.C.-Edm.	1967-81
110 -	Sam Etcheverry, Mtl.	1952-60
104 -	Warren Moon, Edm.	1978-83
75 -	Roy Dewalt, B.C.	1980-87
72 -	Kenny Ploen, Wpg.	1957-67
65 -	Russ Jackson, Ott.	1958-69

MOST PASSES ONE GAME:

56 -	Danny Barrett,	Cal. vs. Tor.,	Nov. 24, 1991
49 -	Doug Flutie,	Cal. vs. Wpg.,	Nov. 29, 1992
48 -	Jack Jacobs,	Wpg. vs. Ham.,	Nov. 28, 1953

ALL-TIME MOST PASSES COMPLETED:

92 -	Bernie Faloney, Edm.-Ham.-Mtl.-B.C.	1954-67
76 -	Ron Lancaster, Ott.-Sask.	1960-78
68 -	Sam Etcheverry, Mtl.	1952-60
64 -	Tom Wilkinson, Tor.-B.C.-Edm.	1967-81
60 -	Warren Moon, Edm.	1978-83
58 -	Sonny Wade, Mtl.	1969-78
51 -	Matt Dunigan, Edm.-B.C.-Tor.-Wpg.	1983-92
42 -	Roy Dewalt, B.C.	1980-87
39	Damon Allen, Edm.-Ott.-Ham.	1985-93
35 -	Kenny Ploen, Wpg.	1957-67
34 -	Danny Barrett, Cal.-B.C.	1987-92

MOST PASSES COMPLETED ONE GAME:

34 -	Danny Barrett,	Cal. vs. Tor.,	Nov. 24, 1991
33 -	Doug Flutie,	Cal. vs. Wpg.,	Nov. 29, 1992
31 -	Jack Jacobs,	Wpg. vs. Ham.,	Nov. 28, 1953

ALL-TIME MOST YARDS PASSING:

1369 -	Bernie Faloney, Edm.-Ham.-Mtl.-B.C.	1954-67
1244 -	Sam Etcheverry, Mtl.	1952-60
1022 -	Ron Lancaster, Ott.-Sask.	1960-78
994 -	Warren Moon, Edm.	1978-83
780 -	Sonny Wade, Mtl.	1969-78
734 -	Russ Jackson, Ott.	1958-69

MOST YARDS PASSING ONE GAME:

508 -	Sam Etcheverry,	Mtl. vs. Edm.,	Nov. 26, 1955
480 -	Doug Flutie,	Cal. vs. Wpg.,	Nov. 29, 1992
474 -	Kent Austin,	Sask. vs. Ham.,	Nov. 26, 1989

ALL-TIME MOST TOUCHDOWN PASSES:

8 - Bernie Faloney, Edm.-Ham.-Mtl.-B.C. 1954-67
- Russ Jackson, Ott. 1958-69
7 - Ron Lancaster, Ott.-Sask. 1960-78
- Joe Krol, Ham.-Tor. 1945-55
6 - Sam Etcheverry, Mtl. 1952-78
- Warren Moon, Edm. 1978-83

MOST TOUCHDOWN PASSES ONE GAME:

4 - Russ Jackson, Ott. vs. Sask., Nov. 30, 1969
3 - Joe Krol, Tor. vs. Wpg., Nov. 30, 1946
- Sam Etcheverry, Mtl. vs. Edm., Nov. 27, 1954
- Ron Lancaster, Sask. vs. Ott., Nov. 26, 1966
- Sonny Wade, Mtl. vs. Edm., Nov. 27, 1977
- Warren Moon, Edm. vs. Ham., Nov. 23, 1980
- Roy Dewalt, B.C. vs. Ham., Nov. 24, 1985
- Mike Kerrigan, Ham. vs. Sask., Nov. 26, 1989
- Kent Austin, Sask. vs. Ham., Nov. 26, 1989
- Tom Burgess, Wpg. vs. Edm., Nov. 25, 1990

ALL-TIME MOST INTERCEPTIONS:

8 - Sam Etcheverry, Mtl. 1952-78
6 - Ron Lancaster, Ott.-Sask. 1960-78
- Bernie Faloney, Edm.-Ham.-Mtl.-B.C. 1954-67

MOST INTERCEPTIONS ONE GAME:

4 - Sam Etcheverry, Mtl. vs. Edm., Nov. 24, 1956
- Bruce Lemmerman, Edm. vs. Mtl., Nov. 27, 1977
3 - Ron Lancaster, Sask. vs. Ham., Dec. 2, 1967
- Sonny Wade, Mtl. vs. Cal., Nov. 28, 1970
- Dave Marler, Ham. vs. Edm., Nov. 23, 1980
- J.C. Watts, Ott. vs. Edm., Nov. 22, 1981
- Warren Moon, Edm. vs. Ott., Nov. 22, 1981
- Tracy Ham, Edm. vs. Wpg., Nov. 25, 1990
- Danny Barrett, Cal. vs. Tor., Nov. 24, 1991

ALL-TIME MOST INTERCEPTION RETURNS:

4 - Joe Hollimon, Edm. 1976-85
3 - Bruce Coulter, Mtl. 1948-57
- Garney Henley, Ham. 1960-75
3 - Vern Perry, Mtl. 1977-78
- Mike McLeod, Edm. 1980-84

MOST INTERCEPTION RETURNS ONE GAME:

2 - Bruce Coulter, Mtl. vs. Edm., Nov. 24, 1956
- Ray Bawel, Ham. vs. Wpg., Nov. 30, 1957
- Frank Andruski, Cal. vs. Mtl., Nov. 28, 1970
- Al Phaneuf, Mtl. vs. Cal., Nov. 28, 1970
- Garry Lefebvre, Edm. vs. Ott., Nov. 25, 1973
- Vern Perry, Mtl. vs. Edm., Nov. 27, 1977
- Joe Hollimon, Edm. vs. Ham., Nov. 23, 1980
- Greg Battle, Wpg. vs. Edm., Nov. 25, 1990
- Reggie Pleasant, Tor. vs. Cal., Nov. 24, 1991

ALL-TIME MOST YARDS ON INTERCEPTION RETURNS:

116 - Vern Perry, Mtl. 1977-78
88 - Greg Battle, Wpg. 1987-92
54 - Dick Thornton, Wpg.-Tor. 1961-72
43 - Jackie Parker, Edm. 1954-62
39 - Bob Richardson, Ham. 1967-68

MOST YARDS ON INTERCEPTION RETURNS ONE GAME:

88 - Vern Perry, Mtl. vs. Edm., Nov. 27, 1977
- Greg Battle, Wpg. vs. Edm., Nov. 25, 1990
54 - Dick Thornton, Tor. vs. Cal., Nov. 30, 1971
50 - Ed Berry, Tor. vs. Cal., Nov. 24, 1991

LONGEST INTERCEPTION RETURN:

74 - Vern Perry, Mtl. vs. Edm., Nov. 27, 1977
56 - Greg Battle, Wpg. vs. Edm., Nov. 25, 1990
54 - Dick Thornton, Tor. vs. Cal., Nov. 30, 1971

MOST FUMBLES ONE GAME:

4 - Gerry James, Wpg. vs. Ham., Nov. 30, 1957
3 - Johnny Bright, Edm. vs. Mtl., Nov. 24, 1956
- Matt Dunigan, Edm. vs. Ham., Nov. 30, 1986
- Matt Dunigan, Tor. vs. Cal., Nov. 24, 1991

MOST FUMBLE RETURNS ONE GAME:

3 - Phil Minnick, Wpg. vs. Ham., Nov. 27, 1965
2 - Ray Bawel, Ham. vs. Wpg., Nov. 30, 1957
- Ben Zambiasi, Ham. vs. Edm., Nov. 30, 1986
- David Bovell, Wpg. vs. Edm., Nov. 25, 1990
- Keith Castello, Tor. vs. Cal., Nov. 24, 1991

LONGEST FUMBLE RETURN:

90 - Jackie Parker, Edm. vs. Mtl., Nov. 27, 1954 (TD)
75 - Ralph Goldston, Ham. vs. Wpg., Nov. 29, 1958 (TD)
71 - Bill Munsey, B.C. vs. Ham., Nov. 28, 1964 (TD)

ALL-TIME COMBINED YARDAGE ATTEMPTS:
(Rushing, receiving and return of kicks)

91 - Leo Lewis, Wpg. (776 yds) 1955-66
81 - George Reed, Sask. (432 yds.) 1963-75
75 - Normie Kwong, Edm. (329 yds.) 1951-60
75 - Jim Germany, Edm. (324 yds.) 1977-83
53 - Jackie Parker, Edm. (659 yds.) 1954-62
48 - Rollie Miles, Edm. (384 yds.) 1951-60

MOST OFFENSIVE ATTEMPTS ONE GAME:

31 - Normie Kwong, Edm. vs. Mtl., Nov. 26, 1955 (145 yds.)
- Johnny Bright, Edm. vs. Mtl., Nov. 24, 1956 (211 yds.)
27 - Ron Stewart, Ott. vs. Edm., Nov. 26, 1960 (137 yds.)
26 - Derrick McAdoo, Ham. vs. Sask., Nov. 26, 1989 (187 yds.)

ALL-TIME MOST COMBINED YARDAGE:

776 - Leo Lewis, Wpg. (91 att.) 1955-66
663 - Hal Patterson, Mtl.-Ham. (33 att.) 1954-67
659 - Jackie Parker, Edm. (53 att.) 1954-62
462 - Willie Bethea, Ham. (46 att.) 1963-70
448 - Garney Henley, Ham. (38 att.) 1960-75

MOST COMBINED YARDAGE ONE GAME:

316 - Red O'Quinn, Mtl. vs. Edm., Nov. 27, 1954 (13 att.)
266 - Garney Henley, Ham. vs. Wpg., Dec. 1-2, 1962 (14 att.)
234 - Leo Lewis, Wpg. vs. Ham., Dec. 1-2, 1962 (20 att.)

ALL-TIME MOST PUNTS:

64 - Hank Ilesic, Edm-Tor. 1977-92
53 - Joe Zuger, Ham. 1962-71
51 - Cam Fraser, Ham.-Mtl. 1951-69
47 - Sonny Wade, Mtl. 1969-78
35 - Charlie Shepard, Wpg. 1957-62
32 - Garry Lefebvre, Edm.-Mtl. 1966-76

MOST PUNTS ONE GAME:

17 - Charlie Shepard, Wpg. vs. Ham., Nov. 28, 1959
- Joe Zuger, Ham. vs. Sask., Dec. 2, 1967
15 - Cam Fraser, Ham. vs. Wpg., Nov. 28, 1959
- Cam Fraser, Ham. vs. Wpg., Dec. 2, 1961
- Ron Stewart, Cal. vs. Mtl., Nov. 28, 1970
14 - Cam Fraser, Ham. vs. Wpg., Nov. 30, 1957
- Jack Delveaux, Wpg. vs. Ham., Dec. 2, 1961
- Jim Furlong, Cal. vs. Tor., Nov. 28, 1971

ALL-TIME MOST YARDS PUNTING:

2735 - Hank Ilesic, Edm.-Tor. 1977-93
2166 - Joe Zuger, Ham. 1962-71
2092 - Cam Fraser, Ham.-Mtl. 1951-69
1857 - Sonny Wade, Mtl. 1969-78
1551 - Charlie Shepard, Wpg. 1957-62
1340 - Bernie Ruoff, Ham. 1980-87
1329 - Lui Passaglia, B.C. 1976-93
1202 - Bill Van Burkleo, Tor.-Ott.-Ham. 1966-72
1183 - Garry Lefebvre, Edm.-Mtl. 1966-76
1130 - Alan Ford, Sask. 1965-76

MOST YARDS PUNTING ONE GAME:

782 - Charlie Shepard, Wpg. vs. Ham., Nov. 28, 1959
760 - Joe Zuger, Ham. vs. Sask., Dec. 2, 1967
621 - Cam Fraser, Ham. vs. Wpg., Dec. 2, 1961

LONGEST PUNTS:

87 - Alan Ford, Sask. vs. Ham., Dec. 2, 1967
85 - Garry Lefebvre, Edm. vs. Ott., Nov. 25, 1973
84 - Lui Passaglia, B.C. vs. Wpg., Nov. 27, 1988

ALL-TIME MOST PUNT RETURNS:

37 - Ron Latourelle, Wpg. 1955-64
22 - Greg Butler, Edm. 1977-80
20 - Garney Henley, Ham. 1960-75
19 - Tommy Grant, Ham. 1956-68
17 - Gene Wlasiuk, Sask. 1959-67
- Henry Janzen, Wpg. 1959-65

MOST PUNT RETURNS ONE GAME:

13 - Ron Latourelle, Wpg. vs. Ham., Dec. 2, 1961
12 - Darnell Clash, B.C. vs. Ham., Nov. 24, 1985
10 - Gene Wlasiuk, Sask. vs. Ham., Dec. 2, 1967

ALL-TIME MOST YARDS ON PUNT RETURNS:

250 - Ron Latourelle, Wpg. 1955-64
170 - Randy Rhino, Mtl. 1976-80
137 - Garney Henley, Ham. 1960-75
135 - Greg Butler, Edm. 1977-80
126 - Darnell Clash, B.C.-Tor. 1984-87

MOST YARDS ON PUNT RETURNS ONE GAME:

105 - Darnell Clash, B.C. vs. Ham., Nov. 24, 1985
90 - Ron Latourelle, Wpg. vs. Ham., Dec. 2, 1961
88 - Randy Rhino, Mtl. vs. Edm., Nov. 27, 1977

LONGEST PUNT RETURN:

79 - Bill Hatanaka, Ott. vs. Sask., Nov. 28, 1976 (TD)
67 - Raghib Ismail, Tor. vs. Cal., Nov. 24, 1991
52 - Randy Rhino, Mtl. vs. Edm., Nov. 27, 1977
40 - Ken Winey, Wpg. vs. Edm., Nov. 25, 1990
38 - Johnny Rodgers, Mtl. vs. Edm., Nov. 23, 1975

ALL-TIME MOST KICKOFFS:

31 - Dave Cutler, Edm. 1969-84
29 - Don Sutherin, Ham.-Ott.-Tor. 1958-70
23 - Trevor Kennerd, Wpg. 1980-91
16 - Don Sweet, Mtl.-Ham. 1972-85
15 - Hank Ilesic, Edm.-Tor. 1977-92

MOST KICKOFFS ONE GAME:

10 -	Trevor Kennerd,	Wpg. vs. Ham.,	Nov. 18, 1984
-	Paul Osbaldiston,	Ham. vs. Sask.,	Nov. 26, 1989
8 -	Norm Fieldgate,	B.C. vs. Ham.,	Nov. 28, 1964
-	Don Sweet,	Mtl. vs. Edm.,	Nov. 27, 1977
-	Jerry Kauric,	Edm. vs. Tor.,	Nov. 29, 1987
-	Dave Ridgway,	Sask. vs. Ham.,	Nov. 26, 1989
7 -	Joe Mobra,	Edm. vs. Mtl.,	Nov. 24, 1956
-	Dave Cutler,	Edm. vs. Ham.,	Nov. 23, 1980
-	Hank Ilesic,	Tor. vs. Edm.,	Nov. 29, 1987
-	Trevor Kennerd,	Wpg. vs. Edm.,	Nov. 25, 1990

ALL-TIME MOST YARDS ON KICKOFFS:

1623 -	Don Sutherin, Ham.-Ott.-Tor.	1958-70
1412 -	Dave Cutler, Edm.	1969-84
1305 -	Trevor Kennerd, Wpg.	1980-91
871 -	Hank Ilesic, Edm.-Tor.	1977-93
814 -	Don Sweet, Mtl.-Ham.	1972-85
674 -	Jack Abendschan, Sask.	1965-75
626 -	Lui Passaglia, B.C.	1976-93
508 -	Gerry Organ, Ott.	1971-83
433 -	Jerry Kauric, Edm. -Cal.	1987-89
407 -	Bernie Ruoff, Ham.	1980-87

MOST YARDS ON KICKOFFS ONE GAME:

622 -	Paul Osbaldiston,	Ham. vs. Sask.,	Nov. 26, 1989
551 -	Trevor Kennerd,	Wpg. vs. Ham.,	Nov. 18, 1984
440 -	Dave Ridgway,	Sask. vs. Ham.,	Nov. 26, 1989

LONGEST KICKOFF:

100 -	Dave Cutler,	Edm. vs. Tor.,	Nov. 28, 1982
77 -	Peter Kempf,	B.C. vs. Ham.,	Nov. 30, 1963
-	Don Sutherin,	Ham. vs. Wpg.,	Nov. 27, 1965
-	Bernie Ruoff,	B.C. vs. Ham.,	Nov. 24, 1985
75 -	Justin Canale,	Mtl. vs. Cal.,	Nov. 28, 1970

ALL-TIME MOST KICKOFF RETURNS:

11 -	Rufus Crawford, Ham.	1979-85
10 -	Leo Lewis, Wpg.	1955-66
9 -	Tom Richards, Edm.	1986-90

MOST KICKOFF RETURNS ONE GAME:

8 -	Dwight Edwards,	Tor. vs. Edm.,	Nov. 29, 1987
7 -	Obie Graves,	Ham. vs. Edm.,	Nov. 23, 1980
-	Rufus Crawford,	Ham. vs. Wpg.,	Nov. 18, 1984
6 -	Tim McCray,	Sask. vs. Ham.,	Nov. 26, 1989

ALL-TIME MOST YARDS ON KICKOFF RETURNS:

306 -	Leo Lewis, Wpg.	1955-66
187 -	Tom Richards, Edm.	1986-90
183 -	Raghib Ismail, Tor.	1991-92
181 -	Rufus Crawford, Ham.	1979-85
178 -	Carl Brazley, Mtl.-Ott.-Tor.	1980-90
169 -	Tim McCray, Ott.-Sask.	1984-90
134 -	Anthony Drawhorn, B.C.-Ott	1988-93
132 -	Obie Graves, Ham.-Wpg.	1980-82
-	Dwight Edwards, Tor. -Sask.-Ott.-Cal.	1978-88
127 -	Mark Guy, Sask.	1989-90
126 -	Joe Hollimon, Edm.	1976-85

MOST YARDS ON KICKOFF RETURNS ONE GAME:

183 -	Raghib Ismail,	Tor. vs. Cal.,	Nov. 24, 1991
169 -	Tim McCray,	Sask. vs. Ham.,	Nov. 26, 1989
134 -	Anthony Drawhorn,	B.C. vs. Wpg.,	Nov. 27, 1988

LONGEST KICKOFF RETURN:

87 -	Raghib Ismail,	Tor. vs. Cal.,	Nov. 24, 1991 (TD)
78 -	Alan Ford,	Sask vs. Ott.,	Nov. 30, 1969
74 -	Jackie Parker,	Edm. vs. Ott.,	Nov. 26, 1960

ALL-TIME MOST UNSUCCESSFUL FIELD GOAL RETURNS:

2 -	Henry Williams, Edm.	1986-92
1 -	Darnell Clash, B.C.-Tor.	1984-87
-	Wally Zatylny, Ham.	1988-91
-	Carl Brazley, Tor.	1980-91
-	PeeWee Smith, Cal.	1991-92

MOST UNSUCCESSFUL FIELD GOAL RETURNS ONE GAME:

2 -	Henry Williams,	Edm. vs. Tor.	Nov. 29, 1987

ALL-TIME MOST YARDS ON UNSUCCESSFUL FIELD GOAL RETURNS:

143 -	Henry Williams, Edm.	1986-92

MOST YARDS ON UNSUCCESSFUL FIELD GOAL RETURNS ONE GAME:

143 -	Henry Williams,	Edm. vs. Tor.	Nov. 29, 1987

LONGEST UNSUCCESSFUL FIELD GOAL RETURN:

115 -	Henry Williams,	Edm. vs. Tor.	Nov. 29, 1987 (TD)

ALL-TIME MOST QUARTERBACK SACKS:

5.0 -	Tyrone Jones, Wpg.	1983-92
4.5 -	Rick Klassen, B.C.-Sask.	1981-90
4.0 -	Grover Covington, Ham.	1981-91
3.5 -	Dave Fennell, Edm.	1974-83
3.0 -	Kevin Konar, B.C.	1980-89

MOST QUARTERBACK SACKS ONE GAME:

4.0 -	Tyrone Jones,	Wpg. vs. Ham.,	Nov. 18, 1984
3.0 -	Grover Covington,	Ham. vs. Edm.,	Nov. 30, 1986
2.5 -	Dave Fennell,	Edm. vs. Tor.,	Nov. 28, 1982
-	James Parker,	Edm. vs. Tor.,	Nov. 28, 1982
-	Rick Klassen,	B.C. vs. Tor.,	Nov. 27, 1983

ALL-TIME MOST DEFENSIVE TACKLES:

14 -	Greg Battle, Wpg.	1987-93
13 -	Dan Bass, Tor.-Cal.-Edm.	1980-91
10 -	Aaron Brown, Wpg.	1982-84, 1988
9 -	Darryl Ford, Tor.	1990-91
8 -	Willie Fears, Wpg.-Tor.	1988-89
-	Don Moen, Tor.	1982-92
-	Greg Clark, Wpg.	1993
7 -	Richie Hall, Sask.	1988-91
6 -	Jake Vaughan, Tor.	1987-88
-	Stephen Jordan, Ham.	1989-92
-	Elfrid Payton, Wpg.	1991-93
-	Vaughn Booker, Wpg.	1992-93

MOST DEFENSIVE TACKLES ONE GAME:

10 -	Aaron Brown,	Wpg. vs. B.C.,	Nov. 27, 1988
9 -	Darryl Ford,	Tor. vs. Cal.,	Nov. 24, 1991
8 -	Dan Bass,	Edm. vs. Tor.,	Nov. 29, 1987
-	Willie Fears,	Wpg. vs. B.C.,	Nov. 27, 1988
-	Don Moen,	Tor. vs. Cal.,	Nov. 24, 1991
	Greg Clark,	Wpg. vs. Edm.,	Nov. 28, 1993

MOST SPECIAL TEAMS TACKLES ONE GAME:

3 -	Bruce Elliott, Tor. vs. Cal.,	Nov. 24, 1991
-	Greg Knox, Cal. vs. Wpg.,	Nov. 29, 1992
-	Donald Smith, Wpg. vs. Cal.,	Nov. 29, 1992
-	Jason Dzikowicz, Wpg. vs. Cal.,	Nov. 29, 1992
	Chris Tsangaris, Wpg. vs. Edm.,	Nov. 28, 1993

SUNDAY, NOVEMBER 27, 1994

B.C. PLACE STADIUM

VANCOUVER, B.C.

COACHING RECORDS

(based on records since 1950)

ALL-TIME COACHING RECORDS - THE 500 CLUB

(a list of coaches with overall winning percentages over .500 and a minimum of 3 seasons of coaching after 1950)
Legend - A - appearances; L - losses; S - seasons; T - ties; W - wins; % - winning percentage

	REGULAR SEASON					PLAYOFFS				GREY CUP			OVERALL			
	S	W	L	T	%	S	W	L	T	A	W	L	W	L	T	%
Hugh Campbell, Edm. (77-82)	6	70	21	5	.755	6	6	0	0	6	5	1	81	22	5	.773
Frank Ivy, Edm. (54-57)	4	50	14	0	.781	4	8	4	0	3	3	0	61	18	0	.772
Ralph Sazio, Ham. (63-67)	5	49	20	1	.707	5	7	3	1	4	3	1	59	24	2	.706
Wally Buono, Cal. (90-93)	4	50	21	1	.701	4	4	2	0	2	1	1	55	24	1	.694
Bud Grant, Wpg. (57-66)	10	102	56	2	.644	8	16	9	1	6	4	2	122	67	3	.643
Cal Murphy, B.C. (75-76, Wpg. (83-86, 93)	7	67	40	3	.623	5	5	3	0	2	1	1	73	44	3	.621
Don Matthews, B.C. (83-87), Tor. (90), Sask. (91-93)	10	100	60	1	.624	8	4	6	0	2	1	1	105	67	1	.610
Carl Voyles, Ham. (50-53)	6	48	27	1	.638	6	5	9	0	1	1	0	54	36	1	.599
Marv Levy, Mtl. (73-77)	5	43	31	4	.577	5	5	2	0	3	2	1	50	34	4	.591
George Trafton, Wpg. (51-53)	3	28	17	1	.620	3	5	5	0	1	0	1	33	23	1	.588
Frank Clair, Tor. (50-54), Ott. (56-69)	19	147	106	7	.579	17	22	17	1	6	5	1	174	124	8	.582
Bobby Dobbs, Cal. (61-64)	4	38	23	3	.617	4	7	9	0	0	0	0	45	32	3	.581
Mike Riley, Wpg. (87-90)	4	40	32	0	.556	4	5	2	0	2	2	0	47	34	0	.580
Adam Rita, Tor. (90-92)	2	16	13	0	.552	2	1	0	0	1	1	0	18	13	0	.581
Jackie Parker, B.C. (69-70), Edm. (83-87)	7	48	32	1	.599	5	2	4	0	1	0	1	50	37	1	.574
Ray Jauch, Edm. (70-76), Wpg. (78-82), Sask. (93)	13	111	78	4	.585	9	6	7	0	3	1	2	118	87	4	.574
Les Lear, Cal. (48-52)	5	40	30	0	.572	3	3	2	1	2	1	1	44	33	1	.571
Joe Faragalli, Sask. (81-83), Edm. (87-90), Ott. (91)	8	69	52	1	.570	5	4	3	0	2	1	1	74	56	1	.569
Vic Rapp, B.C. (77-82)	6	53	39	4	.573	3	2	3	0	0	0	0	55	42	4	.564
Jerry Williams, Cal. (65-68), Ham. (72-75)	8	70	52	2	.573	6	6	7	0	2	1	1	77	60	2	.561
Eagle Keys, Edm. (59-63), Sask. (65-70), B.C. (71-75)	16	131	107	8	.549	10	15	11	0	4	1	3	147	121	8	.547
Jim Trimble, Ham. (56-62), Mtl. (63-65)	10	77	61	2	.557	9	9	7	0	5	1	4	87	72	2	.547
Lou Agase, Tor. (60-62)	3	17	13	1	.565	2	2	3	0	0	0	0	19	16	1	.542
Peahead Walker, Mtl. (52-59)	8	59	48	1	.551	7	6	6	0	3	0	3	65	57	1	.533
Frank Filchok, Edm. (52), Sask. (53-57)	6	50	41	5	.547	5	7	8	1	1	0	1	57	50	6	.531
John Payne, Sask. (73-76), Ham. (78-80)	7	59	50	3	.540	7	5	5	0	2	0	2	64	57	3	.528
Jim Duncan, Cal. (69-73)	5	38	38	1	.500	3	6	3	0	2	1	1	45	42	1	.517
Bob O'Billovich, Tor. (82-89, 93), B.C. (90-92)	12	98	86	3	.533	8	5	5	0	3	1	2	104	99	3	.512
Joe Restic, Ham. (68-70)	3	22	17	3	.560	3	0	4	0	0	0	0	22	21	3	.511
Joe Scanella, Mtl. (78-81)	4	28	28	2	.500	4	4	1	0	2	0	2	32	31	2	.508
Dave Skrien, B.C. (61-67), Sask. (71-72)	9	59	59	6	.500	4	7	4	0	3	1	2	67	65	6	.507
Jack Gotta, Ott. (70-73), Cal. (77-79, 82-83), Sask. (85-86)	11	83	82	5	.503	6	5	5	0	1	1	0	89	87	5	.506
Al Bruno, Ham. (83-90)	8	53	52	3	.505	7	6	4	0	4	1	3	60	59	3	.504
Al Sherman, Wpg. (54-56)	3	24	22	2	.521	3	4	6	1	0	0	0	28	28	3	.500

REGULAR SEASON

ALL-TIME MOST SEASONS COACHED

19 - Frank Clair, Tor. (1950-54), Ott. (1956-69)
16 - Eagle Keys, Edm. (1959-63), Sask. (1965-70), B.C. (1971-75)
12 - Ray Jauch, Edm. (1970-76), Wpg. (1978-82)
12 - Bob O'Billovich, Tor. (1982-89, 93), B.C. (1990-92)
11 - Jack Gotta, Ott. (1970-73), Cal. (1977-79, 1982-83), Sask. (1985-86)
- George Brancato, Ott. (1974-84)
10 - Jim Trimble, Ham. (1956-62), Mtl. (1963-65)
- Bud Grant, Wpg. (1957-66)

ALL-TIME MOST REGULAR SEASON WINS

147 - Frank Clair, Tor. (1950-54), Ott. (1956-69)
131 - Eagle Keys, Edm. (1959-63), Sask. (1965-70), B.C. (1971-75)
111 - Ray Jauch, Edm. (1970-76), Wpg. (1978-82)
102 - Bud Grant, Wpg. (1957-66)
100 - Bob O'Billovich, Tor. (1982-89, 93), B.C. (1990-92)
- Don Matthews, B.C. (1983-87), Tor. (1990), Sask. (1991-93)
83 - Jack Gotta, Ott. (1970-73), Cal. (1977-79, 1982-83), Sask. (1985-86)
82 - George Brancato, Ott. (1974-84)
77 - Jim Trimble, Ham. (1956-62), Mtl. (1963-65)
70 - Jerry Williams, Cal. (1965-68), Ham. (1972-75)
- Hugh Campbell, Edm. (1977-82)

MOST WINS ONE SEASON

16 -	Joe Faragalli, Edm. (16-2-0)	1990
15 -	Wally Buono, Cal. (15-3-0)	1993
14 -	Frank Ivy, Edm. (14-2-0)	1955
-	Frank Ivy, Edm. (14-2-0)	1957
-	Bud Grant, Wpg. (14-2-0)	1960
-	Eagle Keys, Sask. (14-2-0)	1970
-	Hugh Campbell, Edm. (14-1-1)	1981
-	Bob O'Billovich, Tor. (14-4-0)	1988
-	Cal Murphy, Wpg. (14-4-0)	1993
13 -	Bud Grant, Wpg. (13-3-0)	1958
-	Bud Grant, Wpg. (13-3-0	1961
-	Eagle Keys, Sask. (13-3-0)	1969
-	Hugh Campbell, Edm. (13-3-0)	1980
-	Don Matthews, B.C. (13-3-0)	1985
-	Jackie Parker, Edm. (13-4-1)	1986
-	Adam Rita, Tor. (13-5-0)	1991

ALL-TIME MOST FIRST-PLACE FINISHES

6 - Hugh Campbell, Edm., '77, '78, '79, '80, '81, '82
5 - Jim Trimble, Edm., '57, '58, '59, '61, '62
- Bud Grant, Wpg., '58, '59, '60, '61, '62
- Bob O'Billovich, Tor., '82, '83, '84, '86, '88
4 - Peahead Walker, Mtl., '53, '54, '55, '56
- Frank Ivy, Edm., '54, '55, '56, '57
4 - Ralph Sazio, Ham., '63, '64, '65, '67
- Eagle Keys, Sask., '66, '68, '69, '70

MOST CONSECUTIVE FIRST-PLACE FINISHES

6 - Hugh Campbell, Edm., 1978 to 1982
5 - Bud Grant, Wpg., 1958 to 1962
4 - Peahead Walker, Mtl., 1953 to 1956
- Frank Ivy, Edm., 1954 to 1957

PLAYOFFS

MOST PLAYOFF SEASONS

17 - Frank Clair, Tor.-Ott
10 - Eagle Keys, Edm.-Sask.-B.C.
- George Brancato, Ott.
9 - Jim Trimble, Ham.-Mtl.
- Ray Jauch, Edm.-Wpg.
8 - Bud Grant, Wpg.
- Bob O'Billovich, Tor.-B.C.
- Don Mathews, B.C.-Tor.-Sask.
7 - Peahead Walker, Mtl.
- John Payne, Sask.-Ham.
- Al Bruno, Ham.

MOST CONSECUTIVE PLAYOFF SEASONS

14 - Frank Clair, Ott., 1956 to 1969
10 - George Brancato, Ott., 1974 to 1984
7 - Peahead Walker, Mtl., 1953 to 1959
- Al Bruno, Ham., 1983 to 1989
6 - Carl Voyles, Ham., 1950 to 1955
- Bud Grant, Wpg., 1957 to 1962
- Hugh Campbell, Edm., 1977 to 1982
5 - Jim Trimble, Ham., 1961 to 1962 and Mtl., 1963 to 1965
- Leo Cahill, Tor., 1967 to 1971

ALL-TIME MOST PLAYOFF WINS

22 - Frank Clair, Tor. (1950-54), Ott. (1956-69)
16 - Bud Grant, Wpg. (1957-66)
15 - Eagle Keys, Edm. (1959-63), Sask. (1965-70), B.C. (1971-75)
9 - Jim Trimble, Ham. (1956-62), Mtl. (1963-65)
8 - Frank Ivy, Edm. (1954-57)

GREY CUP

MOST GREY CUP APPEARANCES

6 - Frank Clair, Tor. '50, '52, Ott. '60, '66, '68, '69
- Bud Grant, Wpg. '57, '58, '59, '61, '62, '65
- Hugh Campbell, Edm. '77, '78, '79, '80, '81, '82
5 - Billy Hughes, Queen's U. '22, '23, '24, Ham. '32, Ott. '36
- Lew Hayman, Tor. '33, '37, '38, Tor. RCAF '42, Mtl. '49
- Reg Threlfall, Wpg. '38, '39, '41, '42, '43
- Jim Trimble, Ham. '57, '58, '59, '61, '62
4 - Mike Rodden, U. of Tor. '20, '27, '28, '29
- Al Ritchie, Reg. '29, '30, '31, '32
- Eagle Keys, Edm. '60, Sask. '66, '67, '69
- Ralph Sazio, Ham. '63, '64, '65, '67
- Al Bruno, Ham. '84, '85, '86, '89

MOST CONSECUTIVE GREY CUP APPEARANCES

6 - Hugh Campbell, Edm., 1977 to 1982
4 - Al Ritchie, Reg., 1929 to 1932
3 - several tied

MOST GREY CUP WINS

5 - Lew Hayman, Tor. '33, '37, '38, Tor. RCAF '42, Mtl. '49
- Frank Clair, Tor. '50, '52, Ott. '60, '68, '69
- Hugh Campbell, Edm. '78, '79, '80, '81, '82
4 - Billy Hughes, Queen's U. '22, '23, '24, Ham. '32
- Bud Grant, Wpg. '58, '59, '61, '62
3 - Frank Ivy, Edm. '54, '55, '56
- Ralph Sazio, Ham. '63, '65, '67
- Ted Morris, Tor. '45, '46, '47

MOST CONSECUTIVE GREY CUP WINS

5 - Hugh Campbell, Edm., 1978 to 1982
3 - Billy Hughes, Queen's U., 1922 to 1924
- Ted Morris, Tor., 1945 to 1947
- Frank Ivy, Edm., 1954 to 1956

OFFICIATING STAFF

DIRECTOR OF OFFICIATING: DON BARKER

NEIL PAYNE - REFEREE/OFFICIATING SUPERVISOR
Born July 10, 1939 in Winnipeg, Manitoba. Payne was appointed the League's Assistant Director of Officiating in April, 1985. During the '88 and '89 seasons he assumed a supervisory position, returning to the assistant director's position in January, 1990. Payne is one of the CFL's two Officiating Supervisors. He worked 155 regular season and playoff games and in addition appeared in two Grey Cup finals. He resides in Winnipeg, Manitoba.

ROSS PERRIER - REFEREE/OFFICIATING SUPERVISOR
Born June 26, 1934 in Toronto, Ontario. Perrier officiated for eighteen seasons including 335 regular season and playoff contests. In addition he appeared in 7 Grey Cup finals. He retired from active service after the 1990 season and stepped into the position of officiating supervisor. Perrier is one of the CFL's two Officiating Supervisors. He resides in Scarborough, Ontario.

DON AIKIN
LEAGUE REPRESENTATIVE & GAME OBSERVER
Born January 9, 1928 in Loveland, Colorado. Has spent a total of 25 seasons officiating football including Division I service with the Big Sky Conference and the Western Athletic Conference. He resides in Las Vegas, Nevada.

HANK DELOTTY
LEAGUE REPRESENTATIVE & GAME OBSERVER
Born March 22, 1930 in San Francisco, California. Officiated 25 seasons of High School Football in Northern California plus twelve seasons of University Football to the Division 1-A level. Hank's officiating career included in excess of 800 contests at various levels of play. He resides in Stockton, California

GORD JOHNSON
LEAGUE REPRESENTATIVE & GAME OBSERVER
Born January 7, 1931 in Winnipeg, Manitoba. In 16 seasons as a game official (1970 to 1985), he worked in 192 regular season and playoff games including four Grey Cup Games. Become a Supervisor in 1986. He lives in Winnipeg, Manitoba.

VERN HEATH
LEAGUE REPRESENTATIVE & GAME OBSERVER
Born August 30, 1942 in Banff, Alberta. Worked 8 seasons as a game official with his last on-field campaign occurring in 1986. He served as a Supervisor in 1985 before returning to field duty. He worked 135 games as a game official. He resides in Calgary, Alberta.

LARRY HILL
LEAGUE REPRESENTATIVE & GAME OBSERVER
Born July 20, 1930 in Washington, D.C. Worked for thirty years as a football official in the U.S.F.L., the Arena Football League and the Atlantic Coast Conference and as a Supervisor of Officials in the Mid-Eastern Athletic Conference. He also served as a U.S. college basketball official for 12 seasons in the Atlantic Conference, the Big East Conference and the Mid-Eastern Athletic Conference. He resides in Baltimore, Maryland.

MURRY MULHERN
LEAGUE REPRESENTATIVE & GAME OBSERVER
Born July 14, 1927 in Vancouver, British Columbia. He is in his seventh season as a CFL Officiating Supervisor following an 18-year career as an official between 1964 and 1981. He resides in Richmond, B.C.

CHUCK PAUL
LEAGUE REPRESENTATIVE & GAME OBSERVER
Born August 16, 1930 in Ottawa, Ontario. Worked for one year as a CFL Supervisor following a 28-year career as an Official, which included 465 Regular Season and Playoff games and 8 Grey Cup games. He lives in Ottawa, Ontario.

CHRIS SIDARIS
LEAGUE REPRESENTATIVE & GAME OBSERVER
Born June 17, 1929 in Kansas City, Kansas. Spent 36 seasons officiating football at the Division I level in the Southland Conference and the Gulf States Conferences. Was a professional baseball player at the AAA level followed by an Umpiring career at the collegiate level. He resides in Shreveport, Louisiana.

JOHN STROPPA
LEAGUE REPRESENTATIVE & GAME OBSERVER
Born January 2, 1926 in Winnipeg, Manitoba. Worked for six seasons as a Supervisor. As an official between 1967 and 1981 he worked in 240 regular season and playoff games including 1 Grey Cup. He resides in Edmonton, Alberta.

1994 CFL OFFICIALS *Listed Alphabetically - CFL Total Service includes Regular Season, Playoff and Grey Cup Games*

RON ARTELLE Line Judge - No. 76
Born - January 7, 1955 in Ottawa, Ontario
Residence - Ottawa, Ontario
CFL Total Service - 8 seasons, 104 games
Grey Cup Service - 1 game

GEORGE BLACK Field Judge or Referee - No. 58
Born - June 27, 1948 in Toronto, Ontario
Residence - Islington, Ontario
CFL Total Service - 15 seasons, 300 games
Grey Cup Service - 5 games

HEINZ BRADERMANN Line Judge - No. 40
Born - January 28, 1948 in Arnstein, Germany
Residence - Sherwood Park, Alberta
CFL Total Service - 3 seasons, 46 games
Grey Cup Service - 0 games

DON CARMICHAEL Back Judge - No. 21
Born - January 29, 1958 in Pembroke, Ontario
Residence - Stouffville, Ontario
CFL Total Service - 1 season, 8 games
Grey Cup Service - 0 games

FRANK CHAPMAN Line Judge - No. 43
Born - January 10, 1958 in Ottawa, Ontario
Residence - Ottawa, Ontario
CFL Total Service - 4 seasons, 51 games
Grey Cup Service - 0 games

MURRAY CLARKE Side Judge - No. 22
Born - January 1, 1961 in Camrose, Alberta
Residence - Victoria, B.C.
CFL Total Service - 2 seasons, 24 games
Grey Cup Service - 0 games

JACQUES DECARIE Field Judge - No. 20
Born - January 26, 1945 in Montreal, Quebec
Residence - Montreal, Quebec
CFL Total Service - 24 seasons, 434 games
Grey Cup Service - 9 games

DON ELLIS Field Judge - No. 70
Born - October 1, 1950 in Toronto, Ontario
Residence - Scarborough, Ontario
CFL Total Service - 12 seasons, 231 games
Grey Cup Service - 4 games

JACK EWATSKI Back Judge - No. 69
Born - March 14, 1952 in Winnipeg, Manitoba
Residence - Winnipeg, Manitoba
CFL Total Service - 2 seasons, 32 games
Grey Cup Service - 0 games

JIM FARMER Field Judge - No. 23
Born - March 4, 1954 in Los Angeles, California
Residence - Irvine, California
CFL Total Service - 1 season, 16 games
Grey Cup Service - 0 games

BILL HAGANS Head Linesman - No. 24
Born - April 11, 1956 in Belfast, Ireland
Residence - Scarborough, Ontario
CFL Total Service - 5 seasons, 62 games
Grey Cup Service - 2 games

BILL HARCOURT Line Judge - No. 25
September 17, 1953 in Toronto, Ontario
Residence - Mississauga, Ontario
CFL Total Service - 5 seasons, 74 games
Grey Cup Service - 0 games

BRUCE HAWKSHAW Line Judge - No. 78
Born - January 6, 1945 in Vancouver, B.C.
Residence - North Vancouver, B.C.
CFL Total Service - 3 seasons, 47 games
Grey Cup Service - 0 games

DAVE HUTTON Umpire - No. 41
Born - January 24, 1949 in Hamilton, Ontario
Residence - Ancaster, Ontario
CFL Total Service - 8 seasons, 135 games
Grey Cup Service - 3 games

JOHN (JAKE) IRELAND Referee - No. 62
Born - December 1, 1946 in Hamilton, Ontario
Residence - Townsend, Ontario
CFL Total Service - 15 seasons, 293 games
Grey Cup Service - 8 games

GLEN JOHNSON Field Judge - No. 32
Born - May 25, 1961 in Winnipeg, Manitoba
Residence - Winnipeg, Manitoba
CFL Total Service - 4 seasons, 65 games
Grey Cup Service - 0 games

JAMIE KRAEMER Field Judge - No. 35
Born - December 1, 1956 in Winnipeg, Manitoba
Residence - Winnipeg, Manitoba
CFL Total Service - 6 seasons, 90 games
Grey Cup Service - 0 games

KEN LAZARUK Referee - No. 53
Born - February 28, 1947 in Winnipeg, Manitoba
Residence - Winnipeg, Manitoba
CFL Total Service - 17 seasons, 323 games
Grey Cup Service - 6 games

JIM LENAU Line Judge - No. 42
Born - June 4, 1956 in Sacramento, California
Residence - Sacramento, California
CFL Total Service - 1 season, 15 games
Grey Cup Service - 0 games

BILL MacDONALD Head Linesman - No. 72
Born - April 27, 1948 in Edmonton, Alberta
Residence - St. Albert, Alberta
CFL Total Service - 11 seasons, 201 games
Grey Cup Service - 2 games

ART McAVOY Back Judge - No. 57
Born - June 12, 1943 in Moose Jaw, Saskatchewan
Residence - Winnipeg, Manitoba
CFL Total Service - 16 seasons, 316 games
Grey Cup Service - 6 games

AL McCOLMAN Field Judge - No. 54
Born - September 19, 1949 in Hamilton, Ontario
Residence - Hamilton, Ontario
CFL Total Service - 17 seasons, 311 games
Grey Cup Service - 6 games

RICK McFADYEN Line Judge - No. 26
Born - September 2, 1952 in Winnipeg, Manitoba
Residence - Sherwood Park, Alberta
CFL Total Service - 5 seasons, 67 games
Grey Cup Service - 0 games

KEN PICOT Umpire - No. 80
Born - July 8, 1948 in Regina, Saskatchewan
Residence - Regina, Saskatchewan
CFL Total Service - 10 seasons, 143 games
Grey Cup Service - 3 games

BERNIE PRUSKO Field Judge - No. 79
Born - October 1, 1949 in Smoky Lake, Alberta
Residence - Edmonton, Alberta
CFL Total Service - 10 seasons, 202 games
Grey Cup Service - 4 games

BOB REDDEKOPP Line Judge - No. 39
Born - January 25, 1955 in Calgary, Alberta
Residence - Calgary, Alberta
CFL Total Service - 2 seasons, 24 games
Grey Cup Service - 0 games

RICH ROSE Line Judge - No. 36
Born - May 29, 1946 in Berkeley, California
Residence - Lafayette, California
CFL Total Service - 1 season, 15 games
Grey Cup Service - 0 games

ROSS SAUNDERS Umpire - No. 67
Born - November 29, 1956 in Ottawa, Ontario
Residence - Ottawa, Ontario
CFL Total Service - 13 seasons, 236 games
Grey Cup Service - 3 games

BUD STEEN Referee - No. 66
Born - June 21, 1951 in Edmonton, Alberta
Residence - Edmonton, Alberta
CFL Total Service - 13 seasons, 237 games
Grey Cup Service - 3 games

DAVE SUTHERLAND Umpire - No. 37
Born - April 3, 1949 in Brandon, Manitoba
Residence - Calgary, Alberta
CFL Total Service - 5 seasons, 68 games
Grey Cup Service - 0 games

TURK TRTANY Back Judge - No. 31
Born - September 17, 1940 in Kirkland Lake, Ontario
Residence - Burlington, Ontario
CFL Total Service - 8 seasons, 132 games
Grey Cup Service - 2 games

RANDY WARICK Back Judge - No. 27
Born - August 31, 1949 in Bruno, Saskatchewan
Residence - Saskatoon, Saskatchewan
CFL Total Service - 2 seasons, 30 games
Grey Cup Service - 0 games

RAY WILLETT Back Judge - No. 34
Born - March 9, 1946 in Waterville, Maine
Residence - Orangevale, California
CFL Total Service - 1 season, 15 games
Grey Cup Service - 0 games

BILL WRIGHT Umpire - No. 59
Born - September 17, 1943 in Prince Albert, Saskatchewan
Residence - St. Albert, Alberta
CFL Total Service - 15 seasons, 236 games
Grey Cup Service - 1 game

DAVE YULE Referee - No. 64
Born - February 12, 1946 in Lethbridge, Alberta
Residence - Calgary, Alberta
CFL Total Service - 13 seasons, 242 games
Grey Cup Service - 6 games

DENNIS ZWARYCH Side Judge - No. 33
Born - February 12, 1946 in Regina, Saskatchewan
Residence - Regina, Saskatchewan
CFL Total Service - 2 seasons, 17 games
Grey Cup Service - 0 games

FIRST SEASON OFFICIALS

Darryl Baron - No. 49
Residence - Sherwood Park, Alberta

Gary Cavaletto - No. 47
Residence - Goleta, California

Boris Cheek - No. 55
Residence - Hyattsville, Maryland

Dan Dooley - No. 61
Residence - Lisle, Illinois

James Jackson - No. 52
Residence - Washington, D.C.

Stanley Johnson - No. 56
Residence - Triangle, Virginia

Bill Laude - No. 60
Residence - Frankfort, Illinois

Chuck Miers - No. 51
Residence - Shreveport, Louisiana

Kim Murphy - No. 48
Residence - Grimsby, Ontario

Carl Paganelli - No. 45
Residence - Grand Rapids, Michigan

Lea Rutter - No. 50
Residence - Thibodaux, Louisiana

Marvin Shade - No. 63
Residence - Hazel Crest, Illinois

Brian Small - No. 65
Residence - Edmonton, Alberta

Bill Vinovitch - No. 46
Residence - Lake Forest, California

TOUCHDOWN OR FIELD GOAL
Both arms extended above head

SAFETY TOUCH
Palms together above head

SINGLE POINT
One arm extended above head and indicating one point

TIME IN
Downward rotation of arm

TIME OUT
Hands crisscrossed above head

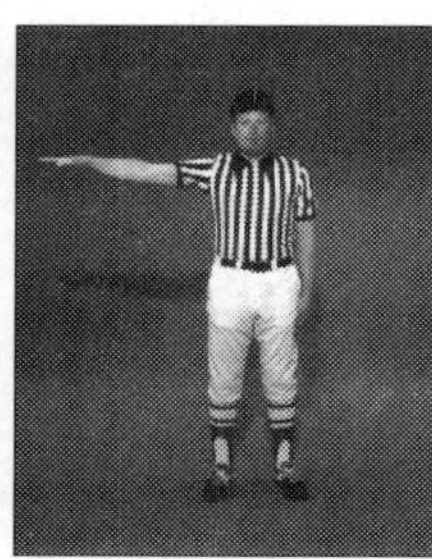

TIME COUNT VIOLATION
Arm extended in a circular motion

OFFSIDE
Hands on hips

PROCEDURE
Hands rotated in forward motion

ILLEGAL KICK-OFF
Same signal followed by Swinging leg

HOLDING
Grasping wrist at chest level

NO YARDS
Arms folded at chest

ILLEGAL PASS
Horizontal arc of arm

CLIPPING
Striking back of knees

ILLEGAL INTERFERENCE
Pushing arms forward from shoulders

ILLEGAL SUBSTITUTION -ILLEGAL PARTICIPATION
One hand on top of head

TOO MANY PLAYERS
Both hands on top of head

INTENTIONAL GROUNDING
Passing motion and pointing at ground

OBJECTIONABLE CONDUCT
One hand behind back

DELAY OF GAME
Both hands behind back

ILLEGAL BLOCK
Arm extended and grasp wrist

CONTACTING KICKER
Touch raised leg below knee

ILLEGAL CRACKBACK
Strike thigh with open hand

DISQUALIFICATION
Chopping action on wrist

PENALTY DECLINED
Swinging arms at hip level

TRIPPING
A chopping action on both knees

INELIGIBLE RECEIVER
Both arms extended sideways

MAJOR FOUL
Pumping motion of arm sideways

ILLEGAL CONTACT ON RECEIVER
One arm extended with open hand

SPEARING
Chopping motion above head

FACE MASK

PILING
Vertical chopping motion

CHOP OR CUT BLOCK
Horizontal chopping motion

ROUGHING PASSER
Passing motion

ROUGHING KICKER
Kicking motion

SUMMARY OF ABBREVIATIONS

AFD	Automatic First Down	L25	Loss of 25 yards
AR	Approved Ruling	LB	Loss of Ball
1D	First Down	LD	Loss of Down
12D	First or Second Down	LS	Line of Scrimmage
3D	Third Down	PBD	Point Ball Dead
Team A	Team Putting Ball Into Play	PBH	Point Ball Held
		PF	Point of Foul
Team B	Other Team	PLS	Point of Last Scrimmage
DR	Down Repeated	PPG	Point Possession Gained
L5	Loss of 5 yards	YG	Yards Gained or Goal-Line Reached
L10	Loss of 10 yards		
L15	Loss of 15 yards	YNG	Yards Not Gained

PLAN OF FIELD

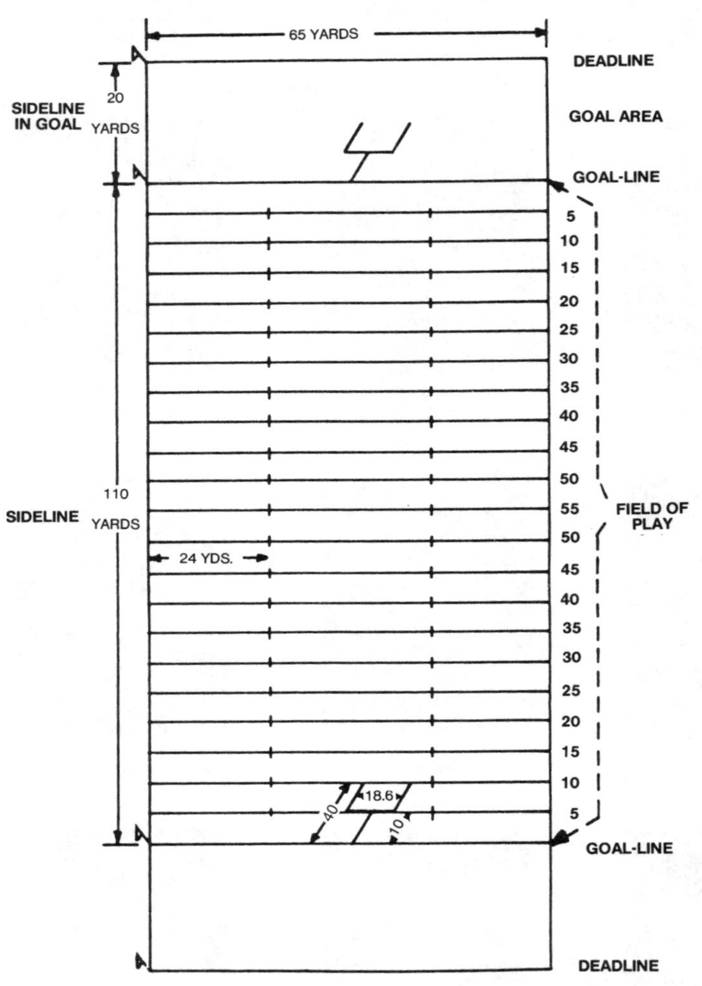

RULE 1 *Conduct of the Game*

SECTION 1: THE FIELD

Article 1: Regulation Fields

The field shall be 110 yards long by 65 yards wide. It shall be distinctly marked as indicated herein.

The lines marking the sides of the field shall be named Side-Lines.

The lines marking the ends of the field shall be named Goal-Lines.

The area bounded by these two sets of lines shall be called the Field-of-Play.

Twenty yards behind each goal-line, and parallel to it, shall be marked a line named the Dead Line.

The Side-Lines extended from Goal-Line to Dead-Line shall be named the Side-Lines-in-Goal.

The area bounded by the Goal-Line, the Dead-Line, and the Side-Lines-in-Goal shall be named the Goal Area.

The Bounds shall be defined as the "inside" of the side-lines, side-lines-in-goal, and dead-lines.

The field-of-play shall be marked every 5 yards with lines extending from side-line to side-line and parallel to the goal-lines.

Twenty-four yards in from each side-line each 5 yard stripe shall be marked by a short cross stripe parallel to the side-lines (Hash Marks).

Markers shall be placed opposite each 5 yard line from the goal-line, indicating the distance of each such line from the goal-line toward the centre of the field.

The four intersections of goal-lines and sidelines and the four intersections of deadlines and sidelines-in-goal shall be indicated by flexible markers which must be so placed that they are not touching the surface of the playing field.

Vertical posts (goal posts) shall be placed and centred on each goal line. The distance between the posts shall be 18 feet 6 inches. The goal posts shall extend 40 feet above ground level and shall be joined by a crossbar parallel to the ground at a height of 10 feet. The diameter of each post above the crossbar shall be not less than 3 inches or greater than 4 inches. At the extreme top of each post there shall be attached a coloured ribbon 4 inches wide and 42 inches long. A wishbone type or single shaft goal post assembly may be used provided that it complies with the above standards, and the base of the assembly is not further than 75 inches from the goal line.

Article 2: Fields Less Than Regulation Size

If the regulation length of a field is not available because of a fence, a running track or any other object, a clear line of demarkation shall be established at least one foot toward the playing surface from such fence, track or object. A line shall be painted on the playing surface and shall be considered as the boundary line. A player who touches this line, the surface outside the line or any object outside the line shall be ruled as having gone out of bounds.

SECTION 2: THE BALL

The game is played with a ball made of Horween Red leather in four panels which shall be inflated to a pressure not less than 12 1/2 psi nor greater than 13 1/2 psi. The circumference of the long axis shall be not less than 27 3/4 inches nor greater than 28 1/4 inches. The circumference of the girth or short axis shall be not less than 20 7/8 inches nor greater than 21 1/8 inches. The length of the long axis shall be not less than 11 inches nor greater than 11 1/4 inches. The total weight of the ball shall not be less than 14 ounces nor greater than 15 ounces.

The ball shall be painted with 1 inch white stripes around the short axis commencing 3 inches away from the point of greatest circumference of the short axis.

A minimum of seven balls shall be used in a game and changed at the discretion of the Referee. The balls shall be kept clean and in playable condition.

The official football for a Canadian Football League game shall be the Spalding J5V football, which shall be inscribed with the signature of the Commissioner.

SECTION 3: POSSESSION

Possession means having the ball firmly held in hand or hands, arm or arms, leg or legs, or under the body.

When players of the opposite teams have possession of the ball it shall belong to the player who first gained possession and who has not lost possession.

If players of both teams legally gain possession of the ball simultaneously it shall belong to the team which last previously had possession.

A ball not in possession of a player is still in play. A ball shall be considered to have been fumbled if the player last in possession has lost control of it.

SECTION 4: DEAD BALL

The ball is dead:

When ever a field official blows his whistle;

When an official has signalled a score;

When the ball goes out-of-bounds;

When a forward pass is declared incomplete;

When a kicked ball strikes the opponent's goal post assembly in flight, without first touching the ground, a player or an official;

When the ball carrier is tackled and his forward progress has been halted;

(tackling is defined as the act of grasping or encircling a ball carrier with hands and arms);

When the ball carrier behind the line of scrimmage is firmly in the grasp and control of a tackler to the extent that he cannot throw the ball.

When a ball carrier is tackled and driven back towards his own goal-line an official must assume that he was attempting to advance the ball and that only the actual contact with an opponent prevented such advance. Therefore, the most forward point of advance shall be considered the point where the ball became dead;

When the ball carrier is contacted by an opponent and loses his balance so that a portion of his body, other than his hands or feet touches the ground, the ball shall be dead at the point where it was held when he so touched the ground, or the point where the ball was held when he was contacted, whichever is the furthest point of advance;

When the quarterback, in possession of the ball, intentionally kneels on the ground during the last three minutes of a half;

When the quarterback, in possession of the ball dives in a feet first sliding motion the ball shall be declared dead at the point it was held when another part of the quarterback's body, other than his hands or feet, touches the ground.

When a player, having possession of the ball in his own goal area, intentionally kneels on the ground;

When a ball carrier is on the ground and, in the judgment of the official, is not attempting to advance the ball the official shall immediately declare the ball dead.

Note: A ball lying on the ground and not in possession of a player is not dead.
A ball striking an official is not dead except on a forward pass.

SECTION 5: TEAMS

For reference hereinafter the team which puts the ball in play shall be identified as Team A and the other team shall be named Team B. The game is played by teams of 12 men of each team.

SECTION 6: TEAM CAPTAINS

At all times each team must have on the field a player designated as captain, and so identified to the referee.

The captain shall be the sole communicator between his team and the officials (through the referee) and he may appeal to the referee only on questions of interpretation and application of rules. Such consultations should be held apart from other players on the field.

The captain may request the referee to call in the yardsticks to determine whether a first down has been made, or how much distance is required. If in the judgment of the referee the position of the ball is within one yard of the first down marker he shall signal time out and call for the measure, otherwise he shall refuse the request and order play to continue.

The referee's decision cannot be disputed. A captain is entitled to an explanation of any decision but no prolonged argument is to be allowed. When the yardsticks are called in from the sidelines to determine whether a first down has been gained the on-field captain for each team shall be the only players permitted in the vicinity of the measurement.

In case of a foul the captain of the non-offending team shall be given the choice of the penalty or the option provided.

SECTION 7: STARTING AND TIMING

Article 1: Starting

The game shall start promptly at the time prescribed by the Commissioner. If the team is late appearing on the field at the start of the first or third periods—

Penalty: L10

At the start of the game the captains of both teams shall meet the referee at centre field. The referee shall toss a coin with the visiting team captain making the call. The captain of the team winning the coin toss shall declare whether he wishes to have first choice at the start of the first or second half.

The captain of team having first choice at the start of the first half shall choose between

(a) kicking off or receiving the kickoff, or
(b) which end of the field to defend.

The captain of the other team shall have first choice at the start of the second half when both captains shall again meet the referee at centre field to inform him of their choices.

Article 2: Playing and Rest Periods

The length of game shall be 60 minutes of actual playing time, divided into four periods of 15 minutes each. The scoreboard clock shall be the official time for the game, and shall be operated under the direction and control of the Timekeeper. (See Rule 2, Section 2, Article 9).

Goals shall be changed at the end of the first and third periods. At the start of the second and fourth periods the ball shall be put into play at a point corresponding exactly to the point at the other end of the field where the ball became dead at the end of the previous period. It shall be put into play in exactly the same manner as if play had not been interrupted.

The kickoff to start the second half shall take place at exactly fourteen minutes after the conclusion of the first half and a team shall be subject to penalty if the players are not lined up on the field ready to start the second half at that time.

Article 3: Time Out

Time shall start when the ball is touched following the kickoff at the start of a half, or after a scoring play, and shall continue until the ball is ruled dead and an official signals to the timekeeper that time shall stop for any of the following reason:

When a score has been made;
When the ball goes out-of-bounds;
When a forward pass is incomplete;
For the application of penalties;
For player substitution;
For delay caused by player injury;
When time expires at the end of each period;
When the ball becomes dead after the three minute warning has been given in any half.
When a player requests a team time-out.
For a convert attempt during the last three minutes of a half or during overtime.
When the referee deems it necessary to suspend play.

If in any period the ball becomes dead with only a short period of time remaining, the team in possession shall be entitled to one complete play even though that play may extend beyond the normal termination of that period.

If a touchdown is scored on the last play of a period the period shall be extended to include the convert attempt.

If in any period time expires during a play in which a foul occurs, the non-offending team may

(a) accept the penalty in which case the team entitled to possession shall be required to put the ball into play, or
(b) decline the penalty and accept the play as it terminated to end the period, or
(c) elect to have the penalty applied on the first play of the following period, if the foul was a Major Foul.

Note: For the purpose of this rule an Offside Pass shall not be considered to be a foul.

Should the play be terminated by an official's whistle prior to the ball being put into play the penalty shall be applied and the period extended for another play.

Article 4: Time In

After a "time out" for any reason, time shall start again on the signal of the referee:
When the ball is touched following a kick-off; or
When it is ready to be scrimmaged; or
When it is snapped immediately after a "time count" foul; or
When it is snapped on the play immediately following a "time out" due to crowd noise; or
When it is snapped following a team time out
When it is snapped on the play immediately following a kick-off or a kick from scrimmage or an open field kick during the last three minutes in any half.
When it is snapped immediately following a play during which possession changed in the last three minutes in any half.
When it is snapped immediately following an incomplete legal forward pass in the last three minutes in any half.
When it is snapped immediately following a time out caused by the ball being carried out of bounds during the last three minutes in any half.
When it is snapped immediately following a score during the last three minutes in any half.
When it is snapped immediately following the application of a penalty for a foul which occurs after the three minute warning signal has been given in any half—however the non-offending team may decline the penalty and permit time to resume as though a foul had not occurred.
When it is snapped immediately following the application of dual penalties during the last three minutes of a half.

If, during the last three minutes of a half, an infraction is committed before the ball can be snapped the non-offending team may;

(a) accept the penalty, in which case time shall resume on the snap, or
(b) decline the penalty and elect whether time shall resume on the snap or when the Referee declares the ball in play.

After a touchdown time shall stop and shall resume when the Referee declares the ball in play for a convert attempt, except during the last three minutes of a half or during overtime when time shall resume when the ball is touched on the ensuing kickoff.

Article 5: Team Time-Out

During a half a team shall be permitted to call one time out, subject to the following:

(a) The time out may be requested by any player on the field and may be directed to any official on the field.
(b) The time out shall be 30 seconds in duration.
(c) The game time will resume on the snap.

Article 6: Ball in Play

The ball shall be considered in play until an official stops the game by sounding his whistle.

The game shall not be stopped because of player injury until the ball is dead.

The referee shall not stop the game to impose a penalty until the ball is dead.

Article 7: Delay of Game

The game shall not be delayed except by permission of the Referee. Any unauthorized delay shall be subject to penalty.

(a) If the Referee finds it necessary to suspend play while a player in the game has repairs to his equipment that player shall be required to leave the game for a minimum of three plays.
(b) If the Referee finds it necessary to suspend play while an injured player receives medical attention on the field that player shall be required to leave the game for a minimum of three plays, except when the injury had occurred as a direct result of an infraction for which the opponent was penalized, in which event the Referee may waive the requirement for the player to leave the game.
(c) On a kickoff Team A shall be required to kick the ball within 20 seconds of notification by the Referee that play is to commence.
(d) If a Team B player interferes with the placement of the ball after it has been declared in play by the Referee his team shall be penalized.

Penalty: L10

Article 8: Crowd Noise

The Team A captain may request the referee to stop the game if excessive crowd noise prevents Team A from putting the ball into play. The referee may, if he agrees with the captain, permit Team A to return to its huddle. The referee shall allow reasonable time but under no circumstances shall he permit that play to be delayed more than three times.

Article 9: Ball in Goal

The ball is in goal if it is on or behind the goal-line, even in the air.

SECTION 8: TIE GAME

If the score is tied at the end of the second half there shall be a two minute intermission followed by an overtime period consisting of two five minute halves. Prior to the start of the overtime period the captains of both teams shall meet the Referee at centre field to inform him of their choices. The referee shall toss a coin with the visiting team captain making the call. The captain of the team winning the coin toss shall declare whether he wishes to have first choice at the start of the first or second half of the overtime period.

The game timing rules that apply in the last three minutes of a half shall apply during the last minute of each half of the overtime period. There shall be an interval of 90 seconds at the end of the first half of the overtime period.

In the event that the score is tied at the end of the overtime period the game shall be declared over and each team shall be awarded one point in the standings.

If the game is a playoff or championship game and a winner must be determined, the same procedure shall continue in consecutive ten minute overtime periods until a winner is declared. There shall be a ten minute intermission before the start of overtime and between any subsequent overtime periods.

SECTION 9: OUT OF BOUNDS

Article 1: Definitions

The ball is out of bounds when it touches a side-line, side-line-in-goal, dead-line, or the ground or any other object beyond these lines.

The ball is out of bounds when a player in possession of the ball touches a side-line, side-line-in-goal, dead-line, or the ground or any other object beyond these lines.

Note: The ball shall remain in play when it is knocked or batted back into the field of play by a player who is off the ground and who has not touched the ground or any object out of bounds.

Note: If a player gains possession of the ball while off the ground in bounds and is contacted by an opponent in a manner which causes him to land out of bounds in possession of the ball such player shall retain possession.

Note: If a player gains possession of the ball near the sideline and touches the ground in bounds with his first step he shall retain possession even if his next step takes him out of bounds.

Article 2

When the ball is kicked out of bounds it shall belong to the opposite team, subject to the penalty applicable on a kick-off.

Article 3

When, on any play, the ball is fumbled out of bounds, or touches a player in the field of play and then goes out of bounds, it shall belong to the team which last touched the ball in the field of play.

The ball shall next be scrimmaged:
(a) at the point where the ball went out of bounds, or
(b) at the point where the ball was last touched in the field of play;
whichever point is closer to the goal line of the team entitled to possession.

Article 4

When a player directs the ball, other than by kicking, from the field of play over the opponent's goal line and hence out of bounds in the goal area without the ball touching an opponent, it shall be ruled as a fumble out of bounds in the field of play, with the ball declared dead at the point where it was last touched in the field of play.

Article 5

When a player fumbles or directs the ball from the field of play into his own goal area, where the ball goes out of bounds without possession being gained by either team, a safety touch score shall be awarded.

Article 6

When a player directs the ball other than by kicking, from the field of play over the opponent's goal line where it is recovered by an opponent, or is touched by an opponent before going out of bounds in the goal area, there shall be no score and the ball shall be awarded to the opponent's team at its 25 yard line. If in attempting to run the ball out of the goal area the opponent's team commits an infraction the penalty shall be applied from the 25 yard line.

Article 7

When a player in his own goal area fumbles or directs the ball, other than by kicking, across the goal line and out of bounds in the field of play without touching an opponent the non-offending team may:

(a) Accept a two point score if the offending team had previously directed the ball into its own goal area, or
(b) Accept a one point score if the non-offending team had kicked the ball into the goal area, or
(c) Decline the score and require the team entitled to possession to scrimmage the ball 24 yards in from the point where the ball went out of bounds.
(d) If prior to the fumble or offside pass out of bounds the player's team had gained possession in its goal area by intercepting a forward pass or recovering an opponent's fumble from the field of play it shall be awarded the ball at its 25 yard line without option.

Article 8

A player of either team who goes out of bounds, except as a result of bodily contact, must remain out of that play.

Penalty: L10

Article 9

When a player in his own goal area kicks the ball out of bounds in his goal area, the ball shall be awarded to the opponent at the 10 yard line.

If the ball was in the goal area as the result of an opponent's kick the opponent may elect to take a single point score. If the ball had been carried, passed or kicked into the goal area by the player's team the opponent may elect to take a safety touch score.

Article 10

When a player in the opponent's goal area kicks the ball out of bounds in the opponent's goal area the ball shall be awarded to the opponent at the 25 yard line.

SECTION 10: PLAYING UNIFORMS

Article 1: Equipment

No player shall wear or use equipment or clothing which in the opinion of the officials endangers or confuses his opponents.

No player shall wear metal in or on any part of his uniform other than such metal as may be necessary in the regular manufacture of the uniform, such as metal eyelets and nails, such as are used fastening cleats.

Where a cleat comes in contact with the playing surface, it must measure not less than three-sixteenths of an inch across any dimension and it must not be concave or hollow.

A cleat made of metals is illegal but a composition cleat with a metal tip which conforms to all other requirements shall be permitted.

Penalty: The offending player shall be removed from the game until illegal equipment is removed. Substitution shall be allowed but the game shall not be delayed.

Article 2: Helmets

A player shall be required to wear his helmet when on the field of play and shall not voluntarily remove it while the play is in progress.

The use of helmets or other objects to deceive opponents as to the whereabouts of the ball is prohibited.

Penalty: L5

Article 3: Numbering of Players

Each player shall be conspicuously numbered on the front and back of his jersey, and on his upper arms or shoulders. Such number must correspond with that listed with the scorer. A player shall retain the same number throughout the game except when permission to change is given by the referee. Such change shall be reported to the scorer.

In the event that a Team A player is required to change his playing number in order to play at a different position he must change his jersey in the team bench area and enter the game properly numbered. Under no circumstances shall he be permitted to change his jersey while on the playing field.

Penalty: The offending player shall be removed from the game until his proper playing number is determined. Substitution shall be allowed.

Article 4: Illegal Substance

A player shall not be permitted to apply or have applied on his uniform, his equipment or his body;

(a) an adhesive substance which, in the sole judgment of the referee, has made the game ball unsuitable for play as a result of direct or indirect contact with that player, and/or

(b) a greasy substance which, in the sole judgment of the referee, has the potential to give that player an unfair advantage.

Penalty: L10 The offending player shall be required to leave the game and shall not be permitted to return until the substance has been removed. Substitution for the player shall be allowed.

Article 5: Hazardous Equipment

A player shall not be permitted to wear equipment which, in the sole judgment of the Referee, has the potential to cause injury to an opponent.

Penalty: L15 The offending player shall be required to leave the game for a minimum of three plays, and not permitted to return until the hazardous equipment has been removed.

Article 6: Dress Code

A team is required to dress in a professional manner and shall be subject to penalty if a player fails to comply with the following requirements:

(a) The team jersey shall be tucked inside the top of the pants and shall remain tucked in throughout the game. If the jersey is pulled out during the game the player shall be required to tuck it in during a break in the play.

(b) Uniform stockings shall be worn in such manner that no part of the player's knee or leg is exposed.

(c) Protective gear shall be worn underneath the team jersey, pants and stockings. When a short-sleeved jersey is worn, the colour of protective gear on the elbow or lower arm shall be the same as one of the basic colours of the team.

(d) The team uniform shall not be cut away or altered in any manner whatsoever.

(c) White tape may be used on wrists and hands but tape used on stockings or any part of the uniform shall be the same colour as the uniform or equipment it covers.

Penalty: L10 The offending player shall be required to leave the game for a minimum of three plays and shall not be permitted to return until the dress code violation has been remedied.

SECTION 11: TEAM PERSONNEL

Article 1: Bench Area

The team bench area shall be a rectangular area situated not closer to the sideline than 6 feet and extending for a distance of 20 yards parallel to the sideline. During a game the area may be occupied only by substitute players in uniform and other accredited persons including coaches, doctors, trainers, equipment assistants and water carriers. All such personnel are required to remain within the rectangular area with the exception of the coaches who may take positions between the bench area and the sideline. The coaches shall not be permitted on the playing field at any time during the game, except with the permission of the referee.

Penalty: L10

Article 2: Official Time Out

When the referee has called an official time out not more than one player of each team may proceed to the sideline to talk with the coach.

Penalty: L10

Article 3: Trainers and Injured Players

During a stoppage in play, for injury or other reason, not more than two representatives of each team other than medical personnel shall be allowed to enter the field.

The referee need not permit the attendants of both teams to enter the field in case of injury to a player of one team only. He shall indicate his permission to the attendants of one or both teams.

When time out has been called for player injury or equipment repair that player shall be required to leave the game for a minimum of three plays, except when the injury had occured as a result of an infraction for which the opponent was penalized.

Penalty: L10 PLS DR or L10 PBD or option.

Article 4: Substitution Procedure

A substitute may enter the field of play at any time the ball is dead and only at that time.

If the substitute enters the game to the extent that he can communicate with a teammate on the field he must remain in the game for at least one play.

A player leaving the game shall proceed directly to the side-line on which his bench is located and, thence, outside the field of play to his bench.

A team shall not be permitted to use player substitution as a means of deceiving the opponents.

The side official (head linesman or line judge) shall monitor the team bench on his side of the field and, when the ball becomes dead, shall observe the sideline for possible substitutions. When Team A breaks the huddle or, if no huddle, the Referee declares the ball in play, the side official shall turn his back to the sideline and raise his arms to shoulder level. After he has assumed this position further substitution shall not be permitted.

Penalty: L10

Article 5: Sleeper Play

A sleeper play is a play in which a pass is thrown to a player who, by use of substitution procedures and his proximity to his team bench area, has disguised his presence on the field and his eligibility as a potential pass receiver.

Team A shall not use a player substitution as a means of disguising a sleeper play. If following a substitution a Team A player does not participate in the team huddle and positions himself within eleven yards of the sideline adjacent to his team bench area when the ball is put into play he shall be deemed ineligible as a pass receiver.

Penalty: L10

Article 6: Error in Number of Players

If through error in substitution or otherwise, a team has more than twelve players on the field the offending team shall be penalized.

Penalty: L10

SECTION 12: OTHER PERSONNEL

Article 1

If a person entitled to be in a team bench area (i.e. a substitute player in uniform or one of the other accredited persons) interferes with the play in progress, his team shall be subject to penalty as follows:

(a) If the opponent had possession of the ball the referee shall award an automatic touchdown to the opponent.

(b) If the offending person's team had possession it shall be penalized for illegal interference (L10 PBH or PBD) while the downs shall continue without interruption.

(c) If neither team had possession the ball shall be awarded to the opponent at the point of recovery with a penalty of half the distance to the goal-line and the opponent shall be permitted a series of three downs regardless of the time remaining in the half.

Furthermore, the offending person shall be disqualified from the game immediately, and subject to disciplinary action by the Commissioner. There shall not be any additional yardage penalty by reason of the disqualification.

Article 2

If a person other than one described in Article 1 should interfere with the play in progress the penalty shall be;

(a) If such person interfered to the advantage of the team in possession that team shall be penalized for illegal interference at the point where the ball was held when the interference occurred.

(b) If such person interfered to the advantage of the team not in possession the team in possession shall be awarded

(i) a touchdown score if, in the judgment of the referee, a touchdown would have been scored on the play, or

(ii) a penalty of half the distance to the goal line from

1. the point where the ball was held when the interference occurred, or
2. the point where the ball became dead, or
3. the point where the ball was put into play, or the team gained possession

whichever is the greater advantage to the team in possession, plus a series of three downs regardless of the time remaining in the half.

(c) If such person interferes with the play when the ball is not in possession of either team the referee shall whistle the play dead immediately. The entire play shall be repeated at the point the ball was previously put into play, with the down, yardage, score and time remaining the same.

(d) If such person interferes with a forward pass play in the goal area the ball shall be awarded to

(i) Team A at the one yard line if the interference was to the advantage of Team B, or

(ii) Team B at the ten yard line if the interference was to the advantage of Team A.

RULE 2 *Officials*

SECTION 1: DESIGNATION OF OFFICIALS

Article 1: Field Officials

1. Referee
2. Umpire
3. Back Judge
4. Side Judge
5. Field Judge
6. Head Linesman
7. Line Judge

Article 2: Side Line Officials

Downsman
Yardsmen
Communications
Co-ordinator
Timekeeper
Scorer

SECTION 2: JURISDICTION & DUTIES OF OFFICIALS

Article 1: General

All field officials are equally responsible for the conduct of the game and no agreement shall be undertaken that would prevent the calling of any foul, against either team, by an official.

Each field official shall be equipped with a whistle and a coloured marker to be used to indicate a foul.

The sounding of the whistle shall stop the game.

The throwing of a marker indicates that a foul has been committed, but play shall continue until its termination.

The signal of "time in" shall be a clockwise sweep of the referee's arm from the overhead position, and the sounding of the referee's whistle.

Article 2: The Referee

The referee shall take primary charge of the game and shall guide and direct the efforts of the other officials. He shall enforce the rules and he only shall apply the penalties and adjudicate upon disputes or cases unprovided for by the rules. He may overrule any other official. He may cause to be removed any of the side-line officials, if he considers it necessary, and immediately require the replacement of the official(s) so removed.

Subject to check with the head linesman he shall keep count of the downs.

He shall be notified by the head linesman (or line judge) when three minutes remain to play in each half, and shall so notify the captain of each team.

He shall take primary charge of the play of Team A and for this purpose should position himself behind Team A so that he can clearly see that the ball is put in play legally and can judge its position and progress.

He shall cover the actions of kickers and passers and the defensive actions of their opponents.

He is primarily responsible for marking balls out of bounds in flight.

He shall cover onside (lateral) passes behind the line of scrimmage and onside players in an "onside kick" situation.

Article 3: The Umpire

The umpire shall have jurisdiction over the conduct and actions of players on the scrimmage lines of both teams and shall position himself behind the defensive linemen (Team B).

Article 4: The Back Judge

The back judge shall have jurisdiction over the conduct and actions of players of both teams on Team B's side of the line of scrimmage and shall be responsible for sideline violations downfield.

Article 5: The Side Judge

The duties of the side judge shall be identical to those of the back judge.

Article 6: The Field Judge

The field judge shall have jurisdiction over the conduct and actions of players of both teams on Team B's side of the line of scrimmage and shall position himself downfield between the hash marks.

Article 7: The Head Linesman

The head linesman shall supervise and control the yardsmen and their actions in the placement and movement of the yardsticks, under the direction of the referee.

He shall record the number of each down and assist the referee in this respect.

He shall systematically check his side-line for player substitutions and ensure that only approved substitution procedures are used.

Article 8: The Line Judge

With the exception of (a) the supervision and control of the yardsmen, and (b) the recording of downs, the jurisdiction and duties of the line judge are identical to those of the head linesman.

Article 9: Downsman and Yardsmen

Under the direction of the head linesman the downsman shall place his marker at the forward point of gain or loss after each play and shall indicate the number of each down on the marker provided.

Two yardsmen shall function on one side-line under the direction of the head linesman. They shall remain outside the field-of-play unless called to assist in measuring for a possible first down. They shall be equipped with two pickets, connected near the lower ends by a chain. The distance between these pickets shall measure ten yards.

A third yardsman shall be used to hold a single picket on the opposite sideline to mark ten yard objective line. However such picket shall not be used to determine whether a first down has been gained.

Article 10: Timekeeper and Scorer

Prior to the game the scorer shall be provided with a complete list of the eligible competing players and the starting line-ups. He shall keep a record of all scoring plays in the game.

The timekeeper shall keep the time according to Rule 1, Section 7 and 8. He shall notify the head linesman or line judge when three minutes remain in each half.

If the scoreboard clock should fail to operate the timekeeper shall, prior to the last minute of play in each quarter, take a position so that he will be clearly visible to the referee. At the commencement of the last minute of play he shall raise a flag and continue to hold it in a raised position until time has expired in that quarter.

RULE 3 *Scoring*

SECTION 1: TABLE OF SCORES

Touchdown	6 Points
Field Goals	3 Points
Safety Touch	2 Points
Rouge	1 Point
Convert	1 Point or 2 Points

The team scoring the majority of points shall be the winner.

SECTION 2: DEFINITIONS

Article 1: Touchdown

A touchdown is scored when the ball in possession of a player is in his opponent's goal area, or when the ball in the possession of a player crosses or touches the plane of the opponent's goal-line. Should the ball subsequently be fumbled, or the player in possession forced back into the field of play, the touchdown shall score.

After a touchdown the team scored against may kick-off from its own 35 yard line, or require the scoring team to kick-off from its (scoring team's) 35 yard line.

Article 2: Field Goal

A field goal is scored by a drop kick or place kick (except on a kick-off) when the ball, after being kicked and without again touching the ground goes over the cross bar and between the goal posts (or goal posts produced) of the opponent's goal.

The ball shall be dead immediately, i.e. it crosses the cross bar.

After a field goal the team scored against may kick-off or scrimmage the ball as first down at its own 35 yard line or require the scoring team to kick-off from its 35 yard line.

AR Team A attempts field goal. After ball is kicked and before crossing line of scrimmage it touches or is touched by a player of either team and then proceeds through the uprights and over the crossbar in flight. Ruling - Field Goal.

AR Team A attempts field goal. After the ball has crossed line of scrimmage it touches or is touched by a Team B player before it proceeds through the uprights and above the crossbar in flight. Ruling - Field Goal.

Article 3: Safety Touch

A safety touch is scored when the ball becomes dead in the possession of a team in its own goal area, or touches or crosses the dead-line or a side-line-in-goal as a result of the ball having been carried, kicked, fumbled or otherwise directed from the field of play into the goal area by the team scored against, or as a direct result of a kick from scrimmage having been blocked in the field of play or goal area.

After a safety touch, the scoring team may elect to have the ball next put into play as follows:

(a) By scrimmaging the ball at its own 35 yard line, or
(b) By kicking off from its own 35 yard line, or
(c) By requiring the team scored against to kick off from its 35 yard line.

When a Rough Play or Unnecessary Roughness foul is committed on a play during which a safety touch is scored by the non-offending team, the score shall be allowed and the penalty assessed from the point where the ball is next put in play.

Article 4: Rouge or Single Point

If the ball is kicked into the goal area by an opponent, a rouge is scored (1) when the ball becomes dead in possession of a player in his own goal area or (2) when the ball touches or crosses the deadline, or a side-line-in-goal, and touches the ground,a player, or some object beyond these lines.

AR Team A kicks to Team B. B1 attempting to catch the ball on his 3 yard line, fumbles it and is tackled with the ball in his possession in his goal area. Ruling - rouge (ball considered kicked into goal area by Team A).

AR Team A kicks to Team B. B1 catches ball in field of play while moving toward his goal line and, in the judgment of the official, his momentum carries him into his goal area. Ruling - possession deemed to have been gained in the goal area.

After a rouge the team scored against shall next put the ball into play by a scrimmage as first down at any point between the hash marks on its 35 yard line.

If the single point was scored as the result of an unsuccessful field goal attempt the team scored against may elect to scrimmage the ball at its own 35 yard line or at the point of last scrimmage.

Article 5: Convert

A team scoring a touchdown may attempt to add to its score by means of a scrimmage play from any point between the hash marks on or outside the opponent's five yard line, as follows:

1 point - By kicking a field goal.

or

2 points - By scoring a touchdown by means of a ball carrying or passing play.

The ball shall remain in play until a score is made or the play has been terminated.
If Team B legally gains possession during an unsuccessful convert attempt (i.e. interception of forward pass, recovery of fumble or blocked kick), it may score two points by advancing the ball across Team A's goal line. If the play terminates with Team B in possession in its own goal area, there shall be no score.
If the play terminates with Team A legally in possession in Team B's goal area, Team A shall be awarded two points if the ball had been carried or passed across the line of scrimmage, but no points if the ball had been kicked across the line of scrimmage.

Note: For infraction on convert attempt, see Rule 8, Section 5.

SECTION 3: TERMINATING A PLAY IN GOAL

A player in possession of the ball in his goal area may terminate the play by dropping to the ground on one knee. The official shall immediately declare the play dead.

SECTION 4: MISCELLANEOUS

No score can be made from a kick-off unless the ball, after it is kicked off, is touched by a player of either team within bounds.

RULE 4 *Scrimmage*

Note: Where a violation under this Rule occurs before the ball has been snapped the officials are empowered to stop the play and apply the penalty. Such penalty shall apply without option, however the yardage may be declined. For a violation during the last three minutes of a half see Rule 1, Section 7, Article 4.

SECTION 1: DEFINITIONS

Article 1: Line of Scrimmage

The line of scrimmage is an imaginary line, extending from side-line to side-line, parallel to the goal-line, and passing through the point of the ball farthest from Team A's goal-line.

Article 2: Line and Backfield

Players of Team A who are within one yard and on their own side of the line of scrimmage, and formed in a single line when the ball is put in play, shall be considered scrimmage line, or line players. A player is on the line if the most forward part of his body is within one yard of the line of scrimmage.
A player of Team A is considered to be in his backfield if he is clearly back of the line when the ball is put in play. This will also include the player occupying the position of quarterback.
No player of Team A shall be in a position that will create doubt as to whether he is on the line or in the backfield, when the ball is put in play.

Penalty: L5

Article 3: Scrimmage Zone

The scrimmage zone is the area extending one yard on each side of the line of scrimmage and from side-line to side-line.

Article 4: Defensive Line

On a play from scrimmage, players of Team B must line up at least one yard back of, and on their own side of the line of scrimmage until the ball is put in play. This includes the player giving defensive signals.

Penalty: L5

SECTION 2: METHOD OF SCRIMMAGE

Article 1: The Centre

At the commencement of a scrimmage play one Team A player (the centre) shall take up his position facing the opponent's goal-line with the ball on the playing surface immediately in front of him. He shall put the ball in play by snapping it back between his legs in one continuous motion to another Team A player behind the line of scrimmage. The ball must leave the centre's hands and he shall not touch the ball again until it has been in the possession of another player.

Team A shall be subject to penalty for attempting to draw an opponent offside if,

(a) the centre fakes a snap, without snapping the ball, or
(b) the centre, having assumed his stance holding the ball, bobs his head, moves his shoulders or flexes his knees without snapping the ball.

Penalty: L5

Note: On a Team A kicking formation the centre shall be permitted to move his head for the purpose of checking the position of an opponent prior to snapping the ball.

Article 2: Illegal Movement

Team A shall be subject to penalty for attempting to draw an opponent offside if,

(a) the quarterback makes a quick movement towards the centre position without the ball being snapped immediately, or
(b) the quarterback, having assumed his stance with his hands under the centre, bobs his head, moves his shoulders or flexes his knees in a jerking motion without the ball being snapped, or
(c) the quarterback, having assumed his stance with his hands under the centre, moves away without the ball being snapped.

Penalty: L5

Either team shall be subject to penalty for attempting to draw an opponent offside if a player makes a motion or voices a signal which, in the judgment of the official, is intended to draw an opponent offside.

Penalty: L5

Article 3: Offside - At The Snap

Team A players must be completely behind the line of scrimmage, except that the head, arms, and hands of the centre may be in advance of the line of scrimmage.

Penalty: L5

If a Team B player is offside on his own one yard line.

Penalty: Team A shall be awarded a first down or score made.

If a Team B player goes offside and breaks the plane of the line of scrimmage before the ball is snapped, the officials shall stop the play immediately and award the penalty, subject to the right of Team A to decline the yardage penalty and order the same down to be repeated as though a foul had not occurred.

If players of both teams are offside on the same play, the same down shall be repeated without penalty from the point of last scrimmage.
A player of either team who is offside and contacts an opponent, even though he recovers his onside position prior to the snap, shall be penalized for being offside.
Team A may put the ball into play without waiting for Team B players to be onside, but an offside penalty cannot be claimed against Team B. Such an offside player shall not interfere with the play in any manner.

Penalty: L5

Article 4: Time Count

The referee shall allow Team A 20 seconds in which to put the ball into play. If the stadium countdown clock is not in operation he shall be the sole judge as to when the time count shall commence, after allowing both teams reasonable time in which to line up after the preceding play.

Penalty: L5DR - Yardage penalty may de declined.

Note: After the three minute warning has been given in a half the penalty shall be 12D - LD, 3D- L10 DR.

Note: The penalty for a time count violation on a convert attempt shall be L5 DR at any time during the game.

Note: If in the opinion of the referee Team A is taking a deliberate third down time count penalty the referee may order Team A to put the ball in play legally within 20 seconds or forfeit possession to Team B.

SECTION 3: INTERFERENCE

Article 1: General Definition

Interference takes place when a player obstructs, blocks, screens, or charges towards an opponent, with or without direct contact, in such a manner that he prevents the opponent's approach to the ball carrier, potential ball carrier or the ball.

Article 2: By Team A

(a) On a play from scrimmage, a Team A player may interfere with an opponent from deadline to deadline commencing from the instant the ball is snapped, except in the case of:
(i) A play during which a forward pass is thrown across the line of scrimmage, or
(ii) A play during which the ball is kicked across the line of scrimmage.
(b) For interference on a forward pass play see Rule 6, Section 4, Article 8(a).
(c) On a kicking play a Team A player may interfere with an opponent up to one yard in advance of the line of scrimmage.
(d) A Team A player may use his hands, open or closed, and may thrust them forward to contact an opponent provided that his hands are kept inside his elbows and contact is made from the front or side of the opponent within the frame of the opponent's body that is presented to the blocker.

Penalty: L10

Article 3: By Team B

(a) On any play from scrimmage a Team B player may use his hands and arms to reach the ball carrier, but shall not hold or encircle any Team A player, other than the ball carrier.

Penalty: L10

(b) For interference on a forward pass play see Rule 6, Section 4, Article 8(b).
(c) For interference on a kicking play see Rule 5, Section 4, Article 3.

SECTION 4: PLACEMENT OF BALL

Article 1: After a Score

When the ball is placed in play by the referee after a scoring play, after the ball has been declared dead in the end zone, or following the application of a penalty for a foul in goal or a foul on a convert, Team A may elect to scrimmage the ball at any point between the hash marks.

Article 2: Within Twenty-Four Yards of a Side-Line

If the ball becomes dead within twenty-four yards of either side-line, or goes out-of-bounds, it shall next be scrimmaged twenty-four yards in from such side-line at the yardage point where it becomes dead.

Article 3: Within One Yard of Goal Line

If Team A has possession of the ball within one yard of either goal-line, it shall be scrimmaged one yard out from such goal-line.

Article 4: Within Fifteen Yards of Own Goal

When, on third down, Team A scrimmages on or within its own 15 yard line, Team A may position the ball away from the goal posts towards the closest side-line, but not closer than 24 yards to such side-line.

Article 5: Within Five Yards of Own Goal

If Team A is scrimmaging within 5 yards of its own goal line it shall be permitted to have the ball moved out to the nearest hash mark.

SECTION 5: PLAYER RESTRICTIONS

Article 1: Seven Players on Line

At the instant the ball is put in play at least seven players of Team A must be within one yard, and on their own side of the line of scrimmage. (This does not include the player in the position usually occupied by the quarterback.) Conversely, Team A can never have more than five players, including the quarterback, in backfield positions.

Penalty: L5

Article 2: Stance

No line player of Team A, except the centre, having assumed a three or four point stance, may legally move his head, body, arms, hand, legs, or feet until the ball is snapped.

Penalty: L5

Article 3: Identification and Positions

On all scrimmage plays at least five line players, including the centre, shall be identified as ineligible pass receivers and must be positioned in a continuous, unbroken line. In addition, one player at each end of the line shall be identified as an eligible pass receiver.

Any other Team A player is an eligible pass receiver, provided he is so identified by his playing number and, at the snap of the ball, is occupying a backfield position at least one yard back of the line of scrimmage.

Note: Team A Players shall be identified by numbering as follows:

Eligible Receivers	00 to 39
	and 70 to 99
Ineligible Receivers	40 to 69

Note: Notwithstanding this article a Team A player wearing an eligible receiver number may, upon notification to the Referee, enter the game at an ineligible receiver position under the following circumstances;
(a) On a third down play, or
(b) On a convert attempt, or
(c) On a first or second down kicking formation in the last minute of a quarter, on the understanding that he shall not be eligible as a pass receiver.

Penalty: L5

Article 4: Linemen in Motion

No player of Team A, who is within one yard of the line of scrimmage, shall be moving towards his opponent's goal-line when the ball is put in play.

All Team A players positioned in the scrimmage zone from offensive tackle to offensive tackle inclusive or having assumed a three or four point stance within one yard of the line of scrimmage shall be required to remain motionless for at least one second immediately prior to the snap of the ball.

Article 5: Designated Quarterback

Prior to the game a team is required to designate three players who shall be permitted to alternate for each other during the game at the quarterback position exclusively. The three players can never be in the game at the same time and neither can enter the game as a member of Team B. A player shall be deemed to be playing at the Team A quarterback position if:
(a) he is positioned as the team punter or place kicker, or
(b) at the snap of the ball he is in position to receive the ball directly from the centre.

If a designated quarterback participates in the game at another position.

Penalty: L25 PLS DR or L25 PBD or option.

Article 6: Designated Import

If a team is using its full complement of import players it shall, prior to the game, designate one import player as a special teams player, who shall be permitted to enter the game at another position only on the understanding that another import player is required to leave the game for that play. Such player may enter the game on an unrestricted basis only if another import player is removed for the balance of the game.

If a designated import participates in the game illegally.

Penalty: L25 PLS DR or L25 PBD or option.

SECTION 6: SERIES OF DOWNS

Article 1: Ten Yards on Three Downs

Team A shall have three downs in which to gain the required distance of ten yards. A down may be repeated following the application of a penalty against either team. If in a series of three downs Team A has not gained the required ten yards, the ball shall be awarded to the opponents as first down at the point where the ball becomes dead. If the required ten yards are gained a new series of downs begins.

Article 2: Consecutive Downs

"Consecutive" shall mean possession in a continuous series of downs in which the ball is in possession of the one team.

Article 3: Continuity of Downs

The continuity of downs is interrupted:
(a) When the ball, having been kicked, other than dribbled, crosses the line of scrimmage.
(b) When on a scrimmage play the ball is dribbled by Team B.
(c) When the ball definitely passes into possession of opponents. (Touching the ball by opponents is not possession.)
(d) When the required distance is gained.
(e) When the ball is kicked out of bounds.

Article 4: Position of Ball in Measuring

In measuring for downs the forward point of the ball, and not its centre, shall be the determining point and the ball, before measuring, shall be rotated so that its long axis is parallel to the side-lines. A touchdown cannot be awarded as a result of such rotation.

Note: When Team A has failed to gain the distance required for a first down and the ball is awarded to Team B the referee shall reverse the ball in order to have the forward point facing in the opposite direction.

RULE 5 *Kicking*

SECTION 1: DEFINITIONS

Article 1: Kicked Ball

A kicked ball is one struck by a player's foot, or leg below the knee.

Note: If the ball accidentally strikes a player's leg or foot it shall not be ruled as a kicked ball.

Article 2: Drop Kick

A drop kick is made by dropping the ball from the hands kicking it with the foot just as it rises from the ground.

Article 3: Place Kick

A place kick is made by kicking the ball after it has been placed on the ground and held by a Team A player who shall be considered "offside" with reference to the position of the ball.

On a kickoff the ball may be held, placed on the ground, or placed on a tee, provided that the lowest part of the ball shall be raised not more than three inches above the playing surface.

On a field goal or convert attempt a kicking tee may be used provided that the ball shall be raised not more than one inch above the playing surface.

Article 4: Punt

A punt is made by letting the ball fall from the hands and kicking it with the foot before it touches the ground.

Article 5: Dribbled Ball

A dribbled ball occurs when the ball is kicked while not in possession or control of a player, i.e. a loose ball following a fumble, a blocked kick, a kickoff, or a kick from scrimmage. Such a dribbled ball may be touched by the kicker or an onside player without penalty.

If touched by an offside player,

Penalty: Ball awarded to opponents at point ball touched, or option.

If touched by an offside player in the opponent's goal area,

Penalty: Ball awarded to opponent at its 25 yard line, or option.

If touched by an offside player in his own goal area,

Penalty: Ball awarded to opponent at 10 yard line, or option.

Note: A ball dribbled by Team A across the line of scrimmage does not interrupt the continuity of downs.

Note: A dribbled ball which strikes a goal post shall remain in play.

Article 6: Onside and Offside

An onside player is a member of the kicker's team who is behind the ball at the instant it is kicked towards the opponent's deadline.

An offside player is a member of the kicker's team who is not onside.

An offside player becomes an onside player when the ball, after being kicked towards the opponent's deadline, touches or is touched by an opponent, the kicker or another onside player.

Exception: On a kick from scrimmage if a Team B player touches the ball before it crosses the line of scrimmage such touching does not put an offside player of Team A onside.

Article 7: Application of Penalties

Under this Rule 5, the penalty for any infraction which occurs after the ball has been kicked and before possession has been gained by the receiving team shall be applied as follows:

(a) Foul by kicking team, (Other than "No Yards" to kick receiver or failure to kick off ten yards)

— At point of last scrimmage, or point of kickoff, or point of actual kick on an open field kick, as the case may be. If the open field kick originates in the goal area, the penalty shall be applied at the 10 yard line.

(b) Foul by receiving team. (Other than Contacting the Kicker, or illegal Blocking of the kicker or an onside player)

— At point receiving team gains possession or is entitled to possession. If possession gained in goal area penalty shall be applied from the receiving team's 10 yard line.

SECTION 2: KICK-OFF

Article 1: Points of Kick-off

The ball shall be kicked-off, by a place kick, from any point between the hash marks on Team A's.

(a) 35 yard line—at the start of the game, or any half, or after a touchdown;

(b) 35 yard line—after a score of 3 points by the kicking team; or the team scored against may elect to put the ball in play by kick-off or scrimmage from its own 35 yard line.

(c) 35 yard line—after a score of two points against the kicking team; or the scoring team may elect to put the ball in play by kickoff or scrimmage from its own 35 yard line.

Article 2: Legal Kick-off

(a) The ball, unless touched by an opponent, must be kicked more than ten yards towards the opponent's goal line before it may be legally touched by a member of Team A.

Penalty: L5 kickoff repeated or Team B may take possession at the point the ball was first touched by Team A or option.

(b) The ball, unless touched, shall not go out of bounds in the field of play.

Penalty: L5 kickoff repeated or Team B may take possession at its 35 yard line or at the point where the ball went out of bounds.

(c) Should the ball be kicked out of bounds in the receiving team's goal area without being touched by a player of either team there shall be no penalty and the ball shall next be put in play by the receiving team at its 25 yard line.

(d) Should the kicked ball strike the goal post assembly in flight it shall be declared dead immediately and awarded to the receiving team at its 25 yard line.

(e) If the kicked ball is simultaneously recovered by players of both teams, or is simultaneously touched by players of both teams before going out of bounds, the kickoff shall be repeated.

Article 3: Offside on Kick-off - Team A

At the instant the ball is kicked-off no player of the kicking team shall be in advance of the ball, except the player who may be holding the ball for such kick-off.

Penalty: L5 - kick-off repeated, or option.

Article 4: Offside on Kick-off - Team B

Players of the receiving team must stand at least ten yards on their own side of the line of kick-off when the ball is kicked.

Penalty: L5 - kick-off repeated, or option.

Article 5: Interference by Team B

On a kick-off a player of the receiving team may interfere with an opponent anywhere within bounds commencing from the moment the ball is kicked, provided that contact is made only above the waist of the opponent.

Penalty: L10 PBH or PPG

Article 6: Interference by Team A

(a) Before gaining possession - A player of the kicking team shall not be permitted to interfere with an opponent until his team has gained possession.

Penalty: L10 - kick-off repeated, or option

(b) After gaining possession - If a player of the kicking team recovers the ball on the kick-off his team may then interfere with opponents anywhere within bounds, provided that contact is made only above the waist of the opponent.

Penalty: L10 - PBH

SECTION 3: BLOCKED KICK

Article 1: Definition

A blocked kick is a kick from scrimmage in which, after being kicked, the ball is prevented from crossing the line of scrimmage because of contact with an opponent or a player of the kicking team who is offside.

It is not a blocked kick if, on a kick from scrimmage, the ball is touched by, or touches, an opponent or a player of the kicking team who is offside and then crosses the line of scrimmage. Such touching of the ball shall be disregarded.

If the kicked ball, after being so touched prior to crossing the line of scrimmage, should strike any part of the goal post assembly in flight without touching the ground, an official or a player, it shall be declared dead immediately and awarded to the receiving team on its 25 yard line.

Article 2: Recovery of Blocked Kick

If the ball is blocked, without going out of bounds, it may legally be recovered by a player of either team. If, however, the ball is recovered by a player of the kicking team the continuing play shall be considered as any other play from scrimmage.

Article 3: Blocked Out-of-Bounds

Where a kick is blocked and the ball goes out-of-bounds:

(a) On first and second down it shall belong to the team last touching it in the field-of-play 24 yards in from the side-line
  (1) at the point where the ball left the field-of-play, or
  (2) at the point where the ball was last touched in the field-of-play - whichever point is closer to the goal-line of the team entitled to possession;

(b) On third down it shall belong to the non-kicking team at either of the points set out in (a) above.

Article 4: Blocked Through Goal Area

When a kick is blocked in the field of play or goal area and without again being touched the ball goes directly out of bounds in the goal area possession shall be awarded to the opponent's team as first down at the point of last scrimmage, or the option of two points.

Note: This article shall also apply if immediately prior to the ball going out of bounds in the goal area, it is last touched by Team B in the goal area.

AR Team A punt from scrimmage is blocked on A5 yard line. Team B player touches the ball, without gaining possession, on A2 yard line before ball crosses goal line and out of bounds in the goal area. Ruling - Team B has option of 1st down at A2 or a two point score.

SECTION 4: KICK FROM SCRIMMAGE AND OPEN FIELD KICK

Article 1: Restriction on Offside Player (No Yards)

(This article does not apply to a "dribbled ball".)

When on a kick from scrimmage (ball crosses line of scrimmage), or on an open field kick, a player is "offside" in relation to his kicker;

(a) He shall not touch the ball, or interfere with an opponent attempting to gain possession of the kicked ball.

Penalty: (1) In field of play - scrimmage by non-offending team 15 yards in advance of point where ball was first touched.
(2) In goal area - scrimmage by non-offending team on its 35 yard line.

(b) He shall allow five yards to an opponent attempting to gain possession of the kicked ball. The five yard zone is determined by a circle of radius five yards, with the centre point being the ball at the instant it is first touched by an opponent.

Penalty: (1) In field of play - scrimmage by receiving team 15 yards in advance of the point where the ball was first touched, OR 5 yards in advance of that point if the kicked ball had struck the ground before being touched by the receiving team.
(2) In goal area - scrimmage by receiving team after penalty applied from the goal line.

(c) The kicker or an onside player may enter the restraining zone and legally recover the kicked ball, but shall not interfere with an opponent attempting to recover the ball.

Penalty: Ball awarded to receiving team at point of foul or at its 25 yard line if the foul occurred in the receiving team's goal area.

(d) If the kicked ball has not yet been touched and a player of the receiving team fakes an attempt to recover the ball he may be tackled without penalty. If an offside player touches the ball there shall be no penalty and the ball shall be awarded to the receiving team.
(e) If the kicked ball has not yet been touched and, in the judgment of the official, no effort is being made by either team to recover the ball, he may declare the ball dead and award possession to the receiving team.

Article 2: Kicked Ball Striking Goal Post Assembly

(a) If the ball after being kicked should strike the opposing team's goal post assembly in flight the ball shall be declared dead immediately and awarded to the receiving team as first down at its 25 yard line.
(b) A kicked ball striking the goal post assembly after having touched an official, the ground, or a player shall remain in play.
(c) A kicked ball striking the kicking team's goal post assembly shall remain in play.
(d) If the kicked ball on a field goal or convert attempt should strike the goal post assembly in flight and then proceed through the uprights above the crossbar the score shall count.

Article 3: Interference on Kick from Scrimmage

(a) A player of the receiving team may interfere with any player of the kicking team who has crossed the line of scrimmage provided that contact is made only above the waist. Such interference shall be permitted from the instant the ball is snapped.

Penalty: L10 PBH or PPG

(b) The kicker or an onside player may not be contacted until he has reached the line of scrimmage, or until the receiving team has touched the ball.

Penalty: L10 PLS

Article 4: Interference on Open Field Kick

A player of the team receiving an open field kick may commence interfering with an opponent at the instant the ball is kicked, provided that such contact is made only above the waist of the opponent.

Penalty: L10 PBH or PPG

Article 5: Interference by Kicking Team

On a play from scrimmage in which the ball is kicked across the line of scrimmage a player of the kicking team may interfere with an opponent up to one yard in advance of the line of scrimmage. After the ball is kicked he may use his hands and arms to ward off a blocker interfering with his approach to the ball carrier.

Penalty: L10 PLS

Article 6: Recovery of Own Kick

The kicker or an onside player may recover the kick across the line of scrimmage, in which case the ensuing down shall be first down whether or not the original yardage has been gained.

Following such recovery by the kicker or an onside player, a player of the kicking team may interfere with an opponent provided that contact is made only above the waist of the opponent.

Penalty: L10 PBH

Article 7: Kick That Fails to Cross Line of Scrimmage

When a ball kicked from scrimmage fails to cross the line of scrimmage and is recovered by an onside player of the kicking team, the series of downs shall not be interrupted unless after recovery the yardage required for a first down is gained.

If touched by offside player

Penalty: Ball awarded to opponent at point ball touched, or option

If touched by offside player in his own goal area:

Penalty: Ball awarded to opponent at 10 yard line, or option

RULE 6 *Passing*

SECTION 1: LATERAL OR ONSIDE PASS

A lateral or onside pass is one thrown, handed, knocked, batted or fumbled by a player parallel to or in the direction of his own dead ball line.

A player shall be considered onside in relation to a team-mate in possession of the ball if he is not closer to the opponent's deadline than such player in possession.

The point at which the ball is caught, strikes another player, an official, or the ground, or goes out of bounds is the factor which determines whether it is a lateral or an offside pass, regardless of the direction in which it goes afterwards.

A lateral pass striking the ground is not dead and may be recovered by either team without penalty.

When a lateral pass goes out of bounds in the field of play, the ball shall be put in play by scrimmage at a point twenty-four yards in from the point where the ball went out of bounds.

SECTION 2: HAND-OFF PASS

A hand-off pass is made on a scrimmage play when the ball is handed, but not thrown, by one Team A player to another behind the line of scrimmage. There is no restriction on the number of hand-off passes on any one play.

The player receiving the hand-off pass must not be occupying the position of an interior lineman at the instant he receives the ball

Penalty: L5 PLS DR

SECTION 3: OFFSIDE PASS

Article 1: Definition

An offside pass is made when the ball is directed towards the opponent's deadline in any manner other than by being kicked.

A team making an offside pass shall not be permitted to advance the ball or retain possession beyond the point of origin of the pass.

Penalty: Next scrimmage at point of origin of pass, or option.

Exceptions: Hand-off Pass (Rule 6, Sec. 2)
Forward Pass (Rule 6, Sec. 4)

Article 2: Offside Pass in Field-of-Play

An offside pass shall be ruled as having occurred in the following situations:

(a) On a scrimmage play, a Team A player makes an offside pass after he has crossed the line of scrimmage.
(b) On a play, other than from scrimmage (e.g. kick return, kick-off return, interception return, fumble return, recovery of onside kick or kickoff), a player makes an offside pass.
(c) In attempting to catch a forward pass, a Team A eligible receiver tips, deflects, knocks or bats the ball in an offside direction where it is caught by another Team A player who is not eligible as a receiver.

Penalty: Ball to team making offside pass, at point of origin of pass (downs continue unless yards gained at that point - or option).

Article 3: Not an Offside Pass

An offside pass shall be ruled not to have occurred in the following situations:

(a) On a scrimmage play, before the ball crosses the line of scrimmage, a Team A player in possession of the ball makes an offside pass - rule as a forward pass.
(b) On a forward pass play, an eligible Team A receiver, in attempting to catch the ball, tips, deflects, knocks or bats the ball in an offside direction where it is caught by another eligible Team A receiver.
(c) In attempting to intercept a forward pass, a Team B player directs the ball in an offside direction where it is caught by another Team B player.
(d) On any play where the ball carrier, or a player attempting to catch a kicked ball, unintentionally drops or fumbles the ball forward and it is recovered by a player of the same team.

Article 4: Offside Pass in Goal Area

(a) If Team A makes an offside pass in its own goal area and retains possession of the ball, Team B shall be awarded 2 points or option.

(b) If Team B makes an offside pass in its own goal area after gaining possession from a Team A kick, Team A shall be awarded one point or option.
(c) If Team B makes an offside pass in its own goal area after gaining possession by interception of a Team A forward pass, or by recovery of a Team A fumble, it will scrimmage at its own 25 yard line, or option.
(d) If a player deliberately throws the ball out of his own goal area and it is touched or goes out to bounds in the field of play, the play shall be ruled as an offside pass in the goal area and the opponent shall have the option to accept a one or two point score, as applicable, or to accept the play as it terminated.

Note: This article applies to a ball fumbled from the goal-area, into the field-of-play, and out-of-bounds without touching an opponent.

SECTION 4: FORWARD PASS

Article 1: Definition & Possession

A legal forward pass is thrown by any Team A player from a point behind the scrimmage line, towards the opponent's dead-line, to any eligible receiver or receivers. The ball shall not touch the ground, a goal post or cross bar, an official or any other object. It shall not go out-of-bounds. The ball is considered to be in the possession of Team A until the pass is ruled completed or incompleted.

Article 2: One Forward Pass on Any Down

Only one forward pass shall be thrown on any down. If a second pass is thrown:

Penalty: L10 DR

Article 3: Eligibility of Passer

A pass may be thrown by any Team A player who was behind the scrimmage line when he passed the ball. The passer need not be the first player to receive the ball from the centre.

If pass thrown from point across line of scrimmage:

Penalty: L10 DR

Article 4: Eligibility of Receivers

The following players are eligible receivers:
(a) Any Team A player who is identified by number as an eligible receiver and who, at the snap of the ball, is occupying a position either at the end of the line of scrimmage or in the backfield at least one yard back of the line of scrimmage.
(b) Any player of Team B, whether or not the pass is legally thrown.

Note (1) If a ball is touched by, or touches, a Team B player before it crosses the line of scrimmage, such touching does not affect the number of Team A eligible receivers. However, if after crossing the line of scrimmage the ball is touched by, or touches, a Team B player all players of both teams become eligible receivers.
Note (2) Team A players shall be identified by numbering as follows:

Eligible Receiver	00 to 39 and 70 to 99
Ineligible Receivers	40 to 69

Note (3) Notwithstanding this article a Team A player wearing an eligible receiver number may, upon notification to the Referee, enter the game at an ineligible receiver position under the following circumstances;
(a) On a third down play, or
(b) On a convert attempt, or
(c) On a first or second down kicking formation in the last minute of a quarter, on the understanding that he shall not be eligible as a pass receiver.
Note (4) As an alternative to Note (3) a Team A player wearing an ineligible receiver number may be declared eligible as a receiver provided that -
(a) he reports to the Referee immediately prior to each play in which he is to be declared eligible, and
(b) he occupies an eligible receiver position on the line of scrimmage, and
(c) at the instant the ball is snapped he is positioned within three yards of the position occupied by the Team A tackle.

When an ineligible receiver is the first player of Team A to catch or deliberately touch the ball.

Penalty: L10

Article 5: Completed Forward Pass

A pass is completed under the following conditions:
(a) When caught by a Team A eligible receiver, or by two or more such receivers simultaneously;
(b) When caught by a player or, simultaneously, by players of Team B or when such a pass is touched by, or touches B1 and then is caught by B2;
(c) When caught simultaneously by players of both teams who maintain possession until the play is terminated the ball shall be awarded to Team A.
(d) If an eligible receiver of either team catches a pass while off the ground and inbounds, but is carried or pushed by the opponent in a manner which causes him to land out of bounds in possession of the ball, pass shall be ruled complete at the furthest point of advance.
(e) If an eligible receiver of either team catches a pass near the sideline and touches the ground in bounds with his first step he shall retain possession even if his next step takes him out of bounds.

Article 6: Incomplete Forward Pass

A forward pass shall be declared incomplete and the ball next put in play at the point of last scrimmage with downs continuing:
(a) When the ball strikes the ground, goal post assembly, an official, or any object on or back of the goal-line or out-of-bounds (even if previously touched by a player).
(b) When the ball goes out-of-bounds, even though touched by a player in the field-of-play.
(c) When the ball is caught by en eligible player of either team while off the ground who, on landing, touches a side-line, a side-line-in-goal, a dead-line, or any object or ground beyond such lines.
(d) When the passer has commenced with his forward passing motion with the ball moving forward and, as a result of contact with an opponent, the ball leaves the passer's hand and strikes the ground.

Article 7: Intentional Grounding

If a Team A passer deliberately, in the official's opinion, throws the ball out of bounds or to an area in which there is not an eligible Team A receiver for the purpose of avoiding loss of yardage his team shall be penalized.

Penalty: LD at point from which pass was thrown. If pass thrown from goal area a safety touch score shall be awarded to Team B subject to the right of Team B to decline the score and accept the play as it terminated.

Article 8: Interference

(a) By Team A - A player of Team A may interfere with an opponent anywhere within bounds after the pass has been completed. Prior to the pass being completed or declared incomplete a Team A player may interfere with an opponent anywhere within bounds provided that the pass is thrown to a receiver behind the line of scrimmage. If the pass is thrown to a receiver beyond the line of scrimmage, any interference which has occurred more than one yard beyond the line of scrimmage shall be ruled to have been illegal.

Penalty: L10

(b) By Team B - A player of Team B may interfere with a player of the passing team in a zone one yard in depth on his own side of the line of scrimmage. However, prior to the pass being thrown, a Team B player occupying a position behind the line may use his hands or arms to ward off an opponent who as a potential blocker threatens his defensive position. Such Team B player shall not be permitted to interfere with a potential pass receiver who is not threatening his defensive position. A Team B player shall not be permitted to interfere illegally with a Team A eligible receiver in his attempt to catch the ball.

Penalty: (i) if interference is ruled accidental — L10 PLS and AFD for Team A.

(ii) if interference is ruled deliberate — AFD awarded to Team A, at PF of 10 yards in advance of PLS (whichever is closer to Team B goal line). If the infraction occurs in the Team B goal area — AFD for Team A at Team B's one yard line.

Note: Yardage penalties will be subject to Rule 8, Section 4, Article 1. (Restricted penalties)

(c) If a Team B player interferes illegally with an eligible receiver of Team A, behind the line of scrimmage, in his attempt to catch the ball.

Penalty: 1D to Team A, 10 yards in advance of PLS.

(d) By Team B on a convert attempt.

Penalty: Attempt repeated by Team A at Team B's one yard line.

(e) Interference on Intercepted Passes - when a pass has been intercepted any player of Team B may interfere with an opponent anywhere within bounds provided that contact is made only above the waist of the opponent.

Note: Pass interference shall not be penalized if, in the judgment of the official
(i) players of Team A and Team B make contact in a simulanteous attempt to catch or bat the ball, or
(ii) the ball has previously been touched by an eligible receiver, or
(iii) the ball is clearly uncatchable.

Article 9: Interception in the Goal Area

Pass intercepted by Team B in its goal area.
If B in possession of ball is "held" within his goal-area, the ball is dead without score.
If B intercepts and then fumbles in attempting to run the ball out of the goal area, the ball may be legally recovered by Team A.
When the ball is dead without score, B shall scrimmage it at its 25 yard line, first down.
If Team B, while in possession in its goal area following an interception in goal

commits any infraction in the goal area or in the field of play, the penalty shall be applied from the 25 yard line, or option.

If Team B intercepts a pass in its goal area and the play is ruled dead in B's goal area and Team A is called for Rough Play or Unnecessary Roughness in the field of play or in the goal area, the penalty shall be applied from Team B's 25 yard line.

Note: If a Team B player intercepts a pass in the field of play while moving toward his goal line and his momentum carries him into his goal area the play shall be ruled as an interception in goal.

Note: The only score that can result from a Team B interception in its goal area, while the ball remains in the goal area, is a touchdown by Team A following recovery of a Team B fumble.

RULE 7 *Fouls and Penalties*

SECTION 1: ILLEGAL TACTICS

Article 1: Holding

Holding is defined as the use of the hands and/or arms to grasp or encircle an opponent. It is illegal at all times, except when a player tackles the ball carrier. Holding hands and locking arms during a scrimmage is prohibited.

Penalty: L10 PLS PBH PPG

Article 2: Clipping

Clipping means blocking an opponent, other than the ball carrier, from the rear in such a manner that the player charges into the opponent's back, or falls across the back of his legs. The application of a penalty is determined by the initial contact, which must be observed by the official, and shall not be called if, in the judgment of the official.

(a) The block occurs in the area between the offensive tackles within two yards of either side of the line of scrimmage and is executed by a Team A player who at the snap of the ball was positioned within this area, or
(b) The initial contact is made on the side of the opponent, or
(c) The opponent could see the blocker approaching and deliberately turned his body in order to be contacted from behind.

Penalty: L15

Article 3: Crackback Blocking

A Team A player who, at the snap of the ball,
(a) is positioned more than three yards outside the offensive tackle, or
(b) is in motion towards the ball within three yards of the offensive tackle from a point more than three yards outside the offensive tackle

shall not be permitted to move laterally toward the ball and contact an opponent below the waist in the area up to five yards in advance of the line of scrimmage from sideline to sideline.

Penalty: L15

Article 4: Chop Blocking

Chop blocking means contacting an opponent at or below the knees at the time that opponent is already being engaged by another player.

Penalty: L15

Article 5: Cut Blocking

It shall be illegal to contact an opponent at or below the knees when that opponent is:
(a) in a backfield position blocking for the passer or kicker, or
(b) Blocking for the ball carrier on a kick return play, or
(c) a potential pass receiver on the line of scrimmage.

Penalty: L15

Article 6: Contacting the Kicker

It shall be illegal to touch the kicker when he is in the act of kicking from scrimmage, subject to the following conditions:
(a) If prior to kicking the ball the kicker had recovered a loose ball on the ground or made a motion to pass the ball or run with the ball he shall NOT be entitled to protection under this Article.
(b) An opponent who blocks or touches the ball shall not be penalized for contacting the kicker.
(c) An opponent shall not be penalized when a blocker of the kicker's team causes him to contact the kicker.
(d) If, in the referee's opinion, a defensive player attempting to block the kick makes slight and incidental contact which does not affect the play, he shall not be penalized.
(e) This section does not supply to a "quick" kick or to an "open field" kick.
(f) The act of kicking shall begin when the kicker's kicking foot leaves the ground, and shall terminate when his foot returns to the ground after kicking, or attempting to kick, the ball.

Penalty: L10 PLS

Article 7: Pyramiding

It shall be illegal for a player to use the body of another player or the goal post assembly in any way to elevate himself in an attempt to block a field goal or a convert attempt.

Penalty: L5

Article 8: Illegal Blocking

(a) After a change in possession during a play, or the recovery of a kicked ball by either team, a player of the team in possession shall not be permitted to contact an opponent below the waist in any manner whatsoever.

Penalty: L10 PBH

(b) During any play a player of the team in possession shall not be permitted to contact an opponent from behind in a manner that interferes with the opponent's approach to the ball carrier.

Penalty: L10

Article 9: Tripping

A player shall not use his leg below the knee to hinder the progress of an opponent.

Penalty: L10 PLS, PBH or PPG

Article 10: Tandem Blocking

It shall be illegal to assist the forward progress of a ball carrier by providing impetus from behind.

Penalty: L10 PLS or PBH

SECTION 2: MAJOR FOULS

Note: The Rules Committee has declared its total abhorrance of Rough Play and Unnecessary Roughness. Officials are instructed that no tolerance whatsoever is to be given to infractions under this Section.

Article 1: General Application

(a) The penalty for a major foul shall be applied in addition to:
  i) any other penalty for any other foul, and
  ii) the advantage of any distance gained or score made.
(b) If the foul occurs during a scrimmage play prior to a first down being gained the non-offending team may elect to have the penalty applied
  i) from the point of the last scrimmage with the same down repeated, or
  ii) from the point where the ball became dead on the play with the downs continuing.
(c) If the foul occurs during a scrimmage play after a first down has been gained the non-offending team may elect to have the penalty applied.
  i) from the point where the ball was held when the foul occurred, or
  ii) from the point where the ball became dead on the play.
(d) If the foul occurs after a change in possession the non-offending team may elect to have the penalty applied
  i) from the point where the ball was held when the foul occurred, or
  ii) from the point where the ball became dead on the play.
(e) If the foul occurs when neither team is in possession the non-offending team may elect to have the penalty applied
  i) from the point where possession was gained or deemed to have been gained, or
  ii) from the point where the ball became dead on the play.
(f) If the foul occurs after the play has been terminated the penalty shall be applied from the point where the ball became dead on the play.
(g) If the foul occurs after a scoring play the score shall count and the penalty shall be applied from the point where the ball would normally next be put into play. If the scoring play was a touchdown the penalty shall be applied on the convert or subsequent kickoff at the option of the non-offending team. If the foul occurs after a convert attempt the penalty shall be applied on the subsequent kickoff.

Article 2: Rough Play

A player shall be penalized and subject to disqualification for any act of rough play against an opponent, including but not limited to:
(a) Striking an opponent with the fist, hand, knee or elbow in an excessively rough manner.
(b) Kicking an opponent.
(c) Any other act of excessive roughness considered by the referee to warrant disqualification.

Penalty: L25 and disqualification of offending player
If Team B is the offending team on a play from scrimmage Team A shall be awarded a first down in addition to the yardage penalty.

When a player has been disqualified the referee shall inform the coaches of both teams and the official scorer.

In the event of dual fouls under this Article 2 the offending players shall be disqualified and penalties balanced at the point of application. If the fouls occur on a scrimmage play Team A shall not be awarded a first down by virtue of the penalty against Team B.

Article 3: Unnecessary Roughness

A player shall be penalized for any act of unnecessary roughness against an opponent, including but not limited to:

(a) Piling by a player who, in an unnecessarily rough manner, falls upon the ball carrier after the play has been terminated.
(b) Contacting an opponent out of bounds in an unnecessarily rough manner.
(c) Contacting the passer in an unnecessarily rough manner.
(d) Unnecessary roughness against the punter, or kicker or the ball holder on a place kick.
(e) Grasping an opponent's face guard.
(f) Using the helmet to butt, ram or spear an opponent, including but not limited to, a passer, a receiver in the act of catching a pass, a ball carrier in the grasp of another tackler, or a ball carrier on the playing surface not attempting to advance.
(g) Contacting an opponent above the shoulders in an unnecessarily rough manner.
(h) Any other act of roughness or unfair play, provided it is not considered excessive enough to warrant disqualification.

Penalty: Team A - L15
Team B - L15 and 1D to Team A
If both teams offend the penalties shall be applied against each other but Team A shall not be awarded a first down by virtue of the penalty to Team B.

Article 4: Disqualification

A player shall be disqualified from the game, and substitution permitted, for any act of serious misconduct, including but not limited to:

(a) Rough Play against an opponent.
(b) Physical abuse of an official.
(c) Excessive objectionable conduct against an opponent or an official.

A player who has been disqualified from the game shall be required to leave the bench area and not permitted to return.

Article 5: Objectionable Conduct

A player shall be penalized for any act of objectionable conduct, including but not limited to:

(a) verbal abuse or objectionable gesture directed at an opponent, official or spectator, or
(b) throwing the ball at an opponent, official or occupant of the team bench area, or
(c) interfering with the placement of the official's flag marking the spot for a penalty.

Penalty: L10

If a team continues with objectionable conduct after a penalty has been applied a further penalty may be assessed.

Penalty: L10

For physical abuse of an official in any manner whatsoever.

Penalty: L25 plus disqualification of the offending player.

RULE 8 *Application of Penalties*

SECTION 1: DEFINITIONS

Article 1: Loss of a Down

In any penalty "loss of a down" means that the down upon which the foul occurred has used up one of the permissible series of consecutive downs.

Article 2: Loss of Yards

In any penalty where there is a loss of yardage there shall be no loss of down.

Exception - Major foul
(See Rule 7, Section 2)

Article 3: Option Provided

When a foul has been committed on any play, the non-offending team shall be entitled to the penalty, or the option of declining the penalty to take any advantage of position, score, down, time, etc. The non-offending team may decline a score to take advantage of a penalty or may decline a penalty to permit a score by the offending team to stand.

In certain cases, where so stated, a penalty shall be applied without option.

SECTION 2: FOULS AND LEGAL GAINS

Article 1

Should any foul be committed on a play from scrimmage after the yardage necessary for a first down has been gained the penalty shall be applied from the point where the ball was held when the foul occurred.

Article 2

Should any foul be committed on a play from scrimmage during which the yardage necessary for a first down was gained, but the foul occurred prior to the necessary yardage being gained the penalty shall be applied from the point of last scrimmage.

Article 3

Should any foul be committed after a team has gained possession by a pass interception, a fumble recovery or a kick the penalty shall be applied from the point where the ball was held when the foul occurred.

SECTION 3: DUAL AND DOUBLE FOULS

Article 1

Double fouls occur when the same team commits one or more fouls on the same play.

The non-offending team shall have the option of accepting either penalty, or may decline the penalties to take advantage of the play as it is terminated. If one of the fouls is a major foul that penalty shall be applied whether or not the non-offending team accepts the penalty for the other foul.

Article 2

Dual fouls occur when each team commits one or more fouls on the same play. If one of the dual fouls is a minor foul (not U.R. or R.P.) and the applicable penalty is or includes A.F.D. or L.B. it shall be deemed to have the same yardage as the other foul in the event that the penalties are balanced. An automatic first down shall not be awarded.

If U.L. of R.P. is one of the dual fouls the yardages shall be deemed equal however a first down may be awarded subject to normal application.

Article 3

When on a play from scrimmage not involving a change in possession dual fouls are committed, the following rules shall apply.

(a) If both fouls are committed prior to yards being gained the referee shall cancel the play. If the fouls are of equal value the down shall be repeated at the point of last scrimmage. If the fouls are not of equal value the referee shall apply the penalties for both fouls balancing one penalty against the other from the point of last scrimmage. No option.
(b) If both fouls are committed after yards have been gained the penalties shall be applied at the point the ball was held at the time of the first foul. However the non-offending team on the first foul shall have the right to decline the penalty against the opponent and accept the play as it was completed subject to the penalty against itself for the second foul at the normal point of application.
(c) If the first foul is committed before yards have been gained and the second foul after yards have been gained the penalties shall be balanced and applied from the point of last scrimmage. However the non-offending team on the first foul shall have the right to decline the penalty against the opponent and accept the play as it was completed subject to the penalty against itself for the second foul at that normal point of application.
(d) If one of the dual fouls involves a non-yardage penalty (e.g. AFD or LD) it shall be deemed to have the same yardage value as the other foul, in which event the two penalties shall be balanced against each other at the point of last scrimmage. No option.

Article 4

When on a play from scrimmage involving a change in possession (i.e. a kicking play or a forward pass interception, or a play in which a fumble is lost) dual fouls are committed, the following rules shall apply. For the purposes of this Article 4 "possession" shall be deemed not to have changed until the second team has gained possession. A "No Yards" or "Loose Ball Interference" infraction shall be deemed to have occurred after the change in possession.

(a) If both fouls are committed before the change in possession the penalties shall be applied as provided in Article 3.
(b) If both fouls are committed after the change in possession the penalties shall be applied and balanced at the point the ball was held at the time of the first infraction. The non-offending team on the first foul shall have the right to decline the penalty against the opponent and accept the play subject to the penalty against itself for the second foul at that normal point of application.
(c) If the first foul is committed before the change in possession and the second foul after the change in possession, the penalties shall be applied and balanced at the point of application for the first foul. The non-offending team on the first foul shall have the right to decline the penalty against the opponent and accept the play as it was completed subject to the penalty against itself for the second foul at the normal point of application.
(d) If both fouls are committed in goal after the second team has gained possession in its own goal area the penalties shall be applied and balanced from the second team's ten yard line, or the twenty-five yard line if possession had

been gained by an interception or a fumble. No option.

(e) If the first foul is committed in goal after the change in possession and the second foul in the field of play the penalties shall be applied and balanced from the ten yard line. The non-offending team on the first foul shall have the right to decline the penalty against the opponent and accept the play as it progressed subject to the penalty against itself at the normal point of application.

Article 5

When on a kickoff play dual fouls are committed, the following rules shall apply:

(a) If both fouls are committed before possession has been gained the penalties shall be applied and balanced at the point of kickoff with the kickoff repeated. No option.

(b) If both fouls are committed after possession has been gained the penalties shall be applied and balanced at the point of application for the first foul. The non-offending team on the first foul may decline the penalty against the opponent and accept the play subject to the penalty against itself for the second foul at the normal point of application.

(c) If the first foul is committed before possession has been gained and the second foul after possession has been gained the penalties shall be applied and balanced at the point of kickoff with the kickoff repeated. The non-offending team on the first foul may decline the penalty against the opponent subject to penalty against itself for the second foul at that normal point of application.

SECTION 4: RESTRICTION NEAR A GOAL LINE

Article 1

If a distance penalty is applied within 30 yards of the offending team's goal line it shall not exceed one half the distance between the point from where the penalty is applied and said goal line. In no case shall the ball be scrimmaged within the one yard line.

Article 2

In no case shall a distance penalty applied from a point outside the offending team's 30 yard line bring the ball closer to the goal line than the offending team's 15 yard line. (This applies to a 25 yard penalty).

Article 3

Where an unrestricted penalty would have resulted in yards gained or goal line reached by Team A, a first down shall be awarded.

Article 4

If double fouls are called against the same team, one of which is for a major foul, the penalties shall be applied consecutively. The normal penalty shall be applied first, followed by the penalty for the major foul. Each penalty shall be subject to the limitation of half the distance to the goal line although the aggregate of the two penalties may be greater than half the distance to the goal-line from the point of application of the first penalty.

SECTION 5: FOUL ON CONVERT

Article 1

If a foul is committed during a convert attempt the following shall apply:

(a) If either team commits a foul (except a Major Foul or Defensive Off-side) prior to the ball being snapped or during a convert attempt the non-offending team may elect to have the penalty appied from PLS or accept the play as it terminated

(b) If the foul is a Major Foul or Defensive Off-side the non-offending team may elect to have the penalty applied from PLS or accept the play as it terminated and apply the penalty on the subsequent kick-off.

(c) If the time has expired in the period the kickoff will take place at the start of the following period. If game time has expired no further play shall be permitted

Article 2

If either team commits a Major Foul after the convert attempt the penalty shall be applied on the subsequent kickoff.

Article 3

If time has expired in the period the kickoff will take place at the start of the following period. If game time has expired no further play shall be permitted.

SECTION 6: FOUL IN GOAL

Article 1: Foul in Own Goal

(a) If Team A commits a foul while in possession of the ball in its goal area, the penalty shall be applied from PLS or option.

Exception - See Intentional Grounding - Rule 6, Section 4, Article 7, Offside Pass - Rule 6, Section 3, Article 4.

(b) If Team B commits a foul in its goal area while in possession of the ball in its goal area, Team A may elect to
  i) accept the one or two point score, if applicable, or
  ii) decline the penalty and accept the play as it terminated, or
  iii) decline the score and require the penalty to be applied against Team B from its 10 yard line.

If the foul is committed outside the goal area while Team B is in possession of the ball in its goal area the penalty shall be applied from Team B's 10 yard line or option.

Exception - See interception in goal area - Rule 6, Section 4, Article 9, and recovery of opponent's fumble in goal area - Rule 1, Section 9, Article 7.

Article 2: Foul in Opponent's Goal

If a team commits a foul in the opponent's goal area the penalty shall be applied as though the foul had occurred in the field of play. However, where a yardage penalty would otherwise be applicable in the goal area it shall be applied as follows:

(a) If the foul occurs before a score is made, the score shall be disallowed and the penalty shall be applied from the goal line.

(b) If the foul occurs after a score is made, the score shall count and the penalty shall be applied from the point where the ball is next put into play. If the scoring play was a touchdown the non-offending team may elect to have the penalty applied on the convert or subsequent kick-off.

(c) If foul occurs after interception in goal area see Rule 6, Section 4, Article 9.

(d) If Team A makes an offside pass in Team B's goal area in the act of completing a forward pass, i.e. the ball is touched by an eligible Team A receiver in Team B's goal area, and deflected in an offside direction where it is caught by another Team A player who is not eligible as a receiver, the pass shall be ruled as caught by the second Team A player at the point where it was touched by the first Team A player.

RULE 9 *Interference*

SECTION 1: GENERAL DEFINITION

Interference takes place when a player obstructs, blocks, screens or charges towards an opponent, with or without direct contact, in such a manner that he prevents the opponent's approach to the ball carrier, potential ball carrier or the ball.

SECTION 2: INTERFERENCE ON SCRIMMAGE PLAYS

Article 1: By Team A

(a) On any play from scrimmage, except one in which a forward pass is thrown or the ball is kicked across the line of scrimmage, a player of Team A may interfere with an opponent from dead-line to dead-line, commencing from the instant the ball is snapped.

(b) After a forward pass has been completed a player of Team A may interfere with an opponent anywhere within bounds. Prior to the pass being completed or declared incomplete Team A may interfere with an opponent anywhere within bounds provided that the pass is thrown to a receiver behind the line of scrimmage. If the pass is thrown to a receiver across the line of scrimmage any interference which has occurred more than one yard beyond the line of scrimmage shall be ruled to have been illegal.

Penalty: L10

(c) On a play from scrimmage in which the ball is kicked across the line of scrimmage a player of Team A may interfere with an opponent up to one yard in advance of the line of scrimmage.

Penalty: L10

Article 2: By Team B

(a) On any play from scrimmage a Team B player may use his hands and arms to reach the ball carrier, but shall not hold or encircle any Team A player, other than the ball carrier.

Penalty: L10

(b) On a play from scrimmage in which a forward pass is thrown a Team B player may, prior to the pass being thrown, use his hands and arms to ward off a Team A player who, as a potential blocker, threatens his defensive position. However he shall not be permitted to interfere with a potential pass receiver who is not threatening his defensive position.

Penalty: L10 PLS and AFD at PF if, in the judgment of the official, the interference had been deliberate.

(c) After the pass is thrown a Team B player shall not be permitted to interfere with a Team A receiver in his attempt to catch the ball.

Penalty: AFD at PF, or AFD 10 yards in advance of PLS if infraction took place on Team A's side of line of scrimmage.

(d) On a play from scrimmage in which the ball is kicked across the line of scrimmage a Team B player shall be permitted to interfere with any Team A player who has crossed the line of scrimmage provided that contact is made only above the waist of the Team A player.

Penalty: L10 PBH or PPG

(e) The kicker or an onside player of Team A may not be contacted until he has reached the line of scrimmage, or until the ball has been touched by Team B.

Penalty: L10 PLS

SECTION 3: INTERFERENCE AFTER GAINING POSSESSION WITHOUT SCRIMMAGE

Interference from dead-line to dead-line shall be permitted for the team gaining possession of the ball without scrimmaging it, provided that such interference shall be restricted to contact above the waist of the opponent.

Penalty: L10 PBH

SECTION 4: INTERFERENCE ON LOOSE BALL

Article 1

A player shall not deliberately interfere with an opponent attempting to recover a loose ball following a blocked kick, a dribbled ball, or a wild snap from the centre.

Penalty: LB at PF

If foul occurs in the goal area the ball shall be awarded to the non-offending team.

(a) at the 10 yard line if the foul occurred in the offending team's goal area, or
(b) at the 25 yard line if the foul occurred in the non-offending team's goal area.

Article 2

If in attempting to recover a loose ball two or more players come into contact the play shall not be ruled as illegal interference.

Article 3

A team having fumbled shall not be penalized if its blockers continue to carry out the normal assignments which they would have been entitled to carry out if the ball had not been fumbled.

GLOSSARY OF CFL TERMS

IMPORT - A player who played football outside of Canada and who did not play football in Canada prior to his seventeenth birthday.

NON-IMPORT - A player who has spent a total of five of his first fifteen years in Canada, or who has never played football outside of Canada.

GAME ROSTER - In 1994 the Game Roster for the Canadian-based clubs shall consist of 14 imports, 20 non-imports and 3 quarterbacks. U.S.-based clubs may consist of 34 imports and 3 quarterbacks.

RESERVE LIST - Players on a Club's roster who are not dressed for a game are carried on the Reserve List. The Reserve List shall consist of up to two players.

SPECIALTY TEAMS PLAYER - When a team dresses 14 imports one must be designated as a specialty teams player who is used on a restricted basis.

WAIVERS - Before a Club may terminate a player's contract it must give other Clubs the opportunity to claim the player's services.

WAIVERS WITH RECALL - A Club has the right to recall a player from waivers twice in a calendar year.

OPTION CLAUSE - Each player contract contains a clause which gives the Club the option to renew the contract for another season.

ROSTER QUOTA - The League annually determines the number of players a Club may have on its roster, the number that may dress for a game, and how many may be imports.

NON-ACTIVE LIST - Players not under contract who are permitted to practice with a Club are declared on the Non-Active List.

ROSTER CUTDOWN - The date determined by the League when a Club is required to establish its roster within the prescribed limits. In 1994 the date is Sunday, July 3.

RETIRED LIST - A player who elects to retire may, at the request of the Club, be placed on the Retired Players List.

SUSPENSION LIST - A player who violates his contract with the Club may, upon application by the Club to the Commissioner, be placed on the League Suspension List.

DISABLED LIST - A player who is judged unfit to play for reasons other than a football related injury may, at the request of the Club, be placed on the Disabled List.

COLLEGE DRAFT - The annual draft of Canadian players graduating from universities in Canada and the United States.

GRADUATING JUNIOR - A junior player who attains the age of 23 during the current calendar year.

ROOKIE - A player who has not been named on any CFL Club's active roster, reserve, injured or disabled list, or the equivalent category of a team in any other professional league at the time a game was played in a previous season.

NEGOTIATION LIST - A Club may claim exclusive negotiation rights to a specified number of players on its Negotiation List, and may make changes daily.

INJURED LIST - A player who has been injured may, at the request of the Club, be placed on the Injured Players List for a minimum period of 30 days or for one game after clearing waivers while identified as "injured".

TIE-BREAKING PROCEDURE

The top four teams in each Division will qualify for post-season play.

NOTE: When two or more member Clubs are tied in the final Division standings at the conclusion of the regular season schedule preferential ranking for playoff purposes shall be determined on the basis of the following priorities and shall be awarded to the club which

a) has won the greater number of games played against the other tied Club(s), or
b) has scored the higher net aggregate of points (i.e. points scored for less points scored against) in games played against the other tied Club(s), or
c) has scored the higher net quotient of points (i.e. points scored for divided by points scored against) in games played against the other tied Clubs(s), or
d) has won the greater number of games (or percentage of games) played against all member Clubs of the Division, or
e) has scored the higher net aggregate of points in games played against all member Clubs of the Division, or
f) has scored the higher net quotient of points in games played against all member Clubs of the Division, or
g) has won the greater number of games played against all member Clubs of the League, or
h) has scored the higher net aggregate of points in games played against all member Clubs of the League, or
i) has scored the higher net quotient of points in games played against all member Clubs of the League.

STATISTICAL AND SCORING RULES

SECTION 1 - FIRST DOWNS

A first down shall be recorded whenever the yardsticks are ordered forward by the officials on a sequence of downs, whenever a touchdown is scored on an offensive play from scrimmage, and whenever a gain from scrimmage is made on the last play in a half that would have resulted in a first down being awarded had time not run out. However a first down shall not be awarded when a team first gains possession as a result of a kick, a fumble, a pass interception, or a penalty.

First downs gained are subdivided to show the type of play responsible for the gain, as follows:

(a) *By Rushing* - means that the play that resulted in a new first down being awarded was a rushing play, even though a different type of play may have accounted for most of the yardage in that series of downs.

(b) *By Passing* - means that the play that resulted in a new first down being awarded was a passing play, even though a different type of play may have accounted for most of the yardage in that series of downs.

(c) *By Penalty* - means that the yardsticks were ordered forward as a result of the application of penalty.

SECTION 2 - TOTAL OFFENCE

(a) Total Offence represents the aggregate of all net gains from scrimmage, and includes the following:

(1) Net yards on rushing plays where the gains and losses are chargeable to individual players. (See section 3)

(2) Net yards on passing plays. (See section 4)

(3) Yardage losses chargeable against the team record but not against individual players. (See section 5)

(b) Total plays from scrimmage consists of all plays where a team puts the ball into play by a scrimmage, including those nullified by penalty, and including convert attempts.

SECTION 3 - RUSHING PLAYS

(a) Every play from scrimmage is to be ruled as a rushing play except:

(1) A passing play as described in Section 4, or

(2) A team loss play as described in Section 5, or

(3) A kicking play as described in Section 8.

(b) Rushing yardage is measured from the line of scrimmage to the point where the ball is declared dead, or is recovered by the opponents in the case of a fumble.

(c) The rushing total is a net figure. All rushing losses must be recorded to account for the net figure. Such losses will also be taken into account in determining the rushing records of individual players.

(d) The player charged with the carry will be the player who carries the ball across the line of scrimmage, or is the man responsible for a fumble, or the man in possession, whichever is applicable, when the play is stopped behind the line of scrimmage.

(e) All gains on lateral passes which originated or grew out of a rushing play are included in rushing yardage. (See Section 7)

SECTION 4 - FORWARD PASS PLAYS

(a) Forward passing gains or losses are measured from the scrimmage line to the point where the ball is declared dead or is recovered by opponents in the case of a fumble. Both the length of the pass and the running advance after completion are included in the total gain. All yards gained or lost on a completed pass play are credited to both the passer and receiver.

(b) The passer is charged with all forward passes thrown by him whether complete or incomplete, EXCEPTING those on which an interference penalty is called. It will also include all passes intercepted. Those passes ruled as intentionally grounded will be recorded under penalties, under team losses and under quarterback sacks but the yardage lost will be recorded only under team losses.

(c) If the passer has commenced his forward throwing motion with the ball moving forward and he is contacted with the ball becoming loose, the play will be regarded as an incomplete forward pass unless the Referee rules the play to be a fumble.

(d) The receiver is credited only with the number of passes caught and total yards gained. Where a pass is touched by two receivers the player making the final catch will be credited.

e.g. - Team A has ball on 30 yard line. Quarterback passes to A1 on 40 yard line who tips the ball forward to A2 on the 43 yard line. The referee will declare the pass complete on the 43 and A2 shall be credited with the catch.

(e) Loss from a completed forward pass play which did not advance to the line of scrimmage is a yardage charge against both the passer and receiver.

(f) A passer is not a passer until he throws the ball, so, if he is caught behind the line of scrimmage it is either a loss by rushing under Section 3 or a team loss under Section 5.

(g) There is no pass completed by penalty. A gain through interference on a passing play is a penalty against the defending team. The passer is not charged with a pass attempt nor credited with a completion or the yards gained, nor is the intended receiver credited with a pass caught. The passing team is credited only with a first down gained by penalty. The defending team is charged with a penalty, and the distance from the line of scrimmage to the penalty spot is recorded under Yards Lost Penalties.

(h) Great care must be taken to distinguish between forward passes behind the line of scrimmage and lateral passes behind the line of scrimmage. Since there is no distinction under the playing rules, other than the eligibility of the receiver, there will be no ruling by the referee unless such pass falls incomplete. If he waves it incomplete, it was a forward, if he declares it a free ball it was a lateral.

SECTION 5 - TEAM LOSSES

This category covers yardage losses suffered by a team which are not chargeable against the rushing records of individual players, or the team's rushing or passing records for that game. Such losses are, however, included in determining a team's total offence for the game and the season.

The following are examples of losses which belong in this category:

(a) A player drops back or rolls out with the intention of throwing a pass, but is thrown for a loss before he can get the pass away. Where, however, upon finding his receivers covered he makes a positive attempt to run with the ball, as distinct from taking normal evasive action, any such loss incurred will be treated as an ordinary rushing loss under Section 3. In case of doubt, rule as a team loss.

(b) Team A has 3rd down on its own 20, and is in punt formation. The would-be kicker catches the ball and retreats behind his goal-line to concede a safety touch. The 20 yard loss will be charged to the player under team losses.

(c) Similar situation as above, the centre makes a wild snap and the ball goes into the end zone where it is recovered by either team. The centre will be charged with a fumble and the 20 yard loss will be charged to him under team losses.

(d) A third down kick is blocked and recovered by either team 10 yards behind the line of scrimmage. In this case the kicker is charged with a fumble and the 10 yard loss is charged to him under team losses.

(e) When a quarterback voluntarily drops to one knee and concedes yards in an effort to run out the clock, the yards lost will be charged to him under Team Losses.

Note - No quarterback sack will be given in this situation.

(f) Team A scrimmages on its own 25 yard line. Team A quarterback drops back to pass, but is tackled on the Team A 20 before he can throw the ball.

Note - The Team A quarterback is charged with a Team Loss of 5 yards.

(g) Same situation as (f). Team A quarterback fumbles the ball while attempting to handoff to the Team A running back. The ball is finally recovered by Team B on the Team A 20 yard line.

Note - The Team A quarterback is charged with a fumble, fumble lost and a Team Loss of 5 yards.

(h) Team A kicker stands on Team A 10 yard line to receive the ball from centre. Instead of kicking the ball, he retreats into the Team A end zone to run out the clock, and eventually runs over the dead ball line conceding a safety.

Note - The Team A kicker is charged with a Team Loss of 10 yards from the line of scrimmage to the goal line. The other distance he retreated into the end zone shall be disregarded.

SECTION 6 - INTERCEPTION RETURNS

(a) Runbacks on interception of forward passes shall be measured from the point of interception to the point where the ball is declared dead, or is recovered by opponents in case of a fumble. Such gains are, of course, *not* included in Yards Gained Passing.

(b) Where a pass is intercepted in the goal area and the interceptor is not successful in running out of the goal area he will still be credited with the yards returned to the point where the ball is declared dead.

SECTION 7 - LATERAL PASSES

(a) A lateral pass is always a component part of the play during which it occurs. The only laterals that are recorded are those that occur -

(1) After a forward pass has been completed.

(2) After the ball crossed the line of scrimmage on a rushing play.

(3) On returns or runbacks of punts, kickoffs, pass interceptions and fumbles.

(b) Pitchouts, handoffs and other laterals behind the line of scrimmage are not recorded.

(c) Examples showing how laterals are recorded:

(1) Player A catches a forward pass for a gain of 10 yards then laterals to B who goes for 5 more. A is credited with a pass caught and 10 yards gained. B is not credited with a catch but is credited with 5 yards gained. The passer is credited with a completed pass and 15 yards gained.

(2) A takes a lateral from the quarterback and crosses the line of scrimmage for a gain of 10 yards, then laterals to B who gains another 5. Player A is charged with a carry and credited with 10 yards gained rushing. B is *not* charged with a carry but is credited with 5 yards.

Note - The gain made by B starts only when he reaches the line where A made the pass. If in Example 2 above A made 10 yards then passed backward to B who was only able to advance within one yard of A, the net gain would be nine yards all of which should be credited to A. B will not be charged with a one-yard loss.

(3) A catches a punt and returns it 10 yards before lateralling to B who goes for another 5. A is charged with a punt return and credited with 10 yards. B is not charged with a punt return but is credited with 5 yards.

(d) Incomplete lateral passes are scored as fumbles and yards lost are charged against the player who, in the statistician's opinion was responsible for the failure of the pass, subject to the provision of Section 5.

(e) Intercepted lateral passes are scored as fumbles and the passer is charged with a fumble lost.

SECTION 8 - KICKING PLAYS

(a) *Kicks that cross line of scrimmage*

1. Punts are measured from the line of scrimmage to the point where the ball is recovered by a player, goes out of bounds, or is otherwise declared dead.
2. If the ball is punted over the goal line the distance into the goal area will be included in the length of the punt.
3. If the receiver touches the ball but it continues to roll past him, the point of ultimate recovery will determine the distance of the punt.
4. Should the receiver lose yards in attempting to run back a kick, his loss will be charged as a loss on punt returns (See Section 10). Where, however, the momentum of the kick forces the receiver backwards, such yardage lost in this manner will be added to the length of the kick. In cases where a receiver concedes a rouge by running back across the deadline, the kick will be measured only to the point possession was gained by the receiver.
5. If the receiver should kick the ball back to his opponents this will count as a punt and will be measured from the point of kick. This does not apply to dribbled balls which are dealt with in Section 11 on fumbles.
6. If the kicker should recover his own kick, or another onside player of his team should do so, the kick will count as a punt, and the yardage measured to the point of recovery. Yards gained subsequent to the recovery will be recorded separately under Own Punts Recovered.
7. An attempted field goal which fails to score becomes a punt and is subject to the section. For individual record purposes, however, unsuccessful field goal attempts are recorded separately from normal punts.
8. Punts partially blocked that cross the line of scrimmage are treated as ordinary punts.
9. An attempted punt which fails for any reason to cross the line of scrimmage will not be recorded as a punt since it could still evolve into a rushing or passing play. See Subsection 8(b).
10. Distance of successful field goals are recorded on the scoring summary.

(b) *Kicks that do not cross scrimmage line*

1. If a kicker should attempt a kick from scrimmage and the ball fails to cross the line of scrimmage, this will not count as a punt but will be considered the same as a lateral pass behind the line of scrimmage. If legally recovered by a player on the kicker's side the eventual outcome of the play will determine the way it should be recorded, that is, if a forward pass is thrown it will become a passing play; otherwise, it is a rushing play.
2. If recovered by the defending side, the kicker will be charged with a fumble lost and the yards lost from the line of scrimmage to the point of recovery will be charged as a team loss.

3. If a blocked kick is recovered by the kicking team, the kicker will be charged with a fumble. The events after recovery will determine whether the play shall be recorded as a rushing play, passing play, or team loss play.
4. If such blocked kick is recovered by a defending player, the kicker will be charged with a fumble lost. The yards lost from the line of scrimmage to the point of recovery will be charged as a team loss under Section 5. Yards gained by the blocking team after recovery will be recorded under Fumble Returns (section 11).
5. The name of the defending player blocking the kick will be recorded in the space provided on the statistics reporting forms. The type of kick attempt blocked should also be indicated (punt, convert, field goal).

SECTION 9 - KICKOFFS

(a) Kickoffs are measured from the kickoff line to the point of recovery. If kicked over the deadline or out of bounds in the goal area without being touched by any player, the yardage will be recorded in the same manner as a punt into the end zone. If kicked out of bounds in the field of play, the receiving team has the option of taking the ball at that point or having the kickoff repeated. If the receiving team elects to take the ball at the point it went out of bounds, the kickoff shall be recorded to that point and the kicking team charged with a penalty declined. If the kickoff has to be repeated the kicking team will be charged with a penalty of 5 yards.
(b) The same rules for statistics purposes apply to kickoffs that apply to punts.

SECTION 10 - KICK RETURNS

(a) Kick returns are recorded in three separate categories.
(1) Returns of punts; (2) Returns of unsuccessful field goal attempts; (3) Returns of kickoffs.
(b) Kick returns are measured from the point where the receiver gains possession of the ball to the point where the ball is declared dead or is lost by fumble or is kicked back. If the receiver loses yards on a kick return after gaining possession such losses will be charged against his kick return yardage.
(c) When a penalty is called on a kick return for an offense such as clipping or illegal interference, the return will be measured to the point from which the penalty is applied.
(d) A receiver will not be charged with a kick return if he concedes a single point without attempting to advance the ball, or if a penalty is applied from the point he gained possession of the ball, such as a No Yards penalty.
(e) Returns of unsuccessful field goal attempts are to be treated in the same manner as punt returns, since they are identical under the playing rules, but are to be recorded separately from punt returns.

SECTION 11 - FUMBLES

(a) On any play terminated by a fumble the yards gained or lost to the point of recovery are credited or charged to the player who fumbled, regardless of which team recovers the ball. Examples of this type of play are:
(1) Player A carried the ball for five yards, is tackled and then fumbles. The ball goes forward for another three yards and is recovered by the opposition. A is credited with an eight yard gain and charged with a fumble lost.
(2) Same play but ball goes backward three yards and is recovered by a player of A's team. A is credited with a two-yard gain and charged with a fumble recovered.
(b) A player generally should not be charged with a fumble if he recovers the ball himself. However, if it is a flagrant fumble and opposing players have an opportunity to recover it, a fumble should be charged.
(c) The act of merely touching the ball is not necessarily possession. On the greased-pig type of scrambling for a fumbled ball, charge the original player for the fumble and credit the eventual recovery to the man who winds up with the ball. Ignore all momentary touching in between.
(d) The player who fumbles a ball out of bounds is to be charged with a fumble and an own-team-fumble recovery.
(e) Yards gained by a player subsequent to recovery of a team-mate's fumble will remain as part of the play giving rise to the fumble, and will be regarded as the nature of a gain after a lateral pass.(See Section 7). However the player recovering such fumble will also be credited under Own Fumbles Recovered on the statistics reportform.
(f) Yards gained by a player subsequent to recovery of an opposition fumble is covered under Fumble Returns. (Section 12).
(g) When a player fumbles the ball and it is recovered by another player of the same team the continuing action shall be regarded as part of the same play leading up to the fumble. For Example:
(1) Team A running back carries the ball for 10 yards, fumbles and it is recovered by a Team A lineman who then carries the ball for 7 more yards before the play is stopped.
Note - This was a 17 yard rushing play. The running back is charged with 1 carry for 10 yards while the lineman is not charged with a carry, but is given credit for 7 yards rushing.
(2) Team A has the ball on Team B's 30 yard line. Team A quarterback throws a pass to the Team A receiver, who carries the ball to the Team B five yard line where he fumbles. The ball continues on into the Team B end zone where it is fallen on by a Team A player.
Note - Team A quarterback is credited with a completed TD pass for 30 yards. The receiver is credited with a catch for 30 yards, but no TD. The Team A player who recovered the ball is credited with a TD receiving, but with no catch or yards.
(3) Team A punts to Team B on third down. The Team B player returns the ball for 10 yards, fumbles and the ball is picked up by another Team B player who carries it for 15 more yards.
Note - The Team B punt return is 25 yards. The first Team B player is credited with a return and 10 yards. The second Team B player is not credited with a return, but is credited with 15 yards.

SECTION 12 - FUMBLE RETURNS

(a) This category deals with the recovery and returns of opposition fumbles including these situations:
(1) Yards gained following recovery of a blocked punt or field goal attempt.
(2) Yards gained following interception of a lateral pass.
(b) Fumble returns are measured from the point of recovery to the point the play becomes dead or possession is lost on a subsequent fumble.
(c) Dribbling a loose ball downfield will be considered a fumble return.

SECTION 13 - PENALTIES

(a) Five items are recorded with regard to penalties:
(1) Times Penalized; (2) Yards Penalized; (3) First Downs Gained by Penalties; (4) Penalties Declined By; (5) Gains Forfeited on Penalties.
(b) Times Penalized include those penalties declined by the opposition, double penalties against both teams which are often cancelled out against each other, and multiple penalties called against one team on a single play.
(c) Yards Penalized are measured from the point of penalty to the point where the ball is next put into play.
(d) Refer to Section 1 for treatment of first downs gained by penalties.
(e) Gains Forfeited on Penalties are the yardage gains which would normally be recorded in total offence categories and have been nullified by application of a penalty.

SECTION 14 - SCORING PLAYS

(a) Touchdowns (six points) will be credited to the player scoring it. Yardage gained on a scrimmage play, or the return of a punt, kickoff, interception, or fumble which resulted in the score will also be recorded in the appropriate category.
(b) Converts or Points-After-Touchdown will be credited to the player completing the play. They may be scored in three ways:
(1) By kicking a field goal, in which case the kicker receives credit for one point.
(2) By completing a forward pass, in which case the receiver gets credit for two points. The pass attempt and yards gained will be included in the game totals for passing and in the individual records of the passer and receiver.
(3) By carrying the ball across the goal line. The ball carrier will be credited with two points as well as with the yards gained rushing.
(4) A defensive player may score a two-point convert by legally gaining possession of the ball and advancing it across his opponent's goal line. The yardage gained or lost will be recorded in the appropriate category (unsuccessful field goal return, interception return and/or fumble return).
(c) Field goal (three points) is credited to the kicker. The yardage on successful field goals is recorded from the point the ball was held to the goal line.
(d) Safety Touch (two points) is credited as a team score only and no individual credit is to be given to any player.
(e) Single (one point) is credited to the player who kicked the ball across the goal line.
(f) When a score is made on the final play of any quarter, it shall be timed at 15:00.

SECTION 15 - GOAL AREA

Distance into the goal area is measured only in the following circumstances:
(1) Team A kicks the ball into the goal area where it is recovered by Team B receiver 10 yards deep. The 10 yards is included in the total length of the punt or kickoff measured from the line of scrimmage or the line of kickoff.
(2) In the above example, Team B receiver runs the ball out of the end zone to his own 5 yard line. He is credited with a kick return of 15 yards.
(3) In the same example, Team B receiver immediately concedes a single point. He shall not be charged with a return.
(4) In the same example, Team B receiver runs around in the end zone and eventually concedes a single point. In this case, he shall be charged with a return and the yards gained or lost since he gained possession of the ball.

SECTION 16 - QUARTERBACK SACKS

Whenever the Team A quarterback is tackled with the ball in his possession behind the line of scrimmage for a loss of yardage, Team B or an individual Team B player shall be credited with a quarterback sack as follows:
(a) SOLO SACK - means the player tackled the quarterback behind the line of scrimmage and prevented him from passing the ball resulting in a loss of yardage under Team Losses. The yards lost shall also be credited to the Team B player.
(b) TEAM SACKS - If two or more players are equally responsible for the sack, no individual credit will be given and the team will be credited with the sack.

If a Team A player other than the quarterback is attempting to pass but is tackled behind the line of scrimmage with the ball in his possession for a yardage loss the play will not be regarded as a sack.

A quarterback sack does not necessarily have to relate to a Team Loss.

SECTION 17 - DRIBBLED BALL

A dribbled ball occurs when the ball is kicked while not in the possession or control of a player, i.e. a loose ball following a fumble, a blocked kick, a kickoff or a kick from scrimmage. Such a dribbled ball may be legally touched or recovered by the kicker or an onside player.

Net yards gained or lost, or points scored will be recorded in the same manner as the play in which the dribbing occurred.

SECTION 18 - TACKLES

Whenever a player is tackled with the ball in his possession, only one opponent shall be credited with a solo tackle. Tackles will be recorded on all plays. Defensive and Special Teams tackles will be recorded separately. The yards lost shall be credited to the player making the tackle and will be identified as a Tackle for Loss.

SECTION 19 - RATINGS

Rushing Average Leaders are based on a minimum of 10 carries in a game, 100 for a season and 500 for a career.

Pass Reception Average Leaders are based on a minimum of 3 catches in a game, times the number of games played in a season by a team in season and 200 catches for a career.

Punting Average Leaders are based on a minimum of 5 punts in a game, 100 for a season and 1,000 for a career.

Passing Percentage Leaders based on a minimum of 20 passes per game for a single game, a season and a career.

Passing Efficiency Leaders based on a minimum of 20 passes per game, 300 passes for a season and 2,000 passes for a career.

SECTION 20 - NET PUNTING AVERAGE

Net Punting Average shall be calculated by dividing the total number of punt attempts into the total number of punting yards, minus the punt return yards. Leaders are based on 5 punt attempts in a game, 100 for a season and 1,000 for a career.

1994 CANADIAN FOOTBALL HALL OF FAME INDUCTEES

Bill Baker - Player

Born on April 23, 1945 in Sheridan, Manitoba. Baker participated in high school football at Notre Dame College in Wilcox and with the Scott Collegiate "Blues" in Regina. He played junior football with the Regina Rams in 1963 while still eligible to play at the high school level. He attended Otterbein College in Ohio on a football scholarship, majoring in Political Schience, and for four years was a member of the first team at the offensive and defensive tackle and linebacker positions. He was an Ohio Conference All-Star in his junior and senior years and was voted MVP in 1967.

Baker joined the Saskatchewan Roughriders of the Canadian Football League in 1968 and remained with the squad until '73. In 1974, he was part of a three-team trade involving Toronto and B.C., ending up with the Lions, where he stayed through the '76 season. He returned to Saskatchewan in 1977 via a pre-season trade for Frank Landy and Jesse O'Neal and retired following the '78 season, playing a career total 174 games.

Baker's credo was "Your opponents are only as tough as you let them be" and throughout his career, "The Undertaker" was known for his ferocious pass rush. A Baker forearm to the head was respected by his teammates during practice, but especially by the opposing quarterbacks who came within range.

In December 1988, Bill Baker was named the CFL's President and Chief Operating Officer in Toronto, serving for one year.

His awards and honours included being named the Schenley Outstanding Defensive Player in 1976, winner of the Dr. Beattie Martin Trophy as the Outstanding Canadian Player in the West in 1976, winner of the Norm Fieldgate Trophy as the Outstanding Defensive Player in the West in 1975 and '76, All-Western All-Star defensive end in 1971, '72, '73, '75, '76 and CFL All-Star in 1972, '73, '75, '76. Baker also participated in the 1969 and '72 Grey Cup Championships and was inducted to the Saskatchewan Roughriders' Plaza of Honour.

Tom Clements - Player

Born on June 18, 1953 at McKees Rocks, Pennsylvania. For three years, Clements was the starting quarterback at the University of Notre Dame. He was selected All-American three times and was fourth in the balloting for the Heisman Trophy.

Clements began his Canadian professional career with the Ottawa Rough Riders of the CFL, playing with the club from 1975 to '78. In early '79, he was traded to the Saskatchewan Roughriders for Steve Dennis, Bob O'Doherty and a 1980 draft choice. In September '79, he was traded to the Hamilton Tiger-Cats for Lawrie Skolrood and future considerations. He spent 1980 with the Kansas City Chiefs of the NFL, but played sparingly, and requested his release. He re-signed with Hamilton in April, 1981 and stayed until he was traded to the Winnipeg Blue Bombers for quarterback Dieter Brock in September '83. He was sidelined with a shoulder separation nine games into the '86 season, but returned to championship form the following year. Clements provided outstanding leadership on and off the field until his retirement after the 1987 season.

Clements had a career total 2,807 completions out of 4,657 attempts for 39,041 years, 252 TDs and a 60.3% completion rate. He led his division in attempts and completions in 1981 and '82 and the League leader in 1987, when he also had the most passing yardage. He holds the League record for best pass completion average for one season with 67.58% in 1986.

He participated in the Grey Cup game in 1976 and '84, being victorious on both occasions, and in each game, was selected the Outstanding Offensive Player. His awards in the CFL include: All-Eastern All-Star in 1975, '76, '77, '79, '81; All-Western All-Star in 1984 and '87; CFL All-Star in 1984 and '87; winner of the Most Outstanding Player Award in 1987, Runner-up as the League's Outstanding Player Award in 1981 and 1987, and runner-up as the CFL Rookie of the Year in 1975.

Gene Gaines - Player

Born on June 26, 1938 in Los Angeles, California. Gaines attended L.A. Jordan High School then studied at UCLA, playing football under the direction of coach Bill Barnes. He was drafted by both San Diego Chargers and Pittsburgh Steelers, but he and teammate Marv Luster opted for careers in Canada.

Gaines began his Canadian professional career with the Montreal Alouettes in 1961. He was the starting wing back on offence and a defensive halfback. In 1962, he was traded to the Ottawa Rough Riders for Angelo Mosca, and remained in the nation's capital through the '69 season. In Ottawa, he played offensive and defensive halfback and was considered the "quarterback" on defence. Away from the gridiron, he taught in an Ottawa school.

Gaines played out his option in Ottawa and returned to the Alouettes in 1970, via a trade for Rod Woodward and John Kruspe, to play defensive back and become Montreal's defensive backfield coach. Many credit Gaines' hard work on and off the field for the Alouettes' Grey Cup victory in 1970, a rebuilding year. In '73, he was sidelined by a leg fracture, but returned to form in '74 and continued in the dual role of player/coach through the 1976 season.

Gaines played 217 games, 161 of them consecutive, over a 16-season period. Among his statistics, he intercepted 42 opposition passes for 679 yards and had 14 fumble recoveries for 44 yards. In the playoffs, Gaines had 429 kickoff return yards, 237 of those in 1964 alone. He holds the CFL record for the longest kickoff return with a 128-yard run for an Ottawa touchdown in the November 14, 1964 final against Hamilton.

In total, he appeared in six Grey Cup championships, three with each club. The Rough Riders were victorious in 1968 and '69; while the Alouettes won the national championship in '70 and '74.

Gaines was named an All-Eastern linebacker in 1963, All-Eastern defensive back in '65, '66, '67 and '71, and a CFL All-Star DB in '65, '66 and '67. He was also the recipient of the Jeff Russel Memorial Trophy in 1966 as the Eastern Division's Most Outstanding Player.

Since 1977, Gene Gaines has coached defence with Montreal Alouettes, Edmonton Eskimos, Los Angeles Express (USFL), Houston Oilers (NFL), Winnipeg Blue Bombers, and joined the B.C. Lions' coaching staff in 1991.

Donald W. McNaughton - Builder

Born in Montreal, Quebec and is a graduate of Loyola College. He has been a member of the Board of Governors for Loyola College and is Past-President of the Loyola Alumni Association. He is a former Director of the Montreal Sportsmen's Association and a former Director of the Cerebral Palsy Association of B.C.

Following graduation, McNaughton was employed by Trans Canada Airlines. From 1957-63, he worked for Carling in advertising, public relations and sales for the Montreal and Quebec City regions. In 1963, he joined Canadian Schenley Distilleries as Director of Advertising, a position which included the duties of Awards Coordinator for the Schenley Football Awards. The Schenley Football Awards, presented at both the professional and amateur levels, symbolized excellence in football from 1953 until 1988. He was the coordinator of the awards from '63 to '66.

McNaughton moved to Vancouver in 1966 and the following year, became General Manager of Park-Tilford, a Schenley subsidiary. In 1969, he was appointed President of Park-Tilford and also became President and Chief Executive Officer of Canadian Schenley. In his capacity as President and CEO, and later as Chairman, he met annually with the Board of Trustees and the Awards Coordinator to discuss policy and finance, and to ensure the continued growth of the Awards.

McNaughton, noted for his creative, analytical mind, devoted considerable time to the Awards. He travelled across the country discussing the concept with knowledgable football people, both at the club level and in the private sector. Over the years, he increased the involvement duties of the Board of Trustees of the Awards and set guidelines for the continuing improvements of every aspect of the awards procedure. The Schenley Awards quickly became an eagerly awaited event during the Grey Cup Week festivities.

From 1969 through '88, Donald W. McNaughton presented the Most Outstanding Player Award to the Canadian Football League's finest participant, and he is respected nationally for his hard work and devotion to the Schenley Football Awards.

CANADIAN FOOTBALL HALL OF FAME

(* - deceased)

The list of those honoured in the Canadian Football Hall of Fame presently is now at 168 (53 Builders and 115 Players) since charter membership to the Hall occurred on June 19, 1963.

The Canadian Football Hall of Fame and Museum officially opened on November 28, 1972. Conveniently located next to City Hall in downtown Hamilton, the Canadian Football Hall of Fame and Museum is open from Monday to Saturday year-round from 9:30 a.m to 4:30 p.m. From June to November, it is open on Sundays from noon to 4:30 p.m. There is a small admission fee.

Directions to the Hall are as follows: from Toronto, take the QEW to Highway 403 to the Main Street East off ramp and proceed one mile east to City Hall Plaza; from Niagara Falls, take the QEW, cross the Skyway Bridge, take 403 to Main Street East to City Hall Plaza.

Commissioner Larry Smith is Chairman of The Canadian Football Hall of Fame Selection Committee and Ed Chalupka and Janice Smith are the Secretaries. Others on the Hall's Selection Committee are: Jim Coleman (Vancouver), Johnny Esaw (Toronto), Ralph Sazio (Burlington), Bryan Hall (Edmonton), John Lynch (Regina), Jack Matheson (Winnipeg), Russ Jackson (Mississauga), Doug Mitchell (Calgary), Terry Kielty (Ottawa), Paul Dojack (Regina), Jim Taylor (Vancouver), John Michaluk (Hamilton) and Greg Fulton (Toronto).

Here is a look at inductees in The Canadian Football Hall of Fame:

ATCHISON, RON, Elected as a Player, June 24, 1978. He starred with the Saskatchewan Roughriders from 1952 to 1968, earning All-Western All-Star honours at Middle Guard in 1956, 1960, 1961, 1962 and 1963 plus All-Western All-Star Defensive Tackle in 1964.

***BACK, LEONARD P.,** Elected as a Builder, November 25, 1971. A head injury in 1919 curtailed his playing to two seasons with the Hamilton Tiger Juniors but he returned to become manager of that team in 1920. Back became synonymous with Hamilton football clubs managing Junior, Intermediate, Senior and Pro teams in his native Hamilton.

BAILEY, BYRON L. BY, Elected as a Player, June 28, 1975. Recruited by Annis Stukus, By Bailey was with the B.C. Lions when they debuted in the CFL in 1954, scored their first TD and starred for eight seasons at Fullback and three more at Defensive Back for them.

***BAILEY, HAROLD,** Elected as a Builder, November 25, 1965. For 30 years he served as Secretary-Treasurer of the Ontario Rugby Football Union; he was President of the Canadian Rugby Football Union in 1941 and member of the CRU Rules Committee from 1931 through 1950. As head of the ORFU during the Second World War, he kept football alive in difficult days.

***BALLARD, HAROLD E.,** Elected as a Builder, May 2, 1987. The President and majority shareholder of Maple Leaf Gardens Limited purchased the Hamilton Tiger-Cats in 1978, keeping the strong tradition of pro football in that City. Also a member of the Hockey Hall of Fame.

BARROW, JOHN, Elected as a Player August 5, 1976. In 14 years with the Tiger-Cats he earned All-Star status 16 times because for four consecutive years (1957-8-9-60) he was an All-Star Tackle on offence and defence. He helped Hamilton to nine Grey Cup Games and in 1962 he was selected as the CFL's top lineman.

***BATSTONE, HARRY L,** Elected as a Player, June 19, 1963. Of medium height and only 155 pounds, he was nonetheless a triple threat Halfback who could run and kick. He and Lionel Conacher made the end run play a success especially in winning the first East-West Grey Cup Game in 1921 when the Argonauts beat Edmonton. Later at Queen's, Batstone starred often through a string of 26 consecutive victories which included three Grey Cups in a row.

***BEACH, ORMOND,** Elected as a Player, June 19, 1963. A great Fullback and Linebacker, The Sarnia Imperials watched him lead them to four Senior ORFU titles from 1934 to 1937 plus two Grey Cup Championships.

***BERGER, SAMUEL,** Elected posthumously as a Builder on June 26, 1993. He was President and Director of the Ottawa Football Club which won the Grey Cup Championship on four occasions. Sold his interest in the Ottawa team and purchased the Montreal Alouettes in 1969. He revitalized the team which won the Grey Cup in 1970, 1974 and 1977. He was President of the CFL in 1964 and 1971 and was instrumental in drafting the League's first T.V. contract.

BOX, AB, Elected as a Player, November 25, 1965. A tremendous Halfback who could run as well and punt 60 yards often, he starred for Balmy Beach and the Argos, winning the Jeff Russel Trophy in 1934.

***BREEN, JOSEPH M.,** Elected as a Player, June 19, 1963. After scoring football playing honours with the University of Toronto, Parkdale Canoe Club and the Argos, he coached the University of Western Ontario to its first Intercollegiate football championship in 1931. A member of the Canadian Sports Hall of Fame.

***BRIGHT, JOHNNY,** Elected as a Player, November 26, 1970. This powerful Fullback gained 10,909 yards in 13 CFL seasons with Calgary and Edmonton. He was top rusher in the West four times; a Western All-Star seven times and the Most Outstanding Player in the CFL once and along with Jackie Parker and Normie Kwong, Bright and the Eskimo backfielders charged to three straight Grey Cup wins in the mid-1950's.

***BROOK, T.L. TOM,** Elected as a Builder, June 28, 1975. He vetoed a CRU movement to establish a two-game Grey Cup series and he strongly emerged as one of the first to push the interlocking schedule. Brook kept the Calgary Stampeders alive in low times in 1948 and that club responded with a 12-0 record in 1948, another two wins and a tie in the playoffs plus 10 straight wins in 1949 for a 25-game unbeaten streak.

***BROWN, D. WES,** Elected as a Builder, June 19, 1963. For more than 40 years he served as the Director of the Ottawa Football Club. He was Director, Treasurer and Secretary with Ottawa and became Secretary of the CFL's Eastern section in 1948.

BROWN, TOM, Elected as a Player, April 3, 1984. Although a neck injury ended his career, for five years he starred for the B.C. Lions playing Middle Guard, Linebacker and Defensive End. Twice he was the CFL's Lineman of the Year with Schenley Awards; he was an All-Canadian and an All-Western All-Star three times as the Lions made two Grey Cup appearances during his time, winning in 1964.

CASEY, TOM (CITATION), Elected as a Player, November 26, 1964. Enjoyed a splendid CFL career, with the Hamilton Wildcats (1940) and the Winnipeg Blue Bombers (1950-55), earning All-Western All-Star honours at Running Back three times and Defensive Back three times.

CHARLTON, KENNETH (KEN), Elected as a player on October 24, 1992. The Regina native joined the Roughriders in 1941, only to spend the next two years playing for military teams due to the Second World War. Following the War, he played in both Regina and Ottawa until he retired at the conclusion of the 1954 season. He earned All-Star honours in 1941, 1945, 1946, 1948 and 1949 at flying wing, running back and halfback.

CHIPMAN, ARTHUR, Elected as a Builder, November 28, 1969. Helped save the game during the Second World War Years in the West, he joined the executive of the Winnipeg Football Club in 1936 and was President from 1944 to 1948. In 1949, he was President of the Western Interprovincial Rugby Union and, in 1952, he was President of the Canadian Rugby Union.

CLAIR, FRANK, Elected as a Builder, January 6, 1981. He came to Canada in 1950 and started with a Grey Cup victory with the Argos. The professor coached in five more Grey Cup Games after that, winning four of those to tie Lew Hayman's Grey Cup record of five all-time victories. He won 174 games in 19 years as a Coach before retiring in 1969 with a Grey Cup victory with Ottawa.

COFFEY, TOMMY JOE, Elected as a Player, June 25, 1977. Seven times an All-Canadian All-Star, four times an Eastern All-Star and three times a Western All-Star, the Pass Receiver-Kicker finished with 10,320 yards on pass receptions and 971 points. After two seasons with Edmonton, T.J. left football in 1961 but returned to shine for the Eskimos (1962-66), Hamilton (1967-72) and Toronto (1973) before retiring in 1973.

***CONACHER, LIONEL,** Elected as a Player, June 19, 1963. Acclaimed as Canada's greatest all-round athlete and football player of the 1900-1950 era. The unbelievable Back not only tasted Grey Cup victory but he also played on two Stanley Cup teams and played professionally in five different sports. In the Argos' 23-0 Grey Cup victory over Edmonton in 1921, The Big Train, as he was known, scored 15 points.

COOPER, RALPH W., Elected as a builder on October 24, 1992. The Hamilton native was responsible for merging the Hamilton Tigers and the Hamilton Wildcats into the Hamilton Tiger-Cats. He served as Club President, was a member of the Board of Directors and served on the team's Board of Governors. Was a member of the committee responsible for recommending a draft system for university players. Helped devise the interlocking schedule which still stands today.

COPELAND, ROYAL, Elected as a Player on March 5, 1988. Played from 1944 to 1956. He and Joe Krol were known as the Gold Dust Twins during their days with the Argos. An Eastern All-Star Running Back in 1945-46-47-49 and Jeff Russel Memorial Trophy winner in 1949. Only player to score a TD in 3 consecutive Grey Cup games.

CORRIGALL, JIM, Elected as a player on April 28, 1990. He played his entire career (1970 to 1981) with the Toronto Argonauts. Corrigall was an Eastern All-Star as a Defensive End eight times and was also honoured four times as a CFL All-Star. His best season was in 1975, when he was chosen the Most Outstanding Defensive Player in the League and was the Argonauts' nominee for Most Outstanding Player and Canadian.

***COX, ERNEST,** Elected as a Player, June 19, 1963. Many regarded him as the greatest Snapback (Centre) in the late 1920s. He was the first winner of the Jeff Russel Memorial Trophy and a member of the Hamilton Tigers' Grey Cup squads in 1928, 1929 and 1932.

***CRAIG, ROSS,** Elected as a Player, November 26, 1964. A powerful lineman who scored consistently as a ball carrier he played from 1906 to 1920 beginning in his native Peterborough and on to Dundas, Hamilton Rowing Club, Hamilton Alerts and Hamilton Tigers. He scored 15 points in the 1913 Grey Cup Game.

***CRIGHTON, HECTOR NAISMITH HEC,** Elected as a Builder August 17, 1985. Crighton was elected to the Canadian Rugby Union Rules Committee in 1947 and five years later rewrote their rules. He is best remembered as the author of the revised Intercollegiate Rule Book, development of the College Bowl and the Hec Crighton Trophy presented annually to the Most Outstanding Canadian Intercollegiate football player.

***CRONIN, CARL,** Elected as a Player, November 30, 1967. The first American import brought into Winnipeg in 1932, this excellent Passer and hard-hitting Linebacker was a fiery leader. As a playing-Coach in 1933, he led Winnipeg to the Western Canadian title. He later served as Coach of the Calgary Bronks and made them a gritty club, typical of his character.

***CURRIE, ANDREW,** Elected as a Builder, May 6, 1974. This distinguished player and high school football Coach eventually launched a successful career in Officials' Associations in Manitoba and B.C. He served on the CFL's Rules Committee from 1957 to 1970. In 1965 he was named Chairman of a sub-committee of the Rules Committee and was responsible for revising and rewriting the rule book which was adopted in 1967.

***CUTLER, WES,** Elected as a Player, November 28, 1968. An All-Star End from 1933 to 1938, he assisted the Argos to Grey Cup wins in 1933, 1937 and 1938. He won the Jeff Russel Trophy in 1938.

DALLA RIVA, PETER, Elected as a player on June 26, 1993. He played 14 seasons with the Montreal Alouettes from 1968 to 1981. This tight end led the team in receiving 5 seasons and is the franchise's all-time leader in TD catches; 2nd in receptions and yardage; 3rd in TDs scored and 5th in scoring. His play earned him All-Star honours in 1972, 1975 and 1976 and All-Canadian honours in 1972, 1973 and 1975. He played in six Grey Cup games, winning three. The Montreal franchise retired his number 74 in 1981.

***DAVIES, DR. ANDREW P.,** Elected as a Builder, November 28, 1969. A player with McGill and Ottawa, he served as player, Officer and Physician of the Ottawa Club from 1915 to 1948. In 1940, he served as President of the Canadian Rugby Union.

***DeGRUCHY, JOHN,** Elected as a Builder, June 19, 1963. Until his death in 1940, he served football in many capacities for half a century. President of the Canadian Rugby Union in 1925, 1930 and 1935, he was father of the Toronto city series between the Argos, Varsity and Balmy Beach.

***DIXON, GEORGE,** Elected as a Player, May 6, 1974. Winner of the Schenley Award as the CFL's Most Outstanding Player in 1962, he averaged 6.3 yards per carry in seven seasons with the Montreal Alouettes. Following a series of injuries, this dynamic Running Back retired in 1965.

DOJACK, PAUL, Elected as a Builder, June 24, 1978. He ended a 23-year Officiating career in 1970. During his time, Dojack worked in 15 Grey Cup Games, eight as the Referee including back-to-back assignments as Referee, the first time the tradition of alternating between an Easterner and a Westerner had been broken.

***DUGGAN, ERIC WILWIN THOMAS (ECK),** Elected as a Builder, January 6, 1981. Involved in Canadian football for close to 60 years, he Quarterbacked and later served on the executive of the Edmonton Eskimos, officiated in a Grey Cup Game, served as President of the CFL and virtually provided his services to many other areas of foot- ball.

***DuMOULIN, SEPPI,** Elected as a Builder, June 19, 1963. As a Backfielder for the Hamilton Tigers (1894 to 1906) and later Coach of Hamilton and Winnipeg teams he went on to serve football for close to 70 years. It was, he said, for the love of football that he gave the sport so much of his life.

***ELIOWITZ, ABE,** Elected as a Player, November 28, 1969. The first Ottawa player to win the Jeff Russel Trophy, this Fullback-Halfback was four times an All-Star with Ottawa in 1934 and 1935 along with Montreal in 1936 and 1937.

***EMERSON, E.K. EDDIE,** Elected as a Player, November 27, 1963. He served the Ottawa Football Club as a player for 23 seasons (1912 to 1937) and was President of the Rough Riders in 1930-31 along with 1947-48-49-50-51.

ETCHEVERRY, SAM, Elected as a Player, November 28, 1969. The Rifle, as he was known, set assorted passing records in nine seasons with the Montreal Alouettes. In seven years of recorded statistics, he passed for 25,582 yards and 174 touchdowns, winning the Schenley Award in 1954 and the Jeff Russel Trophy in 1954 and 1958.

EVANSHEN, TERRY, Elected as a Player, March 16, 1984. This sure-handed Wide Receiver, Split End and Flanker spent 14 seasons with Montreal, Calgary, Hamilton and Toronto, catching 600 passes for 9,697 yards and 80 TDs. He twice won the Schenley as the CFL's Most Outstanding Canadian, earned All-Conference All-Star honours six times and All-Canadian selection once.

FALONEY, BERNIE, Elected as a Player, May 6, 1974. His CFL career began in 1954 when he and Jackie Parker quarterbacked Edmonton to the Grey Cup victory. From 1957 to 1964 he led Hamilton to seven Grey Cup finals, winning the Schenley as the CFL's Most Outstanding Player in 1961. Faloney moved to Montreal in 1965 and ended his career two years later with B.C.

***FEAR, A.H. (CAP),** Elected as a Player, November 30, 1967. Another all-round athlete, this Outside Wing earned All-Star honours six times in a standout career with the Argos (1919 to 1926), Montreal (1926 to 1928) and Hamilton (1928 to 1932).

FENNELL, DAVE, Elected as a player on April 28, 1990. "Doctor Death" was a stalwart on the Edmonton Eskimos' Defensive Line from 1974 to 1983. He was a major cog on the Eskimo team that won five consecutive Grey Cups from 1978 to 1982 as well as one in 1975. He was the Defensive Star of the 1978 Grey Cup, and the Defensive and Canadian Star of the 1982 Championship. He was a CFL and Western All-Star at Defensive Tackle from 1977 to 1981 and the Most Outstanding Defensive Player in 1978. He won the Most Outstanding Canadian Award in 1979 and was Runner-up in 1980.

***FERRARO, JOHN,** Elected as a Player, November 24, 1966. He excelled as a Punter, Place-kicker, Quarterback, Fullback, Defensive specialist and Coach with Hamilton and Montreal from 1934 through the early 1940s. His play did not escape the eye of Lew Hayman who selected Ferraro to his All-Canadian Team of that era.

FIELDGATE, NORM, Elected as a Player, June 30, 1979. He played for the B.C. Lions from 1954 to 1967 - the lone Lion original in 1954 to celebrate the club's first Grey Cup victory in 1964. An All-Canadian once and All-Western All-Star three times, he played more than 200 games as Offensive End, Defensive End, Corner Linebacker and Defensive Back.

FLEMING, WILLIE, Elected as a Player, May 28, 1982. Willie The Wisp earned All-Western All-Star honours three times and All-Canadian Team recognition once. He is the first CFLer to rush for a career mark in excess of seven yards per carry and in 1963 he rushed for a 9.7-yard average as the Lions reached their first Grey Cup Game.

***FOULDS, WILLIAM C.,** Elected as a Builder, June 19, 1963. A brilliant player with the University of Toronto in 1909 and 1910 and excellent Coach of the Grey Cup bound Argonauts in 1911 and 1914, it was Foulds who put up $4,000 to make the first East-West Grey Cup Game in 1921 possible. He unselfishly also served the Canadian Rugby Union in many capacities over a long period of time.

GABRIEL, TONY PETER, Elected as a Player, August 18, 1984. His remarkable 11-year career ended in 1981 with eight All-Canadian and All-Eastern honours to his credit. He ranks fourth in pass receptions and pass reception yardage. This determined Tight End with Hamilton and Ottawa was Schenley winner as the CFL's Most Outstanding Player in 1978 and four times he won the Schenley as Most Outstanding Canadian.

***GALL, HUGH,** Elected as a Player, November 27, 1963. He could kick with either foot and from 1908 through 1912 this Backfielder with the University of Toronto earned his place into the Hall of Fame. In the 1909 inaugural Grey Cup against Parkdale, Gall scored one touchdown and kicked eight singles.

GAUDAUR, JACOB GILL JAKE, Elected as a Builder, March 16, 1984. For almost 50 years, he has given much to Canadian football at the Senior and Professional levels. He spent 16 years as Commissioner of the CFL after a long association as player and executive with the Hamilton Tiger-Cats. He was also one of the key figures in the founding of The Canadian Football Hall of Fame and Museum.

GOLAB, TONY, Elected as a Player, November 26, 1964. For a decade he was the Golden Boy of Canadian football with the Ottawa Rough Riders. One of the game's great Backfielders, he won the Jeff Russel Trophy in 1941 and was a Big Four All-Star three times. Despite suffering serious wounds to the arms and legs during World War II, Golab returned to star with Ottawa until 1950.

GRANT, HARRY PETER BUD, Elected as a Builder, May 13, 1983. The first pro football coach to win 100 games in his first 10 years of coaching became a force in the CFL and NFL. An All-Star Offensive End with Winnipeg on three occasions, he also picked off five interceptions in one game. He coached Winnipeg to six Grey Cup Games, winning four times, before becoming Head Coach of the Minnesota Vikings in 1967.

GRAY, HERBERT, Elected as a Player, June 23, 1983. This Offensive and Defensive Lineman played beside and for Bud Grant in Winnipeg. He was a Western Conference All-Star Defensive End six times and Western All-Star Guard once. In 1960 he became the first defensive player to win the Schenley Most Outstanding Lineman Award and in 1962 he earned All-Canadian honours.

***GREY, LORD EARL,** Elected as a Builder, June 19, 1963. Appointed Governor-General of Canada on December 10, 1904, Lord Grey donated the Lord Earl Grey Cup in 1909 as a trophy for the amateur rugby football championship of Canada. The $48 trophy went on to become the symbol of the championship pro football team in Canada.

GRIFFING, DEAN, Elected as as Player, November 25, 1965. This daring Centre loved to ride rival players and fans. But he backed any challenges with determination and thus became one of the most valuable contributors to the growth of football in Regina and Calgary from 1936 to 1956.

***GRIFFITH, DR. HARRY CRAWFORD,** Elected as a Builder, November 27, 1963. The Coach of the first official Grey Cup champion in 1909, the University of Toronto. In fact, the University of Toronto under Dr. Griffith won again in 1910.

***HALTER, G. SYDNEY,** Elected as a Builder, November 24, 1966. In 1934 he helped Joe Ryan and Frank Hannibal organize the Winnipeg Football Club. Eighteen years later, Halter was named Deputy Commissioner of the Western Interprovincial Football Union and Commissioner in 1953. Several years later, officials of the WIFU and the Big Four amalgamated with Halter becoming first Commissioner of the CFL in 1958, a post he held until retiring in 1966. Member of Canada's Sports Hall of Fame.

***HANNIBAL, FRANK,** Elected as a Builder, June 19, 1963. One of the great builders of Western Canada Football, he was Vice-President of Winnipeg in 1934 and President in 1935-36, the final year of which marked the first time a Western Club won the Grey Cup. For nearly 30 years he served football in several capacities.

HANSON, FRITZ, Elected as a Player, June 19, 1963. This slightly built flash from North Dakota returned punts for more than 300 yards on seven returns including a 78-yard TD run when Winnipeg won the West's first Grey Cup, 18-12 over the Hamilton Tigers in 1935 right in Hamilton. He starred in many more fine hours for Winnipeg.

HARRIS, WAYNE, Elected as a Player August 5, 1976. His career spanned from 1961 to 1972 and for 11 consecutive seasons the Calgary Middle Linebacker was a Western Conference All-Star. He was an All-Canadian eight times. After losses in two Grey Cup appearances, Harris was MVP in 1971 when Calgary finally won, beating Toronto in the Grey Cup Game.

HARRISON, HERMAN, Elected as a player on June 26, 1993. Nicknamed "Ham", he played tight end for the Calgary Stampeders from 1964 to 1972 and garnered All-star honours in 1965 and from 1967 to 1971. He was named All-Canadian from 1968 to 1970. He participated in three Grey Cup games, winning the last one in 1971.

***HAYMAN, LEW,** Elected as a Builder, June 28, 1975. He gave a half century of his life to football service in Canada. As a 25-year-old in 1933, he coached his first of five Grey Cup victories when Toronto edged Sarnia, 4-3. Hayman never lost in a Grey Cup appearance as Head Coach.

HELTON, JOHN, Elected as a Player August 17, 1985. Signed by the Calgary Stampeders in 1969, the nine-time CFL All-Star played 14 seasons in the league, 10 of them with Calgary. Twice he was named the Schenley Most Outstanding Defensive Player (1972 and 1974) and in Winnipeg in 1979 he was the runner-up. Helton was a Western All-Star 12 times and a member of two Grey Cup winners.

HENLEY, GARNEY, Elected as a Player, June 30, 1979. For 16 seasons until retiring in 1975, he starred with the Tiger-Cats initially as a Defensive Back and later as a Wide Receiver. After nine consecutive seasons as an All-Canadian Defensive Back, Henley became an All-Canadian Wide Receiver truly indicative of one of the CFL's All-Time most versatile stars.

HINTON, TOM, Elected as a Player on May 11, 1991. Played his entire Canadian professional career with the B.C. Lions, a career which spanned 136 games from 1958 through 1966. Made the Western all-star team in his rookie season and was B.C.'s nominee for the Schenley Most Outstanding Lineman Award. In 1963, the country's number one guard became a Canadian citizen, made both the All-Western and All-Canadian All-Star teams and participated in B.C.'s first Grey Cup contest.

***HUFFMAN, DICK,** Elected as a Player, May 2, 1987. A versatile two-way Lineman, he was voted All-Western All-Star eight times - five with Winnipeg and three with Calgary.

***HUGHES, W.P. BILLY,** Elected as a Builder, May 6, 1974. He made his mark at Queen's as Head Coach where his clubs won three consecutive Grey Cup Games and 26 league and exhibition games in a row. He coached Hamilton in 1932 and 1933, Ottawa in 1935 and 1936 and Quebec RCAF in 1942-43.

***ISBISTER, BOB Sr.,** Elected as a Player, November 25, 1965. From 1905 to 1919 he was a solid performer for the Hamilton Tigers and renowned for his all-round ability, defensive qualities and sportsmanship. Following his playing days he became a Referee in the Interprovincial and Intercollegiate Unions, President of the Big Four and later a member of the Board of Governors for Hamilton in 1933.

JACKSON, RUSS, Elected as a Player, May 16, 1973. A three-time Schenley Winner as Most Outstanding Player, a four-time Schenley Winner as Most Outstanding Canadian, a six-time All-Eastern All-Star and a three-time All-Canadian All-Star Jackson was instrumental in Ottawa reaching the Grey Cup finals four times, winning three of them including his farewell game in 1969.

***JACOBS, JACK,** Elected as a Player, June 19, 1963. He came to Winnipeg in 1950 and earned All-Western All-Star honours as Quarterback in 1950 and 1952. He gave Winnipeg a decade of excitement and rewrote Western Canada records completing 710 passes for 11,094 yards and 104 touchdowns.

***JAMES, EDDIE,** Elected as a Player, June 19, 1963. Dynamite, as he was called, was a 60-minute player who was at ease either on Offence or Defence. He was a star with Winnipeg, the Regina Pats, Winnipeg St. Johns and the Regina Roughriders through the 1920s and early 1930s.

JAMES, GERRY, Elected as a Player, January 6, 1981. Son of Eddie Dynamite James, Gerry joined the Blue Bombers as a 17-year-old and was a regular the next season. The first winner of the Schenley All-Canadian Award, he won it again in 1957. A talented rusher, he combined his football career with several seasons of hockey with the Toronto Maple Leafs.

***KABAT, GREG,** Elected as a Player, November 24, 1966. Another prominent figure in Winnipeg's first Grey Cup victory in 1935. This Quarterback, Guard, Flying Wing and Fullback also was an expert place-kicker and blocker. Kabat later coached the Vancouver Grizzlies in 1941.

KAPP, JOE, Elected as a Player, March 16, 1984. Twice an All-Canadian All-Star Quarterback and twice an All-Western All-Star, Kapp played eight years in the CFL initially with Calgary and for almost six seasons with B.C. He passed for 22,925 yards and guided the Lions to their first Grey Cup win in 1964.

KEELING, JERRY, Elected as a Player, June 3, 1989. Played 15 consecutive seasons in the CFL and 229 games as a Defensive Back and Quarterback with Calgary (1961-72), Ottawa (1973-75) and Hamilton (1975). Was a CFL All-Star at Defensive Back in 1964, 1965 and 1967 and a Western All-Star from 1964 to 1968. Led his club to four Grey Cups, winning two (1971, 1973) and losing the others (1968, 1970). Combined with fellow Hall of Famer, Terry Evanshen, to tie the CFL record for the longest completed pass, 109 yards, at Winnipeg, in 1968.

KELLY, BRIAN, Elected as a Player May 11, 1991. The clever wide receiver, affectionately called "Howdy Doody" by his team mates, was a 5'9" dynamo during his career which lasted though the 1987 season. During his nine-year career, Brian Kelly caught 575 passes for a CFL record 11,169 yards and scored 586 points. His 97 career touchdowns are second only to George Reed's all-time TD total of 137 in the CFL record book.

KELLY, ELLISON, Elected as a Player on October 24, 1992. He joined the Hamilton Tiger-Cats during the 1960 season. He was an All-Eastern All-Star from 1961 to 1964 and was selected All-Canadian guard in 1964. He also received All-Star honours at tackle from 1968 to 1971, earning All-Canadian honours in 1969 and 1970. The Tiger-Cats won three Grey Cup Championships during his tenure in Hamilton. During his 13-year career, he never missed a game, playing in 175 consecutive regular season games.

KEYS, EAGLE, Elected as a builder on April 28, 1990. He came to the Canadian Football League as a Player in 1949 and remained involved with the League for more than a quarter century. Best remembered as a player for his final game (the Eskimos' 1954 Grey Cup triumph) when he played on a broken leg. He coached Edmonton from 1959 until 1963, became an assistant coach with Saskatchewan in 1964 and was promoted to Head Coach in 1965. He was picked as Coach of the Year in 1968. In 1970, the Roughriders finished with a mark of 14 wins and 2 losses, a CFL record that stood until 1989 when Edmonton went 16-2. Keys resigned at the end of that season and coached B.C. from 1971 until partway through the 1975 season.

KIMBALL, NORMAN H., Elected as a Builder, May 11, 1991. His affiliation with the Edmonton Eskimos began in 1961 when he became their minor football coordinator and continued through the 1985 season. Was Chairman of the CFL General Managers for three years, beginning in 1971, and as a senior league executive made a significant contribution while serving on numerous standing committees. From 1975 he headed the Player Relations Committee which negotiated agreements with the Canadian Football League Players' Association. On March 4, 1986 became part owner, President and Chief Operating Officer of the Montreal Football Club and Company Limited. Kimball remained with the Montreal organization until the team folded on June 24, 1987.

***KRAMER, R.A. (BOB),** Elected as a Builder, May 2, 1987. He guided the Saskatchewan Roughriders through some of their most trying times, serving as President from 1951-53 and 1961-65, leaving the Club much stronger through his leadership.

KROL, JOE, Elected as a Player, November 27, 1963. One of Canada's greatest players in a career which went from 1932 to 1953. Joe King Krol to Royal Copeland became a well-known one-two punch often referred to as the Gold Dust Twins, Krol, a precision pivot starred in high school and university ball. He joined the Argos in 1945 and played on five Grey Cup winners to go along with one in '43 with Hamilton.

KWONG, NORMIE, Elected as a Player, November 28, 1969. The China Clipper played 13 seasons with Calgary and Edmonton. In 11 years of recorded statistics, he gained 9,022 yards with a 5.2-yard average. Combined with another great, Johnny Bright, Kwong gave the Eskimos a dynamic backfield which resulted in three consecutive Grey Cup wins (1954-55-56).

LANCASTER, RON, Elected as a Player, May 28, 1982. Four times an All-Canadian All-Star and seven times an All-Western All-Star, this Quarterback starred 19 seasons in the CFL, three with Ottawa and 16 with Saskatchewan. Winner of the Schenley Award as Most Outstanding Player in 1970 and 1976 he holds scores of passing records.

***LAWSON, SMIRLE,** Elected as a Player, June 19, 1963. This great plunging Halfback was hailed as the Original Big Train. He starred for the University of Toronto's Grey Cup victories in 1909 and 1910 and later stood out for the Big Four Argos in their win in 1914.

***LEADLAY, FRANK R. PEP,** Elected as a Player, June 19, 1963. He captained Queen's and the Hamilton Tigers in a dynamic career which brought this Backfielder joy with five Intercollegiate championships and three successive Grey Cups with Queen's plus two more Grey Cups with the Tigers, the last of which came in 1929.

***LEAR, LES,** Elected as a Player, May 6, 1974. The first Canadian developed player to go to the NFL (he played Guard with Cleveland, LA Rams and Detroit), he was also a member of three Grey Cup winners (Winnipeg in 1939 and 1941 and Calgary in 1948). Lear coached the unbeaten Stampeders to their first Grey Cup win in 1948.

LEWIS, LEO, Elected as a Player, May 16, 1973. The Lincoln Locomotive played 11 seasons with the Blue Bombers ending in 1965. The six-time All-Star rushed for 8,861 yards and averaged 6.6 yards. He also returned kick-offs for 5,444 yards and a 29.1-yard average.

***LIEBERMAN, M.I. MOE,** Elected as a Builder, May 16, 1973. Active in football for more than 60 years as a player, manager, official and executive, he made his mark with the Eskimos. As President of the Eskimos, they won the Grey Cup in 1955 and 1956. He also was active in the formation of the Edmonton Alumni Club.

LUNSFORD, EARL, Elected as a Player, May 13, 1983. The Earthquake as this Fullback was called played six seasons for the Calgary Stampeders and became the first player in the history of pro football to rush for a mile in one season (1,794 yards in 1961). He was an All-Western All-Star three times and an All-Canadian All- Star once.

LUSTER, MARV, Elected as a player on April 28, 1990. He began his career with the Montreal Alouettes in 1961, then joined the Toronto Argonauts midway through 1964 and played there until '72. He rejoined the Alouettes until the end of his career in 1974. He was an Eastern All-Star in 1961-62. Throughout his career he played Defensive Back and received Eastern All-Star recognition from 1966 to '72 and was a CFL All-Star six times. In the final game of his career he suited up for Montreal's 1974 Grey Cup winning team. As a testament to the tremendous respect he had earned, Montreal Head Coach Marv Levy dressed Luster for the '74 Grey Cup Championship even though he had not played since the 11th game of the regular season.

LUZZI, DON, Elected as a Player August 17, 1985. An inspirational leader of the Calgary Stampeders from 1958 to 1969, Luzzi was a three-time CFL All-Star. He was named a Western All-Star seven times. The 1958 winner of the Schenley Most Outstanding Lineman award, Luzzi played both as an offensive and defensive tackle.

***McBRIEN, HARRY,** Elected as a Builder, June 24, 1978. An original member of the Canadian Football Hall of Fame Selection Committee, he had early involvements in basketball and football through officiating. He served the Canadian Rugby Union as a Secretary-Treasurer for many years and later became Grey Cup Co-Ordinator for the CFL. Is also a member of the Canadian Sports Hall of Fame.

***McCAFFREY, JIMMY P.,** Elected as a Builder, November 30, 1967. One of the most respected General Managers in Canadian Football, he took over the Ottawa Club in 1923 and turned it into a unified success after almost folding. He won four Grey Cups with Ottawa and lost in the final three times.

***McCANCE, CHESTER CHES,** Elected as a Player August 5, 1976. A colourful character and two-way End, he was an All-Western All-Star in 1940 and 1941. He was one of few players to play for Grey Cup winners in the West and the East (Winnipeg in '39 and '41; Montreal in '49).

***McCANN, DAVE,** Elected as a Builder, November 24, 1966. An outstanding Quarterback and Halfback with Ottawa from 1907 to the War Years, he later coached Ottawa to Grey Cup wins in 1925 and 1926 before turning to the executive level as Chairman of the Canadian Rugby Union Rules Committee.

***McGILL, FRANK,** Elected as a Player, November 25, 1965. One of Montreal's outstanding all-round athletes in the early 1900s when he starred in football, swimming and hockey. In football, he shone with Montreal high school, McGill and the Winged Wheelers, winners of the 1919 Big Four title.

***McPHERSON, DON,** Elected as a Builder, May 13, 1983. A driving force behind the Saskatchewan Roughriders, the Canadian Rugby Union and the Western Football Conference. He was appointed a Director of the Roughriders in 1949; became President in 1956-57 and served on the Club's Management Committee until his death in 1973.

McQUARTERS, ED, Elected as a Player on March 5, 1988. Played with Saskatchewan from 1966 to 1974. A CFL and Western All-Star in 1967-68-69, Schenley Award Winner as Most Outstanding Lineman in 1967. Lost his left eye in a home workshop accident in 1971 but courageously returned to action on August 27, 1971.

***METRAS, JOHNNY,** Elected as a Builder, May 24, 1980. Came to Canada in 1933 to attend St. Michael's College. After two years at Centre he moved to the University of Western Ontario as an Assistant Coach. In 1940 he became Head Coach at Western and in 30 years captured nine league championships with a 106-76-11 record.

MILES, ROLLIE, Elected as a Player, May 24, 1980. A splendid 11-year performer with the Edmonton Eskimos ending in 1961. He was an All-Western All-Star eight times, three at Running Back, three at Defensive Back and two at Linebacker. He also played in five Grey Cup Games, playing for the winning side three times.

***MOLSON, PERCY,** Elected as a Player, November 27, 1963. An amazing all-round athlete whose life was cut short in the First World War. He starred for Montreal High School, McGill and the Winged Wheelers and, after graduating from McGill in 1913, he set up a committee to build Graduates Stadium. The venue became Molson Stadium in honour of a great athlete and soldier.

***MONTGOMERY, KENNETH G.,** Elected as a Builder, November 26, 1970. An avid sportsman with involvement in hockey and horse racing. he was one of the founders and road secretary of the Edmonton Eskimo Football Club (1938-39), as well as President of the Eskimos (1952-53-54) during which time the Club won its first Grey Cup.

MORRIS, FRANK, Elected as a Player, May 13, 1983. As a tremendous Guard and Defensive Tackle, he played on two teams (the Argos and the Eskimos) who put together three consecutive Grey Cup victories. He served the Eskimos as Director of Player Development from 1973 to 1988 and celebrated six more Grey Cup wins including five in a row.

***MORRIS, TED,** Elected as a Player, November 26, 1964. A staunch Canadian who merited entry into the Hall of Fame as a Player and Builder. He starred nine years for the Argos and later coached them to three consecutive Grey Cup victories (1945-46-47).

MOSCA, ANGELO, Elected as a Player, May 2, 1987. He played 15 CFL seasons, including nine times in the Grey Cup Game (emerging a winner five times). A CFL All-Star in 1963 and 1970, he was an Eastern All-Star Defensive Tackle five times.

NELSON, ROGER, Elected as a Player August 17, 1985. One of the most consistent offensive tackles ever to play in the Canadian Football League, he made consistency his byword. Through the course of his career he gained the reputation of never missing an assignment and four times was named a Western All-Star. In 1959 he was named the Schenley Most Outstanding Lineman. He played 13 seasons for the Edmonton Eskimos between 1954 and 1967.

NEUMANN, PETER, Elected as a Player, June 30, 1979. His career with Hamilton began in 1951 and ended in 1964. This masterful Defensive End was nine times named an All-Eastern All-Star including a stretch of seven years in a row. He was also an All- Canadian in 1964.

***NEWTON, JACK,** Elected as a Builder, November 26, 1964. Another Canadian football great who qualified as a Player-Builder based on more than 50 years of service to the sport. Noted as a leader, his part in the University of Toronto's 1909 Grey Cup win merely proved success followed him wherever he went.

O'QUINN, JOHN RED, Elected as a Player, January 6, 1981. An All-Eastern All-Star five times, he set numerous pass catching records with the Montreal Alouettes despite the fact statistical records were not available for the 1952 and 1953 seasons. In six seasons records were kept he averaged 62.8 receptions per year.

PAJACZKOWSKI, TONY, Elected as a Player on March 5, 1988. Played with Calgary from 1955 to 1965; spent 1966-67 with the Montreal Alouettes. Paj was a CFL All-Star Guard in 1962-63-64-65 and had six Western All-Star honours plus one Eastern Division All-Star honour. Schenley Most Outstanding Canadian in 1961.

PARKER, JACKIE, Elected as a Player, November 25, 1971. The Fast Freight from

Mississippi State or Ole Spaghetti Legs starred for the Edmonton Eskimos from 1954 to 1962, the Argos from 1963 to 1965 and B.C. Lions from 1966 to 1968. He played on three Grey Cup winners with Edmonton, won the Schenley as the CFL's top player three times was an All-Star for eight straight years and scored 750 points including that dramatic 84- yard TD run in the 1954 Grey Cup game. He starred at Quarterback, Halfback and Defensive Back. Member of Canada's Sports Hall of Fame.

PATTERSON, HAL, Elected as a Player, November 25, 1971. Prince Hal possessed a lot of charisma and provided 14 unbelievable seasons for CFL fans. After playing with Montreal from 1953 to 1960, he was traded to last-place Hamilton and the gifted receiver helped put them into the Grey Cup Game in 1961-62-63-64-65. He scored 75 TDs in his splendid career.

PERRY, GORDON, Elected as a Player, November 26, 1970. Captain of the Montreal Winged Wheelers who went through the 1931 season unbeaten and untied en route to the Grey Cup win. A speed merchant who was difficult to tackle, this Back was also a fine hockey and baseball player.

***PERRY, NORMAN,** Elected as a Player, June 19, 1963. The Norm Perry Memorial Stadium in Sarnia is named after this immortal Halfback who captained Sarnia's 1934 Grey Cup victory. He later devoted his efforts to the Canadian Rugby Union of which he was elected President in 1953.

PLOEN, KEN, Elected as a Player, June 28, 1975. He played in the Rose Bowl Game and the Grey Cup Game in 1957. He starred 11 seasons with Winnipeg which included six Grey Cup finals, four of them victories. An All-Western All-Star Quarterback in 1957 and 1965, he was also an All-Canadian in 1965. In the 1958 Grey Cup Game, Ploen moved from QB to Halfback and Safety. He was an All-Star Defensive Back in 1959.

***PRESTON, KEN,** Elected as a builder on April 28, 1990. Was known as the 'Dean' of General Managers during his stint at the helm of the Saskatchewan Roughriders from 1958-77. During this time the Roughriders compiled more wins than any other club in the CFL with 172. Preston's clubs were in the playoffs 15 times, finished first on five occasions, were in the Grey Cup Game five times and won it in 1966. He also is credited with developing the minor football program in Saskatchewan as he initiated clinics and staged annual tryout camps for graduating high school players.

***QUILTY, S.P. SILVER,** Elected as a Player, November 24, 1966. From 1907 to 1912, he was the prime ball-carrier for the University of Ottawa. In 1908-09, he also handled kicking duties. From a star player, he later became a football Official, a member of the Rules Committee and Coach.

REBHOLZ, RUSS, Elected as a Player, November 27, 1963. One of the first two imports to play football in Winnipeg. An all-round Backfielder, The "Wisconsin Wraith" threw TD passes to Joe Perpich and Bud Marquardt to give Winnipeg the first Grey Cup for a Western team in 1935.

REED, GEORGE, Elected as a Player, June 30, 1979. Through 13 seasons of standout service with the Saskatchewan Roughriders ending in 1975, he became the No. 1 rusher of All-Time Pro Football. This durable Fullback rushed for 16,116 yards, rushed for 134 TDs, was an All-Canadian All-Star nine times, an All-Western All-Star 10 times and once was selected the Schenley winner as Most Outstanding Player.

***REEVE, TED,** Elected as a Player, June 19, 1963. The Moaner as the beloved Reever became known to his many friends and readers, was a fine soldier, excellent lacrosse player, superb football player and winning football Coach. He played for the Argos and Balmy Beach and became known for blocking kicks and stopping plungers as they tore through the line.

RIGNEY, FRANK JOSEPH, Elected as a Player, August 18, 1984. He anchored Winnipeg's offensive line for 10 seasons from 1958 to 1967. He was an All-Canadian Tackle three times and an All-Western All-Star seven times. In 1961 he was the CFL's Outstanding Lineman. In four or five Grey Cup appearances, Rigney celebrated victories.

***RITCHIE, ALVIN,** Elected as a Builder, June 19, 1963. The Silver Fox was instrumental in the formation of the Regina Football Club. Through the years under Ritchie, Regina became a force in Western Canada but he died nine months before Saskatchewan brought the Grey Cup to Regina in 1966.

***RODDEN, MICHAEL J.,** Elected as a Player, November 26, 1964. A player of All-Star ability at the University of Ottawa and Queen's plus the Argos, he became a superb Coach with future Hall of Famers Conacher, Batstone, Breen, Timmis, Cox, Leadlay, Reeve, Fear, Welch and Sprague among his proteges. Coached Hamilton to Grey Cup wins in 1928 and 1929.

***ROWE, PAUL,** Elected as a Player, November 26, 1964. One of the greatest plunging Fullbacks in Canadian football history, he starred 12 seasons for Calgary and was an All- Western All-Star five times. He was part of Calgary's 1948 Grey Cup winning team and twice led the West in scoring. Member of Canada's Sports Hall of Fame.

RUBY, MARTIN, Elected as a Player, May 6, 1974. He was one of the last excellent two-way linemen in Canadian football. He signed with Saskatchewan in 1951 and in seven years he was an All-Star seven times including three years when he was chosen both offensively and defensively.

***RUSSEL, JEFF,** Elected as a Player, June 19, 1963. Killed tragically in 1926 repairing a power line in a driving rainstorm, the Jeff Russel Memorial Trophy was established to honour the Eastern player who was as gifted an athlete and sportsman like Russel. A great competitor, Russel starred for the famous Winged Wheelers (1922 to 1925).

***RYAN, JOSEPH B.,** Elected as a Builder, November 28, 1968. Rendered his services and helped construct strong franchises in Winnipeg, Montreal and Edmonton. He engineered the amalgamation of the Winnipeg Rugby Club and St. John's so that by 1935 the Grey Cup went to Winnipeg.

SAZIO, RALPH, Elected as a Builder on March 5, 1988. Joined Hamilton as a player in 1950. Was Head Coach of the Hamilton Tiger-Cats from 1963-67 and during his tenure registered a 49-20-1 record, four Eastern Conference Championships (1963-64-65-67) and three Grey Cup victories (1963-65-67). Became General Manager in 1968 and President in 1972, a year in which Hamilton hosted and won the Grey Cup. Became President of the Argonauts on August 6, 1981. His teams had first-place Eastern Division finishes in 1982-83-84-86-88 and Grey Cup appearances in 1982-83-87 with a triumph in '83.

***SCOTT, VINCE,** Elected as a Player, May 28, 1982. Joined the Hamilton Wildcats in 1949 and ended his spectacular Tiger-Cat career in 1962. He was selected an All-Eastern Guard 10 times, was voted to Hamilton's Fabulous Fifties Team and played in the first four CFL All-Star Games.

SHATTO, DICK, Elected as a Player, June 28, 1975. After 12 seasons with the Argos, he retired in 1965 and, at that time, had scored more touchdowns, caught more passes and accounted for more offensive yardage than any other player in the history of Canadian football. Eastern All-Star on eight occasions.

***SHAUGHNESSY, FRANK SHAG,** Elected as a Builder, November 27, 1963. An accomplished player, owner, manager and executive, he achieved success in baseball, hockey and football. As a Coach, he won, too, and also helped introduce new tactics to Canadian football. His McGill teams were perennial Intercollegiate champions with him at the helm.

***SHOULDICE, W.T.H. HAP,** Elected as a Builder, June 25, 1977. In 1929, he first officiated in the Ottawa High School League and in 1935 he was appointed to the Big Four. He officiated in nine Grey Cup Games and went on to become the CFL's first Director of Officiating.

***SIMPSON, BENJAMIN L.,** Elected as a Player, November 27, 1963. An outstanding Kicker who played with the Hamilton Tigers from 1904 to 1910. He later served as President of the Big Four and President of the Tiger Football Club. Member of Canada's Sports Hall of Fame.

SIMPSON, BOB, Elected as a Player August 5, 1976. A swift runner who gave many superb performances for the Windsor Rockets in 1949 plus the Ottawa Rough Riders from 1950 to 1962. Sixty-five of his 70 touchdowns came on pass receptions but apart from starring as an Offensive End, he also shone as Offensive Back and Defensive Back, making All-Star at all three.

***SIMPSON, JIMMY,** Elected as a Builder August 17, 1985. A genuine builder of the game, Simpson appeared in approximately 19 Grey Cup Games, six as a player with the Hamilton Tigers and Wildcats, three as an official and 10 as a trainer of the Hamilton Tiger-Cats. His career in Canadian football began in 1928. Simpson's four touchdowns in Grey Cup Games ranks second to the all-time record of five by fellow Hall of Famer, Hal Patterson.

***SLOCOMB, KARL,** Elected as a Builder, June 3, 1989. Served on the executive of the Winnipeg Blue Bombers before becoming Vice-President and, in 1953, President of the Grey Cup Finalists. He served as President of the Western Interprovincial Football Union in 1956 after serving as Vice-President. President of the Canadian Rugby Union in 1960 and the Intermediate Section of the CRU in 1961.

***SPRAGUE, DAVID S.,** Elected as a Player, June 19, 1963. A perennial All-Star in his 15-year career with Hamilton and Ottawa he ran to fame in a sport he truly loved. Like so many others of his day, he played despite injuries.

***SPRING, HARRY C.,** Elected as a Builder August 5, 1976. One of the fathers for the Vancouver franchise, he was an original Director of the Lions in 1954. Treasurer in 1955 and 1956, Vice-President in 1957 and President in 1958 and 1959.

STEVENSON, ART, Elected as a Player, November 28, 1969. At Quarterback or Halfback, he made his mark in Canadian football leading Winnipeg to many victories in the late 1930s and early 1940s. He was also an accomplished Kicker and booted the winning point in Winnipeg's 1939 Grey Cup win over Ottawa.

STEWART, RON, Elected as a Player, June 25, 1977. He was 5-foot-8 but his CFL accomplishments made him a giant with Ottawa from 1958 to 1970 following impressive careers at Toronto Riverdale High and Queen's. He set the single game rushing mark of 287 yards in 1960, shared in three Grey Cups and took many individual honours.

STIRLING, HUGH BUMMER, Elected as a Player, November 24, 1966. One of the best ever triple threat Backfielders and finest Kickers in Canadian football, he starred for Sarnia from 1929 to 1938. He was an ORFU All-Star six times, and ORFU MVP once. In 1938 was first football player to be picked as Canadian Press Athlete of the Year.

STUKUS, ANNIS, Elected as a Builder, May 6, 1974. A versatile player with the Argos which included Grey Cup wins in 1937 and 1938, Stuke went on to assist new franchises in Edmonton and Vancouver. Despite low budgets, Stuke promoted like a genius and made sure the Eskimos and the Lions were quicky in the black.

SUTHERIN, DON, Elected as a Player on October 24, 1992. He joined the Tiger-Cats in 1958 and left the following year for the NFL. He returned to the Tiger-Cats in 1960 and remained with the Club until 1966 when he joined the Ottawa Rough Riders. He was an All-Eastern defensive back six times, and was All-Canadian on three occasions. He led the Eastern Conference in scoring four times and in interceptions twice. He participated in eight Grey Cup games, winning two with Hamilton and two with Ottawa.

***TAYLOR, N.J. PIFFLES,** Elected as a Builder, November 27, 1963. After a playing career with Regina, he became President of the Regina Roughriders from 1934 to 1936 and became President of the Canadian Rugby Union in 1946. He is credited with helping develop football in Western Canada.

THELEN, DAVE, Elected as a Player, June 3, 1989. Rushed 1,530 times for 8,463 yards and 47 TDs in a nine-year career with Ottawa and Toronto. Earned All-Eastern All-Star honours in 1959, 1960 and from 1963 to 1966. Led the East in rushing three times as well as leading the CFL in 1960. In addition to his offensive exploits, he earned praise as being one of the finest blocking backs in CFL history.

***TIMMIS, BRIAN,** Elected as a Player, June 19, 1963. He often sacrificed his body to make the big play for Hamilton. He played helmetless and he played with determination. Three times he helped the Hamilton Tigers to Grey Cup wins (1928, 1929 and 1932). He made a comeback at age 38 for a playoff game in Ottawa and played 58 minutes despite a bad shoulder. Member of Canada's Sports Hall of Fame.

TINDALL, FRANK, Elected as a Builder, August 18, 1984. Recruited by the Argonauts, Tindall was a Star Tackle in 1933 and later earned selection to the All-Time Argo squad (1921-1941). After taking over as Coach at Queen's in 1939, he became full-time Head Coach in 1948 until 1975 leading Queen's to a 112-84-2 record, eight intercollegiate and one National championship.

TINSLEY, ROBERT PORTER BUDDY, Elected as a Player, May 28, 1982. He spent 11 seasons with Winnipeg going both ways at Tackle and occasionally carrying on short-yardage situations. He was an All-Western All-Star eight times, five of those occasions on offence.

***TOMMY, ANDREW J.,** Elected as a Player, June 3, 1989. Starred both ways, at Flying Wing/Running Back with Ottawa from 1933 to 1941 as well as in 1946-47 and with Toronto from 1942 to 1945. Eastern All-Star Running Back in 1936 and Flying Wing in 1940, he won the Jeff Russel Trophy in 1940. Is a Member of the Canada Sports Hall of Fame and is remembered for returning a fumbled ball 123 yards for a TD at a time when official statistics were not kept.

***TRAWICK, HERB,** Elected as a Player, June 28, 1975. The first player in the East to make the East All-Star team seven times he was recruited by Montreal in 1946 when Lew Hayman and Leo Dandurand started to build the Alouettes. A big man, he was a swift Offensive Lineman.

***TUBMAN, JOE,** Elected as a Player, November 28, 1968. Captain of Ottawa's Grey Cup victories in 1925 and 1926, he gave the Rough Riders 13 seasons before retiring in 1931. He later served as Referee in ORFU and Big Four matches until 1944.

TUCKER, WHITMAN (WHIT), Elected as a Player on June 26, 1993. As a member of the Ottawa Rough Riders from 1962 to 1970, he earned All-Star recognition in 1966, 1967 and 1968 and was All-Canadian in 1967. Was also runner-up as the Most Outstanding Canadian in 1968. Registered 53 TD receptions during his career. Played in three Grey Cup games, winning the Championship in 1968 and 1969.

URNESS, TED, Elected as a Player, June 3, 1989. Anchored the Saskatchewan Roughriders' splendid Offensive Line from 1961 to 1970. Was an All-Canadian and All-Western All-Star from 1965 to 1970. Honoured with a Schenley Award as the CFL's Most Outstanding Lineman in 1968. Upon his arrival, the Club went from a fourth-place finish in 1961 to the start of a string of 15 consecutive playoff years.

VAUGHAN, KAYE, Elected as a Player, June 24, 1978. Quick and versatile, he gave the Ottawa Rough Riders 12 star-studded seasons ending in 1964. He was an Eastern Conference All-Star 10 times and on more than one occasion he was an All-Star offensively and defensively because he also stood out at the Tackle, Guard and Middle Guard positions.

WAGNER, VIRGIL, Elected as a Player, May 24, 1980. An original Alouette, he played with Montreal from 1946 to 1954 but the absence of statistics during that time prevented numerical recollections of this brilliant Running Back. The four-time Eastern Running Back tied Joe Krol for one scoring title before winning three in a row.

***WARNER, CLAIR,** Elected as a Builder, November 25, 1965. He played eight seasons with Alvin Ritchie's strong Regina Roughrider teams which played in four Grey Cup finals. Later he served the Regina Club in several capacities including President as well as on the executive of the Western Interprovincial Union and the Canadian Rugby Union Rules body.

***WARWICK, BERT,** Elected as a Builder, November 26, 1964. A leader and contributor to Canadian football for more than 50 years, he was Head Coach of the Western champion Winnipeg Blue Bombers in 1945. He later served as Chairman of the CFL's Rules Committee.

***WELCH, HAWLEY HUCK,** Elected as a Player, November 26, 1964. A great kicking Halfback, he played on Grey Cup winners with the Hamilton Tigers (1928 and 1929) and the Montreal Winged Wheelers in 1931. He won the Jeff Russel Trophy in 1933 and made All-Star five times.

WILKINSON, TOM, Elected as a Player, May 2, 1987. A three-time CFL All-Star through 15 seasons, he never missed a game in his 10 years with Edmonton which included five wins in eight Grey Cup Games.

***WILSON, SEYMOUR,** Elected as a Builder, March 16, 1984. His Officiating career began in 1930. For more than 30 years he was involved in Officiating with the Canadian Rugby Union and the CFL. His Officiating assignments included 10 Grey Cup Games of which he was most familiar because, as a player with Hamilton, he played in the 1932 and 1935 Grey Cup Games.

WYLIE, HARVEY, Elected as a Player, May 24, 1980. An exceptional Defensive Back and Kickoff Return specialist he spent nine years with the Calgary Stampeders ending in 1964. For five consecutive seasons he was an All-Western All-Star and twice he was an All-Canadian All-Star.

YOUNG, JIM, Elected as a Player, May 11, 1991. Played two years with the Minnesota Vikings of the National Football League before joining the B.C. Lions for his entire Canadian professional career, 197 games from 1967 to 1979. The Toronto Argonauts, who held his Canadian rights, traded him to B.C. in 1967 in exchange for Dick Fouts and Bill Symons. Young was B.C.'s nominee for the Schenley Most Outstanding Player Award in 1967, 1969, and 1972, and was their nominee for the Schenley Most Outstanding Canadian Award in 1967 and then every year from 1969 to 1972, winning in 1970 and 1972. Spent from 1989 to 1992 working in the Lions' front office.

***ZOCK, WILLIAM,** Elected as a Player, August 18, 1984. He was all heart in his 18-year career, 10 with the Argos, four with Balmy Beach and four with Edmonton. The Guard and Tackle celebrated Grey Cup victories with the Argos (1937, 1938, 1945, 1946 and 1947) and with Edmonton (1954) while losing in only one Grey Cup Game (1952 when Edmonton lost to Toronto).

FOOTBALL REPORTERS OF CANADA - CANADIAN FOOTBALL HALL OF FAME

The Football Reporters of Canada annually select inductees for their section in the Canadian Football Hall of Fame and Museum. The following are the 1994 FRC Executive:

President - John Wells
1st Vice-President - Darrell Davis
2nd Vice-President - Mark Lee
3rd Vice-President - J. Paul McConnell
Secretary-Treasurer - Rick Cluff
Past President - Cam Cole

The following is the list of FRC Hall of Famers:

1979 - Ivan Miller, Baz O'Meara, Ted Reeve, Hal Walker
1980 - Jim Coleman, Andy O'Brien, Annis Stukus, Henry Viney
1981 - Tony Allen, Vern de Geer, Dave Dryburgh, Jack Wells
1982 - Rheaume (Rocky) Brisbois, Bill Good Sr., Maurice Smith, Gord Walker
1983 - Gorde Hunter, Hal Pawson, Doug Smith
1984 - Johnny Esaw, Erwin Swangard, Bill Westwick
1985 - Eddie MacCabe, Wes McKnight, Bob Moir, Pierre Proulx
1986 - Austin 'Dink' Carroll, Milt Dunnell, Jack Matheson, Lloyd Saunders
1987 - Eric Bishop, Trent Frayne, Jim Hunt, Gillis Purcell
1988 - Ernie Afaganis, George Kent, Scotty Melville, Bill Stephenson
1989 - Bryan Hall, Pat Marsden, Norm Marshall, Jim Taylor, Fred Sgambati
1990 - Ralph Allen, R.J. "Bob" Frewin, Bob Hughes, Don Wittman
1991 - Terry Kielty, Ken Newans, Perc Allen
1992 - Bob Hanley, Jim Proudfoot, Bob Picken

1993 INDUCTEES

Al McCann - Born in Lethbridge, Alberta, Al "lucked" into the radio business in his home town, leading to the position of sports director of CJOC from 1955 to 1963. He then moved on to run the sports department at CFRN for 30 years. Saw his first Grey Cup in 1956 at old Varsity Stadium, starting a string of 29 visits to The Big One. He also conducted a weekly Football Huddle with various Eskimo coaches for 28 years. This is his third Hall of Fame induction - Al has already been saluted by the city of Lethbridge and the province of Alberta.

Jim Kearney - Born in Calgary, Alberta, Jim grew up in Victoria, and went straight from high school to the Victoria Times as a copy boy in 1940. He moved to the Vancouver Sun as a sports writer three years later. Kearney then crossed the street to the Province later and got the Lions' beat three days before they were born in 1954. He covered the Leos through the formative, toddling years before moving up in 1962 to columnist, where like all sports columnists, he knew everything.

- CANADIAN FOOTBALL -
PAST TO PRESENT

Here is a brief look at some highlights in 131 years of Canadian Football:

1861 - Saturday, November 9th, first documented football game was played at the University of Toronto on the present site of University College (400 yards west of Queen's Park). One of the participants in the game involving University of Toronto students was (Sir) William Mulock, later it's Chancellor.

1868 - First written account of a football game played in Quebec on Saturday, October 10th, 1868, was by R. Tait Mackenzie. It was between a team of officers from the English troops garrisoned in Montreal and a team of civilians, mainly from McGill University, and was played on the St. Catherine Street cricket grounds.

1869 - The Hamilton Foot Ball Club was formed on Wednesday, November 3rd in a room over George Lee's Fruit Store and adopted the colours of black and orange. Games were played on the Maple Leaf Baseball Club Grounds on Upper James Street. The first game for the HFBC was on Saturday, December 18th against the 13th Battalion (now Royal Hamilton Light Infantry) at the Baseball Grounds. No score was reported. According to the Hamilton Spectator of Tuesday, November 30th the HFBC had more than 100 members.

1872 - The Montreal Foot Ball Club was organized on Monday, April 8th in one of the lower rooms of the Mechanics Hall building. The first game played in Quebec occurred when the Montreal FC played Quebec City on Saturday, October 12th at the Esplanade in Quebec City. The two teams met again on Saturday, October 26th at McGill University. Both games ended in 0-0 ties.

1873 - The Toronto Argonaut Rowing Club formed the Toronto Argonaut Football Club on Saturday, October 4th and played its first game against the University of Toronto on Saturday, October 11th. The University of Toronto won by a Goal and a Try to Nil. The Argonauts adopted dark blue as the team colour. The first meeting of the Argonauts and HFBC was on Saturday, October 18th at the University of Toronto. Toronto won by a Goal and a Try to Nil. The HFBC wore yellow and black for the first time in this game. The following Saturday, the two clubs met in Hamilton at the Cricket Ground (later Hamilton A.A.A. Ground). Hamilton won by a Goal and Try plus a Touch In Goal to two Goals and two Trys. It was in the reporting of this game that the HFBC was first referred to as the Tigers.

1874 - The rules of a hybrid game of English rugby devised by the University of McGill were first used in the United States in a game at Boston between McGill and Harvard. On Thursday, May 14th, Harvard won 3-0 using Harvard rules. The next day, the teams tied 0-0 while playing Canadian rules. Harvard liked the new game so much they introduced it into the Ivy League. Both U.S. and Canadian football evolved from these games.

1875 - The first inter-provincial game was played between Ontario and Quebec on Saturday, October 16th at the Toronto Cricket Grounds. Ontario won on a Goal from a Try.

1876 - The Ottawa Football Club was formed on Wednesday, September 20th at the Russell House and played the Aylmer Club at Jacques Cartier Square on Saturday, September 23rd. (Sir) Percy Sherwood kicked a Goal from a Try for the winning point. Ottawa team colours were cerise (moderate red), French grey and navy blue.

1877 - The Ottawa and Britannia Football Clubs played their first game at Montreal. Britannia won 2 Trys and 3 Rouges to 1 Rouge.

1878 - Second inter-provincial game is played to a scoreless draw on Monday, October 28th between an "All-Ontario" team and a team from Montreal at Montreal.

1879 - The University of Michigan played a game against the University of Toronto. The Winnipeg Rugby Football Club was formed.

1880 - The "Open Formation" was introduced for the first time. Both teams were required to lineup across from each other.

1883 - The Ontario Rugby Football Union was formed on January 6th; 10 days later the Quebec Rugby Football Union was formed. The ORFU played a Tie Schedule with teams of 15-men per side. Team A played Team B and the winner played Team C until only one team remained undefeated. Three divisions were formed in the ORFU. Referees were used for all games. A point-scoring system was put into place with 6 points for a Goal from the Field (field goal); 4 points for a Try (touchdown), Goals from a Try, Penalties and Free Kicks; 2 points for Safety Touches; and 1 point for Kicks to the Deadline, Rouges and Touch in Goals. The Quebec Union adopted the Challenge System with Scoring by Goals and Trys. This format required the previous year's champion to defeat all challengers. The Toronto Argonauts defeated the Ottawa FC 9-7 in the first ORFU Championship on Saturday, November 10th.

1884 - The Canadian Rugby Football Union was formed on Thursday, February 7th at the Montreal Gymnasium and used the ORFU and New English Rugby Union Rules to form the Code of Rules for Canadian football. The QRFU adopted the OFRU system of scoring and the Tie Schedule. The Montreal Foot Ball Club (QFRU) defeated the Toronto Argonauts (ORFU) 30-0 on Thursday, November 6th in the first CRFU Championship game.

1885 - The ORFU divided into City and College groups. The CRFU stated that the playing field should be as close to 100 yards in length as practical by 65 yards wide. A combined team from the Montreal and Britannia Football Clubs (QRFU) defeated an Ontario Combined Team (ORFU) 3-0 on Wednesday, November 12th in the CRFU Championship game. The CRFU ruled the game was a draw because the Montreal team did not score 4 points.

1886 - The CRFU ruled that a quarterback could run or kick the ball only after the defenders had pushed the ball through the scrimmage. The ORFU objected to the CRFU rules governing championship games and refused to participate. No championship game was played.

1887 - The ORFU withdrew from the CRFU and the governing body ceased to function. The ORFU adopted "heeling" the ball as a method of putting it into play. They also began using a 5-man scrimmage. Goals from the Field were reduced to 5 points. At the end of the season, team executive members arranged a Dominion Championship game at McGill University in which Ottawa College (ORFU) defeated the Montreal Football Club (QRFU) 10-5 on Saturday, November 5th.

1888 - ORFU aligned into one unit and competed in a Challenge System. Penalty Kicks were lowered in value to 2 points. Hamilton Tigers introduced the 3-man scrimmage. ORFU and QRFU executives arranged a Dominion Championship at Ottawa. Ottawa College (ORFU) and the Montreal Football Club played to a scoreless tie. This was the last title match until 1892. Winnipeg Football Club, St. John's College and the Royal School of Infantry formed the Manitoba Rugby League.

1889 - ORFU lowered the value of a Goal from Field to 5 points. Intercollegiate teams used a 2-point Goal from a Try. The QRFU adopted a Challenge System.

1890 - ORFU returned to the Tie Schedule. All teams adopted the 2-point Goal from a Try. QRFU adopted the 3-man scrimmage. First game in Alberta, as Edmonton and Clover Bar played to a scoreless tie. In October, Regina North West Mounted Police played the Winnipeg Football Club twice in Winnipeg with each side winning once.

1891 - At a meeting of delegates of the Quebec and Ontario Rugby Unions at the Windsor Hotel in Montreal on Saturday, December 19th, the Canadian Rugby Union was formed. Games were to consist of two 45-minute halves, scoring values: Goal from the Field 5 points; Try 4 points; Goal from a Try 2 points; Penalty Kick and Free Kick 4 points each Safety Touch 2 points and a Rouge 1 point. ORFU rules were adopted by the CRU including an increase in the height of the goalposts to 20 feet from 13; the Scrimmage had to release the ball before the lines could come together and games were to be won by a majority of points scored. Edmonton defeated Calgary 6-5 in the Alberta Total-point Challenge Series.

1892 - The first CRU championship game was played on Thanksgiving Day, Thursday, November 10th at Toronto's Rosedale Field with Osgoode Hall of ORFU defeating the Montreal Foot Ball Club of the QRFU 45-5. ORFU assigned Umpires for all games. QRFU adopted a a Balanced Schedule (all teams played the same number of games) and lowered the value of a Goal from a Try to 2 points. The Manitoba Rugby Football Union was formed on Monday, February 22nd and played Fall and Spring Schedules.

1893 - QRFU assigned Umpires for all games and returned to the Challenge System format.

1894 - Ottawa College and the Ottawa AAA joined the QRFU. QRFU adopted the Balanced Schedule.

1895 - Timekeepers were appointed for the first time to relieve the referees of that duty. ORFU and QRFU lowered the value of Penalty Kicks to 2 points.

1896 - CRU game length was reduced to two 40-minute halves and the size of a field was set at 110 yards by 65 yards. CRU published the first "Constitution, Rules of the Championship Competitions and Rules of the Game". MRFU adopted the CRU rules. QRFU introduced 5-yard Punt Returns.

1897 - On Wednesday, November 24th, the Canadian Intercollegiate Rugby Football Union was organized in Kingston, Ontario. CRU changed the length of a game to two 35-minute halves. The QRFU lowered the Free Kick to 2 points and adopted a three-team playoff format. Ottawa FC was suspended by the QRFU executive for excessive rough play.

1898 - First Intercollegiate game was played at Kingston on Saturday, October 8th between McGill and Queen's. McGill won by 3 Rouges to 2. McGill then played the University of Toronto on Saturday, October 15th. The U of T won 11-5 in the rain. Toronto went on to win the Yates Trophy as Intercollegiate champions. The CIRFU was accepted into the CRU, but left later in the year. Ottawa FC re-organized as the Rough Riders on Friday, September 9th and adopted the colours of the Canadian Regiment in the Spanish-American War - red and black. Ottawa joined the ORFU which adopted the Balanced Schedule of play. The CRU again changed the length of a game to two 30-minute halves.

1900 - The ORFU prohibited the use of CIRFU players and the CRU stated that players must block with their bodies and not hold opponents with their arms or hands.

1901 - The ORFU stated that all players must sign amateur cards. CRU rules that the ball was to placed on the ground in line with the front foot of the Scrimmage before the lines could come together. John Thrift Meldrum Burnside's revised football rules were put into play in University of Toronto Inter-faculty games, and later in the Mulock Cup championship games.

1903 - The ORFU adopted the Burnside Rules which reduced teams to 12 men per side, put into play the Snap-Back system of moving the ball, required the offensive team to gain 10 yards on three downs, abolished the Throw-In from the sidelines, permitted only six men on the line, stated that all Goals by Kicking were to be worth 2 points and the opposition was to line up 10 yards from the defenders on all Kicks. The Rules were to be made uniform across the country as quickly as possible. The CIRFU, QRFU and CRU refused to adopt the new Rules. QRFU and CRU reduced their rosters from 15 to 14 players. CRU ruled that possesion could not go beyond 3 scrimmages unless during the third scrimmage the ball was moved 5 yards on a run or a kick. Ottawa returned to the QRFU and MRFU moved to a fall schedule.

1904 - The value of a Try (touchdown) was increased to 5 points and Goals from a Try was reduced to 1 point in the ORFU. QRFU adopted a rule by Tom (King) Clancy of Ottawa that a team must make 5 yards on its third scrimmage to keep possesion of the ball.

1905 - The Intercollegiate and Quebec Unions refused the Burnside Rules. For championship games, the CRU ruled the teams would use QRFU rules for the first half and the Intercollegiate rules for the second half. QRFU moved to four 15-minute quarters; Trys worth 5 points and Goals from Trys worth 1 point. CIRFU adopted 10-yard rule for 3 downs and the ORFU gave captains the option of playing four 15-minute quarters. Goals from the Field were increased to 3 points and the Fair Catch rule was replaced by a 3-yard Punt Return rule.

1906 - Specifications first laid down for the size of football - 11 inches long, 23 inches in circumference and 13-3/4 ounces in weight. Goals from the Field and Free Kicks were increased to 4 points in the ORFU. Games were four 15-minute quarters in length. CIRFU lowered Goals from the Field to 4 points and Free Kicks to 3 points. Calgary City Rugby Foot-ball Club was formed Wednesday, March 14th at Calgary City Hall.

1907 - The Interprovincial Rugby Football union (Big Four) grew out of an amalgamation between the Hamilton Tigers, Toronto Argonauts of the ORFU and the Ottawa Rough Riders and the Montreal Foot Ball Club of the QRFU on Friday, September 13, 1907. The QRFU withdrew from senior competition. The Ottawa entry was the result of the amalgamation of the Ottawa St. Pats and Rough Riders. Montreal won the Big Four's first game, 17-8 over Toronto and subsequently became the league's first championship team. Calgary City Rugby Foot-ball Club played its first game on Thursday, October 31st and defeated the Strathcona Rugby Foot-ball Club 15-0 at Calgary. The CRU adopted the Intercollegiate rule of 1 yard between opposing lines and stated that the lines could not move until the ball was put into play by the Scrimmage. Teams had to gain 10 yards in 3 downs; a Try was 5 points; a Goal from a Try was 1 point; a Goal from the Field was 4 points; a Free Kick was 3 points and a Penalty Kick was worth 2 points. The ORFU adopted the CRU rules. The Edmonton Rugby Foot-ball Club was formed on Wednesday, April 10th and adopted the uniform colours of black with yellow facings. Edmonton played its first game on Saturday, November 9th and defeated the Calgary City Rugby Foot-ball Club 26-5 at the Edmonton Exhibition Grounds. The Saskatchewan Rugby Football League was furmed.

1908 - Calgary City Rugby Foot-ball Club was re-organized as the Tigers on Thursday, August 27th and adopted yellow and black as the team colours. Calgary Rugby Football Union was formed on Tuesday, September 29th in the offices of the Sovereign Life Insurance Company. The Caledonia and Hillhurst Football Clubs play for the championship of the Central Alberta Rugby Football League on Friday, September 4th. The Edmonton Rugby Foot-ball Club was re-organized as the Esquimoux on Friday, October 16th. Goals from the Field were reduced to 3 points by the CRU.

1909 - Albert Henry George, the fourth Earl of Grey and the Governor General of Canada, donated a trophy to be awarded for the Rugby Football Championship of Canada. Only teams registered with the Canadian Rugby Union were eligible to compete for the trophy. The 1st game was played in Toronto at Rosedale Field on Saturday, December 4th between the University of Toronto and the Parkdale Canoe Club with the University of Toronto winning 26-6 before 3,807 fans. Hugh Gall kicked a record eight singles in the game for the U of T. The gross revenue was $2,616.40. On Sat., Dec. 11th, following an invitation from the New York Herald newspaper, Hamilton Tigers and Ottawa Rough Riders played a CFL exhibition game in New York City at Van Cortland Park. Tigers won 11-6 before 15,000 fans.

1910 - Regina Rugby Club was formed on Tuesday, September 13th at the Regina City Hall and adopted the colours of old gold and purple. On Thursday, September 22nd the Saskatchewan Rugby Football Union was organized in the Flanagan Hotel at Saskatoon. SRFU adopted the CRU rules. Regina played Moose Jaw Tigers in its first game on Saturday, October 1st at the Moose Jaw Baseball Grounds. The Tigers won 16-6. Edmonton changed its name to the Eskimos.

1911 - Manitoba, Saskatchewan and Alberta Unions formed the Western Canada Rugby Football Union on Saturday, October 21st. Regina RC changed its colours to blue and white. Winnipeg realtor Hugo Ross donated the championship trophy bearing his name, he subsequently drowned in the sinking of the S.S. Titanic in April, 1912. Calgary Tigers won the Western Championship and challenged for the Grey Cup, but the CRU would not accept the challenge because the WCRFU was not a full member of the CRU. University of Toronto defeated the Argonauts 14-7 on Saturday, November 25th to win its third consecutive Grey Cup championship.

1912 - Regina Rugby Club adopted the colours of the Canadian contingent in the Spanish-American War - red and black. Hamilton Alerts were suspended by the ORFU on Saturday, November 23rd for flaunting the authority of the Union. Toronto Rowing and Athletic Club had protested a penalty call which had resulted in a victory for the Alerts. The ORFU ordered the game be re-played on the 23rd, but the Alerts refused to field a full team. The Alerts lost to Toronto 39-7 while the main squad lost a regularly scheduled match in Hamilton to the Tigers 12-8. The Alerts went on to defeat the Toronto Argonauts 11-4 in the Grey Cup Game. Many of the players joined the Tigers of IRFU the following season.

1913 - Hamilton Tigers played four exhibition matches in Western Canada defeating Winnipeg 26-1, Regina 26-4, Moose Jaw 25-1 and Calgary 19-2. This is the first documented East-West series of games. On Saturday, September 6th the Hamilton Alerts applied for reinstatement in the ORFU under the name of the East Hamilton Athletic Association, but the request was denied. The Hamilton Rowing Club, however, was accepted.

1914 - The remnants of the Hamilton Alerts operated separately from any Union for several seasons before fading from the scene. The CRU appointed Head Linesmen and the CIRFU adopted a 3-yard Interference rule. IRFU adopted a Residence Rule.

1916-1918 - No games because of the First World War.

1919 - No playoff games because of a rules dispute with the CRU in the West, lack of interest in the East and student studies to the Intercollegiate Union which were more important.

1920 - CIRFU and IRFU adopted a 4-yard Interference rule while the CRU opted for 3 yards of Interference.

1921 - Western Canada Rugby Football Union joined the CRU and challenged for the Grey Cup. Edmonton Eskimos, first Western team to play in a Grey Cup game, lost to Toronto Argonauts 23-0. Rule changes included reducing players from 14 to 12 per side; putting ball into play by snapping it back; limit of 18 players with substitutes permitted freely.

1923 - Calgary Tigers renamed the 50th Battalion. Queen's defeats Regina 54-0 as Queen's scored a record nine touchdowns on Saturday, December 1st. Edmonton withdrew from competition.

1924 - Coach Bill Hughes of Queen's introduced the use of films as a coaching technique. Numbering of players, although used for years was made compulsory. The Regina Rugby Club became the Regina Roughriders.

1925 - McGill coach Frank Shaughnessy introduced the "huddle" system to Canadian football. It was at first called the "Conference System". Calgary 50th Battalion became the Tigers. Ottawa changed its name to the Senators.

1926 - British Columbia Rugby Football Union was formed on Wednesday, September 1st.

1927 - Western Canada Intercollegiate Union was formed. Ottawa reverted to the name Rough Riders.

1928 - Tri-City Rugby Football Union was formed on Saturday, August 25th and consisted of Moose Jaw, Regina and Winnipeg. The Union disbanded the following year because of travel expenses. Saskatchewan and Winnipeg re-formed their unions. First radio play-by-play broadcast of a Grey Cup Game was on Sunday, December 1st. Hamilton Tigers shutout Regina Roughriders 30-0 before a crowd of 4,767 at the Hamilton Amateur Athletic Association Grounds.

1929 - CRU adopted use of the forward pass on a limited basis in Junior, Interscholastic, Western Canada Rugby Union, Western Intercollegiate Union and the Grey Cup final. First legal pass in Canada was thrown by Gerry Seiberling and the first reception was by Ralph Losie of Calgary Altomah-Tigers against Edmonton on Saturday, September 21st. Jersey Jack Campbell of Regina threw the first forward pass in a Grey Cup game and Jerry Erskine made the first reception. First TD pass was by Edmonton's Joe Cook to Pal Power in the second quarter of a game against the University of Alberta on Saturday, September 28th. The first interception return for a touchdown was by Joe Hess of the University of Alberta in the same game when he caught a pass by Cook.

1930 - On Tuesday, June 10th, the Winnipeg Winnipegs Rugby Football Club was formed and adopted the colours of green and white. Winnipeg played its first game against St. John's Rugby Club at Carruthers Park on Saturday, September 13th. St. John's won 7-3. On Monday, September 29th in the first game played in Canada under floodlights, the Hamilton Tigers defeated University of British Columbia in an exhibition game at Athletic Park. The first game in Eastern Canada under floodlights was on Wednesday, October 29th, between Oshawa and Toronto Balmy Beach in Toronto's Ulster Stadium. The Convert kicking spot was moved from the 35-line to the 25, but only drop kicks were allowed.

1931 - CRU approved the forward pass for all leagues and the first TD pass in Grey Cup history was a Warren Stevens to Kenny Grant play in Montreal's 22-0 win over Regina. Convert scrimmage line was moved to the 5-yard line, and the point could be scored by a drop-kick, place kick, run or pass.

1932 - Calgary Altomah-Tigers became the Altomahs. Winnipeg and St. John's amalgamated to field a stronger team, and adopt the colours of blue and gold.

1934 - Edward (Red) Tellier of Montreal, who had been suspended for life for attacking George Gilhooley of Regina in the 1931 Grey Cup final, was re-instated. Eastern Intercollegiate Union formally withdrew from Grey Cup competition. The horn was introduced to officiating.

1935 - For the first time a Western team won the Grey Cup. Winnipeg 'Pegs (they weren't Blue Bombers for another year) defeated Hamilton Tigers 18-12 at Hamilton. Calgary became the Bronks.

1936 - Teams were restricted to a maximum of five imports and only players who had lived in Canada for a full year could compete in the Grey Cup Game. The Western Interprovincial Football Union (WIFU) was formed with Winnipeg Blue Bombers, Calgary Bronks and Regina Roughriders. IRFU and WIFU adopt playoff format of a two-game total-point series between 1st and 2nd place teams. A white ball was used for games played under floodlights in Western Canada. Intercollegiate teams stop competing for the Grey Cup.

1937 - The Quebec Rugby Football Union discontinued challenging for the Grey Cup.

1938 - Edmonton Eskimos joined the Western Interprovincial Football Union and adopted the colours of blue and white, but withdrew in 1940.

1940 - The only two-game total point series in Grey Cup history was played. Ottawa defeated Toronto Balmy Beach 8-2 and 12-5. The series was arranged by the Canadian Rugby Union when it refused to allow Winnipeg Blue Bombers, the Western winners, to compete in the final because the West had played its season under rules which varied from rules in the East.

1941 - Calgary left the WIFU and Vancouver Grizzlies joined. IRFU was renamed Eastern Canada Union for one season.

1942 - WIFU and IRFU suspended operations for the duration of War.

1945 - Calgary Bronks changed its name to Stampeders on Friday, September 28th and adopted the colours of blue and gold. IRFU resumed play.

1946 - Montreal Alouettes were organized. WIFU resumed play. Regina Roughriders were renamed Saskatchewan Roughriders. Air travel in football was used for first time. Argos flew to Winnipeg for pre-season games.

1948 - Hamilton Tigers of the IRFU (Big Four), joined the ORFU, and the Hamilton Wildcats of the ORFU joined the Big Four on Friday, April 9th. Saskatchewan Roughriders adopted the colours of green and white. Calgary Stampeders introduced pagentry to the Grey Cup Game with saddle horses and chuck wagons. Calgary reverts to the colours of red and white. Stampeders defeated Ottawa 12-7 for their first Grey Cup victory.

1949 - Edmonton Eskimos rejoined the WIFU and adopted the colours of green and gold. Wearing of helmets was made compulsory. Western Canada Rugby Football Union ceased to exist.

1950 - Hamilton Tigers and Hamilton Wildcats amalgamated to form Hamilton Tiger-Cats. Regina officially its changed its name to Saskatchewan Roughriders on Saturday, April 1st. WIFU gave the 3rd place team in standings a playoff berth. The first professional playoff game was played at night under lights - Winnipeg at Edmonton. Grey Cup attendance - 27,101 at Varsity Stadium.

1951 - The B.C. Lions were formed in January at the Arctic Club. E. Kent Phillips of Saskatoon was appointed Commissioner of WIFU.

1952 - Television revenue for the first time. CRU was paid $7,500 by CBC for Grey Cup TV rights. CBLT Toronto was only station to carry game live.

1953 - Three television stations carried the Grey Cup game live, and the CRU was paid $20,500 for the rights. Billy Vessels won the first Schenley Award. G. Sydney Halter, QC was named Commissioner of WIFU.

1954 - B.C. entered the WIFU and adopted the colours burnt orange and brown. B.C. played its first game at Empire Games Stadium against the Montreal Alouettes on Wednesday, August 11th. The Alouettes won 22-0. IRFU (Big Four) games were televised on the NBC national network.

1955 - IRFU awarded the 3rd place team a playoff berth. The Grey Cup Game was played in the West for the first time in Vancouver's Empire Stadium, attendance 39,500, gross revenue $198,000. ORFU withdrew from Grey Cup competition.

1956 - Canadian Football Council was formed Sunday, January 22nd at Winnipeg and national negotiation lists were introduced. Value of a touchdown was increased from 5 to 6 points. Television rights were sold for $101,000. G. Sydney Halter, QC was named Commissioner of Canadian Football Council.

1957 - Interference by eligible blockers legal up to third 5-yard stripe. First Grey Cup Game telecast live from coast to coast in Canada. TV rights brought $125,000.

1958 - Canadian Football Council withdrew from Canadian Rugby Union. CFC was renamed the Canadian Football League on Sunday, January 19th at the Royal Alexandra Hotel in Winnipeg. G. Sydney Halter, QC of Winnipeg was appointed Commissioner. The CFL opened on Thursday, August 14th as the Blue Bombers defeated the Edmonton Eskimos 29-21 at Winnipeg before 18,206 spectators.

1960 - Interprovincial Rugby Football Union (Big Four) changed name to Eastern Football Conference. Unlimited blocking was allowed on interception returns. McMahon Stadium in Calgary was built in 103 days and the Stampeders moved in Monday, August 15th.

1961 - Western Canada Intercollegiate Rugby Union merged with the Canadian Intercollegiate Athletic Union. Western Interprovincial Football Union changed name to Western Football Conference. Partial interlocking schedule introduced between Eastern and Western Conference. First Grey Cup Game to go into overtime was 21-14 Winnipeg victory over Hamilton at CNE Stadium, Toronto. Four backs were permitted unlimited blocking on rushing plays if they lined up outside the ends. The tackle -eligible play was made illegal.

1962 - Canadian Football Hall of Fame was established and Hamilton was named the site. Grey Cup Game stopped by fog on Saturday, December 1st and the final 9 minutes and 29 seconds were played the next day. Winnipeg edged Hamilton 28-27.

1963 - Charter Membership into Hall of Fame.

1965 - CFL commissioned an economic study of all aspects of Canadian football. Canadian Football Players Association was organized. First meetings were May 15th to 16th in Toronto.

1966 - Unlimited blocking on rushing plays was legalized. Rule book rewritten and reduced in size. Trusteeship of Grey Cup turned over by CRU to CFL. Goose-necked goalposts were introduced.

1967 - CFL office set up in Toronto with Senator Keith Davey as Commissioner. Senator Davey was succeeded on Thursday, February 23rd by Ted Workman and then Allan McEachern. Recommendations of Committee On One League (COO) approved to bring operating matters under control of the League. Players' Pension Fund established. CRU became the CAFA on Sunday, January 1st and turned over the Grey Cup trophy to the CFL. CFL League Office took up residence at 11 King Street West in Toronto in Montreal Trust Building.

1968 - J.G. (Jake) Gaudar was appointed Commissioner and CFL adopted new Constitution.

1969 - Although the 1962 game was completed on a Sunday, the 1969 game was the first Grey Cup game to start and finish on a Sunday and the first Grey Cup game in Montreal since 1931.

1970 - 3m Tartan Turf was installed in Vancouver's Empire Stadium. First sod was turned for Hall of Fame building in Hamilton. First All-Star Game since 1958.

1971 - Grey Cup Game was played on artificial turf for first time in Vancouver, Calgary defeated Toronto 14-11.

1972 - Canadian Football Hall of Fame opened in Hamilton. Grey Cup was played on Astroturf in Hamilton's Ivor Wynne Stadium.

1973 - Both Conferences adopted standard playoff procedure.

1974 - Eastern Conference adopted 16-game schedule. ORFU ceased to exist.

1975 - For the first time, a Grey Cup final on the Prairies - in Calgary. Blocking above waist was permitted on punt-returns; 2-point convert was introduced.

1976 - The Canadian Football League attracted more than 2 million fans for the first time as 2,029,586 people attended its games.

1977 - Grey Cup Game was played before record crowd (68,318) which paid record receipts ($1,401,930) at Montreal's Olympic Stadium. Montreal Alouettes set CFL attendance record of 476,201.

1979 - Edmonton Eskimos set single season attendance record of 340,239 for Western Conference.

1980 - CFL signed record television contract with Carling-O'Keefe Breweries for $15.6 million to cover 3-year period (1981-83).

1981 - Eastern, Western Conference dissolved and renamed East and West Divisions. Board of Governors replaced Executive Committee and Management Council replaced General Managers Committee. Complete interlocking schedule for first time.

1982 - CFL granted a new franchise to Montreal, called the Concordes. The Grey Cup Game attracted the largest television audience in the history of Canadian television as 7,862,000 viewers watched Edmonton extend their record to five consecutive Grey Cup victories.

1983 - CFL signed record television agreement with Carling O'Keefe Breweries for $33 million over a 3-year period (1984-86). League attendance reached an all-time high of 2,856,031 for all games. The 71st Grey Cup Game was played before 59,345 fans in B.C. Place Stadium and was the first CFL championship game to be played indoors. The Game provided the League with its first $2 million gross gate. Television coverage on CBC, CTV and Radio-Canada of the Grey Cup Game attracted the largest viewing audience in television history for a Canadian sports program as 8,118,000 people watched Toronto edge B.C. 18-17.

1984 - On Friday, June 1st, Douglas H. Mitchell, Q.C. of Calgary became the sixth Commissioner of the CFL. In the fall, a market research study was done with fans in the CFL cities. The League moved to make the 1985 Canadian College Draft 'Open' and eliminated Territorial Exemptions. Edmonton played host to its first Grey Cup Game.

1985 - The CFL moved to adopt overtime in the Regular Season which consisted of two five-minute halves (no-sudden death) and would be implemented in 1986. The CFL changed the overtime format for Playoff Games from two 10-minutes halves (with no sudden-death) to two 5-minute halves (no sudden-death).

1986 - The CFL moved to an 18-game (per Club) Regular Season schedule. The Playoff structure was revised permitting a fourth place team from one division to qualify for post-season play providing it had more points in the Regular Season standings than the third place team in the other division. The CFL and the CFLPA agree to a new three-year agreement. The Alouettes were re-born as the Montreal Football Club changed its name from the Concordes to the Alouettes, on the 40th anniversary of the founding of the Alouettes. The Sports Network carried live coverage of the first round of the 1986 Canadian College Draft from coast-to-coast Winnipeg Blue Bombers and Montreal Alouettes played the first pre-season game in the Canada Games Stadium at Saint John, New Brunswick. Winnipeg won 35-10. The CFL amended the quota to 35-man game rosters (13 Imports, 19 Non-imports and 3 Quarterbacks). The Designated Import rule was eliminated. End zones were reduced from 25 to 20 yards. The Canadian Amateur Football Association changed its name to Football Canada in June.

1987 - The CFL celebrated the 75th Grey Cup Championship Season with the milestone Game at B.C. Place Stadium on Sunday, November 29th. The Canadian Football Network, a syndicate of Canadian television stations was formed. The CFL experimented with the TV blackout policy as four games (two in Hamilton and two in Toronto) are televised in the Hamilton-Toronto market. Game rosters were revised from 35 to 34 (19 Non-Imports, 13 Imports and 2 Quarterbacks) the reserve list was increased from three to four. The Montreal Alouettes folded on June 24th; the schedule was revised and the Divisions realigned with the Winnipeg Blue Bombers moving to the Eastern Division. The Playoff format reverted to pre-1986.

1988 - The CFL's agreement with CFN was extended through to 1990. Game rosters were to consist of 20 non-imports, 14 imports and 2 quarterbacks, the reserve list consisted of up to 2 players. When a team dressed 14 imports, one had to be designated as a specialty teams player. On Monday, December 12th, Roy McMurtry was appointed Chairman-Chief Executive Officer and Bill Baker President-Chief Operating Officer, both appointments were effective Sunday, January 1, 1989. The Board of Governors also approved the sale of the Toronto Argonauts from Carling O'Keefe to Harry Ornest.

1989 - On Friday, February 24th, the Board of Governors approved the sale of the Hamilton Tiger-Cats from Harold E. Ballard-Maple Leaf Gardens Limited to David Braley. Two months later, the CFL announced a two-year television agreement with Carling O'Keefe for $12 million plus an additional $3 million in Club promotional support. Hamilton hosted the CFL Annual Meetings-Canadian College Draft for the second consecutive year. The Argos began play at the SkyDome, which would play host to the 77th Grey Cup Championship on Sunday, November 26th. Saskatchewan defeated Hamilton 43-40. Murray Pezim purchased the B.C. Lions in September. The Canadian Interuniversity Athletic Union moved its championship, the Vanier Cup, from Varsity Stadium to the SkyDome. The University of Western Ontario defeated the University of Saskatchewan 35-10 in the Silver Anniversary game. Bill Baker resigned as President-Chief Operating Officer effective Sunday, December 31st.

1990 - J. Donald Crump was appointed the eighth Commissioner of the CFL on Friday, January 5th. The CFL Annual Meetings-Canadian College Draft were held in Hamilton for the third consecutive year. Rosters were increased to 37 players including 20 non-imports, 14 imports and 3 quarterbacks. The reserve list remained at 2 players. Toronto and B.C. set a record for most points in a game when they combined to score 111 on Saturday, September 1st at Toronto. Argonauts won 68-43. B.C. added silver to its colours. Vancouver played host to the Grey Cup Game for the 11th time.

1991 - The Toronto Argonauts were sold by Harry Ornest to Bruce McNall, Wayne Gretzky and John Candy on Monday,February 25th. Ottawa Rough Riders Board of Directors resigned on Wednesday, July 24th and two days later the CFL assumed ownership of the franchise. On Saturday, October 19th, Bernie and Lonnie Glieberman purchased the club from the CFL. Five days later, Larry Ryckman purchased the Calgary Stampeders from the Stampeder Football Club Limited. The eight clubs combined for a record 64.2 points per game and attendance figures broke 2 million (2,001,858) for the 10th time. Winnipeg played host to the Grey Cup Game for the first time on Sunday, November 24th. Toronto defeated Calgary 36-21 before a crowd of 51,985 fans. The Game was the most-watched Canadian TV show with an audience of 3,531,000 viewers. J. Donald Crump resigned as Commissioner on Tuesday, December 31st.

1992 - Larry Smith, former running back and tight end with Montreal Alouettes was named the ninth Commissioner of the CFL on Thursday, February 27th. CFL celebrates 100 years of football in Canada, commemorating the formation of the Canadian Rugby Union in 1892, the forerunner of Football Canada and the CFL. Calgary Stampeders sign free agent quarterback Doug Flutie in March, 1992. On August 27, the League revokes the franchise of B.C. Lions owner Murray Pezim and assumes control after his refusal to pay club bills. Bill Comrie purchases the B.C. franchise on September 23 from the CFL. At CFL's Outstanding Player Awards during Grey Cup Week, Flutie is named the Most Outstanding Player for the second consecutive year, only the third player in League history to win back-to-back awards. Toronto hosts the Grey Cup for the 45th time, more than any other city. The 80th Grey Cup is played at SkyDome as Calgary defeats the Winnipeg Blue Bombers 24-10 for their third Grey Cup win and first since 1971, ending the longest drought of any CFL team.

1993 - At the League's Annual Meetings on February 23 in Hamilton, the Sacramento Gold Miners are admitted as the CFL's ninth franchise, to begin play in 1993 in the Western Division. Sacramento becomes the League's first franchise based in the United States and is the first addition since the B.C. Lions in 1954. The Annual Canadian College Draft is held in Calgary on March 6, the first time it has been held in a Western Division city since 1971 in Winnipeg. Calgary's McMahon Stadium will be the site of the Grey Cup for the second time in history with the 81st Grey Cup Championship to be played on Sunday, November 28.

1994 - The Las Vegas Posse, Shreveport Pirates and Baltimore CFL Colts became the Canadian Football League's tenth, eleventh and twelfth members respectively with all beginning play in the 1994 season. Las Vegas joins the Western Division while Baltimore and Shreveport will participate in the Eastern Division bringing the number of teams in each Division to six. Bruce M. Firestone purchased the Ottawa Rough Riders Football Club from former owner Bernie Glieberman in February, 1994. B.C. Place Stadium will play host to the 82nd Grey Cup Championship on Sunday, November 27. This marks the twelfth time the game has been played in Vancouver. The first ever CFL game between two American teams will be played on Friday, July 8 when Las Vegas travels to Sacramento to take on the Gold Miners.

CANADIAN FOOTBALL LEAGUE

(Established January 17, 1958)

COMMISSIONER

1994 - Larry W. Smith, Montreal
1993 - Larry W. Smith
1992 - Larry W. Smith
1991 - J. Donald Crump, C.A., Toronto
1990 - J. Donald Crump, C.A.
1989 - Bill Baker, Regina*
1988 - Douglas H. Mitchell, Q.C., Calgary
1987 - Douglas H. Mitchell, Q.C.
1986 - Douglas H. Mitchell, Q.C.
1985 - Douglas H. Mitchell, Q.C.
1984 - Douglas H. Mitchell, Q.C.
1983 - J.G. (Jake) Gaudaur, Hamilton
1982 - J.G. Gaudaur
1981 - J.G. Gaudaur
1980 - J.G. Gaudaur
1979 - J.G. Gaudaur
1978 - J.G. Gaudaur
1977 - J.G. Gaudaur
1976 - J.G. Gaudaur
1975 - J.G. Gaudaur
1974 - J.G. Gaudaur
1973 - J.G. Gaudaur
1972 - J.G. Gaudaur
1971 - J.G. Gaudaur
1970 - J.G. Gaudaur
1969 - J.G. Gaudaur
1968 - J.G. Gaudaur
1967 - Keith Davey, Toronto
- Ted Workman, Montreal
- Allan McEachern, Vancouver
1966 - G. Sydney Halter, Q.C., Winnipeg
1965 - G. Sydney Halter, Q.C.
1964 - G. Sydney Halter, Q.C.
1963 - G. Sydney Halter, Q.C.
1962 - G. Sydney Halter, Q.C.
1961 - G. Sydney Halter, Q.C.
1960 - G. Sydney Halter, Q.C.
1959 - G. Sydney Halter, Q.C.
1958 - G. Sydney Halter, Q.C.

*Note: Bill Baker held the title of President/Chief Operating Officer

BOARD OF GOVERNORS

	Chairman	Secretary-Treasurer
1994 -	John H. Tory, Toronto	Gregory B. Fulton, Toronto
1993 -	John H. Tory	Greg. Fulton
1992 -	John H. Tory	Greg. Fulton
1991 -	Phil Kershaw, Regina	Greg. Fulton
-	R. Roy McMurtry, Q.C., Toronto	
1990 -	R. Roy McMurtry, Q.C.	Greg. Fulton
1989 -	R. Roy McMurtry, Q.C.	Greg. Fulton
1988 -	Hon. William G. Davis, P.C., C.C., Q.C., Brampton	Greg. Fulton
1987 -	Hon. William G. Davis, P.C., C.C., Q.C.	Greg. Fulton
1986 -	Ronald M. Jones, Vancouver	Greg. Fulton
1985 -	L. Edmond Ricard, Montreal	Greg. Fulton
1984 -	Dallas Gendall, Edmonton	Greg. Fulton
1983 -	Ralph Sazio, Toronto	Greg. Fulton
1982 -	Gordon Staseson, Regina	Greg. Fulton
1981 -	Terry Kielty, Ottawa	Greg. Fulton
	President	**Secretary-Treasurer**
1980 -	R. Ross Smith, Winnipeg	Greg. Fulton
1979 -	David Berger, Montreal	Greg. Fulton
1978 -	Jack Farley, Vancouver	Greg. Fulton
1977 -	W.R. (Bill) Hodgson, Toronto	Greg. Fulton
1976 -	W.R. (Roy) Jennings, Calgary	Greg. Fulton
1975 -	Ralph Sazio, Hamilton	Greg. Fulton
1974 -	Jim Hole, Edmonton	Greg. Fulton
1973 -	David Loeb, Ottawa	Greg. Fulton
1972 -	W.E. (Bill) Clarke, Regina	Greg. Fulton
1971 -	Sam Berger, Montreal	Greg. Fulton

	President	Secretary-Treasurer
1970 -	Dr. Neville Winograd, Winnipeg	Greg. Fulton
1969 -	Lew Hayman, Toronto	Greg. Fulton
1968 -	Allan McEachern, Vancouver	Greg. Fulton
1967 -	Allan McEachern, Vancouver	Greg. Fulton
1966 -	M.E. (Ted) Workman, Montreal	R.H. (Bob) Gillies, Regina
1965 -	Patrick Mahoney, Calgary	R.H. Gillies
1964 -	Sam Berger, Ottawa	R.H. Gillies
1963 -	E.M. (Eck) Duggan, Edmonton	R.H. Gillies
1962 -	J.G. (Jake) Gaudaur, Hamilton	R.H. Gillies
1961 -	Ralph Parliament, Winnipeg	R.H. Gillies
1960 -	Ralph Cooper, Hamilton	R.H. Gillies
1959 -	Don McPherson, Regina	R.H. Gillies
1958 -	G. Sydney Halter, Winnipeg	D. Wes Brown, Ottawa and R.H. Gillies, Regina

CANADIAN FOOTBALL COUNCIL

(Established January 22, 1956)

	Chairman	Secretary-Treasurer
1957 -	Ralph Cooper, Hamilton	Brown and Gillies
1956 -	Ralph Cooper, Hamilton	Brown and Gillies

FOOTBALL CANADA

CANADIAN AMATEUR FOOTBALL ASSOCIATION

	President	Executive Director
1993 -	Joe Pistilli, Montreal	Jack Jordan, Ottawa
1993 -	Joe Pistilli, Montreal	Jack Jordan, Ottawa
1992 -	Barry Wright, Kingston	Jack Jordan, Ottawa
1991 -	Barry Wright, Kingston	Bob O'Doherty, Ottawa
1990 -	Richard Criddle, Halifax	Bob O'Doherty, Ottawa
1989 -	Richard Criddle, Halifax	Bob O'Doherty, Ottawa
1988 -	Richard Criddle, Halifax	Bob O'Doherty, Ottawa
1987 -	Richard Criddle, Halifax	Bob O'Doherty, Ottawa
1986 -	Jerry Zbytnuik, Regina	Bob O'Doherty, Cam Innes, Ottawa
1985 -	Jerry Zbytnuik, Regina	Cam Innes, Ian Inrig, Ottawa
1984 -	Don Henderson, Edmonton	Bob Larose, Ottawa
1983 -	Don Henderson, Edmonton	Bob Larose, Ottawa
1983 -	Jerry Joynt, Calgary	Bill Robinson, Ottawa
1982 -	Jerry Joynt, Calgary	Bill Robinson, Ottawa
1981 -	Len Trudel, Ottawa	Bill Robinson, Ottawa
1980 -	Len Trudel, Ottawa	Bill Robinson, Ottawa
1979 -	Len Trudel, Ottawa	Bill Robinson, Ottawa
1978 -	T. Brian Prentice, Burnaby	Bill Robinson, Ottawa
1977 -	T. Brian Prentice, Burnaby	Bill Robinson, Ottawa
1976 -	Dr. Robert Ripley, Ottawa	Bill Robinson, Ottawa
1975 -	Dr. Robert Ripley, Ottawa	Peter Mercer, Ottawa
1974 -	Dr. Robert Ripley, Ottawa	Peter Mercer, Ottawa
1973 -	David Rothstein, Winnipeg	Peter Mercer, Ottawa
1972 -	David Rothstein, Winnipeg	Peter Mercer, Ottawa
1971 -	Jack Rockett, Mississauga	William Leveridge, Toronto
1970 -	Jack Rockett, Mississauga	William Leveridge, Toronto
1969 -	Gordon Ingram, Edmonton	William Leveridge, Toronto
1968 -	Gordon Ingram, Edmonton	William Leveridge, Toronto
1967 -	William McEwen, Ottawa	William Leveridge, Toronto

1936/1993
YEAR-BY-YEAR STANDINGS

The James S. Dixon Trophy which is presented annually to the champion of the Eastern Division of the Canadian Football League is one of the oldest trophies still active in the League. It was first presented by Mr. Dixon of Hamilton to the Inter-Provincial Rugby Football Union champion in 1912. The Western counterpart to this trophy, the Hugo Ross was first presented in 1911 and retired in 1942. In 1948, the Ross Trophy was replaced by the N.J. "Piffles" Taylor Trophy named in honour of the former president and one of the founders of the Western Inter-Provincial Football Union.

1993

WESTERN DIVISION

	W.	L.	T.	F.	A.	Pts.
Cal.	15	3	0	646	418	30
Edm.	12	6	0	507	372	24
Sask.	11	7	0	511	495	22
B.C.	10	8	0	574	583	20
Sac.	6	12	0	498	509	12

EASTERN DIVISION

	W.	L.	T.	F.	A.	Pts.
Wpg.	14	4	0	646	421	28
Ham.	6	12	0	316	567	12
Ott.	4	14	0	387	517	8
Tor.	3	15	0	390	593	6

Semi-Finals - Saskatchewan 13, Edmonton 51
- B.C. 9, Calgary 17,
Final - Edmonton 29, Calgary 15

Semi-Final - Ottawa 10, Hamilton 21
Final - Hamilton 19, Winnipeg 20

Grey Cup - Edmonton 33, Winnipeg 23

1992

WESTERN DIVISION

	W.	L.	T.	F.	A.	Pts.
Cal.	13	5	0	607	430	26
Edm.	10	8	0	552	515	20
Sask.	9	9	0	505	545	18
B.C.	3	15	0	472	667	6

EASTERN DIVISION

	W.	L.	T.	F.	A.	Pts.
Wpg.	11	7	0	507	499	22
Ham.	11	7	0	536	514	22
Ott.	9	9	0	484	439	18
Tor.	6	12	0	469	523	12

Semi-Final - Saskatchewan 20, Edmonton 22
Final - Edmonton 22, Calgary 23

Semi-Final - Ottawa 28, Hamilton 29
Final - Hamilton 11, Winnipeg 59

Grey Cup - Calgary 24, Winnipeg 10

1991

WESTERN DIVISION

	W.	L.	T.	F.	A.	Pts.
Edm.	12	6	0	671	569	24
Cal.	11	7	0	596	552	22
B.C.	11	7	0	661	587	22
Sask.	6	12	0	606	710	12

EASTERN DIVISION

	W.	L.	T.	F.	A.	Pts.
Tor.	13	5	0	647	526	26
Wpg.	9	9	0	516	499	18
Ott.	7	11	0	522	577	14
Ham.	3	15	0	400	599	6

Semi-Final - B.C. 41, Calgary 43
Final - Calgary 38, Edmonton 36

Semi-Final - Ottawa 8, Winnipeg 26
Final - Winnipeg 3, Toronto 42

Grey Cup - Toronto 36, Calgary 21

1990

WESTERN DIVISION

	W.	L.	T.	F.	A.	Pts.
Cal.	11	6	1	588	566	23
Edm.	10	8	0	612	510	20
Sask.	9	9	0	557	592	18
B.C.	6	11	1	520	620	13

EASTERN DIVISION

	W.	L.	T.	F.	A.	Pts.
Wpg.	12	6	0	472	398	24
Tor.	10	8	0	689	538	20
Ott.	7	11	0	540	602	14
Ham.	6	12	0	476	628	12

Semi-Final - Saskatchewan 27, Edmonton 43
Final - Edmonton 43, Calgary 23

Semi-Final - Ottawa 25, Toronto 34
Final - Toronto 17, Winnipeg 20

Grey Cup - Winnipeg 50, Edmonton 11

1989

WESTERN DIVISION

	W.	L.	T.	F.	A.	Pts.
Edm.	16	2	0	644	302	32
Cal.	10	8	0	495	466	20
Sask.	9	9	0	547	567	18
B.C.	7	11	0	521	557	14

EASTERN DIVISION

	W.	L.	T.	F.	A.	Pts.
Ham.	12	6	0	519	517	24
Tor.	7	11	0	369	428	14
Wpg.	7	11	0	408	462	14
Ott.	4	14	0	426	630	8

Semi-Final - Saskatchewan 33, Calgary 26
Final - Saskatchewan 32, Edmonton 21

Semi-Final - Winnipeg 30, Toronto 7
Final - Winnipeg 10, Hamilton 14

Grey Cup - Saskatchewan 43, Hamilton 40

1988

WESTERN DIVISION

	W.	L.	T.	F.	A.	Pts.
Edm.	11	7	0	477	408	22
Sask.	11	7	0	525	452	22
B.C.	10	8	0	489	417	20
Cal.	6	12	0	395	476	12

EASTERN DIVISION

	W.	L.	T.	F.	A.	Pts.
Tor.	14	4	0	571	326	28
Wpg.	9	9	0	407	458	18
Ham.	9	9	0	478	465	18
Ott.	2	16	0	278	618	4

Semi-Final - B.C. 42, Saskatchewan 18
Final - B.C. 37, Edmonton 19

Semi-Final - Winnipeg 35, Hamilton 28
Final - Winnipeg 27, Toronto 11

Grey Cup - Winnipeg 22, B.C. 21

1987

WESTERN DIVISION

	W.	L.	T.	F.	A.	Pts.
B.C.	12	6	0	502	370	24
Edm.	11	7	0	617	462	22
Cal.	10	8	0	453	517	20
Sask.	5	12	1	364	529	11

EASTERN DIVISION

	W.	L.	T.	F.	A.	Pts.
Wpg.	12	6	0	554	409	24
Tor.	11	6	1	484	427	23
Ham.	7	11	0	470	509	14
Ott.	3	15	0	377	598	6

Semi-Final - Edmonton 30, Calgary 16
Final - Edmonton 31, B.C. 7

Semi-Final - Toronto 29, Hamilton 13
Final - Toronto 19, Winnipeg 3

Grey Cup - Edmonton 38, Toronto 36

1986

WESTERN DIVISION

	W.	L.	T.	F.	A.	Pts.
Edm.	13	4	1	540	365	27
B.C.	12	6	0	441	410	24
Wpg.	11	7	0	545	387	22
Cal.	11	7	0	484	380	22
Sask.	6	11	1	382	517	13

EASTERN DIVISION

	W.	L.	T.	F.	A.	Pts.
Tor.	10	8	0	417	441	20
Ham.	9	8	1	405	366	19
Mtl.	4	14	0	320	500	8
Ott.	3	14	1	346	514	7

Semi-Final - B.C. 21, Winnipeg 14
Semi-Final - Edmonton 27, Calgary 18
Final - Edmonton 41, B.C. 5

Final - Game 1 - Toronto 31, Hamilton 17
Final - Game 2 - Hamilton 42, Toronto 25
(Hamilton won 2 game tl.-points series 59-56)

Grey Cup - Hamilton 39, Edmonton 15

1985

WESTERN DIVISION

	W.	L.	T.	F.	A.	Pts.
B.C.	13	3	0	481	297	26
Wpg.	12	4	0	500	259	24
Edm.	10	6	0	432	373	20
Sask.	5	11	0	320	462	10
Cal.	3	13	0	256	429	6

EASTERN DIVISION

	W.	L.	T.	F.	A.	Pts.
Ham.	8	8	0	377	315	16
Mtl.	8	8	0	284	332	16
Ott.	7	9	0	272	402	14
Tor.	6	10	0	344	397	12

Semi-Final - Winnipeg 22, Edmonton 15
Final - B.C. 42, Winnipeg 22

Semi-Final - Montreal 30, Ottawa 20
Final - Hamilton 50, Montreal 26

Grey Cup - B.C. 37, Hamilton 24

1984

WESTERN DIVISION

	W.	L.	T.	F.	A.	Pts.
B.C.	12	3	1	445	281	25
Wpg.	11	4	1	523	309	23
Edm.	9	7	0	464	443	18
Sask.	6	9	1	348	479	13
Cal.	6	10	0	314	425	12

EASTERN DIVISION

	W.	L.	T.	F.	A.	Pts.
Tor.	9	6	1	461	361	19
Ham.	6	9	1	353	439	13
Mtl.	6	9	1	386	404	13
Ott.	4	12	0	354	507	8

Semi-Final - Winnipeg 55, Edmonton 20
Final - Winnipeg 31, B.C. 14

Semi-Final - Hamilton 17, Montreal 11
Final - Hamilton 14, Toronto 13 (overtime)

Grey Cup - Winnipeg 47, Hamilton 17

1983

WESTERN DIVISION

	W.	L.	T.	F.	A.	Pts.
B.C.	11	5	0	477	326	22
Wpg.	9	7	0	412	402	18
Edm.	8	8	0	450	377	16
Cal.	8	8	0	425	378	16
Sask.	5	11	0	360	536	10

EASTERN DIVISION

	W.	L.	T.	F.	A.	Pts.
Tor.	12	4	0	452	328	24
Ott.	8	8	0	384	424	16
Ham.	5	10	1	389	498	11
Mtl.	5	10	1	367	447	11

Semi-Final - Winnipeg 49, Edmonton 22
Final - B.C. 39, Winnipeg 21

Semi-Final - Hamilton 33, Ottawa 31
Final - Toronto 41, Hamilton 36

Grey Cup - Toronto 18, B.C. 17

1982

WESTERN DIVISION

	W.	L.	T.	F.	A.	Pts.
Edm.	11	5	0	544	323	22
Wpg.	11	5	0	444	352	22
Cal.	9	6	1	403	440	19
B.C.	9	7	0	449	390	18
Sask.	6	9	1	427	436	13

EASTERN DIVISION

	W.	L.	T.	F.	A.	Pts.
Tor.	9	6	1	426	426	19
Ham.	8	7	1	396	401	17
Ott.	5	11	0	376	462	10
Mtl.	2	14	0	267	502	4

Semi-Final - Winnipeg 24, Calgary 3
Final - Edmonton 24, Winnipeg 21

Semi-Final - Ottawa 30, Hamilton 20
Final - Toronto 44, Ottawa 7

Grey Cup - Edmonton 32, Toronto 16

1981

WESTERN DIVISION

	W.	L.	T.	F.	A.	Pts.
Edm.	14	1	1	576	277	29
Wpg.	11	5	0	517	299	22
B.C.	10	6	0	438	377	20
Sask.	9	7	0	431	371	18
Cal.	6	10	0	306	367	12

EASTERN DIVISION

	W.	L.	T.	F.	A.	Pts.
Ham.	11	4	1	414	335	23
Ott.	5	11	0	306	446	10
Mtl.	3	13	0	267	518	6
Tor.	2	14	0	241	506	4

Semi-Final - B.C. 15, Winnipeg 11
Final - Edmonton 22, B.C. 16

Semi-Final - Montreal 16, Ottawa 20
Final - Ottawa 17, Hamilton 13

Grey Cup - Edmonton 26, Ottawa 23

1980

WESTERN DIVISION

	W.	L.	T.	F.	A.	Pts.
Edm.	13	3	0	505	281	26
Wpg.	10	6	0	394	387	20
Cal.	9	7	0	407	355	18
B.C.	8	7	1	381	351	17
Sask.	2	14	0	284	469	4

EASTERN DIVISION

	W.	L.	T.	F.	A.	Pts.
Ham.	8	7	1	332	377	17
Mtl.	8	8	0	356	375	16
Ott.	7	9	0	353	393	14
Tor.	6	10	0	334	358	12

Semi-Final - Calgary 14, Winnipeg 32
Final - Winnipeg 24, Edmonton 34

Semi-Final - Ottawa 21, Montreal 25
Final - Montreal 13, Hamilton 24

Grey Cup - Edmonton 48, Hamilton 10

1979

WESTERN DIVISION

	W.	L.	T.	F.	A.	Pts.
Edm.	12	2	2	495	219	26
Cal.	12	4	0	382	278	24
B.C.	9	6	1	328	333	19
Wpg.	4	12	0	283	340	8
Sask.	2	14	0	194	437	4

EASTERN DIVISION

	W.	L.	T.	F.	A.	Pts.
Mtl.	11	4	1	351	284	23
Ott.	8	6	2	349	315	18
Ham.	6	10	0	280	338	12
Tor.	5	11	0	234	352	10

Semi-Final - B.C. 2, Calgary 37
Final - Calgary 7, Edmonton 19

Semi-Final - Hamilton 26, Ottawa 29
Final - Ottawa 6, Montreal 17

Grey Cup - Edmonton 17, Montreal 9

WESTERN DIVISION **EASTERN DIVISION**

1978

	W.	L.	T.	F.	A.	Pts.		W.	L.	T.	F.	A.	Pts.
Edm.	10	4	2	452	301	22	Ott.	11	5	0	395	261	22
Cal.	9	4	3	381	311	21	Mtl.	8	7	1	331	295	17
Wpg.	9	7	0	371	351	18	Ham.	5	10	1	225	403	11
B.C.	7	7	2	359	308	16	Tor.	4	12	0	234	389	8
Sask.	4	11	1	330	459	9							

Semi-Final - Winnipeg 4, Calgary 38
Final - Calgary 13, Edmonton 26

Semi-Final - Hamilton 20, Montreal 35
Final - Montreal 21, Ottawa 16

Grey Cup - Edmonton 20, Montreal 13

WESTERN DIVISION **EASTERN DIVISION**

1977

	W.	L.	T.	F.	A.	Pts.		W.	L.	T.	F.	A.	Pts.
Edm.	10	6	0	412	320	20	Mtl.	11	5	0	311	245	22
B.C.	10	6	0	369	326	20	Ott.	8	8	0	368	344	16
Wpg.	10	6	0	382	336	20	Tor.	6	10	0	251	266	12
Sask.	8	8	0	330	389	16	Ham.	5	11	0	283	394	10
Cal.	4	12	0	241	327	8							

Semi-Final - B.C. 33, Winnipeg 32
Final - Edmonton 38, B.C. 1

Semi-Final - Ottawa 21, Toronto 16
Final - Montreal 21, Ottawa 18

Grey Cup - Montreal 41, Edmonton 6

WESTERN DIVISION **EASTERN DIVISION**

1976

	W.	L.	T.	F.	A.	Pts.		W.	L.	T.	F.	A.	Pts.
Sask.	11	5	0	427	238	22	Ott.	9	6	1	411	346	19
Wpg.	10	6	0	384	316	20	Ham.	8	8	0	269	348	16
Edm.	9	6	1	311	367	19	Mtl.	7	8	1	305	273	15
B.C.	5	9	2	308	336	12	Tor.	7	8	1	289	354	15
Cal.	2	12	2	316	442	6							

Semi-Final - Edmonton 14, Winnipeg 12
Final - Saskatchewan 23, Edmonton 13

Semi-Final - Hamilton 23, Montreal 0
Final - Ottawa 17, Hamilton 15

Grey Cup - Ottawa 23, Saskatchewan 20

WESTERN DIVISION **EASTERN DIVISION**

1975

	W.	L.	T.	F.	A.	Pts.		W.	L.	T.	F.	A.	Pts.
Edm.	12	4	0	432	370	24	Ott.	10	5	1	394	280	21
Sask.	10	5	1	373	309	21	Mtl.	9	7	0	353	345	18
Wpg.	6	8	2	340	383	14	Ham.	5	10	1	284	395	11
Cal.	6	10	0	387	363	12	Tor.	5	10	1	261	324	11
B.C.	6	10	0	276	331	12							

Semi-Final - Saskatchewan 42, Winnipeg 24
Final - Edmonton 30, Saskatchewan 18

Semi-Final - Montreal 35, Hamilton 12
Final - Montreal 20, Ottawa 10

Grey Cup - Edmonton 9, Montreal 8

WESTERN DIVISION **EASTERN DIVISION**

1974

	W.	L.	T.	F.	A.	Pts.		W.	L.	T.	F.	A.	Pts.
Edm.	10	5	1	345	247	21	Mtl.	9	5	2	339	271	20
Sask.	9	7	0	305	289	18	Ott.	7	9	0	261	271	14
B.C.	8	8	0	306	299	16	Ham.	7	9	0	279	313	14
Wpg.	8	8	0	258	350	16	Tor.	6	9	1	281	314	13
Cal.	6	10	0	285	305	12							

Semi-Final - Saskatchewan 24, B.C. 14
Finals - Edmonton 31, Saskatchewan 27

Semi-Final - Ottawa 21, Hamilton 19
Finals - Montreal 14, Ottawa 4

Grey Cup - Montreal 20, Edmonton 7

WESTERN DIVISION **EASTERN DIVISION**

1973

	W.	L.	T.	F.	A.	Pts.		W.	L.	T.	F.	A.	Pts.
Edm.	9	5	2	329	284	20	Ott.	9	5	0	275	234	18
Sask.	10	6	0	360	287	20	Tor.	7	5	2	265	231	16
B.C.	5	9	2	261	328	12	Mtl.	7	6	1	273	238	15
Cal.	6	10	0	214	368	12	Ham.	7	7	0	304	263	14
Wpg.	4	11	1	267	315	9							

Semi-Final - Saskatchewan 33, B.C. 13
Finals - Edmonton 25, Saskatchewan 23

Semi-Final - Montreal 32, Toronto 10 (overtime)
Finals - Ottawa 23, Montreal 14

Grey Cup - Ottawa 22, Edmonton 18

WESTERN DIVISION **EASTERN DIVISION**

1972

	W.	L.	T.	F.	A.	Pts.		W.	L.	T.	F.	A.	Pts.
Wpg.	10	6	0	401	300	20	Ham.	11	3	0	372	262	22
Edm.	10	6	0	380	368	20	Ott.	11	3	0	298	228	22
Sask.	8	8	0	330	283	16	Mtl.	4	10	0	246	353	8
Cal.	6	10	0	331	394	12	Tor.	3	11	0	254	298	6
B.C.	5	11	0	254	380	10							

Semi-Final - Saskatchewan 8, Edmonton 6
Finals - Saskatchewan 27, Winnipeg 24

Semi-Final - Montreal 11, Ottawa 14
Finals - Hamilton 7, Ottawa 19
Finals - Ottawa 8, Hamilton 23

Grey Cup - Hamilton 13, Saskatchewan 10

WESTERN DIVISION **EASTERN DIVISION**

1971

	W.	L.	T.	F.	A.	Pts.		W.	L.	T.	F.	A.	Pts.
Cal.	9	6	1	290	218	19	Tor.	10	4	0	289	248	20
Sask.	9	6	1	347	316	19	Ham.	7	7	0	242	246	14
Wpg.	7	8	1	366	349	15	Ott.	6	8	0	291	277	12
B.C.	6	9	1	282	363	13	Mtl.	6	8	0	226	248	12
Edm.	6	10	0	237	305	12							

Semi-Final - Winnipeg 23, Saskatchewan 34
Finals - Saskatchewan 21, Calgary 30
Finals - Calgary 23, Saskatchewan 21

Semi-Final - Ottawa 4, Hamilton 23
Finals - Toronto 23, Hamilton 8
Finals - Hamilton 17, Toronto 17

Grey Cup - Calgary 14, Toronto 11

WESTERN DIVISION **EASTERN DIVISION**

1970

	W.	L.	T.	F.	A.	Pts.		W.	L.	T.	F.	A.	Pts.
Sask.	14	2	0	369	206	28	Ham.	8	5	1	292	279	17
Edm.	9	7	0	282	287	18	Tor.	8	6	0	329	290	16
Cal.	9	7	0	293	209	18	Mtl.	7	6	1	246	279	15
B.C.	6	10	0	295	384	12	Ott.	4	10	0	255	279	8
Wpg.	2	14	0	184	332	4							

Semi-Final - Calgary 16, Edmonton 9
Finals - Calgary 28, Saskatchewan 11
Finals - Saskatchewan 11, Calgary 3
Finals - Calgary 15, Saskatchewan 14

Semi-Final - Montreal 16, Toronto 7
Finals - Hamilton 22, Montreal 32
Finals - Montreal 11, Hamilton 4

Grey Cup - Calgary 10, Montreal 23

WESTERN DIVISION **EASTERN DIVISION**

1969

	W.	L.	T.	F.	A.	Pts.		W.	L.	T.	F.	A.	Pts.
Sask.	13	3	0	392	261	26	Ott	11	3	0	399	298	22
Cal.	9	7	0	327	314	18	Tor.	10	4	0	406	280	20
B.C.	5	11	0	235	335	10	Ham.	8	5	1	307	315	17
Edm.	5	11	0	241	246	10	Mtl.	2	10	2	304	395	6
Wpg.	3	12	1	192	359	7							

Semi-Final - B.C. 21, Calgary 35
Finals - Calgary 11, Saskatchewan 17
Finals - Saskatchewan 36, Calgary 13

Semi-Final - Hamilton 9, Toronto 15
Finals - Ottawa 14, Toronto 22
Finals - Toronto 3, Ottawa 32

Grey Cup - Saskatchewan 11, Ottawa 29

WESTERN DIVISION **EASTERN DIVISION**

1968

	W.	L.	T.	F.	A.	Pts.		W.	L.	T.	F.	A.	Pts.
Sask.	12	3	1	345	223	25	Ott.	9	3	2	416	271	20
Cal.	10	6	0	412	249	20	Tor.	9	5	0	284	266	18
Edm.	8	7	1	228	288	17	Ham.	6	7	1	262	292	13
B.C.	4	11	1	217	318	9	Mtl.	3	9	2	234	327	8
Wpg.	3	13	0	210	374	6							

Semi-Final - Edmonton 13, Calgary 29
Finals - Calgary 32, Saskatchewan 0
Finals - Saskatchewan 12, Calgary 25 (overtime)

Semi-Final - Hamilton 21, Toronto 33
Finals - Ottawa 11, Toronto 13
Finals - Toronto 14, Ottawa 36

Grey Cup - Calgary 21, Ottawa 24

WESTERN DIVISION **EASTERN DIVISION**

1967

	W.	L.	T.	F.	A.	Pts.		W.	L.	T.	F.	A.	Pts.
Cal.	12	4	0	382	219	24	Ham.	10	4	0	250	195	20
Sask.	12	4	0	346	282	24	Ott.	9	4	1	337	207	19
Edm.	9	6	1	266	246	19	Tor.	5	8	1	252	266	11
Wpg.	4	12	0	212	414	8	Mtl.	2	12	0	166	302	4
B.C.	3	12	1	239	319	7							

Semi-Final - Edmonton 5, Saskatchewan 21
Finals - Saskatchewan 11, Calgary 15
Finals - Calgary 9, Saskatchewan 11
Finals - Saskatchewan 17, Calgary 13

Semi-Final - Toronto 22, Ottawa 38
Finals - Hamilton 11, Ottawa 3
Finals - Ottawa 0, Hamilton 26

Grey Cup - Saskatchewan 1, Hamilton 24

WESTERN DIVISION **EASTERN DIVISION**

1966

	W.	L.	T.	F.	A.	Pts.		W.	L.	T.	F.	A.	Pts.
Sask.	9	6	1	351	318	19	Ott.	11	3	0	278	177	22
Wpg.	8	7	1	264	230	17	Ham.	9	5	0	264	160	18
Edm.	6	9	1	251	328	13	Mtl.	7	7	0	156	215	14
Cal.	6	9	1	227	259	13	Tor.	5	9	0	182	271	10
B.C.	5	11	0	254	269	10							

Semi-Final - Edmonton 8, Winnipeg 16
Finals - Winnipeg 7, Saskatchewan 14
Finals - Saskatchewan 21, Winnipeg 19

Semi-Final - Montreal 14, Hamilton 24
Finals - Ottawa 30, Hamilton 1
Finals - Hamilton 16, Ottawa 42

Grey Cup - Saskatchewan 29, Ottawa 14

WESTERN DIVISION **EASTERN DIVISION**

1965

	W.	L.	T.	F.	A.	Pts.		W.	L.	T.	F.	A.	Pts.
Cal.	12	4	0	340	243	24	Ham.	10	4	0	281	153	20
Wpg.	11	5	0	301	262	22	Ott.	7	7	0	300	234	14
Sask.	8	7	1	276	277	17	Mtl.	5	9	0	183	215	10
B.C.	6	9	1	286	273	13	Tor.	3	11	0	193	360	6
Edm.	5	11	0	257	400	10							

Semi-Final - Saskatchewan 9, Winnipeg 15
Finals - Winnipeg 9, Calgary 27
Finals - Calgary 11, Winnipeg 15
Finals - Winnipeg 19, Calgary 12

Semi-Final - Montreal 7, Ottawa 36
Finals - Hamilton 18, Ottawa 13
Finals - Ottawa 7, Hamilton 7

Grey Cup - Winnipeg 16, Hamilton 22

1964

WESTERN DIVISION

	W.	L.	T.	F.	A.	Pts.
B.C.	11	2	3	328	168	25
Cal.	12	4	0	352	249	24
Sask.	9	7	0	330	282	18
Edm.	4	12	0	222	458	8
Wpg.	1	14	1	270	397	3

EASTERN DIVISION

	W.	L.	T.	F.	A.	Pts.
Ham.	10	3	1	329	201	21
Ott.	8	5	1	313	228	17
Mtl.	6	8	0	192	264	12
Tor.	4	10	0	243	332	8

Semi-Final - Calgary 25, Saskatchewan 34
Semi-Final - Saskatchewan 6, Calgary 51
Finals - B.C. 24, Calgary 10
Finals - Calgary 14, B.C. 10
Finals - Calgary 14, B.C. 33

Semi-Final - Montreal 0, Ottawa 27
Finals - Hamilton 13, Ottawa 30
Finals - Ottawa 8, Hamilton 26

Grey Cup - B.C. 34, Hamilton 24

1963

WESTERN DIVISION

	W.	L.	T.	F.	A.	Pts.
B.C.	12	4	0	387	232	24
Cal.	10	4	2	427	323	22
Sask.	7	7	2	223	266	16
Wpg.	7	9	0	302	325	14
Edm.	2	14	0	220	425	4

EASTERN DIVISION

	W.	L.	T.	F.	A.	Pts.
Ham.	10	4	0	312	214	20
Ott.	9	5	0	326	284	18
Mtl.	6	8	0	277	297	12
Tor.	3	11	0	202	310	6

Semi-Finals - Saskatchewan 9, Calgary 35
Semi-Finals - Calgary 12, Saskatchewan 39
Finals - B.C. 19, Saskatchewan 7
Finals - Saskatchewan 13, B.C. 8
Finals - Saskatchewan 1, B.C. 36

Semi-Final - Montreal 5, Ottawa 17
Finals - Hamilton 45, Ottawa 0
Finals - Ottawa 35, Hamilton 18

Grey Cup - B.C. 10, Hamilton 21

1962

WESTERN DIVISION

	W.	L.	T.	F.	A.	Pts.
Wpg.	11	5	0	385	291	22
Cal.	9	6	1	352	335	19
Sask.	8	7	1	268	336	17
B.C.	7	9	0	346	342	14
Edm.	6	9	1	310	346	13

EASTERN DIVISION

	W.	L.	T.	F.	A.	Pts.
Ham.	9	4	1	358	286	19
Ott.	6	7	1	339	302	13
Mtl.	4	7	3	308	309	11
Tor.	4	10	0	259	378	8

Semi-Finals - Saskatchewan 0, Calgary 25
Semi-Finals - Calgary 18, Saskatchewan 7
Finals - Winnipeg 14, Calgary 20
Finals - Calgary 11, Winnipeg 19
Finals - Calgary 7, Winnipeg 12

Semi-Final - Montreal 18, Ottawa 17
Finals - Hamilton 28, Montreal 17
Finals - Montreal 21, Hamilton 30

Grey Cup - Winnipeg 28, Hamilton 27

1961

WESTERN DIVISION

	W.	L.	T.	F.	A.	Pts.
Wpg.	13	3	0	360	251	26
Edm.	10	5	1	334	257	21
Cal.	7	9	0	300	311	14
Sask.	5	10	1	211	314	11
B.C.	1	13	2	215	393	4

EASTERN DIVISION

	W.	L.	T.	F.	A.	Pts.
Ham.	10	4	0	340	293	20
Ott.	8	6	0	359	285	16
Tor.	7	6	1	255	258	15
Mtl.	4	9	1	213	225	9

Semi-Finals - Edmonton 8, Calgary 10
Semi-Finals - Calgary 17, Edmonton 18
Finals - Winnipeg 14, Calgary 1
Finals - Calgary 14, Winnipeg 43

Semi-Final - Toronto 43, Ottawa 19
Finals - Hamilton 7, Toronto 25
Finals - Toronto 2, Hamilton 48 (overtime)

Grey Cup - Winnipeg 21, Hamilton 14 (overtime)

1960

WESTERN DIVISION

	W.	L.	T.	F.	A.	Pts.
Wpg.	14	2	0	453	239	28
Edm.	10	6	0	318	225	20
Cal.	6	8	2	374	404	14
B.C.	5	9	2	296	356	12
Sask.	2	12	2	205	422	6

EASTERN DIVISION

	W.	L.	T.	F.	A.	Pts.
Tor.	10	4	0	370	265	20
Ott.	9	5	0	400	283	18
Mtl.	5	9	0	340	458	10
Ham.	4	10	0	273	377	8

Semi-Finals - Calgary 7, Edmonton 30
Semi-Finals - Edmonton 40, Calgary 21
Finals - Winnipeg 22, Edmonton 16
Finals - Edmonton 10, Winnipeg 5
Finals - Edmonton 4, Winnipeg 2

Semi-Final - Montreal 14, Ottawa 30
Finals - Toronto 21, Ottawa 33
Finals - Ottawa 21, Toronto 20

Grey Cup - Edmonton 6, Ottawa 16

1959

WESTERN DIVISION

	W.	L.	T.	F.	A.	Pts.
Wpg.	12	4	0	418	272	24
Edm.	10	6	0	370	221	20
B.C.	9	7	0	306	301	18
Cal.	8	8	0	356	301	16
Sask.	1	15	0	212	567	2

EASTERN DIVISION

	W.	L.	T.	F.	A.	Pts.
Ham.	10	4	0	298	162	20
Ott.	8	6	0	275	217	16
Mtl.	6	8	0	193	305	12
Tor.	4	10	0	192	274	8

Semi-Finals - Edmonton 20, B.C. 8
Semi-Finals - B.C. 7, Edmonton 41
Finals - Winnipeg 19, Edmonton 11
Finals - Edmonton 8, Winnipeg 16

Semi-Final - Montreal 0, Ottawa 43
Finals - Hamilton 5, Ottawa 17
Finals - Ottawa 7, Hamilton 21

Grey Cup - Winnipeg 21, Hamilton 7

1958

WESTERN DIVISION

	W.	L.	T.	F.	A.	Pts.
Wpg.	13	3	0	361	182	26
Edm.	9	6	1	312	292	19
Sask.	7	7	2	320	324	16
Cal.	6	9	1	314	312	13
B.C.	3	13	0	202	399	6

EASTERN DIVISION

	W.	L.	T.	F.	A.	Pts.
Ham.	10	3	1	291	235	21
Mtl.	7	6	1	265	269	15
Ott.	6	8	0	233	243	12
Tor.	4	10	0	266	308	8

Semi-Finals - Edmonton 27, Saskatchewan 11
Semi-Finals - Saskatchewan 1, Edmonton 31
Finals - Winnipeg 30, Edmonton 7
Finals - Edmonton 30, Winnipeg 7
Finals - Edmonton 7, Winnipeg 23

Semi-Final - Ottawa 26, Montreal 12
Finals - Hamilton 35, Ottawa 7
Finals - Ottawa 7, Hamilton 19

Grey Cup - Winnipeg 35, Hamilton 28

1957

WESTERN DIVISION

	W.	L.	T.	F.	A.	Pts.
Edm.	14	2	0	475	142	28
Wpg.	12	4	0	406	300	24
Cal.	6	10	0	221	413	12
B.C.	4	11	1	284	369	9
Sask.	3	12	1	276	438	7

EASTERN DIVISION

	W.	L.	T.	F.	A.	Pts.
Ham.	10	4	0	250	189	20
Ott.	8	6	0	326	237	16
Mtl.	6	8	0	287	301	12
Tor.	4	10	0	274	410	8

Semi-Finals - Calgary 13, Winnipeg 13
Semi-Finals - Winnipeg 15, Calgary 3
Finals - Edmonton 7, Winnipeg 19
Finals - Winnipeg 4, Edmonton 5
Finals - Winnipeg 17, Edmonton 2 (overtime)

Semi-Finals - Montreal 24, Ottawa 15
Finals - Hamilton 17, Montreal 10
Finals - Montreal 1, Hamilton 39

Grey Cup - Winnipeg 7, Hamilton 32

1956

WESTERN DIVISION

	W.	L.	T.	F.	A.	Pts.
Edm.	11	5	0	358	235	22
Sask.	10	6	0	353	272	20
Wpg.	9	7	0	315	228	18
B.C.	6	10	0	251	361	12
Cal.	4	12	0	229	410	8

EASTERN DIVISION

	W.	L.	T.	F.	A.	Pts.
Mtl.	10	4	0	478	361	20
Ham.	7	7	0	383	385	14
Ott.	7	7	0	326	359	14
Tor.	4	10	0	331	413	8

Semi-Finals - Winnipeg 7, Saskatchewan 42
Semi-Finals - Saskatchewan 8, Winnipeg 19
Finals - Edmonton 22, Saskatchewan 23
Finals - Saskatchewan 12, Edmonton 20
Finals - Saskatchewan 7, Edmonton 51

Semi-Final - Ottawa 21, Hamilton 46
Finals - Montreal 30, Hamilton 21
Finals - Hamilton 41, Montreal 48

Grey Cup - Edmonton 50, Montreal 27

1955

WESTERN DIVISION

	W.	L.	T.	F.	A.	Pts.
Edm.	14	2	0	286	117	28
Sask.	10	6	0	270	245	20
Wpg.	7	9	0	210	195	14
B.C.	5	11	0	211	330	10
Cal.	4	12	0	209	299	8

EASTERN DIVISION

	W.	L.	T.	F.	A.	Pts.
Mtl.	9	3	0	388	214	18
Ham.	8	4	0	271	193	16
Tor.	4	8	0	239	328	8
Ott.	3	9	0	174	337	6

Semi-Finals - Winnipeg 16, Saskatchewan 7
Semi-Finals - Saskatchewan 9, Winnipeg 8
Finals - Edmonton 29, Winnipeg 6
Finals - Winnipeg 6, Edmonton 26

Semi-Final - Toronto 32, Hamilton 28
Final - Toronto 36, Montreal 38

Grey Cup - Edmonton 34, Montreal 19

1954

WESTERN DIVISION

	W.	L.	T.	F.	A.	Pts.
Edm.	11	5	0	255	163	22
Sask.	10	4	2	239	204	22
Wpg.	8	6	2	202	190	18
Cal.	8	8	0	271	165	16
B.C.	1	15	0	100	345	2

EASTERN DIVISION

	W.	L.	T.	F.	A.	Pts.
Mtl.	11	3	0	341	148	22
Ham.	9	5	0	275	207	18
Tor.	6	8	0	212	265	12
Ott.	2	12	0	129	337	4

Semi-Finals - Winnipeg 14, Saskatchewan 14
Semi-Finals - Winnipeg 13, Saskatchewan 11
Finals - Winnipeg 3, Edmonton 9
Finals - Edmonton 6, Winnipeg 12
Finals - Winnipeg 5, Edmonton 10

Finals - Montreal 14, Hamilton 9
Finals - Montreal 24, Hamilton 19

Grey Cup Semi-Final - Edmonton 28, K-W Dutchmen 6
Grey Cup - Edmonton 26, Montreal 25

1953

WESTERN DIVISION

	W.	L.	T.	F.	A.	Pts.
Edm.	12	4	0	276	157	24
Sask.	8	7	1	243	239	17
Wpg.	8	8	0	226	226	16
Cal.	3	12	1	190	313	7

EASTERN DIVISION

	W.	L.	T.	F.	A.	Pts.
Mtl.	8	6	0	292	229	16
Ham.	8	6	0	229	243	16
Ott.	7	7	0	266	238	14
Tor.	5	9	0	172	249	10

Semi-Finals - Saskatchewan 5, Winnipeg 43
Semi-Finals - Winnipeg 17, Saskatchewan 18
Finals - Winnipeg 7, Edmonton 25
Finals - Edmonton 17, Winnipeg 21
Finals - Winnipeg 30, Edmonton 24

Finals - Hamilton 37, Montreal 12
Finals - Hamilton 22, Montreal 11

Grey Cup Semi-Final - Winnipeg 24, Toronto Balmy Beach 4
Grey Cup - Hamilton 12, Winnipeg 6

1952

WESTERN DIVISION

	W.	L.	T.	F.	A.	Pts.
Wpg.	12	3	1	394	211	25
Edm.	9	6	1	291	280	19
Cal.	7	9	0	293	340	14
Sask.	3	13	0	216	363	6

EASTERN DIVISION

	W.	L.	T.	F.	A.	Pts.
Ham.	9	2	1	268	162	19
Tor.	7	4	1	265	191	15
Ott.	5	7	0	200	238	10
Mtl.	2	10	0	136	278	4

Semi-Finals - Edmonton 12, Calgary 31
Semi-Finals - Calgary 7, Edmonton 30
Finals - Winnipeg 28, Edmonton 12
Finals - Edmonton 18, Winnipeg 12
Finals - Edmonton 22, Winnipeg 11

Finals - Toronto 22, Hamilton 6
Finals - Hamilton 27, Toronto 11
Finals - Toronto 12, Hamilton 7
East Final - Toronto 34, Sarnia 15

Grey Cup - Toronto 21, Edmonton 11

1951

WESTERN DIVISION

	W.	L.	T.	F.	A.	Pts.
Sask.	8	6	0	277	219	16
Edm.	8	6	0	306	262	16
Wpg.	8	6	0	303	311	16
Cal.	4	10	0	205	299	8

EASTERN DIVISION

	W.	L.	T.	F.	A.	Pts.
Ott.	7	5	0	218	197	14
Ham.	7	5	0	229	131	14
Tor.	7	5	0	226	205	14
Mtl.	3	9	0	146	286	6

Semi-Final - Winnipeg 1, Edmonton 4
Finals - Saskatchewan 11, Edmonton 15
Finals - Edmonton 5, Saskatchewan 12
Finals - Edmonton 18, Saskatchewan 19

Semi-Final - Hamilton 24, Toronto 7
Semi-Final - Toronto 21, Hamilton 7
Finals - Ottawa 17, Hamilton 7
Finals - Ottawa 11, Hamilton 9
East Final - Ottawa 43, Sarnia 17

Grey Cup - Ottawa 21, Saskatchewan 14

1950

WESTERN DIVISION

	W.	L.	T.	F.	A.	Pts.
Wpg.	10	4	0	221	156	20
Sask.	7	7	0	207	177	14
Edm.	7	7	0	201	197	14
Cal.	4	10	0	152	251	8

EASTERN DIVISION

	W.	L.	T.	F.	A.	Pts.
Ham.	7	5	0	231	217	14
Tor.	6	5	1	291	187	13
Mtl.	6	6	0	192	261	12
Ott.	4	7	1	182	231	9

Semi-Final - Edmonton 24, Saskatchewan 1
Finals - Winnipeg 16, Edmonton 17
Finals - Edmonton 12, Winnipeg 22
Finals - Edmonton 6, Winnipeg 29

Finals - Hamilton 13, Toronto 11
Finals - Toronto 24, Hamilton 6
East Final - Tor. Argos 43, Tor. B.B. 13

Grey Cup - Toronto 13, Winnipeg 0

1949

WESTERN DIVISION

	W.	L.	T.	F.	A.	Pts.
Cal.	13	1	0	270	77	26
Sask.	9	5	0	235	102	18
Edm.	4	10	0	93	235	8
Wpg.	2	12	0	74	258	4

EASTERN DIVISION

	W.	L.	T.	F.	A.	Pts.
Ott.	11	1	0	261	170	22
Mtl.	8	4	0	295	204	16
Tor.	5	7	0	209	254	10
Ham.	0	12	0	147	284	0

Finals - Calgary 18, Saskatchewan 12
Finals - Saskatchewan 9, Calgary 4

Finals - Montreal 22, Ottawa 7
Finals - Montreal 14, Ottawa 13
East Final - Montreal 40, Ham. Tigers 0

Grey Cup - Montreal 28, Calgary 15

1948

WESTERN DIVISION

	W.	L.	T.	F.	A.	Pts.
Cal.	12	0	0	218	61	24
Sask.	3	9	0	133	137	6
Wpg.	3	9	0	81	234	6

EASTERN DIVISION

	W.	L.	T.	F.	A.	Pts.
Ott.	10	2	0	264	130	20
Mtl.	7	5	0	221	172	14
Tor.	5	6	1	160	191	11
Ham.	1	10	1	88	240	3

Finals - Calgary 4, Saskatchewan 4
Finals - Saskatchewan 6, Calgary 17

Finals - Montreal 21, Ottawa 19
Finals - Ottawa 15, Montreal 7
East Final - Ottawa 19, Hamilton Tigers 0

Grey Cup - Calgary 12, Ottawa 7

1947

WESTERN DIVISION

	W.	L.	T.	F.	A.	Pts.
Wpg.	5	3	0	83	83	10
Cal.	4	4	0	79	93	8
Reg.	3	5	0	78	64	6

EASTERN DIVISION

	W.	L.	T.	F.	A.	Pts.
Ott.	8	4	0	170	103	16
Tor.	7	4	1	140	122	15
Mtl.	6	6	0	164	164	12
Ham.	2	9	1	119	204	5

Finals - Calgary 4, Winnipeg 16
Finals - Winnipeg 3, Calgary 15
Finals - Calgary 3, Winnipeg 10

Finals - Toronto 3, Ottawa 0
Finals - Toronto 21, Ottawa 0
East Final - Toronto 22, Ottawa Trojans 1

Grey Cup - Toronto 10, Winnipeg 9

1946

WESTERN DIVISION

	W.	L.	T.	F.	A.	Pts.
Cal.	5	3	0	60	37	10
Wpg.	5	3	0	69	46	10
Reg.	2	6	0	46	92	4

EASTERN DIVISION

	W.	L.	T.	F.	A.	Pts.
Mtl.	7	3	2	211	118	16
Tor.	7	3	2	140	124	16
Ott.	6	4	2	175	128	14
Ham.	0	10	2	78	234	2

Finals - Winnipeg 18, Calgary 21
Finals - Calgary 0, Winnipeg 12

Final - Toronto 12, Montreal 6
East Final - Tor. Argos 22, Tor. B.B. 12

Grey Cup - Toronto 28, Winnipeg 6

1945

WESTERN DIVISION

	W.	L.	T.	F.	A.	Pts.

NO LEAGUE PLAY

EASTERN DIVISION

	W.	L.	T.	F.	A.	Pts.
Ott.	5	1	0	105	40	10
Tor.	5	1	0	92	44	10
Ham.	1	5	0	36	68	2
Mtl.	1	5	0	32	113	2

Semi-Finals - Calgary 3, Regina 1
Semi-Finals - Regina 0, Calgary 12
Final - Calgary 6, Winnipeg 9

Finals - Toronto 27, Ottawa 8
Finals - Toronto 6, Ottawa 10
East Final - Tor. Argos 14, Tor. B.B. 2

Grey Cup - Toronto 35, Winnipeg 0

1944 Grey Cup Game - Montreal Navy 7, Hamilton Wildcats 6

1943 East Final - Hamilton Wildcats 7, Lachine RCAF 6
Grey Cup Game - Hamilton 23, Winnipeg RCAF 14

1942 East Final - Toronto RCAF 18, Ottawa RCAF 13
Grey Cup Game - Toronto RCAF 8, Winnipeg RCAF 5

1941

WESTERN DIVISION

	W.	L.	T.	F.	A.	Pts.
Wpg.	6	2	0	92	19	12
Reg.	5	3	0	64	43	10
Van.	1	7	0	15	109	2

EASTERN DIVISION

	W.	L.	T.	F.	A.	Pts.
Ott.	5	1	0	72	21	10
Tor.	5	1	0	66	42	10
B.B'ch	2	4	0	27	34	4
Mtl.	0	6	0	12	80	0

Finals - Winnipeg 6, Regina 8
Finals - Regina 12, Winnipeg 18
Finals - Regina 2, Winnipeg 8

Finals - Toronto 16, Ottawa 8
Finals - Ottawa 10, Toronto 1
East Final - Ottawa 7, Ham. Wildcats 2

Grey Cup - Winnipeg 18, Ottawa 16

1940

WESTERN DIVISION

	W.	L.	T.	F.	A.	Pts.
Wpg.	6	2	0	108	58	12
Cal.	4	4	0	79	76	8
Reg.	2	6	0	39	92	4

EASTERN DIVISION

	W.	L.	T.	F.	A.	Pts.
Ott.	5	1	0	116	40	10
Tor.	4	2	0	58	79	8
Ham.	2	4	0	45	73	4
Mtl.	1	5	0	39	66	2

Finals - Winnipeg 7, Calgary 0
Finals - Calgary 2, Winnipeg 23

Finals - Ottawa 12, Toronto 1
Finals - Ottawa 8, Toronto 1

Grey Cup - Ottawa 8, Balmy Beach 2
Ottawa 12, Balmy Beach 5
Ottawa won round 20-7

1939

WESTERN DIVISION

	W.	L.	T.	F.	A.	Pts.
Wpg.	10	2	0	201	103	20
Reg.	6	6	0	84	136	12
Cal.	4	7	0	144	123	8
Edm.	3	8	0	80	147	6

EASTERN DIVISION

	W.	L.	T.	F.	A.	Pts.
Ott.	5	1	0	145	44	10
Tor.	4	1	1	58	43	9
Ham.	2	4	0	29	84	4
Mtl.	0	5	1	23	84	1

Semi-Final - Calgary 24, Regina 17
Finals - Calgary 13, Winnipeg 7
Finals - Winnipeg 28, Calgary 7

Finals - Ottawa 11, Toronto 0
Finals - Ottawa 28, Toronto 6
East Final - Ottawa 23, Sarnia 1

Grey Cup - Winnipeg 8, Ottawa 7

1938

WESTERN DIVISION

	W.	L.	T.	F.	A.	Pts.
Cal.	6	2	0	50	27	12
Wpg.	6	2	0	114	63	12
Reg.	4	4	0	69	55	8
Edm.	0	8	0	29	117	0

EASTERN DIVISION

	W.	L.	T.	F.	A.	Pts.
Ott.	5	1	0	141	41	10
Tor.	5	1	0	151	52	10
Ham.	2	4	0	61	122	4
Mtl.	0	6	0	30	168	0

Semi-Final - Regina 0, Winnipeg 13
Finals - Winnipeg 12, Calgary 7
Finals - Calgary 2, Winnipeg 13

Finals - Toronto 9, Ottawa 1
Finals - Toronto 5, Ottawa 3
East Final - Toronto 25, Sarnia 8

Grey Cup - Toronto 30, Winnipeg 7

1937

WESTERN DIVISION

	W.	L.	T.	F.	A.	Pts.
Cal.	5	3	0	47	70	10
Wpg.	4	4	0	57	47	8
Reg.	3	5	0	58	45	6

EASTERN DIVISION

	W.	L.	T.	F.	A.	Pts.
Tor.	5	1	0	72	43	10
Ott.	3	3	0	52	46	6
Ham.	2	4	0	42	63	4
Mtl.	2	4	0	35	49	4

Finals - Calgary 13, Winnipeg 10
Finals - Winnipeg 9, Calgary 1

Finals - Ottawa 15, Toronto 11
Finals - Toronto 10, Ottawa 1
East Final - Toronto 10, Sarnia 6

Grey Cup - Toronto 4, Winnipeg 3

1936

WESTERN DIVISION

	W.	L.	T.	F.	A.	Pts.
Wpg.	5	2	1	104	37	11
Reg.	3	2	1	52	42	9
Cal.	1	5	0	17	94	4

EASTERN DIVISION

	W.	L.	T.	F.	A.	Pts.
Tor.	4	2	0	74	37	8
Ott.	3	3	0	49	63	6
Ham.	3	3	0	62	71	6
Mtl.	2	4	0	45	59	4

Calgary-Regina games worth 4 points
Semi-Finals - Winnipeg 7, Regina 4
Semi-Finals - Regina 20, Winnipeg 5
Final - Regina 3, Calgary 1

Semi-Final - Ottawa 3, Hamilton 2
Finals - Ottawa 5, Toronto 1
Finals - Ottawa 17, Toronto 5

Grey Cup - Sarnia 26, Ottawa 20